T5-CCX-011

Auditing

Auditing

Wanda A. Wallace

Ph.D., CPA, CMA, CIA
The Deborah D. Shelton Systems Professor of Accounting
TEXAS A & M UNIVERSITY

MACMILLAN PUBLISHING COMPANY
NEW YORK
COLLIER MACMILLAN PUBLISHERS
LONDON

Printed in the United States of America

Macmillan Publishing Company
866 Third Avenue, New York, New York 10022

Collier Macmillan Canada, Inc.

Library of Congress Cataloging-in-Publication Data

Wallace, Wanda A.,
Auditing.

Includes index.
1. Auditing. I. Title.
HF5667.W2123 1986 657'.45 85-15601
ISBN 0-02-423940-2

Printing: 1 2 3 4 5 6 7 8 Year: 6 7 8 9 0 1 2 3 4 5

Grateful acknowledgment is made for permission to reprint from the following:

Material from CIA Examination Questions and Answers, copyright © 1972–1985 by the Institute of Internal Auditors, is reprinted with permission.

Material from Uniform CPA Examination Questions and Unofficial Answers, copyright © 1960–1985 by the American Institute of Certified Public Accountants, Inc., is reprinted with permission.

ISBN 0-02-423940-2

DEDICATION

To my husband Jim,
a colleague, friend, and partner

Preface

I have always found the topic of auditing to be fascinating, and I hope the enthusiasm that permeates these pages will make auditing interesting and real to readers. Beyond the traditional coverage of introductory auditing books, this text interweaves anecdotes from practice, news events, research findings, dilemmas presently faced by practitioners, and unresolved issues and challenges with which the profession is grappling. The intent is to nurture the reader's appreciation for society's demands of the auditing profession, the evolution of the audit process, current practices, new technology, areas of controversy, and responsibilities commensurate with being an audit professional.

The reader is encouraged to think and discuss issues, to consider research results that provide insights on the evolving nature of the profession, and to learn to "think as an auditor" by considering actual audit judgments and dilemmas. While much debate centers on the type of instruction likely to be most effective in both accounting and auditing, consensus exists that students must be able to (1) learn to exercise judgment; (2) appreciate that a rule book with all of the answers does not exist; and (3) communicate well, both orally and in writing. The text examples and chapter-end materials are directed at these three concerns. One example of how the book addresses these concerns is the litigation chapter. This chapter goes beyond merely stating the key legal decisions and develops the case setting, the auditor's actions, the rationale for judgments reached, and, at times, the discrepancies in such judgments and generally accepted standards of practice. This permits far better understanding of how practice has evolved and the present litigious environment in which CPAs practice.

Throughout the manuscript, both the how and the why of the audit process are stressed, with ample references to professional pronouncements, existing literature, and gray areas of practice in which audit judgment becomes particularly crucial. An attempt is made to present the audit process as a coherent whole. The early chapters on the basic topics of evidence also include detailed coverage of internal control, EDP, and sampling. Later descriptions of the audit process for each major operating cycle use these tools to demonstrate how an audit is actually performed, including the interaction of its component parts.

Recent developments in practice have focused on risk assessment, the use of analytical review procedures, and EDP, both as a control problem and as an audit tool. Microcomputers are increasingly important audit tools that have facilitated the application of both sampling and regression analysis. An emphasis is placed on objectives, problems, and procedures that are unique to the auditor when applying both statistical and nonstatistical auditing tools, rather than merely emphasizing pure statistical theory.

Another unique aspect of this book is a separate chapter on special audit risk areas, such as revenue recognition, unrecorded liabilities, and related party transactions. These issues have been the Achilles heel to practitioners, and they warrant special attention.

If I were asked to describe the philosophy of this text in five words or less, I would respond that it is intended "to excite, challenge, and inform."

Organization

Each chapter begins with an introductory case based on actual news events or audit experiences. These are intended to whet the students' appetite for that chapter's subject matter. The content of each case will be revisited at various points throughout the chapter and should be an impetus to students' discussion of key issues. The cases can be used by instructors to build lecture material and begin class discussion. Many exhibits appear in each chapter illustrating, summarizing, and highlighting key concepts, as well as empirical evidence. Italicized terms introduce the "jargon" of auditors and are intended to focus students' attention. Cross references to professional pronouncements are provided throughout the text to facilitate more in-depth review of technical literature. These citations also serve to emphasize when certain subject matter stems directly from professional pronouncements. Periodically, illustrative CPA exam questions, with solutions, are provided within the text of the chapter both to demonstrate the application of concepts discussed and to familiarize students with professional examinations.

At the end of each chapter, this exposure to professional examinations is further supported by a rich set of adapted questions in both essay and multiple-choice form. In addition to these adapted materials, there are a wide variety of review questions, exercises, and cases for discussion written by the author specifically for this text. The extensive set of original chapter-end material is intended to encourage students' development of analytical, verbal, and writing skills.

Chapter 1 of the text emphasizes both the nature and economic role of the audit. The general standards are introduced, as is an overview of the audit process. The simplified outline of the audit process provides a framework that can be used by students in organizing their understanding of auditing. Materials in an appendix to Chapter 1 describe career opportunities and the sizable problem of turnover in public accounting. Throughout the text, issues specific to internal auditing are explored.

Chapter 2 provides an initial introduction of audit reports. Since most students have seen an auditor's report in earlier course work, they are initially curious about its meaning and purpose. This text takes advantage of this natural inquisitiveness by introducing report forms in Chapter 2, using simple examples. Chapter 17 extends the discussion of accountants' reports and incorporates more complex issues. Exhibit 2-1 provides a historical perspective on the development of the auditor's report, and Exhibit 2-9 summarizes the primary report forms, with examples of the wording of each type of variation from a standard clean opinion. Reporting standards are described in Chapter 2, as are research findings related to users' understanding of auditors' reports. Comparisons are made between internal and external auditors' reports.

Chapter 3 describes the structure and standards of the auditing profession. The organization of a typical public accounting firm, the structure of the auditing standards board, the role of the public oversight board and peer review activities, and the standards of field work are a sample of the topics discussed. An appendix to Chapter 3 provides details on various requirements of the state boards of accountancy with respect to obtaining a CPA.

In Chapter 4 the code of professional ethics is described with examples of unethical behavior, current controversies, and a historical account of how the code has evolved to its present form. The text discusses such fascinating issues as how confidentiality can be interpreted in light of the *Fund of Funds* litigation and how efforts by the Internal Revenue Service to gain access to auditors' working papers that relate to tax accruals have affected practice. Research concerning ethics, particularly the differing perspective on independence of the profession relative to the Securities and Exchange Commission, is summarized. An appendix to Chapter 4 compares codes of ethics of other countries, as well as other professions, to that of CPAs and internal auditors.

Chapter 5 provides a detailed account of litigation cases, emphasizing the circumstances involved in each case and the lessons to be learned from each case. Exhibit 5-6 summarizes legal responsibilities. The nature of the litigious environment in which the auditor practices is described, including litigation experiences in other countries and liability insurance considerations.

Chapter 6 describes the economics of operating a public accounting firm and issues related to accepting and reassessing the continuation of services to a particular client. The "red flag" literature is reviewed, as well as specific prescriptions for quality control within CPA firms. Engagement letters and audit fee determinants are among the topics explored.

Chapter 7 presents theories underlying the collection and documentation of audit evidence. The capabilities of various audit procedures to gather audit evidence are detailed (see Exhibit 7-4), with in-depth coverage of analytical review techniques (see Exhibit 7-5) and the strength of a business approach to auditing. Attention is given to how audit procedures are directed by audit objectives.

Chapter 8 describes how to prepare an audit program, including examples of alternative approaches to writing a program. It discusses risk analysis in detail, including the use of risk worksheets used in making an evaluation of control risk. Reporting issues and letters of audit inquiry to clients' lawyers are discussed. Care is taken to recognize administrative aspects of an audit engagement such as time budgets and performance evaluations.

Chapter 9 provides an intuitive approach to both designing and evaluating existing and proposed controls. Critical concepts underlying the evaluation of control and the tools of flowcharting, narratives, checklists, and walk-throughs are explained, with several examples from practice. The interrelationship of control objectives and control procedures is stressed.

In Chapter 10 the effect of electronic data processing on controls and its use as an audit tool are detailed. A dual emphasis is placed on possible controls in an EDP environment and the losses that each control is intended to reduce. Exhibit 10-1 familiarizes students with the major types of EDP environments. These are then compared from the perspective of relative risk exposure and related controls. Past EDP frauds are described, to ensure that students acquire an adequate appreciation of inherent risk, control risk, and the relative effectiveness of various audit procedures in EDP environments.

In Chapter 11 sampling concepts are introduced, which relate to both attribute and variables sampling. However, a detailed discussion of attributes testing is found in Chapter 11, with variables sampling emphasized in Chapter 12. The use of regression analysis as an analytical review tool is introduced in Chapter 12. The usefulness of simple descriptive statistics, easily obtained from microcomputer applications, is emphasized. Exhibit 11-3 reconciles traditional statistical concepts with Statement on Auditing Standards No. 39, to facilitate students' application of tools already acquired from basic quantitative coursework. Tables for determining sample size are placed in an appendix. A detailed description of ratio and difference estimation is provided in Chapter 12, with examples presented in Exhibits 12-3 and 12-4.

Chapters 13, 14, and 15 are cycle chapters that integrate the key concepts presented in prior chapters. The use of generalized audit software and the application of statistical and nonstatistical sampling in both an attributes and variables setting are illustrated in the cycle chapters. Exhibit 13-1 details the audit process that is described in each cycle chapter.

First, a typical flowchart of each cycle is presented, followed by a summary of the forms that are commonly used to document that cycle. The "things that could go wrong" are detailed. An emphasis is placed on the types of questions that are likely to be useful in gaining an understanding of an auditee's business, within the context of each major cycle: revenue, cost of sales or production, and financing. Then ways in which risks can be addressed via segregation of duties and control procedures are detailed. Auditors' control evaluations, compliance tests, and linkages to substantive tests are emphasized. (See Exhibits 13-10 and 13-14 as examples.)

Chapter 16 necessarily overlaps with the cycle chapters, as its central purpose is to highlight special audit risks. Contingencies, revenue recognition, going concern assessments, and related party concerns are among the topics described.

Chapter 17 discusses the other types of engagements accepted by CPAs, including compilation and review engagements, special reports, comfort letters, reports on internal accounting controls, and services related to forecasting. Operational auditing reports are described. An appendix to Chapter 17 presents the Standards for Audit of Governmental Organizations, Programs, Activities, and Functions.

Chapter 18 discusses issues facing the profession. The placement of an in-depth discussion of the Metcalf Report, Moss Commission, Cohen Commission, Dingell Commission, and related regulatory pressures in the final chapter reflects my belief that students are better able to appreciate the issues involved in such literature after obtaining an understanding of the audit process, particularly the economics of the profession, the role of litigation, and the way in which audit procedures are applied. This chapter also describes the proposed attestation standards that may eventually replace present general, reporting, and field work standards. The differences in these proposed standards and present standards require an understanding of the broad range of reporting services that accountants have begun to provide, so they naturally follow Chapter 17. Details regarding the Cohen Commission and the Private Practice Section of the AICPA appear in an appendix to Chapter 18.

An appendix to the text presents an outline of Statements on Auditing Standards. This summary of key aspects of the professional pronouncements is intended as a handy reference for students that should encourage more in-depth reading of relevant technical literature, as the auditing course progresses.

Supplemental Items

The *Instructor's Manual* accompanying this text provides detailed solutions to all chapter-end material, outlines of each chapter's content to facilitate lecture preparation, and extra resource materials in the form of a case and possible approaches to classroom discussions.

The text also has a *Test Bank* available for instructors. The text of the test bank is available on floppy disk. These disks can be used with compatible word processing programs to help in the preparation of printed tests. For more information on these disks please contact Chip Price, Accounting Editor, Macmillan Publishing Co., 866 Third Ave. New York, NY 10022.

For the student, two supplements are available. The first is entitled *Auditing Monographs,* which contains two monographs: "The Economic Role of the Audit in Free and Regulated Markets" and "A Synopsis of Selected Audit Research Findings." The first monograph develops the ideas outlined in Chapter 1 of this text in far greater depth, describing auditing as an economic service and linking both the economics and finance training of students to their detailed study of auditing. The second monograph provides auditing students with a small sample of some of the interesting audit research performed to date. The second supplement, *An Audit Practice Set,* will help students apply the concepts they have learned from the text.

Acknowledgments

Many individuals have influenced my understanding and attitudes about auditing and the profession. However, I want particularly to thank Geraldine F. Dominiak (Texas Christian University); Sheridan Biggs, Ralph Hoffman, Walter Pugh, and Joe Croteau (all of Price Waterhouse); James DeLoach, Jack Lathrop, Mark Bronson, Dick Kreutzfeldt, Brad Porter, and Dan Haley (all of Arthur Andersen); Abe Akresh (Laventhol & Horwath); Bob Elliott, John Willingham, Nancy Grimes, and Jerry Snyder (all of Peat, Marwick, Mitchell & Co.); and Bob Kay and Henry Korff (both of Touche Ross & Co.). All of these individuals have affected the manner in which I analyze current auditing issues. Of course, all of my associates in academia who share my fervor for audit research have had an indelible effect on this manuscript; I regret that the list of those individuals is far too lengthy to give an exhaustive account. Yet many of you will find yourselves prominently displayed in the authors' index to this text. I appreciate your contribution.

This manuscript was significantly enhanced by the review efforts of W. Steven Albrecht (Brigham Young University), Richard J. Asebrook (University of Massachusetts), Van Ballew (San Diego State University), R. Glen Berryman (University of Minnesota), James Collins (University of East Carolina),

Gere Dominiak (Texas Christian University), S. Michael Groomer (Indiana University), William F. Messier, Jr. (University of Florida), Henri C. Pusker (Youngstown State University), Randolph A. Shockley (University of Georgia), Ira Solomon (University of Illinois), Maurice Stark (Kansas State University), Richard Tabor (Auburn University), Robert W. Vanesse (California State University, Fullerton), and Carl Warren (University of Georgia). The detailed input by Steve Albrecht and Richard Asebrook was particularly valuable and is greatly appreciated. I am indebted to the American Institute of Certified Public Accountants, The Institute of Internal Auditors, and many other publishers for granting permission to reprint excerpts from professional publications, past examinations, and journals.

Typing support for this project has been extensive. David Guisinger, Edith Benham, Madelon Gafford, Wanda Hanson, Teresa McGee, and Bess Vick (all of Southern Methodist University), and Sindy Rabold (Texas A & M University) did a superb job in preparing the manuscript. David Guisinger assisted administratively at several stages of the project, and, as usual, his work was of the highest quality.

My primary "sounding board" for ideas, readability, and teaching effectiveness issues is my husband, James J. Wallace (Texas A & M University). His patience with my often repetitious inquiries, long hours, and anxious moments and his immeasurable contributions via formal suggestions on the manuscript are deeply appreciated.

No set of acknowledgments would be complete without expressing my ever-growing appreciation of my parents' encouragement to ask questions, analyze issues, and enjoy learning.

To all of these individuals I extend my thanks.

W. A. W.

About the Author

The author has public accounting experience and presently consults with the national office of Price Waterhouse concerning the application of regression analysis as an audit tool and with Arthur Andersen concerning audit methodology. In the past she has consulted with the national office of Peat, Marwick, Mitchell & Co. concerning internal control and the training of senior auditors. Her research on auditing topics has been supported by Deloitte Haskins & Sells; Ernst & Whinney; Peat, Marwick, Mitchell & Co.; Price Waterhouse; Touche Ross; and The Institute of Internal Auditors (IIA). Professor Wallace is an active member of the AICPA, American Accounting Association (AAA), Auditing Section of the AAA, and IIA, among other organizations. She has served as chairman of the Auditing Standards Committee, an officer of the Auditing Section, and a member of the board of regents of the IIA. She is presently a member of an AICPA Task Force, a joint project with the Canadian Institute. Dr. Wallace holds three certifications and was awarded the gold medal for her performance on the international Certified Internal Auditor Examination, as well as a Certificate of Distinguished Performance on the Certified Management Accounting Examination. Although her teaching experience spans the full extent of accounting course offerings at both the undergraduate and graduate levels, Dr. Wallace has primary teaching interests in auditing. Her publications appear in numerous academic and professional journals and have been recognized by four national literary awards, including the Wildman medal.

Contents

Exhibits

1

What Is Auditing?

Having boarded a flight for home, after doing some business in New York City, Professor Stephanie Parish found herself seated next to a businessman, who immediately introduced himself:

Bob Caraway. How do you do? I'm Bob Caraway of Caraway Motors.

Professor Parish. My name is Stephanie Parish. I'm glad to meet you.

Bob Caraway. Were you in the city on business?

Professor Parish. Oh, I teach accounting at the university and do some consulting work with one of the auditing firms in the city.

Bob Caraway. You don't say! Do you know Tom Hill by any chance? He's our accountant.

Professor Parish. No, but being new to the area, I haven't yet had much of an opportunity to meet the local CPAs. Does he audit your company?

Bob Caraway. Yes, Tom comes out to the dealership every year-end and prepares our financials.

Professor Parish. I teach auditing to MBAs and I'm always interested in the reasons that local businesses decide to be audited.

Bob Caraway. Frankly, our bookkeeper can handle our day-to-day activities just fine, but he has no training in preparing financial statements. So when my banker said he'd need financial statements before he'd extend my line of credit, I decided that I needed a CPA.

Professor Parish. But why an audit?

Bob Caraway. Well, I figure if you're going to have a CPA, you might as well go the whole route and have an audit, too. Besides, my banker liked the idea of having someone outside our business prepare the financial statements.

Professor Parish. How did you happen to select Tom Hill?

Bob Caraway. Oh, Tom plays golf in our foursome. So I had no problem at all in finding a CPA. He's really a nice guy, too; I've known him for better than twenty years. In fact, his daughter's our assistant bookkeeper and receptionist.

Professor Parish. Has the audit been useful to you?

Bob Caraway. Yes. I'm not really sure what Tom does, but it's always a relief to get a clean bill of health on the business. We run a pretty loose shop, and it's nice to know that nobody's ripping us off, if you know what I mean.

Professor Parish. How long does the audit take?

Bob Caraway. Tom comes out for two or three days every year-end and collects all the information that he needs. Of course, he prepares and audits our tax returns, too. Last year he came up with a real brainstorm that saved time on our record keeping for inventory; I think he called it a pegboard system. He's also started helping me with my cash flow planning. As interest rates have been climbing, it's become a real problem. . . .

The conversation then turned to economics, politics, and current events. Later, when Professor Parish reflected on the conversation, it became clear to her that Bob Caraway's CPA was probably providing write-up, tax, and accounting services and not audit services. The time frame Bob described and his loose use of the term *audit* with respect to the tax returns were clues that there was some misunderstanding regarding what the CPA was really doing. Tom Hill's independence also could be questioned, making it unlikely that he would serve as an auditor. What's more, Bob Caraway had the wrong impression of CPAs' ability to detect fraud or other kinds of embezzlement. Stephanie was reminded of an article she had recently read about some survey results. A local CPA firm surveyed 299 clients, regarding their perceptions of audits and found a general lack of understanding of what they really are. After arriving home that evening she reread the following passage from the article:

> In a question dealing with services performed for clients, the term "certified audit" was used in an effort to be sure clients were differentiating audits from other services provided by the firm. Nevertheless, a substantial number of clients in each of the five groups, ranging from 7.8 percent in tax to 60 percent in accounting services, believed they had an audit performed when no such services were being provided. Conversely, 16 percent of respondents known to be audit clients replied they did not have an audit performed.[1]

Stephanie smiled at herself for being surprised at Bob Caraway's comments; she'd simply collected some additional evidence that her profession had a monumental education problem. The public, and particularly the auditors' clients, need to be made aware of what CPAs do and what an audit is. How else can clients be certain that they are receiving the desired and required services for their company? How can they possibly know who they should hire as a CPA if they do not understand the services provided? Stephanie remembered an MBA student who had come by the other day and asked, "I don't plan on being a public accountant, so is there any reason for taking an auditing course? Would I get anything out of it? I plan on starting my own business down the line."

[1]Dan M. Guy, Patricia E. Harris, and Doyle Z. Williams, "Client Perceptions of a Local CPA Firm," *CPA Journal*, March, 1979, p. 18.

The answer to the student's question of whether to take an auditing course is definitely yes; learning about auditing can be useful to people other than public accountants, as this chapter will explain. This knowledge is useful to those preparing to be internal auditors for the private and public sectors, to those who use audit reports, to those who must select an auditor (as well as auditing and related services), and to those who work with auditors. First, we shall review the audit process and describe the general standards, including relevant economic and financial concepts. The intent is to develop a strong theoretical foundation for your understanding of the audit product. In the Appendix, we shall explore career planning, especially the available opportunities and recent research on who stays in public accounting.

General Definition

An *audit* is an examination to determine the propriety of representations. Typically, these representations are financial, and an *external auditor* issues an independent report on the fairness with which the management's financial statements have been presented ***[SAS 1, Section 110]***. The more traditional definition of auditing is the process by which competent, independent individuals collect and evaluate evidential matter to form an opinion as to the degree of correspondence between what is observed and established criteria. This definition indicates that an audit process can be applied to nonfinancial data and does not require that an external party be involved. *Internal auditors* are employees of an entity who audit an entity's operations and overall control system as a service to its management. In addition to performing financial audits, internal auditors often perform *operational audits,* which assess the efficiency and effectiveness of the entity's operations, focusing on nonfinancial statistics and procedures. Internal auditors also do a great deal of *compliance auditing,* which pertains to financial accounting systems. The purpose of such audits is to test whether the auditees are complying with the prescribed policies and procedures.

Why Study Auditing?

An understanding of auditing is essential to the accounting major intending to pursue public accounting as a career. Accounting curricula usually require an introductory auditing course, and the Certified Public Accountant (CPA) Examination has a section on auditing. Furthermore, most entry-level public accountants are expected to have had some training in basic auditing. Aside from such practical considerations, however, are there other reasons for studying auditing?

Preparing to Be an Auditor

Without the recognized certifications that symbolize professional expertise and knowledge of the audit process, an auditor's professional practice opportunities are limited. Besides the CPA exam, an auditor can sit for the Certified Internal Auditor (CIA) and Certified Management Accounting (CMA) exams, which require a thorough understanding of auditing and systems, respectively. These certifications are for internal auditing and internal accounting positions in controller departments and cost accounting systems and much more. Any businessperson who wants to obtain professional certification in accounting must study auditing and systems. Beyond the basic job training and certification, a knowledge of auditing will improve job efficiency; for example, the external auditor's and the internal auditor's ability to coordinate their activities will reduce the external auditor's fees. This coordination requires an understanding of both external and internal auditing.

Other people, who do not consider themselves auditors, nevertheless may have occasion to use a knowledge of auditing. For example, suppose that you, a manager, suspect that a clerk in your department who is supposed to check the mathematical accuracy of your invoices (billings from suppliers) is not doing his job. Based on your study of auditing, you should know how to draw a statistical sample (a subset of billings typical of all invoices) and how to audit the clerk's compliance with his job responsibilities. Similarly, assume that you had reason to believe that the edit checks that were supposed to be in the computer program to avoid payments to unauthorized parties were not operating effectively. For example, if a payment were made to a supplier who was not on an approved listing, the computer would be expected to report that payment as an exception. Your knowledge of auditing in regard to test data and other audit tools for examining EDP systems could prove invaluable in confirming your suspicions. For instance, you could submit test data, including some payments to unauthorized suppliers, in order to see whether or not an exception report were generated. If it were not, your suspicions would be confirmed. In other words, you need not be a full-time auditor to find auditing skills useful in your career.

Using Audit Reports

Audit reports (introduced in Chapter 2) are a common sight to investors, creditors, and government officials, as they appear in the annual reports of all companies regulated by the Securities and Exchange Commission (SEC) and with the financial statements of many municipalities, privately owned corporations, partnerships, and nonprofit enterprises. If "properly" interpreted, audit reports help investors, creditors, and donors in the decision-making process. You probably already know that the purpose of an external audit is to verify independently an entity's financial statements. But you probably do not yet know how this is done. Auditors perform tests of transactions rather than examine all transactions. For example, by recomputing the depreciation expense for a sample of assets, the auditor can draw a conclusion regarding the total depreciation expense.

You may not yet know, either, that auditors cannot ensure that any defalcations, or fraud, will be disclosed by an audit. In evaluating risk, an astute investor who has a basic knowledge of auditing will understand that the probability of fraud is greater than zero, despite the existence of an auditor's report. Yet the reliability of the information can be expected to be greater, owing to the performance of an audit, than it would have been otherwise. Any information that can improve the estimation of risk can enhance the return from investment decisions. According to finance theory, better risk estimates permit investors to diversify more wisely their portfolio of investments and thus to earn a higher return for a given level of risk.

Bankers also may find it useful to know something about auditing. Banks are subject to regulations regarding what documentation must be retained to support lending decisions. Such regulations may require different types of CPA services, including an audit report. Trustees who are responsible for investing other people's funds in venture capital projects or private companies often require audited financial statements from such investment (or credit) prospects. To interpret existing regulations and the public's expectations and to determine whether they are being met, such users of financial statements must be able to discern the difference between audited and unaudited financial statements and to interpret managements' and auditors' disclosures. If a company is discredited because its audit report contains a qualification that is not understood by the user, the company may be needlessly penalized. And a banker or trustee may forgo higher earnings by excluding that company. On the other hand, if a disclaimer, or a qualified audit report (described in Chapter 2), is accepted when an unqualified, or "clean," report is required, the user of the auditor's report may be liable for the consequences of not complying with the regulations.

Consider an analogy with the user of a realtor's appraisal of some property. The appraisal's usefulness or reliability is likely to depend on both the realtor's reputation and the procedures used in making the appraisal. The typical user of such an appraisal may well require that the realtor

- Visit the property.
- Document transactions involving adjacent or similar properties.
- Review surveyors', engineers', buyers', and other professionals' reports concerning the possible and allowable uses of the property.
- Submit a detailed report regarding the basis for the appraisal.

The user of an audit report may find the same sort of detail in regard to the particular procedures performed by the auditors to be helpful when interpreting their findings. And of course, one means of understanding auditors' reports on companies in which resources may be invested is to study auditing. CPAs report their use of generally accepted auditing standards (GAAS), which will mean very little to a person who has not studied the audit process. In the case of the property appraisal, based on an understanding of what the realtor did and did not do, the user of the appraisal can augment the information set used for the investment decision from other sources. Without an understanding of what an auditor does or does not do, it is difficult for the report user to determine what other information should be acquired for an investment decision. For example, a long-term creditor may want assurance that the internal accounting control system of a company is adequate to produce reliable monthly financial statements. If that creditor has studied auditing, (s)he knows that the auditor may have chosen not to rely on controls of the company. In fact, the auditor may have located material weaknesses in the control system and, nevertheless, could have issued an unqualified ("clean") audit report. A *material weakness* is a condition in which specific control procedures do not reduce to a relatively low level the risk that material errors could occur and not be detected on a timely basis. A sophisticated creditor would know that (s)he should require a CPA's report as to whether any material weaknesses were communicated to the company and should consider requiring the company to engage a CPA to report on the adequacy of the internal accounting control system. While reports on internal control are not commonly required by creditors, the point being made is that users of audit reports need to understand what can and cannot be assumed based on an unqualified audit report. With no knowledge of auditing, the user might assume that controls were adequate and inappropriately rely on monthly financial statements in decision making; the consequence could very well be a significant loss of funds and/or reputation by the user of the audit report.

The users of audit reports are frequently subject to regulations that require the use of audited financial statements as input to the decision process. For example, Florida's Department of Transportation requires that audit reports be provided by contractors who are submitting competitive bids to do construction work. Unless decision makers at such governmental agencies can read and interpret such reports appropriately, the department could forgo a savings due to erroneously rejecting a low bidder. For example, some qualifications of audit reports do not reflect adversely on an auditee. Yet an operating rule that only contractors with "clean" reports be accepted could evolve out of ignorance, leading to the rejection of financially sound low bidders. One means of avoiding such errors is to acquire an understanding of the audit function.

Selecting an Auditor

In the introduction to this chapter, Bob Caraway stated that he had selected his CPA from his golf foursome, that he had known him for years and had employed his daughter as an assistant bookkeeper and receptionist. Social contacts are one means of finding a CPA, but certainly, friendship alone is not an appropriate criterion for establishing a professional relationship. Just as a patient needing cardiac bypass surgery is unlikely to entrust her operation to her friend the podiatrist, a business person should not assume that his company can be best served by his friend the CPA. Just as physicians' practices vary, CPAs' practices also vary. For example, a particular CPA firm may prepare only unaudited financial statements, service only non-SEC clients, offer only tax or estate tax services, or otherwise restrict the firm's practice.

Had Bob Caraway studied auditing, he would have been aware of the differences in CPAs' services. He also would have realized that Tom Hill might not have been a good choice as the auditor for Caraway Motors, because he could not claim independence from the company, as his daughter worked there as an assistant bookkeeper. If Bob Caraway's banker knew that Tom Hill's daughter worked as an assistant bookkeeper for Bob Caraway, he probably would not consider Tom sufficiently independent to render an audit report on Caraway Motors. The banker most likely would prefer another CPA, one who had no family tie to members of Caraway Motors' accounting department. Had Bob Caraway been more aware of the purpose of the audit, he would have recognized the possible adverse consequences of hiring a CPA who did not appear to be independent. A CPA who is deemed to be lacking in independence is required to issue a *disclaimer* (a report stating that the auditor is unable to express an opinion on the financial statements) rather than an audit report, which, by definition, is intended to be an independent CPA's attestation. However, many CPA services, other than an audit, can be provided by a CPA who is not independent, although such a lack of independence must often be disclosed. The point of our example is to illustrate that without some understanding of auditing, decision makers will find it difficult to select the best CPA.

You may wonder who typically selects the independent auditor. A survey[2] of 1,979 companies reported that 73 percent of the 239 companies that had an audit committee used this special committee of the board of directors to select or recommend the CPA firm to be employed. Audit committees of boards of directors are usually made up of board members who are not officers or employees. In this survey, of the remaining sample without audit committees, the CPA firm was selected or recommended by

- The board of directors in 29 percent of the companies.
- The chief financial officer in 23 percent of the companies.
- The president or chairperson in 10 percent of the companies.
- The treasurer in 9 percent of the companies.
- The controller in 9 percent of the companies.
- The president and chief financial officer together in 10 percent of the companies.
- Other combinations of executives in 10 percent of the companies.

For smaller businesses, the management often chooses the CPA firm. Hence, numerous business people may be asked at some point in their careers to select a CPA firm. Exhibit 1-1 summarizes those factors that have been cited as affecting the selection and retention of CPAs. Other studies have cited recommendations from the Internal Revenue Service.[3] Larger CPA firms are reportedly selected on account of their national coverage, international facilities, and company and industry knowledge (in addition to the factors cited in Exhibit 1-1).[4] Exhibit 1-2 lists the principal reasons that enterprises gave for switching auditors. Survey research in 1967 indicated that from 1955 to 1963, management change and the need for additional services accounted for over 63 percent of the seventy-six auditor switches by the *Fortune* 500

EXHIBIT 1-1

Factors Affecting the Selection and Retention of CPAs

	% of Small Business Respondents*	% of Practitioner Respondents*
Personal Contact (Accessibility)	41	30 (2)
Reputation (Competence, Quality, Integrity, Creativity)	36	17 (5, 4, 1, 1)
Prior Relationship (Timely Completion)	25	3 (1)
Recommended by Banker or Attorney	21	---
Recommended by Other Clients	16	---
Location	13	---
Range of Services	12	13
Industry Expertise (Experience, Adequacy of Trained Personnel)	9	5 (16, 2)
Fee	7	---
Small Business's Parent Company	3	---

*Total exceeds 100 percent because of multiple responses.

Note: The basis for selecting an outside accountant was reported by 993 small businesses (average annual sales of $5.1 million) and compared with the criteria proposed by 440 practitioners (having a median number of clients of 269).

From Bradford W. Ketchum, Jr., "You and Your Accountant," *Inc.*, March 1982, pp. 84, 86.

[2] George Hobgood and Joseph A. Sciarrino, "Management Looks at Audit Services," *Financial Executive*, April 1972, pp. 26–32.

[3] Dan M. Guy, Patricia E. Harris, and Doyle Z. Williams, "Client Perceptions of a Local CPA Firm," *CPA Journal*, March 1979, p. 18.

[4] Robert W. Taylor and G. Clark Thompson, "Company Relationships with Public Accountants," *Journal of Accountancy*, October 1962, pp. 67–69.

EXHIBIT 1-2
Principal Reasons for Switching Auditors

Explanation	Percentage of clients reporting this explanation (the sum of these percentages could exceed 100 per cent, as some companies gave more than one explanation)
Change in management or corporate ownership	22.8%
Change in audit fee	18.4%
Change in auditing firm, including	13.7%
-firm dissolved	
-firm set policy of accepting no SEC clientele	
-individual auditor changed and CPA firms and client followed	
-a question concerning independence had arisen	
Need for larger firm, often a "Big 8" firm	10.5%
Desire for a "fresh look" (i.e., the desire to rotate auditors)	9.7%
Dispute between auditor and client, including	7.8%
-accounting issues	
-the audit opinion	
-fees	
Smaller firm preferred, often a local firm	6.5%
Physical move by client	4.9%
Bankruptcy of client	2.7%
Creditor encouraged move; creditors mentioned included underwriters, bankers, venture capitalists, primary lenders, and mortgagors	1.7%
Nonpayment of audit fee	1.3%

Note: An additional 40 clients, beyond the 474 analyzed above, reported that the CPA firm's industry expertise with respect to tax, management, or SEC-related services was a consideration in changing auditors. If these 40 companies were added to the original sample, they would represent 7.8 percent of the total number of auditor changes for which explanations were provided. The rationale for changing auditors is based on 474 explanations reported by clients in *The Public Accounting Report* from May 1978 to January 1980.

companies that were analyzed.[5] The management change factor similarly dominated through 1980.

Selecting Auditing and Related Services

Once the CPA firm has been selected, the client company must determine what services it wants performed. Again, in the introduction to this chapter, Bob Caraway noted, "It's nice to know that nobody's ripping us off." If Bob Caraway suspected fraud or defalcation, he should not rely on the audit to detect such problems, for that is not its purpose. Instead, he could hire a CPA to perform a special investigation intended to detect fraud. CPAs offer many services beyond audits and fraud investigations, and Exhibit 1-3 lists some of them.

Unfortunately, as reported in Exhibit 1-4, many clients are unaware of the services that their CPAs offer. Consequently, a company may forgo cost savings available from utilizing the management advisory services department of the company's CPA firm. These cost savings come from the knowledge that the CPA firm has already accumulated through its auditing activities regarding the company's operations.

Exhibit 1-5 summarizes companies' proxy disclosures regarding the percentage of audit fees expended for various types of tax and management advisory engagements. This exhibit refers to ASR No. 250, the now discontinued Accounting Series Release of the Securities and Exchange Commission (SEC) which was issued June 29, 1978, entitled "Disclosure of Relationships with Independent Public Accountants." ASRs (now known as FRRs) were the official pronouncements of the *SEC*, which regulates securities markets in the United States. ASR No. 250 required each SEC registrant to disclose the services provided to the company during the last fiscal year by its principal independent accountant and the percentage relationship of fees for nonaudit services to audit fees, individually (if over 3 percent) and in the aggregate. But this disclosure requirement recently was removed because of its questionable information content; nonetheless, these statistics reveal the extent to which the CPA firm performing a company's audit was also used to perform tax and management service engagements. The variety of services offered by CPAs is also apparent from such disclosures.

Working with Auditors

Auditors perform their field work at the client's place of business and work with operating personnel and employees at all levels of management. If you take a job in the business, government, or nonprofit sector, it is highly likely that you will work with auditors—external CPAs, regulators' auditors and inspectors, auditors from the *General Accounting Office (GAO)*, and/or internal auditors. The

[5] John C. Burton and William Roberts, "A Study of Auditor Changes," *Journal of Accountancy*, April 1967, p. 34.

EXHIBIT 1-3
The Mix of Services by CPAs

	Total staff of less than 40	Total staff of 40 to 149	Total staff of 150 to 399	Total staff of 400 to 2,499	Total staff of 2,500 or More
	Smaller CPA firms		Medium-sized CPA firms		Large CPA firms
Other accounting services: nonopinion and write-up work	20%	27%	15%	31%	6%
Opinion Audits	37%	42%	48%	36%	66%
Subtotal	57%	69%	63%	67%	72%
Tax	29%	21%	27%	25%	18%
MAS	14%	10%	10%	8%	10%
Total	100%	100%	100%	100%	100%

Note: Average percentage of fees derived from opinion audits, other accounting services (nonopinion and write-up work), tax, and management advisory services (MAS), for a sample of 50 CPA firms. Adapted from statistics presented by Harold E. Arnett and Paul Danos, *CPA Firm Viability* (Ann Arbor: University of Michigan Press, 1979), p. 66.

GAO is the "watchdog of Congress" and audits governmental operations, particularly objectives, effectiveness, efficiency, compliance, and financial matters. Part of your performance evaluation may depend on how effectively you can work with different types of auditors. By gaining some understanding of the audit process, you will be better able to work with them and to carry out their requests. Without such an understanding, particularly if the auditors give incomplete or erroneous instructions, costly mistakes could be made. For example, if you (1) scheduled and performed a physical inventory count without notifying the external auditor, (2) destroyed voided checks without regard for the *audit trail* (that documentary evidence that permits an auditor to reconstruct transactions and

EXHIBIT 1-4
Clients' Awareness of Services Available

Type of service	Percentage of clients unaware that such service was offered by their CPA firm
Insurance Analysis	72%
Data-processing Feasibility Studies	73%
Help in Securing Financing	73%
Product Costing and Profitability Analyses	68%
Tax Shelter Analyses	46 to 70%
Estate Planning	46 to 70%
Real Estate Investment Advice	46 to 70%

Constructed from data reported by Dan M. Guy, Patricia E. Harris, and Doyle Z. Williams, "Client Perceptions of a Local CPA Firm," *CPA Journal,* March 1979, pp. 17-22; and based on 299 survey responses from the clientele of a CPA firm located in Lubbock, Texas, which has twenty-five professional staff members and one support personnel.

the related control procedures that have been performed), or (3) mailed out confirmations to customers rather than permitting the CPA to maintain control over the mailing, the consequences would be costly. Most likely, (1) the inventory would have to be recounted, (2) the auditors' procedures would have to be extended with respect to cash disbursements, and (3) the confirmations would have to be remailed. Had you pursued the study of auditing in preparation for your business career, such mistakes might not have been made.

Not only can costly errors be avoided, but means of increasing the efficiency of an audit can be learned through the study of auditing. For example, homogeneity of units of operations may permit cost savings from sampling plans or from the application of the statistical tool of *regression analysis.* By modeling how you expect each unit of operation to perform based on all other operating units, regression analysis can flag unexpected operating results that require investigation. You could realize cost savings by suggesting that such tools be applied similarly by the auditors. You may be aware of a preferred way of defining the *sampling unit* that would make it easier for your company to retrieve requested documents. For example, the auditor might test disbursements by sampling from the paid invoice file or from the canceled check file. You can provide information as to which is likely to be more efficient. Because of your in-depth knowledge of the company's accounting and filing system, as well as your understanding of the auditing objectives of the statistical sampling plan, you would have a comparative advantage in identifying a variety of means by which audit effectiveness and efficiency could be improved.

A final aspect of interfacing with the auditor concerns your evaluation of the CPA's performance. Most companies continually review the CPA's activities and decide, on an annual basis, whether or not they wish to retain their auditors. Although changes in auditors are infrequent, as reported in Exhibit 1-2, reasons do arise for changing auditors. A basic understanding of the audit process provides a basis for evaluating whether or not an auditor is doing a good job.

An Overview of the Audit Process

To this point, the emphasis has been upon why the study of auditing should be pursued. Only a very general definition of auditing has been provided. Now an overview of the audit process will be outlined as a means of suggesting the potential value of this type of "examination." The perspective of the public accountant will dominate the overview, although many facets of the process relate to internal auditing as well.

Understanding the Client's Operations

The first step in any audit engagement is understanding your client's operations. What is your client's business, and how are current economic conditions likely to affect it? What are the key financial statement items, and how well supported are management's dollar representations? Which financial and nonfinancial statistics does your client routinely maintain? How is your client organized physically and organizationally? Has your client been in a growth trend or in a slump, and what problems do such trends suggest?

EXHIBIT 1-5
Evidence From ASR No. 250 Disclosures in Proxy Statements Issued October 1, 1978

Type of nonaudit services disclosed	Percentage of *Fortune* 1,300 companies reporting such services		Percentage of 3,019 companies not in *Fortune* 1,300 reporting such services	Percentage of audit fees expended for such services
Employee benefit plan audit, including actuarial services (total sample)		1%		2%
Tax (total sample)		77%		10%
– Corporate tax return, preparation, and review	56%		61%	
– Corporate planning and consultation	61%		39%	
– Other corporate tax services	37%		23%	
– Individual tax services:				
– For expatriate employees	14%		1%	
– For U.S. employees	14%		4%	
Management advisory services (total sample)		36%		8%
– Management planning* and organizational controls	29%		13%	
– Financial and accounting systems and controls	22%		11%	
– Data systems consulting	18%		8%	
– Human resource systems	16%		7%	
– Operational systems and controls	10%		4%	
– Actuarial services	2%		1%	
– Other (acquisition, merger, and divestiture programs; expert testimony; special investigations; and comprehensive operations analysis)	—		—	1%

*Included assistance in developing financial projections, forecasts, feasibility evaluations, and modeling systems,as well as advice or assistance related to the application of quantitative methods. Statistics, statistical sampling, probability, simulation methods, and operations research are commonly used to evaluate quantitatively management decision alternatives.

From Scott S. Cowen, "Nonaudit Services: How Much Is Too Much?" *Journal of Accountancy*, December 1980, pp. 51–56.

Assessing Risk Exposure

Because of such inquiries as those in the preceding paragraph, the auditor is able to make an initial assessment of risks and to rank the various sources of the risk exposure ***[SAS 47, Section 312]***. *Audit risk* is the risk that the auditor may unknowingly fail to modify the auditor's opinion regarding financial statements that are materially misstated. *Materiality* is a professional judgment regarding the magnitude of omission or misstatement that would be likely to change or influence the judgment of a reasonable person relying on the information. Audit risk and materiality are important considerations in planning an audit and evaluating its results.

As an example of an indicator of risk exposure, consider a client with both a growth in recorded receivables and an increase in the age of these receivables. Such a client may have a collectibility problem. The risk of an understated allowance for doubtful accounts could be significant. Similarly, if interest expense has increased recently without adequate working capital arrangements, the client's risk of becoming insolvent is greater. Often managers' and employees' incentives are clues to potential risks. For example, the presence of profit-sharing plans that have a floor and a ceiling on profit-based bonuses can create incentives to "smooth." *Smoothing,* which has also been termed *window dressing,* means that numbers are slightly distorted in order to achieve a steady trend, such as a slow upward growth line. In this way, the managers can maximize the bonuses received and not forgo bonuses because a ceiling has been exceeded. If a ceiling is reached, efforts are made to "smooth" the growth by deferring the revenue to a future period. The auditor's concern is whether such "smoothing" practices will result in significant misstatements.

Besides employees' incentives—which may come from union activities, merger negotiations, or other similar events—investors' incentives may also cause concern. Whenever a client suffers a misfortune, investors have a greater incentive to try to recoup their losses, by claiming, for example, a misstatement of the financial statements or an "audit failure." The auditor must be alert to risks that stem from the various user groups of an entity's financial statements. Generally, a public company is expected to pose a greater risk because it has a more diverse group of users than a private company does. Auditors' reports on public companies are regularly read by the SEC, bondholders, stockholders, prospective creditors and investors, underwriters, and the general public. In contrast, private companies tend to limit the distribution of their auditors' reports, and many of their users are familiar with the company's operations.

The auditor's tools to investigate a client's operations include the observation of physical facilities and available documentation concerning operations, as well as inquiry procedures regarding the client's management, employees, creditors, and numerous other third-party relationships with professional advisers, competitors, and customers. Observation requires sufficient expertise to determine whether assets are what they are claimed to be. Hence, an auditor of a jewelry shop may need to hire a gemologist to assist in observation procedures. Inquiry procedures, when directed toward managers, are corroborated by other audit steps. For example, an auditor may review a Dun & Bradstreet credit report on a client. The use of ratio analysis and both regression analysis and similar time series or trend analysis techniques can be helpful in determining a client's risk exposure due to unusual changes in operations or financial representations. *Ratio analysis* compares data interrelationships across time and across industry competitors; for example, the return on sales, the level of working capital, and the percentage of bad debts might be analyzed. Some CPAs have used bankruptcy prediction models as a means of assessing the risk of insolvency.

Studying and Evaluating Internal Accounting Control

The second phase in the audit process is studying and evaluating the internal accounting controls. The concept of control spans from having competent employees who are aware of their respective responsibilities, to the actual compliance of an individual employee with a single prescribed duty, such as checking the math on an invoice before forwarding it to the department responsible for paying it. The *control environment* encompasses the enterprise's organizational structure, the methods used to communicate responsibility and authority, and the methods used for supervision, including an internal audit function, if present. A good internal accounting system will be designed to maintain a complete and accurate accounting system and to safeguard assets and records, establishing accountability for all of the entity's assets. The second standard of field work requires that the system of internal accounting control be studied and evaluated. By this means, the auditor can judge the control environment and the flow of transactions but need not document the general design of those controls if no reliance is planned ***[SAS 43, Section 1010].*** The only documentation required is a record of the reasons that the auditor has decided not to extend the minimum required review of controls. This decision commonly rests on an assessment of the efficiency of relying on designed checks and balances within the control system, as compared with the efficiency of testing the financial statement balances being represented. If the reliance on control is thought to be cost justified, detailed documentation of the controls will be prepared. For example, the auditor could test the controls of fixed assets by reviewing the authorization procedures for asset disposals. Or, the auditor could count the physical assets to ensure that there are no unrecorded disposals. The auditor will decide which is the more efficient means for gathering evidence. To make sure that the auditor understands the flow of data through a transaction-processing system and the subsequent appearance of these data in the form of information on the aggregate financial statements, a *walk through* is frequently performed. Just as the name implies, the auditor "walks through" the system, following the documents through the processing trail, until the raw data reach the general ledger of the client's accounting system. The auditor needs to have a general understanding of the various classes of transactions and their methods of authorization, execution, initial recording, and subsequent processing. Based on the study of control design and the walk through, an auditor determines the extent to which the controls must be tested to support the decision to rely on control. In a sense, this is the initial point at which the auditor plans the extent, nature, and timing of the tests of both controls and financial statement transactions and balances. *Extent* refers to the scope of the testing, and *nature* refers to the type of procedures applied. *Timing* pertains to whether some of the audit work can be performed before year-end (this is referred to as *interim work*). Their determination rests on the evaluation of risk and materiality.

When Relying on Controls, Performing and Evaluating Compliance Tests

The third phase, evaluating controls, is the testing of the client's compliance with internal accounting controls. This phase is optional, as no compliance testing is required if the auditor decides not to rely on controls. The *compliance testing* is based on a sampling, which means that only some of the total number of transactions are selected for testing. For example, the auditor might examine fifty purchase orders to see whether they have been initialed to indicate that they were properly approved. If five documents were not initialed, the auditor would have evidence that the client was not complying with prescribed authorization procedures. If the controls have not been followed to the extent expected, the auditor will have to alter plans for testing the financial statement balances and to do more work in the areas of purchases, accounts payable, and inventory.

Testing Financial Statement Balances

A *direct test of balances* at year-end evaluates the validity and propriety of the accounting treatment of balances and seeks to uncover any material errors and irregularities. For instance, a direct test of cash on hand would count the cash and tie it to the recorded balance. To illustrate how tests of controls mesh with tests of balances to form a total picture, consider a simple review of fixed assets. Compliance tests would focus on the authorizations for and controls over asset additions and disposals. Tests of balances might include a physical inventory of fixed assets (observing and counting assets) and tracing such totals to the recorded assets. *Tracing* means comparing detailed documents, in this case the count sheets, with the accounting records, in this case the fixed assets subsidiary ledger. If the controls are satisfactory, the sampling plan for the physical inventory will yield a lower sample size than that required if there were no controls or if controls were weak. Instead of counting two hundred pieces of equipment, fifty pieces may be deemed to be sufficient. A *sampling plan* outlines the determinants of the sample size and the means by which the sample is to be selected. The results of the compliance and balance tests together provide the basis for judging the fairness of the recorded fixed assets.

Making the Final Review

Once the controls and balances have been tested, there is a basis for a final review of the overall reasonableness of the client's financial statements. An overall review compares the current statements with those of previous years and industry competitors, taking into account any relevant changed conditions.

Tying Up Loose Ends

Tying up the "loose ends" of an audit means documenting the client's and the client's lawyer's representations. This is typically done through formal letters that state what has been said to the auditor and that there has been full disclosure. "To do" points relating to missing steps along the audit process must be completed, and any subsequent events that may require disclosure must be reviewed. For example, if a customer were bankrupt as of year-end and this were not discovered until a date after the year-end, the financial statements would have to be adjusted for material effects. Typically, the auditor will analyze the financial statements at the end of field work (the collection of evidence at the client's premises) in a manner similar to that of the first review of the management's preaudit representations. In other words, ratio analysis, regression analysis, account interrelationships, and the matching of numbers with expectations, in light of the auditor's understanding of the business, are all common audit approaches.

Forming an Audit Opinion

The audit opinion relates to the set of financial statements and is communicated in a standardized report form. The audit process is illustrated in Exhibit 1-6. The diagram is overly simple, though it does outline the auditor's approach and the capability of the audit process to enhance the reliability of financial statements. And in order to understand the audit process, you need to be aware of the framework of generally accepted auditing standards within which that process is applied.

EXHIBIT 1-6
The Audit Process

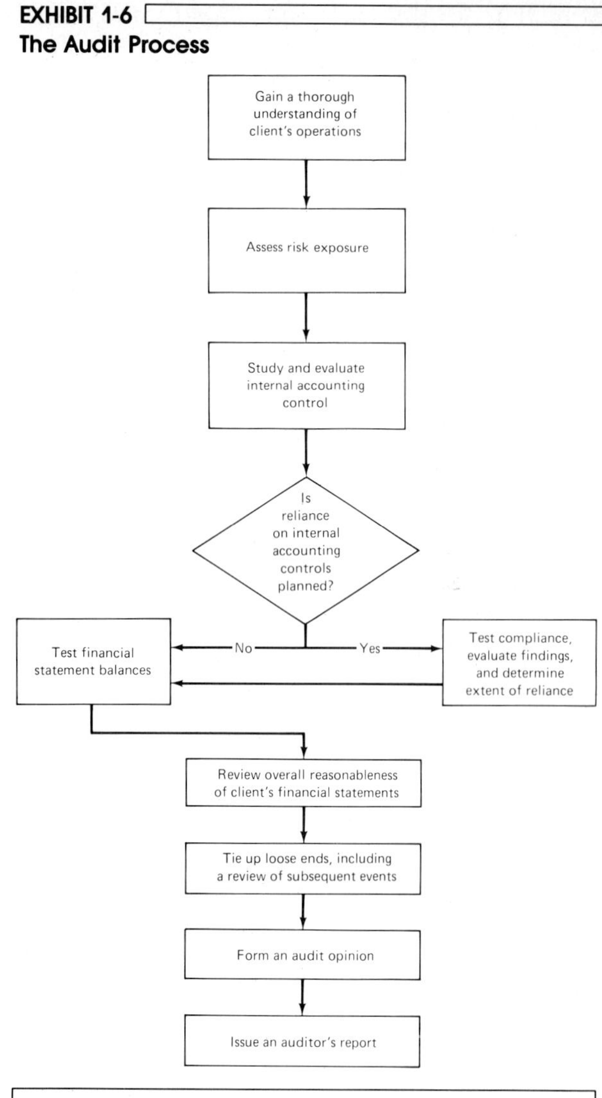

Standards

Standards are benchmarks by which the quality of performance can be measured and the achievement of objectives can be documented ***[SAS 1, Section 201]***. By using standards, an auditor can determine the professional qualities necessary for effective audit performance, the judgments by which the conduct of the examination will be planned and will progress, and the means by which the findings of the audit can be effectively communicated. Personal, or *general standards* are directed at the professional's personal characteristics and emphasize the auditor's qualifications and quality of audit work. It is assumed that generally accepted auditing procedures will be applied with professional competence by properly trained persons.

Procedures are the particular acts or methodologies that skilled accountants use to gather audit evidence. *Procedural standards* refer both to the broad objectives obtained by applying particular audit procedures and to reporting responsibilities. The auditing standards that control the nature and extent of the evidence obtained through audit procedures by means of the field work and the examination are the *standards of field work.* Those auditing standards that refer to the reports on field work are called *standards of reporting.*

General Standards

The first general standard states that the examination is to be performed by a person or persons having adequate technical training and proficiency as an auditor ***[SAS 1, Section 210].*** No matter how talented a businessperson may be, if that person is to be an auditor, training and experience in the field of auditing are essential. A rigorous course of professional study will encompass technical training as well as an adequate amount of general education. Obviously, the requisite experience is generally unavailable to the newly hired staff auditor, yet the competency standard can be met through proper supervision and review of the new assistant's work by an experienced auditor.

The professional certification process is expected to ensure that this standard will be met. You must satisfy both educational and experience requirements in order to be licensed to practice as a CPA. However, the first general standard also envisions the continuing education of professionals, in order that their training can be maintained at an adequate level after the initial certification.

The second general standard states that in all matters relating to the assignment, the auditor or auditors must maintain an independent mental attitude ***[SAS 1, Section 220].*** In order for auditors to be independent, they must be unbiased with respect to their clients and objectively consider facts as the determinants of an audit opinion. Intellectual honesty is the essence of independence; the traditional signal of independence used to be the CPAs' working for themselves (i.e., "hanging out their shingles"), rather than being hired as employees of their clients. But beyond being independent in fact, CPAs must also be recognized by others as being independent. The profession has established certain guidelines that state when a CPA is presumed to lack independence. For example, CPAs should not have a financial interest in a client's business and should not perform services on a contingent fee basis. Statement on Auditing Standards No. 1 explains the meaning of independence:

> Independence does not imply the attitude of a prosecutor, but rather a judicial impartiality that recognizes an obligation for fairness not only to the management and owners [shareholders] of a business, but also to creditors and those who may otherwise rely (in part, at least) upon the independent auditor's report, as in the case of prospective owners or creditors.[6]

The third general standard states that due professional care is to be exercised in performing the examination and preparing the report ***[SAS 1, Section 230].*** *Due audit care* includes both what the auditors do and how well they do it. In large part, their performance will be evaluated in regard to the procedural standards governing field work and reporting responsibilities. In exercising due care, both the work performed and the supervision of that work at all levels must be critically reviewed, with emphasis on the judgment of those involved in the examination. The importance of the review reflects the relationship of responsibility to authority, as well as the value of audit experience as a quality control over the examination.

As each of the procedural standards is considered throughout your study of auditing, keep in mind that the auditor's concern for due care requires assurance that the proper procedures have been employed, that such procedures were tailored to the circumstances and were properly applied and coordinated, and that the client's accounting procedures and disclosures are appropriate and adequate. Beyond a focus on audit procedures and reporting, the due audit care standard applies to the *working papers* that document the audit process. The design, format, substance, and control of working papers help demonstrate that the due audit care standard has been met.

Why Audit?

Microeconomics suggests that a commodity is produced as a consequence of the market forces that reflect the consumers' valuation of that good.

[6] AICPA, "Independence," SAS 1 (New York: AICPA, November 1972), AU§220.05.

Regulations can influence or alter these market forces. If you are familiar with the Securities & Exchange Commission (SEC), you are probably aware that preparation and certification of financial statements are required by the Securities Act of 1934.

Many people have asserted that auditing exists solely because of such SEC regulation. Yet this assertion can be refuted by observing the free market before the SEC's requirements for certification of financial statements and by focusing on the unregulated sectors of today's economy, including both private and public entities.

Evidence of Demand

The accounting profession easily dates back to the first exchange transaction, and auditing has been traced back to as early as 500 B.C. In the Greek city-state of Athens, revenues and expenditures were verified by three boards of accountants. Later, auditing developed in Italy as a means of verifying the accountability of the ship captains returning to Europe from the Old World with their riches. Without auditing, trade would have developed much more slowly, and without some means of ensuring the accountability of their agents, most traders would have been hesitant to entrust their resources to others. (An *agent* is any individual who is entrusted with another's—the principal's—resources.) This historical profile speaks to the audit's economic role even in the absence of regulation. Indeed, before such regulation, in the United States, as early as 1899, over 183 public accountants were practicing in New York City, and 71 were practicing in Chicago, all primarily involved in performing audits.[7]

Although the auditor's role may seem obvious, it is a concept that has been overshadowed by misconceptions concerning the establishment of the SEC. The SEC was created in the aftermath of the Great Depression, as the government's "solution" to the problem that created the Depression. It was claimed to be an agency that would initially force businesses to provide audited information to investors and thus that would effectively curb the reporting scandals of the past. Yet not only did legislators fail to include evidence of one so-called reporting scandal in the voluminous testimonies directed at the "need" for a SEC, they also managed to ignore an empirical fact: In 1926, according to *Moody's Manuals*, 82 percent of the firms traded on the New York Stock Exchange had already been audited by the CPAs, and this percentage grew to 94 percent before the federal legislators had even commenced their deliberations on the proposed SEC. Although the SEC is widely acclaimed as having been the impetus for fair reporting practices, before regulation, the free market alone had led to the prevailing business practice of presenting audited financial statements.[8]

Currently, the evidence of a market demand for audits is that audits are common in segments of the economy that are not subject to the SEC. For example, 80 percent of the corporate audit clients of Price Waterhouse are not registered with the SEC. As Price Waterhouse is one of the so-called Big Eight accounting firms, this statistic points to the great number of voluntary audits. Similarly, in the municipal sector, which is not subject to SEC requirements, audits are common. One research study investigating over one thousand municipalities found that over half had contracted for their initial audit before 1955,[9] that is, well before the recent audit-related requirements of the Federal Revenue Sharing Act. This evidence leads to questions about both the sources of and the rationale for this demand. Why has the market created a demand for audits even when the government has not required them?

Sources of Demand

Economic, finance, and accounting theory help explain why audits are valued in the marketplace. Exhibit 1-7 depicts the four major sources of the

[7]See C. A. Moyer, "Early Developments in American Auditing," *Accounting Review* (January 1951), pp. 3–8.

[8]There is a full report on these findings by George Benston, "The Value of the SEC's Accounting Disclosure Requirements," *Accounting Review,* July 1969, pp. 515–532.

[9]Wanda A. Wallace, "The Timing of Initial Audits of Municipalities: An Empirical Test," *Research in Governmental and Nonprofit Accounting* (forthcoming).

EXHIBIT 1-7
Determinants of Demand

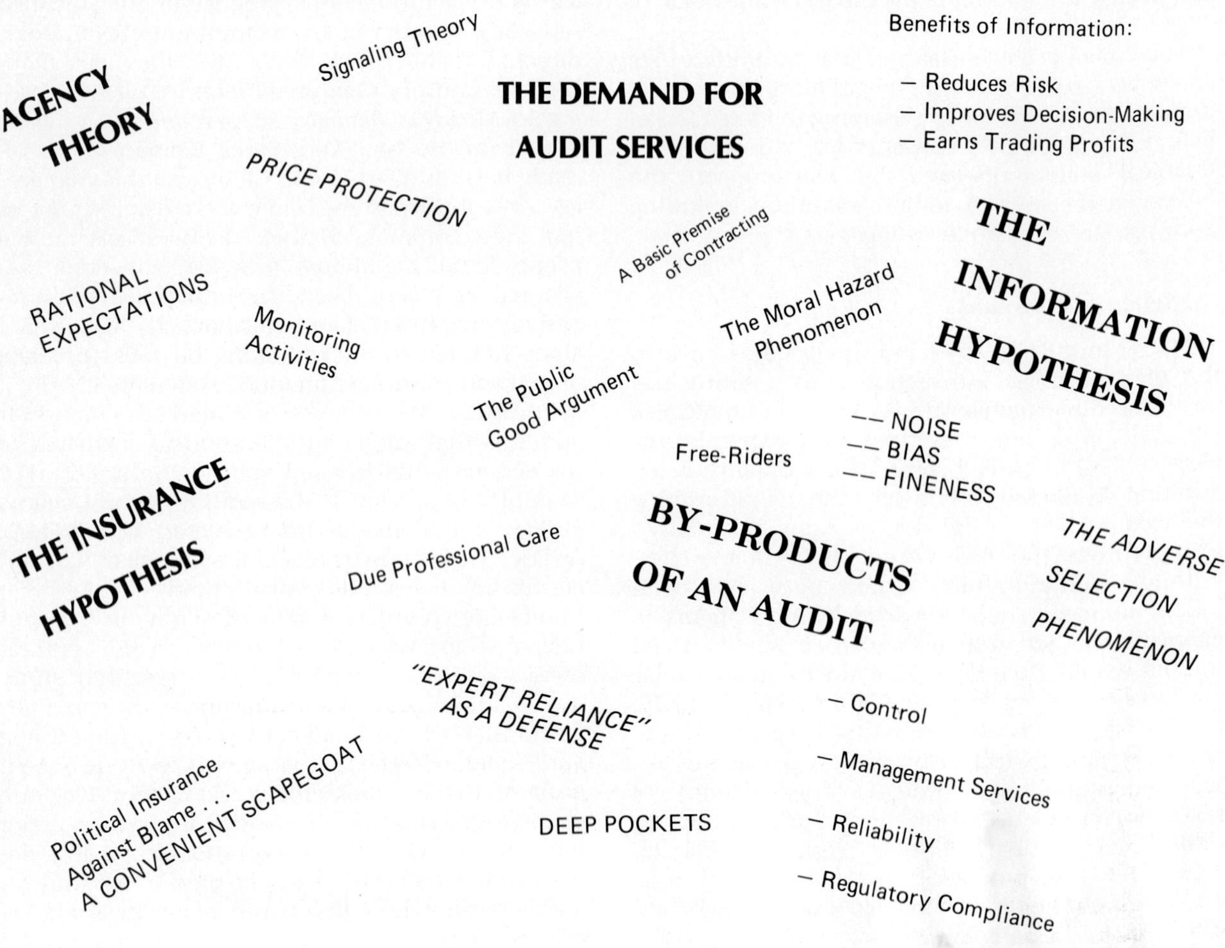

"The origin of auditing goes back to times scarcely less remote than that of accounting. . . . Whenever the advance of civilization brought about the necessity of one man being entrusted to some extent with the property of another the advisability of some kind of check upon the fidelity of the former would become apparent." Richard Brown, *A History of Accounting and Accountants* (London: T.T. and E.C. Jack, 1905), p. 75.

demand for audits and the related theoretical jargon pertaining to each source.[10] *Agency theory* refers to the stewardship function of handling others' resources on their behalf. It is closely related to the

[10] Additional development of these concepts appear in Wanda A. Wallace, *The Economic Role of the Audit in Free and Regulated Markets* (Touche Ross & Co. Aid to Education Program, 1980).

economic theory of *rational expectations,* which formalizes the idea that people learn from their past experiences and mistakes and, therefore, cannot be repeatedly "fooled" or "ripped off." It is assumed that the market will analyze all of the information available to it and create a "rational expectation" of values. This implies that if a company disseminated fraudulent reports, their users might be "fooled" once, but thereafter they would never again accept any information provided by that entity. Similarly, in any principal/agent relationship, the principal will use all available information to predict the agent's actions. Based on this expectation, the principal (such as the owner of a company) will set a compensation level or wage for the manager, or agent, that will *price-protect* the principal from any future adverse actions by the agent. Because the agent is thereby penalized for this "expected divergent behavior," regardless of his or her intentions, the agent has reason to make information available to the principal that will ensure that the agent has not and will not take such adverse actions. An example of divergent behavior is a manager's acceptance of unrecorded "kickbacks" from suppliers or the purchase of elaborate furnishings for the manager's office. But one means of providing assurance to the principal that such actions will not be taken is to undergo an audit.

Besides the agency-related cost savings that accrue from audits, audits also provide information. The role of information theory in our society is evident: it is the core of decision making, and efforts are constantly being made to upgrade the quality of information. The attributes of information, as cited in the collage, include noise, bias, and fineness. *Noise* is essentially an error in measurement; *bias* is a one-sided misstatement; and *fineness* is the extent to which the information measures the substance of the relevant subject in a manner that can be analyzed and compared. The nature of the audit process is conducive to minimizing the errors and hence the noise in reported financial numbers. An auditor's objectivity can be expected to offset the natural optimism, or bias, that can result from unmonitored disclosures by managers. The fineness, or information content of financial disclosures, can be enhanced by using standards and consistency in measuring performance, through the audit process. The auditor's practice of testing to ascertain that a client's financial statements comply with generally accepted accounting principles (GAAP) is one means of improving the information content of annual reports.

Despite such information advantages, the theory of information economics identifies certain barriers to the production of information that can carry over to the production function for auditing. A *public good* is said to exist whenever one person's consumption of a good does not reduce another person's consumption. In economics, a common example is national defense as a public good. Similarly, audited financial statements have public-good characteristics: An individual's use of information to rebalance an investment portfolio does not diminish the value of that same information to other users for rearranging their portfolios. The public-good argument is that no user of financial statements should be excluded from access to such statements once they are produced. But, if no users are excluded, then a *free-rider problem* can arise. Who will incur the initial cost of producing information if all are guaranteed the use of that information once it is produced? An example is public television. Because everyone has free access to public television, there is no means to ensure that all individuals will pay their "fair share," and doubtlessly some will "free-ride." If one were to base the decision of whether or not public television should exist, or even be expanded, on the total contributions made by viewers, "underproduction" would be the result. This would be because the benefits accruing to the noncontributors would not be considered in the decision. This free-rider problem, coupled with the desirability of unlimited access to public goods, is often cited as a rationale for regulation.

The claim that businesses were not producing enough information was the primary rationale for creating the SEC, even though no one knew by how much this information was underproduced. The pre-1934 market evidence suggests that financial data were often audited voluntarily. In fact, information economics provides no less than four reasons that despite free-rider problems, companies voluntarily offer substantial financial disclosures.

Perhaps the most telling rationale is known as the *adverse selection phenomenon,* often referred to as the "market for lemons." This is an economic theory that describes why used cars can be sold for so much less than new cars can. Most car purchasers assume that cars enter the used car market largely because they caused problems for the current owner. Thus the expectation is that most used cars are lemons, and this prediction forces used car prices downward. If you own a "good used car," you are unlikely to be tempted to sell it because of the low average price in the market, but if you have a real lemon, you will readily sell it and consider yourself "way ahead." Hence, there is adverse selection in the used car market. To reverse the phenomenon, it must be possible for the seller of the high-quality used car to demonstrate that his car is different from those low-quality cars generally believed to dominate the market. This used car example can easily be transferred to the stock market. Rather than experience some "average deflated stock price," businesses, in general, have incentives to provide information.

Signaling theory describes how, in regard to the quality of the item being sold, the *asymmetry of information* between the buyer and the seller can be balanced. Signaling includes the issuance of audited financial statements and is one way of improving the buyer's information set (that is, making the availability of information for buyers less asymmetrical or unbalanced in relation to that for sellers).

There may be problems with false signaling. A classic story involves the Rothschild banking interests who, needless to say, were greatly interested in the outcome of the Battle of Waterloo and its effects on the prices of securities traded on the London Stock Exchange.[11] The effect of the battle clearly would be cataclysmic, and it was well known that the Rothschilds would be the first to find out who the victor was. The dilemma facing the Rothschilds was how they could be assured of benefiting from the information they obtained. The answer was to induce the market to go in the wrong direction, relative to the true direction. By selling some investments, the Rothschilds deceived the market into selling and so then were able to make substantial returns on the true information by buying investments at very deflated values. The "false signal" problem illustrated by this story can permeate financial statements if the signals that the statements disclosed cannot be verified. Hence, the audit has evolved as a signal that is available to business to demonstrate its fairness of financial statement presentation and overall quality.

If information signals were not produced, the overall volume of business could be expected to decline geometrically. The *theory of contract* requires that the service contracted be described in a manner that permits the parties to observe whether or not the contract has been fulfilled. The role of audited financial statements in facilitating contractual terms with creditors and employees is apparent from the many *bond convenants* and management compensation plans that are based on audited financial numbers. Bond covenants are restrictions placed on the borrower by the bondholders. A typical covenant is a restriction on the amount of dividends that can be declared by a corporation. Despite the principal's ability to price-protect against an agent's divergent actions, the *moral hazard phenomenon* suggests that some monitoring still is necessary. This phenomenon is usually applied to the insurance industry, in which the fear is that the manager of an insured company will expend less effort or money on safety precautions, simply because he or she has insurance. Unless the manager has incentives to take precautions and the insurer has some means to monitor the precautions taken, they cannot draw up a mutually agreeable contract. For example, higher insurance premiums are levied against those types of construction that are more prone to damage by fire, and lower rates may be offered to those installing certain types of fire or burglary alarms. Yet, without monitoring, the insured individuals may fail to maintain such systems properly. Perhaps the best way to understand the implications of the contracting and agency dimensions of the demand for auditing is to picture the modern corporation without monitoring activities. What is to prevent a manager—the agent—from selling all of the assets with which he or she has been entrusted, pocketing the proceeds, and claiming that there were "huge business losses" when ques-

[11] Cited by Robert E. Verrecchia, "The Rapidity of Price Adjustments to Information," working paper at the University of Chicago, November 1979.

tioned by the creditors and stockholders? If this could be done easily, absentee ownership would have been unlikely to develop, and today's technology could easily have been postponed for decades, if not centuries. As information capabilities and monitoring techniques improve, the ability to pool and administer effectively large amounts of resources also increases. One element of this information and monitoring capability is the audit process.

Beyond the implications of agency and information theory for the demand for audits, an *insurance hypothesis* has descriptive power. Perhaps foremost, should litigation occur, is the ability of creditors, owners, or other third parties to apply the defense of "expert reliance," thereby shifting the liability to the auditor. *Expert reliance* simply means that the parties claim to have relied on the expert, who in this setting is the CPA. The auditor often has special appeal in such a case, because of the perception that auditing firms have "deep pockets." In other words, they have a lot of money available for their claimants, including large amounts of professional liability insurance coverage. But, the most intriguing aspect of the insurance hypothesis addresses the political insurance provided by the audit process.

When the SEC was established, the government could have become the target for criticism whenever a fraud was discovered in the securities market or a large corporation failed financially. Instead, the SEC prescribed audits by independent public accountants, and by doing so, it effectively shifted the responsibility for politically costly events to the private sector. Through the years, auditors have served as convenient scapegoats whenever there has been a financial scandal. Instead of asking, "Why wasn't the SEC aware of the situation?" people wonder, "Why didn't the auditor discover and reveal the problems?" Government regulators and politicians can insure themselves against blame by requiring that the SEC companies be audited by public accounting firms. Note that this added insurance benefit to politicians is distinct from the impetus for audits that stems from the private sector.

The final source of audit demand, cited in Exhibit 1-6, stems from the product attributes of the audit itself, sometimes referred to as *by-products.* Audits enhance controls, often reduce the costs of such complementary services as tax work or the filing of regulatory reports, and improve the reliability of financial numbers. Of course, the most obvious by-product of the audit is the ability to comply with the regulation requiring such audits! However, the question is which came first, the chicken or the egg? Historically, the audits preceded regulation.

The Role of Regulation

Although many people would insist that the SEC's requirements increase the overall demand for audits, they fail to recognize the cost of regulations. The SEC's statutes increase the cost of producing audit services, as one set of professional standards of auditing guides the examination process for both SEC and non-SEC clients. Companies can avoid the statutes requiring audits by not "going public." When audit costs are increased to the point that their price is not cost beneficial to potential voluntary auditees, the demand by these parties will decline, and the incentive for SEC companies to "go private" will rise. In other words, the higher audit costs that result from regulation may offset the additional demand from SEC clients that is generated by the statutes. But the number of non-SEC companies that might have undergone an audit had it been priced in the absence of regulations cannot be determined. Thus, in light of the cost effect of regulation, in addition to the demand effect, it is unclear whether regulation has increased or decreased the total demand for audits.

External Auditing

The demand for audits has been answered differently in the private and public sectors. Whereas the external certified public accountant (CPA) performs audits in the private sector, the General Accounting Office (GAO) generally performs the federal government's audit. The degree of independence is somewhat different, as the CPA cannot be an employee of the entity being audited, whereas the GAO technically has an employee–employer relationship with the federal government. Other public sectors vary in their use of external CPAs, as opposed to governmental auditors. For example, most states have state auditors. Although some states restrict local governments to state audits unless they obtain special permission to hire a CPA (such as in Ohio), other states encourage local governments to undergo audits by independent CPAs and to submit their reports at the state level (such as in Florida, where state audit activities focus on counties rather than cities). Certain agencies of the federal government have similarly opted for audits by independent CPAs in lieu of, or in addition to, GAO audits. This has, in part, been due to shortages of GAO staff, which preclude an annual review of all federal government operations.

The audit performed by CPAs and the GAO is often complemented by an entity's establishment of an internal audit department. Though intended to be independent to a degree that is analogous to the GAO's status, internal auditors are employees whose responsibility is to audit operations continuously as a service to management. By acting as the constant monitor of an entity's control system, the internal auditor enhances the overall control environment and contributes to a more efficient audit by CPAs and/or the GAO (or similar governmental auditors at the state level).

This text will emphasize external auditing, the service provided by CPAs. The main distinction between the CPA's service and that provided by other professionals is that the CPA performs an attestation on behalf of the public. Although the CPA is hired by the board of directors and management, the auditor's professional responsibilities are to third parties. The CPA has legal responsibilities to creditors, investors, and other users of the auditor's report. The value of the CPA certification is linked to the CPAs' reputation for being independent skilled professionals who apply a set of generally accepted auditing standards in order to ensure that an enterprise's financial statements have been prepared according to a set of generally accepted accounting standards.

The individual who chooses to pursue a public accounting career has elected to serve the marketplace as an independent expert on financial statement and related reporting issues, rather than to serve management. This profession's service orientation to a diverse set of user groups has been a constant challenge to standard-setting bodies and to professionals who strive to provide useful information. Generally, the profession has focused on the investors in business entities who have exercised due care in evaluating the operations of the enterprise in which they are investing, as well as appreciating the various accounting principles that apply to that entity's financial statements. The *due care* or *prudent man* concept recognizes the users' responsibility for exercising reasonable care in collecting and evaluating information; this users' knowledge is assumed when evaluating disclosure needs. In the nonprofit sector, the primary user group to which disclosures are directed tends to be more diverse, including both those who provide the capital for operations and those who utilize its services and facilities. External auditors in the public sector are similarly concerned with a diverse set of users, ranging from the taxpayers to the city council members who are entrusted with budgeting and operational decision making. The recent formation of the Governmental Accounting Standards Board (GASB) is expected to ensure some consistency in reporting practices and to clarify the objectives of financial statements for the public sector.

Regardless of the group to which the auditor's report is directed, it will be an independent review of financial statements for a third party other than the auditee's management. An auditor's report may be addressed to the management of an entity, indicating that the audit was performed on another entity, on behalf of the management, when mergers are being considered. The management of Company A will hire an independent CPA to audit Company B. In such a situation, the auditor's report would appropriately be addressed to the management of Company A—that "third party" to whom the CPA has reporting responsibility. However, such reports are the exception; typically, the auditor's report is addressed to the stockholders.

Internal Auditing

The internal auditor's primary reporting responsibility is to management. In this service capacity, internal auditors perform many audits other than financial statement audits. For example, *operational audits* that focus on the effectivensss and efficiency of operations are common. Internal auditing might be asked to evaluate the purchasing department's activities, with special attention to the department's competitive bidding practices and whether they meet objectives (effectiveness) in an efficient (low cost) manner. If management suspects that there has been fraud, the internal auditors may be asked to perform a *fraud investigation.* This type of investigation is more extensive than an audit, as it may require reconstructing unrecorded transactions. External auditors can also be hired to perform operational and fraud audits. But generally, external auditors perform financial statement audits, and internal auditors perform compliance and operational audits.

Internal auditors oversee the entire control system, rather than the controls related to financial statement representations. They are often concerned with engineering, marketing, distribution, and personnel issues that require backgrounds beyond a basic understanding of accounting and auditing. The continuous nature of the internal audit calls for an in-depth knowledge of total operations not asked of the external auditor who performs periodic reviews and audits of the financial statements of the entity.

General Accounting Office

The GAO is generally recognized as the key innovator in defining and developing the concept of operational auditing. It was created to oversee such diverse activities as those of the Environmental Protection Agency (EPA) and the Federal Bureau of Investigation (FBI). Net income is not a relevant measure to the GAO, whereas the efficiency with which generally accepted objectives (often expressed in nonfinancial terms) are achieved is relevant information.

Consider a report issued by the comptroller general to the Congress concerning "The FBI's System for Managing Investigative Resources and Measuring Results."[12] Traditionally, the FBI allocated resources to various field offices based on average case load statistics, regardless of the nature or importance of its investigations. As a means of emphasizing quality over quantity, a new resource allocation system was planned, which would give more credit to those offices that concentrated on the most serious crime problems in each geographic area. Although this plan had advantages, its implementation had been faulty, as reported by the GAO. The auditors found that there were no criteria for the field offices' identification of "quality" or priority cases. Furthermore, the FBI did not have adequate data to measure the effectiveness of its resource allocation. The GAO report specifically outlined the shortcomings of the "accomplishment statistics" in use, including the mixing of estimates with actual dollars, the duplication of statistics, and the inclusion of investigations in which other law enforcement agencies made major but unrecognized contributions. Examples of the failure of the FBI and the U.S. attorneys to coordinate their selection of criminal and security problems for priority investigative and prosecutive attention were provided. One recommendation by the GAO was that the "U.S. attorneys and FBI field office personnel establish and pursue mutual priorities."[13] The GAO report described the scope of the review and the audit methodology, including the statistical sample sizes and interview techniques applied. The report acknowledged that the auditors did not see investigative files or original file documents, because of their confidential/sensitive nature. The agency's comments and the auditors' reactions were also reported, with special consideration given to the cost-benefit dimensions of the GAO's recommendations.

The diversity of operations within the federal government makes such tailored audit and reporting approaches essential to the GAO's effective performance of its responsibilities, as outlined by Congress. Similar to the internal auditor's reporting responsibility to management, the GAO's reporting responsibility is to Congress. Yet, the makeup of Congress is intended to ensure representation of the taxpayer and other interested parties. It would be fair to say that the GAO concentrates on operational audits, although financial statement objectives are often part of an examination. An interesting aspect of the GAO's function is the loan of its personnel to various

[12] GGD-78-1, February 15, 1978. [13] Ibid., p. 44.

congressional committees that are considering changes in agency programs. Frequently, GAO auditors are treated as experts who can advise legislators as to the effectiveness of past decisions and the probable results of proposed legislation. This active role as consultant is analogous to the advisory capabilities of internal and external auditors but is likely to represent a relatively larger percentage of the GAO auditor's time.

Appendix: Career Planning

Although the focus of our discussion has been on careers in auditing, it is also important to realize the many careers that are related to accounting. A knowledge of auditing can be useful in any accounting-related profession.

Alternatives Available

The spectrum of career opportunities and professional activities is illustrated in Exhibit 1-A. Although external auditing has been emphasized as the career of public accountants, most CPA firms have departments specializing in tax and management advisory services. Moreover, in many CPA firms, these services are growing faster than their audit services are. Far beyond preparing tax returns, the responsibilities of a tax professional will concentrate on tax planning to assist clients in avoiding taxes through sound business strategies.

EXHIBIT 1-A
The Spectrum of Opportunities

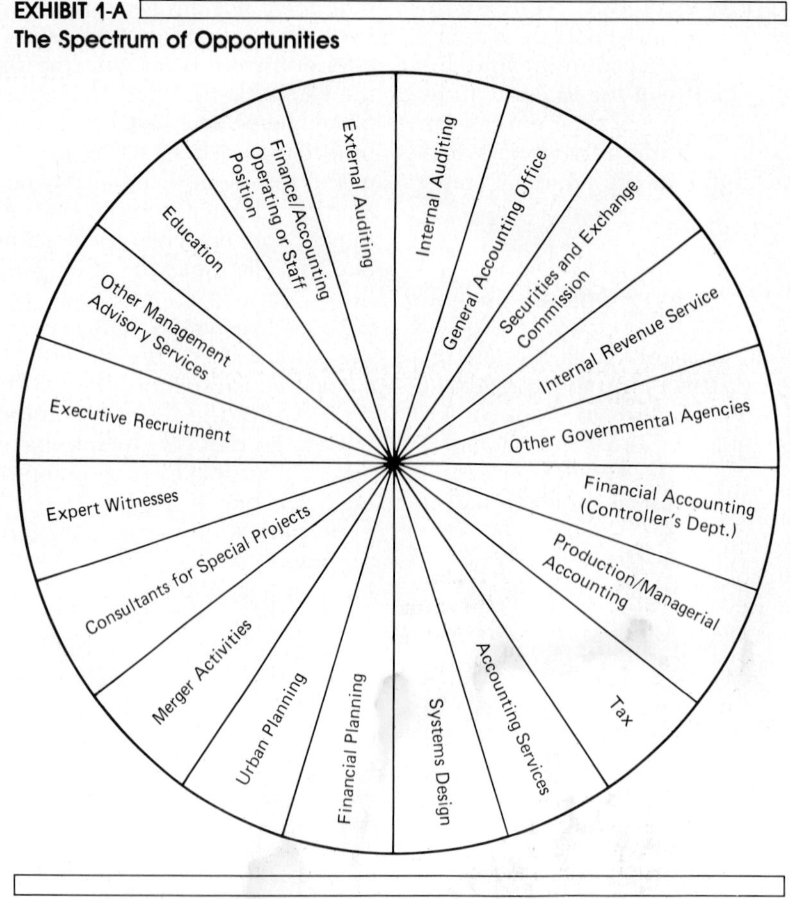

(Note that tax avoidance is a legal and acceptable objective of business, as distinct from tax evasion, the illegal nonpayment of taxes.) Merger activities, acquisition policies, charitable contribution practices, and employee benefit plans are only a few of the numerous business decisions that involve tax planning. The management service departments will include systems design, accounting services, financial planning, cost accounting systems, merger investigations, and special projects such as the preparation of a rate regulation case for a utility client. CPA firms also recruit executives for nonaudit clients.

There also are many so-called industry positions for auditors, including financial accounting, managerial accounting, and internal auditing. These positions are also available in the governmental sector, in addition to special jobs in investigative and regulatory agencies. For instance, urban planning requires the joint efforts of sociologists, public administrators, engineers, politicians, accountants, and numerous other professionals.

Teaching future accountants, business professionals, and non-business-oriented students who nevertheless need a basic understanding of accounting and auditing principles is another career alternative. The demand for professors of accounting is enormous, with a shortage of qualified academicians projected over the next ten to twenty years. There are many opportunities for continuing education as well as for writing educational books and monographs for the college and professional markets.

Consulting has become a rather nebulous term; yet some have created specific accounting-related careers by establishing their own consulting firms. The services offered often entail expert witness responsibilities regarding accounting and auditing practices, software development, and forecasting assistance to companies and governmental entities. Professional board members who devote their time to service on three to seven companies' boards of directors are responding to industry's increased demands of directors, particularly audit committee members. With the annual compensation per board often exceeding $15,000, this career alternative has become even more attractive.

From Auditing to Other Careers

Many college graduates initially pursue an auditing career, although they intend to end up in one of the other careers shown in Exhibit 1-A. Consider the turnover statistics for public accounting firms:

- A study of employees from forty-two CPA firms found that after four years, 75 percent of the firms retained fewer than half of their initial employees.[14]
- A study of 7,500 employees entering one CPA firm from 1945 to 1966 indicated that 85 percent were still employed one year later, 38 percent five years later, and only 18 percent ten years later.[15]
- Another study noted that many CPA firms retained only 4 to 16 percent of their personnel over a ten-year period.[16]

Although the reasons for the turnover are diverse, it is likely that many of the professionals entering public accounting have no intention of pursuing an external auditing career. So why is initial employment in auditing sought? The answer appears to be the added flexibility gained from initial experience as an auditor. Many employment ads specify "Big 8 experience," "2 to 3 years public accounting desired," "CPA preferred," or "CPA, CIA, or CMA required." (CIA refers to Certified Internal Auditor, and CMA refers to Certified Management Accountant.)

Why is an auditing background valued by employers? As you will appreciate when you have completed this text, auditing requires an understanding of controls, operating efficiency, monitoring effectiveness, reporting and disclosure issues, ethical considerations, and regulatory compliance. The ability to get along with people, to communicate ideas, to document the rationale for profes-

[14] H. I. Grossman, "Public Accounting Employee Turnover," unpublished report to the 1967 Annual Meeting of the American Institute of Certified Public Accountants, New York.

[15] R. S. Capin, "How to Cope with the Staff Man Shortage," *The Practical Accountant,* 1969, p. 22.

[16] Park E. Leathers, "Staff Retention in Public Accounting Firms," *Journal of Accountancy,* January 1971, p. 87.

sional judgments, and to make difficult decisions is developed as one obtains auditing experience. In public accounting, one's exposure to a wide variety of clients, industries, control settings, and operating innovations is an important resource for future employers. In addition, public accounting firms are well known for the quality of their continuing education programs. Basically, public accounting can be viewed as an investment in human capital. Similarly, employment as an internal auditor can be an effective means of gaining an overview of operations and an in-depth knowledge of controls that can prepare professionals for positions as financial managers. In fact, many companies have a rotational plan that brings line managers into the internal audit department for a two-year training period, in preparation for promotions that will entail greater responsibility and knowledge of the business.

Many consultants advertise their previous experience with the Internal Revenue Service or other governmental agencies as a means of establishing their knowledge of governmental policies that could affect clients. Again, an investment in human capital is often made by first working as a governmental auditor.

All of the auditing careers are noted for the continuing education training provided by employers. Such training tends to be rewarded by subsequent employers in the form of increased salary. Given the advantages of auditing to subsequent career endeavors, why do some individuals remain in auditing positions—particularly public accounting? What factors determine when others leave?

Who Stays in and Who Leaves Auditing Careers

When asked what the best- and least-liked qualities of CPA firm work were, ninety-eight staff auditors gave the following responses:

Best-Liked Qualities (Rank)

- Diversity of work situations (1)
- Challenging work, enjoyable work (2)
- Personal development, learning and work experience, training (3)
- Responsibility, recognition (4)
- Professionalism (5)

Least-Liked Qualities (Rank)

- Dull work, not requiring brains or education (1)
- Long or irregular hours (2)
- Time constraints and budgetary pressure (3)
- Office politics and rules (4)
- Firm attitudes toward personnel, attitudes required of personnel, and professionalism (5)

When sixty-eight staff members who voluntarily left public accounting were asked their reasons for leaving, they mentioned

- Feeling that your job tended to interfere with your family life;
- Working more hours than you preferred;
- Not having the chance to use your skills and abilities;
- Desiring some understanding people around you who are sympathetic to the problems of your position and upon whom you can rely for assistance and advice;
- Feeling that your progress on the job was not what it should be;
- Feeling that your salary compensation was inadequate; and
- Having more to say in the way you accomplish your work (e.g., procedures, routine, pace).[17]

In another study of a nonturnover group of 133 and a turnover group of 67 (with about five years of experience), "The non-turnover group exhibited a preference for analytic or scientific orientations, and the turnover sample leaned toward people- or sales-related vocations."[18] The nonturnover group displayed several characteristics with more intensity than did the turnover group, including a tendency to be more responsible, obliging, tolerant, persistent, foresighted, alert, and socially adept (as well as being able to demonstrate coping behavior).

When another survey of fifty-one staff auditors

[17] John Grant Rhode, James E. Sorensen, and Edward E. Lawler III, "Sources of Professional Staff Turnover in Public Accounting Firms Revealed by the Exit Interview," *Accounting, Organizations and Society* 2(1977):165–175.

[18] John Grant Rhode, James E. Sorensen, and Edward E. Lawler III, "An Analysis of Personal Characteristics Related to Professional Staff Turnover in Public Accounting Firms," *Decision Sciences* 7(1976):797.

asked for details on job satisfaction, the greatest satisfaction was cited as the prestige of the job outside the firm, the opportunity for growth, and the opportunity to do challenging work. The most dissatisfaction with the job was cited as not having a feeling of security, an opportunity to help others, or an opportunity for close friendship. Uncertainty was cited as present in making decisions, in evaluating the effects of environmental factors, and in measuring the loss that would result from a wrong decision. All such perceived uncertainty was reported to increase the level of job dissatisfaction.[19]

What Is Available for Those Who Leave. The job opportunities shown in Exhibit 1-A are available to the staff auditor who chooses to leave public accounting. The transition is typically very smooth, as many public accountants are later employed by former audit clients. In fact, a discussion with CPA firm partners will quickly reveal that because of training investments, little return is earned on staff accountants, whereas managers can earn reasonable returns for the CPA firm but are often tempted away by clients. Managers admit that they are at the career stage of "investing" in the CPA firm in which they wish to be made partners. But turning down lucrative offers by clients is difficult.

Some public accountants switch CPA firms, most often for reasons of geographical preference. CPA firms are trying to halt the loss of good professionals. For example, some firms are using more paraprofessionals, computer auditing, and statistical sampling procedures in order to reduce the amount of uninteresting work entailed in external audits. Others have expanded internship programs to provide previous work experience so that prospective employees can better understand the nature of a public accounting career and decide whether they want to pursue it. In planning audit assignments, individuals' preferences regarding travel and overtime are also considered.

Yet, the "infamous busy season" (when the fiscal year-ends, the calendar year-ends, and tax time all meet) is unlikely to be altered substantially. In contrast, the national CPA firms' tendency to increase the number of their offices, geographically dispersed and extending to those international offices required for servicing clients, has helped curb the extent of out-of-town travel. With the replacement cost of entry-level staff accountants being estimated to exceed $10,000 beyond base salary, CPA firms have real incentives to address the problems commonly associated with auditing careers.

Moreover, the strong points of public accounting can be further strengthened by constantly improving training programs and the diversity of job experiences.

An Image Problem

Although the research on staff retention and turnover emphasizes the prestige of public accounting, accounting is also perceived as being boring. Indeed, students do not expect their work to be interesting and challenging. The dull image of accounting is really a problem. Contrary to the popular portrayals of "dry, tedious accountants" by both Charles Dickens and Monty Python, the dynamic business and governmental environment, the sophisticated audit technology that is evolving, the ever-increasing breadth of CPAs' services, and the diversity of client portfolios combine to make accounting careers some of the most interesting and challenging careers to pursue.

Yet it is only fair to acknowledge that the image problem will likely persist until a prime-time series focuses on the adventures, trials, and tribulations of a CPA, in a manner that is analogous to famous doctor and lawyer depictions of "Trapper John" or "Perry Mason"! So you may as well start to learn patience in facing the "accountants' image" and other "common misconceptions."

Exhibit 1-B is a collage of phrases that accountants are likely to hear, especially at cocktail parties. You will find that all CPAs are expected to know about income taxes; few people distinguish between a bookkeeper and an accountant; and you are in a very select group if the term CIA is understood to mean Certified Internal Auditor!

Because only 10 percent or so of candidates for the CPA exam pass the first time, some of you are

[19] Kenneth R. Ferris, "Perceived Uncertainty and Job Satisfaction in the Accounting Environment," *Accounting, Organizations and Society* 2(1977):23–28.

EXHIBIT 1-B
Likely to Be Overheard . . .

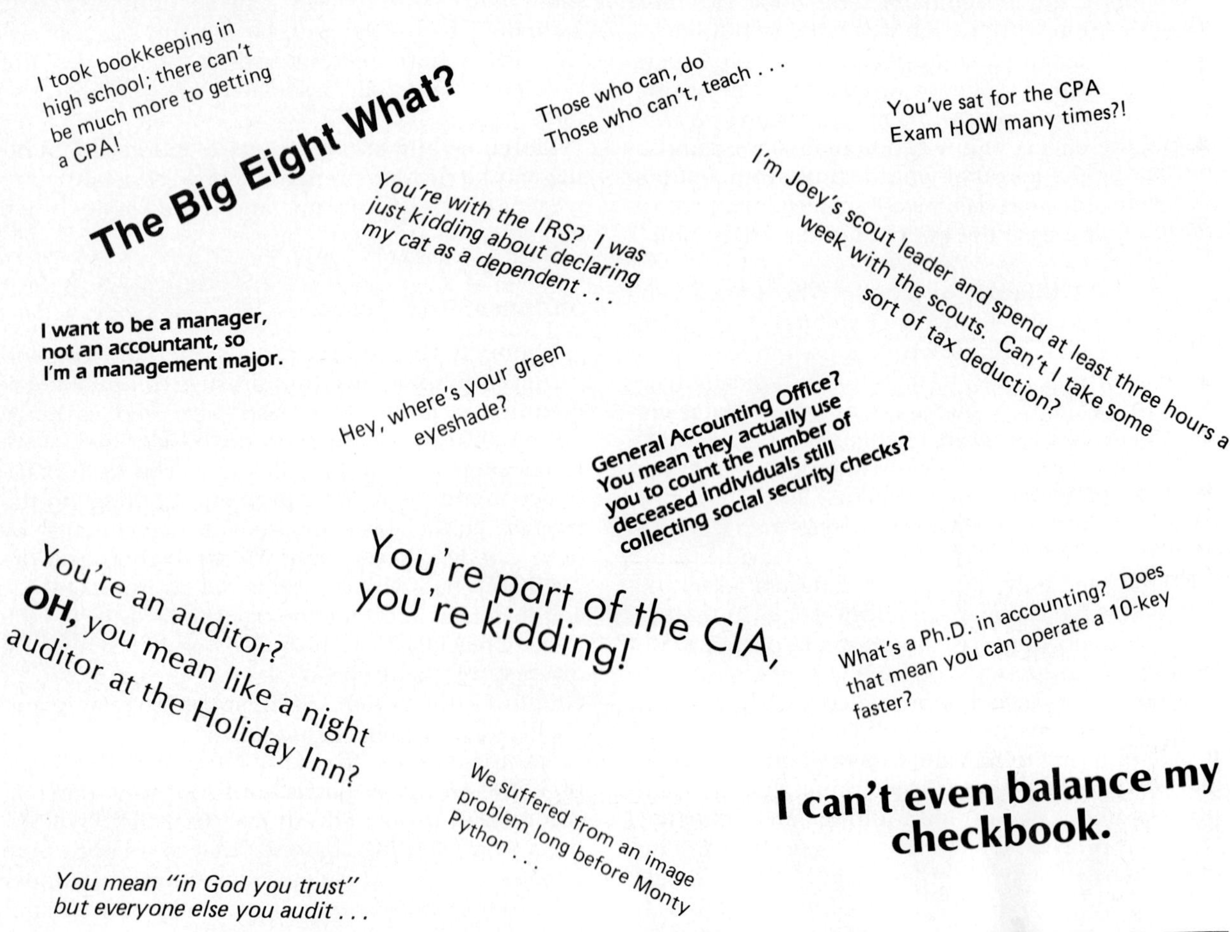

likely to be repeat candidates, in which case you'll have to tolerate the "superior" attitude of those who are fortunate enough to pass the first time! Hence, the collage in Exhibit 1-B cites the dreaded question: "You've sat for the CPA Exam HOW many times?!" Don't get discouraged! Take heart in the statistic provided by the Federal Trade Commission that serious candidates who take the exam up to six times experience an overall pass rate of 80 to 90 percent. Remember that the professional examinations, which will be discussed in greater depth in a later chapter, are the hallmark of the profession and can help to objectively demonstrate your professional competency in those areas of accounting in which you plan to pursue a career.

I took bookkeeping in high school; there can't be much more to getting a CPA!
The Big Eight What?
Those who can, do
Those who can't, teach . . .
You've sat for the CPA Exam HOW many times?!
You're with the IRS? I was just kidding about declaring my cat as a dependent . . .
I'm Joey's scout leader and spend at least three hours a week with the scouts. Can't I take some sort of tax deduction?
I want to be a manager, not an accountant, so I'm a management major.
Hey, where's your green eyeshade?
General Accounting Office? You mean they actually use you to count the number of deceased individuals still collecting social security checks?
You're an auditor? OH, you mean like a night auditor at the Holiday Inn?
You're part of the CIA, you're kidding!
What's a Ph.D. in accounting? Does that mean you can operate a 10-key faster?
We suffered from an image problem long before Monty Python . . .
I can't even balance my checkbook.
You mean "in God you trust" but everyone else you audit . . .

REVIEW QUESTIONS

1. Why do you think businesspersons are frequently confused as to whether their CPA has or has not performed an audit?
2. Define auditing, and explain how your definition applies to **(a)** external auditing, **(b)** internal auditing, and **(c)** the General Accounting Office.
3. You have a colleague who plans to pursue a career as a loan officer. When selecting an elective, your colleague asks which courses you are taking and whether any of them might be useful to a future loan officer. What can you tell him about the advantages of an auditing course?
4. What is the first step in the audit process? Explain how this step is performed.
5. Is the testing of internal controls a required step in the audit process? Why or why not?
6. Describe the general standards.
7. What evidence is there that audits would be demanded even without regulation?
8. Assume that you are an agent of a principal who is financing your way through school. The financing will continue only as long as you make "satisfactory progress." What incentives do you have to provide information on your progress? Could an auditor help you in providing information to the principal? Why or why not?
9. The "market for lemons" can be applied to a variety of settings. In part, it helps explain why grades are an integral part of the educational process. Assume that you have just attended the first class of a course in which the professor has announced that all students will receive an A. Describe how the adverse selection phenomenon is likely to be revealed in the students' course performance.
10. What qualities of information are valued, according to information theory? Compare and contrast the cash basis of accounting with the accrual basis of accounting, in terms of their relative information value.
11. Some insurance companies reduce the premium on homeowners' insurance if the insured has installed a burglar alarm or smoke alarm. Explain how the moral hazard problem applies to this practice.
12. In discussing the audit function, one practitioner asserted, "The audit is basically an insurance policy for creditors and investors." Comment on the accuracy of this statement.
13. Correspondence with individuals working for the state of Michigan indicated that the state law that mandated that municipalities be audited had had little or no opposition. Further inquiries found that one of the reasons for the lack of opposition was that the municipalities were already being audited. Then what is likely to have been the purpose of such a law?
14. If an audit focuses on the fairness of management's financial representations, why should the auditee expect any improvement in operating efficiency as a result of being audited?
15. "It cannot be denied that regulation has increased the overall demand for audits." Comment on the validity of this claim.
16. To whom is the external auditor primarily responsible?
17. To whom is the internal auditor primarily responsible? Compare this responsibility with that of the General Accounting Office.
18. Describe the main type of audits performed by the General Accounting Office.

(Questions 19 through 23 refer to the Appendix.)

19. Classified ads in the *Wall Street Journal* and professional journals often state: "Public accounting experience desired." This is common in ads for controller positions, internal audit positions, and other financial management positions. Why?
20. What advantages are there in gaining experience as an external, internal, or governmental auditor?
21. Based on past research, what are the most-liked and most-disliked attributes of public accounting?
22. What general statements can be made about those individuals who leave public accounting, in comparison to those who stay?
23. What actions can CPA firms take to reduce turnover?

EXERCISES

1. You were recently hired as the controller of a small business that intends to undergo its first audit next year. The president has asked you to help the business evaluate CPA firms, in order to select one as its external auditor. Prepare such a plan, in a form suitable to submit to the president.
2. Your business has had difficulty in discovering an efficient inventory system that can guard against inventory stock-outs, yet can ensure minimal inventory storage costs. A decision has been made to hire a consulting firm to evaluate the situation and make

recommendations. You have suggested that the company consider hiring the CPA firm that performs its annual audit. Explain why this is a good suggestion.

3. You are a loan officer, authorized to make only one more loan of $50,000 before the fiscal year-end. You have two prospective borrowers' loan applications, and their financial statement positions appear to be similar in terms of credit worthiness. You have just outlined your comparison of the two prospects to a fellow loan officer, who immediately asks: "Who prepared the financial statements? Have the statements been audited?" You respond that the controller prepared one statement, and a certified public accountant (CPA) prepared the other. Although the CPA is known to perform annual audits, that borrower's fiscal year-end differs from your bank's, and so you received an unaudited interim financial statement from the CPA. Your colleague declares: "Well, I think you have your answer."
   a. What does your colleague mean?
   b. Assume that you were given approval to make both loans. Would you charge the same interest rate to both borrowers? Why or why not?
   c. You decide to call the borrower who submitted the financial statement that was prepared by the controller and to request that a statement be submitted by a CPA. When you make the request, the prospective borrower responds: "I'd be happy to, as long as you pick up the bill!" What would be an appropriate response to this prospective borrower, and why?

4. You are a member of a board of directors that has recently decided to form an audit committee. This committee will be responsible for overseeing both the internal and the external auditors' activities. The members of this committee believe that they need to understand the basic auditing process in order to discharge their duties effectively. As chairperson of the new committee, you have been asked to give an overview of the audit process. Prepare your presentation to the committee in written form. (Be prepared to make an oral presentation during the next classroom session of your auditing course.)

5. The following summary report was issued by the comptroller general of the United States for an examination entitled "Farmers Home Administration and Small Business Administration Natural Disaster Loan Programs, Budget Implications and Beneficiaries" (CED 79-111; August 6, 1979):

> The volume of Farmers Home Administration and Small Business Administration loans for disaster assistance surged to almost $6 billion in fiscal year 1978. This was due largely to widespread drought conditions, low interest rates, and broadening of the Small Business Administration's disaster assistance loan program to include farmers.
>
> Loans were made in every state. Farmers were the principal borrowers, accounting for 88 percent of the amount loaned. GAO believes many loan recipients could get credit from other sources. Generally, there is no assurance the loans were used for disaster-related needs.

   a. Describe the purpose of the audit that generated this report.
   b. On what type of an audit process would such a report be based?
   c. Compare and contrast the general form of this GAO report with the CPA reports that you have read.

(Exercise 6 refers to the Appendix.)

6. During slack time, you are asked to help the personnel director evaluate the CPA firm's turnover and draft a proposed strategy to reduce this loss of talented professionals.
   a. Outline the statistics that you would use to evaluate the turnover. What benchmarks are available to you for determining the severity of the turnover problem?
   b. Propose a strategy to resolve the turnover problem. Be specific, giving your reasons for each part of the strategy.

QUESTIONS ADAPTED FROM PROFESSIONAL EXAMINATIONS

1. Internal auditing is a staff function found in virtually every large corporation. The internal audit function is also performed in many smaller companies as a part-time activity of individuals who may or may not be called internal auditors. The differences between the audits by independent public accountants and the work of internal auditors are more basic than is generally recognized.

Required:
Briefly discuss the auditing work performed by the independent public accountant and the internal auditor with regard to the
   1. Auditing objectives.
   2. General nature of the auditing work.

(CPA exam adapted)

2. The following statement is representative of attitudes and opinions sometimes encountered by CPAs in their professional practices:

> An audit by a CPA is essentially negative and contributes to neither the gross national product nor the general well-being of society. The auditor does not create; he or she merely checks what someone else has done.

Required:
Regarding the above statement, indicate

a. Areas of agreement with the statement, if any.

b. Areas of misconception, incompleteness, or fallacious reasoning included in the statement, if any.

(CPA exam adapted)

3. Feiler, the sole owner of a small hardware business, was told that the business should have its financial statements examined by an independent CPA. Feiler, having had some bookkeeping experience, personally prepared the company's financial statements and does not understand why such statements should be examined by a CPA. Feiler discussed the matter with Farber, a CPA, and asked him to explain why an audit is important.

Required:

a. Describe the objectives of an independent audit.

b. List ten ways in which an independent audit may help Feiler.

(CPA exam adapted)

4. In order to function effectively, the internal auditor must often explain to auditees and other parties the nature and purpose of internal auditing.

Required:

a. Define internal auditing.

b. Briefly describe five possible benefits from a program by an internal auditing department to teach auditees and other parties the nature and purpose of internal auditing.

(CIA exam adapted)

5. Multiple-Choice: Role of an Audit and Definition of Terms

Select the one answer that best completes the statement or answers the question.

5.1 The securities of Ralph Corporation are listed on a regional stock exchange and registered with the Securities and Exchange Commission. Ralph's management engages a CPA to perform an independent audit of its financial statements. The objective of this audit is to provide assurance to the

a. regional stock exchange.

b. Board of directors of Ralph Corporation.

c. Securities and Exchange Commission.

d. Investors in Ralph securities.

(CPA exam adapted)

5.2 Which of the following best describes the operational audit?

a. It requires the internal auditors' constant review of the administrative controls as they relate to the company's operations.

b. It concentrates on implementing financial and accounting control in a newly organized company.

c. It attempts and is designed to verify the fair presentation of the results of a company's operations.

d. It concentrates on seeking out aspects of operations in which waste would be reduced by introducing controls.

(CPA exam adapted)

5.3 As generally conceived, the audit committee of a publicly held company should be made up of

a. Representatives from the client's management, investors, suppliers, and customers.

b. The audit partner, the chief financial officer, the legal counsel, and at least one outsider.

c. Representatives of the major equity interests (bonds, preferred stock, common stock).

d. Members of the board of directors who are not officers or employees.

(CPA exam adapted)

5.4 Which of the following best explains why an independent auditor is asked to express an opinion on the fair presentation of financial statements?

a. It is difficult to prepare financial statements that fairly present a company's financial position and changes in financial position and operations without the expertise of an independent auditor.

b. It is management's responsibility to seek available independent aid in appraising the financial information shown in its financial statements.

c. The opinion of an independent party is needed because a company may not be objective with respect to its own financial statements.

d. It is a customary courtesy that all stockholders of a company receive an independent report on management's stewardship in managing the company's affairs.

(CPA exam adapted)

5.5 An investor is reading the financial statements of the Stankey Corporation and observes that the statements are accompanied by an auditor's unqualified report. From this the investor may conclude that.

a. Any disputes over significant accounting issues have been settled to the auditor's satisfaction.

b. The auditor is satisfied that Stankey is financially sound.

c. The auditor has ascertained that Stankey's financial statements have been prepared accurately.
d. Informative disclosures in the financial statements but not necessarily in Stankey's footnotes are to be regarded as adequate.
(CPA exam adapted)

5.6 Operational audits generally have been conducted by internal auditors and governmental audit agencies but may be performed by certified public accountants. The main purpose of an operational audit is to provide
a. A means of assurance that internal accounting controls are functioning as planned.
b. Aid to the independent auditor, who is conducting the examination of the financial statements.
c. The results of internal examinations of financial and accounting matters to a company's management.
d. A measure of management's performance in meeting organizational goals.
(CPA exam adapted)

5.7 Which of the following best explains why publicly traded corporations have the outside auditor appointed by the board of directors or elected by the stockholders?
a. To comply with regulations of the Financial Accounting Standards Board.
b. To emphasize the auditor's independence from the corporation's management.
c. To encourage a policy of rotating the independent auditors.
d. To give the corporate owners an opportunity to voice their opinion concerning the quality of the auditing firm selected by the directors.
(CPA exam adapted)

5.8 The essence of the attest function is to
a. Detect fraud.
b. Examine individual transactions so that the auditor may certify their validity.
c. Determine whether the client's financial statements are fairly stated.
d. Assure the consistent application of correct accounting procedures.
(CPA exam adapted)

6. Multiple-Choice: Audit Process

Select the one answer that best completes the statement or answers the question.

6.1 An auditor evaluates the existing system of internal control in order to
a. Determine which substantive tests must be performed.
b. Determine which compliance tests must be performed.
c. Ascertain whether irregularities are probable.
d. Ascertain whether any employees have incompatible functions.
(CPA exam adapted)

6.2 Which of the following determines the specific audit procedures necessary to give an independent auditor a reasonable basis to express an opinion?
a. The audit program.
b. The auditor's judgment.
c. Generally accepted auditing standards.
d. The auditor's working papers.
(CPA exam adapted)

6.3 **Most** of the independent auditor's work in formulating an opinion on financial statements consists of
a. Studying and evaluating internal control.
b. Obtaining and examining evidential matter.
c. Examining cash transactions.
d. Comparing recorded accountability with assets.
(CPA exam adapted)

6.4 The principal purpose of performing compliance tests is to offer reasonable assurance that
a. Accounting control procedures are being applied as prescribed.
b. The flow of transactions through the accounting system is understood.
c. Transactions are recorded at the amounts executed.
d. All accounting control procedures leave visible evidence.
(CPA exam adapted)

6.5 Before expressing an opinion concerning the results of operations, the auditor can best examine the income statement by
a. Applying a rigid measurement standard designed to test for understatement of net income.
b. Analyzing the beginning and ending balance sheet inventory amounts.
c. Making net income comparisons with published industry trends and ratios.
d. Examining income statement accounts concurrently with the related balance sheet accounts.
(CPA exam adapted)

6.6 In the context of an audit of financial statements, substantive tests are audit procedures that
a. May be eliminated under certain conditions.
b. Are designed to discover significant subsequent events.

c. May be tests of transactions, direct tests of financial balances, or analytical tests.
d. Will increase proportionately with the auditor's reliance on internal control.

(CPA exam adapted)

6.7 The early appointment of the independent auditor will enable
a. A more thorough examination to be performed.
b. A proper study and evaluation of internal control to be performed.
c. Sufficient competent evidential matter to be obtained.
d. A more efficient examination to be planned.

(CPA exam adapted)

6.8 The independent auditor should understand a client's internal audit function in order to decide whether the work of internal auditors will be a factor in determining the nature, timing, and extent of the independent auditor's procedures. The work performed by internal auditors might be such a factor when the internal auditor's work includes a
a. Verification of the invoices' mathematical accuracy.
b. Review of administrative practices to improve efficiency and achieve management objectives.
c. Study and evaluation of internal accounting control.
d. Preparation of internal financial reports for management purposes.

(CPA exam adapted)

7. Multiple-Choice: General Standards

Select the one answer that best completes the statement or answers the question.

7.1 The first general standard of the generally accepted auditing standards, which states in part that the examination is to be performed by a person or persons having adequate technical training, requires that an auditor have
a. Education and experience in the field of auditing.
b. Ability in the planning and supervision of the audit work.
c. Proficiency in business and financial matters.
d. Knowledge in the areas of financial accounting.

(CPA exam adapted)

7.2 The third general auditing standard requires that due professional care be exercised in performing the examination and preparing the report. The matter of due professional care refers to what is done by the independent auditor and how well it is done. For example, due care in the working papers requires that its
a. Format be neat and orderly and include both a permanent file and a general file.
b. Content be sufficient to support the auditor's report, including the auditor's representation as to compliance with auditing standards.
c. Ownership be determined by the legal statutes of the state in which the auditor practices.
d. Preparation be the responsibility of assistant accountants whose work is reviewed by senior accountants, managers, and partners.

(CPA exam adapted)

7.3 The first general standard requires that a person or persons have adequate technical training and proficiency as an auditor. This standard is met by
a. An understanding of business and finance.
b. Education and experience in auditing.
c. Continuing professional education.
d. A thorough knowledge of the Statements on Auditing Standards.

(CPA exam adapted)

7.4 The third general standard states that due care should be exercised in performing the examination. This should be interpreted to mean that a CPA who undertakes an engagement will perform
a. With reasonable diligence and without fault or error.
b. As a professional who will assume responsibility for losses consequent upon error of judgment.
c. To the satisfaction of the client and third parties who may rely on it.
d. As a professional possessing the degree of skill commonly possessed by others in the field.

(CPA exam adapted)

7.5 Which of the following best describes what is meant by generally accepted auditing standards?
a. Acts to be performed by the auditor.
b. Measures of the quality of the auditor's performance.
c. Procedures to be used to gather evidence to support financial statements.
d. Audit objectives generally determined on audit engagements.

(CPA exam adapted)

7.6 A CPA certificate is evidence of
a. Recognition of independence.

b. Basic competence at the time the certificate is granted.
c. Culmination of the educational process.
d. Membership in the AICPA.

(CPA exam adapted)

CASES FOR DISCUSSION

1. As the manager of a regional CPA firm, you have just been handed a special assignment. The partner-in-charge of your office recently read a survey showing that clients are usually unaware of services that are available from CPA firms. She has resolved to make this firm's clients aware of such services by having an attractive, informative brochure prepared for distribution by the firm. Recognizing your six years of experience with the firm and your diverse background in management advisory services, she has asked you to prepare a brochure that she and her fellow partners can discuss at the partners' meeting next month.

Design a brochure, assuming that your regional firm offers the typical CPA services and has a diverse set of clients.

2. (This case refers to the Appendix.) A local professional organization is planning a career day and has asked you to serve on a panel to explain the various accounting career alternatives. During the panel discussion, you were asked the following questions:

a. As an auditor, don't you get tired of being treated like the plague? I mean, does anybody like auditors; why should they?
b. What's the difference between a CPA and the numerous "tax advisers" that publicize their services during tax season? My aunt does tax work, yet she's no CPA! Why study taxes in college if the career can be pursued with a high school diploma?
c. I remember hearing that a staff auditor spent all afternoon looking up customers' names in the telephone book and verifying their addresses. Now what possible purpose could that have served? Is most of an auditor's work that boring?
d. I don't understand the difference between external and internal auditors. If a business has one, does it really need the other?
e. I've heard that most people don't stay in public accounting for more than a couple of years. How do you explain this?
f. I've heard that CPA firms have a separate department for management advisory services. Exactly what does this department do, and how easy is it to be hired directly into such a department?
g. People tell me that even if you want to specialize in taxes, many public accounting firms require their staff first to join the auditing group. Two years later, a transfer onto the tax staff can be arranged. What purpose does this policy serve?
h. I'm thinking about going to graduate school and pursuing a career as a professor of accounting. Are there many such positions available?
i. I want to start my own CPA firm, but I've been told to get a job with an established CPA firm first. Why?

Explain how you would respond to each of these questions. Label your answers using the letter of the question. Assume that at the end of the question-and-answer session, each of the panel members is asked to give a five-minute talk regarding career opportunities in their respective professions. Outline your talk.

2

The Auditor's Report—The "Product"

Five auditing students in their senior year are discussing a group project.

Terry. "I don't see how we can be expected to critique the auditor's standard report in the second week of the course. We don't know anything about auditing yet!"

Matt. "Remember, most people who use the report aren't auditors. So if the report's unclear to us, how can we expect other people to understand it?"

Heather. "You've got a point. After all, the auditor's standard report is our main product and is supposed to show what we've done."

Jim. "As I understand it, we're supposed to review Exhibit 2-1 that the professor gave us, which traces the development of the auditor's report over time. We're supposed to analyze these developments, including the proposed revisions that have been rejected. Then, it's our job to propose a new auditor's report, based on our critique of the strengths and weaknesses of the current report form. Right?"

Pat. "Right."

Terry. "About the only thing obvious to me is that since 1917, the auditor's report has gotten a lot longer!"

Heather. "I think we should outline the main changes over time. We'll set up the contents of the report before 1917 vertically and the date of the changes horizontally."

Heather proceeded to prepare Exhibit 2-2, based on her colleagues' observations.

Matt. "Exhibit 2-2 suggests that we've used both the terms *EXAMINED* and *AUDITED*. In some years there was no description of the nature of the exam, but later the testing and the judgment involved in selecting procedures were emphasized. Once

EXHIBIT 2-1

A Historical Perspective of the Auditor's Report

Report Before 1917 (Based on British reports)

We have examined the above accounts with the books and vouchers of the company, and find the same to be correct. We approve and certify that the above balance sheet correctly sets forth the position of the company.

(Price Waterhouse opinion on St. Louis Breweries Ltd.)

Standard Report Recommended in Federal Reserve Bulletin of 1917

I have audited the accounts of Blank and Co. for the period from . . . to . . . and I certify that the above balance sheet and statement of profit and loss have been made in accordance with the plan suggested and advised by the Federal Reserve Board and in my opinion set forth the financial condition of the firm . . . and the results of its operations for the period.

("Uniform Accounting," *Federal Reserve Bulletin*, Federal Reserve Board, 1917)

Verification of Financial Statements 1929 Revision by Federal Reserve

I have examined the accounts of . . . company for the period from . . . to . . . I certify that the accompanying balance sheet and statement of profit and loss, in my opinion, set forth the financial condition of the company at . . . and the results of operations for the period.

("Verification of Financial Statements," *Federal Reserve Bulletin*, Federal Reserve Board, 1929)

Typical Report After 1931

We have examined the accounts of . . . for the year ended. . . . In our opinion the accompanying balance sheet and statement of profit and loss set forth the financial condition of the company at . . . and the results of its operations for the year then ended that date.

1934 Report Stemming from the Profession's Cooperation with the New York Stock Exchange

We have made an examination of the balance sheet of the XYZ Company as of December 31, 1933, and of the statement of income and surplus for the year 1933. In connection therewith, we examined or tested accounting records of the company and other supporting evidence and obtained information and explanations from officers and employees of the company; we also made a general review of the accounting methods and of the operating and income accounts for the year, but we did not make a detailed audit of the transactions.

In our opinion, based upon such examination, the accompanying balance sheet and related statements of income and surplus fairly present, in accordance with accepted principles of accounting consistently maintained by the company during the year under review, its position at December 31, 1933, and the results of its operations for the year.

(Audits of Corporate Accounts, "Correspondence between the special committee on cooperation with Stock Exchanges of the American Institute of Accountants and the Committee on Stock List of the New York Stock Exchange," AICPA, 1934, pp. 30-31)

1939 Report Revised by the Accounting Profession

We have examined the balance sheet of the ABC Company as of December 31, 1939, and the statements of income and surplus for the fiscal year then ended; have reviewed the system of internal control and the accounting procedures of the company, and, without making a detailed audit of the transactions, have examined or tested accounting records of the company and other supporting evidence by methods and to the extent we deemed appropriate.

In our opinion, the accompanying balance sheet and related statements of income and surplus present fairly the position of ABC Company at December 31, 1939, and the results of its operations for the fiscal year, in conformity with generally accepted accounting principles applied on a basis consistent with that of the preceding year.

(Statements on Auditing Procedure No. 1, "Extensions of Auditing Procedure," Committee on Auditing Procedure, AIA, September 1939, p. 4)

1948 Report Revision

We have examined the balance sheet of ABC Company as of December 31, 1949, and the related statements of income and surplus for the year then ended. Our examination was made in accordance with generally accepted auditing standards, and accordingly included such tests of the accounting records and such other auditing procedures as we considered necessary in the circumstances.

In our opinion the accompanying balance sheet and statements of income and surplus present fairly the financial position of ABC Company at December 31, 1949, and the results of its operations for the year then ended, in conformity with generally accepted accounting principles applied on a basis consistent with that of the preceding year.

(Committee on Auditing Procedure, AIA, October 1948)

EXHIBIT 2-1 (continued)

Proposed Change in Auditor's Report in 1972—Rejected

We have audited the accompanying balance sheet of XYZ Company as of December 31, 1972, and the related statements of income, shareholders' equity, and changes in financial position for the years then ended. These statements are based on the company's records and other representations of the company's management. Our audit was made in accordance with the generally accepted auditing standards of the American Institute of Certified Public Accountants. Accordingly, we applied auditing procedures to the financial statements and to the underlying data and transactions selected by us from the company's records; we consider the auditing procedures to be of the nature and to the extent sufficient to provide a basis for our opinion expressed below.

In our opinion, the financial statements mentioned above present in all material respects the financial position of XYZ Company at December 31, 1972, and the results of its operations and the changes in its financial position for the years then ended in accordance with generally accepted accounting principles applied on a consistent basis.

("Proposed Statement on Auditing Procedure, The Independent Auditor's Short-Form Report," March 2, 1972 draft, p. 3)

1977 Revision of Report Form

We have examined the balance sheets of ABC Company as of December 31, 19X2 and 19X1, and the related statements of income, retained earnings, and changes in financial position for the years then ended. Our examinations were made in accordance with generally accepted auditing standards and, accordingly, included such tests of the accounting records and such other auditing procedures as we considered necessary in the circumstances.

In our opinion, the financial statements referred to above present fairly the financial position of ABC Company as of December 31, 19X2 and 19X1, and the results of its operations and the changes in its financial position for the years then ended, in conformity with generally accepted accounting principles applied on a consistent basis.

(Statement on Auditing Standards No. 15, "Reports on Comparative Financial Statements," AICPA, December 1976, p. 3)

Proposed Change in the Independent Auditor's Report in 1979—Rejected

The accompanying balance sheet of X Company as of December 31, 19XX, and the related statements of income, retained earnings, and changes in financial position for the year then ended are management's representations. An audit is intended to provide reasonable, but not absolute, assurance as to whether financial statements taken as a whole are free of material misstatements. We have audited the financial statements referred to above in accordance with generally accepted auditing standards. Application of these standards requires judgment in determining the nature, timing and extent of tests and other procedures and in evaluating the results of these procedures.

In our opinion, the financial statements referred to above present the financial position of X Company as of December 31, 19XX, and the results of its operations and the changes in its financial position for the year then ended in conformity with generally accepted accounting principles.

("Proposed Statement on Auditing Standards, The Auditor's Standard Report," September 10, 1980 draft, p. 112)

From D. R. Carmichael and Alan J. Winters, "The Evolution of Audit Reporting," *Audit Symposium VI,* edited by D. R. Nichols and H. F. Stettler (Proceedings of the 1982 Touche Ross/University of Kansas Symposium on Auditing Problems), pp. 1-20. Also see George Cochrane, "The Auditor's Report: Its Evolution in the U.S.A.," *The Accountant,* November 4, 1950, pp. 448-460.

the concept of certifying was dropped, our professional opinion was stressed. Rather than stating that something was correct, we stated its accordance with certain standards and its fair presentation. The proposed changes that were rejected (1972 and 1979) would have dropped the "fairly" wording and used either a materiality concept or a single reference to the entity's financial position. The consistency of presentation, introduced in 1934, has continued in all of the report forms. The 1977 version seemed to emphasize two years over the single-year focus in earlier periods."

Terry. "I think that's a pretty good summary for our report, but is the meaning of everything clear?"

Heather. "I understand why the "material respects" wording of the 1972 proposal failed; that's a judgment that accountants don't seem to be able to define. Imagine what trouble nonaccountants would have when they tried to interpret the concept."

EXHIBIT 2-2
Analysis of Report Changes

Content Before 1917	Date of Change								
	1917	1929	1931	1934	1939	1948	1972	1977	1979
We have examined accounts . . . of the company.	I have audited the accounts . . . for the period from . . .	I have examined	We have examined	We have made an examination . . . as of . . . for the year	We have examined . . . have reviewed	similar	We have audited. . . . These statements are based . . .	We have examined . . . as of December 31, 19X2 and 19X1	The accompanying balance sheet . . . are management's representations. The audit . . . we have audited
With the books and vouchers	deleted	deleted	deleted	We have examined or tested accounting records of the company . . . transactions	Without making a detailed audit of the transactions . . . appropriate	Our examination was made . . . circumstances	Our audit was made . . . below	Our examinations were made . . . circumstances	in accordance . . . requires judgment . . . procedures
Correct	made in accordance with . . .	Set forth the . . .	similar	fairly present, in accordance . . .	present fairly	similar	present in all material respects the financial position	present fairly the financial position	present the financial position
Approve and certify	certify . . . in my opinion	similar	In our opinion	In our opinion, based on such examination	In our opinion	similar	similar	similar	similar
Position of the company	financial condition . . . and the results	similar	similar	consistently maintained . . . and the results of its operations . . .	The position of . . . and the results of its operations . . . in conformity	the financial position	similar	as of December 31, 19X2 and 19X1, and the results . . . for the years	as of December 31, 19XX, and the changes . . . for the years . . .

Pat. "That's true, but how much better is "present fairly"? It seems like a rather ambiguous concept. I'm also curious as to how users are supposed to appreciate the references to generally accepted auditing standards and generally accepted accounting principles."

Jim. "I think the idea is to let the user know that the profession has reached a consensus regarding how audits ought to be performed and what measurement rules are acceptable. The auditor is simply stating that those guidelines have been met. I think the general concept's clear without knowing the details of either the standards or the principles."

Pat. "I guess the main question is how well the testing concept is understood. Only the 1979 proposal attempted to explain this idea with the phrase "REASONABLE, but not absolute, assurance," and it keeps the "material misstatements" idea. I always thought that auditors performed fairly extensive examinations; I'm not sure of the idea of "reasonable" or "material" as used in testing. For example, is it true that an audit ensures that fraud has not occurred or only that material fraud has not occurred? If the latter, what is material?"

Terry. "I have some more questions: Why do we stress the phrase "as we considered necessary in the circumstances"? Isn't that implicit in the generally accepted auditing standards? Why did the 1979 proposal stress management's representations? What does "consistently" mean, and how long were the procedures applied consistently?"

Heather. "I think we've done a fair job—no pun intended—of asking the right questions, but now we've got to give some answers."

Matt. "Yeah, it's always easier to criticize than it is to be constructive. Drafting a new auditor's report is going to be tough."

The group's deliberations in this case highlight the main areas of controversy concerning the content and meaning of the auditor's report. The group's apprehensions as to whether the report can be revised effectively may help explain why there have been no significant improvements or changes in the audit report in over thirty-three years. This chapter's purpose is to explain the meaning of the standard auditor's report and to introduce the major variations from the short-form report. We also shall review the profession's history in providing negative assurance, with an emphasis on current attention to the reporting practices that offer various levels of assurance to report users. The relationship of the auditor's report to clients' annual reports will be described. In addition, the external auditor's report will be compared with the typical reporting practices of internal auditors. Detailed discussion of reporting practices in other than an external audit setting is deferred to a later chapter. That separate discussion of "Other Types of Engagements" will provide examples of other forms of communication by CPAs and internal auditors. It is intended that this chapter's material will address the numerous questions that are raised in the introductory case.

Purpose

Before analyzing the content of the auditor's report, we shall examine its purpose, which is linked to the demand for audits discussed in Chapter 1. Management prepares financial statements and related representations for use by investors, creditors, regulators, and other third-party users. Because the interests of the managers and owners, as well as other user groups, are not necessarily the same, the unmonitored financial representations may lack credibility. Thus the CPA acts as an intermediary between the preparers and the users of financial statements, and the auditor's report is the CPA's product, which is intended to describe the results of the examination.

The CPA is expected to remove any biases of management that are incorporated in the accounts, by examining the selection and application of accounting principles and enforcing standards for the preparation and presentation of financial information. The CPA expresses a considered, professional, and independent opinion as to the overall fairness of the financial statements. As an objective party whose opinion is directed to the public, the CPA provides assurance and guidance as to the strength of the financial statements and their use in decision making. Thus the auditor's report is an information source that can influence the allocation of resources.

Related Research

A recent research study[1] questioned CPAs and bankers about the significance of CPA reports to credit decisions. Both groups acknowledged that an unqualified opinion made financial statements more reliable and less biased, acting as a check on the integrity of the company's management. Although both agreed that the quality of the company as a loan prospect was affected by the report, the bankers perceived the CPA report as a more important variable in the credit decision than the CPAs did. In fact, though the CPAs stated that the company's riskiness was not affected by the report, the bankers said that it was. Most likely, the

[1] Thomas P. Edmonds, Mattie C. Porter, and Ira R. Weiss, "Do Bankers and CPAs Have Different Views on Reports of Financial Statements?" *Journal of Commercial Bank Lending*, June 1981, pp. 52–62.

CPAs were emphasizing business risk, and the bankers were viewing the total risk picture, comparing that of a borrower with audited financial statements with that of a borrower without audited financial statements.

Historical Perspective

Before 1934, the auditors' report, as illustrated in Exhibit 2-1, read, "We certify that in our opinion . . ." and this led to reports being referred to as *auditors' certificates.* However, the word *certificate* seemed to imply more exactness than could be achieved in the financial statements, and so the profession has shifted to the more appropriate term *auditor's report,* which is more consistent with the idea that the auditor is expressing an opinion on, rather than certifying, the financial statements.

The term *judgment* means that one single precise determination of the correct financial statement representations is not possible. But by permitting the auditors to exercise oversight as to the "fairness" of financial statements, the users can expect to be able to rely on the auditors' reports as providing reasonable assurance that no material misstatements have been included in the accounts. *Material misstatements* are those errors that are sufficiently important that they could alter a prudent investor's decision. Materiality pertains to both quantitative and qualitative judgments.

Legal Perspective

Obviously, the audit report cannot provide absolute assurance; it is not a guarantee. Rather, it reflects the legal undertaking of a professional who is committed to act responsibly:

> Every man who offers his services to another and is employed assumes the duty to exercise in the employment such skill as he possesses with reasonable care and diligence. In all those employments where peculiar skill is requisite, if one offers his services, he is understood as holding himself out to the public as possessing the degree of skill commonly possessed by others in the same employment and if his intentions are unfounded, he commits a species of fraud upon every man who employs him in reliance on his public profession. But no man, whether skilled or unskilled, undertakes that the task he assumes shall be performed successfully and without fault or error. He undertakes for good faith and integrity but not for infallibility and he is liable to his employer for negligence, bad faith, or dishonesty, but not for losses consequent upon mere errors of judgment.[2]

The audit report thus attests to the fairness of the client's set of financial statements, based on an examination performed with due audit care, as generally defined by the accounting profession.

The General Format of an Auditor's Report

The most common standard *(short-form)* audit report has two components: the *scope* section, which is the first paragraph, and the *opinion* section, which is typically the second paragraph ***[SAS 15, Section 505].*** An example of the auditor's standard report on comparative financial statements is shown in Exhibit 2-3.

Addressing the Report

The auditor's report may be addressed to the company whose financial statements are being examined, but it is usually addressed to the company's stockholders, board of directors, or both ***[SAS 2, Section 509].*** This practice acknowledges the auditor's primary obligation to the owners and to the directors elected by those owners. Because a corporation's stockholders are generally asked to ratify the appointment of the external auditors, this approach appropriately emphasizes that the auditor's client is not the management but the owners of the company.

Scope Paragraph

The first sentence of the standard report, as shown in Exhibit 2-3, states which financial statements were audited. For example, an audit report

[2] Reprinted with permission from *A Treatise on Law of Torts: or the Wrongs Which Arise Independently of Contracts, 4th Edition* (pp. 335, Vol. 3, 1932), by Thomas M. Dooley, published by Callaghan & Co., 3201 Old Glenview Rd., Wilmette, IL 60091.

EXHIBIT 2-3
Auditors' Standard Report on Comparative Financial Statements

To the Stockholders of ABC Company:

We have examined the balance sheets of ABC Company as of (at) December 31, 19X2 and 19X1, and the related statements of income, retained earnings, and changes in financial position for the years then ended. Our examinations were made in accordance with generally accepted auditing standards and, accordingly, included such tests of the accounting records and such other auditing procedures as we considered necessary in the circumstances.

In our opinion, the financial statements referred to above present fairly the financial position of ABC Company as of (at) December 31, 19X2 and 19X1, and the results of its operations and the changes in its financial position for the years then ended, in conformity with generally accepted accounting principles applied on a consistent basis.

New York, N. Y. John Doe & Co.
February 15, 19X2

From SAS No. 15, "Reports on Comparative Financial Statements" (New York: AICPA, December 1976).

may cover only the balance sheet. The key word of that sentence is the first "of", as that indicates whose financial statements were audited ***[SAS 1, Section 110].*** In other words, the company prepares the financial statements and footnotes, which are a *representation by management.* The auditors can influence these financial statements by requiring that certain principles be used and certain disclosures be made in order for them to be able to express an unqualified opinion. The principal responsibility for the financial statements, nonetheless, rests with the management, regardless of whether or not an auditor's report is issued.

Many CPAs state not only the name of the client but also the type of entity being audited. If it is a corporation, the client's state of incorporation is often noted. In this case, Exhibit 2-3 would read: "of ABC Company (a Delaware Corporation)." The state reference is a reminder of the state laws that govern corporate matters, including the payment of dividends. In addition, as different states may house corporations with the same name, the state reference can help identify the client being audited. The parenthetical comment may also disclose a significant relationship of the client, for example, "and a wholly owned subsidiary of ———."

Applicable Dates and Periods of Financial Statements

The report is typically issued for *comparative financial statements,* as reflected by the dates of the reports cited in the first sentence of the scope paragraph ***[SAS 15, Section 505].*** The profession's reporting standards require an expression of opinion regarding the financial statements *taken as a whole.* This phrase applies to the financial statements for the current period and for all prior periods that are presented on a comparative basis. A *continuing auditor*—one who has examined the financial statements for the current year and for at least one earlier year—should update these earlier audit reports. An *update* is a re-expression of a previous opinion or a revision of that report based on information available from the current year's examination. If an uncertainty was resolved, a new uncertainty was identified, or an event took place after the year-end that resulted in a restatement, the previous audit report(s) must be changed. This restatement of the earlier financial statements may be made, for example, in order to comply with GAAP. This practice of reporting on comparative financial statements can, of course, produce an audit report with differing opinions for the two or more years involved. Instructions on how these reports are drafted are given in SAS No. 15, "Reports on Comparative Financial Statements."[3]

A *predecessor auditor* (an auditor who has been replaced) can be asked to *reissue* the previous auditor's report, based on a reading of the current period's financial statements, a comparison of those statements with the earlier period's, and the receipt of a *letter of representation* from the *successor auditor* stating whether the current examination revealed any matters that might materially affect the earlier financial statements. If the predecessor auditor's report is not presented, the successor auditor must revise the scope paragraph of his or her report, indicating that other auditors (unnamed) examined the earlier period's financial statements and issued their report on a specified

[3]SAS No. 15 (New York: AICPA, December 1976).

date with a specified type of opinion expressed. The successor auditors also must give the reasons for the predecessor auditors issuing other than an unqualified report.

Exhibit 2-3 shows an auditor's report on comparative financial statements. Note that comparative statements can be presented for any number of years, with the report altered to reflect the appropriate quantity (for example, "for each of the five years in the period ended———").

Generally Accepted Auditing Standards (GAAS)

The beginning of the second sentence refers to *generally accepted auditing standards* ***(GAAS).*** This term encompasses all of the standards that have evolved over the years and have been approved and adopted by the membership of the American Institute of Certified Public Accountants (AICPA). These standards take into account the CPA's training, proficiency, and independence, as well as the manner in which an examination is to be performed. In addition, they include reporting standards, all of which are incorporated in the standard report in Exhibit 2-3. The generally accepted auditing standards are rather general in nature, whereas the auditing procedures are more specific and are tailored to the particular client setting. To emphasize this fact, the end of the second sentence refers to those other procedures deemed to be necessary in the circumstances, stating the importance of the auditors' judgment in selecting the auditing procedures for conducting an examination.

"As We Considered Necessary"—An Example

Not only is judgment used in selecting audit procedures, it is also essential to applying these procedures. For example, one required audit procedure is the observation of physical inventory. However, how the observation of inventory is performed can differ widely. Thus an auditor must make sure that the approach selected fits the circumstances and can provide sufficient evidence of the propriety of the client's representations regarding inventory.

As an example, imagine an auditor who intends to observe a cattle rancher's inventory. One option would be to count the client's steers as they are herded through a gate. However, to most of us, each steer would look like every other steer. What would prevent a client from circling some of the steers already counted through the pasture and back through the gate where the auditor is making the count? This could result in double or even triple counting, thereby greatly misrepresenting the actual inventory on hand.

An auditor who is responsible for observing a mobile inventory therefore must use observation techniques that will prevent such a misrepresentation. Remember that with mobile inventory, miscounts can also occur by accident, with no intended fraud by the client. An employee may be unaware that the steers from one pasture had already been counted and may inadvertently double count that portion of the inventory. To prevent either intentional or unintentional error, the auditor should use a technique like aerial photography. By photographing all the pastures and corrals at one time, the steers are unlikely to be counted twice. The auditor merely needs to count the steers in the photograph. But then, trees or shelters could hide some of the steers, a possibility that must be taken into account.

Other Adjustments

After the phrase "in the circumstances," some CPAs will add references to work done in subsidiary companies, whose financials are not included but whose importance to the valuation of assets is significant. The usual phrasing is "including a similar examination of the financial statements of each subsidiary."

Generally accepted reporting standards do not require disclosure of the omission of customary auditing procedures, as long as the auditor can get satisfaction by applying alternative audit procedures. Alternative procedures must be reported only when the confirmation of receivables or the observation of the physical inventory reported on the latest balance sheet has been omitted. It is acceptable, however, to apply alternative procedures to beginning inventories in a first-time audit, with no mention of them in the scope paragraph. Sometimes, when very material assets have had to be tested by alternative procedures, the auditor will choose to disclose this fact, without indicating an exception to the generally accepted auditing standards. In this case, the phrasing might be "We were unable to obtain confirmation of receivables from the United States government; however, we have applied other auditing procedures to these receivables." This sentence would come at the end of the scope paragraph.

Middle Paragraph(s)

The auditor's standard report presented in Exhibit 2-3 has only two paragraphs: the scope paragraph and the opinion paragraph. However, it is common to see reports with more than two paragraphs. The *middle paragraph* typically explains either a scope-related or an opinion-related event that is thought to be important to the user's interpretation of the auditor's report, in which case, it is required. But if the middle paragraph only emphasizes a matter, with no effect on either the scope or the opinion paragraph, it is optional and is included at the auditor's discretion. The unqualified opinion then would appear as shown in Exhibit 2-3, with the addition of a middle paragraph.

Examples of the type of explanatory information that may be presented in a separate paragraph in order to emphasize a matter are (1) a reference to the entity's status as a component of a large business enterprise, (2) an acknowledgment of significant transactions with related parties (such as subsidiaries or large stockholders), (3) an emphasis on an unusually important subsequent event, or (4) an emphasis on an accounting matter affecting the comparability of financial statements with those of the preceding period.

Though not necessary, the CPA may prefer an emphasis on certain disclosures. Typically, the footnotes will already cite the information, and so there will be a cross reference to the footnote. For example, the middle paragraph might read as follows:

> As stated in Note 2 to the balance sheet, the corporation is negotiating for the reacquisition of one-half of its outstanding common stock at a price substantially equivalent to the book value plus two-thirds of the excess of appraised values over the book value of the property. The means of financing this reacquisition has not yet been determined.

Note that several "middle paragraphs" may be inserted, depending on the number of issues that the CPA wishes to emphasize.

Opinion Paragraph

The phrasing "in our opinion" stresses that a professional opinion rather than a statement of fact is being provided. In no way is the opinion intended to be a stamp of approval for either a creditor or an investor. Rather, the CPA expresses an opinion on the fairness of the financial statements, not on the client's investment or credit risk.

Other Auditors' Involvement

Modifying the opinion paragraph to indicate that other auditors' reports have been incorporated into the opinion being issued is not considered to be a qualification of the opinion. It simply divides responsibility for the audit work. All other modifying phrases in the second paragraph, however, are considered to be qualifications.

As an example of dividing responsibility, consider a situation in which other auditors examine consolidated subsidiaries that are a significant part of the client's financial representations. In this case, both the scope and the opinion paragraphs should be adjusted. At the end of the first paragraph, therefore, is inserted a sentence indicating the basis for sharing responsibility, such as

> The financial statements of certain consolidated subsidiaries, ———, whose assets represent approximately 30 percent of the total consolidated assets, were examined by other auditors, and we were furnished with their reports on such financial statements.

At the beginning of the second paragraph, there could be a sentence like "In our opinion, based on our examination and the reports of the other auditors referred to above, . . . " According to the standards, only the first paragraph has to be altered. Note that the scope paragraph's adjustment is not a scope limitation; the report could be unqualified and still contain such a reference.

The percentage statistics are unnecessary if the *principal auditor* (the auditor who has performed the more material portion of the financial statements' examination and is familar with the financial statements taken as a whole) is willing to use the other auditors' reports ***[SAS 1, Section 543].*** This means that the principal auditor is responsible to third parties for the other auditors' work. No reference is made to that part of the examination being made by another auditor. If the examination by others is insignificant, this would be the typical approach to reporting.

Meaning of "Financial Statements"

The phrase "financial statements" refers to the financial data and related footnotes that are derived from the client's accounting records to represent his or her financial position or changes therein. Besides the statements cited in the scope paragraph of Exhibit 2-3, the summary of operations, statement of operations by product lines, and statement of cash receipts and disbursements are financial statements that may be presented ***[SAS 29, Section 551].*** The term *basic financial statements* is used in the professional literature to refer to the four main statements cited in the scope paragraph, descriptions of accounting policies, notes to financial statements, and schedules and explanatory material that are identified as being a part of the basic financial statements ***[SAS 21, Section 435].*** Segment information is part of the financial statements to which the audit opinion applies. Specifically, the auditor determines whether such information conforms with GAAP in regard to the financial statements taken as a whole. There is no separate opinion on segment information; therefore, the materiality of such information is determined relative to the financial statements as a whole rather than to the segment information alone.

Meaning of "Present Fairly"

The phrase "present fairly" refers to an objective, candid, and equitable representation of financial position. It is not intended to be a hedge that the presentations are tolerable but, rather, an opinion that fairness may mean some imprecision within the framework of the generally accepted accounting principles (GAAP). Yet the user is assured that the presentation of financial statements, within such a framework, is impartial.

But a controversy arose over whether the report meant that the financial position was presented fairly *and* was in accordance with GAAP, was presented fairly *because of* its being in accordance with GAAP, or was presented fairly *despite* its accordance or nonaccordance with GAAP. On rare occasions, noncompliance with GAAP is required in order to present a financial position fairly ***[SAS 5 Section 411].*** Finally, the auditing standards board clarified the report's intention:

> The independent auditor's judgment concerning the "fairness" of the overall presentation of financial statements should be applied within the framework of generally accepted accounting principles. . . .
>
> Rule 203 . . . provides that an auditor should not express an unqualified opinion if the financial statements contain a material departure from such pronouncements unless, due to unusual circumstances, adherence to the pronouncement would make the statements misleading.[4]

Rule 203 thus puts the burden of proof on the auditor. The report is required to present in a separate paragraph a description of the departure, its approximate effects if practicable, and the reasons that the departure is necessary to prevent the financial statements from being misleading. But this is seldom used, given the presumption that officially established accounting principles will not be misleading in their effects.

Sometimes, however, the selection of a particular accounting principle makes misleading the financial statements taken as a whole. For example, there are various accounting techniques for recording long-term construction contracts, some of which might produce misleading financial statements. In this case, other GAAP should be selected for the client's representations.

[4]SAS No. 5, "The Meaning of 'Present Fairly' in Conformity with Generally Accepted Accounting Principles," in *The Independent Auditor's Report* (New York: AICPA, July 1975), par. .03, .06.

Meaning of Generally Accepted Accounting Principles (GAAP)

GAAP include accounting principles and practices as well as the methods of applying them. Professional judgment is required to determine whether the principles employed have found general acceptance. Such acceptance may be present even if its usage is limited. GAAP are officially defined as "those principles which have substantial authoritative support."[5]

SAS No. 43 Section 1010, "Omnibus Statement on Auditing Standards" explains the order of authority of sources of GAAP:

a. Pronouncements of an authoritative body designated by the AICPA Council to establish accounting principles, pursuant to Rule 203. . . . (FASB, APB, ARB pronouncements, and FASB interpretations)
b. Pronouncements of bodies composed of expert accountants that follow a due process procedure, including broad distribution of proposed accounting principles for public comment, for the intended purpose of establishing accounting principles or describing existing practices that are generally accepted. (AICPA Industry Audit Guides and Accounting Guides and AICPA Statements of Position)
c. Practices or pronouncements that are widely recognized as being generally accepted because they represent prevalent practice in a particular industry or the knowledgeable application to specific circumstances of pronouncements that are generally accepted. (FASB Technical Bulletins and AICPA Accounting Interpretations, as well as industry practices)
d. Other accounting literature (e.g., AICPA Issues Papers, textbooks, and articles). (par. .05, .06, .07, .08)[6]

Generally accepted accounting principles emphasize substance over form, and so the auditor is responsible for detecting significant differences between the actual substance of transactions and their recorded form.

When an auditor reports on financial statements prepared in accordance with a comprehensive basis of accounting other than GAAP, the auditor must disclose in his or her report that the statements are not intended to conform to GAAP and then express an opinion or disclaimer with respect to whether the financial statements conform to the comprehensive basis of accounting used. This is an example of a special report, such as one issued for an insurance company that complies with the reporting rules of a state insurance commission. Special reports are the subject matter of a later chapter.

Meaning of "Applied on a Consistent Basis"

The phrase "applied on a consistent basis" ensures that the financial statements presented are comparable and have not been materially affected by changes in the accounting principles used or in the method used to apply such principles. Although some events other than a change in principles can affect comparability, they are not consistency qualifications; if material, they will be disclosed in the footnotes. Examples of such events are technological effects on assets' useful lives, the effects of acquisitions, and the disposal of a line of business.

If the report covers less than two years, the consistency phrasing should refer to the fiscal year preceding the period presented. If the report covers two years or more, the CPA need not disclose any inconsistency with a period before the first year presented. Note that no consistency reference is appropriate for the first accounting period of a new company.

Date of Report and Its Relationship to Legal Responsibilities

The report will be dated as of the last day of field work, which will extend beyond the date of the financial statements being examined. The last day of field work is essentially the last day that the auditor collects evidence concerning the client's representations. For a calendar-year client, field work often extends to the beginning of February. The auditor is responsible for performing a review for

[5] Resolution of the AICPA Council, October 2, 1964.
[6] New York: AICPA, August 1982.

subsequent events that have occurred since the date on the financial statements (such as 12/31/x7) but before or on the date that the field work is completed (such as 2/2/x8). The idea of this review is to discover information that would have affected the financial statements had it been available earlier ***[SAS 1, Section 530].*** In addition, information that could be significant to assessing the entity's financial position, even though it has no direct effect on the financial statements, may require disclosure in footnotes to the financial statements.

Two types of subsequent events and examples of each type are given in Exhibit 2-4. The auditor's legal responsibilities for non-SEC clients generally extend to the date of the audit report ***[SAS 1, Section 560].*** An exception occurs when a subsequent event requiring disclosure is discovered after the field work has been completed but before the auditor's report has been issued. One alternative available to the auditor is *dual dating.* The first date represents the last day of field work and is qualified by the phrase "except for Note——as to which the date is ———," thereby extending the auditor's responsibility for subsequent events that are related only to the specific event cited.

It is permissible to extend the report date beyond the original completion of field work, provided that the auditor's review of subsequent transactions is extended through the later date. Hence, instead of dual dating the auditor's report, CPAs can extend their review to the later date. It is important to recognize that this also extends the legal responsibility for all subsequent events to that later date.

Unqualified Opinions

So far, we have not discussed any modifications of the auditor's report that would constitute a

EXHIBIT 2-4

Subsequent Events That Can Affect the Dating of the Auditor's Report

Type 1	Type 2
Basic Definition	**Basic Definition**
"Those events that provide additional evidence with respect to conditions that existed at the date of the balance sheet and affect the estimates inherent in the process of preparing financial statements. . . . The financial statements should be adjusted for any change in estimates resulting from the use of such evidence."	"Those events that provide evidence with respect to conditions that did not exist at the date of the balance sheet being reported on but arose subsequent to that date. These events should not result in adjustment of the financial statements. Some of these events, however, may be of such a nature that disclosure of them is required to keep the financial statements from being misleading."
Examples	**Examples**
• Loss on uncollectible trade receivables as a result of customers' deteriorating financial condition leading to bankruptcy subsequent to the balance-sheet date would be indicative of conditions existing at the balance-sheet date. • Settlement of litigation for an amount different from recorded liability, if the events giving rise to the litigation (e.g., personal injury or patent infringement) took place prior to the balance-sheet date.	• Sale of a bond or capital stock issue. • Purchase of a business. • Settlement of litigation when the event giving rise to the claim took place subsequent to the balance-sheet date. • Loss of plant or inventories as a result of a fire or flood. • Losses on receivables resulting from conditions (such as a customer's major casualty) arising subsequent to the balance-sheet date.

From SAS No. 1, "Codification of Auditing Standards and Procedures" (New York: AICPA, November 1972), AU §560.06.

qualification; Exhibit 2-3 shows an unqualified, or "clean," audit report.

Short-Form Report and the Four Generally Accepted Reporting Standards

Exhibit 2-3 is called a short-form report and is the most common report issued for inclusion in clients' annual reports. The short-form report fulfills the profession's four reporting standards ***[SAS 1, Section 150]***.

1. The report shall state whether the financial statements are presented in accordance with generally accepted principles of accounting.
2. The report shall state whether such principles have been consistently observed in the current period in relation to the preceding period.
3. Informative disclosures in the financial statements are to be regarded as reasonably adequate unless otherwise stated in the report.
4. The report shall contain either an expression of opinion regarding the financial statements taken as a whole or an assertion to the effect that an opinion cannot be expressed. When an overall opinion cannot be expressed, the reasons therefore should be stated. In all cases where an auditor's name is associated with financial statements, the report should contain a clear-cut indication of the character of the auditor's examination, if any, and the degree of responsibility he is taking.

All four standards are included in the opinion paragraph of the auditor's report. The phrase in the fourth standard "the financial statements taken as a whole" applies equally to a complete set of financial statements and to an individual financial statement ***[SAS 2, Section 509]***. But an auditor can express an unqualified opinion on one financial statement and another type of opinion on another financial statement. The fourth standard requires only that the auditor's report clearly indicate the degree of responsibility that he or she is assuming. In other words, whenever an auditor's name is associated with a financial statement, either an opinion must be expressed or a disclaimer of an opinion must be issued, with the reason for the disclaimer clearly stated. Remember that a disclaimer is a statement by the auditor that he or she is unable to express an opinion on the financial statements.

Although the reason for a disclaimer must be stated, the explanation should be concise and written in a manner that does not shift to the user the responsibility for determining the appropriate type of opinion to be issued. For example, if a CPA issues a disclaimer because he or she lacks independence, that fact should be stated. But the reason that the CPA is not independent should not be stated, because that may lead the user to think: "Oh, that's not a substantial dependence, and so I can still rely on these statements." CPAs are responsible for assessing their own independence, and it is a yes or no judgment, based on professional standards. Only the result of the judgment is to be disclosed. Similarly, the reason for any type of qualification of the short-form report is to be communicated clearly.

Information Accompanying Financial Statements in Auditor-Submitted Documents

An unqualified report can be expanded from Exhibit 2-3 to provide details regarding (1) line items (for example, percentage breakdown of governmental versus nongovernmental receivables or an aging of the accounts receivable), (2) statistical data (for example, the number of employees hired or covered by a pension plan), and (3) scope of the examination (for example, specific reference to the confirmation of receivables and tests for unrecorded liabilities). Sometimes nonaccounting data and explanatory comments in response to the client's request for information are included in the auditor's report; that is, the reports can be tailored to fit the needs of the report users. Often, the additional disclosure is directed to the creditors' needs. The auditor must indicate the character of the examination of any additional data presented that was not included (not needed) for fair presentation in the short-form report. If the auditor does not intend to limit his or her responsibility, the report may include a paragraph like the following:

> Our examination was made for the purpose of forming an opinion on the basic financial statements taken as a whole. The data included in Exhibits —— through —— of this report are presented for purposes of addi-

tional analysis and are not a required part of the basic financial statements. Such information has been subjected to the auditing procedures applied in the examination of the basic financial statements and, in our opinion, is fairly stated in all material respects in relation to the basic financial statements taken as a whole ***[SAS 29, Section 551]***.

The auditors can assume either no responsibility or limited responsibility if they so choose. In the former case, the information should be marked as "unaudited" or refer to the auditor's disclaimer.

The term *long-form reports* was used before 1980 but was deleted from the professional literature in order to focus on *auditor-submitted documents.* Any document that the auditor submits to the client or others that contains information in addition to the client's basic financial statements and the auditor's standard report thereon must clearly describe the character of the auditor's examination and the degree of responsibility taken with respect to the accompanying information. Note that *client-prepared documents* such as annual reports entail different responsibilities, which will be considered at the end of this chapter. Auditor-submitted documents may contain information from sources outside the accounting system or outside the entity. They often include a brief history and description of the auditee, its officers and directors, and general information concerning insurance coverage. Additional information about various items in the financial statements and about statistics in the appendices is common. For instance, historical comparisons of financial data can be valuable in analyzing trends. General comments often discuss aging, turnover, credit terms, inventory turnover, inventory obsolescence or shrinkage experiences, credit agreements, contingent liabilities, and similar information that would be relevant to evaluating a client's liquidity. Major changes in operations may also be detailed, such as the acquisition of other companies' capital stock, new product lines, and unusual business activity. An example of the types of statistics presented is the following list of tables included in the audit report of a large automobile manufacturer:

- Number of cars sold by type.
- Average price realized per type of car.
- Average cost per type of car, before inventory adjustments.
- Average gross profit per type of car.
- Ratio of sales to selling expense.
- Ratio of sales to general and administrative expense.
- Gross profit percentages.
  —per type of car.
  —parts and accessories.
- Ratio of factory overhead expense to productive labor by plant.[7]

When an auditor-submitted document includes supplementary information required by the Financial Accounting Standards Board (FASB) that is presented outside the basic financial statements, the auditor should disclaim an opinion on that information, unless specifically engaged to examine and express an opinion on it. The form of such disclaimers will be described later in this chapter.

Qualified Opinions

Reporting standards require the auditor's report to contain either an expression of opinion regarding the financial statements taken as a whole or a statement that an opinion cannot be expressed and the reasons. After reviewing the clean opinion in Exhibit 2-3, it is easy to identify what might go wrong in an audit that would preclude issuing a clean opinion. First, in the scope paragraph, you may have failed to follow the generally accepted auditing standards, or you may not have performed all tests considered necessary. In the opinion paragraph, you may find that the financial statements are not fairly presented, are not in conformity with GAAP, and/or are not consistent in their application of GAAP. Moreover, there may be some uncertainty that makes determining fair presentation contingent upon particular events. The extent to which each of these possibilities affects the audit report depends on the level of each problem's

[7]Adapted from Hugh Jackson, "Audit Certificates and Reports," *Accounting Review*, September 1926, pp. 45–63.

materiality. If the problem is *pervasive* or so severe as to cause uncertainty concerning the fairness of the overall financial statements, a disclaimer can be issued. (However, GAAS permits use of the "subject to" qualification even in this circumstance.) If the problem is so severe that the overall financial statements are not believed to result in fair presentation, an adverse opinion is required. But if the overall financial statements are fairly presented yet there is a problem that is material (such as noncompliance with GAAS), a qualified audit report form is appropriate. Besides the problem's level of materiality, it is useful to consider the type of problem: Is it an accounting, an auditing, or an uncertainty problem? Accounting problems can result in qualified or adverse opinions, whereas auditing problems can result in qualified opinions or disclaimers. *Qualified opinions* disclose problems that are not so material as to make the overall financial statements unfair, whereas *adverse opinions* state that the financial statements are not fairly stated. It is not possible for an accounting problem to result in a disclaimer or for an auditing problem or uncertainty to result in an adverse opinion. An overview of the different types of audit reports is shown in Exhibit 2-5.

The four major conditions that can lead to a qualification, disclaimer, or adverse opinion follow ***[SAS 2, Section 509].***

1. The scope of an examination can be insufficient as a source of competent evidential matter on which a clean opinion can be issued, because of
   - conditions that have precluded the application of particular auditing procedures that are considered necessary in the circumstances, or
   - restrictions by the client on the scope of the exam. *(auditing problem)*
2. The financial statements may not fairly present the financial position because of
   - a departure from generally accepted accounting principles, the effect of which is material, or
   - inadequate disclosure. *(accounting problem)*
3. The presentation may be inconsistent because of a material change between periods in
   - accounting principles or
   - the method of their application. *(accounting problem)*
4. The financial statements may be affected by significant uncertainties about the future, and the uncertainty
   - cannot be resolved because the outcome depends on future events, or
   - the effect cannot be estimated or reasonably provided for in the accounts. *(uncertainty problem)*

All modifying phrases in the opinion paragraph, except for a reference to the report of other auditors, are considered to be qualifications. All reasons for the qualification, with the exception of an opinion's being modified because of a change in accounting principles, are to be disclosed in a separate explanatory paragraph in the auditor's report. The explanatory paragraph should state: the subject matter of the qualification; the effects of the qualification on each financial statement, if determinable; and, when applicable, a statement that the effects of the qualification are indeterminable. The explanatory paragraph should be cited in the opinion paragraph (and in the scope paragraph if the problem is a limitation on scope).

"Except for" Qualifications

Auditing Problem. An "except for" phrase is appropriate when a scope limitation results in the auditor's report being qualified. In the scope paragraph, the exception is commonly phrased as "Except as explained in the following paragraph, our examination. . . . " Then a middle paragraph explains the limitations; the scope limitations should not appear in footnotes, as these are the auditor's representations, not the client's. The explanation should describe the circumstances causing the limitation. For example, if the client imposed the restriction, the report should state "as instructed," or if the timing of the engagement precluded certain procedures, the report should state "we were appointed as auditors after the date of the inventory." The discussion should clarify the client's limiting instructions or the impracticality of applying procedures, in order to ensure that the users

EXHIBIT 2-5
Overview of Audit Reports

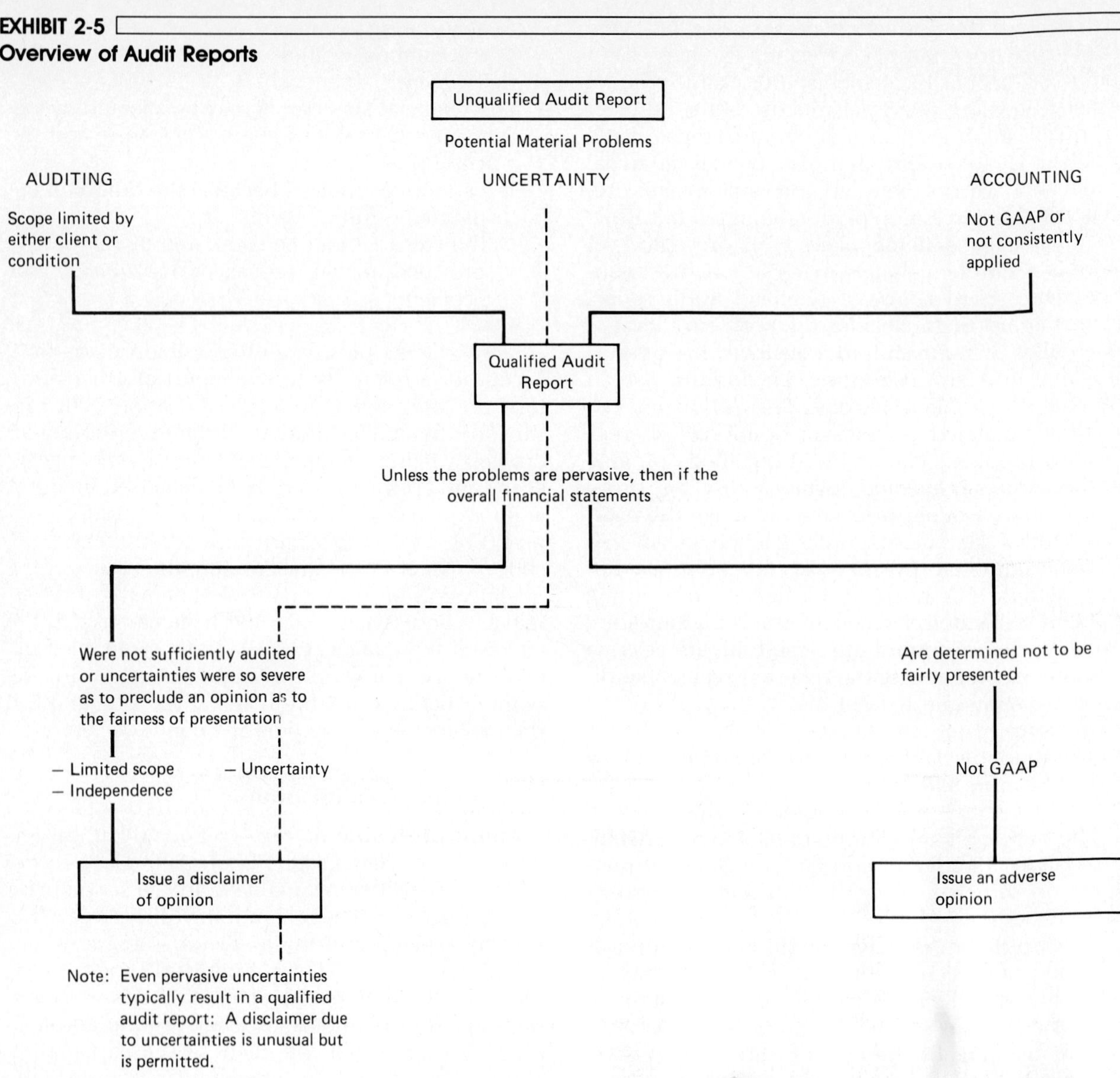

understand that the auditor did not make the omission by choice.

Whenever a CPA is asked to examine the financial statements of a company whose fiscal year has ended, he or she is required to ascertain whether the circumstances are likely to permit an adequate examination and expression of an unqualified opinion. If not, the CPA should discuss the likely qualifications with the client before accepting the engagement. An explanatory paragraph often used in auditors' reports for municipalities is

Detailed property records have not been maintained to enable us to obtain sufficient evidence to form an opinion as to whether at December 31, 19XX, property, plant, and equipment ($——) are stated at cost and as to the adequacy of the accumulated depreciation ($——) at December 31, 19XX or the depreciation expense ($——) for the year then ended for enterprise funds.

The following opinion paragraph is common:

> In our opinion, except for the effect of any adjustments which might be required with respect to property, plant, and equipment and related depreciation accounts, the accompanying . . . .

The opinion paragraph is thereby able to emphasize that the scope limitation is not of primary concern; rather, the potential effect of that limitation on the financial statements is the key matter.

Accounting Problem: GAAP. Another type of "except for" qualification refers to accounting principles. If the auditors believe that one of the client's accounting principles deviates from the generally accepted accounting principles, they must explain the reason for the qualification, including the approximate amount involved and its effect on the financial statements. Consider the following middle paragraph:

> As explained in Note 1 to the financial statements, operating equipment was sold on January 5, 19XX for $——, which is $——less than that equipment's value on the books. No provision for this loss has been made in the accompanying financial statements.

Such a paragraph can incorporate a footnote reference, whereas the acceptable disclosure of scope limitations is in the auditor's report only. No reference to the noncompliance with generally accepted accounting principles is required in the scope paragraph. In fact, the scope paragraph is never concerned with GAAP; it is directed at GAAS. Noncompliance with GAAP is reported in the opinion paragraph: "In our opinion, except for the effect of not providing for the loss described in the preceding paragraph. . . . " Common types of exceptions are valuation accounts like depreciation, warranties, reserves, contingencies, and tax deferral accounts. Inventory pricing and cash-based versus accrual-based statements are other areas that are frequently included in "except for" qualifications. Omission of the statement of changes in financial position when an entity issues financial statements that purport to present its financial position and results of operations will normally require an "except for" qualification ***[SAS 1, Section 545].*** When the disclosure in the financial statements is inadequate, those financial statements are not in conformity with GAAP ***[SAS 32, Section 431].*** The auditor should provide the information required by GAAP in his or her report, if practicable. This means that the information can be obtained reasonably easily from management's accounts and records and that providing the information does not require the auditor to become the preparer of financial information. For example, the auditor would not be expected to prepare segment information that had been omitted by the client. The auditor should be careful not to disclose confidential information that is not required by GAAP.

Accounting Problem: Consistency. A change in accounting principle that has a material effect on the financial representations is the third type of "except for" qualification and must be stated as a consistency qualification in the auditor's reports. Details concerning the change must be given in the footnotes to the financial statements, in accordance with GAAP. Its effect on the financial statements may be explained by the auditor in either a footnote or a middle paragraph. However, the opinion paragraph should still indicate the nature of the change and cite where the details can be found. The qualification ought to read ". . . generally accepted accounting principles that, except for the change . . . , as indicated in note——, were applied on a basis consistent with that of the preceding year." Remember from your intermediate accounting course that changes in accounting principles include changes in a reporting entity and the correction of errors, if these errors involve accounting principles or their application. When the effect of a change in accounting principle is inseparable from the effect of a change in estimate, it is accounted for as a change only in estimate, but because it also is a change in principle, a consistency qualification is required as well.

Any changes made in the terms used to express changes in financial position (such as cash, cash and cash equivalents, or working capital) between periods do not require consistency qualifications, provided that the changes have been applied retroactively to the earlier periods presented and are adequately disclosed ***[SAS 43, Section 1010].*** This means that the apparent trend toward cash basis statements of changes in financial position will not require that auditors' reports be qualified.

"Subject to" Qualifications

Whenever future developments or decisions outside the control of the client's management will determine the outcome of a material unresolved matter, a "subject to" opinion may be expressed. Such unresolved matters are not susceptible to audit verification; hence the auditor can only state the unresolved matter and, possibly, the aggregate amount involved, though the latter is often not available. The current literature requires auditors to qualify their opinion when an adverse resolution that would have a material effect on the financial statements is considered to be a probable future occurrence. Essentially, the opinion does no more than explicitly recognize uncertainties that could affect the client's financial position. The "subject to" qualification in no way impugns the adequacy or quality of management's disclosures.

Examples of "subject to" qualifications are the uncertainties related to lawsuits, tax matters, or other contingencies. The going concern qualification is one type of "subject to" opinion that signals some uncertainty as to the client's solvency. The recovery of investments in certain assets or the attainment of an adequate credit line may be critical uncertainties. In evaluating the breadth of the "subject to" opinion's effects, the uncertainty must be considered with respect to each financial statement. For example, a concern over the realization of asset values will raise questions about the adequacy of provisions for depreciation, amortization, depletion, and losses. Consequently, the wording of the auditor's report will reveal the auditor's opinion as to the reasonableness of the provision, as distinct from any determination of its adequacy. For example, a possible phrase is: "Our examination indicated that the reserve may not be sufficient." Then the "subject to" phrasing in the opinion ought to be very direct, such as "Subject to the effects on the financial statements of such adjustments, if any, as might have been required had the outcome of the uncertainty referred to in the preceding paragraph been known . . . " ***[SAS 43, Section 1010].***

A middle paragraph is required for all qualifications other than a change in accounting principle ***[SAS 2, Section 509].*** This explanatory paragraph should disclose all of the substantive reasons for the qualification and its principal effects, if determinable (or a statement that the effects cannot be easily determined).

Current Controversy. The auditing profession is currently reconsidering the "subject to" form of reporting. Many have noted that a qualified opinion is not appropriate if the disclosure in the body of the financial statements is judged to be complete and the qualification is cited to be both misleading and redundant. But others have claimed the "subject to" qualification to be an important, attention-directing "flag" for users. Still others question the redundancy of such qualifications: The footnotes clearly represent management's view of contingencies and uncertainties, and the auditor's judgment as to the material effects of such uncertainties can be stated in the "subject to" qualification option.

Despite proposals in the past to eliminate "subject to" reports, the profession's recent exposure drafts suggest that this type of qualification will be retained, at least over the short term. Nonetheless, the guidelines determining when a "subject to" report is to be issued are likely to be altered. Exhibit 2-6 summarizes the various criteria for issuing a "subject to" opinion. Although all of these criteria are likely to affect the auditor's judgment, their importance in leading to the expression of a qualified opinion is unclear in both theory and practice. At this time, the literature requires auditors to qualify their opinion when an adverse resolution that will have a material effect on the financial statements is probable of occurrence. The requirement holds even if the resolution is not expected to be disruptive.

Adverse Opinions

Whereas material uncertainties and scope limitations may lead to "subject to" qualifications and

EXHIBIT 2-6

Various Criteria Considered As Potential Guidelines for Determining the Appropriateness of a "Subject to" Audit Report

Probability of an Adverse Outcome

Management's probability assessment can be used; remote items require no qualification. Probable outcomes are most important. FASB 5 has been cited as providing criteria for disclosure.

Materiality of Potential Effects

The significance of the potential disruption of operations, financial structure, and operating control is critical, with an emphasis on liquidity, when evaluating disclosure requirements. The super materiality concept has been defined as a serious item with a dollar amount that can exceed several times the materiality used on the financial statements. A "subject to" opinion would be issued for "super material" items.

Variability of Potential Effects

The range of potential loss warrants attention. Potential disruptive effects are also important. "What if" is the focal point for evaluation. Some claim that only the most severe potential outcome deserves attention, whereas others encourage an emphasis on possible outcomes.

Imminence

Though likely to refer to the variability of potential effects, the idea that the closer it is to the outcome, the more certain will be its effect is communicated via the imminence criterion. The longer the time period is before resolution, the more time management will have to prepare to absorb the outcome; hence, the less disruptive the outcome will be and the less likely a qualification will be. One proposed definition is that an event must be expected to be resolved before the issuance of the subsequent audited financial statements.

Impact on Pattern of Cash Flows

Liquidity and cash flow projections are more relevant measures of future potential effects than are accounting earnings projections.

Expected Value Predictions

Possible losses can be assigned weights to reflect their probability of occurrence. Once a certain materiality for the expected value estimate is reached, disclosure is appropriate.

A Worst-Case Prediction

If the worst possible case is not material, then nothing is. The maximum potential loss must be assessed. FASB 5 allows accrual at the lowest point of the range of estimated losses from contingencies; the auditor must consider the materiality of the potential loss in excess of the accrued amount if the chance of an adverse outcome is considered probable.

"except for" qualifications, respectively, very material conditions will lead to an adverse opinion or a disclaimer. An adverse opinion states that the financial statements do not present fairly the financial position or results of operations in conformity with generally accepted accounting principles. When exceptions to the financial statements are so material that this judgment is made, either the client must be persuaded to adjust the financial statements or an adverse opinion must be expressed. When possible, the nature and effect of the misstatement should be clearly delineated. If this is not possible, the report should state that the effects cannot be easily determined. Exhibit 2-7 offers an example of a middle paragraph for an adverse opinion, as well as the opinion paragraph that is required. The opinion paragraph must include a direct reference to the separate paragraph that describes the basis for an adverse opinion. Note that whenever an adverse opinion is issued, no consistency statement should be made, as it is no longer relevant, unless a specific exception requires disclosure.

EXHIBIT 2-7

Adverse Opinions: An Example of Required Disclosure

As discussed in Note 7 to the financial statements, the company carries its property, plant, and equipment accounts at appraisal values and provides depreciation on the basis of such values. Generally accepted accounting principles, in our opinion, require that property, plant, and equipment be stated at an amount not in excess of cost, reduced by depreciation based on that amount. Because of the departures from generally accepted accounting principles described above, as of December 31, 19XX, inventories have been increased $__ by inclusion in manufacturing overhead of depreciation in excess of that based on cost; property, plant, and equipment less accumulated depreciation is carried at $__ in excess of an amount based on the cost to the company. The effect on retained earnings is $__. For the year ended December 31, 19XX, cost of goods sold has been increased $__ because of the effects of the depreciation account, resulting in a decrease in net income and earnings per share of $__ and $__, respectively.

In our opinion, because of the effects of the matters discussed in the preceding paragraph, the financial statements referred to above do not present fairly in conformity with generally accepted accounting principles, the financial position of the company as of December 31, 19XX, or the results of its operations and changes in its financial position for the year then ended.

Adapted from SAS No. 2, "Reports on Auditing Standards" (New York: AICPA, 1974), AU §509.43.

Adverse opinions are rarely issued, as clients can usually be persuaded to make the required adjustments. But if no adjustments are made, the auditor must disclose the significant deficiencies.

Disclaimer of Opinion

An auditor may not have collected sufficient evidence to form an opinion on the financial statements; in such a case, a disclaimer of opinion is appropriate. The disclaimer of an overall opinion ought to include the reasons for the disclaimer. Typical reasons include extensive limitations on scope, inadequate records to the point that the audit cannot be performed, and uncertainty about the future that is so material that it would negate any overall opinion. If the auditor lacks independence, he or she is required to issue a disclaimer. Scope limitations may be imposed by the client or by the circumstances. An example of the latter is the initial audit engagement's review of inventory in which a physical inventory of beginning balances was impossible and the auditors were unable to satisfy themselves by applying other auditing procedures. If the inventory amounts could significantly affect financial representations, a disclaimer would be appropriate. Such a circumstance is reflected in Exhibit 2-8, which is an example of a disclaimer that results from the inability to obtain sufficient competent evidence. Note that the scope and opinion paragraphs have been adjusted and that the middle paragraph explains why the disclaimer was issued.

When exceptions to the financial statements are sufficiently material that an adverse opinion would be required but, concurrently, there are major uncertainties concerning other matters that would call for a disclaimer even if adjustments were made for the known exceptions, the auditor must decide which opinion should be issued. Generally, an adverse opinion will be issued, emphasizing the uncertainties. A disclaimer should be used only when the auditor cannot form an opinion on the fairness of the financial statements taken as a whole. The disclaimer report form should not be used to avoid the disclosure of information that would be required had either a qualified or an adverse opinion been issued.

EXHIBIT 2-8
Disclaimers—One Example

Except as set forth in the following paragraph, our examination was made in accordance with generally accepted auditing standards and accordingly included such tests of the accounting records and such other auditing procedures as we considered necessary in the circumstances.

The company did not take a physical inventory of merchandise, stated at $____in the accompanying financial statements as of December 31, 19X2, and at $____as of December 31, 19X1. The company's records do not permit the application of adequate alternative procedures regarding the inventories.

Because the company did not take physical inventories and we were unable to apply adequate alternative procedures regarding inventories, as noted in the preceding paragraph, the scope of our work was not sufficient to enable us to express, and so we do not express, an opinion on the financial statements referred to above.

Adapted from SAS No. 2, "Reports of Auditing Standards" (New York: AICPA, 1974), AU §509.47.

Synopsis

A summary of report forms is presented in Exhibit 2-9. Note the distinction between the terms *departure* and *modifications*. Modification implies either a qualified or an adverse opinion, whereas departure does not.

Negative Assurance

The term *negative assurance* is often stated as the auditors' acknowledgment that "nothing came to their attention which caused them to believe that . . . " concerning any event of interest. For example, there is no evidence of noncompliance with GAAP or with certain bond covenants. Negative assurance is distinguished from *limited assurance statements* in the professional literature, with the latter including positive opinions about specific findings based on agreed-upon procedures.

A Historical Perspective

In the past, accountants were permitted to make very sketchy examinations and give an opinion such as: "Subject to the qualifications in the foregoing comments, in my opinion the attached statements fairly reflect . . . " Such practices inspired satirical verses like the following, which dates back to before 1930:

The Accountant's Report

We have audited the balance sheet and here is our report:
The cash is overstated, the cashier being short;
The customers' receivables are very much past due,
If there are any good ones they are very, very few;
The inventories are out of date and practically junk,
And the method of their pricing is very largely bunk;
According to our figures the enterprise is wrecked . . .
But subject to these comments, the balance sheet's correct.[8]

In 1939, the profession's first action to avoid such abuse of the auditor's reporting alternatives was to amend Rule 5 of the Rules of Professional Conduct of the American Institute of Accountants to read:

> In expressing an opinion on representations in financial statements which he has examined, a member shall be held guilty of an act discreditable to the profession if . . . his exceptions are sufficiently material to negative the expression of an opinion.

In 1949, Statement on Auditing Procedure No. 23 extended the accountants' responsibility to state in any report whether or not they could express an opinion. At this time, disclaimers became common. But many accountants held that *piecemeal opinions* (those expressing positive opinions on particular items in the financial statements despite an overall adverse opinion or disclaimer) could enhance the information value of an auditor's report, as long as the assurances in the report did not obscure the importance of the general disclaimer. Each section of a piecemeal opinion must identify those items to which it refers and then state its fairness, using phrases like "In our opinion, however, the amounts shown therein for cash, accounts receivable . . . are presented fairly." The flag, presumably, is the *however,* which would be repeated in each piecemeal attestation following an overall disclaimer or adverse opinion.

[8] I. B. McGladrey, "The Audit Report," *Accounting Review,* April 1951, pp. 197–198.

EXHIBIT 2-9
A Summary of Report Forms

Departures from Auditor's Standard Report That Are Not Considered to Be Qualified		Examples of the phrasing of such report forms
• The predecessor auditor's report is not presented.	Scope ¶:	The financial statements of Z Company for the year ended 19X6, were examined by other auditors whose report dated March 1, 19X7, expressed an unqualified opinion on those statements.
• The auditor's opinion is based in part on the report of another auditor.	Scope ¶:	We did not examine the financial statements of Z Company, a consolidated subsidiary, whose statements reflect total assets and revenues constituting 18 percent and 20 percent, respectively, of the related consolidated totals. These statements were examined by other auditors whose report thereon has been furnished to us. and our opinion expressed herein, insofar as it relates to the amounts included for Z Company, is based solely on the report of the other auditors.
	Opinion ¶:	In our opinion, based on our examination and the report of other auditors, the accompanying . . .
• The auditor wishes to emphasize a matter regarding the financial statements.	Middle ¶: [No reference is made in either the scope or the opinion ¶]	Effective January 1, 19X5, the company revised its estimates of the obsolescence rate of inventories, as discussed in Note 4. This revision reflects a change in conditions and not a change in accounting principles. As a result of this revision, with which we concur, net income for the year ended December 31, 19X5, was reduced by $700,000.
• Rule 203 application is appropriate.	Middle ¶: [No reference is made in either the scope or the opinion ¶]	In October 19X8, the company extinguished a substantial amount of debt through a direct exchange of new equity securities. Application of Opinion No. 26 of the Accounting Principles Board to this exchange requires that the excess of the debt extinguished over the present value of the new securities should be recognized as a gain in the period in which the extinguishment occurred. Because the terms and conditions of the new equity securities are substantially similar to those of the debt securities extinguished, it is the opinion of management, with which we agree, that no realization of a gain occurred in this exchange. For that reason, the $2,000,000 gain that would be recorded under GAAP is not recognized.

Modifications of the Auditor's Standard Report (Modifications refer to reporting situations that would result in a qualified opinion or an adverse opinion)		Examples of the phrasing of such report forms
Qualifications		
Auditing Problems	Scope ¶:	Except as explained in the following paragraph, our examination . . .
– "Except for" scope limitations	Middle ¶:	We did not observe the taking of the physical inventories as of December 31, 19X5 (stated at $___) and December 31, 19X4 (stated at $___), as those dates came before the time we were initially engaged as auditors for the company. Because of the nature of the company's records, we were unable to satisfy ourselves as to the inventory quantities by means of other auditing procedures.
	Opinion ¶:	In our opinion, except for the effects of such adjustments, if any, as might have been determined to be necessary had we been able to observe the physical inventories. . .*
Accounting Problems – "Except for" noncompliance with GAAP	Middle ¶:	The company has excluded from property and debt in the accompanying balance sheet certain lease obligations that, in our

EXHIBIT 2-9 (continued)

Modifications of the Auditor's Standard Report (Modifications refer to reporting situations that would result in a qualified opinion or an adverse opinion)		Examples of the phrasing of such report forms
	[No reference is made in the scope ¶, as GAAS are not involved]	opinion, should be capitalized in order to conform with generally accepted accounting principles. If these lease obligations were capitalized, property would be increased by $____, long-term debt by $____, and retained earnings by $____, as of December 31, 19X7, and net income and earnings per share would be increased (decreased) by $____ and $____, respectively, for the year then ended.
	Opinion ¶:	In our opinion, except for the effects of not capitalizing lease obligations, as discussed in the preceding paragraph, the financial statements. . .†
Accounting Problems —"Except for" inconsistencies	Opinion ¶: [No reference is made in the scope ¶, as GAAS are not involved]	. . . applied on a basis consistent with that of the preceding year after giving retroactive effect to the change, with which we concur, in the method accounting for long-term construction contracts as described in Note X to the financial statements.‡
Uncertainties —"Subject to" outcome of future events	Middle ¶: [No reference is made in the scope ¶, as GAAS are not involved]	As discussed in Note X to the financial statements, the company is a defendant in a lawsuit alleging infringement of certain patent rights and claiming royalties and punitive damages. The company has filed a counteraction, and preliminary hearings and discovery proceedings on both actions are in progress. The ultimate outcome of the lawsuits cannot presently be determined, and no provision of any liability that may result has been made in the financial statements.
	Opinion ¶:	In our opinion, subject to the effects on the financial statements of such adjustments, if any, as might have been required had the outcome of the uncertainty referred to in the preceding paragraph been known, . . .§
Adverse Opinion		
Accounting Problems: So pervasive as to make the financial statements as a whole misleading.		See Exhibit 2-7 for an example of an adverse opinion.

	Examples of the phrasing of such report forms
Auditing Problems:	
• So severe a scope limitation that the examination was insufficient to enable the auditor to form an opinion.	See Exhibit 2-8 for a disclaimer on scope limitation.
• A lack of independence precludes the issuance of an audit opinion.	We are not independent with respect to XYZ company, and the accompanying balance sheet as of December 31, 19X9, and the related statements of income, retained earnings, and changes in financial position for the year then ended were not audited by us, and accordingly, we do not express an opinion on them. (signature and date) ‖
Uncertainties: So severe an uncertainty that the auditor declines to express an opinion.	Note: GAAS states that the explanation of the uncertainties and the qualification of the auditor's opinion are expected to inform users of even pervasive uncertainty. However, the auditor is permitted to decline to express an opinion in cases involving uncertainties, stating why and disclosing the nature and possible effects of the uncertainties.

Adapted from Hortense Goodman and Leonard Lorensen, *Illustrations of Departures from the Auditor's Standard Report, Financial Survey 7* (New York: AICPA, 1975), p. 97.

*SAS No. 2, "Reports on Audited Financial Statements" (New York: AICPA, October 1974), AU § 509.40.

†Ibid., AU § 509.36.

‡SAS No. 1, "Reporting on Inconsistency" (New York: AICPA, November 1972), AU § 546.02.

§SAS No. 43, "Omnibus Statement on Auditing Standards" (New York: AICPA, August 1982), AU § 1010.06.

‖SAS No. 26, "Association with Financial Statements" (New York: AICPA, November 1979), AU § 504.10.

Piecemeal opinions were criticized for overshadowing the opinion expressed on the financial statement when taken as a whole, and as of January 31, 1975, the generally accepted auditing standards eliminated piecemeal opinions from the realm of acceptable practice.

Current Practices

Even though piecemeal opinions were eliminated, negative assurance has persisted since the mid-1960s with "comfort letters" to the underwriters. As already explained, negative assurance means that the CPAs apply specific procedures as a basis for stating that nothing came to their attention that caused them to believe that specified matters did not meet particular standards ***[SAS 26, Section 504].*** (The issuance of comfort letters to underwriters will be discussed in Chapter 17 dealing with types of engagements other than audits.)

By 1974, limited review reports had become commonplace, and by 1982, over nineteen different limited assurance engagements were recognized by generally accepted auditing standards. (Review engagements are one of the subjects of Chapter 17.) The various report forms for the nineteen limited assurance engagements in GAAS include

- Disclaimers, with statements as to specific findings, limited assurance that "no adjustments are necessary," or no additional disclosures.
- Negative assurance, with no disclaimer or findings or with a disclaimer.
- Silence as to findings or assurance.
- Positive opinions.[9]

Note that negative assurances are a subset of limited assurance engagements. The basis for these reports may be an audit, review procedures, a set of agreed-upon procedures, or a careful reading of the financial statements. This basis may or may not be identified and the report may or may not be restricted to specific parties' use.

Current AICPA Investigation of "Levels of Assurance"

The AICPA is currently reviewing the different expressions of limited assurance, in the hope of establishing more consistency and eliminating ambiguities. The AICPA investigation is addressing issues related to (1) the accountant's scope of involvement, (2) the criteria to which limited assurance refers (for example, generally accepted accounting principles or contractual and regulatory requirements), (3) user restrictions and responsibilities, and (4) reporting requirements.

Forecast Reviews

One type of limited assurance engagement that is being used more and more is known as a forecast review (discussed in detail in Chapter 17). CPAs are required to disclose in their forecast reviews:

- the sources of information they use.
- the major assumptions underlying the forecasts.
- the kind of work the CPA performs.
- the degree of responsibility being assumed.

CPAs cannot, however, reveal whether they think the forecast will be achieved. Rather, the purpose of the review is to provide a basis for a report on the proper preparation and presentation of the forecast, as well as the reasonableness of the underlying assumptions.

The Report's Relationship to Information Accompanying Financial Statements

Aside from the auditor's report on the financial statements, the profession has acknowledged a related reporting obligation. The CPA should make

[9] Alan J. Winters, "An Analysis of Professional Standards for Limited Assurance Engagements" (Prepared for the Planning Subcommittee of the Auditing Standards Board of the AICPA from 1981 to 1982).

clear what responsibility he or she is assuming with respect to the *supplementary information that accompanies the financial statements.*

As noted earlier, the information that accompanies the basic financial statements in auditor-submitted documents may be subject to audit or be reported as unaudited ***[SAS 29, Section 551].*** If the information is audited and not found to be materially misstated, an unqualified report should be issued. But if any supplementary information required by the FASB (such as price level–adjusted data or mineral reserve disclosures) is omitted or materially departs from the measurement or presentation guidelines set by the FASB, the report should be extended. If a modified opinion or adverse opinion is issued on the financial statements, the effect of such qualifications on the accompanying information should be disclosed, without contradicting or overshadowing the opinion issued on the financials. If the accompanying information is materially misstated and is not revised, a modified report must be issued describing the misstatement. This is necessary whether or not the FASB requires the accompanying information to be presented and whether or not the information has been subjected to an audit. But, the CPA must state whether or not the accompanying information was audited and what effects the modifications would have on the auditor's report.

If the accompanying information is not known to be materially misstated and is unaudited, a disclaimer of opinion should be issued on both the information required by the FASB and the information not required by the FASB. Exhibit 2-10 shows

EXHIBIT 2-10

Reporting Excerpts Regarding Information in Auditor-Submitted Documents

I. Report on Unaudited Unrequired Information

Our examination was made for the purpose of forming an opinion on the basic financial statements taken as a whole. The (identify accompanying information) is presented for purposes of additional analysis and is not a required part of the basic financial statements. Such information has not been subjected to the auditing procedures applied in the examination of the basic financial statements, and accordingly, we express no opinion on it.

II. Report on Unaudited Required Supplementary Information

The (identify the supplementary information) on page XX is not a required part of the basic financial statements but is supplementary information required by the Financial Accounting Standards Board. We have applied certain limited procedures, which consisted principally of inquiries of management regarding the methods of measurement and presentation of the supplementary information. However, we did not audit the information and express no opinion on it.

III. Omission of Required Supplementary Information

The company has not presented (describe the supplementary information required by the FASB in the circumstances) that the Financial Accounting Standards Board has determined is necessary to supplement, although not required to be part of, the basic financial statements.

IV. Departure from FASB Guidelines

The (specifically identify the supplementary information) on page XX is not a required part of the basic financial statements, and we did not audit and do not express an opinion on such information. However, we have applied certain limited procedures, which consisted principally of inquiries of management regarding the methods of measurement and presentation of supplementary information. As a result of such limited procedures, we believe that the (specifically identify the supplementary information) is not in conformity with guidelines established by the Financial Accounting Standards Board because (describe the material departure(s) from the FASB guidelines).

V. Prescribed Procedures Not Completed

The (specifically identify the supplementary information) on page XX is not a required part of the basic financial statements, and we did not audit and do not express an opinion on such information. Further, we were unable to apply to the information certain procedures prescribed by professional standards because (state the reasons).

From SAS No. 29, "Reporting on Information Accompanying the Basic Financial Statements in Auditor-submitted Documents" (New York: AICPA, 1980), pars. 12, 13, and 15, applying to Excerpts I and II; and SAS No. 27, "Supplementary Information Required by the Financial Accounting Standards Board" (New York: AICPA, December 1979), sec. 553, applying to Excerpts III, IV, and V.

examples of the phrasing of that section of audit reports that pertain to unaudited supplementary information. The first (I) disclosure refers to unrequired information, and the second (II) report excerpt refers to unaudited supplementary information required by FASB. Excerpts III, IV, and V are passages used when required supplementary information is omitted, when it materially departs from prescribed guidelines, and when prescribed procedures were not completed.

As suggested by Excerpt III, the generally accepted auditing standards require the CPA to perform limited procedures with respect to FASB-required disclosures ***[SAS 27, Section 553].***[10] These tend to be inquiry and limited analytical review procedures, such as comparing information obtained for consistency with the auditor's knowledge of operations and the evidential base collected with respect to the financial statements. If the auditor is unable to complete these prescribed procedures, his or her report must be expanded to indicate that they were not performed and to give the reason, as shown in Exhibit 2-10.

Information in annual reports (client-submitted documents) should be read by the auditor who then should decide whether such information or the manner of its presentation is materially inconsistent with the financial statements ***[SAS 8, Section 550].*** If it is materially inconsistent, the appropriate revisions should be made. Should the client refuse to do this, the auditor may (1) include an explanatory paragraph, describing the material inconsistency; (2) withhold the use of the auditor's report in the document; and/or (3) withdraw from the engagement. The action taken will depend on the circumstances and on the significance of the inconsistency.

Should a reading of other information uncover a material misstatement of fact that is not a material inconsistency, the auditor should discuss the matter with the client, suggesting that the client consult with other advisers such as legal counsel. If not corrected, the auditor should consider notifying the client in writing as to his or her views. The auditor may also wish to seek legal counsel.

Research on Users' Comprehension of Auditors' Reports

Any discussion of the auditor's report (the "product") would be incomplete without directing some attention to the users' understanding of such reports. Of particular interest is the fact that certain banks have adopted a requirement in their standard loan agreement that audit reports submitted contain "no qualifications unacceptable to the bank." The only available assurance that prospective borrowers will not be overly penalized by variations in the standard unqualified auditor's report is the bankers' understanding of the meaning of various types of qualifications. Evidence that bankers do, in fact, perceive audit reports in a manner that is similar to CPAs' perceptions is available from a study of twenty-eight commercial loan officers from five large banks and thirty audit partners of five "Big Eight" CPA firms, all from Chicago.[11] They were given ten audit reports, including variations of unqualified, qualified, and disclaimer reports based on uncertainty caused by asset realization or litigation and scope limitations, imposed by either circumstances or the client. The perceptions of the users and the preparers of the audit reports were remarkably similar; the only difference was that the bankers' perceptions made a greater distinction between client-imposed and circumstance-imposed scope limitations. The research results supported the similarity of qualified and unqualified reports as information for loan decisions, whereas disclaimers appeared to differentially affect the bankers' evaluation. The qualified reports were perceived to increase the riskiness of loan prospects and to create a need for additional information. Disclaimers and qualified reports with client-imposed scope limitations tended to be comparable in terms of the message conveyed as to the company's risk and quality as a loan prospect. Overall, the research suggested that there was fairly accurate communication between the accounting and banking professions with respect to the interpretation of auditors' reports.

[10] See SAS No. 27, "Supplementary Information Required by the Financial Accounting Standards Board" (New York: AICPA, December 1979).

[11] Robert Libby and Daniel Short, "A Review and Test of the Meaning of Audit Reports from the Perspective of Bankers," *Journal of Commercial Bank Lending*, August 1980, pp. 48–62.

From 1967 to 1975, there was a fourfold increase in the number of "subject to" opinions issued, with 15 percent of the 9,500 companies filing 10-K reports containing uncertainty qualifications. When asked which type of opinion should be expressed in order to ensure appropriate communication to the users of financial reports, 58.2 percent of the 232 randomly selected partners of international CPA firms indicated that asset realization, litigation, going concern, and other uncertainties required either a qualified opinion or a disclaimer.[12] This evidence supports the idea that "subject to" opinions are a useful extension of the auditor's reporting function, despite past controversy as to whether such a report form should be retained.

The usefulness of "subject to" opinions is likely to depend in part on the consistency with which they are issued. A study of 1,226 annual reports in 1976 found 12 percent qualified opinions, with some striking dilemmas regarding the appropriateness of the disclosures. For example, out of six major cigarette companies involved in class action antitrust lawsuits, only three had qualified opinions. Similarly, three major armored car companies were investigated for possible antitrust violations by a federal grand jury in 1975, and although one audit firm served all three clients, only one client received a qualified opinion. Only in 1976 did all three receive qualified opinions, and these did not carry through to the financial statements of the parent company.[13] This type of research evidence suggests that the users' comprehension of the auditors' reports is likely to be enhanced through more consistent application of reporting standards. The fact that observed inconsistencies are found in litigation is not by chance. "Subject to" qualifications most commonly pertain to litigation: The 1978 edition of *Accounting Trends and Techniques*[14] reports that out of six hundred companies sampled, sixty-two to forty-seven received "subject to" opinions from 1974 to 1977 and that about one-half of these were related to litigation. This tendency has continued through the 1980s.

One research study surveyed 207 financial analysts and asked them to predict which type of auditors' disclosure would appear in annual reports for a set of asset realization, litigation, going concern, and less severe uncertainty situations. Only 39 percent of their predictions were accurate, with 16 percent expecting a more severe or higher level of disclosure and 45 percent expecting a less severe or lower level of disclosure.[15] Apparently, there is an education gap, suggesting an opportunity for the profession to improve the financial statement readers' comprehension of report qualifications.

Regardless of how well specific disclosure practices are understood, there is evidence that the form of disclosure can make a difference in the users' decisions. A survey of 198 randomly selected financial analysts with expertise in financial statement use and analysis asked for the price at which an entity's stock would represent an attractive investment, based on a packet of information, including financial statements, footnotes, descriptive information, a cover letter, and an auditor's report. The technical departure from the equity basis of accounting, required by generally accepted accounting principles was disclosed in all of the packets distributed, although half contained a qualified "except for" opinion, and the remainder contained an unqualified opinion. The price estimate for the group receiving the qualified auditor's report was significantly lower than the price estimate for those receiving the clean audit report ($15.33 versus $17.27). The evidence suggests that a qualified "except for" auditor's report has a negative effect on financial analysts' attitudes toward the reporting company, quite apart from the effect of the basis for the exception, such as the dollar effect of not complying with the equity basis of accounting. Rather, the form of the report appears to

[12] Jesse F. Dillard, Richard J. Murdock, and John K. Shank, "CPAs' Attitudes Toward 'Subject to' Opinions," *CPA Journal*, August 1978, pp. 43–47.

[13] William C. Norby, "Accounting for Financial Analysis," *Financial Analysts Journal*, May–June 1978, pp. 18–19.

[14] New York: AICPA, 1978.

[15] John K. Shank, Jesse F. Dillard, and Joseph H. Bylinski, "What Do 'Subject to' Auditors' Opinions Mean to Investors?" *Financial Analysts Journal*, January–February 1979, pp. 41–45.

have a separate impression on the users of financial statements.[16]

Comparison of External Auditors' Reports with Internal Auditors' Reports

All external auditors' (CPAs') reports tend to be boiler-plate reports, with similar paragraphing, phrasing, and reporting guidelines. In contrast, internal auditors' reports can take a variety of forms and are often long, with an executive summary prepared for management's quick perusal.

The last chapter quoted from reports issued by the General Accounting Office. In the report concerning the Federal Bureau of Investigation, no standard wording is required, and the main objective is to communicate the results effectively. This is done by describing the scope of the audit, the measurement tools used, often the precise audit procedures (including sample sizes), and the manhours expended. The scope is followed by a report of the findings which, again, are reported in far greater detail than in the external report forms. Often, a point-by-point itemization of key findings is included in the internal auditor's report. An important part of most internal audit reports is the set of recommendations proposed by the internal auditors. There is often a formal feedback requirement, whereby the auditees respond to the internal audit report and describe their reactions and intentions with regard to the various findings and recommendations.

The internal auditing literature recognizes six components in an audit report: an overall summary, an introduction, a statement of purpose, a statement of scope, a statement of opinion, and the findings. The reporting standards prescribed for the GAO are shown in Exhibit 2-11, and they bear out the emphasis on effective communication.

The preparation of internal audit reports, by other than GAO auditors, can be flexible, with some professionals opting (1) to exclude recommendations, (2) to express their scope and findings without any opinion expressed as such, and (3) to quantify the cost savings that would accrue from implementing suggestions—as a means of encouraging acceptance of the internal auditors' recommendations. Because the internal auditors' primary responsibility is to serve management—particularly the audit committee of the board of directors—it is only appropriate that their reports be tailored to the board's use and be prepared in a manner that is deemed to be most effective in communicating the results.

REVIEW QUESTIONS

1. When a middle paragraph is added to a standard auditor's report in order to emphasize a matter, phrases like "with the foregoing explanation" should not be used in the opinion paragraph. Why not?

2. "The auditor may express an unqualified opinion on one of the financial statements and express a qualified or adverse opinion or even disclaim an opinion on another, if the circumstances call for this treatment" (SAS No. 2, AU§509.05). How can this fact be reconciled with the concept of reporting on statements "taken as a whole"?

3. The "subject to" and "disclaimer" qualifications indicate that the auditor totally agrees with the presentation of the financial statements. Is this assertion correct? Explain your reasoning.

4. In 1958, at least one accounting firm adopted a variation of the standard form of the auditor's report which read: ". . . present fairly . . . and were prepared in conformity with generally accepted accounting principles. . . ."[17] What are the implications of this report? How has the profession addressed these implications since 1958? Assume that your client uses the LIFO method of inventory valuation but that you believe that the FIFO method would result in a fairer presentation. What, then, are your responsibilities?

5. Rule 203 of the Code of Ethics of the AICPA states

[16] Ralph Estes and Marvin Reimer, "An Experimental Study of the Differential Effect of Standard and Qualified Auditors' Opinions on Investors' Price Decisions," *Accounting and Business Research*, Spring 1979, pp. 157–162.

[17] "Implications of 'Present Fairly' in the Auditor's Report," edited by Carman G. Blough, *Journal of Accountancy*, March 1958, pp. 76–77; and "More About 'Present Fairly' in the Auditor's Report," edited by Carman G. Blough, *Journal of Accountancy*, May 1958, pp. 73–75.

EXHIBIT 2-11

Reporting Standards for Audits of Governmental Organizations, Programs, Activities, and Functions

1. Written audit reports are to be submitted to the appropriate officials of the organizations requiring or arranging for the audits. Copies of the reports should be sent to other officials who may be responsible for taking action on audit findings and recommendations and to others responsible or authorized to receive such reports. Unless restricted by law or regulation, copies should also be made available for public inspection.

2. Reports are to be issued on or before the dates specified by law, regulation, or other arrangement and, in any event, as promptly as possible so as to make the information available for timely use by management and by legislative officials.

3. Each report shall:

   a. Be as concise as possible but, at the same time, clear and complete enough to be understood by the users.

   b. Present factual matter accurately, completely, and fairly.

   c. Present findings and conclusions objectively and in language as clear and simple as the subject matter permits.

   d. Include only factual information, findings, and conclusions that are adequately supported by enough evidence in the auditor's working papers to demonstrate or prove, when called upon, the basis for the matters reported and their correctness and reasonableness. Detailed supporting information should be included in the report to the extent necessary to make a convincing presentation.

   e. Include, when possible, the auditor's recommendations for actions to effect improvements in problem areas noted in his audit and to otherwise make improvements in operations. Information on underlying causes of problems reported should be included to assist in implementing or devising corrective actions.

   f. Place primary emphasis on improvement rather than on criticism of the past; critical comments should be presented in balanced perspective, recognizing any unusual difficulties or circumstances faced by the operating officials concerned.

   g. Identify and explain issues and questions needing further study and consideration by the auditor or others.

   h. Include recognition of noteworthy accomplishments, particularly when management improvements in one program or activity may be applicable elsewhere.

   i. Include recognition of the views of responsible officials of the organization, program, function, or activity audited on the auditor's findings, conclusions, and recommendations. Except where the possibility of fraud or other compelling reason may require different treatment, the auditor's tentative findings and conclusions should be reviewed with such officials. When possible, without undue delay, their views should be obtained in writing and objectively considered and presented in preparing the final report.

   j. Clearly explain the scope and objectives of the audit.

   k. State whether any significant pertinent information has been omitted because it is deemed privileged or confidential. The nature of such information should be described, and the law or other basis under which it is withheld should be stated.

4. Each audit report containing financial reports shall:

   a. Contain an expression of the auditor's opinion as to whether the information in the financial reports is presented fairly in accordance with generally accepted accounting principles (or with other specified accounting principles applicable to the organization, program, function, or activity audited), applied on a basis consistent with that of the preceding reporting period. If the auditor cannot express an opinion, the reasons therefor should be stated in the audit report.

   b. Contain appropriate supplementary explanatory information about the contents of the financial reports as may be necessary for full and informative disclosure about the financial operations of the organization, program, function, or activity audited. Violations of legal or other regulatory requirements, including instances of noncompliance, and material changes in accounting policies and procedures, along with their effect on the financial reports, shall be explained in the audit report.

From Comptroller General of the United States, *Standards for Audit of Governmental Organizations, Programs, Activities, and Functions* (Washington, D.C.: U.S. General Accounting Office, 1972).

that "the proper accounting treatment is that which will render financial statements not misleading." The existing literature has interpreted this as implying a "fairness test" on a negative basis to encompass (a) concern over the users' understanding, (b) responsibility for not leading the users to forecast incorrect or unlikely events, and (c) determination that the disclosure is sufficient. An example of (b) is a situation in which substantially all sales made during a year were made under a contract that was later canceled.[18] This fact should be presented on the face of the income statement. Give examples of (a) and (c).

6. Statement on Auditing Procedure No. 22 addresses the technical authorship of financial statements:

> The accountant's representations are confined to and expressed in his report, or opinion, upon the statements. The transactions with which the accounting records have to do, and the recording of those transactions in the books and accounts are matters within the direct or primary knowledge of the company. The accountant's knowledge of them is a secondary one, based on his examination. Accordingly, even though the *form* of the statements may show the influence of the accountant, it can only do so if the company accepts, and adopts, the form of disclosure advised by the accountant—the *substance* of the financial statements of necessity constitutes the representations of the company.[19]

How can auditors communicate this technical authorship? How else can they clarify this point?

7. The standards of reporting are the same whether an auditor's report is a short-form report or refers to information accompanying the basic financial reports in auditor-submitted documents. How does the report on such accompanying information differ from the short-form report?

8. One client capitalizes certain minor, relatively short-lived items of plant and equipment and then depreciates the amount so capitalized. Another client charges off such items, expensing them when purchased or installed. How can an auditor attest to both clients' compliance with the depreciation requirement of the generally accepted accounting principles?

9. Indicate whether the following statements are true (t) or false (f). Rewrite any false statements to make them true.

- **a.** An accounting principle may be found to have only limited usage but still have general acceptance.
- **b.** The omission of the confirmation of receivables will require disclosure in both the scope and the opinion paragraphs.
- **c.** When a qualification pertains to the amount of a provision for losses, the auditor should state "It is not possible to determine the losses."
- **d.** Very material scope limitations will result in an "except for" qualification of the auditor's report.
- **e.** A CPA's review of a client's forecast constitutes an attestation as to the achievability of that forecast.

10. The proverbial expression of "circumstances alter cases" has been cited as peculiarly fitting the auditor's function, making inevitable the need for an auditor to exercise his or her judgment. How does the auditor's report communicate this judgment?

11. "Sometimes it would appear that auditors sign certificates which, if read carefully, mean nothing at all, and in which little or no responsibility is assumed concerning the financial position of the company whose accounts have been audited."[20] Comment on the historical and current validity of this assertion.

12. Some of the alternative phrases for the "subject to" audit report include

- "subject to the foregoing comments."
- "subject to the explanation in the preceding paragraph."
- "subject to the effect of such adjustment, if any, that may be required as a result of the matter referred to in the preceding paragraph."
- "subject to this uncertainty which has been appropriately disclosed in the financial statements."

Explain the advantages and disadvantages of each alternative.

13. Under what circumstances must inquiry and limited analytical review procedures be applied to supplementary information in auditor-submitted documents? How should the audit report read in such a circumstance? State all of the assumptions you made in answering this question.

14. Compare and contrast internal auditors' and external auditors' reports.

EXERCISES

1. The following auditor's report was common in England in 1862:

> I have examined the above balance sheet with the books of the company, and certify that in my opinion the bal-

[18] J. Burton, "Fair Presentation: Another View," *CPA Journal*, June 1975, pp. 17–18.

[19] Special Report by the Committee on Auditing Procedure, "Tentative Statement of Auditing Standards—Their Generally Accepted Significance and Scope" (New York: AICPA, 1947), p. 35.

[20] J. Hugh Jackson, "Audit Certificates and Reports," *Accounting Review*, September 1926, p. 47.

ance sheet, containing the particulars required by the first Schedule of the Companies Act, 1862, and properly drawn up so as to exhibit a true and correct view of the state of the company's affairs.[21]

Compare this report with the various reports presented in Exhibit 2-1. What are its relative strengths and weaknesses?

2. Indicate whether the following statements are true (t) or false (f). Make any false statements into true statements.
   a. Engagements in which the auditor is asked to report on one financial statement and not the others involve scope limitations.
   b. When auditors decide to refer to the report of another auditor as a partial basis for their opinion, these references do not constitute a qualification of the auditor's opinion.
   c. Restrictions on the scope of an auditor's exam constitute a scope limitation if imposed by the client but not if caused by circumstances such as the timing of the audit work.
   d. When restrictions that significantly limit the scope of the audit are imposed by the client, the auditor generally should qualify an opinion on the financial statements.
   e. A middle paragraph indicates a qualified audit opinion.
   f. A client whose annual report includes four years' audited financial statements, all of which received unqualified opinions, will be representing that accounting principles are consistently applied for five years—the four years presented and the preceding year.
3. The modification of an auditor's report with respect to consistency would be required in which of the following settings?
   a. Change in estimated residual value for equipment.
   b. Disposition of a subsidiary.
   c. Change in the basis of accounting for an investment from the cost basis to the equity basis of accounting.
   d. Correction of the reported balance of marketable securities owing to a typographical error in preparing the financial statements for the preceding year.
   e. Adoption of the percentage-of-completion method for a newly established line of business—the entity's first construction-related operation.
   f. Change in accounting for inventory from FIFO to weighted average.
4. The auditors are discussing their report with their client's audit committee, explaining that both the prior and the current year's reports will have to include qualified opinions. One of the directors exclaims, "But last year we had an unqualified opinion. I understand that our legal exposure under this pending workmen's compensation case is uncertain and potentially material, requiring a qualified opinion for the current year. But why is last year affected?" Explain the conditions that have made it necessary for the auditors to express a qualified opinion for the current and the prior year. Can any other reporting approaches be used?
5. The auditor's practice of emphasizing a matter in a middle paragraph has been criticized as a source of ambiguity. The emphasis is cited as effectively suggesting that an auditor is unhappy with management's disclosure. The idea of introducing that paragraph with such phrasing as "we draw attention to . . . " and then not referring to that middle paragraph in the opinion paragraph is cited as having the practical effect of leaving the middle paragraph "floating in limbo." The current literature emphasizes that users are left with a sense of uneasiness. How valid is such criticism? Do you believe that the "emphasis of matter" reporting practice ought to be continued? Why or why not?
6. According to the British Standards for Chartered Accountants, a distinction should be made between *material* and *fundamental*. Specifically, when there is a disagreement between the auditor and the client concerning a material but not a fundamental matter, an "except for" opinion is appropriate. But when the matter is fundamental, an adverse opinion is required, in which chartered accountants state that in their opinion, the financial statements do not give a "true and fair" view. Similarly, if financial statements are affected by uncertainty on a particular matter that is material but not considered fundamental, a "subject to" opinion is issued. When a fundamental matter is at hand, involving uncertainty, a disclaimer of opinion is required in which the chartered accountants state their inability to form an opinion as to whether the financial statements give a "true and fair" view.

   How do the concepts of fundamental and material in the British standards compare with the U.S. reporting standards for qualified opinions? Give two examples of what you believe would be a material versus a fundamental matter for both uncertain and disagreement circumstances. How distinct do you perceive those classifications to be in practice? What are the ramifications of your perception?

[21] Francis W. Pixley, *Auditors: Their Duties and Responsibilities* (London: Henry Good and Son, 1906), p. 444.

7. In 1938, the point was raised that footnotes belonged to the client and therefore should contain explanatory material but that qualifications and exceptions belonged in the accountants' report: "The company cannot take exception to its own presentation." One year earlier, the issue had been similarly cited:

> While explanatory footnotes are sometimes necessary, an accountant has not lived up to his full professional obligation if he accepts an unsatisfactory method, explained in a footnote, in any case in which by the exercise of courage and persuasion he might have brought about the adoption of a more satisfactory method which would have rendered the footnote unnecessary.[22]

Should the accountant be unable to persuade the client to change, then a qualification of the auditor's report is appropriate. Consider the "subject to" reporting controversy in light of these assertions.

8. In 1938, the phrase "subject to the foregoing" commonly appeared in the last paragraph of a certificate with reference to the preceding paragraphs. Some accountants stated:

> No, we are not taking exception; we are merely calling attention to the fact that the foregoing comments must be read in order to get an intelligent picture of the financial condition of the company or the results of its operations; they are explanatory in nature and not qualifications.

Other accountants said:

> Most assuredly we intend to take exception. When we have stated a practice followed by the client and then say "subject to the foregoing," we mean to say that our certificate is qualified by the matters previously recited.[23]

How has the profession responded to this problem?

9. An auditor's report was drafted as follows:

> Pursuant to instructions received and in continuation of previous audits, we have made an audit of the books and accounts of the Blank Company for the year ended December 31, 19——, and supplementing the certified accounts already furnished you, we now submit our detailed report thereon. We have not attempted to make a detailed check of all cash or other transactions within the period under review. However, the broader examination necessarily brought to our attention a large number of these transactions and we are pleased to report that so far as our examination extended the accounts were found in order.[24]

Comment on the report's clarity.

10. A study of auditors' reporting practices before 1926 indicated that three out of thirty-eight firms printed statements warning against the fraudulent use of the reports on audited statements. An example of these statements, which appeared in italics at the bottom of the first page of the audited report and set of financial statements, is as follows:

> Our certificate or report upon an audit or examination is delivered to client with the distinct understanding that any advertisement, publication, or copy therefrom in full or in part, of such certificate or report, shall be in the form to be approved by us. As a preventive against fraud, attention is directed to the fact that all pages in this report should bear our watermark.[25]

What is your reaction to this warning? Who owns the auditor's report?

11. The claim that "subject to" opinions ought to be retained for attention-directing purposes has been cited as a troublesome premise. Should other items also be included in the audit report as "flags"? What if the auditor fails to include a flag? In what sense does the "subject to" qualification differ from the use of a middle paragraph to emphasize a matter?

Many believe that "subject to" opinions are useful flags for the users. What other flags would you suggest for disclosure in the auditor's report, and why? Compare and contrast the emphasis of a matter disclosure approach with the "subject to" report form.

QUESTIONS ADAPTED FROM PROFESSIONAL EXAMINATIONS

1. Presented below are three independent, unrelated auditor's reports. The corporation being reported on, in each case, is profit oriented and publishes general-purpose financial statements for distribution to owners, creditors, potential investors, and the general public. Each of the reports contains deficiencies.

Auditor's Report I

We have examined the consolidated balance sheet of Belasco Corporation and subsidiaries as of December 31, 19X5, and the related consolidated statements of income and retained earnings and changes in financial position for the year then ended. Our examination was made in accordance with generally accepted auditing standards and accordingly included such tests of the accounting records and such other auditing procedures as we considered necessary in the circumstances. We did not examine the financial statements of Seidel Company, a major consolidated

[22] Carman G. Blough, "Accountants' Certificates," *Journal of Accountancy*, February 1938, p. 111.
[23] Ibid., p. 112.
[24] J. Hugh Jackson, "Audit Certificates and Reports," *Accounting Review*, September 1926, p. 52.
[25] Ibid., p. 62.

subsidiary. These statements were examined by other auditors whose report thereon has been furnished to us, and our opinion expressed herein, insofar as it relates to Seidel Company, is based solely upon the report of the other auditors.

In our opinion, except for the report of the other auditors, the accompanying consolidated balance sheet and consolidated statements of income and retained earnings and changes in financial position present fairly the financial position of Belasco Corporation and subsidiaries at December 31, 19X5, and the results of its operations and the changes in its financial position for the year then ended, in conformity with generally accepted accounting principles applied on a basis consistent with that of the preceding year.

Auditor's Report II

The accompanying balance sheet of Jones Corporation as of December 31, 19X5, and the related statements of income and retained earnings and changes in financial position for the year then ended were not audited by us; however, we confirmed cash in the bank and performed a general review of the statements.

During our engagement, nothing came to our attention to indicate that the aforementioned financial statements do not present fairly the financial position of Jones Corporation at December 31, 19X5, and the results of its operations and the changes in its financial position for the year then ended, in conformity with generally accepted accounting principles applied on a basis consistent with that of the preceding year; however, we do not express an opinion on them.

Auditor's Report III

I made my examination in accordance with generally accepted auditing standards. However, I am not independent with respect to Mavis Corporation because my wife owns 5 percent of the outstanding common stock of the company. The accompanying balance sheet of December 31, 19X5, and the related statements of income and retained earnings and changes in financial position for the year then ended were not audited by me; accordingly, I do not express an opinion on them.

Required:

Describe the reporting deficiencies in each auditor's report, explain the reasons therefore, and briefly discuss how the report should be corrected. Each report should be considered separately. When discussing one report, ignore the other two. Do not discuss the addressee, signatures, and date, and do not rewrite any of the auditor's reports. Organize your answer as follows:

Report No.	Deficiency	Reason	Correction

(CPA exam adapted)

2. The following tentative auditor's report was drafted by a staff accountant and submitted to a partner in the accounting firm of Better & Best, CPAs:

To the Audit Committee of
American Widgets, Inc.

We have examined the consolidated balance sheets of American Widgets, Inc., and subsidiaries as of December 31, 19X5 and 19X4, and the related consolidated statements of income, retained earnings, and changes in financial position, for the years then ended. Our examinations were made in accordance with generally accepted auditing standards as we considered necessary in the circumstances. Other auditors examined the financial statements of certain subsidiaries and have furnished us with reports thereon containing no exceptions. Our opinion expressed herein, insofar as it relates to the amounts included for those subsidiaries, is based solely upon the reports of the other auditors.

As discussed in Note 4 to the financial statements, on January 8, 19X6, the company halted the production of certain medical equipment as a result of inquiries by the Food and Drug Administration, which raised questions as to the adequacy of some of the company's sterilization equipment and related procedures. Management is not in a position to evaluate the effect of this production halt and the ensuing litigation, which may have an adverse effect on the financial position of American Widgets, Inc.

As fully discussed in Note 7 to the financial statements, in 19X5 the company extended the use of the last-in, first-out (LIFO) method of accounting to include all inventories. In examining inventories, we engaged Dr. Irwin Same (Nobel Prize winner 19X3) to test-check the technical requirements and specifications of certain items of equipment manufactured by the company.

In our opinion, except for the effects, if any, on the financial statements of the ultimate resolution of the matter discussed in the second preceding paragraph, the financial statements referred to above present fairly the financial position of American Widgets, Inc., as of December 31, 19X5, and the results of operations for the year then ended, in conformity with generally accepted accounting principles applied on a basis consistent with that of the preceding year.

To be signed by
Better & Best, CPAs

March 1, 19X6, except for
Note as to which the date
is January 8, 19X6

Required:

Identify the deficiencies in the staff accountant's tentative report that depart from the generally accepted standards of reporting.

(CPA exam adapted)

3. About two years ago you were engaged to conduct an annual audit of Pierson Company. This was shortly after the majority stockholders assumed control of the company and discharged the president and several other corporate officers. A new president canceled a wholesaler's contract to distribute Pierson Company products. The wholesaler is a Pierson Company minority stockholder and was one of the discharged officers. Shortly after you commenced your initial audit, several lawsuits were filed against Pierson Company by the wholesaler. Pierson Company filed countersuits.

None of the suits has been decided. The principal litigation is over the canceled contract, and the other suits are claims against the company for salary, bonus, and pension fund contributions. Pierson Company is the plaintiff in suits totaling approximately $300,000 and the defendant in suits totalling approximately $2,000,000. Both amounts are material in relation to net income and total assets. Pierson's legal counsel believes that the outcome of the suits is uncertain and that all of the suits are likely to be "tied up in court" for an extended time.

Each year you are instructed by the board of directors to issue an audit report only if it contains an unqualified opinion. Pierson Company refuses to provide for an unfavorable settlement in the financial statements because legal counsel advised the board of directors that such a provision in the financial statements could be used against Pierson by the opposition in court. The pending litigation was fully disclosed in a footnote to the financial statements, however.

You did not issue a report on the completion of your audit one year ago, and you have now completed your second annual audit. The scope of your audits was not restricted in any way, and you would render unqualified opinions if there were no pending litigations. You have attended all meetings of the stockholders and the directors and answered all questions directed to you at these meetings. You were promptly paid for all work completed to the current date. The board of directors of Pierson Company invited you to deliver to them an audit report containing an unqualified opinion or to attend the annual meeting of the stockholders one week hence to answer questions concerning the results of your audit if you are unwilling to render an unqualified opinion.

Required:

a. Discuss the issues raised for the CPA by the fact that he or she attended the stockholders' and directors' meetings and answered all questions addressed to him or her. Do not consider the propriety of the CPA's failure to issue a written audit report.

b. Should a CPA issue his or her audit report right after completing the examination? Why or why not?

c. **(1)** What kind of auditor's opinion would you render on Pierson Company's financial statements for the year just ended? Why? (You need not write an auditor's opinion.)

(2) Informative disclosures are usually contained in the middle paragraph of the short-form auditor's report. Write the middle paragraph that you would include in your short-form auditor's report for Pierson Company's financial statements for the year just ended.

(CPA exam adapted)

4. The auditor's report must contain an opinion or a statement to the effect that an opinion cannot be expressed. Four types of opinions that meet these requirements are generally known as

a. Unqualified opinions.
b. Qualified opinions.
c. Adverse opinions.
d. Disclaimers of opinion.

For each of the following situations indicate the type of opinion that you would render by selecting the appropriate letter from this listing. Select the one best answer choice for each item.

Unless indicated to the contrary, you may assume that the examination was made in accordance with generally accepted auditing standards, that the financial statements present fairly the financial position and results of operations in conformity with generally accepted accounting principles applied on a consistent basis, and that the statements include adequate informative disclosure necessary not to be misleading.

(1) During the course of an examination, the CPA suspects that a material amount of the assets of the client, Ash Corporation, have been misappropriated through fraud. The corporation refuses to allow the auditor to expand the scope of the examination sufficiently to confirm these suspicions.

(2) Balsam Corporation is engaged in a hazardous trade and cannot obtain insurance coverage from any source. A material portion of the corporation's assets could be destroyed by a serious accident. The corporation has an excellent safety record and has never suffered a catastrophe.

(3) The CPA is examining the Chestnut Corporation's financial statements for the first time. Earlier financial statements carry the unqualified opinion of a CPA who is unknown to the CPA currently conducting the examination. The CPA believes the balance sheet fairly presents the corporation's financial position, but the CPA was not authorized to test the activity of earlier periods and is unwilling to assume any responsibility for the work performed by the previous CPA.

(4) Dogwood Corporation owns properties that have substantially appreciated in value since the date of purchase. The properties were appraised and are reported in the balance sheet at the appraised values with full disclosure. The CPA believes that the values reported in the balance sheet are reasonable.

(5) The CPA is examining the financial statements that are to be included in the annual report to the stockholders of Elm Corporation, a regulated company. Elm Corporation's financial statements are prepared as prescribed by a regulatory agency of the United States government, and some items are not presented in accordance with generally accepted accounting principles. The amounts involved are material and are adequately disclosed in footnotes to the financial statements.

(6) The CPA was engaged to examine the Fig Wholesale Corporation's financial statements after the close of the corporation's fiscal year. On completing the examination, the CPA is satisfied that the corporation's financial statements are presented fairly, except that the CPA is not satisfied that the Fig Wholesale Corporation's inventory is fairly stated on the balance sheet date. The amount of the inventory is material.

(7) The CPA has examined Ginkgo Corporation's financial statements for many years. During the year just ended a service bureau was employed to process by computer the corporation's financial data. The CPA knows very little about computers and does not wish to conduct the audit for the year just ended. The CPA and the president of the corporation are old friends, however, and the president persuaded the CPA that she should not withdraw from the engagement. After glancing at the records and comparing the current year's statements with those of earlier years, the CPA believes that the statements prepared by the service bureau are stated fairly.

(8) After the close of the Holly Corporation's fiscal year, a major debtor was declared bankrupt owing to a rapid series of events. The debtor had confirmed the full amount due to Holly Corporation at the balance sheet date. Because the account was good at the balance sheet date, Holly Corporation refuses to disclose any information in regard to this subsequent event. The CPA believes that all accounts were stated fairly at the balance sheet date.

(9) Ivy Corporation has a subsidiary company in a foreign country. An independent auditor in that country issued an unqualified opinion on the subsidiary's financial statements. Although the CPA is unaware of the standards of the practice of public accountancy in the foreign country, (s)he is willing to accept full responsibility for the independent auditor's opinion on the subsidiary company's financial statements because (s)he believes Ivy Corporation's internal audit staff performed an adequate check on the operations of the subsidiary company during the year. The CPA would be willing to express an unqualified opinion on the financial statements of Ivy Corporation alone, but (s)he must also express an opinion on the consolidated financial statements of Ivy Corporation and its subsidiaries.

(10) For many years the CPA has examined the Juniper Corporation's financial statements and has always been able to render an unqualified opinion. Seven months ago the membership of the AICPA, in consensus with the authoritative organizations responsible for financial reporting standards, adopted (effective ninety days after adoption) only one of two procedures as proper for reporting a particular financial transaction. The Juniper Corporation has applied the previously acceptable procedure for many years and consistently applied that procedure during the year just ended. The corporation disclosed through footnotes to the current financial statements that the procedure employed now differs from the procedure adopted by the AICPA. The corporation feels that lack of consistency is an overriding factor because the change in procedure would require it to report a material loss for the current year.

(11) Kapok Corporation is a substantial user of electronic data-processing equipment and has used an outside service bureau to process the data in years past. During the current year the client adopted the policy of leasing all hardware and expects to continue this arrangement in the future. This change in policy is adequately disclosed in footnotes to the client's financial statements, but uncertainty prohibits either the client or the CPA from assessing the effect of this change on future operations.

(12) Linden Corporation has material investments in stocks of subsidiary companies. Stocks of the subsidiary companies are not actively traded in the market, and the CPA's engagement does not extend to any subsidiary company. The CPA is able to satisfy himself or herself that all of the investments are carried at original cost, and (s)he has no reason to suspect that the amounts are not stated fairly.

(13) Maple Corporation has large investments in stocks of subsidiary companies, but the investments are not material in relation to the corporation's financial position and results of operations. Stocks of the subsidiary companies are not actively traded in the market, and the CPA's engagement does not extend to any subsidiary company. The CPA is able to satisfy himself or herself that all investments are carried at original cost, and (s)he has no reason to suspect that the amounts are not fairly stated.

(14) Pecan Corporation has material investments in stocks of subsidiary companies. Stocks of the subsidiary companies are actively traded in the market, but the CPA's engagement does not extend to any subsidiary company. Management insists that all investments be carried at original costs, and the CPA is satisfied that the original costs are fairly stated. The CPA believes that the client will never realize a substantial portion of the investments, but there is no disclosure to this effect in the financial statements.

(15) Quassia Corporation has material investments in stocks of subsidiary companies. Stocks of the subsidiary companies are actively traded in the market, but the CPA's engagement does not extend to any subsidiary company. Management insists that all investments be carried at original costs, and the CPA is satisfied that the original costs are fairly stated. The CPA believes that the client will never realize a substantial portion of the investments, and the client has fully disclosed the facts in footnotes to the financial statements.

(CPA exam adapted)

5. The following report was drafted by an audit assistant at the completion of an audit engagement and was submitted to the auditor with client responsibility for review. The auditor reviewed the matters thoroughly and properly concluded that the scope limitation was not client imposed and was not sufficiently material to warrant a disclaimer of opinion, although a qualified opinion was appropriate.

To Carl Corporation Controller:

We have examined the accompanying financial statements of Carl Corporation as of December 31, 19X6. Our examination was made in accordance with generally accepted auditing standards and accordingly included such auditing procedures as we considered necessary in the circumstances.

On January 15, 19X7, the company issued debentures in the amount of $1,000,000 for the purpose of financing plant expansion. As indicated in Note 6 to the financial statements, the debenture agreement restricts the payment of future cash dividends to earnings after December 31, 19X6.

The company's unconsolidated foreign subsidiary did not close down production during the year under examination for physical inventory purposes and took no physical inventory during the year. We made extensive tests of book inventory figures for accuracy of calculation and reasonableness of pricing. We did not make physical tests of inventory quantities. Because of this, we are unable to express an unqualified opinion on the financial statements taken as a whole. However:

Except for the scope limitation regarding inventory, in our opinion the accompanying balance sheet presents the financial position of Carl Corporation at December 31, 19X6, subject to the effect of the inventory on the carrying value of the investment. The accompanying statements of income and of retained earnings present the incomes and expenses and the result of transactions affecting retained earnings in accordance with generally accepted accounting principles.

December 31, 19X6

Pate & Co., CPAs

Required:
Identify all of the deficiencies in the above draft of the proposed report.

(CPA exam adapted)

6. Multiple-Choice: Reporting Issues
Select the one answer that best completes the statement or answers the question.

6.1 The accuracy of information included in the footnotes that accompany the audited financial statements of a company whose shares are traded on a stock exchange is the primary responsibility of:
a. The stock exchange officials.
b. The independent auditor.

c. The company's management.
d. The Securities and Exchange Commission.

(CPA exam adapted)

6.2 With respect to issuing an audit report that is dual dated for an event occurring after the completion of field work but before the issuance of the auditor's report, responsibility for those events occurring after the completion of fieldwork is

a. Extended to include all events occurring until the date of the last subsequent event referred to.
b. Limited to the specific event referred to.
c. Limited to all events occurring through the date of the report's issuance.
d. Extended to include all events occurring through the date that the report is submitted to the client.

(CPA exam adapted)

6.3 Internal audit reports can be structured to motivate management to correct deficiencies. Which of the following report writing techniques is likely to be the most effective?

a. List the deficiencies found so as to provide an easy-to-follow checklist.
b. Suggest improvements for the currently used procedures after indicating the audit findings.
c. Point out the procedural inadequacies and resulting improprieties.
d. Recommend changes and state the punitive measures that will follow if the recommendations are not implemented.
e. Direct that the corrective action be taken.

(CPA exam adapted)

6.4 The auditor's best course of action with respect to "other financial information" included in an annual report containing the auditor's report is to

a. Indicate in the auditor's report that the "other financial information" has not been audited.
b. Consider whether the "other financial information" is accurate, by performing a limited review.
c. Obtain written representations from management as to the material accuracy of the "other financial information."
d. Read and consider the manner of presenting the "other financial information."

(CPA exam adapted)

6.5 When comparative financial statements are presented, the fourth standard of reporting, which refers to financial statements "taken as a whole," should be considered to apply to the financial statements of the

a. Periods presented plus the one preceding period.
b. Current period only.
c. Current period and those of the other periods presented.
d. Current and immediately preceding period only.

(CPA exam adapted)

6.6 On February 13, 19X6, Fox, a CPA, met with the audit committee of the Gem Corporation to review the draft of Fox's report on the company's financial statements as of and for the year ended December 31, 19X5. On February 16, 19X6, Fox completed all remaining field work at the Gem Corporation's headquarters. On February 17, 19X6, Fox typed and signed the final version of the auditor's report. On February 18, 19X6, the final report was mailed to Gem's audit committee. What date should have been used on Fox's report?

a. February 13, 19X6.
b. February 16, 19X6.
c. February 17, 19X6.
d. February 18, 19X6.

(CPA exam adapted)

6.7 Which of the following actions should be taken by a CPA who has been asked to examine the financial statements of a company whose fiscal year has ended?

a. Discuss with the client the possibility of an adverse opinion because of the late engagement date.
b. Decide whether circumstances are likely to permit an adequate examination and expression of an unqualified opinion.
c. Inform the client of the need to issue a qualified opinion if the physical inventory has already been taken.
d. Determine whether a proper study and evaluation of internal control can be conducted after completion of the field work.

(CPA exam adapted)

6.8 Before reissuing a report that was previously issued on the financial statements of an earlier period, a predecessor auditor should

a. Review the successor auditor's working papers.
b. Examine significant transactions or events since the date of the previous issuance.
c. Obtain a signed engagement letter from the client.
d. Obtain a letter of representation from the successor auditor.

(CPA exam adapted)

6.9 The auditor's judgment concerning the overall

fairness of the presentation of financial position, results of operations, and changes in financial position is applied within the framework of

a. Quality control.
b. Generally accepted auditing standards which include the concept of materiality.
c. The auditor's evaluation of the audited company's internal control.
d. Generally accepted accounting principles.

(CPA exam adapted)

6.10 When reporting on financial statements prepared on a comprehensive basis of accounting other than generally accepted accounting principles, the independent auditor should include in the report a paragraph that

a. States that the financial statements are not intended to be in conformity with generally accepted accounting principles.
b. Justifies the comprehensive basis of accounting being used.
c. Refers to the authoritative pronouncements that explain the comprehensive basis of accounting being used.
d. States that the financial statements are not intended to have been examined in accordance with generally accepted auditing standards.

(CPA exam adapted)

6.11 When comparative financial statements are presented but the predecessor auditor's report is not presented, the current auditor should do which of the following in the audit report?

a. Disclaim an opinion on the prior year's financial statements.
b. Identify the predecessor auditor who examined the financial statements of the prior year.
c. Make no comment with respect to the predecessor auditor's examination.
d. Indicate the type of opinion expressed by the predecessor auditor.

(CPA exam adapted)

6.12 For reporting purposes, the independent auditor should consider each of the following types of financial presentation to be a financial statement, except the statement of

a. Changes in owners' equity.
b. Operations by product lines.
c. Changes in the elements of working capital.
d. Cash receipts and disbursements.

(CPA exam adapted)

6.13 It is not appropriate for the auditor's report to refer a reader to a financial statement footnote for details regarding

a. A change in accounting principle.
b. A limitation in the scope of the audit.
c. An uncertainty.
d. A related party transaction.

(CPA exam adapted)

6.14 When the financial statements of a previous period are compared with the financial statements of the current period, the continuing auditor is responsible for

a. Expressing dual-dated opinions.
b. Updating the report on the previous financial statements only if there has not been a change in the opinion.
c. Updating the report on the previous financial statements only if the previous report was qualified and the reasons for the qualification no longer are valid.
d. Updating the report on the previous financial statements regardless of the opinion previously issued.

(CPA exam adapted)

6.15 Which of the following best describes the reference to the expression "taken as a whole" in the fourth generally accepted auditing standard of reporting?

a. It applies equally to a complete set of financial statements and to each individual financial statement.
b. It applies only to a complete set of financial statements.
c. It applies equally to each item in each financial statement.
d. It applies equally to each material item in each financial statement.

(CPA exam adapted)

6.16 If the information accompanying the basic financial statements in an auditor-submitted document has been subjected to auditing procedures, the auditor may express an opinion that states that the accompanying information is fairly stated in

a. Conformity with generally accepted accounting principles.
b. Terms of negative assurance.
c. All material respects in regard to the basic financial statements taken as a whole.
d. Conformity with principles for presenting accompanying information.

(CPA exam adapted)

7. Multiple-Choice: Types of Reports

Select the one answer that best completes the statement or answers the question.

7.1 If the auditor believes that significant required disclosures have been omitted from the financial statements under examination, the auditor should issue either

a. A qualified opinion or an adverse opinion.
b. A disclaimer of opinion or a qualified opinion.
c. An adverse opinion or a disclaimer of opinion.
d. An unqualified opinion or a qualified opinion.

(CPA exam adapted)

7.2 In which of the following circumstances would an auditor be required to issue a qualified report with a separate explanatory paragraph?

a. The auditor satisfactorily performed alternative accounts receivable procedures because scope limitations prevented the performance of normal procedures.
b. The financial statements reflect the effects of a change in accounting principles from one period to the next.
c. A particular note to the financial statements discloses a company accounting method that deviates from generally accepted accounting principles.
d. The financial statements of a significant subsidiary were examined by another auditor, and a reference to the other auditor's report is to be made in the principal auditor's report.

(CPA exam adapted)

7.3 When financial statements are prepared on the basis of a going concern and the auditor believes that the client may not continue as a going concern, the auditor should issue

a. A "subject to" opinion.
b. An unqualified opinion with an explanatory middle paragraph.
c. An "except for" opinion.
d. An adverse opinion.

(CPA exam adapted)

7.4 When an adverse opinion is expressed, the opinion paragraph should include a direct reference to

a. The footnote to the financial statements that discusses the basis for the opinion.
b. The scope paragraph that discusses the basis for the opinion rendered.
c. A separate paragraph that discusses the basis for the opinion rendered.
d. The consistency or lack of consistency in the application of generally accepted accounting principles.

(CPA exam adapted)

7.5 In the auditor's opinion, which of the following requires recognition as to consistency?

a. Changing the salvage value of an asset.
b. Changing the presentation of prepaid insurance from inclusion in "other assets" to disclosing it as a separate line item.
c. Division of the consolidated subsidiary into two subsidiaries that each are consolidated.
d. Changing from consolidating a subsidiary to carrying it on the equity basis.

(CPA exam adapted)

7.6 Jones, a CPA, is the principal auditor for his client's consolidated financial statements. Jones plans to refer to another CPA's examination of the financial statements of a subsidiary company but does not wish to present the other CPA's audit report. Both Jones and the other CPA's audit reports have noted no exceptions to generally accepted accounting principles. Under these circumstances the opinion paragraph of Jones's consolidated audit report should express

a. An unqualified opinion.
b. A "subject to" opinion.
c. An "except for" opinion.
d. A principal opinion.

(CPA exam adapted)

7.7 In a first audit of a new company, the auditor's report will

a. Remain silent with respect to consistency.
b. State that the accounting principles have been applied on a consistent basis.
c. State that accounting principles have been applied consistently during the period.
d. State that the consistency standard does not apply because the current year is the first year of audit.

(CPA exam adapted)

7.8 An auditor is confronted with an exception considered sufficiently material as to warrant some deviation from the standard unqualified auditor's report. If the exception refers to a departure from generally accepted accounting principles, the auditor must express either

a. An adverse opinion and a "subject to" opinion.
b. An adverse opinion and an "except for" opinion.
c. An adverse opinion and a disclaimer of opinion.
d. A disclaimer of opinion and a "subject to" opinion.

(CPA exam adapted)

7.9 A continuing auditor updates his or her opinion on earlier financial statements by issuing a "subject to" opinion for the

a. Subsequent resolution of an uncertainty in the current period.
b. Discovery of an uncertainty in the current period.
c. Discovery of an uncertainty in the current period that relates to the prior-period statements being reported on.
d. Restatement of prior-period statements in conformity with generally accepted accounting principles.

(CPA exam adapted)

7.10 Thomas, a CPA, has examined the consolidated financial statements of Kass Corporation. Jones, another CPA, has examined the financial statements of the sole subsidiary which is material in relation to the total examined by Thomas. It would be appropriate for Thomas to serve as the principal auditor, but it is impractical for him to review Jones's work. Assuming that Jones has expressed an unqualified opinion, you would expect Thomas to
a. Refuse to express an opinion on the consolidated financial statements.
b. Express an unqualified opinion on the consolidated financial statements and not refer to Jones's work.
c. Express an unqualified opinion on the consolidated financial statements and refer to Jones's work.
d. Express an "except for" opinion on the consolidated financial statements and refer to Jones's work.

(CPA exam adapted)

7.11 The management of Stanley Corporation has decided not to account for a material transaction, in accordance with the provisions of a recent statement of the FASB. They have set forth their reasons in note "B" to the financial statements which clearly demonstrates that because of unusual circumstances the financial statements would otherwise have been misleading. The auditor's report will probably contain
a. A consistency exception and a reference to Note "B."
b. An unqualified opinion and an explanatory middle paragraph.
c. A "subject to" opinion and an explanatory middle paragraph.
d. An "except for" opinion and an explanatory middle paragraph.

(CPA exam adapted)

7.12 An auditor includes a middle paragraph in an otherwise unqualified report in order to emphasize that the entity being reported on is a subsidiary of another business enterprise. The inclusion of this middle paragraph
a. Is appropriate and will not negate the unqualified opinion.
b. Is considered a qualification of the report.
c. Is a violation of generally accepted reporting standards if this information is disclosed in footnotes to the financial statements.
d. Necessitates a revision of the opinion paragraph to include the phrase "with the foregoing explanation."

(CPA exam adapted)

7.13 Under which of the following set of circumstances might an auditor disclaim an opinion?
a. The financial statements depart from generally accepted accounting principles, the effect of which is material.
b. The principal auditor decides to refer to the report of another auditor who audited a subsidiary.
c. There has been a material change between periods in the method of the application of accounting principles.
d. There are significant uncertainties affecting the financial statements.

(CPA exam adapted)

7.14 Which of the following should be recognized as a consistency modification in the auditor's report, whether or not the item is fully disclosed in the financial statements?
a. A change in accounting estimate.
b. A change from an unacceptable accounting principle to a generally accepted one.
c. Correction of an error not involving a change in accounting principle.
d. A change in classification.

(CPA exam adapted)

CASES FOR DISCUSSION

1. Financial statements are always affected by the uncertainty of future events, as reflected by the prevalence of estimates throughout the accounts. The allowance for bad debts, provisions for warranties, and recorded contingencies are examples of the primary role of estimates in the financial presentation.

The auditor is in no better position to evaluate the outcome of litigation than any other user is. Moreover, the going concern qualification is a prime example of the auditor's assumption of a risk that should be taken by the user of the financial statements. Auditors are cited as not being particularly good at foreseeing company liquidations.

In fact, research has shown that an analysis of financial statements, using certain simple financial ratios, is a better indicator of a company's future prospects than noting whether the auditor had expressed a qualified opinion or an unqualified opinion.[26]

Yet the expression of doubt about a company's continued existence can have some important effects. An interesting analogy with the "subject to going concern" qualification has been presented in the literature:

> Compare it, though, to getting a car back from a garage with a note saying, "subject to the fact that the engine is about to blow up, this car is in good condition." And in exactly the same way that you would have great difficulty selling a car with that comment attached to the windscreen, it is difficult for a company to raise additional finance with a going concern qualification in its audit report. So it becomes a self-fulfilling prophecy—the auditor stands back and says, "I told you so."[27]

These considerations have led to the claim that "subject to" opinions create confusion and ought to be eliminated. Only those situations in which the auditor disagrees with management's disclosures are cited as appropriate circumstances for issuing a qualified audit report. The AICPA actually proposed, in 1977, to do away with the "subject to" opinion and the separate paragraph describing unresolved matters such as pending lawsuits that could have a material effect on the financial statements. But the proposal was not adopted.

Discuss the justification of "subject to" reports or lack thereof. Tie your analysis to each of the points frequently raised by those who oppose this reporting alternative.

2. An article appearing in 1926 addressed the meaning of certification:

> The position of an accountant in certifying to statements seems to me to be in many respects similar to his position as witness in court. He may be called to present figures as they appear in the books and records and he may encounter little difficulty so long as he confines his testimony to the presentation of the exact book entries. But let the questioning once turn to his opinion of the correctness, the meaning or the propriety of entries or accounts, and the court will insist on his being duly qualified to give expert testimony on those questions and will draw a careful line between the facts to which he can testify from personal knowledge and the opinions which he may express as a qualified expert. Nothing will more promptly discredit his testimony than confusion of fact and opinion.[28]

Comment on the appropriateness of this analogy of the attest function with the role of an accountant as a witness in the courtroom. In what sense does an auditor make representations concerning the financial statements' presentation of property, plant, and equipment? Consider those representations that might be relevant to a courtroom controversy over the valuation of capital contributions by two partnerships to a third entity—a newly formed corporation. With respect to which of these representations would an auditor's testimony likely be relevant?

3. The *Journal of Accountancy* of August 1926 reported on an interesting audit report of the 1800s:

> "Port Allen, La., Dec. 29, 1874.
>
> "We, the undersigned, having been appointed a committee to audit the books of the treasurer of the Poydras fund, hereby certify that we have examined all his books and accounts and find them correct in every particular.
>
> "Peter (X) Washington.
> (his mark)
>
> "George (X) Steptoe.
> (his mark)"
>
> The auditors, Messrs. Washington and Steptoe, being unable to read or write affixed their respective marks. It will be noted that they certified that they had examined all books and accounts. This was probably a perfectly correct statement, but it does not affirm that they have read any portion of the books or accounts. If their certificate had ever been called in question it would have been possible for them to say that being illiterate they had done all that was possible to protect the interests of their client. If the client wanted men who could really understand the records in the books, other auditors should have been engaged. (p. 122)

What is the meaning of "we have examined"? In the past, the phrase changed from examined to audited, referring to both audit certificates and opinions. Which term is more precise? Could the 1874 report be issued today? What reporting practices would permit or forbid its issuance?

4. A *Wall Street Journal* headline read "General Tire's Auditor Qualifies Its Opinion Seventh Year in a Row," followed by a description of a number of uncertainties.[29] Arbitration proceedings, a civil antitrust action,

[26] *Commission on Auditors' Responsibilities: Report on Tentative Conclusions* (New York: Commission on Auditors' Responsibilities, 1977), p. 30.

[27] Les Adey, "The Audit Report 'Subject to' . . . Misunderstanding?" *Accountancy*, July 1981, p. 58.

[28] Henry B. Fernald, "Accountants' Certificates," *Journal of Accountancy*, October 1926, p. 255.

[29] February 25, 1982, p. 16.

actions of the California Regional Water Quality Control Board to gain a subsidiary's compliance with regulation, private personal injury suits tied to the alleged contamination of ground waters, the potential requirement to reimburse the U.S. Environmental Protection Agency for the cost of cleanup, and the resolution of judicial and administrative reviews of the Federal Communications Commission all are cited in the fiscal year 1981 report, and most were also in the 1980 report. The *Wall Street Journal* stated:

> Price Waterhouse in its opinion asserted that the "ultimate outcome" of these uncertainties "cannot be determined and no provision of losses, if any, that may result has been made" for potential liabilities. General Tire also doesn't estimate any potential losses, but does say its liabilities in cases involving Cordova "could be substantial." (p. 16)

What appears to be the information value of these disclosures and the auditor's report? Why would the *Wall Street Journal* run this type of story? Does your response have implications for the "subject to" reporting controversy?

5. In his book *Accountants' Legal Responsibility*, Saul Levy described the independent auditor's report as "an expert, independent, informed, technical, and candid opinion."[30] *Webster's New International Dictionary*, 2nd ed., unabridged, defines the exercise of judgment as "the operation of the mind, involving comparison and discrimination, by which knowledge of values and relations is mentally formulated." R. K. Mautz in an article entitled "Evidence, Judgment, and the Auditor's Opinion," elaborated on the certainty of judgments.

> When a man says, "I know," he means merely that he is convinced. And how many of us at one time or another have found our firmest convictions in error? Whether it be politics, the anticipated outcome of athletic contests, or expected business results, most of us have had the experience of being absolutely sure—and also dead wrong. Even sensory perceptions are not always reliable. We see a friend in a crowded room, slap him on the shoulder, and find he is a complete stranger. Eyewitnesses to a crime or an accident often differ considerably in their descriptions of what happened.[31]

In light of these insights into the definition of an auditor's report, the meaning of judgment, and limitations in terms of anyone's "certainty," explain how you would evaluate the essence of the auditor's report. Assume that your auditor's report has just been proved to be inaccurate, as a fraud has been uncovered at a past client's operations. Does such an inaccuracy mean that you have failed to fulfill your responsibilities? Justify your response.

6. In an article entitled "What Does 'Subject to' Mean in an Audit Report?" the following arguments are made for eliminating "subject to" qualifications:

a. A "subject to" qualification is not consistent with an auditor's primary responsibility and is redundant.
b. All firms face uncertainties—it is the reader's responsibility to evaluate them.
c. A "subject to" qualification may be an unfair, self-fulfilling prophecy.
d. Auditors have been unable to isolate "subject to" situations effectively.
e. "Subject to" qualifications are confusing to readers.[32]

Arguments for retention include:

a. "Subject to" qualifications direct readers' attention to unusual uncertainties.
b. Auditor access to inside information should help in the assessment of uncertainty.
c. "Subject to" qualifications need not confuse readers.
d. "Subject to" qualifications may limit auditor liability.[33]

Which of these arguments do you find persuasive, and why? Draft a presentation that you might make before the Auditing Standards Board in support of your views as to whether "subject to" opinions should be retained or eliminated.

[30] New York: AICPA, 1954, p. 7.
[31] *Journal of Accountancy*, April 1959, p. 41.
[32] Kurt Pany and Ralph E. Smith, *Journal of Commercial Bank Lending*, November 1979, p. 39.
[33] Ibid., p. 40.

3

Structure and Standards of the Auditing Profession

John Langley and Wayne Wolfson, two CPAs who are partners of small CPA firms and long-time friends, are meeting for lunch.

John. Did you see that Statement on Auditing Standards (SAS) No. 46 on omitted procedures? What's the purpose of such a pronouncement? I mean, we're really suffering from a standards overload!

Wayne. I know, the tons of paper that we're expected to absorb is getting ridiculous. It's not so bad for the larger firms, as they can afford to assign professional staff members to siphon through it, release information to the staff, and coordinate training sessions. But our staff is operating at 95 percent billable hours.

John. I read SAS No. 46, and it seems to say that if you leave out some audit procedure that should have been performed, you're supposed to go back and do it. Now why did the AICPA waste its paper on so much common sense?

Wayne. Oh, I do have some information about that particular SAS. Apparently, peer review has uncovered noncompliance with auditing standards that suggests there is an inadequate evidential base on which an opinion can be expressed. The AICPA and SEC wanted the profession to remedy this situation, if there are individuals relying on the outstanding reports.

John. You mean that this is our "nonintervening" SEC? I can't tell who's issuing the standards anymore, but as my stack of pronouncements increases, I feel more sure the government's involved.

Wayne. I know a member of the Auditing Standards Board who made an interesting comment regarding the "standards overload" complaints. He pointed out that "overload" to one practitioner is "service" to other practitioners. For example, the "Supplementary Oil and Gas Reserve Information" provision of the 1983 "Omnibus

Statement" (No. 45) is a great help to CPAs servicing that industry, though it's nothing but more paperwork to us!

John. I've been thinking. Maybe we ought to consider merging our firms. We could gain some efficiencies in sorting through technical pronouncements and offering training programs. Plus I think our staffs would complement each other pretty well.

Wayne. We couldn't merge even if we wanted to. Have you forgotten about your partner Merv? He's the brother-in-law of the chief executive officer of our largest client!

John. You're right. But we may have to find another small firm to merge with, because I'm getting concerned about our ability to meet the general standards. Our only choice may be to get out of the auditing business and offer only accounting and tax services.

Wayne. The more I read about the software that those Big Eight firms are producing, the more I wonder about what the audit process will be like by the 1990s.

This discussion between two professionals is typical of the controversy and misunderstanding that often arise in audit standard setting, like that in accounting standard setting. It also points out the difference in the support services available for the small CPA firms and those for larger CPA firms. The "behind the scenes" insight into the standard-setting process bears out the large number of participants that influences the standards-setting process. The mixed reactions to the profession's cooperation with regulators that are reflected in the case just cited are realistic in describing professionals' preference for self-regulation while perceiving the reality of having to operate in a regulated business environment. The impetus to the merger phenomenon that has been observed in the market for auditing services is captured by the observation that increased firm size can increase operating efficiency—essentially the economies to scale principle of microeconomics. Yet, professional standards raise considerations such as the independence of staff, which can operate as barriers to merger that are rather peculiar to the auditing market. The case similarly alludes to changes in the nature of the audit process which could change the future structure of the profession. This chapter will address these various issues raised in the case. After describing public accounting firms, with a profile of the Big Eight firms, the typical organizational structure of practicing units is described. Then the history of the standard-setting process and the current and potential changes in the structure of the Auditing Standards Board are outlined. The field work standards of the profession are described. The many organizations with which the AICPA interacts are discussed. Further evidence of the increased technical knowledge base of accounting professionals is provided by a description of the various types of specialized certifications which are available. Finally, the possible shifts in the profession's structure that could evolve from the merger phenomenon, specialization, and changes in the nature of the auditing process are acknowledged.

Public Accounting Firms

In the early 1980s the number of CPAs grew by 10 percent annually.[1] In 1984, the American Institute of Certified Public Accountants had 218,855 members, 112,673 of which were in public practice.[2]

The Big Eight Firms

The accounting firms that traditionally have been referred to as the Big Eight are

[1] "Choosing the CPA Firm That's *Right* for You" (New York: AICPA, 1981).

[2] "An Updated Look at the AICPA Membership," *The CPA Letter* (New York: AICPA, October 22, 1984), p. 4.

- Arthur Andersen
- Arthur Young
- Coopers & Lybrand
- Deloitte, Haskins & Sells
- Ernst & Whinney
- Peat, Marwick, Mitchell
- Price Waterhouse
- Touche Ross

However, these are no longer in actuality the largest eight public accounting firms. K. M. G. Main Hurdman was the seventh largest accounting firm in 1983, based on total revenue, and the mergers that have recently been discussed may further alter the size rankings.[3] Nevertheless, the Big Eight firms' clients account for at least 94 percent of all sales, profits, and employment in the United States and pay 90 percent of all income taxes.[4] The fact that fewer than 1,000 CPA firms audit the approximately 10,000 corporations registered with the SEC has been cited as troublesome by regulators. Yet, the accounting profession is far less concentrated among the Big Eight than are many key industrial sectors of the economy. For example, of 450 manufacturing industries, 36 had eight-firm concentration ratios from 90 to 100 percent (i.e., exceeding that observed in the public accounting profession.)[5]

As an example of the individual firms' size, Peat, Marwick, Mitchell's 1983 revenue was $1.23 billion, and it had over 1,300 partners and 12,500 staff members in one hundred domestic offices.[6] The 1983 revenue for all of the Big Eight firms was about $8 billion.[7] Or, consider Price Waterhouse's 1976 financial report. The balance sheet's total assets were $75.5 million, and total liabilities were $14.3 million, leaving $61.2 million as the partners' capital account. The auditing, accounting, and other consulting service fees totaled $221.5 million, with expenses of $169 million. Of the expenses, almost 75 percent represented compensation to employees other than partners. Over $9 million was reported for continuing education expenses, and over $4 million was reported for liability insurance and expenses related to litigation. The 378 active partners' average earnings were $128,000, with the top three executives each earning about $330,000. These figures would undergo substantial adjustment to reflect 1983's total worldwide revenue of $1.01 billion, the 17,419 professionals, and the 1,751 partners worldwide.[8]

The auditing firms' size is in large part due to the enormous size of many of their clients. Just to audit General Motors (currently a client of Deloitte, Haskins & Sells) requires fourteen hundred accountants around the world; this represents an audit team that is larger than 99 percent of all the accounting firms in the world. Exhibit 3-1 gives the statistics for the Big Eight firms for the 1930s, 1970s, and 1980s. Although such statistics are constantly changing in the competitive market for audit services, the exhibit shows the long-term stability of each of the Big Eight firms as the dominant suppliers of audit services.

Most of the Big Eight firms are organized as partnerships with no immunity available for the partners' assets. Once the partners' capital is taken, their personal assets are at risk. Thus, it is not surprising that each of the Big Eight firms carry between $60 and $100 million of liability insurance, with double that amount in coverage.

Medium-sized Firms

Although considerably smaller than the Big Eight, some medium-sized firms represent large and, in many cases, national practices. These firms include (in alphabetical order)

Alford, Meroney & Company
Altschuler, Melvoin and Glasser
Baird, Kurtz & Dobson

[3] *Public Accounting Report,* cited in Gary Klott, "Merger Moves in Accounting," *New York Times,* October 3, 1984, pp. D1, D5.

[4] U.S. Senate, Subcommittee on Reports, Accounting and Management of the Committee on Government Operations, *The Accounting Establishment: A Staff Study* (Washington, D.C.: U.S. Government Printing Office), December 1976, known as the Metcalf Report.

[5] "CPAs Suggest the Watchdogs They Want," *Business Week,* May 23, 1977, pp. 94–96.

[6] "Peat Marwick Partners Elect a New Chairman," *New York Times,* October 11, 1984, p. D2.

[7] Klott, "Merger Moves in Accounting," op. cit.

[8] Ibid.

EXHIBIT 3-1

The Big Eight: Descriptive Statistics for the 1930s, 1970s, and 1980s

CPA firm names 1932	Number of companies listed* on New York Stock Exchange audited by each CPA firm in 1932	Total companies audited in 1978† (percentage of auditees with sales over $1 billion audited by each firm in 1978)	Worldwide revenues in 1983 (in millions)
Price Waterhouse & Co.	146	783 (19.4)	$1,013
Haskins & Sells	71	618 (12.1)	$ 894
Ernst & Ernst	71	922 (9.8)	$ 972
Peat, Marwick, Mitchell & Co.	56	1,007 (14.6)	$1,230
Arthur Young & Co.	49	516 (7.9)	$1,003
Lybrand, Ross Bros. & Montgomery	48	848 (9.2)	$1,100
Touche Niven & Co.	27	651 (7.6)	$ 845
Arthur Andersen & Co.	24	1,106 (15.8)	$1,238

* Total listings on the New York Stock Exchange in 1932 were 1,056 companies.
† More than 95 percent of the corporations listed on the New York Stock Exchange were audited by Big Eight firms in 1978.

From "Certified Public Accountants: Architects of the U.S. Balance Sheet," *Fortune*, June 1932, p. 63; Peter W. Bernstein, "Competition Comes to Accounting," *Fortune*, July 17, 1978, p. 91; Steven S. Anreder, "Profit or Loss? Price-Cutting Is Hitting Accountants in the Bottom Line," *Barron's*, March 12, 1979, p. 9; N. Dopuch and D. Simunic, "Competition in Auditing: An Assessment," *Illinois Audit Symposium*, October 1980; *Public Accounting Report*.

Brout & Company
Cherry, Bekaert & Holland
Clifton, Gunderson & Co.
Crowe, Chizek & Co.
Eide, Helmeke, Boelz & Pasch
Eisner & Lubin
John F. Forbes & Company
Fox & Co.
Galusha, Higgins & Galusha
Alexander Grant & Company
Laventhol & Horwath
Kenneth Leventhal & Co.
Mann Judd Landau
May, Zima & Co.
McGladrey, Hendrickson & Co.
Moss, Adams & Co.
Murphey, Jenne & Jones
Geo. S. Olive & Co.
Oppenheim, Appel, Dixon & Co.
Pannell, Kerr, Forster
Plante & Moran
A. M. Pullen & Co.
Seidman & Seidman
Lester Witte & Co.

In 1984, Alexander Grant (the eleventh largest CPA firm) had fifty-nine offices, 2,565 employees, and $146 million of revenue from domestic operations, and Fox & Co. (the thirteenth largest CPA firm) had fifty-two offices, 1,500 employees, and $90 million revenue.[9]

Local Firms

In 1981, there were about thirty thousand CPA firms, and approximately two-thirds of the ninety thousand certified public accountants that were in public practice were with local firms.[10] In 1984, about 57 percent of the 112,673 AICPA members in public practice were with firms with 9 or fewer AICPA members.[11] Note that the partners in CPA firms are the owners and that other professional staff are employees. Partners of local CPA firms often prefer to offer a broad range of business services to a diversified portfolio of clients of various sizes, with an emphasis on smaller emerging businesses. Generally, small CPA firms can provide a more informal work environment for employees, constant interaction with partners, total client responsibility more quickly along one's career path, and fewer out-of-town demands than large CPA firms can. In the first few years of employment, the professional staff members of smaller CPA firms are more likely to have a variety of job assignments, ranging from auditing to consultation regarding clients' financial matters, design and implementation of

[9] Gary Klott, "Accounting Firms Discuss Tie," *New York Times*, October 2, 1984, pp. D1, D8 (from the *Public Accounting Report*).

[10] "Choosing the CPA Firm That's *Right* for You" (New York: AICPA, 1981).

[11] "An Updated Look at the AICPA Membership," *The CPA Letter*, October 22, 1984, p. 4.

accounting systems, tax services, and nonaudit write-up and management advisory services, than are the professional staff members of larger firms. Moreover, the staff accountants in the smaller CPA firms are likely to have more direct contact with the owners and presidents of the medium and small businesses.

The Typical Firm's Structure

Most CPA firms have new staff assistants, senior accountants, managers, and partners. Some firms add an "in-charge" accountant step before the senior phase, and others have senior managers as a step before gaining partner status. These staff classifications usually apply to the CPA firm's auditing, tax, and management advisory service units.

The staff assistant has entry-level responsibilities, and the in-charge accountant may supervise two to five staff assistants on intermediate-level duties. The senior accountant has primary field supervision responsibilities. Day-to-day decisions in the course of an audit usually are a senior's responsibility, with the manager participating in the engagement's planning and final review phase. Similarly, the partner works mainly on the planning and review phase of an engagement. The partner also has more of an oversight role, whereas the manager will probably perform many of the review activities in the field.

In the past, the CPA firm was viewed as a pyramid, with a rather large number of staff accountants, a smaller number of seniors and managers, and fairly few partners. One means of achieving such a structure is through the turnover of larger firms. At Arthur Young & Co. over the past ten years, about 70 percent of the company's new employees left the firm within five years from the date they were hired, and at Peat, Marwick, Mitchell & Co. over the past ten years, an estimated ten thousand professional employees left, with about 20 percent leaving in their first year of employment.[12] Most firms apply an "up or out" philosophy; that is, the professional employees are expected to ascend in rank to partner at a reasonable rate, or they will eventually be "counseled out" of the firm.[13] But most firms view their turnover as excessive and wish to lessen it. This has become an increasing concern as firms hypothesize that the traditional pyramid needs to be narrowed at its base. With the advent of electronic data processing (EDP), microcomputers, and generalized audit software tools (the use of EDP in auditing), there is less demand for inexperienced assistants to perform mundane tasks like footing (adding figures or checking extensions). In contrast, more senior-level staff are needed who can perform more sophisticated audit procedures. Therefore, means of retaining a larger percentage of a smaller number of hirees need to be identified.

Studies of turnover have indicated that departing professionals are usually dissatisfied with supervision and coworkers and are frustrated or discontented with their work. One study, based upon a random sample of 651 professional employees, comparing the attitudes of employees who intended to stay with their employers for at least the next five years with those planning to leave during that period, identified certain personality traits that were more common in those staying in public accounting: a greater amount of cautiousness and emotional stability. Partners tended to score higher than managers or seniors on "vigor, ascendance, and sociability and about the same on original thinking." Of course, this difference in scores may merely reflect the career evolution that takes place from manager to partner. The implication of this survey data, assuming its validity, is the need for increased attention to timely performance evaluations, the weeding out of less qualified staff, the awarding of assignments commensurate with abilities and past performance, and the aggressive attention by firms to using paraprofessionals or clients' staff for more mundane tasks, to ensure rewarding work experience.[14]

[12] Ralph L. Benke, Jr. and Claire B. Arguala, "Why Do Professional Employees in CPA Firms Leave?" *The Virginia Accountant,* March 1982, pp. 7–10.

[13] Harold E. Arnett and Paul Danos, *CPA Firm Viability* (Ann Arbor: Paton Accounting Center, University of Michigan, 1979), p. 116.

[14] Ralph L. Benke, Jr. and Claire B. Arguala, "Why Do Professional Employees in CPA Firms Leave?" *The Virginia Accountant,* March, 1982, pp. 7–10, direct quote from p. 9.

As CPA firms respond to research findings and the changing business environment, the staff levels of the CPA firms are likely to become more equal across staff assistant, in-charge, and senior classifications, with an increasing amount of responsibility placed upon each member of the professional staff.

Companies' Views of CPA Firms

A survey asked 648 chief executive officers or presidents of large companies to evaluate CPA firms and to list those firms' civic responsibilities. Three-fourths of the respondents felt that a CPA firm's independent status was not threatened by its offering of management advisory services. In selecting a CPA firm, the firm's general reputation was the most frequently cited factor, followed by "experience with government regulatory matters" and "experience with companies in your industry/specialization." Stockholders' familiarity with the name and reputation of the company's CPA firm was considered to be very important. Almost half of the companies sampled had retained their CPA firms for fifteen or more years.

The nonaudit services most frequently performed by CPA firms are the evaluation of EDP systems, preparation or verification of government reports, and accounting systems design and analysis. Half of the respondents rated as excellent or good, the CPA firm's ability to help a company save money, but half gave a rating of fair to poor.

More than 90 percent of the survey respondents believed that it was appropriate for a CPA firm to speak out publicly on issues affecting their profession or the financial community.

The respondents noted that certain audit team members were particularly valuable, that changing the audit team's composition (often because of turnover in the CPA firm's staff) was undesirable to a point and then became desirable on a periodic basis and that CPAs' ability to stand up against the clients' demands was important.[15] These views as to factors affecting the selection of a CPA firm can be expected to influence the manner in which CPA firms organize their operations and interact with clients. Another key influence will be generally accepted auditing standards.

The AICPA and the Auditing Standards Board

In January 1939 the Institute [now the American Institute of Certified Public Accountants (AICPA)] officially began to draw up generally accepted auditing standards. Its Special Committee on Auditing Procedure was charged with examining current auditing procedures in light of a widely publicized fraud. The result was the "Extensions of Auditing Procedure" which required direct confirmation of accounts receivable with debtors and the observation of the taking of physical inventories ***[SAS 2, Section 509]***. *Confirmations* are written communications directly from the auditor, requesting that certain information be provided. The *observation of inventory counts* was intended to ensure that the inventory did exist in the quantity reported on the financial statements. The committee, delayed by World War II, eventually issued a report entitled "Tentative Statement of Auditing Standards—Their Generally Accepted Significance and Scope" in October 1947. In 1949, this report was combined with a portion of the Statement on Auditing Procedure No. 23 and ten broad requirements for audits were adopted, which were termed "generally accepted auditing standards" ***[SAS 1, Section 150]***. The three general standards were described in Chapter 1 and the four reporting standards in Chapter 2. The remaining field work standards will be introduced in this chapter. The pronouncements were first called Statements on Auditing Procedures but are currently referred to as Statements on Auditing Standards.

The *AICPA* is the professional organization responsible for promulgating auditing standards, and it has taken an active self-regulation role on behalf of CPAs and a strong support role in continuing education and practice guidance. The organizational chart for the AICPA's activities in standard setting as of April 1983 is presented in Exhibit 3-2.

[15] *Wall Street Journal, The Balance Sheet: Top Executives Speak Out About CPA Firms* (New York: Dow Jones, 1978).

EXHIBIT 3-2
Organizational Chart for the AICPA's Activities Related to Standard Setting

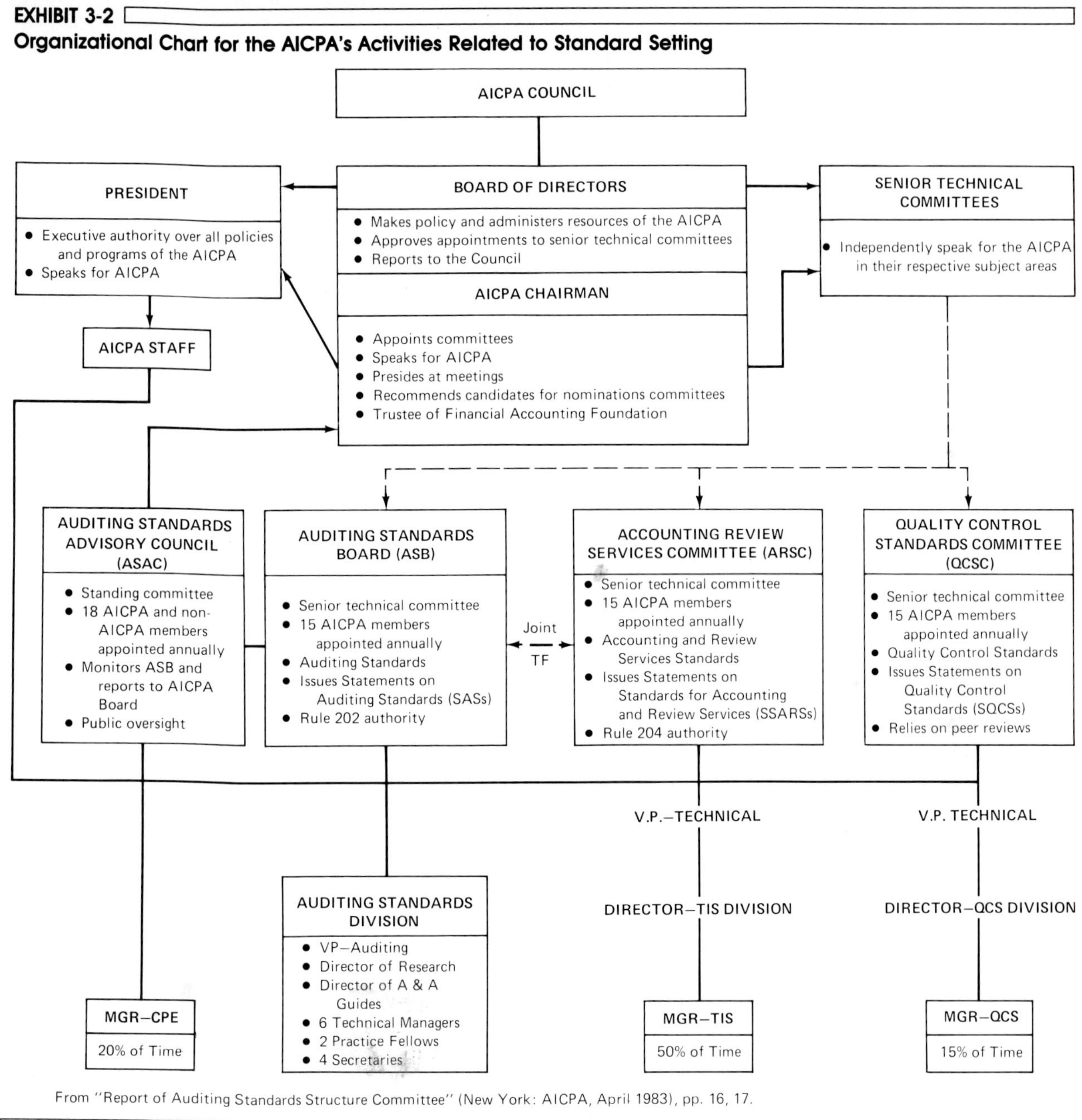

From "Report of Auditing Standards Structure Committee" (New York: AICPA, April 1983), pp. 16, 17.

The Auditing Standards Board's (ASB) purpose and responsibilities are as follows:

> The Auditing Standards Board shall be responsible for the promulgation of auditing standards and procedures to be observed by members of the AICPA in accordance with the Institute's rules of conduct.
>
> The Board shall be alert to new opportunities for auditors to serve the public, both by the assumption of new responsibilities and by improved ways of meeting old ones, and shall as expeditiously as possible develop standards and procedures that will enable the auditor to assume those responsibilities.
>
> Auditing standards and procedures promulgated by the Board shall:
>
> **a.** Define the nature and extent of the auditor's responsibilities.
> **b.** Provide guidance to the auditor in carrying out his duties, enabling him to express an opinion on the reliability of the representations on which he is reporting.
> **c.** Make special provision, where appropriate, to meet the needs of small enterprises.
> **d.** Have regard to the costs which they impose on society in relation to the benefits reasonably expected to be derived from the audit function.
>
> The Auditing Standards Board shall provide auditors with all possible guidance in the implementation of its pronouncements, by means of interpretations of its statements, by the issuance of guidelines, and by any other means available to it.[16]

The ASB is a part-time, volunteer, standard-setting group that requires, on the average, eight hundred hours a year of professional service, per member.

Of the fifteen members of the Auditing Standards Board, no more than five can represent the Big Eight firms. One member is from academia. The board is intended to have a balanced representation from large, medium, and small firms. A three-year rotational policy is used for board members. The ASB's voting procedures require nine affirmative votes for the exposure of a proposed Statement on Auditing Standards (SAS) or for the issuance of a final SAS.

Statements on Auditing Standards (SASs) are enforceable under *Rule 202* of the AICPA's Rules of Conduct:

> A member shall not permit his name to be associated with financial statements in such a manner as to imply that he is acting as an independent public accountant unless he has complied with the applicable generally accepted auditing standards promulgated by the Institute. Statements on Auditing Procedure [now Statements on Auditing Standards] issued by the Institute's Committee on Auditing Procedure [now the Auditing Standards Executive Committee] are, for purposes of this rule, considered to be interpretations of the generally accepted auditing standards and departures from such statements must be justified by those who do not follow them.

In addition to SASs, the Auditing Standards Division of the AICPA issues auditing interpretations which are issued by the staff to provide timely information on the application of SASs, as problems arise in practice. Industry audit guides, prepared by the AICPA's subcommittees or task forces, address auditing and reporting issues that pertain to particular industries.

Exhibit 3-2 also depicts two related standard-setting groups. The *Accounting and Review Services Committee (ARSC)* was established in 1977 to set guidelines for engagements involving unaudited financial statements. This was done, in part, because of criticism that the AICPA had been preoccupied with the problems of large, publicly traded companies that were CPA clients but gave little attention to engagements involving unaudited financial statements. The ARSC has fifteen members, nine from small local CPA firms (firms with fewer than fifty professionals). As of April 1983, five Statements on Standards for Accounting and Review Services had been issued, with fourteen related Interpretations.

The *Quality Control Standards Committee (QCSC)* was formed in September 1977, with the objective of developing standards, promoting understanding and compliance with such standards, and administering consulting reviews of firms concerning quality controls of CPA firms. Unlike the ASB and ARSC, the QCSC's standards and interpretations are not enforceable under the AICPA's Rules of Conduct of the Code of Professional Ethics. But firms that are members of the AICPA division for CPA firms and those that are participants in the AICPA voluntary quality control review program are re-

[16] "Report of Auditing Standards Structure Committee" (New York: AICPA, April 1983), pp. 16, 17.

quired to abide by these standards and interpretations ***[SAS 25, Section 161]***. Although GAAS must be followed in audit engagements, quality control standards must be followed in conducting a firm's audit practice as a whole. Quality control policies and procedures can provide reasonable assurance of conforming with GAAS in audit engagements. These policies and procedures should be tailored to the firm and reflect cost-benefit considerations.

In 1981, the AICPA Management Advisory Services Executive Committee issued the Statement on Standards for Management Advisory Services No. 1, entitled "Definitions and Standards for MAS Practice." AICPA members who depart from this or subsequent statements may be called on to justify such departures.

AICPA Division for CPA Firms

In 1977, the AICPA Division for CPA firms was established, which is credited with making the profession pay more attention to *quality control* and peer review, including the creation of the QCSC. *Peer reviews* are examinations by other CPAs of a firm's quality controls. Special attention is given to the firm's practices with respect to ensuring its independence, the careful evaluation of whether to accept new clients or to continue providing services to present clients, the hiring of competent personnel, the development of professional staff, the appropriate assignment of personnel to engagements, and adequate supervision and consultation. Firms are expected to reward their personnel's satisfactory performance and establish an internal inspection program to monitor their quality controls. Independent peer reviewers examine the work performed for a sample of the CPA firm's audit and accounting clients. Financial statements, the auditor's report that was issued, and the work papers supporting that report are examined to determine whether the firm's personnel complied with professional standards in performing their work. Before 1978, the AICPA could discipline individual CPAs but had no means of disciplining CPA firms. The profession thus initiated a self-regulatory program that created two practice sections: *private practice* and *SEC practice*. All members of the sections are to undergo a peer review of their audit quality controls at least once every three years. Members of the SEC section are also required

- To report to the client's audit committee or board of directors any disagreements with management concerning auditing or accounting matters that would have resulted in a qualified opinion had they not been resolved.
- To give the audit committee or board of directors an annual report on consulting services rendered and the related fees.
- To rotate the partner in charge of an audit at least once every five years.
- To have a second partner review of audit work before issuing an annual audit report.

Review of the Standard-setting Process

The AICPA periodically creates committees to review the structure for establishing auditing standards. For example, the Commission on Auditors' Responsibilities, which is known as the Cohen Commission, proposed a full-time, paid auditing standards board. The AICPA Special Committee Regarding the Commission on Auditors' Responsibilities, known as the Derieux Committee, was later assigned responsibility for reviewing the standard-setting process and rejected the Cohen Commission's proposal. The AICPA Special Committee to Study the Structure of the Auditing Standards Executive Committee, known as the Oliphant Committee, issued its report in 1978, which is essentially the current standard-setting structure. On March 1982, the Auditing Standards Structure Committee was appointed, and it issued its report in April 1983. One of the main changes it proposed was to discontinue the Auditing Standards Advisory Council and, instead, to have the AICPA strengthen its liaison with outside groups like the

- Financial Executive Institute (FEI).
- Robert Morris Associates (RMA, representing banking professionals).
- Financial Analysts Federation (FAF).
- American Accounting Association (AAA, representing university educators).

- American Bar Association (ABA).
- Securities and Exchange Commission (SEC).

An annual symposium has been suggested as a means of encouraging an interchange of ideas. Representation from AICPA members in industry is also cited as being desirable.

The structure committee proposed that the QCSC be discontinued and the ARSC be reduced from fifteen members to perhaps seven to nine members. To avoid a standards overload, the committee's report suggested that pronouncements other than SASs be emphasized, such as recent auditing procedures, studies on confirmations, small business audits, and special reports.

The review of standard setting is an ongoing process, presenting a real possibility for change. The past reviews support the profession's capabilities to react to the practice of public accounting, as well as the AICPA's interest in establishing the most effective standard-setting framework.

Standards of Field Work

The first standard of field work states ***[SAS 1, Section 150]***: "The work is to be adequately planned, and assistants, if any, are to be properly supervised." In planning an examination, an auditor should prepare a written audit program to help instruct assistants in the work to be done ***[SAS 22, Section 311]***. In order to prepare such a program, an auditor should understand the client's business, especially those events, transactions, and practices that may affect the financial statements. Audit risk and materiality should be considered in determining the nature, timing, and extent of the auditing procedures. When planning the audit, the auditor is required, for audit purposes, to form a preliminary judgment about the materiality levels. This judgment need not be quantified. With the focus upon risk, an auditor can be described as exercising healthy professional skepticism in approaching the audit.

Interim work, before closing the account balances, can lead to substantial benefits at a reduced cost, if it is done before the public accounting firms' infamous "busy season." Careful planning is essential to ensure adequate audit coverage and control over operations, account balances, and related assets from the interim date to year-end. Planning is also important to both the timeliness and orderliness of applying audit procedures. With respect to timeliness, the issue of *cutoff*, in which only assets in a particular fiscal period are included in the financial statements of that period, frequently will require simultaneous timing of the audit of liquid assets. With respect to orderliness, to ensure that the physical inventory procedures used during the auditor's observation will be effective, the CPA will need to review the instructions to be distributed to employees and make sure that the arrangements are in order for handling the goods received and shipped during the count and other inventory-related matters ***[SAS 45, Section 1020]***. The planned timing of audit procedures necessarily considers whether related auditing procedures are properly coordinated.

The competency standard within the three general standards described in Chapter 1 applies to the supervision requirement. Assistant auditors obtain their professional experience by having experienced auditors supervise and review their work. This supervisory process is the essential follow-through of planning an audit engagement, with various levels of experienced staff being assigned appropriate audit responsibilities.

The second standard of field work states: "There is to be a proper study and evaluation of the existing internal control as a basis for reliance thereon and for the determination of the resultant extent of the tests to which auditing procedures are to be restricted." The system of *internal accounting control* rather than *administrative control* is intended to be within the scope of this field work standard: "The system of internal accounting control comprises the plan of organization and the procedures and records that are concerned with the safeguarding of assets and with the reliability of financial records produced by the accounting system."[17] Administrative controls refer to operations not covered by the accounting-related controls; an ex-

[17] "Statement on Auditing Standards No. 43—Omnibus Statement on Auditing Standards" (New York: AICPA, April 1982), footnote 1.

ample of an administrative control is a monitoring system for evaluating salespersons' performance.

As described in Chapter 1, the review of internal accounting controls is intended to help the auditor understand the control environment and the flow of transactions ***[SAS 43, Section 1010]***. Based on this understanding, the auditor can determine whether the control procedures' design justifies reliance on internal accounting control as a means of altering the nature, extent, and timing of substantive tests. If it does not, the auditor's familiarity with the control design nevertheless will help in the design of substantive tests. Any test of balances, as distinct from tests of controls, is referred to as a *substantive test.*

The *control environment* encompasses organizational structure, the methods by which an entity communicates responsibility and authority, and the means by which the entity supervises the system, including the creation of an internal audit department. The review of transaction flows gives the auditor information about the types of transactions processed and the entity's authorization, execution, recording, and processing activities with respect to the various classes of transactions. Often these activities will include electronic data-processing considerations. If the review of controls leads to a decision not to rely on controls, the only documentation required under the second field standard is a record of the auditor's reasons for not extending the review of the system of internal accounting control past the minimum level. This is referred to as the preliminary phase of an auditor's review of internal accounting controls and is the sole requirement of the second standard of field work.

If reliance on controls is planned, the auditor must not only understand the prescribed procedures and methods but must also be reasonably assured that they are in use and are operating as planned. *Compliance tests* are necessary for those prescribed procedures on which the auditor intends to rely ***[SAS 1, Section 320]***. As the name suggests, these tests are capable of providing assurance that employees are complying with prescribed accounting control procedures. But the second standard of field work does not assume that reliance on internal accounting controls will be warranted; that is an auditor judgment which depends upon the quality of control design and expected compliance, as well as the economic consequences of relying on controls rather than performing certain substantive tests.

The third standard of field work states: "Sufficient competent evidential matter is to be obtained through inspection, observation, inquiries and confirmations to afford a reasonable basis for an opinion regarding the financial statements under examination." The audit process centers on the collection of evidential matter; the evaluation of the reliability, validity, and relative weight of the various types of evidential matter collected; and the judgment that such matter is sufficient to support an audit opinion. The standard cites the procedures applied to confirm receivables and observe inventories. But it also recognizes that these procedures are appropriate only when they are practicable and reasonable and when the amounts of receivables and inventory are material.

The term *practicable* is defined as "capable of being done with the available means," and *reasonable* is defined as "sensible in light of the surrounding circumstances." If an audit engagement is initiated after the fiscal year-end, the observation of physical inventory may be effectively prevented. Similarly, if certain customers fail to return confirmation requests, *alternative procedures* may be required. For example, the auditor may test to see whether subsequent cash receipts match the recorded receipts.

In deciding on the degree of testing, the auditor should ask whether the tests can be relied on at a reasonable level of confidence to reveal any errors in about the same proportion as would be found if a 100 percent audit were practical. The competency of applied procedures should be continually evaluated. For example, if the auditors are concerned about unrecorded liabilities, the evidence they collect through a 100 percent confirmation of all recorded payables will not reveal unrecorded claims by third parties. Similarly, if the auditors examine investment securities without checking their numerical identity, they will have no evidence of whether the securities have been improperly substituted. The *sufficiency of evidence* is determined according to its persuasiveness regarding assertions in the financial statements; the evidence is not expected to be convincing ***[SAS 31,***

Section 326]. This standard is met through compliance test work and substantive test work, with the latter including detailed tests and analytical review procedures. Ratio analyses, trend analyses, and industry comparisons are examples of analytical review procedures used in the evidential basis for expressing an opinion.

The AICPA and the SEC

The SEC has a stated policy of relying on the AICPA to establish auditing standards:

> Until experience should prove the contrary, we feel that this program is preferable to its alternative—the detailed prescription of the scope of and procedures to be followed in the audit for the various types of issuers of securities who file statements with us—and will allow for further consideration of varying audit procedures and for the development of different treatment for specific types of issuers.[18]

Similarly, ASR No. 4 in 1938 and No. 150 in 1973 (ASRs are now known as Financial Reporting Releases, or FRRs) confirm the SEC's policy of having the profession set its accounting principles. Yet there is little doubt as to the SEC's influence on standard setting. For example, in February 1941, ASR No. 21 required auditors to state whether an audit had been made in accordance with the generally accepted auditing standards (GAAS) appropriate in the circumstances, thereby influencing the content of the GAAS approved by the AICPA's membership in 1949. More recently, ASR No. 153 (February 1974) noted that the communication of the successor auditor with the predecessor auditor when the latter had resigned was inadequate. The profession then responded in October 1975 with SAS No. 7, "Communications Between Predecessor and Successor Auditors," which requires inquiry procedures and provides guidance regarding the significance of the communication and the form it should take. Despite the AICPA's and the SEC's cooperation, the responsibility for audit standard setting is maintained by the private sector, with oversight by the SEC.

In the capacity of regulator, the SEC has the power to issue rules to limit the scope of services. Under *Rule 2E* of the SEC's Rules of Practice and Investigation, the SEC can hold administrative hearings concerning complaints of CPAs' improper practices under the federal securities laws. This rule gives the SEC the power to suspend a firm from practicing before the commission.

The AICPA and Congress

When it adopted the Securities Acts, Congress also considered the alternative of the federal chartering of auditors, as well as having audits made by a corps of government auditors.[19] More recently, in overseeing the SEC and the accounting profession, Congress carried out two major investigations, commonly known as the Moss Committee and Metcalf Committee (at the time of this writing, the Dingell investigation is in progress),[20] leading to recommendations that the government reconsider having the government set accounting and auditing standards. However, the success of cooperative efforts of the SEC and the AICPA has been the basis for rejecting such proposals.

In addition to an oversight function directed at protecting the public interest, Congress has an information-seeking relationship with the profession. For example, Congress recently considered bail-out programs for troubled companies and sought CPAs' assistance.

Ernst & Whinney was asked by the assistant secretary of the treasury to project Chrysler's sales through the 1983 model year and to perform several "what if" analyses to assist the government in deciding whether Chrysler Corporation should be bailed out. The congressional approval of a $1.5 billion financial aid package was clearly influenced by the audit firm's analysis.

[18] SEC Accounting Series Release No. 19, "In the Matter of McKesson & Robbins, Inc.," December 5, 1940.

[19] J. Wiesen, *The Securities Acts and Independent Auditors: What Did Congress Intend?* Commission on Auditors' Responsibilities Research Study No. 2 (New York: AICPA, 1978).

[20] These committees were named after Representative John E. Moss, who chaired the House Commerce Committee's Oversight and Investigations Subcommittee, and Senator Lee Metcalf, who chaired the Subcommittee on Reports, Accounting and Management of the Senate Committee on Government Operations.

The AICPA and the Public Oversight Board

The Public Oversight Board (POB) is a "sounding board" for the public, Congress, the SEC, and federal agencies in their interaction with the accounting profession. It was created as part of the AICPA's SEC practice section to serve as an independent monitoring link between the profession and the public. The POB's first meeting was held in March 1978, and it had five members, including two former SEC chairmen, two retired CEOs of large companies, and a distinguished lawyer. The POB is a self-perpetuating body that can appoint, remove, and set the terms of its members, after consulting with and gaining the approval of the AICPA's board of directors. Its activities are monitoring the AICPA's peer review program and being a liaison between that program and the SEC. In addition, the POB analyzes the scope of CPAs' services and related independence issues.

Peer Review

Voluntary peer review was proposed in 1974, but there was controversy over whether the reviewers' findings should be made public. It was not until 1976 that the council of the 118,000-member AICPA approved such a program. But many firms had already taken voluntary actions before the AICPA's program. For instance, early in 1976 Price Waterhouse hired Deloitte, Haskins & Sells (then named Haskins & Sells) for a review, and Arthur Andersen hired Deloitte, Haskins & Sells to audit its 1976–1977 financials.[21]

The POB is supposed to ensure (1) that the peer review is conducted according to the standards, (2) that the reviewers are competent, and (3) that the public files of reports and letters are consistent with the reviewers' findings. At first, in organizing the peer review program and the oversight function, the SEC opposed *firm-on-firm reviews,* insisting that they were really mutual back scratching. The SEC wanted review teams with members drawn from several firms, but the profession felt that such an approach would be too costly. The SEC then accepted the firm-on-firm reviews but also required a *quality control review panel* that would issue an opinion on the quality control system of the reviewed firm. In a sense, a double review was performed. The SEC initially opposed the firms' right to select their own reviewers but eventually agreed that this selection process was acceptable, provided that the reviewers met the qualifications set forth in the standards.

One problem has been the extension of the peer review program to international engagements. Client confidentiality, laws, and differences in auditing standards and national pride all complicate the problem. Nevertheless, the POB and SEC are trying to address these issues.

Probably the most difficult aspect of the peer review program has been the SEC's insistence on having direct access to the peer review process and, in particular, the reviewer's work papers, as it did not want to rely completely on the POB. But the profession feared that the information obtained by the chief accountant's office would be shared with the SEC's enforcement division and that their clients would refuse the reviewers' access to their work papers if the SEC were to be given access to them. The initial compromise was for the POB to prepare the work papers, concealing the client's identity, and to give them to the SEC for review.

In its 1979 report to Congress, the SEC still pushed for access to peer reviewers' working papers but did give a qualified endorsement to the peer review committee. However, it did express concern that in 1979, only 20 percent of the CPA firms practicing before the SEC had undergone a peer review. By 1982, an arrangement was made for the SEC to examine a sample of certain working papers of peer reviewers. In 1982, the Quality Control Review Panel was eliminated for cost-effectiveness reasons, and so the second check would no longer be needed. The POB's annual reports in 1981 and 1982 concluded that "the self-regulating structure is sound and is functioning properly"—conclusions also cited by the SEC in its 1982 report to Congress. According to the POB's 1983–1984 report, the number of peer reviews performed for the total division for CPA firms was 1,389; of these, 529 were for the SEC practice section.

[21] Frederick Andrews, "Accounting Profession Moves to Promote Good Auditing and to Help Its Credibility," *Wall Street Journal,* May 4, 1976, p. 6.

About 87 percent of the peer review reports have been unqualified.

The State Boards of Public Accountancy

In addition to the AICPA's quality enforcement activities, the state boards of accountancy are active in monitoring CPAs' practice. State boards enforce laws regulating public accounting and have the power to revoke, suspend, or refuse to renew a permit to practice. In addition, they can suspend the CPA's certificate and censure permit holders. These powers apply to both individual CPAs and CPA firms, although no state has suspended or revoked a firm's permit. To enforce professional standards, some state boards have hired investigators to review auditors' work and, when deficiencies are noted, make agreements as to the CPA's continuing education needs or quality control reviews.

State boards set the criteria for becoming a CPA, although the Uniform CPA Examination is used across the states to measure professional competency. The variability of requirements can be seen in the Appendix. It should be noted that some states accept a master's degree in lieu of one year of experience. Although many state boards require the first-time application for the exam by either February 1 or September 1 and reexamination applications by March 31 or September 30, the application deadlines do vary. Similarly, the first-time exam fee varies from $25 in the Virgin Islands to $140 in New York. The Uniform CPA Examination has four parts, with a two-part accounting practice section:

Accounting Practice—Part I
Part II
Accounting Theory
Auditing
Business Law

The exam lasts two and a half days, with nine hours for accounting practice and three and a half hours for each of the other three parts. Once the exam has been passed and the state board's requirements regarding experience or other qualifications have been met, a permit to practice can be issued.

The State Societies and Associations of CPAs

The state boards' continuing education requirements are met, in part, through programs of the AICPA, its affiliated State Societies of CPAs, and voluntary associations of CPA firms. The latter groups are regional groups or national groups of firms of similar size with common interests. The state societies have established quality control policies and procedures, intended to encourage professionals' compliance with GAAS. Both the societies and the associations are professional organizations that often sponsor journals (such as the New York State Society of CPAs' publication, *The CPA Journal*), professional seminars, lobbying activities on behalf of its membership before the state board and state legislators, and service and civic activities, frequently tied to university relations or charitable professional services. In addition, societies and associations offer social activities. Some associations have organized peer review programs.

The Institute of Internal Auditors (IIA)

The Institute of Internal Auditors (IIA) serves a role analogous to that of the AICPA and has local chapters that are comparable to the state societies of CPAs in their objectives and activities. The IIA issues professional standards and has adopted a code of ethics, and it has a *Certified Internal Auditor (CIA)* program that was begun in 1972. Eligibility for the certified internal auditor designation requires that candidates (1) possess a baccalaureate degree or its equivalent; (2) be of good character, as documented by a letter of reference by a certified internal auditor or a supervisor; (3) pass a twelve-hour, four-part examination covering the theory and practice of internal auditing, principles of management, information systems, and numerous disciplines related to internal auditing; and (4) meet a work-experience requirement that includes two years of internal auditing or public accounting experience or four years of full-time teaching experience at the university level in the area of auditing, computer systems, finance, accounting, or management. Advanced academic degrees can substitute for one year of the experience requirement, and no experience is required in order to sit for the exam.

Other Certification Programs

There are several certification programs besides those for the certified public accountant and the certified internal auditor. The *Certificate in Management Accounting (CMA)*, offered since 1972, is sponsored by the Institute of Management Accounting, which is a branch of the National Association of Accountants, an organization of, primarily, internal accountants such as controllers and their department's professionals. The exam covers economics and business finance; organization and behavior; public reporting, auditing, and taxes; periodic reporting; and decision analysis. It lasts seventeen and a half hours, and certification requires a baccalaureate or its equivalent and two years of experience.

Other certifications include the Chartered Bank Auditor (CBA), awarded through the Bank Administration Institute; the Certificate in Data Processing, sponsored by the Data Processing Management Association; Certified Information Systems Auditor (CISA), awarded through the EDP Auditors Foundation; and Enrolled Agent (to practice before the U.S. Internal Revenue Service).[22]

All of these certifications are intended to test professional competency; they differ from the CPA in that a license to practice as a CPA is granted by individual jurisdictions which give the individual the capability of serving in the attestation function for the public. Independence is not a presumption of the other certifications which are mainly for the internal accountant, systems designer, internal auditor, or revenue agent.

The Governmental Accounting Office (GAO)

The GAO is the auditor of governmental agencies and Congress. It has been largely responsible for developing methodologies for operational auditing, directed at assessing the effectiveness and efficiency of various operations. The GAO has had a substantial effect on philosophies and approaches to auditing nonfinancial information and in performing compliance audits. The GAO's standards for operational auditing are likely to affect the form of future pronouncements by the AICPA that may be directed toward operational auditing considerations.

The Financial Accounting Standards Board (FASB) and Other Standard Setters

An auditor must first be an accountant, because attestation that financial statements are in accordance with generally accepted accounting principles (GAAP) requires an in-depth understanding of such principles. Because the FASB is the standard-setting body for GAAP, it is in continuous communication with the public accounting profession. CPA firms sponsor rotational tours by their professional staff to interact as SEC fellows and AICPA fellows, analyzing, researching, and responding to professional pronouncements. In addition, they maintain in-house technical groups whose chief responsibility is to submit response letters as to their firm's position on various exposure drafts.

In the past, in addition to the FASB, the Cost Accounting Standards Board (CASB), which focused on standards related to governmental contracts, had similar interactions with the profession. The CASB is no longer in existence, although its standards are still applied. In the future, the Governmental Accounting Standards Board (GASB), the newly created standard-setting group for governmental accounting, is expected to have substantial interaction with the practice community.

Possible Changes in the Profession's Structure

Both the structure of the auditing profession and the standard-setting may change over time. In particular, the phenomena of mergers, specialization, and changes in the nature of the auditing process

[22] Linda H. Kistler and Joseph F. Guy, "An Evaluation of Professional Certification Programs in Accounting," *Journal of Accountancy*, September 1975, pp. 104–108.

are likely to cause future shifts in the profession's structure.

The Merger Phenomenon

In 1979, an estimated 10 percent of the nation's local public accounting firms were investigating or negotiating mergers.[23] The reasons for these mergers were the acknowledgment that very small firms have difficulty keeping up with the quantity of new professional pronouncements and regulations and the desire to increase firms' present billings and reduce the cost of insurance and practice administration.

Of course, mergers are not new. In fact, the so-called merger fever of the fifties and sixties reappeared in 1977 and has persisted to date. In 1977, Touche Ross merged with J. K. Lasser combining $410 million and $40 million of revenue, respectively. But the merger's success has been questioned, as by 1981, of the 130 J. K. Lasser partners joining Touche Ross, only 44 remained in the firm.[24] The problem was apparently a lack of attention to the emotional and human problems of a merger. There is also the danger of losing control over the firm's practice when both professional staff and clients are obtained through the merger. A former manager of Alexander Grant reported that almost every problem with litigation that the firm faced arose from audits that spanned a period in which there were eighty mergers.[25] Nevertheless, headlines in 1984 discussed possible mergers between Alexander Grant & Co. and Fox & Co., as well as Price Waterhouse and Deloitte, Haskins & Sells.

For small firms, personnel acquisition and retirement considerations and technical and regulatory incentives are the key rationales for merging. For medium-sized firms, geographical coverage and competitive pressures are the main reasons.[26] The profession's structure has and will continue to change toward larger CPA firms. Some even predict that the day of the lone public accountant will come to an end as the complexity of the profession increases. Yet, voluntary associations of CPA firms represent just one of the alternative approaches to addressing such complexity, in lieu of merging.

Specialization

Another development that may change the profession's structure is the increasing specialization within the accounting profession. Computer, statistical, industry-related, and regulatory expertise have become valued more and more as necessary ingredients for the breadth and complexity of the client services being demanded. If this trend continues, means of organizing firms, audit teams, and other engagement teams may change to facilitate access to experts within and across firms. The AICPA has periodically considered the designation of specialists within the profession. Proposals have included tax, management advisory service, audit expertise, and industry-concentrated experience designations. Though not currently available, except in certification programs related to computers, management, and internal audit capabilities, the professional designation of specialists could alter the structure of auditing practice in the future.

The Auditing Process

The auditing process itself is most likely to influence professional standards and the structure of the auditing profession. The scope of audits and the methodologies applied are evolving in line with technological developments. As already noted, the base of the typical accounting firm's pyramid has begun to shrink in terms of personnel demands related to audit engagements. Beyond a shift in the levels of staff used in the typical audit, the specialized knowledge base of staff, the degree to which professional judgments are aided by decision support systems, and the appropriateness of such specific audit requirements as confirmation pro-

[23] Sidney F. Jarrow, "Mergers—Mystique, Myopia or Missed Opportunity," *Practicing CPA*, June 1979, pp. 1–3.

[24] *Fortune*, May 18, 1981, pp. 103–107.

[25] "To Merge or Not to Merge, That Is the Question," *Forbes*, December 1, 1977, pp. 58–59.

[26] Harold E. Arnett and Paul Danos, *CPA Firm Viability* (Ann Arbor: Paton Accounting Center, University of Michigan, 1979).

cedures and the observation of physical inventory taking are likely to change significantly within the next decade.

Appendix: State Board Requirements

Exhibit 3-A (p. 92) presents the requirements of various boards of accountancy.

REVIEW QUESTIONS

1. What are the names of the Big Eight firms? Why do you believe such large multinational auditing firms have evolved? Does auditing appear to be a heavily concentrated industry? Support your response.
2. Would you describe the auditing profession as labor intensive or capital intensive? In what sense is it both? Do you expect any shift in the labor-capital mix in the future?
3. Why do some CPA firms choose not to grow?
4. Describe the organizational structure of the typical firm. What is meant by the pyramid structure? Has it changed, or is it likely to change?
5. What have studies of turnover in public accounting indicated? What are the implications of the findings?
6. How do companies' managements select a CPA firm?
7. What are SAPs and SASs?
8. Describe the structure and charge of the Auditing Standards Board.
9. What is the significance of Rule 202 of the AICPA's Rules of Conduct?
10. What is the purpose of the (a) Accounting and Review Services Committee and (b) the Quality Control Standards Committee?
11. What is the AICPA Division for CPA Firms? What is its significance?
12. What is peer review? What quality controls are of interest to peer reviewers?
13. List the standards of field work.
14. Distinguish between administrative and internal accounting control.
15. Define a control environment.
16. What are substantive tests? Compliance tests?
17. Describe the relationship of the public accounting profession to **(a)** the SEC, **(b)** Congress, **(c)** the Public Oversight Board, **(d)** state boards of public accountancy, and **(e)** the Financial Accounting Standards Board and other standard setters.
18. What is the function of state societies of CPAs and associations of CPA firms?
19. Describe the available certification programs for accounting professionals.
20. What is the merger phenomenon and what are its causes?

EXERCISES

1. In an audit engagement, the CPA tested well over a third of the aggregate value of inventories in the year-end physical observation. Because the complexity of records and the arrangements of goods made testing the inventory held at a warehouse rather difficult, the auditors decided against including it in the testing program. Later, a shortage was discovered at the warehouse, which had previously been concealed by manipulations of the records, before the client's eventual bankruptcy. All of the omitted items were part of the inventory in the warehouse. With the benefit of hindsight, it is easy to recognize that

   > The very fact of those difficulties, entailing the possibility of serious discrepancy should, of course, have given that warehouse a definite preference in the selection of items for testing.[27]

   What is the appropriate role of "difficulty in testing" in deciding which auditing procedures to apply? What is the concept of "practicable and reasonable"?
2.
   > In the broadest sense, the discipline of accounting includes auditing. However, accounting can be described as measuring and reporting the effects of economic activities of individual entities. Auditing, on the other hand, involves an independent examination to determine the propriety of accounting processes, measurement, and communication. Stated simply, the accountant prepares financial information. The auditor checks it.
   >
   > The distinction, however, cannot be made in practice. To perform his function, the auditor must continually evaluate accounting activities and presentations; he must be, and is, trained as an accountant and an auditor.[28]

   Do you agree with this assertion? Support your response by citing the professional standards.
3. A 1971 survey of one thousand people from the metropolitan Chicago and Cleveland areas indicated a big information gap between the profession and the general public. When asked, "What services does a CPA perform?" 90 percent of the respond-

[27] Committee on Auditing Procedure, "Tentative Statement of Auditing Standards—Their Generally Accepted Significance and Scope" (New York: AICPA, 1947), p. 28.

[28] Commission on Auditors' Responsibilities, *Report of Tentative Conclusions* (New York: Commission on Auditors' Responsibilities, 1977), p. xii.

EXHIBIT 3-A

Requirements of Various Boards of Accountancy as of May 1, 1981

State Board (Address)	Number of Years of Higher Education Required	Number of Parts, Specific Parts, and Minimum Scores on Parts Failed (P = Practice)	Life of the Condition (Y = years) (NE = Next Exams)	Years of Experience	Continuing Education Requirements (Hours Within a Set Number of Years)
Alabama (1103 S. Perry St., Montgomery 36104)	4	2 or P	4NE	2-3	40 in 1 year
Alaska (Pouch D, Juneau 99811)	2-4	2 or P	5Y	2-4	60 in 2 years
Arizona (1645 W. Jefferson St., Phoenix 85007)	4	2 or P	3Y	2	
Arkansas (1515 W. Seventh St., Suite 320, Little Rock 72202)	4	2 or P	5NE	1-2	120 in 3 years
California (2135 Butano Dr., Suite 112, Sacramento 95825)	0-4	2 or P	3Y	2-4	80 in 2 years
Colorado (600A State Services Bldg., Denver 80203)	4	2 or P	5NE	0-1	120 in 3 years
Connecticut (20 Grant Street, Hartford 06106)	4	2 or P	3Y	2	120 in 3 years
Delaware (P.O. Box 121, Newark 19711)	2	2 or P, 50%	5NE	2-4	Yes
Washington, D.C. (614 H St. NW, Rm. 109, Washington, D.C. 20001)	4	2 or P	5NE	2	Yes
Florida (P.O. Box 13475, Gainesville 32604)	4 (now 5)	2 or P, 50%	5NE	0-1	16-64 in 2 years
Georgia (166 Pryor St. SW, Atlanta 30303)	4	2, 40%	3Y	2-5	60 in 2 years
Guam (P.O. Box P, Agana 96910)	4	2 or P, 50%	6NE	1-2	
Hawaii (P.O. Box 3469, Honolulu 96801)	5	2 or P, 50%	6NE	0	80 in 2 years
Idaho (P.O. Box 2896, Boise 83701)	4	2 or P, 50%	6NE	1-2	
Illinois (10 Administration Bldg., 506 S. Wright, Urbana 61801)	4	2 or P, 50%	3 or N6E	0	
Indiana (912 State Office Bldg., Indianapolis 46204)	4	2	6NE	2-6	80 in 2 years
Iowa (904 Grand Ave., Des Moines 50309)	4	2 or P, 50%	5NE	1-3	120 in 3 years
Kansas (503 Kansas, Rm. 236, Topeka 66603)	4-5	2, 50%	4 of N6E	0-2	80 in 2 years
Kentucky (310 W. Liberty, Louisville 40202)	4	2 or P, 50%	5NE	2-5	

EXHIBIT 3-A
(Continued)

State Board (Address)	Number of Years of Higher Education Required	Number of Parts, Specific Parts, and Minimum Scores on Parts Failed (P = Practice)	Life of the Condition (Y = years) (NE = Next Exams)	Years of Experience	Continuing Education Requirements (Hours Within a Set Number of Years)
Louisiana (1109 Masonic Temple Bldg., New Orleans 70130)	4	2, 50%	1 of N4E	1-3	60 in 3 years
Maine (84 Harlow St., Bangor 04401)	4	2 or P	3Y	1-2	
Maryland (One S. Calvert Bldg., 8th Fl., Baltimore 21202)	4	2 or P, 50%	5NE	0	40 in 1 year
Massachusetts (100 Cambridge St., Rm. 1524, Boston 02202)	4	2 or P, 50%	6NE	2-9	
Michigan (905 South Land, P.O. Box 30018, Lansing 48909)	4	2 or P, 50%	5NE	2	40 in 1 year
Minnesota (Metro Square Bldg., 5th Fl., St. Paul 55101)	0-5	2, 50%	5NE	1-6	120 in 3 years
Mississippi (P.O. Box 16261, Jackson 39206)	4	2 or P, 45%	10NE	1-4	
Missouri (P.O. Box 613, Jefferson City 65102)	4	2 or P, 50%	Unlimited	0	
Montana (Lalonde Bldg., Helena 59620)	4	2 or P	5NE	1	120 in 3 years
Nebraska (P.O. Box 94725, Lincoln 68509)	0	2 or P, 50%	5NE	2-4	120 in 3 years
Nevada (1 East Liberty St., Suite 614, Reno 89501)	4	2 or P	6NE	1-4	80 in 2 years
New Hampshire (One Tremont St., Concord 03301)	4	2	5Y	1-3	
New Jersey (1100 Raymond Blvd., Rm. 507-A, Newark 07102)	4	2 or P	6NE	2-4	
New Mexico (401 San Pedro NE, No. 6, Albuquerque 87108)	4	2	3Y	1	120 in 3 years
New York (Cultural Education Center, Albany 12230)	4	2 or P	Unlimited	1-2	
North Carolina (P.O. Box 2248, Chapel Hill 27514)	2	2 or P	5NE	1-2	
North Dakota (Box 8104, University Station, Grand Forks 58202)	0	2 or P	5NE	0-4	120 in 3 years
Ohio (65 S. Front St., Suite 222, Columbus 43215)	4	1	8Y	1-4	120 in 3 years

EXHIBIT 3-A
(Continued)

State Board (Address)	Number of Years of Higher Education Required	Number of Parts, Specific Parts, and Minimum Scores on Parts Failed (P = Practice)	Life of the Condition (Y = years) (NE = Next Exams)	Years of Experience	Continuing Education Requirements (Hours Within a Set Number of Years)
Oklahoma (265 West Ct., 4545 Lincoln Blvd., Oklahoma City 73105)	4	2 or P	1 of 3 N6E	0-3	24 in 1 year
Oregon (Labor & Industries Bldg., 4th Fl., Salem 97310)	4	2 or P, 50%	6NE	1-2	40 in 1 year
Pennsylvania (P.O. Box 2649, Harrisburg 17120)	4	20%		1-2	80 in 2 years
Puerto Rico (Box 3271, San Juan 00904)	0	2	Unlimited	0-6	
Rhode Island (100 N. Main St., Providence 02903)	4	2 or P	Unlimited	1-2	120 in 3 years
South Carolina (P.O. Box 11376, Columbia 29211)	4	2 or P, 40%	3NE	2	60 in 2 years
South Dakota (SFC, 1501 S. Prairie Ave., Sioux Falls 57101)	2	2 or P	4Y	1	96 in 3 years
Tennessee (Capitol Hill Bldg., 7th & Union, Nashville 37219)	4	2 or P	6NE or 3 yr	1-2	120 in 3 years
Texas (330 Northulund Dr., Suite 500, Austin 78731)	2	2	5Y	1-6	
Utah (330 East 4th South St., Salt Lake 84111)	4	2	6NE	1-4	
Vermont (109 State St., Montpelier 05602)	0	2	5 yrs. or 5E	2	80 in 2 years
Virgin Islands (Royal Strand Bldg., Christiansted, St. Croix 00820)	0	2		2-6	
Virginia (2 South 9th St., Richmond 23219)	4	2 or P, 50%	5NE	2-4	
Washington (210 E. Union, Suite H, EP-21, Olympia 98504)	4	2 or P	3Y	1-3	120 in 3 years
West Virginia (825 Charleston National Plaza, Charleston 25301)	4	1	3Y	0	
Wisconsin (1400 E. Washington Ave., Madison 53702)	4	2, 50%	2 of N4E	1 1/2	
Wyoming (Barret Building, 3rd Fl., Cheyenne 82002)	4	2 or P, 50%	3Y	0	120 in 3 years

Adapted from Alvin M. Stenzel, Jr., *Approaching the CPA Examination: A Personal Guide to Examination Preparation,* "State Board of Accountancy Requirements" (New York: John Wiley, 1981), app. A, pp. 69-70.

ents indicated that a CPA's work was restricted to "bookkeeping" and "preparation of tax returns."[29] Why do you believe this image problem exists? How might the profession improve its image?

4. The audit process itself has been cited as a likely source of change in the future structure of the auditing profession and professional standards. How is the audit process likely to change? How would these changes affect the profession's structure? Do you believe that such effects are desirable?
5. A point of contention in the initial peer review program was whether a reviewed firm should have the right to exclude certain engagements from the review process. Critics alleged that this would reduce the credibility of the review process and that requests for exclusion were likely to be excessive.[30] However, the right was acknowledged, though there have been few requests for exclusion. Why do you suppose that, to date, the critics have been proved wrong by the experience?
6. Research[31] concerning sources of CPA revenue has offered the following comparison:

Percent of Revenue Generated

	1977		1984	
	Large Firms	**Small Firms**	**Large Firms**	**Small Firms**
From Audits	29.3%	15.0%	25.7%	11.4%
From Tax Work	34.8%	34.9%	35.8%	40.7%
From MAS	5.0%	6.9%	8.2%	8.1%
Unaudited Financial Statements	13.4%	14.4%	17.4% *	21.5%
Other	17.5%	28.8%	12.9%	18.3%

*In 1984 CPAs also offered review and compilation services.

How do such figures, based on a national sample of 2,400 firms, show that the profession has changed?

QUESTIONS ADAPTED FROM PROFESSIONAL EXAMINATIONS

1. Ray, the owner of a small company, asked Holmes, a CPA, to conduct an audit of the company's records. Ray told Holmes that the audit should be completed in time to submit the audited financial statements to a bank as part of a loan application. Holmes immediately accepted the engagement and agreed to provide an auditor's report within three weeks. Ray agreed to pay Holmes a fixed fee plus a bonus if the loan was granted.

   Holmes hired two accounting students to conduct the audit and spent several hours telling them exactly what to do. Holmes told the students not to spend time reviewing the controls but instead to concentrate on proving the mathematical accuracy of the ledger accounts and summarizing the data in the accounting records that supported Ray's financial statements. The students followed Holmes's instructions and after two weeks gave Holmes the financial statements, which did not include footnotes. Holmes reviewed the statements and prepared an unqualified auditor's report. The report, however, did not refer to generally accepted accounting principles nor to the year-to-year application of such principles.

   Required:
   Briefly describe each of the generally accepted auditing standards and indicate how Holmes failed to comply with each standard.

   Organize your answers as follows:

Brief Description of Generally Accepted Auditing Standards	Holmes's Failure to Comply with Generally Accepted Auditing Standards

   Note: You will need to refer back to Chapters 1 and 2 and review the general standards, along with the standards introduced in this chapter.

   (CPA exam adapted)
2. XYZ Manufacturing is a large diversified conglomerate with more than 800 operating facilities and annual sales in excess of $15 billion. To provide adequate audit coverage of such an organization, twenty-five regional audit offices, employing 210 internal auditing professionals, have been established throughout the world.

   To promote consistency and quality in the work of its professional employees, the management of XYZ's internal auditing department developed and

[29]Kenneth I. Solomon, "What Others Think of Us: The CPA's Public Image," *The Practical Accountant,* January–February 1971, pp. 29–33.

[30]Adapted from Louis W. Matusiak, "The Role of the Public Oversight Board in the Accounting Profession's Self-regulatory Program," *Ohio CPA,* Autumn 1979, pp. 144–152.

[31]Sanoa Hensley and Carlton Stolle, "How Does Your Firm Stack Up?" *CPA 84,* December–January 1984, p. 16.

disseminated a uniform technical audit manual containing standards and instructions related to each major component and phase of the overall audit process.

Required:
State seven other actions the management of the internal auditing department should take to promote consistency and quality in its professional employees' work.

(CPA exam adapted)

3. Multiple-Choice Questions
Select the one answer that best completes the statement or answers the question.

3.1 Which of the following is mandatory if the auditor is to comply with generally accepted auditing standards?
- **a.** Adequate technical training.
- **b.** Analytical review on audit engagements.
- **c.** Statistical sampling whenever feasible on an audit engagement.
- **d.** Confirmation by the auditor of material accounts receivable balances.

(CPA exam adapted)

3.2 Which of the following best describes what is meant by generally accepted auditing standards?
- **a.** Acts to be performed by the auditor.
- **b.** Measures of the quality of the auditor's performance.
- **c.** Procedures used to gather evidence to support financial statements.
- **d.** Audit objectives generally determined on audit engagements.

(CPA exam adapted)

3.3 Which of the following underlies the application of generally accepted auditing standards, particularly the standards of field work and reporting?
- **a.** Materiality and relative risk.
- **b.** Internal control.
- **c.** Corroborating evidence.
- **d.** Reasonable assurance.

(CPA exam adapted)

3.4 The first standard of field work, which states that the work should be adequately planned, and assistants, if any, should be properly supervised, recognizes that the
- **a.** Early appointment of the auditor is advantageous to the auditor and the client.
- **b.** Acceptance of an audit engagement after the close of the client's fiscal year is generally not permissible.
- **c.** Appointment of the auditor after the physical count of inventories requires a disclaimer of opinion.
- **d.** Performance of substantial parts of the examination is necessary at interim dates.

(CPA exam adapted)

3.5 An auditor's examination performed in accordance with generally accepted auditing standards should
- **a.** Ensure that illegal acts will be detected when internal control is effective.
- **b.** Disclose violations of truth in lending laws.
- **c.** Encompass a plan to seek out illegalities regarding operations.
- **d.** Not be relied on to ensure that illegal acts will be detected.

(CPA exam adapted)

3.6 An auditor who accepts an audit engagement and does not possess the industry expertise of the business entity, should
- **a.** Engage financial experts familiar with the business.
- **b.** Study the enterprise's business.
- **c.** Refer a substantial portion of the audit to another CPA who will act as the principal auditor.
- **d.** First inform management that an unqualified opinion cannot be issued.

(CPA exam adapted)

3.7 The third standard of field work states that sufficient competent evidential matter may be obtained in part through inspection, observation, inquiries, and confirmations to afford a reasonable basis for an opinion regarding the financial statements under examination. The evidential matter required by this standard may in part be obtained through
- **a.** Auditors' working papers.
- **b.** Proper planning of the audit engagement.
- **c.** Analytical review procedures.
- **d.** Review of the internal control system.

(CPA exam adapted)

3.8 Which of the following statements best describes the primary purpose of Statements on Auditing Standards?
- **a.** They are guides intended to set forth auditing procedures that apply to a variety of situations.
- **b.** They are procedural outlines intended to narrow the areas of inconsistency and divergence of auditors' opinion.
- **c.** They are authoritative statements, enforced

through the code of professional ethics, and are intended to limit the degree of auditor judgment.

d. They are interpretations intended to clarify the meaning of generally accepted auditing standards.

(CPA exam adapted)

3.9 The independent auditor's plan for an examination in accordance with generally accepted auditing standards is influenced by the possibility of material errors. The auditor will therefore conduct the examination with an attitude of

a. Professional skepticism.
b. Subjective mistrust.
c. Objective indifference.
d. Professional responsiveness.

(CPA exam adapted)

3.10 The auditor's review of the client's system of internal accounting control is documented in order to substantiate

a. Conformity of the accounting records with generally accepted accounting principles.
b. Compliance with generally accepted auditing standards.
c. Adherence to management's requirements.
d. The fairness of the financial statement presentation.

(CPA exam adapted)

3.11 Williams & Co., a large international CPA firm, is to have an "external peer review." The peer review will most likely be performed by the

a. Employees and partners of Williams & Co. who are not associated with the particular audits being reviewed.
b. Audit review staff of the Securities and Exchange Commission.
c. Audit review staff of the American Institute of Certified Public Accountants.
d. Employees and partners of another CPA firm.

(CPA exam adapted)

3.12 The preliminary phase of the auditor's review of internal control is designed to provide information on three matters. Which of the following is not a purpose of the preliminary review?

a. Determining the extent to which EDP is used in significant accounting applications.
b. Understanding the flow of transactions in the system.
c. Comprehending the basic structure of accounting control.
d. Identifying the controls on which reliance is planned.

(CPA exam adapted)

CASES FOR DISCUSSION

1. The one-act play *An Ideal Accountant* discusses, in part, accountants' competency. The characters include the parents (the Chilterns), whose son (Lord Goring) is considering an accounting profession, and three guests.

Mrs. Marchmont. Lord Goring was just saying that he intended to be an Accountant. . . .

Lady Chiltern. Is academic knowledge, as opposed to knowledge gained from experience, essential? . . .

Sir Robert Chiltern. Yes, I think so. An Accountant, if he is to be successful, must have the basic theory of the many subjects with which he will have to deal. Once the theory, gained from intensive study, is firmly rooted it can sprout and grow on the fertile ground of experience. It is, in my opinion, essential for an Accountant to have a retentive memory.

Lady Markby. I quite agree. But a man can't know everything, and if an Accountant can't immediately give an authoritative answer to a point there is no harm in his admitting it. The essential thing is that he should know where he can find the answer, and only constant reading and theoretical delving can provide this.

Lord Goring. I think an Accountant would be well advised to admit frankly that he doesn't immediately know the answer if that is the case, or to say that he would like time to give a considered opinion. I feel also that he should not hesitate to advise his client to have a second adviser on a particularly obscure point, where they find the issue is likely to be shrouded in doubt. I should have far more confidence in someone who was that frank, rather than someone who was obviously trying to bluff his way through.

Mrs. Cheveley. Some people say that the professions are openly frank, but that trade is cunningly candid. How does one become an Accountant?

Sir Robert Chiltern. One takes the examination or otherwise of the various bodies governing the profession. There seem to be several bodies all having almost the same objectives and no doubt all having worthy and highly experienced, qualified and capable members.

Mrs. Marchmont. How odd. One would have thought that one society would have been sufficient.

Mrs. Cheveley. Ah! They are so busy putting other people's houses in order that they have neglected their own, although to be fair I imagine that the fault does not lie with the average member of these societies. They would, no doubt, support any reasonable scheme to eliminate this unfortunate state of affairs. It is surely for the officers or leaders to sink their differing opinions and possibly personal interests for the good of the Accountancy profession and also the public.

Lord Goring. That's a rather sweeping remark Mrs. Cheveley. But I wonder how true it is.

Mrs. Cheveley. The truth will depend on whether you are an officer or just a member of the society. But I have no doubt that it will not be a popular remark. . . .

Lady Markby. I suppose an Accountant should mix as much as possible amongst fellow members of the profession.

Lord Goring. I think so, for surely that's the only way to keep abreast of things, and to obtain new ideas and information. It can't all be read in books and Finance Acts. . . .

Lady Chiltern. This has been a most interesting discussion. Now what do you think about becoming an Accountant, Lord Goring?

Lord Goring. Obviously one has to be cut out for the profession and of course it's a lifetime study. Before coming to a decision I think I will consult some of the examination papers. I feel that they may be a deciding factor in the first instance.[32]

Discuss the viewpoints expressed here. How do these individuals' opinions correspond to the profession's concept of competency? Describe your reaction to Mrs. Cheveley's remarks regarding the accounting profession's neglect of its own house. What evidence can you provide that the profession has not been guilty of such neglect? What additional actions should the profession take?

2. An article entitled "Accounting Odyssey—2080" examined the future of auditors.

> Looking a century ahead is very difficult. For instance, clearing out the attic, I stumbled upon a copy of the very first edition of *The Auchenbothie Accountant*, and in that issue there was an article entitled "A Hundred Years On," part of which predicted:
>
> "By rubbing a piece of amber over the Day Book and the Ledger, Electrick Vapours attached to each figure will be released into the Aether and friendly vapours will be attracted to each other so that when a figure in the Day Book encounters its mate in the ledger a small Bolt of Lightning would be set off: The Selection of the Fittest and Prudent Breeding will produce a race of Bonded Bairns specialised in their crafts, with those bred for their loud voices engaged in Calling and those with neat hands used in Ticking: The Proper Study of Physiognomy will allow the Master to know which clients are Deceitful and which are Honest, so that he can better direct his Bonded Bairns to check the books of Deceitful clients and spare Honest men from worry."
>
> The lesson from that for the accountant of 1980 is that the long-term shift will not be in how we will do what we currently do, but in what we will be required to do.[33]

In what sense has the development of the auditing profession followed this historical projection? Does the "lesson" for the accountant of 1980 appear to be accurate? Provide evidence to support your response.

[32]Michael Locke, "An Ideal Accountant," *Accountants Record*, February 1981, pp. 26, 27. By kind permission of *Accountants Record*, the official Journal of the Society of Company and Commercial Accountants, February 1981 edition.

[33]*Journal of Accountancy*, May 1980, p. 65.

4

The Code of Professional Ethics

John and Sam were old friends. They'd gone to the same university and had joined the same public accounting firm five years ago. Now John confided to Sam, "I'm thinking of leaving our firm."

Sam. Why? Where do you plan to go, to one of those clients who made a "fat offer"?

John. No, I like public accounting, but my real interest is in hospitals, and you know who has most of the hospital clients in this locale!

Sam. Have you told anyone else here that you're thinking about moving?

John. No, I want everything lined up first; then I'll give my notice.

Sam. Did they approach you, or vice versa?

John. They approached me, why?

Sam. It's a good thing for you that our code of ethics was changed a few years back. The old Rule 402 required a member in public practice to inform other public accountant employers before making a direct or indirect offer of employment to the others' employees.

John. Yeah, I remember the old code of conduct—a rule that had no other purpose than to take away people's freedom of choice.

Sam. You know, I would've agreed with you a few days ago, but did you read the front page of yesterday's *Wall Street Journal?*

John. No, I was tied up all day with a client. I didn't get home until almost midnight.

Sam. Well, let me fill you in. One of the Big Eight firms brought four partners from a highly successful local firm into their partnership. Using the new partners' knowledge of the local firm's client list, the Big Eight firm immediately sent letters to hundreds of the local firm's clients, soliciting their business and asking them to fill out a form to release their files from the smaller firm to the Big Eight firm.

John. I bet a lot of those clients thought the smaller firm had merged with the Big Eight firm. They probably felt obligated to sign the release forms. But hadn't the smaller firm foreseen the problem and told their clients that although the four partners were leaving, it had hired replacements and that their firm would continue to do business with them?

Sam. The problem was that the small firm didn't know the four were leaving. Even though the four included the partner for whom the small firm was named, they didn't give any advance notice. The four partners submitted resignations, effective immediately, on a Monday at 5 P.M. You're right about the small firm's claims. They reported that their clients were confused and kept asking if they were going out of business. Not only were the clients lost, but a lot of the professional staff quit. They were afraid that the firm would fail and they'd be out of a job.

John. Exactly what was the damage to the smaller firm?

Sam. Would you believe that its 1,403 clients dropped to 961! Billings dropped $800,000, and uncollectibles soared to $600,000, double that of last year. Remember that when the trouble began, all the competing CPA firms in the area declared open season on the smaller firm's client list. The professional staff of thirty-one fell to fourteen, and the rest of the partners had to chip in $200,000 to keep the firm going.

John. My gosh, wasn't anything done in advance to prevent this?

Sam. Well, it turns out that the partners' agreement required a ninety-day notice, which might have permitted the smaller firm to take preventive actions. But in the words of one of the remaining partners of the smaller firm, "there was conspiracy," with the pirating of key employees and no advance warning. The smaller firm has held up the capital payments to the four partners who left and even filed a complaint with the state's board of accountancy about the letter mailed by the Big Eight firm to the smaller firm's clients. But the complaint was dismissed, because the letter was found not to have violated any of the board's rules.

John. What does the Big Eight firm say in its defense?

Sam. It offered to send a second letter to clarify the first, but the smaller firm said no, because it felt the move would just give the bigger firm another crack at its clients. A spokesman for the Big Eight firm said it denied having done anything wrong. The firm really believes that it acted ethically and legally throughout.

John. Maybe the AICPA shouldn't have repealed the rules restricting competition among firms, if this is our new definition of ethical behavior.

Sam. A lawsuit has been filed for the Big Eight firm's so-called anticompetitive practices. I guess we'll soon get a working definition of competition. But as the article reported, this case is by no means a unique event. A senior partner at another Big Eight firm reported, "The big firm's point of view is watch out for yourself." The competitiveness of the accounting profession was compared to the marketing battles between Pepsi and Coke!

John. I hate having our profession get that kind of an image. I guess I didn't realize why the original code of ethics was adopted.

Sam. You realize, though, if it were still in place, you wouldn't be as free to get a job with another public accounting firm, because they'd have to notify your firm first.

John. All things considered, I'd be willing to give up a little personal freedom to help our profession. With CPA firms' dependence on personnel, they can't afford to be left in the lurch. Besides, I'm going to be difficult to replace," he said with a smirk, as the two headed out the door.[1]

This dialogue illustrates some of the recent changes in the AICPA's Code of Professional Ethics that have affected practice. Despite the media's reports of the fierce competition among accountants, the code still maintains guidelines for ethical behavior in advertising and rulings on other professional activities. Yet the recent changes that are only now being interpreted in practice pose some interesting questions as to what really is and is not ethical behavior. In this chapter, the profession's code of ethics will be described, as well as the dilemmas that can arise as the professional attempts to comply with these rules. Some areas of practice in which numerous questions arise as to what is ethical will be described with some attention given to current court cases that relate to these practice areas. For example, the confidentiality of auditors' workpapers has been challenged by the Internal Revenue Service, by clients, and by customers of clients. These points will be developed, integrating some issues from the introductory case whenever applicable. Beyond external auditors' code of ethics, the code of ethics for internal auditors is presented. An appendix to this chapter discusses other professionals' codes of ethics, comparing the provisions to the AICPA Professional Code of Ethics.

Indeed, a 1932 issue of *Fortune* noted:

> Today, it is no overstatement to say that there are preeminently three professions upon whose ethics as well as upon whose skill modern society depends: Law, Medicine, and Certified Public Accounting . . . upon the expert opinion of [CPAs] . . . who pit their judgment against the unbelievably subtle economic forces of this generation—the financial structure of our greatest industries is founded.[2]

The CPA performs the attest function to protect the interests of the investing public and society as a whole, and he or she is responsible to the public, the profession, the client, and the practitioner.

Marcus Aurelius said, "A man should *be* upright; not be *kept* upright."[3] No code of ethics can be sufficiently definitive to serve the latter purpose; its intent is always to guide the former. The concept of ethics is a pragmatic, essential part of the public accountant's practice. The code has the practical purpose of striving to induce that behavior which is capable of maintaining public confidence. The distinguishing mark of professionals is their acceptance of responsibility to the public including an obligation to uphold that profession's principles. The AICPA Code of Professional Ethics requires an unswerving commitment to honorable behavior, even at the sacrifice of personal advantage.

The General Concepts of Ethics and the Professional Code

The ethical principles on which the AICPA's Code of Professional Ethics is constructed are a combination of the so-called *golden rule* and the *organization ethic*. The former stresses the idea that decision makers place themselves in the shoes of those affected by their actions and try to determine the best responses. The latter acknowledges that the individuals' needs should be subordinated to the greater good of the organization in order to produce the desired benefits, an idea commonly attributed to Peter Drucker. These two concepts are best understood in regard to (1) how

[1] Adapted from Sanford L. Jacobs, "CPA Quarrel: Big 8 Accounting Firm Is Blamed by Small One for All of Its Troubles," *Wall Street Journal*, July 28, 1983, pp. 1, 10.

[2] Cited by Mark Stevens, *The Big Eight* (New York: Macmillan, 1981), p. 7.

[3] *AICPA Professional Standards, Volume 2, Ethics & Bylaws* (July 1, 1977).

materiality is defined and (2) the extent to which the code stresses an appearance of independence.

All materiality ideas are tied to whether certain information is likely to affect the users of financials. In other words, putting yourself in the shoes of the investor, would this information alter your decision or actions?

The appearance of independence is emphasized mostly to protect the profession's reputation. Little doubt exists that one might be able to demonstrate that independence existed, for example, in spite of a commission being received from a supplier of goods which a CPA recommended, in a single individual setting. However, the repeated incidence of such settings in which the public at large does not realize, for example, that the professional service was performed without knowledge of a commission and hence was "in fact, independent," clearly would tarnish the reputation of the total profession. The code has numerous requirements that underscore the importance of the entire profession, apart from individual practitioners' preferences. Rather than relying on individuals' judgment, the AICPA uses a sort of *utilitarian rule*. With respect to the profession and the public it serves, what is the greatest good for the greatest number? This general concept of ethics is attributed to philosophers like John Stuart Mill and is often referred to as the *democratic ethic*.

The Organization of the Code of Professional Ethics

The AICPA's Code of Professional Ethics has four parts: (1) concepts that describe general ideas and goals; (2) enforceable rules of conduct; (3) interpretations, which are explanatory rulings by the AICPA's Division of Professional Ethics; and (4) ethics rulings, or formal rulings made by the professional ethics division's executive committee, summarizing the application of the rules of conduct and interpretations to certain circumstances. All rules of professional conduct must be observed by AICPA members in public practice. Those not in public practice are required to comply only with those rules relating to integrity and objectivity (Rule 102) and acts that would discredit the profession (Rule 501). Members are also not permitted to let others perform on their behalf, either with or without compensation, any act that, had they performed it, would have violated the rules of conduct.

The chapter discussion will first focus on independence issues and then proceed to rules related to competency, advertising, confidentiality, and other ethical provisions. The applicable Rule of Conduct will be described, along with issues related to each rule. In addition to the AICPA's Code of Professional Ethics, the state societies of CPAs and state boards have codes of ethics which may add requirements to those of the AICPA's Code. Since these provisions vary by state, this chapter will do no more than provide an example of more stringent provisions that appear in various states' code of ethics. The Uniform CPA Examination is based upon the AICPA's Code, which will be our focal point.

INDEPENDENCE

Rule 101—Independence

A member of a firm of which (s)he is a partner or shareholder shall not express an opinion on financial statements or an enterprise unless (s)he and his or her firm are independent with respect to such enterprise. Independence will be considered to be impaired if, for example:

A. During the period in which the CPA is actually working on the engagement, or at the time of expressing an opinion, (s)he or the firm

1. a. Had or was committed to acquire any direct or material indirect financial interest in the enterprise; or

b. Was a trustee of any trust or executor or administrator of any estate if such trust or estate had or was committed to acquire any direct or material indirect financial interest in the enterprise; or

2. Had any joint closely held business investment with the enterprise or any officer, director, or principal stockholder thereof which was material in relation to the individual's or firm's net worth; or

3. Had any loan to or from the enterprise or any officer, director, or principal stockholder thereof, other than the following loans from a financial institution (when made under normal lending procedures, terms, and requirements):

a. Loans obtained by a member of the firm which are not material in relation to the net worth of such borrower.

> **b.** Home mortgages.
> **c.** Other secured loans, except loans guaranteed by a member's firm which are otherwise unsecured.
>
> **B.** During the period covered by the financial statements, during the period the CPA is actually working on the professional engagement, or at the time of expressing an opinion, (s)he or the firm
> **1.** Was connected with the enterprise as a promoter, underwriter, or voting trustee, a director or officer or in any capacity equivalent to that of a member of management or of an employee; or
> **2.** Was a trustee for any pension or profit-sharing trust of the enterprise.
>
> The above examples are not intended to be all-inclusive.[4]

This means that if a CPA had a financial interest in an enterprise during an audit period, yet disposed of that interest before undertaking the engagement, the CPA would be independent. The SEC had taken a more restrictive view of this until a July 1972 change in S-X Rule 2.01 resulted in agreement on this issue with the AICPA's Code of Professional Ethics.

The ethical rule that a CPA cannot have any direct financial interest or indirect material financial interest, or be committed to acquire such an interest, distinguishes between both direct and indirect and material and immaterial. The direct–indirect concept does allow a relative who does not share the same household to have a financial interest in a client. The materiality criterion permits a partner to own shares in a mutual fund that, in turn, owns stock in a company audited by the partner's CPA firm. But, neither of these distinctions has been accepted by all state societies. For example, the Illinois Society of Certified Public Accountants forbids its members to have any financial interest in an audit client, direct or indirect.

Although CPAs can have a financial interest in their clients during the period covered by the financial statements—as long as they are disposed of before the audit—CPAs cannot serve as either an officer or a director for their clients during the period covered by the financial statements. This is because the CPAs would be effectively auditing their own work.

An exception to this rule is made with respect to honorary directorships of charitable, religious, civic, or other nonprofit organizations. The CPA can still express an independent opinion if the directorship is more of a figurehead than a decision-making position. The purpose of this exception is to allow CPAs to lend their name to worthy causes of nonprofit organizations, to aid in fund raising. A good example of how independence influences the CPA's year-to-year relationship with his or her client is the issue of audit fees. If a client has not paid the previous year's fees by the time of the next engagement, the CPA must inform the client that such nonpayment means that the CPA now lacks independence.

Rule 101 covers the CPA and his or her spouse (whether or not dependent) and dependent persons (whether or not related). *Nondependent close relatives* include children, brothers, sisters, grandparents, parents, parents-in-law, and their respective spouses. Independence is impaired if a proprietor, partner, shareholder, or professional employee participating in the engagement or located in an office participating in a significant portion of the engagement has a close relative who can (1) exercise significant influence over the client's operating, financial, or accounting policies, (2) is otherwise employed to perform "audit sensitive" activities—the duties of cashiers, internal auditors, general accounting clerks, purchasing agents, and inventory warehouse supervisors—or (3) is known to have a financial interest in the client that is material to the close relative.

This meaning of independence applies to members, full-time and part-time professional and managerial employees of a firm, and the proprietor or all partners or shareholders of a firm. Beyond the circumstances specified, the member is expected to consider whether third parties might question one's independence because of family or dependent person relationships, particularly personal and business relationships. According to Ethical Interpretation No. 101–9, effective after December 31, 1983, the CPA must consider whether

> a reasonable person aware of all the facts and taking into consideration normal strength of character and normal

[4] "Bylaws and Rules of Conduct" (New York: AICPA, 1981).

behavior under the circumstances [would be led] to conclude that the situation poses an unacceptable threat to the member's objectivity and appearance of independence.[5]

Underlying Concepts

Independence is recognized as the foundation of the public accounting profession. All relationships that could even subconsciously impair one's objectivity, appear to create a conflict of interest, or represent any obligation to or interest in the client, its management, or its owners must be avoided. The stated standards are in no way comprehensive but merely permit the investigation, adjudication, and discipline of an individual's behavior that deviates from the profession's accepted conventions. In large part, members' reason, instinct, common sense, and conscience are expected to guide them in judging right from wrong.[6]

The close tie-in of independence and objectivity requirements and the existence of additional Rules of Conduct with a primary objective of ensuring an appearance of independence suggests the propriety of considering Rules 102, 302, and 503 at this juncture.

INTEGRITY AND OBJECTIVITY

Rule 102—Integrity and Objectivity

A member shall not knowingly misrepresent facts and when engaged in the practice of public accounting, including the rendering of tax and management advisory services, shall not subordinate his or her judgment to others. In tax practice, a member may resolve doubt in favor of his or her client as long as there is reasonable support for that position.[7]

Both the fact and the appearance of integrity and objectivity are important when expressing an opinion on financial statements. For this reason, both financial relationships and those in which a CPA appears to be part of management should be avoided. Rule 102 applies not only to members who knowingly misrepresent facts but also to those who permit or direct others, such as subordinates, to make false or misleading entries in the entity's financial records. This concept of being responsible for the direction of subordinates' actions contrary to the Rules of Conduct permeates the entire Code of Professional Ethics.

CONTINGENT FEES

Rule 302—Contingent Fees

Professional services shall not be offered or rendered under an arrangement whereby no fee will be charged unless a specified finding or result is attained, or where the fee is otherwise contingent upon the findings or results of such services.

Fees are not regarded as being contingent if fixed by courts or other public authorities or, in tax matters, if determined based on the results of judicial proceedings or on the findings of governmental agencies.[8]

According to Rule 302, the CPA's advice can never even appear to be influenced by the contingent fee arrangement. In order to be perceived as objective, the CPA should not benefit more from one outcome than another. An exception is possible only when a CPA is representing a client in proceedings in which the public is represented by a third party. In this case, the CPA's apparent advocacy role is acceptable. Note that tax planning or the preparation of tax returns cannot be performed on a contingent basis by claiming that the IRS automatically represents the public. The incidence of tax audits clearly shows that the public is not represented in the same way that a CPA represents a client. Only in court hearings or proceedings of public authorities are contingent fees permitted.

COMMISSIONS

Rule 503—Commissions

A member shall not pay a commission to obtain a client, nor shall (s)he accept a commission for a referral to a client of products or services of others.[9]

The Code of Ethics Rule 503 expressly prohibits kickbacks, as they might be interpreted to have in-

[5] AICPA, Ethics Interpretation No. 101–9, "The Meaning of Certain Independence Terminology and the Effect of Family Relationships on Independence."

[6] Adapted from Statement on Auditing Procedure No. 33 and an official 1947 Statement on Independence of the Council of the American Institute.

[7] "Bylaws and Rules of Conduct" (New York: AICPA, 1981).

[8] Ibid. [9] Ibid.

fluenced the CPA's objectivity. The result would be that the profession's image would be tarnished. Hence, it becomes irrelevant whether the kickback was known or not at the time of a decision; the question is not one of factual effect but is one of the possible appearance of an effect.

Rule 503 also prohibits fee splitting, again with the intent that references not be made based on a commission but, rather, on the qualifications of the professional colleague. By prohibiting such payments, clients do not incur fees for which commensurate services are not received. Interpretation 503–1 does permit the payment of fees to a referring public accountant for professional services actually rendered to either the client or the successor firm, though the mere act of referral is not deemed to be a professional service.

Appearance

The appearance of independence is based on individuals' perceptions, which has given rise to much debate. One such issue is the desirability of competition in the market for audits and Management Advisory Services (MAS). The Metcalf Subcommittee (cited in Chapter 3) claimed that the lack of competition permitted the Big Eight accounting firms to establish accounting principles, thereby exercising excessive control. In contrast, the Cohen Commission cited possible excessive competition as a problem because of its effects on the quality of services. However, the more significant problem is the CPA's worry that clients will discharge them and hire others who are more "cooperative." Competition is worse for smaller firms because of their smaller resource base.

Independence has been discussed in considerable depth with respect to the size of CPA firms. Since each client represents a greater proportion of smaller CPA firms' resources, those firms are expected to face a greater risk of losing independence. Furthermore, the close, personal relationships of smaller CPA firms with clients has been cited as increasing this risk. With respect to MAS, smaller firms are less likely to be capable of separating the audit staff from the MAS staff, and therefore are expected to face a greater risk of independence problems.

Long associations with clients have been claimed to threaten independence and lead to complacency or an excessive level of confidence in the client. On the other hand, a long association may lead to greater familiarity with the client's operations, requiring less reliance on management and providing the CPA with an increased capability of withstanding client pressures.

A study of the perceptions of ninety-two certified public accountants and eighty-four financial statement users indicated that audit firms are perceived as being more apt to lose independence when they operate in highly competitive environments, provide management advisory services, or are smaller in size. The length of time that the CPA had been an auditor was not seen as significantly affecting his or her independence.[10] The greater expertise of a partner, commonly obtained through long-term client relationships, may outweigh the threat of becoming "too close" to a client.

Management Advisory Services

In its Statement on Management Advisory Services No. 1, the AICPA's Committee on Management Services defines *MAS* as the consulting services that are intended to improve the client's use of its capabilities and resources so as to achieve the organization's objectives. MAS No. 2 states that an *MAS engagement* applies an analytical approach and process to a study or project. Activities include determining clients' objectives, fact finding, opportunity or problem definition, evaluation of alternatives, formulation of proposed action, communication of results, implementation, follow-up, or some combination thereof. MAS No. 3 defines an *MAS consultation* as typically being oral advice based on the CPA's knowledge of the client, the circumstances, and the technical matters obtained from the concurrent offering of professional services. Professional advisory services will probably include

- ○ Management functions of analysis, planning, organizing, and controlling.

[10] Randolph A. Shockley, "Perceptions of Auditors' Independence, An Empirical Analysis," Working Paper #80–004 (Athens: University of Georgia, Center for Audit Research, 1980).

- Introduction of new ideas to management.
- Improvement of procedures, systems, and organizational relationships.
- Application and use of managerial accounting, control systems, data processing, and mathematical techniques.
- Special studies, recommendations, plans, and technical assistance.

The Public Oversight Board (POB) lists the benefits of nonaudit services as

1. Cost savings due to familiarity with clients, such as minimal start-up costs.
2. Quality improvements based on the auditor's understanding of operations.
3. CPA firms' capability to attract MAS professionals, increasing the possibility of more innovative audits.
4. Enhancement of controls, thereby improving the quality of financial statements and the ease of performing audits (and decreasing audit costs).
5. More effective response to weaknesses or defects detected in the audit.

The POB also noted that for smaller businesses, requiring separate firms for audits and MAS could be too expensive, leading to either no MAS or to lower-quality services.[11]

Yet despite the benefits of MAS, critics have asserted that such services might impair the auditor's independence. But, some research has shown that management advisory services can actually enhance an audit firm's independence.[12] That is, by offering nonroutine services, the audit firm can demonstrate its indispensability and help the client resist pressures that might threaten the CPA's independence.[13] The Cohen Commission, after studying the Metcalf Subcommittee's claims that nonaudit services impaired independence, concluded that there was no evidence that this claim was valid.[14]

In contrast, some claim that CPAs who provide MAS (1) may become the client's advocate, (2) may thereby develop a stake in their client since their reputation as effective advisers becomes tied to the client's success, (3) may make decisions that they are later required to audit, and (4) may become too close to management. All four would presumably threaten independence. The larger fees from MAS could also increase the CPA's financial dependence on a particular client.

Accounting Series Releases (ASR) No. 250 and No. 264 (now known as FRRs) issued by the SEC reacted, in part, to this contention and deepened the concern over the profession's offering of MAS. After September 30, 1978, ASR No. 250 mandated disclosure of (1) the types of nonaudit services performed by the principal accountant, (2) the proportion of such fees to the audit fee, and (3) whether either the board or the audit committee had both reviewed and approved the nonaudit services. These reporting requirements, however, have since been repealed.

A random sample of 100 SEC registrants' proxy statements that included disclosure of nonaudit services were examined to estimate the average level of nonaudit services that clients received from their auditing firm. The average was 32 percent, with a median (or halfway) level of 17 percent. To assess the perceptions of user groups as to the meaning of such disclosures, a case study involving 50 chartered financial analysts and 50 unsophisticated and less knowledgeable subjects (MBA students) was performed. The CFAs did not question auditor independence when aggregate nonaudit services were varied from 8% to 49% of the audit fee, across a diverse set of services. Only 40 percent questioned such independence when the percentage reached 51% and included a search for merger or acquisi-

[11] Tom Herman, "Accounting Oversight Board Doesn't See Need for Major New Limits on Consulting," *Wall Street Journal*, March 15, 1979, p. 19.

[12] A. Schulte, "Compatibility of Management Consulting and Auditing," *Accounting Review*, July 1965, pp. 587–593; and R.H. Hartley and T.L. Ross, "MAS and Audit Independence: An Image Problem," *Journal of Accountancy*, November 1972, pp. 42–52.

[13] This concept is developed in greater depth by A. Goldman and B. Barlev, "The Auditor-Firm Conflict of Interests: Its Implications for Independence," *Accounting Review*, October 1974, pp. 707–718.

[14] Commission on Auditors' Responsibilities, *Report of Tentative Conclusions* (New York: Cohen Commission, 1977), p. 92.

tion candidates. The less knowledgeable group had lower confidence and rejected the independence of CPAs under 6 more circumstances than CFAs, lending credibility to the claim that education of the public is needed.[15]

In the fall of 1966 the AICPA had an *ad hoc* committee investigate the propriety of CPAs rendering management services. In its report, the committee noted that it had not found any instance in which independence had been impaired. Inquiries to 44 state boards and the SEC indicated they had never had such a case. But the committee did conclude that there was a need for long-range education. This same call for the education of users also appeared in reports of the Cohen Commission and the Public Oversight Board. In particular, the main problem was the imprecision of the term *management services*, and the AICPA's statements on MAS were seen as helpful in this area. Peripheral MAS, that is, those services not logically related to either the financial process or broadly defined information and control systems, was reported as most likely to hurt the image of the CPA as an auditor. The committee encouraged practitioners to limit voluntarily the extent of such services. Statement on Management Advisory Services No. 3 emphasizes that CPAs should be aware of others' views of their role and should not permit themselves to be put in a position that would endanger their objectivity and independence, an admonition that the committee endorses. CPAs are encouraged to exercise greater care the greater the economic consequence of a decision by management.[16]

Decision Making. Independence includes attitudes and judgments as well as appearance. With respect to MAS work, the distinction between decision making and recommendations is critical. If the CPA becomes the decision maker, he or she will be put in the position of auditing his or her own decisions. But if the client makes the decision based on the CPA's recommendations, this problem will not arise. But even in this latter case, the CPA should consider the magnitude of the capital expenditures in relation to the MAS work. The likelihood of the CPA's independence being violated appears to rise as that magnitude increases. CPAs are expected to exercise self-restraint and judgment when evaluating the propriety of their dual role in audit and MAS engagements.

Examples. Rule of Conduct 101 B.1 permits CPAs to draw up position descriptions and candidate specifications, seek and initially screen candidates, and recommend qualified candidates to a client. But the client's management must be responsible for any final hiring decision if the CPAs are to remain independent.[17]

Similarly, when a CPA firm is asked to help an audit client implement an information and control system, including arranging interviews for hiring new personnel and instructing and overseeing the training of new personnel, the firm must be careful to avoid direct supervision of operations or undue involvement in management functions. Under Rule of Conduct 101, the CPA firm's independence would not be impaired if (1) management made all of the decisions related to both hiring and system implementation and (2) supervisory activities were restricted to initial instruction and training.[18]

Whenever CPAs are asked to evaluate their services, for example, service bureaus for processing the client's accounting records, they should not accept that engagement if they have a financial interest in one of the service bureaus that are available for consideration. This could violate Rule 102, as the CPA's objectivity could be questioned. If they were to recommend that bureau, the firm's CPAs may appear to have subordinated their judgment to those partners having a financial interest in the service bureau. On the other hand, client service could be impaired if that bureau was not recommended merely because of the financial interest, as it might well be the best service bureau for the

[15] Philip M.J. Reckers and A.J. Stagliano, "Non-Audit Services and Perceived Independence: Some New Evidence," Working Paper, University of Maryland.

[16] Ad Hoc Committee of Independence, "Final Report," *Journal of Accountancy*, December 1969, pp. 51–56.

[17] "Under Rule of Conduct 101: Executive Search," *Journal of Accountancy*, January 1977, p. 98.

[18] "Under Rule of Conduct 101: Independence During MAS Systems Implementation," *Journal of Accountancy*, January 1977, p. 98.

client. Hence, the client's financial interests can constrain the firm's ability to perform certain MAS engagements.[19]

SEC Considerations. Accounting Series Release 264 (now a FRR) states:

> While hard-and-fast lines cannot be drawn, any firm which finds that a substantial portion of its aggregate revenues arise from nonaudit engagements should seriously evaluate the resulting impact on its image as a professional accounting firm and from the standpoint of the potential for impairment of its independence. Similarly, where the firm's revenues from a given audit client are heavily weighted towards MAS, the impact on both the fact and appearance of independence merits thoughtful review.

The SEC continued by cautioning CPAs to be particularly careful to avoid accepting engagements that would require CPAs to audit their own work, such as a comprehensive review of internal accounting controls engagement when those controls were designed by the MAS group of the same firm.

Accounting Series Release 264, which was essentially a threat of future restrictions on MAS practices by CPAs, is claimed to have had adverse effects on the growth of MAS. Some directors prefer to avoid any potential claims of conflict of interest, and so they do not consider their auditors when assigning MAS work.

The SEC's 1980 annual report to Congress on the accounting profession and the commission's oversight role, offers an additional interpretation of Accounting Series Release No. 264:

> While the Commission agrees that independence is primarily dependent on the nature of the accountant's relationship with individual audit clients, it disagrees with the notion that the profession may disregard the magnitude of MAS activities on a firm-wide basis. Undue emphasis on MAS could ultimately have an unfavorable effect on the quality of audit work performed.

Such statements ignore the benefits to CPAs from their provision of MAS. From the MAS engagement, a deeper knowledge of the client is obtained and the CPA becomes a better auditor. Futhermore, recruiting is more effective, and ways of enhancing controls to reduce the cost of future audits can be identified and implemented. Managers have repeatedly demonstrated their confidence in CPAs' ability, in spite of such a stance by the SEC, as they repeatedly select the auditor to perform MAS.

In its response to Accounting Series Release 264, Deloitte, Haskins & Sells noted: "We do not and have not provided services such as psychological testing, public-opinion polls, plant layout, merger and acquisition assistance for a finder's fee or actuarial services." Obviously, care has been exercised on a voluntary basis in the marketplace by CPAs, in order not to injure their independent and professional appearance.

The SEC's Perspective. The SEC's position on independence is expressed in Rule 2–01(b) of Regulation S–X:

> The Commission will not recognize any certified public accountant or public accountant as independent who is not in fact independent. For example, an accountant will be considered not independent with respect to any person or any of its parents, its subsidiaries, or any other affiliates, (1) in which, during the period of his professional engagement to examine the financial statements being reported on or at the date of his report, he or his firm or a member thereof had, or is committed to acquire, any direct financial interest or any material indirect financial interest; or (2) with which, during the period of his professional engagement to examine the financial statements being reported on, at the date of his report or during the period being covered by the financial statements, he or his firm or a member thereof was connected as a promoter, underwriter, voting trustee, director, officer, or employee, except that a firm will not be deemed not independent in regard to a particular person if a former officer or employee of such person is employed by the firm and such individual has completely disassociated himself from the person and its affiliates and does not participate in auditing financial statements of the person or its affiliates covering any period of his employment by the person. For the purposes of Rule 2–01, the term "member" means all partners in the firm and all professional employees participating in

[19] Rule of Conduct 505 and Interpretation 505–1 are also relevant to this setting. See "Under Rule of Conduct 102: MAS Engagement to Evaluate Service Bureaus," *Journal of Accountancy*, January 1977, p. 98.

the audit or located in an office of the firm participating in a significant portion of the audit.[20]

This rule does not distinguish between independence in fact and the appearance of independence. The Securities and Exchange Commission narrows the AICPA's definition of independence. A CPA lacks independence if he or she has participated in *any* business transactions, even if there is no direct financial interest. For example, in ASR No. 97, the SEC found that a CPA would not be independent if he or she were one of three stockholders and an officer and comanager of a finance company that made loans to customers and employees of a client who was a registered broker-dealer. ASR No. 126 states that independence is an objective analysis of a situation by a disinterested third party. With respect to MAS,

> the basic consideration is whether, to a third party, the client appears to be totally dependent upon the accountant's skill and judgment in its financial operations or to be reliant only to the extent of the customary type of consultation or advice.[21]

The SEC stated that it would consider a number of nonaudit services to be improper if it were asked to judge them formally in an enforcement action, including (1) actuarial services to calculate insurance reserves and the like, (2) plant surveys, (3) consulting on employee benefits and compensation, (4) consumer surveys, (5) public opinion polls, and (6) psychological testing. The basis for these categories, according to the SEC, is that they are not expected to produce any cost advantages, whereas internal control reviews and tax services clearly do. The SEC's chief accountant, Clarence Sampson, explained that the question of independence will grow as MAS work occupies a larger share of the total payments to the CPA firm that is performing an audit. But despite such statements, the SEC did not ban any of the services in question.[22] The profession responded to these concerns, and now SEC Practice Section firms are not to engage in activities that obviously compromise their independence: predominantly commercial services, psychological testing, public opinion polls, merger and acquisition assistance for a finder's fee, marketing consultations, and plant layout services.

Examples of Specific Rulings. In 1962, the SEC decided that a CPA firm was not independent because one of its partners also acted as the client's legal counsel.[23] This has been cited as a ruling related to the SEC's concerns over independence in regard to MAS.

In regard to EDP and bookkeeping services, the SEC's ASR No. 126 states:

> Systems design is a proper function of the qualified public accountant. Computer programming is an aspect of systems design and does not constitute a bookkeeping service . . . where source data is provided by the client and the accountant's work is limited to processing and production of listings and reports, independence will be adversely affected if the listings and reports become part of the basic accounting records on which, at least in part, the accountant would base his opinion.[24]

One example of an EDP situation that impairs independence is considered by the SEC in ASR No. 126 as follows:

> A client prepared and forwarded to the CPA printed tapes to be read on an optical scanner. The CPA merely sent those tapes to a service bureau and forwarded print-outs of the financial statements and general ledgers back to the client. Due to the appearance that the service bureau was acting as the CPA's agent, independence is impaired. If instead, the client dealt directly with the service bureau, no such impairment would result.

The SEC opposes the joint provision of write-up and audit services. Regardless of whether books are kept manually or on computers, the CPA is placed in a

[20] Securities and Exchange Commission, "Qualifications of Accountants," Regulation S–X, Article 2–01.

[21] Now FRR, July 5, 1972.

[22] "SEC to Warn Accounting Firms, Clients That Nonaudit Jobs May Be Violations," *Wall Street Journal,* June 14, 1979, p. 6.

[23] News Report, "SEC Rules CPA Who Is Client's Attorney Is Not Independent," *Journal of Accountancy,* May 1962, p. 14.

[24] Now FRR, July 5, 1972.

EXHIBIT 4-1

Situations in Which Independence Might Be Questioned—Research Findings

	Consensus Response	AICPA	SEC
1. An accounting firm had its office in a building owned by a client. The accounting firm occupied approximately 25 percent of the available office space in the building, and the client occupied the remainder.	Independent	Not Independent	Not Independent
2. In addition to the audit, an accounting firm provided services for the client that included maintaining the journal and ledgers, making adjusting entries, and preparing financial statements.	CPAs – Not Independent Users – Independent	Independent	Not Independent
3. In order to keep certain information confidential, the client had the accounting firm perform the following services in addition to the audit: (a) prepare the executive payroll and (b) maintain selected general ledger accounts in a private ledger.	Independent	Independent	Not Independent
4. A partner in an accounting firm managed a building owned by an audit client.	Not Independent	Not Independent	Not Independent
5. From the books of original entry, client personnel prepared printed tapes that could be read on an optical scanner and sent the tapes to the accountant's office. The accountants forwarded the tapes to a service bureau. The accountants received the printouts of the financial statements and general ledgers and sent them to the client. The accountants did not edit the data before transmitting them to the service bureau. The accountants provided this service in addition to the audit.	Independent	Independent	Not Independent
6. According to a plan of recapitalization, the company's existing debt was exchanged for five-year promissory notes. The accounting firm received the same kind of promissory notes in payment of its audit fee.	CPAs – No consensus Users – Not Independent	Not Independent	Not Independent
7. A was the controller of Company Z. He was not an elected officer, nor did he have any stock holdings in Company Z. A's brother, B, was a partner in the public accounting firm that audits Company Z's books. However, B was not the partner in charge of the audit.	Independent	*	Not Independent
8. A partner in a public accounting firm had a brother-in-law who was the sales vice-president for a recently acquired client. The brother-in-law was not directly involved in the company's financial affairs, and the partner was not in any way connected with the audit.	Independent	Independent	Independent
9. An accounting firm rented block time on its computer to a client when the client's computer became overburdened.	Independent	Independent	Not Independent
10. Four partners in an accounting firm were among the six founders of a company engaged in the same type of business and directly competing with an audit client. In addition to owning stock, they also served as directors and officers of this company. The accountants informed the president of the client-company of their investment in a business competitor, but he did not object to the business venture and permitted them to continue as auditors. Both companies were located in the same geographical area.	Not Independent	Not Independent	Not Independent

* If the auditors are from a different office, they are independent. But if the auditors are from the same office, they are not independent. Adapted from David Lavin, "Perceptions of the Independence of the Auditor," *Accounting Review*, January 1976, pp. 41–50.

position of evaluating and attesting to his or her own record keeping. Similarly, renting computer time to a client is deemed to be a business transaction beyond the normal professional relationship and so adversely affects independence. Note that the AICPA see no impairment of independence in offering either bookkeeping or electronic data-processing services. The AICPA considers bookkeeping as a summary or translation service separate from decision making.

Related Research. In its Accounting Series Release No. 126, the SEC listed thirty-nine situations in which an auditor either was or was not independent. Because this differed from the AICPA's Code of Professional Ethics, third parties' and CPAs' opinions on auditor independence were sought. A total of 202 CPAs, 114 loan officers, and 74 research financial analysts was surveyed. A sample of their decisions, compared with the AICPA's official stance under the 1972 Code of Professional Ethics and the SEC's position, is shown in Exhibit 4-1. Overall, the users and CPAs agree more with the AICPA position than with the SEC's.

Write-up Services. Holding that write-up work causes a CPA to lose independence, the SEC referred particularly to a CPA's original work on the accounting records and postings to the general ledger and the preparation of closing entries. However, if a sudden resignation or death of key accounting personnel creates an emergency, the SEC permits auditors to help maintain the client's records. The rationale for the general ruling is that a CPA who writes up the books must also decide on the classification and allocation of various transactions and therefore cannot provide a second independent check of "management's" accounting.

Although the AICPA states that members may write up clients' accounting records, it has simultaneously recommended that audits be conducted by staff members who are not associated with the original accounting work. CPAs are asked to consider their independence, in fact, and the AICPA holds that a CPA is not independent if he or she (1) is a resident auditor for the client, (2) is authorized to sign checks, (3) approves vouchers, (4) recommends personnel changes, and (5) performs other management functions.[25]

It should be reemphasized, however, that the AICPA permits CPAs who have performed write-up services to consider themselves independent for the purpose of performing an audit. In fact, most small accounting firms regularly offer bookkeeping services to their audit clients, and these are an important part of their professional practice.

One Proposed Model

A model for analyzing auditors' deviant behavior—in particular, for determining the likelihood of not being independent or lacking objectivity and integrity—is illustrated in Exhibit 4-2. The model summarizes the competing pressures on an auditor in decision making that may enhance the risk of deviant behavior. One way of increasing auditors' power or freedom from excessive pressure by management is the client's use of audit committees. Recall that only outside directors can be appointed to such committees. Others have suggested that auditors' power would be enhanced by

- Offering the auditor more discretionary options to impose sanctions on clients, such as required communication between predecessor and successor auditors or the filing of *8–K reports* with the SEC whenever companies change auditors (8–K reports should be filed whenever there are significant events that affect SEC-registered companies' operations).
- Reducing the auditor's and/or client's flexibility of action by increasing the cost of inappropriate behavior (such as greater specification of auditing and accounting standards).
- Changing the structure of auditor–client contractual relationships as a means of decreasing the discretionary options available to the company (such as longer-term engagements).[26]

In Accounting Series Release No. 123,[27] the SEC endorses the establishment of standing audit committees composed of outside directors as a means of protecting investors relying on financial statements. This may well be one of the more effective means of enhancing auditors' independence.

[25] AICPA, "Special Reports—Application of Statement on Auditing Procedure No. 28."

[26] Donald R. Nichols and Kenneth H. Price, "The Auditor–Firm Conflict: An Analysis Using Concepts of Exchange Theory," *Accounting Review*, April 1976, pp. 335–346.

[27] Now FRR, March 23, 1972.

EXHIBIT 4-2
A Model for Analyzing Auditors' Deviant Behavior

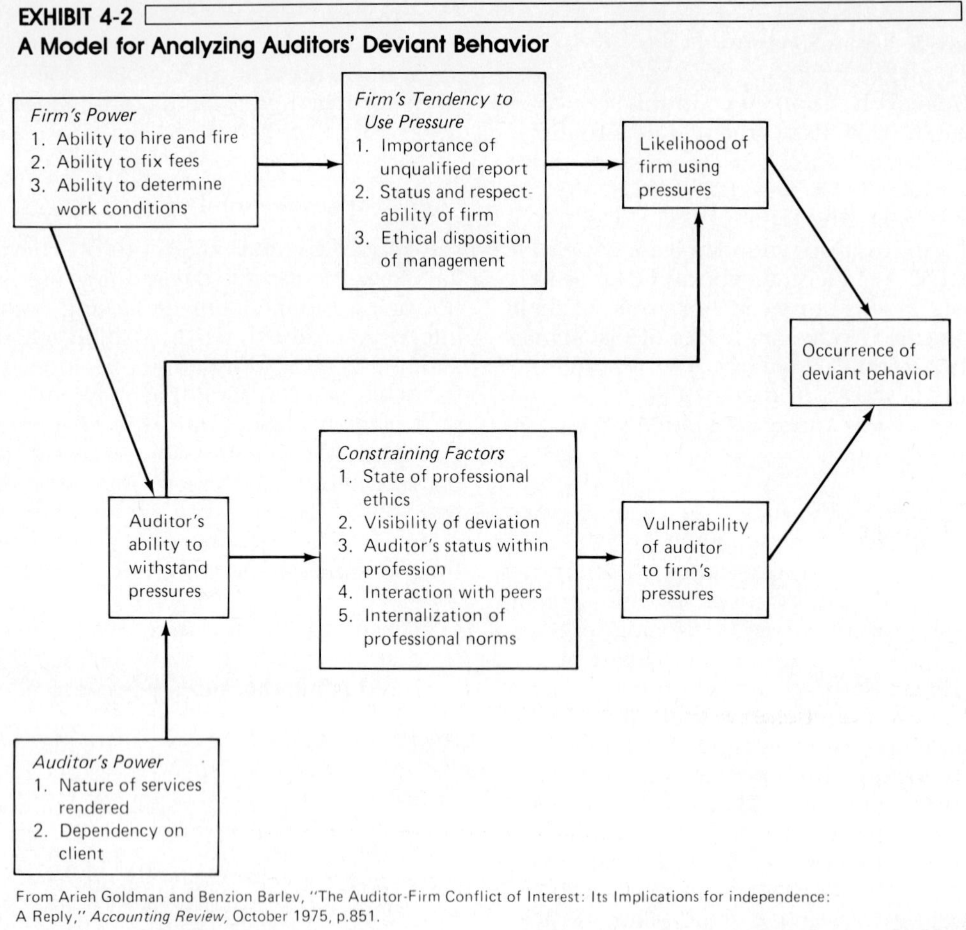

From Arieh Goldman and Benzion Barlev, "The Auditor-Firm Conflict of Interest: Its Implications for independence: A Reply," *Accounting Review,* October 1975, p.851.

Reporting Considerations

When lacking independence, a CPA should issue a disclaimer like that presented in Chapter 2:

> Inasmuch as we . . . are not . . . independent, our examination of the accompanying financial statements was not conducted in accordance with generally accepted auditing standards. Accordingly, we are not in a position to and do not express an opinion on these financial statements.[28]

Note that the CPA should not give the reasons for the lack of independence, as the judgment that independence is lacking is made by the CPA, not the user of financial statements. Furthermore, no matter what procedures have been performed, they are not to be reported, as, by definition, they could not have been performed in accordance with generally accepted auditing standards.

Both the SEC and AICPA permit the reissuing of a previously expressed opinion, despite the subsequent loss of independence. The critical time period is when the opinion was first expressed; nevertheless, the CPA is responsible for reviewing subsequent events, a topic introduced in Chapter 2 that will be discussed further in Chapter 8.

[28] AICPA, Opinion No. 15.

COMPETENCY

Rule 201—General Standards

A member shall comply with the following general standards and must justify any departures therefrom.

A. *Professional competence.* A member shall undertake only those engagements which (s)he or the firm can reasonably expect to complete with professional competence.

B. *Due professional care.* A member shall exercise due professional care in the performance of an engagement.

C. *Planning and supervision.* A member shall adequately plan and supervise an engagement.

D. *Sufficient relevant data.* A member shall obtain sufficient relevant data to afford a reasonable basis for conclusions or recommendations in relation to an engagement.

E. *Forecasts.* A member shall not permit his or her name to be used in conjunction with any forecast of future transactions in a manner which may lead to the belief that the member vouches for the achievability of the forecast.

Rule 202—Auditing Standards

A member shall not permit his or her name to be associated with financial statements in such a manner as to imply that (s)he is acting as an independent public accountant unless (s)he has complied with the applicable generally accepted auditing standards promulgated by the Institute. Statements on Auditing Standards issued by the Institute's auditing standards executive committee are, for purposes of this rule, considered to be interpretations of the generally accepted auditing standards, and departures from such statements must be justified by those who do not follow them.

Rule 203—Accounting Principles

A member shall not express an opinion that financial statements are presented in conformity with generally accepted accounting principles if such statements contain any departure from an accounting principle promulgated by the body designated by Council to establish such principles which has a material effect on the statements taken as a whole, unless the member can demonstrate that due to unusual circumstances the financial statements would otherwise have been misleading. In such cases his or her report must describe the departure, the approximate effects thereof, if practicable, and the reasons why compliance with the principle would result in a misleading statement.

Rule 204—Other Technical Standards

A member shall comply with other technical standards promulgated by bodies designated by Council to establish such standards, and departures therefrom must be justified by those who do not follow them.[29]

The Institute states that CPAs must observe the profession's technical standards, continually striving to improve both their competence and the quality of their services. The CPA is expected to determine whether he or she has the competency required by each engagement. Unfamiliar problems may be approached competently through research, study, or consultation with a practitioner who possesses the necessary competence. However, if unable to gain sufficient competency via these alternatives to experience, in fairness to the client and the public, the CPA should suggest that someone who meets the competency requirements be hired. Acceptance of an engagement assumes that one has the ability to carry it out. The forecast provision now under Rule 201 used to be Rule 204 of the 1973 Code of Ethics. It states, as mentioned in Chapter 2, that a member cannot in any sense guarantee that a forecast will be met. According to Interpretation 204–1, this rule does not prohibit members from preparing or helping clients prepare forecasts. Disclosures accompanying such forecasts are expected to include the sources of information used, the major assumptions underlying the forecast, the character of work performed, and the degree of responsibility assumed.

Rules 202 and 203 bind the CPA to GAAS and GAAP. Rule 202 does not prohibit a member from being associated with unaudited financial statements; it simply stresses that if an audit is implied, generally accepted auditing standards must be met. Rule 202 enforces compliance with GAAS. Rule 203, cited in Chapter 2, recognizes that in unusual circumstances, the literal application of pronouncements on accounting principles would make financial statements misleading. In such a situation, the proper accounting treatment is whatever makes the financial statements not misleading. New legislation or a new form of business transactions are cited in Interpretation 203-1 as justifying such a departure. Rule 203 enforces compliance with GAAP.

[29] "Bylaws and Rules of Conduct" (New York: AICPA, 1981).

ADVERTISING AND SOLICITATION

.01 Rule 502—Advertising and other forms of solicitation. A member shall not seek to obtain clients by advertising or other forms of solicitation in a manner that is false, misleading, or deceptive. Solicitation by the use of *coercion, overreaching* or *harassing conduct is prohibited.* [Effective January 6, 1983.]

Interpretations Under Rule 502—Advertising and Other Forms of Solicitation

.02 502-1—Informational advertising. Advertising that is informative and objective is permitted. Such advertising should be in good taste and be professionally dignified. There are no other restrictions, such as on the type of advertising media, frequency of placement, size, artwork, or type style. Some examples of informative and objective content are—

1. Information about the member and the member's firm, such as—
   - **a.** Names, addresses, telephone numbers, number of partners, shareholders or employees, office hours, foreign language competence, and date the firm was established.
   - **b.** Services offered and fees for such services, including hourly rates and fixed fees.
   - **c.** Educational and professional attainments, including date and place of certifications, schools attended, dates of graduation, degree received, and memberships in professional associations.
2. Statements of policy or position made by a member or a member's firm related to the practice of public accounting or addressed to a subject of public interest.

.03 502—False, misleading, or deceptive acts. Advertising or other forms of solicitation that are false, misleading, or deceptive are not in the public interest and are prohibited. Such activities include those that—

1. Create false or unjustified expectations of favorable results.
2. Imply the ability to influence any court, tribunal, regulatory agency, or similar body or official.
3. Consist of self-laudatory statements that are not based on verifiable facts.
4. Make comparisons with other CPAs that are not based on verifiable facts.
5. Contain testimonials or endorsements.[30]

After the AICPA ban on advertising was lifted, Arthur Young ran some institutional ads, but Deloitte, Haskins & Sells was the first to launch what was termed by its managing partner as "a national hard-sell campaign." The ad slogan "Beyond the Bottom Line" was emphasized.[31] Ads for Peat, Marwick, Mitchell & Co., Ernst & Whinney, and Cooper and Lybrand have appeared in *Business Week, Forbes,* and other trade journals. Peat, Marwick even had an office building in Chicago named after it.[32]

Advertising: A Historical Perspective and Perceptions

A 1976 survey of 636 accountants, attorneys, dentists, and physicians in Denver, Kansas City, and Memphis, showed that these professionals have similar attitudes toward advertising. They indicate only limited agreement as to the value of advertising, and they oppose advertising without restrictions. They question whether advertising would increase the public's awareness of professionals' qualifications or assist them in choosing services. Similarly, they question whether bans on advertising have lessened competition. All groups believe that advertising would increase the prices of their services and would adversely affect the public image of practitioners.[33]

The pros and cons of advertising were widely discussed before the AICPA changed its Code of Professional Ethics. The pros were: (1) the advent of competitive pricing; (2) increased information to the public about services available, individual firms, and practitioners; and (3) the public's "right to know." The cons were: (1) the poor service to consumers caused by exaggerations and misrepresentations of professionals' skills; (2) deceptive advertising of fees, as each job is different and low

[30] AICPA Professional Standards, Section 502 (New York: AICPA, 1982).

[31] Mark Stevens, *The Big Eight* (New York: Macmillan, 1981), p. 44.

[32] Margaret Yao, "Fierce Competition Forces Auditing Firms to Enter the Alien World of Marketing," *Wall Street Journal,* March 18, 1981, p. 31; and personal observation.

[33] John R. Darling, "Attitudes Toward Advertising By Accountants," *Journal of Accountancy,* February 1977, pp. 48–53.

hourly rates in no way ensure lower costs, because inexperienced professionals can take longer to do an engagement; (3) destruction of some of the AICPA members' professionalism; and (4) problems in trying to prevent false advertising.[34] Because CPAs' clients cannot usually evaluate such services, advertising has been criticized as merely commercializing the profession. In addition, many argued that because of larger firms' ability to advertise more, the smaller firms would be hurt.

In 1978, the Justice Department recommended that a complaint be filed against the AICPA seeking removal of two sections of its code of ethics: (1) the ban on direct, uninvited solicitations of specific potential clients and (2) the encroachment rule, including the requirement that (a) members first consult with the current CPA if asked by another's audit client for professional advice on accounting or auditing matters in connection with an audit report and (b) accountants who get work through referral from another accountant should not seek an additional engagement from that client and not accept the client's request to extend services beyond the specific assignment without first notifying the referring accountant. (Recall that this rule was the main point of this chapter's introductory dialogue.)

Other professions have similarly faced government's opposition to restrictions on advertising. For example, the medical profession's restrictions on advertising and patient solicitation were cited as violating federal antitrust laws in a ruling by a Federal Trade Commissioner Administrative Law Judge in 1978, in support of a three-year-old charge against the American Medical Association. The Supreme Court has overturned restrictions on advertising governing lawyers, based on the First Amendment right of the public to commercial information.[35] The National Society of Professional Engineers tried to defend its competitive bidding ban as reasonable due to its intent to minimize the risk that competition would produce inferior engineering work thereby endangering the public safety. However, the Sherman Act prevailed. The American Institute of Architects had a similar experience.

A case upholding the constitutionality of a ban on lawyer solicitation stressed the protection of the public against those aspects of solicitation potentially involving fraud, undue influence, intimidation, overreaching, and other forms of vexatious conduct. Since the lawyer in the case solicited two injured parties in an automobile accident while still in the hospital and one shortly thereafter, the abusive setting accounts for the Court's ruling.[36] After being advised by legal counsel that the AICPA was "unlikely" to win in court, a referendum of the 145,000 members was held, resulting in 71,271 votes—69% voted to eliminate bans on solicitation and 72% voted to eliminate the encroachment rule. The effect of this referendum is debatable since the rules were often evaded by creative approaches to getting an invitation from some potential clients to bid for their business.[37]

After a fifty-year ban on advertising, in April 1978 the AICPA voted to allow advertising that was not false, misleading, or deceptive. In 1979, the restriction against "a direct uninvited solicitation of a specific potential client" was eliminated.

The Designation of Specialists

Several events point to the probability of more specialization designations in the future. These include such a trend in medicine, law, and engineering and the belief of regulators and professionals that the tradition of public service can best be served by helping clients identify specialized practices. However, past survey research has found that despite 71 percent of 638 CPAs—from a sole practitioner to the Big Eight firms in Illinois—identifying themselves as functional specialists, only half actually endorsed the formal recognition of

[34] Ronald D. Willyard, "Advertising and the CPA . . . ," *Texas Society of CPAs News,* February 1977, pp. 1–3.

[35] "AMA, Ired by FTC Judge's Ruling, Vows Appeals Will Reach Congress if Needed," *Wall Street Journal,* November 30, 1978, p. 12.

[36] Willkie Farr & Gallagher, "Blanket Ban on Solicitation—Antitrust Considerations," Memorandum of Law distributed to members of the AICPA, October 6, 1978.

[37] Tom Herman, "Accountant Group Votes Change in Code to Allow Direct Solicitation of Clients," *Wall Street Journal,* April 30, 1979, p. 12.

specialties. According to this Illinois study, the larger CPA firms are more apt to want professional specialty designations, through the AICPA. Smaller firms seem to fear the competitive effect of such designations and, if granted, would want the individual firms, rather than the AICPA, to certify such specialties. The fear is that the CPAs' prestige could be damaged and that the profession would become segmented. Less public visibility of specialist designations is preferred; in other words, stationery, business cards, and the yellow pages were acceptable to the majority of the Illinois respondents, whereas press releases were favored by only a third. Mandatory continuing professional education for such designations was favored, though less by sole practitioners than others. Approximately 80 percent of the respondents opposed the formal recognition of industry specialties like insurance, stating that this would limit firms' practices to particular industries and have adverse effects on smaller firms. The profession must decide whether such designations are to apply to firms or individuals.[38] Currently, any claim of professional attainments must be verifiable. However, more direction in terms of specialists' designations would be desirable for the profession as a whole in avoiding some of the ills feared during past disputes over advertising. As will be discussed, under Rule 505, members are prohibited from using a firm name that indicates specialization.

One current practice is specifying particular types of CPA firms in loan agreements. For example, some loan agreements were reported as naming Big Eight auditors. The AICPA felt that this was an arbitrary size distinction that implied differential quality within the profession. In response, the AICPA published the policy statement presented in Exhibit 4-3.

CONFIDENTIALITY

Rule 301—Confidential Client Information

A member shall not disclose any confidential information obtained in the course of a professional engagement except with the consent of the client.

This rule shall not be construed (a) to relieve a member of his or her obligation under Rules 202 and 203, (b) to affect in any way his or her compliance with a validly issued subpoena or summons enforceable by order of a court, (c) to prohibit review of a member's professional practice as a part of voluntary quality review under Institute authorization, or (d) to preclude a member from responding to any inquiry made by the ethics division or trial board of the Institute, by a duly constituted investigative or disciplinary body of a state CPA society, or under state statutes.

Members of the division and trial board of the Institute and professional practice reviewers under Institute authorization shall not disclose any confidential client information which comes to their attention from members in disciplinary proceedings or otherwise in carrying out their official responsibilities. However, this prohibition shall not restrict the exchange of information with an aforementioned duly constituted investigative or disciplinary body.[39]

Rule of Conduct 301 requires that any confidential information obtained while performing an engagement not be disclosed without the client's consent. Special knowledge and expertise, however, can be offered to other clients. A scenario discussed in the literature is whether a CPA should apply a newly developed electronic ticketing system used for one client to a similar engagement for another client. In addition, if the first engagement gave the CPA sufficient expertise as to have reservations as to the system's desirability for the second client, can he or she state such reservations? The key consideration is whether the new client would recognize the origin of the information on which the reservations are based and whether such information is sensitive. If the answer is yes, the CPA should get permission from the first client to accept the new client. But if the circumstances do not create these problems, the CPA can communicate his or her reservations to the prospective client, providing that the details of the other client's engagement are not disclosed.[40]

The AICPA has held that an independent public accountant can accept accounting and auditing engagements on behalf of government agencies and others that involve a client's accounts, provided that

[38] Gary Siegel, "Specialization and Segmentation in the Accounting Profession," *Journal of Accountancy*, November 1977, pp. 74–80.

[39] "Bylaws and Rules of Conduct" (New York: AICPA, 1981).

[40] Special Supplement, *The CPA Letter* (New York: AICPA, September 28, 1981).

EXHIBIT 4-3

Policy Statement on Discriminatory Clauses in Loan Agreements

The special committee on small and medium-sized firms of the American Institute of Certified Public Accountants recommended the issuance of a resolution opposing clauses in loan or other agreements which discriminate in favor of, or against, any particular group or type of accounting firm.

The resulting resolution adopted by the AICPA's board of directors follows:

> With increasing frequency, credit grantors, underwriters, and others requiring professional accounting services have been limiting firms from whom they will accept such services to those which are one of the "Big 8" or which are "nationally recognized." The American Institute of Certified Public Accountants deplores this practice since it is not in the best interests of either the accounting profession or the public it serves.
>
> Certified public accountants, no matter what the size of the firms with which they practice, must meet the same standard of competence for admission to the profession and licensure to practice. And all practitioners, regardless of the size of their firms, must adhere to the same auditing and accounting rules adopted by the profession, and regulations adopted by the state boards of accountancy.
>
> Hence, practitioners in general are qualified to meet the needs of those seeking professional accounting services, and the size of the firms in which they practice becomes important only when, for example, the size of the engagement would require more manpower than a local firm could provide. But that circumstance is a fact which should be determined in negotiations following a request for proposal—not in an arbitrary policy decision limiting performance of the engagement to "Big 8" or "nationally recognized" firms.
>
> Selection of auditors by use of such terms provides no assurance that management has appropriately discharged its responsibility to select an accounting firm which will offer quality accounting services at a reasonable price.
>
> The Institute strongly recommends, therefore, the legal instruments or forms providing that only accounting services of a "Big 8" or "nationally recognized" firm are acceptable should be modified to provide that the needed accounting services will be performed by "an accounting firm mutually acceptable to the parties." This change will provide assurance that no firm is arbitrarily eliminated on the basis of its size and will afford clients the opportunity of broad selection among all firms competing in the marketplace.

From Special Supplement, *The CPA Letter* (New York: AICPA, September 28, 1981).

the CPA's relationship to the various parties is fully disclosed.

The concept of "privileged communication," that is, the idea that professionals cannot reveal information given to them by the client, even in the courtroom, has not been extended to CPAs. Unlike the relationship between husband and wife, attorney and client, medical doctor and patient, and priest and parishioner, the CPAs must reveal information concerning their clients when required to do so in judicial proceedings. Nevertheless, in 1970, fifteen states and one territory were reported to have statutes conferring such privileged communication status in certain circumstances,[41] though these statutes have been cited as being inconsistent with the auditor's concept of independence. If the auditor's primary responsibility is to the public, then the privileged communication appears to contradict this role. Outside the courtroom, CPAs are expected to maintain a confidential relationship with their clients. But they can make the disclosures necessary for GAAS compliance, without fear of claims under a privileged status.

Work Papers: Access Sought by the IRS

One area of dispute concerning the accountant–client privilege is the Internal Revenue Service's (IRS) access to accountants' work papers, especially the tax accrual files in the work papers that document the adequacy of a corporation's provision for income taxes. These files traditionally have contained estimates of contingent tax liabilities, as well as the accountants' own evaluations of tax issues that may be sensitive to Internal Revenue Service inquiry. The papers have been compared to a road map, capable of leading the IRS to weak spots in the return with respect to contingent tax liabilities and also revealing the client's negotiating posture on these questions.

[41] "Earlier Similar MAS Study with Negative Outcome," *Journal of Accountancy*, January 1977, p. 98.

The accounting profession has pointed out that clients are also unlikely to be candid with their accountants if the IRS is granted access to such work papers. A 1982 court case balanced two public policies: the enforcement of revenue laws and the maintenance of fair and honest securities markets. The Arthur Young case[42] decided that with respect to tax accrual files, IRS access would interfere substantially with and undermine the audit process. The court stressed the damage to the corporation's negotiating position with the IRS. Despite this victory, several earlier and later cases (including an appeal of the AY case) have gone the other way, granting access, and with no clear privileged communication protection. Interviews with practitioners suggest that they are therefore altering their approach to documenting their work in the tax accrual files, in light of the possibility that the IRS will be given access to such files.[43]

Confidentiality Concerns Involving Clients' Requests and the Information Flow Across Offices Within a Single Firm

Fund of Funds will be discussed in Chapter 5, as will the financial difficulties faced by *Penn Square*. Each of these settings involve issues related to confidentiality. The former case involves investors of a mutual fund who suffered losses due to investments in overvalued assets of another client of its auditor. The claim was made that the CPA firm should have shared its knowledge of such overvalued assets with the mutual fund investors. Since this case has been settled out-of-court, after a finding against the CPA, its implications for the profession are unclear. Similarly, a bank client of the auditors of Penn Square (Chase Manhattan Bank) who was participating in loans made by the latter requested the CPA to provide information as to the quality of such loans. Since the auditors' response to the request is not public information, the sole implication of this setting is that pressures to reveal information concerning other clients can be expected to be exerted.[44]

While the stance in the Penn Square setting may be obvious, consider the dilemma faced within a single firm. If auditor A discovers information while conducting an examination of client A that would materially change the financial position of client B, can auditor A use such information while auditing client B? What if a different office audits client B? Can auditor A make auditor B, within the same firm, aware of the situation? After all, the auditing firm is liable for the fairness of presentation of both client A's and client B's financials.

The current Code of Professional Ethics requires primary responsibility to the public, and secondary responsibility to the client. Yet is it reasonable for a client to be granted confidential information merely because its auditors happened to examine the financials of some party which had an effect on its business? Consider the business ramifications for both clients and auditors. How could an international CPA firm effectively "share" all relevant client information in a manner that would ensure disclosure to interested parties such as the Fund of Funds investors? Would such sharing be desirable? How could the confidentiality of the client-accountant relationship be maintained?

These issues are introduced to emphasize the role of judgment when applying professional standards and the possible liability exposure that can arise, in spite of compliance with the Code.

Other Provisions

The AICPA has stressed that CPAs are to conduct themselves in a manner that will enhance the stature of the profession and its ability to serve the public. To this end, several provisions besides those related directly to independence, competency, advertising, and confidentiality are included in the AICPA's Code of Professional Ethics.

INCOMPATIBLE OCCUPATIONS

Rule 504—Incompatible Occupations

A member who is engaged in the practice of public accounting shall not concurrently engage in any business

[42] 677 F. 2d 211, 1982, cert. granted, 51 U.S.L.W. 3611 (U.S. Feb. 22, 1983) (No. 82–687)

[43] John R. Robinson and Clyde D. Stoltenberg, "Privilege and Accountants' Workpapers," *American Bar Association Journal*, October 1982, pp. 1248–1250.

[44] "Penn Bank's Secret Loan Pact," *New York Times*, August 17, 1982, pp. 1, 4.

or occupation which would create a conflict of interest in rendering professional services.[45]

The institute has not actually made a list of incompatible professions. In the past, the reason for this rule was both a concern for the CPA's independence and a desire to prevent the CPA's participation in a so-called *feeder practice.* For example, if a CPA sold insurance or securities, these occupations would involve solicitation and promotional activities that might promote a public accounting practice, and this would not be permitted because of the advertising prohibition. Today, however, the concern is only whether the CPA's appearance of independence might be jeopardized. For example, if a CPA told a client that increased insurance coverage would be appropriate and also happened to be in the insurance sales business, the objectivity of such advice might well be questioned.

Before 1951, practicing both law and accounting was deemed to be unethical and led to litigation involving accountants who were charged with the unauthorized practice of law.[46] But, over the years the prohibitions against dual practice have become more lenient, and so dual practice is growing. Its advocates stress the improved service capabilities of a professional who is familiar with both the legal and the accounting literature. But its opponents assert that it is practically impossible to be competent in both professions, staying up-to-date on current developments.[47]

Incompatibility is based on whether the CPA's objectivity is impaired, there are conflicts of interest, and the public image of the profession is likely to be tarnished. For example, in general, there is no objection to a CPA's participating in a nonprofessional commercial enterprise providing computerized bookkeeping services if the CPA's participation is purely as an investor and is not material to the corporation's net worth. But, the organization must be in the form of a professional corporation and must operate in accordance with professional standards and ethics if the CPA is an active participant in operations and policy setting.

ACTS DISCREDITABLE TO THE PROFESSION

Rule 501—Acts Discreditable

A member shall not commit an act discreditable to the profession.[48]

Rule 501 permits members to be held grossly negligent if they make, direct, or permit another to make false or misleading entries in financial records or statements. This can occur even without the member's knowing about it, as such a lack of knowledge could have resulted from the member's gross negligence.

The code's prohibition of discreditable acts can be thought of as a "catchall" that empowers the AICPA to take action against members committing acts not specifically included in the code, yet nonetheless deemed to be discreditable to the profession.

Interpretation 501-1 notes that retaining a client's records after he or she asks for them is an act that discredits the profession. Even the fact that a state's statute may permit a lien to be placed on the client's records in the member's possession does not negate this provision. Records also cannot be retained to enforce payment. Remember that the client's records are not the property of the auditor, but of the client.

Rule of Conduct 501 also applies to confidential relationships with nonclients. If the CPA acquires information from a third party that is pertinent and is likely to affect his or her conclusions and recommendations, formal approval from the client is necessary in order to use such confidential outside sources—even if it is understood that its source will remain undisclosed. If the CPA cannot get approval, he or she should withdraw from the engagement, as he or she can neither violate a confidence nor omit such information from a final recommendation.[49]

[45] "Bylaws and Rules of Conduct" (New York: AICPA, 1981).

[46] "Lawyers and Certified Public Accountants: A Study of Interprofessional Relations," *Journal of Accountancy,* August 1970, pp. 62–66.

[47] See Burt A. Leete and Stephen E. Loeb, "The Dual Practitioner: CPA, Lawyer or Both?" *Journal of Accountancy,* August 1973, pp. 57–63 for a related discussion.

[48] "Bylaws and Rules of Conduct" (New York: AICPA, 1981).

[49] "Use of Confidential Information on MAS Engagements," *Journal of Accountancy,* January 1977, p. 98.

FORM OF PRACTICE AND NAME

Rule 505—Form of Practice and Name

A member may practice public accounting, whether as an owner or employee, only in the form of a proprietorship, a partnership, or a professional corporation whose characteristics conform to resolutions of Council.

A member shall not practice under a firm name which includes any fictitious name, indicates specialization, or is misleading as to the type of organization (proprietorship, partnership, or corporation). However, names of one or more past partners or shareholders may be included in the firm name of a successor partnership or corporation. Also, a partner surviving the death or withdrawal of all other partners may continue to practice under the partnership name for up to two years after becoming a sole practitioner.

A firm may not designate itself as "Members of the American Institute of Certified Public Accountants" unless all of its partners or shareholders are members of the Institute.[50]

The characteristics of a professional corporation or association as referred to in Rule 505 of the code of professional ethics are as follows:

- *Name.* The name under which the professional corporation or association renders professional services shall contain only the names of one or more of the present or former shareholders or of partners who were associated with a predecessor accounting firm. Impersonal or fictitious names, as well as names which indicate a specialty, are prohibited.
- *Ownership.* All shareholders of the corporation or association shall be persons engaged in the practice of public accounting as defined by the code of professional ethics. Shareholders shall at all times own their shares in their own right and shall be the beneficial owners of the equity capital ascribed to them.
- *Directors and Officers.* The principal executive officer shall be a shareholder and a director, and to the extent possible, all other directors and officers shall be certified public accountants. Lay directors and officers shall not exercise any authority whatsoever over professional matters.
- *Liability.* The stockholders of professional corporations or associations shall be jointly and severally liable for the acts of a corporation or association or its employees—except where professional liability insurance is carried, or capitalization is maintained, in amounts deemed sufficient to offer adequate protection to the public. Liability shall not be limited by the formation of subsidiary or affiliated corporations or associations each with its own limited and unrelated liability.[51]

Interpretation 505-1 holds that a member may have a financial interest in a commercial corporation that performs for the public the services of a type performed by public accountants and whose characteristics do not conform to the resolutions of the AICPA's council if such interest is immaterial to the corporation's net worth and the member is solely an investor in that corporation. The purpose of this ruling is to prevent misleading designations or descriptions of accounting firms, as well as organizational forms that fail to protect the public interest (that is, that attempt to limit the firms' liability).

Enforcement Procedures

Violation of the code can lead to admonishment, suspension, or expulsion from membership in the AICPA. Note that if a member is suspended or expelled by the AICPA's trial board, that individual may still practice as a public accountant. The AICPA has no legislative authority for licensing; rather, it is the state board of accountancy that can temporarily or permanently revoke a CPA license or certificate.

As stated earlier in this chapter, many state societies of CPAs and state boards of accountancy have adopted their own codes of ethics which often differ from the AICPA's. For example, the Texas Society's Code of Professional Ethics (June 18, 1973), which prohibited competitive bidding, and Florida's Board of Accountancy (July 1, 1977), with a similar restriction, were actively enforced beyond the time that such a provision was part of the national body's code (1972). This diversity complicates enforcement.

The SEC's Rule 2-01 of Regulation S-X recognizes CPAs only if "duly registered and in good standing as such under the laws of the place of his residence or principal office." Hence, if a CPA were suspended because of a violation of the state's code of ethics, he or she would be prohibited from practicing before the SEC.

[50] "Bylaws and Rules of Conduct" (New York: AICPA, 1981).
[51] Appendix C of "Bylaws and Rules of Conduct" (New York: AICPA, 1981).

One study of CPAs in Wisconsin identified nineteen CPAs who were thought by their peers to be highly unethical and twenty-two CPAs who were believed to be highly ethical, in order to determine how they would behave in various ethical conflict situations. Some of these situations are reported in Exhibit 4-4, listing the type of conflict and the percentage of each set of CPAs who performed unethically, based on the code of ethics at that time. Those CPAs identified as unethical reported unethical behavior more frequently, thus permitting each item to distinguish between types of behavior. These situations were then tested on fifty-nine large offices, thirty medium offices, and thirty-three small offices of CPAs in Milwaukee, Wisconsin, with the resulting reported incidence of unethical behavior that is presented in Exhibit 4-4.

The most common complaints regarding ethics that have been referred to state societies are:

- Clients' claims that the records they ask to be returned to them are not returned. Note that the working papers belong to the CPA, but the clients' records in those working papers—not duplicated but removed from the clients' records—should be made available to the clients on request, as they are the clients' books.
- CPAs' practice of continuing to provide services to clients who have not paid for the previous year's services, resulting in a lack of independence under Rule 101.
- CPAs' acceptance of commissions from organizations marketing tax shelters as a fee for introducing such investments.
- Provision of services on a barter basis, creating problems regarding when income is earned on both sides. Note that none of the conduct rules makes bartering illegal unless it is done to conceal income.
- CPAs' acceptance of contingent fees.
- Unfair advertising such as listing oneself in the directory entitled *The Best Accountants in America.*
- Acceptance of an engagement in which the CPA has no expertise.
- Lack of familiarity with the code of professional ethics.[52]

Membership in the AICPA is suspended without a hearing if a CPA is convicted of a felony, willfully fails to file a required income tax return, files a false or fraudulent return either for himself or herself or a client, and willfully aids in the preparation and presentation of a false and fraudulent income tax return. Similarly, suspension of a member's certificate will automatically suspend membership in the institute, just as revocation of the certificate will terminate membership. The latter can be considered by the trial board if the member supplies a timely written petition. All other complaints against a member are investigated by the ethics committee of a state society, and if a case is established, they are referred to the secretary of the joint trial division. The member involved is asked to appear at a regional trial board or panel of the National Review Board. The Joint Ethics Enforcement Program is a means for state societies and the AICPA to cooperate in achieving compliance with the code of ethics. Beyond such efforts, positive enforcement programs have been established by various state boards of accountancy. As one example of their activities, a study of 48 state accounting boards reported that from 1962 to 1967 there were 375 violations for which punishments were imposed, 64 of which were expulsions and 105 suspensions. Of particular interest is a later study of 1,639 complaints made in 7 states from 1980 to 1982. Only 7 cases involved independence. The issues of primary concern were practicing without adequate expertise for the specific client or industry, retention of client records, and not meeting the state's continuing education requirements.[53]

Internal Auditing

The Institute of Internal Auditors (IIA) has its own code of ethics, as presented in Exhibit 4-5. The IIA

[52] Maureen O'Riordan and Arthur S. Hirshfield, "Aspects of the Profession's Code of Ethics," *CPA Journal,* August 1982, pp. 30–33.

[53] Adapted from Stephen E. Loeb, "Enforcement of the Code of Ethics: A Survey," *Accounting Review,* January 1972, pp. 1–10 and Kent S. Pierre, "Independence and Auditor Sanctions," *Journal of Accounting, Auditing, and Finance,* Spring, 1984, pp. 257–263.

EXHIBIT 4-4
Unethical Behavior by CPAs as Reported by Practitioners

Item	Type of Item	Summary of the situation	Percentage of CPAs who perform unethical acts		Percentage of accountants reporting unethical behavior: Sizes of CPA Offices		
			Unethical	Ethical	Large	Medium	Small
1.	Colleague	*Incompatible occupation.* CPA J is in public practice. He is also an officer and stockholder in a finance company. J does not audit the books of the finance company.	90	59	69	90	97
2.	Client	*Confidential relation.* CPA J is approached by a prospective client employed by an existing client corporation. The employee discloses that key personnel of the organization are planning to form their own corporation in competition with their employer. CPA J reveals the scheme to his client.	53	36	--	--	--
3.	Client	*Merger information.* CPA R is considering a merger with CPA J. To facilitate the negotiations, R gives J access to R's files of client work papers, income tax returns, and correspondence. CPA R's clients are unaware of the proposed merger.	53	36	8	17	24
4.	Public	*Independence of staff man.* A staff man of CPA J & Co. is a member of the board of directors of a federal savings and loan association. He has no proprietary interest in the accounting firm. The firm is conducting negotiations with the savings and loan association that may lead to the performance of an opinion audit. If the engagement materializes, the firm will not use the staff member on the audit.	63	14	35	50	70
5.	Client	*Conflict of interest.* CPA J serves as the auditor for Widget & Co. Widget's market share has declined dramatically, and J knows that Widget will soon be bankrupt. Another of CPA J's audit clients is Solid Company. While auditing Solid's accounts receivable, J notes that Widget & Co. owes Solid $100,000.	42	19	10	27	33
6.	Public	*Family relationship.* Joe Doe, CPA, is the senior partner of the accounting firm of John Doe & Co., CPAs. John's broker, Sam Doe, is the treasurer and a 26 percent stockholder of an audit client of the firm.	47	32	52	53	61
7.	Public	*Inside information.* CPA T is associated with the firm of I, J & K, CPAs. During the annual audit of Jones, Inc., CPA T sees that reported earnings will be substantially more than in the previous year. CPA T buys 100 shares of Jones, Inc., in his wife's name.	26	9	2	33	27
8.	Public	*Trustee.* CPA J agrees to serve as trustee for the Alpha Trust. J is presently the independent auditor for the Alpha Corporation. The Alpha Trust owns 50 percent of the common stock of the Alpha Corporation.	42	5	7	27	33
9.	Colleague	*Client kickback.* A client of CPA J refers another client to J and indicates that he expects some small compensation from J for his service. J gives the client a small amount of money, a small gift, takes him out to dinner, and reduces the client's fee for the current year.	74	32	29	43	45
10.	Client	*Fees.* CPA J loses a client. The client still owes J $3,000. CPA J still has many of the client's records. When the client refuses to pay the fee, J refuses to return the client's records until the $3,000 is paid.	74	50	17	53	40

Adapted from Stephen E. Loeb, "A Survey of Ethical Behavior in the Accounting Profession," *Journal of Accounting Research*, Autumn 1971, pp. 287–306.

EXHIBIT 4-5

The Institute of Internal Auditors, Inc. Code of Ethics

INTERPRETATION OF PRINCIPLES: The provisions of this Code of Ethics cover basic principles in the various disciplines of internal auditing practice. Members shall realize that individual judgment is required in the application of these principles. They have a responsibility to conduct themselves so that their good faith and integrity should not be open to question. While having due regard for the limit of their technical skills, they will promote the highest possible internal auditing standards to the end of advancing the interest of their company or organization.

ARTICLES:

I. Members shall have an obligation to exercise honesty, objectivity, and diligence in the performance of their duties and responsibilities.

II. Members, in holding the trust of their employers, shall exhibit loyalty in all matters pertaining to the affairs of the employer or to whomever they may be rendering a service. However, members shall not knowingly be party to any illegal or improper activity.

III. Members shall refrain from entering into any activity which may be in conflict with the interest of their employers or which would prejudice their ability to carry out objectively their duties and responsibilities.

IV. Members shall not accept a fee or a gift from an employee, a client, a customer, or a business associate of their employer without the knowledge and consent of their senior management.

V. Members shall be prudent in the use of information acquired in the course of their duties. They shall not use confidential information for any personal gain nor in a manner which would be detrimental to the welfare of their employer.

VI. Members, in expressing an opinion, shall use all reasonable care to obtain sufficient factual evidence to warrant such expression. In their reporting, members shall reveal such material facts known to them, which, if not revealed, could either distort the report of the results of operations under review or conceal unlawful practice.

VII. Members shall continually strive for improvement in the proficiency and effectiveness of their service.

VIII. Members shall abide by the bylaws and uphold the objective of *The Institute of Internal Auditors, Inc.* In the practice of their profession, they shall be ever mindful of their obligation to maintain the high standard of competence, morality, and dignity which *The Institute of Internal Auditors, Inc.* and it members have established.

also has its Statement of Responsibilities, shown in Exhibit 4-6, which is effectively inseparable from Exhibit 4-5, detailing such concepts as independence.

Independence

Independence for internal auditors differs from that for external auditors. For example, internal auditors are employees of the entity that they are expected to audit, and so in that sense they are not financially independent. However, other than the salary relationship, the internal auditors' economics are expected to be independent of the operations that are audited and the auditees. For example, internal auditors cannot accept gifts without explicit approval by management, nor can they participate in businesses or activities that pose a conflict-of-interest problem.

The key concern with respect to internal auditors' independence is their reporting relationship. Obviously, if an internal auditor had to report directly to the auditee and depend on that auditee for performance evaluations and raises, the likelihood of independent reviews that are thorough and that clearly set out the shortcomings of the auditee's operations would diminish. To ensure open and complete lines of communication, the internal auditor should report to a high enough level of management that the internal audit reports can be expected to receive the appropriate attention. This often includes a reporting link to the chief executive officer or chief financial officer, with periodic reporting responsibility directly to the audit committee of the board of directors.

EXHIBIT 4-6
Statement of Responsibilities of Internal Auditors

Nature

Internal auditing is an independent appraisal activity within an organization for the review of operations as a service to management. It is a managerial control which functions by measuring and evaluating the effectiveness of other controls.

Objective and Scope

The objective of internal auditing is to assist all members of management in the effective discharge of their responsibilities by furnishing them with analyses, appraisals, recommendations, and pertinent comments concerning the activities reviewed. Internal auditors are concerned with any phase of business activity in which they may be of service to management. This involves going beyond the accounting and financial records to obtain a full understanding of the operations under review. The attainment of this overall objective involves such activities as:

- Reviewing and appraising the soundness, adequacy, and application of accounting, financial, and other operating controls, and promoting effective control at reasonable cost.
- Ascertaining the extent of compliance with established policies, plans, and procedures.
- Ascertaining the extent to which company assets are accounted for and safeguarded from losses of all kinds.
- Ascertaining the reliability of management data developed within the organization.
- Appraising the quality of performance in carrying out assigned responsibilities.
- Recommending operating improvements.

Responsibility and Authority

The responsibilities of internal auditing in the organization should be clearly established by management policy. The related authority should provide the internal auditor full access to all of the organization's records, properties, and personnel relevant to the subject under review. The internal auditor should be free to review and appraise policies, plans, procedures, and records.

The internal auditor's responsibilities should be

- To inform and advise management, and to discharge this responsibility in a manner that is consistent with the Code of Ethics of The Institute of Internal Auditors.
- To coordinate internal audit activities with others so as to best achieve the audit objectives and the objectives of the organization.

In performing their functions, internal auditors have no direct responsibilities for nor authority over any of the activities reviewed. Therefore, the internal audit review and appraisal does not in any way relieve other persons in the organization of the responsibilities assigned to them.

Independence

Independence is essential to the effectiveness of internal auditing. This independence is obtained primarily through organizational status and objectivity:

- The organizational status of the internal auditing function and the support accorded to it by management are major determinants of its range and value. The head of the internal auditing function, therefore, should be responsible to an officer whose authority is sufficient to assure both a broad range of audit coverage and adequate consideration of and effective action on the audit findings and recommendations.
- Objectivity is essential to the audit function. Therefore, internal auditors should not develop and install procedures, prepare records, or engage in any other activity which they would normally review and appraise and which could reasonably be construed to compromise the independence of the internal auditor. The internal auditor's objectivity need not be adversely affected, however, by determining and recommending standards of control to be applied in the development of the systems and procedures being reviewed.

The Statement of Responsibilities of Internal Auditors was originally issued by The Institute of Internal Auditors in 1947. The continuing development of the profession has resulted in three revisions: 1957, 1971, and 1976. The current statement embodies the concepts previously established and includes such changes as are deemed advisable in light of the present status of the profession.

Other Provisions

Issues of loyalty, confidentiality, competency, and due audit care also are addressed by the IIA's code. The Certified Internal Auditor Code of Ethics (almost identical to Exhibit 4-5) is enforceable, and violations, as determined by the IIA's board of directors, can lead to forfeiture of the professional certification designation.

Responsibilities Regarding Tax Services

Specific exceptions to the AICPA's Code of Ethics relate to CPAs in tax practice:

- Tax returns and supporting schedules are not financial statements.
- The statement, affidavit, or signature of preparers on tax returns does not represent an opinion on financial statements and does not require a disclaimer.
- The judgment of a member is not to be subordinated to that of others, but the member may resolve doubt in favor of a client if there is reasonable support for that position.
- Fees are not considered to be contingent if determined on the basis of the results of judicial proceedings or the findings of government agencies.

Advisory opinions guiding tax practitioners have been formulated by the AICPA's Division of Federal Taxation. The AICPA's Statement on Responsibilities in Tax Practice No. 1 requires that CPAs sign as the preparer of any federal tax return prepared, whether or not compensation for the tax service was received. The AICPA Committee on Responsibilities in Tax Practice was asked: If a CPA prepares an estate tax return but the client's attorney wants to sign as the preparer, can the CPA release the return without signing it as the preparer? The committee's response was that as long as the CPA is assured that another practitioner who can practice before the IRS signs the return as the preparer, such subcontracting is permissible, and the return can be released to the attorney without a signature.[54]

Statement on Responsibilities in Tax Practice No. 2 states that a CPA may sign as the preparer if a review is performed that gives the CPA knowledge equivalent to what he or she would have obtained from preparing the return himself or herself. The same level of responsibility is assumed whether a CPA is the preparer or the reviewer.

Statement on Responsibilities in Tax Practice No. 3 requires that a CPA sign as the preparer only if he or she is satisfied that a reasonable effort has been made to answer all questions pertaining to the taxpayer, even if the answers are disadvantageous to the taxpayer.

Statement on Responsibilities in Tax Practice No. 4 holds that (1) a CPA may sign as the preparer of a return that does not treat in the same way an item involved in an administrative proceeding regarding an earlier year's return and (2) a CPA does not need to disclose such a departure, provided that it is justified by the facts and rules as they are evaluated at the time the return is prepared.

Statement on Responsibilities in Tax Practice No. 5 permits the CPA to use reasonable estimates if they are generally acceptable and are presented in a manner that does not imply greater accuracy than is present. If it is not practical to obtain exact data, reasonable estimates are similarly permitted.

Statement on Responsibilities in Tax Practice No. 6 requires that a CPA inform a client either orally or in writing of any error in previously filed returns or any information acquired in regard to the client's failure to file a required return, along with recommendations of measures that should be taken. The CPA may not inform the IRS without the client's permission, nor is he or she obligated to do so. If a CPA prepares a later year's return and is aware of a client's failure to correct an earlier year's error, he or she may prepare the later return, provided that reasonable steps are taken to ensure (1) that the error that would or may result in a material understatement of the tax liability is not repeated and (2) that inconsistent double deductions, carry-overs, or similar items related to that uncorrected earlier error are not permitted to reduce the tax liability other than is provided by the Internal Revenue Code, regulations, pronouncements, and court decisions. This provision regarding the prep-

[54] Walter C. Frank, "The CPA and Ethics in Tax Practices," *The Tax Adviser,* December 1973, pp. 716–722.

aration of later years' returns does not apply when a method of accounting is continued under circumstances believed to require the permission of the Commission of Internal Revenue to change the manner of reporting the item involved.

Assessing the materiality of an understatement is likely to mean considering (1) the size of the error itself, (2) the size of the error in relation to the total taxable income, (3) the effect of the error on the current tax liability, and (4) the cumulative effect (including carry-back and carry-over consequences) of the error.

Statement on Responsibilities in Tax Practice No. 7 requires that a CPA who is aware that there is an error in a client's tax return that has resulted or may result in a material understatement of tax liability and who is asked to represent that client in an administrative proceeding get permission from the client to disclose the error to the IRS. If permission is not granted, the CPA may have to withdraw from the engagement.

Statement on Responsibilities in Tax Practice No. 8 emphasizes the CPA's use of judgment when giving tax advice to a client. It acknowledges that without a specific agreement, the CPA does not have a continuing responsibility to communicate later developments affecting past advice on significant tax matters except when he or she is helping the client implement procedures or plans associated with the advice provided.

Statement on Responsibilities in Tax Practice No. 9 states that a CPA should use clients' past returns whenever feasible and encourage a client to provide supporting data when appropriate. If the information presented appears incorrect or incomplete, he or she is required to make reasonable inquiries. Ordinarily, information furnished by the client can be relied on, and so there is no requirement to examine or review documents or other evidence in support of the client's information. When signing as the preparer, a CPA is not permitted to modify the preparer's declaration.

Statement on Responsibilities in Tax Practice No. 10 stresses that in all cases there must be reasonable support for the CPA's position. If that position contradicts a specific section of the Internal Revenue Code, the treatment must be disclosed. If it contradicts only the Treasury Department or IRS interpretations of the code, no disclosure is required.

The CPA cannot deliberately fail to recognize the obvious implications of the things he or she sees. That is the essence of the "due diligence" requirement in Circular 230 of the Treasury Department regarding tax practice. Though not obligated to investigate and verify the authenticity of information furnished, the CPA is not warranted in ignoring indications that something is wrong with the figures provided.

Responsibilities Regarding Management Services

The CPA's responsibilities with respect to MAS merit special attention, and the AICPA has drawn up MAS practice standards:

1. *Personal Characteristics.* In performing management advisory services, a practitioner must act with integrity and objectivity and be independent in mental attitude.
2. *Competence.* Engagements are to be performed by practitioners having competence in the analytical approach and process, and in the technical subject matter under consideration.
3. *Due Care.* Due professional care is to be exercised in the performance of a management advisory services engagement.
4. *Client Benefit.* Before accepting an engagement, a practitioner is to notify the client of any reservations (s)he has regarding anticipated benefits.
5. *Understanding with Client.* Before undertaking an engagement, a practitioner is to inform his or her client of all significant matters related to the engagement.
6. *Planning, Supervision, and Control.* Engagements are to be adequately planned, supervised, and controlled.
7. *Sufficient Relevant Data.* Sufficient relevant data are to be obtained, documented, and evaluated in developing conclusions and recommendations.
8. *Communication of Results.* All significant matters regarding the results of the engagement are to be communicated to the client.[55]

[55] AICPA Professional Standards, MAS Sections 101, 110, 120, 130, 140, 150, 160, 170, 180 (New York: AICPA, 1981).

Like the Code of Professional Ethics, these standards emphasize independence, competency, and service to the public and client.

Appendix: Other Codes of Ethics

A review of the independence standards in the United Kingdom, Australia, France, West Germany, and Canada indicates that those of the United States are the most restrictive. For example, immaterial direct financial interest or indirect financial interests would not cause difficulties in these countries. Only in Australia, as of 1972, were material indirect financial interests proscribed by ethical rulings. Hence, for international engagements, foreign auditors must be careful to comply with American rules if reliance on their work is planned.[56]

Some countries establish ethics for industry accountants; an example is given in Exhibit 4-A. Such a code is far more comprehensive than the AICPA code's applicability to CPAs not in public accounting. Another interesting code of ethics is the Association of Government Accountants Code of Ethics, shown in Exhibit 4-B.

The structure of accountants' Code of Ethics is similar to the Model Code of Professional Responsibility of the American Bar Association. It has three parts: Canons, Ethical Considerations, and Disciplinary Rules. The canons are axiomatic Norms describing in general terms the standards of professional conduct. The Ethical Considerations are a body of principles intended to provide guidance. The Disciplinary Rules state the minimum level of conduct below which no lawyer can fall without being subject to disciplinary action. Exhibit 4-C presents the Canons. Note the similarity of the ethical considerations underlying the practice of accounting and law. The key differences relate to Canon 7. While similar to ethics for tax practice, the CPA as an auditor serves the public first and foremost when exercising judgment. In addition, it is well known that the confidential relationship of a lawyer enjoys "privileged communication" which is not available to the CPA.

REVIEW QUESTIONS

1. The CPA may not say with Hamlet,

"Seems, madam! Nay, it is; I know not seems!"[57]

Why?

2. How do the golden rule, the organization ethic, and the democratic ethic apply to the AICPA's Code of Professional Ethics?

3. Describe the parts of the AICPA Code of Professional Ethics.

4. The bank at which you hold a mortgage and a personal loan to finance your purchase of some land is also your audit client. Does this relationship destroy your independence? Why or why not? Do you need additional information in order to make a judgment? If so, what questions would you like to have answered?

5. Assume that you are a new senior accountant and have been working particularly hard to meet the time budget agreed upon at the start of the audit. It becomes apparent to you that you are not going to finish in time. While driving home late on the second straight day, it occurs to you that one way of meeting the deadline would be to work straight through the upcoming weekend but to not record the time on your report.

Would doing this violate the AICPA Code of Professional Ethics? Would it matter if you discussed it with your superior, an audit manager, who gave you her tacit consent? What if you knew that you had not been working at top speed early in the audit, taking longer than usual to complete the earlier phases? Would such action be justified if this were an audit of the Red Cross? How might your decision affect next year's audit?[58]

6. **a.** May an AICPA member determine his or her fee for services rendered in connection with a bond issue as a percentage of the total amount of the bond issue? Why or why not?

[56] Adapted from William K. Grollman, "Independence of Auditors and Applicability to International Engagements," *CPA Journal*, April 1973, pp. 286–291.

[57] Adapted from John L. Carey and William O. Doherty, "The Concept of Independence—Review and Restatement," *Journal of Accountancy*, January 1966, pp. 38–48.

[58] Adapted from Floyd W. Windal and Robert N. Corley, *The Accounting Professional: Ethics, Responsibility, and Liability* (Englewood Cliffs, N.J.: Prentice-Hall), 1980.

EXHIBIT 4-A
Another Country's Actions to Set Ethics for Industry Accountants

The Council of the Institute (following proposals by the CCAB Ethics Committee) has given approval to the incorporation within the Guide to Professional Ethics of some additional (paragraphs). The purpose of these additions is to introduce guidance on specific areas of difficulty with which the member engaged in industry, commerce and the public sector may be confronted but which are unlikely to confront the member in professional practice in the same way.

Integrity

1. A member, including one working outside the areas normally associated with accountancy, must maintain a high standard of conduct. In conforming with this standard, a member should not knowingly mislead or misrepresent facts to others and should use due care to avoid doing so unintentionally. At all times, a member should be conscious that integrity must be an overriding principle.

Independence & Objectivity

2. A member has a duty to be objective in carrying out professional work, and should maintain an independent approach to that work. Thus a member performing professional work in commerce, industry or the public sector, should recognize the problems created by personal relationships or financial involvements which by reason of their nature or degree may threaten his objectivity.

Confidentiality—Disclosure of Information

3. Confidentiality should be preserved both within and outside a member's organization.
4. However, in the course of his work a member may find himself faced with conflicts between his loyalty to his employers or colleagues on the one hand and his duties as a member of a profession or as a citizen on the other hand. When faced with such conflict a member should make disclosure only with proper authority or where there is a professional obligation, a right, a legal requirement or a public duty to disclose.
5. Where a member is in doubt as to whether he has a right or duty to disclose he should, if appropriate, initially discuss the matter fully within the organization in which he works. If that is not appropriate, or if it fails to resolve his problem, he should take legal advice and/or consult his professional body.

Confidentiality—Mis-use of Information

6. Information acquired by a member in the course of his duties and to which he would not otherwise have access should not be used for personal advantage nor for the advantage of a third party. When a member changes his employment he must distinguish between experience he has gained in his previous employment and confidential information acquired there.

Published Information

7. When a member has sole responsibility for the preparation and approval of information, including management information which is to be made public or is to become available, on however restricted a basis, outside the organization to which it refers, he should ensure that such information complies with professional pronouncements or if it does not so comply, that the reasons for non-compliance are stated truthfully, unambiguously and fairly.
8. When his is not the sole responsibility he should use his best endeavours to achieve compliance or, if the information does not comply with professional pronouncements that the reasons for non-compliance are stated truthfully, unambiguously and fairly.
9. Professional pronouncements include, for example, Statements of Standard Accounting Practice, the City Code and Take-overs and Mergers and the Rules and Regulations of the Stock Exchange.

Conflict of Interest

10. A member should always make full and proper disclosure of any conflict of interest unless to do so would be inconsistent with the advice given under the heading Confidentiality—Disclosure of Information.

Trade Union Membership

11. It is recognized that a member has a statutory right to belong to a trade union. He should not, however, take part in industrial action which is a contravention of the law or puts him in conflict with the provisions of the Guide to Professional Ethics.

Share Dealings

12. Subject to:
(a) relevant legislation.
(b) Stock Exchange and other non-statutory requirements.
(c) his own terms of service, and
(d) awareness of the risks attendant on financial involvement referred to in para 2 hereof,
a member may own and deal in shares in any organization in which he is employed or holds office.

Gifts

13. A member should be aware of the difficulties which may arise from the offer or the acceptance of any gift, favour or hospitality which may be interpreted as intended to influence the recipient.

From "Ethical Guidelines for Members Engaged in Industry, Commerce and the Public Sector," *Accountancy*, July 1982, p. 87.

EXHIBIT 4-B

Association of Government Accountants Code of Ethics

Introduction

The Association of Government Accountants is a national professional organization most of whose members are primarily engaged in government accounting, auditing, budgeting, and related financial management activities.

The membership represent most government agencies as well as industrial, education, and private personal service organizations having an interest in government programs.

The Association of Government Accountants' major program objectives are to:

Unite professional financial managers in government service to perform more efficiently for their own development and for the benefit of the government.
Encourage and provide an effective means for interchange of work and related professional ideas.
Aid in providing financial management techniques and concepts.
Improve financial management education in the government and universities.

Purpose of the Code

In order to foster the highest professional standards and behavior, and exemplary service to the governments, this Code of Ethics has been developed as a guidance for the members of the Association of Government Accountants, and for the information of their employers.

Definitions

In instances where reference is made to a member, it is intended to include all classes of membership. Where reference is made to employer, it is intended to apply to a government agency as an entity, and to a non-government organization where the principle is considered applicable.

Ethical Principles

Personal Behavior

1. The member shall adhere to the Standards of Conduct promulgated by his employer. (This principle for example, endorses the commitment of Federal employees to recognize the Standard of Conduct prescribed by their government agencies pursuant to Executive Order 11222 or May 8, 1965, (30 F.R. 6469), and the Code of Ethics for government service adopted by the Congress on July 11, 1958).
2. A member shall not engage in acts or be associated with activities which are contrary to the public interest or discreditable to the Association of Government Accountants. (This principle cautions members to avoid actions which adversely affect the public interest and the professional image of the Association).
3. A member shall not engage in private employment or hold himself out as an independent practitioner for remuneration except with the consent of his employer, if required. (This principle identifies a restriction against earnings which result from the use of a member's professional qualifications, without the express approval of his employer, if required).
4. A member shall not purposefully transmit or use confidential information obtained in his professional work, for personal gain or other advantage. (This principle prohibits the improper use of official position or office for strictly personal purposes, monetary or otherwise.)

Professional Competence and Performance

5. A member shall strive to perform the duties of his position and supervise the work of his subordinates, with the highest degree of professional care. (This principle emphasizes the requirement for a member to give special attention to the professional aspects of his work, and not to condone substandard performance at any level within his responsibility.)
6. A member shall continually seek to increase his professional knowledge and skills, and thus to improve his service to employers, associates and fellow members. (This principle stresses the importance of professional development and the use of professional skills in helping his colleagues and employers.)
7. A member shall render opinions, observations or conclusions for official purposes only after appropriate professional consideration of the pertinent facts. (This principle stresses the importance of avoiding unsupported opinions involving professional judgments which could cause inappropriate official actions.)
8. A member shall exercise diligence, objectivity and honesty in his professional activities and be aware of his responsibility to identify improprieties that come to his attention. (This principle places the responsibility upon a member to exercise moral and independent judgment and to disclose illegal, improper or unethical practices noted in the course of his work.)
9. A member shall be aware of and strive to apply requirements and standards prescribed by authorized government agencies, which may be applicable to his work. (This principle recognized that special professional criteria are promulgated by authorized government agencies—e.g., U.S. General Accounting Office, the Office of Management and Budget, the Treasury Department, and others—which require attention in certain assignments.)

Responsibilities to Others

10. In the performance of any assignment, a member shall consider the public interest to be paramount. (This principle stresses a member's foremost concern for the public interest in any specific work situation involving competing interests.)
11. A member shall not engage in any activity or relationship which creates or gives the appearance of a conflict with his responsibilities to his employer. (This principle cautions against becoming involved in situations where a member's official or personal activities are inconsistent with his responsibilities to his employer.)
12. In speaking engagements or writings for publication, a member shall identify personal opinions which may differ from official positions of his employer. (This principle stresses the need to avoid inappropriate interpretations by the public from speeches or articles by members which reflect personal rather than official viewpoints of their employers.)

EXHIBIT 4-C

Canons Promulgated by the American Bar Association from Which Ethical Considerations Are Derived

Canon 1	A Lawyer Should Assist in Maintaining the Integrity and Competence of the Legal Profession
Canon 2	A Lawyer Should Assist the Legal Profession in Fulfilling Its Duty to Make Legal Counsel Available
Canon 3	A Lawyer Should Assist in Preventing the Unauthorized Practice of Law
Canon 4	A Lawyer Should Preserve the Confidences and Secrets of a Client
Canon 5	A Lawyer Should Exercise Independent Professional Judgment on Behalf of a Client
Canon 6	A Lawyer Should Represent a Client Competently
Canon 7	A Lawyer Should Represent a Client Zealously Within the Bounds of the Law
Canon 8	A Lawyer Should Assist in Improving the Legal System
Canon 9	A Lawyer Should Avoid Even the Appearance of Professional Impropriety

From ABA Canon of Professional Ethics, Canon 45 (1908), as amended. (As reported in *Martindale-Hubbell Law Directory* Vol. VII Law Digests Uniform Acts ABA Codes Adopted Jan. 1, 1970)

b. May an AICPA member as an expert witness in a damage suit receive compensation based on the amount that is awarded to the plaintiff?

c. If a CPA were sent a payment from a tax shelter investment group, in recognition of the three clients of that CPA who had invested in the shelter, could the CPA keep that payment and still be in compliance with the Code of Professional Ethics?

7. What factors have been cited in the literature as potential determinants of the public's perception of CPAs' independence? What has research suggested about such determinants?

8. Define MAS. What are the benefits of MAS, according to the Public Oversight Board? In what sense might MAS work be detrimental to CPAs' independence?

9. Of what importance to the CPA is the action of recommending, as distinct from decision making?

10. How do the SEC's definitions of independence differ from the AICPA's definitions? Be specific.

11. Of what importance are audit committees with respect to the AICPA's Code of Professional Ethics?

12. How can the lack of independence influence a CPA's audit report? How can it influence the reexpression of a previously issued opinion?

13. What is a CPA permitted and not permitted to do with respect to forecasts?

14. What is the rationale for Rule 203? Do you suspect that it is invoked frequently? Why or why not?

15. Describe the pros and cons frequently debated as the profession made the transition from no advertising to the current provisions of the Code of Professional Ethics. When did this transition occur, and why?

16. What problems are feared as specialists are designated more and more often?

17. What is "privileged communication"? Do accountants have it? Do they want it? Should they want it?

18. Describe the dispute with the IRS involving confidentiality. What are the confidentiality concerns related to Fund of Funds and Penn Square? How are these issues likely to affect practice?

19. If three CPA firms decided to form an association—not a partnership—to be known as "Wilson, Wallace & Associates," would there be an impropriety under the code of ethics? In what sense?

20. What are the ramifications of not complying with the Code of Professional Ethics? What are the effects for SEC client settings?

21. Compare and contrast the internal auditor's code of ethics with that of the AICPA.

22. Describe a CPA's responsibilities when providing tax services.

23. Describe a CPA's responsibilities when performing MAS work.

EXERCISES

1. A popular anecdote tells of a company president who interviewed several prospective independent auditors, asking "How much is three plus four?" All who answered "Seven" were rejected. Finally, one asked, "How much do you want it to be?" and received the appointment. What prevents such a cooperative arrangement between CPAs and clients under the Code of Professional Ethics?

2. Accounting Series Releases (now FRRs) No. 47 and 81 list certain situations in which certifying accountants are considered to lack independence:

a. An accountant's settlement of his or her fee by taking an option for the shares of the client's common stock.

b. An accountant's spouse owns stock in a proposed registrant.

c. Using their own funds, the spouses of partners in an accounting firm purchased the client's stock just before registration.

d. The spouse of an accountant had a 47.5 percent interest in one of the three principal underwriters of a proposed issue by the registrant.

e. A partner of the CPA firm acted as the registrant's controller.

f. The auditor was the father of the registrant's secretary-treasurer.

g. The partner of an accounting firm acted as one of three executors of the will of one of the registrant's principal officers and one of three trustees of a trust established under the will. The trust's principal asset was a substantial proportion of the registrant's voting stock.

h. An auditor organized a corporation that purchased property from the registrant by issuing a purchase money mortgage.[59]

Would the AICPA agree with each of these SEC examples? In your response, tie each item to the relevant section of the AICPA's Professional Rules of Conduct.

3. At a bank's annual meeting, a minority shareholder sharply criticized a $1,600,000 loan by the bank to the company's auditors on the grounds that it was a conflict of interest and jeopardized the auditor's independent status.[60] Evaluate the minority stockholder's contention, using the Code of Professional Ethics as support.

4. To say that the performance of management services and independent auditing for the same client is incompatible with the auditor's independence is not the same as saying that the auditor has lost his independence.[61]

This is like saying that a house is combustible is not the same as saying that it is burning. How do these observations relate to current practice under the Code of Professional Ethics?

5. A survey[62] of 155 trust officers, loan officers, investment officers of mutual funds and large financial institutions, and financial analysts produced the findings reported in the next column.

How would you evaluate these survey results? How do you explain the varying reactions (that is, the 32 percent to 8 percent range)? What are the implications of this research?

Type of Service	Percentage of 155 Who Thought There Might Be Loss of Audit Independence from Providing This MAS	Percentage of 155 Who Thought This MAS Should Be Prohibited for Auditor
Mergers and business acquisitions	32%	17%
Executive recruitment	27%	15%
Policy determination	27%	12%
Personnel appraisal and/or selection	23%	11%
Executive and wage incentive plans	21%	10%
Management audits	19%	12%
Financial budgeting	17%	10%
Assistance on specific accounting problems	17%	8%
Capital budgeting	17%	10%
Inventory control	12%	6%
Computer systems and applications	11%	5%
Plant layout	10%	4%
Material handling	8%	2%

6. The legal profession requires that a lawyer should not serve two clients whose interests conflict. Yet, CPAs commonly serve competitors in the same industry.

a. Do you consider this practice appropriate? How does the Code of Professional Ethics affect this practice?

b. A CPA firm has a client relationship with a company in a bankruptcy proceeding and with the creditors in that same proceeding. Comment on the propriety of such a scenario.

7. It has been proposed that offers of employment made on behalf of a client be reported to practitioner employers as part of the code of ethics. What would be the reason for such a proposal?

8. Problems with interpreting confidentiality guidelines are not limited to the accounting profession. On February 8, 1983, the *Wall Street Journal* had headlines reading "IBM's Court Squabble with NCR Focuses on What a Consultant Should Tell a Client." The story was about a computer industry consult-

[59] John L. Carey and William O. Doherty, "The Concept of Independence—Review and Restatement," *Journal of Accountancy*, January 1966, pp. 38–48.

[60] "Security National Seeks to End a Loan Made to Its Auditor," *Wall Street Journal*, April 10, 1974, p. 24.

[61] D. R. Carmichael and R. J. Swieringa, "The Compatibility of Auditing Independence and Management Services—An Identification of Issues," *Accounting Review*, October 1968, p. 705.

[62] Adapted from Pierre L. Titard, "Independence and MAS—Opinions of Financial Statement Users," *Journal of Accountancy*, July 1971, pp. 47–52.

ing firm that had reported program infringements by NCR to IBM. IBM requested permission to defend the consultants, indicating that it had the right to protect its interest in the freedom of honest people to report apparent thefts of IBM property. If a CPA has two clients, one of which invests in the other's assets, which are known by the CPA to be overpriced, what actions should and can the CPA take? Compare and contrast those actions with the actions claimed to have been taken in the IBM and NCR dispute.

9. The American Bar Association's delegates approved an ethical ruling prohibiting lawyers, once a trial has begun, from concealing evidence of their client's perjury, other crimes, or fraudulent actions. If this rule were adopted by the states, it would change the privileged communication rule. Why do you think the ABA sees this rule as desirable? Compare this rule with the accountants' rules on confidentiality and their position with respect to privileged communication.[63]

10. Indicate whether the following activities are likely to be incompatible (i) or compatible (c) with the practice of public accountancy:

____ **(1)** Being a mutual fund salesperson.
____ **(2)** Being a real estate broker.
____ **(3)** Conducting a CPA coaching course, promoting it through mailings to practitioners, bookkeepers, and related personnel.
____ **(4)** Performing actuarial and administrative services in connection with employee benefit plans.
____ **(5)** Sending collection letters to clients' customers.
____ **(6)** Conducting an investment service.
____ **(7)** Being a silent limited partner in a stock brokerage firm.
____ **(8)** Acting as a broker in handling industrial and commercial loans.
____ **(9)** Engaging in an employment agency that services non-CPAs.
____ **(10)** Being an officer or director of a consumer credit company that purchases installment sales contracts from retailers and receives payments from consumers.[64]

11. In 1975, abut 34,000 members of the AICPA were employed in industry and required to comply with only Rules 102, 501, and Bylaw 7.4 (requiring expulsion if convicted of a felony or if failing to file a personal income tax return). Can these AICPA members tell management that they are required to follow Rule 203 on accounting principles? If management issues misleading financial statements, should the members inform the AICPA or other authorities? In what sense can AICPA members in industry serve as a first line of defense against misleading financial statements?[65]

12. The prevailing ethic required of lawyers is to assert any position on behalf of the client unless the lawyer is absolutely convinced that the position is frivolous or fraudulent. However, this ethic has been cited as encouraging groundless litigation. Hence it has been reevaluated in light of the observed "countersuit phenomenon," and there seems to be a shift toward a standard akin to that of gross negligence or recklessness.[66] How do these developments in the legal profession compare with CPAs' responsibility in tax practice? Support your comments.

13. **a.** A client has a chain of stores, each of which it wants to incorporate in order to take advantage of the tax consequences. The client asks you: "Can't we think up a good business purpose for separate corporations per store?" How should you respond? Comment on the propriety of the question and the ethics reflected in your response.

b. You tend to be conservative in handling tax clients, as you enjoy a reputation for never having had an IRS audit performed on one of your clients. Because taking chances increases the risk of controversy and you think that the client is likely to believe that you were negligent if he or she were called in, you think it makes sense to be careful and conservative.[67] Comment on the propriety of such an approach to tax service, and support your position.

[63] Adapted from Stephen Wermiel, "Lawyers' Group Adopts Toughened Rule for Telling Court of Client's Misconduct," *Wall Street Journal* (February 9, 1983), p. 19.

[64] Adapted from John L. Carey and William O. Doherty, *Ethical Standards of the Accounting Profession* (New York: AICPA, 1966), pp. 249–256.

[65] Adapted from Rex B. Cruse, Jr., "Ethics for the CPA in Industry," *Journal of Accountancy*, June 1975, pp. 71–73.

[66] Richard H. Underwood, "Curbing Litigation Abuses: Judicial Control of Adversary Ethics—The Model Rules of Professional Conduct and Proposed Amendments to the Rules of Civil Procedure," *St. John's Law Review*, Summer 1982, pp. 625–628.

[67] Adapted from William L. Raby, "Ethics in Tax Practice," *Accounting Review*, October 1966, pp. 714–720.

14. CPAs are acknowledged as assuming more of an advocate's than a judge's role in tax practice, but it has been argued that such an advocacy role impairs an auditor's independence. Using your knowledge of the Statements on Responsibilities in Tax Practice, discuss the propriety of referring to the CPA who provides tax service as an advocate. In your opinion, do tax services impair a CPA's independence in fact or appearance? Support your opinion.

QUESTIONS ADAPTED FROM PROFESSIONAL EXAMINATIONS

1. Auditors must not only appear to be independent; they must also be independent in fact.

Required:

a. Explain the concept of auditors' independence as it applies to a third party's reliance on financial statements.

b. (1) What determines whether or not auditors are independent in fact?
(2) What determines whether or not auditors appear to be independent?

c. Explain how an auditor may be independent in fact but not appear to be independent.

d. Would a CPA be considered independent for an examination of financial statements of a
(1) church for which he is serving as treasurer without compensation? Explain.
(2) women's club for which his wife is serving as treasurer-bookkeeper, even if he is not to receive a fee for the examination? Explain.

e. Write a disclaimer of opinion such as should accompany financial statements examined by a CPA who owns a material direct financial interest in his audit client.

(CPA exam adapted)

2. An auditor's report was appended to the financial statements of Worthmore, Inc. The statements consisted of a balance sheet as of November 30, 19X4, and statements of income and retained earnings for the year then ending. The first two paragraphs of the report were like those of a standard unqualified short-form report, and the third paragraph read as follows:

> The wives of two partners of our firm owned a material investment in the outstanding common stock of Worthmore, Inc. during the fiscal year ending November 30, 19X4. The aforementioned individuals disposed of their holding of Worthmore, Inc. on December 3, 19X4, in a transaction that did not result in a profit or a loss. This information is included in our report in order to comply with certain disclosure requirements of the *Code of Professional Ethics* of the American Institute of Certified Public Accountants.
>
> Bell & Davis
> Certified Public Accountants

Required:

a. Was the CPA firm of Bell & Davis independent with respect to the fiscal 19X4 examination of Worthmore, Inc.'s financial statements? Explain.

b. Do you find Bell & Davis's auditor's report satisfactory? Explain.

c. Assume that no members of Bell & Davis or any members of their families held any financial interest in Worthmore, Inc. during 19X4. For each of the following cases, indicate whether Bell & Davis would lack independence, assuming that Worthmore, Inc. is a profit-seeking enterprise. In each case, explain why independence would or would not be lacking.
(1) Two directors of Worthmore, Inc. became partners in the CPA firm of Bell & Davis on July 1, 19X4, also resigning their directorships on that date.
(2) During 19X4 the former controller of Worthmore, now a Bell & Davis partner, was frequently asked by Worthmore for assistance. He made decisions for Worthmore's management regarding fixed asset acquisitions and the company's product marketing mix. In addition, he conducted a computer feasibility study for Worthmore.

(CPA exam adapted)

3. The attribute of independence has been traditionally associated with the CPA's function of auditing and expressing opinions on financial statements.

Required:

a. What is meant by "independence," as applied to the CPA's function of auditing and expressing opinions on financial statements? Discuss.

b. CPAs have imposed on themselves certain rules of professional conduct that encourage their members to remain independent and to strengthen public confidence in their independence. Which of the rules of professional conduct are concerned with the CPA's independence? Discuss.

c. The Wallydrag Company is indebted to a CPA for unpaid fees and has offered to issue to him unsecured interest-bearing notes. Would the CPA's acceptance of these notes have any bearing on his independence in his relations with the Wallydrag Company? Discuss.

d. The Rocky Hill Corporation was formed on October 1, 19X3, and its fiscal year will end on September 30, 19X4. You audited the corporation's opening balance sheet and rendered an unqualifed opinion on it.

A month after issuing your report, you are offered the position of secretary of the company, because of the need for a complete set of officers and for convenience in signing various documents. You will have no financial interest in the company through stock ownership or otherwise, will receive no salary, will not keep the books, and will not have any influence on its financial matters other than occasional advice on income tax matters and similar advice normally given a client by a CPA.

(1) Assume that you accept the offer but plan to resign from the position before conducting your annual audit, with the intention of again assuming the office after rendering an opinion on the statements. Can you render an independent opinion on the financial statements? Discuss.

(2) Assume that you accept the offer temporarily until the corporation has gotten under way and can employ a secretary. In any event you would permanently resign the position before conducting your annual audit. Can you render an independent opinion on the financial statement? Discuss.

(CPA exam adapted)

4. Shortly before the due date, Daniel Burr requested that you prepare the 19X4 federal income tax return for Burr Corporation, a small, closely held, service corporation that he controlled. Burr placed a package on your desk and said, "Here is all the information you need. I'll pay you $300 if you prepare the return in time for filing by the deadline with no extension—and if the tax liability is less than $2,000, I'll increase your fee to $500." The package contained the corporation's bank statements and paid checks, prior years' tax returns prepared on the accrual basis, and other financial and tax information. The books of account were not included because they were not posted up to date.

You found that deposits shown on the bank statements substantially exceeded Burr's sales figure and that the expenses listed seemed rather large in relation to sales. Burr explained that he had made several loans to the corporation during the year and expenses just seemed to "mount up."

Required:

a. What ethical issues should you consider before deciding whether to prepare the federal income tax return for Burr Corporation?

b. If you prepare this return, must you sign it? Explain.

c. If you sign the return, what does your signature imply?

(CPA exam adapted)

5. Part a. During 19X4 your client, Nuesel Corporation, requested that you conduct a feasibility study to advise management of the best way the corporation could utilize electronic data-processing equipment and which computer, if any, would best meet the corporation's requirements. You are technically competent in these areas and accept the engagement. After completing your study, the corporation accepts your suggestions and installs the computer and related equipment that you recommended.

Required:

(1) Discuss the effect the acceptance of this management services engagement would have on your independence in expressing an opinion on the financial statements of the Nuesel Corporation.

(2) A local printer of data-processing forms customarily offers a commission for recommending him as supplier. The client is aware of the commission offer and suggests that you accept it. Would it be proper for you to accept the commission with the client's approval? Discuss.

Part b. Your CPA firm decides to form a partnership with Fred Reitz, a non-CPA management consultant, which would result in a "mixed partnership" of a CPA and a non-CPA.

Required:

Under what circumstances, if any, would it be ethically proper for a CPA to form a "mixed partnership?" Discuss.

Part c. Alex Pratt, a retired partner of your CPA firm, has just been appointed to the board of directors of Palmer Corporation, your firm's client. Pratt is also a member of your firm's income tax committee which meets monthly to discuss income tax problems of the partnership's clients. The partnership pays Pratt $100 for each committee meeting he attends and a monthly retirement benefit of $1,000.

Required:

Discuss the effect of Pratt's appointment to the Palmer Corporation's board of directors on your partnership's independence in expressing an opinion on the corporation's financial statements.

(CPA exam adapted)

6. Gilbert and Bradley formed a corporation called Financial Services, Inc., each taking 50 percent of the authorized common stock. Gilbert is a CPA and a member of the American Institute of CPAs. Bradley is a CPCU (Chartered Property Casualty Underwriter). The corporation performs auditing and tax services under Gilbert's direction and insurance services under Bradley's supervision. The opening of the corporation's office was announced by a three-inch, two-column "card" in the local newspaper.

One of the corporation's first audit clients was the Grandtime Company. Grandtime had total assets of $600,000 and total liabilities of $270,000. In the course of his examination, Gilbert found that Grandtime's building, with a book value of $240,000, was pledged as security for a ten-year-term note in the amount of $200,000. The client's statements did not mention that the building was pledged as security for the ten-year-term note. However, as the failure to disclose the lien did not affect either the value of the assets or the amount of the liabilities and his examination was satisfactory in all other respects, Gilbert rendered an unqualified opinion on Grandtime's financial statements. About two months after the date of his opinion, Gilbert learned that an insurance company was planning to lend Grandtime $150,000 in the form of a first-mortgage note on the building. Realizing that the insurance company was unaware of the existing lien on the building, Gilbert had Bradley notify the insurance company that Grandtime's building was pledged as security for the term note.

Shortly afterwards, Gilbert was charged with a violation of professional ethics.

Required:

Identify and discuss the ethical implications of Gilbert's acts that were in violation of the AICPA Code of Professional Ethics.

(CPA exam adapted)

7. Savage, a CPA, has been requested by an audit client to perform a nonrecurring engagement involving the implementation of an EDP information and control system. The client requests that in setting up the new system and during the period before conversion to the new system, Savage:

- Counsel on potential expansion of business activity plans.
- Search for and interview new personnel.
- Hire new personnel.
- Train personnel.

In addition, the client requests that during the three months after the conversion, Savage:

- Supervise the operation of the new system.
- Monitor client-prepared source documents and make changes in basic EDP-generated data as Savage may deem necessary without the client's concurrence. Savage responds that he may perform some of the services requested but not all of them.

Required:

a. Which of these services may Savage perform, and which of these services may he not perform?

b. Before undertaking this engagement, Savage should inform the client of all significant matters related to the engagement. What are these matters?

c. If Savage adds to his staff an individual who specializes in developing computer systems, how much does Savage himself need to know in order to supervise the specialist's activities?

(CPA exam adapted)

8. a. Your client is a small college in a small town. The college has recently elected as treasurer the president of the local bank in which the college keeps its cash funds. The bank is also the custodian of the college's endowment fund securities. Furthermore, certain short-term securities are held at the bank in a safe deposit box to which the president has access.

Confirmation requests to the bank in the past have been signed by the former college treasurer, and the bank's replies have been signed by the bank president.

Required:

(1) What should you do about direct confirmations for the current fiscal year?

(2) What effect would these circumstances have on your opinion?

b. CPAs often have continuing engagements during which they write up the client's books, make numerous adjusting entries, and prepare financial statements.

Required:

(1) What effect do these circumstances have on the CPA's opinion and report if the client requests the auditor's opinion on the financial statements?

(2) What disclosure should be made, if any?

(CPA exam adapted)

9. Certified public accountants have imposed on themselves a rigorous code of professional ethics.

Required:

a. Discuss the reasons for the accounting profession's adopting a code of professional ethics.

b. A rule of professional ethics adopted by CPAs is that a CPA cannot be an officer, director, stockholder, representative, or agent of any corporation engaged in the practice of public accounting, except for the professional corporation form expressly permitted by the AICPA. List the arguments supporting this rule that a CPA firm cannot be a corporation.

(CPA exam adapted)

10. In a recent management letter, the external auditors for Holten Services, Inc. questioned the effectiveness of the internal auditing department. Management was concerned and retained a retired internal auditing practitioner to review the department's operations. The review revealed that

(1) Several of the company's internal auditors had relatives or close friends employed by Holten in various operating positions. The director of internal auditing was unaware of some of these relationships. The relationships often were not considered when assigning audit personnel, resulting in many instances when an auditor's judgment could have easily been compromised.

(2) The director of internal auditing requires his employees to work in Holten's operations for at least one year before joining the audit staff so as to give the staff the insight it needs to perform effective audits.

(3) Whenever possible, the director arranges with the line managers for a temporary exchange of their operating staff for auditing staff. The director has discovered that operating personnel can perform more efficient audits of the units from which they are borrowed.

(4) To promote consistency and continuity in audits, lead auditors are required to review the same activities for at least five consecutive years. This strategy has virtually eliminated auditee complaints about the auditors' not understanding the nature and objectives of the unit's activities.

(5) To improve audit staff morale, the director enriches the jobs of his employees by giving them more responsibility for audit reporting. He never challenges the information contained in the audit reports. In fact, he seldom reviews them or the supporting documentation.

Required:
For each of the five observations listed above, state whether the condition is a violation of one of the specific guidelines within the objectivity standard. Justify your answers.

(CIA exam adapted)

11. You are approached by the president of the Hopewell Mfg. Company to audit the company's financial statements. You have no knowledge of the Hopewell Mfg. Company other than that it is a medium-sized company.

Required:
From an ethical standpoint, what should you learn about the Hopewell Mfg. Company before you agree to accept the engagement? Discuss. (Because you have not yet been engaged, do not discuss the auditor's survey of the company's system to determine audit programs.)

(CPA exam adapted)

12. The following cases relate to the CPA's management of his or her accounting practice:

Case 1

Tom Jencks, a CPA, conducts a public accounting practice. In 19X4 Jencks and Harold Swann, a non-CPA, organized the Electro-Data Corporation to specialize in computerized bookkeeping services. Jencks and Swann each supplied 50 percent of Electro-Data's capital, and each holds 50 percent of the capital stock. Swann is the salaried general manager of Electro-Data. Jencks is affiliated with the corporation only as a stockholder; he receives no salary and does not participate in the day-to-day management. However, he has transferred all of his bookkeeping accounts to the corporation and recommends its services whenever possible.

Required:
Organizing your presentation around Jencks's involvement with Electro-Data Corporation, discuss the propriety of:

a. A CPA's participation in an enterprise offering computerized bookkeeping services.
b. The use of advertising by an enterprise in which a CPA holds an interest.
c. A CPA's transfer of bookkeeping accounts to a service company.
d. A CPA's recommendation of a particular bookkeeping service company.

Case 2

Judy Hanlon, a CPA, was engaged to prepare the federal income tax return for the Guild Corporation for the year ended December 31, 19X4. This is Hanlon's first engagement of any kind for the Guild Corporation.

In preparing the 19X4 return, Hanlon finds an error on the 19X3 return. The 19X3 depreciation deduction was overstated significantly—accumulated depreciation brought forward from 19X2 to 19X3 was understated, and thus the 19X3 base for declining balance depreciation was overstated.

Hanlon reported the error to Guild's controller, the officer responsible for tax returns. The controller stated: "Let the revenue agent find the error." He further instructed Hanlon to carry forward the material overstatement of the depreciable base to the 19X4 depreciation computation. The controller noted that this error also had been made in the financial records for 19X3 to 19X4 and offered to give Hanlon a letter assuming full responsibility for this treatment.

Required:

a. Evaluate Hanlon's handling of this situation.

b. Discuss any additional actions that Hanlon should now take.

Case 3

Fred Browning, a CPA, has examined the financial statements of the Grimm Company for several years. Grimm's president now has asked Browning to install an inventory control system for the company.

Required:

Discuss the factors that Browning should consider in determining whether to accept this engagement.

(CPA exam adapted)

13. Multiple-Choice: Code of Ethics, Other Than Those Dealing with Tax Services and Independence Issues

Select the one answer that best completes the statement or answers the question.

13.1 The AICPA Code of Professional Ethics requires compliance with the accounting principles promulgated by the body designated by the AICPA council to establish such principles. The pronouncements covered by the code include all of the following except

a. Opinions issued by the Accounting Principles Board.

b. AICPA Accounting Research Studies.

c. Interpretations issued by the Financial Accounting Standards Board.

d. AICPA Accounting Research Bulletins.

(CPA exam adapted)

13.2 A CPA's retention of client records as a means of enforcing payment of an overdue audit fee is an action that is

a. Considered acceptable by the AICPA Code of Professional Ethics.

b. Ill advised, as it would impair the CPA's independence with respect to the client.

c. Considered discreditable to the profession.

d. A violation of generally accepted auditing standards.

(CPA exam adapted)

13.3 The AICPA Code of Professional Ethics states, in part, that a CPA should maintain integrity and objectivity. Objectivity in the code refers to a CPA's ability

a. To maintain an impartial attitude on all matters that come under the CPA's review.

b. To distinguish independently between accounting practices that are acceptable and those that are not.

c. To be unyielding in all matters dealing with auditing procedures.

d. To choose independently between alternative accounting principles and auditing standards.

(CPA exam adapted)

13.4 During an audit, an auditor required additional research and consultation with others. This additional research and consultation is considered to be

a. An appropriate part of the engagement's professional conduct.

b. A responsibility of the management, not the auditor.

c. A failure by the CPA to comply with generally accepted auditing standards because of a lack of competence.

d. An unusual practice that indicates that the CPA should not have accepted the engagement.

(CPA exam adapted)

13.5 An auditor should not render a report on

a. The achievability of forecasts.

b. Client internal control.

c. Management performance.

d. Quarterly financial information.

(CPA exam adapted)

13.6 The AICPA Code of Professional Ethics recognizes that the reliance of the public, the government, and the business community on sound financial reporting imposes particular obligations on CPAs. The code derives its authority from

a. Public laws enacted over the years.

b. General acceptance of the code by the business community.

c. Requirements of governmental regulatory agencies such as the Securities and Exchange Commission.

d. Bylaws of the American Institute of Certified Public Accountants.

(CPA exam adapted)

13.7 Richard, a CPA, performs accounting services for the Norton Corporation. Norton wishes to offer its shares to the public and asks Richard to audit the financial statements prepared for registration purposes. Richard refers Norton to Cruz, a CPA, who is more competent in the area of registration statements. Cruz performs the audit of Norton's financial statements and subsequently thanks Richard for the referral by giving Richard a portion of the audit fee collected. Richard accepts the fee. Who, if anyone, has violated professional ethics?

a. Only Richard.
b. Both Richard and Cruz.
c. Only Cruz.
d. Neither Richard nor Cruz.

(CPA exam adapted)

13.8 A CPA, who is a member of the American Institute of Certified Public Accountants, wrote an article for publication in a professional journal. The AICPA Code of Professional Ethics would be violated if the CPA allowed the article to state that the CPA was

a. A member of the American Institute of Certified Public Accountants.
b. A professor at a school of professional accountancy.
c. A partner in a national CPA firm.
d. A practitioner specialized in providing tax services who has a good rapport with the regional Internal Revenue Service agents.

(CPA exam adapted)

13.9 A CPA can accept an engagement for a professional service without violating the AICPA Code of Professional Ethics if the service involves

a. The preparation of cost projections for submission to a governmental agency as an application for a rate increase, and the fee will be paid if there is a rate increase.
b. Tax preparation, and the fee will be based on whether the CPA signs the tax return prepared.
c. A litigatory matter, and the fee is not known but is to be determined by a district court.
d. Tax return preparation, and the fee is to be based on the amount of taxes saved, if any.

(CPA exam adapted)

13.10 A CPA's report on a client's balance sheet, income statement, and statement of changes in financial position was sent to the stockholders. The client now wishes to present only the balance sheet, along with an appropriately modified auditor's report, in a newspaper advertisement. The auditor may

a. Permit the publication as requested.
b. Permit only the publication of the originally issued auditor's report and accompanying financial statements.
c. Not permit publication of a modified auditor's report.
d. Not permit publication of any auditor's report in connection with a newspaper advertisement.

(CPA exam adapted)

13.11 With respect to records in a CPA's possession, the rules of conduct state that

a. Copies of client records incorporated into audit workpapers must be returned to the client upon request.
b. Worksheets in lieu of a general ledger belong to the auditor and need not be furnished to the client upon request.
c. An extensive analysis of inventory prepared by the client at the auditor's request are work papers that belong to the auditor and need not be furnished to the client upon request.
d. The auditor who returns copies of client records must also return the original records upon request.

(CPA exam adapted)

13.12 The AICPA Code of Professional Ethics states that when a CPA is required to express an opinion on a combined or consolidated financial statement that includes a subsidiary, branch, or other component audited by another independent public accountant, the CPA may

a. Insist on auditing any such component that the CPA judges necessary to warrant the expression of an opinion.
b. Insist only on reviewing any such component.
c. Not insist on auditing any such component but may request copies of all work sheets relevant to the other independent public accountant's examinations.
d. Not insist on auditing any such component or reviewing work sheets belonging to the other independent public accountant.

(CPA exam adapted)

13.13 The AICPA Code of Professional Ethics states that a CPA should not disclose any confidential information obtained in a professional engagement except with the client's consent. This rule should be understood as preventing a CPA from responding to an inquiry made by

a. The trial board of the AICPA.
b. An investigative body of a state CPA society.
c. A CPA-shareholder of the client corporation.
d. An AICPA voluntary quality review body.

(CPA exam adapted)

13.14 Inclusion of which of the following statements in a CPA's advertisement is not acceptable according to the AICPA Code of Professional Ethics?

a. Paula Fall
Certified Public Accountant
Fluency in Spanish and French
b. Paula Fall
Certified Public Accountant
J.D., Evans Law School 1964
c. Paula Fall
Certified Public Accountant
Free Consultation
d. Paula Fall
Certified Public Accountant
Endorsed by AICPA

(CPA exam adapted)

13.15 Which of the following is required for a firm to designate itself as a member of the American Institute of Certified Public Accountants on its letterhead?

a. At least one of the partners must be a member.
b. The partners whose names appear in the firm name must be members.
c. All partners must be members.
d. The firm must be a dues-paying member.

(CPA exam adapted)

13.16 According to the AICPA rules of conduct, the auditor's responsibility to the profession is defined by

a. The AICPA Code of Professional Ethics.
b. Federal laws governing licensed professionals who are involved in interstate commerce.
c. Statements on Auditing Standards.
d. The AICPA's bylaws.

(CPA exam adapted)

13.17 When management refuses to disclose illegal activities identified by the independent audit, the independent auditor may be charged with violating the AICPA Code of Professional Ethics for

a. Withdrawing from the engagement.
b. Issuing a disclaimer of opinion.
c. Failing to uncover the illegal activities during earlier audits.
d. Reporting these activities to the audit committee.

(CPA exam adapted)

13.18 In performing an audit, Jackson, a CPA, discovers that he does not have the professional competence necessary for the engagement. Jackson informs management of the situation and recommends another local CPA firm, and management engages this other firm. Under these circumstances.

a. Jackson may request compensation from the other CPA firm for any professional services rendered to it in connection with the engagement.
b. Jackson may accept a referral fee from the other CPA firm.
c. Jackson has violated the AICPA Code of Professional Ethics because of nonfulfillment of the duty of performance.
d. Jackson's lack of competence violates generally accepted auditing standards.

(CPA exam adapted)

14. Multiple-Choice: Tax Services

Select the one answer that best completes the statement or answers the question.

14.1 While performing tax services for a client, a CPA may learn of a material error in a previously filed tax return. In such an instance, the CPA should

a. Prepare an affidavit with respect to the error.
b. Recommend compensating for the earlier year's error in the current year's tax return when such action will mitigate the client's cost and inconvenience.
c. Advise the client to file a corrected return, regardless of whether or not the error resulted in an overstatement or understatement of tax.
d. Inform the IRS of the error.

(CPA exam adapted)

14.2 In tax practice, which of the following would not be considered reasonable support for taking a position contrary to the Internal Revenue Code?

a. Proposed regulations advocated by the IRS.
b. Legal opinions as to the constitutionality of a specific provision.
c. Possible conflicts between two sections of the Internal Revenue Code.

d. Tax court decisions not accepted by the IRS.

(CPA exam adapted)

14.3 In accordance with the AICPA's Statements on Responsibilities in Tax Practice, if after having given tax advice to a client, there are legislative changes that affect this advice, the CPA

a. Is obligated to notify the client of the change and its effect.

b. Is obligated to notify the client of the change and its effect if the client was not told that the advice was based on existing laws that are subject to change.

c. Cannot be expected to notify the client of the change unless the obligation is specifically undertaken by agreement.

d. Cannot be expected to have knowledge of the change.

(CPA exam adapted)

14.4 In accordance with the AICPA Statements on Responsibilities in Tax Practice, when a question on a federal income tax return has not been answered, the CPA should sign the preparer's declaration only if

a. The CPA can provide reasonable support for this omission upon examination by the IRS.

b. The information requested is not available.

c. The question is not applicable to the taxpayer.

d. The reason for the omission is given.

(CPA exam adapted)

14.5 The preparer of a federal income tax return signs a preparer's declaration that states: "Under penalties of perjury, I declare that I have examined this return . . . and to the best of my knowledge and belief, it is true, correct, and complete." A CPA who signs this declaration as preparer of a client's tax return warrants that

a. Information furnished by the client was relied on in preparing the tax return unless it appeared incorrect or incomplete.

b. Information furnished by the client was examined in accordance with generally accepted auditing standards.

c. All available evidence in support of material assertions on the tax return was examined in accordance with generally accepted auditing standards.

d. All available evidence in support of material assertions on the tax return was documented in the CPA's working papers.

(CPA exam adapted)

14.6 Which of the following is implied when a CPA signs the preparer's declaration on a federal income tax return?

a. The tax return is not misleading based on all information of which the CPA has knowledge.

b. The tax return and supporting schedules were prepared in accordance with generally accepted accounting principles.

c. The tax return was examined in accordance with standards established by the AICPA's Federal Tax Division.

d. The tax return was prepared by a CPA who maintained an impartial attitude.

(CPA exam adapted)

14.7 A member of the AICPA should sign the preparer's declaration on a federal income tax return

a. Only when the CPA prepares a tax return for compensation.

b. Only when the CPA can declare that a tax is based on all information of which the CPA has knowledge.

c. Whenever the CPA prepares a tax return for others.

d. Only when the income tax regulations allow the CPA to sign the preparer's declaration.

(CPA exam adapted)

15. Multiple-Choice: Independence Issues

Select the one answer that best completes the statement or answers the question.

15.1 An independent auditor must be unbiased with respect to a client's financial statements, in order to

a. Comply with the laws established by governmental agencies.

b. Maintain the appearance of separate interests by the auditor and the client.

c. Protect against criticism and possible litigation from stockholders and creditors.

d. Ensure the impartiality necessary for an expression of the auditor's opinion.

(CPA exam adapted)

15.2 The AICPA Committee on Management Services stated that a CPA should not undertake a management advisory service engagement to implement the CPA's recommendations unless

a. The client has made a firm decision to proceed with implementation based on a complete understanding and consideration of alternatives.

b. The client does not understand the na-

ture and implications of the recommended course of actions.
c. The client does not have sufficient expertise in its organization to comprehend the significance of the changes being made.
d. The CPA withdraws as the client's independent auditor.

(CPA exam adapted)

15.3 A firm of CPAs may use policies and procedures such as notifying professional personnel of the names of audit clients having publicly held securities and confirming periodically with such personnel that prohibited relations do *not* exist. This is done to achieve effective quality control in which of the following areas?
a. Acceptance and continuance of clients.
b. Assigning personnel to engagements.
c. Independence.
d. Inspection.

(CPA exam adapted)

15.4 Which of the following most completely describes how independence has been defined by the CPA profession?
a. Performing an audit from the public's viewpoint.
b. Avoiding the appearance of significant interest in the affairs of an audit client.
c. Being able to act with integrity and objectivity.
d. Accepting the responsibility to act professionally and in accordance with a professional code of ethics.

(CPA exam adapted)

15.5 A CPA examines the financial statements of a local bank. According to the AICPA Code of Professional Ethics, the appearance of independence ordinarily would not be impaired if the CPA
a. Served on the bank's committee that approves loans.
b. Owned several shares of the bank's common stock.
c. Obtained a short-term loan from the bank.
d. Used the bank's time-sharing computer service to solve client-related problems.

(CPA exam adapted)

15.6 While performing an audit, a CPA strives to achieve independence in appearance in order to
a. Reduce risk and liability.
b. Maintain public confidence in the profession.
c. Become independent in fact.
d. Comply with the generally accepted standards of fieldwork.

(CPA exam adapted)

15.7 A CPA who performs primary actuarial services for a client would normally be precluded from expressing an opinion on the financial statements of that client if the
a. Fees for the actuarial services had not been paid.
b. Actuarial services were a major determinant of the pension expense.
c. Client was an insurance company.
d. Actuarial assumptions used were not in accordance with generally accepted auditing standards.

(CPA exam adapted)

15.8 When a computer-based management information system is being designed and implemented, what internal auditor involvement is most appropriate? The internal auditor should be:
a. Involved in the design of the system to ensure that the system includes adequate control procedures.
b. Consulted on the auditability of data to be processed during the testing stage.
c. Involved in the start-up phase to ensure that the controls are operating efficiently.
d. Involved in maintaining the system documentation during the design stage.
e. Concerned during the design and implementation stage with processing transactions with outside parties.

(CIA exam adapted)

15.9 In determining independence with respect to any audit engagement, the decision as to whether or not the auditor is independent must be made by the
a. Auditor.
b. Client.
c. Audit committee.
d. Public.

(CPA exam adapted)

15.10 A CPA should not undertake a management advisory service engagement that includes continued participation through implementation, unless
a. The CPA accepts overall responsibility for implementation of the chosen course of action.
b. The CPA acquires an overall knowledge of the client's business that is equivalent to that possessed by management.
c. Upon implementation, the client's person-

nel will have the knowledge and ability to maintain and operate the systems.

d. Upon implementation, the system of internal control is studied and evaluated again.

(CPA exam adapted)

15.11 In which of the following instances would the CPA's independence not be considered to be impaired? The CPA has been retained as the auditor of a brokerage firm

a. That has owed the CPA audit fees for more than one year.

b. In which the CPA has a large active margin account.

c. In which the CPA's brother is the controller.

d. That owes the CPA audit fees for current-year services and has just filed a petition for bankruptcy.

(CPA exam adapted)

15.12 In which of the following instances would the CPA's independence not be considered to be impaired? The CPA has been retained as the auditor of a

a. Charitable organization in which an employee of the CPA serves as treasurer.

b. Municipality in which the CPA owns $25,000 of its $2,500,000 indebtedness.

c. Cooperative apartment house in which the CPA owns an apartment but is not part of the management.

d. Company in which the CPA's investment club owns a one-tenth interest.

(CPA exam adapted)

15.13 Mavis, a CPA, has audited the financial statements of South Bay Sales Incorporated for several years and had always been paid promptly for services rendered. Last year's audit invoices have not been paid because South Bay is experiencing cash flow difficulties, and the current year's audit is scheduled to commence in one week. With respect to the past due audit fees, Mavis should

a. Perform the scheduled audit and allow South Bay to pay when its cash flow difficulties are alleviated.

b. Perform the scheduled audit only after arranging a definite payment schedule and securing notes signed by South Bay.

c. Inform South Bay's management that the past due audit fees are considered an impairment of audit independence.

d. Inform South Bay's management that the past due audit fees may be considered a loan on which interest must be computed for financial statement purposes.

(CPA exam adapted)

15.14 An audit independence issue might be raised by the auditor's participation in management advisory services engagements. Which of the following statements is most consistent with the profession's attitude toward this issue?

a. Information obtained as a result of a management advisory services engagement is restricted to that specific engagement and should not influence performance of the attest function.

b. The decision as to loss of independence must be made by the client based on the particular case.

c. The auditor should not make management decisions for an audit client.

d. The auditor who is asked to review management decisions is also competent to make these decisions and can do so without loss of independence.

(CPA exam adapted)

CASES FOR DISCUSSION

1. A one-act play entitled *An Ideal Accountant,* discusses the role of monetary incentives in determining how accountants perform their duties. The characters include the parents (the Chilterns), whose son (Lord Goring) is considering an accounting profession, and three guests.

Mrs. Marchmont. Lord Goring was just saying that he intended to be an Accountant, Mrs. Cheveley.

Mrs. Cheveley. How interesting. And do you intend to be a conscientious one or a prosperous one?

Mrs. Marchmont. Surely, that is not a proper thing to say, although I suppose there is an element of truth in it. . . .

Lord Goring. It would seem then, that an Accountant should never give advice unless he would be prepared to carry out that advice if he were the Client.

Mrs. Cheveley. Accountants never give advice they always sell it. . . .

Lady Markby. I have always wondered how Accountants arrive at their fees.

Sir Robert Chiltern. I think in the main they charge on a time occupied basis. That is to say, if a principal is engaged for a day on a particular case it would obviously cost more than say, the junior clerk. Nevertheless, they do charge, I am told, for advice and consultations, the knowledge for which can only be obtained from years of experience, and on such occasion a client will pay for that experience as well as for the time involved.

Mrs. Marchmont. That seems rather unfair since somebody else has already paid the accountant for gaining that experience.

Lord Goring. Quite so, but this experience, which after all is really knowledge in knowing how, when, and why, or why not, is stored in the brain, and I understand that brain storage space is a most expensive commodity. . . .

Mrs. Cheveley. I have often wondered if it is proper for an Accountant to profit by the advice which he gives, such as instructing a Client to take out an Endowment Policy and then receiving the commission thereon.

Lady Chiltern. In my opinion, an accountant is wise if he sticks purely to his profession and leaves Insurance to those who thoroughly understand its complications. Whatever advantages he receives from the advice he gives should always be disclosed to his client. I think this should be done for the Accountant's protection and also as a matter of courtesy to the Client.

Mrs. Cheveley. I would never take advice from somebody who stands to gain substantially by the advice which he gives.[68]

Comment on the characters' viewpoints. How has the accounting profession addressed these issues? How do the profession's actions compare with other means of addressing them? Would you suggest any alterations in either the code of ethics or the general way in which accountants practice their profession?

2. The basic question to be resolved in dealing with an appearance criterion is whether appearance should be examined on the basis of that which would be perceived by an informed person with a knowledge of the facts or by a person with no understanding of the audit process or the nature of relationships that conventionally exist. Most reported surveys of perceptions of independence indicated that the greater the degree of knowledge about the profession and auditing, the less concern there is about threats to independence emerging from the scope of services performed. On the other hand, those without information or background of this sort are inclined to perceive a problem.

If the pursuit of the appearance of independence is to continue and is to be expressed in terms of the suspicions of uninformed persons, there seems to be no way in which the current structure of auditing and the accounting profession can be sustained. No uninformed and suspicious citizen who views the world through skeptical eyes could be expected to be convinced of an auditor's independence when the auditor is paid for his services by the client.[69]

In addition to educating the public, monitoring the quality control of CPA firms, and disclosing all aspects of the auditor–client relationship, including the fees charged, the author suggests that a concerted effort be made to replace the term *independence* with *professional, unbiased, and objective* in order to clarify the auditor's role.

Evaluate the author's argument and suggestions. Do you believe that the entire system requires change in order to address adequately the critic's comments regarding independence? What changes would you suggest?

3. It has been stated that you should not enter public accounting practice without having a good understanding of:

- how far you are willing to go in satisfying each client.
- to what extent you would subordinate your personal preference.
- how much you can compromise.
- beyond what point you would refuse to go, with a polite statement of the reasons.[70]

Write a scenario involving contingent fees in a tax situation that illustrates your understanding of how you should handle the threshold point for the above situations, activities, or concerns.

4. Statistical decision models have been outlined as including:

a. The determination of the nature of the possible decision.

b. The determination of the events that could occur.

c. The determination of expected profit or loss per combination of events.

d. The determination of each event's probability of occurrence.

e. Selection of the act with the highest expected value.

This outline has been applied to the analysis of MAS activities. Specifically, it has been contended that the CPA would still be independent if advice were confined to items a, b, and c, and would probably be in-

[68] Michael Locke, "An Ideal Accountant," *Accountants Record,* February 1981, pp. 26, 27. By kind permission of *Accountants Record,* the official Journal of the Society of Company and Commercial Accountants, February 1981 edition.

[69] John C. Burton, "A Critical Look at Professionalism and Scope of Services," *Journal of Accountancy,* April 1980, p. 51.

[70] Adapted from John L. Carey, "The Realities of Professional Ethics," *Accounting Review,* April 1947, pp. 119–123.

dependent even if advice were given on item d.[71] Do you agree? Explain the reasons for such an analysis of independence as it relates to MAS.

5. In *The Philosophy of Auditing,* Robert K. Mautz and Hussein A. Sharaf stated:

> Management, of course, is at liberty to accept, modify, or reject a given piece of expert advice. But advice is requested because management feels its own inability to know all the alternative solutions to the problem at issue and to evaluate them and choose from among them. Management wants the advice and intends to use it: advice is sought and paid for to be followed, not to be ignored. It seems folly indeed to separate advising and judgment making. This is true whether the advice is concerned with income tax, systems, or general business decisions.[72]

Discuss this view. How would you justify current practice in light of such a perspective?

6. The American Bar Association considered a proposal that would have permitted a lawyer to disclose to stockholders and prosecutors information about corporate officials enriching themselves at the company's expense or acting in other ways against the company's best interests. A vote of 207 to 129 defeated the proposal, adopting instead a guideline permitting disclosure only if "imminent death or substantial bodily harm" might be involved. Another proposal considered would have permitted lawyers representing a corporation to blow the whistle on "looting" by corporate officials at the company's expense, once they had complained to the company's top officials, as the lawyer's going public could show his or her loyalty to the company rather than to the officers.[73]

Explain why the ABA most likely rejected the proposed ethics guidelines. Compare its position with accountants' responsibilities.

7. The *American Bar Association Journal* cited the dilemma under its ethics rules of trying to sell a law firm. In substance, there is nothing to sell, as its files belong to the client, not the lawyer. In transferring a practice, the confidentiality of clients also could be damaged. There is another interesting confidentiality and conflict-of-interest problem in which a California Supreme Court (*Maxwell* v. *Superior Court of Los Angeles County* [639 P. 2d 248]) upheld the practice of selling the rights to a client's life story to raise attorney fees. Past court claims involved the assertion by Patricia Hearst Shaw that her attorney jeopardized her defense in order to protect a literary contract.[74] Does an accountant face any similar confidentiality and conflict-of-interest problems? Give examples.

8. Based on a 1983 Gallup poll[75] conducted for the *Wall Street Journal,* the overall level of ethics in American society was thought to have declined by 65 percent during the past decade. But, a survey of executives indicated that only 23 percent believed that business ethics had declined, and 31 percent believed that they had risen. The statistics suggested that lying and pilfering were common. The percentage of respondents who reported they had carried out certain unethical activities was substantial:

	% of Business Executives	% of General Public
Have taken home work supplies	74	40
Have called in sick to work when not ill	14	31
Have used company telephones for personal long-distance calls	78	15
Have overstated deductions somewhat on tax form	35	13

What are the implications of such survey results for the CPA? How might the AICPA more actively encourage its membership to comply with the Code of Professional Ethics, in light of apparent changes in society's values?

[71] Adapted from John L. Carey and William O. Doherty, "The Concept of Independence—Review and Restatement," *Journal of Accountancy,* January 1966, pp. 38–41.

[72] Monograph No. 6 (Sarasota: American Accounting Association, 1961), p. 221.

[73] Adapted from Stephen Wermiel, "ABA Rejects Proposed Ethics Guideline Designed to Encourage Whistle Blowing," *Wall Street Journal,* February 8, 1983, p. 6.

[74] "Ethics," Lawscope, *American Bar Association Journal,* April 1982, pp. 406–407.

[75] Roger Ricklefs, "Executives and General Public Say Ethical Behavior Is Declining in U.S.," *Wall Street Journal,* October 31, 1983, Sec. 2, p. 25.

5

The Auditor and Litigation

An auditor should remember that the day may arise when an engagement will undergo legal scrutiny. The professional judgment and procedures performed will be second-guessed with the benefit of hindsight. Picture a courtroom setting in which the CPA is on the witness stand.

Attorney. In what line of business does your client operate?
CPA. Real estate investment trusts, primarily.
Attorney. Would you say that it is a rather specialized industry?
CPA. Yes, I would.
Attorney. You were the manager on the engagement, correct?
CPA. Yes.
Attorney. Did you have previous experience in this specialized industry?
CPA. No, but our firm has special reference manuals concerning the industry, which I read.
Attorney. So you had no professional experience in this line of business. I understand that your firm has designated industry specialists, is that correct?
CPA. Yes, we do, but not in our office.
Attorney. So nobody on the engagement was an industry specialist?
CPA. No, but again, we do feel that our training manuals develop sufficient expertise.
Attorney. Yet as I understand it, one of the key issues in this case is that a highly unusual and complicated transaction was accounted for improperly.
CPA. That has not been determined.
Attorney. Are you suggesting that the accounting that resulted in a healthy finan-

cial position's being reported, with a clean audit opinion for an entity that went bankrupt one month later, could have been proper?

CPA. Accounting is historical, not future oriented, and we believe that the inherent risk of that industry should be recognized and assumed by the investor.

Attorney. However, we've had experts testify that alternative valuations would have been more appropriate, and you have testified that no similarly qualified individuals were on the actual engagement. In fact, we're all curious. You've admitted that your firm had experts in other offices. Did you consult with such specialists during the audit?

CPA. No, we did not see the need.

Attorney. So you did not see that due professional care implied the oversight of specialized accounting issues by a recognized industry expert with experience? Well, let's shift to the work that you did perform. Did you confirm accounts and loans receivable?

CPA. Yes.

Attorney. Did you confirm *all* such receivables?

CPA. No.

Attorney. Is it not true that generally accepted auditing standards, the guidelines for the practice of your profession, require that receivables be confirmed with debtors?

CPA. Yes, but it is acceptable to do so on a test basis.

Attorney. Did this test basis include the ten largest receivable balances?

CPA. No, but it included five of those ten.

Attorney. Did those five debtors respond?

CPA. Not all five; only one returned the confirmation requested.

Attorney. So how could you possibly conclude that receivables were properly stated when the four largest receivable balances were not confirmed?

CPA. We used alternative procedures, as suggested by generally accepted auditing standards.

Attorney. What were these alternative procedures?

CPA. We examined the sales contracts, reviewed past and subsequent cash receipts for those contracts, and performed some other reasonableness checks.

Attorney. I trust that these procedures are documented in detail in your work papers; would you show me that documentation?

CPA. Let me turn to our loan receivable files. No, I don't see our documentation here. Let me take a look at our audit program. I guess we failed to note it there either, but I am certain that those procedures were performed.

Attorney. Let's go on to another subject. . . .[1]

Nothing seems to awaken the sensitivity of professional practice to liability exposure quite as effectively as imagining oneself in the courtroom, faced by a skillful lawyer, who repeatedly questions one's professional judgment and the adequacy of work performed. In this chapter, the types of liability exposures faced, past court cases that have particularly affected the development of auditing standards and practices, and the overall role of litigation in the profession will be explored.

[1]Adapted from Charles Chazen and Kenneth I. Solomon, "The Art of Defensive Auditing," *Journal of Accountancy*, October 1975, pp. 66–67; and from training films prepared by various CPA firms.

Legal Liability Consequences

As in all professions, public accountants are faced with liability consequences whenever they perform their duties in a manner judged to be inadequate for the circumstances at hand. The duties performed result in a broad spectrum of liability suits, as shown in Exhibit 5-1. The AICPA's Professional Liability Insurance Plan tracked the most common causes of claims against CPAs since 1974, resulting in nine categories, with claims ranging from under $5,000 to over $35,000. Considering that these claims were mainly made against smaller CPA firms, including one-person operations, this shows how quickly the fees earned in one year can be offset by a single liability suit.

Common Law

Common law is based on judicial precedents and changes in response to shifts in societal expectations and demands. Professionals now can be held liable for their actions in regard to both clients and third parties.

Privity

Privity refers to the contractual relationship between two or more contracting parties. For the CPA, it is the contract for professional services. A contract for an audit by a CPA means that the audit will be performed in accordance with generally accepted auditing standards. Hence if this is not done or if it has not been completed by the date agreed upon by the contractual parties, the contract will have been breached. And because the auditor is understood to have a confidential relationship with the client, any violation of the code of ethics provisions regarding confidentiality would also be a breach of contract.

Upon payment of a client's loss, the insurer becomes entitled to any right of action that client had against the one who caused the loss. Hence an insurer has the right to proceed against the auditor if recovery cannot be made from the primary cause of the loss; that is, if the embezzler cannot cover the loss, the auditor can be sued for negligence in not discovering the embezzlement.

Tort

Tort is a wrongful act that injures another person's property, body, or reputation. *Tort liability* is the failure to carry out a duty that was created by social policy. For CPAs, it is generally held that the profession has a social contract for exercising due professional care and, therefore, that CPAs are liable not only to the parties in privity but also to third parties.

Causes of Action

Disputes involving parties in privity of contract or those not in privity are based on one of three causes:

1. *Ordinary negligence,* which is the failure to exercise the due care that a reasonable, prudent person would exercise in the same circumstances.
2. *Gross negligence,* which is the failure to use even slight care.
3. *Fraud,* which is the intentional deception of others, resulting in injury.

In 1919, the case of *Landell* v. *Lybrand* held that parties not in privity could not hold a CPA liable for negligence; fraud would have to be proved. However, by 1931, *Ultramares Corp.* v. *Touche* found that liability for fraud could be inferred from gross negligence (for example, negligence so gross that it constitutes fraud). The auditors failed in this case to discover fictitious accounts receivable and other assets. But, liability to third parties for ordinary negligence was not recognized unless those parties had been identified at the time of the audit to be so-called primary beneficiaries of the audited information. A *primary beneficiary* is that party who is to be the primary recipient of the auditor's report, as identified by name to the auditor before the audit. The primary beneficiary issue often comes up when an audit is being performed to acquire financing from a particular lender. In his reasons for thus limiting auditors' exposure for negligence to primary beneficiaries, Judge Cardozo in the *Ultramares* case wrote: "If liability for negligence exists, a thoughtless slip or blunder, the failure to detect a theft or forgery beneath the cover of de-

EXHIBIT 5-1

AICPA Professional Liability Insurance Plan: Most Common Causes of Claims in the Plan Since 1974

1. Tax Matters

   Claims arising from late filing of returns and from underpayment of estimated tax because of alleged negligence of the accountant, which results in penalties, interest and other serious harm to the client. Some claims also arise because of items reported on the tax return prepared by the accountant.

2. Audit Services

   Claims alleging that a CPA firm did not properly discharge its obligations in an engagement to examine books and records of a company in accordance with Generally Accepted Auditing Standards (GAAS) and to report whether the financial statements are presented in conformity with Generally Accepted Accounting Principles(GAAP).

3. Accounting Services

   Claims alleging improper execution of an engagement to provide accounting services (referred to as "writeup," "unaudited financial statement work," or "compilation and review") and although no opinion was expressed, assurance was given that nothing came to the accountants' attention during the limited review to indicate that Generally Accepted Accounting Principles (GAAP) were not being followed.

4. Client's Counterclaims

   Claims arising as the result of an accountant's suit to collect fees from a client.

5. Defalcations

   Claims arising because of the accountant's failure to detect embezzlement during an audit or other engagement.

6. SEC and Stockholder Suits

   Claims by third parties (parties not privy to the engagement contract, such as stockholders and/or the Securities & Exchange Commission) which involve high-dollar liabilities and defense costs.

7. Business and Investment Advice

   Involves audit or accounting services as well as tax and MAS advice. This category is basically comprised of claims relating to business acquisition evaluations and projections, and such things as advising on a suitable mix (equity vs. debt) of portfolio investments for business and funds. Not included are financial management or handling of funds which are primarily fiduciary responsibilities.

8. Fiduciary Responsibilities

   Claims brought under the ERISA law and under the expanded definition of "Fiduciary" in the 1974 revised SEC Rule 10b.

9. Management Advisory Services

   Claims alleging that advice given by an accountant to a business in order to improve its efficiency and/or to make maximum use of its resources was incorrect.

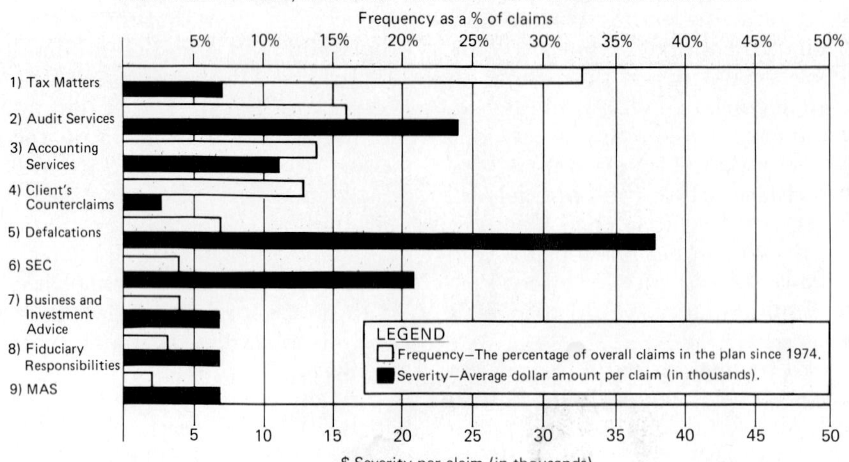

From "Be Alert," Number 3 in a series prepared by AICPA Professional Liability Insurance Plan Committee (New York: Rollins Burdick Hunter).

ceptive entries, may expose accountants to a liability in an indeterminate amount for an indeterminate time to an indeterminate class." The *State Street Trust Co.* v. *Ernst* case in 1938 involved the auditors' failure to assess adequately the collectibility problems. This case recognized that liability to third parties did arise from gross negligence, stressing reckless misstatement and flimsy grounds for expressing an opinion as evidence of such gross negligence. Hence, it translated the "could" language of *Ultramares* to "did."

The primary beneficiary distinction emphasized in *Ultramares* dimmed in importance after a 1968 case, *Rusch Factors, Inc.* v. *Levin,* as it held auditors to be responsible to "foreseen and limited classes" when ordinary negligence is proved. These third parties may include individuals not named or identified though entitled to receive an audit report in fulfillment of some business transaction, such as a financing venture. Shareholders and bondholders are not included, however; the emphasis was on lenders.

The *Rusch Factors, Inc.* v. *Levin* case noted:

> The wisdom of the decision in Ultramares has been doubted . . . and this court shares the doubt. Why should an innocent reliant party be forced to carry the weighty burden of an accountant's professional misconduct? Isn't the risk of loss more easily distributed and spread by imposing it on the accounting profession, which can pass the cost of insuring against the risk onto its customers, who can in turn pass the cost onto the entire consuming public?

From this stance, liability to *foreseeable parties* was created. The *Escott* v. *BarChris Construction Corp.* (1968) case is often cited as effectively acknowledging that the public's reliance on the CPA's report is foreseeable and that the report's "end and aim" are the transactions in the marketplace. In other words, the consumer is the investor and is foreseeable.[2]

The *Rhode Island Hospital Trust National Bank* v. *Swartz* (1972) case demonstrates a more recent application of the foreseeable parties concept, despite the CPA's expression of a disclaimer. The problem was that the reasons offered for the disclaimer were found to be misleading because they referred to nonexistent leasehold improvements as though they existed. As a result, the CPA was found to be culpable for ordinary negligence to foreseeable parties. Generally, the initial idea of ordinary negligence leading only to liability to a client, as opposed to third-party liability, shifts so often that the CPA cannot rely on it. Ordinary negligence can and has led to CPAs' liability to third parties. The current law seems to emphasize the class of user and type of transaction as being foreseeable, although some interpret "foreseeable" rather broadly.

Burden of Proof

Under common law, the burden of proof is placed on the plaintiff. Specifically, the plaintiff is expected to demonstrate that

1. Damage was suffered.
2. The financial statements were materially misleading.
3. The accountant was negligent, grossly negligent, deceitful, or otherwise responsible for the unlawful behavior.
4. He or she relied on those financial statements (that is, that there is a causal connection between negligence and injury).

Damages for breach of contract are limited to those foreseeable at the time of contract, whereas tort action damages are limited to those resulting from the "proximate cause" of negligence, which has been defined, in part, by the foreseeability of the consequences from the negligent act. To summarize, under common law, the plaintiff's demonstration of ordinary negligence is sufficient for clients, primary beneficiaries, and foreseen third parties, to hold auditors liable, whereas gross negligence is required for ordinary third parties to hold auditors liable.

Auditors' Defenses

When confronting a client's or a third party's claim of malpractice, CPAs will try to demonstrate that they were not negligent. And incorrect judgment does not constitute negligence; rather, CPAs

[2] A. A. Sommer, Jr., "Financial Reporting: Who Is Liable?" *Financial Executive,* March 1974, pp. 19–25.

must demonstrate that they took reasonable care and were competent. A second defense is to demonstrate that whatever negligence there was did not cause the loss that the client or third party is claiming. For example, if a plaintiff has other information concerning a problem, reliance may not be demonstrable. A third defense is to show that the client's or a third party's negligence contributed to the loss; this is called a *contributory negligence* defense. An example of a circumstance in which this defense would apply is the performance of an audit in which the client or third party limited the audit scope, thereby making detection of the problem unlikely. Similarly, if an auditor reported material weaknesses in a client's internal control system that the client failed to correct, the CPA could claim contributory negligence. The final defense available to the CPA is the *general law of single recovery,* which means that by demonstrating the client's or the third party's recovery of the claimed loss from another source, the CPA can prevent any additional recovery by that plaintiff.

A CPA who is found guilty may be able to shift part of the responsibility for the losses suffered. Such *partial indemnity* can be proved if others have taken wrongful actions that, together with those of the auditor, caused the loss. The share for each party may be equal or may be based on the defendants' proportion of fault. (For example, *McLean v. Alexander,* 1976, resulted in 90 percent of the fault being allocated to management, and 10 percent to the auditor.)

Securities Act of 1933

The Securities Act of 1933, known as the "truth of securities" law, requires audited financial statements in registration statements. Section 11(a) essentially allows any individual acquiring a security to sue the accountant, among others, for untrue statements or omissions of material fact in a registration statement. The plaintiff need only show that damages were suffered and financial statements were misleading. Section 11(e) holds the accountant liable for (1) the difference between the purchase price and the market value of the security at the time of the suit or (2) the sales price if the security has been sold, with a ceiling on the recovery equal to the security's original offering price. If more than twelve months have elapsed since the financial statements were issued, the burden of proof is extended, and the plaintiff has additional responsibility for proving reliance on those statements. Otherwise, the burden of proof is on the accountant. In other words, the CPA must establish that due care was exercised and must show that there was no negligence or fraud. The CPA must demonstrate that the audit was performed with reasonable care and in good faith and that he or she had no knowledge of any material misstatement. In addition, the auditor may try to demonstrate that the plaintiff's losses were attributable to other causes.

Section 13 of the 1933 act contains a *statute of limitations* which requires that action be brought within one year after the false statement or omission was or should have been discovered, but no more than three years after the effective date of the public offering's registration statement. The 1933 act can result in convictions for both civil and criminal liability.

Securities Exchange Act of 1934

The Securities Exchange Act of 1934 required audited annual statements by public companies, and it established the Securities and Exchange Commission to carry out the requirements of the 1933 and 1934 acts. Section 18 of the 1934 act made CPAs liable to both purchasers and sellers (the latter were excluded from the 1933 act). The plaintiff must prove, however, that personal reliance on the financial statements was the actual cause of the losses, resulting in a greater burden of proof than typically called for by the 1933 act. But the courts have not been very demanding in terms of the proof of negligence. For example, in class action suits, the courts have held that because financial analysts and other informed investors can be expected to have justifiably relied on such statements and have affected existing market prices, all parties thereby effectively relied on the statements. Although the CPA can be liable for ordinary negligence under the 1933 act, the 1934 act requires only that the CPA acted in good faith and had no knowledge that the financial statements were misleading. Either gross negligence or fraud must be established for the CPA to be liable. The 1934 act has the same statute of limitations as the 1933 act does, and Section 32 of the 1934 act allows for criminal penalties, with fines up to $10,000 and/or imprisonment up to five years.

Rule 10b-5

In 1942, Rule 10b-5 was promulgated as a section of the 1934 act, ruling that is it "unlawful to make any untrue statement of a material fact necessary to make the statements made, in the light of the circumstances under which they were made, not misleading." This rule contains none of the ordinary restrictions, as it applies to both the new and secondary market, can be applied to defendants who did not make any securities transactions, and can involve a plaintiff who did not engage in any securities transactions. No express statute of limitations applies to Rule 10b-5, and court cases in 1967 made it clear that privity was not required in 10b-5 cases.

In 1966, Rule 23 of the Federal Rules of Civil Procedure was revised so that class action suits would bind all who were in the class and had not requested exclusion, thereby enabling a contingency fee basis for the filing of suits. This revision, in combination with Rule 10b-5, was recognized as a threat to corporate existence. By 1968, a third of all securities actions were Rule 10b-5 cases. The potential liability exposure under this rule is perhaps best captured by the experience of Texas Gulf Sulphur Co., which was faced with possible claims (due to misleading press releases) adding up to $150,000 more than its entire net worth. Class action suits have sought damages equal to the decline in the market value of all of an issuer's outstanding shares.

CPAs' Defenses

Similar to common law, the SEC's acts under Section 11(b) provide for a *due diligence defense*, whereby CPAs must attempt to demonstrate that they exercised due diligence or adequate care in performing an audit. By showing that after a reasonable investigation, a CPA had reason to believe and did believe that the statements were true without material omission, he or she can avoid liability. *Reasonable investigation* is defined in terms of that standard of reasonableness that a prudent person would exercise in the management of his or her property (see Section 11[e]). In addition, a *causation defense* is recognized under Section 11(e) whereby a CPA can claim that other events caused the loss. For example, if a decline in stock price is the basis for a claim, the CPA may try to show that a general decline in the economy and the industry accounts for a considerable portion of the decline in stock price and thus can be separated from the error or omission in dispute. Section 11(a), imposing liability, contains the exception: "unless it is proved that at the time of such acquisition he knew of such untruth or omission." In other words, the CPA can use as a defense the claim that the plaintiff had prior knowledge of the falsity or misrepresentation.

Obviously, the CPA can also try to prove that a misstatement was immaterial and, as provided under Section 11(f), can claim contribution from other parties in order to share the responsibility for the losses claimed.

Indemnity, or the shifting of an entire loss from one person to another for reasons of equity, has been denied to accountants in such cases as *State Mutual Life Assurance Company* v. *Peat, Marwick, Mitchell & Company*, in which the court noted:

> There exists yet another reason for striking the third party complaint [of the public accountants]. To permit public accounting firms to escape liability for misconduct in the performance of their duties by obtaining indemnity from the alleged participants in the misconduct would be violative of both the public policy embodied in the federal securities legislation and the public faith reposed in these firms. If accountants could escape liability for their own misfeasance by obtaining indemnity from the officers of the corporation which financial statements they have fraudulently prepared, there would be much less incentive to be thorough in examination and truthful in reporting.

In contrast, the concept of *contribution*—in which losses are distributed among those persons who are jointly and severally liable, by requiring each to pay a proportionate share based on fault, unjust enrichment, or degree of participation in the wrongful action—has been generally recognized as available, even to intentional tortfeasors.[3]

For 10b-5 cases, the CPA's defenses can include a demonstration that *scienter* has not been proved, that is, that no intent to deceive, manipulate, or defraud has been proved. The necessity of scienter was upheld by the U.S. Supreme Court in *Ernst & Ernst* v. *Hochfelder*.

The SEC Injunction and Accounting Series Releases (Now FRRs)

SEC investigations are quasi-judicial proceedings that are intended to be nonadversary, similar to a grand jury investigation. To take evidence, the staff need not show probable cause that a violation has or is about to occur, and it has subpoena power, without geographical restrictions. Information can be obtained from such parties as other governmental agencies, self-regulatory bodies, and bankruptcy trustees. There is clearly a difficulty in fighting the government with all of its resources, as explained by an experienced securities attorney:

> I believe that the question is raised as to why are there so many consent injunctions. Why do so many defendants simply agree to sign up and not fight? . . .
>
> There is a feeling on the part of counsel in many injunctive cases that if the case were vigorously defended by the defendant that the case would be won or would likely be won. Now, if that is so, why not fight? Well, we all know the reasons why cases are not fought. They're not fought primarily because it's not easy to fight the Federal Government. . . . The fact is that when you go to court against the SEC you are going to court against the Federal Government, and there is no effective limit to the resources available in their behalf.
>
> The private defendant, on the other hand, has to pay the costs of defending the case; has to suffer the adverse publicity and charges that are involved in the adversary proceeding. And in an adversary proceeding both the SEC and, of course, the defendants often go to extremes of advocacy within the bounds of professional limitations, which means that name calling is not ruled out entirely. Accordingly, even though respondents very often feel that they might win a case, it is often by far the wiser choice for counsel to advise settlement, especially when, in the eyes of many, the settlement of an injunctive proceeding involves no more in some cases than a promise not to do it again.[4]

By settling an SEC action before formal proceedings begin, the language of the settlement and the consent decree can be negotiated, including a statement that the defendant "neither admits nor denies" the allegations. This can help avoid class action suits and other ill effects of formal proceedings by the SEC.[5]

If the SEC investigates and finds that the acts have been violated, it can institute civil injunctive actions. Such cases are tried in public before federal district judges. There are three types of injunctions under Rule 65 of the Federal Rules of Civil Procedures: (1) a temporary restricting order (ten days in duration), (2) a preliminary injunction, and (3) a permanent injunction. The third is a court order that requires a defendant to comply with a law or to refrain from violating a law; violation can result in civil or criminal contempt proceedings with imprisonment.

Under its *Rule 2(e)*, the SEC may bar or suspend an individual or firm from practice before the commission.[6] Once the firms show that they are fit to practice, reinstatement is possible. The SEC's chief accountant has emphasized that the permanent bar from practice is not often used because of the commission's belief that a professional firm

[3] James M. Fischer, "Contribution in 10b-5 Actions," *The Business Lawyer*, April 1978, pp. 1821–1844.

[4] Remarks by Kenneth Bialkin, ABA Annual Convention, reprinted in Program of the Committee on Federal Regulation of Securities, *Business Lawyer*, July 1975, pp. 1317–1318. Copyright 1975 by the American Bar Association. All rights reserved. Reprinted with the permission of the American Bar Association and its section of Corporation, Banking and Business Law.

[5] Lewis B. Merrifield III, "Investigations by the Securities and Exchange Commission," *The Business Lawyer*, July 1977, pp. 1583–1631.

[6] SEC Rules of Practice 2(e), 17 C.F.R. § 201.2(e) (1974).

can take actions to improve its performance, reach an acceptable level, and demonstrate this achievement to the SEC.[7]

Beyond Rule 2(e) action, the SEC may use sanctions in consent situations. Quality control and inspection and the limiting of new firm business have been used as sanctions. Any hearing that is held on a temporary suspension assumes that the professional is guilty even if a consent decree was entered without admission or denial of the charges. Mitigating circumstances intended to prevent censure or disqualification from practice are considered, however. SEC civil injunctions involving national CPA firms are typically settled with a consent judgment, and the firm or office of the firm is given a short suspension from accepting new clients. The SEC issues Accounting Series Releases (ASRs, now FRRs) discussing the problems in its injunctive actions, such as

- ASR 153: In the Matter of Touche Ross & Co.
- ASR 157: In the Matter of Arthur Andersen & Co.
- ASR 173: In the Matter of Peat, Marwick, Mitchell & Co.
- ASR 238: Litigation Involving Price Waterhouse & Co.
- ASR 241: In the Matter of Haskins & Sells (now Deloitte, Haskins & Sells)
- ASR 248: In the Matter of Ernst & Ernst (now Ernst & Whinney)

Legal Perils of Engagement Withdrawal

Walking away from a client can result in the client's suing for breach of contract. Therefore, CPAs report that they put themselves in a position to be fired when they judge it to be desirable. This way they can choose who is going to sue them, at least in some cases. But not surprisingly, there is a controversy over the CPAs' responsibility for whistle blowing after they walk away from a client. CPAs have resisted any pressures to reveal incriminating information, emphasizing the confidentiality of client relationships. But there is little doubt that liability exposure is possible.

Liability for Accounting and Review Services

Less responsibility is assumed when CPAs perform write-up work or prepare unaudited financial statements; yet there has been liability to clients and third parties. It is expected that the CPA understands the economic substance of the transactions recorded; if he or she does not, negligent misrepresentation can be claimed. It is also expected that the CPA will talk to the client about any suspicious events. The CPA does not have the prerogative to be silent simply because the engagement is not an audit. The CPA must indicate clearly in all reports his or her examination and the degree of responsibility accepted. Hence, unaudited financial statements should be clearly marked as such. The use of a CPA's letterhead implies audited financials with the related liability exposure, if there is no clear communication to the contrary.

Court cases have found that there was no third-party liability for financial statements prepared "For Internal Use Only" and not given to third parties. Hence it has been suggested that CPAs do compilations (preparation of financial statements) only for internal use. Compilations of financial statements may have several known material departures from generally accepted accounting principles. If these compilations were disseminated and third parties misled, the CPAs could be held liable for being reckless. *Review engagements* (limited assurance based on analytical review procedures) are fairly new reporting alternatives that are not subject to legal precedents concerning unaudited financials. But even ordinary negligence in performing reviews may lead to liability to clients and foreseen third parties.

To encourage accountants' participation in the issuance of interim statements, the SEC adopted a rule to exclude such statements from a securities law provision that makes accountants automatically liable for a client's false and misleading finan-

[7] John C. Burton, "SEC Enforcement and Professional Accountants: Philosophy, Objectives and Approach," *Vanderbilt Law Review* 28 (1975):19–29.

cial statements unless they can prove that they have been diligent. The accountants are still liable under the antifraud provisions of the federal securities law, but under all other sections, all damages would be paid by the directors.[8]

Court Cases That Have Influenced Auditing Standards and Practices

Several court cases have attracted publicity and have affected both the development of auditing standards and practices and the CPAs' liability exposure.

Effects on Audit Procedures

In the 1930s, audit procedures were not spelled out in the generally accepted auditing standards. The emphasis was on professional standards, which were seen as a general guide for the auditor as he or she gathered enough evidence to express an audit opinion. However, a case known as *McKesson & Robbins* called into question the adequacy of these general standards of practice.

A company that had been audited for several years had repeatedly insisted that it had a warehouse full of inventory. Accepted auditing practices did not require that physical inventory taking be observed, and so the auditors had used paper documentation to verify the reasonableness of the recorded inventory balance. The folklore story of how the client's fraud came to light goes something like this:

> One of the audit partners happened to be on vacation, not far from the client's warehouse location. Being the typical auditor, with a professional interest in and curiosity about business associates, even during vacations, he decided to drive by the warehouse site. However, when he reached the claimed location, he found nothing but an empty field—no sign of a warehouse or any inventory. Bewildered, the partner called his firm's office to double-check the address for the client's warehouse. Indeed, he had the correct address, but there was no inventory and no warehouse.
>
> When the dust had settled, a huge paper fraud was uncovered which had essentially been the basis for taking advantage of the "float" on funds that would have been required to finance the level of documented paperwork transactions. The problem was that the paperwork did not refer to real transactions.

Although it makes an interesting story, in actuality the treasurer and director discovered the facts and brought them to the attention of the president, who instigated a stockholder suit that claimed waste, mismanagement, and fraudulent assets exceeding $10 million. The auditors investigated and found that $10 million of inventory and $9 million of accounts receivable were fictitious (note that consolidated assets were $87 million in 1937, the year in which the fraud was discovered). The perpetrator of the fraud was, in fact, the president, who shot himself on December 16, 1938, when his true identity and the fictitious assets were revealed. It seems that he had a history of fraud, prison terms, and enough experience with business to have learned about the auditing practices of those days—particularly that physical inventories were not observed unless the auditors were specifically requested to do so. It may be somewhat comforting to CPAs that *Who's Who in America* was similarly duped as to this man's (Philip Musica's) identity. It seems that by growing a mustache and changing his name, he made the 1938–1939 edition.[9]

The auditors settled the trustee's claim for the reorganization of McKesson & Robbins without litigation, by refunding the total audit fees, ($522,402.29) paid by McKesson & Robbins after January 1, 1933.[10] The SEC issued Accounting Series Release No. 19, "In the Matter of McKesson & Robbins, Inc." (1940). This case posed the interesting questions of why the auditors had not observed the inventory counts and why the client's customers had not been asked to confirm the balances they owed. Obviously, either procedure would have discovered the fraud, as neither the inventory

[8] "SEC Votes to Limit Accountants' Liability for Misleading Interim Fiscal Statements," *Wall Street Journal*, December 13, 1979, p. 5.

[9] "The 'Who's Who' Hoax," *Parade Magazine*, January 22, 1984, p. 18.

[10] Robert Shaplen, "Annals of Crime, the Metamorphosis of Philip Musica," *New Yorker*, October 22, 1955, and October 29, 1955; and Robert Shaplen, "America's Boldest Swindler," *Saturday Evening Post*, February 28, 1953, pp. 34–35.

nor the customers existed, except on paper. With the public's attention on such a perceived lack of care in assessing the value and accuracy of reported balances, the auditing profession decided to adopt both the observation of physical inventory and the sending of confirmations to customers, as required procedures according to generally accepted auditing standards. Of particular interest is the SEC's suggestion in 1940 that auditors investigate the management of new clients. Some CPA firms even hire private investigating firms to screen new clients in order to detect the use of an alias (as was done by the president of McKesson & Robbins) or other attributes of management that might make the prospective client unacceptable as an auditee.

Effects on Communication

The next case that had strong implications for public accounting was *Yale Express (Fischer* v. *Kletz).* This case involved a question as to the reporting responsibility of professional accountants who discovered a financial misstatement in an earlier year's audited report while performing a management advisory service (MAS). The MAS team did not disclose the new information, and the audit team for the client merely waited until the normal timing of the following year's audit to follow up on the problem. The magnitude of the financial statement error was clearly material (changing reported net income from a profit of $1,140,000 to a loss of $1,254,000 and charging retained earnings for an additional $629,000), and the discovery was finally reported in March 1965.

When the public became aware of the historical developments that could have meant the dissemination of corrected financial statement figures at a far earlier date, it demanded the timely disclosure of such discoveries and that CPAs be held liable for not doing so. The suit was filed under Section 18(a) of the 1934 act and Rule 10b-5.

The AICPA modified its rules in October 1969 to require that when a CPA becomes aware of information that could have affected a report, there must be an investigation. In other words, *Fischer* v. *Kletz* led to the AICPA's Statement on Auditing Procedure No. 21, which provides that errors discovered after the completion of an audit are not to be concealed by the auditors' silence. If it is determined that the report would be affected and parties are currently relying on such reports, the auditor should prepare a revised report and see that the client sends it to those relying on the earlier report, including the regulators. Should the client refuse to cooperate, he or she should be notified not to associate the audit report with the financial statements. In addition, the CPA must report the situation to regulators and other known users. Obviously, to ensure this disclosure capability, CPA firms have had to establish effective communication links among all of the various engagement teams that might be performing services for a particular client. In addition, policies must be established for handling that information affecting the reasonableness of past disclosures.

Effects on Audit Approach

Two litigation cases were the major determinants of the audit approach that appears in the current professional literature and is known as the *business approach.* Both of these cases were massive frauds involving such great growth in the clients' operations that an astute business analysis would have raised the question of how such growth was possible. In the first case, the reported inventory balance, if tied to industry statistics, would have been most of the world's supply of salad oil. In the second case, the growth rate, if extended, would have implied that Equity Funding could literally have taken over the reinsurance industry, despite its numerous competitors. The business approach to auditing presumably would have questioned the plausibility of the reported figures.

Other aspects of the *"Salad Oil King"* and *Equity Funding* cases are of special interest because of their implications for varied audit approaches. The so-called Great Salad Oil Swindle was perpetrated in 1963 through

1. The use of a respected name—American Express (specifically, American Warehousing Ltd., a small subsidiary of American Express).
2. The placement of inventory in an independent public warehouse.
3. The application of two fairly simple principles:
   a. Oil floats on water.

b. What is underground is not evident from above ground.

The first step—using a respected name—may have put the auditors at ease, so that they expected to find a sound business, and the second step—using an independent public warehouse—provided paper documentation of inventory moving in and out of a location that did not appear to be under the client's control. The problem was that although the public warehouse was tied to an established, well-regarded business, the controls at that particular warehouse were loose. In fact, inventory receipts were handed out on what almost seemed to be a "by request" basis.

Knowing the requirements that stemmed from McKesson & Robbins, you may wonder what the real problem was in this case, as the auditor was required to observe the inventory and surely then could have detected the inventory overstatements. Now the ingenious yet simple strategy of those perpetrating the fraud comes into play. Many of the vats were filled with water, with only a top layer of oil. In addition, pipes connected the vats underground, permitting the layer of oil to be shifted across the vats as needed during the inventory observation procedure. It was reported that the auditors would climb up, look into the vat, and then measure its level. Adding a story-telling dimension to the events, folklore has it that one year a particularly enterprising auditor climbed up to the vat, looked in, and then requested a stick. His intention was to dip the stick into the vat in order to measure the depth of the oil. But when he took the stick out, it had not one but two lines—one made by the water level and one made by the salad oil level. And this is what led to further investigation.

Allied Crude Vegetable Oil Refining Corporation, headed by Anthony "Tino" DeAngelis, had sublet a tank farm in Bayonne, New Jersey and secured receipts of the American Express warehouse for vast quantities of salad oil, soybean oil, and fish oil. Exporters paid for merchandise purportedly represented by these receipts and financed their purchases through foreign and domestic banks and other lenders who never questioned the receipts' validity. Interestingly, the receipts issued exceeded the total capacity of the Bayonne tank farm and even the total amount of salad oil in the country. But no exporter or lender had all of the receipts outstanding.

As a result of this salad oil fraud, the SEC turned its attention to audit procedures involving public warehouses and to analytical review methodologies that would stress the reasonableness of clients' representations. Also at issue was the effectiveness with which new audit clients were evaluated. It seems that the perpetrator of the fraud, similar to that of the McKesson & Robbins case, had a history of difficulty with regulators, yet somehow was able to use the warehouse business affiliation to assure the auditors of the quality of the inventory storage facilities.

The Equity Funding case caused such a media sensation that it was later made into a movie for television. Equity Funding found itself in a slight working capital crunch in 1964 and so developed a plan to solve the short-term problem. The company was in the reinsurance business, whereby one insurance company sells policies to customers and then resells the present policy for the value of future premiums—slightly reduced by a service charge—to a second insurance company, who then receives all of the premiums and is responsible for honoring any claims by the insured. The short-term solution to the working capital squeeze was to create some bogus life insurance policies and to sell their equivalent present value to other insurance companies. Of course, Equity Funding had to mail the premiums owed to these other companies, as there were no real customers. The plan was expected to work, because it was not an industry practice to confirm policies purchased from insurance companies, such as Equity Funding, with the original policyholders. In other words, the internal controls over reinsurance transactions were rather loose.

As in many reported frauds, the perpetrators found that their plan worked so well that they decided to use it to secure a strong leadership position in the industry and, later, to use it as a "growth policy." But, as the volume of bogus policies grew, some means had to be developed to ensure that other companies did not find such policies unusual, thereby prompting an investigation. The computer provided this means. Actuarial tables were used to transfer the past experiences with real insurance policies to the bogus policy files. This also meant that some bogus policyholders "died" and that Equity Funding was then able to collect the insurance proceeds!

Having ensured that the companies' experiences with the bogus policies would be similar to the industry's experience with life insurance, Equity Funding still faced one other potential source of risk—that the external auditors might discover the bogus policies. The auditors were known to apply statistical sampling in their tests of policies and thus asked for files documenting a sample of policies. At first, Equity Funding was able to claim that a file had been lost or misplaced, but as the company grew, the auditors requested a larger proportion of policies. If the documentation could not be produced, the auditors would become suspicious. But, it would take time to "manufacture" supporting documentation, and there was no way of knowing which files the auditors would request.

Again, the client planned a strategy. Top management unexpectedly invited all of the external auditors on the job for lunch but stressed that they must hurry to get in line early and avoid the rush. In their haste, as expected, the external auditors did not secure their work papers. While the auditors were having a long lunch, an employee of the client found the sampling plan for reinsurance policies, made a copy, and then returned the sampling plan to its original location. At this point, the infamous "midnight parties" began. Groups of employees worked together late at night to produce policies, including death certificates, in support of those policies to be tested by the external auditors. Thus when the external auditors requested particular files, they were ready and were immediately turned over to the audit team.

The growth in assets, income, and stock price for Equity Funding was enormous. About half of the policies on the books were bogus. During this time, one of the Big Eight auditing firms was asked to review Equity Funding as a merger prospect. It was later publicized in the press that the firm advised its client not to make the acquisition, because "it looked too good to be true." But as yet, there was no solid evidence of a fraud.

So how did the bubble burst? Disgruntled ex-employees who had been fired told the story to a Wall Street analyst, and the Securities and Exchange Commission was called, with the suggestion that the SEC check out Equity Funding, particularly its "midnight parties." Rumors started on March 19 when Equity Funding's stock price was $24.875, and by the time trading was halted on March 27, it had dropped to $14.375.[11] The SEC froze Equity Funding's operations, suspended all trading in any of the company's securities, and started to uncover the breadth of the fraud. Out of 99,000 policies representing $3.5 billion of insurance on the books, 56,000 policies representing $2 billion of insurance were fictitious. In addition, management had created some fictitiously valued or nonexistent holdings on the books. After adjustments, the December 31, 1972, reported net worth of $143.4 million was restated to a negative, or deficit, net worth of $42.1 million. The accounting firms involved are reported to have settled the claims against Equity Funding for almost $44 million.[12]

Two important lessons were learned from the Equity Funding experience. The first was the importance of securing sampling plans and working papers in order to ensure that such tests remain secret and also that the samples are really representative of the population of interest. The second was the possibility of widespread fraud within a client's business. Auditors believe that the necessity of collusion decreases the probability of fraud. Yet at Equity Funding, many employees knew about and even participated in the "midnight parties." The ramifications of such collusive fraud for building control systems and analyzing risk had to be evaluated. The presumption that there was no conflict of interest between management and the auditor had to be reconsidered. In particular, auditing firms paid more attention to "whistle-blowing" activities and the means by which they might be encouraged. Much of the literature on "red flags" was written in the aftermath of Equity Funding.

A third rather harsh, yet humorous, lesson regarding the importance of preparing working paper documentation in a professional manner was

[11] William E. Blundell, "A Scandal Unfolds: Some Assets Missing, Insurance Called Bogus at Equity Funding Life," *Wall Street Journal,* April 12, 1973, pp. 1, 14.

[12] "News Report," *Journal of Accountancy,* July 1978, p. 12, and Soble and Dallos, *The Impossible Dream* (New York: G. P. Putnam's Sons, 1975).

learned in the course of the Equity Funding litigation. A small subsidiary of Equity Funding was a ranch operation, audited by one of the "Big Fifteen" CPA firms. A full year before the fraud was uncovered at the parent company, an attribute of the ranching client struck one of the staff auditors as funny, and this humor worked its way into the documentation of the field work. After summarizing the work performed and the conclusions drawn, the staff auditor noted that an opportunity seemed to exist for the client to make a fortune from the large amount of "by-product" (often referred to with a four-letter word that appropriately means waste) that was routinely generated by the steers. An exposé on such a possibility was presented, in jest, in the working papers. The reviewer of these papers shared the staff auditor's sense of humor and noted: "Pass further work, as this whole thing is full of_____" (expletive deleted).

Well, you can imagine the fun that opposing counsel had with this 1971 working paper excerpt throughout the course of the trial! I have been told that it was the most commonly quoted phrase, taken out of context, and stated as support of the fact that auditors had known about the Equity Funding fraud and that the financial statements were, in fact, "full of_____" (expletive deleted)!

The point of sharing this experience is to emphasize that the preparer of working papers ought to remember that those documents could some day find their way into the courtroom setting. They are not the appropriate place for humor; they are support for the evidential matter on which an opinion is to be expressed.

One other factual detail of Equity Funding which did not help the CPA firm was that from 1964, the year that the company went public and for the four years prior to the company's collapse, the man in charge of the audit was not a CPA until 1972. When you consider how this was most likely interpreted in the courtroom, you may gain an understanding of why the passage of the CPA exam is deemed essential by public accounting firms in order for professional staff members to progress.

Effects on GAAP Reliance

A case that is commonly cited as evidence that an auditor is not "protected" merely because the financial statements on which an audit opinion is expressed have been prepared in accordance with generally accepted accounting principles (GAAP) is *Continental Vending* (*United States* v. *Simon,* 1969). This case focused upon three parties: (1) a major stockholder of (2) a company that had (3) a subsidiary with which two distinctly different types of transactions were common—one that generated receivables and one that generated payables. An overview of these transactions is shown in Exhibit 5-2. There were two accounting issues. The first was the client's practice of netting the receivable and payable, thereby camouflaging the magnitude of the related-party transactions. The second was the fact that receivables to the major company were mainly backed by collateral of that company's stock. The marketable securities held as collateral, according to GAAP, did not have to be described in a footnote. But if something happened to the large company's financial position, its stock would also be

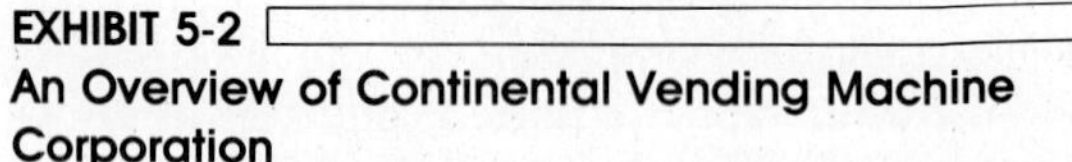

EXHIBIT 5-2
An Overview of Continental Vending Machine Corporation

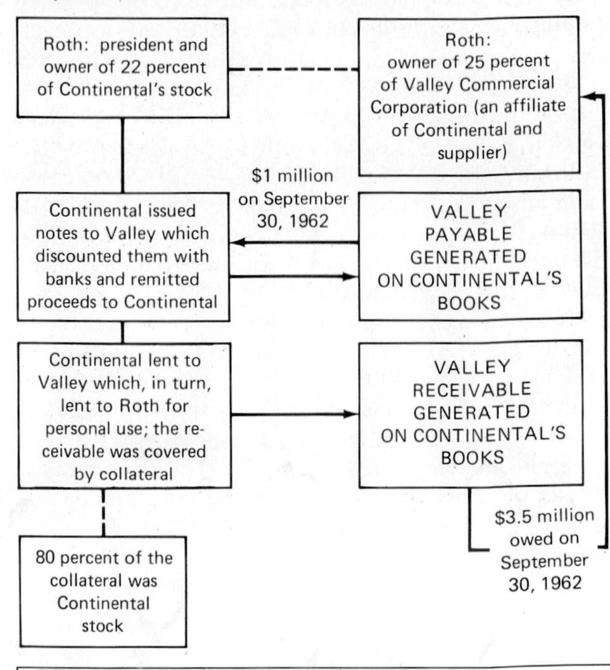

affected, suggesting that there was no real collateral protection. In fact, when the company's stock did plunge, the value of the collateral evaporated. The judge in this case held that the profession must be held to a higher standard than GAAP. In 1962, two partners and a manager were fined $17,000, and the settlement of the civil suit by the CPA firm cost $1,960,936. The message was that auditors should evaluate the probable effect of disclosures on stockholders' investment decisions, and if the disclosures are likely to affect such decisions, disclosure is appropriate, regardless of GAAP's requirements. In addition, this case reminds auditors that they should be familiar with the financial affairs of affiliated companies and perhaps even insist on auditing them directly: Ethics Rule 401 provides for such a practice. If this had been done, the loans by Valley to insoluble Mr. Roth would have been discovered.

The *Simon* case was claimed to have caused many CPA firms to institute a procedure called *cold review,* in which, just before the public release of the financial statements, a partner who is not involved in the audit decides whether they could be understood by a lay man. Often such reviews include both a work paper and report review as a quality control measure of the firm.[13]

BarChris. An example of auditors' difficulty in applying generally accepted accounting principles to reflect the economic substance of transactions is the *Escott* v. *BarChris Construction Corp.* case. This 1968 case involved the recording of a sale and a leaseback as a sale. Note that the transaction occurred in 1960 and that the Accounting Principles Board issued its first pronouncement on sale and leaseback transactions in 1964. Essentially, several bowling alleys, which included bar and restaurant facilities, were constructed and sold, but economic conditions forced a sale and leaseback arrangement to keep the facilities in operation. As a result, the sales and gross profit were overstated, and the recorded receivable was not actually current. This led to a 15 percent error in earnings per share and a 19 percent error in the current ratio; the recorded receivable was deemed material, but the sales and gross profit were not.

BarChris is often cited as providing materiality guidelines, because a $600,000 overstatement of current assets was deemed material in its alteration of the current ratio from 1.9 to 1, down to 1.6 to 1; and yet a 14 percent misstatement of sales and an earnings per-share change from $0.75 to $0.65 were deemed immaterial.

Although the judge in this case is widely quoted to have said, "Accountants should not be held to a standard higher than that recognized in their profession," the court found the CPAs to be liable to third-party investors under Section 11 of the 1933 act, because the audit program had not been followed properly and the basis of all GAAP, that is, the communication of economic substance, was lacking, regardless of the dispute over specific accounting rules.

Effects on Contracting for an Engagement

A case that has been cited as exemplifying CPAs' potential liability exposure in engagements involving unaudited financial statements is 1136 Tenants'. The CPA documented in the work papers some missing invoices, yet did not investigate them because of the engagement's limited scope. Specifically, a work paper entitled "Missing Invoices 1/1/63–12/31/63" disclosed missing invoices totaling more than $44,000. Later a fraud was discovered, and the CPA was sued. The client claimed that the CPA had been asked to perform an audit and therefore was responsible for investigating the apparent alteration of the books. The CPA denied this claim, but his case was hurt because the financial statements he reviewed had a separate line item, reporting "audit fee" as an expense. Similarly, the managing agent's monthly statements reported an expense category of "audit." In addition, the 1968 case reported that one of the defendant's senior partners admitted that the defendant performed services for the plaintiff that went beyond the scope of a write-up, including audit procedures. Bank statements, invoices, and bills were examined. There was no engagement letter to clarify the understanding between the CPA and the client regarding the scope of work to be performed. Furthermore, the CPA had not issued a clear disclaimer of opin-

[13] A. A. Sommer, Jr., "Financial Reporting: Who Is Liable?" *Financial Executive,* March 1974, pp. 19–25.

ion. The judgment in 1972 was for $232,278 in damages, even though the accountant's fee had been only $600.

It was not then, nor is it currently, required under generally accepted auditing standards that a formal engagement letter be obtained. However, it is strongly recommended, and it is clear from the 1136 Tenants' case why it is. The *1136 Tenants' Corp.* v. *Max Rothenberg & Co.* case is not generally thought to demonstrate an increased level of liability for engagements involving unaudited financial statements, because of the case's unique and conflicting facts. But it is difficult not to see that there can be a considerable liability risk in engagements other than audits. The case clearly established a duty for CPAs doing "write-up" work to disclose to their clients any suspicious circumstances that may suggest the existence of fraud.

Responsibility for Detecting Errors and Irregularities

The *Hochfelder* case is widely recognized as an example of the profession taking a stance and trying to draw the line as to what constitutes a reasonable level of responsibility for external auditors. Briefly, the case was a fraud perpetrated on many large customers of an investment banking firm, First Securities Company of Chicago. Leston B. Nay, president of the firm and the owner of 92 percent of its stock, told these customers that he had a special investment opportunity that he would manage on their behalf but that the opportunity could be offered to only a select group of investors and therefore must be kept confidential. He further informed them not to expect a typical statement for this investment account and to forward to him any related correspondence, writing "private and personal" on the envelope.

Nay had in fact pocketed the investment principal sums and forwarded periodic monetary returns to the investors. This was facilitated by the fact that the investors made out their personal checks to Nay or a designated bank, for his account. Eventually, having lost most of the proceeds from the fraud, Nay committed suicide in 1968, and the investors' losses came to light. In fact, Nay left a note that described the company as bankrupt and the special escrow accounts as "spurious." The auditors were sued, the main contention being that they should have tested and reviewed the mail marked "private and personal" and addressed to either Nay or to Nay's attention, much as they tested the controls over cash receipts. The auditors argued that this would have been an invasion of privacy and outside the purview of the controls. The case went back and forth in court. The affidavit of Fred J. Duncombe, the past president of the Illinois Society of CPAs, stated:

> If I had discovered in making an audit of a brokerage company that the President of the Company had established an office rule that all mail addressed to him or to the company for his attention should not be opened by anyone but him; and that when he was away from the office for a few days, the mail addressed to him or to the Company for his attention piled up on his desk, I would not have regarded that brokerage firm as having adequate internal control and would not have certified that a report based on such an audit fairly represented the financial position of the Company.[14]

This affidavit reflects the disagreement among auditors over their duty of inquiry. In *Hochfelder* v. *Ernst & Ernst* (503 F. 2d 364 [7th Cir. 1974]), the court stated:

> Although the defendant [Ernst & Ernst] correctly stated that generally accepted auditing standards do not ordinarily require such investigation, we do not find that entirely compelling . . . we are not constrained to accept faulty standards of practice otherwise generally accepted in an industry or profession.[15]

One interesting aspect of the audit was that none of the "selected investors" commented on the incompleteness of the confirmations that they received from the auditors. The Supreme Court ruled in favor of the auditors, focusing on the statutory wording and the legislative and administrative history of Section 10(b). The *Ernst & Ernst* v. *Hochfelder* 1976 decision held that in order to sue for damages under Rule 10b-5, the defendant must be proved to have knowingly and willfully misrepresented the report. This permits auditors to make "honest" mistakes without incurring liability. How-

[14] *Hochfelder* v. *Ernst & Ernst*, 503 F. 2d 1100, p. 1110.

[15] Ibid., p. 1113.

ever, a reading of the opinion indicates that the Court did not set too broad a precedent. Although many believe that if the auditor's negligence is to be claimed, scienter, or the auditor's knowledge of fraud, is required, others do not recognize such a clear-cut requirement. One open question is whether the presence of gross negligence or recklessness is sufficient to satisfy the scienter requirement.[16]

Effects on Liability Exposure

The most optimistic interpretations have cited *Hochfelder* as an end to most 10b-5 cases. The burden of demonstrating scienter was cited as so great that it would deter case filings. But, other SEC provisions provide opportunities for filing in the absence of scienter, and a comparison of later decisions by lower courts supports the varied opinions of *Hochfelder* as a precedent.

Alternatives to Section 10(b) include Section 18(a) of the Securities Exchange Act and Section 17(a) for purchasers. Some have cited Section 11(a) of the Securities Act of 1933 as an alternative, except that the "due diligence" defense can be considered as a negligence standard. Of course, the SEC can also bring in its Rule 2(e) if the professional's fitness to practice before the commission is questioned. The *Hochfelder* case implicitly recognized that scienter is not a necessary element in an injunctive action under Section 10(b), as discussed in "Office Memorandum, Securities and Exchange Commission" (August 27, 1976, from the Harvey L. P. H., General Counsel).

Responsibility for Detecting Fraud

A prominent headline in the *New York Times* and *Wall Street Journal* concerned Saxon Industries. A fraud lasting from 1968 to 1981 padded the company's books with about $75 million in nonexistent inventory, according to a SEC complaint. The company's auditors, Fox and Company, were replaced by Touche Ross because of "unanswered questions" about past audits. After the fraud was discovered, reported steady profits through the third quarter in 1981 were lowered to an estimated loss of $47 million for the year.[17] There is little doubt that this case will have ramifications for the profession, and it has already called into question the level of service provided by auditors in the presence of fraud.

The courts have often debated CPAs' responsibility for detecting management fraud. The jury verdict in favor of Seidman & Seidman against Cenco Inc. (that is, the new management at Cenco) found that the accounting firm was not negligent for failing to uncover inventory fraud by Cenco's former management. The case supported the idea that if management defrauds its auditors, it cannot seek damages against those auditors for not detecting such fraud. Judge Posner noted in the court's decision that "auditors aren't detectives hired to ferret out fraud." Although auditors should investigate if fraud is suspected, top management's involvement makes such detection extremely difficult. Of particular interest is the court's allowing Seidman & Seidman to sue Cenco for an amount equal to the $3.5 million that the accounting firm had paid to Cenco's shareholders following a 1980 class action dispute. The idea underlying such a case is that Cenco's management, by means of misinformation and fraud, had effectively led the CPA firm into issuing a clean report.[18]

Touche Ross successfully defended itself in litigation involving Cedars of Lebanon Hospital Corp. in Miami, noting, "There was collusive fraud at the top. The evidence will show . . . that there is no way that an outside auditor can catch collusive fraud at the top."[19] The case, filed by the hospital and its board of directors, involved the auditors' failure to detect an embezzlement scheme carried out by the corporation's administrator. Of partic-

[16] For a discussion of such issues, see Nathan S. Slavin, "The Elimination of 'Scienter' in Determining the Auditor's Statutory Liability," *Accounting Review*, April 1977, pp. 360–368.

[17] Agis Salpukas, "U.S. Cites Saxon for False Data," *New York Times*, September 10, 1982, pp. D1, D10; and Thomas J. Lueck, "Sorting Out the Saxon Tangle," *New York Times*, July 15, 1982, p. D1.

[18] "Two Jury Verdicts Limit Accountants' Liability in Respect to Negligence," *Journal of Accountancy*, May 1982, p. 12.

[19] Ibid.

ular interest was the award made to Touche Ross for legal and accounting fees, as well as $500,000 in punitive damages from Cedars of Lebanon Hospital.

A recent case that was settled for almost $7 million concerned the fraud-riddled Frigitemp as it filed for bankruptcy in 1979. When in January 1978, the chairman's office of Arthur Andersen & Co. received an anonymous letter warning of "dirty deeds" at Frigitemp Corp., in the words of that client's assistant controller, "AA came in like the Gestapo." Their investigations uncovered

- a series of notes from Frigitemp to an obliging supplier for $4.2 million in deck planking that in fact was still in the form of trees growing in forests.
- a set of phony records to support inflated expenditure claims, created by six employees who even rubbed the paper with cigar ashes to make it look old.
- punched stacks of phony time cards, creating an "audit trail" of high labor costs being shifted across projects.
- fictitious addresses and phone numbers for suppliers who sent false invoices.
- recycling of receipts in order to achieve lapping (that is, crediting old accounts with recent payments, and removing or improperly using and inaccurately recording earlier cash receipts).

Allegations included independence issues regarding the engagement team's audit partner's active involvement in acquisition and borrowing transactions and his use of the client's Manhattan apartment. In addition, that partner reportedly encouraged the very liberal application of "cost-to-cost percentage-of-completion" accounting. The audits pointed out that one of the bigger auditing problems was that over half of Frigitemp's business was with federal agencies who rarely answer auditors' letters inquiring about an account. Recall the introductory dialogue's emphasis on confirmations, and consider the irony of such obstacles as the government's lack of cooperation. Andersen's legal adviser observed, "We were really a victim of collusive activity." Yet the legal costs and concern over the public's expectations of the auditors' responsibility for detecting fraud have prompted this type of settlement. And this concern appears to be warranted in light of a 1983 decision by the New Jersey Supreme Court regarding a suit against Touche Ross for the audit of Giant Stores, which went bankrupt. This case established that auditors are liable to "third parties" for fraudulent information in their audit reports.[20] Clearly, liability exposure is always present, and despite the profession's belief that its responsibility for detecting fraud is limited, it has had to pay substantial settlements.

One means of ensuring recognition of CPAs' limited responsibility for detecting fraud or for other aspects of a client's financials—particularly when offering less than a full-scope audit—is to issue a formal engagement letter. Although this point was made in the Tenants' case, a comparison of two cases involving fraud, with the key difference in the factual settings being the existence or nonexistence of an engagement letter, clarifies the point further.

Maryland Casualty Co. v. *Jonathon Cook* involved a city treasurer's embezzlement of funds and a dispute over the CPAs' scope of work. Had there been an engagement letter that clearly limited the scope of the claimed cash audit, there would not have been any liability. Verbal discussions with the city of Flint's director of finance were not adequate to support either the scope of work contracted with the city or its director. Hence the bonding company was reimbursed $11,169.09, that part of the total loss of $12,969.15 that occurred after the audit.

In contrast, the *O'Neil* v. *Atlas Automobile Finance Corporation* case was resolved in favor of the auditors, as their correspondence with the client established that the reports were not audited, and so they could not have detected the bookkeeper's fraud.

[20] John J. Fialka, "Why Arthur Andersen Was So Slow to Detect Chicanery at Frigitemp," *Wall Street Journal*, September 21, 1984, pp. 1, 14. Other facts of the fraud were detailed by Edward T. Pound and Bruce Ingersoll, "Tale of Deceit: How Frigitemp Sank After It Was Looted by Top Management," *Wall Street Journal*, September 20, 1984, pp. 1, 23. The Touche Ross case was discussed by Lee Berton, "Insurers Tell Big Accounting Concerns Liability Rates May Rise, Sources Say," *Wall Street Journal*, November 8, 1984, p. 4.

The Question of Confidentiality

Fund of Funds Ltd. was a 77,000-shareholder mutual fund that from 1968 to 1970 had paid $90 million for natural resource properties that were later discovered to be overvalued. The auditors for the mutual fund also happened to be the auditors for the party from which the properties were purchased. Because the seller of the properties was bankrupt, the auditors were sued, with the investors in Fund of Funds claiming that the auditors should have revealed that the assets were overvalued. As discussed in Chapter 3, the auditors' defense was that client privilege prevented them from doing so. In November 1981, a federal jury in New York ordered Arthur Andersen & Co. to pay $80 million to the shareholders. The case was finally settled for a little less than that amount (the judge's reduction was at least $9.6 million), meaning that appeals will not be heard and the case's precedent value is unclear. However, the case has posed this question: What are CPA firms expected to disclose to each of its clients, as they interact with many clients with whom a business is likely to have transactions? The only lesson learned from the *Fund of Funds* case is to seek a lawyer's counsel when information gained from one audit engagement is known to affect another client.[21]

Other Lessons

Two fairly recent bank failures were given press coverage unfavorable to the auditors of the *Penn Square Bank* and the *United American Bank of Knoxville.* Exhibit 5-3 presents some facts about Penn Square and the United American Bank of Knoxville, as well as the banking industry as a whole. [Those interested in further details on Penn Square may wish to review "Annals of Finance: Funny Money—I, II, and III," *The New Yorker* (April 22, 1985, pp. 51–103; April 29, 1985, pp. 42–91; May 6, 1985, pp. 49–109).]

The first similarity between the two banks is the extent to which both were involved in related-party transactions. Both made large transactions with members of the boards of directors, officers, brothers, stockholders, and "special friends"—transactions with inferior documentation and collateral levels. And there seemed to be cooperation between the parties to cover up the collectibility problems known to exist with some of the loans.

Both banks had been visited an unusual number of times by representatives of the comptroller of the currency. In fact, the United American Bank is reported to have changed its structure largely as a means of avoiding certain regulators' intervention. Neither bank met the requirements regarding insider or related-party transactions or the limits on the size of transactions in relation to the bank's capital base.

But the main warning signal seen in Exhibit 5-3 is the presence of many so-called red flags that might have been noticed had the audit used a business approach with an emphasis on analytical review tests. For example, standard banking practice is to hold diversified portfolios. Yet Penn Square made primarily energy-related loans, and United American concentrated its holdings in World's Fair–related projects. Furthermore, industry statistics and competitors' experience suggested that the energy field had reached its peak price and was likely to turn back down, and World's Fair revenue clearly should have been viewed as a risky potential inflow.

In regard to collateral practices, the banks' competitors granted only one-half of their claimed reserves as an acceptable basis for determining collateral value and then applied a 30 percent weight to that. But this 15 percent collateral equivalent was far below Penn Square's policies. Similarly, a guaranteed buy-back of troubled loans for pooling arrangements is definitely unusual and, given Penn Square's capital base, should have been highly suspect.

A business approach to the audits of these two entities would have produced a high risk profile for each entity and perhaps have led to some limited footnote disclosures that would have communicated more effectively the entities' investment risk. In the United American case, it appears that audi-

[21] Paul A. Gigot, "Big Fraud Verdict Against Andersen Shakes Up Accounting Profession," *Wall Street Journal*, February 3, 1982, p. 27; and Tamar Lewin, "Arthur Andersen Liability Is Reduced," *New York Times*, July 20, 1982, p. 4.

EXHIBIT 5-3

United American and Penn Square—Could Analytical Review Have Detected These Debacles?

Industry Knowledge

- The comptroller of the currency ranks banks on a 1 to 5 scale in which 1 and 2 are sound, 3 is weak, 4 is unsafe, and 5 is a serious risk of failing. About 92 percent of national banks are ranked 1 and 2. In October 1982, 15 banks were ranked 5, 49 were ranked 4, 299 were ranked 3, and 4130 were ranked 1 and 2.
- In the recent past, the number of bank examiner positions has declined by 12 percent, causing banks with less than $1 billion in assets to receive less coverage by examiners. Yet all troubled banks are examined at least once a year, with a follow-up on progress concerning examiners' comments within that same year.
- Federal Banking Law in 1978 restricted direct loans to executives, setting limits of
  - $60,000 for mortgages
  - up to $20,000 for educational purposes
  - $10,000 for consumer loans

  Under this regulation, each bank designates which officers come under this lending limit restriction.
- Another overall restriction is that banks may not lend more than 10 percent of their capital to any one party.

United American Bank of Knoxville, Tennessee

- $178.3 million of the bank's problem loans, according to the FDIC, were not correctly classified as partly or totally uncollectable; a substantial number were related to World's Fair-related projects.
- In 1976, the bank changed from a national to a state bank; both state and federal regulators say that Jake F. Butcher (chairman of the World's Fair and head of United American), with his brother's help, often tried to foil regulators by bouncing loans among their institutions, e.g., by transferring some problem loans to a related institution not being examined.
- On November 1, the day after the fair closed, more than 100 FDIC examiners descended on Butcher's banks.
- After closing the bank on February 14, 1983, state banking commissioner revealed that "about $337 million, or roughly half its assets in loans" were partly or totally uncollectable; nearly 43 percent of these had not been on the books in November 1981 during a FDIC exam, according to regulators.
- More than 40 percent of loans were reported to have been made to 8 Butcher associates and their interests.
- Poor documentation and scant collateral are reported for "parachute loans" from Jake's office; one borrower did not own 4 of the 58 lots listed as collateral.

Penn Square

- Penn Square had capital of $35 million and from 1974 to 1981 experienced a growth from $35 million in assets to $525 million; 80 percent of the loans were energy related.
- $2.5 billion of energy-related loans were made with $2 billion sold to major "upstream" banks with the tacit guarantee that they would be repurchased on demand.
- Loans were based on 75 percent of the gross value of claimed proven reserves of oil and gas as collateral.
- Some problem loans were sold to Clifford Resources to whom, concurrently, new loans were extended. As problem loans proliferated, the bank made principal and interest payments on behalf of delinquent borrowers to large correspondent banks. In 1981, $2 million in payments were made; in 1982, $10 million in payments were made.
- All directors had loans; one had $200 million in loans.
- An estimated 20 percent of problem loans involved insiders.
- In January 1981, Penn Square was classified as number 3; from the beginning of 1980 through July 1982, the comptroller's office performed 5 exams.
- Top management instructed its own internal auditors not to review many of the energy-related loans.
- The comptroller said that instead of 15 percent, the external auditors should have looked at 80 percent of the outstanding loans.

Note: Case facts are adapted from media coverage in *The Wall Street Journal* and *The New York Times.*

tors' inquiries directed toward regulators, prompted by the regulators' unusually high number of reviews, might have uncovered the breadth of the problem and led to a qualified audit opinion. The research to date supports the CPAs' expectation that the issuance of "subject to" opinions when contingencies are resolved unfavorably for the client should at least moderately improve an auditor's defensive position.[22]

A long-term trend analysis of interest expenses for Penn Square might have identified the increasing loan payments to other banks, intended to cover up its collectibility problems. Shortly after the World's Fair opened, there was evidence available to the public that a shortfall from projected revenues was likely. Yet the loss reserves in the statements issued just before the bank's failure did not reflect this. The lesson from these two engagements is that CPAs should give more consideration to a business approach to audits, the use of analytical review tools, and the role of related parties as a means of reducing both audit and litigation risk.

The message stressed herein is a need for a more rapid evolution of auditing technology, as will be discussed in later chapters. Such techniques can be directed at assessing aggregate reasonableness through such modeling approaches as regression analysis and tie-in to industry data bases. The increasing availability of EDP hardware and software facilitates such evolution. However, the points of contention in the pending litigation are far more traditional in nature and merit a review.

The Federal Deposit Insurance Corporation (FDIC) is now suing Peat, Marwick, Mitchell & Co. for more than $130 million, charging that the firm failed to conduct a proper audit of the Penn Square Bank. The claim involves an ethical question, as the charges cite that the partners in Peat Marwick's Oklahoma City office compromised the firm's independence by accepting, directly and indirectly, more than $1 million in loans from Penn Square. Peat Marwick officials point out that the loans were made before the firm was retained as the bank's accountants and that Penn Square was advised to sell these loans to other banks and did so. The FDIC's other complaints criticize the auditors' evaluation of Penn Square's lending policies, the audit team's size and experience level, and the fact that the audit team did not urge the bank to set up a sufficiently large reserve against loan losses. The FDIC has declined the audit firm's offer to settle the dispute by binding arbitration or to have its work on the loan-loss reserve reviewed by another major accounting firm.[23]

Besides this litigation directed at Penn Square, a shareholder derivative suit against Continental Illinois Bank for its reckless handling of lending and misleading financials, tied to its relationship with the Penn Square Bank, led to Judge Grady's "tentative finding" that Ernst & Whinney, its auditor, should be included as a defendant. This finding was made despite an investigation by Price Waterhouse that gave Ernst & Whinney a relatively clean bill of health for its performance.[24]

The Benefit of Hindsight in Reviewing Past Court Cases

As litigation cases are reviewed, there is a tendency to be extremely critical of the audit team and to think that you would never make such a mistake. Yet hindsight is twenty-twenty vision, much as the Monday morning quarterback always would play a better game than did the real quarterback the day before. One way of appreciating the problems that auditors have faced is to consider the problems that auditors now face largely because of current business developments that have posed new accounting questions for which there are, as yet, no generally accepted accounting principles.

[22] This perception was held by 80.1 percent of the 232 responding CPAs. See Jesse F. Dillard, Richard J. Murdock, and John K. Shank, "CPAs' Attitudes Toward 'Subject to' Opinions," *CPA Journal*, August 1978, pp. 43–47.

[23] Edwin A. Finn, Jr., "FDIC Sues Peat Marwick for $130 Million over Its Audit of Failed Penn Square Bank," *Wall Street Journal*, December 13, 1984, p. 6.

[24] John Helyar, "Continental Illinois Holder Suit May See Two Bankers, Auditor Added As Defendants," *Wall Street Journal*, July 1, 1983, p. 2.

Health Spa Revenue Realization

Many business failures and related litigation concern questions of revenue realization. In hindsight, they look obvious in substance, and accountants have been criticized for their apparent attention to mere form. Yet, envision yourself as the auditor of various clients in the health spa industry. The common industry practice is to book revenue when it is collected, when customers "join" the health spa. But this practice makes you feel uneasy when you notice that a few clients appear to have "overbooked" their facilities. If all their members used the services to which they were entitled through membership, the health spa would not be able to meet its commitments. In fact, the members could not even fit in the spa, let alone enjoy its equipment and sauna. When the auditor realizes this and asks the client about the reasonableness of the revenue realization practice, the client may answer, "But, it's normal industry practice, and so it's unfair for you to ask that I use some other valuation approach." How should or can the CPA react? It's been reported that a stand was taken by some CPAs which led to their loss of several health spa clients—such loss is sometimes interpreted as clients "shopping around for an auditor," thereby impugning the standards and the consistency of their application by the profession. Yet the basic problem is often the absence of standards or principles, as reflected by the BarChris and Continental Vending cases described earlier.

The strategy that some CPA firms followed was to limit the number of health spa clients they accepted, in order to control any risk exposure stemming from the industry's revenue realization practices. At the same time, they urged the American Institute of Certified Public Accountants (AICPA) and the Financial Accounting Standards Board to establish guidelines that would support a shift toward what appeared to be a more reasonable revenue realization approach to accounting for health spa revenue. Eventually, the AICPA issued a Statement of Position, and the generally accepted accounting principles for the health spa industry shifted toward recognizing revenue with the passage of time, as it was earned. This approach to health spa revenue is analogous to that commonly used for newspapers' subscription revenue and appears to be more in line with the substance of the earnings process. The question to contemplate is what position you would have taken before the development of official guidance.

Product Financing and Repurchase Arrangements

There is a similar problem in defining an accounting treatment that would be consistent with the substance of transactions in the area of product financing and repurchase arrangements. For example, assume that a producer of goods decides that it wants to subcontract some of the production of its goods. The company thus draws up a sales agreement to transfer the necessary raw materials with a repurchase commitment, thereby financing the subcontractor's work. The agreement's sales form is used as a basis for recording current revenue, although the alternative revenue stream of interest is the final sale of the goods. In form, the accounting treatment seems clear; yet in substance a sale has not occurred. The whole funding transaction was intended to facilitate the production of required goods and was part of the company's whole financing plan. The repurchase agreement seems to clarify this fact. But once again, there was a gap between when the policy setters' pronouncements were issued and when practitioners had to decide on the propriety of the reported numbers. Pretend that you are a CPA, without a FASB statement as support, and then consider the innovative approaches to designing repurchase agreements that appeared to have enough risk to the seller and buyer that a sale could be claimed to have occurred. It should now be clear that deciding what a "fair" presentation is, is not easy.

GAAP Compliance As a Defense

There are conflicting precedents for relying on GAAP as the auditor's defense. Complying with GAAP seems to have been accepted as a complete defense in *Shahmoon* v. *General Development Corp.* And not complying with GAAP did not result in liability for the accountants in *Franklin Supply Co.* v. *Tolman* and *Bunge* v. *Eide*. Yet the *Herzfeld* opinion emphasized that full disclosure duties "cannot be fulfilled merely by following generally accepted accounting principles." The court quoted from an article by a SEC staff member which stated: "While adherence to generally accepted accounting principles is a tool to help achieve that end, it is not necessarily a guarantee of fairness."[25] This finding is consistent with those for the *BarChris* and *Simon* cases. Similarly, "In the Matter of Associated Gas & Electric Company," 1942, the SEC stated:

> Each of the accountants' certificates in question contained the opinion that subject to various qualifications therein, the financial statements fairly presented the financial condition of the registrant, in accordance with generally accepted accounting principles. If that basic representation was not accurate as to the financial statements as a whole, no weight of precedent or practice with respect to the minutiae of the statements could justify the accountants' certificates. . . . For the average investor the financial statements of this system contain not a hint of the rot hidden beneath the surface of this holding company system.[26]

A Case Example

To stress the difficulty of uncovering those problems that lead to unfavorable press coverage for auditors and, perhaps, to litigation, consider the widely publicized case of H. J. Heinz. A synopsis of the problem is presented in Exhibit 5-4. In addition, the exhibit cites the critical press coverage and the substantive tests an auditor would be likely to apply in such an audit and yet still not discover the improprieties that were present. With the benefit of hindsight, I suggest in the exhibit some audit procedures that might have revealed the problem. However, if you objectively consider the information you would have gathered, it is probable that you'll realize that you could very well have been the auditor that "missed" the defalcation from 1971 to 1979. To reiterate a point that has been apparent in numerous court cases and is stressed in Exhibit 5-4, a business approach to a client, emphasizing analytical review procedures, holds much promise for the auditor in controlling both audit and litigation risk.

The Role of Litigation

Litigation has influenced the standards of audit practice, has communicated society's expectations, and has led to reforms in accounting disclosure policies. Many consider it an important quality control over the profession, although some suits that have attempted to make CPAs responsible for business losses because of their deep pockets—as distinct from an audit failure—have been cited as threatening the profession's existence. The principal categories of plaintiffs have been (1) shareholder suits—both individual and class action; (2) derivative suits—by the shareholder on behalf of the company; (3) client suits, including trustees in bankruptcies; (4) creditor litigation, with banks, like surety and fidelity companies, becoming more aggressive; (5) governmental groups like state boards of accountancy; and (6) the SEC.[27]

A Historical Perspective

Much of American law has English precedents. The first English case involving an auditor is reported to have been *Leeds Estate Building and Investment Co.* v. *Shepherd*, decided in 1887, which essentially held that auditors are responsible for checking the substance of transactions, not merely their arithmetical accuracy. The earliest American case dealing with a CPA's liability to a third party was in 1919: *Landell* v. *Lybrand*. This case held that negligence without an intent to deceive was not sufficient as a basis for a third party to receive damages from an auditor.[28] Since then the number of law suits against auditors has risen sharply. In 1966, it was reported that in the United States about

[25] *Herzfeld* v. *Laventhol, Krekstein, Horwath & Horwath*, 540 F. 2d 27 (2d Cir. 1976).

[26] *SEC Decisions and Reports* (Washington, D.C.: Government Printing Office), vol. 11, pp. 1058–1059.

[27] Carl Liggio, "Litigation and the Accounting Profession," seminar sponsored by Arthur Young, Chicago, 1979.

[28] Denzil Y. Causey, Jr., *Duties and Liabilities of Public Accountants* (Homewood, Ill.: Dow Jones–Irwin, 1979), pp. 63, 113.

EXHIBIT 5-4

H. J. Heinz Case: With the Advantage of Hindsight. . . .

Synopsis

By colluding with at least 6 suppliers, legal fees, advertising, and market research expenses were manipulated from 1971 to 1979. Bogus invoices were prepared upon request. If services were not subsequently rendered, prior cash payments were returned to Heinz. Sales cutoff was also manipulated by adjusting internal documentation. Over 325 employees were aware of the impropriety, perpetrated in large part for the purpose of maximizing managers' bonus-incentive awards.

The Dilemma

The Wall Street Journal reported

> "... it is unclear how the improper accounting practices escaped the notice of ..., Heinz's auditors for the entire period of the improprieties"
>
> (November 23, 1979)

Which Substantive Tests Could Not Discover These Improprieties?

- Confirmations to vendors
- Normal cutoff tests
- Tests directed at overstatement of revenues and income and understatement of expenses
- Inquiry and observation procedures
- Those tests emphasizing large account balances, such as inventory
- Year to year comparisons from 1972 through 1979

What Analytical Review Procedures, Outlined in SAS 23, Might Have Detected the Improprieties?

- Ratio analysis, comparing the percentage relationship of marketing, advertising, and legal expenses to sales across divisions, as well as comparing such divisional ratios to industry statistics
- In 1971 and possibly 1972, a comparison of multi-year historical patterns, pre-1971
- In the course of formulating structural models, the five-year business plans may have been reviewed by the CPA, offering the chance of detecting one strong clue of the problem: "Pre-billed Advertising Invoice" for services it paid for but did not receive, on Ore-Ida's 1974, 1975, and 1976 reports
- Comparison to budget at the end of the first two months of each quarter could indicate much more variance on a monthly basis than a quarterly basis
- A comparison of the division's pattern of payment practices across vendors
- The business background required for analytical review procedures would increase the CPA's awareness of the smoothing incentives and division's autonomy in reporting, thereby encouraging two-sided check of balances in miscellaneous accounts which have a weaker audit trail, i.e., purchases of services, which typically lack shipping and receiving documentation, and the use of data external to a single division when performing analytical review

From Wanda A. Wallace, "Analytical Review: Misconceptions, Applications, and Experience – Part II," *CPA Journal*, February 1983, p. 22.

100 lawsuits were pending against CPA firms,[29] and in June 1968, *Fortune* magazine[30] reported that the number of suits filed against auditors in the past twelve months equaled the total for the previous twelve years. Between 1972 and 1975, 60 percent of the 237 cases surveyed for the Cohen Commission were stockholder suits; 8 percent were creditor suits; 6.4 percent involved acquiring corporations; 8 percent were individual stockholder suits; 4 percent were trustees in bankruptcy; 10 percent were client suits; and the remainder were difficult to classify. More than 70 percent were 10b-5 cases (seventy-eight were filed under the 1933 act): 74 percent attacking audited financial statements, 5 percent involving unaudited financial statements, 16 percent involving prospectuses, 13 percent annual reports, and 10 percent proxies. Improper acts of management were claimed not to have been disclosed in 30 of the 237 cases studied by the Cohen Commission.[31] Consider Exhibit 5-5. These

[29] "Auditors' Critics Seek Wider, Faster Action in Reform of Practices," *Wall Street Journal*, November 15, 1966, p. 13.

[30] Arthur M. Louis, "The Accountants Are Changing the Rules," *Fortune*, June 15, 1968, p. 177.

[31] Cohen Commission "Survey Claim Summary" (New York: Crossley Surveys, Inc., August 1975)—File #15503.

EXHIBIT 5-5

A Sample of Auditor-Related Litigation Attracting Wide Media Attention

Case	Claim
U.S. Financial Inc. (1974)	Auditor was negligent in failing to discover management fraud; mandatory peer review was required; and the SEC stressed the importance of communication between predecessor and successor auditors.
Four Season Nursing Centers (1972)	Misleading financial reports were issued.
National Student Marketing (United States v. *Natelli)* (1975)	False statements appeared in a 1969 proxy statement: failure to disclose the write-off of uncollectable accounts.
Franklin Supply Co. v. *Tolman* (1972)	Nondisclosure of audit supervisor's membership on the acquired firm's board of directors and alternate directorship of the selling firm, as well as nondisclosure of the meaning of current replacement value, constituted fraud. (Judgment: no legal fraud, only negligence – fees returned as damages.)
Gulf & Western Ind. Inc. v. *Great Atlantic & Pacific Tea Co., Inc.* (1973)	Nondisclosure of unasserted claims, i.e., potential violation of antitrust laws, affected fairness of presentation.
Herzfeld v. *Laventhol, Krekstein, Horwath & Horwath* (1974)	A "subject to realization" qualification was not a satisfactory communication as to the doubtful collectability of receivables.
McLean v. *Alexander* (1979)	Receivables reported as "Considered Fully Collectable" were really consignment sales, almost 90 percent of which were not confirmed, making statements misleading. (1977 judgment concluded that scienter was not present.)
United States v. *Benjamin* (1964)	Due diligence was not exercised in reviewing pro forma financial statements (case filed under Section 24 of 1933 act and represented a criminal conviction).
Westec Corporation (Ernst & Ernst) (1967)	Independence of auditors was questioned, as was the application of GAAP, owing to auditors' heavy involvement in structuring the pooling that led to over 100 percent of reported earnings.
Ryan v. *Kanne* (1969)	Accountants were liable to party, whom they knew intended to rely on the accounting statement, for negligent failure to determine amount of accounts payable in manner agreed upon, though statement was not certified.
White v. *Guarente* (1977)	Accountant retained by a limited partnership to perform auditing and tax return services is responsible for negligence to an identifiable group of limited partners, as they are foreseeable users of the information provided.
Bonhiver v. *Graff* (1976)	Accountant was liable under 10(b) for unaudited financials to the client and a nonclient insurance agent for unaudited financials that disclosed liability for the financing of equipment without revealing that the equipment was unusable and a judgment against the seller was uncollectable.

cases have been diverse, involving claims of nondisclosure, misrepresentation, inadequate audit or specified procedures, and a lack of auditor independence. The expense items emphasized in the 237 suits studied by the Cohen Commission were bad debts and the cost of goods sold (39 and 23 cases, respectively), with unrecorded liabilities at issue in 24 cases and contingent liabilities at issue in 25 cases. In the *Adams* v. *Standard Knitting Mills, Inc.* case, the court found Rule 10b-5 liability because of the auditors' failure to disclose EDP deficiencies, even though the financial statements were not themselves misleading. Although this decision was changed on appeal, it implies future responsibility related to controls. One Big Eight firm estimated in 1979 that about 115 lawsuits had been filed against it since 1969, claiming some sort of malpractice. At one time the claimed amounts for these suits totaled $589 million. About 80 of these suits were dismissed without any contribution by the CPA firm. Six cases were tried and won; four cases were settled for a total of $1.8 million. Three were settled without the CPAs' contribution, and three were dismissed but are being appealed by the plaintiffs. Others were still in process. Survey results collected by the Cohen Commission reflect the growing number of lawsuits during the 1970s: in 1972, 27 were reported, in 1973, 59 were reported, in 1974, 86 had been filed, and in the first six months of 1975, 65 had been filed, with the peak occurring in 1976. Of course, while most were single cases, some cases had three or more suits filed. In fact, a total of 117 suits were eventually filed related just to Equity Funding.[32]

After 1976, the number of claims began to level off. One reason claimed to be a contributor to the decline in the number of cases is the increasing willingness of CPAs to "fight back" against the litigious trends of investors filing suits to recover business losses and regulators filing apparent nonsense suits.

The Advent of In-House General Counsel: "Fighting Back"

The larger CPA firms have formed in-house legal departments to help defend them against litigation. The first in-house lawyer was hired by Peat, Marwick in 1968, and Arthur Young reported a growth in its legal department from one lawyer in December 1972 to four lawyers in a department of forty by 1979. Instead of merely turning over all working papers when a subpoena is served, CPA firms now require that the issues being raised be specified, so that only relevant working papers are made available. This helps deter the plaintiffs from going on "fishing expeditions" through the working papers, looking for something unclear or in error.

The harassment element of subpoenas (in the late 1970's one Big Eight firm reported that it averaged 200 subpoenas per year) has also been responded to by the profession. One story that has been told at seminars on litigation-related matters is of a request by a regulator that all workpapers be made available, three days before the close of the audit. The CPA explained that meeting such a request would mean that the filing requirements of the client would not be met and that the causes of the delay would be made public by the client and the CPA firm, in order to ensure that the regulators were held responsible for the results of their actions. On second thought, the regulators decided to adjust the subpoena to permit the working papers to be submitted after the audit had been completed.

While very few firms contested charges leveled against them by the SEC in the past, by 1979 a discernible increase in the amount of contested litigation was reported. Some firms have decided that they would rather fight than settle. Causes of this attitude were cited to be losses by the SEC in trying to get novel interpretations of the securities laws accepted by the courts, as well as the Commission's efforts to extract tougher settlements, thereby raising doubts about the conventional wisdom that firms are better off settling. Of course, the firms' win–loss record's mixed, but court findings have included such statements as "there is a wide gap between the SEC's claim and the proof" (Federal Court case in Washington D.C. involving Mr. Wills, a former GAC executive). This GeoTek victory of Arthur Young exemplified firms' capability of demonstrating that charges did not constitute guilt.[33]

Another aggressive move by CPA firms has been to sue its clients in order to recover suit costs and damages, based on management's giving materially wrong information to the auditors. It appears that these actions, exemplified by Arthur Young's case against SCA Service, Inc., have dampened the clients' tendency to file suits against their CPA firms.

However, the most vivid evidence of CPAs "fighting back" can be seen in the filing for indemnification from plaintiffs for their costs and expenses of litigation. This is permitted under laws of Kansas, the Bahamas, the federal securities laws, and in some states besides Kansas. Arthur Young was awarded $466,260.65 indemnity in *Koch Industries v. Vosko* (1974).

From 1973 to 1975, the total number of security suits were 2,000 and of those involving financial data, 60 percent involved the CPA firm. In 1979, it was far less common for CPA firms to be named. In-house legal departments claim that CPAs' rep-

[32] Ibid.

[33] Stan Crock, "Fighting It Out: More of SEC's Targets Are Going Into Court Rather Than Settling," *Wall Street Journal*, July 16, 1979, p. 1.

utation for litigating rather than settling is a primary reason for such a shift.

Projections

In the future, the legal environment will be largely determined by society's demands. Some have noted that social and economic philosophies toward consumerism have set into motion legal liability by any expert involved to the consuming group. The *Herzfeld* v. *Laventhol, Krekstein, Horwath & Horwath* case has been cited as favoring consumers, because—despite the plaintiff's statement that the auditor's report and footnote had not been read and, in fact, were not available on the investment date—the court ruled that the auditors were the probable cause of the damage.[34]

The courts have increasingly socialized risks and harms, protecting consumers against losses. They are prone to place the risk of error in certified financial statements on those who are able to "socialize" the fees or insurance premium. In fact, by the end of 1984, some observed that recent court decisions may be spurring more liability suits against CPA firms. In particular, a 1983 decision by the New Jersey Supreme Court involving a suit against Touche Ross for their audit of Giant Stores Corp. (cited earlier) has been interpreted by the general counsel of Arthur Young & Co. as saying that the existence of liability insurance justifies pursuing a claim against the accounting firm.[35]

The *BarChris, Continental Vending, Yale Express,* and *Westec* cases are cited as being likely to give to those plaintiffs not in a contractual relationship with accountants easier access to accountants than they had under common law. These cases' commentaries on officers', directors', and other professionals' responsibility for financial statements appearing in prospectuses and related documents are expected to increase awareness of such responsibilities and risks and lead to requests for accountants to expand their attest function.[36]

One legal counselor to a Big Eight firm noted his belief that Statement on Auditing Standards No. 16 calling for a search for irregularities increases the possibility of auditor suits and even described the pronouncement as the "death wish of the accounting profession." It is clear that the role of standards is debatable.

Auditing standards or procedures were contested in 91 of the 267 cases studied by the Cohen Commission. Litigation has influenced GAAS, as has the SEC; a review of U.S. Financial (ASR [now FRR] No. 153), as an example, has led to more awareness of related party and affiliated transactions.

Precedents are established when compliance with generally accepted auditing standards has been accepted as a complete defense. Such precedents are also established when a demonstrated noncompliance with GAAS and/or GAAP has not led to liability. But if professional standards are judged to be insufficient or if financial statements are deemed to be materially misleading, it is clear that mere compliance with GAAS and GAAP cannot be relied on to save the auditors from liability.

One probable source of increased litigation are surety companies' claims. In 1979, one CPA firm reported that a third of its claims were by surety companies. Similarly, more banks are filing suits against CPAs, and whenever economic conditions worsen, these types of suits tend to grow.

Often, the best indicators of the future are experiences of the past. Research of 334 errors in 129 cases filed from 1960 to 1976 resulted in the following summary analysis:

Errors involving disclosure	60
Errors involving GAAP	49
Errors involving GAAS	51
Errors involving audit procedures	97
Errors involving client fraud	42
Errors involving auditors' fraud	24
Other	11
	334

Only 5 percent of the errors were caused by poor estimates, while 48 percent were errors of inter-

[34] Carl D. Liggio, "Expanding Concepts of Accountant's Liability," *California CPA Quarterly,* September 1974, pp. 18–23.

[35] Lee Berton, "Insurers Tell Big Accounting Concerns Liability Rates May Rise, Sources Say," *Wall Street Journal,* November 8, 1984, p. 4.

[36] Henry B. Reiling and Russell A. Taussig, "Recent Liability Cases—Implications of Accountants," *Journal of Accountancy,* September 1970, pp. 39–53.

pretation. Problems with overreliance on management were identified. The researchers stressed that a general attitude of skepticism and caution in dealing with management representations can be recommended based on an analysis of past legal cases.[37]

Past research involving 236 Rule 10b-5 class action suits filed after 1967, identified 67 cases involving one predominant reporting error. In analyzing these errors, 43 percent involved misrepresentations, while 57 percent involved misestimations. The average error size per share for the types of errors analyzed ranged from $.40 to $9.81. The types of errors analyzed indicated that 31 percent failed to disclose fraud, 25.5 percent involved the over-valuation of assets, 10.5 percent related to overstated revenues, and 21 percent involved inadequate loan loss reserves. A study of the market effects of litigation related to failures of reported financial information in reflecting accurate estimates of future events indicated that there were considerable declines in the market values of defendant firms during the period of the errors, as well as the public announcement of such errors. These findings have been tied to auditors' apparent "deep pocket" insurance-type role, as well as to auditors' preference for historical cost-based reports over movements away from historical cost valuation.[38]

Auditors must strive not to place excessive reliance on management, to maintain their objectivity, and to understand affiliates' transactions. Consultations and audit work should be documented, because even if an audit conclusion is wrong, if it was done in good faith, it is expected to be an effective defense (at least in 10b-5 cases).

In describing good faith duty, *SEC* v. *Republic National Life Insurance Co.* (378 F. Supp. 430, 440 (S.D.N.Y., 1974)) states that an "accountant is not a guarantor of the reports he prepares and is only duty bound to act honestly in good faith and with reasonable care in the discharge of his professional obligations."

Perhaps the best advice was offered by Arthur Andersen, as reported in *The First 50 Years:* "When confronted with the necessity for a decision on a difficult question of policy with respect to financial statements, the accountant should search his conscience rather than the statutes."[39] This realization, coupled with complete and well-organized documentation, is most likely to offer an effective defense to professionals involved in future litigation.

The International Scene

Liability exposure is not limited to the United States as a concern of professionals. In fact, insurance companies ranked countries in the late 1970's and indicated that Australia had the highest liability exposure, the United States was second, the United Kingdom was third, and Canada assumed the fourth position. Many Big Eight firms stress that they are world-wide firms and, as a result, are being sued by international banks in cases involving independent operating sections of the firms.[40] At least 260 legal opinions outside of the United States have involved auditors.

The Size of Claims

In analyzing cases surveyed by the Cohen Commission for the 1972 to 1975 time period, more than 60 of the 237 cases claimed punitive damages. Three of these cases sought damages of under $100,000, thirty-two claimed between $100,000 to $500,000, forty-three claimed one-half to $2 million, sixty claimed $2 to $10 million, thirty claimed $10 to $30 million, 19 claimed $30 million to $100 million, and 14 claimed over $100 million.

Beyond dollar claims is the exposure faced in the form of defense costs. Arthur Young estimated that its defense in the GeoTek Resources case cost $3.5 million. Of this, $2.2 million were for outside legal costs, and the remainder involved identifiable time spent internally and charged at normal billing rates.

[37] Kent St. Pierre and James Anderson, "An Analysis of Audit Failures Based on Documented Legal Cases," *Journal of Accounting, Auditing & Finance,* Spring, 1982, pp. 229–247.

[38] Robert L. Kellogg, "Thesis Proposal: An Empirical Study of Rule 10b-5 Buyers' Suits Based Upon Accounting Errors," Graduate School of Management, University of Rochester, January, 1979.

[39] Arthur Andersen & Co., 1963, p. 110.

[40] For example, see Jim Drinkhall, "Suit Prompted by Failure of Bahamas Bank Puts Accounting Industry on Trial," *Wall Street Journal,* February 17, 1981, pp. 33, 39.

One problem is that small CPA firms can have the same exposure as the big CPA firm due to the way damages are determined. An example of a good-sized client involved in a 10b-5 case with a smaller CPA firm that had limited liability coverage was Sheffield Watch Corporation. The class claimed an $8 million loss, with three lending institutions having losses of $4 million. The CPA firm had fewer than 7 partners. Similarly, Generics involved four banks' claims of $14 million, and Amer Bio involved $11 million of claims against smaller CPA firms. Beyond the problem of the size of claims, are the manpower difficulties of small accounting firms in facing claims. Time is not available to maintain one's practice and concurrently prepare to battle litigation. In addition, defense can be more difficult due to the impression of a lack of independence. For example, in the Amer Bio case, 6 auditing problems were resolved in favor of the client, which represented 60 percent of the CPA firm's income.

Obviously, claims, in part, are determinants of liability insurance premiums; however, what factors seem to drive these claims? Research concerning actuaries' perceptions of what affects auditors' liability indicates strong consensus that the risk of litigation increases when CPAs' clients have a weak financial condition. A positive relationship between increased risk of lawsuits and the size of both the accounting firm and the client was also detected. No significant effects on such risk were indicated for the CPA firm's practice of rotating auditors among clients or the relative amount of write-up work performed. These findings, in part, provide a rationale from more rigorous quality standards in larger firms and within any firm, more rigorous standards for larger clients. The latter is likely to be warranted due to the role of SEC-related litigation.[41]

Professional Liability Insurance and Self-insurance

The professional liability insurance market is rather limited, and so there is no insurance for some kinds of suits. For example, in 1979, domestic insurance companies did not cover SEC-related litigation costs, and many policies excluded punitive damages and fraud. Carriers want to use the past to predict future claims, but because of the irregularity of large and catastrophic losses, many insurers have gotten out of the market. For example, how does one forecast an Equity Funding? Originally, insurance policies applied to acts committed during the coverage period, but owing to the time lag in filing suits and its effects on projection, such acts were not well defined, and there were disputes over whether an act resulted in a claim. The insurance companies thus shifted to insuring only "claims made" during the period of coverage. In other words, there is no insurance for unasserted claims, which has become a big problem for smaller CPA firms but helps the insurance companies both evaluate and control the "long-tail" liability business. And a discovery clause can be added to cover unasserted claims for a set period beyond the date when a policy is terminated. Most CPA firms begin with a policy of $10 million to $20 million and then buy separate policies to supplement this. Lloyd's of London is usually the insurance carrier for larger CPA firms, and state-sponsored society programs are offered to smaller CPA firms. An idea of the professional liability coverage of large firms and its related cost is provided by the reported experience of Arthur Young. The firm emphasizes that the premiums collected by insurers did not cover the claims for accountants through 1978 and that a major reason why insurance is available at all is that self-insurance is a common practice, helping to level off the claims against insurance companies. In 1968, a $5,000 deductible Lloyds of London Policy cost $60,000 in premiums for $20 million of coverage, and Arthur Young also invested $30,000 to $40,000 in legal fees. By 1978, a $929,000 deductible was set, with a $3.3 million dollar premium, and $5 million self-insurance was established beyond the deductible. Over $1.2 million was spent on internal legal costs, and up to $2.8 million on outside legal fees. In 1979, the premium was adjusted to $2.1 million dollars with an $800,000 deductible. This provides $60 million liability coverage. The decrease in premium was, in

[41] Joseph J. Schultz, Jr. and Sandra G. Gustavson, "Actuaries' Perceptions of Variables Affecting the Independent Auditor's Legal Liability," *Accounting Review*, July, 1978, pp. 626–641.

part, attributed to the firm's experience, quality controls, client portfolio, and investment in its legal defense.[42] The maximum coverage by the Big Eight firms in 1979 was reported to be $100 million, with most firms carrying around $75 million in coverage. In 1984, it was reported that in addition to the primary layer of $10 to $20 million coverage from Lloyd's, added "excess" layers of as much as $200 million or more are written by Lloyd's, U.S., or European insurers for the Big Eight accounting firms. The cost of such excess lines has been projected as possibly doubling in 1985, with some firms' loss of as much as 25 percent of their excess coverage, due to the tightening capacity for all liability and casualty insurance.[43] Given a 1979 premium for $60 million liability coverage, with an $800,000 deductible of $2.1 million,[44] this increase significantly affects the cost structure of public accounting firms.

The AICPA Committee on Insurance in the late 1970's suggested that CPA firms with fewer than 5 SEC clients maintain $2 million coverage. A recent brochure on available professional liability policies indicated that for a staff of 31, a $2 million liability limit with a $5,000 deductible per claim would cost from $3,155 to $6,649 annually, assuming that substantial SEC services are not provided. The 15-man accounting firm would be expected to carry $5 to $10 million coverage with a deductible of about $2,500. One survey conducted in 1973 reported that 681 of 2,191 firms with a staff of 50 or less carried only $100,000 of insurance; only 250 had over a million dollars of coverage.[45] A professional involved in defending claims against CPA firms said that the generic problem of smaller firms is that they have no realization of the dollar amount of exposure. Generically, the situation faced was $1 million coverage with total losses claimed of $14 million.

In addition to professional liability insurance, self-insurance is a necessary cost of doing business. In order to ensure their firms' financial viability, CPAs must be familiar with past liability consequences and variations in the insurance coverage provided by various professional liability policies. Many smaller firms, in light of such knowledge, have stopped servicing SEC clients and have even stopped offering audit services, because they have decided that liability exposure from tax, advisory, and nonaudit services is a more manageable cost than is that from auditing.

A Summary

Exhibit 5-6 summarizes auditors' responsibilities and lists a few of the key litigation cases that influenced such legal exposure. These legal responsibilities also relate to nonaudit services.

COURT CASES CITED

In order of appearance:

Landell v. *Lybrand,* 264 Pa. 406, 107 Atl. 783 (1919)
Ultramares Corp. v. *Touche,* 255 N.Y. 170, 174 N.E. 441 (1931)
State Street Trust Co. v. *Ernst,* 278 N.Y. 104, 15 N.E. 2d 416 (1938)
Rusch Factors, Inc. v. *Levin,* 284 F. Supp. 85(D.R.I. 1968)
Escott v. *BarChris Construction Corp.,* 283 F. Supp. 643, 703 (S.D.N.Y., 1968)
Rhode Island Hospital Trust National Bank v. *Swartz,* 455 F. 2nd 847 (4th Cir. 1972)
McLean v. *Alexander,* 420 F. Supp. 1057 (D.Del. 1976)
SEC v. *Texas Gulf Sulphur Co.,* 401 F. 2d 833 (2d Cir. 1968) cert. denied, 349 U.S. 976 (1969)
State Mutual Life Assurance Company v. *Peat, Marwick, Mitchell & Company,* 49 F.R.D. 202, 213 (S.D.N.Y. 1969)
Ernst & Ernst v. *Hochfelder,* 425 U.S., 185 (1976)
SEC Accounting Series Release No. 19, "In the Matter of McKesson & Robbins, Inc." (1940)

[42] Verbal Presentation in Chicago at a Symposium sponsored by Arthur Young, "Litigation and the Accounting Profession," 1979.

[43] Lee Berton, "Insurers Tell Big Accounting Concerns Liability Rates May Rise, Sources Say," *Wall Street Journal,* November 8, 1984, p. 4.

[44] Verbal Presentation in Chicago at a Symposium sponsored by Arthur Young, "Litigation and the Accounting Profession," 1979.

[45] Richard S. Helstein, "Guidelines for Professional Liability Insurance Coverage," *CPA Journal,* October, 1973, pp. 849–857.

EXHIBIT 5-6
The Accountant's Legal Exposure

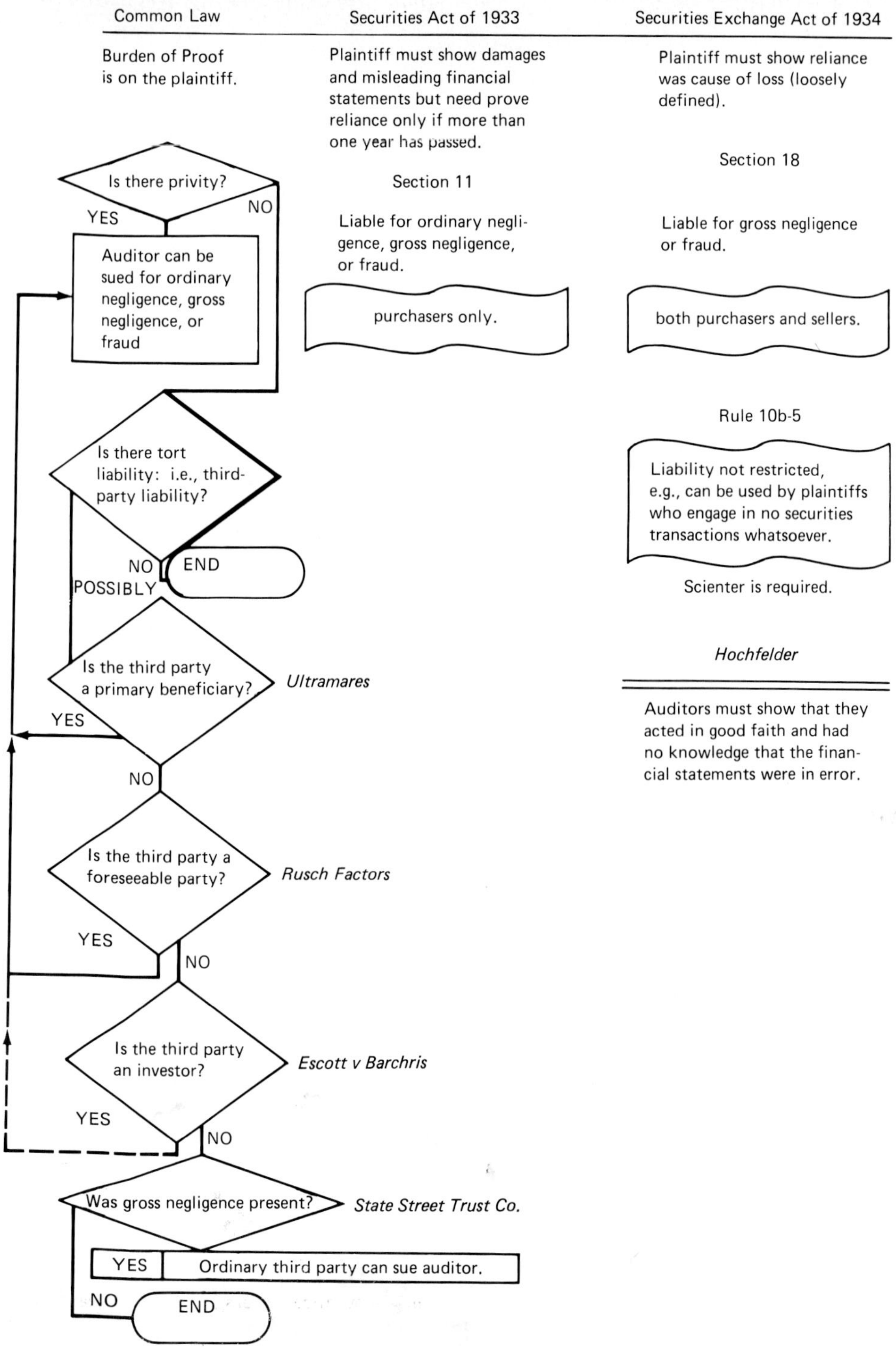

Common Law	Securities Act of 1933	Securities Exchange Act of 1934
Burden of Proof is on the plaintiff.	Plaintiff must show damages and misleading financial statements but need prove reliance only if more than one year has passed.	Plaintiff must show reliance was cause of loss (loosely defined).

Is there privity?
YES
NO
Auditor can be sued for ordinary negligence, gross negligence, or fraud
Is there tort liability: i.e., third-party liability?
NO
END
POSSIBLY
Is the third party a primary beneficiary?
Ultramares
YES
NO
Is the third party a foreseeable party?
Rusch Factors
YES
NO
Is the third party an investor?
Escott v Barchris
YES
NO
Was gross negligence present?
State Street Trust Co.
YES
Ordinary third party can sue auditor.
NO
END
Section 11
Liable for ordinary negligence, gross negligence, or fraud.
purchasers only.
Section 18
Liable for gross negligence or fraud.
both purchasers and sellers.
Rule 10b-5
Liability not restricted, e.g., can be used by plaintiffs who engage in no securities transactions whatsoever.
Scienter is required.
Hochfelder
Auditors must show that they acted in good faith and had no knowledge that the financial statements were in error.

Fischer v. *Kletz*, 266 F. Supp. 180 (S.D.N.Y., 1967)
"Great Salad Oil Swindle" (see *Wall Street Journal*, "The Case of the Phantom Salad Oil," December 1963, for a detailed discussion)
Equity Funding [see *U.S.* v. *Weiner*, 578 F. 2nd 757 (9th Cir. 1978); also see AICPA, "Report of the Specific Committee on Equity Funding," 1975]
United States v. *Simon*, 425 F. 2d 796 (1969)
1136 Tenants' Corp. v. *Max Rothenberg & Co.*, 27 App. Div. 2d 830, 277 N.Y.S. 2d 996 (1967), aff'd, 21 N.Y. 2d. 995, 290 N.Y.S. 2d 919, 238 N.E. 2d 322 (NY Ct. App. 1968)
Maryland Casualty Co. v. *Jonathon Cook*, 35 F. Supp. 160 (E.D. Mich. 1940)
O'Neil v. *Atlas Automobile Finance Corporation*, 139 Pa. Super. 346, 11A. 2d 782 (1940)
Penn Square (see "U.S. Examines Troubled National Banks More Often Since Demise of Penn Square," *Wall Street Journal*, December 13, 1982, p. 12)
United American Bank of Knoxville (see Gregory Stricharchuk and Damon Darlin, "Ernst & Whinney's Audit of Bank That Failed Puzzles Investigators," *Wall Street Journal*, March 4, 1983, p. 21; J. Ernest Beazley and Jim Montgomery, "Knoxville Bank's Fall: Fair Had a Hand in It, As Did Lending Policy," *Wall Street Journal*, March 15, 1983, p. 22)
Shahmoon v. *General Development Corp.* (CCH Fed. Sec. L. Rep. ¶94, 308 (S.D.N.Y., 1973)
Franklin Supply Co. v. *Tolman*, 454 F. 2d 1059 (9th Cir., 1972)
Bunge v. *Eide*, 372 F. Supp. 1058 (D.N.D., 1974)
Leeds Estate, Building and Investment Co. v. *Shepherd*, 36, Ch.D. 787 (1887)
Adams v. *Standard Knitting Mills, Inc.* (CCH Fed. Sec. L. Rep. ¶95, 863 [E.D. Tenn. 1976])
Securities and Exchange Commission v. *U.S. Financial, Inc., et al.* 74 Civil 92-S (S.D. Cal., February 25, 1974, and Accounting Series Release No. 153, February 25, 1974)
Four Seasons (see *Wall Street Journal*, "Eight Are Cited in Four Seasons Fraud Indictment," December 21, 1972, for further details)
United States v. *Natelli*, 527 F. 2d 311 (2d Cir. 1975), Cert. Denied, 425 U.S. 934 (1976) (also, see ASR No. 173, "In the Matter of Peat, Marwick, Mitchell & Co.," July 2, 1975)
Gulf & Western Ind. Inc. v. *Great Atlantic & Pacific Tea Co., Inc.*, 476 F. 2d 687 (2d Cir. 1973)
Herzfeld v. *Laventhol, Krekstein, Horwath & Horwath*, 540 F. 2d 27 (2d Cir. 1976)
McLean v. *Alexander*, 599 F. 2d. 1190 (1979)
United States v. *Benjamin*, 328 F. 2d 854, 863 (2d Cir. 1964)
Westec Corporation (Ernst & Ernst, 1967; original complaint filed in U.S. District Court, Houston, August 23, 1968—*Carpenter* v. *Hall*, C. A. No. 68-H-738)
Ryan v. *Kanne*, 170 N.W. 2d 395 (Iowa, 1969)
White v. *Guarente*, 43 N.Y. 2d 356, 372 N.E. 2d 315 (N.Y. Ct. App. 1977)
Bonhiver v. *Graff*, 248 N.W. 2d 291 (S. Ct. Minn. 1976)
SEC v. *Arthur Young & Co.*, F. 2d. (D.C. Cir. 1978)
Koch Industries, Inc. v. *Vosko*, 494 F. 2d 713 (10th Cir. 1974)

REVIEW QUESTIONS

1. What are the most common causes of claims, as reported by the AICPA Professional Liability Plan?
2. What does common law encompass? Has it been reasonably consistent over time?
3. What is meant by "privity" and "tort"? How do they affect CPA liability? Distinguish among the three major causes for action and how they relate to privity and tort circumstances.
4. Define primary beneficiary. How does it affect CPAs' liability exposure?
5. Describe the findings of *Ultramares Corp.* v. *Touche*, *State Street Trust Co.* v. *Ernst*, *Rusch Factors, Inc.* v. *Levin*, and *Rhode Island Hospital Trust National Bank* v. *Swartz* and their implications for CPAs.
6. Describe the burden of proof under common law.
7. What defenses are available to CPAs in common law actions?
8. Describe the provisions of the Securities Act of 1933 and the Securities Exchange Act of 1934. Compare and contrast their liability implications for CPAs.
9. What is Rule 10b-5, and how does it differ from the 1933 and 1934 acts?
10. What was the significance of Rule 23 of the Federal Rules of Civil Procedure?
11. What defenses are available to CPAs in actions under the SEC acts, including Rule 10b-5?
12. What is meant by scienter?
13. Describe SEC injunctions. Where are these actions documented?
14. What legal problems might a CPA encounter when withdrawing from an engagement?
15. What is a CPA's general liability for accounting and review services?
16. Describe the influence on auditing standards and practices of each of the following court cases:
    a. McKesson & Robbins, Inc. (1940)
    b. Yale Express (*Fischer* v. *Kletz* (1967)
    c. "Great Salad Oil Swindle" (1963)
    d. Equity Funding (1973 discovery)
    e. Continental Vending (*United States* v. *Simon*, 1969)
    f. BarChris (*Escott* v. *BarChris Construction Corp.*, 1968)
    g. 1136 Tenants' (*1136 Tenants' Corp.* v. *Max Rothenberg & Co.*, 1972)

h. Hochfelder (*Ernst & Ernst* v. *Hochfelder,* 1976)
i. Fund of Funds Ltd. (1981)

17. What are the lessons of the experience with the Penn Square Bank and the United American Bank of Knoxville?

18. Provide some examples of where hindsight is 20:20, but the audit judgments are unclear when made in practice. Your examples should consider both past litigation and recently resolved accounting issues.

19. Describe the main categories of plaintiffs involved in litigation suits with CPAs.

20. Explain the significance of the *Herzfeld, Ryan, White,* and *Bonhiver* cases, outlined in Exhibit 5-5.

21. In what sense has the profession "fought back" against the litigious trend involving CPAs? Be specific.

22. Comment on the international scene with respect to CPAs' liability exposure.

23. How large are the claims filed in CPA litigation suits?

24. What is the cost of professional liability insurance for CPA firms, and what are the determinants of such costs?

EXERCISES

1. You operate a small CPA firm. One of your clients, who has been informed of material weaknesses in controls in past audit engagements, has recently hired you to prepare audited financial statements for the current year for the purpose of securing a bank loan. The client is involved in a joint venture with six limited partners for which statements are to be compiled. These also will be submitted to the bank. In preparing the unaudited statements for the joint venture, you discover that certain documentation is missing for the valuation of some fixed assets, and so you use management's representations for reporting purposes. One year later, the joint venture fails. Although its reported operations were immaterial to the client's major operations, the actual operations, discovered only after the venture's loss, would have had a material effect on the audited financial statements, which reflected the client's ownership of an interest in the joint venture. Suits are filed by both the bank, and the participants in the joint venture against the CPA for failing to uncover the fraud in the joint venture operations or its effect on total reported client operations.

a. What are your defenses in this case? Cite relevant court cases that support or contradict your position.

b. What actions might you have taken to place yourself in a better position in defending against the claims?

2. In a symposium concerning CPAs' liability, one speaker commented that many cases arise from professionals' not exercising simple common sense. The so-called business approach to auditing was noted to be a formalization of common-sense precepts, and then the speaker proceeded to cite litigation cases in support of these claims, tying in the effects that might have been observable had a business approach to auditing been used.

a. As the speaker, prepare examples of litigation cases that would prove your point, including the effects of a business approach on the cases you cite. Describe how you would apply the recommended business approach.

b. Now assume that as a member of the audience, you believe the speaker has been overly simplistic and wish to make that point evident during the discussion period following the presentation. Prepare your comments, assuming that the speaker developed the points you outlined in (a) during the formal presentation.

3. Assume that you work for a fidelity bonding company that has just suffered a loss of $8 million from a defalcation perpetrated by a bonded employee. Because the company was audited, you decide to file a suit against the CPAs in an attempt to recover damages. Assume that the $8 million fraud resulted in a material misstatement of that company's financial statements that are contained in a 10-K annual report filing with the SEC. It is your responsibility to determine the most appropriate type of suit to file on behalf of the bonding company.

a. Describe the alternative types of litigation that you could file.

b. Outline the advantages and disadvantages to the plaintiff in each type of suit identified under (a).

c. What are likely to be the issues that will determine whether the CPA is held liable for the $8 million loss?

4. The U.S. Financial Inc. case resulted in a $30 million award against Touche Ross & Co. In 1977, this was the largest civil verdict against any one accounting firm. But in 1981, the Fund of Funds case resulted in an $80 million award by the federal jury, although settlement was for an undisclosed smaller amount. Because the industry norm of liability coverage in the early 1970s was about $50 million, the insurance coverage for the latter claim may well be inadequate. Smaller CPA firms have faced claims of $14 million, yet would find it difficult to make a reasonable profit in their practices if they were forced to pay the premiums for more than $2 million of liability coverage. How can and have CPA firms tried to address such a litigation environment?

CASES FOR DISCUSSION

1. It has been held that an accountant is not independent if he or she has entered into a contract with a client that indemnifies the accountant for any losses, claims, damages, or liabilities arising from the filing of false or misleading financial statements. In Accounting Series Release No. 22, March 14, 1941, the chief accountant stated:

> When an accountant and his client, directly or through an affiliate, have entered into an agreement of indemnity which seeks to assure the accountant immunity from liability for his own negligent acts, whether of omission or commission, it is my opinion that one of the major stimuli to objective and unbiased consideration of the problems encountered in a particular engagement is removed or greatly weakened. Such condition must frequently induce a departure from the standards of objectivity and impartiality which the concept of independence implies.

A question that has been raised regarding this point is whether an accountant who has entered into a contract with an insurance company that protects him or her from liability—either from the client for undetected losses on embezzlement or from creditors and security holders for misleading statements—also loses his or her independence. How would you respond? Support your answer, making comparisons with the chief accountant's position.[46]

2. In discussing Stirling Homex Corp., a former maker of prefabricated houses, and the two sets of records that the corporation maintained in order to inflate revenue and profit by bogus land sales—leading to a rise in the Stirling brothers' net income from $50,000 in 1962 to $3 million in 1967, of which $15 million was for fraudulent sales—the assistant U.S. attorney observed: "Even the companies' auditors were defrauded by the deliberate falsification of entries in the companies' books."[47]

In responding to the SEC's accusations in an administrative proceeding, the managing partner of a Big Eight firm noted that the SEC's charges were "unfounded" and that the commission was resorting to administrative proceedings because it could not hope to win in court. The CPA firm said it had been the victim of "pervasive criminal fraud" by management, in collusion with outside parties. The SEC allegations were characterized as "irresponsible second-guessing." Although the courts have repeatedly rebuffed the commission's efforts to hold auditors responsible for management fraud, the SEC continues to act as prosecutor, judge, and jury in administrative proceedings, according to that partner speaking on behalf of the firm.[48]

Accountants were absolved from blame for the GeoTek oil drilling ventures case in which $30 million was raised based on false financial statements. The SEC had contended that the accountants were guilty of "intellectual dishonesty" in failing to observe the generally accepted accounting standards. The appeals court said that acceptance of the SEC's position "would go far toward making the accountant both an insurer of his client's honesty and an enforcement arm of the SEC. . . . We can understand why the SEC wishes to so conscript accountants," as they are often in the best position for early detection of wrongdoing. However, the securities laws do not allow for such conscription. The accountants were found to have complied in good faith with existing standards.[49]

In light of these commentaries, discuss (a) the auditors' responsibility for fraud detection and (b) the role of the SEC in enforcing auditors' responsibilities.

[46] Adapted from Richard N. Owens, "What Is an Independent Accountant?" *Accounting Review*, December 1941, pp. 394, 395.

[47] "Stirling Homex Kept Two Sets of Records, Prosecution Charges," *Wall Street Journal*, December 23, 1976, p. 8; and July 28, 1976, p. 17.

[48] "Touche Ross Audit Practices Sloppy, Improper in Two Clients' Cases," *Wall Street Journal*, September 3, 1976, p. 4.

[49] "Ruling That Absolved GeoTek Accountants from Blame Is Upheld," *Wall Street Journal*, February 7, 1979, p. 26.

6

Engagement Planning

You are a new staff accountant working for a local CPA firm. It's 8:00 in the morning, and you're the only professional staff member in the office. The receptionist asks you to take a phone call from a potential new client. You agree and find yourself in the following conversation with the president of a local manufacturing concern that you know nothing about:

President. Hello, this is John Smith. I am the president of the Spoonaker Company. My banker wants our company to have its books reviewed by a CPA. A good friend of mine—Joe Dukes—does business with your firm, recommended your services, and thought that you would be able to do the work for us right away.
Staff accountant. We're glad to hear that; when do you want the audit performed?
President. I'd like to have it completed by January, which is when my banker says he'll approve our loan—if we get a clean report from you.
Staff accountant. Today is December 10, but I'm certain that we'll be able to do it.
President. Great. Then I'll tell the bank that everything's set and that your firm will be doing the work. When will you start?
Staff accountant. By December 15, if that's all right.
President. That sounds fine. In fact, a lot of our office personnel will be going home for the holidays, so you'll have the place almost all to yourselves. I've got a call on another line, so I'll expect you on the fifteenth.

As the phone clicks, you hear the partner-in-charge coming into the office, and so you tell him about the new client. As you talk, you note that he looks rather unenthusiastic, if not distressed. He asks you to come into his office to discuss the matter and then says:

I appreciate, as my partners do, your enthusiasm in getting new business; however, our firm does have a review process to evaluate new business. This we find necessary for both professional and business reasons. Let me suggest that in the future you follow our procedures for investigating new clients. This time, I will call John Smith and explain that there was a misunderstanding in your conversation and that we'll have to get some information and discuss the engagement before making any commitment. I will, of course, emphasize that such a policy is in his best interests as well as ours, as we'll find out whether we can offer him what he wants, and we may also suggest additional or alternative services that he may not know about.

After you leave the partner's office, while it is still fresh in your mind, you jot down the details of your telephone conversation. As you read over your notes, it dawns on you why the news of your talk with the president of Spoonaker didn't please the partner. You quickly outline the following points:

1. I assumed an audit engagement when the prospective client merely referred to review work and a clean report, which could mean various types of accounting services.
2. I implicitly agreed that the prospective client would get a clean report, by not reacting to Smith's comment about his banker's requirements.
3. I committed the firm to a January 31 deadline without knowing anything about the client, the nature of the engagement, or our other staff commitments.
4. I let the prospective client think that we could easily come into his business, without any of his main staff to help us, and perform a review or audit. Instead, I should have objected to performing the audit while the office personnel were on vacation.

These points showed your disregard for both professional standards and client service. How can the staff's ability to perform the engagement be assessed when the CPA firm knows nothing about the prospective client? What if a client's computer center demands expertise beyond that available to the CPA firm, either in-house or on a consulting basis? Furthermore, how can the CPA firm be certain that it is, in fact and appearance, independent with regard to the client, unless the firm knows something about the client's management? If the client tells the banker that we have agreed to deliver a clean report, how independent does the firm appear? How can we be sure that we will have enough staff resources to supervise the engagement, comply with field standards, and collect sufficient evidential matter in that length of time? Indeed, a date cannot be "guaranteed," because the professional standards require that audit work be extended when necessary to provide an adequate evidential base, and this could require audit work beyond January 31.

Then there is the issue of client service: Does the client need and/or want an audit; is the client aware of the different services that are available; does the client know what an audit engagement can and cannot provide and the special concerns in a first-year audit engagement that may make it impossible to issue "a clean report"; and does the client have any concept of audit fees? Finally, there are business concerns: Does the auditing firm have any clients who might object to its accepting this new client; will the new client be able to pay us; and finally, how does the new client fit into our firm's portfolio of clients and future plans?

This case situation highlights the importance of exercising due professional care in the initial contact with and evaluation of prospective clients.

Engagement planning is deciding whether or not to accept a client and formalizing an understanding between the auditors and the client. While many of you will be entry-level professional staff of large CPA firms, it is important that you understand the business side of the firms which you will be joining. Shortly into your professional careers, you will be involved in evaluating prospective clients and the advisability of retaining current clients. You may also be asked to arrange an engagement with a client, once accepted. These topics are the subject matter of this chapter. In later chapters, the theory of evidence will be elaborated upon, as will the detailed planning of CPAs' engagements. In the hypothetical discussion with a prospective client, what can go wrong is illustrated and, more importantly, its ramifications in ethical, legal, economic, practical, and related professional terms are suggested. These ramifications will now be discussed in detail, as will the means by which such concerns can be addressed in practice, i.e., through the use of a formal evaluation process.

Ethical Considerations

The AICPA's Code of Professional Ethics requires that auditors be independent in both fact and appearance. When considering potential clients, CPAs must determine their independence. Although certain engagements can be performed without it, such as compiling financial statements, the prospective client must be told that the CPA firm does not consider itself independent and must state this in any reports that it issues.

Many CPA firms retain an investment banker to supervise stock portfolios for those of their professionals who want to invest in the stock market. Then when the firm decides to accept a new client, it gives the banker twenty-four hours to sell any stock in the new client's company. This ensures that the firm will not have any direct financial interests in the client's company. Indirect financial interests and any other relationships that the CPA firm might have with the client must still be investigated. Furthermore, if the client is registered with the SEC, the CPA who does the bookkeeping during the audit period will not be considered independent in regard to performing an audit.

Another ethical consideration in evaluating prospective clients is confidentiality: The CPA is expected not to divulge the client's proprietary information. But there is a fine line between a CPA's industry experience and firm-specific information, and so confidentiality may become an issue when a CPA firm is considering accepting a prospective client who is a competitor of an existing client. Though not required to do so, some CPAs find it to be a good business practice to confer with existing clients who might have reservations about their accepting a particular new client.

A third ethical responsibility is the issue of competency. A prospective client may be in an industry unfamiliar to a CPA firm, have a sophisticated computer system that requires a high level of expertise, need a complex multistage sampling plan, and be subject to regulatory agencies whose requirements are not known to the firm's CPAs. All of these can raise questions of competency, unless the firm can demonstrate the availability of in-house resources or external consultants to provide the necessary expertise. In order to find out the requirements of a prospective engagement, the CPA should meet with the prospective client and its former CPAs to discuss the client's operations and the proposed engagement. Then the CPA firm will decide whether it can perform the requested services.

In the interest of efficiency, a CPA firm will typically have personnel files on all its accountants. These files will include the person's industry experience and areas of specialization. This information would be augmented by data concerning consultants with which the firm has worked. An important consideration in practical terms is whether the staff members and consultants who have the qualifications to perform the proposed engagement will be available during the relevant time frame. In other words, what are their existing time commitments prior to accepting the new client?

Time and Other Limitations

The time commitments of the specialists, staff assistants, and support staff must also be considered. Can the engagement be completed within a reasonable time period, given the available hours of professional staff time, computer resources, and typing and related support services? As a labor-intensive product, auditing requires that a pool of resources be available during a particular time frame, and without such resources, new client commitments are precluded. Although the infamous "busy season" hours of CPAs, the change from calendar fiscal year-ends by clients, and the increasing levels of *interim work* (i.e., work in the middle of the year, rather than at year-end) have provided CPA firms with increased flexibility in responding to client demands, staff constraints do become binding at some point and are a relevant consideration in accepting new clients.

Other constraints to be considered include those likely to be affected by complementary CPA services, such as tax and debt compliance reports, and by the expected growth of existing and prospective clients. The relationship between a CPA firm and its clients is typically a long-term commitment. The client presumes that a high level of service will be provided over a reasonably long period of time, accruing the advantage of economies of scale and past audit experience with the client; the client certainly does not expect a CPA firm to face staffing limitations which restrict the alternative services which it can offer.

Economic Considerations

The prior discussion raises the question: why not expand the staffing and CPA firm's facilities to fulfill all prospective clients' demands? The answer is twofold: (1) some professionals prefer a smaller CPA firm as the desirable work environment and do not wish to grow; and (2) fluctuations in the pattern of services within the year and the effect of economic growth cycles upon the demand for CPA services suggest that a direct reaction to current demand can lead to an over-expansion of the professional staff, which causes overhead costs to be excessive and firm operations to be inefficient. CPA firms' limited resources force them to evaluate carefully the economic effects of accepting or rejecting a prospective client. For example, certain types of clients are known to rotate their auditors, perhaps every two to three years. Because the first year of auditing is expensive, some auditing firms will decide not to take on the costs of becoming familiar with those industries. But if the potential client demand from that industry or economic sector is believed to be substantial and/or growing, the CPA firm may be happy to accept such a short-term arrangement in order to train personnel, acquire industry expertise, and increase the firm's market opportunities.

Peat, Marwick, Mitchell & Co. (PMM & Co.) had success in being awarded the initial audit of New York City with a three-year audit assignment, based on a low competitive bid of $1 million annually (with the next lowest being $1.5 million, for slightly different services, by Deloitte, Haskins & Sells). This bid was cited by its competitors as being likely to produce a financial loss for PMM & Co.; the bid was described as being a third of what the audit should cost. "One accountant estimated the real cost of the audit at $4 million, the same as the annual audit fee General Motors pays. 'It would take a million dollars just to understand New York City,' he quipped."[1] Yet, conversations with the professional staff of PMM & Co. not only cite the obvious experience gained in the municipal sector and the prestige obtained from auditing such a visible municipal unit (with concurrent recognition by the market of PMM & Co.'s "industry" knowledge of the municipal sector), but also claim that a profit was earned on the audit engagement. The concept of penetrating a new market by lowering prices and of accepting lower returns in order to gain business experience is a well-known means of diversifying business and gaining an increased market share.[2] When the typical fiscal year-end of June for municipal units is considered, along with the decreased likelihood of a constraining regulatory deadline for the completion of an audit engagement, the attractiveness of municipal clients to CPA firms, as a way of stabilizing the demands on professional staff time throughout the year, becomes apparent.

[1] Peter W. Bernstein, "Competition Comes to Accounting," *Fortune*, July 17, 1978, pp. 89–96.

[2] Steven S. Anreder, "Profit or Loss? Price-Cutting Is Hitting Accountants in the Bottom Line," *Barron's*, March 12, 1979, p. 20.

Hence the economic considerations in accepting an audit engagement are a prediction of growth in the client's industry, a promise of training opportunities, and the timing of the professional services. Another factor is the amount of industry expertise required for a particular engagement and the extent to which such knowledge can be used for other clients. For example, heavily regulated industries require the CPA to be familiar with regulations, accounting systems, and accounting control and valuation problems that pertain only to that particular industry's operations. Banking, oil and gas, utility, investment banking, and life insurance companies are industries that are likely to demand a substantial amount of industry-specific knowledge that is of limited use to the CPA in auditing other clients, such as those in manufacturing and retailing. To invest resources in learning the uniform accounting system for utilities in a particular state, as well as the procedures of the rate regulators, and the applicable legislation on required pollution equipment and safety standards for nuclear plants, the CPA must either expect other utility companies to be obtained as clients, or expect that a sufficiently high fee will be earned from the single utility client to reimburse the costs incurred in obtaining industry expertise. Given that some competitors already have such industry knowledge, the latter is highly unlikely. It is not surprising, therefore, that many CPA firms specialize in certain industries and often enter relatively new markets by submitting low competitive bids. Exhibit 6-1 offers some statistics concerning a few industry groupings of clients of the "Big 8" CPA firms.

EXHIBIT 6-1
Industry Groupings of Clients of the "Big 8" CPA Firms

Industry	CPA Firm	Percentage of Audited Companies 1975 Sales* (No. of Companies in Industry Sample)
Autos	Coopers & Lybrand	30.4% (8)
	Deloitte, Haskins & Sells	48.0% (8)
Auto Parts	Ernst & Whinney	32.3% (14)
Electronics	Peat, Marwick, Mitchell & Co.	28.9% (34)
Office Equipment	Price Waterhouse	69.5% (10)
Rail Equipment	Arthur Young & Co.	42.0% (6)
Utilities – Gas	Arthur Andersen & Co.	41.5% (11)
		No. of Audited Companies 1964 Assets† (No. of Companies in Industry Sample)
Retail Trade – Dept. Stores, Mail Order, etc.	Touche Ross & Co.	66.1% (15)

*This column reports firm market shares over 25 percent based on percentage of audited companies' sales for the *Fortune* 650 companies classified by industry in 1975. See N. Dopuch and D. Simunic, "Competition in Auditing: An Assessment," *Fourth Symposium on Auditing Research* (University of Illinois at Urbana-Champaign, 1982), pp. 401-450.

†This column reports firm market shares over 25 percent on percentage of audited companies' assets for the companies listed in the *Fortune Directory* of August 1965. The sample is classified into 38 industry categories based on *Standard & Poor's Industry Surveys* and auxiliary information sources. Further details are available from the source of this data: Stephen A. Zeff and Robert L. Fossum, "An Analysis of Large Audit Clients," *Accounting Review*, April 1967, pp. 298-320.

Note: Other studies of auditors' market shares report later statistics, replicating the Zeff and Fossum study: e.g., see John Grant Rhode, Gary M. Witsell, and Richard L. Kelsey, "An Analysis of Client-Industry Concentrations for Large Public Accounting Firms," *Accounting Review*, October 1974, pp. 772-787.

There is also the issue of liability exposure. First is the legal exposure due to the number of potential litigants and the legal framework. CPAs are generally thought to be more vulnerable to liability in regard to public companies, as opposed to private companies, because of stockholders' class action claims, the precedent of tying monetary responsibility to stock price movements, and the SEC's injunctions and similar regulatory actions that may provoke litigation. Although the 10b-5 cases waned slightly after the *Hochfelder* case, the 1933 and 1934 Securities and Exchange Acts continue to offer more liability exposure than do common law obligations. A prospective client's ownership structure and the intended use of the audit reports also are relevant to the auditor in deciding whether a lawsuit might be filed.

Second is the CPA's inevitable legal involvement in business failures. Although an audit failure is not usually the cause of a client's failing for purely business reasons, investors and creditors obviously will try to blame those parties that can compensate for their losses, and one of those parties is likely to be the CPA. Even if the CPA successfully defends the professional work performed, the cost of legal fees, the time of the professional staff, and the adverse publicity can be substantial. Consequently, a CPA firm will try to diversify its client portfolio as one means of avoiding excessive liability owing to business failures that coincide with industry-specific economic problems. For example, real estate investment trusts (REITs) have faced economic difficulties as an industry, posing potentially significant liability problems for those CPAs with several REIT clients. High-technology companies and the auto industry also have "slumps," during which marginal companies either are forced out of business or must reorganize, and consequently a CPA with a client portfolio that includes a number of high technology or auto industry companies will have an increased probability of being involved in litigation during such industry "slumps." Of course, a related problem with having a client portfolio that is concentrated in an economically troubled industry can be in fee collection difficulties, as well as the reduction of audit services which results from the shrinking of business operations.

The economic considerations of selecting a client portfolio are thus rather complex. The positive aspects of having public companies as audit clients include a probable increase in the quantity of services due to the clients' size, as well as the frequent SEC filings and the advantages of efficient audit plans facilitated by good systems of control. The main drawback is, again, the increased liability exposure. The issue of industry expertise has to be balanced with the business desire of the CPA to have a reasonably diversified portfolio. Otherwise, practical problems are likely to arise, such as the high probability that companies within an industry will have similar year-ends and similar time demands on CPAs for assistance in financing and regulatory filings. The CPA firm will want a work schedule as even as possible during the year and thus will try to diversify its clients' industry representation. To effectively select a client portfolio a CPA must jointly consider business, auditing, legal, and practical issues.

Special Concerns in an Initial Audit

A prospective client's initial audit raises basic questions as to its *auditability* ***[SAS 31, Section 326].*** That is, the third standard of field work, pertaining to the accumulation of sufficient competent evidence, requires (1) records supporting account balances and transactions for the most recent year; (2) records supporting long-term accounts that cannot be verified through other available information, for example, the ownership and acquisition cost of fixed assets; and (3) minutes of the board of directors' meetings, because some of the information in the minutes often preclude alternative means of verification.

Beyond ascertaining the existence of such an "audit trail," the prospective auditor must determine the propriety of the accounting principles applied in previous years. A review of the company's "Summary of Significant Accounting Policies" (discussed in APB No. 22) can be helpful in checking for compliance with generally accepted accounting principles (GAAP), although the auditor should also test several earlier transactions to gain further assurance. GAAP compliance is critical to evaluating the effects of the previous year's balance sheet on the current period's income calculation. Common problem areas are inventory valuation and accumulated depreciation accounts, both of which may have material effects on cost of goods sold and depreciation charges in the current period. For example, if in an earlier period, a company recorded its ending inventory at retail instead of cost, then its ending inventory would be overstated. Assume this overstatement were $300,000. It would affect the current period, as beginning inventory is added to purchases and then netted with ending inventory to calculate cost of goods sold. The current period's income thus would be overstated by $300,000 because of the prior period's noncompliance with GAAP. Furthermore, if the CPA is asked to perform an audit after the client's current balance sheet date, audit procedures such as the physical examination of inventory and the confirmation of receivables often cannot be performed. The auditor sometimes may be able to obtain satisfaction, by using alternative procedures (such as testing for subsequent collections), that the financial statements are fair. But if the amounts are material and such satisfaction cannot be obtained, a scope qualification with an "except for" opinion, or possibly a disclaimer of opinion, is required ***[SAS 1, Section 310]***. The prospective client should be told that the auditor probably will have to give an unqualified opinion when earlier years' financial statements, current accounting and record-keeping practices, the timing of the present audit, or the absence of an earlier year's audit make it unlikely that sufficient evidence can be obtained. In addition, the client's accounting practices may require a consistency qualification if the accounting principles applied in previous years differ from those currently used.

The propriety of GAAP compliance and the prospective auditor's ability to gather sufficient evidential matter both rely on the company's maintaining a relationship with an attorney that permits the proper evaluation of claims, litigation, and assessments to determine the necessary disclosures under FAS No. 5 ***[SAS 12, Section 337]***. This attorney–client relationship is normally required before an auditor can express an unqualified opinion on financial statements, because of the provisions of SAS No. 12, "Inquiry of a Client's Lawyer Concerning Litigation, Claims, and Assessments."

The second standard of field work, pertaining to the study and evaluation of controls, is related to SAS No. 16 (Section 327), which deals with the subject of errors and irregularities. *Errors* are defined as unintentional mistakes, whereas *irregularities* are intentional distortions, including fraud and misrepresentations by management. How effective the established controls are will depend largely on management's integrity. This fact points out the importance of investigating, before an initial engagement, the client's history and current financial circumstances that may create incentives for misstating financial statements. Indicators of possible trouble include (1) management's inaction with respect to material weaknesses in internal control that are practicable to correct, (2) a high turnover rate in top financial positions, and (3) understaffing of accounting and financial functions. SAS No. 16 discusses the higher-than-normal risk of irregularities that exists whenever working capital is inadequate or the client's industry experiences several business failures.

Related-Party Considerations

A *related party* is defined in the professional literature as

> the reporting entity; its affiliates; principal owners, management, and members of their immediate families; entities for which investments are accounted for by the equity method; and any other party with which the reporting entity may deal when one party has the ability to significantly influence the management or operating policies of the other, to the extent that one of the transacting parties may be prevented from fully pursuing its own separate interests. Related parties also exist when another entity has the ability to significantly influence the management or operating policies of the transacting parties or when another entity has an ownership interest in one of the transacting parties and the ability to significantly influence the other, to the extent that one or more of the transacting parties might be prevented from fully pursuing its own separate interests.[3]

There is a higher risk of misrepresentation or error in related-party transactions because of (1) the non-arm's-length basis on which the transactions may be negotiated; (2) the related parties' joint and overlapping incentives; (3) the informality that may shroud the clarity and documentation of the transaction's substance; and (4) the accounting necessity of identifying transactions with related parties in order to facilitate either elimination, when consolidated financial statements are prepared, or adjustment for other presentations.

SAS 45 (Section 1020) discusses related-party transactions and the risks and problems that can

[3]Statement on Auditing Standards No. 6, "Related Party Transactions" (New York: AICPA, July 1975), par. .02.

arise from economic dependence on one or a few customers or suppliers. Such problems would not necessarily be apparent from a review of past years' financial statements and hence require investigative procedures by the prospective auditor. The problems cited in SAS No. 16 and SAS No. 45 have been termed "red flags," indicating increased audit risk.

Predecessor Auditors

Although the special considerations in an initial audit that have been discussed can involve both clients being audited for the first time and clients acquired after being audited by another CPA, a consideration that applies only to the latter is described in SAS No. 7, "Communications Between Predecessor and Successor Auditors" (Section 315). The prospective CPA is required to communicate with the previous period's auditor. The initiative for communicating rests with the new auditor and may be written or oral. Any such communication should be treated as confidential. Although the prospective CPA should talk to the predecessor auditor before accepting an engagement, he or she may do so afterward. The main purpose of such communication is to find out any information that is relevant to deciding whether or not to accept a particular client, although it can also be of use to a new auditor in assessing risk. Of course, the predecessor auditor is subject to the confidentiality requirement of the code of ethics and must obtain the client's permission before giving out any information to the prospective auditor. The successor auditor also should request the client's permission to talk to the predecessor auditors, explaining the need for such communication. The client must explain a refusal of such permission to the successor auditor, who in turn should consider the refusal's implications.

If the client refuses to give such permission, the previous period's auditor is required to tell the prospective auditor that no information can be given. If the client does give permission, the predecessor auditor is required to respond to the request for information. In the former case, the CPA may be willing to conduct alternative forms of investigation in order to decide whether or not to accept the client and may, in fact, decide to accept the client, despite the added risk exposure implied by the absence of open communications with the former auditor. When the predecessor auditor is permitted to communicate with the successor auditor, they probably will discuss past disputes over accounting principles, audit procedures, fees, and past problems with misrepresentation or fraud. Issues of interest include facts bearing on (1) management's integrity, (2) disagreements as to accounting principles, auditing procedures, or other significant matters, and (3) the reason for the change of auditors, as understood by the predecessor auditor. The predecessor auditor is expected to provide prompt and full replies unless he or she specifically indicates that the response is limited (for example, because of litigation claims). The successor auditor is to evaluate the implications of any limited replies.

Often, the predecessor's working papers will be made available, assuming the client has granted permission to do so and that business reasons do not preclude such access. These work papers can help the successor auditor determine risks and the required audit time for significant accounts. However, the successor auditor's report should not refer to the predecessor auditor's work or report. If a successor auditor discovers that an earlier year's statements need revision, he or she should ask the client to set up a meeting to resolve the matter.

Material Weaknesses

Also of interest are reports on material weaknesses in internal accounting control and the client's subsequent actions to correct them ***[SAS 20, Section 323].*** Recall that a material weakness is a condition in which errors and irregularities in amounts that would be material to the financial statements may occur and not be expected to be detected within a timely period by employees in the normal course of performing their assigned functions. A client's unwillingness to respond to practical suggestions concerning material weaknesses is typically thought to be indicative of increased *audit risk.* Recall that audit risk refers to the auditor's failure to appropriately modify his or her opinion on financial statements that are materially misstated.

The "Red Flag" Literature

The "red flag" literature discusses observable characteristics of the client that are likely to signal increased audit risk. The literature has been created, in part, by applying theoretical concepts. In addition, past experiences with fraud and bankruptcy offer some empirical evidence that certain signs do indeed point to trouble. Exhibit 6-2 summarizes these signs, commonly referred to as "red flags," grouping them according to the auditor's reason for reading them as danger signals. Indeed, many CPA firms have drawn up audit risk questionnaires to alert the audit teams to such red flags. Much of the "red flag" literature ignores this criterion and would augment Exhibit 6-2 to include such signals as the "honesty of managers," which clearly is rather difficult for the auditor to assess through other than fairly indirect and potentially ineffective modes of investigation. As it is, the potential use of the flags in Exhibit 6-2 may well depend upon the CPA's willingness to use investigative agencies or similar means of analysis. In addition, without a weighting of a priority scheme, what does the CPA do once information is obtained regarding the flags listed in Exhibit 6-2? Surely many CPAs have clients with financial difficulties who nonetheless are considered to be of low audit risk; at what point is concern for the danger signals appropriate?

The "red flag" literature is summarized in Exhibit 6-2 primarily to provide the reader with an idea of the type of factors which may be relevant to deciding whether to accept a new client or to retain an existing client. However, unless such lists can be fine-tuned and an effective means of utilizing the lists can be developed, the flags are likely to serve only as memory joggers, as opposed to effective audit tools. Of course, judgment is a familiar and critical aspect of the audit process, so the mere lack of structure to the application of red flag checklists in no way precludes their use in evaluating such risks; the lack of structure merely reduces the extent to which such checklists are likely to influence the CPA's decision process. Note that many CPA firms have designed audit risk questionnaires for the express purpose of alerting the audit team to the presence of "red flags" in a particular client setting.

One method of detecting red flags is reading trade journals pertaining to the client's industry and keeping abreast of economic and legislative changes affecting that industry. A second method is to use the same type of current information sources that clients use to evaluate their customers. Credit ratings on prospective clients, the Better Business Bureau's records, and the company's reputation with its competitors all should be investigated. A third method is to expand the amount of contact with the client's personnel and physical operations. When you speak with practitioners about what the future has in store, some will speculate that the theoretical possibility exists of doing an entire audit from the CPA firm's office, seated at a computer terminal. Yet, inevitably, another practitioner will comment, "Field visits are essential; they're the best source of information and provide the basis for understanding the client." The highly regarded concept that some people make good auditors because they have accurate "gut feelings," depends upon client contact to formulate such a "gut feel" for that client. By observing the comings and goings of personnel, customers, and suppliers, the work habits of employees, and the general orderliness of operations, the auditor can evaluate the likelihood of many of the flags cited in Exhibit 6-2. Face-to-face inquiries and interactions with the auditees at the work place, during breaks, and after hours all combine to form a profile of the employees' probable competence, life-style, attitude, and personal habits. Auditors will commonly work later than the typical auditees do, in part, to observe the operations after hours. For example, cash receipts left on desk tops may indicate poor control; disorderly behavior, revealing remarks, and candor noticed after hours may identify trouble spots. A fourth approach is to follow up on hunches. For example, if one of the auditee's managers is observed hastily putting away papers when the auditor enters the office, an investigation of those papers may be warranted. Similarly, if an employee's life-style seems too grand for the salary earned, a detective agency may be able to find out whether there are any problems regarding the client's risk exposure. A fifth approach is to apply preliminary analytical review tools. A comparison of prospective and existing clients' liquidity positions and various operating ratios and statistics with

EXHIBIT 6-2
"Red Flags"—Danger Signals to Auditors

Financial Flags

Incentives Due to Personal Habits:

- Spending patterns
- Gambling activities
- Alcohol use
- Drug use
- Involvement in sexual relationships
- Associating with questionable characters

Incentives Due to Personal Financial Stress:

- High personal debts
- Severe illness of family members
- Inadequate compensation

Incentives Due to Company's Financial Condition:

- Increased competition, particularly from low-priced imports
- Economic slump
- Narrowed profit margin
- Reduction in sales order backlogs
- Difficulty in collecting customers' receivables
- High indebtedness
- Limited sources of capital
- Restrictive debt covenants
- Past losses from operations
- Inadequate liquid resources
- Insufficient collateral
- Dependence on a limited market (i.e., high undiversified risk)
- Uncontrolled expansion
- Excessive inventory buildup relative to sales, particularly if obsolescence risks are great
- Contingent liabilities such as litigation
- Regulators' threats to suspend or terminate operations

Incentives Due to Motivational Factors:

- Compensation tied to reported financial statistics
- Compensation tied to specific transactions over which management has either actual or implied control
- Job security threatened by proxy contests for control or by pending mergers

Risk Exposure Flags

Lack of Environmental Control:

- Poor hiring practices
- Noncompetitive salaries
- Insufficient training programs
- Inadequate documentation of policies and procedures
- High staff turnover
- No requirement of annual vacation or periodic rotation in key areas of operations
- Working overtime regularly so that custody of records is constantly maintained and ample privacy is available for employee's handling of records
- Unreasonable performance standards
- Staff shortages, particularly in accounting and finance areas
- Inadequate involvement by management in design and monitoring of controls

Circumstances That Increase the Opportunities for Defalcations:

- Related parties
- Complex multicompany affiliations
- Decentralized banking relationships
- Extensive integration of computers into operations and the accounting system
- Poor control systems
- Absence of internal auditing function
- Managers' ability to override control system (typically greater when management is dominated by one or two individuals)
- Trusted employee's familiarity with all operations
- Frequent rotation of auditing firms
- Changes in banking relationships and legal counsel
- No effective oversight by board of directors

"Sour Notes"

Audit Evidence

- Significant fluctuation, detected through analytical review procedures, cannot be reasonably explained
- Reluctant or untimely cooperation with external auditors
- Unwillingness to disclose additional information to clarify financial statements
- Accounting changes that lower quality of earnings made for no obvious "business" purpose
- Managers particularly inquisitive as to earnings-per-share effect of accounting alternatives
- Use of unduly liberal accounting practices
- Large, unusual year-end transactions
- Numerous adjusting entries identified during audit
- Litigation, particularly between management and stockholders
- Unusually large expenditures to lawyers, consultants, agents, and employees, relative to the normal level of service of such parties
- Client's pressures on auditor to complete the engagement in unusually short time
- Unwillingness to correct material weaknesses in control system detected by either management or external auditor, despite justification of such improvements in cost-benefit terms

Events with Economic Consequences

- Trading of stock suspended or removed from stock exchange
- Significant tax adjustments made by IRS
- Continual problems with regulators

Managers and Their Actions

- Managers known to have criminal or questionable backgrounds
- Fraud perpetrators, upon discovery, not disciplined, a fact well known to company employees

Note: References providing similar "red flag" checklists include:

American Institute of Certified Public Accountants' Standing Committee on Methods, Perpetration, and Detection of Fraud, "Warning Signals of the Possible Existence of Fraud" (discussed in *CPA Letter*, October 23, 1978; and published as a red flag checklist by New York: AICPA, 1979).

Robert K. Elliott and John J. Willingham, *Management Fraud: Detection and Deterrence* (New York: Petrocelli Books, 1980), especially W. Steve Albrecht, David J. Cherrington, I. Reed Payne, Allan V. Roe, and Marshall B. Romney, "Auditor Involvement in the Detection of Fraud," pp. 207-261; and James E. Sorensen and Thomas L. Sorensen, "Detecting Management Fraud: Some Organizational Strategies for the Independent Auditor," pp. 195-206.

those of their competitors can often reveal potential problems or possible areas of misstatement caused by errors or irregularities. Trend analysis of the past three to five years of a client's operations can offer some idea of the likely direction of a client's operations, for example, extent of growth, need to expand facilities, and the likelihood of going public.

Suggestions in the literature range from administering lie detector and psychological tests to formulating a "typical profile" for the fraud perpetrator as means of assessing or controlling the risk of defalcation. However, since few generalities can be drawn as to how a criminal "looks" and many negative reactions to testing arise from prospective employees, the red flag detection capabilities of auditors are likely to continue to be largely dependent upon the quality of individuals' judgments. Note that although red flags apply mainly to fraud, they also may indicate the risk of error. For example, lax hiring practices, insufficient compensation, and understaffing can increase the risk of error.

Alternative Approaches to Evaluating Whether to Accept New Clients and Whether to Retain Existing Clients

CPA firms' methods of evaluating new and continuing clients vary with respect to (1) the types of information considered relevant to selecting or retaining a client, (2) the sources used to obtain the desired information, and (3) the extent to which the acceptance or retention decision process is formally documented. Exhibit 6-3 presents one approach to documenting this process. The AICPA's 1981 Peer Review Programs ***[SAS 25, Section 16]*** state:

> A member firm should establish policies and procedures for deciding whether to accept or continue a client in order to minimize the likelihood of association with a client whose management lacks integrity. The firm does not vouch for the integrity or reliability of a client nor does it have a duty to anyone but itself with respect to the acceptance, rejection, or retention of clients. However, the firm should consider that the reputation of a client's management could reflect on the reliability of representations and accounting records and on the firm's own reputation. In making decisions to accept or continue a client, a firm should also consider its own independence and its ability to service a client properly with particular reference to industry expertise, size of engagement, and manpower available to staff the engagement.[4]

Although the emphasis in Exhibit 6-3 is on new clients, this approach can also be used periodically for existing clients. For example, a client may acquire a business by merger, and so the CPA would have to decide whether to accept the audit engagement of the acquired company. Such procedures should be in writing and should be used to reconsider an engagement not only when there are mergers, but also when key events occur, such as (1) changes in management, ownership, legal counsel, financial condition, litigation status, nature of business, or scope of engagement or (2) conditions that would have caused rejection of a client had they existed when the client was initially accepted. Responsibility for performing the evaluation process for new, as well as existing clients should be assigned to a particular individual or group at an appropriate level in the CPA firm that is commensurate with such responsibility. The professional personnel of the CPA firm should be informed of the policies and procedures relating to new and continuing clients to assure compliance. If effective communication had been present, the new assistant in the case that introduced this chapter would have known better than to commit the CPA firm to a new audit engagement; the assistant would have been aware of the appropriate procedures for client acceptance and would have referred the new client to that member of the firm who is responsible for evaluating new clients.

Exhibit 6-3 summarizes the alternative information sources which can prove to be useful in evaluating new and existing clients. In the process of accepting a new client, the audit firm will make a preliminary visit to the client organization before preparing a proposal. This visit is usually made by the partners and managers who will be involved

[4]AICPA Division for CPA Firms Peer Review Program, *Compliance Review Program Guidelines for Firms with Generally from 2 to 20 Professionals* (New York: AICPA, 1981), p. 61.

EXHIBIT 6-3
New Client Evaluation

Name of Prospective Client ____________

Location ____________

Nature of Business ____________

____

____

____

Ownership Structure ____________

____

____

Top Managers/Directors ____________

____

Stability of Management ____________

Public or Private Company ____________

Subject to SEC Regulation ____________

Subject to Other Regulatory Agencies ____________

Describe ____________

____

Type of Services Desired

Intended Use of Reports ____________

(Consider the effect of such use on the auditor's legal liabilities)

Fiscal Year End ____________

Banker ____________

Legal Counsel ____________

Predecessor Auditor ____________

Operating and Financial Statistics:

Number of Employees ____________

Total Assets ____________

Total Liabilities ____________

Total Revenue ____________

Net Income ____________

(Attach Financial Statements & SEC Form 10-K and/or tax returns, if available, for the past 3 years.)

Credit Rating ____________

(Attach Dun & Bradstreet or other credit agency's report)

Note: Consider arranging a tour of the prospective client's plant and offices. Information concerning physical operations, the control system, the quality of client personnel, and potential problems can often be learned from such a tour. It is common for the individuals expected to be assigned as the partner and manager on a prospective client's engagement to visit the client's premises before accepting that engagement.

Prepare a Brief Memo Documenting Your Evaluation of the

- Integrity and competence of both management and owners,
- Financial position and earnings history of the Client and prospects for growth,
- Client's relationships with related parties and their effects on the engagement,
- Legal status of the Client,
- Client's relationship with the previous auditors,
- Ability of the company to pay for services,
- Prospects for a continuing relationship with the Client, as well as the prospects for offering other services in such areas as tax and management advisory services,
- Maintenance of accounting standards by the Client, with emphasis on GAAP compliance, and
- Public relations effects of accepting the Client.

Attach supporting evidence such as working papers prepared (1) to analyze the financial position of the client or (2) to document (a) the results of a tour of the plant and offices of the prospective client, (b) correspondence with the company's legal counsel, commercial bankers, investment bankers, and previous auditors, (c) reports by security firms performing client investigative work, and (d) press releases, trade publications, or other published information from or about the client.

NOTE: Some firms utilize audit risk questionnaires for documenting these risk factors.

Is the CPA firm able to act independently with respect to this client? ____

If not, explain ____________

____

Does a potential conflict of interest exist with current clients? ____________

If so, describe actions taken and attach supporting documentation (such as correspondence with other audit clients) ____________

____

____

Does expertise in the client's industry exist in the local office, is it available from another office, or can it be acquired prior to initiating the engagement (e.g., on a consulting basis or through educating the professional staff)?

____

____

Does adequate personnel exist to enable the services to be performed in compliance with Firm Standards?

____

____

Provide an analysis as to whether, from a business perspective, it is desirable to accept this prospective client. Consider the firm's

- existing portfolio,
- market opportunities related to this engagement (such as those arising from the acquisition of industry expertise),
- the mix of time that will be required on the engagement and its effect on the profit contribution of the engagement (i.e., is an inordinate amount of manager or partner time expected to be required), and
- the challenge that is provided by the engagement (an essential element in maintaining the morale of the firm's professional staff).

AICPA, Division for CPA Firms Peer Review Program: Compliance Review Program Guidelines for Firms with Generally from 2 to 20 Professionals (New York: AICPA, 1981). Also see Statement on Quality Control Standard No. 1 and AU Section 315 (SAS No. 7); J. W. Grimsley, "Client Evaluation," *CPA Journal*, March 1975, pp. 57–59; Edward J. Lusk, "Evaluation of Prospective Audit Clients: An Eigenvalue Priority Assignment Model, *"Symposium on Auditing Research II* (University of Illinois at Urbana-Champaign, 1977), pp. 19–35; and commentaries thereon by Daniel M. Guy (pp. 36–41) and Harold H. Hensold, Jr. (pp. 42–49).

with the client if the engagement becomes a reality.

As indicated earlier, some CPA firms employ detective agencies such as Pinkerton's, Inc. or Intertel, Inc. to check out executives in companies that are not well-known to the firm.[5]

If the CPA firm decides to investigate a prospective client, the investigation is usually of the chief executive and one or two other top managers, along with the chief executives of any subsidiaries. As reported by Marshall Romney and Steve Albrecht in their article "The Use of Investigative Agencies by Auditors":

> Although the specific information is confidential, we are aware of at least four instances where CPA firms did not accept a client, based on the recommendations of an investigative agency. These clients were subsequently picked up by other major CPA firms that did not use investigative agencies. A short time thereafter, all four clients were sued for fraud (e.g., offering false securities), and the CPA firms experienced significant losses through litigation.[6]

The conclusion drawn in the article cited is that an investigation costing from $200 per person investigated to $1,000 for an entire review of a prospective client is cost-beneficial relative to the substantial costs of litigation, undesirable clients, and uncollectible audit fees. Of particular interest are the reasons identified by investigative agencies for reporting to CPA firms that certain potential clients are undesirable. Pinkerton's, Inc. in a letter to prospective CPA clients provides the following examples: (1) unsettled civil suits, (2) pending litigation, (3) state tax evasion, (4) involvement in illegal business practices, (5) suspected criminal relationships, (6) under investigation by government authorities, and (7) failure to file income taxes. Although professional detective agencies are likely to have many information sources that may not be easily accessible to CPA firms, many National Offices of CPA firms have invested in data bases which include media coverage of *The New York Times, The Washington Post,* and similar newspapers, as one means of performing their own investigation of potential clients. Such characteristics as "syndicate connections" or "questionable business practices" may be identified by utilizing such information sources.

Hence, alternative approaches exist for evaluating new clients and for determining whether existing clients should be retained. These approaches span a wide range of methods, from confirmations with the financial and legal community to the hiring of investigative agencies to gather information on prospective clients. Although Exhibit 6-3 stresses a formalized decision process, many smaller firms may utilize a similar approach to evaluation, with no formal documentation whatsoever. If you recall the case which introduced this chapter, the new assistant might be asked to review firm policies regarding the acceptance of new clients and to orally summarize these requirements for the benefit of other recently hired professional staff members. Presumably, the firm's policies will parallel those discussed herein, and the CPA firm's compliance with such policies will be enhanced by assuring that the professional staff are familiar with the firm's client evaluation process. An important point to be stressed in such educational seminars with professional staff is that the evaluation process is not limited to new clients but is also an ongoing decision process with existing clients. The primary difference in evaluating new and existing clients is the availability of substantially more in-depth information concerning existing clients, as a result of prior years' engagements.

The Engagement Letter

Once a CPA firm has decided to accept a client, it is important that the CPA and the client both understand the nature of the engagement and their responsibilities, and this is the purpose of the engagement letter. Though not required by generally accepted auditing standards, the use of engagement letters is a common business practice.

Exhibit 6-4 outlines the contents of an engagement letter, and Exhibit 6-5 provides a sample letter. Once the client signs the engagement letter, it becomes a contract between the auditor and the client. Before sending the letter, the CPA will dis-

[5] As reported by *Business Week*, reprinted in *CPA Journal*, October 1975, pp. 83–85.
[6] *Journal of Accountancy*, October 1975, p. 63.

EXHIBIT 6-4
Components of an Engagement Letter

-Normally addressed to the chairman of the board of directors, the chairman of the audit committee, or the chief executive officer
-Name of entity
-Fiscal year-end
-Financial statements to be prepared and/or examined
-Scope of services to be provided
-Scope limitations set by client
-Purpose of engagement
-The necessity of hiring an independent specialist to observe specialized inventories and how the charges for the specialist's services are to be handled in the billing
-Disclaimer of responsibility for detection of fraud
-Timing of services, including target dates for completion of field work and delivery of audit report
-Type of report expected to be issued, i.e., audit opinion, disclaimer, report on internal accounting control
-Intended use of reports, e.g., to be used in negotiating renewal or extension of a significant loan, to be mailed with proxies, a prospectus, or the offering of securities for sale, etc.
-Requirement that accountant approve all printed materials in which CPA reports appear
-Obligations of client's staff regarding the preparation of schedules and statements and cooperation with the auditor in locating documents and responding to inquiries
-CPA's responsibility for the preparation or review of tax returns and subsequent tax examinations
-Fee or method for fee determination
-Specifications regarding how expenses incurred by the audit staff are to be handled in billing the client
-Frequency of billings and the client's obligation to pay
-Intention to notify client if circumstances arise that could significantly affect the initial estimate of audit fees
-Client's signature with date of acceptance of the engagement letter
-Request that client return the signed duplicate copy of the letter to the CPA (Note, however, that some CPAs merely retain a copy of the letter in their files and do not ask for a signature.)
-Expression of thanks for being selected as the CPA for the client's operations
-In a new engagement, reminder that the cooperation of the prior accountant with the new CPA is to be obtained by the client

From American Institute of Certified Public Accountants, *Sample Engagement Letters for an Accounting Practice* (New York: AICPA, 1978); and related professional literature.

cuss with the client the nature and purpose of the desired services, including the fee. Frequently, if the client is undergoing an initial audit, the CPA will describe the audit process, its objectives, and its limitations. He or she will also explain alternative and complementary CPA services. Because the initial audit of a company with material inventory levels will often result in the issuance of a disclaimer on the income statement, owing to the auditor's inability to obtain satisfactory evidence of the beginning inventory balance, the CPA must be sure to tell the client that an unqualified opinion is unlikely to be issued in the first year. The CPA should explain that disclaimers are common in initial audits and should make sure that the client does not expect or need an unqualified report (for example, because of creditors' specifications).

Another topic of discussion with an initial-audit client is that the audit fee for the first examination will probably be much higher than that for later years' engagements. Not only are there start-up costs for assimilating permanent audit files on the client and documenting its control system, but the opening balances for the year also have to be verified by analyzing previous years' transactions.

Competitive Bidding and Audit Fees

One component of the engagement letter outlined in Exhibit 6-5 was the audit fee. Clients typically want an initial estimate of the audit or other engagement fee for planning purposes, as well as for comparison to other CPAs' fee proposals. While the CPA profession historically banned advertising, including competitive bidding, the revised Code of Ethics, discussed in Chapter 4, has resulted in extensive advertising and competitive bidding. In fact, the competitiveness of the market for CPA services has increased the importance of formulating rea-

EXHIBIT 6-5

An Example of an Engagement Letter

Hawkins & Hawkins
Certified Public Accountants
359 Park Lane
Boston, Massachusetts 10689

November 15, 19X3

Mr. John Jeffries
Chairman of the Audit Committee
Cruxco, Incorporated
1944 Frontage Road
Boston, MA 10910

Dear Mr. Jeffries:

This letter is intended to confirm our arrangements with you to audit the financial statements of Cruxco, Incorporated for the year ended December 31, 19X3, as we discussed yesterday morning.

We are to examine the balance sheet at December 31, 19X3, and the related statements of income, retained earnings, and changes in financial position for the year then ended in accordance with generally accepted auditing standards, including such tests of the accounting records and such other auditing procedures as we consider necessary to enable us to express our opinion on the financial statements. The audit will not include a detailed examination of all transactions and is not primarily or specifically designed, and cannot be relied on, to disclose defalcations or other similar irregularities, should any exist. Primary reliance for the prevention and detection of errors and irregularities must be placed on the company's existing system of internal control, although it should be acknowledged that no system of control can eliminate the possibility of errors or irregularities. Of course, we shall advise you of any unusual or abnormal matters that come to our attention during the course of our examination. The audit is designed to provide reasonable, but not absolute, assurance as to the fairness of the presentation of management's financial statements taken as a whole; hence, the examination focuses on events that would have a material effect on the financial statements.

Our examination will include a study and evaluation of the company's system of internal accounting control, as well as tests of those aspects of the control system on which we choose to rely in performing the audit. We shall prepare a letter with our recommendations for correcting the control weaknesses that are identified during the course of the audit engagement.

We shall prepare the federal and state income tax returns of Cruxco, Incorporated for the year ended December 31, 19X3, and we shall advise you concerning those income tax matters regarding which you specifically request our advice.

Our examination is scheduled as follows:

-Begin field work	November 28, 19X3
-Observation of physical inventory	December 30, 19X3
-Mailing of confirmations	January 4, 19X4
-Completion of field work	February 22, 19X4
-Delivery of audit report and tax returns	March 1, 19X4

These should be regarded as target dates, not guaranteed dates, as the timing of the issuance of our report is largely dependent on our findings during the examination.

The primary responsibility for maintaining adequate accounting records and preparing proper financial statements rests with officials of the company. Such statements are the representations of management. To facilitate our timely audit of these representations, you have agreed to provide us with a year-end trial balance by January 12, 19X4. Other assistance that we expect your accounting staff to provide, in order for our firm to perform efficiently the audit of your company, includes

- the preparation of customer statements for mailing by the morning of January 4, 19X4 (we will insert our confirmation requests with these statements and control their mailing);
- the performance of account analyses, including prepaids, a listing of all fixed asset additions and retirements, and details concerning accumulated depreciation;
- the preparation of an aging of accounts receivable, a control listing of individual marketable securities and their location, and similar schedules upon request; and
- the location of vouchers, invoices, contracts, minutes, and other corporate documents requested by our audit staff.

You have told us that our audit opinion is not intended to be issued now or in the future in conjunction with any public offering of securities and that if the company should decide to do otherwise, you will contact our firm well in advance of such action. The printer's proof of any publication of your company's financial statements that are accompanied by our auditor's report will be submitted for review and approval by our firm before the final printing.

EXHIBIT 6-5 (continued)

Mr. John Jeffries
November 15, 19X3
page two

Our fees for these services will be computed at our standard rates for the various professional personnel engaged on the job, plus travel expenses and other direct costs. We estimate that our fee will be $28,000. Should we find conditions indicating that additional audit time is necessary and therefore a higher fee, we shall notify you immediately. Of course, if you request additional services, the related fees will be agreed upon and billed separately. Our practice is to bill for our services as the work progresses, with final billing upon completion of the engagement. Bills for services are due when rendered.

We are pleased that you selected our firm as auditors for Cruxco, Incorporated and shall be happy to discuss this letter further, as well as other desired services, upon request. You may be certain that every phase of the engagement will receive our most careful attention and that the entire resources of our firm will be made available to your company in addressing any accounting, auditing, tax, regulatory, and management service issues that may arise.

If the foregoing is in accordance with your understanding, please sign the enclosed copy of this letter in the space provided to indicate your agreement with the arrangements, and return it to us at your earliest convenience. We appreciate this opportunity to be of service to your company.

Sincerely,

____
Hawkins & Hawkins
Certified Public Accountants

The terms of this letter
constitute our agreement.

Accepted by: ____________________________
Chairman, Board of Directors
Cruxco, Incorporated

Date: ____________________________

Note: Other relevant literature includes

Earl F. Davis and James W. Kelley, "The Engagement Letter and Current Legal Developments," *Journal of Accountancy*, December, 1972, pp. 56-57.

AICPA, *Guide for Engagement of CPAs to Prepare Unaudited Financial Statements* (New York: AICPA, 1975), pp. 13-14.

AICPA, Statement on Standards for Accounting Review Services No. 1 (New York: AICPA, 1979).

sonable fee estimates which, from a business perspective, earn an adequate return for the firm. Some insight as to the relative importance of the audit fee as a motivation for changing auditors is provided by a perusal of *The Public Accounting Report* from May 1978 to January 1980; 18.4% of the 474 companies changing auditors and providing explanations for the change reported that audit fees were a primary reason for hiring the new CPA firm.

Only limited information is available to the public concerning audit fees. A 1972 study reported that average audit fees paid by U.S. manufacturing companies in 1971 were .04% of annual sales volume, although smaller companies with under $100 million in annual sales were at least *double the average*.[7] A 1978 study reported average audit fees of .033% of annual sales for U.S. manufacturing concerns, and .03% of annual sales volume for all U.S.

[7] G. Hobgood and J. A. Sciarrino, "Management Looks at Audit Services," *Financial Executive*, April 1972, pp. 26–32.

companies in the sample of 1,305 respondents.[8] A 1980 study reported that the audit of Boston, MA required 73,000 hours at a fee of $500,000.[9] Exhibit 6-6 presents a summary of those factors that determine audit fees, and Exhibit 6-7 reports aggregate statistics that demonstrate the broad range of audit fees paid by clients of similar size (in terms of sales). Fee statistics for smaller entities are reported, some of which relate to nonaudit services. It is interesting to note that the second biggest gripe concerning accountants is the lack of a "reasonable and clear fee structure." This suggests an area for future improvement but also reflects, in part, the complexity of the process by which fees are determined.

Competitive bidding is common in the municipal sector. Sometimes the submitted bids are made public, and invariably the range of bids is very wide:

> . . . one state government, according to Richard S. Hickok, managing partner of Hurdman & Cranstoun, on a proposal attracted bids from 10 firms, most of them in the neighborhood of $300,000. A Big Eight CPA firm offered to do the job for $45,000. "There's no way," says Hickok, "the others could have been that far off."[10]

An extremely low bid may be justified for a particular job if the CPA firm has (1) excessive unbillable professional staff time in the summer, owing to the predominance of calendar year-end corporate clients; (2) staff who are interested in the governmental sector; and (3) growth opportunities with other municipal clients. But some CPA firms have been openly critical of such price cutting and fear for the quality of the professional services. Yet, when one recognizes the advantages of developing a client base, the liability and professional consequences of doing inadequate work, and the effect of legal troubles or adverse publicity on a CPA firm's existing client portfolio, one can expect that quality services will be provided despite the price-cutting tactics.

Identifying Unique Aspects of an Engagement

Part of planning an audit engagement is identifying the unique aspects that are likely to affect the timing and nature of particular procedures. For example, if a client performs a cycle count of inventory locations at staggered times throughout the period, the auditor must coordinate his or her inventory observation procedures throughout the fiscal year. Similarly, if the client has inventory that requires the use of an appraiser, such as for a diamond or jewelry retailer, then the auditor must ensure that there will be a competent observation of inventory.

When planning an audit, the auditor must determine whether system changes have occurred or are scheduled to occur before the fiscal year-end. Using compliance tests as a basis for relying on controls and reducing substantive tests will depend partly on such changes. The inefficiency of having to test two systems in one period may thus point to a more substantive testing approach to the engagement.

If a client has international operations, the auditor may have to arrange with other CPA firms with offices at the various foreign locations to perform audit work for the primary auditor. At a minimum, the auditor should study the business, accounting, auditing, and sociological characteristics of the country in which the audit will be performed. If subsidiaries are to be consolidated, the various subsidiaries' auditors should be coordinated to provide a basis for an audit opinion on the consolidated entity. Whenever multilocation or multientity audits are involved, the planning phase must consider the entire audit plan; coordinate activities, with continuous monitoring of the audit work schedule; and tailor the audit instructions to facilitate on-location supervision, with an information link to the engagement's coordinator.

[8] J.A. Sciarrino, edited by Daniel E. Miller, "The Annual Audit Revisited," *Financial Executive,* March 1978, pp. 38–44.

[9] Charles F. Feeney, "Competition in an Emerging Governmental Audit Market," *Massachusetts CPA Review,* March–April 1980, pp. 20–22.

[10] Steven S. Anreder, "Profit or Loss? Price-Cutting Is Hitting Accountants in the Bottom Line," *Barron's,* March 12, 1979, p. 18.

EXHIBIT 6-6
Determinants of Audit Fees

Financial Characteristics

- Revenue
- Income
- Assets
- Foreign Assets
- Equity
- Expenditures to Operate and Enhance the Internal Accounting Control System
- Receivables/Total Assets
- Inventory/Total Assets
- Audited vs. Unaudited Prior Years' Financial Statements

Operating Characteristics

- Industry
- No. of Locations
- No. of Consolidated Subsidiaries
- No. of Product Lines
- Legal Complexity
- Degree of Automation of Accounting Records
- Degree of Centralization of Accounting & Financial Controls
- Public vs. Private Company
- Nature of Internal Auditor's Activities
- Past Problems With Fraud or Bankruptcy
- Audit Committee
- Qualifications of Financial and Accounting Personnel

Environmental Factors

- Competition Among CPA Firms
- Legal Environment
- Market for Professional Staff
- Regulatory Requirements Affecting Form of Audit Services

External Auditors' Activities

- Extent to Which They Rely on Internal Auditors
- Extent of Reliance on Internal Control
- No. of Separate Audit Reports Issued Annually
- Past Experience With Client
- Past Experience With Other Clients in the Same Industry
- Extent of Experience Including Length of Auditor/Client Relationship
- Extent of Interim Work
- Timing of Completion of Audit Work
- Urgency With Which Work Had to Be Completed
- Past "Subject to" Audit Opinion
- Practice Development Objectives of the CPA
- Requirement for Overseas Service
- Type of CPA Firm and Office Location
- Level of Audit Staff on the Job
- Services Rendered, i.e., Issuance of a Management Letter and Provision of Complementary Tax and Management Advisory Services

From Wanda A. Wallace, *A Time Series Analysis of the Effect of Internal Audit Activities on External Audit Fees* (Altamonte Springs, Fla.: Institute of Internal Auditors, 1984), pp. 43-51.

EXHIBIT 6-7
The Relationship of Audit Fees to Client Size

1981 Operating Revenue	Range of Audit Fees Paid*		
	Low	High	Average
Under $500 million (42 entities)	$12,500	$3,900,000	$ 218,354
Over $500 million (29 entities)	$40,000	$4,379,500	$1,104,830

1981 Sales Volume (in Millions of Dollars)	Average Annual Accountants Fee†
Under $1	$ 3,000
$1 - $2.9	$ 5,300
$3 - $4.9	$10,600
$5 - $24.9	$16,600
$25+	$42,600

*Wanda A. Wallace, "Judging the Reasonableness of External Audit Fees – One Useful Benchmark," *Financial Executive,* March-April 1984, p. 37.
†Only one-third of entities with sales less than $1 million undergo an audit, whereas one-half in the $3 million to $5 million category are audited, 70 percent of the $5 million to $25 million category, and virtually all of the over $25 million category are audited. Bradford W. Ketchum, Jr., "You and Your Accountant," *INC.*, March 1982, pp. 81-90.

Selecting the Audit Team

Once the fee is determined and the engagement is accepted, the next step is to select the audit team. The team usually will contain a partner, manager, senior, and one or more staff auditors. The many considerations in selecting them include (1) the professional staff's industry training and experience; (2) the client's computer environment and the need for a computer specialist; (3) the planned use of statistical sampling and the possible need for a statistical sampling specialist if the sampling applications are expected to be complex; (4) the intention to use innovative analytical review techniques, such as regression analysis, and the need for personnel trained to use such audit tools; (5) the professional staff's interests and career development objectives; (6) convenience factors such as the client's geographical location relative to the staff members' residences; (7) commitments to other clients; and (8) the desire for continuity and the expected effects of staff turnover. This final consideration warrants discussion, as most auditor–client relationships are long term. "Only 13 percent of . . . [the 620 companies appearing in the *Fortune* list of the 500 largest industrial companies from 1955 to 1963] switched auditors in a 13-year period, an average of 1 percent per year.[11] Research which surveyed ninety-five companies indicated that they had retained their CPA as their external auditor for an average of twenty-two years, as of year-end 1981.[12] But despite the client's apparent wish for a continuing relationship with the audit team and the audit firm, there are sometimes two obstacles that may prevent this: staff turnover and the SEC's Practice Section requirement of rotating the partner in charge of an audit at least every five years.[13] Despite the advantages claimed for rotation policies, such as the ability of the new partner or professional staff member to take a "fresh look" at the engagement, few clients are enthusiastic about "training" a new audit team each year. Therefore the engagement planning process should consider the long-term involvement of each staff member with a particular client and strive to retain some continuity. For example, if a senior accountant is to be changed for next year's engagement, then this year's manager should be kept on the team.

The selection of the audit team must reflect professional standards and firm policies. In addition to complying with partner rotation requirements, the competence of the audit staff is extremely important. The team should be balanced to permit the training of inexperienced staff by experienced staff and to assure that the special needs of the client can be met.

Beyond audit team considerations are client service team considerations. In other words, representatives from the tax, consulting functions, or other special outside sources can provide a multidisciplined approach to improving CPA firms' service to clients. Beyond those technical skills already mentioned in the areas of computers, sampling, and regression analysis, the following examples of technical skills of use in today's auditing environment are cited in the literature: "Quantitative analysis; Systems analysis; Industrial engineering; Federal and state regulation and compliance; Tax analysis and planning; Financial analysis; Employee benefits; Organization planning."[14] Of course, the members of a particular service team or audit team should reflect the client's point of view in regard to its needs, as well as cost-benefit considerations. The costs of the client getting upset at having to serve as a training ground for new professional staff members must be balanced with the benefits of training new staff and developing industry expertise. Similarly, the cost of paying professionals for overtime must be balanced with the benefit of not having to rotate additional staff on and off various engagements. The benefits from using a specialist in the area of employee benefits, in the form of improved client service and increased billings, must justify the cost of that specialist's services.

In selecting an audit team, the engagement planner must be mindful of potential effects of the selection process on the manageability of the team. For example, known personality conflicts should be avoided, and input from the senior or manager on the job should be considered when choosing the staff assistants for an engagement. Of course, satisfying requests may require the "juggling" of schedules which can be difficult to manage with a large staff. By publicizing staff availability through long-range scheduling, managers can be given the opportunity to choose and to negotiate for particular audit team members. Morale can be affected by sending auditors from the west-side of town to east-side engagements, or vice versa, or by assigning what appears to be an excessive number of out-of-town engagements to some individuals, if the rationale for assignments is not communicated to the professional staff. Similarly, if an assignment is

[11] John C. Burton and William Roberts, "A Study of Auditor Changes," *Journal of Accountancy*, April 1967, p. 33.

[12] Wanda A. Wallace, *A Time Series Analysis of the Effect of Internal Audit Activities on External Audit Fees* (Altamonte Springs, Fla.: Institute of Internal Auditors, 1984), p. 252.

[13] AICPA, "Report of Progress" (New York: AICPA, 1978), p. 9.

[14] W. F. Crouse, M. C. Paradis, and John C. Shaw, "The Client Service Team Approach to Auditing," *Journal of Accountancy*, August 1979, p. 53.

made upon a client's request, despite the known conflict of such an assignment with the career development objectives of an individual, communicating the rationale for the assignment can deter staff turnover or morale problems. The complexity of staff assignments has led to the use of mathematical programming models, although they are typically augmented by subjective factors not easily captured by such models.[15]

The managing of an audit team for a new client can be expected to differ from the managing of the team for a continuing engagement. Specifically, more preliminary planning and review of the client's operations are necessary in the former case, and special care not to harass the client with endless, and possibly repetitive, questions must be exercised. Often a policy whereby one or two members of the audit team are responsible for interacting with the client at different management levels is an effective management tool. In a continuing audit engagement, new staff members can review the client's permanent file and the prior year's working papers, often eliminating the necessity of holding a formal preliminary conference with the audit team members. Of course, some discussion of changes in the client's operations and the audit approach is required, and for efficiency, clear instructions to team members as to their individual responsibilities are essential. Frequently, this can be done most effectively by arranging a brief preliminary conference with the audit team. Whether a new or existing client is involved, the audit team is likely to include some professional staff members who are new to the engagement. Therefore, the preliminary conference should include a discussion of the client's business, personnel, idiosyncrasies of employees with whom the auditors will be interacting, particular risk exposures, and the planned audit approach. Trouble-spots from prior years should be highlighted, as should key environmental and industry-related changes that are likely to affect client operations. The planning and supervisory responsibilities of both the audit and the client service teams are described in SAS No. 22, "Planning and Supervision,"[16] as well as Statement on Quality Control Standards No. 1, "System of Quality Control for a CPA Firm,"[17] and will be discussed in Chapter 8.

Communication Between Client and Audit Team

Rapport with the client and the timely communication of audit findings or problems are essential to an efficient audit approach. The client should be told that the external auditor would prefer not to disrupt the client's operations but will need several employees' time and cooperation in order to obtain records and documents for examination and to answer questions that arise during the audit. Advance planning should indicate the records that will be needed for the auditor's review, the schedules that the client should prepare, and the timing of procedures that will require the employees' assistance, such as the application of EDP auditing tools. A communication link, whereby the client can inform the auditors of employees' complaints during the course of an audit, can ensure the timely resolution of problems and the circumvention of personality conflicts that are slowing down the progress of the engagement.

There may be surprises during the audit that adversely affect the work schedule, fee, or form of the auditor's reports. The CPA should immediately inform the client of such events, so that he or she is not taken unawares at the audit's completion. Indeed, the client may be able either to minimize or even resolve such problems. For example, the client could authorize extended work by the internal audit department, a detailed analysis and correction of errors stemming from a programming or control problem, or the timely installation of a control procedure. A good way of encouraging communication is for the client and the CPA firm to designate a liaison for each side. The CPA should stress to the client the importance of discussing any planned changes in the accounting practices and system controls. And if the client has an internal audit department, the CPA should arrange to receive the internal audit reports (or, at least executive summaries) on a routine basis.

[15]Approaches to staff assignments are discussed in *Journal of Accountancy*, April 1979, pp. 42–46, by Miklos Vasarhelyi; those readers with particular interest in this topic are encouraged to investigate such literature.

[16]New York: AICPA, March 1978. [17]New York: AICPA, November 1979.

The Management Letter

The CPA's management letter lists the CPA's recommendations to the client regarding internal control and operations. Many CPAs discuss their findings in person with their clients, eliciting management's comments, and then putting all of this into a letter at both an interim date and after the conclusion of the audit. Such an approach gives the client an opportunity to improve controls and also to give the CPA his or her reactions and suggestions. Some CPAs have found that such discussions with clients uncover impractical suggestions and misinterpreted findings, saving both from misunderstandings later on. Exhibit 6-8 shows a suggested form for a management letter. The suggestions need to be tailored to the particular client, but the general content of the letter should include a statement of the problem, its materiality, its effects, and some means of resolving the problem.[18]

The Audit Committee

Finally the engagement-planning process usually includes a report to the board of directors or the audit committee regarding the general audit approach and the required cooperation of the client's personnel. A meeting permitting the directors to ask about the audit approach and the effectiveness of coordinating the internal and external auditors will confirm to the auditor what the client expects and to the client the means by which the professional standards will be met.

REVIEW QUESTIONS

1. We audit six of the eight banks in town. But when we asked to submit a competitive bid on one of the other two banks, the chairman of the bank's board of directors stated that the bank was not interested in its competitor's auditor. Explain the probable reasons for the chairman's response. Can you offer any arguments as to why the bank should consider hiring our CPA firm to perform its annual audit?
2. A partner of a local CPA firm indicated that all inquiries from prospective clients were being forwarded to a competing firm unless they had fiscal year-ends in the summer. "We're splitting at the seams," he explained. Comment on why the partner decided to do this.
3. A local utility company asked several CPA firms in the area to submit competitive bids for the next three years' audits. One CPA firm declined. What are the probable reasons?
4. A national CPA firm had a client portfolio that included several clients in real estate investment trusts (REITs). The national office therefore ruled that in the future, before they are accepted, all prospective REIT clients be reviewed by two partners who are real estate specialists. What is the reason for such a policy?
5. You call a client's predecessor auditor who refuses to discuss the previous year's engagement. What should you do next?
6. A common red flag is inadequate compensation. How can the auditor discern its presence?
7. "Once a prospective client has been evaluated and accepted, that client should be viewed as a permanent member of the CPA's client portfolio." Comment on this statement.
8. How can a CPA investigate the integrity of both the management and the owners of prospective clients?
9. Generally accepted auditing standards do not require engagement letters. Why, then, are they commonly used by CPAs?
10. Recall the dialogue that introduced this chapter and assume that you have made an appointment with the president to discuss a potential engagement. Outline the issues you should bring up at the meeting.
11. What should be the contents of an engagement letter? To whom should it be addressed? Who should sign the letter? At what point in the engagement should the letter be prepared? What is the main purpose of an engagement letter?
12. What is the typical relationship between audit fees and client size? Why?
13. Exhibit 6-6 cites several financial, operating, and environmental factors that affect audit fees, including those external audit activities that are likely to influence the fee's size. Which of the characteristics listed in Exhibit 6-6 would probably reduce the fees if either present or increased?

[18] For those readers wanting more elaboration on how to construct management letter suggestions, see Wanda A. Wallace, "More Effective Management Letters," *CPA Journal*, December 1983, pp. 18–28.

EXHIBIT 6-8
An Introduction to Specific Management Letter Recommendations

February 20, 19X4

Dear (president's name and possibly the board of directors):

In accordance with generally accepted auditing standards, we have reviewed and evaluated existing internal accounting controls to establish a basis for reliance thereon in determining the nature, timing, and extent of the audit tests that were necessary to express an opinion on the 19X3 financial statements.

Our study and evaluation of the entity's system of internal accounting control were not designed for the purpose of making detailed recommendations and would not necessarily disclose all weaknesses in the existing system. Our audit procedures have been appropriately adjusted to compensate for any observed weaknesses. Although we have recommendations concerning various procedural, control, and general matters, our review did not disclose any weaknesses in internal accounting control that we consider to be material weaknesses. A material weakness is defined for our purposes as

> a condition in which we believe that the prescribed procedures or the degree of compliance with them does not provide reasonable assurance that error or irregularities in amounts that would be material in the financial statements being audited would be prevented or detected within a timely period by employees in the normal course of performing their assigned functions. (AU § 320.69)

We have not reviewed the internal control and accounting procedures subsequent to February 2, 19X4, the date of our accountants' report.

As the primary purpose of our exam is to form an opinion on the financial statements, you will appreciate that reliance must be placed on adequate methods of internal control as your principal safeguard against irregularities which a test exam may not disclose. The objective of internal accounting control is to provide reasonable, but not absolute, assurance that assets are safeguarded against loss from unauthorized use and that financial records are reliable for preparing financial statements in accordance with generally accepted accounting principles and for maintaining the accountability for assets. The concept of reasonable assurance recognizes that the cost of a system of internal accounting control should not exceed the related benefits; to operationalize this concept, management is required to formulate estimates and judgments of the cost/benefit ratios of alternative controls.

There are inherent limitations that should be recognized in considering the potential effectiveness of any system of internal accounting control. Errors can result from misunderstanding of instructions, mistakes of judgment, carelessness, fatigue, and other personnel factors. Control procedures whose effectiveness depends upon the segregation of duties can be circumvented by collusion or by management. What's more, any projection of internal control evaluations to future periods is subject to the risk that the procedures may become inadequate because of changes in conditions or due to the deterioration of the degree of compliance with control procedures.

As an adjunct to our audit we remained alert throughout for opportunities to enhance internal controls and operating efficiency. These matters were discussed with management as the audit progressed and have subsequently been reviewed in detail to formulate practical recommendations. Our suggestions should not be construed as a criticism of or a reflection on the integrity of any officer or employee of the company. In fact, the involvement with management at all levels provided an excellent opportunity to exchange ideas and formulate these recommendations. The courtesies and cooperation of employees facilitated the efficient performance of audit procedures, particularly the assistance by your internal audit department. In reviewing this report, it is important to remember that your company's many sound controls that exist are not recited; this letter by nature is critical for the purpose of suggesting means of improving control and operations. Not only can the adoption of our suggestions enhance the audit trail and reduce audit fees, but more importantly, incorrect business decisions that could result from the use of inaccurate and incomplete data can be avoided.

This letter has been prepared solely for your information and may be distributed at your discretion to your employees, regulatory authorities, and your bonding company; we request that you confer with us prior to distributing the report to other third parties. In this manner, we can communicate with creditors and other parties who you may desire to review the report, to ensure that its contents are understood.

We welcome discussion of the ideas expressed herein and would be pleased to assist in the implementation of any desired actions. Let us now turn to our specific suggestions. . .

From Wanda A. Wallace, *Handbook of Internal Accounting Controls* (Englewood Cliffs, N.J.: Prentice-Hall, 1984), pp. 378-379.

14. Exhibit 6-7 shows that audit fees do not always depend on a client's total sales dollars (or revenue). Why not?

15. Exhibit 6-7 reports the percentage of small businesses that undergo an audit. Why do only one-third of entities with sales of less than $1 million and one-half of those with sales from $3 to $5 million undergo an audit, when neither is subject to regulation by the Securities and Exchange Commission? (Hint: You may wish to refer back to Chapter 1 when responding to this question.)

16. What special problems for engagement planning are posed by clients with international operations?
17. Some believe that a CPA firm's independence would be enhanced if all its clients rotated auditors every three to five years. Do you agree? What are the costs and benefits to both sides of such a policy? What have clients, given the choice in the marketplace, in the absence of regulation, opted to do with respect to the length of time that they are associated with a single auditor? What does this "typical practice" imply as to the assertion being made? (Again, a review of Chapter 1 may be useful in responding to this question.)
18. A newly hired staff auditor has just reviewed the staff assignments for the next six months and complains to a colleague: "You get all the jobs on my side of town, and I get all the jobs on yours. What do you say we look into switching our assignments?" Comment on the advisability of the staff auditor's suggestion.
19. Having just been promoted to manager, you are planning your first preliminary conference with the audit team members for a client on whose audit you have worked for the past three years. Outline the topics that you should address at the conference.
20. You just received an irate call from a client who said that the audit fee was three times higher than what was initially quoted in the engagement letter. Surely, there must have been an error. How could the creation of communication channels between the client and the audit team have avoided this? Can this higher fee be justified? Must the CPA stick to the fee quoted in the engagement letter?

EXERCISES

1. It has been suggested that a five-point scale, with five being the best and one the worst, be used to evaluate existing clients on five variables:
   1. Value of services rendered (in the client's judgment).
   2. Development potential.
   3. Client cooperation.
   4. Economic stability (ability to pay).
   5. Timeliness of payment.[19]

   Comment on this scale, the variables, and its usefulness to a CPA who is evaluating the firm's client portfolio.
2. Accounting Series Release (ASR) No. 196 (now referred to as FRRs), "In the Matter of Seidman & Seidman, et al.," includes a reminder by the SEC that CPAs should investigate their clients, especially those acquired by merger. According to ASR No. 196, when Seidman & Seidman acquired a smaller CPA firm that had Equity Funding Corporation of America as a client, it did not investigate the smaller firm's clients.

   Comment on the special problems created by the merger of CPA firms with respect to client evaluation. Based on Chapter 5 material pertaining to Equity Funding, how should Seidman & Seidman have evaluated the risk exposure from its newly acquired client portfolio?
3. The "right to an audit" is an issue that has not yet come up in the United States, although it has in other countries. In one country, a business that was unable to get a properly certified accountant to agree to perform an audit appealed its case to the government. Because neither debt nor stock could be issued without an auditor's attestation, the business claimed that the accounting profession was infringing on its rights to pursue its commercial activities. But the auditors' refusal to accept the engagement appeared to be justified, as all of the officers in the business had criminal records. Nevertheless, the government declared that businesses had a "right to be audited" and that past records must not preclude such an attestation process. Under this pressure, representatives of the country's various accounting firms met and, it was reported, literally drew straws. Ironically, a partner of the firm that drew the shortest straw reported that the audit actually went quite well: "We went in with our eyes wide open and pounded every number into the ground!"

   Comment on the client evaluation issues that arise in this type of situation and the effects on the profession from this government ruling.
4. A small CPA firm recently established a policy of circulating a memo to its professional staff asking for a list of any current clients that the auditors believed should be dropped from the client portfolio. A partner of that firm reported that as a result of terminating these clients, the firm earned higher net returns from total revenue.

   What do you think of the policy? Why may it produce higher net returns? What attributes would lead you to recommend that a particular client be dropped?
5. Damages for liability cases, filed under the Securities and Exchange Regulations, often are deter-

[19] See James W. Grimsley, "Client Evaluation," *CPA Journal*, March 1975, pp. 57–59.

mined by computing the decline in the market price of common stock for that company being sued for false or misleading financial disclosures. Knowing this, what type of information should a CPA firm examine when evaluating both prospective and current clients?

6. In the industry's initial growth stage, many health spas adopted a revenue recognition practice of recording total revenue when memberships to the spa were sold, rather than deferring the revenue to a later point in the year or years when the members actually used the spa facilities. One CPA firm, having acquired several health spa clients, reviewed the industry's accounting practices, appealed to the American Institute of Certified Public Accountants, and was instrumental in drawing up a Statement of Position that held that some of this revenue should be deferred. As a result, the CPA firm lost several of its health spa clients. Why, then, did the firm take these actions?

QUESTIONS ADAPTED FROM PROFESSIONAL EXAMINATIONS

1. When a CPA has accepted an engagement from a new client who is a manufacturer, it is customary for the CPA to tour the client's plant facilities.

Required:
Discuss the ways in which the CPA's observations made during the plant tour would be of help to him or her when planning and conducting the audit.

(CPA exam adapted)

2. Jones, a CPA, is approached by a prospective client who wants Jones to perform an audit that in previous years was performed by another CPA.

Required:
Identify the procedures that Jones should follow in accepting the engagement.

(CPA exam adapted)

3. In late spring of 19X6 you are advised of a new assignment as the in-charge accountant of your CPA firm's annual audit of a major client, the Lancer Company. You are given the engagement letter for the audit covering the calendar year ending on December 31, 19X6, and a list of the personnel assigned to this engagement. It is your responsibility to plan and supervise the field work for the engagement.

Required:
Discuss the necessary preparation and planning for the Lancer Company's annual audit before beginning the field work at the client's office. Include the sources you should consult, the type of information you should seek, the preliminary plans and preparation you should make for the field work, and any actions regarding the staff assigned to the engagement. Do not write an audit program.

(CPA exam adapted)

4. A company has been paying $500,000 in fees per year for the last three years for an audit by its public accounting firm. The company has four manufacturing locations and operates seven distributing warehouses in five states. Each location maintains its own accounting records. The company has an internal auditing department of which the president is proud. He believes it is competent and independent and is even considering whether the internal auditing department can take over some of the functions performed by the external auditors, in order to reduce the external audit fee.

Required:

a. List five different types of tasks that the internal auditing department might undertake to reduce those fees.

b. Describe the criteria or considerations applicable to the decision as to whether the internal auditing department should assume responsibility for these tasks.

(CIA exam adapted)

5. A CPA has been asked to audit for the first time the financial statements of a publicly held company. All preliminary verbal discussions and inquiries have been completed among the CPA, the company, the predecessor auditor, and all other relevant parties. The CPA is now preparing an engagement letter.

Required:
List the items that should be included in the engagement letter, and describe the benefits of such a letter.

(CPA exam adapted)

6. Multiple-Choice: Quality Control
(Note: You may need to refer back to Chapters 3 and 4.)
Select the one answer that best completes the statement or answers the question.

6.1 In pursuing its quality control objectives with respect to independence, a CPA firm may use policies and procedures such as

a. In the firm's training programs, supervision, and review of work, emphasizing an independent mental attitude.

b. Prohibiting employees from owning shares of publicly traded companies' stock.
c. Suggesting that employees conduct their banking transactions with banks that do not maintain accounts with client firms.
d. Assigning those employees who may lack independence to research positions that do not require participation in field audit work.

(CPA exam adapted)

6.2 In pursuing its quality control objectives with respect to assigning personnel to engagements, a CPA firm may use policies and procedures such as

a. Randomly rotating employees from assignment to assignment to expand their training.
b. Requiring timely identification of the staffing requirements of specific engagements so that enough qualified personnel can be made available.
c. Allowing staff members to select their own assignments so as to promote better client relationships.
d. Assigning more employees to each engagement than needed so as not to overburden the staff and lower the quality of the audit work.

(CPA exam adapted)

6.3 The main reason that a CPA firm establishes quality control policies and procedures for its staff accountants is to

a. Comply with the state's continuing educational requirements for all staff accountants in CPA firms.
b. Establish, in fact as well as in appearance, that staff accountants are increasing their knowledge of accounting and auditing matters.
c. Provide a forum for staff accountants to exchange their experiences and views concerning firm policies and procedures.
d. Ensure that staff personnel will have the requisite knowledge to fulfill responsibilities.

(CPA exam adapted)

6.4 Which of the following is not an element of quality control that a firm of independent auditors should consider:

a. Assigning personnel to engagements.
b. Consultation with appropriate persons.
c. Keeping records of quality control policies and procedures.
d. Supervision.

(CPA exam adapted)

6.5 In pursuing its quality control objectives with respect to acceptance of a client, a CPA firm is not likely to

a. Question the proposed client's legal counsel.
b. Review the proposed client's financial statements.
c. Question the proposed client's previous auditors.
d. Review the proposed client's personnel practices.

(CPA exam adapted)

6.6 A CPA establishes quality control policies and procedures for deciding whether to accept a new client and to continue to perform services for a current client. The primary purpose for establishing such policies and procedures is

a. To enable the auditor to attest to a client's integrity or reliability.
b. To comply with the regulatory bodies' quality control standards.
c. To minimize the likelihood of associating with clients whose managements lack integrity.
d. To lessen the exposure to litigation resulting from not detecting irregularities in the client's financial statements.

(CPA exam adapted)

6.7 Which of the following is not an element of quality control?

a. Documentation.
b. Inspection.
c. Supervision.
d. Consultation.

(CPA exam adapted)

6.8 In pursuing its quality control objectives, a CPA firm may maintain records indicating which of its partners or employees were previously employed by the CPA firm's clients. Which quality control objective would this be most likely to satisfy?

a. Professional relationship.
b. Supervision.
c. Independence.
d. Advancement.

(CPA exam adapted)

6.9 Dickens, a CPA firm's personnel partner, periodically studies the firm's personnel advancement experience to ascertain whether those individuals meeting the stated criteria are assigned increased degrees of responsibility. This is evidence of the CPA firm's adherence to prescribed

a. Standards of due professional care.

b. Quality control standards.
c. Supervision and review standards.
d. Standards of fieldwork.

(CPA exam adapted)

6.10 An individual just entering an auditing career must gain professional experience mainly to achieve
a. A positive quality control review.
b. Seasoned judgment.
c. A favorable peer review.
d. A specialty designation by the AICPA.

(CPA exam adapted)

7. Multiple-Choice: Engagement Analysis and Planning

Select the one answer that best completes the statement or answers the question.

7.1 It is important for the CPA to consider the competence of the audit clients' employees, because their competence directly affects the
a. Internal control system's cost-benefit relationship.
b. Achievement of the internal control system's objectives.
c. Comparison of recorded accountability with assets.
d. Timing of the tests to be performed.

(CPA exam adapted)

7.2 Hawkins requested permission to communicate with the predecessor auditor and review certain portions of the predecessor auditor's working papers. The prospective client's refusal to permit this will bear directly on Hawkins's decision concerning the
a. Adequacy of the preplanned audit program.
b. Ability to establish consistency in applying accounting principles over the years.
c. Apparent scope limitation.
d. Integrity of management.

(CPA exam adapted)

7.3 Preliminary arrangements agreed to by the auditor and the client should be put in writing by the auditor. The best place to list these arrangements is in
a. A memorandum to be placed in the permanent section of the auditing working papers.
b. An engagement letter.
c. A client representation letter.
d. A confirmation letter attached to the constructive services letter.

(CPA exam adapted)

7.4 Engagement letters are widely used for professional engagements of all types. The main purpose of the engagement letter is to
a. Remind management that it has the primary responsibility for the financial statements.
b. Satisfy the requirements of the CPA's liability insurance policy.
c. Provide a starting point for the auditor's preparation of the preliminary audit program.
d. Provide a written record of the agreement with the client regarding the services to be provided.

(CPA exam adapted)

7.5 In determining estimates of fees, an auditor may take into account each of the following, except the
a. Value of the service to the client.
b. Degree of responsibility assumed by undertaking the engagement.
c. Skills required to perform the service.
d. Discovery of specific findings.

(CPA exam adapted)

7.6 A CPA may reduce the audit work on a first-time audit by reviewing the predecessor auditor's working papers. The predecessor should permit the successor to review working papers relating to matters of continuing accounting significance, such as those pertaining to the
a. Extent of reliance on specialists' work.
b. Fee arrangements and summaries of payments.
c. Analysis of contingencies.
d. Staff hours required to complete the engagement.

(CPA exam adapted)

7.7 When a CPA is approached to perform an audit for the first time, the CPA should talk to the predecessor auditor. This is a necessary procedure because the predecessor may be able to give the successor information that will help in determining
a. Whether the predecessor's work should be used.
b. Whether the company follows a policy of rotating its auditors.
c. Whether the predecessor believes that the company's internal control has been satisfactory.
d. Whether the engagement should be accepted.

(CPA exam adapted)

7.8 In an audit situation, communication between successor and predecessor auditors should be
a. Authorized in an engagement letter.

b. Acknowledged in a representation letter.
c. Either written or oral.
d. Written and included in the working papers

(CPA exam adapted)

7.9 If during an audit examination, the successor auditor becomes aware of information that may require that the financial statements reported on by the predecessor auditor be revised, the successor auditor should

a. Ask the client to arrange a meeting among the three parties to discuss the information and attempt to resolve the matter.
b. Notify the client and the predecessor auditor of the matter and ask them to attempt to resolve it.
c. Notify the predecessor auditor, who may be required to revise the previously issued financial statements and the auditor's report.
d. Ask the predecessor auditor to arrange a meeting with the client to discuss and resolve the matter.

(CPA exam adapted)

7.10 What is the responsibility of a successor auditor with respect to communicating with the predecessor auditor about a prospective new audit client?

a. The successor auditor has no responsibility to contact the predecessor auditor.
b. The successor auditor should obtain permission from the prospective client to contact the predecessor auditor.
c. The successor auditor should contact the predecessor, regardless of whether the prospective client authorizes contact.
d. The successor auditor need not contact the predecessor if the successor is aware of all available relevant facts.

(CPA exam adapted)

7.11 An independent auditor has the responsibility to plan the audit examination to search for errors and irregularities that might have a material effect on the financial statements. Which of the following, if material, would be an irregularity, as defined in Statements on Auditing Standards?

a. Misappropriation of an asset or groups of assets.
b. Clerical mistakes in the accounting data pertaining to the financial statements.
c. Mistakes in the application of accounting principles.
d. Misinterpretation of facts that existed when the financial statements were prepared.

(CPA exam adapted)

7.12 Although there is no professional requirement to do so on audit engagements, CPAs normally issue a formal "management" letter to their clients. The purpose of this letter is to provide

a. Evidence indicating whether the auditor is reasonably certain that the system of internal accounting control is operating as prescribed.
b. A permanent record of the internal accounting control work performed by the auditor during the engagement.
c. A written record of discussions between auditor and client concerning the auditor's observations and suggestions for improvements.
d. A summary of the auditor's observations resulting from the auditor's special study of the internal control system.

(CPA exam adapted)

CASES FOR DISCUSSION

1. The H. J. Heinz case received national publicity. By colluding with at least six suppliers, Heinz's legal fees, advertising, and market research expenses were manipulated from 1971 to 1979. Bogus invoices were prepared upon request by the suppliers of such services. If the services were not subsequently rendered, any advance cash payments were returned to Heinz. Sales cutoff was also manipulated by adjusting internal documentation. Over 325 employees were aware of the impropriety, based on reports in the *Wall Street Journal*. Upon investigation, it became evident that all this had been done mostly to maximize the managers' bonus-incentive awards. What implications does the Heinz case have for the client evaluation process? Be specific.

2. Risk evaluation models, commonly referred to as bankruptcy prediction models, assign values to a company's various financial attributes so as to create an index that can be compared with those of other companies to discover the relative inability of certain entities to meet their obligations. These models generally use variables related to profitability, debt service, liquidity, size, capital structure, and stability. Arthur Andersen & Co. announced it would use such a model to screen its prospective clients. Other firms, however, have noted that these models were formulated to meet investors', not auditors', objectives and that when applied to a client portfolio, if the model indicated that a significant percentage of the clients were in "trouble," it did not tell them what to do. Why do CPAs use bankruptcy prediction models? Analyze the problem presented by "mixed objectives" of such models and by "false alarms."

3. Multiple regression analysis, also referred to as *ordinary least squares,* is a means of modeling or explaining one variable by using a set of descriptor or explanatory variables. For example, one simple regression model formulated to estimate or explain external audit fees is

$$\text{External Audit Fee} = -60{,}565 + .0000616\,(\text{Operating Revenue}) + 2{,}032{,}517\left(\frac{\text{Foreign Assets}}{\text{Total Assets}}\right) + 46{,}432\left(\begin{array}{c}\text{Square Root of the No.}\\ \text{of Separate Locations}\end{array}\right)$$

This model can be applied by multiplying each coefficient (for example, the .0000616 value) by the variable described in parentheses (for example, the operating revenue) and then adding the numbers to the constant term (−60,565), in order to estimate the total fees. Assume that an entity had $11,873 million of operating revenue, $12,496 million of total assets, $5,800 million of foreign assets, and 170 locations.

a. Compute the estimated audit fee for the entity.

b. Coefficients are generally interpreted as a measure of the change in the average value of the variable being described, per unit change in the explanatory variable, holding all other variables constant. Explain how each of the model's coefficients is interpreted. What does the model say about the interrelationship of its variables?

c. Describe the probable usefulness of the regression model in estimating a particular entity's audit fee.

d. If you could change the model, how would you change it?[20]

4. You asked a staff auditor to draft an engagement letter for a new client. The following rough draft was just submitted:

Mr. Jake Smith
Controller
Axin, Inc.
796 Park Road
Chicago, IL 76302

Dear Mr. Smith:

This letter is intended to confirm our arrangements with you concerning our services to Axin. Inc., which we have discussed.

We shall perform an audit that will result in an attestation as to the fairness of your annual report. Our examination will begin in August and should be completed by February. We understand that you are planning a debt issue for April and need a clean audit report for the underwriters. To meet this time commitment, we shall require some assistance from your employees throughout the course of the audit.

Our fee will be as agreed upon yesterday, and our firm is pleased to be serving you.

Sincerely,

____

Comment on this rough draft. Prepare review notes for the staff auditor. What changes would you make? Write a final draft to send to the client.

[20] Adapted from Wanda A. Wallace, "Judging the Reasonableness of External Audit Fees—One Useful Benchmark," *Financial Executive,* March–April 1984, pp. 34–39.

7

Audit Evidence

It's about 6 P.M., and two senior auditors run into each other in the professional staff room at the CPA firm, where they are both loading up their audit trunks with supplies for field use.

Lynda. Matt, do you have a minute to talk?

Matt. Sure, what's up?

Lynda. Well, this afternoon I came to a conclusion that I find very disconcerting: In spite of what all the textbooks claim, our confirmation procedures are of little evidential value!

Matt. What made you decide that?

Lynda. The client I'm working on has an open invoice system. Most of our confirmation requests come back with this note: Cannot confirm this balance because of our accounting system. As always, government won't confirm anything, and 35 percent of the client's business is with the government.

Matt. You've got a point, but you've had open invoice systems before. Why are you so upset this time?

Lynda. It's bad enough that most clients won't respond to our confirmations, but it's far worse when they give wrong responses. When we were auditing claims and disputed items, we found several dollars involved, on which we received "clean" confirmations with no mention of the pending claim. But even the correspondence in the claim files states those same parties' intention not to pay! I even heard a call to the client's controller from a customer involved in some dispute who apparently asked how he should complete the confirmation. The controller told him just to sign it and send it in!

Matt. Your point's clearer now, but I still don't see anything new.

Lynda. I guess what really destroyed my illusions about the value of confirmations was my review this afternoon of the allowance for doubtful accounts. I went into the controller's office and was given a list of known troubled accounts. Recognizing several of the names as parties who had returned "clean confirmations" on fairly current accounts, I asked the controller about the basis of this account classification. He explained that these customers had filed under Chapter 11. The hard economic times had affected several customers' solvency, and their confirmations of their balances owed weren't worth the paper they'd been written on!

Matt. It's true; confirmations aren't worth the same today as they used to be. But we're pretty well locked in under generally accepted auditing standards, and so we've got to send out confirmations.

Lynda. I realize that, but I think we ought to cut back as far as possible. Sample sizes should be reduced, and a cost-benefit framework should determine how we combine our compliance and other substantive test work with our confirmation procedures. We're wasting a lot of time on alternative procedures for unreturned confirmations. Those procedures usually mean that we confirm a cash receipt. But this proves very little, since checks aren't examined and Account A could easily be receiving credit for some payment on Account B, and so on. I think we're fooling ourselves and ought to rethink our approach!

Matt. I think you've got something. We've got a staff meeting in two weeks. Why don't you ask for some time on the agenda to discuss the evidential value of confirmations? Maybe that will lead to some changes.

Lynda. O.K., I will. And thanks for listening—I needed a second opinion.

Matt. In fact, I think I'll add the topic of the timing of audit work. I'm a bit confused as to when we should mail confirmations and how interim work should be tied to year-end balances.

Lynda. That's not too much of a problem if you're going to rely on controls.

Matt. But what if you think that because of bad financial conditions, the client's management might be predisposed to misstate the financial statements in the remaining period? Or, more commonly, what if business conditions are changing quickly?

Lynda. Then you'd have to wait until the balance sheet date.

Matt. Then is it a choice of yes or no? Either controls are excellent and interim work is fine, or they are poor and everything has to wait for busy season?

Lynda. No, I'm sure that GAAS permits substantive work at interim even if you don't rely on controls. The main consideration is risk. For a calendar-year client, there would be greater risk if you confirmed balances in June than if you waited till September.

Matt. Well, that's exactly what I think should be discussed. When can we schedule work in May? How do we tie interim work to the balance sheet date?

Lynda. You know, you're right; the timing affects all of our audit procedures. I'm certain that all of us would benefit from talking about such timing.

This dialogue points out some of the practical shortcomings of confirmations as a source of audit evidence. Despite the traditional emphasis on third-party confirmations as being strong audit evidence, today's business conditions alter the validity of such evidence. Besides the practical issues raised in the dialogue, the possibility of fraudulent collusion of clients with third parties, though rare, further devalues the confirmation procedure. The dialogue also raises the question of when evidence should be collected and its relationship to risk. This chapter will describe alternative approaches to gathering and documenting audit evidence and will provide a framework which can be useful in evaluating the relative strength of the evidence that is gathered. This relative strength of evidence is influenced by its source, the manner in which it is collected, its extensiveness, the period of time to which it relates, and when it is obtained.

The Auditor's Objective

The auditor's principal objective in an attestation engagement on financial statements is to determine whether those statements are fairly presented. Because the financial statements themselves are management's representations, this objective can be analyzed in relation to management's various assertions about account balances and overall operations. The main financial statement assertions ***[SAS 31, Section 326]*** are that

- The recorded assets and liabilities actually existed at a given date and the recorded transactions occurred during a given period of time (*existence* or *occurrence*).
- All transactions and accounts that should be in the financial statements are included (*completeness* of the records and financial statements).
- All assets are the rights of the entity and all liabilities are the obligations of the entity at a specified date (*rights* and *obligations,* including all ownership rights).
- All amounts reported in the financial statements are appropriate (*valuation* or *allocation* is proper and representations are reasonable).
- Each of the items in the financial statements is properly classified, described, and disclosed (*presentation* and *disclosure*).

The auditor's objective, then, is to test the validity of each of these assertions to the extent deemed necessary to form an audit opinion on the financial statements as a whole.

A Conceptual Foundation

The auditor's objective is a *general proposition* concerning the fairness of the financial position. It is not a statement of fact but of general knowledge that cannot be proved but must be recognized through its *elementary propositions*. These elementary, or specific, propositions can be formulated in a manner conducive to testing. They also can often be proved as true or false, which means that they are essentially statements of fact containing proper names or unique descriptive phrases. For example, "One hundred units of finished goods were shipped to a company in New York this November." It is possible to examine the shipping documents, to confirm delivery with the company, to test the cash receipts, and to check the quantity, date, and destination specifications on all such documentary proof. Yet, the auditor's orientation is toward more general assertions such as: all shipments are recorded. This type of specific proposition is not self-evident but must be analyzed in terms of probability.

Any judgment about the relative frequency of an event is considered to be a *probability assessment. Relative frequency* means the number of times that an event takes place. In the example, the auditor would determine the number of times that shipments have been recorded. Such *demonstrable propositions* cannot be labeled as true or false but only as probable. The auditor's task, then, is to calculate the degree of likelihood: high or low.

A very intuitive example of how an evidential finding or fact can affect a probability assessment is provided by considering the following two statements:

Statement 1: He speaks English.
Statement 2: He is British.

If one were concerned with proving that an individual were British, the evidence that he spoke English would be supportive. Yet, since most English-speaking people are not British, this fact by no means confirms Statement 2. Clearly, the likelihood of being British is greater if the individual speaks English than if he does not speak English. Nevertheless, the probability is not sufficiently high to draw a conclusion in the absence of additional supporting evidence as to the individual's nationality. In stark contrast, if one were interested in proving that an individual spoke English, the finding that he was British would be viewed as *con-*

firming evidence. This is because it is more probable that he speaks English, given he is British, than it is that he does not speak English. Yet, one cannot deny that some possibility exists of the British citizen not speaking English. This bears out the inevitability of the audit process being a process of *persuasion,* as distinct from a process of proof. Generally, auditors will have an idea of probable transactions and related representations, and relative consensus will exist as to the direction of any given piece of evidence, i.e., whether the event is more or less probable as a result of that finding. The key role of judgment enters into the evaluation of the strength of that evidence in moving the auditor toward a conclusion with respect to that assertion or event.

The auditor's reasoning process is known as *heuristic reasoning,* which simply means that the auditor determines probabilities, rather than proving or disproving some fact. An interesting characteristic of heuristic reasoning is that the evidence supporting less probable results will be weighted more heavily than will the evidence supporting highly probable results. For example, misstatements in accounts are generally expected to be less probable than are appropriately stated balances. Hence if there is an unexpected fluctuation that is detected by an attention-directing device such as analytical review, that variation will receive more attention because of its potential strength in disproving the auditor's expectation that the balances are appropriately stated. This explains why much of the audit process emphasizes exceptions from the norm or from expectations. It also explains why a decision can be reached more efficiently without evidence to the contrary than when unexplained variations are detected. This is the "principle of diminishing marginal weight of evidence," which suggests that when an outcome is determined to be more and more probable, the persuasiveness of marginal evidence further supporting its probability will decline. In other words, such additional evidence is not needed, as its value is much lower than its cost. This is simply a different way of explaining how risk is related to gathering evidence. When the risk of misstatement is greater, additional evidence is required to reach a conclusion regarding that assertion. The entire audit process is a probability assessment that focuses on individual detailed audit objectives and procedures. All evidence represents surrogates for facts or assertions that together indirectly support the broader proposition of fairness.[1]

The auditor should evaluate the persuasiveness of audit evidence by asking whether a similarly qualified individual would reach the same audit conclusion based on the evidence collected. Thus *reasonable assurance* (persuasive evidence) is sought, not absolute assurance (convincing evidence) ***[SAS 31, Section 326].*** Reasonable means that cost-benefit evaluations should be made to assess risk exposure and select the auditing tools to collect the evidence. There are generally accepted schema to evaluate the strength of evidence and its relevance to particular types of assertions. These schema pertain to the source of the evidence, the means by which it was collected, and the conditions under which it was produced.

Classifying Evidence by Source

In considering the source of evidence, the auditor asks who created the evidence, who processed it after it was created, and who had access to it.

Internal Evidence

Any information created and processed by the client is *internal evidence.* For example, cost-accounting documents like materials requisition records are internal evidence. Generally, internal evidence is not as valuable as is evidence either created or processed by an external party. The issue raised is how objective is internal evidence when all parties involved in its processing are under the auditee's auspices?

The primary risk of internal data is in the control system's quality. Poorly controlled data can present risks of loss, duplication, and inaccuracy. Unauthorized data may enter the system, or data may be inadvertently destroyed. For example, when

[1] This discussion is adapted from Yoshihide Toba, "A General Theory of Evidence As the Conceptual Foundation in Auditing Theory," *Accounting Review,* January 1975, pp. 7–24.

the auditor examines time cards to test the reasonableness of recorded payroll, they are considered internal evidence. Without effective control, these cards could be incomplete, could include duplicates, and could report unauthorized hours. Thus without referring to another source of evidence, the auditor would have difficulty determining the fairness of recorded payroll expense or related liabilities.

Internal-External Evidence

If data are generated internally and given to an independent third party for processing, that information source is *internal-external*. For example, if a client prepares invoices, mails them to customers, and then requires that a copy be remitted with payment, then that copy is internal-external evidence. Similarly, checks written by a client and then processed by a bank create canceled checks that the auditor can examine when testing cash disbursements. The check's clearing assures the auditor that sufficient funds were on deposit at the bank to cover the expenditure. The internal-external information is generally acknowledged to have greater evidential weight than does purely internal information, even though both are initiated by the client.

Internal-external data have the same risks that internal data have with respect to a poorly controlled system, but because of the independent check provided by the external party, any problems are more likely to be detected in internal-external data than in data never leaving the client's system. Of course, the effectiveness of the evidence's external dimension depends on how independent the external party is and what procedures that external party performs with respect to the evidence. The auditor therefore must be wary of relying on related parties or of presuming that a check has been performed.

External-Internal Evidence

Information generated by third parties and then either processed or maintained by the client is *external-internal* evidence. Additional weight is given to such evidence because of the third party's initial involvement. For example, an invoice from a supplier that the client processes for payment is external-internal evidence. The likelihood of a valid transaction's having occurred is deemed greater because of the other party's involvement in the billing process. But because the bill does pass through the client's system, there is a risk that it may have been altered in some manner, misplaced, or duplicated. This type of evidence is exposed to any control problems that the client may have, and this internal dimension weakens its value relative to that of external evidence.

External Evidence

Data that have not entered the client's operations are *external evidence*. When externally generated, received directly by the auditor—not having passed through the client's hands—and relevant to an auditor's objective, this evidence carries the greatest weight. Both confirmations and deeds of trust filed at the county courthouse and examined by the auditor are considered to be external evidence.

Classifying Evidence by Means of Collection

Besides the effects of the source of evidence on its strength are the effects from how such evidence was obtained. Various audit procedures are available to an auditor, each with different advantages in addressing particular types of assertions regarding the financial statements.

Inquiry

Whenever an auditor has discussions with a client or other third parties, he or she is said to be applying *inquiry* procedures. Often these interviews are most effective at helping the auditor understand operations, key risk areas, and problems that the auditee currently faces in both control over operations and reporting the results of these operations. Effective communication skills should be developed in order to avoid biasing the interviewee's comments, yet still obtain the information necessary to proceed with the audit. In evaluating oral evidence, the auditor should consider the interviewee's competence concerning the topic, his

EXHIBIT 7-1
An Example of an Accounts Receivable Positive Confirmation

Control No. ____________

WAJAW CORPORATION
Anywhere, USA

July 12, 19X7

Customer XX
Somewhere, USA

To Whom It May Concern:

In connection with an examination of our financial statements, please confirm *directly* to our auditors

CPAs
Location, USA

the correctness of the balance of your account with us as of June 30, 19X7, as shown below. If exceptions are noted, please furnish any information that you may have that will assist the auditors in reconciling the difference.

Your timely attention to this request will be most appreciated. Please sign and date your reply and mail it directly to our CPAs. A stamped, addressed envelope is enclosed for your reply.

____
Controller

_____CPAs
Location, USA

The balance of the receivable from us of $3,619 as of June 30, 19X7, is correct except as noted below:

Date ____________ By ____________

or her level of interest, and the responses' logic and reasonableness; that is, is the response pattern internally consistent? When the inquiry procedures are directed at management, the auditor generally must obtain corroborating (supporting) evidence in order to rely on the information gathered in the interviews. In contrast, inquiry-based evidence from third parties may be a sufficient basis for the auditor to make a particular financial statement assertion. Most often, if it concerns a material matter, such evidence will be formally communicated in the form of a confirmation.

Confirmation

A written representation, often prepared by the auditor, that is completed by a third party and then is delivered directly to the auditor is a *confirmation.* A required audit procedure is to confirm accounts receivable. CPAs must mail the requests for confirmation and have them returned directly to them; this maintains the requests' status as external evidence. Exhibit 7-1 shows an accounts receivable positive confirmation. This should be returned by the customer, who also should indicate whether the balance is correct or incorrect. The auditor then follows up any exceptions.

If a client has several relatively small balances, the auditor may use a negative confirmation, such as the form shown in Exhibit 7-2. In order to use such forms, the auditor should have reason to believe that the persons receiving the requests are likely to consider them, as no reply is assumed to mean that the balance is correct.

Formal documentation of confirmations is typically sought from banks with regard to account

EXHIBIT 7-2
An Example of an Accounts Receivable Negative Confirmation

AUDITOR'S CONFIRMATION REQUEST

Please examine this statement with care. If it does NOT agree with your records, please report any exceptions directly to our auditors

_______ CPAs
Location, USA

who are examining our financial statements. For your convenience in replying, an addressed envelope is enclosed; it is important that your reply be mailed directly to our CPAs as indicated.

DO NOT SEND YOUR REMITTANCE
TO OUR AUDITORS.

balances, credit lines, collateral arrangements, compensating balances, and similar matters. A *standard bank confirmation inquiry form* is presented in Exhibit 7-3. Note that along with the items already mentioned, it requests information on contingent liabilities related to notes receivable that the bank has discounted. A type of confirmation, in the form of a letter of representation, is also requested from lawyers regarding pending litigation and related contingency estimates. The external nature of these written representations and the competency and independence of the individuals completing the confirmations add to the strength of the evidence attributed to confirmations. Note this general acceptance that confirmations have substantial evidential value, even though the numerous flaws in the confirmation procedure—cited in the introductory dialogue—cannot be denied. As long as the auditor is aware of each procedure's strengths and weaknesses, he or she can take advantage of the former, compensate for the latter, and thereby ensure the collection of an adequate evidential base from which the auditor can determine the fairness of the financial statements as a whole.

Observation and Inspection

Any physical evidence that the auditor examines is given fairly heavy weight since, as the saying goes, "seeing is believing." The term *observation* applies when the auditor is watching an activity, such as the performance of particular internal control procedures, and the term *inspection* is used when the CPA examines legal documents or physical assets on hand. Yet whether "seeing" is in fact a sufficient basis for "believing" depends on the nature of what is being observed, the qualifications of the observer or inspector, and the absence of fraud. If the inventory were precious gems, then the inspector would need to be a gemologist and would have to be competent and independent of the client. Moreover, mere physical existence does not constitute ownership—other audit procedures are required to confirm such assertions. The inspection of supporting documents to gain assurance of ownership rights will be effective if the documents are not forgeries or have not been fraudulently prepared or altered. Fortunately for auditors, the forgery practices used by Equity Funding are rare.

Scanning

One audit procedure is known as *scanning* and means that the auditor reviews information sets while watching for any unusual values. For example, the auditor may scan a set of adjusting entries and look for amounts over $100,000, as such large dollar entries are unexpected. Similarly, the auditor may scan the accounts receivable subsidiary ledger for credit balances in order to identify accounts requiring reclassification as current liabilities. The effectiveness of scanning relies on the ease with which unusual values can be detected and the auditor's abilities. Computerized audit tools, however, are far more effective than an auditor is at generating listings of "unusual values" based on easily definable criteria such as dollar amount. Nevertheless such tools currently lack the auditor's ability to "discern the unusual when he or she sees it."

Detailed Testing

Whenever an auditor examines documentary evidence, he or she is said to be performing *detailed test work*. Inspection is one aspect of the detailed test, another is *recomputation*. This merely refers to the auditor's testing the mathematical accuracy of various calculations such as interest expense and depreciation. Although recomputation may well be the most factual, objective, and competent audit procedure, it has an extremely narrow scope. The usefulness of a recomputation relies on the input's accuracy and validity. For example, a client's interest income may be accurately recorded based on available information but the client may later be discovered to have not recorded $300,000 of loans and to have a false interest rate because of the presence of a related-party transaction. This suggests that the initial recomputation evidence had an extremely limited value.

Besides recomputation evidence, the auditor often applies the audit procedures of vouching and tracing to documentary evidence. *Vouching* means to test documents supporting recorded balances and demonstrates that recorded transactions are valid.

EXHIBIT 7-3
Bank Confirmation

STANDARD BANK CONFIRMATION INQUIRY
Approved 1966 by
AMERICAN INSTITUTE OF CERTIFIED PUBLIC ACCOUNTANTS
AND
BANK ADMINISTRATION INSTITUTE (FORMERLY NABAC)

Dear Sirs: ____________________ 19____

Your completion of the following report will be sincerely appreciated. IF THE ANSWER TO ANY ITEM IS "NONE," PLEASE SO STATE. Kindly mail it in the enclosed stamped, addressed envelope direct to the accountant named below.

Report from

(Bank) ____________________

Yours truly, ____________________

(ACCOUNT NAME PER BANK RECORDS)

Bank customer should check here if confirmation of bank balances only (item 1) is desired. ☐

NOTE: If the space provided is inadequate, please enter total hereon and attach a statement giving full details as called for by the columnar headings below.

Dear Sirs:

1. At the close of business on ____________ 19____ our records showed the following balance(s) to the credit of the above customer. In the event that we could readily ascertain whether there were any balances to the credit of the customer not designated in this request, the appropriate information is given below.

AMOUNT	ACCOUNT NAME	ACCOUNT NUMBER	SUBJECT TO WITHDRAWAL BY CHECK?	INTEREST BEARING? GIVE RATE
$				

2. The customer was directly liable to us in respect of loans, acceptances, etc., at the close of business on that date in the total amount of $ ________, as follows:

AMOUNT	DATE OF LOAN OR DISCOUNT	DUE DATE	INTEREST		DESCRIPTION OF LIABILITY COLLATERAL, SECURITY INTERESTS, LIENS, ENDORSERS, ETC.
			RATE	PAID TO	
$					

3. The customer was contingently liable as endorser of notes discounted and/or as guarantor at the close of business on that date in the total amount of $ ____________, as below:

AMOUNT	NAME OF MAKER	DATE OF NOTE	DUE DATE	REMARKS
$				

4. Other direct or contingent liabilities, open letters of credit, and relative collateral, were

5. Security agreements under the Uniform Commercial Code or any other agreements providing for restrictions, not noted above, were as follows (if officially recorded, indicate date and office in which filed):

Yours truly, (Bank) ____________________

Date ____________________ 19____

By ____________________
Authorized Signature

Additional copies of this form are available from the American Institute of CPAs, 1211 Avenue of the Americas, New York, N.Y. 10036-8775

For example, recorded sales are expected to be supported by a sales order, shipping documents, billings to customers, and cash receipts. *Tracing* begins with the original documents, such as the shipping documents and then traces them to recorded balances to make sure that all valid transactions were in fact recorded. Tracing addresses management's assertion of completeness. These two audit procedures point out the importance of considering the audit objective when selecting a procedure. For example, vouching cannot provide any relevant evidence for a test of the completeness assertion. Whether vouching or tracing is appropriate is determined by whether understatement or overstatement is of interest. For example, to ascertain whether all of the purchases made were recorded, an understatement is of concern, and so tracing would be appropriate. It would be initiated from the data file of purchase orders, matched with receiving reports and invoices from suppliers, and then traced to purchase journal entries and the perpetual inventory files. In contrast, to ascertain that recorded purchases were actually made, the key concern is overstatement, and so vouching would be applied from the purchase journal entries to the supporting data files of purchase orders, receiving reports, and vendors' invoices.

Other detailed testing is performed on a sampling basis and entails combinations of procedures such as examining documents, vouching, and retracing in order to form conclusions about tests of transactions. Statistical sampling's main advantage is that it quantifies sampling risk, which simplifies the auditor's evaluation of such evidence and the appropriate weight to place on sampling results. Exhibit 7-4 shows which audit procedures achieve which audit objectives. The audit process tends to combine the varied procedures so that they can be integrated to offset the others' weaknesses and optimize their evidential value. Audit judgment is the critical determinant of how the audit plan is prepared and executed to gather the necessary support for an auditor's report.

It is useful to shift attention from detailed procedures to classes of procedures, as such a general classification scheme is common in the audit literature and will lead to an in-depth discussion of one of the procedures noted in Exhibit 7-4, yet not discussed to this point: comparison with related information (more commonly referred to as analytical review procedures).

Classifying Audit Procedures

Audit procedures can be classified as either substantive tests (or tests of balances and/or transactions), which test the fairness of financial statement representations, or compliance tests, which test whether the client is complying with designed controls. The rationale for compliance testing, within an audit's framework, is to reduce the extent of substantive tests. A well-controlled system is more likely to produce a set of fairly presented financial statements. Hence by gathering evidence that a well-designed system is actually in operation, the auditor can justify reducing the substantive testing. Only those compliance tests that cost less than those substantive tests that can be reduced should be performed. In other words, the auditor's mix of substantive and compliance tests is a cost–benefit-based decision. The only constraint is that some substantive tests must be performed; current professional standards do not permit a 100 percent compliance-test audit. This is due in part to the inherent limitations of internal control and the ever-present risk of management override (or circumvention) of an otherwise effective control system.

Substantive Tests

Substantive tests are intended to obtain evidence of the validity and propriety of the accounting treatment of transactions and balances ***[SAS 1, Section 320]***. Because balances are typically composed of several transactions, many of the tests of balances are more accurately described as "tests of transactions." For example, a test of the accounts receivable balance will need to consider sales on account and cash collections, in order to ensure the propriety of the ending receivables balance. To consider those activities affecting each account, an auditor may choose to perform analytical review procedures and/or tests of details.

Analytical Review Procedures. Analytical review procedures are a particular type of substan-

EXHIBIT 7-4

Considering the Capabilities of Various Procedures to Gather Audit Evidence

Procedure	Capabilities
Observation	Can provide evidence only for the time that the observation occurs. Usually is less desirable than inspection and typically requires the concurrent use of inquiry procedures to provide useful information. Is often considered a compliance procedure.
Inquiry	Can suggest explanations for transactions and balances but must be corroborated to justify reliance by an auditor.
Inspection*	
— of assets:	Can provide evidence of physical existence, but ownership, valuation, and completeness of recorded numbers cannot be assessed. May indicate overstocked inventory and/or damaged or obsolete assets.
— of documentation:†	Can provide evidence of ownership and valuation; with other procedures can help check completeness and determine appropriate presentation.
Recomputation‡	Can check arithmetical accuracy but provides no evidence as to the validity, propriety, completeness, or accuracy in terms other than mathematics.
Confirmation	Can only provide evidence of matters confirmed, so tends to be a one-sided test of existence and ownership. Cannot provide other than limited negative evidence of valuation or collectibility.
Reconciliation	Can verify the amount of a balance (for example, reconciling the books to a bank statement) but cannot verify what the balance should be; can demonstrate the integrity of the double-entry accounting system through tie-in of subsidiary records to control accounts.
Comparison with Related Information	Can show the reasonableness of balances relative to expectations, history, and external benchmarks.
Scanning	Can draw attention to unusual entries or balances relative to expectations or other recorded values.
Testing	Sampling and tests of transactions are sometimes viewed as distinct audit procedures, although they involve the above steps and thereby have similar capabilities; the unique aspect of statistical sampling is its capability of quantifying sampling risk.

*Often referred to as physical examination and count.

†Includes retracing and vouching – tracing bookkeeping procedures, checking data-processing flow, matching evidence to records, and checking audit trail, among other procedures.

‡Includes footings, cross-footings, extensions, recalculations, etc.

tive test ***[SAS 23, Section 318]***. These have been emphasized to be overall reasonableness tests, as they usually are directed at aggregate balances rather than individual transactions. However, analytical review procedures are frequently applied to disaggregated balances such as monthly data and the information for each separate operating location (for example, analysis per plant, evaluation per store, or consideration of line-of-business statistics). What type of data is analyzed is decided by the information that the analytical review tools can elicit.

There are three types of analytical review procedures commonly used. The first is the judgmental reasonableness test, which tends to be heavily dependent on the auditor's industry expertise and experience with the client. The judgmental approach is typically applied at the beginning and end of the audit as a means of determining the audit risk for planning an engagement and the overall reasonableness of the final set of financial statements on which the auditor's report will be issued. Based on experience, an auditor can review a client's initial unadjusted trial balance and decide how much "sense" the numbers make. Both industry and economic effects and known operating changes over the past year are considered. Most likely, some of the changes from previous years' balances will be unexpected, and those will be given special attention in the audit plan, in accordance with their significance to the client's overall financial position. When the audit is completed, the final review is intended to ensure that the auditor has not "missed the forest for all the trees"! For example, the auditor may consider the final inventory balance and sales figures and decide that these numbers are plausible, given the client's productive capacity and operating levels. Although the emphasis on judgmental techniques appears in the initial and closing stages of an audit, this reasonableness check, based on experience, is also applied throughout the course of the audit. In performing all types of audit procedures, the auditors must judge whether the evidence collected makes sense in light of their understanding of the client's operations.

The second type of analytical review procedures, which is sometimes referred to as the more traditional tests, encompasses both trend and ratio analyses, incorporating comparisons of budgeted, historical, and industry data. The most commonly applied technique is *flux analysis*, which essentially studies the magnitude of fluctuations since the earlier period. According to SAS No. 23, "Analytical Review Procedures,"[2] the auditor should form an "expected fluctuation" for each account and ask about the cause of any unexpected fluctuations. The auditor then should corroborate these explanations to form an evidential base for the reasonableness of recorded balances.

But rather than emphasizing the previous year, some auditors will focus on trends, analyzing the reasonableness of the current period's changes relative to those in the last three-, five-, or even ten-year period. In this approach, cyclical movements can be considered, and a long-term picture of operations can be obtained. Experimental research found that 75 percent of the forty-four managers and seniors from a Big Eight public accounting firm chose trend analysis as the key analytical tool for reasonableness tests of payroll.[3]

Budgeted data can also be used to assess the reasonableness of a client's recorded balances. Assuming the client has a reasonable budgetary system, how well the client performed in reaching expectations can determine (1) how well-controlled the operations are likely to be, (2) what incentives there might be for management to distort the actual performance, (3) the extent to which the client was affected by unexpected events, and (4) those accounts with a greater risk of misstatement. Of course, the auditor must be wary of budgets that do not reflect a reasonable yet challenging goal or that might be padded, adjusted too frequently, or otherwise distorted in a way that limits their usefulness as a reasonably reliable benchmark.

Besides focusing on historical and budgeted data, the auditor may find ratio analysis to be useful in understanding the relationships among the client's account balances. Measures of the client's liquidity, activity, financing, and profitability can be computed and compared over time. If the gross profit margin has slumped recently, if receivables have grown in relation to sales, or if a client's ability to meet current cash commitments is questionable, that client's audit risk may have increased. By identifying such variations in accounts' interrelationships and investigating their cause, errors can be more readily detected and risk areas can be identified for audit testing. Because industry statistics are averages and can be influenced by changes in accounting practices, differing rates of inflation, and the age of individual companies' assets, they should be interpreted with extreme care.

Or, rather than concentrating on the entity's financial data, nonfinancial data may be considered. For example, production statistics will be expected to have a particular association to cost of sales, and the number of employees should be related to recorded payroll expense. Often, nonfinancial data are generated outside the accounting department and therefore can be a more objective

[2] New York: AICPA, October 1978.

[3] Edward Blocher, Robert S. Esposito, and John J. Willingham, "A Study of Auditor Judgments Concerning the Nature and Extent of Analytical Review in Auditing Payroll," Working paper from the audit conference, University of North Carolina, Chapel Hill, 1981.

barometer for evaluating financial numbers than merely comparing financial accounts, all of which were assimilated by a single department.

To enhance the analysis's objectivity, the auditor can compare trends, budgeted-to-actual performance, and ratios with industry and economic statistics. Externally generated data can be a useful benchmark in assessing a client's operations. If competitors have been troubled by the economic recession, but the client has experienced a steady 10 percent growth, the auditor should find out how the client's operations differ from its competitors'. A clue that there might be misstatements can be discovered in such an industry comparison, if no other explanation can be found. One point to keep in mind is that a major client may comprise a large percentage of an industry and therefore be capable of influencing industry statistics. The auditor thus should also attempt to analyze industry performance separate from the effect of the client's operations.

One purpose of analytical reviews is to enable the auditor to ask the right questions. By directing the auditor's attention to unusual account balances, analytical review procedures are likely to make audit tests more cost beneficial. Analytical reviews can also provide evidence that accounts are reasonable and require little, if any, additional testing. For example, in a very stable environment, a client's accounts may represent effectively identical relationships with those of the previous year, and controls may be excellent. By means of compliance testing and performing analytical review procedures, with detailed test follow-up on the few items appearing unreasonable, the auditor may be able to collect enough evidence to express an audit report. Why test the details if the aggregate numbers can be determined as reasonable at the desired level of accuracy?

The main difficulty in evaluating analytical review procedures is that most do not produce any dollar measure of accuracy or precision. How close is the client's recorded sales figure to expectations, if the observed fluctuation is 10 percent from last year? What confidence can the auditor have in the recorded balances? In order to answer these questions, a third type of analytical review has become increasingly common: structural modeling, or a mathematically based technique known as regression analysis, used to quantify auditors' expectations in dollar terms, with measurable confidence (reliability) and precision (accuracy) levels.

Structural models can also be simple mathematical relationships that are expected to estimate actual account balances with reasonable accuracy. For example, if the auditors gather reliable evidence of the number of employees hired and terminated, the timing of pay changes, and the effect of vacation and sick days, they should be able to extend the previous year's audited payroll expense to the current year's reported balance within a fairly narrow dollar range. Similarly, the interest revenue for a banking client can be tested by focusing on either internally or externally generated data on interest rates for various classes of investments.

Exhibit 7-5 summarizes the broad continuum of available analytical review procedures. The left of the continuum lists the more simplistic approaches to analytical review, and the right shows the more sophisticated techniques. However, the left's approaches are not necessarily cheaper to perform than are the right's. For example, if a client has a computerized data base, the right's structural modeling approaches can be particularly economical to apply. Similarly, regulated industries have an abundant amount of industry data readily available for the auditor's use. The box in Exhibit 7-5 explains how the points on the continuum differ from one another. The key determinants of that point on the continuum at which the auditor will stop are (1) the audit objective, (2) the quality of evidence that the auditor expects to obtain from the selected procedures, (3) the sufficiency of the evidence gathered from alternative audit procedures, and (4) the cost-benefit advantages of a particular point on the continuum, relative to alternative audit procedures. Besides demonstrating the range of available analytical review procedures, Exhibit 7-5 notes some possible sources of data to be used in performing such procedures. The on-line data bases are often accessible through the national offices of CPA firms, libraries, and clients or through connection fees for an initial tie-in to the on-line data bases. The NAARS system focuses on financial statement disclosures; the *New York Times* Information System organizes the topics of articles appearing in major newspapers; and Citibank has assimilated a broad variety

EXHIBIT 7-5

The Continuum of Available Analytical Review Procedures

A Comparison of 2 Points in Time	Use of a Single Benchmark	Use of Historical Data for a Single Account	Use of a Small Set of Internal Data
% Change from Prior Period % Change from Similar Period in Prior Year What Were the Risk Areas Last Period? In Which Accounts Were Adjustments Booked Last Period?	Budgeted Amount Industry Rate of Return Chief Competitor's Performance A Turnover Ratio or Similar Operating Statistic	Time Trend Extrapolations – graphical – regression – other ARIMA techniques Useful Rules of Thumb from Past Experience, Such As Known Cyclical Patterns	Ratio Analysis on Three to Five Years of Annual Data Variance Analysis over the Recent Past Extrapolations from a Short Historical Base Period, Such As the Gross Profit Rate for Three Years Implying a Rate for Next Year Comparison of One Unit of Operation to Other Similar Units of Operation

Use of a Small Set of Internal/External Data	Use of a Large Number of Data Points Generated Internally	Use of a Large Number of Data Points Generated Internally and Externally
Comparison of Recent Experience to the Industry, Including Ratio Analysis Market Share Performance Economic Benchmarks – for the industry – for the company – for particular regions Operating Statistics' Comparison to the Environment, e.g., a Utility's Comparison to Weather Statistics Extrapolations from a Short Historical Base Period, Such As the Relationship of Degree Days to Gas Production Statistics for Three Years, Implying a Relationship for Next Year	Structural Regression Models – time series comparisons of accounts and internal operating statistics – cross-sectional comparisons of units of operation Judgmental Comparisons	Structural Regression Models – time series comparisons of accounts, internal operating statistics, industry statistics, environmental attributes, and economic barometers Judgmental Comparisons

Attributes That Differ Across Available Procedures	Sources of Data for Use in Analytical Review Procedures
– Ease of use – Number of data points utilized – Source of data integrated – Business approach facilitated – Historical perspective provided – Objectivity of inferences drawn – Reliability of projections formulated	– Accounting Department – Client's long-range forecasting department – Marketing, production, and other operating departments – Government – Trade journals, Moody's, Standard & Poor's, Value Line, and similar services – On-line data bases, including • NAARS • DISCLO • NEXIS • Dialog & Orbit • The *New York Times* Information Bank • The Dow Jones News/Retrieval System • Citibank

From Wanda A. Wallace, "Analytical Review: Misconceptions, Applications and Experience—Part I," *CPA Journal*, January 1983, p. 30.

of economic and industry data for easy and timely access.

The effectiveness of analytical review procedures relative to alternative audit approaches has been investigated by examining 281 errors requiring financial statement adjustment on 152 audits. The researchers were able to infer that 27.1 percent of the errors were detected using analytical review procedures, and 20 percent were detected through discussions with client and prior-year expectations.[4] Analytical review procedures included typical analytical review steps:

- comparison of balances with prior year,
- prediction of current balances based on external data,
- analysis of interrelationships among account balances,
- reasonableness tests,
- estimates of account balances, and
- initial cursory reviews of financial statements in the early planning stages of an audit.

These procedures were able to signal more errors than by any other single class of audit procedures (such as detailed testing, other than scanning). Hence, the research indicates that analytical review procedures can be extremely powerful tools in an audit engagement. This research study concentrated on tools at the left end of the continuum in Exhibit 7-5. Given the effectiveness of these rather simplistic techniques, the auditor can expect the more sophisticated procedures to offer a means by which even stronger audit evidence can be obtained that is capable of identifying errors in the accounts with even greater effectiveness. Measurable precision and statistical modeling techniques can provide a more objective and verifiable evidential base.

Test of Details of Transactions and Balances. The test of details generally moves in a direction opposite to that of analytical review ***[SAS 23, Amended Section 320 of SAS 1].*** Whereas analytical review emphasizes various aggregations of data and investigates detail only when necessary, based on unexplained differences in expected and recorded balances, the test of details presumes that if a set of detailed transactions or items comprising an account is reasonably accurate, then the aggregation of these transactions is also likely to be reasonable. An example of a substantive test is the observation of physical inventory. Typically, the auditor observes the client's inventory procedures and takes *test counts* on only a small sample of the inventory items on hand. The presumption is that if the auditor's test counts (that is, the actual recounts of a sample of inventory) match the client's count of a small set of individual inventory items, then they are likely to match for the whole set of inventory, had it been cost beneficial to test all of the client's count.

Another example of a test of details is the confirmation of cash balances in the client's various bank accounts. Two procedures are often used. The first is to mail a letter of confirmation to the bank, as shown in Exhibit 7-3, second is to request a *"cutoff" bank statement* from the banks with which the client does business. A cutoff bank statement is the typical documentation of banking transactions and the bank statement for the first two to three weeks after the fiscal year-end (the "cutoff date"). This statement tells the auditor that deposits in transit, outstanding checks, or other large reconciling items cleared the bank when expected. If the auditor does not have this statement, the risk exists that the client's cash balance has been misstated.

Any audit procedure that asks, "Is this balance reasonable?" is a substantive test. Often analytical review procedures identify transactions that require detailed tests, and sometimes analytical review procedures will eliminate the need for detailed testing. The overall level of substantive tests is largely dependent on the extent and findings of the compliance tests.

Compliance Tests

Tests that ask whether employees are performing their duties as prescribed are compliance tests and provide support for relying on controls ***[SAS 1, Section 320].*** Reliance on internal accounting control is an important kind of audit evidence, as it permits the reduction of substantive test work. To understand why this reliance can support the validity of financial statement assertions, it is helpful to consider the specific control objectives that are tested to support such reliance. These are summarized in Exhibit 7-6. The presumption is that, for example, if transactions are properly authorized, it

[4] R. E. Hylas and R. H. Ashton, "Audit Detection of Financial Statement Errors," *Accounting Review*, October, 1982, pp. 751–765.

EXHIBIT 7-6
Key Dimensions of Specific Control Objectives

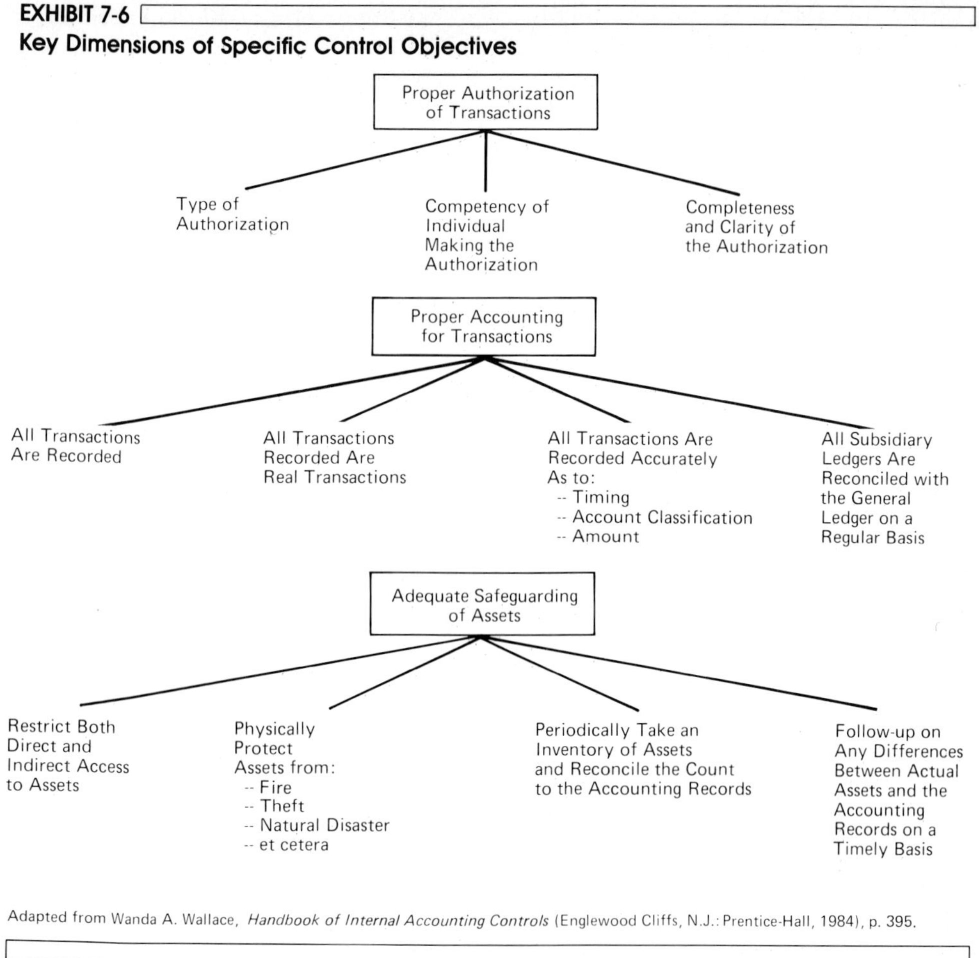

Adapted from Wanda A. Wallace, *Handbook of Internal Accounting Controls* (Englewood Cliffs, N.J.: Prentice-Hall, 1984), p. 395.

is highly likely that those transactions will be valid. If those transactions are both properly authorized and recorded, then it is even more probable that the financial statements will reflect complete, reasonably stated account balances. If assets are adequately safeguarded, it is more likely that the balances on the financial statements will reflect the actual assets and liabilities as of the balance sheet date. Each control objective pertains to the financial statement assertions forming the testable propositions. Substantive tests offer direct evidence of the balances' propriety, whereas compliance tests offer only indirect evidence of the numbers reported in the financial statements.

Assume that an auditor is reviewing accounts payable and is concerned that only the authorized suppliers be paid and that the related disbursement is for an amount actually owed. The internal accounting control system over payables requires that (1) all purchases be made from an authorized vendor; (2) no disbursements be made until a receiving report is on file, documenting that the goods have been delivered as ordered; and (3) invoices be checked for mathematical accuracy, agreement with purchase order and receiving report, and inclusion of the vendor's name on the authorized listing and be initialed by the party performing such a check. Rather than confirming the accounts payable balances, the auditor wants to rely on the control system over accounts payable to ensure the propriety of the recorded balances.

To test compliance, the auditor draws a sample of paid invoices, rechecks them, looks at the initials that document the earlier check, and compares the findings of the tests performed. Presumably, if the auditor's tests reveal no discrepancies, the employee was carrying out the prescribed duties, suggesting that reliance on this aspect of the system is warranted.

Note that a compliance test in this setting includes the reperformance of prescribed duties. Past literature has suggested that an auditor may merely check that all invoices have been initialed, as evidence of control compliance. However, imagine the worst case. Assume this client is involved in litigation that claims that there was an audit failure and that the plaintiff's attorney has the sample of invoices that the auditor tested, pulled, and reviewed. Assume also that the employee entrusted with checking the invoices often, at the end of the day, simply initialed any remaining invoices, without checking them. The party perpetrating the fraud was aware of this employee's habits and so put several unauthorized purchases at the bottom of a stack of several days' invoices. The plaintiff's attorney was therefore able to identify those invoices that had been incorrectly initialed but had not yet been noted as exceptions by the CPA who had actually examined that invoice while performing compliance tests. How could the CPA possibly claim that he or she had taken due audit care, by accepting "superficial initials" as evidence of compliance with prescribed procedures? A proposed interpretation of SAS No. 1, §320 recognizes that the selection of inquiry, observation, inspection, reperformance, and other compliance test procedures is a matter for the auditor's judgment. The nature of the audit trail, the capability of the procedure to detect deviations, the availability of corroborating evidence, and the planned degree of reliance on internal accounting controls are all cited as relevant factors in determining whether reperformance is required.

Unless substantive tests in an audit engagement can be reduced, the compliance test should not be performed. Furthermore, unless the auditor has reason to expect compliance, he or she should not waste time testing what is expected to be a poor control system. The auditor must decide that the controls are good enough to justify reliance, if implemented. Then he or she must compare the cost of testing compliance with the cost of substantively testing the balance of interest. Those deviations from prescribed duties that are likely to reveal problems with the control system must be identified in advance. If the results of the audit tests are not sufficient to support reliance on internal accounting controls, then the substantive tests cannot be reduced.

Dual-Purpose Tests

Although the substantive and compliance test procedures are usually described as separable audit approaches, the results of a particular audit procedure often provides evidence relevant to the questions being addressed by each type of test ***[SAS 1, Section 320]***. For example, the compliance test described included verifying the invoice's mathematical accuracy and producing a dollar test result that is substantive test evidence concerning accounts payable. Similarly, confirmations to banks can reflect the adequacy of controls over cash, just as the counting of inventory provides evidence of adequate control over inventory.

Some would contend that most, if not all, audit tests are dual purpose in nature. However, the term *dual-purpose tests* is most often applied to tests that the auditor specifically designs to meet both substantive and compliance test objectives. The objective of dual-purpose tests is to save money because of the more efficient auditing which can result. Instead of pulling two samples of invoices—one for substantive testing and one for compliance testing—only one sample is required, though it must be big enough to meet each test's evidential requirements. Because examining detailed documents can take a long time, being able to examine fewer documents in slightly greater depth (that is, to meet both testing objectives) can mean substantial cost savings. A proposed interpretation of SAS No. 1 § 320 acknowledges that substantive tests typically will not provide evidence about the operation and effectiveness of the controls throughout the period being audited and restricts the use of the term dual-purpose tests to those that accomplish the purpose of both substantive and compliance tests *concurrently*.

The following examples illustrate the relationship of audit objectives to different testing approaches:

Audit Objective	Likely Audit Test
To ascertain the credit department is approving all sales before the goods are shipped.	Compliance Test
To determine that there is petty cash.	Substantive Test
To determine whether all existing trade accounts payable are recorded.	Dual-Purpose Test

Despite these distinctions, it is possible to address any audit objective with each of the possible audit approaches, and so dual-purpose testing is very common.

Classifying Evidence Based on the Environment in Which It Was Produced

As suggested in the earlier discussion of sources of evidence, the controls of the client are important determinants of the audit value of internal evidence. More satisfactory internal accounting controls will generate more reliable accounting data, which means that such data will have greater evidential value. In contrast, information generated under a system of unsatisfactory control conditions is far more likely to produce unreliable financial statements, as well as poor quality audit evidence. While the environment in which evidence is generated focuses on the client's operations, it is also relevant to external sources of evidence.

What are the auditor's expectations regarding the suppliers' and customers' operations and related controls? When they confirm a particular balance, is that confirmation likely to be accurate? Are the employees in the financial and accounting areas likely to be capable of providing adequate representations to serve the auditor's needs? Is the supplier or customer independent? A lack of independence may result from related-party status or merely from heavy dependence on the client's business or supplies.

Classifying Evidence by Legal Rules

Auditors are not bound by legal rules of evidence in conducting an engagement, yet find useful to their evaluation the evidentiary weight accorded in a courtroom to types of evidence. For example, *direct evidence* legally means that the party offering the evidence acquired it directly, and so it is the strongest form of evidence. The person who was an eyewitness or who inspected particular documents testifies to the actions taken and/or observed. In contrast, *hearsay evidence* is a second-hand account which usually is dismissed in the courtroom because the party who allegedly collected the direct evidence cannot be cross-examined. An example of hearsay evidence is a client's employee telling the auditor that he heard from another employee that a vice-president signed blank checks. Obviously, this evidence would not carry the same weight as it would if the other employee who had witnessed the blank authorization had reported what he had seen to the auditor. Of course, the obvious advantage of the auditor in such a setting is that (s)he can investigate the allegation and presumably collect direct evidence as to the legitimacy of the claim, whereas the courtroom itself tends to have to rely on the facts as presented or to discount them as deemed appropriate under the legal rules of evidence.

In a courtroom, the term *documentary evidence* is any original record, deed, contract, or similar written instrument. The documents must be originals unless it can be demonstrated that the originals are no longer available—perhaps because they were destroyed by fire.

In a courtroom, the emphasis is on fact rather than opinion, with the exception of an *expert's opinion* in areas requiring special expertise. Whenever expert witnesses are used, their credentials and objectivity must be established. This is similar to an auditor's actions when utilizing specialists, as described later in this chapter. However, an auditor can never shift his or her responsibility onto the specialist; rather, he or she must assume responsibility for relying on the specialist.

When there is no direct evidence, *circumstantial evidence* is often offered as being consistent with a particular set of inferences; yet by definition it can be only supportive, not persuasive. And corroborative evidence must also be provided. Any evidence that supports other evidence is said to be corroborative, and the more there is of such evidence, the greater its weight will be. For example, if four individuals testify to the same fact, that information is given more weight than if only one individual so testified. Through corroboration, it is possible to narrow competing explanations that are consistent with circumstantial evidence, to presumably infer what has actually occurred. When evidence is *conclusive,* it means that it cannot be disputed. Circumstantial evidence cannot be conclusive, but direct evidence that is well corroborated is very likely to be conclusive.

Auditors cannot rely on unconfirmed news stories or on common gossip any more than courts can rely on hearsay evidence. Cumulative evidence is thus stressed, focusing on the available corroborating evidence, including the number of sources providing that evidence. Whenever original documents are not available, they must either be found or be found to exist no longer. The chances of any copies having been altered in some manner must also be considered. The legal rules of evidence thus are more stringent than are the evidential guidelines for auditors. The objectivity and competency of evidence is evaluated in a similar manner, though the auditor must also consider their sufficiency in light of the audit objective which is executed in a cost/benefit framework that reflects the value placed upon the audit function by society. Audit evidence is generally persuasive, but it is not expected to be conclusive in a legal sense.

When to Collect Evidence

As suggested in the introductory dialogue, the nature, timing, and extent of evidence all affect its value ***[SAS 45, Section 1020].*** The time between the date that the evidence was compiled and the examination date must be evaluated. Audit risk tends to increase as the lapse of time lengthens but can be controlled through tests of that period. For example, if a physical inventory is taken before year-end, the CPA must consider the effect of the transactions in the intervening period so as to extend the audit conclusions from the earlier date to the balance sheet date. Tests to link interim work to the balance sheet date ordinarily include comparing interim balances and related information with year-end figures, identifying and investigating unusual amounts, and performing other analytical review procedures and/or substantive tests of details deemed necessary.

In planning when to collect audit evidence, the auditor should compare the cost of the interim work, with the substantive tests required to extend the audit conclusions to year-end, to the cost of performing that work as of the balance sheet date. Reliance on internal accounting controls is not required, though the auditor should look at the effects of deciding not to rely on substantive tests. If business conditions are rapidly changing or there are circumstances that could tempt management to misstate financial statements in the remaining period—as suggested in the introductory dialogue—the auditor should collect the evidence as of the balance sheet date.

The other aspect of timing is coordinating related audit procedures. For example, audit tests of assets that are readily negotiable, such as cash on hand and in banks, bank loans, and marketable securities, should be simultaneous, or temporary audit control should be established to ensure the equivalent of simultaneous examination.

Strengths of Evidence Sources

SAS No. 31, "Evidential Matter"[5] emphasizes that measuring the validity of evidence concerning the assertions in the client's financial statements "lies in the judgment of the auditor" ***[SAS 31, Section 326].*** After noting that there are important exceptions, SAS No. 31 provides a set of presumptions about the validity of evidence in auditing:

[5] New York: AICPA, August 1980, par. 2.

- Evidential matter from independent sources outside an entity is more reliable than that secured solely within the entity.
- The auditor can have more assurance as to the reliability of accounting data and financial statements that are developed under satisfactory conditions of internal accounting control than when they are developed under unsatisfactory conditions of internal accounting control.
- The independent auditor's direct personal knowledge, obtained through physical examination, observation, computation, and indirect collection of evidential matter, is more likely to ensure reliability.

SAS No. 31 defines *evidential matter* as "the underlying accounting data and all corroborating information available to the auditor" (par. 13). The corroborating evidence includes (1) documentary material; (2) confirmations and other written representations by knowledgeable people; (3) information obtained by the auditor from inquiry, observation, inspection, and physical examination; and (4) other information developed by, or available to, the auditor that permits him or her to reach conclusions through valid reasoning. The last item is a catchall, permitting innovative ways of collecting evidence. To be *competent,* evidence must be valid and relevant. The review and testing of underlying accounting data are discussed in SAS No. 31 and include retracing procedures and reviewing the steps followed in the accounting process; recalculating; *reconciling* related transactions, balances, and accounts; and checking the information system's internal consistency, especially the accounting records.

Very competent evidence, based on SAS No. 31, would include confirmations, an attorney's letter of representation, and documents of title for building, land, and other assets. All of these originate with third parties. Somewhat competent documentary evidence would include bank statements, canceled checks, signed lease agreements, insurance policies in force, and remittance advices, all a combination of external and internal evidence. Less competent documentary evidence would be that generated internally and retained internally, such as subsidiary ledgers, minutes, employment contracts, purchase requisitions, receiving reports, and payroll records.

Practical Considerations

If an auditor fails to get replies from a confirmation procedure, the alternative is usually internal evidence or, at best, external-internal evidence. For example, subsequent cash collections recorded by the client serve as evidence that unconfirmed receivables were legitimate claims.

There is also the problem of erroneous confirmations. As the introductory dialogue suggested, clients may confirm amounts as owed that they have no intention or capability of paying. Similarly, third parties may confer with clients before returning the confirmations and omit information on claims and disputes. Collusion is even possible, whereby third parties endorse whatever amount is represented on the confirmation form. Then there is human error, in which a clean, but incorrect, confirmation is returned; that is, the third parties fail to reconcile the confirmation amounts to their records.

Similar problems can also influence the quality of direct observation procedures. The auditors may think they are looking at Part 2103 when, because they have no engineering expertise, they are really looking at Part 2105. Few auditors can detect forgeries, though the physical observation of marketable securities is a highly valued audit procedure. In the Equity Funding case, described in Chapter 5, auditors were provided with totally bogus insurance files for fictitious policyholders. Yet, the bogus birth and death certificates were not detected. Even a cash count is subject to the criticism that counterfeit bills would be unlikely to be detected.

In fact, the "seeing is believing" attitude had been dangerous in lulling auditors. Consider the faulty observation procedure that satisfied auditors of the "Salad Oil King's" inventory balance (discussed in Chapter 5), in spite of the fact that such inventory would only have been possible had the client owned the entire world's supply of salad oil! Similarly, shell games have been played on inventory like ammonia fertilizer tanks by moving the fertilizer tanks and changing serial numbers on those tanks, when possible, to create an illusion of a greater amount of inventory than is actually on hand. Auditors should be ever cognizant of the potential weaknesses of selected audit procedures.

An Operative Approach

Rather than ranking types of evidence, the auditor should concentrate on the audit objectives and make sure that the evidence collected can either prove or disprove the accuracy of the account balance or the operation of the control procedure. Overall reasonableness should be checked in all cases to confirm that the evidential findings of detailed tests are plausible.

In following SAS No. 31, the auditor should not equate confirmations with external evidence or observation with the direct collection of evidence. Analytical review procedures using both industry and economic data can be external evidence, and if the auditor formulates structural models through regression analysis, direct evidence can be made available by means of objective statistical results. In other words, it is not the procedure that fits the source and type of evidence guidelines in SAS No. 31, but how the procedure is applied.

Consider an audit plan to test recorded sales. One objective would be to assess their validity: Are all recorded sales valid sales? The auditor may vouch a sample of sales to both the customers' orders and shipping documents and the collection experience with those customers. Yet, vouching can be of little help to the auditor who is considering the other side of the audit risk; that is, were some valid sales omitted from the books? The sampling of shipments then would become the focus, with those shipments being traced to recorded sales. Note that vouching can provide no evidence of unrecorded items, and retracing can give only limited evidence of the validity of recorded sales. The reliability of each procedure can be evaluated only within the context of the objective. For example, if the auditor is concerned about the accuracy of billings, a match of invoice prices to authorized price lists and the recalculation of the invoice extensions will be useful. On the other hand, if net sales is questioned, sales returns and allowances should be reviewed.

An auditor must ensure that recorded sales are plausible and so should ask about productive capacity, inventory levels, customer base, market share, industry experience, and economic effects. The auditor's expertise then will help in evaluating these responses. During the course of the year, the auditor will typically have read trade journals, professional publications, and general media coverage of business and the economy. News releases, observation of business changes such as new product introductions, and knowledge of competitors', suppliers', and customers' experiences all may offer corroborative or disconfirming evidence.

Some representations of sales will be factual, such as the introduction of larger trade discounts, while others will be more general claims like the recession's effects. Yet the legitimacy of the varied representations is determined methodically by the auditor through the selection of those procedures likely to give the most reliable, cost-beneficial evidence on each particular representation.

Accumulating Evidence Concerning Management's Assertions

The auditor obviously should use the most economical and effective audit procedures to achieve the objective. For example, if the auditor wished to test the assertion that the inventory balances include all of the client's items that are in transit or are stored at outside locations, several audit procedures could be applied. For inventory stored in outside warehouses, the auditor could use the confirmation procedure. For goods out on consignment, a similar confirmation procedure is possible, or if the balances were substantial, the auditor might believe that observation of an inventory count at those premises was necessary. The in-transit concern raises the question of how effective the client's cutoff is. Detailed tests of shipping and receiving documents around the year-end date, inspecting the dates of delivery and receipt relative to the order dates, can provide evidence that the inventory on which the terms transferring ownership have not yet been fulfilled is retained on the books. Another procedure is to analyze the relationship of inventory balances to recent purchasing, production, and sales activities via analytical review procedures. Tests of internal accounting controls for shipping and receiving operations and controls over goods on consignment can give the auditor a basis for reliance so that substantive test work can be decreased. Usually a combination of compliance, substantive, and dual-purpose tests is used in an audit. Various audit procedures tend to complement one another and the client's circumstances frequently lead to different procedures being more efficient in one setting versus alternative approaches. For example, observing a physical inventory count in outside warehouses in different locations will mean different costs than will that in warehouses near the client. The value of confirmations declines if the warehouse is a related party. The applicability of analytical review may be limited if the client is a new company, with a short track record and in a relatively new industry. Exhibit 7-7 shows the variety of audit procedures that can be directed at a single audit objective. It presents both an essay question and its recommended solution from a past CPA Examination.

Considerations Affecting Audit Risk

Two sources of evidence have special implications for the auditor evaluating audit risk: outside specialists and client representations. Outside specialists offer external, competent evidence and thereby can greatly reduce audit risk. Client representations must be documented to reflect the information provided to the auditor which he or she, in turn, corroborated through the audit examination. The formal evidence of management's assertions, received by the auditor in good faith, is so essential that a scope limitation will result if the auditor does not obtain such documentation. Thus the increased audit risk from a client's refusal to document representations made to the auditor is likely to be so great that the auditor will resign from such an engagement.

The auditor cannot rely on either outside specialists or on the client in the sense of actually shifting responsibility, yet both sources of evidence are an integral part of the evidential base from which (s)he will draw a conclusion as to the fairness of the financial statements, taken as a whole.

Outside Specialists

The auditor frequently turns to outside specialists for advice concerning legal matters, underwriting estimates, and appraisals of difficult-to-value assets (or of assets requiring expertise for their proper identification) ***[SAS 11, Section 336].*** An auditor will routinely request letters of representation from the client's attorneys regarding pending lawsuits, related contingent liabilities, and unasserted claims that may require disclosure. Lawyers may also be used as specialists in interpreting technical requirements, regulations, or agreements and the potential significance of such documents to the client's operations and, in particular, the valuation of assets and liabilities. Insurance clients have numerous reserves based on actuarial science, requiring an underwriter's review. Clients with highly valued inventory like rare gems may require an appraiser's review, and using the lower-of-cost-or-market method for inventory, marketable securities, and other investments may require an appraiser's help. In addition, recent requirements for supplementary disclosures regarding mineral reserves have increased the level of auditors' involvement with geologists and engineers.

According to SAS No. 11, a *specialist* is a person or firm possessing special skills in or knowledge of a field other than accounting or auditing. Generally, the auditors are responsible for finding out the specialist's professional qualifications and reputation. Although the specialists' opinions may be a substantial part of the evidential base for formulating an audit opinion, again, the auditors remain responsible for the auditor's report. Exhibit 7-8 describes the considerations in selecting specialists, documenting the client–specialist–auditor arrangements with respect to the specialist's role, and using the specialist's findings.

Client Representations

In addition to securing written representations by third parties, auditors obtain a client representation letter ***[SAS 19, Section 333].*** This letter reminds the clients that they are responsible for the financial statements and should have disclosed all

EXHIBIT 7-7

Audit Procedures Directed at a Single Audit Objective

Decker, a CPA, is performing an examination of the financial statements of Allright Wholesale Sales, Inc., for the year ended December 31, 19X6. Allright has been in business for many years and has never had its financial statements audited. Decker has gained satisfaction with respect to the ending inventory and is considering alternative audit procedures to gain satisfaction with respect to management's representations concerning the beginning inventory, which was not observed.

Allright sells only one product (bottled brand X beer) and maintains perpetual inventory records. In addition, Allright takes physical inventory counts monthly. Decker has already confirmed purchases with the manufacturer and has decided to concentrate on evaluating the reliability of perpetual inventory records and performing analytical review procedures to the extent that prior years' unaudited records will enable such procedures to be performed.

Required:

What are the audit tests, including analytical review procedures, that Decker should apply in evaluating the reliability of perpetual inventory records and gaining satisfaction with respect to the January 1, 19X6, inventory?

Solution:

The tests, including analytical review procedures, that Decker should apply are as follows:

- Trace entries to perpetual inventory records from receiving reports and shipping reports.
- Trace entries from perpetual inventory records to receiving reports and shipping reports.
- Compare records of monthly physical counts with perpetual inventory records.
- Ascertain whether perpetual inventory records have been adjusted based on physical counts.
- Test arithmetic accuracy of perpetual inventory records.
- Reconcile beginning inventory quantities with ending inventory quantities.
- Ascertain consistency of methods of determining cost and market value.
- Compare unit costs on inventory listings with paid vouchers (purchase orders and vendor's invoices).
- Compare financial information with information for comparable prior periods (for example, inventory turnover, gross profit percentage, dollar and unit sales, and so forth).
- Compare financial information with anticipated results (based upon budgets, forecasts, trends analysis, long-term agreements, commitments, and so forth).
- Study the relationships of elements of financial information that would be expected to conform to a predictable pattern based on the entity's experience (for example, perform a comparison of statistical data from the sales department with accounting records or relationships between changes in sales and changes in account receivable balances).
- Compare the financial information with similar information regarding the industry in which the entity operates (for example, government publications, trade association data, and so forth).
- Study relationships of the financial information with relevant nonfinancial information (for example, relate insurance coverage to inventory amounts, compare inventory quantities with storage capacity of storage facilities, and so forth).
- Apply other appropriate audit procedures that may be deemed necessary in the circumstances.

Adapted from CPA exam, May 7, 1981, question 5.

material matters to the external auditors. One problem is that smaller clients, when asked to acknowledge that their financial statements are in accordance with generally accepted accounting principles (GAAP), often object to having to make such a representation, pointing out that they rely on the auditors to provide the necessary expertise for selecting the appropriate accounting principles. In response, the profession has adapted the more traditional representation to small businesses' needs, thus recognizing the CPA's duty to help the client select the accounting principles.

The letter of representation from the client is considered to be such important evidence that not having it can result in a qualified audit report. As a symbol of good faith, the letter is a means of clarifying the client's understanding of his or her responsibilities. Furthermore, the auditor has a basis for claiming the client's "contributory negligence" role, should there be an audit failure. But

EXHIBIT 7-8

Auditors' Use of Specialists

Selection Procedure—Three Critical Inquiries

I.

Do specialists have professional certification, license, or other recognition of competence as appropriate to their field?

II.

What are specialists' reputations and standing in view of peers and others familiar with their capability or performance?

III.

What is relationship of each specialist to client?

Specialists may have relationship with client, but auditor should be alert to impairment of such specialists' objectivity and should consider need for additional audit procedures related to assumptions, methods, and findings. Outside specialist might be used to determine reasonableness of work.

Formal Documentation of the Role of Specialists Should Include:

- Objectives of work
- Scope of work
- Representations by specialists regarding their relationship to client
- Assumptions to be used
- Methodology(ies) to be applied
- Comparison of approach with that used in prior period
- Comprehension by specialists that auditor will use their findings to corroborate financial statement representations
- Report form to be prepared by specialists

Auditor's Use of Findings

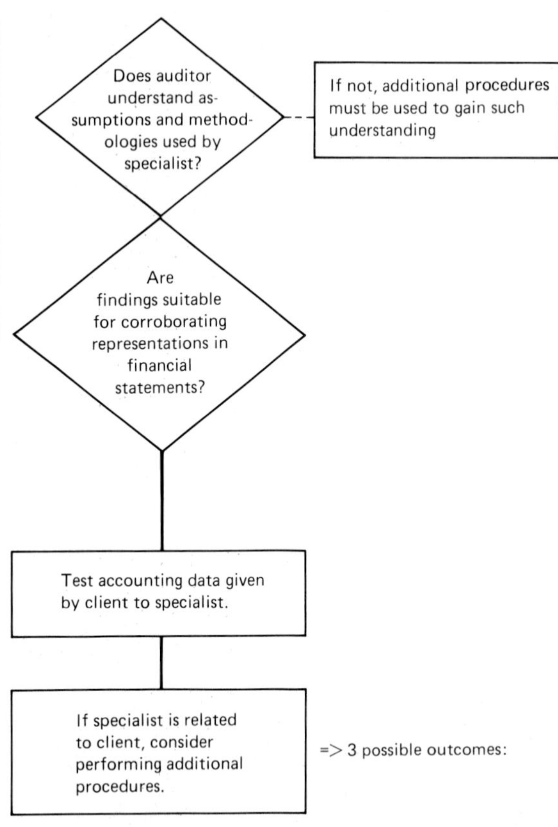
Does auditor understand assumptions and methodologies used by specialist?
If not, additional procedures must be used to gain such understanding
Are findings suitable for corroborating representations in financial statements?
Test accounting data given by client to specialist.
If specialist is related to client, consider performing additional procedures.

=> 3 possible outcomes:

(1) If procedures lead auditor to believe findings are unreasonable, do not use that specialist's work. Apply additional procedures, such as obtaining another specialist's opinion. If matter cannot be resolved, qualified opinion or disclaimer should be issued owing to scope limitation of being unable to obtain sufficient competent evidence on material representation in the financial statements.

(2) If findings are deemed reasonable and support financial statement representations, auditor can conclude that sufficient competent evidential matter has been obtained.

(3) If findings are deemed reasonable and indicate a material difference from financial statement representations, qualified or adverse opinion should be expressed.

Adapted from SAS No. 11, "Using the Work of a Specialist" (New York: AICPA, December 1975).

the letter of representation does not in any way shift the auditor's overall responsibility for collecting a sufficient evidential base to support the auditor's report, nor does it carry much evidential weight. Even though the absence of such a letter can have grave consequences, its presence is unlikely to alter the audit process in any meaningful way. However, management's refusal to provide a representation letter suggests that there may be a problem with respect to management integrity in ensuring a full disclosure relationship with the external auditor. Many CPA firms therefore issue a disclaimer when they cannot get a client's representation letter. In any case, an unqualified opinion would be impossible, as SAS No. 19 rules that the absence of such a letter is a scope limitation.

An example of a client representation letter is given in Exhibit 7-9. For smaller, privately held clients, Point 1 might be adjusted to reflect the CPA's accounting advisory services. A client with material subsidiaries may require a set of such letters, one from each subsidiary. The letters should be adapted to the specific circumstances, although SAS No. 19 requires Points 1, 2, and 3 to be documented formally. Before releasing their audit report, some CPAs require a copy of the final financial statements or a trial balance signed by the client's chief accounting officer, with a note stating that he or she agrees with the books of accounts after posting all adjustments and that the books represent the final statements for the period under audit. In addition, some firms will obtain a separate "minute representation letter," essentially covering part of Point 2 in Exhibit 7-9. Besides meeting the requirements of SAS No. 19, general representation letters confirm that the client officials believe that the financial statements properly and consistently represent the client's financial position and the results of operations; that all reported transactions were "arm's length," with outside parties, unless otherwise indicated; that none of the officers had undisclosed material interests in businesses with which the client had significant transactions; and that there have been no undisclosed subsequent events that could have a material effect or require disclosure.

The existing standards allow the auditor to rely on the truthfulness of management's representation, unless the examination reveals evidential matter to the contrary. The auditor's examination is designed to consider circumstances that might tempt management to misstate financial statements. Auditors are aware of the importance of management integrity and the risk of management override (or circumvention) of established control procedures and so are alert to evidence that suggests that their reliance on management is unwarranted. Even when reliance is appropriate, however, client representations are never a substitute for auditing procedures necessary for an opinion on the financial statements.

Working Papers

Working papers are the auditor's principal record of the work performed and the conclusions reached regarding significant matters. Working papers support the auditor's exercise of due audit care and help the auditor conduct and supervise the audit engagement. Their form and content should match the particular engagement. Those factors that are expected to affect the auditor's judgment concerning the quantity, type, and content of working papers are listed in SAS No. 41, Section 339, "Working Papers":

a. the nature of the engagement,
b. the nature of the auditor's report,
c. the nature of the financial statements, schedules, or other information on which the auditor is reporting,
d. the nature and condition of the client's records,
e. the degree of reliance on internal accounting control, and
f. the needs in the particular circumstances for supervision and review of the work.[6]

All working papers should include records of the audit "procedures applied, the tests performed, the information obtained, and the pertinent conclusions reached in the engagement."[7] These records may be machine readable or in any other useful form.

[6] New York: AICPA, April 1982, par. 4. [7] Ibid., par. 3.

EXHIBIT 7-9

The Client's Representation Letter

Date of Auditor's Report

CPA Firm's Name
Address

Dear Sirs:

We confirm that to the best of our knowledge and belief, the following representations made to you during the course of your examination of the financial statements of ______for the fiscal year ended June 30, 19XX, are accurate and complete:

1. We acknowledge our primary responsibility for the preparation of financial statements in conformity with generally accepted accounting principles.

2. All minutes of the meetings of the board of directors, committees of that board, and stockholders, as well as all financial and accounting records and related data have been made available to you. We are not aware of any transactions, accounts, or material agreements that are not fairly described and properly recorded.

3. We are not aware of any irregularities involving management or employees with significant roles in the internal accounting control system. Nor are we aware of any irregularities involving other employees that could have a material effect on the financial statements.

4. We are not aware of any violations or possible violations of laws or regulations whose effects should be considered for disclosure in the financial statements or as a basis for recording a loss contingency. Nor have we had any communications from regulatory agencies regarding noncompliance or deficiencies that could have a material effect on the financial statements.

5. The company has complied with all aspects of contractual agreements that would otherwise have a material effect on the financial statements.

6. The bases of valuation of all material assets are as represented and satisfactory titles are in our possession. All liens, encumbrances, security interests, and discounts have been disclosed, and adequate valuation reserves and provisions for uncollectibles and obsolete inventory have been recorded.

7. All known liabilities are included in the financial statements. There are no additional material liabilities or contingencies that are required to be accrued or disclosed under FAS No. 5. Nor has our legal counsel advised us of any unasserted claims or assessments that are probable of assertion and must be disclosed under FAS No. 5.

8. We have no future purchase commitments that will result in a loss, nor do they exceed our expected requirements. A provision has been made for any material loss expected on sales commitments due either to our fulfillment or failure to fulfill such commitments.

9. The financial statements, including the footnote disclosures, are in accordance with generally accepted accounting principles and other regulations and laws to which the company is subject. In particular, the following items have been properly presented:

   -- related party transactions included the related amounts of sales, receivables, purchases, payables, loans, transfers, leasing arrangements, and guarantees.

   -- capital stock repurchase options or agreements, as well as restrictions on issuance due to option, warrant, conversion, or similar requirements.

   -- compensating balances, any restrictions on cash balances and line of credit, or similar arrangements with financial institutions.

   -- commitments to repurchase assets that have been sold.

   -- other agreements that are not typical of day-to-day operations.

10. We intend to hold our investment in______; however, we do not exercise significant influence over its operations.

11. We have elected not to amortize goodwill, as it is subject to the grandfather clause of APB Opinion 17.

12. We have no plans or intentions that would materially affect either the valuation or classification of recorded assets and liabilities. No matters have come to our attention since the balance sheet date that have or are likely to have any material effect on the financial statements and related disclosures.

____
Signature of Chief Executive Officer

____
Signature of Chief Financial Officer

____
Signature of Chief Accounting Officer

Preparing the Working Papers

The best way of preparing and evaluating a set of working papers is to consider whether at some future date, a CPA with no previous connection with the engagement could review them and testify as to the audit work performed and the related audit findings. In order to prepare such working papers, the auditor must document information concerning all material facts, the scope of audit work performed, the sources of the information, and the conclusions reached. As a permanent record of the auditor's factual basis for the report, the working papers should follow the style of the CPA firm, in order to facilitate their use and review.

Exhibit 7-10 presents a typical format for a CPA's working paper. The index coding tends to be slightly different for every CPA firm; however, a distinction between alphabetic and numeric indexes is common, one of which corresponds to balance sheet accounts and the other to income statement accounts. In addition, if some working papers are supporting others, a dash followed by numerical codings is used to indicate such relationships. The indication that certain working papers were prepared by the client (PBC) serves two important purposes. First, it documents the efficient coordination of activities with client personnel in preparing the lead schedules (summaries of general ledger accounts) for auditors. Second, the auditors are alerted to their responsibility for testing such schedules and data to gain satisfaction that they have been prepared accurately.

EXHIBIT 7-10
The Structure of a CPA's Working Paper

Index Coding

- When Applicable, Indication of Preparation by the Client with Name of Preparer (e.g., PBC: John Doe)
- Preparer's Name (Signature)
- Date of Preparation
- Reviewer's Name (Signature)
- Date of Review

Client's Name
Title of Working Paper
Audit Engagement: Date of Audit

page___ of ___

Clear Columnar Headings, with Comparison of Prior Year to Current Year

Standards of Preparation:

* Clear, Neat, and Accurate Double-Spaced Content

* Tick Marks Noted in Body of Working Paper

* Cross-references Made to Related Working Papers

* Key to Tick Marks' Meaning Provided

Note: Sources of information and the purpose of collecting such information should be noted. Whenever applicable, conclusions should be carefully stated and supported.

The signatures and date regarding both preparation and review of the working papers facilitates control over the audit process and reflects the responsibility being assumed by the preparer and reviewer of the financial statements.

Each working paper should state the client, type of engagement, and the particular document's purpose. The materials included should serve an audit objective, have been tested, and adequately document the audit process. Loose ends can "hang" an auditor for negligence, just as poor documentation results in no proof that an adequate audit was performed. The auditor should consider means of efficiently setting up working papers, including the borrowing of a company's stamp to label the client name at the top of all documents and photocopying documents of interest in lieu of manually transcribing substantial amounts of information. Microcomputers commonly are used to prepare spread sheets and other working papers, as wordprocessing capabilities of available software can improve overall efficiency.

The page numbering in the "—— of ——" format helps prevent loss or misfiling. All of Exhibit 7-10 to this point should appear on all working papers. In no case should the backs of working papers be used, as they could easily be overlooked by the reviewers and when being duplicated. The remainder of Exhibit 7-10 suggests some useful pointers when preparing working papers. For example, it is helpful to highlight the comparisons with previous years and include documentation of the reasonableness of any observed differences. All contents should be legible, and tick marks are one means of aiding legibility, as well as efficiency. A *tick mark* is any symbol (often a check mark or circled check mark) used to note an explanation or audit procedure related to some piece of information in a working paper. Like footnotes, they prevent clutter in the body of the working paper, yet are always clearly defined in a key, often located at the bottom of the page. It is essential that tick mark keys be clear and complete. For example, to say a number was vouched is incomplete: vouched to which document(s)? The substance of working papers will tend to include the auditors' comments on internal control, the rationale underlying decisions on the scope of the audit exam, audit procedures, and conclusions. As noted in Exhibit 7-10, in addition to tick marks, cross-references to other indexed pages of the working papers can be excellent means of supporting the audit work that has been performed. By organizing working papers in sets with the general trial balances, followed by lead schedules and detailed schedules, their interrelationship will be clearer and easier to review.

For each major part of a cycle, there should be a lead schedule corresponding to the client's working trial balance. The *lead schedule* summarizes the general ledger accounts that tie to a line item in the financial statements. An example of a lead schedule for receivables is illustrated in Exhibit 7-11. The "PBC" notation in the upper right-hand corner shows that the schedule was originally prepared by the client for the auditor's review. The index numbers should tie to *detail schedules* supporting the work performed in each area. The final amount on the detail schedule should match the individual balance on the lead schedule. The detail schedule should also support tests of underlying supporting transactions. Ex-

EXHIBIT 7-11
An Example of a Lead Schedule

PBC
W/P Number
Preparer
Date

WAJAW CORPORATION
Summary of Receivables
Audit 6/30/X6

				6/30/X6			
					Adjustments & Reclassifications		
A/C number		W/P Index	Final 6/30/X5	Per Books	Dr	Cr	As Adjusted
100	Customers' accounts receivable	cross-reference to detail schedule					
200	Employees' accounts receivable						
300	Notes receivable						
	Total receivables						
700	Allowance for doubtful accounts						
	Net Realizable Receivables						

hibit 7-12 gives an example of a detail schedule for notes receivable, and Exhibit 7-13 presents a question asking what is wrong with the working paper. The answer is also given and refers to the technical considerations in preparing documentation so that it will adequately summarize the auditor's evidence. This example is from the Certified Internal Auditor Examination and bears out the similarity in working paper documentation considerations in the internal and external audit settings.

The Relationship of Working Papers to Auditing Standards

The working papers should document the fulfillment of the general and field standards, especially the sufficiency of the evidence. The auditors should not express any conclusions beyond their expertise or leave any questions or notes unanswered. Working-paper memoranda tend to be particularly useful in documenting both the evidence and the conclusions reached. A planning memorandum can document the planning process, and the reviewers' notations help document the presence of supervision.

One means of ensuring adequate documentation of the client's operations is to maintain a separate "permanent and continuing audit file" from the current year's files. The separate file will include information that can be used in all audits, year after year. For example, a client's organizational chart, employees' job descriptions, history of

EXHIBIT 7-12
An Example of a Detail Schedule

W/P Number
Preparer
Date

WAJAW CORPORATION

Notes Receivable
Audit 6/30/X6

Confirmation Number	Maker of Note	Date of Note	Maturity Date	Interest Rate	Face Amount	Balance 6/30/X5	Balance 6/30/X6
001	Zenn. Co.	4/1/X5	4/1/X7	12%	30,000.00	28,692.00	15,442.00 C
					Total	______	______

cross-reference to lead schedule

C = confirmation received: see W/P No. ________

EXHIBIT 7-13
Working Papers: An Example and Critique

G-1

Test of Insurance Coverage For the Year Ending 9-30-X3

Policy Number	Company	Amount of Coverage	Prepaid Balance
12346A	Orange Company	1,500,000/A	3,000 R
84321B	Blue Company	300,000	3,700 R
56371	Green Company	1,000,000/A	2,500
43278	Red Company	5,000,000/A	7,200 R
			16,400 T

T = Totaled
/ = Verified amount of coverage by examining policy
R = Recomputed
A = Adequacy verified

REQUIRED: Evaluate the working paper for its adequacy in meeting audit objectives and documenting findings.

SOLUTION:

Flaws in the working paper include

1. The heading on the working paper should give more information about whether the analysis is company-wide or for a particular division or subsidiary.
2. Whoever prepared this working paper should be clearly identified.
3. The date of the working paper's preparation should be noted.
4. The type of insurance coverage being reviewed should be specified.
5. The replacement cost of the covered assets should be clearly shown, along with a reference to such underlying assets.
6. The period covered by the insurance policy or the policy expiration date should be noted.
7. The working paper should document changes in prepaid insurance for the period of the audit and should reference insurance expense for the period.
8. The premiums paid for the period should be shown.
9. The prepaid balance should be tied to the general ledger or cross-referenced to another working paper (often referred to as a lead schedule) which, in turn, should be tied to the general ledger.
10. The tests that are referenced are not applied to all policies, even though the number of policies is sufficiently small to make such a step viable.
11. The working paper does not contain a conclusion or a recommendation of any sort, nor does it cross-reference another schedule in which such material might appear.

Adapted from the Certified Internal Auditor Examination, Part II, question 44 (November 10, 1983).

operations, press releases, and legal relationships—including the articles of incorporation, bylaws, subsidiaries, and public listing at various exchanges—all are likely to be in the *permanent continuing audit file*. In addition, the file should contain information about accounting policies, valuation bases, mechanization and computerization issues, chart of accounts, control documentation, contracts, and long-term plans. The current working papers then can cross-reference relevant portions of the permanent continuing file. Of course an ongoing responsibility would exist for the auditor to update the entire contents of the continuing file.

The Review Process

When reviewing the working papers, *"to do" points* are prepared by seniors, managers, and partners for follow-up and resolution ***[SAS 22, Section 311]***. Some practitioners refer to such reviews as "grading papers," as they are a reading of the documentation, with review comments made and discussed and implicit grades assigned for incompleteness, inaccuracies, and shortcomings. The experienced auditor, with nothing more than professional expertise and a pencil, can read a set of working papers, assess their reasonableness and capability to support an audit report, and suggest improvements. All "to do" points must be satisfactorily answered, and the disposition of such points is to be adequately documented in the working papers; it is not enough to write *done* beside the review comment. This review process is particularly important when documenting the supervision phase of the audit process. Indeed, many firms have internal programs that have auditors from one of the firm's offices review and critique the working papers of another office. A check on the application of prescribed accounting and auditing guidelines, including working paper techniques, is performed with an emphasis on the overall sufficiency of the work performed. The clear objective of such activities is to improve the overall audit process.

Ownership, Custody, and Retention

As SAS No. 41 Section 339, makes clear, the working papers are the auditor's property, with the rights of ownership being subject to ethical limitations pertaining to confidentiality. Working papers need not be given to either clients or third parties, except under legal demands (for example, subpoenas) in which CPAs' communications are not considered "privileged." Auditors will often, however, permit the client to use the working papers as a reference and will grant access to them to parties designated by the client, such as the successor auditor. The auditor's property, as the record of the audit work performed, should be protected and controlled to ensure its safe custody. This means that working papers should be stored in locked briefcases and trunks to which only the auditor has access. This is necessary not only at day's end but also during lunch time or breaks. Unauthorized access to working papers must be prevented, as confidential information could be divulged. Furthermore, working papers could be altered or information extracted that might invalidate the audit process. The best example of this last circumstance is the Equity Funding case discussed in Chapter 5. The client extracted the statistical sampling plan in order to have sufficient lead time to create bogus files of documentation in support of fictitious insurance policies. Had this information not been extracted, presumably the client would have been unable to supply the requested support documents within a reasonable time period.

SAS No. 41 expressly states that working papers are to be retained

> for a period sufficient to meet the needs of his practice and to satisfy any pertinent legal requirements of records retention. (¶8)

Hence, care must be taken in managing ownership, custody, and retention of working papers.

REVIEW QUESTIONS

1. What are the reasons for performing compliance tests? What conditions warrant the use of compliance tests? Can a 100 percent compliance-test audit be performed? Why or why not?
2. Describe the two major types of substantive tests and give examples of each.
3. What are the advantages and disadvantages of investigating all fluctuations from the past year that exceed 10 percent?
4. Under what conditions is a budget likely to help the auditor evaluate the reasonableness of a client's operations?
5. What kind of nonfinancial data can you use to evaluate the reasonableness of total revenue for an electric utility?
6. What are the advantages of using externally generated data to evaluate the reasonableness of a client's financial statement representations?
7. One auditor asserted, "Analytical review is only use-

ful as an attention-directing tool." Comment on the validity of this assertion.

8. What advantages does the auditor have in using structural modeling (through such tools as regression analysis)?
9. An auditor performing a compliance test on the control over the payment of invoices decides to test that the invoices have been checked appropriately, by examining the initials written on each invoice by the individual who wrote the check. If there are no initials, an exception will be noted. Comment on the acceptability of this audit approach.
10. Give an example of a dual-purpose test. Why do such tests require advance planning?
11. What are the presumptions about the validity of evidential matter in auditing which are delineated in SAS No. 31? Give two examples in which each presumption would be appropriate.
12. Compare and contrast the meaning, risk, and relative evidential value of the following types of information:
    - internal
    - external
    - internal-external
    - external-internal
13. If the auditor uses an underwriter to ensure the reasonableness of actuarially based reserves, should such reliance be expressed in the auditor's report?
14. If there were an audit failure, what evidence would be helpful in establishing the client's contributory negligence?
15. **a.** What are the traditional assumptions concerning the relative strength of various types of audit procedures? What practical considerations call these assumptions into question?

    b. Describe the following audit procedures:
    observation
    inspection
    comparison
    analysis
    computation
    confirmation (both positive and negative)
    inquiry
16. Distinguish between vouching and tracing, and explain each one's audit objective.
17. Distinguish between general propositions and specific propositions. How do they interrelate?
18. Give an example of two statements that have both a confirming and a supporting evidential relationship, depending on which statement is known as a basis for inferring the other.
19. What is heuristic reasoning, and what are its implications?
20. Distinguish between proof and persuasion.
21. Some client representation letters contain the phrase: "Because of our limited expertise with generally accepted accounting principles, including financial statement disclosure, we have engaged you to advise us in fulfilling that responsibility." Why? Is this phrase acceptable to a CPA?
22. What is a tick mark? Some firms make a practice of using standard tick marks. What advantages and disadvantages arise from such a practice?
23. A client who has decided to change auditors has requested that its past CPAs turn over all of their previous years' working papers to the client's financial vice-president. How should the CPA firm react?
24. What purpose is served by "to do" points? How are they to be handled in an audit engagement?
25. The audit team has a habit of leaving their working papers on their desks at the end of each day, ready for the following day. What can be the consequences of such a practice?

EXERCISES

1. To fulfill audit objectives, analytical review techniques are applied to payroll. All monthly payroll figures are as expected except for June's balance. The client has requested that the CPA compliance test the payroll and its tie-in to both the profit-sharing and the pension plans. How can the analytical review results be combined with the planned compliance test procedures?
2. Classify the following items as internal evidence or external evidence, assuming that there are only these two classes of evidence:
   a. checks
   b. bank statements
   c. sales invoices
   d. vendors' invoices
   e. receiving reports
   f. confirmation letters
   g. bill of lading
   Which items represent the more reliable evidence?
3. What is the difference between a substantive test pertaining to the assertion of existence or occurrence and one pertaining to the assertion of completeness?
4. Classify the following assertions, using the codings suggested by SAS No. 31, "Evidential Matter":
   E: existence or occurrence
   C: completeness
   R: rights and obligations
   V: valuation or allocation
   P: presentation and disclosure

——The entity is using the fixed assets on its books.
——The unfunded pension liability is $340,000.
——Inventory is recorded at lower of cost or market.
——There are no unasserted claims.
——All sales are recorded.
——Contingent liabilities refer to guarantees on subsidiaries' loans.
——Major accounting policies are described in footnote 1.
——Subsidiaries in which a controlling interest is held are appropriately consolidated.
——The entity owns the fixed assets on the books.

5. You audit a major oil company and want a specialist's help in evaluating its oil reserve information. Your client employs the best petroleum engineer in the country and has offered his assistance. Should you accept the client's offer? Why or why not?
6. You have just completed the first audit engagement for a new client and have been assigned the task of sorting the working papers into a permanent continuing audit file and a current year audit file.
   a. What is the purpose of sorting the working papers in this way?
   b. What type of information would go into the permanent continuing audit file?
7. You have just started your own CPA firm and want to standardize your working-paper techniques. Design an indexing system for your staff's use that will aid in the orderly filing and handling of their working papers. Provide whatever instructions a new staff member might need to use the system.
8. In reviewing a set of working papers, you come across the sheet presented at the bottom of this page.

   Discuss the format and clarity of the working paper, explaining how the working paper could be improved.
9. A client has complained about audit fees, and you decide to review the working papers to see whether you can use more efficient methods and procedures.

   Generally speaking, what are some likely candidates for such improvement?

QUESTIONS ADAPTED FROM PROFESSIONAL EXAMINATIONS

1. The third generally accepted auditing standard of field work requires the auditor to obtain sufficient competent evidence to express an opinion regarding the financial statements under examination. To decide what constitutes sufficient competent evidence, the underlying accounting data should be distinguished from the corroborating information.

   Required:
   a. Discuss the nature of the evidence that the auditor will consider, in terms of the underlying accounting data, all corroborating information available to the auditor, and the methods by which the auditor tests or gathers competent evidence.
   b. State the three general presumptions regarding the validity of evidence with respect to comparative assurance, persuasiveness, and reliability.

   (CPA exam adapted)
2. In an audit of financial statements, the CPA examines and accumulates accounting evidence.

   Required:
   a. What is the objective of the CPA's examination and accumulation of accounting evidence during the course of an audit?
   b. The source of the accounting evidence is important to the CPA's evaluation of its quality, and the evidence may be classified according to source. For example, one class originates in the client's organization, passes through the hands of third parties, and returns to the client, where it may be examined by the auditor. List the classifications of accounting evidence according to its source, briefly discussing the effect of the source on the evidence's reliability.
   c. In evaluating the quality of the accounting evidence, the CPA also considers factors other than its sources. Briefly discuss these other factors.

   (CPA exam adapted)
3. CPAs accumulate various kinds of evidence on which

Exercise 8. (continued)

PBC
Notes Receivable
12/31

Confirm #	Maker	Date of Note	Maturation	Int.	Face Amount	Balance	Balance
1	Alice's Fashions	7/1/81	7/1/91	15%	100,000	8,000	107,560.20C

they will base their auditor's opinion. Among this evidence are confirmations from third parties and written representations from the client.

Required:

a. 1. What is an audit confirmation?

2. What characteristics must an audit confirmation have for a CPA to consider it as valid evidence?

b. 1. What is a written representation?

2. What information should a written representation contain?

3. How does a written representation affect a CPA's examination of a client's statements?

(CPA exam adapted)

4. When examining financial statements, an auditor must judge the validity of the audit evidence he or she obtains.

Required:

Assume that you have evaluated the client's internal control and found it satisfactory.

a. During the examination, the auditor asks many questions of the client's officers and employees.

1. Describe the factors that the auditor should consider in evaluating oral evidence from the client's officers and employees.

2. Discuss the validity and limitations of oral evidence.

b. An auditor's examination may include computation of various balance sheet and operating ratios for comparison with those of previous years and industry averages. Discuss the validity and limitations of ratio analysis.

c. In connection with an examination of a manufacturing company's financial statements, an auditor observes the physical inventory of finished goods, which consists of expensive, highly complex electronic equipment.

Discuss the validity and limitations of the audit evidence elicited by this procedure.

(CPA exam adapted)

5. The preparation of working papers is an integral part of a CPA's examination of financial statements. On a recurring engagement a CPA reviews his or her audit programs and working papers from the last examination while planning the current examination to determine their usefulness for the current engagement.

Required:

a. 1. What are the purposes or functions of audit working papers?

2. What records may be included in the audit working papers?

b. How does a CPA judge the type and content of the working papers for a particular engagement?

c. To comply with generally accepted auditing standards a CPA includes certain evidence in the working papers, for example, "evidence that the engagement was planned and the work of assistants was supervised and reviewed." What other evidence should a CPA include in the audit working papers to comply with generally accepted auditing standards?

d. What advice should a CPA give a client about discontinuing the use of records needed in an examination, and how should a CPA complete his or her examination when he or she finds that the client has discontinued records that he or she reviewed in earlier examinations?

(CPA exam adapted)

6. Analytical review procedures are substantive tests that are extremely useful in the initial audit planning stage.

Required:

a. Why are analytical review procedures considered substantive tests?

b. How can analytical review procedures be useful in the initial audit planning stage?

c. Which analytical review procedures might a CPA use during an examination performed in accordance with generally accepted auditing standards?

(CPA exam adapted)

7. You are the auditor of Star Manufacturing Company and have obtained the following data:

This is the trial balance taken from the books of Star one month before the year-end:

	Dr. (Cr.)
Cash in bank	$ 87,000
Trade accounts receivable	345,000
Notes receivable	125,000
Inventories	317,000
Land	66,000
Buildings, net	350,000
Furniture, fixtures, and equipment, net	325,000
Trade accounts payable	(235,000)
Mortgages payable	(400,000)
Capital stock	(300,000)
Retained earnings	(510,000)
Sales	(3,130,000)
Cost of sales	2,300,000
General and administrative expenses	622,000
Legal and professional fees	3,000
Interest expense	35,000

There are no inventories consigned either in or out.

All notes receivable are due from outsiders and held by Star.

Required:
Which accounts should be confirmed with outside sources? Briefly describe from whom they should be confirmed and the information that should be confirmed. Organize your answer in the following format.

Account Name	From Whom Confirmed	Information to Be Confirmed

8. In connection with your audit, you request that the management give you a letter or letters containing certain representations. For example, such representations may include the following: (1) the client has satisfactory title to all assets; (2) there are no contingent or unrecorded liabilities except as disclosed in the letter; (3) no shares of the company's stock are reserved for options, warrants, or other rights; and (4) the company is not obligated to repurchase any of its outstanding shares under any circumstances.

Required:
a. Why should you get a letter of representation? (Do not discuss the contents of the letter.)
b. How, if at all, do client representations affect your audit procedures and responsibilities?

(CPA exam adapted)

9. Auditors frequently refer to "standards" and "procedures." Standards refer to measures of the quality of the auditor's performance and specifically to the ten generally accepted auditing standards. Procedures refer to those acts the auditor performs while trying to gather evidence and specifically to the methods or techniques the auditor uses in the examination.

Required:
List at least eight different types of procedures that an auditor would use during an examination of financial statements. For example, an auditor would frequently use the observation of activities and conditions. Do not discuss specific accounts.

(CPA exam adapted)

10. You are an audit supervisor who has just received from an auditor a set of working papers. The auditor has obeyed some of the rules for preparing working papers but has violated others. You plan to compliment the auditor on what was done correctly and explain the reasons for your criticism of what was done incorrectly. Accordingly, you have made the following notes on the review of the working papers:
a. The auditor used only one side of each worksheet.
b. Each worksheet contained, in addition to the test information, a descriptive heading, a legend of tick marks and symbols, and the auditor's initials.
c. The working papers contained the auditor's handwritten transcriptions of pertinent procedures and job instructions.
d. The working papers were made up of 8½″ by 14″ work sheets. When smaller pieces of paper were used, they were clipped to those work sheets.
e. When appropriate information could be obtained, it was included in the working papers. When information was unavailable, the auditor so indicated with a large question mark in red pencil.
f. Copies of all policy statements that had any relationship to the activity being audited were included in the working papers.

Required:
For each of the above items:
a. State the accepted practice for working-paper techniques.
b. Indicate whether the practice was observed or violated.

(CIA exam adapted)

11. Multiple-Choice: Types of Testing
Select the one answer that best completes the statement or answers the question.

11.1 Auditors sometimes use a comparison of ratios as audit evidence. For example, an unexplained decrease in the ratio of gross profit to sales may suggest which of the following possibilities?
a. Unrecorded purchases.
b. Unrecorded sales.
c. Merchandise purchases being charged to selling and general expense.
d. Fictitious sales.

(CPA exam adapted)

11.2 Which of the following best describes the most important stage of an auditor's statistical analysis of significant ratios and trends?
a. Computation of significant ratios and trends.
b. Interpretation of significant variations and unusual relationships.
c. Reconciliation of statistical data to the client's accounting records.

d. Comparison of statistical data with the previous year's statistics and with similar data published by governmental and private sources.

(CPA exam adapted)

11.3 Overall analysis of income statement accounts may reveal errors, omissions, and inconsistencies not disclosed in the overall analysis of balance sheet accounts. The income statement analysis can best be accomplished by comparing monthly

a. Income statement ratios with balance sheet ratios.
b. Revenue and expense account balances with the monthly reported net income.
c. Income statement ratios with published industry averages.
d. Revenue and expense account totals with the corresponding figures for the preceding years.

(CPA exam adapted)

11.4 From which of the following evidence-gathering audit procedures would an auditor obtain most assurance concerning the existence of inventories?

a. Observation of physical inventory counts.
b. Written inventory representations from management.
c. Confirmation of inventories in a public warehouse.
d. Auditor's recomputation of inventory extensions.

(CPA exam adapted)

11.5 Analytical review procedures are

a. Statistical tests of financial information designed to identify areas requiring intensive investigation.
b. Analytical tests of financial information made by a computer.
c. Substantive tests of financial information made by a study and comparison of relationships among data.
d. Diagnostic tests of financial information that may not be classified as evidential matter.

(CPA exam adapted)

11.6 Failure to detect material dollar errors in the financial statements is a risk that the auditor can try to avoid by

a. Performing substantive tests.
b. Performing compliance tests.
c. Evaluating internal control.
d. Obtaining a client representation letter.

(CPA exam adapted)

11.7 One reason that the independent auditor makes an analytical review of the client's operations is to identify probable

a. Material weaknesses in the internal control system.
b. Unusual transactions.
c. Noncompliance with prescribed control procedures.
d. Improper separation of accounting and other financial duties.

(CPA exam adapted)

11.8 Significant unexpected fluctuations identified by analytical review procedures will usually necessitate a (an)

a. Consistency qualification.
b. Review of internal control.
c. Explanation in the representation letter.
d. Auditor investigation.

(CPA exam adapted)

11.9 Which of the following audit tests would be regarded as a test of "compliance"?

a. Tests of the specific items making up the balance in a given general ledger account.
b. Tests of the inventory pricing to vendors' invoices.
c. Tests of the signatures on canceled checks to board of director's authorizations.
d. Tests of the additions to property, plant, and equipment of physical inspections.

(CPA exam adapted)

11.10 How does the extent of substantive tests required to constitute sufficient evidence vary with the auditor's reliance on internal control?

a. Randomly.
b. Disproportionately.
c. Directly.
d. Inversely.

(CPA exam adapted)

11.11 The purpose of tests of compliance is to ensure that the

a. Accounting treatment of transactions and balances is valid and proper.
b. Accounting control procedures are functioning as intended.
c. Entity has complied with disclosure requirements of generally accepted accounting principles.
d. Entity has complied with requirements of quality control.

(CPA exam adapted)

11.12 An auditor decides that it is important and necessary to observe a client's distribution of payroll checks on a particular audit. The client organization is so large that the auditor cannot conveniently observe the distribution of the entire payroll. In these circumstances, which of the following is most acceptable to the auditor?

a. Observation should be limited to one or more selected departments.
b. Observation should be made for all departments, regardless of the inconvenience.
c. Observation should be eliminated, and alternative auditing procedures should be used.
d. Observation should be limited to those departments in which employees are readily available.

(CPA exam adapted)

11.13 A cash shortage may be concealed by transporting funds from one location to another or by converting negotiable assets to cash. Because of this, which of the following is vital?

a. Simultaneous confirmations.
b. Simultaneous bank reconciliations.
c. Simultaneous verification.
d. Simultaneous surprise cash count.

(CPA exam adapted)

11.14 In verifying the amount of goodwill recorded by a client, the most convincing evidence that an auditor can obtain is by comparing the recorded value of assets acquired with the

a. Assessed value as evidenced by tax bills.
b. Seller's book value as evidenced by financial statements.
c. Insured value as evidenced by insurance policies.
d. Appraised value as evidenced by independent appraisals.

(CPA exam adapted)

11.15 As a result of analytical review procedures, the independent auditor determines that the gross profit percentage has declined from 30 percent in the preceding year to 20 percent in the current year. The auditor should

a. Express a qualified opinion because of the client company's inability to continue as a going concern.
b. Evaluate management's performance in causing this decline.
c. Require footnote disclosure.
d. Consider the possibility of an error in the financial statements.

(CPA exam adapted)

11.16 To test for unsupported entries in the ledger, the direction of audit testing should be from the

a. Ledger entries.
b. Journal entries.
c. Externally generated documents.
d. Original source documents.

(CPA exam adapted)

11.17 Internal auditors frequently use the audit technique of observation. Which of the following statements best reflects the auditor's view of observation?

a. It should be carried out separately from any other audit field work.
b. It is related to the review of work flow and plant layout.
c. It is generally considered to be less authentic evidence than are copies of basic documents describing the control process.
d. It can be supported by photography, flowcharts, drawings, and narrative.
e. All of the above.

(CIA exam adapted)

12. Multiple-Choice: Evidence, Working Papers, and Client Representation Letters

Select the one answer that best completes the statement or answers the question.

12.1 Audit evidence can come in different forms with different degrees of persuasiveness. Which of the following is the least persuasive type of evidence?

a. Documents mailed by outsiders to the auditor.
b. Correspondence between auditor and vendors.
c. Sales invoices inspected by the auditor.
d. Computations made by the auditor.

(CPA exam adapted)

12.2 Which of the following is not a factor affecting the independent auditor's judgment of the quantity, type, and content of audit working papers?

a. The needs in the particular circumstances for supervision and review of the work performed by any assistants.
b. The nature and condition of the client's records and internal controls.
c. The expertise of client personnel and their expected audit participation.
d. The type of the financial statements, schedules, or other information on which the auditor is reporting.

(CPA exam adapted)

12.3 During an audit engagement, pertinent data are compiled and included in the audit work

papers. The work papers are mainly considered to be
- **a.** A client-owned record of conclusions reached by the auditors who performed the engagement.
- **b.** Evidence supporting the financial statements.
- **c.** Support for the auditor's representations as to compliance with generally accepted auditing standards.
- **d.** A record to be used as a basis for next year's engagement.

(CPA exam adapted)

12.4 The date of the management representation letter should coincide with the
- **a.** Date of the auditor's report.
- **b.** Balance sheet date.
- **c.** Date of the latest subsequent event referred to in the notes to the financial statements.
- **d.** Date of the engagement agreement.

(CPA exam adapted)

12.5 There will always be a limitation on the scope of the auditor's examination sufficient to preclude an unqualified opinion when management
- **a.** Engages an auditor after the year-end physical inventory count.
- **b.** Refuses to furnish a representation letter.
- **c.** Knows that direct confirmation of accounts receivable with debtors is not feasible.
- **d.** Engages an auditor to examine only the balance sheet.

(CPA exam adapted)

12.6 Audit working papers are used to record the results of the auditor's evidence-gathering procedures. When preparing working papers, the auditor should remember that they should be
- **a.** Kept on the client's premises so that the client can refer to them.
- **b.** The primary support for the financial statements being examined.
- **c.** Considered as a part of the client's accounting records that the auditor keeps.
- **d.** Designed to meet the circumstances and the auditor's needs on each engagement.

(CPA exam adapted)

12.7 To be competent, evidence must be both
- **a.** Timely and substantial.
- **b.** Reliable and documented.
- **c.** Valid and relevant.
- **d.** Useful and objective.

(CPA exam adapted)

12.8 Which of the following ultimately determines the specific audit procedures necessary to provide an independent auditor with a reasonable basis for the expression of an opinion?
- **a.** The audit program.
- **b.** The auditor's judgment.
- **c.** Generally accepted auditing standards.
- **d.** The auditor's working papers.

(CPA exam adapted)

12.9 Which of the following is not a primary purpose of audit working papers?
- **a.** Coordinating the examination.
- **b.** Assisting in preparing the audit report.
- **c.** Supporting the financial statements.
- **d.** Providing evidence of the audit work performed.

(CPA exam adapted)

12.10 A representation letter issued by a client
- **a.** Is essential to the preparation of the audit program.
- **b.** Is a substitute for testing.
- **c.** Does not reduce the auditor's responsibility.
- **d.** Reduces the auditor's responsibility only to the extent that it is relied on.

(CPA exam adapted)

12.11 Which of the following is the least persuasive documentation supporting an auditor's opinion?
- **a.** Schedules of details of physical inventory counts conducted by the client.
- **b.** Notation of inferences drawn from ratios and trends.
- **c.** Notation of an appraisers' conclusions documented in the auditor's working papers.
- **d.** Lists of negative confirmation requests for which the auditor received no response.

(CPA exam adapted)

12.12 Audit evidence can come in different forms with different degrees of persuasiveness. Which of the following is the least persuasive?
- **a.** Vendor's invoice.
- **b.** Bank statement obtained from the client.
- **c.** Computations made by the auditor.
- **d.** Prenumbered client invoices.

(CPA exam adapted)

12.13 Which of the following factors will least affect the independent auditor's judgment of the quantity, type, and content of working papers desirable for a particular engagement?
- **a.** Nature of the auditor's report.
- **b.** Nature of the financial statements, sched-

ules, or other information on which the auditor is reporting.
c. Need for supervision and review.
d. Number of personnel assigned to the audit.
(CPA exam adapted)

12.14 An auditor's working papers will generally be least likely to include documentation showing how the
a. Client's schedules were prepared.
b. Engagement had been planned.
c. Client's system of internal control had been reviewed and evaluated.
d. Unusual matters were resolved.
(CPA exam adapted)

12.15 Which of the following statements pertaining to the competence of evidence is always true?
a. Evidence gathered by an auditor from outside an enterprise is reliable.
b. Accounting data developed under satisfactory internal control are more relevant than are data developed under unsatisfactory internal control.
c. Oral representations made by management are not valid evidence.
d. Evidence gathered by auditors must be both valid and relevant to be considered competent.
(CPA exam adapted)

12.16 Management's refusal to furnish a written representation on a matter that the auditor considers essential constitutes
a. Prima facie evidence that the financial statements have not been presented fairly.
b. A violation of the Foreign Corrupt Practices Act.
c. An uncertainty sufficient to preclude an unqualified opinion.
d. A scope limitation sufficient to preclude an unqualified opinion.
(CPA exam adapted)

12.17 In which of the following instances would an auditor be least likely to require a specialist's assistance?
a. Assessing the valuation of inventories of art works.
b. Determining the quantities of materials stored in piles on the ground.
c. Determining the value of unlisted securities.
d. Ascertaining the assessed valuation of fixed assets.
(CPA exam adapted)

12.18 Which of the following is ordinarily designed to detect possible material dollar errors on the financial statements?
a. Compliance testing.
b. Analytical review.
c. Computer controls.
d. Postaudit working-paper review.
(CPA exam adapted)

CASES FOR DISCUSSION

1. Jack and Tony, two auditing students, were discussing the auditor's relationship with the client. Tony mentioned that she had found an older edition of a standard auditing textbook that stated that there was not necessarily a conflict of interest between the client's management and the auditors. Yet the current textbook makes no similar claim: Why not? How has the profession kept an audit process that depends on the use of client representations, as a practical audit approach, despite the attitudes toward potential conflicts between management and the auditor?

2. Some auditors have claimed that they are "hung" on charges of negligence and fraud much more often by what is included in their working papers than what is excluded from them. This claim is then cited as justifying CPAs' substantial reduction of the volume of their working-paper files. Is this a legitimate claim, and what would be its advantages?

3. FASB Statement of Financial Accounting Concepts No. 2, "Qualitative Characteristics of Accounting Information," defines reliability as the quality of information that ensures that information is reasonably free from error and bias and faithfully represents what it purports to represent. It defines relevance as information that can help users predict the outcomes of past, present, and future events or to confirm or correct past expectations. How are the terms *reliability* and *relevance* applied to the collection of evidence for an audit? Do management's representations meet these qualitative standards? In what sense do compliance tests help the auditor measure the quality of audit evidence?

4. An article entitled "Evidence, Judgment, and the Auditor's Opinion"[8] grades on a three-point scale the

[8] R. K. Mautz, *Journal of Accountancy*, April 1959, pp. 40–44.

persuasiveness of evidence concerning a given proposition:

1. Absolutely convincing.
2. Positively persuasive.
3. Neutrally persuasive (that is, not leading to doubt). There is little evidence that would rank as absolutely convincing, #1, and to some degree, this is preferred:

> a wise auditor recognizes the danger in permitting himself to be absolutely convinced, for to be convinced is often to close one's mind to alternative possibilities. It is the very essence of auditing that the practitioner keep an open mind and strive to obtain any useful evidence available on both sides of every proposition at issue.[9]

What type of evidence is usually obtained through compliance tests? Some auditors view substantive tests as offering the compliance type of evidence as a by-product. Do you agree with this view? If so, how would you rank the compliance type of evidential weight of these substantive tests on the three-point scale, and why?

5. An auditor does not determine truth or falsity but attempts to question financial statement propositions, subject them to testing, and decide whether they are reasonable and conform with expectations. The testing is directed toward the propositions, and then all tests are considered as a basis for forming an opinion on the financial statements as a whole. Often groups of propositions are considered in an audit test. For example, "the apparently simple assertion—'Trade Accounts Payable—$17,000' involves important subsidiary propositions with respect to classification, cut-off, and correlation with inventory and purchases amount."[10] Describe the subsidiary propositions in the following assertions:
   a. Total Sales on Account are $800,000.
   b. Investment in Company X totals $74,000.
   c. Depreciation for the year is $91,500.

[9] Ibid., p. 43. [10] Ibid., p. 42.

8

Preparing the Audit Program

The lead senior, manager, and partner on an engagement meet for a preliminary planning session.

Partner. Things have certainly changed for this client, compared with last year.

Manager. Yeah, last year the pipe for oil and gas drilling was really a seller's market!

Partner. Now, with the industry slump and drilling at a low point, who knows whether there is even a market for our client's inventory.

Lead senior. I've reviewed the available financials for the year to date, and though the reported sales are off a bit, they're only 10 percent lower than last year's.

Partner. Are these arm's length, legitimate sales? In the past, there have been a lot of related-party transactions.

Manager. Apparently the creditors are reevaluating their oil and gas portfolios and, when possible, are reducing their lines of credit. That's an additional consideration.

Partner. From your review of the financials, how does working capital look? Is liquidity a problem?

Lead senior. It seems to me that the answer depends on the collectibility of receivables and the client's ability to realize some profit on its inventory. Quite a few of the company's customers are filing for bankruptcy, and the allowance for uncollectibles appears rather low.

Manager. Do you think we face a risk of litigation this year?

Partner. No suits have been filed yet, and I think the creditors have enough bankruptcies on their hands that they'll work with the client as long as there is no real going concern threat. Of course, an industry in trouble always means more risk of being sued. We have to be realistic about our business risk and be certain that our work reflects it.

Manager. No doubt we're going to have to spend more time on receivables and inventory this year. I also think we'd better move some of our interim work to year-end. The risk exposure from relying on controls is much greater with these economic pressures.

Partner. You're right. We also had better lower our materiality threshold.

Lead senior. Will you give me the necessary time budget and not compare it with last year's? I need to give our staff some figures.

Partner. O.K. I've already spoken with management, and they are expecting us to increase our amount of audit work and, of course, our fees. They're not pleased, but they understand that our risk picture has changed, just as theirs has.

Manager. When writing the audit program, I'd like you to emphasize our risk concerns. The staff should watch for clues of expanded related-party transactions and troubled customers.

Lead senior. We also probably should have a management letter at both interim and year-end. And we may be able to help our client adapt to the market, just as the industry is. For instance, interest rates should be set on receivables outstanding over sixty days. Plus, we should be sure that the purchasing department's adapted to the sales prospects, while the credit department is considering means of enhancing sales, yet controlling risk.

Partner. You're right on target. This is the time that our client can really benefit from our industry expertise. Allow time during planning and interim to call some of our industry specialists to get their input.

Manager. You also better allow for more time in judgmental account areas and for our review of subsequent events. With the industry pressures and state of flux, management will probably make more liberal estimates, and there may also be some rapid unexpected changes.

Lead senior. O.K., I'll have a preliminary draft of the audit program and time budget ready for your review next week, to make certain that I've adequately reflected the concerns we've discussed today.

This case illustrates the role of risk in planning an audit engagement and the likelihood of changes in risk level over time. Materiality decisions, types of procedures applied, and the risk exposure from control reliance, interim work, and related party transactions must be continually reevaluated. This chapter describes overall considerations in preparing an audit program and overseeing the staff on an audit engagement, in addition to key issues of relevance in arriving at a final audit judgment and addressing major reporting responsibilities. The use of other auditors' work, responsibility for detecting and reporting on illegal acts and subsequent events, and SEC required filings are given special attention.

The Walk-Through

One of the best ways that a CPA can become acquainted with a client's information flow and control system is to "walk through" the audit trail ***[SAS 43, Section 1010].*** As the term suggests, the CPA actually follows a set of transactions as they are processed through the system to determine whether day-to-day operations are consistent with the designed system. The effectiveness of the walk-through will depend partly on whether the CPA can do it inconspicuously, so that the employees do not alter their routines.

The walk-through should be done in the early stage of planning an audit because it can help the auditor decide the best way to dovetail the audit procedures with normal operations. For example, if certain documents are routinely filed chronologically rather than numerically, the auditor can design a sample selection approach that accounts for this. And if there is one individual who seems to know a lot about a particular cycle's operations, he or she may be able to help with any problems, such as questions concerning unusual transactions in that cycle.

It is important to remember that a walk-through is a fairly soft technique rather than a definitive test. The sample of transactions that the CPA walks through the system will be very small, often only two or three transactions. Therefore, the technique has little proving power; yet, its disproving capabilities are substantial. A walk-through can reveal a blatant disregard for control procedures, the sloppy application of certain procedures, inefficient redundancy in the system, or variations from prescribed controls, even when using only a very small sample of transactions. The "walk-through" is invaluable as a means of gaining an understanding of clients' systems, as well as assessing the accuracy of one's understanding of how those systems operate. If properly designed, this tracing of one or a few of the different types of transactions may be considered as part of the tests of compliance.

The Business Approach

Earlier chapters have discussed a business approach to the audit process. Essentially, this approach emphasizes that by gaining an understanding of a client's business, the auditor is in a much better position to assess the reasonableness of management's representations and to apply effectively inquiry, observation, and the other audit procedures described in Chapter 7. The line of business in which a client operates will determine many of the key audit risks to which the auditor will need to direct attention. For example, while a manufacturer may face numerous inventory control problems, a service industry is likely to find billings and control over contractual agreements to be key areas requiring emphasis in order to maintain control over operations. These considerations should be an integral part of the audit planning process.

Risk Areas

The first step in understanding a new client's operations and possible risks is to communicate with the predecessor auditors ***[SAS 7, Section 315]***. The types of critical risks of interest would be the "red flags" described in prior chapters, and unexpected fluctuations detected by applying analytical review techniques. A survey of internal auditors identified what factors they considered when evaluating risk; see Exhibit 8-1. These factors are also

EXHIBIT 8-1

Risk Factors of Significance to Internal Auditors When Evaluating the Auditee's Risk Profile

Poor design of internal controls and/or poor past performance of those controls.

Managers that are less competent than would be desired, given their level of responsibility.

Managers of questionable integrity.

Larger operations, since they inherently face larger potential losses.

Recent changes in systems, especially in accounting systems.

Operations that are rather complex.

A greater percentage of assets that is highly liquid.

Discontinuity in key personnel.

Poor economic conditions.

Extensive electronic data-processing (EDP) operations.

Longer time period than typical has elapsed since the last audit.

Increased pressure on managers to meet target objectives.

Greater extent of regulation.

Lower employee morale than desired.

Lack of audit coverage by external auditors.

Greater political exposure.

From James M. Patton, John H. Evans III, and Barry L. Lewis, *A Framework for Evaluating Internal Audit Risk*, Research Report No. 25 (Altamonte Springs, Fla.: Institute of Internal Auditors, 1982), p. 20.

likely to be important to external auditors; however, the audit coverage of particular areas of operations by the internal auditors would be an additional consideration in evaluating risk. These risk factors are rather global and may well be discernible primarily through observation and basic inquiry procedures.

A risk indicator that involves more detailed analysis of cycles and designated groups of transactions is the application of analytical review techniques. As described in an earlier chapter, prior year comparisons, trend analysis, ratios, budget-to-actual comparisons, and modeling can be used to form expectations as to recorded balances. Any large variation of management's representations from recorded balances suggests a higher risk of misstatement and a need for further investigation by the auditor. The broader the scope of information that is incorporated in the analytical review techniques, the more likely those techniques are to be effective as filters, pinpointing high-risk areas of auditees' operations. In evaluating risks, the auditor must try to identify any related parties ***[SAS 45, Section 1020]***; however, an "examination made in accordance with generally accepted auditing standards cannot be expected to provide assurance that all related party transactions will be discovered."[1] Exhibit 8-2 summarizes the types of procedures that are useful in identifying and examining related-party transactions. The auditor must also watch for unreported related-party transactions. If a client is having economic trouble, a related party may provide free services, such as computer time or consultations, thus distorting the entity's financial operating picture.

EXHIBIT 8-2
Identifying and Examining Related Party Transactions

Key Sources of Information

Filings, including proxy material, with the Securities and Exchange Commission and other regulatory bodies.

Information on pension and other trusts established for employees, emphasizing the names of officers and trustees.

Stockholder listings of closely held companies.

Predecessor, principal, or other auditors.

Minutes of board of director meetings, emphasizing material transactions authorized or discussed.

Conflict-of-interest statements completed by management.

Major customer, supplier, borrower, and lender listings.

Large, unusual, or nonrecurring transactions or balances in accounting records.

Confirmations of compensating balance arrangements.

Invoices from law firms.

Confirmations of loans receivable and payable for indications of guarantees.

Contracts involving material transactions.

Management.

Audit Procedures

Review written sources and ask management about related parties and their transactions.

Keep a central listing of related parties in the continuing or permanent audit file, and make certain that all audit staff members are familiar with these names in conducting their audit work, in order to facilitate the identification of related party transactions.

Evaluate the entity's procedures for identifying and properly accounting for related party transactions.

(Exhibit continues on p. 250.)

Related parties increase the likelihood of collusion in order to promote joint interests. For example, property and services may be exchanged or sold at other than their fair market value, or borrowing may be arranged at below market rates with rather vague payment terms. These types of transactions can materially distort financial statements. The form of the related-party transactions must be compared with their substance. If a loan is not supposed to be repaid, then contributed capital may well be the substance of the financing arrangement. Below-market interest rates will distort an entity's true cost of debt, and consequently, the reported return on funds borrowed will not indicate the future expected returns to stockholders. Because of related-party transactions' greater risk, the planning process should allow time to investigate them, in accordance with the overall perceived risk exposure.

[1]Statement on Auditing Standards No. 6, "Related Party Transactions" (New York: AICPA, July 1975), par. .09.

EXHIBIT 8-2 (continued)

Per related party transaction:

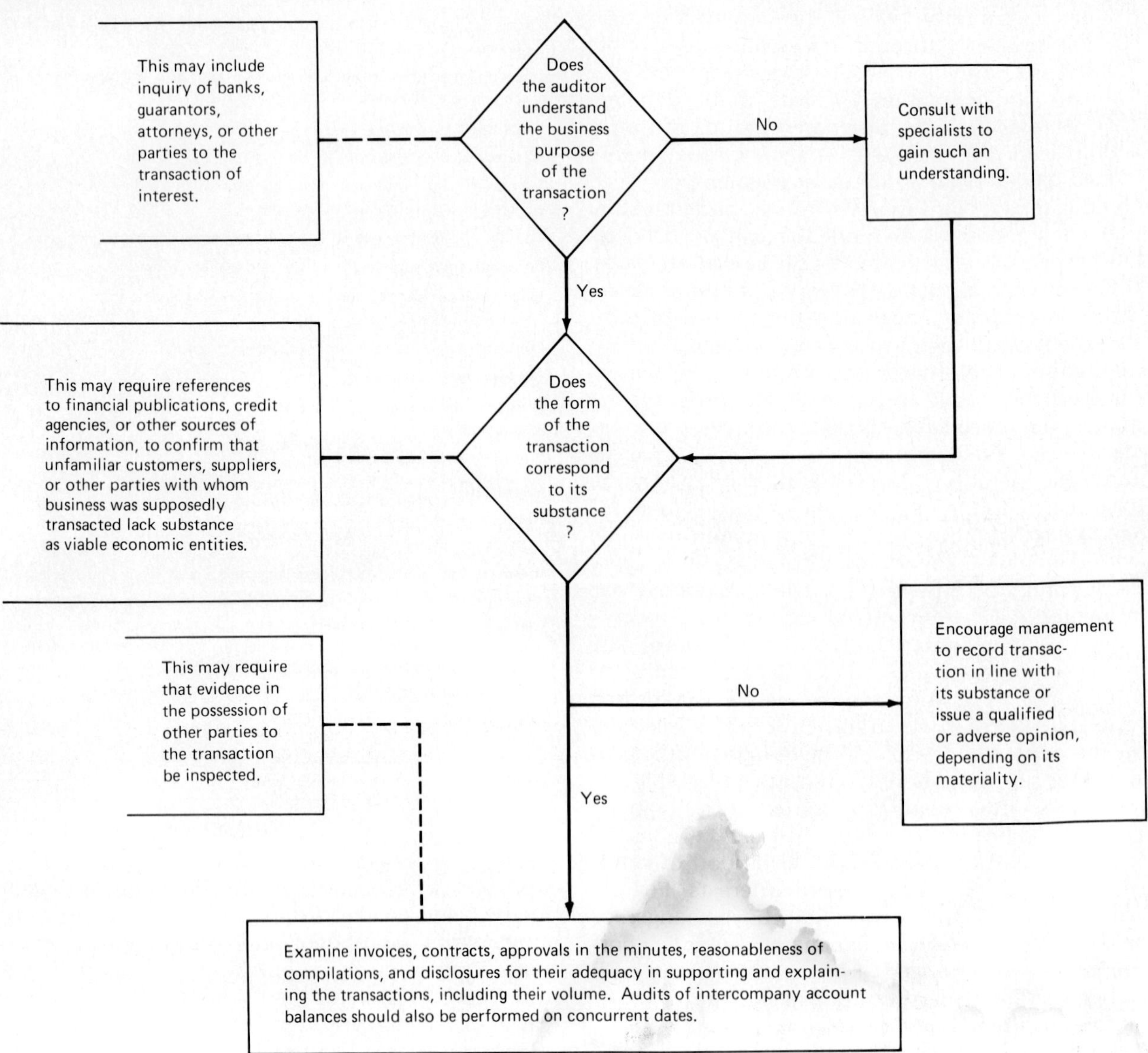
This may include inquiry of banks, guarantors, attorneys, or other parties to the transaction of interest.
Does the auditor understand the business purpose of the transaction ?
No
Consult with specialists to gain such an understanding.
Yes
This may require references to financial publications, credit agencies, or other sources of information, to confirm that unfamiliar customers, suppliers, or other parties with whom business was supposedly transacted lack substance as viable economic entities.
Does the form of the transaction correspond to its substance ?
This may require that evidence in the possession of other parties to the transaction be inspected.
No
Encourage management to record transaction in line with its substance or issue a qualified or adverse opinion, depending on its materiality.
Yes
Examine invoices, contracts, approvals in the minutes, reasonableness of compilations, and disclosures for their adequacy in supporting and explaining the transactions, including their volume. Audits of intercompany account balances should also be performed on concurrent dates.

Past Adjusting Entries

Risk can also be judged according to the CPA's past experience with the client, in particular, the client's past adjusting entries. Assuming that a client has not made any corrections since the preceding year, it seems reasonable to expect similar difficulties in the current year. For example, if last year's inventory was found to be overstated due to poor controls over material requisition and such controls have not been improved, the client's records are likely to contain similar errors this year.

One research project tested the effectiveness of using prior year adjusting entries to signal problems in the current period, in tandem with analytical review flux, trend, and ratio analyses. Specifically, the following six measures were used:

1. The three-year average of audited net income with materiality equal to 10 percent of these "normal earnings."
2. The absolute difference in the balance of individual accounts from one year to the next.
3. The absolute difference in the balance of individual accounts relative to normal earnings.
4. The proportion of each account balance to the total financial statement (a so-called entropy measure).
5. The ratio of account balances.
6. The presence of a material audit adjustment in the preceding year.

Together these measures identified approximately 66 percent of the subsequent year adjustments, although they also produced 16 percent apparent "false alarms."[2]

The Audit Risk Model

An extremely useful means of considering audit risk for planning purposes is to use the audit risk model, which is presented in Statement on Auditing Standards No. 39 (Section 350), "Audit Sampling."[3] The audit risk model defines an auditor's *ultimate risk (UR)*. UR is the risk of a monetary error greater than the tolerable error in the balance or class of transactions remaining undetected after the auditor has completed all of the audit procedures deemed necessary. *Tolerable error* is an error that would not materially misstate the financial statements. Statement on Auditing Standards No. 45 (Section 1020), "Omnibus Statement on Auditing Standards—1983" substituted the term *audit risk (AR)* for ultimate risk (UR).

According to professional standards ***[SAS 47, Section 312]***, the auditor must quantify the AR in light of (1) the risk of material misstatement in the financial statements, (2) the cost of reducing the risk, and (3) the effect of the potential misstatement on the use and understanding of the financial statements.

The risk of material misstatement is generally acknowledged as depending on management's integrity, the entity's internal accounting control system, and the entity's overall economic position. The cost-benefit considerations related to audit risk rest with the CPA, except that professional standards are expected to set some ceiling on the amount of risk that a CPA can accept. Some CPAs avoid high-risk clients, though others are willing to accept such risks, as they believe that the higher audit fees will offset the costs associated with a greater risk of unfavorable publicity or legal sanctions. Of course, factors other than economic considerations influence the acceptance of clients, including a desire to serve the public. The "effect of material misstatement on the users" depends on which user group is involved—for example, public or private companies. A closely held private company may give its financial statements only to its banker and ten stockholders, all of whom will be familiar with its operations, anyway. But a public company sends its financial statements to many users and so is subject to numerous regulatory agencies' reviews. In addition, class action suits can mean big-dollar liability to investors.

With all of these considerations in mind, the CPA will determine the acceptable risk of issuing an opinion on financial statements that may be incorrect because of undetected material errors and irregularities. To plan an audit that can control AR,

[2]William R. Kinney, Jr. "The Predictive Power of Limited Information in Preliminary Analytical Review: An Empirical Study," *Journal of Accounting Research*, supplement, 1979, pp. 148–165.

[3]New York: AICPA, June 1981.

the auditor will rely on internal accounting controls (IC), analytical review procedures (ARP), and substantive tests of details (TD). Professional standards permit any combination of these procedures but do not permit a complete reliance on controls. This audit planning approach is described in the following risk model:

$$AR = IC \times ARP \times TD$$

where IC, ARP, and TD are the risk assessments that each technique would fail to detect errors equal to the tolerable error. The model merely points out that if, for example, internal controls are strong and warrant reliance, then fewer tests of details will be needed. Similarly, extensive use of analytical review should reduce the extent of detailed test work needed. SAS No. 39 offers the following example of how this planning model can calculate the allowable level of risk when performing detailed substantive tests. The phrase "an audit risk level of .05" means that there is a 5 percent risk of incorrectly accepting a balance or, in other words, that the auditor wishes to have 95 percent confidence (100 - .05) that any material error has been identified.

In planning an engagement, if the auditor wants an audit risk level of .05 and believes that internal accounting controls might fail to detect aggregate errors equal to the tolerable error 50 percent of the time, and analytical review procedures might fail to detect such error 30 percent of the time, the allowable risk of incorrect acceptance for a specific substantive test of details would be 33 percent, calculated as follows:

$$TD = \frac{AR}{IC \times ARP} = \frac{.05}{.50 \times .30} = .33$$

If it were possible to reduce ARP to 10 percent, the formula would imply that no substantive tests of detail would be necessary (beyond those tied directly to the analytical review procedures). Just as the above computation solves for TD, the relationship can also be adjusted algebraically to solve for IC, ARP, or the implied AR, depending on how much is known about the effectiveness of various procedures and the planned audit approach.

The professional standards also offer the following assumptions about the audit risk model:

1. The risk factors are assumed to be independent of one another. In other words, it is assumed that there is no significant causal relationship between errors of one type and errors of another. Yet, both ARP and TD are widely acknowledged to depend, in part, on IC.
2. The auditor is assumed to be able to assess IC and ARP subjectively and with reasonable accuracy.
3. Nonsampling risk, such as the auditor's failure to recognize errors or to select the appropriate audit test, is assumed to be negligible, being effectively controlled through planning, supervision, review, and careful selection of audit procedures whenever weaknesses are a concern ***[SAS 22, Section 311].***

Other problems with the model are that other factors may influence the determination of individual risk components. One of these factors is *inherent risk,* or the risk that monetary errors equal to tolerable error would have occurred without internal accounting controls over the account balance or class of transactions. The concept of inherent risk will be developed in the next subsection of this chapter; however, the point raised by those who critique the audit risk model is that if the auditor were given credit for the fact that some clients have less inherent risk, then actual risk would be reduced below the risk calculated in the model's current form. There is also an aggregation problem, in that the model is likely to be applied to sets of transactions and account balances on a disaggregated level, whereas the AR is related conceptually to an aggregate judgment on the set of financial statements. Just as there are no directions as to how to aggregate the audit risk model's various applications, there also are no directions as to how to evaluate audit cost factors when establishing AR. The final warning is the necessity of using the audit risk model solely for planning purposes, as distinct from using it as an iterative evaluation tool. In other words, the AR result would not be accurate if the auditor were to set ARP, IC, and TD; perform ARP, look at the results; and then readjust the ARP value. Every time such a readjustment is made, the audit risk inferred from the model understates the actual risk. At the extreme, if an auditor iteratively evaluated ARP, IC, and TD at all possible levels, the audit risk would actually be .1998 (assuming that the probability of intolerable error is 1), despite the model's computation of a .05 risk.[4]

Inherent Risk

As already noted, inherent risk is the probability that without internal accounting controls, there will be a material error in the accounting process. This probability is likely to be affected by the state of the economy; the client's industry; the turnover of top management; the client's ownership; geographical location; and management's reputation. For example, closely held entities may present more inherent risk with respect to understatements of income, due to tax minimization incentives, and publicly held entities may pose more inherent risk with respect to overstatements of income, due to the structure of incentive plans for top management.

Statement No. 47, Section 312 suggests that an audit risk (AR) model recognize three key components: inherent risk (IR), control risk (CR), and detection risk (DR): AR = IR × CR × DR. *Control risk* is the probability that material errors cannot be prevented or detected on a timely basis by the internal accounting control system. *Detection risk* is the probability that material errors not detected or corrected by the internal accounting control system will also not be detected by the audit procedures. This AR model is an extension of SAS No. 39.

Business Risk

The concept of business risk is the probability that auditors will suffer some loss or injury to their professional reputation as a result of a particular client relationship. In addition, auditors can also lose money because of litigation and/or sanctions imposed by regulators. Business risk thus may also affect insurance coverage and billing rates.[5]

The Permanent Audit File

Since the identification of key risk areas is an integral part of each year's audit, the continuing or permanent audit file should contain the auditor's analysis of the client's risk profile. Industry benchmarks, trends, and related parties would be included, as well as expected future problems based on past experiences. Risk is such a central consideration to audit planning that its inclusion in the permanent audit file makes sense and can facilitate a more efficient assessment of risk, as well as a long-term perspective on how a client's risk profile has changed over time. Obviously, the permanent audit file must be regularly updated to ensure the auditor's consideration of the dynamic operations and business environment of the client.

Risk Work Sheets

One tool that can help assess risk is risk exposure work sheets, which convert risk to a common unit of measure, like dollars, and quantify the worst and the most likely risk exposure for various events, situations, or control configurations. For example, consider evaluating a control system according to (1) the expected error or loss that would arise from one occurrence (like a deviation from designed control) and (2) the frequency of this one occurrence (like the number of control deviations expected).

One approach, which was first used to evaluate computer systems, is to set dollar categories that are distinctive enough to achieve consensus across the control evaluators. These dollar categories are easily derived by taking numbers to a power. As Exhibit 8-3 illustrates, a power of 2 or 10 might be used, depending on the likely size of the operation. This same approach can be used to create distinctive frequency classifications for the rate of occurrence. Although the experts may disagree whether the expected loss would be $80 or $90, they are likely to agree that it is $10, $100, or $1,000. Similarly, the error may be expected to occur fifteen or twenty times per day, though it is gener-

[4]William R. Kinney, Jr., "A Note on Compounding Probabilities in Auditing," *Auditing: A Journal of Practice & Theory*, Spring 1983, pp. 13–22.

[5]See Craig A. Brumfield, Robert K. Elliott, and Peter D. Jacobson, "Business Risk and the Audit Process," *Journal of Accountancy*, April 1983, pp. 60–68.

EXHIBIT 8-3
The Quantification of Risk

(1) Expected Error or Loss from a Single Occurrence

Power of 2 (Likely in Small Entities)	Power of 10 (Likely in Large Entities)
$ 1	$ 1
2	10
4	100
8	1,000
16	10,000
32	100,000

(2) Frequency of the Occurrence

Power of 2	Power of 10
16 per day	10,000 per day
8 per day	1,000 per day
4 per day	100 per day
2 per day	10 per day
1 per day	1 per day
once in 2 days	once in 10 days
once in 4 days	once in 3 1/3 months

ally agreed that the error's frequency is closer to ten than to one hundred occurrences per day. By using the information presented under (1) and (2) of Exhibit 8-3, it is simple to calculate the risk exposure of a certain type of control problem. For example, if the magnitude of the expected loss from not recalculating the mathematical accuracy of billings is found to be in the $10 category and is expected to occur once a day, the calculation will be

$$\$10 \times 1 \text{ time per day} \times 260 \text{ business days} = \$2{,}600$$

Even though this computation is straightforward, there may be some uncertainty about the category of the loss and the frequency of the occurrence. Hence work sheets have been devised to summarize the possible risks, from which the overall assessments can be formulated. Exhibit 8-4 quantifies the various risk exposures that all decision makers agree are possible. They believe that losses over $10,000 or occurrences greater than ten times per day would be detected. Therefore, the maximum risk exposure, or the worst case, based on the completed blocks is $260,000.

Materiality Decisions

Financial Accounting Standards Board Statement of Financial Accounting Concepts No. 2, "Qualitative Characteristics of Accounting Information" defines *materiality* as

> the magnitude of an omission or misstatement of accounting information that, in the light of surrounding circumstances, makes it probable that the judgment of a reasonable person relying on the information would have been changed or influenced by the omission or misstatement.

The discussion explicitly recognizes the importance of making materiality judgments in light of the situation, considering both quantitative and qualitative factors. For example, the possibility of noncompliance with a debt covenant, illegal payments, or inadequate disclosure of related party transactions could influence the qualitative materiality of otherwise quantitatively immaterial errors.

The auditor's consideration of materiality is a matter of professional judgment in the circumstances and will be influenced by his or her perception of the needs of those who will rely on the financial statements. The nature and amount of an error should depend on the nature and amount of items in the financial statements being audited. Materiality thus is recognized as being closely linked to the concept of audit risk in determining the nature, timing, and extent of audit procedures, as well as in evaluating the results of audit procedures in forming an opinion on the financial statements as a whole.

The *objective* of the audit has been described as a search for errors that, either individually or in the aggregate, would be material to the financial statements. Statement on Auditing Standards No. 47 (Section 312), entitled "Materiality and Audit Risk in Conducting an Audit," requires that the auditor obtain a preliminary understanding of materiality (it need not be quantified as a single number) for the financial statements as a whole and use it to plan the audit procedures. The auditor should focus on quantitative material errors and also watch for qualitative factors. The statement requires that any errors be aggregated, including any differ-

EXHIBIT 8-4
Risk Exposure Worksheet—An Illustration

Nature of Cost-Benefit Characteristics:

Possible Risk Exposures:

Frequency of Occurrence

Magnitude of Expected Error or Loss	Once in 3 1/3 months	Once in 10 days	Times per day 1	Times per day 10	Times per day 100	Times per day 1,000
$100,000						
10,000		$260,000				
1,000		$26,000				
100		$2,600		$260,000		
10		$260	$2,600			
1		$26				

Worst Case of Exposure $ ______________
Expected Exposure $ ______________
Further Actions Recommended ______________

ences between an accounting estimate in the financial statements and the closest estimate that the auditor believes is reasonable. Furthermore, errors identified in an earlier period, affecting the financial statements for the current period, should also be included in the aggregate error calculation, as such errors would be relevant to the audit's planning phase. The auditor should also take into account the imprecision of the audit procedures when evaluating the risk of material misstatement. The SAS recommends materiality assessments be made at both the planning and the evaluation phase of the audit. In fact, SAS No. 22 (Section 311), "Planning and Supervision,"[6] recognizes that the audi-

[6] New York: AICPA, 1978.

tor should consider, among other things, preliminary estimates of materiality levels when (s)he plans an audit of financial statements; however, that SAS, similarly, does not require quantification of such an estimate.

One interesting dimension of materiality decisions, recognized in SAS No. 22, is that there may be more than one level of materiality for the financial statements taken as a whole. For example, an account classification error of $200,000 may be immaterial, whereas a $100,000 error affecting net income may be material. Materiality for planning purposes should be set at the smallest aggregate level of errors that could be considered material to any one of the financial statements. Hence if a $300,000 error is judged to be material on the balance sheet, even though $250,000 is material on the income statement, the auditor should not design procedures to detect errors above $300,000. The threshold would need to be set at $250,000 in this instance. The auditor's preliminary estimate of materiality should be based on the components of the financial statements: the size of the entity (measured as assets, total equity, revenue, and average earnings) and the nature of the client's operations and related transactions. For instance:

Tolerable error for a component	=	Preliminary estimate of materiality less expected uncorrected error in the financial statements	×	Square Root of: Amount of component divided by total amount of all components that make up the financial statements to which materiality is being allocated

These tolerable errors would then determine the audit effort.[7]

Coordinating Work with Other Auditors

Other auditors' work may also help determine materiality ***[SAS 1, Section 543]***. Statement on Auditing Procedure No. 45, "Using the Work and Reports of Other Auditors,"[8] discusses whether as the principal auditor, a CPA may use the work and reports of other independent auditors and how the auditor's report should be altered under such circumstances. The first step is determining whether the CPA is in fact the *principal auditor*. If an auditor examines most of the consolidated assets and revenues (or net assets and earnings, if they more clearly reveal the portion of the financial statements examined), is familiar with the financial statements, and decides that the components he or she examined are important to the enterprise as a whole, then he or she is the principal auditor.

The principal auditor can choose to take sole responsibility for the financial statements, in which case no reference is made to other auditors' work in the audit report, or he or she can divide responsibility by referring to the other auditor's examination. Note that even if no reference is made, the other auditor is still responsible for the performance of his or her own work and report and therefore can be held liable by the principal auditor.

Generally, if the work performed by another auditor is immaterial, if that other auditor is retained by the principal auditor and works under his or her guidance and control, or if an associated or correspondent firm is the other auditor, the auditor's report will not refer to that other auditor. But without these three conditions, the principal auditor must assess the risk of assuming sole responsibility. Standards require that the principal auditor be able to determine that the other auditor did essentially the same work and in the same way as the principal auditor would have. Thus the principal auditor must determine the other auditor's technical competence, due care, and independence. Virtual replication of some procedures may be deemed necessary. If the other auditors' work is or is expected to become material, the principal auditor will probably refer to the other auditors' examination in his or her report.

Such a reference should indicate in both the scope and opinion paragraphs the division of re-

[7] George R. Zuber, Robert K. Elliott, William R. Kinney, Jr., and James J. Leisenring, "Using Materiality in Audit Planning," *Journal of Accountancy*, March 1983, p. 50.

[8] New York: AICPA, July 1971.

sponsibility between the principal auditor and the other auditor. The magnitude of each auditor's examination should be stated as dollar amounts or percentages of total assets, total revenues, or, as suggested earlier, other criteria that more clearly reveal the portion of the financial statements examined by the other auditor. Note that the other auditor can be named only if the principal auditor has permission to do so, if that other auditor's report is presented together with the principal auditor's, and if the reference to other auditors' work does not constitute a qualified opinion but merely indicates divided responsibility.

Regardless of whether the other auditors' work is referred to, if it is relied on in gathering the necessary evidential base for the principal auditor's opinion, the other auditor's professional reputation and independence must be established. In particular, the other auditor should write a letter of representation that he or she is independent according to the AICPA's and SEC's (if applicable) standards. Their communications should establish that the other auditor is aware of the principal auditor's reliance, is familiar with the AICPA and applicable SEC standards and will comply with such guidelines, and that those matters affecting the elimination of intercompany transactions or the uniformity of accounting practices will be reviewed. These inquiry procedures are essential unless the other auditors' primary place of practice is in the United States and their professional reputation and standing are already known.

The Study and Evaluation of Internal Control

A later chapter addresses objectives of internal control and approaches to evaluating controls. However, at this juncture, it is important to note that the auditor preparing an audit program must consider the extent to which controls are to be examined. Professional standards only require a basic understanding of information flows. The decision to evaluate controls in depth and to test them for the purpose of relying on controls as a basis for reducing other tests is an audit judgment. Obviously, the audit program must be based on some expectation as to the quality of controls and the feasibility of reliance on controls. Should the expectation prove to be in error, due to later discovery that controls are ineffective or are costly to test, then the audit program would require adjustment. Often, a CPA can reduce audit work by using, to some extent, the work of internal auditors. The competence and objectivity of internal auditors must be evaluated, as must the quality of their work. Substitution of work is not permitted; however, by testing internal audit workpapers, some reliance is warranted by the external auditor and hence a reduction of work is possible.

Costs and Benefits of Various Audit Tests

In spite of excellent controls, an auditor may have substantive tests available which are cheaper to apply than compliance tests in order to reach the desired level of confidence. In this setting, cost considerations could lead to no reliance on controls and total use of substantive test procedures. Although no audit can rely 100 percent on internal accounting controls, it is the case that the percentage weight placed upon controls can be substantial.

In designing an audit program, the auditor will try to achieve the objectives in the most efficient manner. Such cost-benefit considerations may change the allocations of tolerable error across the financial statement components. For example, cash can usually be audited to a tight tolerance at a reasonable cost, whereas the audit of inventory tends to be more expensive. Because fixed assets are largely carried over from earlier years, they may be easily auditable to a tight tolerance. And long-term debt, deferred taxes, common stock, interest expense, and tax provisions can generally be audited 100 percent, with no need to allocate tolerable error.

Sampling Plans and Interim Work

Public accounting's infamous busy season is expensive for professionals, firms, and clients ***[SAS 45, Section 1020]***. Whenever excessive overtime hours are required, fatigue is more likely to result in error. Furthermore, overtime pay is greater than base pay for entry level staff auditors. As a result, an audit efficiency and effectiveness move by many auditing firms is to perform work at an interim date as a means of meeting some of the audit objectives. By audit testing at interim dates, early consideration of significant matters, such as related party transactions and recent system and accounting changes, is possible, and adjustments can be made on a more timely basis. Beyond audit planning and control study and evaluation, substantive tests may be conducted before the balance sheet date, such as tests of details of property, investment, debt and equity accounts, that is, additions and reductions to these accounts; tests of details for income and expense-related transactions; tests of accounts like warranty reserves and defined charges; and analytical review procedures. Yet, as discussed in Chapter 7, this early timing of substantive test work increases audit risk, and additional tests are required to cover the period from interim work to year-end.

Sampling plans will be described in depth in Chapters 11 and 12. However, one decision by the preparer of the audit program when planning interim tests is whether to define the *population of interest* (the total set of transactions being tested) as all of the transactions for the year or as all of the transactions for the year to date. In the former case, the plan is based on the total number of expected transactions. Only the sample units available at interim are examined, and the sampling conclusions are postponed until year-end, when the remaining sample units become available for testing. In the latter case, the sampling plan is carried out, and the results are evaluated at interim. Other tests of details or analytical review procedures are then relied on to extend the audit conclusions to the balance sheet date.

In addition to considering the sampling plans and the mix of procedures from the interim date, the auditor must coordinate the related auditing procedures. SAS No. 45 stresses that the auditor should (1) coordinate audit procedures that are applied to related-party transactions and balances, (2) coordinate the testing of interrelated accounts and their cutoffs, and (3) maintain temporary audit control over readily negotiable assets and simultaneously test such assets and cash on hand in banks, bank loans, and other related items. The auditor must also coordinate the expected degree of reliance on internal controls, the interim work to be performed, and the year-end work to ensure that audit risk is held to a reasonably low level.

Certain audit procedures, such as year-end cash counts, have to be performed at particular times, and some procedures require a lot of time, such as first and second requests for confirmations. Still other procedures are best performed chronologically. For example, internal control review should precede substantive test work, and analytical review procedures often precede detailed test work. *PERT (Program Evaluation Review Technique)* is a management tool that can be used to diagram the sequence of events (commonly using circles connected by arrows) and then to estimate the time required to perform the various concurrent and sequential activities. The costs of any delays in completing these activities on time are also calculated, along with probability estimates of the likelihood of their completion on time. Finally, a "critical path" is laid out for planning purposes and then monitored for variations as the project progresses. Even if an auditor chooses not to formally apply PERT, (s)he may find it useful to informally consider the PERT framework while planning and supervising an audit. Exhibit 8-5 summarizes the various alternatives in planning the audit procedures.

The Initial Audit Plan

The planning of the audit encompasses the nature, timing, and extent of audit procedures. The nature of tests may be compliance, substantive, or dual purpose. Recall that the dual-purpose test provides both compliance and substantive test evidence. The type of evidence to be collected is also a consideration of the auditor who is designing an audit program. The final aspect of the nature of audit procedures is their reliability and relative effectiveness. The client's setting, or audit circumstances, will be influential in the final selection of the nature of audit procedures.

The timing of procedures must consider PERT type constraints, as well as the risk from performing interim work and the benefits of such early timing of substantive tests. The length of time between interim and year-end audit work must be determined.

The final aspect of planning relates to the extent of tests. Substantive test work can be reduced by

EXHIBIT 8-5
Various Alternatives in Planning Nature, Timing, and Extent of Audit Procedures

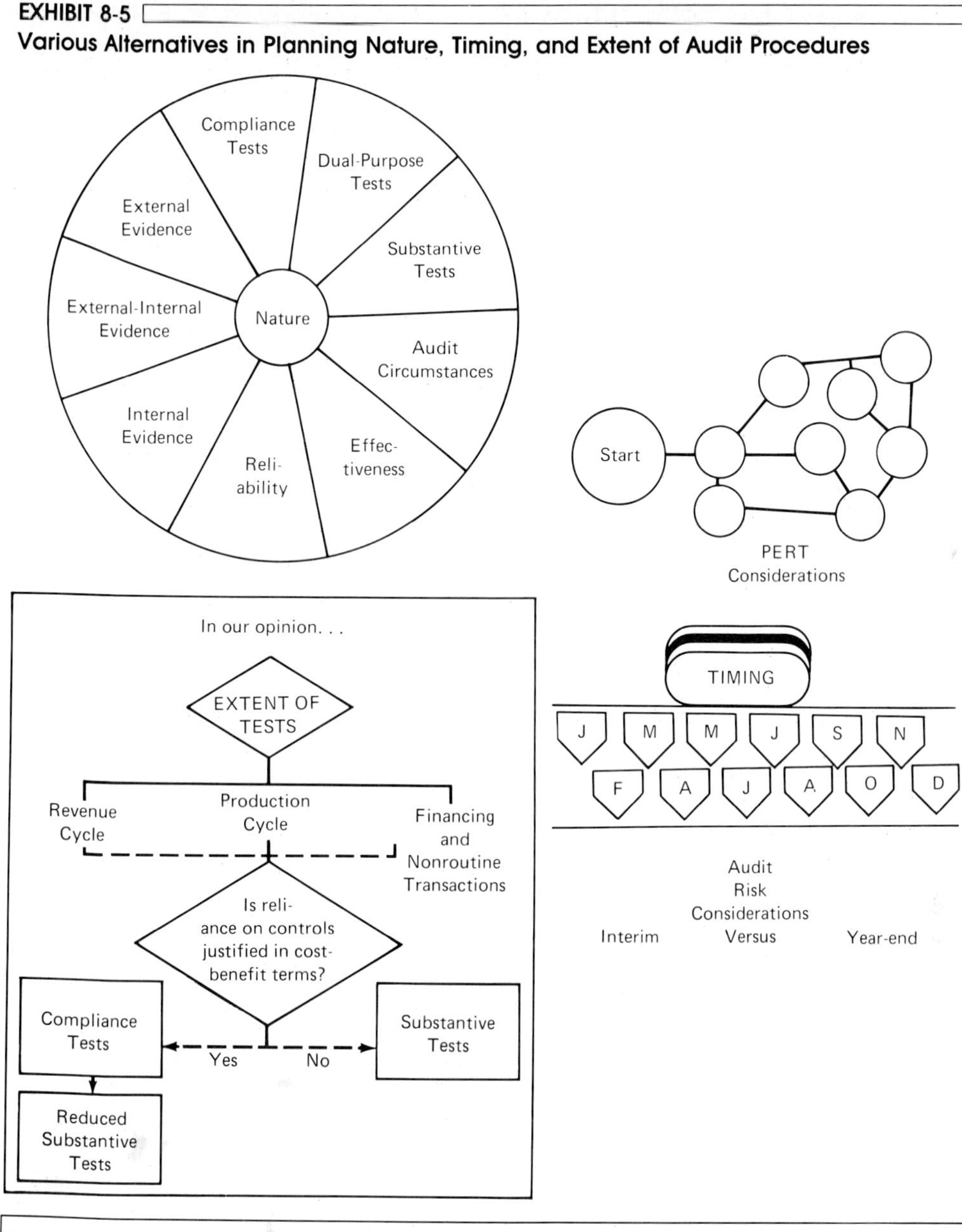

relying on a client's control system. Such reliance requires that the client's controls be designed effectively and that it have less than the tolerable error level, as supported by compliance test work. The critical decision relates to the efficiency of various combinations of compliance and substantive test procedures. Exhibit 8-5 summarizes the various alternatives in planning the nature, timing, and extent of audit procedures, as discussed herein and in prior chapters.

Reacting to the Results of Compliance Tests

If the compliance test results are as expected, the audit program should require little adjustment. But if they are not as expected, the auditor can do one of three things. The first is that some systematic attribute of compliance errors can be detected, corrected, and its effects evaluated to permit the audit plan to proceed with only minor adjustments. The second is to find an alternative control for testing which, if effective, would compensate for that control which is not operating as designed. And the third is not to rely on the controls and to adjust the audit plan to extend substantive test work. Which of the three alternatives is best depends on the circumstances and their relative costs.

Alternative Approaches to Writing Audit Programs

Some auditing firms use standard, often referred to as "canned," audit programs. There are detailed listings of audit procedures that can be tailored to the individual client. The main argument for these canned, *procedure-oriented programs* is that a planned audit step will probably not be inadvertently omitted. On the other hand, many argue that a risk exists that detailed programs will be applied in a routine manner, without careful thought being given to particular audit objectives. This would create the possibility of both inefficient and ineffective audits due to the omission of audit steps which were relevant to particular risks uncovered in the course of the audit work. In particular, some feel that a detailed program is too often accepted as dogma, as opposed to a flexible work plan that is intended to be responsive to the client setting.

Many firms thus stress audit objectives over procedures and encourage their staff to design detailed procedural steps as they became familiar with the client's situation. Exhibits 8-6 and 8-7 give examples of a procedures-oriented audit program and an objectives-oriented program. Both programs address the audit of payroll. The procedures-oriented audit program tells the staff auditor what to do, but not why a particular procedure should be performed. In contrast, the *objectives-oriented program* stresses goals and lets the auditor decide how to achieve them. For example, rather than testing a sample of 40 employees, the auditor may choose to perform analytical review procedures to assess how reasonable recorded payroll is in relation to past periods, production statistics, and industry benchmarks. Perhaps regression analysis would be applied, comparing historical experience, as well as job sites' experiences. By tying related withholding tax and deductions to expected payroll, the reasonableness of net pay may be inferred without detailed testing. The point, of course, is that the auditor is given more latitude in the selection of specific audit procedures when provided a program similar to Exhibit 8-7. However, with this flexibility is the added risk that an important program step will be omitted or that the specific procedures used will not offer sufficient audit evidence. Generally, an objectives-oriented audit program requires closer supervision and more review of the audit field work than does a procedures-oriented program.

Regardless of which approach is taken, it is fair to say that most large CPA firms would include in their audit manuals some standardized program suggestions. Some would make available preprinted programs for adaptation, as a time-saving firm practice. Yet, all practitioners would stress that such standardized programs must be adjusted to "tailor-fit" the client setting, in order for an audit to be both effective and efficient.

Requests to Legal Counsel

Regardless of the type of audit program used, the auditor must request a *letter of representation from the client's legal counsel.* The auditor then uses these letters to assess the adequacy of disclosure. Although lawyers acknowledge that they are the appropriate source of information about actual or threatened claims or litigation involving their clients, they are concerned that their responses to auditors' inquiries about unasserted claims may threaten the confidentiality of the lawyer–client relationship.

In 1975, the AICPA and the American Bar Association (ABA) came to an agreement concerning their policy on cooperating in audit inquiries. This

EXHIBIT 8-6
A Procedurally Oriented Audit Program

Payrolls: Plant and Job Site

Performed by	Date performed	Work paper reference	
________	________	________	1. Select one payroll run for testing.
________	________	________	2. Test the accumulation of hours on the time cards and the transcription by job of total hours on the summary sheet.
________	________	________	3. Compare total hours for the summary sheets with total hours on the payroll register.
________	________	________	4. Compare client tape on the "cut amount" of the checks, for the summary control, with the total for the payroll register by job.
________	________	________	5. Trace totals for payroll register to the payroll journal and totals for the payroll journal to postings in the general ledger.
________	________	________	6. Client does not maintain the payroll bank account on an imprest system. Compare the total on the payroll register with the disbursement from the regular operating account for such payroll.
________	________	________	7. Test the client's reconciliation of the payroll bank account.
________	________	________	8. Investigate the method of handling unclaimed wages.
________	________	________	9. If possible, participate in a surprise "payoff" for one or more job sites.
________	________	________	10. Select forty employees and perform the following:
________	________	________	a. Compare hours on each time card with the hours on the payroll register.
________	________	________	b. Compare rates paid with the authorization in the personnel files and with the preprinted rate on the time cards. Investigate any rates on time cards that were changed by hand.
________	________	________	c. Check deductions from gross pay to authorization forms signed by employees.
________	________	________	d. Test the computation of gross pay, FICA taxes, and the like.
________	________	________	e. Check the personnel records to ascertain whether persons being paid were employees during the period tested.
________	________	________	f. Examine paid payroll checks for employees tested. Compare the endorsement with the W-4 form.
________	________	________	11. Examine termination slips for several employees, and determine the date of deletion from the payroll. Test for reasonableness.

EXHIBIT 8-7
An Objectives-Oriented Audit Program

PAYROLLS: Plant and Job Site

Performed by	Date performed	Work paper reference	
______	______	______	1. Determine that recorded payroll is reasonable.
______	______	______	2. Verify that payroll transactions are recorded on a timely basis and are appropriately classified.
______	______	______	3. Tie recorded payroll into evidence that the related work was actually performed.
______	______	______	4. Make sure that payroll payments are to current employees (i.e., not to fictitious employees).
______	______	______	5. Obtain evidence that recorded payroll is at the appropriate pay rate and extended for the correct number of hours worked and that net pay is properly calculated.
______	______	______	6. Ensure that payroll transactions are being appropriately recorded into employees' records of earnings.
______	______	______	7. Check whether payroll transactions have been properly authorized.

agreement has been criticized for establishing self-protecting positions for CPAs and lawyers and for encouraging more "subject to" opinions, thereby projecting "a seeming deterioration of business conditions which is nonexistent."[9] In any case, Exhibit 8-8 outlines the content of letters of inquiry to the client's lawyer, as suggested in the professional standards ***[SAS 12, Section 337]***. Note that the auditor cannot rely on a lawyer's direct disclosure of unasserted claims, although the lawyer's resignation can be a signal of omissions in a client's disclosure practices. Exhibit 8-9 contains paragraphs 2, 4, and 7 of the "American Bar Association's Statement of Policy Regarding Lawyers' Responses to Auditors' Requests For Information," regarding the limitations of the legal counsel's responses and the use of their responses.

Disclosure Considerations

Research reviewing 249 footnote references to litigation by 198 New York Stock Exchange–listed companies indicated that 71 footnotes did not cite the type of suit and 47 failed to mention loss risk at all. Many feel that companies should disclose the nature of such suits, when they were filed, when they are likely to be resolved, the amount of damages sought, management's views on the materiality of the loss risks, and legal counsel's opinion of the adequacy of available defenses and the materiality of the expected outcomes. But as shown in Exhibit 8-9, a lawyer would have to give his or her permission in order to cite such opinions. An example of the least informative of disclosures found follows: "In the ordinary course of business the

[9] Letter from Joseph A. Sciarrino, technical director, Financial Executive Institute, April 13, 1976.

EXHIBIT 8-8
Content of Letter of Audit Inquiry to Client's Lawyer

Client's name, effective date of inquiry, and desired response date.

List of all pending or threatened litigation, claims, and assessments prepared by management or the client's lawyer.

List that describes and evaluates unasserted claims and assessments that are deemed to be probable of assertion and have at least a reasonable possibility of leading to an unfavorable outcome.

Request that legal counsel

- Describe the nature of each matter that has been asserted, progress of the case to date, and intended action.
- Evaluate the likelihood of an unfavorable outcome for each of these matters, with an estimate of the amount or range of potential loss.
- Identify the omission of any pending or threatened litigation, claims, and assessments.
- Comment on any differences in views from management's.
- State that the listing of asserted matters is complete.
- Confirm that the lawyer has advised the client concerning disclosures required for unasserted or possible claims and assessments.
- Identify the nature of and reasons for any limitation in the lawyer's response.

Note:

If the letter excludes immaterial items, the auditor and client are assumed to have reached an understanding on the limits of materiality for this purpose.

Furthermore, if a lawyer resigns, the auditor should consider the need for inquiries as to the reason, such as possible disregard by the client for a lawyer's advice on disclosure, as this disregard may require such resignation under the lawyer's code of professional responsibility.

If uncertainty is expressed as to the outcome of material litigation, a "subject to" audit opinion is appropriate.

Corporation is involved in routine litigation, none of which is deemed by management to be material." Clearly, the usefulness of this disclosure can be questioned.[10]

It would appear that the clarity of communications to which CPAs attest could be enhanced in a manner that reduces the risk of misleading financials. These issues merit consideration by the auditor in evaluating the adequacy of disclosure and the overall audit risk of the engagement.

Errors or Irregularities

In addition to directing attention to contingencies, the auditor has the responsibility, within the inherent limitations of the auditing process (such as flaws in audit procedures; necessary cost-benefit considerations; and risks created by management override of controls, collusion, forgeries, or unrecorded transactions), to plan the engagement so as to seek out material errors or irregularities.

Statement on Auditing Standards No. 16 (Section 327), "The Independent Auditor's Responsibility for the Detection of Errors or Irregularities" provides guidance to the CPA as to what procedures are to be performed when there is an indication that errors or irregularities may exist. Recall from Chapter 6 that *errors* are defined as unintentional mistakes, while *irregularities* are intentional distortions including misrepresentations by management and fraud. *Professional skepticism* should be the auditor's attitude in setting the audit scope and in gathering evidence. Circumstances outlined in SAS No. 16 that should make the auditor question whether material errors or irregularities exist include affirmative answers to the following: (1) Are there differences in control accounts and subsidiary records, or similar discrepancies within the double-entry accounting system? (2) Are there confirmations that disclose discrepancies in reported accounts and customers' representations? (3) Are there abnormally low response rates to confirmations, relative to the rates expected? (4) Have the transactions been improperly documented? (5) Are some transactions not recorded in accordance with management's general or specific authorization? and (6) Are there unusual transactions at or near the year-end?

If no evidence is obtained to suggest the existence of irregularities, it is reasonable for the auditor to rely on management's representations and on the genuineness of records and documents obtained during the engagement. Professional standards emphasize that the subsequent discovery of errors and irregularities does not, in itself, indicate the auditor's inadequate performance, owing to the audit's own inherent limitations. But if the CPA

[10] David M. Dennis and Robert M. Keith, "Are Litigation Disclosures Inadequate?" *Journal of Accountancy* March 1981, pp. 54–60.

EXHIBIT 8-9

Excerpts from the American Bar Association Statement of Policy Regarding Lawyers' Responses to Auditors' Requests for Information

Limitation on Scope of Response. It is appropriate for the lawyer to set forth in his response, by way of limitation, the scope of his engagement by the client. It is also appropriate for the lawyer to indicate the date as of which information is furnished and to disclaim any undertaking to advise the auditor of changes which may thereafter be brought to the lawyer's attention. Unless the lawyer's response indicates otherwise, (a) it is properly limited to matters which have been given substantive attention by the lawyer in the form of legal consultation and, where appropriate, legal representation since the beginning of the period or periods being reported upon, and (b) if a law firm or a law department, the auditor may assume that the firm or department has endeavored, to the extent believed necessary by the firm or department, to determine from lawyers currently in the firm or department who have performed services for the client since the beginning of the fiscal period under audit whether such services involved substantive attention in the form of legal consultation concerning . . . loss contingencies . . . but, beyond that, no review has been made of any of the client's transactions or other matters for the purpose of identifying loss contingencies to be described in the response. . . .

Limited Responses. Where the lawyer is limiting his response in accordance with this Statement of Policy, his response should so indicate. . . . If in any other respect the lawyer is not undertaking to respond to or comment on particular aspects of the inquiry when responding to the auditor, he should consider advising the auditor that his response is limited, in order to avoid any inference that the lawyer has responded to all aspects; otherwise, he may be assuming a responsibility which he does not intend. . . .

Limitation on Use of Response. Unless otherwise stated in the lawyer's response, it shall be solely for the auditor's information in connection with his audit of the financial condition of the client and is not to be quoted in whole or in part or otherwise referred to in any financial statements of the client or related documents, nor is it to be filed with any governmental agency or other person, without the lawyer's prior written consent. Notwithstanding such limitation, the response can properly be furnished to others in compliance with court process or when necessary in order to defend the auditor against a challenge of the audit by the client or a regulatory agency, provided that the lawyer is given written notice of the circumstances at least twenty days before the response is so to be furnished to others, or as long in advance as possible if the situation does not permit such period of notice

From *The Business Lawyer*, vol. 31 (April 1976): 1709-1715.

EXHIBIT 8-10

Reporting Effects of Illegal Acts

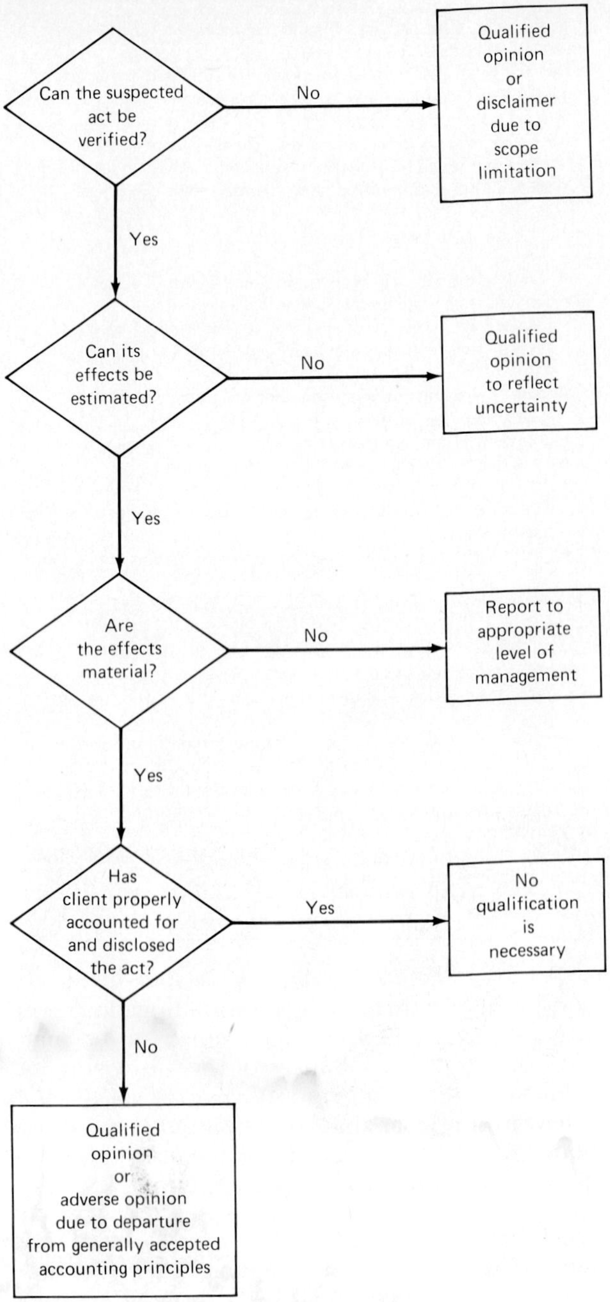

Can the suspected act be verified? — No → Qualified opinion or disclaimer due to scope limitation

Yes ↓

Can its effects be estimated? — No → Qualified opinion to reflect uncertainty

Yes ↓

Are the effects material? — No → Report to appropriate level of management

Yes ↓

Has client properly accounted for and disclosed the act? — Yes → No qualification is necessary

No ↓

Qualified opinion or adverse opinion due to departure from generally accepted accounting principles

discovers irregularities during the audit, he or she should discuss them with a level of management above that involved in the material errors or irregularities. The board of directors or audit committee should also be aware of any material errors and irregularities. The CPA should find evidence of their existence and quantify their effect and perhaps should consult legal counsel. Finally, the auditor may need to qualify his or her report, issue an adverse opinion or a disclaimer, and/or withdraw from the engagement, with a letter to the board of directors of the findings and reasons for the withdrawal. The auditor should also report any immaterial errors and irregularities to a level of management above that involved and evaluate the irregularities' effect on the audit engagement.

Illegal Acts

The auditor must similarly watch for illegal acts (including illegal political contributions, bribes, and other violations of laws and regulations). If an auditor has reason to believe that illegal acts may have been committed, he or she first should gain an understanding of both the nature of the acts and their possible effects on the financial statements ***[SAS 17, Section 328].*** The auditor should do this by talking to management, legal counsel, and other specialists, as is deemed to be necessary. Examples of what might make the CPA suspicious are the client's offering unusual or questionable explanations for certain transactions and the auditor's discovering unauthorized or improperly recorded transactions or untimely or incomplete records of transactions. The CPA then must gauge the illegal acts' materiality, including their effect on the financial statements and any related contingent monetary exposure from fines, penalties, and anticipated damages.

Any material effect will ordinarily require disclosure in the financial statements. All illegal acts should be reported to the client at a level high enough to ensure that there will be remedial actions, adjustments, and disclosure. Furthermore, the CPA must consider the implications of the illegal acts for reliance on management's representations and on internal accounting controls. Exhibit 8-10 tells the reporting consequences of illegal acts. If the client refuses to accept a modified audit report, then the auditor should withdraw from the engagement, document in writing to the client's board of directors the reason for withdrawing, and consult legal counsel.[11]

Tying Up Field Work

As an audit engagement draws to an end, the "to do" points should be resolved. For example, a claims dispute may have required a confirmation by a third party, and if that confirmation has not been received by year-end, the auditor should telephone for the confirmation and/or try alternative procedures. No "to do" points should be left open in the working papers. In addition, the schedule of individually immaterial adjustments, which were "passed" during the audit as not requiring further attention, should be considered in the aggregate ***[SAS 47, Section 312].*** Both known errors and the likely error that the auditor estimates could be in the accounts should be studied when evaluating the reasonableness of the accounts and materiality. If, in total, there is a material quantity, part of the individually immaterial adjustments must be booked so that their aggregate level will be similarly immaterial. Note that if 100 percent examinations were performed, only the known errors would need to be considered. But an audit's sampling nature requires that a projection of likely error be formulated and evaluated.

In evaluating materiality, the previous years' work must also be included. For example, if an understatement of a beginning warranty reserve were known to be $50,000 and an additional $80,000 understatement of the ending warranty reserve were found in the current year's audit, the cumulative effect of the earlier and current periods' findings would be $130,000, a cumulative effect that may well be material.

Obviously, resolution of open points and the proposing of adjustments to the client's books can be time consuming, and the audit plan should allocate sufficient time to ensure that those tasks can be completed in a thorough manner. The planning, administration, and review of an audit are to be well-documented via planning memoranda, risk and materiality assessment working papers, the

[11] Statement on Auditing Standards No. 17, "Illegal Acts by Clients" (New York: AICPA, January 1977).

audit program, and the permanent and current working paper files.

As a CPA finishes the field work, other engagement services need to be considered, to ensure that the information to perform such work will be available. For example, if the CPA firm is to prepare the tax return, some detailed information concerning tax records, beyond the needs of the audit engagement will need to be gathered. Similarly, if a compliance report is to be issued to regulators, it may entail extended procedures in certain operating areas.

Overall Compliance with General and Field Standards

In order to ensure that generally accepted auditing standards are met by the engagement team, attention must be given to planning and effective supervision.

Supervisory Responsibilities

Part of the supervisor's responsibilities is to familiarize the audit team with the client setting, the objectives of the engagement, the risk profile of the client, and the overall audit plan ***[SAS 22, Section 311]***. Beyond this planning phase, the execution of the audit requires continuous monitoring. A supervisor should be available to answer questions that arise during the engagement and should exercise oversight on a daily basis to ensure that new staff members, as well as seasoned professionals, do not get "off track." A new auditor may misinterpret an audit step to mean, for example, draw a sample of 45 vouchers and examine their compliance with stated procedures, *even if* the first 10 are exceptions. If a supervisor were available to provide feedback, the "other 35" vouchers would not be examined, as the sample test results could already be recognized as unacceptable. Similarly, if the supervision of seasoned professionals was lacking, an experienced staff person may proceed with work in the same manner as the prior year, in spite of the potential efficiencies from varying the audit approach due to changes in client operations. For example, a recently established EDP environment can provide cost-saving opportunities through the application of computer-assisted audit tools.

The senior and manager on the job should review working papers as phases of the audit work are completed, in order to identify problems in the execution, interpretation, or documentation of audit findings that may very well require follow up. Review notes tend to produce "to do" points that may require time to follow up, if they are to be resolved before the end of field work. The feedback provided the professional staff via review notes on the working papers is a critical phase of training personnel and ensuring compliance with professional standards.

Performance Evaluation and Time Budgets

The audit's supervisor should prepare a formal performance evaluation form, which indicates the staff's technical competence, quality of work, personality traits that helped or hindered their working relationship with the client and other members of the audit team, and overall potential. Often, areas needing development are cited, as are strengths that are peculiar to the individual staff members. Exhibit 8-11 gives an example of such a performance evaluation form.

In addition to job-oriented performance evaluations, an annual review should be performed that provides staff with constructive suggestions and encouragement regarding professional development and progress within the firm.

The Role of Time Budgets

Another type of feedback which primarily relates to efficiency is the expected versus actual *time budgets* for various phases of the audit work. Time budgets are important to assessing the reasonableness of job performance, as well as supporting the audit fees charged. Of course, the effectiveness with which audit procedures are performed is far more important than the time efficiencies. Hence, if a staff auditor discovers a problem in an area being audited which suggests that additional audit time is warranted, the budgets are intended to be flexible. The important goal is to gather audit evidence that is sufficient for the expression of an opinion. However, since auditing is essentially an audit service

EXHIBIT 8-11

Performance Evaluations—An Illustration

Audit Staff Rating Form
(To Be Completed on a Timely Basis for Each Engagement)

Staff Member Being Rated: ______________________________

Engagement on Which Rating Is Based: ______________________________

Job Title and Related Responsibilities: ______________________________

____

	Poor	Fair	Average	Above Average	Excellent
Technical Competence					
1. Knowledge of Accounting					
2. Knowledge of Auditing					
3. Industry Expertise					
4. Ability to Gain an Understanding of Client's System and Operations					
5. Soundly Approached Problems					
6. Analytical Abilities					
7. Displayed Initiative in Attacking Problems					
Execution					
1. Willing to Follow Instructions					
2. Able to Reach Objective with Minimal Instructions					
3. Capable and Willing to Assume Responsibility					
4. Effective at Supervising Others' Work and Delegating Work When Appropriate					
5. Capable of Adequately Documenting Work					
6. Able to Discriminate Between Important and Unimportant Items					
7. Adequately Planned Work Performed					
8. Carefully Analyzed Findings; Effective Decision Maker					
9. Able to Recognize Significant Findings					
10. Met Reasonable Time Limits on Assignments					
Communication					
1. Oral Presentation Skills					
2. Adequacy of Discussions Regarding Findings					
3. Clarity of Working Paper Documentation					
4. Ability to Write Reports					
Interpersonal Skills					
1. Tactful in Gaining Client's Cooperation in Obtaining Data As Well As the Cooperation of Others					
2. Able to Deal with Management Personnel					
3. Attitude Toward Associates					
4. Attitude Toward Supervisors					
5. Approachable So That Others Can Seek Help As Needed					
6. Can Sustain a Position Without Creating Resentment When Disagreement Occurs					
7. Ability to Stimulate Others to Participate in Decision Making					
8. Can Criticize Others Constructively					
9. Able to Concede Graciously When Shown to Be in Error					
10. Versatile in Handling Unusual Situations					
11. Personal Appearance					
12. Behavior on and Away from Job					
Advancement Potential					
1. Capacity for Growth and Development					
2. Interest in Work					
3. Ability to Accept Increased Responsibility					
4. Understanding and Adherence to Required Standards of Conduct and Ethics					
5. Awareness of Cost/Benefit Dimensions of Audit Work					
6. Leadership Skills					
7. Training Skills					
8. Motivation					

EXHIBIT 8-11 (continued)

Do you feel that this employee is ready for a promotion or increased job responsibility? Justify your recommendations. (For example, does employee possess a CPA certificate for advancement?)

____

____

____

____

Recommendations regarding employee's training and development: ______________________________

____

Other Comments: ______________________________

____

____

____

Evaluated by ______________________________

Date ______________________________

Reviewed by ______________________________

Employee's Comments: ______________________________

____

____

Assignment Preferences: ______________________________

____

Signature of Employee ______________________________

Date ______________________________

Comments on Conference Held With Employee on ______________________________ Date

____

____

____

____

Adapted from William E. Fergusson and Dianne S. Fergusson, *The Internal Audit Training Program*, Research Report 23 (Altamonte Springs, Fla.: Institute of Internal Auditors, 1980), pp. 78–83; and "Compliance Review Program Guidelines," Division for CPA Firms Peer Review Program (New York: AICPA, 1981), pp. 63–72.

which is priced out, in part, based on hours of time expended, tracking audit time, the audit areas to which that time relates, and both budget overages and shortages are important to monitoring audit activities and client services. Exhibit 8-12 presents a typical time budget format for an audit engagement. The audit program usually gives the time spent for each program step, along with the initials of the person who completed the step. Each auditor is responsible for posting such information on a timely basis in order to facilitate the effective supervision of the field work to ensure

EXHIBIT 8-12
Time Budgets—The Typical Format Used

		Staff Classification (Not Including Managers and Partners)				
Audit Area	Interim Work (I) or Year-end Work (Y)	Staff (1 yr. or less experience)	Staff Minimum 2 yrs. experience	Seniors	Lead Senior	Time Budget (Hours)
Planning	I			2	1	40
Cash: Walk Through	I		1			2
Cash Collections	I	1				2
Cash Balances	Y	1				4
Receivables						
Circularization	I	3	1	1		22
Uncollectibles	Y			1	1	3
Other	Y		1			3
Inventory						
Observation	Y	4	1			40
Cost Accumulation	I	3	1			24
Valuation	Y	2	1	1		18
Obsolescence	Y			1	1	4
.	.	.	.	.	.	.
.	.	.	.	.	.	.
.	.	.	.	.	.	.
Total Interim Work		XX	XX	XX	XX	XX
Total Year-end Work		XX	XX	XX	XX	XX
Total		XX	XX	XX	XX	XX
Prior Year Totals		XX	XX	XX	XX	XX
Actual Totals		XX	XX	XX	XX	XX

completion of the engagement within the necessary time frame to meet reporting requirements and other commitments made to the client. The lead senior needs to exercise continual oversight with respect to the progress of the audit work.

The Final Audit Judgment

The final phase of the audit is the expression of an audit opinion. This phase includes (1) the evaluation of the evidence, (2) the selection of an opinion that expresses the fairness of the client's financial representations, (3) an assessment of the adequacy of financial statement disclosures, and (4) the meeting of professional responsibilities for investigating subsequent events.

Sufficiency of Evidence

Evidence is gathered in an audit engagement solely to form an evidential base for expressing an opinion on the fairness of the financial statements ***[SAS 31, Section 326].*** Sufficiency relates to compliance with generally accepted auditing standards, as well as professional judgment. The auditor is not expected to gather enough evidence "to establish beyond a reasonable doubt." Rather, the auditor should meet a standard closer to the concept that the "preponderance of evidence suggests that there is no material error in the financial statements." SAS No. 31 emphasizes that the accumulation of evidence should be persuasive rather than convincing. In other words, a cost/benefit dimension exists for audit services that establishes the market's judgment that "beyond a reasonable doubt" auditing standards would be too costly.

Financial Position

CPAs usually perform a final analytical review of the financials to determine their overall reasonableness ***[SAS 23, Section 318].*** At this phase, the auditor studies the results of clearing the "to do" points, the proposed adjustments that the client did not book, and the client's disclosure practices as they will affect the fairness of disclosure practices. "Subject to" or "except for" qualifications, adverse opinions, or a disclaimer of an opinion may be required.

Adequacy of Disclosure

Many CPA firms have assimilated a disclosure checklist to help assess disclosure practices ***[SAS 5, Section 411].*** Based on generally accepted accounting principles, the required footnote and parenthetical disclosures—for example, for leases, pensions, and marketable securities—are itemized. Although the checklist is helpful, the adequacy of the disclosure is a separate audit judgment. For example, the GAAP checklist might state that footnote disclosure of certain contingencies is required. But those contingencies requiring disclosure and the adequacy of the disclosures are a professional judgment about which the checklist can provide little, if any, information.

Footnotes should summarize significant accounting policies, changes in accounting principles, and subsequent event disclosures. A substantial amount of the audit time on any engagement deals with the evaluation of accounting practices. The type of accounting knowledge needed to evaluate disclosure practices is shown in a typical problem and solution from the auditing part of the CPA Examination, in Exhibit 8-13.

Review of Subsequent Events

The auditor is responsible for reviewing events from the end of the field work to the audit report date ***[SAS 1, Section 560].*** This review is of those events that could affect the fairness of the financial statements. For example, if a key customer went bankrupt, suggesting that collections on accounts receivable would be unlikely, such a subsequent event may require adjustment of the financial statements. Unrecorded liabilities, settlement of pending litigation, and payment of contingent liabilities all are examples of subsequent events that are likely to require adjustments. Disclosure, but no adjustment, is commonly required if bonds or stock has been issued, a business purchased, a casualty loss incurred, or an event subsequent to the balance sheet date has occurred, such as a customer's casualty loss, which will affect receivables. Inquiry procedures, inspection of the client's minutes, and formal representations of the client and legal counsel are the audit procedures typically used for the discovery of subsequent events ***[SAS 12, Section 337].***

Discovery of Facts After the Report Date

If auditors become aware of facts that would make previously issued financial statements misleading, they should immediately contact the client and key users of the financial statements, including regulatory bodies, and they should issue new financial statements that reflect the subsequent events.

Beyond discovering facts as to client operations, auditors via quality review programs may discover that they have omitted required audit procedures on an engagement. Upon such a discovery, generally accepted auditing standards require that the auditor then attempt to gather the audit evidence necessary to form a sufficient basis for an audit opinion ***[SAS 46, Section 390].*** If this is impossible, the auditor should discuss the problem with both the client and the auditor's attorney to determine the extent of required disclosures and the appropriate action. It is likely that key user groups will have to be notified as to existing uncertainties.

Reporting Responsibilities

An auditor must be able to evaluate GAAP and to prepare various accounting analyses in accordance with regulators' and the client's requests. These may include cash flow analyses, acquisition studies, capital budgeting evaluations, and bud-

EXHIBIT 8-13
Accounting Expertise Essential to the Auditor: An Example

Problem: The complete set of financial statements for the Maumee Corporation for the year ended August 31, 19X6, is presented below:

The Maumee Corporation

BALANCE SHEET
(in Thousands of Dollars)
August 31, 19X6

Assets		
Cash		$ 103
Marketable securities, at cost that approximates market value		54
Trade accounts receivable (net of $65,000 allowance for doubtful accounts)		917
Inventories, at cost		775
Property, plant, and equipment	$3,200	
Less: Accumulated depreciation	1,475	1,725
Prepayments and other assets		125
Total assets		$ 3,699

Liabilities and Stockholders' Equity	
Accounts payable	$ 221
Accrued taxes	62
Bank loans and long-term debt	1,580
Total liabilities	$ 1,863
Capital stock, $10 par value (authorized 50,000 shares, issued and outstanding 42,400 shares)	$ 424
Paid-in capital in excess of par value	366
Retained earnings	1,046
Total stockholders' equity	$ 1,836
Total liabilities and stockholders' equity	$ 3,699

The Maumee Corporation

STATEMENT OF INCOME AND RETAINED EARNINGS
(in Thousands of Dollars)
for the Year Ended August 31, 19X6

Product sales (net of $850,000 sales returns and allowances)		$10,700
Cost of goods sold		8,700
Gross profit on sales		$ 2,000
Operating expenses:		
Selling expenses	$1,500	
General and administrative expense:	940	2,440
Operating loss		$ (440)
Interest expense		150
Net loss		(590)
Retained earnings, September 1, 19X5		1,700
		$ 1,110
Dividends:		
Cash – $1 per share	$ 40	
Stock – 6 percent of shares outstanding	24	64
Retained earnings, August 31, 19X6		$ 1,046

Required:

List deficiencies and omissions in the Maumee Corporation's financial statements, and discuss the probable effect of the deficiency or omission on the auditor's report. Assume that the Maumee Corporation is unwilling to change the financial statements or make additional disclosures therein.

Consider each deficiency or omission separately, and do not consider the cumulative effect of the deficiencies and omissions on the auditor's report. There are no arithmetical errors in the statements.

Organize your answer sheet in two columns as indicated below and write your answer in the order of appearance within the general headings of Balance Sheet, Statement of Income and Retained Earnings, and Other.

Solution:

Financial Statement Deficiency or Omission	Discussion of Effect on Auditor's Report
Balance Sheet	
1. Current assets and current liabilities are not shown and cannot be determined from the information presented.	1. The auditor may wish to take exception to this presentation and disclose the amounts of current assets and current liabilities in the auditor's report. This decision will be based on the importance of current position to the readers of the financial statements. The company's large debt position and its net loss for the year (which makes the ability to sustain future losses a significant consideration) make such disclosure desirable.
2. It is not sufficient to state that inventories are stated at cost.	2. The financial statements should state that inventories are presented at the lower of cost or market. If there has been a permanent decline of market value below cost, the company should adjust to the market value. If no adjustment is made, the auditor should take exception and provide appropriate disclosure.
3. The inventory method is not disclosed.	3. There are a number of acceptable inventory methods that the company can use. The method in use should be disclosed. If it is not, the auditor should take exception to the failure to disclose and should provide such disclosure.
4. There is no breakdown of property, plant, and equipment and related accumulated depreciation.	4. It is customary to provide breakdowns of property, plant, and equipment and related accumulated depreciation into

EXHIBIT 8-13
(continued)

Financial Statement Deficiency or Omission	Discussion of Effect on Auditor's Report
	major classes (e.g., land, buildings, vehicles, equipment, other). The auditor must evaluate the importance of the breakdown. If it is considered significant to the readers of the financial statements, the auditor should take exception to the inadequate disclosure and provide pertinent details in the auditor's report.
5. The basis (e.g., cost) for valuation of property, plant, and equipment is now shown.	5. The auditor should be satisfied that the fixed assets are properly stated. If they are not, the auditor should take exception in the auditor's report. If the fixed assets are properly stated at cost, the auditor may conclude that failure to disclose the cost method is so significant as to require an opinion exception for inadequate disclosure.
6. There is no disclosure of the depreciation method in use or the amount of the annual depreciation expense.	6. If the depreciation method in use and the amount of the annual depreciation expense are considered to be significant to the readers of the financial statements, the auditor should take exception because of the inadequate disclosure and provide in the auditor's report the necessary information.
7. There is inadequate disclosure of bank loan and long-term debt information.	7. Considerably more information concerning bank loans and long-term debt should be provided. The nature and amount of each type of debt should be disclosed, together with details of the interest rates, maturity dates, debt subordination, conversion rights, any assets pledged for security, and any restrictions imposed by loan agreements. To the extent these data have not been provided and are considered of significance to users of the financial statements, the auditor should take exception to the inadequate disclosure and make appropriate disclosure in the auditor's report.
8. Prepayments should be shown separately from other assets.	8. Considerably more information about the nature and amount of prepayments and other assets should be provided. Prepayments are usually current, whereas other assets generally

Financial Statement Deficiency or Omission	Discussion of Effect on Auditor's Report
	are long term. To the extent this separation has not been provided and is considered of significance to users of the financial statements, the auditor should take exception to the inadequate disclosure and make appropriate disclosures in the auditor's report.
9. The reference to "capital stock" should be replaced with a reference to the particular class of capital stock (e.g., common stock).	9. Failure to describe more accurately the particular class of capital stock generally would not result in a qualified opinion.
Statement of Income and Retained Earnings	
10. The stock dividend was not properly accounted for, nor was it properly reported.	10. The stock dividend was capitalized at par value (6% × 40,000 shares × $10 = $24,000). When a stock dividend is so small in relation to the shares previously outstanding that there is no apparent effect on the market price of the shares, the stock dividend should be accounted for by transferring from retained earnings to permanent capital an amount equal to the fair value of the additional shares issued. A distribution of less than 20% to 25% generally has little effect on the market price of the shares. Because of the improper treatment of the stock dividend, the auditor should take exception to the presentation because of nonadherence to generally accepted accounting principles and should disclose the proper effect of the stock dividend in the auditor's report.
11. Earnings per share (EPS) is not shown.	11. The presentation of EPS is required by Opinion No. 15 of the Accounting Principles Board. The auditor should take exception because of inadequate disclosure and should disclose the EPS in the auditor's report. (Note: A subsequent removal of such disclosure for certain entities could apply, in which case the exception would not be taken.)

EXHIBIT 8-13 (continued)

Financial Statement Deficiency or Omission	Discussion of Effect on Auditor's Report
12. The tax effects of the operating loss have not been disclosed.	12. Although the company had a loss for the year, it paid dividends out of a sufficient amount of retained earnings, indicating profitable operations in prior years. The reported accounting loss and the loss for tax purposes should not be significantly different, as there are no deferred tax accounts. The operating loss under these circumstances is usually available for carry-back treatment. Because the tax effects of a loss carry-back have not been recorded, carry-back treatment was not usable. The loss, however, can be carried forward. The amounts of any operating loss carry-forwards not recognized in the loss period, together with expiration dates, should be disclosed. If such disclosure is not made and the amounts are material, the auditor should take exception and disclose.
Other	
13. The company has not presented a statement of changes in financial position.	13. In most cases the statement of changes in financial position is required by Opinion No. 19 of the Accounting Principles Board. If the omission of the statement of changes in financial position is not sanctioned by Opinion 19 of the Accounting Principles Board, the auditor should take exception in his or her report to this nonadherence to generally accepted accounting principles. The auditor should not, however, include the statement in his or her report.
14. There are no footnotes to the financial statements.	14. The auditor should determine what disclosure should be required to inform the reader of the financial statements. The auditor should take exception to the lack of disclosure in his or her report and should include therein the required information.
15. There is no summary of significant accounting policies.	15. A summary of significant accounting policies is required by Opinion No. 22 of the Accounting Principles Board. The auditor should determine the accounting policies that are significant and should disclose this information in his or her report and take exception to the inadequate disclosure.

(CPA exam, adapted November 6, 1975, question 7)

gets. SEC clients require numerous filings for annual financial statements, quarterly reviews, proxy statements, and key events such as a change in auditor. The auditor's responsibility for subsequent events varies for such filings. The Securities Act of 1933 (Section 11a) extends the auditor's liability with respect to new securities' registration to the *effective date* of the registration statement, which is the date that the securities are permitted to be sold to the public. Because this date is often weeks after the field work has been completed, auditors should report to the client around that time and conduct another review of subsequent events and read over the entire Form S-1. Exhibit 8-14 summarizes the SEC's required filings and corresponding time limits. In addition to the financial statements and supplementary data, Form 10-K describes the business, its properties, any legal proceedings, directors and officers, management remuneration and security ownership, management's discussion and analysis of financial conditions, and common stock matters.

EXHIBIT 8-14
SEC Required Filings

Securities Act of 1933	
Form S-1 (general form)	Registration
Form S-7 (short form for S-1)	Registration by established companies
Form S-8	Registration for offerings to employees
Form S-14	Registration related to merger or consolidation
Form S-15	Registration related to certain business combinations
Form S-16	Registration option sometimes permitted in lieu of S-7
Form S-18	Registration for small companies
Form 1A	Notification of SEC of offering under Regulation A (exemption for smaller issues)
Securities Exchange Act of 1934	
Form 8-K	Current report on "material" events like acquisition or sale of subsidiary or change in auditors
Form 10	Registration for securities on national exchanges and some issuers over-the-counter
Form 10-K	Annual report (filing due within 90 days of fiscal year-end)
Form 10-Q	Quarterly report (filing due within 45 days of quarter's end)
Form 11-K	Annual report for employee stock purchase and related plans

Tax Services

The audit team is also expected to collect the information necessary for the tax services requested by the client and to watch for tax-related concerns and opportunities. For example, the IRS has been rather strict about the type of documentation required to support travel and entertainment expenditures in order to qualify for tax deductions. Any concern over client practices should be communicated, with suggestions on means of improvement. Tax saving advantages available through tax planning of investment tax credits, equipment replacement policies, inventory valuation practices, and similar issues should be documented and communicated as part of the client service.

Management Advisory Services Considerations

The management letter is often a means by which an auditor expresses the possibility of assisting the client through management advisory services. For example, if the CPA discovers that a client has inadequate computer processing capability, the expertise of the CPA firm in identifying and helping clients to analyze various computer equipment and processing configurations might be highlighted. This potential service capability can then be evaluated by the client.

The audit engagement is a fertile opportunity for identifying opportunities for providing clients with management advisory services. Evaluations of controls, observation of operations, and expertise about industry practices are conducive to the identification of potential cost savings for clients.

Communication Responsibility

Auditors must communicate to their clients, as will be addressed in considerable depth in Chapter 9, the existence of any material weaknesses in the internal accounting controls of which they become aware during the course of the audit. This communication may either be oral or written, but if done orally, ought to be formally documented. Many auditors report material weaknesses within the management letter, clearly distinguishing between material and immaterial findings.

REVIEW QUESTIONS

1. What is a walk-through? What are its objectives and value to an auditor?
2. What is meant by taking a business approach to the audit process?
3. What are the common sources of information about

risk areas in an audit engagement? Explain how the predecessor auditor might be helpful in this regard.
4. What is a related-party transaction? Give two examples of possible problems with such a transaction. How can related-party transactions be detected?
5. What is the audit risk model?
6. Define
   Tolerable error.
   Ultimate risk.
   Audit risk.
   Inherent risk.
   Detection risk.
   Control risk.
   Business risk.
7. Give an example of a business risk. Why is such risk relevant to a CPA firm's decision making?
8. What is a risk work sheet, and how can an auditor use it?
9. What is one way of determining tolerable error for the various parts of the financial statements?
10. What is meant by "principal auditor"? How can a principal auditor effectively coordinate work with other auditors, including taking responsibility for each firm's audit work?
11. What are the various cost-benefit considerations in planning an audit program?
12. Can substantive tests be performed at interim if there is no reliance on internal controls? Explain.
13. How are sampling plans affected by performing interim work?
14. What is PERT, and how can an auditor use it?
15. List, in general terms, the various alternatives in planning the nature, timing, and extent of audit procedures.
16. If compliance test results are other than expected, what are the alternative actions that an auditor might take?
17. Describe the alternative approaches to writing audit programs and the reasons for choosing one over the other.
18. What are "to do" points, and how do they influence the completion of field work?
19. How should time budgets influence the audit process? Why are they maintained?
20. What is meant when an auditor states that the evidence collected is "sufficient"?
21. What might make a CPA suspect the commitment of illegal acts? How is the materiality of such acts evaluated? What might make a CPA suspect material errors or irregularities? How can they affect the audit process?
22. What are the consequences of reporting illegal acts? How should the auditor react to evidence of material errors and irregularities?
23. What are the auditor's responsibilities with respect to subsequent events?
24. What are the typical regulatory filings required for SEC clients?
25. How can the tax services provided by a CPA firm influence an audit engagement?

EXERCISES

1. If the beginning inventory balance were understated by $70,000 and the ending inventory balance were overstated by $40,000, what would be the misstatement of the current period's income statement? What does your answer say about the effect of the preceding years' audit work on an audit program?
2. What is the difference between likely error and known error? Why must likely errors be evaluated? How can audit risk concepts affect the estimation of likely error? How can compliance errors affect the estimation of likely error?
3. It has been asserted that the probability of a material misstatement or inherent risk is likely to depend on the probability that such a material misstatement will be detected—sometimes referred to as control risk. For this reason, some contend that it is impractical to calculate inherent risk separately from control risk. What do you think, and why?
4. You have been asked to conduct an orientation session for newly hired staff regarding the purpose of time budgets and how they should be considered in the execution of an audit, and how the staff will be judged for their performance in each engagement.

   The managing partner of your office is worried that budgets are being overemphasized and that new staff will have difficulty deciding when they should deviate from the budget and/or the designed audit program.

   Outline how you would conduct the orientation session, with detailed point-by-point coverage of your presentation and approach to group discussion. How does your outline address the managing partner's concerns?

QUESTIONS ADAPTED FROM PROFESSIONAL EXAMINATIONS

1. You have been assigned by your firm to complete the examination of the 19X6 financial statements of Carter Manufacturing Corporation, because the senior accountant and his inexperienced assistant

who began the engagement have been hospitalized because of an accident. The engagement is about one-half completed. Your auditor's report must be delivered in three weeks, as agreed when your firm accepted the engagement. You estimate that by using the client's staff to the greatest possible extent you can complete the engagement in five weeks. Your firm cannot assign an assistant to you.

The working papers show the status of work on the examination as follows:

a. *Completed*—Cash, fixed assets, depreciation, mortgage payable, and stockholders' equity.

b. *Completed except as noted later*—Inventories, accounts payable, tests of purchase transactions, and payrolls.

c. *Nothing done*—Trade accounts receivable, inventory receiving cutoff and price testing, accrued expenses payable, unrecorded liability test, tests of sales transactions, payroll deductions test and observation of payroll check distribution, other expenses, analytical review of operations, vouching of December purchase transactions, auditor's report, internal control investigation, internal control letter, minutes, preparation of tax returns, procedural recommendations for management, subsequent events, supervision, and review.

Your review discloses that the assistant's working papers are incomplete and were not reviewed by the senior accountant. For example, the inventory working papers show incomplete notations, incomplete explanations, and no cross-referencing.

Required:

a. What field work standards have been violated by the senior accountant who preceded you on this assignment? Explain.

b. In planning your work to complete this engagement, you should scan the work papers and schedule certain work as soon as possible and also identify work that may be postponed until after the report is to the client.

1. List the areas on which you should work first, and for each area explain why.
2. State which work can be postponed until after the report is rendered to the client, and give the reasons.

(CPA exam adapted)

2. You are meeting with the executives of Cooper Cosmetics Corporation to arrange your firm's engagement to examine the corporation's financial statements for the year ending December 31, 19X6. One executive suggested that the audit work be divided among three audit staff members so that one auditor would examine asset accounts, a second would examine liability accounts, and the third would examine income and expense accounts. Advertising is the corporation's largest expense, and so the advertising manager suggested that a staff member of your firm whose uncle owns the advertising agency that handles the corporation's advertising be assigned to examine the advertising expense account. The staff member has a thorough knowledge of the rather complex contract between Cooper Cosmetics and the advertising agency on which Cooper's advertising costs are based.

Required:

a. Should a CPA follow his or her client's suggestions for the conduct of an audit? Discuss.

b. Discuss the reasons that audit work should not be assigned solely according to asset, liability, and income and expense categories.

c. Should the staff member of your CPA firm whose uncle owns the advertising agency be assigned to examine advertising costs? Why or why not? (*Note:* Refer to Chapter 4 in preparing your response.)

(CPA exam adapted)

3. Evidence supporting the financial statements consists of the underlying accounting data and all corroborating information available to the auditor. In an independent audit of financial statements, the auditor will perform detail tests of samples of transactions from various large-volume populations. The auditor may also audit various types of transactions by tracing a single transaction of each type through all stages of the accounting system.

Required:

What evidence would the auditor expect to find in auditing various types of transactions by tracing a single transaction of each type through all stages of the accounting system?

(CPA exam adapted)

4. The auditor general of a large state government recently decided to audit the state's highway construction and maintenance operation for the last year. The audit will cover highways in selected counties, including land procurement, construction, purchasing, maintenance, and administration. The audit manager in charge has formed a steering committee consisting of senior members of several different audit units. At the committee's first meeting, the chairman (named by the audit manager in charge) proposed that the audit schedule be controlled by the use of Gantt chart techniques. Although several members of the committee agreed with this proposal, the audit manager in charge suggested that the project's complexity required a more sophisticated project control technique such as PERT (Program Evaluation and Review Technique). As many members of the committee were not familiar with PERT as a project control technique, a decision was postponed until the next meeting when the audit manager in charge would explain the PERT technique and its applicability to audit scheduling and control.

Required:
Refer to a reference book which describes the PERT and Gantt chart techniques.

a. Outline the elements of PERT that the director should stress at the next meeting of the steering committee.

b. Name three ways that PERT is superior to Gantt chart techniques in this circumstance.

c. Discuss how PERT would be used in planning the above audit.

(CIA exam adapted)

5. Michael, a CPA, is examining the financial statements of the Diannah Corporation as of and for the period ended September 30, 19X6. Michael plans to complete the field work and sign the auditor's report on November 15, 19X6. Michael's audit work is primarily designed to obtain evidence that will provide a reasonable degree of assurance that the Diannah Corporation's September 30, 19X6, financial statements present fairly its financial position, results of operations, and changes in financial position in accordance with generally accepted accounting principles consistently applied. Michael is concerned, however, about the events and transactions of Diannah Corporation that occur after September 30, 19X6, as he does not have the same assurance for those events as for those occurring before September 30, 19X6.

Required:

a. What is a subsequent event, and what are the two types of subsequent events that the management of Diannah Corporation and Michael should consider?

b. What auditing procedures should Michael use to obtain the necessary assurances concerning subsequent events?

(CPA exam adapted)

6. The independent certified public accountant's report, opinion, or certificate, as it is variously termed, conventionally includes the following: ". . . and accordingly included such tests of the accounting records . . . as we consider necessary in the circumstances."

Required:
Explain how the accountant determines what tests are necessary and the extent to which they are necessary. (CPA exam adapted)

7. In connection with his examination of Flowmeter, Inc., for the year ended December 31, 19X6, Hirsch, a CPA, discovers that the following events and transactions that took place after December 31, 19X6, but before he issued his report dated February 28, 19X7, may affect the company's financial statements:

a. On January 3, 19X7, Flowmeter, Inc. received a shipment of raw materials from Canada. The materials had been ordered in October 19X6 and shipped FOB shipping point in November 19X6.

b. On January 15, 19X7, the company settled and paid a former employee's personal injury claim as the result of an accident that occurred in March 19X6. The company had not previously recorded a liability for the claim.

c. On January 25, 19X7, the company agreed to purchase for cash the outstanding stock of Porter Electrical Co. The acquisition is likely to double the sales volume of Flowmeter, Inc.

d. On February 1, 19X7, a plant owned by Flowmeter, Inc. was damaged by a flood, resulting in an uninsured loss of inventory.

e. On February 5, 19X7, Flowmeter, Inc. issued and sold to the general public $2 million in convertible bonds.

Required:
For each of the above events or transactions, indicate the audit procedures that should have brought the item to the auditor's attention and the form of disclosure in the financial statements, as well as the reasons for such disclosures. Arrange your answer in the following format:

Letter Corresponding to Each Item	Audit Procedure	Required Disclosure

(CPA exam adapted)

8. You are newly engaged by the James Co., a New England manufacturer with a sales office and warehouse located in a western state. The James Co. audit must be made at the peak of your busy season, and you will not have a senior auditor available to travel to the western outlet. Furthermore, the James Co. is reluctant to pay the travel expenses of an out-of-town auditor.

Required:

a. Under what conditions would you, the principal auditor, be willing to accept full responsibility for the work of another auditor?

b. What are your requirements with respect to the other auditor's integrity? To whom would you direct inquiries about the other auditor?

c. What reference, if any, can you make to the other auditor in your report, if you are (1) assuming full responsibility for his or her work or (2) not assuming responsibility for his or her work?

(CPA exam adapted)

9. Multiple-Choice: Errors, Irregularities, and Illegal Acts

Select the one answer that best completes the statement or answers the question.

9.1 With respect to errors and irregularities, which of the following should be part of an auditor's planning of the audit engagement?

a. Plan to search for errors or irregularities that would have a material or immaterial effect on the financial statements.

b. Plan to discover errors or irregularities that are either material or immaterial.

c. Plan to discover errors or irregularities that are material.

d. Plan to search for errors or irregularities that would have a material effect on the financial statements.

(CPA exam adapted)

9.2 Which of the following is not a procedure performed primarily for the purpose of expressing an opinion on the financial statements, but may bring possible illegal acts to the auditor's attention?

a. Study and evaluation of internal accounting control.

b. Review of internal administrative control.

c. Tests of transactions.

d. Tests of balances.

(CPA exam adapted)

9.3 Which of the following conditions would not normally cause the auditor to wonder whether there were any material errors or irregularities?

a. Bookkeeping errors are listed on an EDP-generated exception report.

b. There are differences between control accounts and supporting subsidiary records.

c. Transactions are not supported by proper documentation.

d. Differences are disclosed by confirmations.

(CPA exam adapted)

9.4 The audit client's board of directors and audit committee refused to take any action with respect to an immaterial illegal act that the auditor brought to their attention. Therefore the auditor withdrew from the engagement. The auditor's decision to withdraw was primarily due to doubts about

a. Inadequate financial statement disclosures.

b. Compliance with the Foreign Corrupt Practices Act.

c. Scope limitations resulting from their inaction.

d. Reliance on management's representation.

(CPA exam adapted)

9.5 If as a result of auditing procedures an auditor believes that the client may have committed illegal acts, which of the following actions should he or she take immediately?

a. Consult with the client's and the auditor's counsels to determine how the suspected illegal acts will be communicated to the stockholders.

b. Extend normal auditing procedures to ascertain whether the suspected illegal acts may have a material effect on the financial statements.

c. Consult with the client's management and the client's legal counsel or other specialists, as necessary, to find out the nature of the acts and their possible effects on the financial statements.

d. Notify each member of the audit committee of the board of directors of the nature of the acts and ask that they advise the auditor on what to do.

(CPA exam adapted)

9.6 If an auditor were engaged to discover errors or irregularities and performed extensive detail work, which of the following could he or she be expected to detect?

a. Mispostings of recorded transactions.

b. Unrecorded transactions.

c. Counterfeit signatures on paid checks.

d. Collusive fraud.

(CPA exam adapted)

9.7 An auditor should recognize that auditing

procedures may produce evidence pointing to errors or irregularities and therefore should

a. Design audit tests to detect unrecorded transactions.
b. Extend the work to audit most recorded transactions and records of an entity.
c. Plan and perform the engagement with an attitude of professional skepticism.
d. Not depend on internal accounting control features designed to prevent or detect errors or irregularities.

(CPA exam adapted)

9.8 If an independent auditor's examination leading to an opinion on financial statements points to material errors or irregularities, the auditor should

a. Consider the implications and discuss the matter with appropriate levels of management.
b. Determine whether there have in fact been any errors or irregularities.
c. Ask that the management investigate to determine whether there have been any errors or irregularities.
d. Consider whether the errors or irregularities were the result of the employees' failure to comply with existing internal control procedures.

(CPA exam adapted)

9.9 Which of the following, if material, would be an irregularity, as defined in Statements on Auditing Standards?

a. Errors in the application of accounting principles.
b. Clerical errors in the accounting data for the financial statements.
c. Misinterpretation of facts that existed when the financial statements were prepared.
d. Misappropriation of an asset or groups of assets.

(CPA exam adapted)

9.10 Which of the following statements best describes the auditor's responsibility with respect to illegal acts that do not have a material effect on the client's financial statements?

a. Generally, the auditor does not need to notify parties other than personnel in the client's organization.
b. Generally, the auditor must see that the stockholders are notified.
c. Generally, the auditor must disclose the relevant facts in the auditor's report.
d. Generally, the auditor must compel the client to adhere to the requirements of the Foreign Corrupt Practices Act.

(CPA exam adapted)

9.11 In general, material irregularities perpetrated by which of the following are the most difficult to detect?

a. Cashier.
b. Controller.
c. Internal auditor.
d. Keypunch operator.

(CPA exam adapted)

9.12 Generally, the decision to notify parties outside the client's organization regarding an illegal act is the responsibility of the

a. Independent auditor.
b. Management.
c. Outside legal counsel.
d. Internal auditors.

(CPA exam adapted)

9.13 An auditor has withdrawn from an audit engagement of a publicly held company after finding irregularities that may materially affect the financial statements. The auditor should explain the reasons and findings in correspondence to the

a. Securities and Exchange Commission.
b. Client's legal counsel.
c. Stock exchanges where the company's stock is traded.
d. Board of directors.

(CPA exam adapted)

9.14 The current thinking regarding the concept of materiality as applicable to the reporting of illegal acts is that materiality is

a. An agreed percentage of the total value of the resources exposed to illegal activities.
b. Not a determining factor, in that all illegal acts should be reported by the internal auditor.
c. Normally considered as exceeding a stated amount.
d. Based on a subjective determination of the case's circumstances.
e. Related to the type of illegal act.

(CIA exam adapted)

10. Multiple-Choice: Audit Planning and Execution Select the one answer that best completes the statement or answers the question.

10.1 Which of the following elements ultimately determines the specific auditing procedures that are necessary in the circumstances to afford a reasonable basis for an opinion?

a. Auditor judgment.
b. Materiality.
c. Relative risk.
d. Reasonable assurance.

(CPA exam adapted)

10.2 Taylor Sales Corp. maintains a large full-time internal audit staff that reports directly to the chief accountant. Audit reports prepared by the internal auditors indicate that the system is functioning as it should and that the accounting records are reliable. The independent auditor will therefore probably

a. Eliminate compliance testing.
b. Increase the study and evaluation of administrative controls.
c. Avoid duplicating the work performed by the internal audit staff.
d. Place limited reliance on the work performed by the internal audit staff.

(CPA exam adapted)

10.3 For reporting purposes, subsequent events are defined as events that occur after the

a. Balance sheet date.
b. Date of the auditor's report.
c. Balance sheet date but before the date of the auditor's report.
d. Date of the auditor's report and concern contingencies not reflected in the financial statements.

(CPA exam adapted)

10.4 In an examination of financial statements for the purpose of expressing an opinion thereon, the auditor will normally prepare a schedule of unadjusted differences for which he or she did not propose adjustments when they were uncovered. What is the main purpose for this schedule?

a. To point out to the responsible client officials the errors made by various company personnel.
b. To summarize the adjustments that must be made before the company can prepare and submit its federal tax return.
c. To identify the effects of the errors or disputed items that were considered immaterial when discovered.
d. To summarize the errors the company made so that it can make corrections after the audited financial statements are released.

(CPA exam adapted)

10.5 In connection with the annual audit, which of the following is not a "subsequent events" procedure?

a. Review available interim financial statements.
b. Read available minutes of meetings of stockholders, directors, and committees and, for meetings for which minutes are not available, ask about what was discussed.
c. Ask about the financial statements covered by the auditor's previously issued report if new information has become available during the current examination that might affect that report.
d. Discuss with officers the current status of items in the financial statements that were accounted for on the basis of tentative, preliminary, or inconclusive data.

(CPA exam adapted)

10.6 The concept of materiality would be least important to an auditor in determining the

a. Transactions that should be reviewed.
b. Need for disclosing a particular fact or transaction.
c. Scope of the CPA's audit program relating to various accounts.
d. Effects of direct financial interest in the client on the CPA's independence.

(CPA exam adapted)

10.7 When a contingency is resolved immediately after the issuance of a report that was qualified with respect to the contingency, the auditor should

a. Insist that the client issue revised financial statements.
b. Inform the audit committee that the report cannot be relied on.
c. Take no action regarding the event.
d. Inform the appropriate authorities that the report cannot be relied on.

(CPA exam adapted)

10.8 Karr has examined the financial statements of Lurch Corporation for the year ended December 31, 19X6. Although Karr's field work was completed on February 27, 19X7, Karr's auditor's report was dated February 28, 19X7, and was received by Lurch's management on March 5, 19X7. On April 4, 19X7, Lurch's management asked that Karr approve the inclusion of this report in their annual report to their stockholders, which will also include unaudited financial statements for the first quarter ended March 31, 19X7. Karr approved. Then is he responsible for asking about events occurring through

a. February 27, 19X7?
b. February 28, 19X7?
c. March 31, 19X7?
d. April 4, 19X7?

(CPA exam adapted)

10.9 An example of a transaction that may indicate the existence of related parties is

a. Borrowing or lending at a rate of interest that equals the current market rate.
b. Selling real estate at a price that is comparable to its appraised value.
c. Making large loans with specified terms as to when or how the funds will be repaid.
d. Exchanging property for similar property in a nonmonetary transaction.

(CPA exam adapted)

10.10 Which of the following audit procedures would be likely to disclose a client's related-party transactions during the period under audit?

a. Reading "conflict-of-interest" statements obtained by the client from its management.
b. Scanning accounting records for large transactions at or just before the end of the period under audit.
c. Inspecting invoices from law firms.
d. Confirming large purchase and sales transactions with the vendors and/or customers involved.

(CPA exam adapted)

10.11 An auditor is planning an audit engagement for a new client in an unfamiliar business. Which of the following would be the most useful source of information during the preliminary planning stage, when the auditor is studying the possible audit problems?

a. Client manuals of accounts and charts of accounts.
b. AICPA Industry Audit Guides.
c. The predecessor auditor's previous year's working papers.
d. The client's latest annual and interim financial statements.

(CPA exam adapted)

10.12 Which of the following is the most likely first step of an initial audit engagement?

a. Preparing a rough draft of the financial statements and the auditor's report.
b. Studying and evaluating the internal administrative control system.
c. Touring the client's facilities and reviewing the general records.
d. Consulting with and reviewing the predecessor auditor's work before discussing the engagement with the client's management.

(CPA exam adapted)

10.13 Morgan, a CPA, is the principal auditor for a multinational corporation. Another CPA has examined and reported on the financial statements of a significant subsidiary of the corporation. Morgan is satisfied with the other auditor's independence and professional reputation, as well as the quality of his or her examination. With respect to Morgan's report on the consolidated financial statements, he

a. Must not refer to the other auditor's examination.
b. Must refer to the other auditor's examination.
c. May refer to the other auditor's examination.
d. May refer to the other auditor's examination, in which case Morgan must include in auditor's report on the consolidated financial statements a qualified opinion with respect to the examination of the other auditor.

(CPA exam adapted)

10.14 Each of the following might in itself form a valid basis for an auditor to decide to omit a test, except the

a. Relative risk involved.
b. Relationship between the cost of obtaining evidence and its usefulness.
c. Difficulty and expense in testing a particular item.
d. Degree of reliance on the relevant internal controls.

(CPA exam adapted)

10.15 If the principal auditor decides to refer to the other auditor's examination, the scope paragraph must indicate the

a. Magnitude of the portion of the financial statements examined by the other auditor.
b. Name of the other auditor.
c. Name of the consolidated subsidiary examined by the other auditor.

d. Type of opinion expressed by the other auditor.

(CPA exam adapted)

10.16 With respect to the auditor's planning of a year-end examination, which of the following statements is always true?

a. An engagement should not be accepted after the fiscal year-end.
b. An inventory count must be observed at the balance sheet date.
c. The client's audit committee should not be told of the specific audit procedures that will be performed.
d. It is acceptable to carry out substantial parts of the examination at interim dates.

(CPA exam adapted)

10.17 The plant of an audit client's major customer was destroyed by fire just before completion of year-end field work. The audit client believes that this event could have a significant direct effect on the financial statements. The auditor thus should

a. Advise management to disclose the event in footnotes to the financial statements.
b. Disclose the event in the auditor's report.
c. Withhold the auditor's report until the direct effect on the financial statements is known.
d. Advise management to adjust the financial statements.

(CPA exam adapted)

10.18 An independent auditor finds that Simner Corporation occupies office space, at no charge, in an office building owned by a shareholder. This finding indicates the existence of

a. Management fraud.
b. Related-party transactions.
c. Window dressing.
d. Weak internal control.

(CPA exam adapted)

11. Multiple-Choice: Attorney's Letters

Select the one answer that best completes the statement or answers the question.

11.1 A CPA has received an attorney's letter that noted no significant disagreements with the client's assessments of contingent liabilities. But the resignation of the client's lawyer shortly after receipt of the letter should alert the auditor that

a. There may have been undisclosed unasserted claims.
b. The attorney was unable to form a conclusion about the significance of litigation, claims, and assessments.
c. The auditor must begin a completely new examination of contingent liabilities.
d. An adverse opinion will be necessary.

(CPA exam adapted)

11.2 A lawyer's response to a letter of audit inquiry may be limited to matters that are considered individually or collectively material to the financial statements if

a. The auditor has instructed the lawyer about the limits of materiality in the financial statements.
b. The client and the auditor have agreed on the limits of materiality and the lawyer has been notified.
c. The lawyer and the auditor have agreed on the limits of materiality for this purpose.
d. The lawyer's response to the inquiry explains the legal meaning of the materiality limits and establishes quantitative parameters.

(CPA exam adapted)

11.3 A lawyer's response to an auditor's request for information about litigation, claims, and assessments will ordinarily contain which of the following?

a. An explanation regarding the limitations of the response's scope.
b. A statement of concurrence with the client's determination of which unasserted possible claims warrant specification.
c. Confidential information that if publicized would be prejudicial to the client's defense.
d. An assertion that the list of unasserted possible claims identified by the client represents all such claims of which the lawyer may be aware.

(CPA exam adapted)

11.4 A lawyer limits a response concerning a litigated claim because she is unable to determine the likelihood of an unfavorable outcome. What type of opinion should the auditor express if the litigation is adequately disclosed and the range of potential loss is material in relation to the client's financial statements considered as a whole?

a. Adverse.
b. Unaudited.

c. Qualified.
d. Unqualified.

(CPA exam adapted)

11.5 An attorney is writing to an independent auditor in response to an audit client's letter of inquiry. The attorney may appropriately limit the response to
a. Asserted claims and litigation.
b. Matters to which the attorney has given substantive attention in the form of legal consultation or representation.
c. Asserted, overtly threatened, or pending claims and litigation.
d. Items which have an extremely high probability of being resolved to the client's detriment.

(CPA exam adapted)

11.6 The letter of audit inquiry addressed to the client's legal counsel will not ordinarily be
a. Sent to a lawyer who was engaged by the audit client during the year and soon thereafter resigned the engagement.
b. A source of corroboration of the information originally obtained from management concerning litigation, claims, and assessments.
c. Limited to references to pending or threatened litigation for which the lawyer has been engaged.
d. Needed during the audit of clients whose securities are not registered with the SEC.

(CPA exam adapted)

11.7 When obtaining evidence regarding litigation against a client, the CPA would be least interested in determining
a. An estimate of when the matter will be resolved.
b. The period in which the cause of the litigation occurred.
c. The probability of an unfavorable outcome.
d. An estimate of the potential loss.

(CPA exam adapted)

CASES FOR DISCUSSION

1. It has been asserted that audit programs are most desirable for new staff members who are assigned to an engagement. Experienced auditors, it is claimed, should be able to conduct an examination without referring to an audit program.
   a. Do you agree? Explain.
   b. Other than helping new staff, what are the purposes of an audit program?
   c. After reading this chapter, do you prefer the procedures- or objectives-oriented approach?
   d. Design an audit work program for the petty cash area of a client's operations, using a procedures-oriented approach.
2. For 1 (d), design an objectives-oriented audit program.
3. The sufficiency of audit evidence has been described as a judgment that must reflect
   - the client's attributes and the transactions being audited.
   - the nature of the available evidence.
   - the relative materiality of various financial statement components.
   - the inherent subjectivity of the accounting in particular accounts.
   - the possibility of illegal acts or other irregularities.
   - the degree of audit risk.
   - the circumstances in which the auditor is placed.
   - the cost and time required to perform the work.

   a. Explain how each item affects the "sufficiency" judgment. For each item, give an example of a circumstance leading to more evidence being required and an example of a circumstance leading to less evidence being required.
   b. An auditor reports that a client with good management, stable operations, good internal controls, an internal audit department, and a history of no substantive errors can be "sufficiently" audited by rotating the audit emphasis across time, thereby reducing the extent of auditing in certain material account areas. Do you agree?
   c. Does an auditor assess the sufficiency of evidence for particular accounts or for the financial statements? How can and should this affect the audit program?
4. The exposure draft for the proposed statement on auditing standards, "Materiality and Audit Risk in Conducting an Audit," stated:

   > Inadequate disclosure of certain matters, such as certain related-party transactions and those required by statute or regulatory authority may be considered to be material even though the related amounts are otherwise quantitatively immaterial.[12]

   a. Why is this possible? Comment on the meaning of materiality and how the concept is made operational by practicing auditors.
   b. In a paper regarding materiality, Donald A. Leslie included the following verse:

[12] New York: AICPA, December 6, 1982, p. 5.

Would you tell me please, what number should I consider material?
That depends a good deal on what you want to use this number for, said the cat.
Oh, I don't want to use it for anything; I just want to know what it is.
Then it doesn't much matter what the number is, said the cat. (with apologies to C. L. Dodgson)[13]

Relate this quote to your discussion of the application of materiality concepts in practice, in part (a).

5. Many CPAs include management's reactions to suggestions made in the management letter within the formal communication. Is this desirable? Outline the pros and cons which would affect your decision to integrate management's comments.

[13] Donald A. Leslie, "Materiality in Auditing (Some of the Issues)," *Symposium on Auditing Research II* (Champaign-Urbana: University of Illinois, 1977), p. 83.

9

Internal Control

Chris turned to the small-business column of the *Wall Street Journal* and read the headline: "Firm's Owner Learns Dangers of Growth Without Controls."[1] The story told of a small businessman who almost went bankrupt when a clerk made an error. Apparently, the clerk had jumbled $450,000 in billings in a drawer and forgotten about them for three weeks. Only the lag in the customers' payments caused the owner/manager to make inquiries that uncovered the problem. The business's credit line had to be pushed to its limit in order for the business to survive.

Similarly, a $15,000 shipment went unpaid for forty-five days before it was noticed. Inquiries directed to the customer indicated that the bill had been awaiting approval by a purchasing manager who was out of town. Had inquiries been made earlier, the payment would have already been received!

The final, almost disastrous, error was the ordering of a chemical from a manufacturer that was not one of the business's usual suppliers. The order was made because of the lower price offered. But the chemical, which was delivered directly to the business's customer, had impurities that contaminated that customer's supplies. But worse than the loss of a customer was the damage to the business's reputation.

"Why is it always almost too late when businessmen realize the value of control?" Chris mumbled. "A simple set of checks and balances would have pointed out the lost billings and the slow payment and might have prevented their using an unreliable supplier."

Chris's mind wandered to the many client meetings concerning control suggestions that produced such comments as "My operation is too small to have a control system." or "When I'm running out of time, I do my operating duties . . . my control duties can wait. What I don't need are more cumbersome controls." Must they all

[1]August 15, 1983, p. 17.

have a near disaster before learning about the dangers of operating without effective control?

Chris's attention was then directed to her current audit. Yesterday, a staff auditor had reported that there was virtually no audit trail for cash disbursements. The client used several checking accounts. The checks had not been prenumbered by the printer, and so the cashier numbered the checks as they were issued. Because the voided checks had been discarded, the cashier reused their numbers.

It was obvious to the staff auditor that controls over disbursements could not be relied on. What was not clear was how the audit team could ensure that all disbursements had been recorded and that all expenditures had been appropriate. Obviously, there was more risk in reporting on cash and accounts payable.

The staff auditor suggested testing the bank reconciliations, but the cashier performed such reconciliations, and there seemed no way to test directly the propriety of the outstanding checks that were listed. Therefore an alternative audit approach was necessary.

Chris knew the answer: An extended scope audit would be required, in which the entity's cash disbursements would be made auditable through substantive test work. Chris began to draft the following directions for the staff auditor:

1. Test an extended sample of recorded disbursements:
   Compare the payee with the approved supplier listing.
   Vouch the transaction to supporting purchase documentation for propriety.
2. Mail positive confirmations to suppliers regarding the balance in accounts payable, and include a large sample of suppliers for whom zero balances are recorded in the test.
3. When the cutoff bank statement is received, apply inquiry, confirmation, or other follow-up procedures to test the propriety of outstanding checks.
4. When testing the bank reconciliation procedures, the mathematical accuracy should be calculated, the canceled checks should be tied to recorded disbursements, and the endorsements should be examined for reasonableness. All adjusting journal entries related to outstanding checks should be reviewed. If canceled checks listed on the bank statement are missing, follow them up with the bank unless the disbursements can be found in the books and follow-up procedures applied to the payable.
5. Direct inquiry procedures at the banks are needed to determine whether the authorized check signers and endorsers for checks made payable to the company have been correctly recorded at the banks. The auditor should ask the banks whether they have been instructed not to cash checks made out to cash. The auditor should also confirm with the tellers that the person in charge of disbursements has not cashed checks payable to cash or to the company.
6. Besides these detailed tests and inquiries, analytical review procedures should be used to evaluate the reasonableness of recorded disbursements regarding the level of sales, operating capacity, and competitors' experience.

Reviewing the directions, Chris reflected that her client's experience was like the *Wall Street Journal*'s story. Had the checks been numbered by the printer, issued in sequence, retained when voided, and accounted for periodically, the auditors could have been assured of a complete audit trail. The client would have had better control over its assets, and the extended substantive work could have been avoided. If the reconciliation procedures had been separated from the cashier's duties, the auditor might have been able to rely on controls and reduce substantive test work. The importance of internal control to both the auditor and the client cannot be overstated.

The case bears out the importance of effective controls to both the client and the auditor. The client could be incurring a substantial loss of cash resources in the form of unauthorized disbursements. As important, the efficiency of disbursements would be slowed by the manual prenumbering, and the chance of a misplaced check is greater, creating problems with the client's relationship to its suppliers. The auditor, as a consequence of such risks facing the client, must extend the scope of the engagement in order to estimate these risks. Essentially, the auditor's examination is forced to create an audit trail, due to the inability of the client's control system to create such a trail.

The widely publicized experience of the small businessman is, unfortunately, far from unusual, and it also is common for larger companies, some of which do not appreciate the capabilities of controls, including their exposure to management override. Just the monitoring of operations can be an extremely effective control in avoiding the loss of documents, claims, and assets. The means by which control systems can continuously monitor information flow will be described in this chapter. The limitations of controls will be discussed, as will approaches to documenting and evaluating controls in a manner that can help in the determination of material weaknesses. Finally, the chapter will highlight the influence of the Foreign Corrupt Practices Act. The "why" and "how" underlying those controls that might have prevented or detected the problems cited in the introductory case will be emphasized throughout this chapter.

Before describing the basic concepts which underlie internal control, it is appropriate to consider why control systems are of interest to auditors. Although this should be somewhat implied by the introductory case, it is possible to specifically delineate why the auditor evaluates controls.

Reasons for Evaluating Controls

The reasons for a CPA evaluating an entity's controls depend on the type of engagement. A CPA cannot plan or carry out an audit without understanding the entity's internal accounting system and controls, and the second standard of field work ***[SAS 1, Section 320]*** requires that a study and evaluation of internal accounting control be performed as a basis for determining reliance thereon and the resultant extent of the tests to which auditing procedures are to be restricted.

The CPA first must decide whether an entity is auditable. A reasonably complete and accurate data base must either be available or be able to be created without great expense. Then once a prospective client is deemed to be auditable, the second question is how to perform the audit most efficiently and effectively. A basic economic choice exists for an auditor: which mix of compliance and substantive tests is likely to be an optimum approach to performing the audit examination? Should the client's controls, including the accounting control environment and internal audit department, be relied on, and to what extent? Once this is decided, the CPA should plan the nature, timing, and extent of the audit procedures. The results of the compliance tests of internal accounting controls then may require a reevaluation of the quality of control and an adjustment of the audit plan. The auditor's study and evaluation relates to particular classes of transactions and balances.

If instead of an audit engagement, or as a complement to the audit process, the CPA accepts a comprehensive review engagement, then the reasons for evaluating the controls change ***[SAS 30, Section 642].*** The objective of the review engagement is to express an opinion as to the adequacy of the internal accounting control system taken as a whole. All significant control areas within the system must be reviewed, and all significant control procedures must be compliance tested. A CPA who is requested to provide management advisory services will find it necessary to gain an understanding of controls. As attempts are made to eliminate troublespots and enhance operating efficiency, control ramifications of system changes must be considered. Moreover, in order to identify the cause of problems, the CPA must be familiar with information flows within the organization and the performance of both operating and control duties. Exhibit 9-1 summarizes the CPA's key objectives in evaluating internal accounting controls, as they relate to an external audit engagement, a comprehensive review service, or a management advisory client setting. Control issues permeate all types of CPA engagements and are formalized not only in auditors' working papers, but also in reports known as management letters that tend to be a management advisory by-product of an audit engagement.

EXHIBIT 9-1
Why Does a CPA Evaluate Internal Accounting Controls?

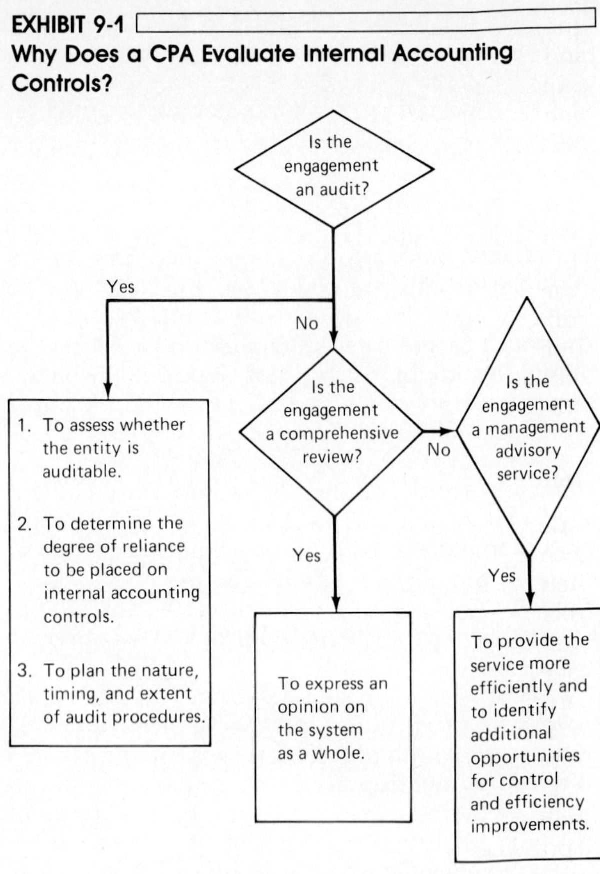

Objectives of Control Systems

An entity's internal control system can be thought of as the nerve center of its operations ***[SAS 1, Section 320]***. Its *administrative controls* are the plan of organization and the procedures and records concerned with the decision processes leading to management's authorization of transactions. This authorization corresponds to management's responsibility for achieving the organization's objectives. *Accounting controls* relate to the plan of organization and the procedures and records concerned with safeguarding the assets against loss from unintentional or intentional errors or irregularities and the reliability of financial records for external reporting purposes. Those controls that affect reported accounting numbers are *internal accounting controls*. Such controls must be able to provide reasonable assurance that some record is made of every transaction in which the entity is involved, so that a reasonably complete information base is available from which financial statements can be prepared and on which managers can rely for decision making. Beyond this requirement, an internal accounting system is expected to provide reasonable, but not absolute, assurance that (1) the assets are being safeguarded (this encompasses restricting access to assets only as authorized and comparing records to existing assets at reasonable intervals, resolving any differences), (2) the transactions are being carried out in accordance with management's general or specific authorization, and (3) the records are being maintained in a manner that will facilitate (a) the preparation of financial statements that follow generally accepted accounting principles or any other criteria applicable to such statements and (b) the maintenance of accountability for assets. The concept of reasonable assurance relates to a materiality threshold. Later in this chapter, material weaknesses will be defined and an example will be provided to help you in judging the overall adequacy of controls. The definitions of administrative and internal accounting controls are by no means mutually exclusive. Regardless of their classification, controls having an important bearing on the reliability of financial records should be evaluated. Yet, generally speaking, CPAs direct their attention to accounting controls. Recall that Exhibit 7-6 describes the specific control objectives that underlie (1), (2), and (3)—the overall objectives of control. Practically, accounting controls encompass any administrative controls or other management functions that achieve, or contribute to the achievement of, specific accounting control objectives.

General Controls

General controls are capable of providing assurance that specific controls are being performed and therefore, should be reviewed first. General controls include the means by which compliance with internal accounting controls is motivated or noncompliance is detected. Any reports that are prepared routinely, reviewed by management, tested by internal auditors, and designed to report on compliance or to detect noncompliance are general controls. These include budgets, variance analyses, operating reports, and monthly financial reports. General controls also include supervision and are the main determinants of the control environment. General controls must be tested for compliance if reliance is planned, and such tests usually include inquiry, observation, and inspection. In an EDP environment, general controls would include control over the development, modification, and maintenance of computer programs and control over the use of and changes to data maintained on computer files.

Specific Controls

Specific controls refer to authorizing, accounting for, and safeguarding assets. The completeness of the accounting records; the propriety of the transactions; the accuracy of amounts, timing, and classifications; and the reconciliation with the general ledger all are specific control objectives. To safeguard assets, (1) their access should be restricted; (2) they should be physically protected; and (3) any discrepancies in their recording should be accounted for and followed up. Specific controls in an EDP environment are referred to as *application controls*. These would relate to individual computerized accounting applications, such as a programmed control step of comparing payables to an authorized vendor file. Exhibit 9-2 offers some examples of control objectives and related control procedures for a commercial bank's lending function. As noted in an earlier chapter, each control objective is related to various management assertions regarding the financial statements.

Preventive Controls

Controls are said to be *preventive* if they are intended to prevent an event from happening. The event to be prevented is typically an error or an irregularity. For example, the requirement that credit checks be performed before extending credit to a new customer is intended to uncover any bad credit risks. Similarly, the use of dual check signers (i.e., two signatures) is expected to prevent unauthorized or inappropriate disbursements. Since preventive controls are a priori, they represent the strongest safeguard approach to designing controls. In fact, generally, if there are preventive controls, they will be the controls that the auditor will test. However, the relative strength comes at a cost; avoiding problems tends to be more expensive than merely detecting problems once they have occurred. For this reason, entities typically design systems that have a mix of preventive and detective controls. Besides, since no preventive control is expected to be 100 percent effective, detective controls are an imperative facet of all control systems.

Detective Controls

Detective controls are used to detect a problem once it has occurred. For example, a test examination of customers' orders after the goods were shipped to verify that credit approval was given is a detective control to locate unapproved sales. Likewise, an examination of checks after they have cleared the bank, to ensure that dual signatures were used, is also a detective control. Bank reconciliations are a particularly important detective

EXHIBIT 9-2
The Interrelationship of Control Objectives and Control Procedures

Setting: The Lending Function in a Commercial Bank

Examples: Objectives and Related Procedures

Control Objectives

A. To ensure that potentially uncollectible amounts are promptly identified, evaluated, and accounted for.

Control Procedures

- Monitoring geographic concentrations in the loan portfolio.
- Periodically reviewing and pricing the value of loan collateral in order to determine its adequacy in protecting the bank's investment.
- Routing a copy of a computer-generated report of all changes made to loan payment-due dates daily, to a high-level, independent official for careful review.

B. To ensure that loan interest, fees, and other charges are recorded correctly as to account, amount, and period.

- Reconciling the totals of the loan interest receivable ledgers to the corresponding control balance, at least quarterly.

C. To ensure that each loan and its terms are reviewed and properly authorized before the transaction is completed.

- Establishing a monitoring of lending limits for all loan officers.
- Requiring that written appraisals be performed by competent, independent individuals to determine the value of real property that will be used to secure a loan.

D. To ensure that the physical loss or misuse of loan documents, collateral, and repossessed property is prevented or promptly detected.

- Assigning responsibilities for maintaining and safekeeping actual loan instruments (notes, collateral receipts, etc.) to individuals who do not receive loan payments.

E. To ensure that all completed lending transactions are recorded correctly as to account, amount, and period.

- Assigning responsibilities for receiving and investigating all customers' inquiries about loan balances to individuals having no control over cash receipts and collection procedures.
- Sending periodic statements of loan activity to all credit customers.
- To ensure that loan interest, fees, and other charges are billed to customers in the correct amounts.
- Requiring an independent officer's approval of all waivers of loan fees.

CIA exam adapted, May 4, 1981, question 36.

control for cash. Periodic aging of receivables is one detective control that would have been of use to the owner-manager in the introductory case setting. The strength of detective controls largely depends upon the *timeliness* with which errors are detected. Obviously, this depends upon how frequently the detective controls are applied and how effective they happen to be.

In a sense, detective controls monitor the effectiveness of preventive controls and can compensate for weak preventive controls. In fact, owing to their usually higher cost, preventive controls may not be used at all in certain areas of operations, and thus the entity relies entirely on detective controls to limit the risk of loss from errors or material irregularities. Interestingly, the threat value of detective controls can help deter individuals who might be contemplating committing a fraud or circumventing the control system, since such controls create a real risk of discovery.

Corrective Controls

Once an error has been detected, the correction of that error must be controlled to the same degree that the original entry is that made the error. An example of a *corrective control* is the requirement that all adjusting journal entries be approved before being included in the accounting records.

Limitations of Control Systems

Why is it unreasonable to expect preventive controls to be 100 percent effective? For the same reason that no control system is expected to be 100 percent effective: *inherent limitations* exist in all control systems. An integral part of control is the individual employee or manager who has prescribed duties intended to prevent and/or detect problems. Yet, human beings can suffer from fatigue, boredom, distractions, ill health, or may simply be sloppy in how they discharge their responsibilities. Errors in judgment or a misunderstanding of instructions can occur, resulting in the ineffective application of control procedures. Beyond the limitations that focus on human error, limitations can exist due to personnel and resource constraints.

For example, employee turnover may delay the application of control procedures; overtime demands may mean that controls are not used when they should be; and any mechanized or computerized information system will have some downtime that will cause both the ineffective and inefficient application of controls. Trade-offs are constantly faced in determining whether or not controls are cost-justified. For example, should the credit check entail the use of Dun & Bradstreet or a set of credit-rating agencies? To build good customer relations, should a nominal amount of credit be extended during the time required to make an adequate credit check? Then the obvious problem exists that the past may not be an effective predictor of the future. A prospective customer who has faced no past problems with credit, could have some economic problems presently, suggesting that the entity should request some current financial statements and, perhaps, some budgeted or forecasted data. No matter how many controls are used, there will always be some risk of loss from extending credit to nonpaying customers. The reasons for having a control system is to control that risk of loss to the extent justifiable in cost-benefit terms.

This past/present comparison of customers' credit standing can also be applied to the evaluation of control systems. Just because a control system has been effective in the past is no guarantee of continued effectiveness. A system of controls, similar to an entity's credit standing, can rapidly deteriorate. The turnover of key employees, a change in operating and control systems that is not understood by those responsible for implementing that change, or a shift in management's emphasis from control duties toward operating duties can all cause the quality of a control system to decline. Hence, a limitation of control systems is that in spite of an effective control system being designed and implemented at one point in time, no assurance exists that controls will continue to be adequate in the future. Continuous monitoring of controls is essential.

These inherent limitations in control systems provide an explanation of why GAAS do not permit 100 percent compliance-test audits. *Full* reliance on controls *in lieu of* substantive test work would never be warranted.

Documenting Controls

A control system can be documented by means of internal control checklists, flowcharting, and memoranda (or descriptive narratives). Often the CPA will find that using a combination of these techniques is the best way to describe a client's control system. Each technique has a comparative advantage in documenting different aspects of a control system.

Internal Control Checklists

For example, a checklist approach is very effective for documenting aspects of the control system that can be described through a yes/no classification scheme: does this control exist, or not? Through the use of preprinted checklists, the CPA has a means of ensuring that a core set of expected controls for all operating entities has been reviewed and that the findings have been documented, thus linking the compliance and the substantive testing and enabling the working papers to be reviewed. Of course, any preprinted checklist also runs the risk of being used mechanically, with ineffective tailoring to client operations and in-

EXHIBIT 9-3
Structuring Internal Accounting Control Checklists

Objective to Be Achieved

Example: Internal Accounting Control related: All receipts are to be accurately recorded and deposited.
Operations related: The collection, recording, and depositing activities are to be performed in an efficient manner.

Potential Errors If Objective Is Not Achieved

Receipts may either be not recorded or not deposited, or if recorded, the amount, account, or period affected could be in error.

Controls Which Are Useful in Achieving the Objective

Working Paper Format

	Are Such Controls Present?					Are Such Controls to Be Tested for Possible Reliance?		Evaluation of Control After Testing		
								Reliance		
Key Controls	Yes	No	N/A	Explanation	W/P Ref.	Yes	No	Yes	No	W/P Ref.
Is the handling of cash receipts segregated from the accounting for such receipts?	√				Flowchart CR 1					
Is a lock box utilized for collecting customers' payments?	√				Flowchart CR 1					
Are cash registers used with controlled-access cash register tapes?			√	Cash sales are rare						
Does one person have responsibility for listing cash receipts by mail for subsequent reconciliation to deposits?	√				Flowchart CR 1	√		√		CR 21

From Wanda A. Wallace, *Handbook of Internal Accounting Controls* (Englewood Cliffs, N.J.: Prentice-Hall, 1984), p. 72.

adequate attention given to the meaning of the individual control points or the clients' responses. Some CPA firms have shifted from checklists of control procedures to checklists of control objectives, requiring the auditor to choose the procedures that meet each objective, while ensuring a fairly complete coverage of the control system.

By tailoring the checklists to operating cycles, or groups of related transaction accounts, the questionnaires can be integrated into the working papers with relative ease. Exhibit 9-3 shows a typical checklist. As illustrated, questions tend to be worded to solicit a yes or no response. Whenever there is a "no" response, it should be followed up, perhaps through inquiry and observation procedures or compensating controls.

As the name suggests, *compensating controls* are intended to compensate for a weakness in one control by adding another control that corrects the particular weakness. The N/A column is appropriate if control attributes are not present due to their inapplicability to the client's line of business. For example, a service industry may have little, if any, inventory on the books, thereby eliminating or reducing the need for certain inventory-related controls.

One well-known drawback of any yes/no standardization of questionnaires where yes always means "good" is the possibility that respondents to that questionnaire will not carefully consider each question. To avoid this pitfall, CPAs will use an interview format and paraphrase items so that "no's" are expected to some questions as "good" responses. For example, instead of questioning the client directly as to whether employees' duties are adequately segregated, the CPA may ask whether one employee performs a set of incompatible duties. If a "no" response is obtained, further inquiry can clarify the exact manner in which tasks are segregated.

As Exhibit 9-3 demonstrates, those controls on which reliance is planned have to be compliance tested. Also depicted is the frequency with which checklists are combined with flowcharts as a means of documenting a client's control system. An example of an internal control questionnaire or checklist and how it is tied to an audit objective is shown in Exhibit 9-4, in the form of a question and answer from a past CPA exam.

Flowcharting

Just as the popular saying asserts that "a picture is worth a thousand words," many CPAs find that flowcharts can most effectively depict the major information flows of a client. A *flowchart* is a dia-

EXHIBIT 9-4
Internal Control Questionnaires: An Example

Problem:

Taylor, a CPA, has been engaged to audit the financial statements of University Books, Incorporated. University Books maintains a large revolving cash fund exclusively for buying used books from students for cash. The cash fund is active all year because the nearby university offers several courses with varying starting and completion dates throughout the year. Receipts are prepared for each purchase, and reimbursement vouchers are periodically submitted.

Required:

Construct an internal control questionnaire to be used to evaluate the system of internal control of University Book's buying segment's revolving cash fund. The internal control questionnaire should elicit a yes or no response. Do not discuss the internal controls over books that are purchased.

Solution:

University Books Incorporated
Revolving Cash Fund
Internal Control Questionnaire

Question	Yes	No
Is responsibility for the fund vested in one person?		
Is physical access to the fund denied to all others?		
Is the custodian independent of other employees who handle cash?		
Is the custodian bonded?		
Is the custodian denied access to other cash funds?		
Are receipts unalterable?		
Are receipts prenumbered?		
Is the integrity of the prenumbered sequence periodically accounted for?		
Does the seller sign receipts?		
Are receipts attached to reimbursement vouchers?		
Are vouchers that are submitted for reimbursement approved by someone other than the custodian?		
Are reimbursement vouchers and attachments (receipts) canceled after reimbursement?		
Is the fund used exclusively to buy books?		
Is the fund periodically counted and reconciled by someone other than the custodian?		
Is the fund maintained on a imprest basis?		
Is the size of the fund appropriate to the purpose intended?		

CPA exam adapted, May 7, 1981, question 4.

gram showing information flow, control duties, the assigned responsibilities for each employee, and processing steps, including the mode of processing. Generally, flowcharts read from left to right and from the top to the bottom of a page. There are uniform symbols for flowcharting, but many CPA firms devise their own symbols. In the process of flowcharting a particular system, it is often the case that new symbols will be developed to capture some unique aspect of the system under study. Auditors, in particular, find it useful to differentiate certain types of documents as having been processed (for example, through a control check such as the examination of invoices for mathematical accuracy) versus those documents that are unprocessed. CPAs also find it to be informative for the later design of audit procedures to note how certain documents are filed: alphabetically or numerically or, possibly, attached to some other primary document. Obviously, the most important objective of a flowchart is to communicate clearly, yet completely. To avoid clutter, flowcharts are commonly drawn on several pages, with "connector symbols" used to make the continuation of the diagram simple to follow. Any obscure symbols should either be avoided or clearly explained in a key to the flowchart. When explanations become lengthy, or the system so complicated that it is not easily captured through flowcharting, memoranda should be used and cross-referenced on the diagram.

Exhibit 9-5 lists some of the more common flowcharting symbols and also demonstrates how the symbols can be tailored to capture additional information concerning processing and filing. The form of the information flow is reflected by the symbols (such as the use of paper documents versus magnetic tape), as is the mode of processing (such as the application of manual systems or online terminals). Flowcharts will tend to focus on operating cycles like revenue-related transactions, rather than accounts, and should be prepared with the intended reader in mind. Sometimes an *overview flowchart* is sufficient, without illustrating detailed document flows, or is used as a sort of summary of system controls, supplementing more detailed flowcharts. In contrast, for significant control positions, a flowchart of that one person's control-related duties may be useful.

Memoranda

Although flowcharts can replace much descriptive material, certain elaboration of controls and complicated information or processing flows can best be presented in memoranda. It may be simple to describe some zig-zag transfers of certain documents across an organization, whereas a diagram of that transfer would be difficult to follow. Similarly, to avoid clutter, extended descriptions of control duties or the personnel who are responsible for particular procedures can best be described in memoranda. The most effective memoranda will be concise and easily interpretable without any additional verbal explanations. Exhibit 9-6 is a description of a client's factory payroll system, and Exhibit 9-7 presents a flowchart that corresponds to this memorandum. These examples bear out the ability to document a single control system in a variety of different ways. The terms in these Exhibits will become more familiar as your study of auditing progresses.

Synopsis

The selection of the means by which controls are to be documented is a cost/benefit choice which may be largely dependent on firm policies and individual choice. Beyond the approaches described herein, decision tables and other forms of documentation are used. Some CPAs are far more comfortable with a template, drawing flowcharts, than they are with a pen, drafting memoranda. Few firms require that only one means be used, although standardized checklists, flowchart formats, and prescribed memoranda are commonly a part of the documentation requirements of CPA firms. Yet, even in such a setting, if a CPA can demonstrate the cost-effectiveness, for example, of integrating the client's documentation of controls into the working papers, most firms would be receptive to such an approach to assembling the evidential base of a control-related or audit engagement.

The Minimum Study and Evaluation of the Internal Accounting Control System

If no reliance on control is intended, the auditor is not required to document an understanding of

EXHIBIT 9-5
Flowcharting Symbols

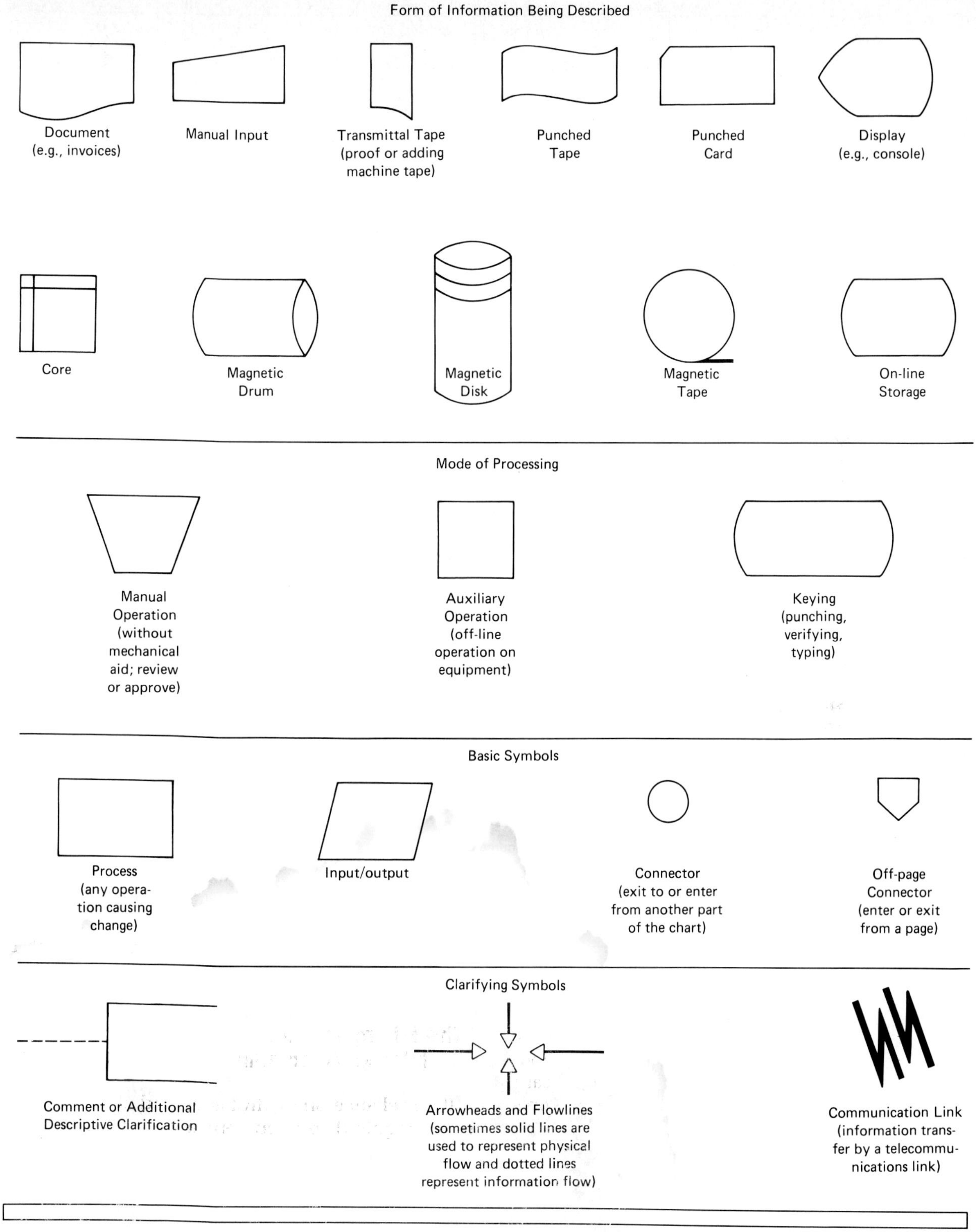

Form of Information Being Described

Document (e.g., invoices)

Manual Input

Transmittal Tape (proof or adding machine tape)

Punched Tape

Punched Card

Display (e.g., console)

Core

Magnetic Drum

Magnetic Disk

Magnetic Tape

On-line Storage

Mode of Processing

Manual Operation (without mechanical aid; review or approve)

Auxiliary Operation (off-line operation on equipment)

Keying (punching, verifying, typing)

Basic Symbols

Process (any operation causing change)

Input/output

Connector (exit to or enter from another part of the chart)

Off-page Connector (enter or exit from a page)

Clarifying Symbols

Comment or Additional Descriptive Clarification

Arrowheads and Flowlines (sometimes solid lines are used to represent physical flow and dotted lines represent information flow)

Communication Link (information transfer by a telecommunications link)

EXHIBIT 9-5
(continued)

Programming Symbols

Decision	Prepare (instruction modification to change the program, e.g., to initiate a routine, originate)	Predefined Process (i.e., specified in another set of flowcharts or in another subroutine)	Stop or Interrupt	Simultaneous or Parallel Operations	Merge

Extract	Collate	Sort	Off-line Storage	Compare or Match	Account

Tailored Control Symbols

To distinguish between processes involving assets, accounting entries, or control events, use a consistent marking within the symbol:

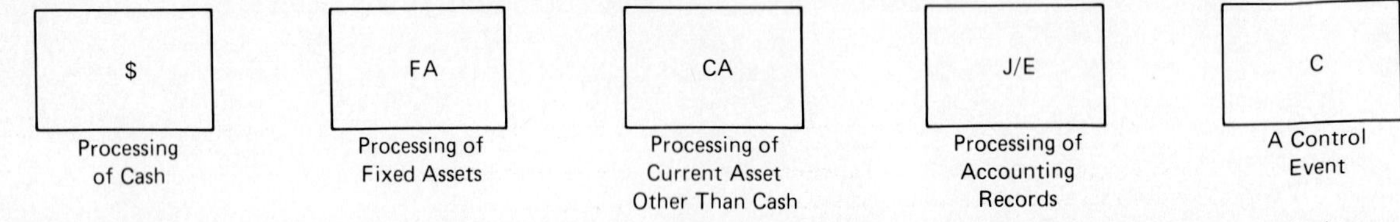

To distinguish between original source documents and those that have been authorized and to indicate those documents that are attached to other documents:

To distinguish between types of files and to signify the manner of filing:

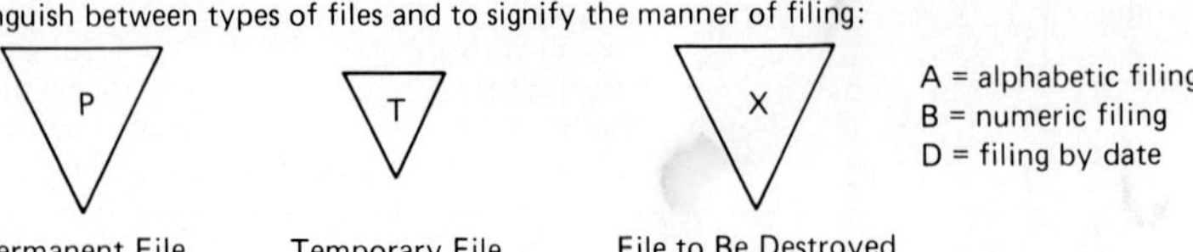

Typically:

- Each vertical column in a flowchart corresponds to an organizational unit.
- The name of each document is included within the document symbol.
- When possible, the names of persons performing the particular processes are shown.
- As the auditor evaluates how the flowchart relates to the internal control checklist, details are recorded as to completeness of documentation, the use of control totals, and the performance of control checks on the flowchart.

Wanda A. Wallace, *Handbook of Internal Accounting Controls* (Englewood Cliffs, N.J.: Prentice-Hall, 1984), pp. 80-81.

EXHIBIT 9-6
Internal Control Memoranda

A narrative description of the Tenney Corporation's factory payroll system

Factory employees punch time clock cards each day when entering or leaving the shop. At the end of each week the timekeeping department collects the time cards and prepares duplicate batch-control slips by department, showing total hours and number of employees. The time cards and original batch-control slips are sent to the payroll accounting section. The second copies of the batch-control slips are filed by date.

In the payroll accounting section payroll transaction cards are keypunched from the information on the time cards, and a batch total card for each batch is keypunched from the batch-control slip. The time cards and batch-control slips are then filed by batch for possible reference. The payroll transaction cards and the batch total card are then sent to data processing, where they are sorted by employee number within each batch. Each batch is edited by a computer program that checks the validity of each employee number against a master employee tape file and the total hours and number of employees against the batch total card. A detail printout by batch and employee number is produced which indicates batches that do not balance and invalid employee numbers. This printout is returned to payroll accounting to resolve all differences.

CPA exam adapted, November 7, 1974, question 7.

the internal accounting control system ***[SAS 43, Section 1010]*** but need only list the reasons for deciding not to extend the review of the internal accounting control system past the minimum level required in the professional standards.

A *preliminary review* is required in order to meet professional standards and includes: inquiry and observation procedures; review of past years' working papers and client-prepared descriptions of the system; previous experience with the client; and the like. Only the accounting system is analyzed during the preliminary review, and an *accounting system* is defined as

> the coordinate functions by which exchange of assets or services with parties outside the business entity and transfers or use of assets or services within it are recognized, and data representing such exchanges, transfers, and uses are assembled, processed, analyzed, and reported.[2]

The objective of the analysis is for the auditor to become familiar with the organization's structure; lines of communication and authority; supervision; the competence and integrity of personnel; operating transactions; means of authorizing, executing, initially recording, and subsequently processing transactions; and principal financial reports. The presence and role of the internal audit department should also be considered. The preliminary review will entail judging whether an entity is auditable and assessing the client's risk profile. The preliminary phase of review should provide the auditor with an understanding of the accounting control environment and the flow of transactions through the accounting system.

Only if reliance on controls is planned would there be a complete or detailed review of controls. Rather than merely focusing on the accounting system, a *detailed review* covers the *internal accounting control system:* "The plan of organization and the procedures and records that are concerned with the safeguarding of assets and with the reliability of financial records produced by the accounting system."[3] Only in this detailed phase would the system have to be documented, according to generally accepted auditing standards.

Evaluating the Control System

An effective way of evaluating a control system is to address the following five questions:[4]

1. Are control and operating responsibilities appropriately segregated?
2. Are all transactions being recorded by the accounting system?
3. Has management established an environment for effective control?
4. Are there adequate checks and balances?
5. Has operating efficiency been appropriately considered in the design and the evaluation of controls?

[2] "The Omnibus Statement on Auditing Standards No. 43" (New York: AICPA, August 1982), p. 3, footnote 1.

[3] Ibid.

[4] For more details, see Wanda A. Wallace, *Handbook of Internal Accounting Controls* (Englewood Cliffs, N.J.: Prentice-Hall, 1984).

EXHIBIT 9-7
Internal Control Flowcharts

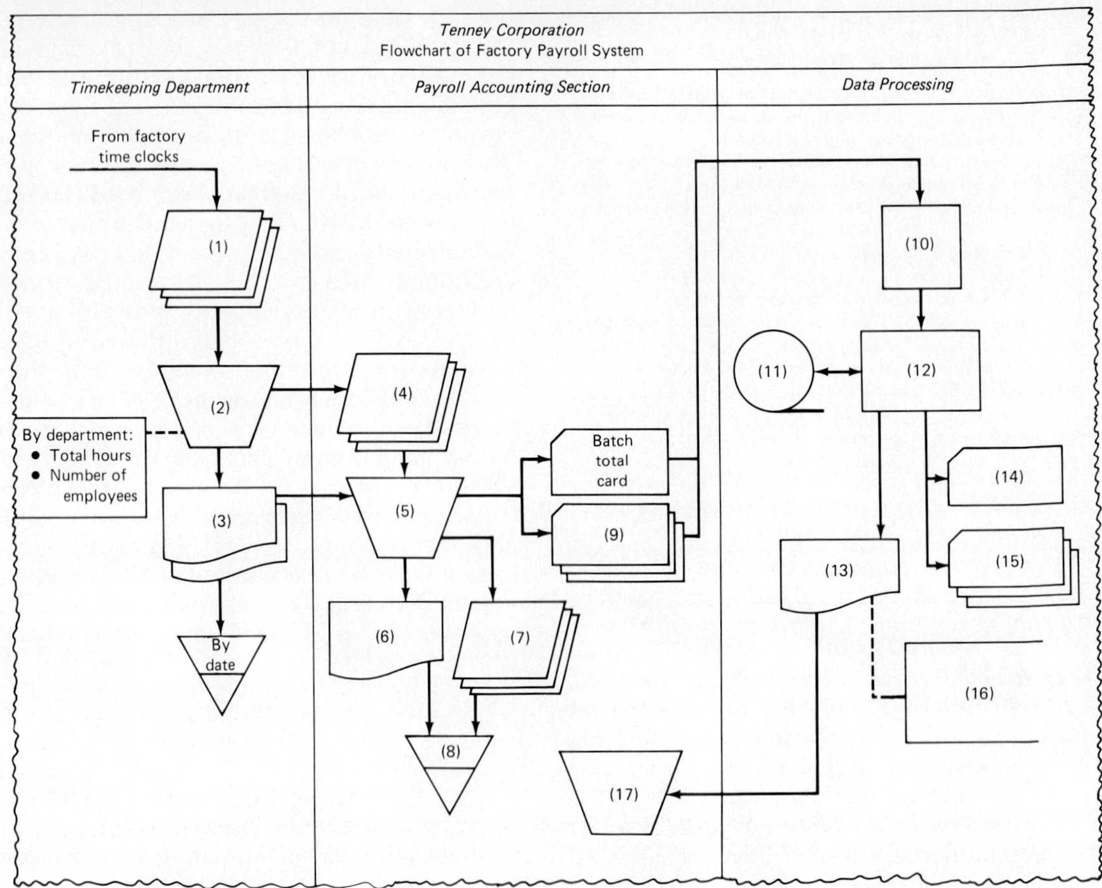

The appropriate labeling (document name, process description, or file order) applicable to each numbered symbol on the flow chart is as follows:

1. Time cards.
2. Preparation of batch-control slips.
3. Batch-control slips (the numbers 1 and 2 should be added to indicate first and second copy).
4. Time cards.
5. Key punch.
6. Batch-control slip (the number 1 should be added to indicate first copy).
7. Time cards.
8. By batch.
9. Payroll transaction cards.
10. Sort by employee number within batch.
11. Master employee file.
12. Editing and comparison of batch total hours and number of employees.
13. Batch listing and exception report.
14. Batch total cards.
15. Payroll transaction cards.
16. Exceptions noted:
    Unbalanced batch.
    Invalid employee number.
17. Resolution of differences.

CPA exam adapted, November 7 , 1974, question 7.

Segregation of Duties

A good internal control system should not give all control over a transaction to a single individual. The authorization of transactions, the custody of assets, and the keeping of accounting records should be assigned to three different people. If this is done, then the three would have to collude in order to commit a fraud. What good does it do to authorize a bogus transaction, if the assets related to that transaction are in another's custody? Why should the storekeeper be tempted to steal inventory, when periodic inventory counts will be reconciled to the accounting records that are being maintained by another employee, ensuring that the theft will be discovered on a reasonably timely basis? Unless one individual can authorize transactions, take custody of assets, and account for the transaction, the single-handed perpetration of a fraud that would not be detected in the normal course of operations is unlikely. CPAs presume that if collusion is required, the probability of fraud is substantially reduced.

As an example of a problem with the segregation of duties, consider a retail operation which permits the accounts payable manager to assign vendor numbers to new vendors as they are needed and to prepare the data to be put onto the master file of approved vendors by the EDP department. As a result of combining authorization and accounting duties in this fashion, it is possible for the accounts payable manager to input a bogus vendor on the master file and structure a means of obtaining cash, even though the manager has no direct access to cash. Note that the lack of segregated duties makes the typical purchase requisition responsibilities, including the check that suppliers are on the approved vendor listing, totally ineffective as an authorization control.

Small-Client Considerations. Responsibilities can even be divided in the smallest operations, although there is more risk because of the generally more informal procedures and the regularity with which practical operating "adaptations" are made in the interest of maintaining smooth and efficient operations. For example, if purchase authorizations are verbal, there is no record to show that the control was used, and if every time the custodian of assets goes to lunch, the accountant "covers" for her, the reason for separating their duties is lost. But the involvement of the *owner-manager* can often control these risks.

The owner-manager understands the entity's operations and can oversee the employees' activities. And he or she has an incentive to safeguard assets and maintain control. By assessing the reasonableness of authorizations, assets-on-hand, and accounting balances, in relationship to the total entity's operations, the owner-manager can serve as an extremely effective detective control over operations.

The extent of the active participation of the owner/manager is an important control environment factor for many companies. His (or her) knowledge of matters such as financial condition, results of operations, inventory levels, major customers and vendors (and transactions reasonable for each) can help prevent or detect errors or irregularities. Owner/manager involvement is most effective when the owner/manager:

- Uses accounting information in both planning and day-to-day managing of the business.
- Is aware of the potential meaning of certain items (such as customer and vendor complaints).
- Seeks explanations for discrepancies between accounting information provided and expectations based on his (or her) knowledge of the business.
- Uses nonaccounting employees (such as receptionists or secretaries) to perform certain accounting control functions where segregation of duties is important.
- Requires his (or her) prior authorization of certain types of transactions or payments (such as those over a certain amount).
- Separates personal transactions from business transactions.

However, owner/managers often are able to override controls for nonroutine transactions and exercise judgment in imprecise areas such as in making valuations or other estimates. This ability to override controls might relate to routine transaction processing as well.[5] Such override possibil-

[5] AICPA, "Proposed Statement on Auditing Standards: The Effects of the Accounting Control Environment on the Examination of Financial Statements" (File Ref. No. 3045, March 4, 1985), paragraph .28d.

ities are a key consideration in evaluating control.

Since an owner-manager knows all employees well and can establish a trust and loyalty relationship that is conducive to effective control, the possibility exists of placing undue reliance on such qualities. Employees can make honest mistakes that result in large losses, or their past loyalties may be altered by a change in personal circumstances. Hence, all entities should carry *fidelity bonding insurance* for employees who handle a significant amount of the entity's assets. This insurance would cover losses incurred if those employees stole the assets they handle. In addition to carrying such insurance, small businesses should establish formalized controls to the extent possible.

Formal Versus Informal Segregation of Duties. Regardless of how formally segregated organizational responsibilities are, the risk of informal day-to-day operations diverging from the formal system is ever present. The problem of lunch time substitutions has already been cited, but less obvious access of individuals to others' assets or records is all too common. For example, an individual entrusted with the keys to a vault containing marketable securities may be known to leave those keys in the unlocked top drawer of a desk which is frequently unmanned. Similarly, bank statements may be left open on a desk, prior to reconciliation, thereby permitting some individual to remove or alter accounting-related documentation.

Employees should be trained to appreciate the importance of their control responsibilities for ensuring that the informal environment corresponds to the formal system design. An understanding of the purpose of controls is often essential to the avoidance of an uncontrolled, informal system. For example, CPAs who are reviewing a system of cash disbursements may be told that the manager who is authorized to sign checks for that client regularly signs a set of blank checks whenever he has to be out of the office. Obviously, the importance of the authorization function being segregated from both custody and accounting duties had not been effectively communicated to that manager.

Electronic Data-processing Implications. The growing computerization of information systems has led to the combination of duties that were traditionally segregated in manual systems ***[SAS 48, Section 320].*** For example, EDP may be used to process all cash disbursement records and to sign checks with a facsimile signature plate. But by assigning key input and output control responsibilities to non-EDP personnel, even this situation can be effectively controlled. A batch control over the total number of documents given to EDP for processing, *dual control* (that is, two individuals required to obtain access) over the facsimile signature plate, and a careful count of the number of checks printed can help minimize risk exposure. These types of controls are examples of compensating controls since they are intended to compensate for the potential problems created by an ineffective segregation of duties.

In evaluating EDP, it is useful to consider the entire process as representing one individual. In this manner, everytime EDP performs incompatible functions, the related risk exposure can be assessed. As EDP becomes more decentralized, with accessibility to almost all areas of operations, compensating controls will become more important controls. For example, passwords to protect accessibility to the EDP system and to particular data files and programs within that system, and computer logs that record who carries out the specific EDP activities can be useful. Edit checks of propriety (for example, all positive balances), accuracy (for example, recalculation of discounts), and completeness (for example, a sequence check), combined with users' feedback on exception reports, can be effective detective controls.

Positional Analysis. The behavioral sciences have suggested some useful techniques for evaluating the organizational aspects of internal control that may not leave a trail of documentary evidence. One of these, *positional analysis,* is asking employees to list the names of fellow employees with whom they spend the most time doing their work and all those employees with whom they came in contact over the past month, with an indication of whether these individuals were or were not under their supervision. This information is then compared with the prescribed relationships and evaluated for conformance.[6] This approach

[6] See Robert A. Swieringa and D. R. Carmichael, "A Positional Analysis of Internal Control," *Journal of Accountancy,* February 1971, pp. 34–43.

appears to be a simple means of extending the one-time observation of segregated duties by an auditor to get a more continuous picture of day-to-day operations.

Completeness

The completeness of recorded transactions is critical to the audit process, as most audit tests focus on recorded transactions. Whenever business transactions occur, evidence that documents the occurrence of those transactions ought to be generated. This documentation should be created for both routine and nonroutine transactions. Representations from management are a part of the evidential matter on completeness but cannot be relied on as sufficient evidence. The risk of omission must be evaluated and tested. While compliance tests can be a part of the evidential matter, some substantive testing must be performed. Detail testing of related populations and analytical review procedures can be useful. For example, do tests of cash disbursements provide evidence that recorded purchases are reasonable?[7] Once assurance is available that some evidence of all transactions exists within an accounting system, the concern shifts to the potential loss of data or the entering of bogus data during processing. The path from an original source document to its final record in the general ledger is referred to as the *audit trail.* Often, document control is attainable through the use of prenumbered forms. Of course, the prenumbering serves no control purpose without a periodic *sequence check.* This means that all voided documents must be retained, and accountability for the consecutive numbers of various documents must be established at several points during processing. This completeness control was needed in the introductory case to avoid an extended scope audit. All documentation should be filed in a manner which facilitates the audit process, and that documentation should be maintained for a sufficient time period to be merged into the audit process.

Not only does an audit trail utilizing prenumbered forms suggest that controls exist over the completeness of documents which are processed, but that trail can similarly support answers to both of the following questions: who processed those documents and how have they been processed? Tangible evidence of approval, accuracy checks, and similar compliance tests has to be obtained. Key controls over completeness include reconciliation of control accounts to detail subsidiary ledgers, periodic comparison of physical assets to recorded balances, and cutoff procedures.

Auditability. If there is an audit trail for all transactions in which the client is involved, the entity is *auditable.* However, often the trail is missing for certain nonroutine transactions. The CPA can address this problem by trying to create an audit trail. This was effectively done in the introductory case by extending substantive testing. As another example, assume that one client persuaded a current creditor to waive a bond convenant provision to enable him to borrow at a better interest rate. In order to document this agreement, the CPA could formally confirm the waiver with the trustee. But sometimes the CPA may not be able to confirm an event with the actual parties and so may have to use other sources of information, such as appraisals from objective and qualified specialists. Further, the CPA who is unable to create an auditable entity by means of extended procedures may be able to provide a professional reporting service by limiting either the scope of the audit or the audit report. First-time auditees often use this alternative. Due to the auditor's inability to verify beginning inventory which is a primary determinant of cost of goods sold, many initial audit clients will request that the auditor report on only the balance sheet. Similarly, cities and towns that have inadequate records of the historical cost of their city hall and similar municipal buildings will report appraised values (which differ from the historical cost principle and thus result in a qualified audit report).

Operating Data. The CPA can ensure that the audit trail is complete also by comparing accounting numbers with operating statistics. For example, normal production levels can be calculated from the number of labor shifts, plant capacity statistics, and storage capabilities, thus showing whether recorded cost of sales is both feasible and reasonable. Industry data on the market share of

[7] AICPA, "Proposed Statement on Auditing Standards: Obtaining Evidential Matter Regarding the Completeness Assertion" (File Ref. No. 2150, August 21, 1984).

the client and competitors' operating performance can similarly help determine the reasonableness of reported sales and cost of sales. The use of analytical review procedures that compare prior year data, historical patterns, budgets, industry statistics, and expectations to current account balances was described in an earlier chapter. Those procedures can be particularly valuable as a check on the completeness of an entity's accounting records.

The Control Environment

The auditor should first review and evaluate the general controls, typically referred to as the entity's *control environment*. Exhibit 9-8 lists the main considerations in such an evaluation. Affirmative answers to this checklist would mean that management has an understanding of control concepts, has communicated the importance of controls to its employees, has monitored key control practices, and has insured against loss of both assets and accounting records. Of central importance to all systems is the *competency* of employees. Not only must *hiring practices* be carefully controlled, but *continuing education policies* and *performance evaluation practices* are important determinants of the professionalism of employees that can serve as deterrents to employees' turnover. Job assignments should be commensurate with employees' skills. Corporate conduct codes and policies can be effective environmental control factors, as can an audit committee. An effective control environment depends on how well management communicates its control policy. Employees will have a tendency to give priority to their operating duties, in spite of the serious operating problems that can arise if control duties are not performed with due care and diligence. Management's expectation that employees conscientiously discharge their control-related responsibilities needs to be made explicit, with a tie-in of that expectation to the performance evaluation system. Operating manuals and job descriptions should formalize responsibilities and lines of authority, as should the client's organizational chart.

The *elements* of any effective system of controls include:

- ○ The appropriate segregation of duties.
- ○ A sufficient audit trail—which includes adequate documentation and complete records.

EXHIBIT 9-8

Evaluating the Control Environment—A Checklist

	Yes	No	Comments
1. Is the organizational structure conducive to control, clearly defining responsibilities and segregating the duties of authorization, custodianship, and record keeping?			
2. Are accounting policies and procedures and job descriptions given in manuals?			
3. Are personnel selection methods, company training programs, supervisory practices, and performance evaluation techniques conducive to control, ensuring that an adequate number of employees are available to perform all of the assigned duties of the vacationing employees?			
4. Are vacations mandatory, and are provisions made for competent replacements to perform all of the assigned duties of the vacationing employees?			
5. For positions of trust, are employees' duties rotated, including those of bookkeepers and cashiers? (Note that before rotation, accountability checks should be performed, such as the counting of cash.)			
6. Is board designation of authorized approvers and handlers of valuable assets required, and are signature files of authorized personnel maintained?			
7. Is fidelity bonding insurance coverage adequate?			
8. Are there provisions for reasonable protection against fire, explosion, other natural disasters, and/or malicious destruction of records or processing facilities, and other assets of the entity? Such provisions should include both adequate loss-of-records insurance coverage and adequate insurance coverage of assets.			
9. Is access to assets, accounting records, and critical forms – both issued and unissued – permitted only in accordance with management criteria that reflect control objectives (i.e., is access limited to those persons whose duties require such access)?			
10. Is record retention adequate?			
11. Are accounting data periodically reviewed, tested, and compared with budgets, variances, and exception reports, and are nonfinancial reports generated outside the accounting department by internal auditors or individuals who do not generate the accounting data? Do operating personnel rely on such data for decision making?			
12. Are recorded balances and related transaction activity periodically substantiated and evaluated through a physical inventory, confirmation, and a review of legal documents? Are the resulting adjusting journal entries consistent with an adequate control environment?			

Adapted from Wanda A. Wallace, *Handbook of Internal Accounting Controls* (Englewood Cliffs, N.J.: Prentice-Hall, 1984), pp. 174–175.

- Physical control over both assets and records, with particular emphasis on limiting accessibility to those who need it to discharge their duties.
- Procedures for authorizing transactions and documenting such authorization.
- Competent personnel who understand their respective duties, authority, and related responsibilities.
- Independent checks on employees' performance.

The means of gaining assurances as to effective segregation of duties tend to be via observation and evaluation of control design. Samples cannot be drawn to compliance test the segregation of duties, but inquiry procedures can be quite effective, as can observation of how procedures are performed and by whom. Auditability and the completeness of documents can be assessed by evaluating control design, testing compliance with that design, and/or performing substantive test work. For example, the auditor can confirm that document logs are in use, that monthly statements are mailed, and that time cards or similar records are used and can test for numerical sequence. Typically, such compliance tests are not based on samples, but rather emphasize inquiry, observation, or a check on the total sequence of documents of interest. The control environment is implied by the design of controls as well as the results of both compliance and substantive test work. Compliance tests of approvals (examination of documents for evidence of approval and tracing of large capital expenditures to the minutes of the board of directors) and compliance tests of the cancellation of documents (examining supporting documentation to ensure proper cancellation to prevent their reuse) can provide relevant evidence as to the quality of authorization and document control. Inquiry and observation can provide insights as to employees' competence and trustworthiness. Documents may be available for examination such as resumés, reference letters, work experience, professional certifications, and files related to hiring practices. A client's compensation practices and turnover experience can be key indicators of the likely competence and experience level of employees. The adequacy of staffing can be inferred through inquiry procedures as to the extent of overtime hours worked by employees, particularly by individuals in the accounting and financial departments. Checking procedures can be tested by recomputing calculations, checking for reconciliations, comparing documents for agreement, and performing such compliance test work as distributing payroll on a surprise basis.

Checks and Balances

The accounting control environment represents the overall attitude, awareness, and actions of management that have a bearing on the effectiveness of specific accounting control procedures. Assured of an effective control environment, the auditor can then consider the specific controls. A very effective means of doing so is the cycle approach of viewing an organization. Despite differing characteristics of accounting and control systems, all organizations share some general operating cycles: a revenue or income-producing cycle, a cost of sales or production cycle, and a financing and nonroutine transaction cycle (a "catchall" cycle). Transactions can be easily classified by cycle and then analyzed to find out those accounts likely to be affected. Rather than focusing on balances, the *cycle approach* follows the normal course of business operations and is fairly generalizable across entities. The CPA can identify the cycle's operating objectives and then decide whether the controls are likely to meet these objectives. Exhibit 9-9 outlines the process required to determine whether checks and balances have been established. The analysis stage can be directed by focusing on what could go wrong and the related controls designed to prevent or detect such occurrences.

Even if a primary preventive or detective control appears weak, a second or third *(redundant)* control may exist which, when combined, can compensate for the observed weakness. The auditor must be alert for this possible role of compensating controls during the evaluation process. For example, an auditor may test purchasing orders to check compliance with prescribed control procedures and find that due to turnover problems, the client had used many unauthorized vendors. However, the second control of having EDP-generated exception reports regarding all purchases made from unauthorized vendors, with the

EXHIBIT 9-9
Determining Whether Checks and Balances Have Been Established

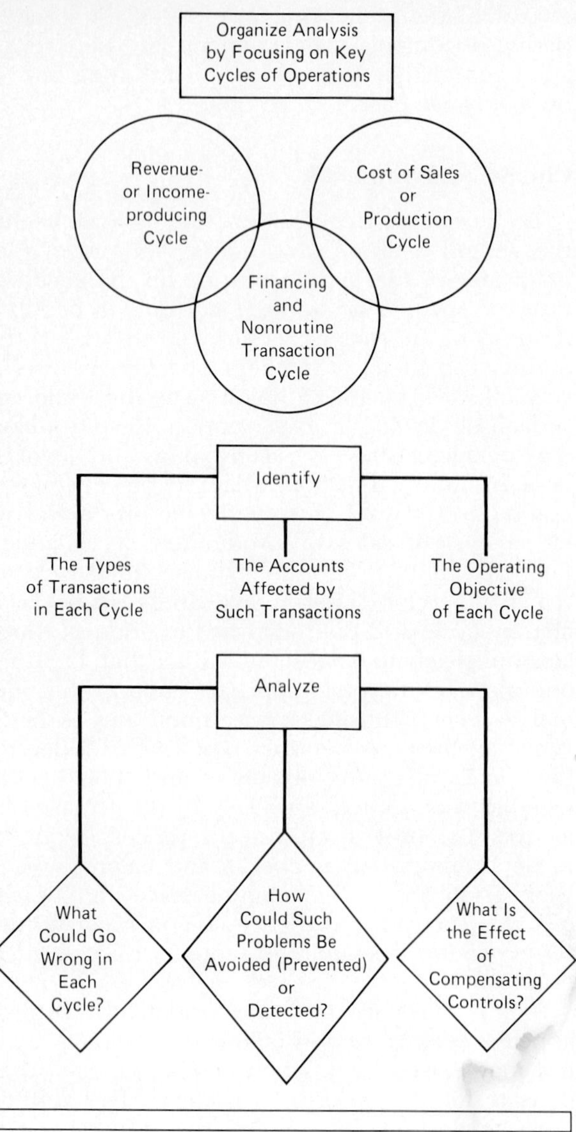

third control that this exception report be reviewed and approved by the purchasing department manager, may be deemed to ensure an adequate level of control over operations. Redundant controls are common, as they are one means of reducing the risk created by employees' fatigue, oversight, or intentional noncompliance with controls and by other inherent limitations of control systems. They can be of particular value to an auditor as alternative controls available for testing, should compliance procedures indicate that a primary control is not operating as prescribed. Note, however, that redundant controls need not be tested if the primary control is operating effectively, although they are likely to lead to an assessment by the auditor that the overall control environment is better than if no such redundancies were included in control design.

Exhibit 9-10 gives an example of the analysis outlined in Exhibit 9-9, by presenting a past CPA exam question and solution. The problem requests that strengths and weaknesses in controls be identified, along with the financial statement effects of any inadequacies. As you review the solution, you'll note: (1) an emphasis on what could go wrong as the primary means for identifying weaknesses; (2) a tie-in of each possible problem to related control procedures that are intended to prevent or detect the problem; and (3) attention to the role of compensating controls. As with earlier CPA exam questions, the terminology in Exhibit 9-10 will become more familiar when you study the key operating cycles in depth in Chapters 13, 14, and 15.

Operating Efficiency

The most effective means of ensuring that prescribed controls are followed is to dovetail accounting controls with operations in a manner that facilitates and, when possible, improves operating efficiency. As an example, consider the design of authorization controls. If control design requires that the assistant manager of the purchasing department approve all orders, but that assistant manager is constantly traveling, leading to large backlogs in unprocessed orders, compliance with prescribed controls is unlikely. Yet, if such approval power is entrusted with the manager of the department, who rarely travels and who can share twenty-five years of experience in analyzing purchase orders, that control duty is likely to be performed. The manager should be encouraged to share the available knowledge regarding suppliers,

EXHIBIT 9-10
Evaluating a Control System

Problem

Dunbar Camera Manufacturing, Inc., is a manufacturer of high-priced precision motion picture cameras. The specifications of the cameras' component parts are vital to the manufacturing process. Dunbar buys valuable camera lenses and large quantities of sheet metal and screws. It also orders screws and lenses and is billed by the vendors on a unit basis. Dunbar orders sheet metal and is billed by the vendors on the basis of weight. The receiving clerk is responsible for documenting the quality and quantity of merchandise received. A preliminary review of the system of internal control indicates that the following procedures are being followed:

Receiving Report

1. Properly approved purchase orders, which are prenumbered, are filed numerically. The copy sent to the receiving clerk is an exact duplicate of the copy sent to the vendor. Receipts of merchandise are recorded by the receiving clerk on the duplicate copy.

Sheet Metal

2. The company receives its sheet metal by railroad. The railroad independently weighs the sheet metal and reports the weight and date of receipt on a bill of lading (waybill), which accompanies all deliveries. The receiving clerk compares the weight on the waybill only with that on the purchase order.

Screws

3. The receiving clerk opens the cartons containing screws and then inspects and weighs the contents. The weight is converted to number of units by means of conversion charts. The receiving clerk then compares the computed quantity with that on the purchase order.

Camera Lenses

4. Each camera lens is delivered in a separate corrugated carton. The cartons are counted as they are received by the receiving clerk, and the number of cartons is compared with the purchase orders.

Required:

a. Indicate whether the internal control procedures are adequate or inadequate for the receiving reports and the receipt of sheet metal, screws, and camera lenses. Do not recommend improvements.

b. What financial statement distortions may arise because of the inadequacies in Dunbar's system of internal control, and how may they occur?

Solution

a. The adequacy of internal control is questionable whenever quantities are not blocked out on the copy of the purchase order that is sent to the receiving department, because this practice may cause the receiving clerk to bypass the counting and inspection procedures. The receiving clerk may compare only the purchase order and the packing slip (or other document accompanying the shipment) and prepare a receiving report based on these documents. As a result of this weakness, incorrect quantities of merchandise or inferior quality merchandise may be received and accepted. However, in the case of Dunbar Manufacturing, Inc., there are compensating controls in certain areas.

   Receipt of sheet metal. Although the receiving clerk may compare only the quantities on the purchase order and the bill of lading, there is a compensating control over the quantities of sheet metal received; the independent verification of weights received and the date of receipt, which are provided on the bill of lading. However, sheet metal with unacceptable quality specifications may still be received and accepted.

   Receipt of screws. Because the receiving clerk weighs the screws upon receipt and the weight is converted to units, the control over the quantities received is adequate. Furthermore, screws of an unacceptable specification may be expected to be detected during the weighing and inspecting process.

   Receipt of camera lenses. Because there are no controls that compensate for the weakness in checking the actual receipt of camera lenses, there is inadequate control over the quantity and quality of lenses received.

b. The inventory may be overstated, and the cost of merchandise sold and income may be misstated because any additions to the inventory may be based on suppliers' invoices, which may include nonusable items or items that were not received. Furthermore, because the company may have erroneously accrued the cost of nonusable items or items not received, accounts payable may be overstated.

Note: The response to (b) should be considered in assessing the required nature, timing, and extent of substantive audit work; for example, more extensive testing of receiving reports may be needed.

CPA exam adapted, November 5, 1981, question 3.

purchase terms, and differential quality standards, as well as expressing any concerns that might arise as to the plausibility of specific orders being filled to meet desired specifications within the necessary time frame. Once the approval process is recognized as providing valuable information concerning operating responsibilities, the control procedure will be viewed as indispensable. While some controls by their nature cannot have such clear operating advantages, in almost every case, the consideration of operating efficiency in both design and implementation of controls can be conducive to obtaining employees' compliance. When an emphasis on both efficiency and effectiveness is combined with a performance evaluation system that penalizes those who circumvent control responsibilities, an effective control environment can be established. Obviously, a primary concern of the auditor is whether the efficiency of designed controls is so poor that compliance with those controls is improbable.

Evaluating an Internal Audit Department

A control environment can be improved by the addition of an internal audit department. This department can be viewed as a control over the entity's control system, as its principal responsibility will be to see that management's control and operating objectives are met. Internal auditors frequently perform audit procedures that are identical with those of external auditors ***[SAS 9, Section 322].*** Recognizing this overlap and an internal audit department's favorable effect on an entity's control environment, the Auditing Standards Board issued Statement on Auditing Standards No. 9, "The Effects of an Internal Audit Function on the Scope of the Independent Auditor's Examination." For clients that have an internal auditing department, CPAs are permitted to reduce their testing by using internal auditors' work, though in order to do so, the CPAs must evaluate the internal auditors' *competency, objectivity*, and *performance* to support the appropriateness of the degree of external audit reliance. Exhibit 9-11 provides an evaluation checklist. As indicated, the primary concerns are over the structural independence of the department, the professionalism of the audit work performed, and both the competency and objectivity of the audit staff members. While internal audit work cannot replace the external audit work, it can support reduction of the latter if, based upon tests of the internal auditors' working papers, the external auditor determines that reliance is warranted.

The Concept of a Material Weakness

A *material weakness* in controls is

> a condition in which the auditor believes the prescribed procedures or the degree of compliance with them does not provide reasonable assurance that errors or irregularities in amounts that would be material in the financial statements being audited would be prevented or detected within a timely period by employees in the normal course of performing their assigned functions.[8]

The auditor must first decide whether there could be a material error because of an identified weakness in the control system and then whether such an error would be detected within a reasonable length of time. Preventive, detective, corrective, and compensating controls all have to be used to calculate the largest possible error, the probability of that error's remaining undetected, and the frequency with which that error could occur. Once the potential for material undetected error is evaluated based on control design, the auditor should investigate the entity's compliance with the control design. Employees' competence and integrity are relevant factors, as well as the organizational reporting structure. For example, an employee who is instructed to check compliance with the credit approval system should not report to the individual who is responsible for credit approval. It is unreasonable to expect employees to point out mistakes of their supervisors.

Example

Material weaknesses often involve a lack of segregated duties, combined with an inadequate au-

[8] "Statement on Auditing Standards No. 20, Section 323, "Required Communication of Material Weaknesses in Internal Accounting Control" (New York: AICPA, 1977), AU § 320.69.

EXHIBIT 9-11

A Checklist for Evaluating an Internal Audit Function

Yes	No	Explanation	
			1. Is the internal audit department relatively autonomous and independent? a. Does it report to top management, the board of directors, or the audit committee? (Top management means vice-president or higher.) b. Does it give such reports regularly? c. Does it have full access to the company's operations and records to perform an unlimited scope audit (i.e., is it permitted to investigate any aspect of the entity's activities)? d. Is there a separate systems and procedures function that is independent of the internal audit department? e. Are temporary assignments of internal audit staff to a line or accounting function prohibited (including substitution for operational responsibilities of vacationing employees)? f. Are professional staff periodically rotated? g. Are individual internal auditors in a position to be independent with respect to the matters that they review?
			2. Does the internal audit department have a statement of responsibility with approved objectives for the department?
			3. Has the organization had an internal audit department for a number of years, providing some assurance of stability and clarity of purpose (the median age of departments is about ten years)?
			4. Is an internal audit schedule covering the scope of internal audit activities established annually? a. Is this schedule approved by top management, the board of directors, or the audit committee? b. Does the schedule reflect an overall audit strategy that is tailored to the critical risk areas, of accounting, auditing, and management concern? c. Is the schedule developed in consultation with the organization's external auditors? d. Are a charter, policies, and budgets formalized for the internal audit department?
			5. Does the internal audit department have adequate staffing? a. Are education and business and audit experience of the professional staff commensurate with responsibilities? b. Are professional staff knowledgeable of company operations, processes, and procedures? c. Do minimum requirements exist with respect to education and experience? d. Do the sources of personnel suggest that hiring practices will provide the necessary expertise for the professional staff's needs? e. Do some of the professional staff have public accounting experience? f. Do some of the professional staff hold professional certifications? g. Are professional staff active in professional organizations? h. Is staff turnover at a reasonable level? i. Does the organization try to avoid fixed or limited terms of duty in the internal audit department, i.e., are career opportunities available within the department? j. Are salaries of professional staff competitive? k. Do the professionals engage in continuing education?
			6. Is the internal audit department adequately supervised? a. Are job descriptions formalized? b. Do job assignments reflect formal job descriptions? c. Are up-to-date audit manuals available? d. Are staff properly instructed prior to commencing an examination? e. Is the work of staff members monitored? f. Is appropriate on-the-job training received? g. Are audits periodically reviewed by superiors and by someone not participating in the particular examination? h. Does the review cited in (g) include a review of: 1. goals 2. personnel 3. documentation 4. whether innovative techniques like computer and statistical auditing procedures are properly controlled and applied, and 5. reports? i. Are periodic performance reviews required? j. Is the internal audit function centralized with the manager of internal auditing coordinating all internal auditing activities?

(Exhibit continues on p. 308.)

EXHIBIT 9-11 (continued)

Yes	No	Explanation	
			7. Do the following requirements exist? a. Internal auditors must follow generally accepted auditing standards. b. Written audit programs must be prepared. c. Audit programs are to be modified to respond to current circumstances. d. Audit program steps are to be initialed at the completion of each test procedure. e. All tests are to be comprehensively documented in the working papers, including the detailed procedure applied and the results of such tests. f. Work is to be adequately supported, particularly with respect to the follow-up work and disposition of exceptions. g. A written report, adequately supported by the working papers and following a prescribed form, is to be prepared for each examination. h. Written reports should summarize all significant matters; no management influence will be permitted to suppress the reporting of audit findings. i. The findings and recommendations of the audit are to be reviewed with management on a higher level than the head of the audited organization. j. Audit reports must be regularly distributed to top executives. k. Mandatory reply procedures exist within the company, whereby auditees formally respond to the internal audit department regarding its reports. l. All reports are subjected to follow-up, with an emphasis on the correction of reported deficiencies and formal responses by affected areas. m. Management relies on the audit reports, encourages corrective action, and regularly provides feedback to the internal audit department. n. All physical facilities are periodically scheduled for review by internal auditing. o. Operational and administrative controls are reviewed on a cyclical basis. p. Periodic reports are to be submitted by the internal auditing department to report its progress with respect to the planning schedule and budget.
			8. Are file retention systems adequate? a. Is there a written description of the filing system? b. Are files organized efficiently? c. Is the retention period for working papers sufficient for external auditors' purposes.

From Wanda A. Wallace, *Handbook of Internal Accounting Controls* (Englewood Cliffs, N.J.: Prentice-Hall, 1984), pp. 76–78.

dit trail. For example, it is far too common for an individual who is responsible for purchasing inventory to also be able to remove inventory from stock, having custody responsibility for the physical control of inventory on hand. Couple this problem of unsegregated duties with a sloppy documentation of purchases, and the entity's risk exposure can be substantial. The absence of control over blank and outstanding purchase orders, the absence of prenumbered forms, and no requirement of independent approval of purchases combine to make the perpetration of a fraud an easy matter. A poorly controlled operation often will permit the party placing an order to receive the goods, upon delivery, and even rely on that party to update perpetual records. When invoices from suppliers are forwarded to the purchaser for matching to purchase orders and receiving documents that happen to be available, prior to forwarding to the accounting department for initial recording, a material problem is evident. Not only could unauthorized purchases be made, but unidentified inventory "shrinkage" easily could occur. The inability to follow-up on outstanding purchase orders, and the virtual absence of reliable purchasing documentation for use in planning cash flows and generating forecasts suggests that operating efficiency will suffer as a result of the poor controls.

The Decision Process

The identification of material weaknesses has two stages. The first stage focuses on control design, while the second stage focuses on compliance tests. The second stage is only performed in those areas of control on which reliance by the external auditor is planned. Of course, if a CPA is asked to express an opinion on the overall system of internal accounting control, stage two would be performed on all significant control areas.

Exhibit 9-12 shows the process of identifying material weaknesses in control, emphasizing the various interpretations of the compliance test findings.

Material weaknesses may be resolved by increasing the audit scope or by issuing either a qualified report or disclaimer. The auditor should document the effect of material weaknesses on the audit scope and the audit report in the working papers. Of particular concern to the CPA making interim statements is the likely effect of observed material weaknesses on interim financial reports. The existence of a material weakness, however, does not mean that there is a material error; it merely implies the possibility of material errors. In that sense, material weaknesses have a futuristic dimension.

Reporting Responsibilities

Professional pronouncements include

> a requirement that the auditor communicate to senior management and the board of directors or its audit committee material weaknesses in internal accounting control that come to his [or her] attention during an examination of financial statements made in accordance with generally accepted auditing standards.[9]

As noted in Chapter 8, communication need not be in writing but, if oral, should be carefully documented in the working papers as to both the time and content of the discussion. No report to the public is required. As already suggested, it is possible for the auditor to adjust audit procedures in order to reflect observed weaknesses in control, including material weaknesses, in order to form an evidential base that can support the issuance of an unqualified or clean audit report. The introductory case provided an example of an extended scope. Since material weaknesses are by no means synonymous with material error, a sufficient amount of substantive test work that provides report users with assurance that no material error exists in the financial statements can support a clean opinion. For example, in spite of the material weakness in purchasing procedures described earlier, a physical inventory count, confirmations with vendors, a testing of cash disbursements, and analytical review procedures are capable of providing sufficient assurance that a material amount of inventory has not been stolen and a material amount of bogus purchases has not been processed.

The CPA may be particularly interested in management's reaction to reported conditions of material weaknesses, as it has implications for the evaluation of the overall control environment. One possible explanation for inaction by management is that a cost/benefit analysis has led to management's judgment that the correction of a material weakness would be more costly than justified by the potential benefits of correcting control conditions. The CPA's disclosure of the material weakness is required regardless of management's judgment; however, the CPA is permitted to include in its report that management believes costs exceed benefits for the particular controls that are involved. In no case can the auditor express an opinion as to the propriety of management's cost/benefit analysis, although an explicit disclaimer can be issued as to the stated belief of management.

The Problem of Management Override

While material weaknesses may occur in control design and compliance with that design, one substantial problem involves the complete circumvention of established control. This action is termed *management override* and is epitomized by the boss asking an employee not to process a particular transaction in the prescribed manner, because it is an unusual business operation that needs "special handling." The manager may process the transaction in a nonroutine manner without involving other employees. This risk is deemed to be substantial in smaller businesses in which the owner-manager has a central role. Employees are likely to fol-

[9] Ibid., ¶ 1.

EXHIBIT 9-12

Identifying Material Weaknesses in Internal Accounting Control

Review Internal Accounting Controls

Is a specific internal accounting control procedure considered necessary by the auditor missing?

Yes

Material weakness

No

Assume that either planned reliance on internal accounting control or the requirements of an opinion on the overall system of internal accounting control cause the auditor to COMPLIANCE TEST INTERNAL ACCOUNTING CONTROLS

Were material audit differences found?

No

Is noncompliance observed?

No

No material weakness

Yes

Are there any mitigating or compensating controls which would prevent the occurrence of undetected material errors?

Yes

No material weakness

No

Could the weakness indicated result in an irregularity?

Yes

Consider aggregate exposure i.e., the maximum possible misstatement or loss that could occur

No

Consider aggregate exposure and the likelihood of exposure

Are errors potentially material?

Yes

Material weakness

No

Consider possibility that the aggregate of such individually immaterial weaknesses are material

Yes

Did the differences arise as a result of differing interpretations of an accounting principle?

Yes

No material weakness

No

Did the differences arise from events related to the system of internal accounting control?

No

No material weakness

Yes

Are the events giving rise to the error isolated?

Yes

No material weakness

No

Would the audit differences have been detected on a timely basis through normal procedures (i.e., through mitigating or compensating controls)?

Yes

No material weakness

No

Material weakness

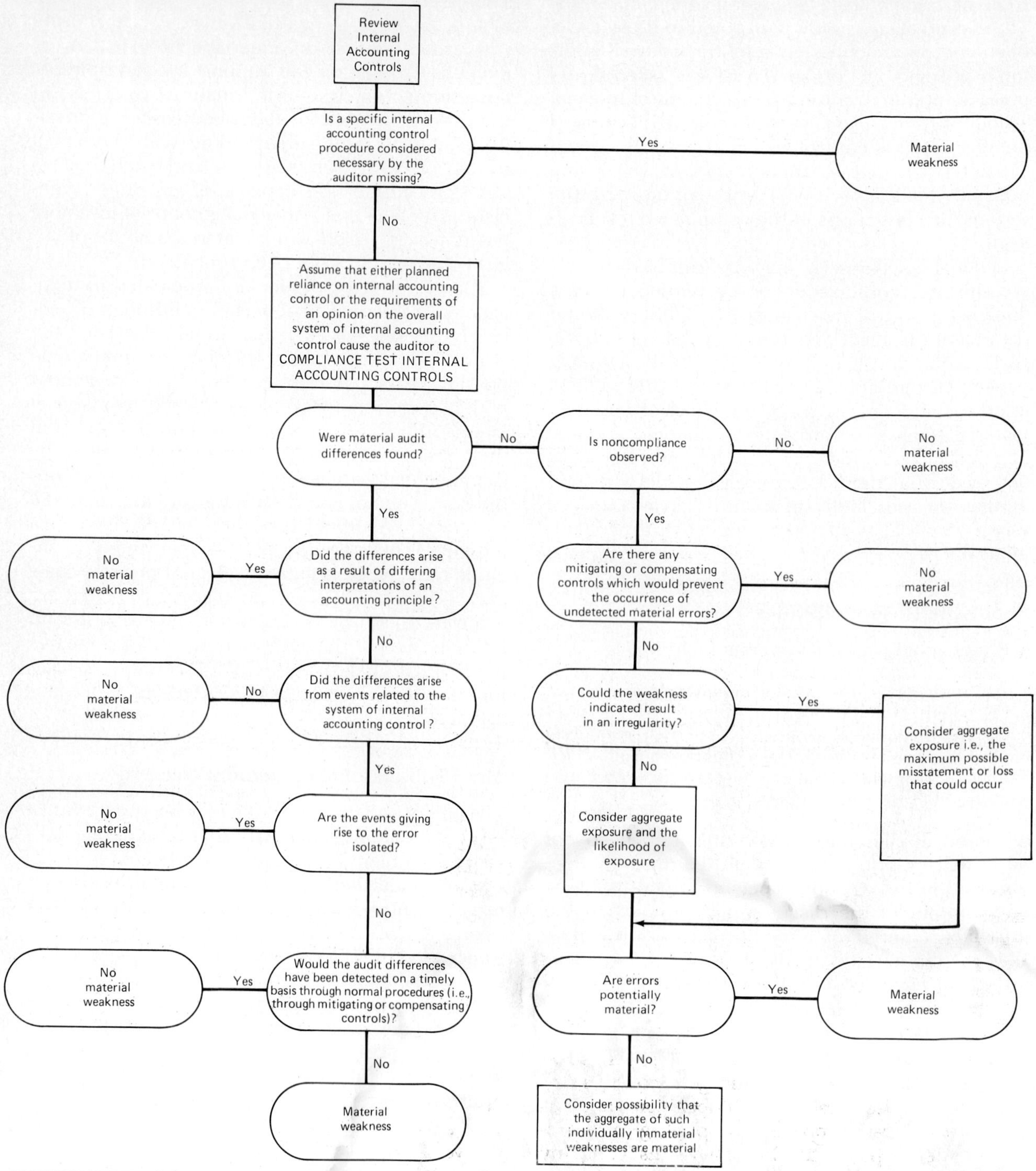

low managers' instructions, and a low probability exists of the request being reported to some third party. Due to owner-managers' excellent knowledge of the business and its controls, they are capable of recognizing the weaknesses of that system and abusing controls at their discretion. Hence, if incentives exist for an owner-manager to abuse controls, the auditor must evaluate the risk of override. Whenever the owner-manager is other than a 100% owner or has credit in any form, some incentive is present for management override. It is possible to benefit from so-called business *perquisites* like plush offices at the disproportionate expense of co-owners, or, possibly, to actually extract assets of the business which, in substance, belong to other owners or creditors. Although the possibility of override is ever present, the CPA's concern is over the probability of management override.

A key issue is how employees have been instructed to react to managers' requests that some aspect of normal processing procedures and controls be circumvented. Ideally, preprinted forms should be available to document any unusual handling of a transaction. Such *exception reporting* can be used to monitor the use of overrides. Of course, the usefulness of these forms will depend upon the setting of clear reporting responsibilities, with set disciplinary action against any employees that fail to comply with the exception-report requirement. Little doubt exists that "blowing the whistle" on one's boss is an unpopular action; as a result, some risk of noncompliance with exception reporting will persist even if top management's expectations are effectively communicated. Those factors that tend to increase the probability of management override are summarized in Exhibit 9-13. Besides system design considerations and the presence of an exception reporting system, the CPA must weigh the degree of decentralization; the potential for collusion with suppliers, customers, or other parties; and the employer's recognition of the controls' importance. The expectation is that:

EXHIBIT 9-13
Factors Affecting the CPA's Assessment of the Probability of Management Override

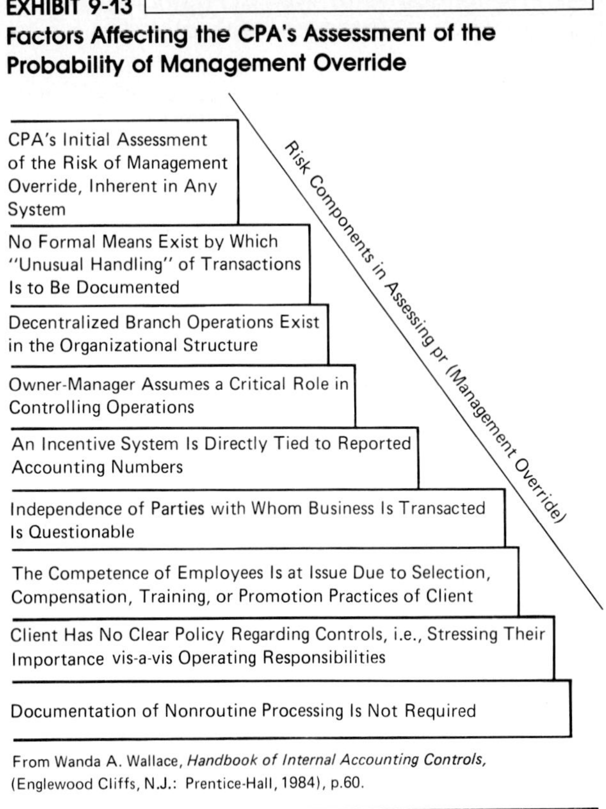

From Wanda A. Wallace, *Handbook of Internal Accounting Controls,* (Englewood Cliffs, N.J.: Prentice-Hall, 1984), p.60.

1. A branch manager can wield more power, is less likely to be subjected to stringent controls owing to the decentralization of operations, and has more persuasive power in appealing to the esprit de corps of the branch versus company loyalty to gain employee cooperation in circumventing control;
2. A single owner-manager does not risk detection by fellow managers when overriding controls and hence is more likely to do so.
3. The incentives to circumvent controls in order to distort performance measures are greater when those measures are used for compensation.
4. The risk of collusion with suppliers or other third parties increases when they are dependent on the entity for a substantial amount of their business.
5. Incompetent or unhappy employees are more likely to abuse controls.
6. A "hole" in the control system, often in the processing of nonroutine transactions, can make overriding the controls easier.

The Influence of the Foreign Corrupt Practices Act

Legislation that may help deter management override and enhance control systems is the Foreign Corrupt Practices Act (FCPA). This legislation was directed at prohibiting companies' making illegal payments, but it also includes a requirement that public companies establish a system of adequate internal accounting control. The rationale of the legislation is that controls will ensure against illegal payments or, as a minimum, will facilitate the detection of illegal payments. In December 1977, the Foreign Corrupt Practices Act (FCPA) became law. Its Antibribery Provisions make it a criminal offense for any domestic concern to pay or offer to pay any foreign official, any foreign political party or official thereof, or any third party who indirectly performs the same functions as the above, in order to obtain, retain, or direct business to any person. Fines of up to $1 million on companies and up to $10,000 for each individual and imprisonment for up to five years were recommended. These provisions have been cited as being responsible for management's increased attention to the development and enforcement of formal codes of conduct.

The Act's second section, the Accounting Standards Provision, requires that entities make and keep records and accounts that are reasonably complete and accurate and devise and maintain a system of internal accounting controls that can provide reasonable assurance that assets are accounted for appropriately, that transactions are recorded in conformity with generally accepted accounting principles, that access to assets is properly controlled, and that periodic comparisons of existing assets to the books are made. The FCPA applies only to companies registered under Section 12 of the 1934 SEC Act, which essentially are those businesses listed on a national stock exchange or those that have at least $1 million in assets and five hundred or more shareholders.

The FCPA is credited with making managers more aware of controls, because of the personal liability of board members and managers should illegal payments be made. Many internal audit departments have since received larger budgets and expanded staffing authorizations.[10] In particular, the FCPA has been cited as the reason for public reporting on the adequacy of internal control systems, including disclosures regarding controls within management reports.

A bill was introduced to the Senate on February 3, 1983, that would modify some of the FCPA's accounting provisions, and other proposals to decriminalize the Act have been discussed.[11] But these proposals are unlikely to alter the effects of the initial act.

REVIEW QUESTIONS

1. What are the differences between internal control and internal accounting control systems?
2. What are the objectives of an internal accounting control system?
3. Give an example of a preventive, a detective, and a corrective control. How are these types of controls similar? Which is usually the most expensive?
4. What are the inherent limitations of an internal accounting control system?
5. How do CPAs typically document controls? What are the advantages and disadvantages of the various approaches to documenting control systems?
6. Internal accounting control checklists are often criticized for their yes/no format. What are the advantages and disadvantages of such a format? Are constructive means available for addressing the disadvantages? Support your answer.
7. Give the flowcharting symbol for the following:
   a. magnetic tape.
   b. document.
   c. input/output.
   d. stop or interrupt.
   e. compare or match.
   f. collate.
   g. sort.
   h. merge.
8. Describe some useful means of tailoring control symbols used in flowcharting to reflect the auditor's special concerns.

[10] Some of the specific actions that have been taken by companies in response to the FCPA are described by Robert K. Mautz et al., *Internal Control in U.S. Corporations: The State of the Art* (New York: Financial Executives Research Foundation, 1980).

[11] See "Reagan Is Urged to Decriminalize Payoffs Abroad," *Wall Street Journal*, January 16, 1981, p. 6.

9. What are the five key questions that can effectively guide the CPA's evaluation of a control system?
10. What are the three responsibilities that should be segregated in any operating entity?
11. What special problems are there in segregating duties in a small business environment?
12. How does EDP affect the evaluation of whether an entity has segregated its duties effectively?
13. What are compensating controls? Describe such controls in an EDP setting when the traditional segregation of duties is lacking.
14. How can a CPA gain reasonable assurance that a client's recorded transactions represent all of the economic transactions for the period?
15. What is a control environment? How does a CPA evaluate a client's control environment?
16. What are the general operating cycles that all organizations have?
17. What are the three questions that help a CPA determine whether checks and balances have been established?
18. How do operating efficiency considerations affect an internal accounting control system?
19. How does the presence of an internal audit department affect controls and an external auditor's examination? Be specific.
20. Describe the various rationales that may exist for a CPA's evaluation of controls.
21. What is a material weakness? Give an example.
22. Is it possible to identify a material weakness without performing any compliance tests?
23. If compliance tests reveal material differences between recorded unaudited numbers and audited balances because of differences in the client's and the auditor's interpretation of an accounting principle, is this a material weakness?
24. What are the auditor's reporting responsibilities with respect to material weaknesses in a client's internal accounting control system? Is public disclosure required?
25. What factors tend to increase the probability of management override?
26. What has been the apparent influence of the Foreign Corrupt Practices Act on clients' internal control system?

EXERCISES

1. "I can't figure out why we bother to look at initials to find out whether the client complied with prescribed authorization procedures. The client could have initialed a set of *blank* forms." What is the validity of this assertion? How does it affect the audit process?
2. As an auditor of a small business, two questions you are likely to ask are (a) What is done when employees are on vacation? and (b) What is done when one employee goes to lunch? Why are these questions asked? What are desirable responses to these questions, from a control standpoint?
3. An employee is entrusted with verifying that purchases are made from authorized vendors and is supervised by the individual who initiated the orders. Comment on the control ramifications of this organizational structure.
4. A material weakness in control does not necessarily mean a material misstatement in financial statements. Why, then, is the auditor concerned about material weaknesses in control? Is the auditor expected to identify all material weaknesses? In your opinion, do auditors have appropriate responsibility for material weaknesses? Explain.
5. Indicate whether the following statements are true (T) or false (F):
   a. The mere knowledge that a large volume of transactions is being subjected to either no control or to an extremely weak control and that no compensating controls are present to offset such design flaws signals a material weakness.
   b. An owner-manager's involvement in operations is considered to be a potential compensating control.
   c. A timely detection capability is not enough to make an otherwise material weakness into an immaterial weakness.
   d. Noncompliance with designed controls is a material weakness even if there are compensating controls that would prevent material errors.
   e. If material audit differences are discovered during compliance testing but are found not to be related to the internal accounting control system, then a material weakness does not exist.
   f. If material audit differences are discovered during compliance testing, there is a material weakness even if isolated events were the cause of those differences.
6. Controls can be designed sequentially, parallel in operation, overlapping, redundantly, or independently with respect to the operation of other controls. Give an example of each type of control, and explain why it might be the best control in certain situations.
7. The following activities need to be carried out in a business that has only three employees:
   a. maintaining the accounts receivable subsidiary ledger.
   b. purchasing of inventory.
   c. hiring employees.

d. paying suppliers.
e. receiving inventory from suppliers.
f. collecting on customers' accounts.
g. preparing customers' statements.
h. accounting for prenumbered receiving reports.
i. shipping inventory to customers.
j. recording accounts payable.
k. paying employees.
l. reconciling the bank statement and tying it to the general ledger.
m. approving credit extensions to customers.
n. making deposits at the bank.

Describe how you would divide these activities (using the letters corresponding to each) to achieve the best possible segregation of duties with only three employees.

8. In describing tools for defensive auditing, the following attributes are of particular use to an auditor:

Curiosity
Inquisitiveness
Skepticism
Imagination
Toughness
Thoroughness

How would such attributes be of use to an auditor in evaluating internal control? Be specific.

9. The exposure draft issued by the General Accounting Office on December 29, 1982, "Standards for Internal Controls in the Federal Government," contained the following definition:

> Internal controls are a plan of organization and all the methods and procedures (techniques) the management of an entity adopts to help it achieve four basic management objectives:
> - Ensure adherence to laws, regulations, and policies.
> - Ensure that reliable data are obtained, maintained, and properly disclosed in reports.
> - Promote economy, efficiency, and effectiveness of operations.
> - Safeguard resources against loss due to errors and irregularities.

Compare and contrast this definition with the internal control concepts emphasized in the generally accepted auditing standards.

10. You own a newspaper stand. Every morning you get deliveries from the six newspaper and magazine companies with which you do business. You have two high school students who help out in the early morning and late afternoon. You have one till into which everyone puts his or her receipts whenever the changeholders are full. At the end of the day, you deposit your receipts at the local bank. Describe a control system that would be useful to you in maintaining control over operations, and prepare a flowchart for your system.

QUESTIONS ADAPTED FROM PROFESSIONAL EXAMINATIONS

1. In conducting an examination in accordance with generally accepted auditing standards, the CPA studies and evaluates the existing internal control of his or her client.

Required:

a. List and discuss the general elements or characteristics of a satisfactory system of internal control.
b. List the purposes for which the CPA reviews his or her client's system of internal control.

(CPA exam adapted)

2. An important procedure in the CPA's audit programs is his or her review of the client's system of internal control.

Required:

a. Distinguish between accounting controls and administrative controls in a properly coordinated system of internal control.
b. List the essential features of a sound system of accounting control.
c. Explain why the CPA is concerned about separating responsibilities for operating custodianship, financial custodianship, and controllership.

(CPA exam adapted)

3. The financial statements of the Tiber Company have never been audited by an independent CPA. Recently Tiber's management asked Anthony Burns, a CPA, to conduct a special study of Tiber's internal control; this study will not include an examination of Tiber's financial statements. After completing his special study, Burns plans to prepare a report consistent with the requirements of Statement on Auditing Standards No. 30, "Reporting on Internal Accounting Control."

Required:

Describe the inherent limitations that should be recognized in considering the effectiveness of any system of internal control.

(CPA exam adapted)

4. On January 2, 19X5, Jordan Finance Company opened four personal loan offices in neighboring cities. Small cash loans are made to borrowers who repay the principal with interest in monthly installments over a period not exceeding two years. Ralph Jordan,

Flowchart to accompany Question 5 on page 316.

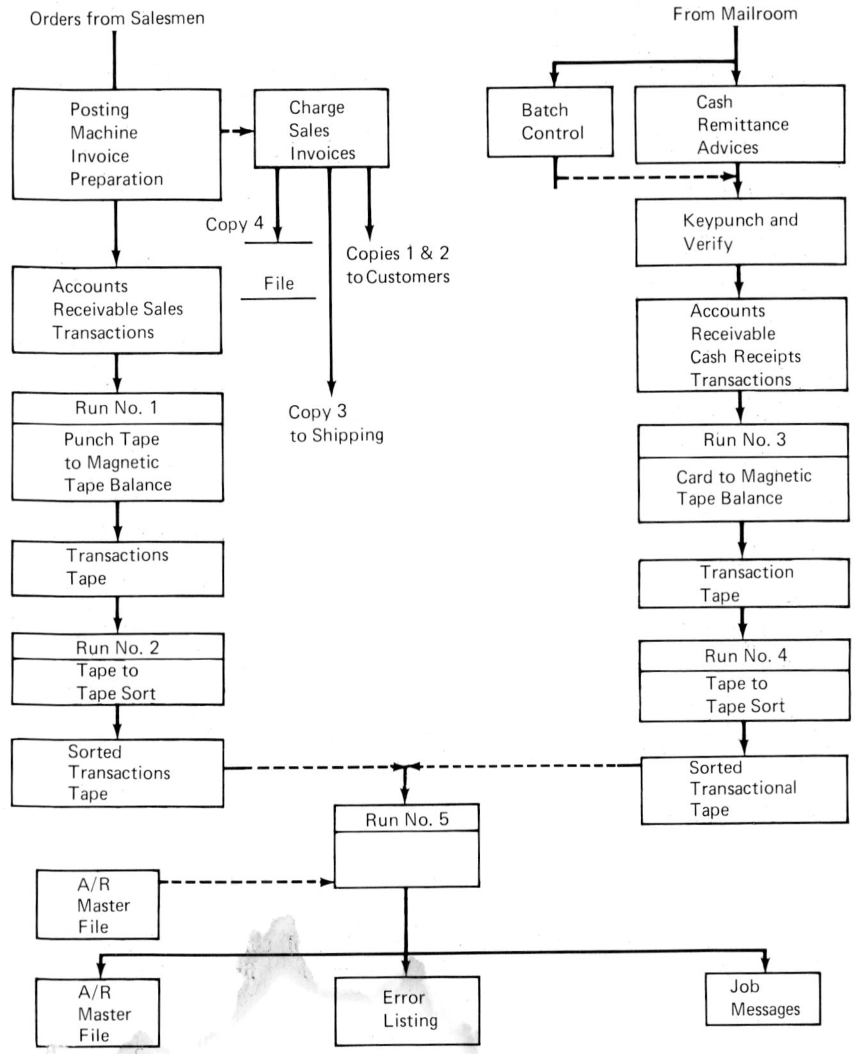

president of the company, uses one of the offices as a central office and visits the other offices periodically for supervision and internal auditing purposes. Jordan is concerned about his employees' honesty. He came to your office in December 19X5 and stated, "I want to engage you to install a system to prohibit employees from embezzling cash." He also stated, "Until I went into business for myself, I worked for a nationwide loan company with five hundred offices, and I'm familiar with that company's system of accounting and internal control. I want to describe that system so you can install it for me because it will absolutely prevent fraud."

Required:

a. How would you advise Jordan about using a large company's system of accounting and internal control for his small firm?

b. How would you respond to Jordan's conviction that the new system will prevent embezzlement?

c. Assume that in addition to undertaking the systems engagement in 19X6, you agreed to examine Jordan Finance Company's financial statements for the year ended December 31, 19X5. No scope limitations have been imposed.

1. How would you determine the scope necessary to complete your examination?
2. Would you be responsible for discovering fraud in this examination? Discuss.

(CPA exam adapted)

5. The independent auditor must evaluate a client's system of internal control to determine the extent to which various auditing procedures must be employed. A client who uses a computer should give the CPA a flowchart of the information-processing system so the CPA can evaluate the system's control features. Page 315 presents a simplified, but incomplete flowchart. Unfortunately the client had only partially completed the flowchart when it was requested by you.

Required:

a. Complete the flowchart.

b. Describe each item in the flowchart, and explain how the data are processed. Your description should be in the following order:

1. "Orders from Salesmen" to "Run No. 5."
2. "From Mailroom" to "Run No. 5."
3. "Run No. 5" through the remainder of the chart.

c. Name each of the following flowchart symbols and describe what each represents.

Flowchart Symbols

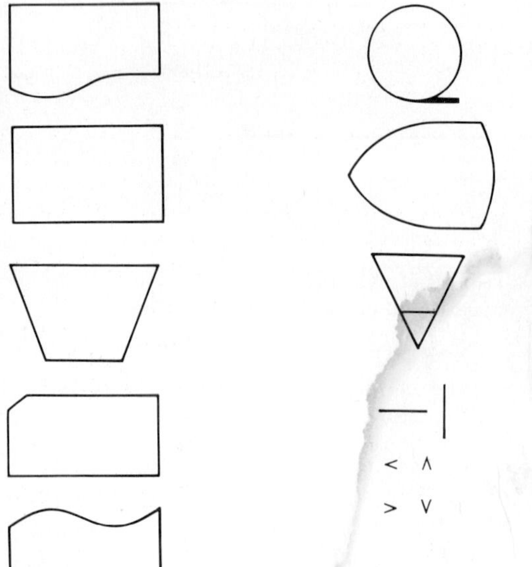

6. A company's system of internal control (which consists of accounting and administrative controls) is strengthened by including specific procedures. For example, the system of internal control may have a voucher system that provides for all invoices to be checked for accuracy, approved for propriety, and recorded before being paid. The system thus reduces the likelihood that an invoice will be mislaid or the discount lost, and it helps prevent improper or unauthorized disbursements.

Required:

Explain the purposes or functions of each of the following procedures or techniques that may be included in a system of internal control, and how each purpose or function may strengthen accounting and administrative internal control.

a. Fidelity bonding of employees.

b. Budgeting of capital expenditures.

c. Listing of mail remittances by the mail department when the mail is opened.

d. Maintaining a plant ledger for fixed assets.

(CPA exam adapted)

7. The Kowal Manufacturing Company employs about fifty production workers and uses the following payroll procedures:

The factory foreman interviews applicants and then either hires or rejects them. If the applicant is hired, he or she prepares a W-4 form (Employee's Withholding Exemption Certificate) and gives it to the foreman. The foreman writes the new employee's hourly rate of pay in the corner of the W-4 form and then gives the form to a payroll clerk as notice that the worker has been employed. The foreman then verbally advises the payroll department of any rate adjustments.

Blank time cards are kept in a box near the entrance to the factory. Each worker takes a time card on Monday morning, fills in his or her name, and notes in pencil on the time card his or her daily arrival and departure times. At the end of the week the workers drop the time cards in a box near the door to the factory.

The completed time cards are taken from the box on Monday morning by a payroll clerk. Two payroll clerks divide the cards alphabetically between them, one taking the A to L section of the payroll and the other taking the M to Z section. Each clerk is fully responsible for his or her section of the payroll. He or she computes the gross pay, deductions, and net pay; posts the details to the employee's earnings records; and prepares and numbers the payroll checks. Employees are automatically removed from the payroll when they fail to turn in a time card.

The payroll checks are manually signed by the chief accountant and given to the foreman. The foreman distributes the checks to the workers in the factory and arranges for the delivery of the checks to those workers who are absent. The payroll bank account is reconciled by the chief accountant who also prepares the various quarterly and annual payroll tax reports.

Required:

Suggest ways of improving the Kowal Manufacturing Company's system of internal control for the factory hiring practices and payroll procedures.

(CPA exam adapted)

8. Orange Corp., a high technology company, is concerned that some parts have been ordered and not used quickly enough to avoid obsolescence. The auditor observed the following procedures for recording raw materials and transferring to work-in-process:
   - Upon receipt of raw materials by stores, the storekeeper writes the part number and quantities on a stock-in report and sends a copy to accounting.
   - Accounting matches the stock-in report with receiving reports and posts the perpetual inventory records, using standard costs.
   - Manufacturing personnel prepare the raw materials requisitions, which show part number and quantity. The supervisor of manufacturing, who is also responsible for job scheduling, approves them. A copy of the requisition is sent to accounting.
   - Accounting reviews the requisitions for completeness and each month transfers the cost from raw materials inventory to work-in-process.

   Required:

   a. Prepare a flowchart describing the current process in the accounting department.
   Use only the following symbols:

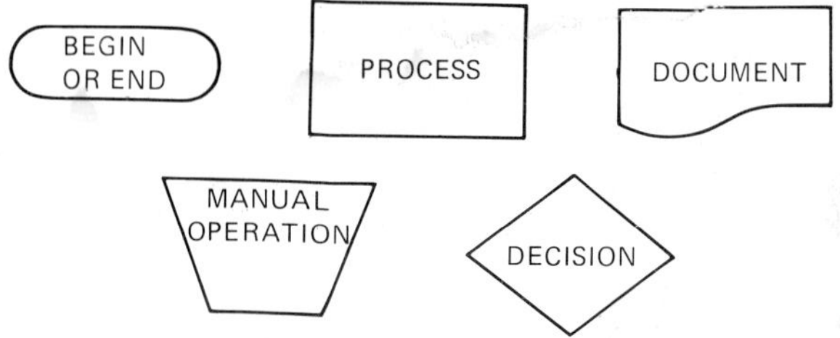

   b. Indicate how the data available should be used to provide monthly reports to management on projected obsolescence.

(CPA exam adapted)

9. **Multiple-Choice: Concepts of Internal Control**
   Select the one answer that best completes the statement or answers the question.

9.1 The concept of internal accounting control that recognizes that the cost of internal control should not exceed the benefits is known as
- **a.** Reasonable assurance.
- **b.** Management responsibility.
- **c.** Limited liability.
- **d.** Management by exception.

(CPA exam adapted)

9.2 Fidelity bonds protect a company from embezzlement losses and also
- **a.** Protect employees who make unintentional errors from possible monetary damages resulting from such errors.
- **b.** Allow the company to substitute the fidelity bonds for various parts of internal accounting control.
- **c.** Reduce the company's need for expensive business interruption insurance.
- **d.** Minimize the possibility of placing persons with dubious records in positions of trust.

(CPA exam adapted)

9.3 Internal accounting control comprises the plan of organization and the procedures and records concerned with the safeguarding of assets and the
- **a.** Decision processes of management.
- **b.** Reliability of financial records.
- **c.** Authorization of transactions.
- **d.** Achievement of administrative objectives.

(CPA exam adapted)

9.4 A secondary objective of the auditor's study and evaluation of internal control is to
- **a.** Suggest improvements in internal control.
- **b.** Provide a basis for relying on the internal accounting control system.
- **c.** Ensure that the records and documents have been maintained in accordance with the company's policies and procedures.
- **d.** Determine the extent of the auditing tests.

(CPA exam adapted)

9.5 The segment of an auditor's internal control work that focuses directly on the purpose of preventing or detecting material errors or irregularities in financial statements is known as
- **a.** Compliance with the existing internal control system.

b. Review of the existing internal control system.
c. Evaluation of the existing internal control system.
d. Study of the existing internal control system.

(CPA exam adapted)

9.6 In general, a material internal control weakness may be defined as a condition in which material errors or irregularities would ordinarily not be detected within a timely period by
a. An auditor during the normal study and evaluation of the internal control system.
b. A controller when reconciling accounts in the general ledger.
c. Employees in the normal course of performing their assigned functions.
d. The chief financial officer when reviewing interim financial statements.

(CPA exam adapted)

9.7 A management information system is designed to ensure that management has the information it needs to carry out its functions, by means of
a. Data gathering, analysis, and reporting.
b. A computerized information retrieval and decision-making system.
c. Statistical and analytical review functions.
d. Production budgeting and sales forecasting.

(CPA exam adapted)

9.8 The auditor's review of the client's system of internal control is documented in order to substantiate
a. Conformity of the accounting records with generally accepted accounting principles.
b. Representation of adherence to requirements of management.
c. Representation of compliance with generally accepted auditing standards.
d. The fairness of the financial statement presentation.

(CPA exam adapted)

9.9 Which of the following is essential to determine whether the necessary internal control procedures were prescribed and are being followed?
a. Developing questionnaires and checklists.
b. Studying and evaluating administrative control policies.
c. Reviewing the system and testing compliance.
d. Observing employees and making inquiries.

(CPA exam adapted)

9.10 The primary purpose of the auditor's study and evaluation of internal control is to
a. Determine whether procedures and records concerned with safeguarding assets are reliable.
b. Suggest improvements in internal control.
c. Determine the nature, extent, and timing of audit tests to be applied.
d. Express an opinion.

(CPA exam adapted)

9.11 After studying and evaluating a client's internal control system, an auditor has concluded that the system is well designed and is functioning as it should. Under these circumstances the auditor would most likely
a. Cease to perform further substantive tests.
b. Not increase the extent of predetermined substantive tests.
c. Increase the extent of anticipated analytical review procedures.
d. Perform all compliance tests to the extent outlined in the preplanned audit program.

(CPA exam adapted)

9.12 The auditor who becomes aware of a material weakness in internal accounting controls is required to communicate this to the
a. Audit committee and board of directors.
b. Senior management and board of directors.
c. Board of directors and internal auditors.
d. Internal auditors and senior management.

(CPA exam adapted)

9.13 Which of the following would be inappropriate during a preliminary evaluation of the system of internal control?
a. Completion of an internal control questionnaire.
b. Use of attribute sampling.
c. Oral inquiries.
d. Review of an accounting manual prepared by the client.

(CPA exam adapted)

9.14 A CPA's study and evaluation of the internal accounting control system in an audit
a. Is generally more limited than that made in connection with an engagement to express an opinion on the internal accounting control system.

b. Is generally more extensive than that made in connection with an engagement to express an opinion on the internal accounting control system.
c. Is generally identical to that made in connection with an engagement to express an opinion on the internal accounting control system.
d. Will generally result in the CPA's expressing an opinion on the internal accounting control system.

(CPA exam adapted)

9.15 A conceptually logical approach to the auditor's evaluation of accounting controls consists of the following four steps:

I. Determine the accounting control procedures that should prevent or detect errors and irregularities.
II. Evaluate any weakness to determine its effect on the nature, timing, or extent of auditing procedures to be applied and suggestions to be made to the client.
III. Determine whether the necessary procedures have been prescribed and are being followed satisfactorily.
IV. Consider the possible types of errors and irregularities.

What should be the order of these four steps?

a. I, II, III, IV.
b. I, III, IV, II.
c. III, IV, I, II.
d. IV, I, III, II.

(CPA exam adapted)

9.16 Internal control is a responsibility of management, and effective control is based on the concept of charge and discharge of responsibility and duty. Which of the following is one of the overriding principles of internal control?

a. Responsibility for accounting and financial duties should be assigned to one responsible officer.
b. Responsibility for the performance of each duty must be fixed.
c. Responsibility for the accounting duties must be borne by the company's audit committee.
d. Responsibility for accounting activities and duties must be assigned only to bonded employees.

(CPA exam adapted)

9.17 Effective internal control in a small company without enough employees to permit the proper division of responsibilities can best be enhanced by

a. Employing temporary personnel to help separate duties.
b. Direct participation by the owner of the business in the recordkeeping activities of the business.
c. Engaging a CPA to perform monthly "write-up" work.
d. Delegating full, clear-cut responsibility to each employee for his or her duties.

(CPA exam adapted)

9.18 A well-designed internal control questionnaire should

a. Elicit "yes" or "no" responses rather than narrative responses.
b. Be a sufficient source of data to evaluate internal controls.
c. Identify internal control system strengths and weaknesses.
d. Be organized by department.
e. Be independent of the audit's objectives.

(CPA exam adapted)

9.19 Which of the following is an administrative control?

a. Authorizing credit terms.
b. Execution of transactions.
c. Recording original data.
d. Accountability over source data.

(CPA exam adapted)

9.20 Assuming an excellent system of internal control, which of the following audit procedures would be least likely to be performed?

a. Physical inspection of a sample of inventory.
b. Search for unrecorded cash receipts.
c. Obtain a client representation letter.
d. Confirmation of accounts receivable.

(CPA exam adapted)

9.21 Which of the following would be least likely to be considered an objective of an internal control system?

a. Checking the accuracy and reliability of accounting data.
b. Detecting management fraud.
c. Encouraging adherence to managerial policies.
d. Safeguarding assets.

(CPA exam adapted)

9.22 The following are steps in the audit process:

I. Prepare a flowchart.
II. Gather exhibits of all documents.

III. Interview personnel.
The most logical sequence of steps is
a. I, II, III.
b. I, III, II.
c. III, II, I.
d. II, I, III.
(CPA exam adapted)

9.23 The auditor observes the clients' employees during the review of the internal control system in order to
a. Prepare a flowchart.
b. Update information contained in the organization and procedure manuals.
c. Corroborate the information obtained during the initial review of the system.
d. Determine the extent of compliance with quality control standards.
(CPA exam adapted)

9.24 The Foreign Corrupt Practices Act requires that
a. Auditors engaged to examine the financial statements of publicly held companies report all illegal payments to the SEC.
b. Publicly held companies establish independent audit committees to monitor the effectiveness of their internal control system.
c. U.S. firms doing business abroad report to the Justice Department any large payments to that country's citizens.
d. Publicly held companies devise and maintain an adequate internal accounting control system.
(CPA exam adapted)

9.25 Which of the following would be least likely to suggest to an auditor that the client's management may have overridden the internal control system?
a. Differences are always disclosed on a computer exception report.
b. Management does not correct internal control weaknesses that it knows about.
c. There have been two new controllers this year.
d. There are numerous delays in preparing timely financial reports.
(CPA exam adapted)

10. Multiple-Choice: Segregation of Duties

Select the one answer that best completes the statement or answers the question.

10.1 Internal control over cash receipts is weakened when an employee who receives customer mail receipts also
a. Prepares initial cash receipts records.
b. Records credits to individual accounts receivable.
c. Prepares bank deposit slips for all mail receipts.
d. Maintains a petty cash fund.
(CPA exam adapted)

10.2 For internal control purposes, which of the following individuals should be responsible for distributing payroll checks?
a. Bookkeeper.
b. Payroll clerk.
c. Cashier.
d. Receptionist.
(CPA exam adapted)

10.3 Proper segregation of functional responsibilities calls for the separation of
a. Authorization, approval, and execution.
b. Authorization, execution, and payment.
c. Receiving, shipping, and custody.
d. Authorization, recording, and custody.
(CPA exam adapted)

10.4 Effective internal control requires organizational independence of departments. Organizational independence would be impaired in which of the following situations?
a. The internal auditors report to the audit committee of the board of directors.
b. The controller reports to the vice-president of production.
c. The payroll accounting department reports to the chief accountant.
d. The cashier reports to the treasurer.
(CPA exam adapted)

10.5 One of the auditor's objectives in observing the actual distribution of payroll checks is to determine that every name on the payroll is that of a bona fide employee. The payroll observation is an auditing procedure that is generally performed for which of the following reasons?
a. The professional standards require the auditor to perform the payroll observation.
b. The various phases of payroll work are not sufficiently segregated for effective internal accounting control.
c. The independent auditor uses personal judgment and decides to observe the payroll distribution on a particular audit.

d. The professional standards are interpreted to mean that payroll observation is expected on an audit unless circumstances dictate otherwise.

(CPA exam adapted)

10.6 There can be effective internal control over purchases in a well-planned organizational structure with a separate purchasing department that
- **a.** Can prepare payment vouchers based on the information on a vendor's invoice.
- **b.** Is responsible for reviewing the purchase orders issued by user departments.
- **c.** Is authorized to make purchases of requisitioned materials and services.
- **d.** Has a direct reporting responsibility to the organization's controller.

(CPA exam adapted)

10.7 Which of the following individuals is the most appropriate to be assigned the responsibility of distributing envelopes that include employee payroll checks?
- **a.** The company paymaster.
- **b.** A member of the accounting department.
- **c.** The internal auditor.
- **d.** A representative of the bank where the company payroll account is maintained.

(CPA exam adapted)

10.8 Which of the following sets of duties would ordinarily be considered incompatible with good internal control?
- **a.** Preparation of monthly statements to customers and maintenance of the accounts receivable subsidiary ledger.
- **b.** Posting to the general ledger and approval of additions and terminations relating to the payroll.
- **c.** Custody of unmailed signed checks and maintenance of expense subsidiary ledgers.
- **d.** Collection of receipts on account and maintaining accounts receivable records.

(CPA exam adapted)

10.9 Which of the following is not a universal rule for keeping strong internal control over cash?
- **a.** Separating cash handling and record keeping.
- **b.** Decentralizing the receipt of cash as much as possible.
- **c.** Depositing each day's cash receipts by the end of the day.
- **d.** Having bank reconciliations performed by employees independent with respect to handling cash.

(CPA exam adapted)

10.10 For effective internal control, billing should be done by the
- **a.** Accounting department.
- **b.** Sales department.
- **c.** Shipping department.
- **d.** Credit and collection department.

(CPA exam adapted)

11. Multiple-Choice: Flowcharting

Select the one answer that best completes the statement or answers the question.

11.1 The normal sequence of documents and operations on a well-prepared systems flowchart is
- **a.** Top to bottom and left to right.
- **b.** Bottom to top and left to right.
- **c.** Top to bottom and right to left.
- **d.** Bottom to top and right to left.

(CPA exam adapted)

11.2 During which phase of an audit examination is the preparation of flowcharts most appropriate?
- **a.** Review of the internal accounting control system.
- **b.** Tests of compliance with internal accounting control procedures.
- **c.** Evaluation of the internal administrative control system.
- **d.** Analytical review of operations.

(CPA exam adapted)

11.3 One reason that an auditor uses a flowchart is to help
- **a.** Evaluate a series of sequential processes.
- **b.** Study the system of responsibility accounting.
- **c.** Carry out important, required, dual-purpose tests.
- **d.** Understand a client's organizational structure.

(CPA exam adapted)

11.4 The program flowcharting symbol for a decision is a
- **a.** Triangle.
- **b.** Circle.
- **c.** Rectangle.
- **d.** Diamond.

(CPA exam adapted)

11.5 Examining the following flowchart of the order-processing cycle shows that this system may result in

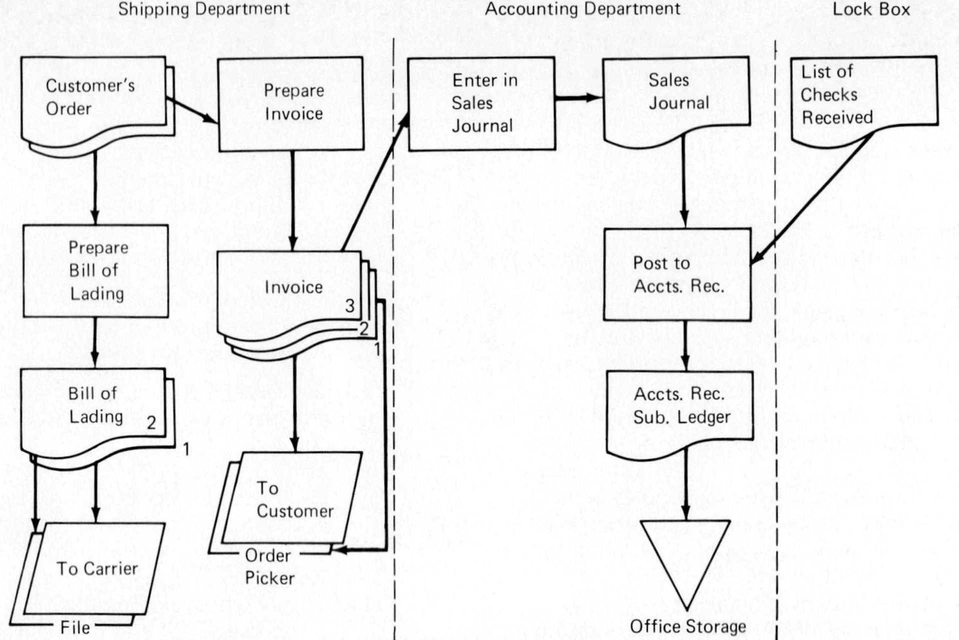

a. Loss of float in handling cash receipts.
b. Errors on invoices.
c. Cash loss.
d. Defalcation in shipping.
e. Merchandise stockouts.

(CPA exam adapted)

CASES FOR DISCUSSION

1. What are the internal control risks created by the following practices?
   a. Bank statements, not yet reconciled, are often left open on desks while the individuals responsible for preparing the reconciliations are away from their desks.
   b. The employee who is entrusted with the one set of keys to the safety deposit box containing marketable securities leaves those keys in the top drawer of his desk.
   c. One of the two individuals required to sign all checks regularly signs blank checks in order to make disbursements more easily.
   d. The requisition clerk for inventory and supplies encourages employees to take whatever they need and to fill out their own requisition slip at the counter.
   e. As cash disbursements are made, the cashier numbers the checks as they are issued, discards voided checks, and simply reuses the check number of any checks that have been voided.
   f. The bookkeeper opens the mail, records cash receipts, and then forwards them to the cashier for deposit in the bank.
   g. Banks regularly cash checks that are made out to Cash.
   h. A company that is initiating its initial lease arrangement has no prescribed procedures for such a transaction. Because the lease involves the use of a word processor on a trial basis, the administrative director merely arranges for the machine's delivery, with a verbal authorization, and informs the disbursement clerk that lease payments will be made out of petty cash over this trial period, so to increase the petty cash balance.
   i. Those authorizing purchase orders have access to blank receiving reports and uncanceled historical documentation of purchases.
   j. Check preparers frequently make mistakes, erase them, and then retype the correct information on the face of the check.
2. Your client has several material weaknesses in internal accounting control. This year, for the first time, your client intends to issue interim financial state-

ments but does not want you to perform a limited review. Does this situation suggest any reporting responsibilities? Assuming that you do not alter your disclosures from earlier periods, what would be the ramifications of your decision? In what sense is your analysis consistent with generally accepted auditing standards?

3. Robert K. Mautz and Hussein A. Sharaf, in *The Philosophy of Auditing,*[12] refer to the people element of control systems:

> To borrow a phrase, "internal control is people." A system of internal control is made up of people and procedures, procedures in which people are expected to perform and report in a normal fashion. But unknown to the reviewer, the pressures which motivate the people in the "system" may change sufficiently that they cease to act in an expected fashion, whereupon the internal control procedure loses its effectiveness.
>
> There are many events and relationships which can work to offset the most effective internal control measures and which at the same time would be neither apparent to nor necessarily discoverable by the independent auditor that acceptance of responsibility for the review of internal control is hazardous at best.

In what sense does the auditor address this "people" problem in both the performance of an audit engagement and the reporting process? Regarding the problems that Mautz and Sharaf described, what do you believe is the appropriate role for internal control evaluations and the reliance on them?

4. Most embezzlement losses are due to breakdowns in the control systems prescribed, not to inefficiency of the system. Most large defalcations are not the work of master minds—they are due to the failure of an employee or auditor to carry out a simple assignment, usually because of an inclination of "let George do it." And right here is where the dishonest employee enters the picture with his offer to take over a part of a fellow worker's duties.[13]

Do you agree? How should a CPA evaluate this sort of risk exposure? What approach to evaluation have the behavioral sciences suggested?

5. The legal profession seems to have supported CPAs' limited responsibility for finding weaknesses and reporting them to management, rather than insisting that such weaknesses be corrected. For example, in an English case,[14] a control problem with short-term receivables was discovered and reported to management. No corrective action was taken, and shortly thereafter, a salesman took advantage of the problem and misappropriated some cash. The auditor was sued for not discovering and reporting on the defalcation but was found not guilty because he had earlier informed his client of the weakness. Similarly, in an American case,[15] a secretary-treasurer embezzled from a company that had not adopted earlier changes to controls that the auditor had recommended, and again the auditor was not held responsible. Do you agree with these decisions? Consider the investors' perspective in your analysis.

[12] Sarasota: American Accounting Association, 1961, p. 145.

[13] Herbert N. Shisler, "Fraud Can Take Place in a Well-Designed System If Working Rules Are Not Followed," *Journal of Accountancy,* February 1953, p. 176.

[14] In re S. P. Catterson & Sons, Ltd., 81 Acct. L. R., 62 (Ch. 1937).

[15] *Bolin, Quinn & Ivy* v. *Lewis Supply Co.,* Chancery Court, Shelby County, Tenn. No. 43687 R. D. (May 27, 1940).

10

Electronic Data Processing

Two managers are discussing some recent findings regarding a client's electronic data-processing (EDP) operation for payroll.

Wayne. I just don't understand how we missed this for so long.

Gere. Well, if you think about it, your team was auditing around the EDP system instead of through it.

Wayne. We recomputed the payroll calculations and tied them to recorded payroll. We checked out the hours worked and pay rate to source documents. The real reason we didn't find the problem was that whoever was taking the funds wasn't greedy and was very clever.

Gere. All that was needed was a minor change to the program. The formula used to calculate the taxes withheld from payroll was set to round up on a random sample of paychecks, and that rounding was siphoned off into a separate bank account. It's been done by others; the twist here was the randomized rounding. Although our calculations were sometimes off by almost a penny, the differences weren't consistent. We had no suspicions whatsoever.

Wayne. Didn't we do a parallel simulation once, using our own EDP program and compare the results with the client's program? Why didn't we find the problem then?

Gere. Remember, we told the client beforehand that we'd be using the EDP system to generate some data for comparison with our program. So it looks as though the program we tested wasn't the one in regular use. At a minimum, the "rounding" routine was circumvented in our runs. That's a constant problem with our "snapshot" approach to testing EDP.

Wayne. Tell me again how we finally did find the problem.

Gere. It was really a fluke. The client has several dormant bank accounts with balances that have been stable for years. We've suggested over and over that they be closed. But this year, instead of just focusing on year-end balances, one of our new staff auditors got creative. She used generalized audit software to count the number of debits and credits booked to the various bank accounts. To her surprise, several transactions had passed through an account number that had been thought to be dormant. By investigating the timing of the entries, it became clear that they were tied to payroll. Because of the client's big payroll, a lot of money passed through the account.

Wayne. As I understand it, you got a copy of the code for the current program, and the rounding subroutine has been identified. Right?

Gere. Yes, but we don't know who did it. Somehow our surprise access to the code was leaked, and rumors are flying. Probably no one will touch the bank account again.

Wayne. You must have *some* suspects?

Gere. We figure it's one of six employees. Whichever one it is has put away a bundle. Surely, they can't be very happy working a forty-hour week at their current pay, with all that money stashed. All we should have to do is sit back and see which one of the six quits!

Wayne. That seems to be a pretty crude way of finding the guilty party.

Gere. True, but at least we've stopped the problem; the culprit isn't stealing any more money. At least, not from that account.

Wayne. But what if this simple "rounding" subroutine has been used elsewhere? How can we know that the EDP operations are in control?

Gere. We're going to have to audit through the computer and time our "snapshots" sporadically, to ensure decent coverage. I've got some ideas. . . .

This introductory case demonstrates how employees can use EDP to commit frauds more easily, in a hard-to-detect style. Merely checking inputs and tying them to outputs, particularly at only a single point in time, does not offer very good audit evidence in an EDP environment. When programs are a "black box," the siphoning, misstatement, and misclassification of transactions can happen with little, if any, chance of detection. The large number of transactions processed means that very minor distortions of individual entries can amass large rewards for the defrauder. The smaller the distortion is, the less likely it will be discovered. For example, what is the likelihood of an employee's complaining about, or even noticing, an extra penny of taxes being withheld?

Periodic testing of continuous processing systems has very real limitations, especially if the periodic test is preannounced. The case bears out the potential payback to innovative testing approaches and the special capabilities of the auditor when the computer is applied as an auditing tool.

The case contains clues of poor control. In addition to the dormant bank accounts being kept open, the fact that six individuals had an opportunity to perpetrate the defalcation suggests poor segregation of duties and restriction of access to both EDP programs and operations. Throughout this chapter, the case will serve as a reminder of why particular EDP controls are useful, why auditing through the computer is essential, and why generalized audit software can be such an effective audit tool.

The Growth of EDP and Its Implications

As the number of microcomputers continues to grow, both control over the data base and the results of computer literacy will become critical issues. Practitioners have told stories of their client calling them for a meeting concerning the end-of-year trial balance, only to observe that the president and controller were holding two different sets of numbers. Invariably, the controller will have made adjustments on a microcomputer and have forgotten to update the central data base, stored on the mainframe or major computer facility of the entity. Such control problems must be recognized as possibilities in a microcomputer environment, and actions must be taken to control the integrity and completeness of the mainframe and key accounting records of the operations. The second critical issue relates to the consequence of computer literacy.

Historically, one of the controls over EDP has been a lack of EDP knowledge by most employees. As the home use of computers increases, however, so does EDP literacy, leading to a key implication: controls must be designed that can be effective even in the presence of knowledgeable employees and other third parties. Recent media coverage has emphasized that employee crime involving computers is a growing problem, ranging from disgruntled employees making up for "passed over" promotions to sabotage (and even related blackmailing) of EDP systems. Ironically, the likelihood of prosecution is inversely proportional to the amount of money involved, due to management's embarrassment at such losses, which means that the scope of computer crime is very difficult to quantify. Computer fraud specialists emphasize that for controls to be effective, secrecy is important—no single programmer or security officer should know all of the security.[1]

The growth in electronic data processing (EDP) systems over the past two decades has been tremendous. In 1970, the number of data communications terminals installed was less than 250,000, yet by 1975, a million were installed,[2] and by 1980, three million. It has been estimated that by 1990, personal computers will be selling at a rate of 11.5 million units annually.[3] Today, it is difficult to conceive of auditing any financial system which does not use a computer; even meter readers and collection agents have hand-held computers to update data bases! While in the 1960's and 1970's, users were commonly separated from the processing activity, the 1980's and 1990's let the users interact with their data. User languages on dispersed micro- and mini-computers have led to distributed systems which often preclude the need for a centralized EDP facility. Instead, a loose networking of local to regional and national systems has evolved, whereby only essential data is processed and filtered upward in the organization. As the equipment has gotten smaller, it has also become easier to gain access to EDP for the purpose of misappropriating assets and more difficult to establish effective controls.

A computer processing department, in contrast to a manual processing system, will alter both the types of errors expected and their magnitude. The random errors expected in manual systems are virtually eliminated in an EDP system. However, a programming error will systematically generate incorrect results for all like transactions that are processed ***[SAS 48, Section 321].*** The potential for errors and irregularities that remain undetected for long periods of time stems from

- permitting unauthorized access.
- the absence of visible evidence that the system, program, or data file has been accessed.
- the decreased involvement of people who might be capable of spotting problems.

Risks that are peculiar to a computerized environment stem from (1) inadequate procedures for controlling program or system changes; (2) undetected hardware or software malfunctions; (3) loss or contamination of data during transmittal; (4) unauthorized access to computer facilities, data files, and programs; and (5) inadequate participation by users, particularly in reviewing output for reasonableness and in maintaining responsibility for authorizations. The so-called audit or account-

[1] Erik Larson, "Crook's Tool: Computers Turn Out to Be Valuable Aid in Employee Crime," *The Wall Street Journal*, January 14, 1985, pp. 1, 8.

[2] William E. Perry and Jerry Fitzgerald, "Designing for Auditability," *Datamation*, August, 1977, pp. 46–49.

[3] This estimate by Dataquest, Inc. is reported by John Naisbitt, *Megatrends* (New York: Warner Books, Inc., 1984), p. 18.

ing trail for transactions, which is intended to document the trail from original transaction to account balances, may only exist in machine-readable form or for such temporary spans of time that its effective use in auditing is precluded. The relative invisibility of information without the use of a computer can be compared with a set of books in a foreign language having to be interpreted before the "represented facts" are visible. In the latter case, the interpreter's objectivity and qualifications would have to be verified before the set of books (translated) could be deemed to be reliable for auditing purposes. Similarly, the auditor must determine that the computer's interpretation of the data files and processing activities are reasonably reliable, in order to use the EDP output. Computers are able to initiate and/or execute transactions automatically. Obviously, the auditor must gain assurance that the EDP system has a sufficient number of controls within application programs to ensure that initiation and execution of transactions are consistent with management's authorizations.

A positive aspect of an EDP system is the capability that management has to exercise greater supervision over operations through the use of analytical tools. Similarly, the auditor is able to apply computer auditing tools that can result in great gains in audit efficiency, as well as audit coverage. Moreover, EDP systems have built-in software and hardware controls that offer advantages over a manual information system.

Organizational Controls

The two bywords of control in an EDP environment are *documentation* and the effective *segregation of duties.* The type of documentation and division of responsibilities that is required is highly dependent on the particular type of EDP system. Exhibit 10-1 describes the variety of EDP environments that an auditor is likely to encounter. Many environments will have a combination of EDP systems; for example, it is common to have real-time systems augmented by batch processing of data for which turnaround does not need to be immediate.

When using a service center, the party(ies) authorizing transactions for the center to process should not be those who are responsible for the user controls. User controls include the comparison of documents submitted to the center with the documents processed and the review of the overall reasonableness of the center's output. Documentation would need to include a contractual agreement with the center, covering

- data ownership.
- data confidentiality.

EXHIBIT 10-1
Major Types of EDP Environments

Service Center	Minicomputer Environment	Batch Systems	Distributed Systems	On-Line and Real-Time Systems	Data Base Systems
Operation external to business does EDP. Third-party reviews of standard packages and systems are typically performed by an auditor engaged by the service center and are made available to user's auditor.	Small computer located in the user department with little physical security. Few staff that have limited EDP expertise operate the minicomputer from on-line terminals, using application systems supplied by manufacturers or software stores.	Information is put into machine readable form, stored, and "batched" together for periodic processing (e.g., daily, weekly, or monthly batching, depending on user's turnaround needs).	Many user sites have a computer and storage devices, can communicate with other computers in the network, and may or may not link to a major host computer.	Equipment and devices are under the control of the computer's central processing unit, with direct communication links. Users have answers immediately displayed at the terminal.	Data are integrated into one "generalized" system that can be accessed by numerous application programs (as distinct from maintaining discrete files that often hold redundant information).

- program access, should the service center terminate its operations or relocate.
- program ownership.
- liability of each party for errors or delays in processing, loss of records, or discontinuance of service center operations.
- backup provisions of the service center.
- movement of data and reports between the entity and its service center.
- insurance coverage maintained by the service center.
- fidelity bond coverage of the service center's employees.
- provisions for the termination of services.
- the privilege of independent or internal auditors to have access to the service center's files and programs.

The documentation should also include a third-party auditor's report on the service center or a report on the center's review by the entity's auditor.

In all computer environments, particularly a minicomputer setting, non-EDP personnel should authorize the transactions, and the EDP personnel should not have access to assets. If they have indirect access, for example, through processing checks, there should be a postreview technique and a third-party control of the critical documents, like blank checks. Finally, the users should reconcile to computer-generated statistics, perform reasonableness checks, and review exception reports and other output. EDP should be documented in detail, establishing an audit trail and program control.

If a batch system has an EDP facility, the entity should also segregate the systems analysts, application programmers, computer operations, file librarian, and *data (input/output) control group*. Such a segregation is based on the concept that if the systems analysts and application programmers were permitted to operate the computer, many of the designed software controls could be circumvented. Similarly, if the operators had access to program documentation, they might be able to alter the processing logic. Finally, not giving the programmers and systems analysts access to data files prevents their tampering with files that might circumvent the software controls. The independent control group should concentrate on maintaining control totals over data entry, processing, and output to users. Documentation will show how batches are controlled and balanced, the control of rejected data, and the programmed controls of input.

Both a distributed system and an on-line and real-time system have segregation and documentation problems shared by minicomputer and batch systems. The adequacy of control procedures over remote processing sites is critical. Responsibility for systems development and program changes must be separated from user groups, and centrally controlled real-time systems require special attention to the accuracy of data transmission and the capability of restoring master files, should the system break down. Access to on-line master files must be effectively restricted, and the prevention of any processing of incomplete or inaccurate data must be the foremost consideration in the design of system controls.

A data base system achieves the effective segregation of duties by establishing the position of the *data base administrator (DBA)*, who defines, organizes, protects, and controls data but does not initiate transactions or operate the computer. In fact, the DBA should not have unsupervised access to the computer. The data base management system (DBMS) librarian documents what programs can access what data and who the authorized users of various programs are.

Beyond the segregation of duties that is tailored to the diverse computer environments cited in Exhibit 10-1, the general principles relevant to the segregation of EDP-related duties in all environments are presented in Exhibit 10-2. *Organizational controls* determine the EDP system's overall control environment. The organizational plan must prohibit EDP from initiating or authorizing transactions or correcting, without authorization, errors that originate outside of EDP. Moreover, there must be procedures for documentation, review, tests, implementation, maintenance, and approval of both manual and EDP systems, particularly changes to systems and programs. Both the supervision and the segregation of duties within EDP, as well as between EDP and the various users of EDP, must be adequate. To limit or control access to equipment,

EXHIBIT 10-2

Checklist of Practices Segregating EDP-related Duties

Principle	Is this principle applied in practice?		
	Yes	No	Comments
1. Data processing should be prohibited from initiating general ledger or subsidiary ledger entries.			
2. The distinction between the custody of data and the accountability for the handling and processing of data should be retained.			
3. Technical people should have restricted access to data files and the computer.			
4. Knowledge of applications, programming, and documentation should be restricted; each person should know only what is required to fulfill his or her job responsibilities.			
5. Live data should not be used in testing.			
6. Personnel involved in sensitive applications should be rotated periodically.			
7. Vacations should be required.			

some entities allow no one except the operator to be in the computer room while a program is being run; this is referred to as the requirement of *closed-shop operations.*

The organizational controls over EDP should include adequate documentation of systems development. Evidence that the users' input has been considered and that the auditors reviewed the adequacy of both controls and the available audit trail should be formally documented. Written specifications approved by management should be formalized as a standard against which existing systems can be evaluated. Exhibit 10-3 outlines the typical phases in system development, the related risks during each phase, and the general controls for these risks. *General control procedures* are those that are designed to contribute to the achievement of *specific control objectives* and tend to be interdependent with specific control procedures. For example, general control over the access to and changing of computer programs determines whether detailed programmed control procedures can be relied on ***[SAS 48, Section 321].***

EXHIBIT 10-3

Typical Phases in System Development, Related Risks, and Controls

Phase	Risks and Controls
Design Phase • Project definition, users' requirements, and uses for system. • System analysis and design: Overall description of system. • Detailed design and programming. • System testing: Check accuracy, completeness, and fulfillment of users' needs.	**Risks** – Will not meet users' needs. – System will be inefficient. – Controls will be inadequate. – Cost overruns will occur. – Errors will exist in system. – Security will be inadequate. **Controls** * Involve auditor, users, design analysts, and EDP personnel in the design phase, with one project leader attuned to each group's concerns. * Plan communication links; personnel, cost, and time demands; testing requirements; and documentation needs.
Conversion and Operation Phase • Place system into operation. • Maintain operations. • Control program changes.	**Risks** – Processing problems will threaten integrity of data base. – EDP will be used inefficiently. – Communications with users will be inadequate. – Security will be inadequate. **Controls** * Have auditor, users, EDP personnel, and project leader review conversion, communicate to top management, and document process and future controls. * Auditor and users should periodically review system regarding specified requirements, stressing the adequacy of documentation.
Postimplementation Phase • Compare system with objectives. • Develop and improve system.	**Risks** – Unmonitored growth. – Behavioral problems. – Inefficient use of EDP. – Obsolescence of EDP facilities. **Controls** * Auditor should examine information regarding applications and procedures as designed and test results of actual performance, with an emphasis on evaluating personnel. * Management plans should be communicated to employees on a timely and factual basis, and good communication should be established among EDP, management, and user groups.

Equipment Controls

The term *equipment controls* can be applied to hardware controls and to those policies regarding the protection, maintenance, replacement, and restriction of access to equipment. *Hardware controls* are built into the EDP equipment by the manufacturer. The hardware should be equipped with automatic error detection features that can signal machine malfunctions and should be regularly maintained. Written procedures tell the operator how to respond to hardware errors or breakdowns. An example of a common built-in hardware control is the *parity check.* This check confirms that data that have been read into the system are transmitted correctly to other components of the computer system. A "bit" is an abbreviation for a binary digit—a 0 or 1 value that represents numbers using base 2 instead of the base 10 that is used in manual systems. A machine will use either an even or odd parity bit, which effectively notes whether a set of data has an even or odd number of ones and matches this parity check for each transmission. For example, assume the data 111110101 was transmitted. This turns on seven bits (a turned-on bit is represented by a 1, and a turned-off bit, by a 0). Each data set will be followed by a parity bit. Assume the machine applies an even parity check. Then the last bit would be a 1, to make the number of ones an even number. The parity check would flag the addition or loss of a bit caused by the equipment's malfunctioning.

In addition to transmitting binary data, the equipment commonly converts data into various codes to facilitate its processing and final output. *Validity checks* are common hardware controls that check the results of encoding and decoding data to make sure that the correct coding scheme is used throughout the transmission and processing. An *echo check* can see that a transmission to another component of the computer system was correctly received. The receiver sends back a message regarding what it received, and if it does not match what was transmitted, an error will be noted. The name of this check is derived from the concept of listening to the echo from one's "transmission" or shout into a valley. Obviously, we expect our echo to match with our initial shout!

Another common hardware control is a *duplication check* which duplicates an operation and then compares the results of the two operations to confirm that they match. If they do not, an error will be signaled. Hardware controls also should include a means of signaling defective components. An auditor should check to see that the hardware monitor (record of level of use, similar to an odometer in an automobile) indicates that the computer is being used as it should. The reliability of the hardware, based on past experience and other available data, should be periodically reviewed. If the hardware is not compatible with particular software programs or data base structures, does not store data efficiently, or produces processing bottlenecks, a change may be necessary. Auditors should also be familiar with the terms *central processing unit* (directs and coordinates the programs' operation), *tape drives* (handle magnetic tapes by reading data from each tape or recording data onto a tape), and *impact printer* (prints output data onto hard copy).

The physical setting of an EDP facility should be conducive to efficient operations. Specifically, the adequacy of space, air conditioning, powerlines and backup power, anti-static floor covering, cleanliness of the environment, location, and protection via fire detectors should be assessed. The location ought to be out of traffic flow and preferably physically secure. The use of guards, alarms, and surveillance devices to detect intrusion and fire ought to be considered. Terminals should be located in supervised areas and should not be left unattended when "logged on." In fact, programs ought to be written which automatically "log off" terminals after so many minutes of inactivity. By physically locking terminals and exercising adequate control over keys, as well as setting a policy that all service personnel and other visitors be accompanied by authorized personnel when they are around the computers, the security of equipment can be greatly enhanced.

An essential means of controlling access is to require a password in order to log on to the terminal and to enter, read, or alter data. Note that an access control can be either hardware or software. Layers of password protection can help prevent against the unauthorized alteration or destruction of data files or programs. Passwords can also be restricted to particular types of data or particular types of activities. For example, one password may grant access to read receivables data and to both read and enter inventory data, while restricting access to marketable securities data. All passwords and keys should be changed periodically.

To assist in maintaining the secrecy of passwords, employees should be educated as to the importance of individual responsibility for an assigned password and the necessity of not making such authorization codes available to fellow employees. The printing of passwords on the terminal screen (or on hard copy) should be suppressed or camouflaged to assist in retaining secrecy. The system can be designed to temporarily *lock out* a terminal on which someone repeatedly attempts to log on with an incorrect password. When these types of access controls are combined with the monitoring of a *usage log* and *console log* that reports all jobs processed by the system, security should be fairly effective and any breach of security should be detectable on a timely basis.

In addition to security concerns, the proper maintenance of computer services is critical to the effectiveness of an EDP system. Obviously, the critical control is to adequately train employees to ensure against accidental destruction of records. *External labeling*, through the use of color codings and disk covers, can assist in ensuring the proper handling of files. Preventive maintenance on computer equipment ought to be performed regularly, and *records of equipment failures* should be maintained in a *log* that shows the time, date, and apparent reason for the equipment failure.

The *method of recovery* from both major and minor interruptions and equipment failures should be carefully planned, documented, tested, and monitored. Assurance should be provided that data files can be reconstructed and processing can be recovered, when necessary. Of particular importance is the entity's establishment of a *disaster plan*. This term is applied when an EDP site is lost, whereas a *back-up plan* is the term applied to short-term recovery problems. The potential risk of disaster is indicated by an IBM study which reported that 352 major data processing disasters occurred from 1967 to 1978:

- 50 percent due to fire
- 13 percent from water and storms
- 17 percent from theft
- 6 percent from loss
- 14 percent from other accidents.[4]

These statistics support the need for both a formal disaster plan and special EDP risk or business interruption insurance.

Important files, programs, and system documentation should be stored away from the EDP facility. The librarian is responsible for making sure that all backup copies are properly maintained off the premises. In a batch EDP environment, the *grandfather-father-son* procedure ensures that destroyed files can be reconstructed. Three versions of a file are available at all times, whereby the father file produces a son, which becomes the father to a third file. The initial file thereby becomes the grandfather and is stored at an off-site location for backup.

In order to read files, all programs, computers, and related supplies must be available in the event of a disaster. Clients should formally arrange for access to compatible computer facilities and periodically review such arrangements to ensure their continued compatibility and sufficiency. Exhibit 10-4 presents the elements of a backup and disaster plan.

Application Controls

Controls designed to achieve specific control objectives, such as the proper recording, processing, and reporting of data, are frequently referred to as specific or *application controls* and often are dependent on general controls ***[SAS 48, Section 321]***. Application controls can be classified as input controls, processing controls, and output controls (some schema further separate file controls, such as external labels from processing controls). However, as on-line, real-time systems become more common in distributed data-processing system configurations, the distinction among these controls becomes blurred. But typically, *input controls*

[4]Stanley D. Friedman, "Contingency and Disaster Planning in the EDP Area," *Today's Executive*, Price Waterhouse, Autumn 1982, pp. 5–10.

EXHIBIT 10-4
Elements of a Backup and Disaster Plan

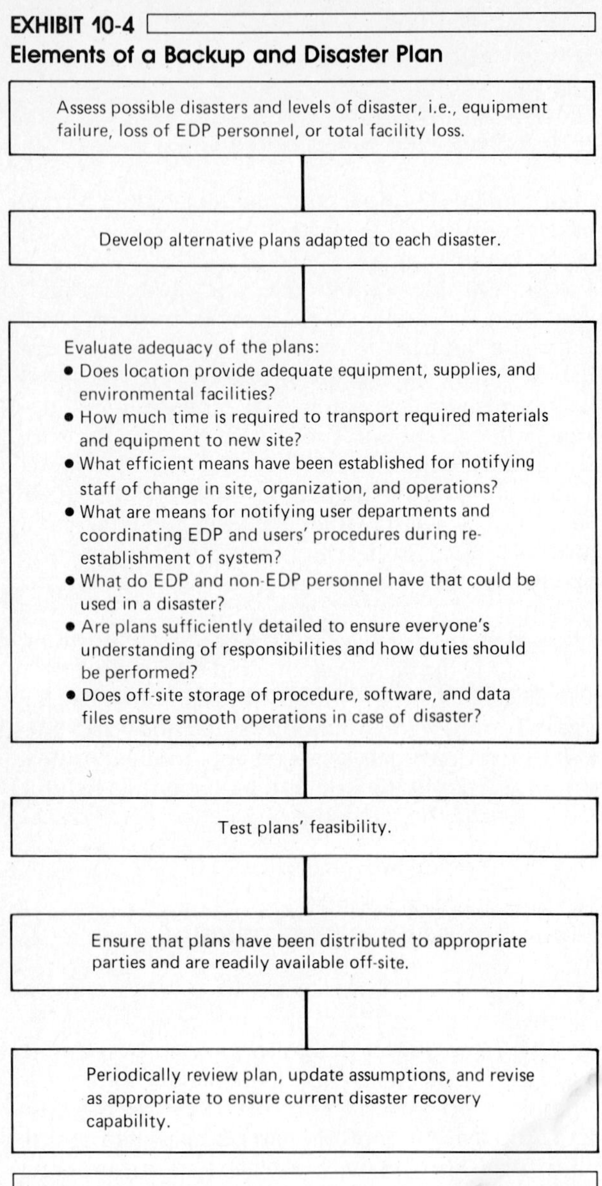
Assess possible disasters and levels of disaster, i.e., equipment failure, loss of EDP personnel, or total facility loss.

Develop alternative plans adapted to each disaster.

Evaluate adequacy of the plans:
- Does location provide adequate equipment, supplies, and environmental facilities?
- How much time is required to transport required materials and equipment to new site?
- What efficient means have been established for notifying staff of change in site, organization, and operations?
- What are means for notifying user departments and coordinating EDP and users' procedures during re-establishment of system?
- What do EDP and non-EDP personnel have that could be used in a disaster?
- Are plans sufficiently detailed to ensure everyone's understanding of responsibilities and how duties should be performed?
- Does off-site storage of procedure, software, and data files ensure smooth operations in case of disaster?

Test plans' feasibility.

Ensure that plans have been distributed to appropriate parties and are readily available off-site.

Periodically review plan, update assumptions, and revise as appropriate to ensure current disaster recovery capability.

cover the authorization process, the conversion of data, and the completeness and accuracy of the data that are to be processed. *Processing controls* ensure that all transactions that are properly authorized are processed correctly. *Output controls* ensure that only authorized parties receive computer reports and also check the accuracy of the processing. However, it is more useful to concentrate on the precise EDP-related task at hand, the problems that might arise from the task, and the particular controls available to address such problems. Using this format will involve joint consideration of input, processing, and output controls under the umbrella of those activities encompassed by EDP.

Exhibit 10-5 defines the main EDP tasks, the attendant risks or problems, and the controls for these problems. It should be apparent from a careful examination of Exhibit 10-5 that each problem described ties back to one of the specific control objectives first introduced in Exhibit 7-6, relating to the more general goals of ensuring the proper authorization of transactions, the proper accounting for transactions, and the adequate safeguarding of assets.

Official Pronouncements

Auditing pronouncements ***[SAS 48, Section 321]*** refer to general controls and application controls. The former would involve organizational controls relating to all EDP activities and intended to provide the basic control environment for effective application controls. General control features include (1) the plan of organization and operation of the EDP activity; (2) the procedures for documenting, reviewing, testing, and approving systems or programs and changes thereto; (3) controls built into the equipment (i.e., hardware controls); (4) controls over access to equipment and data files; and (5) other data and procedural controls affecting overall EDP operations. Any EDP procedure that relates to a specific accounting task is commonly termed an application control. As already noted, these controls are typically classified as input controls, processing controls, and output controls. The pronouncements remind CPAs of the characteristics that are unique to EDP environments that are likely to affect an auditor, the necessity of technical training and proficiency in EDP, and the dependence of application controls upon general controls for their effectiveness. They also clarify that the scope of audit procedures for EDP is the same as that for comparable manual systems.

This chapter has organized controls according to the various phases of an EDP operation, largely

EXHIBIT 10-5

EDP Tasks, Related Problems, and Potentially Useful Controls

EDP Task (Problem)	Control	Control Definition
Initiation of transaction (unauthorized transaction may be entered or inappropriately excluded).	Written authorization by non-EDP personnel.	The segregation of duties is documented to provide an audit trail that approval has been given.
	Restriction of personnel's access to EDP.	The risk of unauthorized transactions is reduced by merely safeguarding the EDP facility.
	Reconciliation of user controls over input with EDP-generated totals for transactions processed.	The number of documents processed and corresponding dollar amounts can often be matched.
Entering data (input can be lost, duplicated, inaccurate, or incomplete).	Preprinted, prenumbered forms.	This allows control over the number of documents issued and processed, to ensure against loss or additions of bogus documents.
	Sequence checks.	All document numbers provide accountability if they are sorted into numerical sequence and checked to see that the document numbers are consecutive.
	Edit and review checks.	Checks typically focus on whether valid characters, field size, field sign and transaction codes are being used (i.e., letter versus numbers; required number of digits; necessity of certain numbers being only positive or only negative; and only certain account transactions being permitted to affect particular master files); whether data are complete, by confirming that all data fields are complete; and information has if-then consistency (for example, <u>if</u> a sale is made and discounts are common, <u>then</u> the recording of a sale will require trade discount information). In addition, redundancy checks should be made, in which processing is repeated and individual results are compared to ascertain that they are equal.
	Hash or related totals.	Hash controls are nonsense totals, like the sum of social security numbers, whereas control totals have some meaning, like the total dollars of sales processed. Record counts are also common controls, such as a batch total of how many invoices are to be processed.
	Default options.	If all transactions are processed in the same way, the program can adjust without redundantly entering the data. For example, if all employees pay $10 a month for parking, the program can automatically make the deduction.
	On-line instruction for untrained users.	The program can be written to "lead the user by the hand." For example, instructions regarding the format for each type of data entry and glossaries to explain the meaning of different commands can be automatically provided.
Use of Codes: – To trigger an automatic check and approval (for example, an automatic credit check or vendor approval verification). – To identify which records and files are affected by the input. –To signal changes to records and instruct how the change is to be made. (Erroneous codes might be used, resulting in a loss of data integrity.)	Logic checks.	Limit checks are common. For example, a payroll check for direct labor not greater than $5,000 could be a built-in limit check. A feasible range of values can be programmed. For example, no payroll checks should be negative values. The propriety of mathematical signs can be checked. For example, all discounts should be subtracted. Zero values may not be permitted for "allowance for doubtful accounts" by any location; hence, the propriety of zero values would be checked and exception reports generated. Nonnumeric checks on data can be performed. For example, none of the characters in a social security number should be alphabetic. Match codings to master file. For example, ensure that all payments reflect vendor codings that are on the approved vendor file listing.

EXHIBIT 10-5
(continued)

EDP Task (Problem)	Control	Control Definition
		Logic checks can be made between fields. For example, a payroll record should have gross pay and withholding deductions, and the latter must not exceed the former. Self-checking digits refer to a digit that is a function of the other digits in a word or number that is used as a means of testing the accuracy of transcribing data. Typically, the digit is computed from a mathematical formula at various stages and checked for consistency as being either even or odd. Cross-footing or extension checks are also common. Cross-footing simply means adding or subtracting horizontally across column totals rather than vertically down the column.
	Master file matching.	Often a numerical coding with the first four letters of a name is required, which is then checked for agreement with the master file data.
	Trailer labels.	This is a record that provides a control total that can be compared with the accumulated totals of the records processed. (These totals may be record counts or dollars.)
	Transaction totals.	For example, a check on the proper coding of personnel might be the total dollar payroll generated.
Translation of data from one medium to another. (During the translation, data errors, loss of data, or additions of bogus data are possible.)	Keystroke verification.	Data are converted on a dual basis and compared for consistency. In other words, redundant entry of data into keyboards to verify the previous entry will result in a mechanical signal whenever a difference is detected.
	Simultaneous preparation by using multiple copies.	In other words, the source data for purchasing, receiving, and accounting are multiple copies of one form.
	One-time recording techniques.	Pegboard systems and similar devices permit one entry to be posted automatically to several records.
Physical and electronic transmission of data. (During the transmission of data, errors, loss of data, or additions of bogus data are possible.)	Transmittal documents.	Signature of party receiving documents is required, with batch totals indicating number of documents transmitted.
	Cancellation of processed documents.	Invoices, once paid, should be perforated to prevent their reuse for unauthorized payments.
	Parity control.	The hardware control already cited that checks whether the number of bits being transmitted is even or odd.
	Echo check.	The hardware control already cited that transmits data received from the output device to the source for comparison with the original data.
	Dual read devices.	For example, data cards are read twice and the results compared for consistency.
	Redundancy checks.	Processing is repeated, with subsequent comparison of results for equality.
	Control register.	Often referred to as a batch control log, it is a record of the values of batches or transactions and their disposition.
	Run-to-run totals.	Each process generates output control totals that become input control totals for the subsequent process, thereby tying one process to another.
	Match of items from parallel systems.	The items from one application's processing are matched with others independently generated in order to flag any unprocessed items.

EXHIBIT 10-5 (continued)

EDP Task (Problem)	Control	Control Definition
	Encrypting or scrambling messages.	Phone lines can be wiretapped to intercept and modify messages. This technique is called piggybacking. By using elaborate encryption schemes and often changing the keys to such encryption, the entity can deter wiretappers. Of course, computers can both scramble and break scrambling schemes quickly, and so frequent changes are imperative for effective control.
Processing of transactions. (Problems may include — use of wrong file or record. — incomplete or incorrect processing. — untimely processing, causing cutoff errors. — loss of files or programs.)	Header labels.	Intended for file control, these are machine-readable records at the beginning of a file used to identify both the file and its date.
	File labels.	Internal or external identification of a file is termed a file label; only the former is machine readable. Disk covers can serve as external labels, often color coded by file type.
	Intermediate check on file.	The operator is informed of the input received for the operator's verification before processing.
	Balancing checks.	The equality of two equivalent sets of items or of one set of items to a control total is tested.
	Overflow checks.	Limit checks that are based on the capacity of the computer's memory or the availability of space to accept certain data are called overflow checks. Often the attempt to divide by zero generates an overflow message.
	Validity checks.	Comparison of characters with a table of acceptable characters on the logical and arithmetic check of subcodes, values, and fields or formats all are termed validity checks.
	Program boundary protection.	This restricts which disks on a disk file can be read from or written on by that application.
	Dates in processing and on files.	By dating files and runs, the misprocessing of old files is less likely.
	Limit checks. Logic checks. Sequence checks. Run-to-run totals. Redundant processing.	Already defined.
	Management review of operator console log.	A review will reveal error messages caused by the operator or indications that label processing and checking are being bypassed.
Correction of errors. (In the correction process, errors may occur.)	Transaction trail for follow-up and correction of errors.	A transaction trail is a manual or machine-readable trail that permits tracing a transaction backward to its source or forward to its final posting.
	Automated error correction.	This automatically corrects errors. For example, if invoices do not match with purchase orders, generate debit memoranda.
	Suspense files for rejected items.	A suspense file, as the name suggests, is a file in "suspense," awaiting further processing. Hence, the file will contain unprocessed or partially processed items that require further action.
	Well-qualified personnel. Same controls as over original data, i.e., upstream resubmission of data requiring correction. Investigation of and attempt to correct cause of error. Maintenance of error source statistics.	Self-explanatory.

EXHIBIT 10-5 (continued)

EDP Task (Problem)	Control	Control Definition
Storage of data. (Data may be accessed by unauthorized parties while stored, and backup may prove to be inaccurate or inadequate to facilitate a recovery from a system breakdown.)	Backup and recovery system. Recovery journals. Off-premise storage (grandfather, father, son file backup) with controlled access. Disaster plan. Data retention policies.	Discussed under organizational and equipment controls.
Preparation of output, including exception reports. (Problems with output can include – untimely reports. – lost reports. – excessive volume of reports, thereby preventing their effective use. – errors in output. – improper distribution of output.)	Documentation of authorized distribution and maintenance of output log to record distribution of all output reports.	A list of who receives which reports should be available.
	Users' review of agings, tickler files, and discrepancy reports.	Tickler files are control files with items requiring follow-up sequenced chronologically. They enable timely oversight. Users' reviews are important to monitoring the overall reasonableness of output. Visual scanning or verification including comparison of master file changes with source documents, and sometimes third-party confirmations are useful in maintaining control.
	Users' reconciliation of output to input and review for reasonableness.	A more detailed review of accuracy is provided by such reconciliations.
	Programming the exception criteria to ensure reports will be useful.	If all purchases over $25,000 result in a 100-page exception report, the $25,000 figure probably warrants adjustment upward, perhaps to $50,000.
Access to data base merely for inquiry purposes. (File security may be lost. Confidentiality is particularly important with respect to data subject to data-protection laws.)	Admission to terminals of only qualified inquiries by authorized parties via passwords and limited access.	This includes the numerous access controls discussed under organizational and equipment controls.
	"Read only" protection for files.	Such protection prevents "writing" on files and so prevents unauthorized alteration.

due to difficulties in classifying controls as input versus processing versus output controls, and the desire to stress the central importance of recognizing which problems each control has been designed to address. For this reason, Exhibit 10-5 reflects general and application controls and shows certain controls as being redundant—capable of addressing difficulties in both the input and processing phase of operations.

Audit Trails

When assessing how EDP is likely to affect the examination process, an auditor should consider the availability of data

- used to enter data.
- retained in data files.
- generated for output.

The data may be available only in machine-readable form and may be accessible for only a brief period. If data are entered directly into the computer, there may not be any input documents. The auditor may thus need to request that particular data be retained for the examination. The seeming invisibility of information also increases the likelihood of errors that would be obvious in a manual system. In addition, in a manual system, initials indicate a mathematical accuracy check, whereas the program edit checks create no visible evidence.

The audit trail is intended to facilitate taking any transaction and following it from the source to its final posting. The control points along the transaction trail are expected to be testable as well. This realization that an audit trail is critical yet does not take its traditional form in an EDP environment has led auditors to the recognition that they must *audit through the computer.* An understanding of organizational, equipment, and processing controls is important. However, the relative timing and importance of these controls is of even greater concern, as is the order in which the auditor considers controls.

The auditor has to obtain reasonable assurance that the computer program for the numerous processing checks has not undergone any unauthorized changes made during the period under review. This assurance must be obtained before reviewing and testing the processing controls. For if no assurance is available that programmed controls have been in operation, what good is a test of those controls today? Therefore, the auditor will review the controls over the access to and changing of computer programs *before* proceeding to review programmed control procedures. If adequate controls exist over the maintenance and processing of computer programs, the compliance test work on detailed procedures can proceed.

An EDP environment often produces computer-generated error listings, for which compliance tests can be used, as for a manual accounting system. When there is no visible evidence, compliance tests will require computer auditing tools. It may be possible to produce an audit trail in hard-copy form, similar to that of a manual system, for the sole purpose of audit testing. But when an error is identified in an EDP environment, tracing it to find who was responsible for making it may be far more difficult than in a manual system, largely because of the multiple records in EDP systems. A client's voucher register can be produced by either ledger account or vendor, and so one may wonder which one is the actual voucher register and whether the various records have identical contents.

Essential to the audit trail are a *systems description* and a *systems flowchart* showing how EDP is designed. The systems flowchart diagrams data flows, paperwork, processing steps, and the relationships of the processing steps and the computer runs. There should also be instructions for data conversion, batch control and transmittal, and the handling, evaluating, processing, and controlling of documents or operations in the EDP system's manual activities. The auditor should review examples of input and output documents, file descriptions, authorizations, and descriptions of control and prescribed standards.

The client should also have narrative descriptions of programs; flowcharts or other details of program logic; source listings (actual listings of computer programs), with a table of code values used in processing; individual program specifications, highlighting special features like error detection routines and program switches; file formats and record layouts (how records are organized and which fields contain what information); test data specifications (indicate the quality of testing before program changes are put on-line); and details of file maintenance transactions. Manuals should be available that describe control features and testing requirements, input/output formats, and operating instructions (including instructions for emergencies). All program changes should be documented with dates and authorizations recorded to show which processing routines were in operation at what time.

Minicomputer-Microcomputer Controls

The control problems of minicomputers and microcomputers typically include a general lack of physical security, uncontrolled access, and a high probability of operating systems and application programs without computerized controls. Often a single user can access an entity's entire data base and can initiate transactions, record transactions, have effective custody of the company's assets, and alter files with no record of having done so. The total absence of segregated duties is analogous to a one-person accounting department in a manual accounting system. As microcomputers become cheaper and acquire greater memory capabilities, these problems can only become worse. The wide diversity of products also makes the absence of computerized controls a very real possibility, suggesting that there must be special care to maintain a reasonable level of control over information systems.

For adequate oversight, the authorization of transactions and the exercise of physical control over assets should be separated from the EDP duties. Users should maintain cumulative totals of master file balances for comparison to the minicomputer's master file balances. If no separate total of input transactions is maintained prior to data entry, some check on a per document basis should be performed. For example, extension checks and overall reasonableness checks should be established. *Exception reports* should be generated for users' review. As an example, reports on all credit customers with balances older than 90 days should be prepared. *Console logs* or *system activity logs* ought to be reviewed by operators' supervisors and maintained over both routine and nonroutine (such as testing) activities. Probably the most critical problem with the minicomputer and microcomputer setting is the lack of EDP expertise commonly available where the computers are located.

The organizational, equipment, and processing controls that have been described apply to all computer environments. However, the luxury of well-segregated EDP operations with well-designed computerized controls is atypical in settings where mini- and microcomputers proliferate. The CPA needs to be particularly attuned to supervisory controls, the restriction of access to accounting records, and user controls to help ensure data integrity. Back-up is often a problem. Diskettes' sensitivity to radios, indentations from writing on top of them in error, and novice users who can easily destroy records creates additional risk.

As minicomputer environments establish improved controls, the auditor must remain alert to the fact that many commercial packages are designed with optional sets of controls. Because of the extra time and cost of control steps when running programs, the designed-in flexibility of optional controls is attractive to a broad range of users. However, such options pose some important audit considerations. Throughout the period under audit, when were the optional controls turned on and off and by whom?

Clients frequently copy data from a mainframe onto a microcomputer for reports, short-term updating, and analysis. This practice poses special control problems for the auditor. Are the micro and mainframe data sets immediately reconciled? Are software applications on the micro reliable? What has been done to ensure that the software is performing as expected and has enough controls to generate meaningful analyses? The commonality of client-written programs or program adaptations on micros can be particularly troublesome, as testing and documentation practices in such a setting are often woefully lacking.

On-line Systems

The primary difference between on-line and other computer systems is the way that records are kept. Management will require an audit trail, but the controls built into the system will be more difficult to test because the actual transaction data base should not be altered by audit tests. As systems change from batch to real time, there are more programmed decisions and internally initiated transactions (for example, in an on-line data base system, automatic inventory reordering is more likely to be programmed). Almost none of the transaction trail is visible, and emphasis has to be placed upon programmed controls rather than user controls. Exception reports are a good monitoring device in such situations. On-line terminals may maintain transaction files, but usually for only a short time. But the system will probably keep storage accessible to the main computer, to answer inquiries. Bank tellers typically have on-line capabilities to check account balances, and such inquiry-only systems have several control problems.

Privacy regulations make businesses responsible for controlling access to information and keeping records on inquiries about particular individuals' data. This issue has been particularly important to credit-rating businesses, and they must even add to their current credit files any information given by the party whose credit is being rated. The problems of inquiry systems include not being totally up-to-date, having erroneous information bases, and being accessed by unauthorized parties.

As the inquiry-only system is complicated by update capabilities, the control problems increase. Data-entry errors, problems with unauthorized access, and the results of system failures can be devastating. As the number of users entering data increases, risks of errors also increase. While systems will strive to use the various organizational, equipment, and processing controls already described, the auditor should be particularly aware of the additional control risks which accompany the more sophisticated on-line systems. The development of on-line computer auditing through continuous and intermittent simulation at the same time the client's program is actually processing transactions may help address some of the special control risks of on-line systems.[5]

Data Base Management Systems

Managers recognize the value of data as a resource for decision making and have started to organize data into a single pool. Instead of having some data files maintained by marketing and others, often redundant, maintained by long-range forecasting, one pool of data is maintained. Any combination of available data can be accessed from these data base systems. The flexibility in both programming and data analyses has led to widespread use of data bases.

A *data base management system (DBMS)* is a group of computer programs designed to manage the data base. The DBMS links the data base with the application programs. The *data dictionary* describes the content of the data base, key relationships in the data, and access authorities. The *data base administrator (DBA)* will be assigned the responsibility of organizing and protecting the data base. The DBA is the only individual with a global picture of the system and therefore should be the one to review all program changes for their potential effect on data and other programs. The earlier discussion of organizational controls suggested the critical role of the DBA and the special concerns for data integrity, restriction of access to data, and effective segregation of duties. *Read only protection* of files is of particular importance, as well as the use of *multilevel passwords*. Logical record locks, area locks, privacy locks, password locks at the transaction level, password protection to the field level, the creation of subschema, and system-level file security are typical means of maintaining data base security. Both the definition of data and access paths to the data need to be protected. As an example, an employee responsible for the inventory subsidiary ledger may not know the password to access purchasing transactions or, in particular, the approved vendor listing. If such access were granted, that employee would have both accounting and authorization power: an unacceptable combination of duties.

The backup of data base systems is more complicated, and thus its exposure to software failure is greater. The grandfather-father-son approach cannot be used, as the data base system requires that all of its files be copied. The cost of storage for backup can be substantial; yet backup is essential because files can be destroyed by system failures or improper use of programs that alter the data base. The concentration of information that is inherent in a data base system increases its potential exposure to destroyed data or effects of unlimited file access.

A 1980 survey of 562 EDP auditors for banks provides some insight as to the use of data base management systems: all but 175 indicated that they either presently used DBMS or planned to in the near future. Heavy use was indicated by 47 and moderate use by 60. Almost half of the respondents had minicomputers, with 5 percent having 5 to 25 minicomputers. All but 157 had some on-line real-time applications. Given that most respondents had from $5 to $50 million in revenue, the unmistakable implication as early as 1980 was that

[5] For a detailed discussion, see Harvey S. Koch, "Online Computer Auditing Through Continuous and Intermittent Simulation," *MIS Quarterly*, March, 1981, pp. 29–41.

DBMS was an important aspect of computer auditing, as were on-line systems, in minicomputer environments.[6] The U.S. computer industry has reported a growth in the number of installed computer bases from 68,000 in 1970 to 100,000 in 1972, to 168,800 in 1974, with the value of the computer base in 1974 being estimated at $33.6 million.[7] By 1980, $75 billion was spent on the computer industry, and a 20 percent growth is predicted.[8] There is little doubt that such growth has continued to be geometric and that data base systems are likely to be a substantial component of total growth. The message is clear: knowledge of the wide variety of potential computer environments and their respective control implications is essential to the auditor and is likely to be a consideration in most engagements.

Computer Service Centers

Many entities use outside computer service centers to process their data. Perhaps most common is the external processing of payroll; however, some entities may have virtually all of their records processed by a service center. The auditor's first question, therefore, will be those data's potential effect on the financial statements. The second question will be whether user controls are adequate to ensure the prompt discovery of errors and irregularities. If the potential effects are considered material, then the auditor must review the controls at the service center, making a walk-through to trace transactions through the system and checking the service center's source data, control reports, error listings, transaction listings, and management reports. Many service centers undergo a third-party review and make their CPA's report on such a review available to the auditors of all their customers ***[SAS 44, Section 324].*** But that report will rarely include enough testing to permit reliance on the service center's controls. A CPA should emphasize user controls over those transactions being processed by the service center.

Computer Frauds—The Lessons Learned

Although computer frauds within an entity are often publicized, the risks that entities face from external parties are not so widely known. Knowledge of computer systems is fairly widespread, which means that parties outside an entity often can take advantage of control weaknesses. An example of how ineffective businesses have been in anticipating these external threats is the banks' experiences when they introduced computerized accounting systems. Account numbers were preprinted in magnetic ink on the deposit slips and checks mailed to each customer. A supply of blank deposit slips was also available at the bank, and some customers intentionally mixed in their coded slips with the blank slips at the bank. Then other customers mistakenly used the defrauders' deposit slips, and so their deposits were credited to the defrauders' accounts. This occurred because the computer automatically made deposits according to the magnetic inscriptions on the deposit slips. The defrauders could periodically confirm their account balance, withdraw "their" funds, and easily steal thousands of dollars. Obviously, this type of fraud has slowly taught client and auditor alike to be alert to fraud by external parties and to develop controls that checked information other than the magnetic coding. Yet as recently as 1972, a man at the Riggs National Bank in Washington, D.C., pocketed all the deposit slips at the writing desks, replaced them with his own coded forms, and disappeared with $100,000 of other customers' deposits three days later.[9]

If someone familiar with computers decides to tamper with an entity's system, the results can be disastrous. This was demonstrated by a twenty-one-year old U.C.L.A. engineering graduate who studied Pacific Telephone and Telegraph's EDP system. He first posed as a journalist and then as a customer and was able to learn enough to place commercial orders for telephone company equipment merely by punching the correct beep tones on his own touch-tone telephone. The defrauder

[6] "Definitions of Bank EDP Auditors," *The Magazine of Bank Administration,* April, 1980, pp. 47–50.

[7] "Information Technology: The Future Is Bright If . . . ," *Government Executive,* February, 1979, pp. 18–24.

[8] *Computerworld,* December 8, 1980, p. 63.

[9] "Key-Punch Crooks," *Time,* December 25, 1972, p. 45.

would order delivery at field locations, including manholes, then he or an employee picked up the equipment in an old phone company truck. He then sold the equipment through a dummy company and, by monitoring Pacific Telephone's inventory, was even able to identify shortages and sell back to Pacific Telephone its own equipment. Pacific Telephone permitted his unpaid bills to accumulate for three years, and the Los Angeles district attorney charged that $1 million worth of goods had been stolen. He was discovered when one of his thirteen employees turned him in after a wage dispute.[10] The lesson from such experiences is that auditors must be involved in the design stage of system development to ensure that adequate controls are built into EDP systems.

The auditor must be particularly alert to ways of covering up frauds. For example, a fraud involving an assistant administrator of the University of Kentucky Medical Center was effectively hidden in "uncollectible," or write-off, entries. That is, the insurance companies' payments to the medical center were collected and deposited in dummy accounts at several banks. By marking the accounts "uncollectible" or removing them from the computer files, the defrauders covered up their activities. They were not discovered until they neglected either to remove or reclassify one of the accounts, and a second billing was sent to an insurance company.[11] The hard lesson for business and auditors is that adjusting entries need special controls to prevent their use in circumventing established controls and procedures that would otherwise detect the defalcation.

A computerized system's risks have been likened to the result of "backing into a buzz saw . . . it is hard to tell which tooth bit you!" However, that buzz saw may be cloaked as a computer fraud which, in reality, is fraud that should have been detectable by applying the basic controls common to a sound manual system. For example, Equity Funding's fraud involved 62% of the company's insurance policies valued at two billion dollars that were fictitious. Phony documents are not an acceptable basis for generating journal entries whether the system happens to be manual or computerized. Similarly, the Westinghouse Electric case which received publicity as a computer fraud case had nothing to do with EDP except that the embezzler used an on-line terminal to report unauthorized payments. The fraud was perpetrated by writing an original check to friends but making out the three copies of the check in the name of a legitimate vendor. It was the absence of control over the documents that facilitated the fraud, rather than the presence of a computer.[12]

Defrauders also take advantage of people's tendency to discount "expected" or "common" computer errors. As an example, a Mr. Slyngstad, a programmer for the state of Washington, wrote checks to Stanley Lyngstad and reported that no bank ever questioned the missing S in his last name.[13] Such a ready waiver of manual controls as tying payee to endorser increases the risk of loss and makes auditors' detection of fraud more difficult. In this case, if an auditor matched the client's EDP employees' names to the listing of recipients of Vocational Rehabilitation checks, no exception would have been noted!

These types of experiences have been a hard lesson that the manual aspects of an EDP system require the same controls as traditional manual systems. Given the magnitude of transactions processed at high speeds, an EDP environment poses greater risks to those entities that fail to establish such controls.

Insiders have been reported to have defrauded businesses of millions of dollars. Computer fraud specialist Donn Parker analyzed 12 bank embezzlements involving EDP that occurred in 1971 and indicated that losses averaged $1.09 million a piece. From 1964 to 1965, data files available on frauds at financial institutions indicate 2,835 reported cases with losses of $20.4 million. In 1974 to 1975, 10,181 cases and $188.7 million of losses are recorded. This was a 400% increase in cases and a 900% increase

[10] "Computer 'Accomplice' in Thefts," *Computerworld*, February 16, 1972, p. 1.

[11] "File Juggling Defrauds State," *Computerworld*, May 17, 1972, p. 3.

[12] Gerald W. Devlin, "EDP Security Control," *The Internal Auditor*, July/August 1974, pp. 16–25.

[13] Erik Larson, "Crook's Tool: Computers Turn Out to Be Valuable Aid in Employee Crime," *Wall Street Journal*, January 14, 1985, p. 1.

in losses. This change is likely to be partially attributed to computerization.[14]

The first federal prosecution for computer fraud occurred in 1966 when a programmer in a Minneapolis bank successfully instructed the computer to ignore all overdrafts from his account. The discovery occurred when the bank returned to manual processing due to a computer failure.[15]

A Union Dime Savings Bank in New York had the chief teller of a branch steal more than $1.5 million from the bank deposits over a three-year period, ending in 1973. By shuffling accounts and feeding false information into the bank's computers, he was able to make accounts appear untampered with whenever quarterly interest payments were due. The teller was a heavy gambler on professional basketball games and horse races and happened to place his bets with a bookmaker who was under police investigation. When detectives found records that the teller was betting $30,000 a day, an investigation was initiated. Morgan Guaranty Trust Co. of New York had a clerk embezzle $33,000 by directing the computer to issue dividend checks in the names of some former shareholders. Morgan had acted as transfer agent for these individuals who had sold their stock. Checks were sent to an accomplice who deposited them. Then, the computer was used to erase all record that the dividend checks had been issued. When the defrauders decided to sell stock rather than settling for dividends, they made an error. Using the former shareholders' names and the accomplice's address, they issued themselves Johnson & Johnson stock after the firm declared a stock split. After selling the stock, the canceled shares came back to the bank since it was the transfer agent. Someone noticed that the new Johnson & Johnson stock had been sent to a "shareholder" who had sold his stock before the split was declared and therefore did not qualify to participate in the split. Follow-up uncovered the fraud.

With such discoveries occurring largely by chance, many have hypothesized that an enormous amount of computer theft has gone undetected and have noted that we can only guess what the very clever people are doing![16] The experiences have led to suggestions that the auditors not only test controls but that they also create a fictitious account for monitoring. Systematic program irregularities might be detectable by applying this technique, since unclaimed allowances, bad debt status, or collection adjustments would immediately flag a potential problem. The point of these experiences with fraud by employees is that auditors must be creative in their attempts to uncover defalcations that may be perpetrated by knowledgeable personnel.

Facing the idea that computer frauds are a fact of life and that no "fool-proof" system exists, General Electric has adopted an interesting policy. As the operator of an extremely large computer time-sharing service utilized by hundreds of customers, GE has offered its employees a $5,000 reward if they can steal information from the computer service. Its objective, of course, is to find loopholes and improve its computer security.[17] Organizations should also maximize the visibility of their security, periodically test it, and adopt the same kinds of security measures used for manual systems. Systems management should be able to detect and report any unscheduled runs, unauthorized access to data files, unauthorized user identification, and misuse of the system during testing. Personnel should be trained as to their security responsibilities, and the company should set an example that demonstrates that it takes security seriously.

Control Evaluation in an EDP Setting

A CPA exam question and its solution are presented in Exhibit 10-6, illustrating how a control system in an EDP setting can be evaluated. In addition to pinpointing weaknesses in the described

[14] *Business Week,* September 8, 1975, p. 30.

[15] Tom Alexander, "Waiting for the Great Computer Rip-Off," *Fortune,* July, 1974, pp. 143–150.

[16] N. R. Kleinfield, "Unsafe Combination: Crooks and Computers," *The Wall Street Journal,* April 26, 1973, pp. 1, 15.

[17] *Buffalo Courier-Express,* November 14, 1971, p. 35.

EXHIBIT 10-6
Evaluating Controls

Problem:

George Beemster, a CPA, is examining the financial statements of the Louisville Sales Corporation, which recently installed an off-line electronic computer. The following comments have been extracted from Beemster's notes on computer operations and the processing and control of shipping notices and customer invoices:

- To minimize inconvenience, Louisville converted without change its existing data-processing system, which utilized tabulating equipment. The computer company supervised the conversion and has trained all computer department employees (except key punch operators) in systems design, operations, and programming.
- Each computer run is assigned to a specific employee, who is responsible for making program changes, running the program, and answering questions. This procedure has the advantage of eliminating the need for records of computer operations because each employee is responsible for his or her own computer runs.
- At least one computer department employee remains in the computer room during office hours, and only computer department employees have keys to the computer room.
- System documentation consists of those materials furnished by the computer company—a set of record formats and program listings. These and the tape library are kept in a corner of the computer department.
- The company considered the desirability of programmed controls but decided to retain the manual controls from its existing system.
- Company products are shipped directly from public warehouses which forward shipping notices to general accounting. There a billing clerk enters the price of the item and accounts for the numerical sequence of shipping notices from each warehouse. The billing clerk also prepares daily adding machine tapes ("control tapes") of the units shipped and the unit prices.
- Shipping notices and control tapes are forwarded to the computer department for key punching and processing. Extensions are made on the computer. Output consists of invoices (in six copies) and a daily sales register. The daily sales register shows the aggregate totals of units shipped and the unit prices which the computer operator compares to the control tapes.
- All copies of the invoice are returned to the billing clerk. The clerk mails three copies to the customer, forwards one copy to the warehouse, maintains one copy in a numerical file, and retains one copy in an open invoice file that serves as a detail accounts receivable record.

Required:

Describe weaknesses in internal control over information and data flows and the procedures for processing shipping notices and customer invoices, and recommend improvements in these controls and processing procedures. Organize your answer sheets as follows:

Weakness	Recommended Improvements

Solution:

Weakness	Recommended Improvements
1. Computer department functions have not been properly separated. Under existing procedures, one employee completely controls programming and operations.	The functions of systems analysis and design, programming, machine operation, and control should be assigned to different employees. This also should improve efficiency, as different levels of skill are required.
2. Records of computer operations have not been maintained.	In order to control usage of the computer, a usage log should be kept and reconciled with running times by the supervisor. The system also should provide for preparation of error lists on the console typewriter. These should be removable only by the supervisor or a control clerk independent of the computer operators.
3. Physical control over computer operations is not adequate. All computer department employees have access to the computer.	Only operating employees should have access to the computer room. Programmers' usage should be limited to program testing and debugging.
4. System operations have not been adequately documented. No record has been kept of adaptations made by the programmer or new programs.	The company should maintain up-to-date system and program flow charts, record layouts, program listings and operator instructions. All changes in the system should be documented.
5. Physical control over tape files and system documentation is not adequate. Materials are unguarded and readily available in the computer department. Environmental control may not be satisfactory.	Programs and tape libraries should be carefully controlled in a separate location. Preferably a librarian who does not have access to the computer should control these materials and keep a record of usage. The company should consult with the computer company about necessary environmental controls.

EXHIBIT 10-6 (continued)

Weakness	Recommended Improvements	Weakness	Recommended Improvements
6. The company has not used programmed controls. Some of the procedures and controls used in the tabulating system may be unnecessary or ineffective in the computerized system.	Programmed controls should be used to supplement existing manual controls, and an independent review should be made of manual controls and tabulating system procedures to determine their applicability. Examples of computer checks that might be programmed include data validity tests, check digits, limit and reasonableness tests, sequence checks, and error routines for unmatched items, erroneous data, and violations of limits.	10. The billing clerk should not maintain accounts receivable detail records.	If receivable records are to be maintained manually, a receivable clerk who is independent of billing and cash collections should be designated. If the records are updated by the computer department, as recommended below, there still should be an independent check by the general accounting department.
		11. Accounts receivable records are maintained manually in an open invoice file.	These records could be maintained more efficiently on magnetic tape.
7. Insertion of prices on shipping notices by the billing clerk is inefficient and subject to error.	The company's price list should be placed on a master file in the computer and matched with product numbers on the shipping notices to obtain appropriate prices.	12. The billing clerk should not receive or mail invoices.	Copies of invoices should be forwarded by the computer department to the customer (or to the mailroom) and distributed to other recipients in accordance with established procedure.
8. Manual checking of the numerical sequence of shipping notices also is inefficient.	The computer should be programmed to check the numerical sequence of shipping notices and to list missing numbers.	13. Maintaining a chronological file of invoices appears to be necessary.	This file's purpose may be fulfilled by the daily sales register.
9. Control over computer input is not effective. The computer operator has been given responsibility for checking agreement of output with the control tapes. This is not an independent check.	The billing clerk (or another designated control clerk) should retain the control tapes and check them against the daily sales register. This independent check should be supplemented by programming the computer to check control totals and print error messages when appropriate.	14. Sending duplicate copies of invoices to the warehouse is inefficient.	The computer can be programmed to print a daily listing of invoices applicable to individual warehouses. This will eliminate the sorting of invoices.

CPA exam adapted, May 11, 1972, question 6.

operation, the solution suggests ways of correcting them.

Once an auditor has completed an evaluation of controls, a decision will be made as to the extent of compliance test work which would be most cost-beneficial in combination with substantive testing. The extent of EDP used in each significant accounting application, the complexity of computer operations, the organizational structure of EDP activities, and the availability of data will all warrant evaluation in planning an audit. Yet, the auditor's specific audit objectives do not change whether accounting data is processed manually or by computer. What is influenced are audit procedures, as described in the next section. It may be difficult or impossible to obtain adequate information in an EDP client setting without computer assistance, i.e., the use of the computer as an audit tool ***[SAS 48, Sections 311, 318, 326]***.

The Computer As an Audit Tool

The computer can be used as an audit tool for testing the system or testing particular controls, processing cycles, or account balances. Although these objectives may overlap, the former relies primarily on system-testing techniques (a compliance test), and the latter relies on generalized audit software (either a compliance or a substantive test). Six key system testing techniques which have been applied by auditors in a compliance-test mode will now be described, with an emphasis placed on the limitations of each technique.

Test Decks or Test Data

In order to test whether a system is operating as designed, auditors commonly create *test decks* (or *test data*, for on-line systems) that trigger various control checks and exception reports. Test decks can be used to create an audit trail. By including both normal and abnormal data, all of a system's key processing and control points can be checked. The test decks are usually created by the auditor and processed by the client's system. Automated methods for creating test decks are called *test data generators*.

Although triggered logic routines provide evidence that processing and control checks are operating as expected, the auditor is unlikely to test all of a program's important logic, because of practical problems in generating test data that capture all possible conditions that could significantly influence the financial statements if an edit check were not operating as designed. Imagine trying to design a test deck to test the detection of all possible combinations of data entry or processing errors. Moreover, different computer programs could generate the same output for a set of test data. Consider the case that introduced this chapter. If the random "rounding" routine were not triggered for a test deck, the output would be identical to that obtained by a program containing no such routine.

The test deck approach takes a *snapshot* of the system for only that time that the test data are processed. The ability to infer that the same program was in operation throughout the period depends upon the client's control over programs and program changes. This reinforces the point made earlier that specific controls are interdependent with general controls.

A test deck approach should begin at the data conversion stage of the client's EDP system and end at the final output stage. Otherwise, the approach is capable of evaluating only a subset of the system's routine. In addition, the test data should be merged with actual data and be indistinguishable by the client's employees. If this is not done, the test deck can be processed apart from the routine data entering the system, thereby destroying the technique's detective powers. Yet, practical problems arise from merging artificial data with actual data, and the result could be a distortion of the actual financial records of the entity. The greatest risk when using test decks is that the system being tested was not operating during the period being audited. The next system-testing technique has evolved as one means of reducing this risk. Moreover, it addresses the fact that test decks are difficult to operationalize in an on-line real-time environment.

Integrated Test Facility (ITF). An *ITF* is a continuous test deck approach. To test a system's performance, test data are continuously processed alongside live data. The test data processed are then documented in order to create a continuous compliance check on the system, which reduces the risk that a program other than the one being tested was in operation during the period.

Other than this single advantage, all of the shortcomings of test decks apply to ITFs. Even so, the practical problems of ITFs are substantially more severe than the problems of test decks. If the test data are not automatically reversed out of the accounting system or captured by a "trap door" technique, the integrity of the accounting records will be threatened. Yet such automatic reversals or capture of data increases the risk that employees will detect the test data, enabling them to process the test data separately. It is difficult to reach a good balance between (1) obtaining sufficient assurance that client data are neither destroyed nor contaminated while processing or adjusting the test files and (2) retaining the camouflaged test data. The next testing technique is able to avoid (1).

Tagging, Tracing, and Concurrent Processing. The auditor can mark (tag) data or classes of transactions so as to trigger the creation of an audit data file. This file then documents the processing of and control checks on the data at various points in the processing. Hence the file traces transactions for the CPA's subsequent review and use in performing data or system tests.

Besides *tracing* "tagged" transactions, the auditor may use *concurrent processing*. A data file can be automatically created for certain classes of transactions. For example, every time a master file is changed, a data file can be created to summarize the change. Examples are adding authorized vendors' names, raising credit limits, or increasing pay rates. Similarly, a limit check can trigger an exception report for the auditor. Perhaps the file is programmed to record all sales over $40,000. The auditor can then test the data files created by concurrent processing, thereby reducing the number of auditing procedures. For example, the stratification (subdividing or sorting) of sales to facilitate 100 percent testing of large transactions is simplified by having such a data file available.

To use concurrent processing, the CPA must help the client design the system. Otherwise, later addition of automatic audit-related data files is likely to be too expensive.

Tagging and tracing procedures and concurrent processing have shortcomings similar to those of test decks and ITFs. That is, all of a program's important logic may not be effectively tested, and clients may be able to identify the tagged data or the points at which data files are created and thus could circumvent the tests. To avoid total dependence on a client's system and employees, an alternative testing approach has evolved.

Parallel Simulation. The auditor creates a program that replicates the primary logic of common computerized edit and control checks and processing routines. Then the data that were processed by the client's EDP system are reprocessed through the CPA's program. The output is expected to match the client-generated output except for certain deviations owing to the CPA's replication of only a subset of the client's program. The CPA's computer system is thus used for testing.

Although the auditor's set of application programs is intended to simulate the client's processing functions on a set of data, the mere comparability of input and output does not necessarily mean the comparability of the processing logic. In addition, inferences cannot be drawn beyond the particular data set analyzed. Hence, the effectiveness of the test is largely dependent on the care with which data sets are selected and the thoroughness with which the system's real control and processing attributes are simulated.

When tailored to a client, *parallel simulation* requires a good knowledge of programming. However, if a less tailored simulation is sufficient, the auditor can use generalized audit software to capture the primary processing logic of the system to be tested. For example, a standard sorting, footing, and recalculation package may be sufficient to test depreciation expense of assets with historical costs exceeding $30,000. In such a setting, the CPA need not be a programmer. All that is required is that the CPA be able to identify the key processing logic which needs to be tested. If computer programming expertise is available, alternative system testing techniques become plausible.

Program Code Checking and Flowchart Verification. The CPA's detailed analysis of the client's process code can reduce the risk that the processing logic is different from that replicated in, for example, a parallel simulation. Instead of depending on the comparison of inputs and outputs, the program logic is reviewed in detail. This review can be automated through a *flowchart verification routine* and the software routine can generate a logic flowchart. An even better technique is to apply software directed at systems analysis that compares audit source to audit object. But, these techniques require programming and flowcharting expertise and can be both time-consuming and inefficient. The combination of human, software, and practical limitations decreases the thoroughness and accuracy of any line-by-line review of a program code. Hence these techniques are unlikely to be used for most audits. Rather, alternative test approaches, which also require programming expertise, are more commonly used.

Mapping and Controlled Processing or Reprocessing. The CPA can use *mapping* to identify logical paths in a process, concentrating on paths that have and have not been crossed in a particular application. Having identified such paths, the client's system is used under the auditor's control to process or reprocess the data. In this way, the CPA can authenticate the consistency of the client's current or past output with expected and actual output from that program. Parallel simulation and *controlled reprocessing* are often compared as similar testing techniques. But, one difference is that the CPA's system is used in simulations, and the client's system is used in reprocessing, though under the auditor's control. Another difference is the expertise involved, as generalized audit software is commonly used for simulations, whereas the combination of mapping and controlled reprocessing is used for detailed logic checks and requires greater programming expertise. Because of these differences, it is also fair to generalize that parallel simulation frequently involves the review of a smaller subsystem of a client's EDP operations than do mapping and controlled reprocessing techniques.

One shortcoming of mapping procedures is the possibility that the client may have earlier introduced a so-called *malicious code* (one intended to perpetrate a fraud) which has been effectively camouflaged in prior processing by the client. Although the comparison of present controlled processing with past processing helps get more than just a single snapshot of coverage, the earlier snapshot, which the auditor cannot control, may not be what it appears to be. In other words, risks do exist that a programmer perpetrating a defalcation is particularly adept at camouflaging unauthorized commands.

Generally, the mapping and controlled processing or reprocessing procedure is constrained to noting only those exceptions that the auditor expects. This persistent risk of all the system techniques, combined with the required programming expertise to apply those particular procedures has meant that they are not applied nearly as frequently as test data and simulation techniques. System testing techniques provide compliance test evidence, determining the propriety of reliance on EDP controls.

General Considerations. Whether the auditor is applying one of these system techniques or generalized audit software, an essential step in the audit process is adequate planning to ensure the effective and efficient execution of the selected procedures. Once the audit objective is defined, the feasibility of applying a selected technique must be investigated. The questions to be answered include:

- What data are available in machine-readable form and can they be easily processed with available audit software?
- Does the client's equipment have sufficient computer time available to perform the tests and is that equipment compatible with the available audit software?
- What alternative arrangements are necessary?

Once these questions are resolved, the planning of the application can proceed, with thorough documentation of data files of interest, their format, the selected technique, and the overall approach.

The planned application ought to be tested by running a small sample of data. In this manner, the CPA can confirm that the processing is being performed as planned and that the output meets the auditor's needs. The CPA should be cognizant of typical audit problems that are created by clients' policies on retaining data files. Actions should be taken to confirm that the necessary files will be available for the time period required for the actual audit application on the computer. Sometimes this may require that the CPA copy a file and save it for later use. Just as important as file retention is the client's assurance that computer time and the assistance of client EDP employees will be available when needed.

When the time comes to apply the computer tools selected, the CPA should maintain control of the actual processing, analyze the results, and carefully document the application, results, follow-up procedures, and conclusions.[18]

Generalized Audit Software (GAS)

Generalized audit software refers to "canned" packages that are easy to use with a minimum amount of computer knowledge. Often, no programming expertise is required unless the auditor wishes to tailor the ready-made application to perform a special-purpose function. Whenever a "canned" routine is modified, expertise in programming and program-testing is critical to ensure that the tailored software meets the auditor's objectives. Although the code is already written and compiled, the auditor still must describe the data to the program. This requires a knowledge of record layouts and is often a major problem in using GAS, particularly in a data base environment.

[18] For more details on available audit testing techniques refer to the article by James I. Cash, Jr., Andrew D. Bailey, Jr., and Andrew B. Whinston entitled "A Survey of Techniques for Auditing EDP-Based Accounting Systems," *The Accounting Review*, October 1977, pp. 813–832.

The obvious advantages of generalized audit software are its adaptiveness to different computer systems and its applicability to several audit procedures. The speed and accuracy of the computer permit 100 percent testing of computations and extensions, whereas such coverage would be practically impossible in a manual system. Its efficiency in following auditors' instructions regarding logic checks, sorting routines, and printing can significantly expedite numerous audit procedures. Consider the payroll case at the beginning of this chapter. Had generalized audit software been applied on a surprise basis to a payroll run, a set of exceptions would have been noted for those random calculations being systematically rounded. Without such a 100% coverage, detection by checking computations would be very unlikely. To clarify the range and capability of generalized audit software packages, the major functions of these packages will be outlined with an example of how an auditor might use each of the functions. Note that GAS may be used in compliance testing, substantive testing, and dual-purpose testing.

Reorganization of Data Files

Numerous audit procedures involve the reorganization of data files. In subsequent chapters, the concept of stratified sampling will be developed. Essentially, this sampling approach strives to ensure adequate dollar coverage by including a greater number of larger dollar items than smaller dollar items. In order to apply the technique efficiently, it is useful to *sort* data files in order from the largest dollar amount to the smallest dollar amount. Similarly, an auditor may wish to sample from all recorded payables on a client's books, in spite of the client's account system which distinguishes payables to the government from payables to business and also separates retail, wholesale, and industrial suppliers. The auditor's sampling procedures could be simplified by merging the payables in the separate account files in order to form one file including all payables.

The auditor's use of confirmations has been discussed in earlier chapters. Frequently, in order for the auditor to use the computer to prepare confirmations, the client's data file containing customers' addresses must be updated to reflect the current account balance per customer. To facilitate the mailing of second requests to customers who fail to respond to the initial inquiry, a copy of the updated file will be saved by the auditor. Sometimes a single customer may have more than one receivable balance; for example, the client may have requested separate billing of industrial supplies from raw material orders. The computer can be useful in combining account balances per customer and summarizing the totals of the accounts for use in preparing confirmations.

In a later chapter, inventory observation procedures will be described in some detail. However, from past chapters you should have a perception of the general way in which physical observations are performed. The client counts and tags inventory, and the auditor checks the accuracy of such procedures by observing the process and by making test counts. A *test count* simply means that the auditor chooses some shelf or bin of inventory to count, with the intention of comparing the count to the client's inventory records. This comparison can be performed by the *matching* capability of generalized audit software, and any differences in test counts and client records can be printed out as exceptions for the auditor's investigation.

Totaling or Subtotaling Within a File. Generalized audit software can also aggregate data within a file by location, division, region, or subsidiary to enable the totals to be used in variance (flux) and ratio analyses. Once regions, for example, are tested and found to be in line, except for two of the eight regions under study, the computer can be used to subtotal the regional data by location for more detailed analysis. By forming subtotals by location and then matching the location codings with a master file of location codings, the auditor can check the completeness of the data (whether each location is reflected in the file being studied). This capability is commonly referred to as determining *levels of totals*.

Mathematical Computations. Not only can subtotals be prepared for analysis, but the computer can also perform the ratio analysis of interest. Through such simple functions as addition, subtraction, multiplication, and division, any ratios can be calculated for analytical review. In addition, the mathematical accuracy of clients' calculations can be verified. Banks' calculation of interest, manufacturers' calculation of depreciation, services' calculation of payroll all can be checked, 100 percent, if desired. Often, an auditor will want to look at a profile of a data file, such as its mean or average value, range (difference in highest and lowest value), standard deviation (dispersion around the mean), variance (another measure of dispersion), and mode (the most common value). These statistical attributes can be easily calculated by applying generalized audit software. The attributes can help in designing sampling plans and finding errors or missing data. For example, a data file listing the allowance for doubtful account estimates of one hundred locations would not be expected to contain a zero value. Hence a range that indicated a low value of zero would suggest that one location had not appropriately estimated its bad debts or had neglected to enter its estimate into the accounts. The computer can also calculate square roots and exponents, which may be helpful in some modeling and quantitative techniques, such as calculating the economic order quantity for a client's inventory.

Extracting Records from Data Files. If there is a change in one facet of the production line, the auditor may wish to test the cost accounting records for that single department. A computer can be used to extract those records of interest in order to facilitate the testing of that data subset. Similarly, the auditor may wish to perform extended procedures on self-constructed assets, and again, generalized audit software can be used to extract those assets and the subset of additions and disposals that relate to those assets.

Logic Functions. Logic functions include (1) determining attributes of the data file, in particular its range (substantive testing), (2) searching files to select unusual items (analytical review or scanning), (3) simulating production program logic (compliance testing), and (4) reviewing both the quality and correctness of data (both compliance and substantive testing). Generally, the computer capability used is the move and conditional operation, whereby greater than, less than, and equal comparisons are made. At times, customers will prepay or will be granted allowances that create credit balances that represent a liability to the client and should be reclassified from the receivable account. Generalized audit software can thus be used to isolate all balances less than zero to enable such a reclassification.

Selecting Records Statistically. In the next chapter, various means of selecting statistical samples will be described, including random sampling, interval sampling, and proportionate to size selection. Generalized audit software is available for making any of these selection techniques operational. In this manner, a sample of shipping reports required to test for the presence of unbilled shipments could be randomly selected from a transaction file.

Printing Reports. When the update capabilities of generalized audit software were discussed, the idea of having the computer print confirmations was suggested. Other desirable printing includes reports for analyzing receivables, bar graphs demonstrating the relationship of the allowance for doubtful accounts to total accounts receivable, and a trend line of sales on account, relative to receivables.

The report-writing capabilities of generalized audit software are substantial. The printing of columns, subheadings, and totals can be specified by the user to create commonly used analyses like an aging schedule for accounts receivable. The computer can identify the age of each account and then summarize balances for 0 to 30, 30 to 60, 60 to 90, 90 to 120, and 120 day and older accounts. Aging schedules can be rather time consuming to prepare manually, yet tend to be irreplaceable as decision aids when analyzing the adequacy of the allowance for doubtful accounts.

Utility Programs. Beyond the capabilities already described, numerous miscellaneous functions are available through general-purpose utility programs. Commonly these include the (1) editing of the user's specifications, (2) editing of input files for data format errors, (3) exits to the user's programmed routines, (4) test options, and (5) multiple-pass capabilities. An example of the first program is a system that requires the user to specify two identification codes, each with six characters—one all numeric and the other all alphabetic. A utility program can do an edit check on the user's specifications to ensure that they comply with these requirements. An example of the second program is its verification that all data fields are complete before it rechecks calculations. For example, if the interest accrual is being verified, the fields should include the date a loan was initiated, the date it was paid off, the interest rate, the principal, and the payment terms. Without this information, the generalized audit software would report that a field was incomplete and the calculation could not be made. The third program simply permits easy integration of user programs into general-purpose programs by allowing an exit from the general routine to the special-purpose subroutine. Test options should be reasonably self-explanatory; ready-made test files help ensure that a program is functioning as intended. This is particularly valuable if the user has altered the code in any way, as the testing can indicate if the programmer has inadvertently changed some aspect of the program. Unintended effects can happen, for example, by using variable names in a subroutine which were used for different purposes in the main program or by failing to initialize some variable's value before returning to the main program. The fourth program enables the computer to make multiple passes, which can be used first to read a data file to detect debit balances and then to read through that same file to select all values greater than $100,000. Utility programs are capable of flexible data management and data analysis.

Statistical Sampling Capabilities. Although the various approaches to statistical sampling are discussed in the next two chapters, it is important to recognize that all of the sampling alternatives to be described can be applied with the use of a generalized audit software package. Statistical selection techniques were cited earlier; the packages of interest at this point are those that determine the appropriate sample size and aid in evaluating the sample results that are obtained. If an auditor wishes to determine the extent to which a client has complied with the policy that all purchases over $25,000 be approved by the manager of the purchasing department, a sample of large purchases would have to be drawn. A computer program could provide the appropriate sample size, based on the auditor's desired parameters. If, out of a sample of 60, one error were identified, the program could evaluate this finding in statistical terms.

Modeling Capabilities. Modeling capabilities are often available through time-sharing programs that analyze trends, relationships, product mix effects, present value, and cash flow. Program package capabilities are commonly cited as linear programming, trend-line analysis, correlation analysis, and regression analysis, and some time-sharing services have decision tree and probability routines. These capabilities are of obvious value to a CPA in providing management advisory services. In addition, the CPA should find these capabilities of use when performing analytical review. Microcomputers currently offer powerful if/then simulation routines which can help a CPA analyze the effects of various accounting changes and, in particular, help the CPA in performing a review of the reasonableness of the client's forecasts—including the assumptions that underlie the forecast.

Synopsis. Exhibit 10-7 summarizes the jargon for the generalized audit software packages' specific capabilities. The capabilities of generalized audit software can be expected to grow in breadth and flexibility as the power of micro-computers continues to increase, as does the availability of simpler programming languages that permit tailoring of existing programs by relatively unsophisticated users. Time-sharing linkages facilitate wide use of diverse programs, as well as the sharing of large data bases for integration in modeling and similar data analyses for which external industry or economic data may prove valuable.

As the auditor plans generalized audit software applications, he or she should also prepare a flowchart of the application. The relevant file information required for the application, as well as the desired format for the reports to be printed, should be delineated. This type of detailed planning ensures the efficient use of EDP facilities and the client's EDP personnel. For example, assume that an auditor wanted to test whether all individuals receiving payroll checks were current employees of the client. This test requires payroll information

EXHIBIT 10-7

Capabilities of Generalized Audit Software

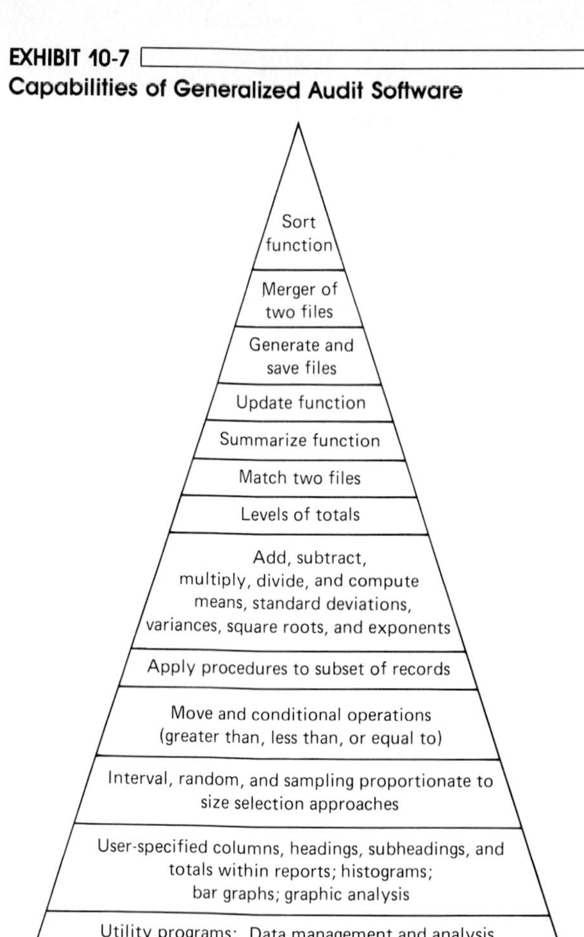

about who was paid, information from the personnel department about the date each employee was hired, and, if applicable, when employees were terminated. The files' layout, with specific columns or fields containing such information, should be documented in the work papers. Exhibit 10-8 shows a flowchart (usually referred to as an *application chart*) that outlines the payroll software application to be performed. Prior to preparing the chart, the auditor had to determine the desired output.

The obvious report to be prepared is the exception report of individuals for whom payroll checks were printed that were not on the personnel file. To make sure that the number of names processed for each file can be reconciled, the exception report should include the total number of employees on each file. Because the application produces such information as a by-product, there should also be a report on those employees hired and terminated during this period. Often an ex-

EXHIBIT 10-8

Payroll Application Chart (Using Generalized Audit Software)

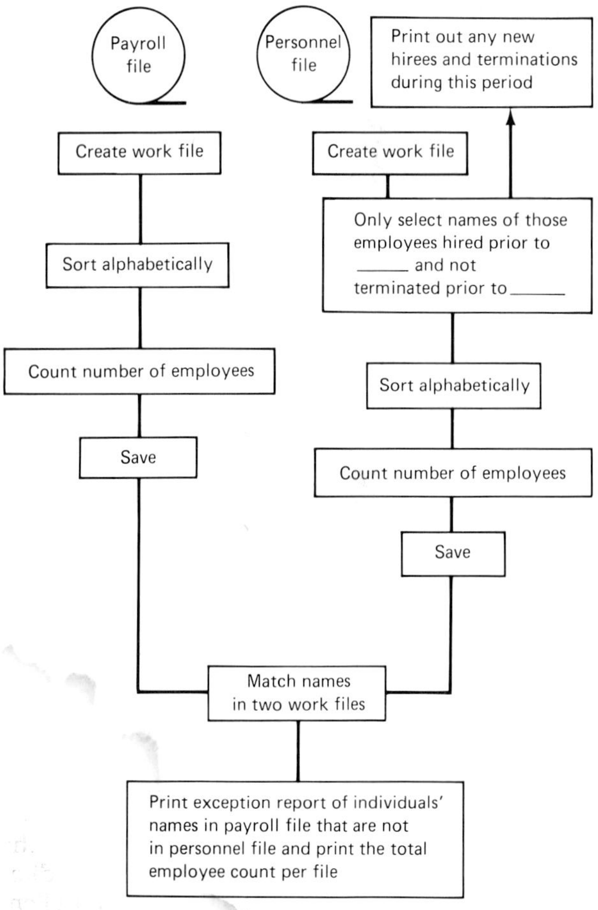

From Wanda A. Wallace, *Handbook of Internal Accounting Controls* (Englewood Cliffs, N.J.: Prentice-Hall, 1984), p. 109.

ception report will reflect a cutoff problem regarding newly hired and terminated employees. The printout of hirees and terminations therefore should be designed to include the employee's name, hire date, and termination date. This printout can then be tied to the exception report as a basis for investigating the probable cause of discrepancies in the payroll and personnel files. Without proper planning, the auditor might have forgotten to request the print-out of new hirees and terminations, resulting in a need to replicate the reading of the personnel file in order to generate the report or a need to resort to manual procedures to investigate the hire or termination date of employees listed on the exception report. Neither alternative is as effective as initially generating the print-out of interest at the same time the exception report is generated.

Exhibit 10-8 demonstrates the joint use of sort, mathematical, save, match, and print capabilities of generalized audit software. Most audit applications will involve a variety of software functions.

Research involving a survey of 39 internal audit departments provides some indication of the extent to which audit software and system testing techniques are applied. The internal auditors' use of audit software to interrogate files (e.g., to select samples, foot populations, etc.) was common in over half of the EDP post-implementation audits. Test data was used to evaluate processing controls one-third to one-half of the time. An integrated test facility was used to monitor processing controls one-third of the time, or less.[19] This same research indicates that external CPAs expect that the use of ITFs and test decks by internal auditors would be likely to have a moderate to significant effect on their audit scope.

The Microcomputer As an Audit Tool

The auditor may also use each of the various procedures described herein on a microcomputer. Microcomputers can generate lead schedules, prepare adjustment/reclassification summaries, write memoranda regarding audit tests performed, prepare debt confirmations, perform trend analysis, prepare projections, and apply statistical packages, including sampling programs and generalized audit software tools. Exhibit 10-9 shows a collage of the type of output that a microcomputer can produce for an audit engagement. The microcomputer is a useful tool in planning an audit engagement—generating budgets and audit programs—and in documenting audit work. Word processing capabilities, as well as spreadsheet software, are familiar to auditors and have become a key complement to the auditor's pencil and frequently, a substitute, due to the ease of use and expedience of microcomputer applications.

A Look to the Future

Software developments are getting sufficiently sophisticated to provide decision support for audit judgments beyond the traditional generalized audit packages already described. For example, a software technology known as TICOM has been developed, using data base management techniques to store an abstract representation of an internal control system. TICOM essentially aids the auditor in evaluating control systems in complex organizations.[20] An entire area of research known as *artificial intelligence* is dedicated to the modeling of decision processes to serve as support systems for professionals' judgments; such software has been effectively applied to modeling medical doctors' diagnoses and is in the developmental stage for audit-related applications.

REVIEW QUESTIONS

1. How do errors generated by manual systems compare with errors generated by an EDP system?

[19] Larry E. Rittenberg and Gordon B. Davis, "The Roles of Internal and External Auditors in Auditing EDP Systems," *The Journal of Accounting*, December, 1977, pp. 51–58.

[20] For further details see James I. Cash, Jr., Andrew D. Bailey, Jr., and Andrew B. Whinston, "The TICOM Model—A Network Data Base Approach to Review and Evaluation of Internal Control Systems," *American Federation of Information Processing Societies Conference, Proceedings, AFIPS*, June, 1977.

EXHIBIT 10-9

How Microcomputers Might Be Applied As Audit Tools

ABESON, INC.

Working Balance Sheet — DECEMBER 31, 19X9

Assets	Final at previous examination 12/31/X8	Per books	Adjustments Reclassifi-cations (12/31/X9)	Final	Variation Analysis	Reference Notes
Current assets:						
Cash						
Marketable securities						
Trade receivables						
Less: Allowances						
Net trade receivables						
Other accounts receivable						
Inventories						
Prepaid expenses						
Total current assets						

ABESON, INC.
Anywhere, USA

SSD Creditors
Somewhere
USA

October 29, 19x9

Gentlemen:

Please confirm our note payable to you to our independent accountants, Rittenberg, CPAs. The information below should be compared with your records and any differences noted. Please mail your reply directly to Rittenberg, CPAs XXX L Street, Anywhere, USA.

DATE OF NOTE:
ORGINAL AMOUNT OF NOTE:
TERMS OF NOTE:
PRINCIPAL BALANCE 10/15/x9:
PRINCIPAL PAYMENTS 1/1/x9 to 10/15/x9
INTEREST PAYMENTS 1/1/x9 to 10/15/x9
COLLATERAL:
COMPENSATING BALANCE AGREEMENTS:

Your expedient response will be most appreciated.

Sincerely,

J. J. Wallach, Treasurer

The information above does agree with our records EXCEPT for the information provided below:

Date: ____________ By: ____________ Title: ____________

ABESON, INC.

Adjusting Journal Entries

Workpaper Ref	Description	AJE Reference	Debit	Credit
	(1)			
	Inventory	D	43,000	
	Accounts Payable Trade	P/L7		43,000
	To adjust book inventory to 12/31/19 physical inventory at MFO cost.			
	(2)			

EB8

I....+....I....+....I....+....I....+....I....+....I
0 2 4 6 8 10
Histogram Frequency

Mean	3982621.58	Std Err	513499.552
Mode	22437.000	Std Dev	3247655.06
Kurtosis	-1.349	S E Kurt	1.960
S E Skew	.374	Range	8774960.00
Maximum	8797397.00	Sum	159304863
Median	3470465.50		
Variance	1.0547E+13		
Skewness	.165		
Minimum	22437.000		

Valid Cases 40 Missing Cases 0

ABESON, INC.

Reclassification Journal Entries

Workpaper Ref	Description	RJE Reference	Debit	Credit
	(A)			
	Notes and loans payable - non current	EE	250,000	
	Notes and loans payable - **current.**	AA8		250,000
	To reclassify current portion of long term debt due to notes and loans payable current			
	(B)			
	Accounts Receivable	C	193,000	
	Cash	A		193,000
	To reclassify accounts receivable mistakenly debited to cash.			

December 31, 19x9

ABESON, INC.

Property, Plant, and Equipment

Generalized Audit Software Application to Recalculation of Depreciation Expense Using Microcomputer--Spreadsheet software

Every asset with an original cost exceeding $30,000 was subjected to a recalculation procedure to check the accuracy of depreciation expense.

All additions to the Property, Plant, and Equipment Account were separately tested as described on PPE4.

J. L. Rittenberg
2/8/x0

ABESON, INC.

Model: Trend Analysis of Revenue

	19x9 actual	19x0 actual	19x1 PROJECTED	19x2 PROJECTED
Average revenue per customer	$150.00	$165.00	$170.00	$185.00
Number of Customers				
Variable Expenses				
Profit (Loss)				
Projected Inflation--			6%	8%

Standardized Scatterplot
Across - IR Down - *RESID
Out 3 2 1 0 -1 -2 -3 Out
-3 -2 -1 0 1 2 3 Out
Symbols:
Max N
1.0
2.0

2. Describe the major types of EDP environment with which an auditor is likely to come in contact.
3. Describe the functions typically performed by a Data Control Group.
4. What items should be included in a contract with a service center?
5. What is a
   - parity check?
   - validity check?
   - echo check?
   - duplication check?
6. The computer control section of the EDP department reconciles certain key user reports and, as part of that reconciliation, creates input data, primarily changes and adjustments. From a control standpoint, what is wrong with this practice?
7. Your client has established a policy that terminated employees may not be given access to the EDP facilities at any time after they have been informed of their termination. Why?
8. A client's formal agreement with the service bureau that processes the plant's payroll does not impose penalties for cancellation or failure to perform. Although the client has an internal audit department, it has not made any periodic reviews of the processing at the outside service bureaus. What are the risks here?
9. When you asked whether your client required EDP personnel to take their vacations, you were assured that they were. But you discover that several employees spread out their vacation days to ensure they are never gone for more than three consecutive calendar days. What effect could this have? What would you suggest to your client?
10. Describe the special concerns of an auditor in the following EDP environments: minicomputers; on-line systems; data base systems; and computer service centers.
11. Some CPAs claim that most computer frauds are really pencil frauds. Do you agree? Why or why not?
12. What advantages do tagging and tracing have over an integrated test facility?
13. What are the differences between parallel simulation and controlled reprocessing?
14. Based on Exhibit 10-7, give an example, other than that in the text, of how each of the capabilities of generalized audit software might be used in an audit setting.
15. What type of information should be included in the planning work papers for a generalized audit software application?
16. Donn Parker, a specialist in research on computer fraud, observed:

    Now the computers are, in a very real sense, the vaults of yesterday. Thus, where entry to the computer is by telephone line, it's like putting a vault in the criminal's bedroom and giving him all kinds of uninterrupted time to figure out how to break in.[21]

    What controls can limit this problem?

EXERCISES

1. What could happen as a result of the following control weaknesses?
   a. Maintenance procedures for application systems permit programmers to move program changes from test to production libraries.
   b. Present policy permits a programmer to schedule hands-on time on the computer. Generally, this time will be scheduled on a weekend when only a part-time operator is on duty. During this period, the programmer has access to all master data files, production codes, and, of course, to the computer hardware.
   c. Files are not locked during nonworking hours, and building maintenance has keys to the computer room.
   d. The computer room doors are secured by locks that require a magnetic card to open them. But at present, there is no master list of such cards.
   e. Access to the data center computer room is controlled by a cipher lock. The combination has not been changed in several months.
   f. EDP operations are not routinely scheduled.
2. The size of the EDP operation of one of your clients makes it impractical to segregate duties adequately. What would you suggest that the client do to enhance control over EDP?
3. Your client has pointed out that its systems and programming department needs to have terminals for testing and that a program is being used to prevent the department's terminals from accessing live files. But this program was written by the systems and programming department. What could this mean?
4. Most of the mechanized applications for one of your clients were developed in the mid-1960s to serve the company as it was then. As your client has grown, the systems have been modified to accommodate business changes and to improve the existing sys-

[21] Donn B. Parker, "Computer Criminals," *Intellect*, November 1977, p. 187.

tems. However, these system changes and improvements have not been made within the framework of an overall systems plan. As a result, your client's business information needs are not being met, and at the same time, there is duplication of information and overlap in several of the existing systems. What advice can you offer?

5. The third stage of an EDP system's growth is exorbitant growth of the computer budget. At this stage, top management commonly overreacts by setting a policy of no additional EDP applications and by implementing stringent controls over the use of EDP. The result is unhappy EDP personnel, underuse of computer facilities, and disruption of operations by management's changes that have been initiated for control purposes.

The alert client and auditor will be cognizant of this common stage in the growth of an EDP system and will take actions to avoid the typical problems of each stage. What suggestions would you make to a client as to constructive ways of avoiding the adverse effects of the third typical stage of EDP growth?

6. A humorous tale of the human foibles that plague small computer centers is worth some analysis. A business just introducing EDP hired one individual to be the system designer/programmer/operator. Suffering from the so-called "I'm-the-only genius-here" (ITOGH) syndrome, the EDP person kept to himself as he worked to deliver his promise of a fully-working receivables system by the end of the month. As month-end approached, the light in his eyes got wilder and wilder as he was on the threshold of success.

> Towards the end, he slept in the computer room, close to his creation. In the morning, our audit staff would find this bushy, unshaven enthusiast excitedly dancing about his equipment like some mad scientist.[22]

The man who was assumed to be the expert was not monitored, as managers felt they were ignorant about computers. "On the fatal day as you might have guessed, the mad scientist's program aborted with a logic error."[23]

Analyze the entity's approach to system development. What recommendations can you offer as to how the business should proceed from this point? What are the control implications of past activities?

7. In 1969, an article on computer security cited the serious problems with computer centers that had arisen because of unrest on college campuses.

- In Montreal, Canada, at Sir George Williams University, students set fire to the computer center, causing an estimated $1 million damage to computer equipment.
- At Brandeis and Northwestern Universities, militant students occupied the computer centers. In both of the latter situations the students held the computer as a hostage, so to speak, and were not destructive.[24]

Comment on the probable effects of these actions. What controls, if established by these universities, would have been capable of addressing these effects?

8. The *Wall Street Journal* reported a case involving a twenty-one-year-old department store sales clerk who had spent $60,000 that was erroneously credited to his account. Apparently, the clerk's account number was nearly the same as that of the Philadelphia Savings Fund Society. Then two numbers were transposed, and a deposit intended for the big mutual savings bank was given to the clerk.

The clerk assumed a "finders-keepers" attitude and became Santa Claus to his friends and family. The clerk claimed to have tried twice to get his bank to correct the mistake before he spent the money. But the jury had little sympathy and convicted the clerk; the possible penalty is seven years' imprisonment and a $15,000 fine.[25]

How could the bank have prevented the error?

The bank claimed to have no record of the clerk's purported attempts to have the error corrected. If you had been a jury member, how would you have voted (note that the actual jury deliberated three hours before reaching a verdict)? Assuming the clerk's claims were honest, what controls might, in the future, prevent the bank from failing to respond to efforts to correct such errors?

9. One author has noted the LITWA mania that has been observed in the computer age. LITWA is an acronym of "Let's-invent-the-wheel-again." As support of the mania, the author cites the 1973 Canadian computer census which indicated that 5,700 computers in Canada had an average of four programmers per installation. This suggests that 114,000 new

[22] R. J. Anderson, "Computer Controls: An Essential Commodity in Computer Systems Development," *The Internal Auditor*, April 1976, p. 43.

[23] Ibid., p. 43.

[24] Joseph J. Wasserman, "Plugging the Leaks in Computer Security," *Harvard Business Review*, September-October 1969, p. 125.

[25] "Sad Tale of a Clerk Who Thought He'd Got $60,000 from Nowhere," *Wall Street Journal*, December 2, 1981, p. 31.

programs were written, if each programmer averaged only five programs a year. The author questioned the likelihood of 114,000 programs being sufficiently unique to warrant starting from scratch per application.

What are the advantages and disadvantages to the LITWA mania? What implications does the mania have for auditors?

10. A bank auditor has prepared the following computer audit application chart:

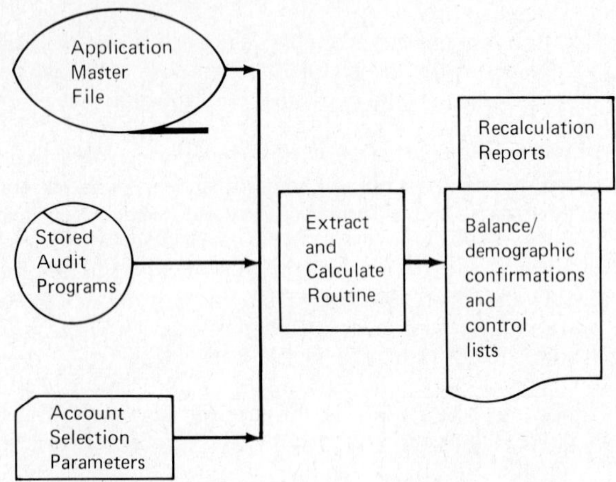

Explain the chart's objective, describing the procedures being performed and the likely use of their output.

11. Airlines' computerized ticket reservation systems are examples of on-line and real-time systems. The seats for upcoming flights represent inventory. The user can randomly access any seat to change it from unsold to sold or "reserved pending sale" status. All locations that sell tickets have on-line connections and can ask about unsold space. Each user can generate input, immediately update the inventory file, and immediately receive an answer.

This computer system is integrated, allowing the recording of a single transaction to initiate numerous other transactions. For example, the selling of a seat will reduce the inventory, price the ticket, prepare the ticket, update sales and receivables, and update the cost records. In contrast, the traditional systems separately maintained sales, inventory, and receivable records.

Analyze the implications of such an integrated EDP system for the auditor. What are the main areas of risk exposure? How can the client control these risks?

12. One difficulty with combating computer fraud is entities' reluctance to report incidents. Companies are embarrassed and fear the loss of public confidence that might result from making computer frauds public. It has been estimated that 85 percent of detected frauds were never reported to law-enforcers.

> What often happens is that the offender, once detected, is required to make restitution and then leave—sometimes even getting severance pay and letters of reference to speed him away. One consequence, no doubt, is a circulating population of unpublished, unrepentant, and unrecognized embezzlers going from company to company.[26]

What special problems are created for the auditor by entities' reluctance to report computer frauds? How might the audit approach be adjusted to resolve such problems?

13. Data protection laws threaten international information flow. The most severe restrictions on data transmissions would be not permitting data to be sent outside a country and the requirement that only the country's own businesses could handle particular types of information and related transactions. Relevant issues include competition, nationalism, protectionism policies, and taxing proposals.[27] Assuming such regulation grows, what would be its implications for the accounting profession and the structure of the market for audit services?

QUESTIONS ADAPTED FROM PROFESSIONAL EXAMINATIONS

1. When auditing an electronic data-processing (EDP) accounting system, the independent auditor should be familiar with its effects on the various characteristics of accounting control and on the study and evaluation of such control. The independent auditor must also be aware of general controls and application controls. General controls refer to all EDP activities, and application controls refer to specific accounting tasks.

Required:

a. What general controls should EDP-based accounting systems have?

b. What are the purposes of each of the following application controls?

[26] Tom Alexander, "Waiting for the Great Computer Rip-Off," *Fortune*, July 1974, p. 145.

[27] David E. Sanger, "Wire Static: Multinationals Worry As Countries Regulate Data Crossing Borders," *Wall Street Journal*, August 26, 1982, pp. 1, 16.

1. Input controls.
2. Processing controls.
3. Output controls.

(CPA exam adapted)

2. You have been engaged by the Central Savings and Loan Association to examine its financial statements for the year ended December 31, 19X6. The CPA who examined the financial statements at December 31, 19X6 rendered an unqualified opinion.

In January 19X7 the association installed an on-line, real-time computer system. Each teller in the association's main office and seven branch offices has an on-line, input-output terminal. Customers' mortgage payments, savings account deposits, and withdrawals are recorded in the accounts by the computer from data input by the teller at the time of the transaction. The teller keys the proper account by account number and enters the information in the terminal keyboard to record the transaction. The accounting department at the main office has both punched card and typewriter input-output devices. The computer is housed at the main office.

In addition to servicing its own mortgage loans, the association acts as a mortgage servicing agency for three life insurance companies. The association maintains mortgage records for them and serves as the collection and escrow agent for the mortgagees (the insurance companies), who pay the association for these services.

Required:
You expect the association to have certain internal controls in effect, because it uses an on-line, real-time computer system. List these controls, i.e., those that should be in effect solely because this system is employed; classify them as

a. Those controls pertaining to input of information.

b. All other types of computer controls.

(CPA exam adapted)

3. Controls over electronic data-processing activities can be classified as preventive, detective, or corrective.

Required:

a. Briefly define each of these three classifications of controls, and give two examples of each.

b. Detective controls are generally considered to be the most important. Give three reasons why.

(CIA exam adapted)

4. Johnson, a CPA, was engaged to examine the financial statements of Horizon Incorporated, which has its own computer installation. During the preliminary review, Johnson found that Horizon had not properly segregated its programming and operating functions. As a result, Johnson intensified his study and evaluation of the internal control system pertaining to the computer and concluded that the existing compensating general controls provided reasonable assurance that the objectives of the internal control system were being met.

Required:

a. In a properly functioning EDP environment, how should the programming and operating functions be separated?

b. What are the compensating general controls that Johnson most likely found? Do not discuss hardware and application controls.

(CPA exam adapted)

5. A CPA's client, Boos & Baumkirchner, Inc., is a medium-sized manufacturer of products for the leisure-time activities market (camping equipment, scuba gear, bows and arrows and the like). During the past year, a computer system was installed, and inventory records of finished goods and parts were converted to computer processing. The inventory master file is maintained on a disk. Each record of the file contains the following information:

item or part number.
description.
size.
unit of measure code.
quantity on hand.
cost per unit.
total value of inventory on hand at cost.
date of last sale or usage.
quantity used or sold this year.
economic order quantity.
code number of major vendor.
code number of secondary vendor.

In preparation for year-end inventory, the client has two identical sets of preprinted inventory count cards. One set is for the client's inventory counts, and the other is for the CPA's audit test counts. The following information has been keypunched into the cards and interpreted on their face:

item or part number.
description.
size.
unit of measure code.

In taking the year-end inventory, the client's personnel will write the actual counted quantity on the face of each card. When all the counts are complete, the counted quantity will be keypunched into the cards. The cards will be processed against the disk file, and quantity-on-hand figures will be adjusted to reflect the actual count. A computer listing will be prepared to show any missing inventory count cards and all quantity adjustments of more than $100 in value. These items will be investigated by client personnel, and all required adjustments will be made. When adjustments have been completed, the final year-end balances will be computed and posted to the general ledger.

The CPA has a general-purpose computer audit software package that will run on the client's computer and can process both card and disk files.

Required:

a. In general and without regard to Boos & Baumkirchner, Inc., list the types and uses of general-purpose computer audit software packages.

b. List and describe at least five ways that a general-purpose computer audit software package can be used to audit the inventory of Boos & Baumkirchner, Inc. (For example, the package can be used to read the disk inventory master file and list items and parts with a high unit cost or total value. Such items can be included in the test counts to increase the dollar coverage of the audit verification.)

(CPA exam adapted)

6. The various data-processing approaches have different advantages or disadvantages.

Required:

List the numbers one through six on your answer sheet, representing the processing approaches in Column 1 below. Select the one advantage or disadvantage from Column 2 that would be the most appropriate for each item in Column 1. Each item in Column 2 can be used only once. Place the appropriate letter from Column 2 beside each number from Column 1.

(CIA exam adapted)

Column 1	Column 2
1. Centralized.	a. Reduces risk of loss or destruction of hardware and critical data.
2. Decentralized.	b. No opportunity for distributed network.
3. Distributed.	c. Dependence on one computer.
4. Both centralized and decentralized.	d. Permits use of data base approach and minimizes duplication of common data.
5. Both decentralized and distributed.	e. Most difficult to maintain overall security of data.
6. Both centralized and distributed.	f. No method for coordinating or exchanging data during processing.

7. The Ultimate Life Insurance Company recently established a data base management system. The company is now planning to provide its branch offices with terminals that have on-line access to the central computer facility.

Required:

a. Define a data base.

b. List one advantage of a data base.

c. Briefly describe three security steps to safeguard the data base from improper access through the terminals.

d. Briefly describe four steps to control the completeness and accuracy of the data transmitted through the terminals to the data base.

(CIA exam adapted)

8. The president of a large utility has asked its internal auditing department to audit the customer payment system, emphasizing the data entry and data transmission functions at local branch offices. Customers may send their payments to the central office or pay in person at any of the company's twenty-four branch offices. When a customer pays a utility bill at a branch office, the payment data are immediately entered into the branch payment system by an employee via a terminal connected to the company's central computer.

In auditing the branch payment system, the internal auditor divided the process into the following three segments:

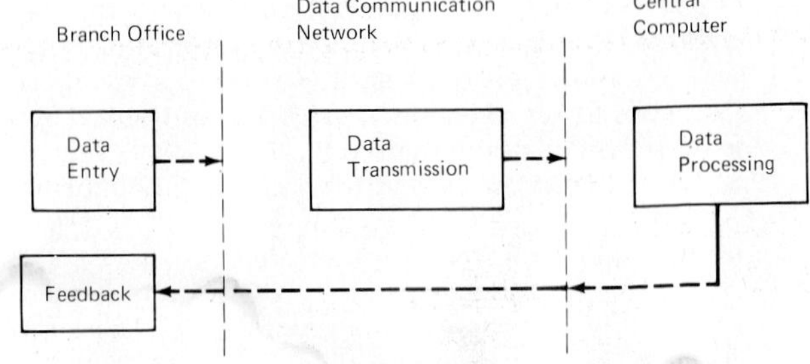

Required:

a. List three major data-entry control objectives that the internal auditor should identify.

b. For each of the three data-entry control objectives listed in your answer, briefly describe two control techniques to achieve them.

(CIA exam adapted)

9. You are involved in the internal audit of accounts receivable, which represents a significant portion of a large retail corporation's assets. Your audit plan requires using a computer, but you encounter the reactions described below.

a. The computer operations manager says that all of the time on the computer is scheduled for the foreseeable future and that it is not feasible to perform the auditor's work.

b. The computer scheduling manager suggests that your computer program be catalogued into the computer program library (on disk storage) to be run when computer time becomes available.

c. You are refused admission to the computer room.

d. The systems manager tells you that it will take too much time to adapt the computer audit program to the EDP operating system and that the computer installation programmers will write the programs needed for the audit.

Required:

For each of the four situations described, state what the auditor should do to proceed with the accounts receivable audit.

(CIA exam adapted)

10. Your company has bought several minicomputers for use in various locations and applications. One of these has been installed in the stores department, which is responsible for disbursing stock items and maintaining stores records. In your audit you find, among other things, that a competent employee, trained in computer applications, receives the requisitions for stores, reviews them for completeness and propriety of approvals, disburses the stock, maintains the records, operates the computer, and authorizes adjustments to the total amounts of stock accumulated by the computer.

When you discuss the applicable controls with the department manager, you are told that the minicomputer is assigned exclusively to that department and that it therefore does not require the same types of controls that the large computer systems have.

Required:

Comment on the manager's contentions, discussing briefly five types of control that would apply to this minicomputer application.

(CIA exam adapted)

11. Your internal auditing department has not performed any audits of the EDP function in your company, nor has it used EDP for auditing purposes. In a recent management letter, the external auditors expressed concern over this situation. The letter was referred to the audit committee of the board of directors. The chairman of the audit committee asked you, as the director of internal auditing, to meet with the committee and present a plan to audit the EDP function. The company has a single computer center, with some divisions doing their own processing through remote job entry (RJE). All of its major financial systems are computer based.

You have listed the following areas of audit concern:

a. Computer operations.

b. Systems under development.

c. Systems in operation.

d. Disaster recovery.

e. Security.

f. Postimplementation review.

Required:

State two reasons that each of these areas should be a cause of audit concern.

(CIA exam adapted)

12. You are assigned to review the documentation of a data-processing function.

Required:

a. List three advantages of adequately documenting a data-processing function.

b. Below are two columns of information. The left column lists six categories of documentation, and the right column lists eighteen elements of documentation related to the categories.

Categories	Elements
A. Systems documentation.	1. Flowcharts showing the flow of information.
B. Program documentation.	2. Procedures needed to balance, reconcile, and maintain overall control.
C. Operations documentation.	3. Storage instructions.
D. User documentation.	4. Contents and format of data to be captured.
E. Library documentation.	5. Constants, codes, and tables.
F. Data-entry documentation.	6. Verification procedures.
	7. Logic diagrams and/or decision tables.
	8. Report distribution instructions.
	9. Messages and programmed halts.
	10. Procedures for backup files.
	11. Retention cycle.
	12. Source statement listings.
	13. Instructions to show proper use of each transaction.
	14. A complete history from planning through installation.
	15. Restart and recovery procedures.
	16. Rules for handling blank spaces.
	17. Instructions to ensure proper completion of all input forms.
	18. List of programs in a system.

Match each of the elements of documentation with the category in which it should be found. List letters *A* through *F* on your answer sheet. After each letter, list the numbers of the elements that best apply to that category. Use each element only once.

(CIA exam adapted)

13. Multiple Choice: Controls in an EDP Environment

Select the one answer that best completes the statement or answers the question.

13.1 In an electronic data-processing system, program controls substitute for human controls in a manual system. Which of the following is an example of a program control?
a. Dual read.
b. Echo check.
c. Validity check.
d. Limit and reasonableness test.
(CPA exam adapted)

13.2 Some electronic data-processing accounting control procedures can be used for all electronic data-processing activities (general controls), and some, for only specific tasks (application controls). General controls include
a. Controls designed to ascertain that all data submitted to electronic data processing for processing have been properly authorized.
b. Controls used to correct and resubmit data that were initially incorrect.
c. Controls to document and approve programs and changes in programs.
d. Controls designed to ensure the accuracy of the processing results.
(CPA exam adapted)

13.3 The machine-language program resulting from the translation of a symbolic-language program is called a (an)
a. Processor program.
b. Object program.
c. Source program.
d. Wired program.
(CPA exam adapted)

13.4 Which of the following disaster recovery measures will help restore an EDP system after the EDP installation has been destroyed?
a. Store the documented recovery plan in the computer facility.
b. Maintain comparable backup physical facilities on a standby basis.
c. Keep backup master and transaction files available in the computer facility.
d. Keep the previous version of the operating system available.
e. Store current versions of programs and program documentation off the premises.
(CIA exam adapted)

13.5 Automated equipment controls in an electronic data-processing system are designed to detect errors caused by
a. Faulty operation of the electronic data-processing equipment.
b. Lack of human alertness.
c. Incorrect input and output data.
d. Poor management of the electronic data-processing installation.
(CPA exam adapted)

13.6 A control feature in an electronic data-processing system requires the central processing unit (CPU) to send signals to the printer to activate the print mechanism for each character. Just before printing, the print mechanism sends a signal back to the CPU verifying that the proper print position has been activated. This type of hardware control is referred to as
a. Echo control.
b. Validity control.
c. Signal control.
d. Check digit control.
(CPA exam adapted)

13.7 An electronic data-processing technique that groups data to permit convenient and efficient processing is known as
a. Document-count processing.
b. Multiprogramming.
c. Batch processing.
d. Generalized audit processing.
(CPA exam adapted)

13.8 The most efficient and least costly method of dumping information in order to maintain a backup file is from disk to
a. Dump.
b. Printout.
c. Cards.
d. Tape.
(CPA exam adapted)

13.9 If a control total were to be computed on each of the following data items, which would be the best hash total for a payroll EDP application?

a. Gross pay.
b. Hours worked.
c. Department number.
d. Number of employees.

(CPA exam adapted)

13.10 Which of the following ascertains whether a given characteristic belongs to the group?
a. Parity check.
b. Validity check.
c. Echo check.
d. Limit check.

(CPA exam adapted)

13.11 In updating a computerized accounts receivable file, which one of the following would be used as a batch control to verify the accuracy of the posting of cash receipts remittances?
a. The sum of the cash deposits plus the discounts less the sales returns.
b. The sum of the cash deposits.
c. The sum of the cash deposits less the discounts taken by customers.
d. The sum of the cash deposits plus the discounts taken by customers.

(CPA exam adapted)

13.12 In a daily computer run to update checking account balances and print out basic details on any customer's account that was overdrawn, the overdrawn account of the computer programmer was never printed. Which of the following control procedures would have been best to detect this irregularity? The auditor's
a. Using the test deck approach to test the client's program and verify the subsidiary file.
b. Using a running control total for the master file to check account balances and compare with the printout.
c. Using a program check for valid customer code.
d. Periodic recompiling of programs from documented source decks and comparing with programs currently in use.

(CPA exam adapted)

13.13 A procedural control used to minimize the possibility of data or program file destruction through operator error includes
a. Control figures.
b. Cross-footing tests.
c. Limit checks.
d. External labels.

(CPA exam adapted)

13.14 Where disk files are used, the grandfather-father-son updating backup concept is relatively difficult to implement because
a. Finding the information points on disks is extremely time-consuming.
b. Magnetic fields and other environmental factors make off-site storage impractical.
c. Information must be dumped in the form of hard copy if it is to be reviewed before being used in updating.
d. The process of updating old records is destructive.

(CPA exam adapted)

13.15 When an on-line, real-time (OLRT) electronic data-processing system is used, internal control can be strengthened by
a. Separating keypunching and error-listing operations.
b. Attaching plastic file protection rings to reels of magnetic tape before new data can be entered on the file.
c. Making a validity check of an identification number before a user can obtain access to the computer files.
d. Preparing batch totals to ensure that file updates are made for the entire input.

(CPA exam adapted)

13.16 More than one file may be stored on a single magnetic memory disk, and several programs may be in the core storage unit at the same time. In both cases it is important to prevent mixing the data. One way to do this is to use
a. File integrity control.
b. Boundary protection.
c. Interleaving.
d. Paging.

(CPA exam adapted)

13.17 Which of the following would weaken internal control in an electronic data-processing system?
a. The computer librarian maintains custody of computer program instructions and detailed program listings.
b. Computer operators have access to operator instructions and detailed program listings.
c. The control group maintains sole custody of all computer output.
d. Computer programmers write and debug programs that perform routines designed by the systems analyst.

(CPA exam adapted)

13.18 One of the biggest problems in an EDP system is that incompatible functions may be performed by the same individual. One compensating control for this is using
a. A tape library.
b. A self-checking digit system.
c. Computer-generated hash totals.
d. A computer log.
(CPA exam adapted)

13.19 As part of internal audit, the auditor studied a computer flowchart that contained the following logic diagram. Which of the controls are represented in this diagram?

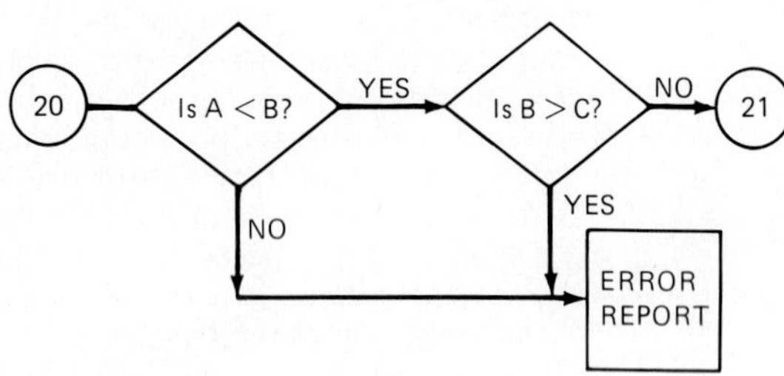

a. Field check.
b. Limit check.
c. Control total.
d. Password check.
e. Numeric check.
(CIA exam adapted)

13.20 A bank's automatic teller machine system (ATM) uses currency dispensing machines to issue cash automatically to customers. ATM uses subsystems connected by data communication networks and data bases. An important edit check in ATM is a validity check, which tests
a. Identification numbers or transaction codes against those known to be authorized.
b. The characters in a field to ensure that they are of the class that the field is supposed to contain.
c. A numerical amount in a record to ensure that it does not exceed some predetermined amount.
d. The logical correctness of relationships among the values of data items on an input record and a file record.
e. None of the above.
(CIA exam adapted)

14. Multiple Choice: Auditing in an EDP Environment

Select the one answer that best completes the statement or answers the question.

14.1 The first step in planning audit activities in a computer environment is to:
a. Develop a detailed program.
b. List the essential internal controls.
c. Obtain detailed information from management about the areas of concern.
d. Select the audit techniques to be employed.
e. Determine the audit's objectives.
(CIA exam adapted)

14.2 When auditing a stand-alone minicomputer, as compared with a large-scale computer system, which of the following will affect the audit program's preparation?
a. The internal auditor will have to perform more substantive tests.
b. The internal auditor will have to tailor the program in order to access data.
c. The internal auditor will have to use audit techniques different from those used in a large computer configuration.
d. The internal auditor should expect to find systems controls different from those found in a larger computer.
e. The internal auditor will have to audit around the computer.
(CIA exam adapted)

14.3 One technique for testing computer application program controls is the test data method. The purpose of this test is to
a. Run data twice through the old and new systems to find unexpected differences.
b. Select and record data for subsequent analysis.
c. Provide the documentation necessary to explain the system of control.
d. Verify the processing logic and controls.
e. Show the trail of instructions executed through an application.
(CIA exam adapted)

14.4 When an EDP auditor performs compliance tests on an inventory file containing over twenty thousand line items, that auditor can maintain independence and perform most efficiently by
a. Employing an independent contractor to write an extraction program.
b. Using a generalized audit software program.

c. Obtaining a printout of the entire file and then selecting each *n*th item.
d. Using the systems department's programmer to write an extraction program.
e. Asking the console operator to print every item that cost more than $100.

(CIA exam adapted)

14.5 Which of the following tasks could not be performed using a generalized audit software package?
a. Recalculations of numbers.
b. Retracing of transactions through calculation and classification operations.
c. Scanning for unusual items.
d. Computation of operating ratios.
e. Physical counts.

(CIA exam adapted)

14.6 A computer service center processes, for an auditor's client, financial data that has a material effect on that client's financial statements. The independent auditor need not review the service center controls if
a. The service center controls have already been reviewed by the client's internal audit team.
b. The service center processes data exclusively for the audit client and its subsidiaries.
c. The user controls relied on, which are external to the service center, are adequate to ensure that errors and irregularities will be discovered.
d. The service center is a partially owned subsidiary of the client company, whose financial statements are examined by another CPA.

(CPA exam adapted)

14.7 Accounting control procedures in the EDP activity may leave no visible evidence indicating that the procedures were performed. In such instances, the auditor should test these accounting controls by
a. Making corroborative inquiries.
b. Observing the separation of the employees' duties.
c. Reviewing transactions submitted for processing and comparing them with related output.
d. Reviewing the run manual.

(CPA exam adapted)

14.8 Compliance testing of an advanced EDP system
a. Can be performed using only actual transactions, as testing of simulated transactions is of no consequence.
b. Can be performed using actual transactions or simulated transactions.
c. Is impractical, as many procedures in the EDP activity leave no visible evidence of having been performed.
d. Is inadvisable because it may distort the evidence in the master files.

(CPA exam adapted)

14.9 One advantage of using generalized audit packages in the audit of an advanced EDP system is that it enables the auditor to
a. Substantiate the accuracy of data through self-checking digits and hash totals.
b. Use the computer's speed and accuracy.
c. Verify the performance of machine operations that leave visible evidence of occurrence.
d. Gather and store large quantities of supportive evidence in machine-readable form.

(CPA exam adapted)

14.10 Which of the following is necessary to audit balances in an on-line EDP system in an environment of destructive updating?
a. Periodic dumping of transaction files.
b. Year-end utilization of audit hooks.
c. An integrated test facility.
d. A well-documented audit trail.

(CPA exam adapted)

14.11 Which of the following is an advantage of generalized computer audit packages?
a. They all are written in one computer language.
b. They can be used for audits and clients that use differing EDP equipment and file formats.
c. They have reduced the auditor's need to study input controls for EDP-related procedures.
d. They can be substituted for a relatively large part of the required compliance testing.

(CPA exam adapted)

14.12 The client's EDP exception reporting system helps an auditor to conduct a more efficient audit because it
a. Condenses data significantly.
b. Highlights abnormal conditions.
c. Decreases the EDP compliance testing.
d. Is an efficient EDP input control.

(CPA exam adapted)

14.13 During the review of an EDP internal control system, an auditor may review decision tables prepared by the client. A decision table is usually prepared by a client to supplement or replace the preparation of

a. An internal control questionnaire when the number of alternative responses is large.
b. A narrative description of a system where transactions are not processed in batches.
c. Flowcharts when the number of alternatives is large.
d. An internal control questionnaire not specifically designed for an EDP installation.

(CPA exam adapted)

14.14 An auditor should be familiar with a client's electronic data-processing hardware and software. One important element of the client's software is the program, and another element of software is the

a. Cathode ray tube (CRT).
b. Central processing unit (CPU).
c. Magnetic tape drive.
d. Compiler.

(CPA exam adapted)

14.15 Which of the following client electronic data-processing (EDP) systems generally can be audited without examining or directly testing the system's EDP computer programs?

a. A system that performs relatively uncomplicated processes and produces detailed output.
b. A system that affects a number of essential master files and produces a limited output.
c. A system that updates a few essential master files and produces no printed output other than final balances.
d. A system that performs relatively complicated processing and produces very little detailed output.

(CPA exam adapted)

14.16 Which of the following is true of generalized audit software packages?

a. They can be used only in auditing on-line computer systems.
b. They can be used on any computer without modification.
c. They each have their own characteristics that the auditor must consider before using.
d. They enable the auditor to perform all manual compliance test procedures less expensively.

(CPA exam adapted)

CASES FOR DISCUSSION

1. You have just completed an EDP system review and have prepared the following comments:

- There is no insurance coverage (other than the usual fire coverage) to protect against accidental losses of records and losses from the manipulation of records.
- No formal background checks are made before employing persons who would have access to sensitive data.
- The organizational structure does not separate programming, computer operation, and manual control duties.
- Entrances to areas where magnetically encoded data are stored are not equipped with devices to detect magnets.
- Key personnel do not know the location of shut-down valves for the main water supply.
- Exit and entry ramps to the EDP facility do not provide access to fire fighting and emergency equipment.
- Duplicate programs are not maintained in another location.
- System and programming documentation is not updated after each change.
- The computer system does not have a console typewriter to control and record the activities performed by the computer and the computer operator.
- Copies of critical data files are not stored at a remote location.

Based on these comments, evaluate the client's risk exposure. How would you explain to the client his current risk picture? Draft a report which could accompany these comments that interprets the meaning of the weaknesses for your client and the consequences of management's decision not to correct such weaknesses.

2. One client's programs seem to be constantly revised. Your investigation has indicated:

- Properly approved written requests are not always required for program revisions.
- When used, written requests frequently do not describe the reasons for the proposed changes.
- A log of program changes indicating the date when the change went into operation is not maintained.
- Program changes are not always developed and programmed by employees other than those assigned to computer operations.
- Computer operators have access to the detailed program documentation both during and after the testing phase.

○ Revisions to programs are not always tested before being used in production.

Discuss the control implications of these findings.

3. Some believe that cathode-ray "controls by code" are foolproof. For example, the purchasing department will have a code like PD-1 which can only be used for procurements. If a user of the PD-1 coding were to try to process a receipt, the screen would flash the message "No possible task." Similarly, a RD-1 code is given to receiving, and an AP-1 code is given to accounts payable. As the user of AP-1 processes the invoice, the check in payment of the purchase is mechanically produced and signed but manually stuffed into an envelope and mailed.

Assume as the internal auditor of an entity with such controls, you suspect that computer programmers and system analysts may not have been sufficiently aware of internal controls as they designed the system. You obtain a list of all cathode-ray tubes in use, their locations, and the identification and process codes. You test all inquiries and identification on each tube. Your test reveals that all cathode-ray tubes can complete transactions and processing for all departments.

Explain what type of fraud could be perpetrated in this situation, and how. What controls would you recommend to the business, besides the cathode-ray "controls by code"?[28]

4. One writer noted that it is possible to hold a sixty-four-kilobyte computer in one's hand and that is exactly the equipment carried by gas meter readers along their route. The 3-pound computer which costs less than $1,000 is capable of

○ telling the meter reader his route for the day.

○ reporting the average gas consumption per month for the past six months for each household.

○ computing and printing the bill.

○ recording the time for each stop.

○ transmitting the day's business to the gas company's computer.

Following this description, the author states: "The best thing about it is that the meter reader can't program it, but just give technology time!"[29]

Why does the author describe the programming limitation of the computer as a "plus"?

Assume that technology now permits such programming, what controls should be established and what risks are present?

Without such technology, discuss the risk exposure of the gas company that exists due to the use of computers, which was not present when a manual system was in place.

5. Banks have particularly vulnerable inventory, as money is homogeneous and highly negotiable. Potential fraud or errors are limitless; however, if material, they should be able to be detected by a well-controlled computer audit program. For each of the following examples of fraud, first list the fraud's effects, and then describe how computer auditing tools and generalized audit software can be used to detect each occurrence:

a. Fraudulent withdrawals.
b. Fraudulent deposits.
c. Transfer of funds from dormant to active accounts.
d. Misstatement of loan interest.
e. Address alterations.
f. Incorrect payment histories.
g. Falsification of collateral.
h. Erroneous savings interest calculation method.
i. Suppression of service charges.
j. Suppression of exception reports.

6. U.S. Steel has reportedly used a modified integrated test facility (ITF) in auditing its multiplant payrolls. Rather than adding test data to real payrolls, a separate payroll cycle for ITF was established that paralleled regular payroll cycles. For ITF payroll processing, all the normal clerical controls were prepared, and all input and output data were balanced or reconciled to predetermined totals. Data for eight hundred of the two thousand employees of one steel plant were converted into ITF files. The output of the ITF processing was reconciled to the live payroll from which input data had been mechanically extracted. The ITF tested 92 percent of the conditions under which an employee could work. Why did U.S. Steel modify the ITF approach? What risks does the modification present that would not have been as great if the usual ITF approach had been used? Comment on the advantages and disadvantages of this ITF approach, compared with other means of testing the EDP system for payroll.[30]

7. An auditor of a public utility intends to pass cus-

[28] Robert E. Booth, "Cathode-Ray Tube Checkmate," *The Internal Auditor*, March-April 1974, pp. 39–41.

[29] Fenwicke W. Holmes, "Distributed Data Processing," *Journal of Systems Management*, July 1977, pp. 10–12.

[30] Adapted from B. L. Thurman, Jr., and Regis C. Cunningham, Jr., "Using an Integrated Test Facility in Audits of Multiplant Payrolls," *The Internal Auditor*, November-December 1974, pp. 50–56.

tomer master file information and the current list of open accounts receivable through generalized audit software and check to see that (a) individual accounts receivable balance with the control total; (b) individual customers' deposits balance with the control total; (c) all company meters are either being billed currently or are recorded as turned off; and (d) the company's credit and collection procedures are being followed. In addition, accounts with unusual consumption patterns, old outstanding balances, credit balances, and no billings for the current billing cycle will be identified for follow-up. Confirmation requests on accounts selected by applying a random sampling technique will also be prepared. What are the specific generalized audit software capabilities that should be used for these checks and audit procedures? Use the jargon introduced in this chapter, and describe the type of data used for the various generalized audit software functions.

8. An article about computer rip-offs discusses Equity Funding as a case that

> pretty well demonstrated that conventional auditing is all but helpless when confronting deception involving computers. The auditors have lost their traditional "paper trail"—the detritus of indelibly inscribed orders, invoices, bills, and receipts that the men in the green eyeshades pore through on the track of irregularity.[31]

In an elaboration of how computer audit software has come into vogue, the article points out that this audit approach "is only as dependable as the computer itself. And unfortunately, computers can be programmed to lie or conceal as easily as they can be programmed for truth."[32] Security specialists point out the absence of external evidence of frauds: "Sherlock Holmes . . . can't come in and find any heel marks. There's no safe with its door blown off."[33] When questioned about auditing software, the specialists respond, "The first thing the interloper would do is corrupt the audit-trail software itself."[34] Research by Computer Fraud Specialist Donn Parker indicated that out of 175 cases of computer crime analyzed, almost all were exposed by happenstance, as opposed to being detected through security precautions or accounting controls. There is also evidence that "a persuasive liar on a telephone can entice employees of a time-sharing system into giving out passwords."[35] Similarly, employees are observed to be careless in writing down passwords or discarding print-outs with legible passwords. The point is that controls pose few real obstacles to the defrauder.

Critique the perspective represented in this article, and evaluate the consequence for the auditor of the various facts that are presented and the arguments that are developed. How can the auditing profession effectively respond to such a setting?

[31] Tom Alexander, "Waiting for the Great Computer Rip-Off," *Fortune*, July 1974, p. 144.
[32] Ibid. [33] Ibid. p. 146. [34] Ibid. [35] Ibid., p. 148.

11

Sampling Concepts and Attribute Testing

A continuing education (CE) course on statistical sampling has just begun, and the instructor, an audit manager who has recently been the national firm's troubleshooter for statistical problems with sampling applications in the field, has just been introduced.

Instructor. Before we get started, I'd like to make a list of your questions or past experiences that have troubled you about statistical theories or practical problems. That way, I'll be certain to cover those topics sometime during this CE session. Who's got something on their mind?

Participant 1. I have yet to figure out sequential sampling. Now, as I understand it, if I begin a compliance test and decide to use sequential sampling, I'll have a smaller initial sample size. But if the results aren't quite as good as I expected, I'll have to draw a larger total sample than would have been necessary had I not used sequential sampling. If I have the same audit objective, and the findings are essentially the same, why am I, in the end, penalized by selecting sequential sampling? I thought the biggest argument for it was its efficiency. . . . You might say that I've missed the logic underlying the determination of sample sizes!

Participant 2. I have a related question. Often, when we select a sample, a couple of those documents are missing. I can't see why we have to assume that those documents are in error! Usually they've just been misplaced; in fact, often they show up before the end of the audit work. As I understand it, a random sample is just an arbitrary selection of documents; so what's so special about the missing ones? Why can't we substitute more randomly selected documents for those that are missing?

Participant 3. Now that we're talking about random sampling, I have a question. How can an "ith sample" or "interval sampling" approach be considered random? For one of our clients, we take every hundredth document as a sample item; yet we know that the client systematically files national suppliers first, then regional, and last local. I'm not even convinced that our interval sampling from alphabetized files is really random! Why, one of our clients makes 40 percent of its sales to three customers, all of whose company names begin with an "E"!

Participant 4. Even if the interval sampling were random, there's no guarantee of audit coverage. I've taken reasonably large samples that represented less than 5 percent of the total dollar transactions for that cycle. The "luck of the draw" simply led to small-dollar transactions.

Participant 1. Well, I can help out there; I think the answer to that is to sample in proportion to size. A lot of firms call it dollar-unit sampling; it ensures that you'll include more large-dollar items in your sample.

Participant 5. Yeah, that sounds great, but you realize then it's not a random selection, and could create some problems. I was reading in the paper the other day about a Las Vegas "skimming" case in which the leader of the defrauders advised stealing "where the auditing is less rigorous."[1]

If our clients find out that we're not paying attention to small-dollar items; then that's where we'll have problems. And, small dollar transactions can add up!

Participant 6. I, for one, am not all that sure that random samples make sense, even when stratified to include larger-dollar items. We know a lot about a client's operations before we ever start sampling. For example, I think we ought to be sampling more transactions that involve related parties. I'd like to hear more about directed sampling.

Participant 7. I was talking to somebody the other day about the tendency to use 95 percent confidence levels in our audit tests. He pointed out that the implication of such tests was 5 percent error and that the level of risk would seem unacceptable in light of the SEC's definition of materiality as 3 percent of net income. I was stymied and unsure of how to reply!

Participant 8. I think I might be in the wrong course. The terms *sequential sampling, random sampling, ith sampling, interval sampling, sampling in proportion to size, dollar-unit sampling, stratified sampling, directed sampling,* and *confidence level* are Greek to me! I vaguely remember some of them, but I thought this was an introductory course!

All of the concepts described in this introductory case are, indeed, introductory concepts, all of which will be described in this chapter or the accompanying Chapter 12. Sampling is such an integral part of the audit process that it is essential for you to gain an intuitive understanding of sampling techniques, as well as an appreciation for problems that you are likely to experience in practice. The questions posed by the participants in the CE course are common theoretical and practice-related issues which will be clarified and resolved, to the extent possible, in the following pages.

This chapter will introduce most of the terminology that is relevant to sampling, including terminology that relates to attribute and to variables sampling. However, the in-depth discussion of

[1] Thomas Petzinger, Jr., "Wiretaps and Informer Helped U.S. Break a Las Vegas 'Skimming' Case," *Wall Street Journal*, August 12, 1983, p. 17.

variables sampling will be postponed to Chapter 12. In that chapter, examples of variables testing will be provided and regression analysis will be described as an auditing tool.

An Intuitive Introduction

Sampling is a very intuitive audit tool, as it allows the auditor to draw inferences from tests of a subset of a client's transactions. Recall from earlier chapters' discussion that it would not be cost/beneficial or practical for the auditor to examine all transactions of an entity during the period under audit. As the auditor's report emphasizes, "tests" are performed to form the basis of the auditor's report. These tests are statistical and nonstatistical tests. *Statistical tests* measure *sampling risk,* or the possibility that the sample or subset of transactions or units tested is not representative of (similar to) the overall population (total number of transactions of interest.) *Nonstatistical sampling* cannot measure sampling risk. A statistical sampling approach relies on generally accepted theory of mathematics and probability to quantify sampling error (sampling risk) by following a specific *sampling plan,* which describes the audit objective, the mode of selection, the number of units to be selected, and the manner of sample evaluation. In particular, the auditor must specify the objective of the sampling application, that is, what is desired of the particular sampling process being used—what *accuracy (precision)* and what *reliability (confidence level)?* These audit judgments will be elaborated upon in further depth throughout this chapter, but intuitively, you should expect that the greater amount of accuracy an auditor desires, the larger the *sample size* required. Similarly, the greater the amount of confidence or reliability the auditor desires in the sample's representativeness of the population, the greater the price (s)he has to pay; that price is greater sample size—more units or transactions would have to be tested to improve reliability. Hence, sample size is critically dependent on these two auditor judgments: reliability and precision.

Sample size is also influenced by two characteristics of the population of interest: *population size* and *population variability.* As your intuition would suggest, larger populations require somewhat larger samples; however, as the chapter will elaborate, this is not a directly proportional effect, as required sampling only increases slightly as a population grows very large. Far more important as a determinant of sample size is the population's variability. If every item in a population were exactly the same, then there would be no variability among the separate items. In this case, a sample of one would suffice because "if you've seen one, you've seen them all!" In contrast, if there was great variability among items in the population, a sample of one could hardly be representative of the population. The typical example used in basic probability courses is an urn full of marbles. If all marbles were white, then a selection of one marble could completely describe the other items in the population. However, if some marbles are white and some are red, more than one marble would need to be selected to form a conclusion as to the proportional mix of colored marbles in the urn. Similarly, an auditor trying to form a conclusion as to reported inventory value may be able to select a very small sample if all inventory items are of one type, have a similar value, and are expected to be in the same condition. Yet, if the client has 100 lines of product, varying from inventory values of $1 to $10,000, it should be very intuitive that you would need to examine a far greater number of inventory items to form an estimate of the total inventory value. The overall moral is simple: the greater the population variability, the greater the required sample size.

The effect of the auditor's judgments as to reliability and precision, as well as population characteristics such as population size and population variability, should be similar no matter what type of sampling is used. The key difference between statistical and nonstatistical tests is whether they are formalized and capable of estimating the sampling risk in statistical terms—a statistical sampling approach—or whether a departure from the formal statistical planning, selection, or evaluation of the sampling items has precluded such a quantitative estimate of sampling risk based on probability theory—a nonstatistical sampling approach.

Before proceeding to a more specific and technical discussion, it is of interest to recognize that regardless of the auditor's approach to sampling, there will be a nonsampling risk that is not quantified by either statistical or nonstatistical audit tools. *Nonsampling risk* exists in all auditing procedures and refers to the chance that an error is made in performing an audit. That error may be caused by improper planning, selecting inappropriate auditing procedures to address a particular audit objective, a mistake in examining a document (e.g., thinking that mathematical accuracy was correct because the auditor made the same error in recalculation as the original preparer), or an error in executing a procedure, perhaps because of incompetence or inadequate supervision during the audit. Despite sampling theory's inability to quantify the effectiveness of audit procedures from the perspective of nonsampling error, it is possible to control the nonsampling risk by complying with generally accepted auditing standards. Most important, adequate planning and supervision can help keep nonsampling risk to a reasonably low level.

Descriptive Statistics

Whenever an auditor is going to test a population, he or she should be familiar with its nature or "profile," which may be learned by scanning raw data. But that can be very time-consuming and may be impractical and ineffective if the population is very large. Instead, the auditor can review the population's *descriptive statistics.* Past statistical courses have introduced descriptive statistics, but we will briefly review them as a reminder of their meaning, their information content, and the manner in which they can be used to describe the nature of both a population and a selected sample.

To determine the appropriate *descriptive statistics,* it is useful to make a picture of the data set, by plotting along the *y*-axis the number of times that a value appears in the data set (with the value plotted along the *x*-axis). If such a plot looks like that in Exhibit 11-1, it is said to be *normally distributed* (symbolized as $\mathcal{N}$). Such a distribution can be described by its mean and its standard deviation. These two statistics and the other descriptive data commonly used to describe a data set are defined in Exhibit 11-2. If a data set is symmetrical and readily available tables describing normally distributed data can be used, then it is simple to determine the range within which stated percentages of the population values are expected to lie. Exhibit 11-2 shows that 67 percent of the data points will lie within 1 standard deviation of the mean. This statement is based on the concept of precision and reliability. Any item selected from a population can be expected to lie between a value of 1.5 and 10.5 about 67 percent of the time an item is drawn (using the example in Exhibit 11-2). Ninety-five percent of the time, the values could be expected to lie within about 2 standard deviations of the data set's mean value. Yet, the appropriateness of such statements depends upon a population being normal.

But many data sets are not normally distributed. The data set in Exhibit 11-2 is symmetric but also flat (has kurtosis) relative to a normal curve. In audits, the populations are often skewed. For example, inventory items are likely to include several small-dollar items and far fewer large-dollar items. However, no matter what the population's shape is, the auditor's focus tends to be upon sampling distributions that display a normal shape whenever the sample size is reasonably large. For this concept to become intuitive, it is necessary to rethink the purpose of a sampling plan.

EXHIBIT 11-1
Illustrating a Data Set

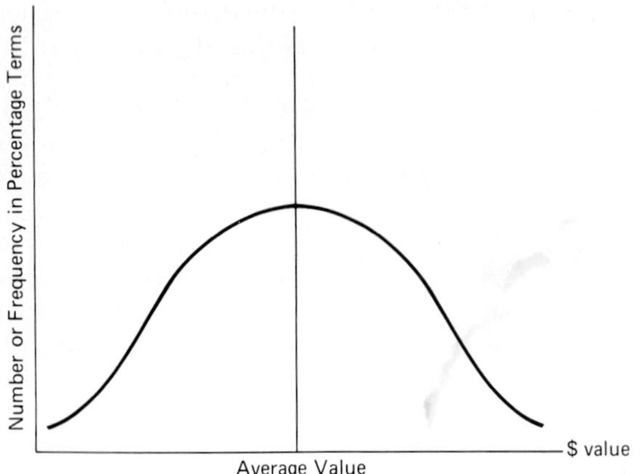

Normal Distribution: Bell-shaped symmetrical distribution that can be totally described by its mean (average value) and standard deviation (scatter).

EXHIBIT 11-2
Descriptive Statistics

Summary measures describing the data base of interest, in lieu of having to review the raw data listings

- **Mean** (1st Moment, μ) — Average or Measure of Central Tendency: Add together all data points' values and divide by the number of data points
  DATA SET: 3, 5, 7, 9
  Computation:
  $$\frac{3+5+7+9}{4} = \underline{\underline{6}}$$

Mean: Graphical Example

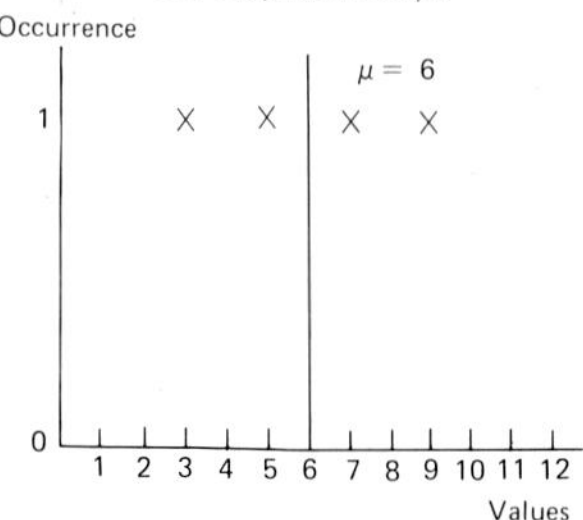

X = data points

- **Standard Deviation** (2nd Moment, σ) — Dispersion around the mean: Take the difference in each value and the mean, square it, then add the squared values, taking the square root of the sum
  DATA SET: 3, 5, 7, 9
  where $\mu = 6$
  COMPUTATION:
  $(3-6)^2 + (5-6)^2 + (7-6)^2 + (9-6)^2 =$
  $9 + 1 + 1 + 9 = 20$
  $\sqrt{20} = \underline{\underline{4.5}}$

Standard Deviation: Graphical Example

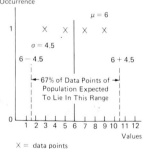

Occurrence
$\mu = 6$
1
X X X X
$\sigma = 4.5$
6 − 4.5
6 + 4.5
← 67% of Data Points of Population Expected To Lie In This Range →
0
1 2 3 4 5 6 7 8 9 10 11 12
Values

X = data points

- **Variance** — Variation around the mean: Square the standard deviation
  DATA SET: 3, 5, 7, 9
  where $\sigma = 4.5$
  COMPUTATION: $(4.5)^2 = \underline{\underline{20}}$

- **Standard Error** — Measures sampling error in estimating mean values: Divide the standard deviation by the square root of the number of data points, as an estimate
  DATA SET: 3, 5, 7, 9
  where $\sigma = 4.5$
  COMPUTATION:
  $$\frac{4.5}{\sqrt{4}} = \underline{\underline{2.25}}$$

- **Minimum** — Smallest value of a variable
  DATA SET: 3, 5, 7, 9
  MINIMUM: $\underline{\underline{3}}$

- **Maximum** — Largest value of a variable
  DATA SET: 3, 5, 7, 9
  MAXIMUM: $\underline{\underline{9}}$

- **Range** — Maximum minus Minimum
  DATA SET: 3, 5, 7, 9
  RANGE: 9 − 3 = $\underline{\underline{6}}$

- **Mode** — The value that occurs most often, or the lowest value that's tied
  DATA SET: 3, 5, 7, 9, 9
  MODE: 9

- **Median** — Middle value or value lying exactly at the 50th percentile, once all values are rank ordered from highest to lowest
  DATA SET: 3, 5, 7, 9, 9
  MEDIAN: 7

Minimum, Maximum, Range: Graphical Example

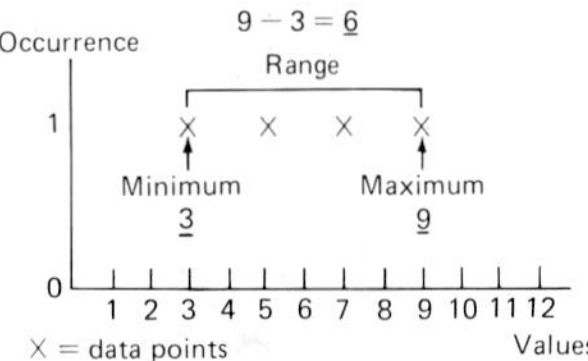

X = data points

Mode & Median: Graphical Example

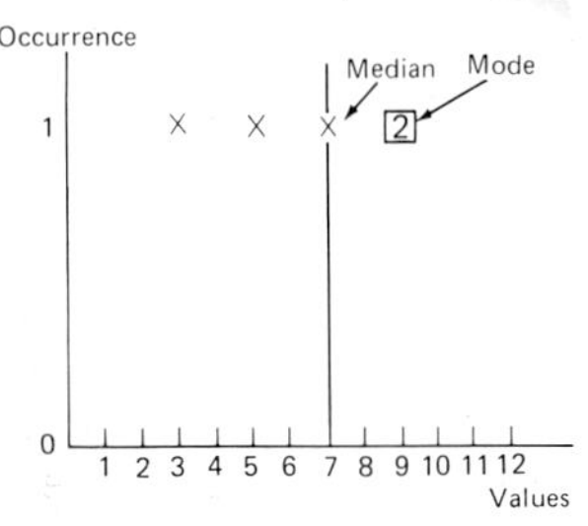

X = data points

[2] = incidence of 2 for this data point value

- **Skewness** (3rd Moment) — Deviation from symmetry: Compute the difference from the mean, divide by the standard deviation, raise the amount to the third power, add those amounts, and then divide the sum by the number of data points
  distribution has a zero value
  positive value
  negative value
  DATA SET: 3, 5, 7, 9 where $\mu = 6$ and $\sigma = 4.5$
  COMPUTATION: $[((3-6)/4.5)^3 + ((5-6)/4.5)^3 + ((7-6)/4.5)^3 + ((9-6)/4.5)^3]/4$
  $= (-.30 + -.01 + .01 + .30)/4 = \underline{\underline{0}}$

  RULES OF THUMB: A skewness coefficient between zero and ±.5 is about normal

Skewness: Graphical Example

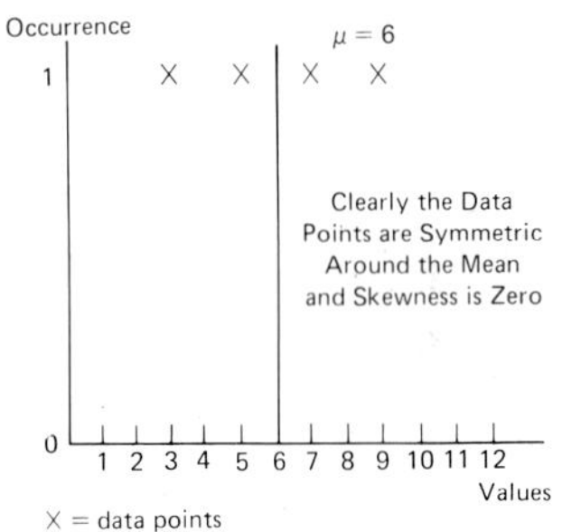

X = data points

- **Kurtosis** (4th Moment) — Relative peakedness or flatness of the curve: Compute the difference from the mean, divide by the standard deviation, raise that amount to the fourth power add those amounts, then divide the sum by the number of data points and subtract 3
  distribution has a zero value
  positive value
  negative value
  DATA SET: 3, 5, 7, 9 where $\mu = 6$ and $\sigma = 4.5$
  COMPUTATION: $([((3-6)/4.5)^4 + ((5-6)/4.5)^4 + ((7-6)/4.5)^4 + ((9-6)/4.5)^4]/4) - 3 = [(.20 .00237 + .20 + .00237)/4] - 3 = .10 - 3 = \underline{\underline{-2.90}}$

  A Kurtosis coefficient between zero and ±1 is about normal

Kurtosis: Graphical Example

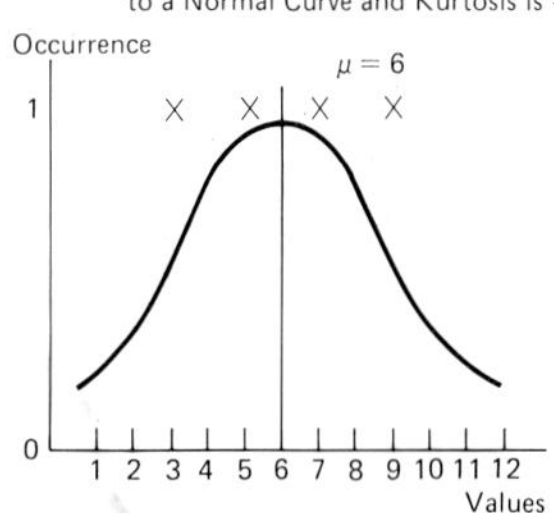

X = data points

Any sample, be it a compliance test to estimate the error rate for a specific control procedure or a substantive test to estimate inventory value, should give an unbiased estimate of the "average value" and, in a compliance test, also give a limit on the expected error rate. To do so, sample items will be drawn, and one could imagine a large number of samples being drawn from any given population. If thirty auditors were to take a similar-sized sample from a population of inventory, we would expect each of their estimated mean values of inventory, when plotted, to form a normal distribution. This plot of sampling means is similar to the plot of raw data, in that it permits the quantification of that range within which any sample mean is likely to fall. However, rather than referring to the measure of dispersion or variability as a standard deviation, it is called a *standard error* to bear out the fact that we're now dealing with sampling results, each based on a number of data points. The definition in Exhibit 11-2 reflects the intuitive notion that the larger the sample size is, the more accurate the estimation will be.

Hence no matter how a population happens to be distributed when it is plotted, repeated samples of the population, when plotted as sampling means, can be expected to form a normal distribution. To prove this fact to yourself, you can design a small population of twenty items, draw twenty samples of five items, calculate the mean value of each sample, and plot those means. For that plot, the standard error will measure the variability of sampling means, and you can calculate the range in which 68.3 percent of the sampling means will lie as ± 1 standard error, the range in which 95 percent of all sample means will fall is ± 1.96 standard errors, and the range in which 99.7 percent of sample means will fall is ± 3 standard errors of the mean. This normality of sampling means tends to be found in samples that have at least thirty data points, and so the above example's smaller population and sample sizes may vary slightly from normality. However, the "area under the curve" defined by standard errors holds for even slight variations of a distribution away from normality. Hence, many of the sampling concepts, particularly those elaborated upon in Chapter 12, will tie back to the normal curve in evaluating sampling results. With this general notion of descriptive measures to be calculated through sampling or modeling procedures, we'll consider concepts and terminology from professional pronouncements. ***[SAS 39, Section 350].***

Statistical and Nonstatistical Sampling

Statement on Auditing Standards No. 39, "Auditing Sampling," defines *audit sampling* as

> the application of an audit procedure to less than 100 percent of the items within an account balance or class of transactions for the purpose of evaluating some characteristic of the balance or class.

Because only a subset of data is collected, there is always a risk that the subset will not represent the characteristics of the entire population of interest and therefore will lead to erroneous conclusions. If this risk is not measured by applying statistical laws of probability to the sample, which has been selected through a generally accepted sampling plan, then that sampling application is referred to as *nonstatistical sampling*. There is no conceptual difference in the design, performance, execution, or evaluation of a nonstatistical and a statistical sampling test. The reason for not measuring risk through probability laws may be the practical difficulties of formulating a sampling plan, selecting the sample, and evaluating the sample results.

Inquiry and observation are nonstatistical sampling procedures; they are informal because the sample size is not computed and the inferences drawn cannot be easily quantified through statistical formulas. Note that if the auditor does not intend to extend conclusions to the remainder of an account balance or class, (s)he is not using audit sampling. Similarly, if the auditor is testing compliance with a procedure which does not provide documentary evidence of performance, (s)he is not applying statistical sampling. **[Proposed Auditing Interpretation, SAS 39].**

Sampling may be inappropriate in some situations. For example, if the audit procedures to be applied are comparisons of monthly financial statements, sampling only two or three months will not achieve the audit objectives of assessing the reasonableness of such summary statements for the entire period under audit. Audit sampling procedures can be applied only to substantive tests of details, not to analytical review procedures. Similarly, if generalized audit software is available to recompute 100 percent of certain calculations, there is no need for sampling. At times, the auditor can define a population to facilitate a 100 percent test (e.g., all expenditures over a specified amount), thereby precluding the need to sample.

Terminology

In order to gain an understanding of how sampling is used as an audit tool, you must learn some basic vocabulary that underlies the study of statistical methods. As previously noted, a population is the universe from which a sample is to be drawn. It is said to be *finite* if it has established boundaries that contain a specified number of items. An example of a finite population is all sales transactions for this year. An example of an *infinite* population is all sales transactions that the system can handle. In other words, an infinite population is a continual process.

A necessary step in sampling is to decide on a real-world referent for the population of interest. For example, the population of all sales transactions may be identified as all shipments. Hence, the total shipments, represented by the shipping documents issued during the period being audited, is the frame. The *frame* is the population actually sampled that is expected to be equivalent to the defined population to which the inferences will be drawn. The auditor must gain assurance that the population and frame are equivalent.

The individual elements in the frame or population to be sampled are the *sampling units.* In the shipping example, these may be copies of bills of lading. Sampling units may be documents, entries, line items, or other elements and should be selected according to the audit objective and efficiency considerations. For example, checks are not always the best sampling unit, because canceled checks are often not filed in sequence by check number but by voucher number or some batch system. This is why voucher tests are a fairly common audit procedure.

Beyond the concepts of population—that account balance or class of transactions of interest to the auditor—and samples—the portion of that account balance or class of transactions examined—the auditor has a number of other technical key terms with which (s)he must become familiar in order to plan and execute a sampling plan.

Since sampling may either be statistical or nonstatistical, the AICPA, in its *Audit and Accounting Guide on Audit Sampling* adopted generic terms to describe the similar concepts underlying these two sampling approaches. Recall that statistical sampling is distinguished by its mathematical measurement of the degree of uncertainty that results from examining only part of a population. Sampling risk is, again, the risk that the characteristic of interest in a randomly selected sample is not representative of the population as a whole. In order to evaluate sampling risk, several statistical concepts are considered. The AICPA's generic terms relate to more traditional statistical language whenever a statistical sample (as distinguished from a nonstatistical sample) has been drawn and evaluated. The relationship of the AICPA's generic language, which applies to all sampling and was introduced by SAS No. 39, to the more traditional statistical language is outlined in Exhibit 11-3. An emphasis will be placed in this chapter upon the statistical terminology in Exhibit 11-3. This is done to tie the instruction to your past training in statistics. However, the auditing literature uses the SAS No. 39 terms in order that the concepts that are effectively the same for statistical and nonstatistical plans can be parsimoniously discussed. It is imperative that you learn all of the terms in Exhibit 11-3 and are able to recognize those which are synonyms.

All statistical terms can be thought of in layman terms, as to what one is trying to quantify. For example, in regard to compliance tests, precision refers to the accuracy or range within which an error rate can be measured. The *error rate* is the frequency of deviations from the prescribed internal control procedures. One cannot expect the sample's error rate to be exactly the same as the error rate of the population. In fact, other than by examining 100 percent of the population, the exact number or proportion of errors present in the accounts cannot be determined. A sample can yield a mean, or average estimate, around which a range can be determined and within which the population value can be expected to lie for a specified percentage of samples. For example, compliance tests may produce a sample average error rate of 3 percent, with a precision of ± 2 percent at 95 percent confidence. This means that the error rate of the population is expected to lie for 95 percent of the samples, between 1 and 5 percent (that is, $3-2=1$ and $3+2=5$). Hence precision is measured as a range of values, plus or minus, around the sample result and quantifies accuracy at a given level of confidence or reliability. The "plus or minus" refers to a *two-tailed test* in which the auditor is interested in both overstatements and understatements. In performing compliance tests, the auditor usually has a *one-tailed* concern (or upper-tail concern) and focuses on the maximum tolerable error rate.

Reliability is the assurance that identically constructed intervals around a sample estimate (referred to as confidence intervals) will contain the "true error rate" with a specified frequency. Reliability thus refers to the process of taking several samples of a given size. The question is whether the sample is large enough to "trap" the true error rate, or what the probability is that the auditor's conclusions will be correct to a specified precision. For example, a 95 percent confidence that the 3 percent sample estimate is precise to ± 2 means that 95 out of 100 samples from the true population, drawn in a similar manner, are expected to include the actual population value within ± 2. As discussed earlier, the ability to express such probabilities stems from statistical theory which describes how population distributions behave. The discussion to this point permits you to anticipate such concepts as: the higher the standard deviation or variability of a set of data points, the less the precision is likely to be at a specified confidence level; and the greater the number of sampling units, the tighter the precision that can be expected.

Precision for substantive tests is commonly stated in dollars and is related to materiality. One common guide used in two-tailed tests is to set precision at one-half of materiality, as then the difference in the limits of confidence intervals will represent materiality, reinforcing the concept that book values within those intervals will be acceptable.

Reliability tends to be related to the reasonableness of the basis for the auditor's opinion. The term *confidence* refers to the percentage of times that a correct decision, within the precision limits specified, will result when reaching a conclusion based on a sample of a given size drawn from a given

EXHIBIT 11-3

Terminology in Statement on Auditing Standards No. 39 Reconciled with Traditional Statistical Concepts

SAS No. 39	Related Statistical Terms
Risk	Reliability Confidence level

Risk is the complement of reliability or confidence level. For example, an auditor who desires a 5 percent sampling risk would specify the reliability, or confidence level, as 95 percent.

SAS No. 39	Related Statistical Terms
Risk of overreliance on internal accounting control for compliance testing	beta risk (β) Risk of Type II errors
Risk of incorrect acceptance for substantive testing	beta risk (β) Risk of Type II errors

A Type II error is the likelihood of thinking that something is true when it is actually false. In an audit context, such a "mistake" in compliance tests is equivalent to believing the controls are operating effectively when, in fact, they are not. This erroneous belief increases the risk of overreliance. Similarly, for a substantive test, the concern is that the auditor will believe an account to be accurately recorded when, in fact, it is materially misstated. Another name for the risk of Type II errors is beta risk (β).

SAS No. 39	Related Statistical Terms
Risk of underreliance on internal accounting control for compliance testing	alpha risk (α) Risk of Type I errors
Risk of incorrect rejection of an account balance for substantive testing	alpha risk (α) Risk of Type I errors

A Type I error is the likelihood of thinking something is false when it is actually true. In an audit context, such a "mistake" in compliance tests is equivalent to believing that controls are poorly designed and/or operating ineffectively when, in fact, they are adequately designed and in operation. This erroneous belief increases the risk of underreliance. Similarly, for a substantive test, the concern is that the auditor will believe an account to be materially misstated when, in fact, it is accurately recorded. Another name for the risk of Type I errors is alpha risk (α).

SAS No. 39	Related Statistical Terms
Tolerable error	Precision
Allowance for sampling risk	Precision

When applied as a planning concept, precision refers to how accurate an estimate is desired, whereas in an evaluation mode, precision reports the accuracy that has been achieved from a given sample. In the planning mode, tolerable error refers to the concept of "acceptable inaccuracy," whereas in the evaluation mode, the allowance for sampling risk refers to the "achieved accuracy" notion.

Adapted from AICPA, *Audit and Accounting Guide: Audit Sampling,* prepared by the Statistical Sampling Subcommittee, 1983.

population. The confidence level for substantive testing then is a measure of risk and should reflect internal control's effectiveness, the auditee's financial condition, and the auditor's knowledge of client operations.

Reliability and precision are interdependent and inseparable. In fact, to cite precision without citing reliability is meaningless. It is likely that six different random samples from the same population will produce six different estimates of the true population mean. So in order to obtain a precision range of ± $0, with 100 percent reliability, a 100 percent sample must be taken. Reliability expresses the mathematical probability of achieving a certain degree of accuracy, expressing the proportion of all possible similar samples of the same size that would include the actual population value within a set range or precision. If sample size were predetermined, the degree of precision desired would vary inversely with the expected confidence level. Assuming the same population size, sample size, and estimated error rate, an increase in the specified confidence level will widen the range of precision.

Auditors use tests of detail and analytical reviews. The tests of detail can range from testing 100 percent of the detail in a particular account, to scanning. The evidence required to form an opinion is a matter of audit judgment, but the ideal sample size must balance the cost of auditing with the risk of not detecting material error. Both *alpha* and *beta risks* described in Exhibit 11-3, are relevant here. Alpha risk, or the risk of a *Type I error,* refers to the audit procedures' efficiency. Alpha risk can lead to overauditing and inefficient audits. Beta risk, or the risk of a *Type II error,* refers to the audit's effectiveness and is the risk of giving the wrong opinion, resulting in an ineffective audit. The means by which these risks are reduced include reliance on internal control, if appropriate, and directing a set of substantive audit procedures toward the same audit objective. The greater the reliance on controls and other related substantive tests is, the higher the acceptable beta risk will be. Obviously, the higher the acceptable risk, the lower the required sample size for a given substantive test. This generic approach to defining alpha and beta risk technically departs from statistical convention.

By statistical convention, a Type I error arises when a true null hypothesis (assertion being tested) is incorrectly rejected and the probability of such an error is alpha risk, while a Type II error is defined to be the incorrect acceptance of a false null hypothesis that has a probability referred to as beta risk. In other words, Type I and Type II terminology, as well as alpha and beta risk, is driven by the null hypothesis being tested, rather than by the nature of the null hypothesis. The AICPA *Guide* presumes that the null hypothesis is always equivalent to the client's true account balance or reliable control system. Yet the statistical tests described in both this chapter and Chapter 12 are sometimes directed at a null hypothesis other than one of these assertions. In particular, the approach of projecting an error value implicitly tests a null hypothesis: Is the account book value misstated by an amount greater than tolerable error? Since this is worded in error terms, traditional statisticians would cite Type I error or alpha risk as being of central concern to the auditor. In other words, incorrectly rejecting that an *error exceeding the tolerable error exists* is the alpha risk yet seems equivalent to what is described in Exhibit 11-3 as "beta risk." Hence, when discussing alpha and beta terminology, it is imperative that you consider whether statistical convention or the AICPA's generic terminology is of interest. In the latter case, the overriding intuitive interpretation intended in the AICPA *Guide* is that auditors' greatest risk is thinking things are all right when they are not. This concern is labeled "beta risk."

One way of reconciling the auditing literature to statistical convention is to view the global null hypothesis of an audit as the clean audit report. Then view every statistical test's null hypothesis as a component of the global hypothesis. Although concerns may vary between alpha and beta terminology at the test level, with respect to the overall audit opinion, the *Guide* effectively interprets alpha

[2]This technical distinction is described in greater depth in Paul J. Beck and Ira Solomon, "Sampling Risks and Audit Consequences Under Alternative Testing Approaches," Working Paper, University of Illinois, May 1985. An example of the "null hypothesis" language, in a setting which is consistent with the language of the AICPA *Guide*'s use of the terms *alpha* and *beta,* is provided in an article by Robert K. Elliott and John R. Rogers, "Relating Statistical Sampling to Audit Objectives," *Journal of Accountancy,* July 1972, pp. 46–55.

and beta as tied to audit efficiency and effectiveness, respectively.[2]

Whenever an auditor is able to gain support for an audit conclusion from independently derived pieces of evidence, confidence is increased by their joint occurrence more than had they been separately collected and evaluated. Thus, a sample may not need to confirm the account under examination as conclusively as it would if no other support were available. This is one of the reasons that Participant 7 in the introductory case could have conducted one particular test at 95 percent confidence, or even at a far lower percent confidence. One test need not stand alone.

Hence the auditor should consider the audit evidence accumulated at a particular point in time as he or she proceeds through the audit, adjusting the timing, nature, and extent of work as deemed to be appropriate. Because internal control is usually evaluated early in the audit, it is commonly recognized as a key determinant of the reliability desired for a particular sample for substantive testing. If controls are thought to be excellent, the auditor might decide that 60 to 70 percent confidence was sufficient in sampling work, whereas only fair controls might suggest a need for 90 to 95 percent confidence. As the confidence level is adjusted, the auditor is effectively measuring the amount of information needed from the sample. This notion of reliability for each sample plan is different from the overall conclusion about the population based on the combined audit evidence.

The Role of Judgment

Professional judgment is required throughout the sampling process. First, the auditor must decide where sampling would be appropriate. Generally there should be one objective and many transactions to which that objective relates. Second, the auditor must make a preliminary evaluation of internal control in planning the type of sampling to be used. Third, previous experience must be weighed to assess its effect on the sample design. Fourth, errors must be defined, and the maximum acceptable rate or amount of error must be decided. Fifth, the risk level or confidence level, which are complements of each other, must be set. ("Complements" means that 1 minus alpha risk yields confidence level.) As already described, confidence level is the probability of a sample estimate falling within some stated range around the true value for the population as a whole. Alternatively, it is the percentage of times that a correct decision will be made within a specified range, based on sample estimates. Risk, on the other hand, is the percentage of times that an incorrect decision will be made. Finally, the auditor must judge the significance of the discovered errors in order to draw conclusions. This significance is based on not only the quantity of the error, but its qualitative nature as well. For example, do the errors form a systematic pattern, and do they appear to have been intentional?

Advantages of Statistical Sampling

In spite of the significant role of judgment, a statistical sampling approach, due to its foundation in mathematics and probability theory, is a very objective tool that will yield essentially the same results no matter who actually applies the procedures. Note that this does *not* deny the critical role of judgment, since specified precision and reliability are the essential judgmental inputs to any statistical application. Yet, if one assumes that judgment as to inputs is identical across two auditors, one can also assume identical results in those auditors' measurement of sampling risk from a given sample. For that reason, statistical sampling inferences are highly defensible. An objective basis exists for estimating the sample size which is drawn.

The greatest value of statistical techniques lies in quantifying sampling risk. As already defined, sampling risk is the risk of reaching a wrong conclusion based on the analysis of a sample rather than examining 100 percent of a population. This quantifying of risk assists the auditor in deciding whether a conclusion based on a sample is sufficiently reliable to warrant its acceptance. Furthermore, one can expect findings to be more accurate from statistical samples because of the reduced chance of auditor error in specifying sample sizes or incorrectly selecting sampling units. Another advantage of statistical sampling is that the deviation of the sample from the population can be projected and different auditors' work at different locations can be combined. The likelihood of oversampling, with its related costs, is reduced due to the objective basis for sample size determination. Furthermore, should an auditor be asked to explain the extent of audit testing performed, the very objectivity of statistical sampling provides a strong basis for justifying the level of testing at a client's, as well as the associated audit costs.

The use of statistical sampling permits better advance planning of an audit, since sample sizes and items to be selected can be specified in advance and set up in worksheet format for use in later field work. Since random samples will tend to include selected items that are scattered across a number of files, an impression will be given that the audit process is very thorough. In contrast, nonstatistical tests, if they do not select a random sample, may not appear as thorough. A related "threat value" accrues to audits that appear more thorough; compliance is likely to be implicitly encouraged due to the fear that deviations will be identified by the auditor.

Overall, statistical sampling methodology assists the auditor in designing an efficient sample, measuring the sufficiency of the evidential matter obtained, and evaluating the sample results. Sampling risk can be quantified to assist in limiting it to an acceptable level.

Audit Objectives

As one selects among alternative sampling plans, attention should be directed at the type of audit objective which the plan is expected to address. Five distinct audit objectives have been cited in past literature[3]: protection, correction, prevention, estimation, and discovery. *Protective sampling* is intended to achieve the maximum total dollar coverage possible for the sample. *Corrective sampling* is intended to find and correct as many errors as possible, given the sample size. *Preventive sampling* is intended to reduce auditees' ability to predict the sampling plan, thereby increasing the chance of error detection. The objectives of *estimation* and *discovery* sampling are self-explanatory. Each of these objectives suggests that certain audit approaches would be more appropriate than others, and, in fact, precludes the applicability of certain sampling plans. The key categories of sampling plans are attribute tests and variables sampling.

An *attribute test* is intended to test for the presence or absence of a specific characteristic (or attribute) of a sampling unit in order to estimate the proportion of population units that either do or do not possess that characteristic. This type of sampling is easily tailored to compliance test objectives. For example, a purchase order either has or has not been approved. An attribute test quantifies the percentage of purchase orders not properly approved. But *variables sampling* quantifies how much, rather than a proportion or a percentage occurrence, and can make dollar or quantity estimates. Variables sampling is generally used for substantive test objectives. For example, a variables sample may estimate the total recorded inventory value.

The difference between variables hypothesis sampling and variables estimation sampling is that in the first, the hypothesis that the book value is correct within a specified range is tested and either accepted or rejected but, in the second, the objective is to project a population value from a sample. In such cases, a book value may be known to be incorrect, making a hypothesis approach totally inapplicable. A common example in statistics courses is of a manufacturer receiving a shipment of twenty thousand lightbulbs, taking a sample of fifty, and, if none is found to be defective, accepting the shipment. Although this type of acceptance sampling is often used in industrial quality control, it has several limitations which make it an infrequently used audit tool. Acceptance sampling establishes a predetermined decision rule, indicating accept or reject, without measuring the actual

[3]Yuji Ijiri and Robert S. Kaplan, "A Model for Integrating Sampling Objectives in Auditing," *Journal of Accounting Research*, Spring, 1971, pp. 73–87.

extent of error. Furthermore, only one characteristic of the data can be tested at a time, whereas other techniques permit the simultaneous inspection of related characteristics.

Further examples of how audit objectives affect sampling plan selection can be provided; however, many of the terms used will not be explained until later in this chapter or in Chapter 12. Recognizing this shortcoming, let's nevertheless review some examples of the mutual exclusivity of several sampling alternatives. Specifically, dollar-unit sampling (which is an attribute-based technique with a variables approach applicability) can be useful in checking the reasonableness of an estimate, but should not typically be used if the auditor plans to have the sampling estimate "booked" or "corrected." This is because the approach does not estimate the "most likely" amount, but focuses on limits on an amount. For such an estimation, a classical variables sampling approach is needed. *Classical variables sampling* estimates the mean value rather than the range or limit of a value and is unbiased. Similarly, if an auditor wishes to discover an unusual event, if present, a discovery sampling plan (a specialized attributes test) is likely to be the most efficient, whereas if errors were expected, the check on the adequacy of a control system in protecting assets would be likely to require compliance tests using more generalized attributes sampling.

Careful consideration of audit objectives is essential to effectively designing a sampling approach. In addition, it is important to realize that sampling conclusions will relate only to the samples that are drawn in the field and that those samples need to be tied to audit risk. For example, if an auditor is concerned with pilferage problems involving employees' or customers' removal of goods by using their lunch boxes or purses, the population of interest would be small tools, as distinct from large inventory items like cranes (unless, of course, the crane were able to be removed one piece at a time, or the employees had very large lunch boxes!). Hence, a sample of all inventory items would fail to tie to that population which is actually considered to be at risk. Risk assessment is a key determinant of audit objectives and, in turn, critical to the direction of planning for sampling applications.

If an auditor is concerned about a rare event, such as the presence of appropriate support in lieu of a receiving report for expenditures for services instead of for the typical expenditure on goods, the definition of a frame may be very difficult, calling into question whether sampling is likely to be an efficient audit procedure. Or if materiality requires assurance of such expenditures, an alternative testing approach should be considered, with the expectation that a voucher test of the entire population of expenditures will provide some limited corroborative evidence concerning purchases of services. Hence the particular audit objective will not only lead to a particular sampling plan, but may also lead to the selection of an audit procedure other than sampling.

Planning a Sample

In planning a sample, the first step is to define the population, its size, and the characteristics that might affect the selection techniques. Attribute testing can be more difficult to apply than variables testing is, as the population may have to be redefined to meet its objective. For example, receiving reports can be used for variables testing but will be inadequate in testing controls over canceled vouchers, because of the vouchers relating to services and similar disbursements for activities that do not require receiving reports. When used for sampling purposes, vouchers require testing so as to ensure coverage of all expenditures.

Population size is often easy to determine because of the many prenumbered forms. In order to estimate the population size, the number of the last document processed in the previous year can be subtracted from the last number processed at the end of the current period of interest. The audit objective will guide the test procedures, including the specific characteristics that will flag errors. In selecting and using an attributes sampling plan, the error that would mean a lack of control documentation or the failure of a control to accomplish its objective must be clearly defined. The auditor must specify the precision and confidence level desired and thus the acceptable maximum error rate. Then he or she can use statistical tables and formulas to determine the required sample size. The sampling

EXHIBIT 11-4
Steps in a Sampling Plan

The steps of any sampling plan are

1. specifying the audit objective to which the sample relates.
2. defining the population and number of population items.
3. specifying the sampling unit.
4. selecting a method of sampling.
5. specifying sample parameters such as confidence level and precision.
6. determining sample size.
7. choosing a sample selection technique.
8. choosing a sample.
9. evaluating a sample.
10. determining whether adjustment to original plan is needed.
11. evaluating any changes.
12. formulating a conclusion.

results will quantify sampling error: the difference between the sample's estimate of the population and the estimate that would have resulted had identical methods been applied to the entire population. The steps of a sampling plan are presented in Exhibit 11-4.

Auditors' Sampling Problems

As illustrated in the introductory case, auditors have difficulty deciding on the appropriate sampling approach and addressing commonplace occurrences such as lost documents. In order for a sample to be *random,* every item in the population and every combination of items in the population must have an equal chance of selection. Although theoretically the most effective means of fulfilling this requirement is to use a *random number generator* (that is, computer software) corresponding to the sampling units, there are many practical problems that can preclude such an approach.

Identifying a Frame

In designing a sampling plan, the frame from which a sample will be drawn must be established. For example, the population of interest may be all suppliers' files, but the frame may be a certain set of file cabinets. Because certain documents may have been removed from those files, the frame will not be equivalent to the population. If estimates are based on only the readily available documents, the projections will be biased. This is why the frame must be tested for its completeness and correspondence to the population of interest. Perhaps the foremost practical issue in sampling as an audit tool is whether assurance can be gained that the population of interest has been appropriately identified and is complete and retrievable.

One means of avoiding such problems as incomplete file drawers from which sampling units are to be drawn is to select a frame other than file drawers: one that is easier to test for completeness. For example, controlled sources like voucher registers or check registers can be reviewed for numerical sequence completeness, footed, and reconciled to the population totals in the control accounts. Then the sample can be selected from the register and traced into the filing drawers.

To ensure that a purchasing-related population is complete, books of entry such as the voucher register, rather than a file cabinet, should be used whenever possible for sampling, so that risk can be controlled. Note that although the full year's vouchers will be tested, the entire voucher register does not need to be footed when checking the frame's completeness. A random test can be used, tracing a sample of the months' totals to the general ledger. The auditor need only obtain reasonable assurance of completeness.

But if filing drawers must be used as the frame, supplemental tests should be performed to assess the equivalency of the frame and the population. These might include reviewing the vouchers in drawers for their numerical sequence or actually footing the vouchers in the drawers so that they can be reconciled to the control. Tests may be performed from vouchers or other supporting documents to the drawers, but these are far less efficient than using a controlled source, should it be available (such as a cash disbursement register).

An Example

If an auditor wishes to determine whether all shipments have been billed, the population of total billings would be incapable of addressing the audit objective. The appropriate population would be total shipments. However, what if shipping documents are not prenumbered or what if they are stapled to customers' order forms and filed alphabetically? These conditions would point to no numerical completeness control and a problem with easily retrieving the population of shipping documents for sampling purposes. The auditor would then try to ensure that customers' orders represented total shipments, which might require compliance test work: Are those working on the shipping dock complying with the prescribed procedure that all shipments be accompanied by a copy of the customer's order? Is there a separate file of customers' orders that have not been shipped? Is there numerical control of customers' orders? Are customers' orders likely to be removed from the files and not correctly refiled? Is there a checkout system for finding out who has which files, should they be selected for testing?

The point, of course, is that practical issues arise in sampling due to the uniqueness of each entity's documentation, filing, and control procedures. If a one-to-one correspondence can be reasonably assumed to exist between customers' orders and shipping documents, then the dilemma becomes one of how to sample from those orders. Practically speaking, use of customer order numbers would be totally inefficient, since files are maintained alphabetically. Yet some customers may place more orders than others or may place orders of higher dollar amounts. (Recall the introductory case's reference by participant 3 to sales made to customers whose names began with an "E".) If the population from which the sample units were drawn happened to be customers' names, the underlying assumption would be that each name had about an equal number of customers' orders. Since this would be unlikely, an alternative approach to sampling would be some sort of interval or "*i*th" sampling plan. This might mean that an auditor chooses customer orders for testing from the alphabetical files by specifying an interval of "every 5 inches of file space." This approach presumes that the alphabetical ordering has no necessary correspondence to the propensity for customers' orders to be shipped and billed. While the approach is not random in the same sense as a random number generator corresponding to customer order number would be, it is expected to behave in a manner that is similar to a random sample in its *representativeness.*

Evaluating samples may also pose practical problems. For example, assume that in testing customers' orders on an *i*th, or interval, basis, the auditor discovers a customer order to which no shipping documents are attached. Upon investigation, he or she finds that the customer was never billed. Does this constitute an "error"? Should the next customer order that is "matched" with a shipping report be selected in lieu of the former order, which was not intended to be part of the population under examination? What if, in evaluating the sample, the auditor becomes aware of an additional ten files that had been taken from the files before sampling and not appropriately checked out? How would this affect the evaluation? What information would the auditor need to evaluate the effects?

The intent of this discussion is to point out that executing a sampling procedure is not without problems that require auditor judgment. That judgment should be driven by a clear understanding of sampling theory. Taking the problems one step at a time, the key concern of the auditor is that the population from which a sample is drawn is *complete.* Hence, additional documents such as the unmatched customer order do not pose a problem, provided (1) the incidence in the files of unmatched customer orders is expected not to relate to shipping and billing practices in any systematic manner and (2) a sampling unit from the appropriate population is selected in lieu of that order. In and of itself, an unmatched customer order that has not been billed or shipped does not constitute an error with respect to the audit objective being tested. It does, however, suggest a related problem that some customer orders received may not be appropriately controlled for processing and follow-through. In other words, shipments are being billed, but orders are not necessarily being shipped! Since the former objective clearly relates to a risk similar to the latter, the finding may suggest alternative audit work to be performed, or different sampling approaches when conducting audit procedures to address other audit objectives.

On the other hand, the ten files missing from the population sampled are not "represented" by the sample. Then, the auditor asks, why were those ten files removed? Are they more likely to have problems? Or perhaps they were pulled to investigate customers' claims. The auditor should first try to make sure that the ten files missing from the checkout register are an exception and not likely to represent a systematic problem regarding the completeness of the frame from which samples were drawn. Then, assuming such assurance is obtained, testing all ten of the ten files as a separate population would be the most conservative means of determining that the conclusion regarding shipping and billing practices is appropriate.

Interim Work

If a sample is drawn during interim work based on the population to date of certain types of transactions, any conclusions will pertain only to the period tested. In other words, statistical conclusions based on interim results cannot be drawn for the whole period. If the auditor wants to draw conclusions for the total year, he or she can (1) take a separate sample from the population of transactions occurring from the interim to the year-end and form a separate statistical conclusion, (2) use a sampling plan at interim that includes sampling items from the estimated full year of transactions and postpone conclusions until year-end when those additional sampling items can be added to the interim sampling units to form a conclusion, or (3) apply alternative auditing procedures to tie interim work to year-end balances, forming a nonstatistical audit conclusion.

The full year should be defined as the relevant population if inferences are intended to relate to the entire year. But if substantive testing is performed at interim that relies on the results of the compliance tests, it may be necessary to draw conclusions at interim. In this case, other tests will have to be performed in order to tie the interim compliance work to the entire year's assurance of effective control.

One practical approach to this type of setting is to intentionally oversample. At interim, the sample size required for the interim period is computed and conclusions are drawn. However, a total sample size is computed for the full-year time period, with a proportionate increase in sample size for the period from interim to year-end. But in estimating the numbering sequence for a full year to enable this sampling approach, errors may be made. If the number of items issued is smaller than estimated, additional random numbers must be used to select replacement items for random numbers that apply to unused documents. In fact, it is always a good practice to draw a larger number of random numbers than the specified sample size in order to enable such sample expansion or extensions necessitated by voided documents. If the actual population of issued documents was significantly larger than the number sequence used for sample selection, the auditor (1) could use the correct number sequence from interim to year-end and perform a stratified sample test (essentially, subsamples of strata are formed from which sampling units are then drawn; this approach will be described in Chapter 12) or (2) could separately select from the numbers initially excluded and perform a test on a stratified or oversampling basis. The only other alternative is to redefine the population tested and separately assess the effect of the population not sampled.

Besides using an estimated total population for the year, then, an alternative is to use stratified sampling, with two separate selections made for the interim period and the total year. At least 30 items need to be selected for the period from interim to year-end. Of course, required sampling at year-end will depend, in part, on how accurate the auditor's expectations were regarding the error rate.

Multilocation Clients

Multilocation clients' operations may be examined with one centralized sampling approach. The relevant questions are whether the multiple locations are similar, whether they have a centralized control design and supervision, and whether the purpose of the engagement is to form an overall opinion or to issue separate reports for each location. When separate reports are required and the control systems differ, some form of multistage sampling, which will be described later in this chapter, may be applicable.

Controlling Risk

The reason for being conservative is to control audit risk—in particular, to control beta risk or the risk of a Type II error. These terms as defined by the AICPA refer to the likelihood of believing something is correct or operating effectively when, in fact, it is misstated or operating ineffectively. In sampling, the auditor controls such risk by carefully selecting the population and sampling plan and conservatively evaluating the sample results. In fact, this is the reason that any "missing document" is commonly assumed to be in error, as was cited in the introductory case to this chapter.

Sometimes there may be an alternative to considering missing documents to be errors. For example, if the auditor wants to examine evidence that goods were in fact received and a receiving report is not attached to a voucher, as expected, inquiry procedures may be used to locate elsewhere in the system where receiving reports are on file, and then a copy of the missing report may be obtained from that department. In particular, the receiving department is likely to maintain its own files. If the concern is whether the goods were in fact received, the auditor may be able to obtain evidence of delivery from the vendor. In other words, both the auditee's information system and sources outside the system should be considered as means of finding out about misplaced documents. Obviously, these steps can only address audit objectives such as "evidence of receipt exists" and could rarely find alternative information sources for objectives like "evidence of approval exists." This would be due to the typical practice of only requiring approval on one copy of a document. Whenever documents are missing, alternative audit procedures should be applied to gain assurance that the recorded transaction is valid. As another example, if a vendor's invoice is unavailable, reference to that vendor's price catalog might provide support for the inventory's cost. If an audited amount is determinable for the unobtained document, it can be used in sample evaluation.

But in most cases, when a document is missing, it must be considered to be an error. An auditor cannot merely substitute another sample item, as suggested by Participant 2 in the introductory case, because that would bias the results, making the sample potentially unrepresentative of the population of audit interest, that is, all documents rather than those that "aren't missing"!

If a selected sampling unit has been voided or was not issued, the auditor should test the propriety of the void and whether the books were adjusted and then must replace the unused sampling numbers with an issued sampling unit. Often voids are strictly clerical and do not affect the books; in such cases, they do not represent errors. Clearly, unused documents could not represent the population of interest and thus would not be proper sampling units.

Nonsampling Risk

The auditor also has to be careful to control nonsampling risk, as noted earlier. Such risk is often referred to as "human error" and can stem from (1) the nature of the audit procedures themselves, (2) their timing, (3) the auditor's skills, (4) the auditor's due audit care, and (5) the system being examined. The proper definition of the audit objective, the appropriate selection of audit procedures to meet that objective, the effective performance of those procedures, and the proper interpretation of findings are all examples of key decision areas that are potential sources of nonsampling risk. Sufficient experience levels of the professional staff performing each audit step and adequate supervisory practices are the primary means of controlling nonsampling risk.

Because sampling applications are often based on recorded populations, there is a risk that some items will be omitted from the population being tested. That risk is addressed through explicit tests for understatement and the complementary nature of many audit procedures. For example, tests of bank reconciliations should reveal understatements in cash disbursements, and confirmation procedures may reveal unrecorded transactions.

Selection Techniques

Although several types of sample selection techniques have been referred to, the specific manner in which each is to be applied has yet to be explored.

The objective of all selection techniques is to draw representative samples, though what is being represented will vary. For example, some samples are intended to represent the characteristics of documents, while others are intended to represent dollars in a population. This distinction will become apparent in the following discussion.

Random Sampling Techniques

Given a specified sample size, a random selection procedure draws a sample such that every possible sample of that size is equally likely to be chosen. Three key procedures are commonly applied to select random samples.

Random Number Tables. Tables of random numbers can be used for selection. Assume that the population of invoices to be tested is numbered from 1 to 4,000 and that sixty items will be sampled. The auditor randomly chooses a starting point in the table, often by looking at the serial number on a dollar bill and using the last few digits to represent particular page numbers, column numbers, and row numbers on the table. Then, four columns in the table would be used to select the first sixty numbers falling between 1 and 4,000. The auditor should move through the table in a predetermined, consistent pattern, typically from the top to the bottom of the column and from the left to the right of the page.

Let us demonstrate, using the following columns of random numbers:

6952	8097
2945	4395
0497	6422
2812	6485
4124	7656
2253	0682
0430	7523

Assuming that 6952 is the starting point, let us choose #2,945, #497, #2,812, #2,253, #430, and #682. Remember that only numbers 1 through 4,000 are valid invoice numbers, leading to omission of values in excess of 4,000, such as 6,952.

If there is great variability in the number of entries on each item to be sampled, it is possible to define the population in order to select a random sample of items and then to select a random sample of one entry from each selected item. For example, a population of invoices can be sampled, and then quantity and/or price and/or amounts can be randomly sampled from each of the selected items.

To illustrate how a random number table is used to correspond to lines on pages, consider the numbers

30247
05051
07032

and assume a population of 350 pages with 50 lines per page. The interpretation of the sampling units could be line #47 on page 302 and line #32 on page 70. Note that 05051 must be discarded because there are not 51 lines.

Documents will often not be prenumbered but will be filed into groups to which numbers can be assigned. For example, assume that an auditor plans to test investments for overstatements through a physical examination of a sample of securities. Those securities are filed in groups of 50, and the total number of groups is 500. A selection approach would be to apply random numbers, with the digits pertaining to each group and then to the security within each group. For example, random number 42,042 would indicate group #420, and the forty-second investment in that group. If a group had more than 50 investments, those unexpected securities should be examined 100 percent, as by definition they are excluded from the sampling plan.

If the items in a population have alphabetic prefixes or suffixes, they can be given the numbers 1 to 26 to convert the letters onto a random number table. Similarly, months can be coded from 1 to 12.

If unnumbered items are stored in a file cabinet, the drawers can be given numbers, and the items within the drawer can be counted to correspond to a random number table. The working papers should describe the correspondence between the population and the random numbers and how the random number table was used. (Each digit in a random number table is unbiased as to its position in the table, and so any consistent pattern through the table can be used to select the numbers.) The starting point in the table and the pattern of selecting the random numbers should also be noted.

Terminal Digits. Rather than drawing random numbers corresponding to a document number, such as a four-digit invoice number, the auditor can randomly select two two-digit numbers and then examine those invoices that end in this number. Then he or she can select a third two-digit number and use it to select every other voucher that ends in this number, randomly choosing the starting point.

Random Number Generator. Or instead of selecting the sample himself or herself, the auditor can use a utility computer program to generate a list of sixty random numbers. This approach is less likely to be unintentionally biased, such as by a left-handed person's tending to point to the left side of a page when selecting a random starting point.

Systematic Sampling Techniques

Though they are not random samples, systematic or interval samples are intended to behave as random samples would. A *systematic sample* selects every *i*th (sometimes referred to as every *n*th or every *k*th) item, beginning with a random start. The likelihood of such a sample's behaving as though it were a random sample depends on the ordering of sampling units within the frame. If an auditor believes that a population is arranged randomly, he or she can evaluate a systematic sample as if it had been selected using a random number generator, though technically, systematic sampling is not random. This is because not every combination of sampling units has the same probability of being selected. For example, two adjacent items cannot be selected in a systematic sample. This technical point addresses the concerns of Participant 3 in the introductory case. The *i*th sampling approach is not random per se but can be expected to behave randomly if the frame for the test objective does not have a pattern which relates to the test objective.

Every *i*th Item. A systematic sample plan must merely define the items to be sampled, for example, individual invoices or so many inches of file drawer space. Then the population of items is divided by the desired sample size to determine the value of *i*, or the interval. Four thousand invoices divided by the planned sample size of 60 items produces an interval of 66.7. Because there are no partial invoices, to be conservative an interval of 66 is used. This means that the auditor must first select a random number from 1 to 66 as the first invoice to examine and then select every sixty-sixth item thereafter. If the first random number selected is 34, then invoices #34, #100, #166, and so on will be included in the sample.

Randomly Varying the Sample Interval. Every combination of numbers does not have an equal chance of selection when every *i*th item is selected. To help increase the likelihood of the systematic sampling plan's behaving as though it were random, the auditor may use a variable sampling interval. If a sample size of sixty invoices is desired, the auditor will first randomly select an initial item between 1 and 60 and then add a second random number between 1 and 60 to the first number, to obtain the number of the second item to be selected. Assume that 34 is the first invoice selected, that 2 is the second random number drawn, then 57, and then 41. Thus the invoices shown will be #34, #36, #93, #134, and so on, varying the sample interval each time.

Every Random *i*th Item. Instead of varying the interval width, the number selected within each interval can be varied. Because the width of the interval in the invoice example is 66, repeated random numbers from 1 to 66 are selected, indicating which item should be drawn from each interval. If the numbers drawn are 65, 3, 17, and 43, then the invoices selected will be #65, #69, #149, and #241. These numbers are generated by adding multiples of 66, thus placing each item within contiguous intervals of 66, or $66+3$, $(66\times 2)+17$, and $(66\times 3)+43$. This selection procedure would continue until 60 items were selected.

Cluster Sampling

In the past, auditors often tested one week's payroll. Such a *block sample*, however, pertains only to that one week of payroll as the population, and so no inferences can be made about the total payroll. Block sampling does not randomize the selection of blocks and is therefore not expected to be representative. SAS No. 1, Section 61, Paragraph 320 states that block sampling is unacceptable, because the entire population ought to be subjected to sampling. But although block sampling can no longer be used, *cluster sampling* can be applied in a less extreme form. Instead of focusing on one week of invoices, or drawing entirely separate random invoices, groups of contiguous invoices can be selected randomly. For example, a random number can be selected to identify pages in an invoice listing, and then all invoices on those pages can be tested. The problem, of course, is that the consecutive invoices on a page of a listing are likely to overlap to some extent. For example, items purchased at about the same time may be similar and thus the sample may not adequately cover the full range of invoices in the population.

Although cluster sampling can save time, as groups of items tend to be easier to collect (for example, pulling files located together), it is much less efficient in regard to total sample size. Because groups of items (clusters of equal size) are drawn at random points, the number of points tends to become the sampling unit, rather than the number of items examined at each of the selected points. The obvious disadvantage is that a greater number of detailed units must be tested, and because of the ease of random sample selection and the client's ability to have personnel obtain the data for the corresponding sampling units, cluster sampling is not used frequently.

Multistage Sampling

Sampling at several levels is termed *multistage sampling*. For example, a random sample of stores or branches, and then of records at each store or branch, would represent a multistage sampling plan. Another example is selecting a sample of vouchers and then a sample of invoices for each selected voucher. The sample estimate then will pertain to the total group of vouchers.

Multistage sampling has both *primary sampling units*, like stores for a retailing client, and *secondary sampling units*, like accounts receivable. It is most effective when the primary sampling units are homogeneous, in part because an overall conclusion is needed rather than a conclusion for each location. The common practice of rotating field visits is a nonstatistical form of stratified multistage sampling. Statistical sampling may be used for a random selection of locations, with the audit's emphasis changing for each location.

Bias

The types of bias that can creep into nonstatistical sample selection include a person's height, affecting which file drawers are used for sample selections, and the form of storage—current documents in hard-copy form versus older, microfilmed documents—affecting which sampling units are identified. A *judgment sample* has been defined as one selected at the discretion of that individual who draws the sample. It is said to be biased by the selector's judgment or preference. A nonstatistical sample that is supposed to mirror a random sample is a *haphazard sample,* meaning that the units are selected with no intended bias as to which units will be tested. Presumably, all units have an equal chance to be selected. The term *haphazard* is in no way intended to mean that the auditor conducts a test without due care or in a haphazard manner; it pertains only to the pattern of selection.

Attribute Sampling

An *attribute sampling plan* is used to determine an estimated rate of occurrence of some specific quality or attribute of a population. When performing attributes sampling, the variability of a population is defined by the proportion of the population having the specific attribute. The attributes of common interest to auditors are incorrect account distributions, lack of adequate supporting documentation, and similar tests of a client's compliance with specific internal control procedures, such as the appropriate approval of all disbursements. In order to determine the sample size, the auditor must identify the population and decide whether there is a single population for the entire period of audit interest. When compliance testing, the auditor must be alert to system changes that produce two distinct populations. A common example is a system's conversion from manual processing to electronic data processing. Conversion often means that different people will handle the processing and the control duties. In addition, it is likely that the two systems' control procedures will differ. Whenever there are thought to be two populations (or more than two, if there are multiple changes), then two (or more) populations should be defined for compliance test purposes.

Once the population is identified, the auditor must specify the expected rate of occurrence in a population. Again, the rate of occurrence in an attribute sampling plan is the frequency with which a certain characteristic occurs within a population. For example, the auditor will decide on a rate of occurrence by considering previous experience with a client, updated to reflect changes in controls and personnel, or by drawing a presample (called a *pilot sample*) of 50 randomly selected items to formulate an initial estimate. If out of the 50 items, there is 1 deviation, the estimated occurrence rate will be 1 divided by 50, or 2 percent. If the 50 items in the presample (or pilot sample) are selected as the first 50 items of a full sampling plan, then they may be included in the final sample evaluation, thereby imposing no incremental cost by having to form a presample for the initial specification of expectations. (The *expected population deviation rate* is also called the *expected error* rate or the *expected rate of occurrence.*) As the expected error rate climbs, the population becomes more variable; this greater variability means that the sample size must be increased. If all other things are held constant, a required sample size of 93 at a 1 percent population deviation rate will grow to 361 at a 3 percent deviation rate. In reconciling a sampling plan to sample results, any difference in estimated and actual variability must be evaluated. If actual is less than estimated, the evidence collected supports a stronger conclusion than implied by the sampling plan; if greater, the evidence is weaker.[4]

The auditor must also determine the *tolerable rate of error* for the population. In other words, what would be the *maximum rate of deviation* from some prescribed control procedure which would be acceptable without having to alter the planned extent of reliance on controls? In deciding on this maximum or tolerable rate, it is important to keep in mind that a deviation from a control procedure does not automatically constitute an error in the accounting records. The key element in the decision is the extent to which the auditor intends to rely on controls. If substantial reliance is planned, the tolerable rate will likely range from 2 to 7 percent (based on AICPA guidelines), whereas little reliance suggests a tolerable rate from 11 to 20 percent. The tolerable error, other things being equal, moves inversely with sample size. If certain conditions remain constant, a 2 percent tolerable rate will require a sample size of 149, whereas if the auditor can tolerate 10 percent error, the required sample will drop to 29 items. It should be obvious, that as the expected error rate approaches the tolerable rate, the required sample size increases, and as they move closer together, more precise information is needed, thus requiring a larger required sample size. In fact, at some point the sample size would become cost-prohibitive, suggesting that there should be no reliance on controls. If the error frequency is expected to be high and the tolerable error rate is low, then an auditor may need to shift from a sampling approach to a 100 percent examination or reevaluate the efficiency of the planned audit approach. In other words, substantive testing may be more cost beneficial than compliance testing.

As with all sampling plans, the auditor must decide how much risk he or she is willing to accept. The principal risk in attributes sampling is the risk of overreliance, a Type II error or a beta risk according to the AICPA's *Guide,* which simply means that the auditor prefers a low risk of overrelying on internal control. Risk can be viewed as the complement of confidence level. Hence a 5 percent risk of overreliance suggests that the auditor can be 95 percent confident that the sample compliance rate does not misrepresent the true compliance rate. In the appendix to this chapter, Exhibits 11-A and 11-B correspond to 5 percent and 10 percent risks of overreliance (or 95 and 90 percent confidence levels), respectively, and can be used to specify sample size.

In regard to the sample plan in which the presample indicates a 2 percent expected population deviation rate, assume that previous audit experi-

[4] Paul J. Beck and Ira Solomon, "Sampling Risks and Audit Consequences Under Alternative Testing Approaches," Working Paper, University of Illinois, May 1985.

ence suggests to you that a moderate amount of reliance can be placed on controls and the tolerable error rate will be 8 percent. If the auditor wishes to assume only a 5 percent risk of overreliance (or 95 percent confidence), Exhibit 11-A indicates a required sample size of 77, meaning that only 2 errors are expected in the sample. Hence, when the 50-unit presample is expanded by 27 sampling units, the auditor will expect to find no more than 1 deviation.

If instead the auditor is willing to accept a 10 percent risk (or 90 percent confidence), Exhibit 11-B will require a sample size of 48, and the presample or pilot sample will have fulfilled the full sample requirements (assuming it has been properly selected). Both Exhibits 11-A and 11-B assume a large population size, and any sample sizes of over 265 units will not be cost effective for most audit applications. According to the two tables, it is clear that the higher the expected error rate becomes, the larger the sample size will be, holding the tolerable rate constant. Similarly, the closer the expected error rate comes to the tolerable rate, the larger the required sample size will be. In contrast, the higher the tolerable rate and the higher the risk that the auditor is willing to accept, the lower the required number of sampling units will be.

Although the required sample sizes increase as the population sizes increase, the effects of population size are slight. To illustrate the nominal effect of population size, consider what happens as the number of items in the population increases from 500 to 1,000,000:

1. The precision interval widens from ±3.83 to 4.27, assuming an occurrence rate of 5 percent, a sample of 100, and a 95 percent confidence level.
2. The confidence level drops from 95.96 to 93.35 percent, assuming an occurrence rate of 5 percent, a sample of 100, and a precision interval of 4 percent.
3. The sample size increases from 93 to 114, assuming an occurrence rate of 5 percent, a 95 percent confidence rate, and a 4 percent precision interval.

The largest effects of population size are for small populations. For example, under certain conditions, a population of 50, will require a sample of 45 to draw the same type of conclusion as will a sample of 87 from a population of 500.

Multipurpose Testing

If the auditor believes that one type of sampling unit can be used in a set of audit tests, each of which requires different sample sizes, then he or she should expect this multipurpose sample to include different stopping points. In other words, 5 attributes may require testing on 50 items; 3 attributes may require testing on 100 items; and 1 attribute may require testing on 150 items. In order to apply the one set of sampling items to the three sampling plans, all items must be examined in the randomly drawn order. As long as this is done, once the auditor reaches 50 items, he or she can stop examining the attributes that required a sample size of 50 and make that particular sampling conclusion.

Sample Evaluation

Now assume that the 5 percent risk level is specified, 27 additional items are tested, and no more deviations are observed. Therefore, the total sample of 77 units has 1 deviation, resulting in a deviation rate of 1 divided by 77, or 1.3 percent. This sample deviation rate is the auditor's best estimate of the population error rate and clearly falls below the 8 percent tolerable error rate. However, the question remains whether the actual rate of deviations in the population can exceed the tolerable rate once an allowance is made for sampling risk. In other words, what is the upper limit of the possible deviation rate, given the sample size and results, at the specified level of risk? Exhibits 11-C and 11-D in the appendix are evaluation tables for compliance tests, and in this example, Exhibit 11-C is used because it gives the upper error limits at the desired 5 percent level. The table does not show a sample size of 77, and so the auditor is always conservative when using the table and will assume a sample size of 75 if he or she does not wish to interpolate. This indicates an upper error limit of 6.2 percent, which is within the 8 percent tolerable error range. The sample result is that 6.2 percent will exceed the true population occurrence rate 95 times out of 100.

Additional Considerations in Sample Evaluation

The sample result must be evaluated both quantitatively and qualitatively. The quantitative evaluation for a compliance test determines the error rate, and the qualitative evaluation determines the type and severity of any errors.

There are three kinds of procedural deviations: (1) accidental, (2) procedural, and (3) deliberate. The first are the inherent limitations of any control system. The second may be a problem with the prescribed procedures and may suggest a systematic error or a lack of control within the system, thus increasing the auditee's risk exposure. The third is, of course, the most severe deviation from an audit risk perspective as it may indicate the presence of fraud or at least a substantial shortcoming in the auditee's control environment.

The auditor should watch for error patterns. For example, five errors arranged in a particular order may have audit risk implications; if grouped in time, they may flag a vacation period in which several similar errors are likely to have occurred.

In all cases, consideration should be given to the effectiveness of other control procedures in serving as secondary or compensating controls. If the error rates are higher than acceptable, the substantive testing will need to be increased, or its timing will have to be shifted to the balance sheet date. In performing compliance test work, the auditor should also watch the deviation rate. If there are too many deviations to justify control reliance, the auditor may as well stop the test and modify the planned substantive tests. This attention to the error rate in the course of performing the tests on the sample can improve audit efficiency. If the observed error rates are not acceptable, or if the qualitative characteristics of errors flag a problem, their effects on subsequent testing must be evaluated. If the problems are so severe as to make the entity unauditable, the auditor should issue a disclaimer. Technically, an alternative exists to the extension of substantive test work. An auditor may believe that the sample drawn was unrepresentative of the population and choose to expand the sample for attributes testing. At a 95 percent confidence level, a 5 percent chance does exist of this occurring. However, the odds are clearly against the possibility, so selection of an extended sample is unlikely to disconfirm the initial sample estimates and is likely to be an inefficient alternative unless some specific information about the initial sample is known which suggests that the sample is indeed highly atypical.

Discovery Sampling

The other method of estimating a population's qualitative characteristics is a type of attributes test known as *discovery sampling.* Its objective is to provide a specified level of assurance that a sample will show at least one example of an attribute if the rate of occurrence of that attribute within the population is at or above a specified limit. In discovery sampling, as soon as the first error is found, no additional sampling is needed, as the decision is made based on that single error. This is a very economical testing approach for low-incidence items. This technique is appropriate when the occurrence rate is low; in fact, it's analogous to attributes sampling with a zero percent or low expected rate of occurrence. To use this approach, *critical rate of occurrence* (the rate that must be present or exceeded in order to provide the desired probability of producing an example) and the *desired probability of producing an example* (the complement of the acceptable risk level) must be specified. Discovery sampling thus yields a conclusion expressed as the rate of error.

Assume that a population of 4,000 items is to be examined for a specific important error. The auditor decides that more than 40 of these errors in the population will indicate that there is a serious problem. (Remember, the auditor expects zero errors; the critical error rate is the maximum rate that, if present, the auditor wants to detect.) Hence the auditor will use a sampling procedure that will give a 90 percent probability of finding at least one error if there are 40 or more in the population. This represents a discovery sampling objective, in a situation in which, the critical occurrence rate is 40 divided by 4,000, or 1 percent, and the desired probability is 90 percent. Exhibit 11-E in the appendix is read by identifying the critical rate of occurrence at the top of the page and the desired probability in the body of the table. Note that discovery sampling tables are based on ranges of population size and that Exhibit 11-E is for populations from 2,000 to 5,000. Starting at the far right column, the auditor stops at 92 percent (more conservative than the 87 figure in relation to the 90 percent desired probability) and settles on a sample size of 240. If one error is found when examining the sample, the auditor will know that the error rate was not at the acceptable level and will probably stop at that point, investigate the error, and extend the related audit work. An alternative option is to examine all 240 items and then project an error rate in the population by using Exhibit 11-D.

Discovery sampling can be used for compliance tests, for ferreting out frauds, and for substantive tests, in which the error of interest is "a type of error having a potentially material effect on an account balance." In each sampling plan, the auditor must make sure to select a table for the appropriate population size. Exhibits 11-F and 11-G are for populations between 5,000 and 10,000 and over 10,000, respectively. Note that discovery sampling is not good for finding a "needle in a haystack," such as a rate of occurrence of 1 in 500 or 1 in 5,000. This is evident from Exhibit 11-E, which shows that for a 0.3 percent upper limit, a sample size of 900 is required to reach 95 percent confidence.

Sequential Sampling or Stop-or-Go Sampling

A *sequential sample,* sometimes called a *stop-or-go sample,* is a sample that can be used in more than one step. Whether the next step is actually taken depends on the results of the previous step. It is most appropriate when the expected deviation rate is 1 to 2 percent. If no deviations are found in the first sample, the auditor can stop. Stop-or-go sampling should not be used if the second sample cannot be practically audited on a timely basis.

If a very low rate of compliance deviations is expected, sequential sampling can be more efficient than the common attributes test. This approach will not produce the large sample sizes that result from purposely overstating the expected error rate, as the typical attributes plan will. In the original attribute sampling example in which the desired reliability is 95 percent (that is, the acceptable risk level is 5 percent) and the tolerable error rate is 8 percent, the auditor used a 2 percent expected occurrence rate. If instead, a zero expected error rate is used in Exhibit 11-A, the smallest sample size is 36 items. Assume that the 1 deviation is observed in the first 36 items examined. What then is the implied upper precision limit (UPL) (or upper error limit)? Using Exhibit 11-H in the appendix, find the desired 95 percent confidence level column and "one" for the number of occurrences row, in order to identify a 4.8 factor to be used in the evaluation. This factor is then divided by the sample size to compute the maximum upper precision limit, $4.8 \div 36 = 13.3$ percent, which clearly exceeds the 8 percent desired limit. The next step is to divide the factor from Exhibit 11-H by the acceptable upper precision limit to find the total sample size required to reach an acceptable UPL, assuming that the original expectation of a low error rate was appropriate. Hence 4.8 divided by 8 percent yields a total sample of 60. This means that an additional 24 units should be tested $(60 - 36)$. If no other errors are found, the auditor can conclude that an acceptable upper error limit was obtained from the total sample of 60. Note that in the original fixed sample approach, 77 items were drawn and thus that 17 fewer items had to be drawn using stop-or-go sampling in order to meet the same audit objective. This is because the error rate for the total sample was lower than that for the presample.

If a sample is drawn that is expected to have different stopping points in a sequential plan, the selected units must be examined in the randomly drawn order.

A sequential sampling plan will generally be more efficient than a simple random sampling plan, either requiring a smaller sample size or offering greater confidence in its results. In sequential sampling, the acceptable risk levels are determined for alpha and beta, and decision limits are established using a chart or table for either acceptance or rejection of a population, based on the acceptable percentile of errors. A minimum sample size is determined and the samples are drawn in sequence. If the error limit is reached before the minimum sample is drawn, the auditor should reject the population. This rejection may require extended work, opinion qualification, or an adverse opinion. If no errors are found, the population can be accepted. If the decision for acceptance or rejection is not reached, the sample size should be increased until it is. For large samples, it is unlikely that the sample error will be greater than the population error, meaning that extended sampling is unlikely to produce an "accept" decision. Sequential sampling is widely used in quality control.

If the error rate is higher than expected, a sequential plan will produce a higher sample size than will a regular attributes single sample approach, as Participant 1 recognized in the introductory case. Essentially, the auditor must "pay" for the ability to examine the sample results mid-way. The one-time use of sample information in a classical mode penalizes users for drawing inferences mid-way. The absence of such a penalty could lead to severe abuse of the stop-or-go sampling approach. At the extreme, envision an auditor who expected to see a 2 percent deviation rate and stopped whenever that was observed. In some sense, results could be "molded" to expectations rather than being permitted to "represent" the total population as intended.

Merging Audit Evidence

When considering attributes sampling, it is important to recognize that the upper precision or error limit is not the same as a complement of the percentage of effectiveness of controls, as a single sample is only one piece of the pool of evidence for control systems. The preliminary survey, walk-through, and related evaluation procedures using internal control checklists, flowcharts, and memoranda all help determine control effectiveness. Furthermore, the compliance deviations themselves do not constitute dollar errors, meaning that some additional judgment is needed if control effectiveness is to be interpreted as preventing material errors from occurring or detecting any such errors in a timely manner through routine procedures. An 8 percent upper precision limit therefore does not translate into a 92 percent effectiveness in controls. Most likely, the effectiveness is superior to a 92 percent level.

Statistical sampling is often used to collect corroborative evidence and therefore may be performed with acceptable reliability levels lower than 95 or 99 percent. For example, when testing additions to property, plant, and equipment, the auditor may want to examine vouchers supporting labor and material charges to an account or work order, perhaps by using tests of material issue tickets and payroll line items. The idea is to determine the appropriateness of charges to property, plant, and equipment. Such a test will serve to corroborate the primary voucher disbursement test (which would have taken samples from the entire population), concentrating on the propriety of various control and operating procedures. Based on the primary test results already obtained, a 70 percent confidence level may be acceptable in the tests on material issue tickets and payroll line items.

There are various ways of blending compliance test results with materiality judgments in order to extend the evidence across attributes compliance testing and substantive testing. One approach is a crude 3-to-1 benchmark, in which an auditor assumes that only one out of three deviations will involve financial statement error, then multiplies the one-third estimate by the average dollar size of transactions to infer the dollar errors.[5]

A second approach is to consider the maximum exposure of book value to be the total dollar amount of the largest population items that would add to the percentage of the population items that corresponds to the upper precision limit. For example, if a population had high-dollar transactions, as well as medium- and low-dollar transactions, the auditor would focus on the high-dollar transactions (and medium, if required to reach, for example, 8 percent of the total transactions). If some of the items contained, for example, in that 8 percent were actually tested and found to be acceptable, then that particular dollar amount would be excluded and the next largest dollar amount added, thereby reducing the maximum exposure in dollars.

The assumption of normality will often not hold in compliance testing, as the error incidence tends to be very small in audits. If the error rate is 50 percent, the distribution of sample means will be normal; however, the smaller error rates create

[5] Donald A. Leslie, Albert D. Teitlebaum, and Rodney J. Anderson, *Dollar-Unit Sampling* (Toronto: Copp Clark Pitman, 1979).

skewed distributions, possibly underestimating the error rates. To illustrate the risk that results from such population tendencies, consider the probabilities of finding various error rates if a sample of 10 items is drawn from a large population having a 20 percent error rate:

Percentage of Error Found in Sample	Probability of Sample Containing This Percentage Error
0	10.7%
10	26.8%
20	30.2%
30	20.1%
40	8.8%
50	2.6%
60	.6%
70	.1%
80	.0%

Although 20 percent is the most probable result, there is a greater probability of underestimating than of overestimating the error rate. This effect of skewness should be considered when determining sample size requirements and the desired confidence level, as well as when interpreting sample results.

The cycle chapters which follow Chapter 12 will present additional sampling applications to further demonstrate how attribute and variables statistical tests and nonstatistical sampling can be useful to the auditor.

APPENDIX

Exhibits 11-A through 11-H present the various tables related to the performance of attribute testing, many of which are cited throughout the chapter.

REVIEW QUESTIONS

1. Match the letters corresponding to the type of question addressed to the four terms noted below. The letters can be used more than once.

Matching Terms	Type of Question Addressed
1. Estimation Sampling	a. What is the frequency of occurrence?
2. Attributes Sampling	b. How much?
3. Discovery Sampling	c. What assurance is there that at least one occurrence of this type will be included when it happens with at least a stated frequency level in the field?
4. Variables Sampling	

2. A payroll run is printed in departmental order, with department heads at the front of each grouping. Can systematic sampling be applied to such a run? Why or why not?

3. An auditor wants to test inventory count sheets. A total of eight hundred prenumbered sheets were prepared, each containing twenty lines. The auditor wants to use the count sheet as a sampling unit. In such an approach, how many lines of the sheet should be tested? Is there a more efficient way to select samples for use in testing the inventory count sheets?

4. Assume that you apply classical variables sampling and calculate a required sample size of 1,000 items. You consider this to be far too large a sample, practically speaking, and revert to nonstatistical sampling, specifying a sample size of 200 units.

Is the shift to nonstatistical sampling an effective way of addressing the problem of too large a sample size when using a statistical approach? What was the likely cause of the problem? What further action would be appropriate?

5. An auditor wants to project the FIFO cost of inventory for a client who maintains records at standard cost. What sampling approach should be used? Why? Which approach(es) could not be used?

6. When performing inventory test counts, auditors will frequently estimate items' value and select more items that are high valued. What type of sampling is being used in this situation? What would be a better approach?

7. If a client had two hundred stores, and the sampling plan for customers' accounts was to test the fiftieth customer on each store's customer list, would such a sampling plan be random? What assumptions are necessary for randomness to hold?

8. Indicate whether the following statements are true or false. Make any false statements into true statements.

a. Increasing the size of the population being sampled requires only a slight increase in sample size.

b. As desired precision limits become tighter, required sample sizes increase proportionately.

EXHIBIT 11-A

Statistical Sample Sizes for Compliance Testing—5 Percent Risk of Overreliance (with number of expected errors in parentheses)

Expected Population Deviation Rate	Tolerable Rate										
	2%	3%	4%	5%	6%	7%	8%	9%	10%	15%	20%
0.00%	149(0)	99(0)	74(0)	56(0)	49(0)	42(0)	36(0)	32(0)	29(0)	19(0)	14(0)
.25	236(1)	157(1)	117(1)	93(1)	78(1)	66(1)	58(1)	51(1)	46(1)	30(1)	22(1)
.50	*	157(1)	117(1)	93(1)	78(1)	66(1)	58(1)	51(1)	46(1)	30(1)	22(1)
.75	*	208(2)	117(1)	93(1)	78(1)	66(1)	58(1)	51(1)	46(1)	30(1)	22(1)
1.00	*	*	156(2)	93(1)	78(1)	66(1)	58(1)	51(1)	46(1)	30(1)	22(1)
1.25	*	*	156(2)	124(2)	78(1)	66(1)	58(1)	51(1)	46(1)	30(1)	22(1)
1.50	*	*	192(3)	124(2)	103(2)	66(1)	58(1)	51(1)	46(1)	30(1)	22(1)
1.75	*	*	227(4)	153(3)	103(2)	88(2)	77(2)	51(1)	46(1)	30(1)	22(1)
2.00	*	*	*	181(4)	127(3)	88(2)	77(2)	68(2)	46(1)	30(1)	22(1)
2.25	*	*	*	208(5)	127(3)	88(2)	77(2)	68(2)	61(2)	30(1)	22(1)
2.50	*	*	*	*	150(4)	109(3)	77(2)	68(2)	61(2)	30(1)	22(1)
2.75	*	*	*	*	173(5)	109(3)	95(3)	68(2)	61(2)	30(1)	22(1)
3.00	*	*	*	*	195(6)	129(4)	95(3)	84(3)	61(2)	30(1)	22(1)
3.25	*	*	*	*	*	148(5)	112(4)	84(3)	61(2)	30(1)	22(1)
3.50	*	*	*	*	*	167(6)	112(4)	84(3)	76(3)	40(2)	22(1)
3.75	*	*	*	*	*	185(7)	129(5)	100(4)	76(3)	40(2)	22(1)
4.00	*	*	*	*	*	*	146(6)	100(4)	89(4)	40(2)	22(1)
5.00	*	*	*	*	*	*	*	158(8)	116(6)	40(2)	30(2)
6.00	*	*	*	*	*	*	*	*	179(11)	50(3)	30(2)
7.00	*	*	*	*	*	*	*	*	*	68(5)	37(3)

*Sample size is too large to be cost effective for most audit applications.

Note: This table assumes a large population.

From AICPA Statistical Sampling Subcommittee, Audit and Accounting Guide: *Audit Sampling* (New York: AICPA, 1983), p. 106.

EXHIBIT 11-B

Statistical Sample Sizes for Compliance Testing—10 Percent Risk of Overreliance (with number of expected errors in parentheses)

Expected Population Deviation Rate	Tolerable Rate										
	2%	3%	4%	5%	6%	7%	8%	9%	10%	15%	20%
0.00%	114(0)	76(0)	57(0)	45(0)	38(0)	32(0)	28(0)	25(0)	22(0)	15(0)	11(0)
.25	194(1)	129(1)	96(1)	77(1)	64(1)	55(1)	48(1)	42(1)	38(1)	25(1)	18(1)
.50	194(1)	129(1)	96(1)	77(1)	64(1)	55(1)	48(1)	42(1)	38(1)	25(1)	18(1)
.75	265(2)	129(1)	96(1)	77(1)	64(1)	55(1)	48(1)	42(1)	38(1)	25(1)	18(1)
1.00	*	176(2)	96(1)	77(1)	64(1)	55(1)	48(1)	42(1)	38(1)	25(1)	18(1)
1.25	*	221(3)	132(2)	77(1)	64(1)	55(1)	48(1)	42(1)	38(1)	25(1)	18(1)
1.50	*	*	132(2)	105(2)	64(1)	55(1)	48(1)	42(1)	38(1)	25(1)	18(1)
1.75	*	*	166(3)	105(2)	88(2)	55(1)	48(1)	42(1)	38(1)	25(1)	18(1)
2.00	*	*	198(4)	132(3)	88(2)	75(2)	48(1)	42(1)	38(1)	25(1)	18(1)
2.25	*	*	*	132(3)	88(2)	75(2)	65(2)	42(1)	38(1)	25(1)	18(1)
2.50	*	*	*	158(4)	110(3)	75(2)	65(2)	58(2)	38(1)	25(1)	18(1)
2.75	*	*	*	209(6)	132(4)	94(3)	65(2)	58(2)	52(2)	25(1)	18(1)
3.00	*	*	*	*	132(4)	94(3)	65(2)	58(2)	52(2)	25(1)	18(1)
3.25	*	*	*	*	153(5)	113(4)	82(3)	58(2)	52(2)	25(1)	18(1)
3.50	*	*	*	*	194(7)	113(4)	82(3)	73(3)	52(2)	25(1)	18(1)
3.75	*	*	*	*	*	131(5)	98(4)	73(3)	52(2)	25(1)	18(1)
4.00	*	*	*	*	*	149(6)	98(4)	73(3)	65(3)	25(1)	18(1)
5.00	*	*	*	*	*	*	160(8)	115(6)	78(4)	34(2)	18(1)
6.00	*	*	*	*	*	*	*	182(11)	116(7)	43(3)	25(2)
7.00	*	*	*	*	*	*	*	*	199(14)	52(4)	25(2)
					*	*					

*Sample size is too large to be cost effective for most audit applications.

Note: This table assumes a large population.

From: AICPA Statistical Sampling Subcommittee, Audit and Accounting Guide: *Audit Sampling* (New York: AICPA, 1983), p. 107.

EXHIBIT 11-C

Statistical Sample Results: Evaluation Table for Compliance Tests—Upper Limits at 5 Percent Risk of Overreliance

	Actual Number of Deviations Found										
Sample Size	0	1	2	3	4	5	6	7	8	9	10
25	11.3	17.6	*	*	*	*	*	*	*	*	*
30	9.5	14.9	19.6	*	*	*	*	*	*	*	*
35	8.3	12.9	17.0	*	*	*	*	*	*	*	*
40	7.3	11.4	15.0	18.3	*	*	*	*	*	*	*
45	6.5	10.2	13.4	16.4	19.2	*	*	*	*	*	*
50	5.9	9.2	12.1	14.8	17.4	19.9	*	*	*	*	*
55	5.4	8.4	11.1	13.5	15.9	18.2	*	*	*	*	*
60	4.9	7.7	10.2	12.5	14.7	16.8	18.8	*	*	*	*
65	4.6	7.1	9.4	11.5	13.6	15.5	17.4	19.3	*	*	*
70	4.2	6.6	8.8	10.8	12.6	14.5	16.3	18.0	19.7	*	*
75	4.0	6.2	8.2	10.1	11.8	13.6	15.2	16.9	18.5	20.0	*
80	3.7	5.8	7.7	9.5	11.1	12.7	14.3	15.9	17.4	18.9	*
90	3.3	5.2	6.9	8.4	9.9	11.4	12.8	14.2	15.5	16.8	18.2
100	3.0	4.7	6.2	7.6	9.0	10.3	11.5	12.8	14.0	15.2	16.4
125	2.4	3.8	5.0	6.1	7.2	8.3	9.3	10.3	11.3	12.3	13.2
150	2.0	3.2	4.2	5.1	6.0	6.9	7.8	8.6	9.5	10.3	11.1
200	1.5	2.4	3.2	3.9	4.6	5.2	5.9	6.5	7.2	7.8	8.4

*Over 20 percent.

Note: This table presents upper limits as percentages and assumes a large population.

From: AICPA Statistical Sampling Subcommittee, Audit and Accounting Guide: *Audit Sampling* (New York: AICPA, 1983), p. 108.

EXHIBIT 11-D

Statistical Sampling Results: Evaluation Table for Compliance Tests—Upper Limits at 10 Percent Risk of Overreliance

	Actual Number of Deviations Found										
Sample Size	0	1	2	3	4	5	6	7	8	9	10
20	10.9	18.1	*	*	*	*	*	*	*	*	*
25	8.8	14.7	19.9	*	*	*	*	*	*	*	*
30	7.4	12.4	16.8	*	*	*	*	*	*	*	*
35	6.4	10.7	14.5	18.1	*	*	*	*	*	*	*
40	5.6	9.4	12.8	16.0	19.0	*	*	*	*	*	*
45	5.0	8.4	11.4	14.3	17.0	19.7	*	*	*	*	*
50	4.6	7.6	10.3	12.9	15.4	17.8	*	*	*	*	*
55	4.1	6.9	9.4	11.8	14.1	16.3	18.4	*	*	*	*
60	3.8	6.4	8.7	10.8	12.9	15.0	16.9	18.9	*	*	*
70	3.3	5.5	7.5	9.3	11.1	12.9	14.6	16.3	17.9	19.6	*
80	2.9	4.8	6.6	8.2	9.8	11.3	12.8	14.3	15.8	17.2	18.6
90	2.6	4.3	5.9	7.3	8.7	10.1	11.5	12.8	14.1	15.4	16.6
100	2.3	3.9	5.3	6.6	7.9	9.1	10.3	11.5	12.7	13.9	15.0
120	2.0	3.3	4.4	5.5	6.6	7.6	8.7	9.7	10.7	11.6	12.6
160	1.5	2.5	3.3	4.2	5.0	5.8	6.5	7.3	8.0	8.8	9.5
200	1.2	2.0	2.7	3.4	4.0	4.6	5.3	5.9	6.5	7.1	7.6

*Over 20 percent.

Note: This table presents upper limits as percentages and assumes a large population.

From: AICPA Statistical Sampling Subcommittee, Audit and Accounting Guide: *Audit Sampling* (New York: AICPA, 1983), p. 109.

EXHIBIT 11-E

Discovery Sampling Tables: Probability in Percentage of Including at Least One Occurrence in a Sample (for Populations Between 2000 and 5000)

Sample Size	Upper Precision Limit: Critical Rate of Occurrence							
	.3%	.4%	.5%	.6%	.8%	1%	1.5%	2%
50	14%	18%	22%	26%	33%	40%	53%	64%
60	17	21	26	30	38	45	60	70
70	19	25	30	35	43	51	66	76
80	22	28	33	38	48	56	70	80
90	24	31	37	42	52	60	75	84
100	26	33	40	46	56	64	78	87
120	31	39	46	52	62	70	84	91
140	35	43	51	57	68	76	88	94
160	39	48	56	62	73	80	91	96
200	46	56	64	71	81	87	95	98
240	52	63	71	77	86	92	98	99
300	61	71	79	84	92	96	99	99+
340	65	76	83	88	94	97	99+	99+
400	71	81	88	92	96	98	99+	99+
460	77	86	91	95	98	99	99+	99+
500	79	88	93	96	99	99	99+	99+
600	85	92	96	98	99	99+	99+	99+
700	90	95	98	99	99+	99+	99+	99+
800	93	97	99	99	99+	99+	99+	99+
900	95	98	99	99+	99+	99+	99+	99+
1000	97	99	99+	99+	99+	99+	99+	99+

Used with permission of the AICPA: "Sampling for Attributes: Estimation and Discovery," Supplementary Section, *An Auditor's Approach to Statistical Sampling*, vol. 2 (New York: AICPA, 1974), Appendix.

EXHIBIT 11-F

Discovery Sampling Tables: Probability in Percent of Including at Least One Occurrence in a Sample (for Population Between 5000 and 10,000)

Sample Size	Upper Precision Limit: Critical Rate of Occurrence							
	.1%	.2%	.3%	.4%	.5%	.75%	1%	2%
50	5%	10%	14%	18%	22%	31%	40%	64%
60	6	11	17	21	26	36	45	70
70	7	13	19	25	30	41	51	76
80	8	15	21	28	33	45	55	80
90	9	17	24	30	36	49	60	84
100	10	18	26	33	40	53	64	87
120	11	21	30	38	45	60	70	91
140	13	25	35	43	51	65	76	94
160	15	28	38	48	55	70	80	96
200	18	33	45	56	64	78	87	98
240	22	39	52	62	70	84	91	99
300	26	46	60	70	78	90	95	99+
340	29	50	65	75	82	93	97	99+
400	34	56	71	81	87	95	98	99+
460	38	61	76	85	91	97	99	99+
500	40	64	79	87	92	98	99	99+
600	46	71	84	92	96	99	99+	99+
700	52	77	89	95	97	99+	99+	99+
800	57	81	92	96	98	99+	99+	99+
900	61	85	94	98	99	99+	99+	99+
1000	65	88	96	99	99	99+	99+	99+
1500	80	96	99	99+	99+	99+	99+	99+
2000	89	99	99+	99+	99+	99+	99+	99+

Used with permission of the AICPA: "Sampling for Attributes: Estimation and Discovery," Supplementary Section, *An Auditor's Approach to Statistical Sampling*, vol. 2 (New York: AICPA, 1974), Appendix.

EXHIBIT 11-G

Discovery Sampling Tables: Probability in Percent of Including at Least One Occurrence In a Sample (for Populations over 10,000)

Sample Size	Upper Precision Limit: Critical Rate of Occurrence							
	.01%	.05%	.1%	.2%	.3%	.5%	1%	2%
50		2%	5%	9%	14%	22%	39%	64%
60	1%	3	6	11	16	26	45	70
70	1	3	7	13	19	30	51	76
80	1	4	8	15	21	33	55	80
90	1	4	9	16	24	36	60	84
100	1	5	10	18	26	39	63	87
120	1	6	11	21	30	45	70	91
140	1	7	13	24	34	50	76	94
160	2	8	15	27	38	55	80	96
200	2	10	18	33	45	63	87	98
240	2	11	21	38	51	70	91	99
300	3	14	26	45	59	78	95	99+
340	3	16	29	49	64	82	97	99+
400	4	18	33	55	70	87	98	99+
460	5	21	37	60	75	90	99	99+
500	5	22	39	63	78	92	99	99+
600	6	26	45	70	84	95	99+	99+
700	7	30	50	75	88	97	99+	99+
800	8	33	55	80	91	98	99+	99+
900	9	36	59	83	93	99	99+	99+
1000	10	39	63	86	95	99	99+	99+
1500	14	53	78	95	99	99+	99+	99+
2000	18	63	86	98	99+	99+	99+	99+
2500	22	71	92	99	99+	99+	99+	99+
3000	26	78	95	99+	99+	99+	99+	99+

Used with permission of the AICPA: "Sampling for Attributes: Estimation and Discovery," Supplementary Section, *An Auditor's Approach to Statistical Sampling*, vol. 2 (New York: AICPA, 1974), Appendix.

EXHIBIT 11-H

Attribute Sampling Table for Determining Stop-or-Go Sample Sizes and Upper Precision Limit of Population Occurrence Rate, Based on Sample Results

Number of Occurrences	Confidence Levels 90%	95%	97.5%
0	2.4	3.0	3.7
1	3.9	4.8	5.6
2	5.4	6.3	7.3
3	6.7	7.8	8.8
4	8.0	9.2	10.3
5	9.3	10.6	11.7
6	10.6	11.9	13.1
7	11.8	13.2	14.5
8	13.0	14.5	15.8
9	14.3	16.0	17.1
10	15.5	17.0	18.4
11	16.7	18.3	19.7
12	18.0	19.5	21.0
13	19.0	21.0	22.3
14	20.2	22.0	23.5
15	21.4	23.4	24.7
16	22.6	24.3	26.0
17	23.8	26.0	27.3
18	25.0	27.0	28.5
19	26.0	28.0	29.6
20	27.1	29.0	31.0
21	28.3	30.3	32.0
22	29.3	31.5	33.3
23	30.5	32.6	34.6
24	31.4	33.8	35.7
25	32.7	35.0	37.0
26	34.0	36.1	38.1
27	35.0	37.3	39.4
28	36.1	38.5	40.5
29	37.2	39.6	41.7
30	38.4	40.7	42.9
31	39.1	42.0	44.0
32	40.3	43.0	45.1
33	41.5	44.2	46.3
34	42.7	45.3	47.5
35	43.8	46.4	48.8
36	45.0	47.6	49.9
37	46.1	48.7	51.0
38	47.2	49.8	52.1
39	48.3	51.0	53.4
40	49.4	52.0	54.5
41	50.5	53.2	55.6
42	51.6	54.5	56.8
43	52.6	55.5	58.0
44	54.0	56.6	59.0
45	55.0	57.7	60.3
46	56.0	59.0	61.4
47	57.0	60.0	62.6
48	58.0	61.1	63.7
49	59.7	62.2	64.8
50	60.4	63.3	65.0
51	61.5	64.5	67.0

Adapted from a table in Marvin Tummins and Robert H. Strawser, "A Confidence Limits Table for Attribute Sampling," *Accounting Review*, October 1976, pp. 907–912.

c. As desired reliability increases, required sample size increases, with progressively greater increases in the required sample size as the reliability level becomes increasingly high.
d. Decreasing the error rate for an attributes sampling plan will require an increase in the sample size, with progressively smaller increases in the required sample size as the error rate for attributes approaches 50 percent.
e. Increasing the variability in the values in a variables sampling plan will require an increase in the required sample size, with progressively larger increases in the required sample size needed as the variability in the values of the variables approaches infinity.
f. If tighter precision is specified, with lower confidence, the required sample size will increase.
g. If an auditor is willing to accept a lower confidence level and an increased required sample size, the resulting precision will be tighter.
h. If the auditor tightens precision and decreases the required sample size, the effect will be a higher level of confidence.
i. If more precision is acceptable with a lower confidence level, the required sample size will be smaller.

9. How might an auditor respond to sample results that indicate that a population has an unacceptably high error rate?

10. What are the differences between statistical and nonstatistical sampling?

11. What are the most relevant population and sampling units for statistical sampling applications that are intended to meet the following audit objectives:
a. to estimate year-end receivables.
b. to test whether short-term security portfolios are overstated.
c. to ensure that all purchases are recorded.
d. to determine that capitalized expenditures should not have been expensed, given a client situation in which all items under $1,000 are automatically expensed.

12. How does sample size relate to
a. population size?
b. reliability?
c. risk?
d. the population's variability?

13. What is the purpose of a pilot sample? What information can be used in lieu of a pilot sample?

14. Based on the AICPA's *Audit and Accounting Guide on Audit Sampling*, does an auditor tend to be more concerned about alpha risk or beta risk? Why?

15. If an auditor used discovery sampling and found one error, what would be the appropriate conclusion?

16. Two auditors are discussing their plans to perform

Random Numbers

	(1)	(2)	(3)	(4)	(5)	(6)	(7)
1	10480	15011	01536	02011	81647	91646	69179
2	22368	46573	25595	85393	30995	89198	27982
3	24130	48360	22527	97265	76393	64809	15179
4	42167	93093	06243	61680	07856	16376	39440
5	37570	39975	81837	16656	06121	91782	60468
6	77921	06907	11008	42751	27756	53498	18602
7	99562	72905	56420	69994	98872	31016	71194
8	96301	91977	05463	07972	18876	20922	94595
9	89579	14342	63661	10281	17453	18103	57740
10	85475	36857	53342	53988	53060	59533	38867
11	28918	69578	88231	33276	70997	79936	56865
12	63553	40961	48235	03427	49626	69445	18663
13	09429	93969	52636	92737	88974	33488	36320
14	10365	61129	87529	85689	48237	52267	67689
15	07119	97336	71048	08178	77233	13916	47564
16	51085	12765	51821	51259	77452	16308	60756
17	02368	21382	52404	60268	89368	19885	55322
18	01011	54092	33362	94904	31273	04146	18594
19	52162	53916	46369	58586	23216	14513	83149
20	07056	97628	33787	09998	42698	06691	76988
21	48663	91245	85828	14346	09172	30168	90229
22	54164	58492	22421	74103	47070	25306	76468
23	32639	32363	05597	24200	13363	38005	94342
24	29334	27001	87637	87308	58731	00256	45834
25	02488	33062	28834	07351	19731	92420	60952
26	81525	72295	04839	95423	24878	82651	66566
27	29676	20591	68086	26432	46901	20849	89768
28	00742	57392	39064	66432	84673	44027	32832
29	05366	04213	25669	26122	44407	44048	37937
30	91921	26418	64117	94305	26766	25940	39972
31	00582	04711	87917	77341	42206	35126	74087
32	00725	69884	62797	56170	86324	88072	76222
33	69011	65795	95876	55293	18988	27354	26575
34	25976	57948	29888	88604	67917	48708	18912
35	09763	83473	73577	12908	30883	18317	28290
36	91567	42595	27958	30134	04024	86385	29880
37	17955	56349	90999	49127	20044	59931	06115
38	46503	18584	18845	49618	02304	51038	20655
39	92157	89634	94824	78171	84610	82834	09922
40	14577	62765	35605	81263	39667	47358	56873
41	98427	07523	33362	64270	01638	92477	66969
42	34914	63976	88720	82765	34476	17032	87589
43	70060	28277	39475	46473	23219	53416	94970
44	53976	54914	06990	67245	68350	82948	11398
45	76072	29515	40980	07591	58745	25774	22987
46	90725	52210	83974	29992	65831	38857	50490
47	64364	67412	33339	31926	14883	24413	59744
48	08962	00358	31662	25388	61642	34072	81249
49	95012	68379	93526	70765	10592	04542	76463
50	15664	10493	20492	38391	91132	21999	59516

From the Interstate Commerce Commission Bureau of Transport Economics and Statistics Table of 105,000 Random Decimal Digits.

inventory test counts. One proposes selecting sampling units from an inventory listing, known to have been tied to the ledger. The other advocates making a physical selection in the storeroom, based on a randomized selection from a floor plan of inventory locations. Which of the two sampling procedures is preferable, and why?

17. The table beginning this page is an excerpt from a random number table. How can this table be used? Give at least five examples of different ways that it can be used to select a sample.

EXERCISES

1. An auditor wants to test whether vouchers have been charged to the proper account. (S)he wishes to test a population of 10,000 transactions expected to have a 1 percent error rate. The maximum tolerable error rate is 5 percent at a 90 percent confidence level.

a. What is the required sample size?

b. Assume that the auditor tested the selected sample and found two errors. Evaluate the sample results.

2. An auditor performs a voucher test of one hundred items and summarizes the results as follows:

Lack of approval	1
Failed to take an allowable discount	1
Improper documentation—copy of support attached in lieu of originals	1
TOTAL	3

What is the rate of occurrence? How would you evaluate these results? What information is necessary to evaluate the results?

3. A client issues ten thousand vouchers in a period. One-half of these vouchers involves the purchase and receipt of materials. Cash discounts are available on one-fifth of the vouchers. If the auditor wants to estimate the rate of occurrence for the absence of receiving reports and the failure to take a discount that was offered, how should (s)he proceed to define a sampling plan?

4. a. If a sample of two hundred items was selected from a population of five thousand items with an actual error proportion of .02, the sample would be expected to include __ errors.

b. If the auditor wanted to improve reliability, would the sample size increase or decrease?

c. If the auditor desired tighter precision, would the sample size increase or decrease?

d. How does the relationship of expected error and tolerable error affect sample size?

QUESTIONS ADAPTED FROM PROFESSIONAL EXAMINATIONS

1. The use of statistical sampling techniques to examine financial statements does not eliminate judgmental decisions.

Required:

a. Describe four areas in which a CPA may use judgment in planning a statistical sampling test.

b. Assume that a CPA's sample shows an unacceptable error rate. Describe the various actions that he or she may take based on this finding.

c. A nonstratified sample of 80 accounts payable vouchers is selected from a population of 3,200. The vouchers are numbered consecutively from 1 to 3,200 and are listed, 40 to a page, in the voucher register. Describe four different techniques for selecting a random sample of vouchers for review.

(CPA exam adapted)

2. In developing an audit program it is determined that to achieve the specified precision and confidence, a sample of 436 items from a population of 10,000 will be statistically adequate.

Required:

a. Briefly define each of the following terms:

1. Population.
2. Sample.
3. Precision.
4. Confidence.

b. If the population is 100,000 and the specifications for precision and confidence are unchanged from the above situation for a population of 10,000, which of the following sample sizes will be statistically correct for the larger population: 436, 454, 3,000, or 4,360? Justify your answer. (Your answer should be based on judgment and reasoning rather than actual calculation.)

c. Statistical sampling techniques are being used in auditing. A sample is taken and analyzed to draw an inference or reach a conclusion about a population, but there is always a risk that the inference or conclusion may be incorrect. What value, then, is there in using statistical sampling techniques?

(CPA exam adapted)

3. You are now conducting your third annual audit of the financial statements of Elite Corporation for the year ended December 31, 19X6. You decide to employ unrestricted random number statistical sampling techniques in testing the effectiveness of the company's internal control procedures relating to sales invoices, which all are serially numbered. In previous years, after selecting one representative two-week period during the year, you tested all invoices issued during that period and resolved to your satisfaction all of the errors which were found.

Required:

a. Explain the statistical procedures you would use to determine the size of the sample of sales invoices to be examined.

b. Once the sample size has been determined, how would you select the individual invoices to be included in the sample? Explain.

c. How would the use of statistical sampling procedures improve the examination of sales invoices, as compared with the selection procedure used in earlier years? Discuss.

d. Assume that the company issued fifty thousand sales invoices during the year and the auditor specified a confidence level of 95 percent with a precision range of plus or minus 2 percent.

1. Does this mean that the auditor is willing to accept the reliability of the sales invoice data if errors are found on no more than four sales invoices out of every ninety-five invoices examined? Discuss.
2. If the auditor specified a precision range of plus or minus 1 percent, would the confidence level be higher or lower than 95 percent, assuming that the size of the sample remains constant? Why?

(CPA exam adapted)

4. Jiblum, a CPA, is planning to use attribute sampling in order to determine the degree of reliance to be placed on an audit client's internal accounting control system for sales. Jiblum has begun to outline the main steps in the sampling plan.

1. State the objective(s) of the audit test (for exam-

ple, the reliability of internal accounting controls over sales).

2. Define the population (the period covered by the test, the sampling unit, and the completeness of the population).
3. Define the sampling unit (for example, client's copies of sales invoices).

Required:

a. What are the remaining steps in the above outline that Jiblum should include in the statistical test of sales invoices? Do not present a detailed analysis of tasks that must be performed to carry out the objectives of each step. Parenthetical examples need not be provided.

b. How does statistical methodology help an auditor develop a satisfactory sampling plan?

(CPA exam adapted)

5. The following are five situations for which you plan to use statistical sampling.
   1. You will observe an annual physical verification of a perpetual inventory. A statistical sample of the inventory will be counted under the internal auditors' observation.
   2. You suspect that prices were deliberately raised on some of the perpetual inventory line items in order to cover inventory shrinkage caused by thefts.
   3. There are several errors in the keypunch operation, and so you recommend the installation of a continuing statistical sample.
   4. Your audit program calls for examining the purchase orders to see whether they were issued within the prescribed time limits. You plan to use minimum audit effort for this test. Your audit objective will be satisfied with a 95 percent probability that not more than 2 percent of the purchase orders were issued late.
   5. You find that material issue documents for the period under audit are stored in a records warehouse in serial number order in boxes containing one thousand documents each. There are nine hundred boxes of documents.

Required:

For each of the above situations

a. Identify the sampling plan or selection technique that would be most appropriate.

b. State why the particular plan or technique should be used.

(CIA exam adapted)

6. Identify the factual error in each of the following three statements:

a. In any normal distribution of population values, the mean of the distribution plus or minus one standard deviation includes 25 percent of the area under the normal curve.

b. To avoid bias when selecting a sample, every item must have a systematic (every *n*th item) chance of selection.

c. Assuming the same population size, sample size, and estimated error rate, an increase in the confidence level will result in a narrowing of the range of precision.

(CIA exam adapted)

7. **Multiple Choice**

Select the one answer that best completes the statement or answers the question.

7.1 Precision is a statistical measure of the maximum likely difference between the sample estimate and the true but unknown population total and is directly related to

a. Reliability of evidence.
b. Relative risk.
c. Materiality.
d. Cost-benefit analysis.

(CPA exam adapted)

7.2 An auditor obtains a magnetic tape that contains the dollar amounts of all client inventory items by style number. The information on the tape is in no particular sequence. The auditor can best ascertain that no consigned merchandise is included on the tape by using a computer program that

a. Statistically selects samples of all amounts.
b. Excludes all amounts for items with particular style numbers that indicate consigned merchandise.
c. Mathematically calculates the extension of each style quantity by the unit price.
d. Prints on paper the information on the magnetic tape.

(CPA exam adapted)

7.3 An important statistic to consider when using a statistical sampling audit plan is the population variability. The population variability is measured by the

a. Sample mean.
b. Standard deviation.
c. Standard error of the sample mean.
d. Estimated population total minus the actual population total.

(CPA exam adapted)

7.4 When using statistical sampling for tests of compliance, an auditor's evaluation of compliance should include a statistical conclusion concerning whether

a. Procedural deviations in the population are within an acceptable range.
b. Monetary precision is over a certain predetermined amount.
c. The population total is not in error by more than a fixed amount.
d. Population characteristics occur at least once in the population.

(CPA exam adapted)

7.5 Which of the following best describes the distinguishing feature of statistical sampling?
a. It requires the examination of fewer supporting documents.
b. It measures mathematically the degree of uncertainty that results from examining only part of a population.
c. It reduces the problems associated with the auditor's judgment concerning materiality.
d. It is evaluated in terms of two parameters: statistical mean and random selection.

(CPA exam adapted)

7.6 Which of the following best describes what the auditor means by the rate of occurrence in an attribute sampling plan?
a. The number of errors that can reasonably be expected to be found in a population.
b. The frequency with which a certain characteristic occurs within a population.
c. The degree of confidence that the sample is representative of the population.
d. The dollar range within which the true population total can be expected to fall.

(CPA exam adapted)

7.7 An internal auditor plans to sample an insurance claims settlement file to ascertain evidence of fraudulent claims. The auditor draws a sample of claims for auditing that will provide a specified confidence level of detecting at least one fraudulent claim if there is a certain rate of fraudulent claims in the population. This type of sampling plan is known as:
a. Acceptance sampling.
b. Stratified sampling.
c. Discovery sampling.
d. Chi-square sampling.
e. Variables sampling.

(CIA exam adapted)

7.8 If certain forms are not consecutively numbered
a. Selection of a random sample probably is not possible.
b. Systematic sampling may be appropriate.
c. Stratified sampling should be used.
d. Random number tables cannot be used.

(CPA exam adapted)

7.9 Which of the following statistical selection techniques is least desirable for an auditor to use?
a. Systematic selection.
b. Stratified selection.
c. Block selection.
d. Sequential selection.

(CPA exam adapted)

7.10 A CPA examining inventory may appropriately use sampling for attributes in order to estimate the
a. Average price of inventory items.
b. Percentage of slow-moving inventory items.
c. Dollar value of inventory.
d. Physical quantity of inventory items.

(CPA exam adapted)

7.11 An accounts receivable aging schedule was prepared on three hundred pages, with each page containing the aging data for fifty accounts. The pages were numbered from 1 to 300, and the accounts listed on each were numbered from 1 to 50.

Godla, an auditor, selected the accounts receivable for confirmation using the following table of numbers:

Godla's Procedures

Select Column from Table of Numbers	Separate 5 digits: first 3 Digits and Last 2 Digits
02011	020--11 x
85393	853--93 *
97265	972--65 *
61680	616--80 *
16656	166--56 *
42751	427--51 *
69994	699--94 *
07942	079--42 y
10231	102--31 z
53988	539--88 *

x Mailed confirmation to account 11 listed on page 20.
y Mailed confirmation to account 42 listed on page 79.
z Mailed confirmation to account 31 listed on page 102.
* Rejected

This is an example of which of the following sampling methods?
a. Acceptance sampling.
b. Systematic sampling.
c. Sequential sampling.
d. Random sampling.

(CPA exam adapted)

7.12 If the size of the sample to be used in a particular test of attributes has not been determined by means of statistical concepts, but the sample has been chosen in accordance with random selection procedures

a. No inferences can be drawn from the sample.
b. The auditor has committed a nonsampling error.
c. The auditor may or may not achieve desired precision at the desired level of confidence.
d. The auditor will have to evaluate the results by referring to the principles of discovery sampling.

(CPA exam adapted)

7.13 When performing a compliance test of control over cash disbursements, a CPA may use a systematic sampling technique that starts with any randomly selected item. The biggest disadvantage of this type of sampling is that the items in the population

a. Must be recorded in a systematic pattern before the sample can be drawn.
b. May occur in a systematic pattern, thus destroying the sample's randomness.
c. May systematically occur more than once in the sample.
d. Must be systematically replaced in the population after sampling.

(CPA exam adapted)

7.14 In which of the following cases would an auditor be most likely to conclude that all of the items in an account should be examined rather than tested on a sample basis?

The Measure of Tolerable Error Is	Error Frequency Is Expected to Be
Large	Low
Small	High
Large	High
Small	Low

(CPA exam adapted)

7.15 Which of the following best illustrates the concept of sampling risk?

a. A randomly chosen sample of the characteristic of interest may not be representative of the population as a whole.
b. An auditor may select audit procedures that are not appropriate to achieve the specific objective.
c. An auditor may fail to recognize errors in the documents examined for the chosen sample.
d. The documents related to the chosen sample may not be available for inspection.

(CPA exam adapted)

7.16 An auditor plans to examine a sample of twenty checks for countersignatures as prescribed by the client's internal control procedures. One of the checks in the chosen sample of 20 cannot be found. The auditor should consider the reasons for this limitation and

a. Evaluate the results as if the sample size had been nineteen.
b. Treat the missing check as a deviation for the purpose of evaluating the sample.
c. Treat the missing check in the same manner as the majority of the other nineteen checks, i.e., countersigned or not.
d. Choose another check to replace the missing check in the sample.

(CPA exam adapted)

7.17 The tolerable rate of deviations for a compliance test is generally

a. Lower than the expected rate of errors in the related accounting records.
b. Higher than the expected rate of errors in the related accounting records.
c. Identical with the expected rate of errors in the related accounting records.
d. Unrelated to the expected rate of errors in the related accounting records.

(CPA exam adapted)

7.18 If all other factors specified in an attribute sampling plan remain constant, changing the specified precision from 6 percent to 10 percent, and the specified reliability from 97 percent to 93 percent, would cause the required sample size to

a. Increase
b. Remain the same.
c. Decrease.
d. Change by 4 percent.

(CPA exam adapted)

7.19 The precision limit for compliance tests necessary to justify reliance on internal accounting control depends primarily on which of the following?

a. The cause of errors.
b. The extent of reliance on the procedures.
c. The number of substantive errors.
d. The limit used in audits for similar clients.

(CPA exam adapted)

7.20 In attribute sampling, a 10 percent change in which of the following factors normally will have the least effect on the size of a statistical sample?

a. Population size.
b. Precision (confidence interval).
c. Reliability (confidence level).
d. Standard deviation.

(CPA exam adapted)

CASE FOR DISCUSSION

A client's purchasing function is computerized. Once the vendors' invoices are received, they are manually matched with purchase orders and receiving reports. And once the vendors' invoices are batched into groups of thirty invoices, edit runs are prepared for each batch. Each run lists the vendor's name, the invoice date, and the invoice amount. During interim work, the auditor notes that in each of the nine months to date, four hundred to five hundred batches of invoices were processed. Because the client's business is expected to be greater in the fourth quarter, it is anticipated that up to seven hundred batches may be used in any of the final three months. As checks are printed by the computer, they are signed by a facsimile signature under the treasurer's control. Checks over $5,000 must be countersigned by a vice-president. Because checks can pay from one to twenty-five invoices, the total number of checks issued as of the interim date was nine thousand, serially numbered from 30000 to 39000. It is expected that another six thousand checks will be issued during the last quarter. Purchase orders numbered from 1001 to 8950 were written in the first nine months.

You want to perform compliance tests during your interim work on control procedures. Prepare a sampling plan that includes all relevant alternatives and considerations.

12

Variables Sampling and Regression Analysis

John. I heard that you were using regression analysis in one of your engagements.

Teresa. Yes, we're using it for a newspaper client of ours. We're using it to substantive-test the total advertising revenue from classified ads.

John. What kind of model are you using?

Teresa. The classified ads are mainly want ads and real estate ads. We have data on the number of new jobs in the metroplex, national figures on unemployment, industry statistics on employment-related ads, real estate figures on the number of sales transactions, and local figures on apartment occupancy.

John. It sounds interesting, but what about its acceptability? I remember reading that courts were skeptical of statistical evidence due to the commonality with which it tends to be misused. In fact, I recall a quote from one court case: "Too many use statistics as a drunk man uses a lamppost—for support, and not for illumination."[1]

Teresa. There's no doubt that all statistics can be abused, as can many other forms of evidence, but one thing is certain: Courts prefer the objectivity of statistics over the so-called "garden variety proposition about who did what, when, and where."[2] There are many cases in which statistical evidence outweighed subjective approaches, and, in particular, a 1976 case explicitly recognized that regression analysis is a professionally accepted method of analyzing data.[3] Regression analysis

[1] *Keeley* v. *Westinghouse Electric Corp.*, cited by David Whitten, "Statistics and Title VII Proof: Prima Facie Case and Rebuttal," *Houston Law Review*, May, 1978, pp. 1030–1053.

[2] *Trans World Airlines, Inc.* v. *Hughes*, 308 F. Supp. 679 (S.D.N.Y. 1969), aff'd, 449 F. 2d 51 (2d Cir. 1971) rev'd sub nom. *Hughes Tool Co.* v. *Trans World Airlines Inc.*, 409 U.S. 363 (1973).

[3] *Brown* v. *Moore*, 428 F. Supp. 1123, 1128 (S.D. Ala. 1976), aff'd, 575 F. 2d 298 (5th Circuit 1978).

is a common type of evidence presented in antitrust, business interruption (lost profits), and discrimination cases. And public utility commissions and other rate hearings and administrative proceedings often use regression.[4] While no case involving an auditing application has appeared in court, ample precedence exists as to the tool's general applicability.

John. How does regression analysis tie into professional standards?

Teresa. SAS No. 23 on analytical review encourages using a historical benchmark for formulating expectations to which recorded balances can be compared. Essentially, regression modeling, in a time series mode, is a formal trend analysis that can also give precision measures at a particular level of confidence. Not only does it tell you whether accounts are reasonable, but it can also provide a good idea as to the source of unreasonable fluctuations.

John. Really? What's an example?

Teresa. For three years, we've been using regression analysis for a retailing client's stores, comparing each store's performance with the "average store performance," as measured by regression analysis. The modeling process found two stores to be very unusual. We then found out that one hadn't estimated uncollectibles and the other had a theft ring in operation. The models we used were simple relationships for receivable and inventory balances, with operating characteristics such as square footage used to describe variations in account balances across stores.

John. It must be expensive to use.

Teresa. Actually, both times I've used it, we spent less time on our initial application than we had spent on analytical review the year before. And in the years afterwards, it's even cheaper.

John. Do you think regression analysis will eventually replace sampling techniques?

Teresa. I think that modeling will cut down sampling needs and help to direct the definition of relevant populations for statistical samples. But I don't think it will ever replace it, since the tools complement one another and proceed with very distinctive differences in terms of the inferences to be drawn. In sampling, you assume that if a sample of component transactions is fair, then the total balance will also be fair, whereas in modeling, you assume that if the total balance is fair, then its underlying transactions will also be fair. Whether you use sampling or modeling then depends on such factors as the explanatory variables available for models and the internal control setting in which sampling data are generated.

John. Is the computer software user-friendly? Can I log onto my micro and make a test run to see how the interactive system works?

Teresa. Yes, let me give you a demonstration.

This case describes the use of a statistically based auditing tool which will be discussed in this chapter and explains that modeling can complement and even direct sampling plans. Most of the underlying concepts for statistical applications were introduced in Chapter 11 and an in-depth discussion of attributes testing was provided. In this chapter, concepts introduced in Chapter 11 which

[4]For an example of such cases, see Wanda A. Wallace, "The Acceptability of Regression Analysis As Evidence in a Courtroom—Implications for the Auditor," *Auditing: A Journal of Practice & Theory*, Spring 1983, pp. 66–90.

relate to variables sampling will be extended. The manner in which an auditor applies sampling to formulate estimates of account balances for the purpose of reaching a substantive test conclusion will be elaborated upon. Regression analysis can be a very useful tool in assessing the reasonableness of management's representations. As with any analytical review tool, beyond its applicability as a substantive testing technique throughout the audit process, it can be particularly useful as a planning tool (e.g., which units of a multilocation client are to be visited) and as a final review tool (including interim review engagements, which will be discussed in a later chapter of this text).

First, we will direct our attention to variables sampling—its purpose, the primary approaches to such testing, and the relative advantages and disadvantages of alternative approaches.

Variables Sampling

When substantive tests are used for quantifying, there is a choice of many variables sampling approaches. Most of them stem from the *mean-per-unit* (or *mean estimation*) or *direct projection approach,* which can help test such items as warranty costs, billing errors, and inventory valuation.

Just as a higher expected population deviation rate (or error rate or rate of occurrence) will increase the required sample size in compliance testing, a higher *standard deviation* increases sample sizes in variables testing. The mean estimation technique will be presented first to clarify the key role which population variability plays in determining sample size and, therefore, in affecting the selection of a sampling approach.

Mean Estimation Technique

A simple way of understanding how the various sampling plan components discussed to this point interact is to study the basic formulas for sample size, confidence level, and precision in a mean-per-unit sampling application. Although in practice, software is widely available to make such calculations, an understanding of the underlying formulas will better equip auditors in planning audit applications and forming reasonable expectations of sample size requirements in various client settings. It should be recognized that mean-per-unit ideas apply to *ratio* and *difference estimation plans,* both of which are variables sampling approaches that will be described later in this chapter.

Four concepts need attention before proceeding: (1) sampling with and without replacement, (2) the finite correction factor, (3) the sample's variability, and (4) the normal curve and its application in defining confidence intervals. *Sampling with replacement* means that, for example, when invoice #75 is examined, it is placed back, or replaced, into the population for possible reselection later in the sampling process. Hence a sample of seventy-seven items could include five repeated items, leading to an examination of only seventy-two different documents. In contrast, *sampling without replacement* means that when invoice #75 is examined, it is removed from the population and cannot be resampled in that particular sampling plan. Obviously, there is greater audit coverage with sampling without replacement, meaning that required sample sizes are smaller without replacement than with replacement.

A *finite correction factor* applies whenever (1) sampling without replacement is used and (2) the sample size divided by the population size is greater than .05. If the sample size does not constitute at least 5 percent of the population, the finite correction factor will be immaterial, thus eliminating any significant differences in the sample sizes with replacement, versus those without replacement.

To assess the variability of a population, the auditor can most easily focus on the range of values in the population of interest. Range, as noted in Chapter 11, is computed as the difference between the highest value and lowest value in the population. However, the variability measure used in sampling plans is the standard deviation. Recall from the discussion in Chapter 11 that the standard deviation is computed by taking the square root of the quotient formed by taking the sum of the squared deviations from the mean divided by the number of units. If sample estimates are used to measure the population's standard deviation, then the mean should be divided by the number of units minus one. The higher the standard deviation is, the greater the variability of the sample and the larger the required sample size will be. The

EXHIBIT 12-1
The Normal Curve and How It Relates to Alpha and Beta Risks

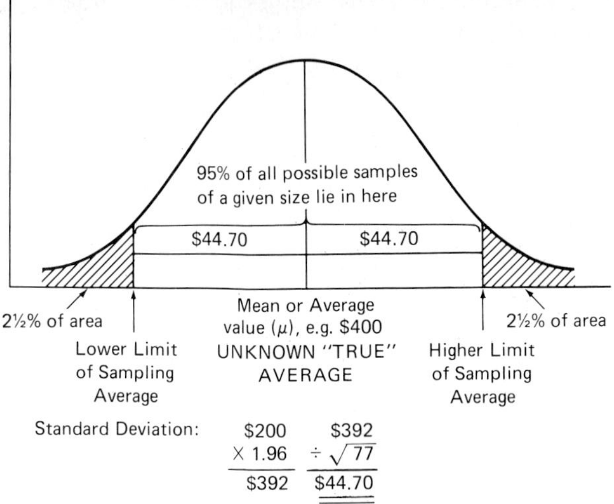

There are 95 chances in 100 that the sample value is no farther from the true value than 1.96 (σ) / $\sqrt{n}$. A sample of 77 items in a large population, with a standard deviation of $200, results in $44.70 as the maximum distance from the true value that a sample estimate of the average (e.g., $372) is expected to lie.

The manner in which the normal curve table lends itself to control of alpha and beta risk is depicted in the following graph of the two sampling distributions: one around the book value and one around the true population value. The area $\alpha/2$ would reject a value that would have been acceptable had the true population distribution been measured, and the β portion under the tail of the true distribution would be a Type II error.

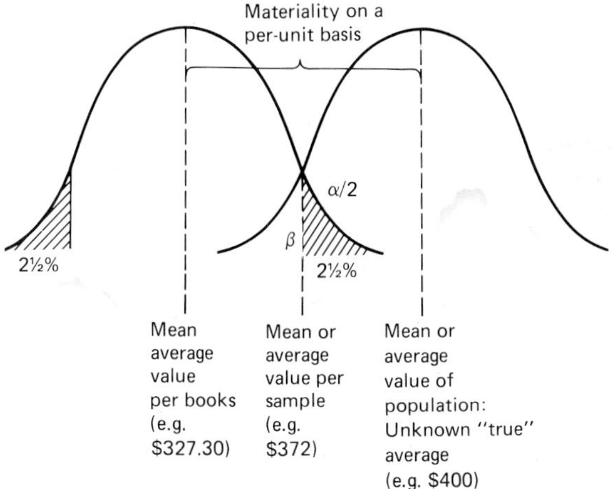

Adapted from Ann B. Puskin, "Presenting Beta Risk to Students," *Accounting Review*, January, 1980, pp.117-122.

standard deviation is useful in predicting the probable range of difference between a sample mean and the population mean. The higher this measure of dispersion is, the wider the expected confidence interval will be. In fact, this can be demonstrated by reconsidering how normal distribution assumptions are applied in the construction of confidence intervals.

Normal Curve. The normal curve describes populations and sampling distributions when classical sampling approaches are used. This assumption is the basis for forming symmetric confidence intervals, that is, the plus and minus precision ranges around the mean estimate. The bell-shaped, symmetric curve shown at the top of Exhibit 12-1 is a *normal curve* in which the values of individual items are concentrated around the mean or average value and the area under the curve is defined in standard tables such as the one in Exhibit 12-A, in the appendix to this chapter. The midpoint of the curve is the mean value of a distribution, meaning that the values are just as likely to be on one side of the mean as on the other. The area under the curve can be measured by relating the standard factors to the amount of standard deviation for that distribution and then adjusting for sample size. In Exhibit 12-A, the .025 risk in either tail (extreme side of the curve) translates into a .5 − .025, or .475, area from the mean for that half of the distribution, yielding a factor of 1.96 (reading from far left to the top of Exhibit 12-A). Exhibit 12-1 illustrates the resulting two-sided 95 percent confidence interval, which leaves a 2.5 percent risk in each tail of the distribution. If the auditor is interested only in a one-sided conclusion, for example, just the overstatement risk, the same tables used for a two-sided interval can be used to adjust from a symmetric risk to a one-tail risk. Then .5 − .05, or .45, will be a factor of 1.645, as .45 lies between .4495 and .4595. That is, a 5 percent two-sided risk translates into a 10 percent one-sided risk, or a one-sided risk doubles the acceptable risk in a single tail of the distribution.

Precision limits are the estimated standard error of the mean times the reliability factors. Remember that the estimated population standard deviation divided by the square root of the sample size is the estimated standard error of the mean. Hence a 95 percent precision limit becomes (rounding to two decimals) 1.65, adjusted for the sample size, 1.65 $(200 \div \sqrt{77})$, which equals \$37.63 in the example from Exhibit 12-1. Any table for the area under a normal curve, as already explained, can be adjusted to either a two-tail or one-tail testing objective; however, the auditor must note which table is being used and adapt it to match the audit objective. For example, a one-tailed table such as that in Exhibit 12-A is read as a .05 level for 95 percent upper limits, but as a .05 divided by 2, or a .025 level, for 95 percent confidence intervals. In contrast, two-tailed tables use .05 for intervals and .10 for one-tailed precision limits.

The second illustration in Exhibit 12-1 shows how precision is related to alpha and beta risks and underlies the formulas for calculating precision, which will be explained in the following example, using a direct projection method.

An Example. In utilizing this simple extension technique, the first assumption is that the number of items in the population is known and that the total book value can be relied on as being arithmetically correct. But the book value of each item in the population is unknown, and so a mean estimate is needed. One situation in which this scenario may occur is the substantive testing of supplies inventory. Mean-per-unit sampling can also be used to determine whether a particular sample is representative of the population. Sometimes it must be used because of practical constraints precluding the application of other, more efficient techniques, such as the ratio or difference methods (which will be discussed following this mean-per-unit example).

When the sample is selected, each item's audited value is determined, and a sample mean estimate is computed, by adding all of the audited values and dividing the sum by the number of sample units. This mean or average value of the sample is assumed to be the best estimate of the average value of the population items. By multiplying the audited average value for the sample by the number of items in the population, a total dollar value of the population can be estimated for comparison with the client's recorded value. This is why this approach is often referred to as the direct projection method; the population values are projected directly from the sample's mean estimate.

Exhibit 12-2 summarizes the variables sampling formulas, the symbols used in each formula, and the finite correction factor for each formula. From studying the formulas, it becomes obvious that sample size increases as one wishes to be more confident, is interested in a population with a higher standard deviation, is estimating larger populations, and prefers tighter precision. Often the sample size formula will be reported as

$$n = \left(\frac{S_{x_j} Z_{\alpha/2}}{A}\right)^2$$

where $Z_{\alpha/2}$ represents the two-sided U_R factor and A is intended to be the precision for each unit, that is, A/N using the notation in Exhibit 12-2. This re-

EXHIBIT 12-2
Formulas for Mean-per-Unit Sampling

Sample Size with Replacement	Sample Size Without Replacement Assuming n/N ≥ .05
$n = \left(\dfrac{U_R * S_{x_j} * N}{A}\right)^2$	$n' = \dfrac{n}{1 + \dfrac{n}{N}}$
Reliability Factor (Confidence Level) with Replacement	**Reliability Factor Without Replacement Assuming n/N ≥ .05**
$U_R = \dfrac{A * \sqrt{n}}{S_{x_j} * N}$	$U_R' = \dfrac{U_R}{\sqrt{1 - \dfrac{n'}{N}}}$
Precision with Replacement	**Precision Without Replacement Assuming n/N ≥ .05**
$A = \dfrac{U_R * S_{x_j} * N}{\sqrt{n}}$	$A' = A\left(\sqrt{1 - \dfrac{n'}{N}}\right)$

Note: All formulas can be derived from the n and n′ relationships.

n = sample size with replacement
n' = sample size without replacement
U_R = reliability factor from which confidence level can be inferred. (see Exhibit 12-A).
S_{x_j} = estimated standard deviation of the population
N = population size (number of items in population)
A = precision

lates to the concept labeled in Exhibit 12-1 on the second illustration, showing how the estimation of materiality *for each unit* can be used to control beta and alpha risks.

To demonstrate the formula's use, assume that the total supplies inventory is $760,000 and is composed of two thousand items and that the $760,000 figure is arithmetically correct. Also assume that a presample of fifty items indicates that the standard deviation of the population is expected to be approximately $200. Because the auditor will accept only a 5 percent risk, he or she wants to be 95 percent confident. This measure must be translated into U_R by using Exhibit 12-A, the normal curve area table. This table, as already explained, depicts one-half of a normal curve, and therefore, the inside of the table is one-half the confidence level. Hence 95 percent divided by 2, or 47.5 percent, is the number to find in the table. The .4750 value can then be read to the left and to the top of the table to obtain the reliability factor of 1.96 to use in the calculations.

To arrive at the desired precision measure, consider materiality and both alpha and beta risk. The alpha risk is reflected in the U_R factor (remember that the confidence level is the complement of alpha). A similar approach is taken to quantify the beta risk, though, before using Exhibit 12-2, the percentage of planned beta risk must be calculated by using the beta formula:

$$\frac{1 - \text{CR}}{(1 - \text{IC})(1 - \text{SP})}$$

where

CR = combined reliability, or the complement of ultimate risk, the chance that a material error will occur and not be detected by internal controls or the auditor's exam.
IC = internal control effectiveness.
SP = supplemental audit procedure effectiveness.

Assume that the auditor believes that the ultimate risk is 5 percent, which is the risk that a material error will occur and not be detected by the client's controls or any audit procedures. A 5 percent ultimate risk leaves a CR of 95 percent. Then assume that the internal controls are 85 percent effective and the supplemental audit procedures are 20 percent effective:

$$\text{beta} = \frac{(1 - .95)}{(1 - .85)(1 - .20)} = .42 \text{ percent}$$

Note that a beta equal to or greater than 1 suggests that the CR has been obtained and that this test is not needed. A beta from .5 to 1.0 is always set equal to .5, on the presumption that a statistical test should not be performed unless it has at least a fifty-fifty chance of detecting a material error.

The beta risk coefficient corresponds to an area under the normal curve of .5 − beta. Because .42 is beta, .5 − .42, or .08, is used to interpret the normal curve table. From Exhibit 12-A, the .08 corresponds to a .0319 beta risk coefficient. Acceptable precision can then be calculated as

$$A = M * \frac{U_R}{U_R + Z_{\text{Beta}}}$$

where

A = precision.
M = materiality.
U_R = reliability factor.
Z_{Beta} = beta risk coefficient.

This calculation controls both alpha and beta risk. Keep in mind that if everything else is held constant, accepting less beta risk will force more alpha risk or vice versa. This trade-off is evident from the second illustration in Exhibit 12-1. Continuing the example and assuming materiality of $35,000, the acceptable precision will be

$$\$35{,}000 * \frac{1.96}{1.96 + .0319} = \$34{,}472.36$$

For ease of computation, we shall round this to $34,500.

Now the desired sample size with replacement can be calculated:

$$\left(\frac{1.96 * 200 * 2{,}000}{34{,}500}\right)^2 = 516.41$$

If the sampling is done without replacement, a finite correction factor may be needed. In this situation, 516 divided by 2,000 obviously exceeds .05 and indicates a need for the correction factor. This then suggests that the sample size can be reduced to

$$\frac{516.41}{1+\frac{516.41}{2,000}} = 409.85$$

This demonstrates the use of the sample size formula. Now, how can the other formulas in Exhibit 12-2 be used?

Imagine that a constraint existed on sample size which made it impossible to sample more than 350 units and as an auditor, you want to find out what reliability can be achieved with the same precision. The computation, assuming sampling with replacement, is

$$\frac{34,500 * \sqrt{350}}{200 * 2,000} = 1.61$$

The 1.61 factor, according to Exhibit 12-A, pertains to a confidence level of .4463, or doubled, .8926. If sampling without replacement is used, the 350 sample size will still represent more than 5 percent of the population items, and the finite correction factor will apply. Note that the sample size is assumed to stay at 350 as the upper limit of interest (although normally it also would be reduced). This yields a reliability factor of

$$\frac{1.61}{\sqrt{1-\frac{350}{2,000}}} = 1.77$$

The 1.77 factor pertains to a .4616, or doubled, a .9232 confidence level.

Now consider another scenario. Assuming that the sample size is 350, with a 95 percent reliability required, then what precision can be assumed? Using the formula in Exhibit 12-2, the precision is

$$\frac{1.96 * 200 * 2,000}{\sqrt{350}} = \$41,902.73$$

If sampling without replacement is used and the sample size is still 350 items, the precision will be tightened to

$$41,902.73\sqrt{1-\frac{350}{2,000}} = \$38,175.20$$

To demonstrate how conclusions can be drawn from the without-replacement sampling plan, assume that 410 items are selected and the average audited value for each item, based on the sample, is \$372. This mean-per-unit sample estimate is multiplied by the number of population items (2,000) to yield the total estimated value of supplies inventory, or \$744,000. This estimate is expected to have a precision of \$34,500 at a 95 percent level of confidence, meaning that ninety-five times out of one hundred, the true population value is expected to lie within the range of \$744,000 ± \$34,500, or from \$709,500 to \$778,500. Because the client's recorded book value is \$760,000 and it lies within this range, it is deemed to be reasonable.

A somewhat more simplistic approach to determining sample size is to compute the estimated average per-unit precision and then to convert this to the maximum dollar value of the allowable standard error of the sample means, by dividing by the number of standard errors of the true mean within which we want the true mean to lie. Remember that this is the U_R factor, that 99.7 percent of the sample means will fall within ± 3, that 95 percent of the sample means will fall within ± 1.96, and that 68.3 percent will fall within ± 1.0 standard errors of the mean. The quotient is then divided into the standard deviation of the population and then squared to determine sample size.

Using the numbers in the first example of how sample size is computed for variables sampling, a ± \$34,500 precision is adjusted by a population size of 2,000 to yield an average per-unit desired precision of \$17.25. Then the deflator factor at 95 percent confidence will be 1.96, yielding a quotient of 8.80. Finally, the standard deviation of \$200 divided by 8.80 and then squared will produce a sample size of 22.73 squared, or 516.65. This approach should further clarify the role of the standard error of sample means and population variability in affecting sample size. Remember, the standard error is a measure of variability of the sample means; it is the standard deviation of the distribution of sample means. It assesses sampling error—that error which statistical sampling techniques are intended to control.

Practically speaking, the implied sample sizes of mean-per-unit estimation result in a very inefficient, almost cost-prohibitive audit tool. The sample sizes do not increase in proportion to the population size but do increase slightly as the population size increases. For example, with the same level of confidence and precision, a population of 100,000, instead of 10,000, will increase a sample about 5 percent; clearly, population has an increasing though slight effect on sample size. But once the size of a population reaches about four hundred units, its size has very little influence on sampling plans. This is evidenced by the fact that many tables are designed for populations of one thousand or more items, treating one thousand as effectively equivalent to an infinite sample size. Although the population size does not account for the large mean-per-unit sample sizes, the variability of populations has a great effect. As a general rule, any change in a population's variability will affect the sample size by the square of the relative change. Hence if standard deviation were doubled, the required sample size would quadruple. This scale of adjustment helps clarify the advantages of ratio, differencing, and stratification techniques (to be described in the following sections of this chapter). Similarly, the sample size increases by the square of the relative change in precision. Hence if desired precision were reduced to one-fourth of its original size, the sample would increase by sixteen times. The tighter the precision is, the greater the increase in required sample size will be.

Another problem is that variations from normality are common. For example, receivable balances are frequently skewed, with a few very large dollar accounts. And skewed distributions usually are better described by median statistics than by mean or average values. The median is the 50 percent location in the distribution and is not as distorted by extreme values as is the average. Whenever the mean differs substantially from the median, a skewed distribution is likely. Although the effect of including skewed items, that is, extremely large or small items, in a random sample can be lessened by increasing the size of the sample, this can be expensive. In order to satisfy the normality assumption, the distribution could be redefined by stratifying the population, often testing 100 percent of the skewed amounts. Stratification forms population subsets or strata from which the sampling units are selected, often in differing proportions for each stratum. In this example, 100 percent of the unusual amounts may be tested, whereas in another stratum 1 percent may be tested.

Fortunately, the simple extension method can be applied to stratified samples, which will be explored later in this chapter. In addition, tools known as difference and ratio estimation are available which produce smaller required sample sizes due to their capability of lowering the effects of one of the terms in each of the formulas presented in exhibit 12-2: S_{xj} or the standard deviation (variability) of what is being estimated.

Ratio and Differencing Methods

One means of reducing the sample size required to estimate an account balance is to reduce the variability of the number being estimated. This can be accomplished by shifting the focus from the total dollars of supplies inventory to the relationship of audited values to book values. Of course, the individual book values must exist in order to have such a focus. The relationship between the audited value and the book value can be measured as the difference between the two amounts or as the ratio of the two. In either case, these measures of interest are likely to have far less variability. The lower standard deviation will decrease the required sample size, as shown in the formulas presented in Exhibit 12-2.

When considering whether to use these techniques, the first question to ask is whether the book values can be expected to differ from the audited values. If they can, these techniques can be used. Generally, a sample size as small as thirty is used in difference estimation, and a minimum of fifty is required in ratio sampling. If the incidence of differences is less than 20 percent, a sample of eighty is typically used. Once the rate of occurrence drops below 5 percent, neither the ratio nor the difference estimation technique is likely to be efficient. Another consideration is the direction of the differences. If the differences go in only one direction, fifty data points are commonly recommended; if they go in both directions, thirty are adequate. The second condition which must be met in order to apply either approach, as noted earlier, is that the recorded book value for each item in the population, the total number of items, and the total book value all be known. Note that these practical guidelines stem from statistical theory and experience in an auditing context.

Ratio Estimation. If the observed differences are expected to be proportional to the book amounts, that is, if the differences become larger as the book values increase, then ratio estimation is more efficient than difference estimation. The pattern of the plot in which the ratio technique is preferred is shown in Exhibit 12-3, in an example of thirty items from a sample containing differences between audited value and book value. It should be obvious that the standard deviation of the book values is larger than the standard deviation of the ratio of audited value to book value.

Difference Estimation. If the observed differences are relatively constant—that is, if their magnitude is about the same, regardless of the size of the book value—the difference estimation technique will be more efficient. As with the ratio technique, the standard deviation of differences between audited value and book value is expected to be smaller than the standard deviation of book values. Exhibit 12-4 shows an example of the difference approach to form a population estimate. Note that the required sample sizes are computed in the same way as in the mean-per-unit approach; the difference is in the standard deviation's influence on the sample size formulas. Probably the biggest practical problem is making sure that the number of differences between the audited value and the book value will not be too small. If at least thirty differences are desired, and some auditors prefer fifty such items, and if only 30 percent of population items are expected to have differences, a sample of at least one hundred items must be drawn to obtain the minimum number of sampling units for computing estimates.

Stratified Sampling

An alternative to ratio and difference estimation approaches—which also effectively reduces the variability of the population to be estimated—is stratified sampling. A *stratified sample* is one drawn from a population that has been divided into subpopulations, or strata, in a manner that selects a predetermined portion of each of the strata. A stratified sampling plan will include certain items in greater proportion, such as large-dollar transactions, so as to improve the probability of including material errors, should there be any. A random stratified sample can be evaluated statistically. The deviation rate, or the rate of errors, is calculated for each stratum. Due to the complexity of computing combined statistical results, computer software is commonly used to provide the overall estimate for the entire population.

Stratification is particularly appropriate when the population's amounts are widely scattered, skewed in one direction, or clustered around a few points. This approach forms population subsets or strata that minimize the variability within each stratum and maximize the variability across strata. These strata are often separated according to the relative dollar size of transactions, for example, all repairs and maintenance over $1,000. The number of items for each stratum should be known; the strata should be defined so that each sampling unit belongs to only one stratum; and it should be possible to sample from each stratum independently in a cost-justified manner. The sample estimates for each stratum can be made and accumulated into a population estimate based on a far smaller number of sampling units than a mean-per-unit sampling plan would require. In fact, stratification can reduce the sample size to a fraction of that required in unstratified sampling, particularly when sampling units are very different in amount, that is, when the population's standard deviation is high.

In terms of sample selection, unrestricted random sampling is applied within each stratum. This selection method draws from separate sections of the field independently. If the strata are not constructed in proportion to the number of items in that section of the population, then obviously, the items selected will not be equally representative of

EXHIBIT 12-3
Ratio Estimation

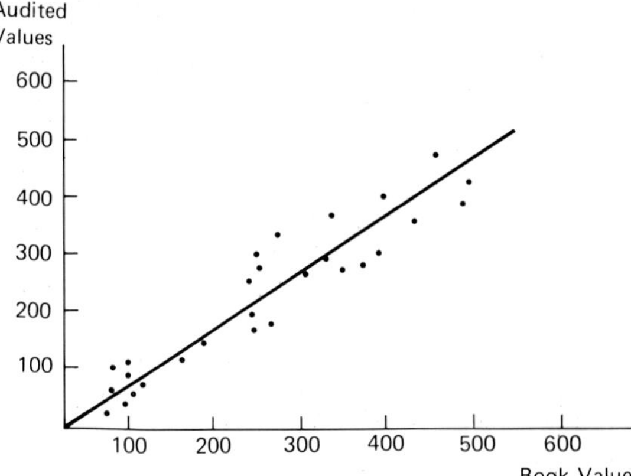

	Audited Values	Book Value
1	10	11
2	20	18
3	30	34
4	32	27
5	45	52
6	57	66
7	61	51
8	73	62
9	81	94
10	90	75
11	102	119
12	150	170
13	200	230
14	205	240
15	210	247
16	300	260
17	310	265
18	317	270
19	350	395
20	362	400
21	371	417
22	360	320
23	370	420
24	390	450
25	450	510
26	470	400
27	500	430
28	510	580
29	515	595
30	600	510
TOTALS	7,541	7,718

Note the similarity of this plot to the following general shape of an appropriate plot for the application of ratio estimation.

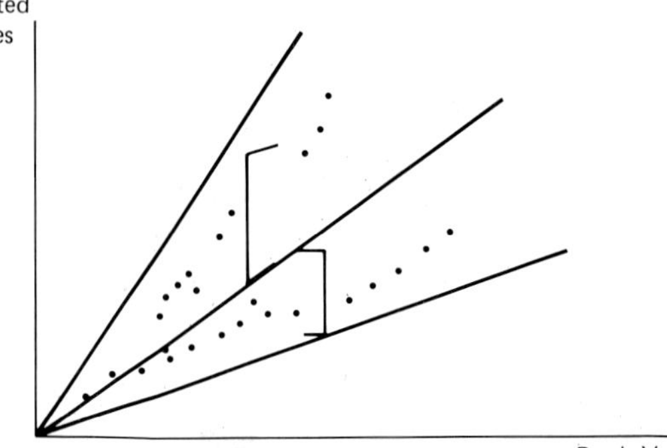

Differences are nearly proportional to the book amounts.

Formula: $\left(\frac{\text{Sum of Audited Values}}{\text{Sum of Book Values}}\right)$ Total Book Value

$= \frac{7{,}541}{7{,}718}$ (\$750,000)

$=$ .977 (750,000)

$=$ $732,750

EXHIBIT 12-4
Difference Estimation

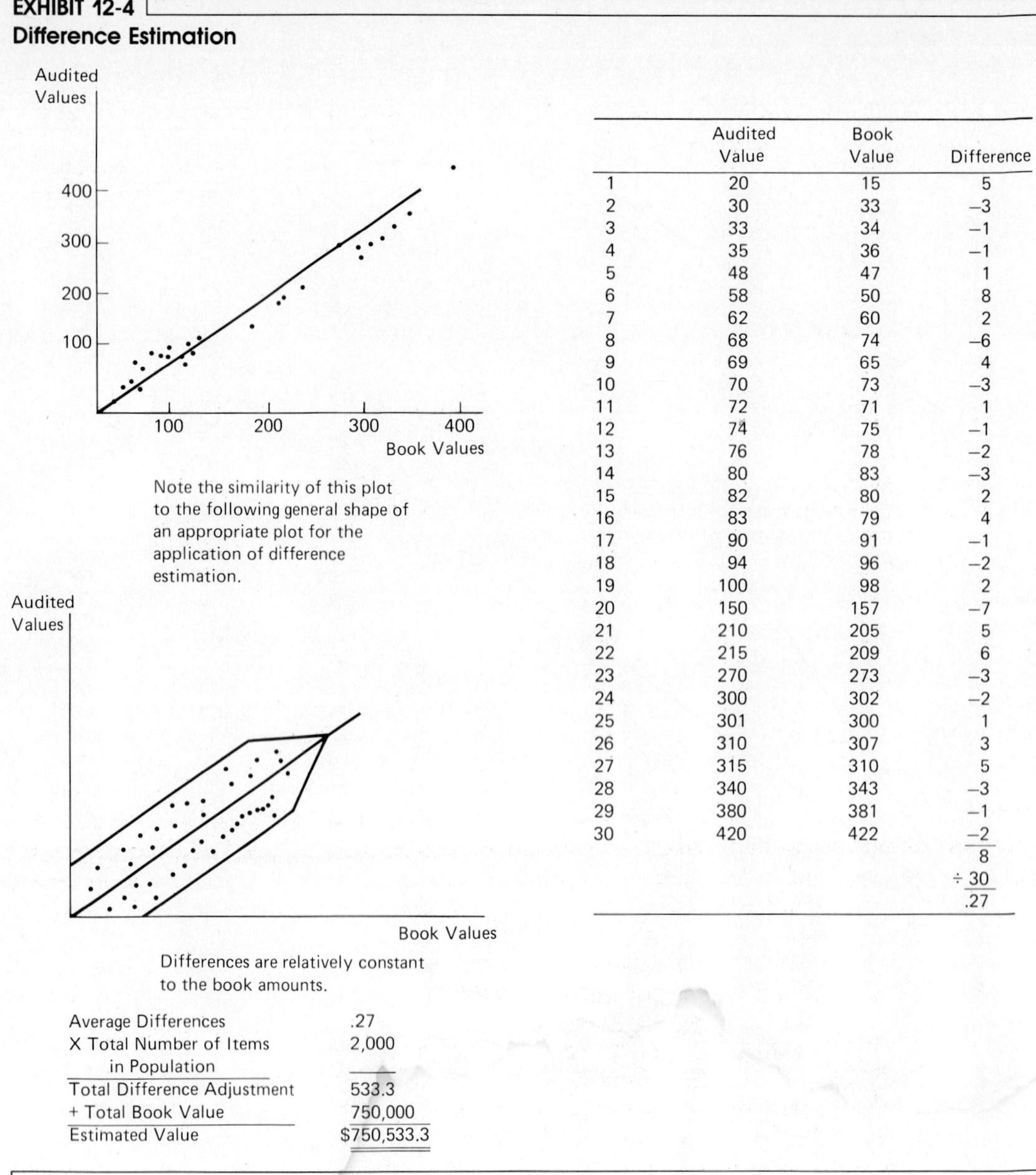

	Audited Value	Book Value	Difference
1	20	15	5
2	30	33	−3
3	33	34	−1
4	35	36	−1
5	48	47	1
6	58	50	8
7	62	60	2
8	68	74	−6
9	69	65	4
10	70	73	−3
11	72	71	1
12	74	75	−1
13	76	78	−2
14	80	83	−3
15	82	80	2
16	83	79	4
17	90	91	−1
18	94	96	−2
19	100	98	2
20	150	157	−7
21	210	205	5
22	215	209	6
23	270	273	−3
24	300	302	−2
25	301	300	1
26	310	307	3
27	315	310	5
28	340	343	−3
29	380	381	−1
30	420	422	−2
			8
			÷ 30
			.27

the population but, rather, will be representative of the defined strata.

When dividing a population into smaller homogeneous segments to enable the auditor to concentrate on certain strata, emphasizing dollar amounts, it is common to pull a third of the sample from items below the mean value and two-thirds from those above. The sample size is commonly allocated based on the proportionate share of total dollars in each stratum. For example:

Stratum 1:	$200,000
Stratum 2:	300,000
Stratum 3:	600,000
Stratum 4:	900,000
	$2,000,000

If the total sample size is estimated as 300 items, the allocation across strata will often be as follows:

Stratum 1: 200,000/2,000,000 * 300 =	30
Stratum 2: 300,000/2,000,000 * 300 =	45
Stratum 3: 600,000/2,000,000 * 300 =	90
Stratum 4: 900,000/2,000,000 * 300 =	135
	300

Often there will be a few very large balances in the population that will be selected for 100 percent examination. If there are 20 such items, the remaining sample size of 280 items must be based on each stratum's dollars relative to the total dollars (already adjusted downward by the amount represented by the 20 items tested 100 percent).

There are no rules governing how many strata should be used in sampling. Typically, two to four strata of approximately equal total dollar amounts are used, although up to six strata can often reduce the required sample size. The rules of thumb are to perform a 100 percent examination of all items over one-half of tolerable error (the auditor's expectation of likely error that will remain uncorrected in the financial statements after the audit is complete *and* an allowance for the risk of possible further error that might not be detected by audit procedures[5]) or, similarly, all items over ten times the estimated population average value. In fact, these rules should be followed even if unstratified sampling will be used for the remaining sample, as they can remove both highly variable items from the population and potentially adverse effects of a population's skewness on sample estimation. However the strata are formed, other than for those strata intended to be audited 100 percent, it is desirable to have at least thirty sampling units for each stratum.

Stratification may be used for other bases than the dollar size of transactions. For example, in testing accounts receivable, an auditor may choose to stratify current accounts receivable from delinquent receivables on the basis of the accounts' age. Populations may be stratified according to characteristics believed to affect the occurrence rate of errors. For example, auditors may form strata based on the age of receivables, under the presumption that there are more likely to be collectibility problems and disputes over claims in older accounts. Similarly, audits of inventory often use strata based on the inventory turnover rate, with more extensive testing of items more exposed to error owing to the higher volume of transactions. Strata based on customer type or inventory classification can often be just as efficient as those based on dollar amounts.

Any stratification that emphasizes particular types of transactions can have behavioral effects on the auditee. For example, if special attention is given to delinquent accounts, auditees are unlikely to perpetrate a fraud—such as recording fictitious accounts—in the set of delinquent accounts. And if any accounts were fraudulent, they would probably be classified as current accounts.

Auditors often test large items 100 percent, for at least two good reasons. First, these items by themselves or in combination may be material; therefore, the audit coverage of dollars is enhanced. In fact, the cutoff as to which items are tested 100 percent is often precision; that is, all items greater than or equal to precision are tested. Second, the variability of the population can be reduced, resulting in smaller required sample sizes. This common practice is effectively a form of stratified sampling.

Note that the concept of stratified sampling was not introduced in the discussion of attribute sampling. This is because generally stratified sampling is not used in attribute testing, since it would require a larger sample size, imply a relationship to dollar amount which does not exist, and imply more than one control system which either does not exist or if it did, would mean that the sampling results per stratum should not be combined. An exception is when attributes sampling is done

[5] AICPA, Proposed Auditing Interpretation, SAS No. 39, Audit Sampling, "Tolerable Error" (1985).

at a multi-location client and the locations represent strata.

Sampling Proportionate to Size (SPS)

An alternative to the classical sampling approaches of direct projection, ratio, difference, and stratified estimation is the variables sampling method (based on attribute sampling theory), called *sampling proportionate to size (SPS)*. This method is useful in substantive testing when an auditor (1) wishes to calculate a maximum dollar overstatement, (2) expects the overstatement to be low, and (3) wishes to base the estimate on a sample selected in proportion to the reported book values, rather than on a sample of items having an equal chance of selection. Because of its one-sided limit estimation and its basis on a sample biased toward larger dollar amounts, this approach is not used to estimate the amount to be adjusted on the books; rather, it should be viewed as a test of reasonableness with respect to overstatement.

In sampling proportionate to size (also referred to as *PPS* sampling, or *probability proportionate to size*), the sampling unit is defined as the monetary or dollar unit (hence, the names *monetary-unit sampling* and *dollar-unit sampling* have evolved). This means that if accounts receivable are being tested, rather than viewing the sampling unit as each of thirty thousand accounts, the total dollar value of $12 million will contain 12 million individual dollar bills, which are the sampling units available for selection. Imagine a stack of 12 million dollar bills, created by accumulating the accounts receivable balances' equivalent value and then selecting dollar bills from the stack. Each dollar selected is tied to an accounts receivable balance, which will be the actual physical unit audited, through, for example, confirmation procedures. Because the larger receivable balances contain more dollar sampling units, their probability of selection is much greater. Hence SPS can be thought of as resulting in an automatic dollar stratification of the population.

To conduct a SPS test, it is necessary to calculate a cumulative amount for the account items of interest and to remove from the population the zero and credit balances for separate testing. This latter step is necessary because, by definition, zero and negative values have no probability of selection using SPS. These values can be "covered" only through separate sampling. The cumulative column for populations of interest has been added to many auditees' accounting systems to facilitate SPS; if it were not available, the method could not be used without generating such information. This cumulative information can be tested by using either systematic selection or a random number table or generator. In the former case, care must be taken to ensure that the ordering of the account's items has no relationship to the audit objective.

Assume that the variation of SPS known as dollar-unit sampling (DUS) is to be used. As already noted, this approach adapts attribute sampling to dollar-value concerns. A random sample of individual dollars in a population is selected, with each treated as being either correct or incorrect. The selected dollar is a "hook" for the entire physical unit being audited. The typical selection technique is to use a random start and then a set sampling interval. The focus on dollars as a hook is thought to deter ill effects of slight patterns in the population, always feared when systematic sampling is used. DUS will select all physical units having book values in excess of the sampling interval, and all other book values have a probability of being selected that is directly proportional to their size. DUS is cited as equivalent to optimal stratification. Because of its focus on overstatements, it is useful in testing asset balances. But it is not useful in tests for understatement, nor is it tolerant of errors. Therefore, DUS is not generally used for liability accounts whose audit risk is tied closely to the possibility of unrecorded liabilities.

Assume that a client has thirty thousand accounts receivable, totaling $12 million. The formula for the average sampling interval is

$$\frac{\text{Tolerable Basic Precision in Dollars}}{\text{Basic Precision Factor * Error Size Limit}} \text{ where}$$

1. The tolerable basic precision in dollars reflects materiality, adjusted for most likely errors and known carry-overs from the previous year, as well as the percentage of each account balance expected to be in error.
2. The basic precision factor depends on the confidence level and is 1.39 at 75 percent, 1.61 at 80 percent, 1.90 at 85 percent, 2.31 at 90 percent,

EXHIBIT 12-5
Selection of a SPS Sample

Accounts Receivable Balance	Cumulative Total	Sample Selection
$20,000	20,000	
400	20,400	
81,000	101,400	X
200	101,600	
1,600	103,200	
6,040	109,240	
300	109,540	
80	109,620	
60	109,680	
2,000	111,680	
1,000	112,680	
8,000	120,680	
12,000	132,680	
4,000	136,680	
30	136,710	
8,060	144,770	
90,000	234,770	
5,000	239,770	
18,010	257,780	
20,012	277,792	
50,015	328,807	
12,000	430,807	X

3.0 at 95 percent, 3.69 at 97.5 percent, and 4.61 at 99 percent.[6]

3. The error size-limit is most conservatively assumed to be 100 percent, as clearly any account balance cannot be overstated by more than its total balance; yet if the overstatement limit is expected to be a percentage of the total balance (such as 50 percent), the sample size will decline substantially.

In the example, let us assume that the tolerable basic precision is $320,000, that a 95 percent confidence level is desired, and that a 70 percent error size limit is expected. This will produce a sampling interval (also known as a cell width) of

$$\frac{\$320,000}{3.00 * 70\%} = \$152,381$$

In dollar-unit sampling, the sampling size can be determined by dividing the sampling interval into the population dollars to be tested. In this case, $12 million divided by $152,381 results in a sample size of seventy-nine. An advantage of DUS is that one does not need to know the population size in order to calculate the sampling interval or to select the sample. If systematic sample selection were to be used, every dollar at an interval of $152,381 would be chosen, after making a random start between the first 1 to 152,381 interval limits. Exhibit 12-5 demonstrates sample selection from the first twenty-two accounts receivable balances. Assume the random starting point is $30,000 and then proceed with intervals of $152,381, yielding $182,381 and $334,762. To prevent selecting a single physical unit more than once, the auditor can simply segregate those items greater than the dollar sampling interval (in this example, greater than $152,381) and then apply the same dollar sampling unit to the remaining population. In other words, whether or not the large amounts are taken out initially, the dollar sampling interval will be the same.

Assume that upon confirmation, no errors are discovered. For sample evaluation, the following formula then can be used:

$$\text{Upper error limit in dollars (UEL)} = \text{Upper error limit factor} \times \text{Average sampling interval}$$

For zero errors, at 95 percent confidence, the basic precision factor is equivalent to the upper error limit factor of 3.0. The average sampling interval is $152,381, yielding an upper error limit of three times this amount, or $457,143. If this is adjusted for the 70 percent error limit for each sampling unit, the computation will yield an upper dollar error limit of $320,000. This 70 percent is often referred to as *tainting*, which is an adjustment based on the ratio of errors to book value. SPS takes into account partial errors, or taintings, in evaluating sample results. For example, if a sampling interval of $20,000 is used and a selected account balance is recorded as $2,000, with an audited value of $1,600, a tainting percentage will be computed: the $2,000 minus $1,600, or the $400 error is divided by the recorded amount of $2,000 to yield a 20 percent

[6] Donald A. Leslie, Albert D. Teitlebaum, and Rodney J. Anderson, *Dollar-Unit Sampling* (Toronto: Copp Clark Pitman, 1979).

tainting. This tainting percentage times the sampling interval is projected to an estimated error for that interval of 20 percent times $20,000, or $4,000. No extension is necessary if the reported balance exceeds the sampling interval. Methods are available for ranking tainted intervals and aggregating the effect of errors.

The UEL increases as the number of detected errors increases; for example, at a 95 percent confidence level, the following factors apply:

Number of Sample Errors	UEL Factor
1	4.75
2	6.30
3	7.76
4	9.16
5	10.52
10	16.97
20	29.07
50	63.29
100	118.07

As this table suggests, the upper error limit grows very quickly as more errors are found, making the technique most helpful when few errors are expected. This is why auditors frequently view DUS sampling as a logical alternative to ratio and difference estimations, which actually require errors in order to be used. (The concepts of tainting and sample evaluation become more complex as errors are discovered, but they are beyond the scope of this discussion.) The only term necessary at this introductory point of your sampling training is "tainting," which as already explained, is a comparison of the amount of error to the book value to which it relates, that is made for the purpose of weighting sampling units for the proportion of observed error. Interested readers are encouraged to utilize the reference cited earlier: *Dollar-Unit Sampling: A Practical Guide for Auditors* by Leslie, Teitlebaum, and Anderson for an in-depth discussion of tainting calculations and the entire DUS approach. To summarize, the statistical evaluation of a sample drawn in proportion to size produces an upper bound of error estimate for the population. If no errors or few errors are expected, SPS will require far smaller sample sizes than other variables sampling approaches will. DUS is a useful alternative to ratio and differencing when there are too few errors to use the latter estimation approaches. Dollar unit sampling is a popular audit tool because of its coverage of high-dollar items; the reduction of cost stemming from focusing on dollars as the sampling unit, which serve as "hooks" for the physical units and thereby permit several sampling units to be used for one physical unit's audit; and the formation of a conclusion in dollar terms.

Overview

Numerous alternatives have been described as to how to perform sampling for the purpose of estimating "how much." Exhibit 12-6 outlines the key decisions in selecting among the various alternatives. The cycle chapters will present additional examples of sampling applications.

Projecting Errors

To project errors for the population, the direct projection method is often used. In a nonstatistical sample for which a ratio of error of 2 percent is estimated, the population error will approach 2 percent.

SAS No. 39, Section 350, states:

> Projected error results from all audit sampling applications and all known errors from nonsampling applications should be considered in the aggregate along with other relevant audit evidence when the auditor evaluates whether the financial statements taken as a whole may be materially misstated.

Errors located in a nonstatistical sample should be extrapolated to the population in a similar manner as statistical sampling for the purpose of evaluating the audit evidence.

The Worst Case

When evaluating the confidence intervals formed in sampling applications, the conservative auditor

EXHIBIT 12-6
Substantive Test Sampling Approaches

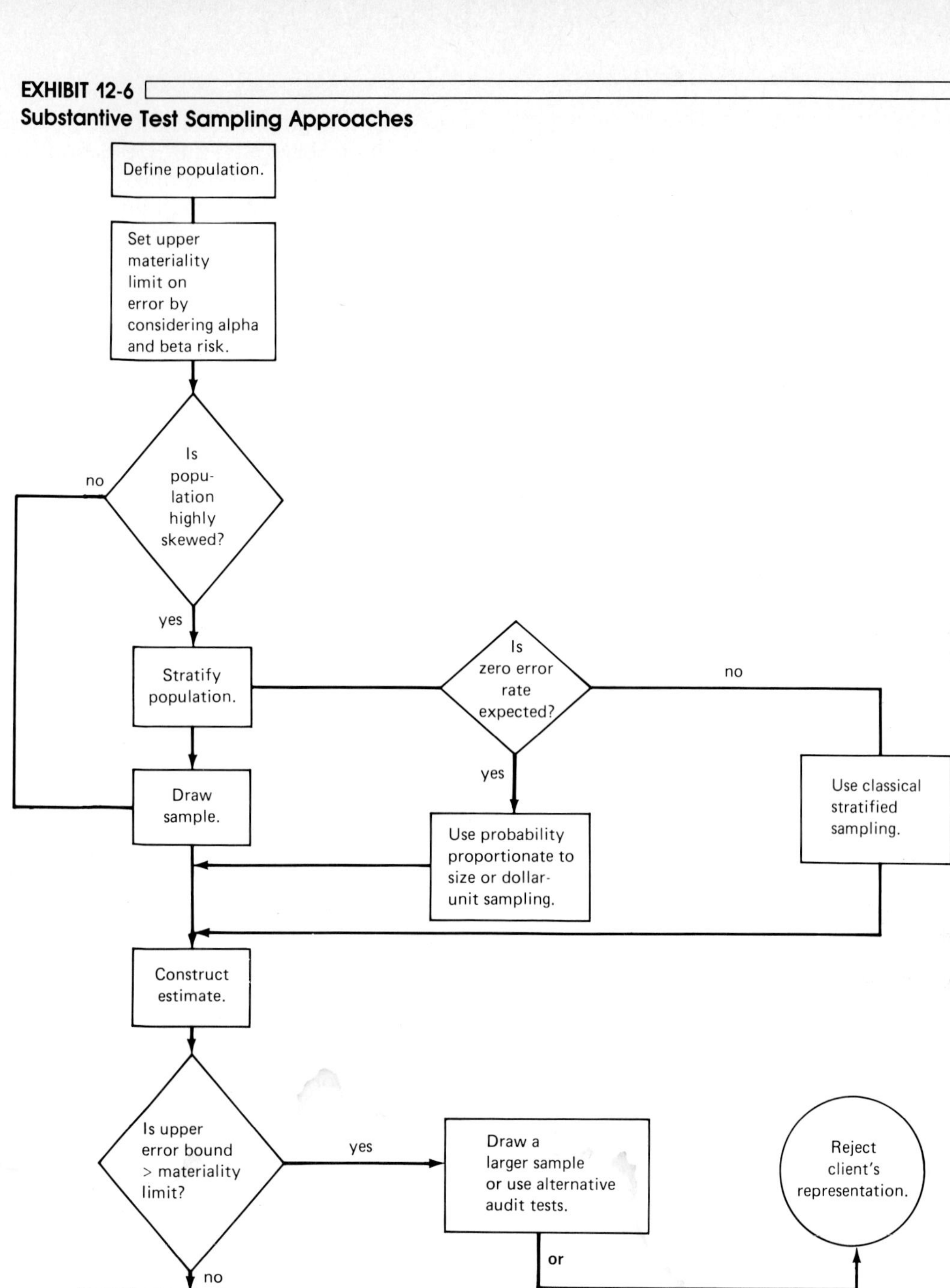

EXHIBIT 12-7
Illustration of the "Worst Case" for Use in Evaluating Risk

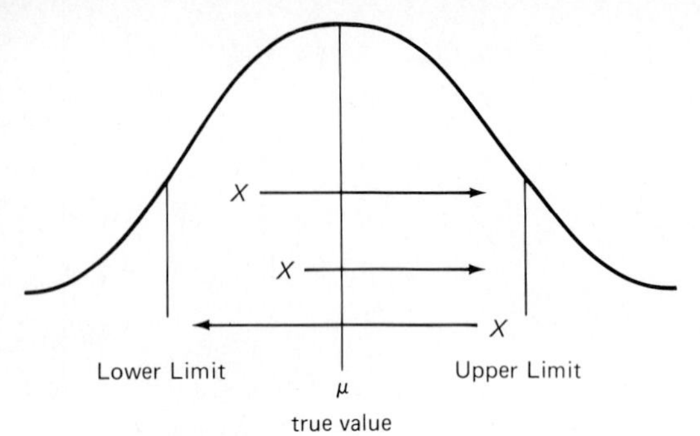

will consider the maximum possible error between a sample-based estimate and the "true" population value. Returning to the normal curve diagram used earlier, Exhibit 12-7 shows the worst case that auditors often consider when assessing risk. The worst case is the distance of any sample estimate (x in the diagram) from the farthest limit or bound of the confidence interval.

Working-Paper Documentation

All sampling plans should be documented in the working papers and include (1) the testing objectives, (2) a definition of the population, (3) a definition of the sampling unit, (4) a definition of the strata when applicable, (5) the means of ensuring that the frame and the population were equivalent, (6) the sample selection technique, (7) the type of sampling approach used, (8) the confidence level selected, (9) the desired precision, (10) details of the pilot sample when applicable, (11) sample size, (12) sample evaluation, and (13) the audit conclusions drawn.

Regression Analysis

Regression analysis is an effective analytical review technique. Whereas statistical sampling focuses on individual transaction items and draws conclusions regarding the population, regression analysis focuses on summary statistics for the population in order to determine the likelihood that individual transactions are reasonably stated. The introductory case for Chapter 11 cited interest by participant 6 in learning about directed sampling. Nonstatistical samples that are not intended to be representative of the entire population but are selected in a manner "directed" by audit knowledge of where problems are likely to occur provide an example of the concept. However, rather than viewing such directed sampling as not being "representative," it can be considered representative of a population different from "all transactions." In other words, by using techniques such as regression modeling, the auditor may define two populations: those accounts that appear to agree with expectations, including all underlying transactions, and those accounts in which unusual unexplained variations are observed. By directing more of the audit tests to that second population, improved coverage of audit risk is likely. But remember that such testing will produce sampling conclusions for only the second population.

Regression analysis is a statistical modeling tool that measures the relationship of a single variable of audit interest (the *dependent variable*) to a variable or set of variables (the set of *independent variable*(s)) that is expected to explain movements in the variable of interest. As a simple example, consider the relationship between a manufacturer's payroll cost and the number of direct labor hours worked. One would expect the payroll cost (the dependent variable) to increase as the number of hours worked (the independent variable) increases.

Scatter Diagram

A *simple regression model* includes only one independent variable, as is the case with the modeling of payroll cost as a function of direct labor hours. To determine the strength of such a relationship, one can plot the dependent, or y-variable, on the y-axis of a graph and the independent variable, or x-variable, on the x-axis in order to depict a *scatter diagram* of the pattern and strength of the association. Possible scatter diagrams are il-

EXHIBIT 12-8
Examples of Scatter Diagrams

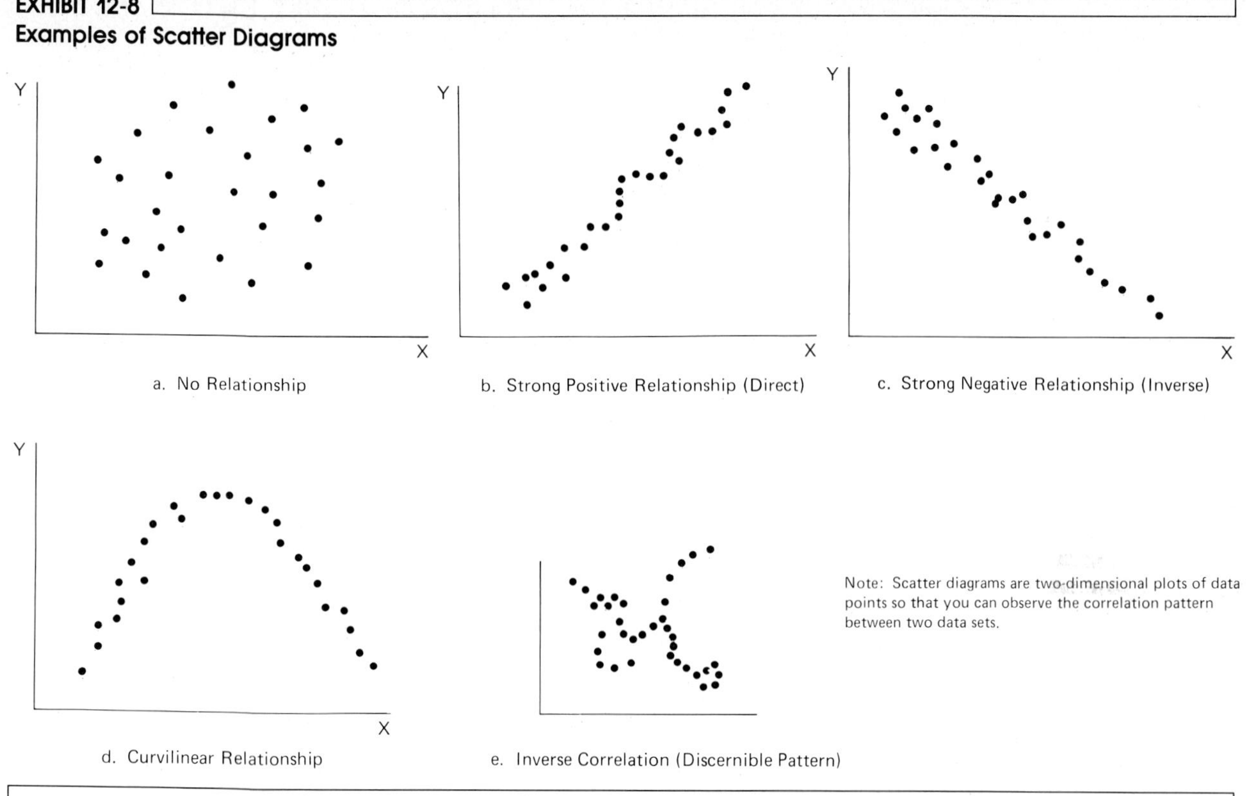

lustrated in Exhibit 12-8. A scatter diagram of payroll cost against direct labor hours would be expected to take the form of graph (b), because as the x variable increases, the y variable also increases. The plot in (b) represents a strong relationship, as a weak relationship would scatter more, rather than form a tight linear pattern. If the plot were so scattered that no pattern was formed, as in plot (a), there would not be a simple regression relationship.

The Form of a Regression Model

A regression model essentially "fits" a single line to the set of points in a scatter diagram. This regression line is called the *best fit* because it minimizes the total sum of squared deviations of the data points from the regression line, as illustrated in Exhibit 12-9. The algorithm, widely available in computer software, will measure the distance of each data point from a fitted line (d in Exhibit 12-9), square that distance (d^2) so that all deviations are positive, and then add those squared deviations (Σd^2). The least sum is then selected as the appropriate line. This is why the regression tool is often called *ordinary least squares.*

Exhibit 12-10 summarizes the concept of regression analysis, as well as the actual approach to calculating simple regression models that would typically be used by computer software. As noted, the availability of software virtually precludes any need for auditors' attention to such calculations. However, it is useful to illustrate how a regression model relates to the mean or average (μ) value of the variable to be explained, since this relationship underlies various measures of goodness of a regression model. The total sum of squares or total variation from the mean value is what we would

EXHIBIT 12-9
Ordinary Least Squares

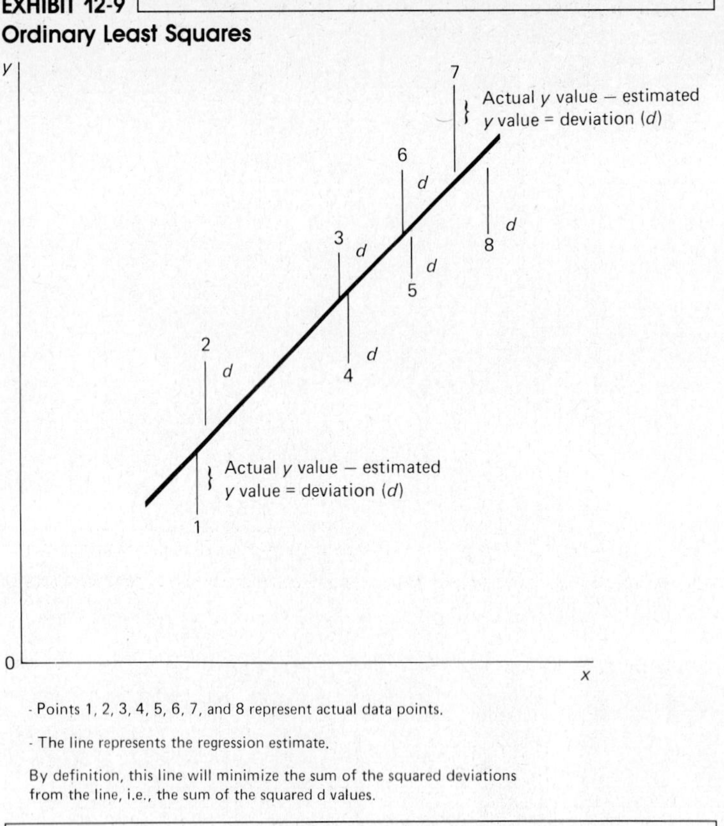

- Points 1, 2, 3, 4, 5, 6, 7, and 8 represent actual data points.
- The line represents the regression estimate.

By definition, this line will minimize the sum of the squared deviations from the line, i.e., the sum of the squared d values.

like to explain through modeling. That portion of the variation actually explained is referred to as the sum of squares for the regression and, as depicted in Exhibit 12-10, is the difference in the regression estimate and the mean. The unexplained variation, referred to as the sum of squares of errors, is the difference between the regression estimate and the actual value of each data point. Hence, the goodness of the model is often measured by R^2, which is essentially the percentage of total variation that has been explained, and by standard error, which is effectively a transformation (square root, after adjusting for the number of data points available for estimation—commonly referred to as the *degrees of freedom*) of the unexplained variation.

Once the line is fitted, it is typically described as

$$y = a + bx$$

where

y = dependent variable of interest.
a = constant or intercept term (y-intercept term).
b = regression coefficient or slope of the line.
x = independent or explanatory variable.

The *constant term* is the number that corresponds to the location on the y axis that is intercepted by the fitted regression line. The *coefficient* measures the change in y for each unit change in x. In the payroll example, a regression model may be estimated as

$$y = \$10{,}000 + \$12x$$

This means that payroll cost has a constant or fixed element that amounts to $10,000 for the relevant

EXHIBIT 12-10
Regression Analysis

A modeling of associations between two or more variables. The intent is to identify descriptor variables that move systematically in relation to a variable you wish to explain. The idea is that by knowing the values of the descriptor variables, you can predict the variable to be explained.

The intuitive basis of a regression modeling approach can be depicted by considering a simple regression model: one descriptor variable explaining a variable of interest.

DEPENDENT VARIABLE (Y)
(vertical axis)
(variable being explained)

The variable that you wish to explain. In a sense, you are measuring the extent to which this variable "depends" on other variables for estimating its own movement.

INDEPENDENT VARIABLE (X)
(horizontal axis)
(descriptor variable)

The variable that you use to describe movements in another variable. How do independent movements of this variable relate to movement in the variable to be explained?

To summarize a scatterplot, you will attempt to fit a line. How well you are able to fit the data will vary with your analytical capabilities. However, an algorithm is possible that can find the "best fit" of these data points with a line. That algorithm is referred to as the ordinary least squares, or regression technique.

The slope of the line is computed as

$$b_1 = \frac{\Sigma(X_i - \overline{X})(Y_i - \overline{Y})}{\Sigma(X_i - \overline{X})}$$

and the intercept of the line is computed as

$$b_0 = Y - b_1 \overline{X}$$

Y is the variable to be explained, and X is the descriptor variable. The bars represent average values of those variables, and Σ denotes a summation.

Such computations do not need to be mastered, as software can quickly compute such a relationship.

The important concepts for the individual who intends to apply regression are the interpretation of estimated values and an appreciation of underlying assumptions.

First, consider the relationship of a regression model to a mere mean extrapolation. Note in particular the basis for the measures to assess the effectiveness of forecasting models and the remaining error in forecasts.

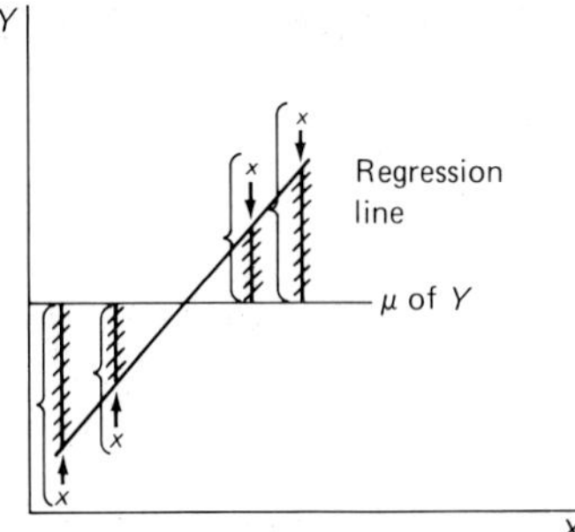

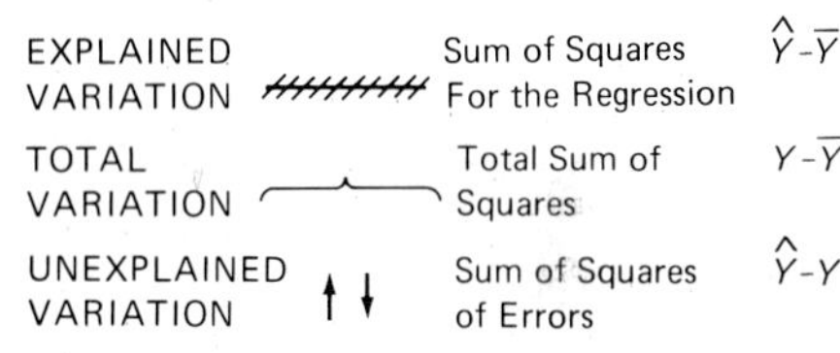

where $\hat{Y}$ = regression estimates
Y = actual data points
$\overline{Y}$ = average value of Y data points

range of operations. The variable element of the cost is \$12 and indicates that for each additional direct labor hour, the payroll cost increases by \$12. This \$12 is expected to correspond approximately to the direct labor rate per hour.

A regression model can also be used to make estimates. For example, if the direct labor hours are 80,000, then the predicted payroll costs will be 10,000 + \$12(80,000), or \$970,000. A confidence interval can be formed around this regression estimate, just as intervals are formed around sample estimates.

The strength of the association of payroll cost and direct labor hours is commonly measured by three indicators (two of which were cited earlier); *t-values* are reported for each regression coefficient and for the constant term, and they represent tests of whether the coefficients differ from zero (as a rule of thumb, *t*-values greater than an absolute value of two represent a strong relationship). For any regression coefficient, it is possible to calculate a standard error (recall that the standard deviation adjusted for those data points used in estimation is called the standard error). The magnitude of the coefficient, divided by the standard error, yields the *t*-statistic. Insignificant *t*-statistics suggest that the corresponding independent variables can be eliminated from a regression model without seriously reducing its explanatory power. *R-squared values* (also known as the coefficient of determination) report the percentage of variability in the y-variable that is explained by the regression model. Finally, the *standard error* is the square root of the sum of the squared deviations, adjusted for the number of data points available for estimating the model, and tells how close estimates of y are likely to be to the actual y-values. Another important way of evaluating regression results is to examine the *residuals*, or the differences between the values predicted or estimated by the regression model and the actual y values. Obviously, the smaller those residuals are, the better the "fit" of the model will be.

Multiple Regression Modeling

When a y variable is expected to be associated with more than one independent variable, the auditor will shift from simple regression modeling to multiple regression modeling. One way to check the possible association of a set of independent variables to the y variable is by creating scatter diagrams or computing *correlation statistics*, which measure the tendency of two variables to move together (positive correlation from 0 to 1.0) or in opposite directions (negative correlation from 0 to −1.0). These can be thought of as percentage measures that correlate two variables' behavior relative to their respective mean or average values. For example, a correlation of .8 suggests that 80 percent of the time that one variable lies above its average value, the other variable also lies above its respective average value. Using the payroll example, when payroll costs are high, direct labor hours will also be high, each relative to its own mean or average value. Any correlation over .10 has a reasonably good chance of being statistically significant; however, for an analysis of around fifty data points, a .1 to .5 correlation is moderate; a .5 to .8 is a definite relationship; and above .8 is a strong correlation. Exhibit 12-11 summarizes the concepts regarding the interpretation of correlation statistics.

Although scatter diagrams provide a picture of correlation statistics that, in turn, summarize that picture, neither is enough when specifying multiple regression models. This is because of multiple regression's ability to estimate "net" relationships. In the earlier example, the direct labor hours used in the simple regression model may have combined two types of employees whose mix has shifted across time. If we could measure the mix

EXHIBIT 12-11
Correlation Statistics

The summary measure that can help rank-order the strength of association between two variables is called the correlation statistic. It answers the question:

To what degree do changes in one variable relate to changes in another variable?

Perfect fit (no error): +1 or −1

Every variable is correlated +1 with itself, by definition.

Positive or direct relationship: $0 < X \leqslant +1$

Variables tend to increase (or decrease) together; in other words, they systematically move in the same direction relative to their own mean values.

Negative or inverse relationship: $-1 \leqslant X < 0$

As one variable increases, the other decreases, and vice versa.

Note: The closer the absolute value is to 1, the stronger the relationship will be. A strong association will also be apparent in the scatterplots.

For technical reference only: To compute the correlation statistic, add the products of the deviation from the mean of each variable and divide the sum by the square root of the product of the sum of the squared deviations for each variable.

of Type A and Type B employees for periods of time that corresponded to each observation of direct labor hours, we would expect the net effect to yield an even stronger descriptive model of how hours relate to payroll cost. As you may expect, in a multiple regression model that takes the form

$$y = a + b_1 x_1 + b_2 x_2 + \ldots$$

the meaning of the regression coefficient changes. The b's can be interpreted as the change in y for a unit change in each x, holding all other x's in the model constant. Hence the coefficients measure net relationships, such as the association of hours to payroll cost, once the mix of employees has been controlled (or adjusted out).

Assumptions

Regression analysis has four key assumptions:

1. The average value of the residuals will be zero, as we expect to form unbiased estimates from the regression model.
2. The standard error or variability of each residual is constant; that is, it is not, for example, higher just because y is higher.

3. The residual values are independent of one another, which means that a positive residual does not change the probability of the next residual's being positive or negative (that is, they are randomly arranged).
4. The residual values are not correlated with any independent variables, because all patterns in the x's are controlled in the model and, therefore, should not remain in the residuals.

We may often add the assumption that the residuals are normally distributed in order to form symmetric confidence intervals around the regression estimates, like those around sampling estimates. Exhibit 12-12 summarizes the key terms and assumptions introduced in this chapter.

Because of auditors' interest in financial and economic activities, a tendency exists for independent variables to be correlated with one another, resulting in a statistical problem known as *multicollinearity*. A good model builder will be alert to x's that are redundant and so intercorrelated that they may create statistical problems. In such situations, only one of these variables should be included in the model, if they overlap extensively.

Also related to the auditor's focus on economic variables is the persistent problem of cyclical patterns appearing in the residuals, a problem termed *autocorrelation*. Exhibit 12-13 shows the types of variation from the random plot of residuals depicted in Exhibit 12-12 that can result from autocorrelation. Yet, for all statistical problems, techniques exist for addressing and correcting them and, very often, improvement of the regression model will eliminate an apparent problem. A good example is provided by the payroll model. It's obvious that we have ignored any changes in pay rates or potential effects of inflation. Hence, residuals may show a pattern tied to this uncontrolled effect until we expand the model to include some rate-related variable.

Audit Objectives

The audit objective will determine the regression model. If fairly wide precision or a low confidence level is acceptable, simple regression models may suffice. On the other hand, multiple regression models that mirror the auditor's understanding of those factors that influence a client's operations are likely to offer tight precision at a high level of confidence.

Two types of regression modeling are commonly used in auditing: time-series and cross-sectional analysis. In the payroll example, we used a time-series model, in which data reporting monthly payroll costs and total direct labor hours per month were collected and analyzed. The *time-series* tool compares historical experience with the unaudited period in order to isolate unexplained fluctuations. Any time period can be used: days, weeks, months, years, or any other chronological unit. The assumption is that the historical experience will be repeated in the future.

In contrast, *cross-sectional applications* focus on a single point in time (though it need not be calendar time—for example, balances and activity measures at the end of a project can be lined up according to completion dates). The relevant benchmark is how the operating units or projects are related to the experience of other units or projects. For example, the payroll example can be altered to create a cross-sectional application. Assume that a client has twenty-five manufacturing plants and that the auditor wants to compare how reasonable the payroll is at each of the plants. Because he or she expects the plants to have similar payroll costs, once the auditor has determined the number of direct labor hours worked at each plant, he or she will collect year-to-year data per plant instead of monthly data. Then a regression line will be fitted to the data set pertaining to each of the twenty-five plants.

If an auditor wants to compare an entity's operations, but there are not enough operating entities to perform cross-sectional regression analysis, another mode of analysis is to split the locations into two similar groups and then compare those groups. The student's t-value can be computed to determine whether the groups are different or are, statistically speaking, equivalent. Those who are interested in such statistics are encouraged to read further in any introductory text on statistical analysis.

Regression analysis is typically introduced into the accounting curriculum in cost accounting, usually in a cost estimation setting. It is an extremely useful audit tool which can both provide substantive test evidence and direct the auditor's attention to key risk areas in which unusual fluc-

EXHIBIT 12-12
Terminology and Assumptions Related to Regression Analysis

Key Terms

R^2: The proportionate reduction of total variation associated with the use of the descriptor variable(s) in the model.

Regression sum of squares = explained variation.

Residual sum of squares = unexplained variation.

$\therefore R^2$ = proportion of total variation explained by the descriptor variables.

"Explain" does not mean a "causality" linkage, however.

Note: A value of R^2 close to 1 does not indicate the precision of inferences about Y based on knowledge of X. The standard error term, which yields the width of the confidence intervals, is the critical determinant of precision.

t-statistics: These measures of statistical significance for regression coefficients depend on the number of degrees of freedom for a regression model.

Degrees of freedom = Number of data points or observations − Number of independent variables plus one

The "plus one" is for the constant term.

Degrees of Freedom	95% Confidence	90% Confidence	50% Confidence
∞	1.960	1.645	.674

Standard error of estimate: The error in estimating the value of y based on a knowledge of *x*.

Intercept or constant term: The point where the regression line intercepts the *y*-axis; the fixed term in a regression model.

Slope or regression coefficient: Change in Y per unit change in X, holding all other variables in the model constant.

Residual: The difference in actual value and that estimated by applying the regression model.

Confidence interval: A reflection of the accuracy with which reliable estimates can be generated; an interval that will contain the true mean a specified percentage of the time.

Random Residuals:

residuals

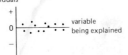

+

0 variable being explained

–

Assumptions

It is important to understand the assumptions underlying regression analysis before proceeding:

1. Each residual has an expected value of zero.
2. The residuals are expected to have a common standard error.
3. The residuals should be statistically independent of one another (i.e., the size or direction of each residual should not affect the size or direction of the other residuals).
4. The residuals should not be related to the descriptor variables (because, theoretically, the effects of these variables have been extracted in producing the residual values).

Note: To make statements based on confidence intervals and prediction intervals, the probability distribution of the residuals must be normal.

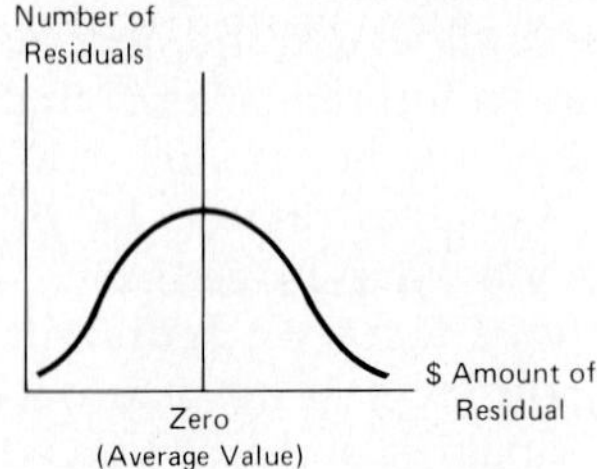

Normal Distribution: Bell-shaped symmetrical distribution that can be totally described by its mean (average value) and standard deviation (scatter).

EXHIBIT 12-13
Autocorrelation Pattern in the Residuals

Economic time series typically have very high serial correlation between adjacent residual values. Residuals that are next to each other in time tend to be very similar because they are acted upon by similar external factors.

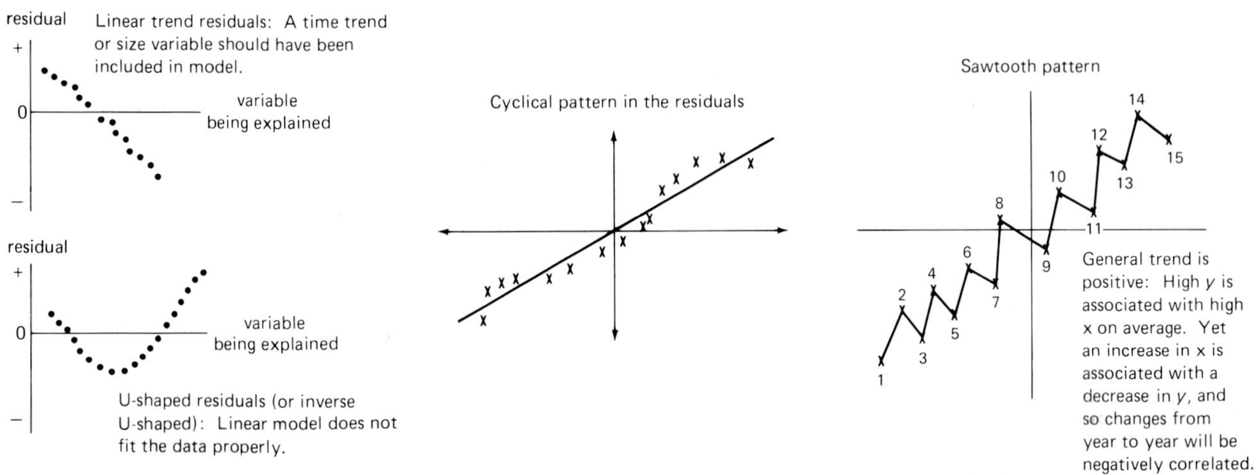

tuations have been observed. As an example, the regression model for the 25 plants' payroll could provide assurance that 23 plants' operations were in line with one another, at a stated precision and confidence level. The other two plants might be reported as *outliers*. This is the term applied to recorded book values that lie outside of the confidence interval that has been formed around the regression estimate. The auditor would proceed to investigate these outliers in order to form an overall conclusion regarding payroll. Those who wish further technical details on regression analysis should refer to courses offered in applied statistical modeling and econometrics.

Directed Sampling

As already suggested, regression analysis can be used in directed sampling. By pinpointing unusual fluctuations, regression analysis directs the auditor's attention to months or locations for testing. Because of the exception basis of sampling, the auditor must remember that results from directed sampling are not expected to be representative of the population but, rather, are intended to explain atypical characteristics of the population.

The idea behind directed sampling is to use all available audit knowledge to control risk and optimize the coverage provided by alternative audit procedures. For example, if certain operating units are located in troubled economic areas, have undergone high turnover, or have experienced unusual growth, focused testing on those units is more likely to be able to reduce audit risk than will tests performed on random samples from all units. Regression analysis is one means of directing the auditor's attention to particular areas of operation for which detailed testing may be appropriate.

APPENDIX

The normal curve area table is presented in Exhibit 12-A on page 426.

REVIEW QUESTIONS

1. Assume the following population:

EXHIBIT 12-A
Normal Curve Area Table

Standard Deviation	.00	.01	.02	.03	.04	.05	.06	.07	.08	.09
0.0	.0000	.0040	.0080	.0120	.0159	.0199	.0239	.0279	.0319	.0359
0.1	.0398	.0438	.0478	.0517	.0557	.0596	.0636	.0675	.0714	.0753
0.2	.0793	.0832	.0871	.0910	.0948	.0987	.1026	.1064	.1103	.1141
0.3	.1179	.1217	.1255	.1293	.1331	.1368	.1406	.1443	.1480	.1517
0.4	.1554	.1591	.1628	.1664	.1700	.1736	.1772	.1808	.1844	.1879
0.5	.1915	.1950	.1985	.2019	.2054	.2088	.2123	.2157	.2190	.2224
0.6	.2257	.2291	.2324	.2357	.2389	.2422	.2454	.2486	.2518	.2549
0.7	.2580	.2612	.2642	.2673	.2704	.2734	.2764	.2794	.2823	.2852
0.8	.2881	.2910	.2939	.2967	.2995	.3023	.3051	.3078	.3106	.3133
0.9	.3159	.3186	.3212	.3238	.3264	.3289	.3315	.3340	.3365	.3389
1.0	.3413	.3438	.3461	.3485	.3508	.3531	.3554	.3577	.3599	.3621
1.1	.3643	.3665	.3686	.3708	.3729	.3749	.3770	.3790	.3810	.3830
1.2	.3849	.3869	.3888	.3907	.3925	.3944	.3962	.3980	.3997	.4015
1.3	.4032	.4049	.4066	.4083	.4099	.4115	.4131	.4147	.4162	.4177
1.4	.4192	.4207	.4222	.4236	.4251	.4265	.4279	.4292	.4306	.4319
1.5	.4332	.4345	.4357	.4370	.4382	.4394	.4406	.4418	.4430	.4441
1.6	.4452	.4463	.4474	.4485	.4495	.4505	.4515	.4525	.4535	.4545
1.7	.4554	.4564	.4573	.4582	.4591	.4599	.4608	.4616	.4625	.4633
1.8	.4641	.4649	.4656	.4664	.4671	.4678	.4686	.4693	.4699	.4706
1.9	.4713	.4719	.4726	.4732	.4738	.4744	.4750	.4758	.4762	.4767
2.0	.4773	.4778	.4783	.4788	.4793	.4798	.4803	.4808	.4812	.4817
2.1	.4821	.4826	.4830	.4834	.4838	.4842	.4846	.4850	.4854	.4857
2.2	.4861	.4865	.4868	.4871	.4875	.4878	.4881	.4884	.4887	.4890
2.3	.4893	.4896	.4898	.4901	.4904	.4906	.4909	.4911	.4913	.4916
2.4	.4918	.4920	.4922	.4925	.4927	.4929	.4931	.4932	.4934	.4936
2.5	.4938	.4940	.4941	.4943	.4945	.4946	.4948	.4949	.4951	.4952
2.6	.4953	.4955	.4956	.4957	.4959	.4960	.4961	.4962	.4963	.4964
2.7	.4965	.4966	.4967	.4968	.4969	.4970	.4971	.4972	.4973	.4974
2.8	.4974	.4975	.4976	.4977	.4977	.4978	.4979	.4980	.4980	.4981
2.9	.4981	.4982	.4983	.4984	.4984	.4984	.4985	.4985	.4986	.4986
3.0	.4986	.4987	.4987	.4988	.4988	.4988	.4989	.4989	.4989	.4990
3.1	.4990	.4991	.4991	.4991	.4992	.4992	.4992	.4992	.4993	.4993

From Donald M. Roberts, *Statistical Auditing* (New York: AICPA, 1978), p. 243.

8	48	98	19	7
60	55	15	33	9
40	63	27	43	71
10	15	29	51	35
5	30	80	63	52

a. From ten different samples of five items, form a mean-per-unit estimate.

b. From ten different samples of ten items, form a mean-per-unit estimate.

c. Quantify the sampling error for (a) and (b). Which is expected to have a lower error? Does it? Why may the expected relationship fail to hold?

2. The internal revenue code's references to statistical sampling in discussions of taxpayers' estimates include: (1) revolving credit for installment accounts receivable, (2) redemption of trading stamps and coupons, and (3) LIFO. What sampling approaches can be used for such estimates?

3. True or false? (Explain your response.) Confirmation replies obtained from a random circularization of one billing cycle of accounts receivable for a client, out of a total of twenty-four cycles, can be reasonably extended as support for the population of billings for the year under audit.

4. Assume that an auditor has calculated the required sample size to be two hundred dollar units for a SPS test of accounts receivable. Further assume that the population has twenty thousand balances, totaling $4.3 million. Describe how a systematic selection of monetary units would be made. Be specific.

5. What is the difference between time-series and cross-sectional regression analysis? Give an example of an audit situation in which an auditor can use each type of analysis.

6. Match the following regression coefficients in a simple regression model explaining sales to the type of business that each coefficient is most likely to describe. Each letter can be used only once.

___	(1) +8,000 number of units sold	a. steel manufacturer
___	(2) +450 number of individual units shipped	b. television retailer
___	(3) +20 number of brown bags used for customers' purchases	c. automobile dealer
___	(4) +48 direct labor hours	d. grocery store
___	(5) −50,000 winter months	e. amusement park

7. What is meant by directed sampling?

EXERCISES

1. Assume that a sample of fifty items was drawn to test depreciation expense and that there is a total of ten differences between recorded depreciation and audited depreciation values.

Sample Unit Number	Difference
7	40.00
15	.25
27	10.12
31	−100.03
32	17.90
40	80.10
43	−13.10
47	4.05
49	70.00
50	−37.19

The total depreciation for the books for the fifty items is $35,690.12. If the total recorded depreciation expense is $5,320,100 for eighteen thousand depreciable assets, what will be the best estimate, based on the auditor's sample results, of total depreciation?

2. An auditor is examining a sample of marketable securities. That auditor expects to find all the securities to be in the client's safety deposit box but wants to be certain that if .5 percent or more of the securities on the list of 5,100 securities are missing, (s)he will note at least one security in the sample that is missing. What sampling approach should be used? What sample size is needed if a 95 percent confidence level is desired?

3. A client has recorded disbursements of $12,500,200 in a voucher register that has thirty items per page and 515 pages. If the auditor wishes to have a 95 percent confidence that the error does not exceed $600,000, what will be the appropriate sampling interval? How would you instruct a staff assistant to draw the systematic sample? Be specific.

4. When auditors are asked to help clients forecast their activities, statistical sampling may sometimes be useful. Give an example of such an application and explain how it differs from the usual auditing application of statistical sampling.

5. A colleague wishes to use regression analysis to predict the expected revenue for a utility client who operates in the northeastern part of the United States, is subject to regulation, and provides both electric and gas services. Describe
   a. the dependent variables of interest.
   b. the likely independent variables that will pertain to the items identified in (a).
   c. the expected correlations between the variables cited in (a) and those matched to each variable in (b).
   d. how the regression results can be used as audit evidence.

QUESTIONS ADAPTED FROM PROFESSIONAL EXAMINATIONS

1. When examining a particular account, the auditor must test certain items in a finite population to form an opinion of the reliability of the account as a whole. In a judgment sample the auditor commonly tests most of the large dollar-amount items and a smaller proportion of the smaller dollar-amount items. A random stratified sample makes the same type of selection but is said to be superior to the judgment sample.

   Required:
   a. Define each of the following and explain how the selection process can be applied to a test of accounts receivable:
      1. A judgment sample.
      2. A stratum in a finite population.
      3. A systematic random stratified sample.
   b. Explain why a random stratified sample is superior to a judgment (nonstatistical) sample.

c. Explain how and why sequential sampling may be more useful to an auditor than simple random sampling is.

(CPA exam adapted)

2. During an audit engagement, a CPA attempts to obtain satisfaction that there are no material misstatements in a client's accounts receivable. Statistical sampling is a tool that the auditor often uses to obtain representative evidence to achieve the desired satisfaction. On a particular engagement an auditor determined that a material misstatement in a population of accounts would be $35,000. To obtain satisfaction the auditor had to be 95 percent confident that the population of accounts was not in error by $35,000. The auditor decided to use unrestricted random sampling with replacement and took a preliminary random sample of one hundred items *(n)* from a population of one thousand items *(N)*. The sample produced the following data:

Arithmetic mean of sample items ($\bar{x}$)	$4,000
Standard deviation of sample items (SD)	$ 200

The auditor also has available the following information:

Standard error of the mean (SE) = SD ÷ $\sqrt{n}$
Population precision *(P)* = *N* × *R* × SE

Partial List of Reliability Coefficients

If Reliability Coefficient (R) is	Then Reliability is
1.70	91.086%
1.75	91.988
1.80	92.814
1.85	93.568
1.90	94.256
1.95	94.882
1.96	95.000
2.00	95.450
2.05	95.964
2.10	96.428
2.15	96.844

Required:

a. Define the statistical terms reliability and precision as used in auditing.

b. If all the necessary audit work is performed on the preliminary sample items and no errors are detected

(1) What can the auditor say about the total amount of accounts receivable at the 95 percent reliability level?

(2) At what confidence level can the auditor say that the population is not in error by $35,000?

c. Assuming that the preliminary sample was sufficient

(1) Compute the auditor's estimate of the population total.

(2) Indicate how the auditor should relate this estimate to the client's recorded amount.

(CPA exam adapted)

3. You want to evaluate the reasonableness of the book value of the inventory of your client, Draper, Inc. You satisfied yourself earlier as to the inventory quantities. While examining the pricing and extension of the inventory, the following data were gathered using appropriate unrestricted random sampling with replacement procedures:

- Total items in the inventory *(N)* 12,700
- Total items in the sample *(n)* 400
- Total audited value of items in the sample $38,400
- $\sum_{j=1}^{400} (x_j - \bar{x})^2$ 312,816
- Formula for estimated population standard deviation $S_{x_j} = \sqrt{\dfrac{\sum_{j=1}^{j=n} (x_j - \bar{x})^2}{n-1}}$
- Formula for estimated standard error of the mean $SE = \dfrac{S_{x_j}}{\sqrt{n}}$
- Confidence level coefficient of the standard error of the mean at a 95 percent confidence (reliability) level ±1.96

Required:

a. Based on the sample results, what is the estimate of the inventory's total value? Show computations in good form where appropriate.

b. What statistical conclusion can be reached regarding the estimated total inventory value calculated in (a) at the confidence level of 95 percent? Present computations in good form where appropriate.

c. Independent of your answers to (a) and (b), assume that the book value of Draper's inventory is $1,700,000, and based on the sample results, the inventory's estimated total value is $1,690,000. The auditor desires a confidence (reliability) level of 95 percent. Discuss the audit and statistical considerations the auditor must evaluate before deciding whether the sampling results support acceptance of the book value as a fair presentation of Draper's inventory.

(CPA exam adapted)

4. The Cowslip Milk Company's principal activity is buying milk from dairy farmers, processing it, and delivering it to retail customers. You are auditing the company's retail accounts receivable and determine the following:

a. The company has fifty retail routes, each of which has one hundred to two hundred accounts, the number that can be serviced by one driver in one day.

b. The driver enters the cash collections from the day's deliveries to each customer directly on a statement form in record books maintained for each route. Mail remittances are posted in the route record books by office personnel. At the end of the month the statements are priced, extended, and footed. Photocopies of the statements are prepared and left in the customers' milk boxes with the next milk delivery.

c. The statements are reviewed by the office manager, who prepares a list for each route of accounts with ninety-day or older balances. The list is used for intensive collection action.

d. The audit program used in previous audits to select retail accounts receivable for confirmation stated: Select two accounts from each route, one to be chosen by opening the route book at random and the other as the third item on each list of ninety-day or older accounts.

Your review of the accounts receivable leads you to conclude that statistical sampling techniques may be used for their examination.

Required:

a. Because statistical sampling techniques do not exempt the CPA from using his or her professional judgment, of what benefit are they to the CPA? Discuss.

b. Why does the audit procedure previously used to select accounts receivable for confirmation (as given in d. above) not produce a valid statistical sample?

c. What are the audit objectives in selecting ninety-day accounts for confirmation? Can statistical sampling techniques help attain these objectives? Discuss.

d. Assume that the company has ten thousand accounts receivable and that your statistical sampling disclosed six errors in a sample of two hundred accounts. Is it reasonable to assume that three hundred accounts in the entire population are in error? Explain.

(CPA exam adapted)

5. The following statements pertain to unrestricted random sampling with replacement. Indicate which are true and which are false.

1. The auditor's previous knowledge of the materiality of the items to be tested may negate the need for random selection.

2. A definition of the population of accounts receivable must specify that only active accounts with balances be included.

3. If a population consists mostly of accounts with large balances, it is acceptable to exclude accounts with small balances from the population to be sampled because the error in a small balance cannot be material.

4. Excluding extremely large items from the definition of the population and evaluating them separately so that they have no chance of being included in the sample would violate the definition of unrestricted random sampling.

5. To be random a sample must be completely unbiased and its selection governed completely by chance.

6. If there is great variability in the number of entries for each item to be sampled, the population can be defined first to select a random sample of items (such as invoices) and then to select a random sample of one entry (quantity and/or price and/or amount) from each item selected.

7. The precision of an estimate of a population mean from a sample mean increases as the degree of confidence in the estimate increases.

8. Five different random samples from the same population will probably produce five different estimates of the true population mean.

9. A 100 percent sample must be taken to attain a precision range of ±$0 with 100 percent reliability.

10. The standard deviation can be used to predict the probable range of difference in a sample mean and population mean.

11. If an auditor wishes to use a table of random digits to select a random sample, he or she must first find a table conforming to the items' numbering in the population to be sampled.

12. If a usable digit appears more than once in the table of random digits during the selection of the sample, the item should be included in the sample only once and another digit selected from the table.

13. A preliminary random sample of at least thirty items must be discarded if it produces one item disproportionately large in relation to the other items selected.

14. The effect of a chance inclusion of a very large or

a very small item in a random sample can be diminished by increasing the sample's size.

15. The reliability specified by the auditor for a sample estimate expresses the degree of confidence that the true value will be within the precision limits determined.

16. The standard deviation measures the variability of items in the universe.

17. The variability of items in a population is a factor that usually causes a sample mean and a population mean to be different.

18. It is necessary to determine the true standard deviation for a population in order to determine the size of the sample to be drawn from that population.

19. The standard error of the mean will always be less than the estimated standard deviation computed from a sample estimate.

20. The standard error of the mean increases as the size of the sample increases.

(CPA exam adapted)

6. The internal auditing staff of Green Lake, Inc. uses regression analysis to review analytically each period's sales expense. Based on data collected over a long period of time, the following statistical regression equation was developed:

Sales expense
($ thousands) = 34.5 + .04 company sales ($ thousands) + .2 shipping costs ($ thousands) + .01 industry sales ($ millions).

The following statistical report was generated by a standard computer program:

	Coefficient	Standard Error	*t*-Statistic
Constant	34.5	.61	56.6
Company sales	.04	.0026	15.4
Shipping costs	.2	.015	13.3
Industry sales	.01	.25	.04
Standard error of regression	10.2		
R^2	70.0		

Required:

a. Identify the dependent and the independent variables in the regression equation.

b. Assume that for the current period, the company incurred sales expense of $400,000 and shipping costs of $800,000 to generate sales of $5 million. Industry sales for the period are estimated to be $2 billion. Based on this information, what point estimate of this period's sales expense would the regression model provide?

c. Indicate how a 95 percent confidence interval for the current period's sales expense point estimate would be constructed. Assume that sales expense is normally distributed.

d. Which variables, if any, in the equation can be eliminated without seriously reducing the regression model's explanatory power?

(CIA exam adapted)

7. An audit of inventory records disclosed that the population has twenty thousand items of inventory. Units within the items vary from 30 to 750.

The values of the units vary from $0.20 to $1,500. The auditor had estimated the error rate at not over 5 percent and because a confidence level of 95 percent and a precision of ±3 percent were desired, the tables used showed a sample of two hundred items. The selection was made from the north end of the storeroom, picking items having one hundred or more units.

In the test, there were forty instances in which the number of units in stock varied by one or more units from the number shown on the inventory records,

The report to management states that the auditor is 95 percent confident that the number of records in the population in error is somewhere between 970 and 1,030.

Required:
Describe five errors in the auditor's technique.

(CIA exam adapted)

8. Multiple Choice
Select the one answer that best completes the statement or answers the question.

8.1 An auditor selects a preliminary sample of one hundred items out of a population of one thousand items. The sample statistics generate an arithmetic mean of $120, a standard deviation of $12, and a standard error of the mean of $1.20. If the sample is adequate for the auditor's purposes and the auditor's desired precision is plus or minus $2,000, the minimum acceptable dollar value of the population will be

a. $122,000. **c.** $118,000.
b. $120,000. **d.** $117,600.

(CPA exam adapted)

8.2 An internal auditor is using variables estimation as the statistical sampling technique to estimate the monetary value of a large inventory of parts. Given a sample standard deviation of $400, a sample size of four hundred, and a 95 percent two-tail confidence level, what precision can the auditor assign to his or her estimate of the mean dollar value of a part?

a. ±$39. **d.** ±$ 4.
b. ±$ 2. **e.** ±$20.
c. ±$52.

(CIA exam adapted)

8.3 A test of two hundred invoices randomly selected by the internal auditor revealed thirty-five that had not been approved for payment. At the 95 percent confidence level, what precision can be assigned?

a. 6.9 percent. **d.** 3.5 percent.
b. 5.3 percent. **e.** 1.7 percent.
c. 9.1 percent.

(CIA exam adapted)

8.4 An auditor's statistical sample drawn from a population of invoices indicates a mean value of $150 and a sampling precision of ±$30 at a 95 percent confidence level. Which of the following statements correctly interprets these sample data?

a. There is a 95 percent probability that the true population mean is $150.
b. There is a 95 percent probability that the true population mean falls between $135 and $165.
c. In repeated sampling, about 95 percent of the intervals with a precision of ±$30 around the sample mean will contain the true population mean.
d. In repeated sampling, the true population mean will fall in the precision range of $120 to $180 about 95 percent of the time.
e. In repeated sampling, the point estimate of the true population mean will be $150 about 95 percent of the time.

(CIA exam adapted)

8.5 The main reason that the difference and ratio estimation methods are expected to produce audit efficiency is that the

a. Number of members of the populations of differences or ratios is smaller than the number of members of the population of book values.
b. Beta risk may be completely ignored.
c. Calculations required in using difference or ratio estimation are fewer and less arduous than those required when using direct estimation.
d. Variability of the populations of differences or ratios is less than that of the populations of book values or audited values.

(CPA exam adapted)

8.6 In estimation sampling for variables, which of the following must be known in order to estimate the appropriate sample size required to meet the auditor's needs in a given situation?

a. The total amount of the population.
b. The desired standard deviation.
c. The desired confidence level.
d. The estimated rate of error in the population.

(CPA exam adapted)

8.7 An auditor initially planned to use unrestricted random sampling with replacement in the examination of accounts receivable. Later the auditor decided to use unrestricted random sampling without replacement. As a result of only this decision, the sample size should

a. Increase.
b. Remain the same.
c. Decrease.
d. Be recalculated using a binomial distribution.

(CPA exam adapted)

8.8 Microtech, Ltd. uses statistical tests to indicate the reasonableness of its sales representatives' monthly expense reports. The relationship between sales revenue and sales representatives' expense was plotted on the following scattergram:

Which of the following statements about this scattergram is correct?

a. Because there is no apparent association, a regression model will not be meaningful.
b. Because there is an apparent association, a regression model cannot assess the reasonableness of a sales representative's expense report.
c. Because there is an apparent association, a regression model can be used to assess the reasonableness of a sales representative's expense report.
d. Because this scattergram is based on past data, it will not be useful in estimating the

reasonableness of current and future relationships.

e. Because there are several regression equations that may explain the relationship between sales representatives' expenses and sales revenues, a regression model should not be used.

(CIA exam adapted)

8.9 Increasing the size of a statistical sample used in an internal audit will

a. Increase the confidence level if the precision is held constant.
b. Decrease the confidence level if the precision is held constant.
c. Widen the precision range if the confidence level is held constant.
d. Narrow the precision range if the confidence level is held constant.
e. (a) and (d).

(CIA exam adapted)

8.10 An internal auditor is using statistical sampling to estimate an inventory's monetary value. Which of the following statistical sampling techniques is not appropriate for estimating monetary value when perpetual inventory records are maintained?

a. Ratio. **d.** Difference.
b. Acceptance. **e.** Regression.
c. Stratification.

(CIA exam adapted)

8.11 The internal auditor's statistical sample of one hundred sampling units indicates an average inventory understatement of $200 with a sampling error of plus or minus $40 at the 95 percent confidence level. To reduce the sampling error to plus or minus $20 at the 95 percent confidence level for the same population would require a statistical sample size in units of about

a. 700. **d.** 400.
b. 200. **e.** 800.
c. 1,200.

(CIA exam adapted)

8.12 In the audit of a population of 100,000 invoices using a sample size of 625, with an average sample unit value of $200 and a sample standard deviation of $100, the lower confidence limit at the 95 percent confidence level for the average sampling unit would be about

a. $180. **d.** $171.
b. $192. **e.** $163.
c. $198.

(CIA exam adapted)

8.13 The auditor can change the standard error of the mean for a statistical sample by

a. Stratifying the population.
b. Increasing the size of the sample.
c. Decreasing the size of the sample.
d. All of the above.
e. (a) and (b).

(CIA exam adapted)

8.14 One measure of the variability among values in a given population is the

a. Arithmetic mean.
b. Median.
c. Range.
d. Mode.
e. Harmonic mean.

(CIA exam adapted)

8.15 The concept of standard deviation is significant in statistical sampling in auditing because

a. The central limit theorem states that repeated samples from a population will produce sample standard deviations that cluster around the population's actual standard deviation.
b. The calculation of sample sizes for variables estimation is directly related to the magnitude of the population standard deviation.
c. The magnitude of the finite population correction factor is directly related to the magnitude of the population's standard deviation.
d. Statistical sampling techniques are inappropriate if a population's standard deviation is very small relative to its mean.
e. The choice between attributes sampling and variables sampling is related to the magnitude of the population's standard deviation.

(CIA exam adapted)

8.16 An auditor wishes to sample statistically a large population of open orders to determine the proportion of backorders on file owing to a lack of stock. This proportion is expected to be 20 percent; accordingly, the auditor draws a sample of 246 open orders, which yields a 95 percent confidence with a precision of ±5 percent. If the auditor wishes to change his or her precision to ±2.5 percent the required sample size will be

a. 174. **d.** 945.
b. 492. **e.** 984.
c. 697.

(CIA exam adapted)

8.17 Sample selection using dollar-unit sampling for inventory valuation will most likely result in a sample with characteristics roughly equivalent to one provided by

a. Judgment sampling plans.

b. Variables sampling plans with substantial stratification by dollar amount.

c. Selection of inventory records using a random starting point for the record selection.

d. Difference or ratio estimation plans on an unstratified basis.

e. Mean-per-unit or direct extension unstratified sampling plans.

(CIA exam adapted)

8.18 Which of the following would be an improper technique when using dollar-unit statistical sampling in an audit of accounts receivable?

a. Combining negative and positive dollar error item accounts in the appraisal of a sample.

b. Using a sample technique in which the same account balance can be selected more than once.

c. Selecting a random starting point and then sampling every *n*th dollar unit (systematic sampling).

d. Defining the sampling unit in the population as an individual dollar and not as an individual account balance.

e. All of the above.

(CIA exam adapted)

8.19 Which of the following statements is correct concerning the appropriate measure of central tendency for the following frequency distribution of loss experience?

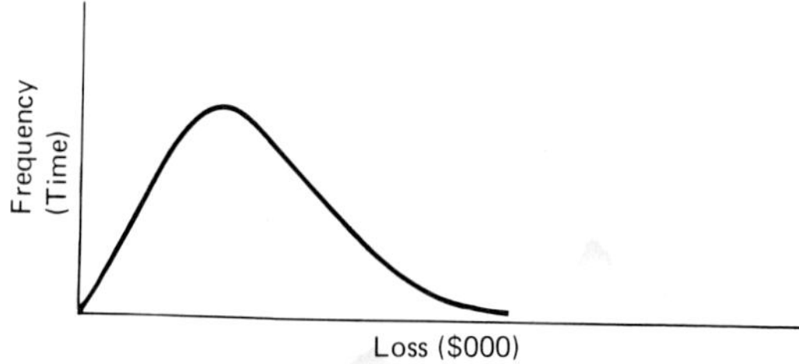

a. The mean should be used because it represents the dollar loss that has occurred most frequently in the past.

b. The mean, median, and mode are equal because the distribution is symmetrical.

c. The mode is the most appropriate measure because it is not affected by the extreme losses.

d. The mean is the best measure of central tendency because it always lies between the median and mode.

(CIA exam adapted)

CASES FOR DISCUSSION

1. Not only have the courts accepted statistical evidence generated by sampling and regression modeling tools, they have also developed substantial expertise. For example, the courts have recognized in a humorous manner their understanding of the difference between correlation and causality:

> [I]t is statistically true that there have been no forest fires on Manhattan Island since the "Smokey the Bear" advertisements have been displayed in New York subways. However, it is not commonly accepted that this statistic proves the value of advertising.[7]

In what sense does this observation relate to the auditor's use of correlation statistics and regression analysis as audit tools?

2. A 1975 survey of 126 auditors reported that those areas in which more than half of the respondents considered using statistical sampling in audits include *Compliance Tests:* Cash disbursements, sales, payroll, cash receipts, voucher system, and purchasing; and *Substantive Tests:* Accounts receivable, inventory, expenses, revenues, and accounts payable.

Fewer than one-half reported using statistical sampling in their audits of notes receivable; property, plant, and equipment; investments in marketable securities; cash; notes payable; accrued expenses; other assets; long-term liabilities; or owners' equity.

When asked about the relative efficiency of statistical techniques, 36 percent indicated greater efficiency for statistical sampling than for nonstatistical sampling, and 36 percent indicated that the two techniques required about the same amount of time.[8]

Why do you suppose that auditors tend not to apply statistical sampling as frequently in those accounts cited by less than one-half of the respondents? Compare and contrast how your response would account for the frequent use of statistical sampling in the other accounts cited.

[7] *Louis* v. *Pennsylvania Indus. Dev. Auth.,* 371 F. Supp. 877, 885 n. 14 (E.D. Pa 1974) cert. denied, 420 U.S. 993 (1974).

[8] Adapted from James P. Bedingfield, "The Current State of Statistical Sampling and Auditing," *Journal of Accountancy,* December 1975, pp. 48–55.

Do you believe that the survey results reflect the relative efficiency of statistical and nonstatistical techniques? Discuss what characteristics of the techniques are likely to affect their relative efficiency.

3. Overhearing a heated debate between two senior accountants, you walk in and ask, "What's the problem?"

Senior 1. I'm planning to use PPS for a compliance test of sales. I'm planning to check invoices, sales orders, credit approval, quantities and prices, extensions, and related journal entries.

Senior 2. And I say that PPS is not a compliance test tool; it's a substantive test tool.

Senior 1. I don't agree, and I don't get decent dollar coverage from attributes testing. What do I say to the board of directors when they ask us what percentage of sales transactions was tested in our evaluation of controls?

Senior 2. How would you ever evaluate the results of PPS in a compliance mode?

Senior 1. What do you mean? It's much easier, 'cause I'll have an estimate of the dollar effect of errors, not just the occurrence rate!

At that moment, the two seniors turn to you, a partner, expecting that you can resolve their debate. Explain to the two seniors the issues relevant to their debates, why each is right or wrong, and how *Senior 1* should proceed.

4. **a.** If correlation analysis, simple regression analysis, or graphical techniques used to establish a gross relationship between two variables fail to indicate an association, does that mean there is no association?

b. In earlier years, the auditor proposed some medium-sized adjustments to a client, who has elected not to book the entries. The auditor waived the adjustments because they did not have a material effect on the financial statements. How will this historical fact affect the auditor if he or she wants to use regression analysis?

c. You estimated the following simple regression model:

Electric Revenue	= 815,520 (t-value = 0.46) Not Significant @ .05 level	+ .08121 Kilowatt Hours (t-value = 3.542) Significant @ .001 level

Achieved precision at 95 percent level of confidence = 24,614,000

How can this regression model be interpreted?

d. Assume the auditor estimates the following regression model:

Electric Revenue	= −29,561,000 (t-value = −3.841) Sign. @ .001	+ .00485 Total KWH's (t-value = 2.683) Sign. @ .01
	+2,200.8 Degree Days (t-value = 3.253) Sign. @ .01	
	+1.0704 (t-value = 9.466) Sign. @ .001	Production Expenses Related to Electric Revenue
	+313,720 (t-value = 6.532) Sign. @ .001	Consumer Price Index

Achieved precision at 95 percent confidence = 3,766,600

Make business sense out of this regression model.

e. The internal controls of a public utility client are excellent except that there is a quarterly, rather than a monthly, cutoff of Accounts Payable. How might this company policy affect regression applications to Accounts Payable or Related Accounts?

13

The Revenue Cycle

"I don't believe it!" exclaimed Mary Anne.

All heads turned in the staff room and saw Mary Anne holding up the local newspaper; the headlines read:

Close to $1 Million Stolen: Guard Thought It Was a Rabbit.

"This used to be our client, and I know the man they think stole the money! He seemed as honest as the day is long, and that past client's controls are excellent!"

Together, several of her colleagues asked, "How did he 'beat the control system'?"

Mary Anne explained, "Well, this Joe Harberg was in charge of undeposited cash receipts. An armored car came for a pick-up late Friday afternoon, so that the company would earn interest over the weekend. On the morning of the robbery, Joe came to work with a wheelbarrow. The security guards have instructions to search anything suspicious either entering or leaving the premises. It seems one guard asked Joe what was in the wheelbarrow. Joe said that he was taking care of his nephew's rabbit, which had babies the night before! The guard looked, and sure enough, there were a bunch of rabbits!

Apparently during the day, Joe filled the wheelbarrow with cash, and he filled up the money bags with coins. After the armored car left, Joe also left, with his wheelbarrow. And naturally the guard waved him through, thinking that he already knew the contents of the wheelbarrow!

This morning, the bank called to confirm the lower than usual deposit, and a bunch of rabbits was discovered in a storeroom. Joe, of course, didn't come to work this Monday morning and seems to have disappeared."

Across the room, David observed, "It just goes to show that every system can be beaten!"

Jan chimed in, "Why do you think we tell our clients to get fidelity bonding insurance?"

Mary Anne observed, "If any of you had met Joe, you'd be surprised!"

Not to be left out, Stan noted, "With cash, it's just too easy and too much of a temptation. Why do you think we have such tight controls over cash, in contrast to those related to fixed assets? We can't rely on human nature and employee loyalty!"

Jan's rejoinder was predictable, "Yeah, but what good are designed controls if the employees fail to comply with the controls? I mean, a million dollars takes up space, and a wheelbarrow certainly merits inspection by a guard!"

David noted, "Whenever people are involved, they can be hoodwinked. I mean, there's always room for a bad judgment call!"

"Well," sighed Mary Anne, "At least they're not our client anymore. We won't be grilled about why the controls didn't work. . . ."

The case illustrates the inherent limitations of control, particularly when dependent on humans who are familiar with their fellow employees. Adding the temptation of an asset that is highly negotiable and virtually untraceable, the revenue cycle poses a particularly high risk area for auditors. With the benefit of hindsight, the client might have required the counting of cash by the armored car employees and the confirmation of the amount by someone who did not have physical access to the cash. This would have required collusion for Joe to have been successful in his plan. In addition, more care in training the guard as to (1) the importance of his procedures, (2) the risk exposure of the client, and (3) the diverse circumstances that can lead even very loyal employees to be tempted to remove highly liquid assets *might* have precluded Joe's success. The case has some implications as to how the auditor ought to evaluate the excellence of controls and what such excellence really means. Moreover, the risk picture in the revenue cycle is made particularly clear, as is the incessant need for fidelity bonding of those who are responsible for highly valued and liquid assets. This case will be revisited at various points throughout the chapter, as the audit approach to the revenue cycle is delineated. The importance of preventive controls and the short-term, timely detective monitoring of revenue transactions will be emphasized.

Introduction to Cycle Chapters

In approaching an audit, alternative strategies for dividing up the audit work are available. Some CPAs may choose an account orientation that focuses on management's representations for each account, relating the relevant controls over that account balance to the level of compliance and substantive testing to be performed. But one disadvantage of this approach is that it does not use the relationships among the accounts when evaluating controls and the extent of work to be performed. In particular, it does not approach a client's organization in the same way that management probably approached its operations when designing its information systems and control procedures. A manager probably considers the organization's information system, to have a cycle orientation. Specifically, a manufacturer would point to his or her income-producing activity, the costs incurred to generate that revenue, and the related financing or treasury type of activities to support operations. The transactions and account balances within each of these major activities (or cycles) are closely related and, if audited as a coherent segment, can streamline the audit procedures. This efficiency stems from (1) an intuitive approach to understanding clients' systems, which follows the entity's operating activities; (2) a more comprehensible basis for communicating with clients—that is, the client tends to think in terms of operating cycles, and so that will be the orientation of the inquiry procedures in conducting the examination; and (3) the ease with which the audit team examining a particular cycle can determine how the evidence relates to different accounts within the cycle, thereby ensuring against overauditing.

Although specific aspects of operating cycles will differ according to the nature of a client's business, there are three generic cycles that capture the overall operations of any entity:

1. The *revenue,* or *income-producing, cycle* includes selecting customers; extending credit; accepting orders; filling orders (shipping); billing credit customers; collecting receivables; handling receipts from cash sales; handling returns and allowances; and earning interest, rental, royalty, and similar income.
2. The *cost of sales* or *production cycle* includes purchasing; transportation; receipt of items purchased; recording and payment of trade payables; manufacturing, including production and conversion, tracing of inventory flows, manufacturing costs, payroll, scrap, and property accounts; and all disbursements.
3. The *financing cycle* includes debt and equity transactions and all related dividend, interest, and miscellaneous expense accounts; and, in the audit, it addresses management functions pertaining to cash balances, financial reporting activities, and general controls over operations, including the maintenance of an internal audit function when applicable.

Even a not-for-profit entity's operations follow these three cycles. The revenue is donations, grants, and outsiders' user charges for services rendered; the cost of sales has inputs similar to those of a profit-oriented operation—other than control over voluntary services rendered at no cost; and the financing cycle covers borrowing and possibly membership dues or other "owners' interests."

Based on the types of transactions recorded in the revenue cycle of a profit-oriented entity, the accounts affected would be revenue, returns and allowances, accounts receivable, allowance for doubtful accounts, cash, and interest, rental, royalty, and miscellaneous income accounts. By grouping the transaction types and their related accounts, similarities among the entities and among the cycles within an entity can be identified, thus simplifying the evaluation of controls. As already noted, the normal course of business processes flow through operating cycles rather than through the accounting system, making the cycle approach an effective framework to apply when determining whether checks and balances have been established for an entity. Then, as described in earlier chapters, this check underlies the planning of compliance and substantive test work. For these reasons, the approach of Chapters 13, 14, and 15 is a description of the audit approach to each cycle of a client's operations. It is important to note that the three cycles used to organize our discussion could be further subdivided; for example, subcycles for payroll and personnel, purchasing and disbursements, and inventory and warehousing could be designated to break down the cost of sales cycle into smaller sets of like transactions to be audited.

As each cycle is explained, an emphasis will be placed upon

1. Description of cycle.
2. Functions involved (e.g., sales, billing, credit approval).
3. Things that could go wrong.
4. Controls that would prevent (or detect) such errors or irregularities.
5. Tests for controls (compliance tests).
6. Accounts involved and transactions.
7. Substantive tests including analytical review procedures.

In addition, a detailed example of the audit of one phase of the cycle, integrating control concerns, EDP use, and statistical sampling tools will be provided. While each cycle chapter may appear somewhat separable from the other cycles, that is not the case during the course of an actual audit. The interface with other cycles is substantial and that, in fact, is the reason that audits are performed by an engagement *team*. Evidence on the handling of goods received clearly relates not only to purchasing but to sales returns and allowances. Cash balances encompass sales, cost of goods sold, and financing activities. Exhibit 13-1 summarizes the audit process and information shared among the cycles. Note the dotted line information flows at each stage of evaluation.

In performing overall risk assessments, users' reliance on financial statements would be considered, as would the likelihood of the client's misstatement of financial statements and the probability of future insolvency. Research utilizing interview techniques to obtain an idea about the Big Eight's efforts to perform risk evaluation has identified the overwhelming consensus that the reputation and stability of client's management is the foremost consideration. Other factors identified in the overall risk evaluation include the

EXHIBIT 13-1
The Audit Process

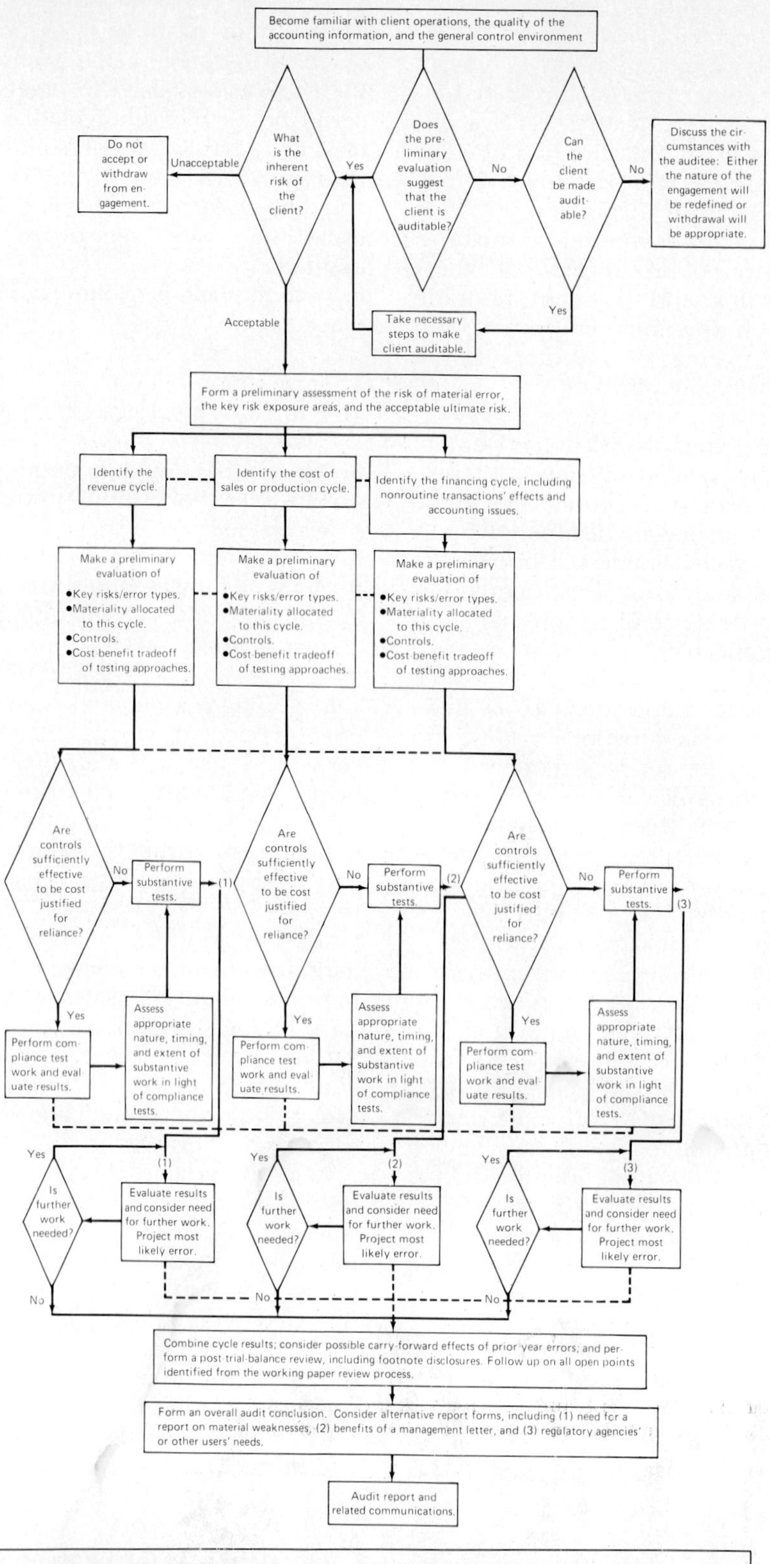

- nature of the client's business.
- rate of growth of the client's business.
- type of financing used by the client.
- client's system of internal control.

Some attention was paid to the client's long-range plans, public status, financial condition, emphasis on earnings per share, and method of growth. Substantial reliance was placed on past experience with the client, although a minority of interviewees noted that the longevity of the engagement did not influence risk (the other 14 were split 50–50 between the responses "influences risk" and "could influence risk"). Perhaps of greatest interest is the firm's reported reliance upon professional judgment as an implicit risk evaluation process, rather than a set of formal procedures intended to evaluate relative risk. Yet firms commonly had prescribed procedures for new client investigation, entailing close personal contacts with bank executives, lawyers, and underwriters. Dun & Bradstreet credit investigations are commonly used. Past auditors are contacted, controls are evaluated, and information from working paper reviews sometimes prompts attention to shortcomings in the approach to risk evaluation. This is particularly so when industry-specific problems arise. Uniformly, the interview demonstrated that attention is paid to pending litigation and its lessons for practitioners.[1] Hence, all of these techniques would be expected to be applied in the first phase of the audit process diagrammed in Exhibit 13-1.

The objectives of internal control are authorization, processing, classification, accuracy, and safeguarding ***[SAS 1, Section 320].*** Each can be tied to assertions about individual account balances. Whenever control objectives are not met, the possibility of financial statement errors is increased. To evaluate this possibility and the role of compensating controls, any possible errors must be identified. Knowing what can go wrong, the possible error or irregularity can be matched with the preventive or detective controls that, if thought to be effective and cost beneficial, can be tested. Exhibit 13-2 illustrates such an analysis for cash receipts. If there are no controls, or if it is not practical to test those controls that are present, it is possible to infer the effect of possible errors on the financial statements and to plan substantive tests of the balances that might be affected. Hence, no matter how objective-oriented an audit firm's methodology appears to be, an error analysis is the critical phase of planning specific steps of the audit process.

Although Exhibit 13-1 separates compliance and substantive tests, their distinction is blurred by dual-purpose testing, an example being the selection of

EXHIBIT 13-2

The Relationship of Management Assertions to Control Objectives, Possible Errors and Irregularities, and Key Controls for Prevention or Detection

Examples for Cash Receipts

Management Assertion: Existence

Cash receipts are actually valid.

Control Objective: To ensure that recorded receipts are valid and properly supported.

Possible Error or Irregularity: Fictitious receipts are recorded.

Key Control(s) to Prevent or Detect Error or Irregularity: Comparison of journal with supporting source documentation by individual with only accounting-related responsibilities. Independent bank reconciliation to ensure that bank's reported balance shows no cash shortage.

Management Assertion: Completeness

All cash receipts are reflected in financial statements.

Control Objective: To ensure that no valid cash receipts are omitted from records.

Possible Error or Irregularity: Cash stolen and not recorded; or cash receipts omitted from the records.

Key Control(s) to Prevent or Detect Error or Irregularity: A cashier has control over cash to be deposited, has no incompatible duties, uses prenumbered sales or receipts books for a sequence check. An independent party retains duplicate deposit slip, checks for agreement of remittance advice with deposit slip, and tests complete sequences for sales and receipts books.

[1] Carl William Brewer, "The Nature of Audit Risk Indicators and Their Effect on the Intensity of Audit Work Performed" (a dissertation presented at the University of Houston, May 1981).

sales invoices for testing in which prices are both checked for approvals and extensions and traced to price catalogues. This latter attention to accuracy would be classified by many as a substantive test procedure.

To illustrate how the error analysis process might be applied to one aspect of the revenue cycle, we shall use interest revenue generated through sales transactions. Assume that the auditor is concerned with the possible error of misstating unearned interest as revenue. The first step is to evaluate the consequences of such a misstatement. Such an error would overstate revenue and receivables and, in later periods, understate revenue. The next step is to decide which controls could prevent such an error. Controls might include

- written procedures for handling time-delayed payments on sales which would ensure that controls had been designed to control interest-related transactions.
- separate handling of those sales that involve interest charges which would make it less likely that interest transactions are improperly stated.

An effective detective control is an independent review of sales invoices to ensure the correct handling of interest charges. If these controls are present, compliance tests should be used, including the examination of written policies, observation of the method used for stating interest revenue, and inspection of initials or working papers documenting the independent review of invoices. These tests indicate whether the designed controls are operating effectively. If the controls are thought to be effective, interim substantive testing may be appropriate. If the controls are weak, the tests should be shifted to year-end.

Substantive testing would likely involve the examination of sales invoices to determine that interest is being added to sales prices, which requires the tie-in of pricing to available price lists. On a test basis, the accounts and notes receivable balances are reviewed to ensure that interest charges are being appropriately handled. Analytical review procedures, comparing the interest revenue to date with that of a similar period in the previous year can also be useful. The extent of the substantive testing will be greater if controls are weak than if the compliance tests indicate that reliance on controls is warranted. At year-end, the final substantive tests should include an analysis of ending accounts receivable balances to ensure separation of the interest portion. This illustration shows how error analysis can direct the audit process.

Another audit concern is whether interest has been earned but not recorded; that is, the client may have forgotten to accrue interest revenue at year-end. The prescribed procedures for accrual adjusting entries should be reviewed to see whether revenues and receivables were likely to be understated despite existing controls. Substantive test reconciliation of notes receivable and interest-bearing sales to the interest revenue account should reveal whether recorded interest has been understated. Generalized audit software can be very effective in performing such a reasonableness test.

The working papers tying together audit objectives, system controls, compliance tests, and subsequent substantive procedures, corresponding to phases (1), (2), and (3) in Exhibit 13-1, are called *bridging working papers* ***[SAS 41, Section 339]***. Exhibit 13-3 shows how such working papers might be prepared for dividend revenue. This exhibit reemphasizes the "sharing" of evidence from tests of transactions to numerous account areas, across all operating cycles. Recall from earlier chapters that documentation would include lead schedules reflecting general ledger balances and detailed schedules relating to such underlying audit work as confirmation procedures. Whenever PBC appears on such working papers, they have been prepared by the client and will be traced back to the books by the auditor before proceeding with the audit.

With this general background on the audit process provided, we will now turn our attention to each of the operating cycles. Initially, we will define the revenue cycle.

A Definition of What Comprises the Revenue Cycle

The revenue cycle includes all income-producing activities: order entry, credit granting, shipping, billing, sales returns and allowances,

EXHIBIT 13-3
Dividend Revenue: Example of a Bridging Working Paper

W/P Ref. No.
Preparer
Date

Bridging Working Paper

Audit Objective:	Reported dividend revenue represents the actual amount earned from investments, is recorded in the proper period, and has been appropriately recorded to reflect dividends receivable and collections of such receivables.
System Controls:	The design of controls over cash receipts is good and encompasses not only receipts from inventory sales but also nonroutine receipts such as investment revenue. A separate investment ledger is maintained that is routinely reviewed and matched with actual receipts. See W/P No. ___.
Compliance Tests:	The investment ledger was tied to the general ledger; controls over cash receipts were tested and found to be effective. See W/P No. ___.
Substantive Procedures:	Investment securities were inspected. Cash balances were confirmed with the bank, and a cutoff bank statement was audited. Dividend revenue was tied to publicly available dividend records printed by Standard & Poor's. See W/P No. ___.
Overall Conclusion:	Dividend revenue is accurately stated in the proper period, and receivables tie to dates of declaration on securities for which the payment date has not yet arrived, whereas all other dividend revenue has been collected, as appropriate.

investment income, and other income transactions. Along with revenue earning is the receipt of assets related to such revenue. The receipts part of the revenue cycle includes credit and collections, maintenance of receivable records, and cash receipts.

Functions Involved in the Revenue Cycle

The typical information flow through the sales cycle for a credit sales operation usually begins with a customer's purchase order. Based on that order, multiple copies of an internal sales order form are prepared. It is useful for later control purposes to send copies of the sales order to the billing department, the shipping department, the credit department, and the customer, filing one copy in the sales order department. After the sales order has been generated, the control procedures include approval by the credit department of the terms of the sale; release of the merchandise to the shipping department; preparation of the bill of lading, with a copy sent to the customer; shipping of merchandise; preparation of the invoice; and posting of the transaction to the sales journal and the customer account. The sales orders should be filed by sales order number, and invoices by payment due date to facilitate control. At this point, the collection phase begins. Exhibit 13-4 shows a flowchart of a typical sales and collection operation.

The information flow can be envisioned by considering the common types of forms which are utilized to document the entire revenue cycle, as summarized in Exhibit 13-5. These forms may be in hard-copy or machine-readable form, depending on the type of processing environment. Each form either documents a transaction or controls the flow of that transaction through the operating cycle into the accounting records.

What Can Go Wrong

When performing an audit, the auditor should consider the types of errors that can occur. Exhibit 13-6 lists the possible errors or irregularities for the revenue cycle. The auditor should be able to pinpoint the client's exposure to such problems by studying the entity's operations. In order to identify which of the items shown in Exhibit 13-6 can actually go wrong for a particular client, the auditor must understand the client's operations. One way to do this is to answer the questions presented in Exhibit 13-7. For example, consider the following credit-granting operation of a client:

Sellmore, Inc. is a retail department store. The store issues credit cards to those customers who meet its credit standards, which are set by the controller who then grants the credit. To encourage sales, credit limits are not imposed until a payment is more than ninety days past due. It is Sellmore's policy to grant a credit card only after a credit check. However, the chief accounts receivable bookkeeper has the authority to waive a credit check

EXHIBIT 13-4

Typical Sales and Collection Flowchart

Order Entry
Credit Department
Shipping Department
Billing Department
Accounting Department
Mailroom
Customer order 1 2 3
Customers' records (credit approval)
Compare order with records for credit approval
Customer order 1 s
Filed (P) by customer (A)
Customer order 2 s
Prepare shipping order and bill of lading
Shipping order documents variations from customer order 1 2
Bill of lading 1 2 3
Shipping order 1
Filed (P) by customer (A)
Bill of lading carrier's copy to obtain customer's signature 1
Bill of lading for customer 2
Customer order 3 s
Shipping order 2
Bill of lading 3
Reconcile documents and prepare invoice
Invoice 1 2 3
Invoice to customer 1
Invoice 3
Filed (P) by customer (A)
Invoice 2
Enter in sales journal and accounts receivable subsidiary ledger
Sales journal
Accounts receivable subsidiary ledger
Invoice 2
Filed by customer
Prelisting with remittance advices when available 2
Reconcile prelisting to remittances. Enter in cash receipts journal and accounts receivable subsidiary ledger
Cash receipts journal
Accounts receivable subsidiary ledger
Prelisting 2
Filed (P) by date (D)
Use updated accounts receivable subsidiary ledger to prepare customers' statement
Customer's statement 1 2
Filed (P) by customer (A)
Checks received
Prepare receipt listing $
Pre-listing 1 2
Prepare deposit slip $
To Bank
Bank validated slip
Prelisting 1
Filed (P) by date (D)
Other activities not shown:
•Returned goods
•Review for uncollectibles
•General ledger postings
Recall: $ = processing of cash
s = signed source document
P = permanent file
A = alphabetic filing
B = numeric filing
D = filing by date
╲ = document attached to another document

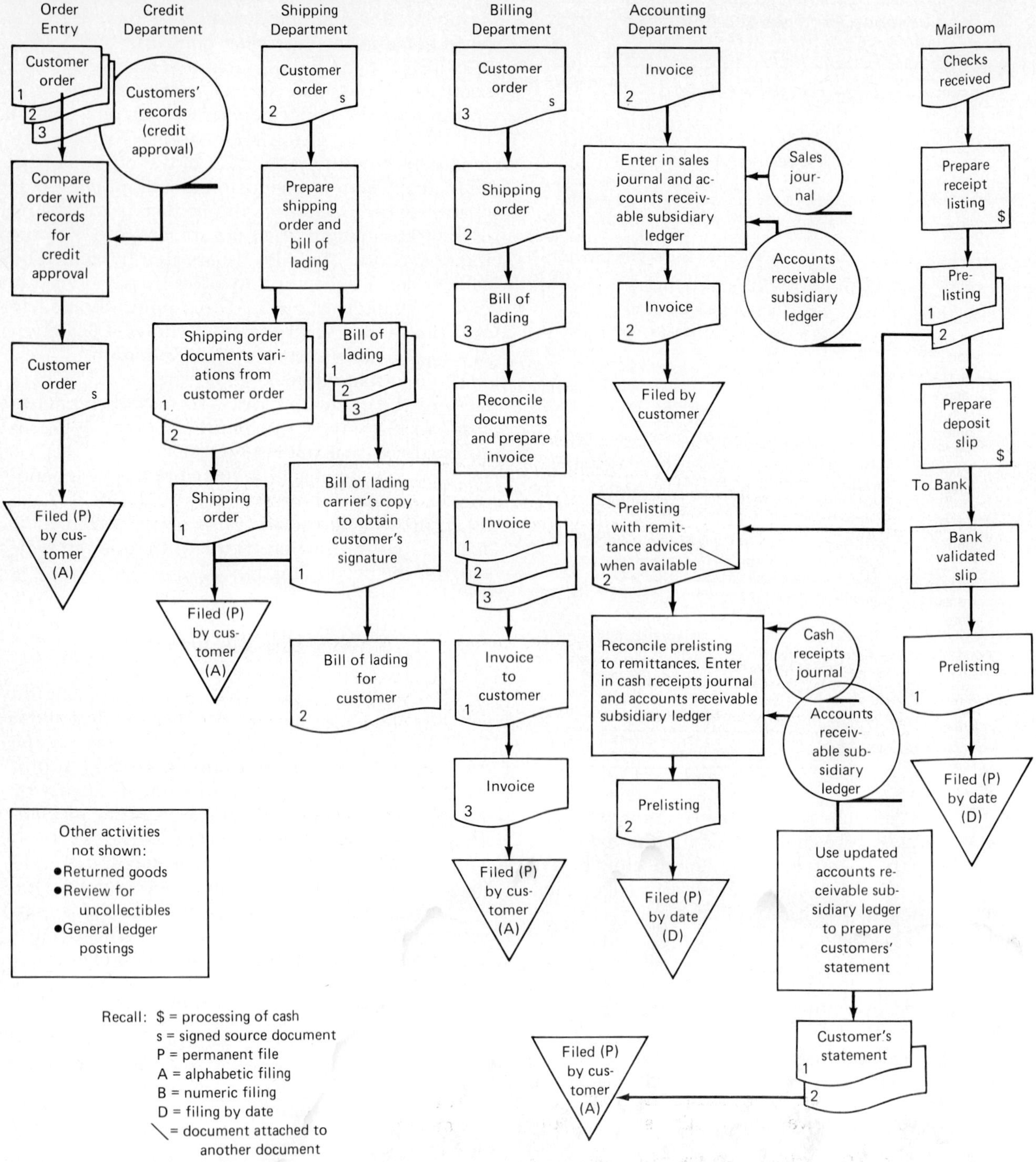

EXHIBIT 13-5

Suggested Forms for Documenting Revenue Cycle

- Customer Order Form: Initially records customers' orders and documents credit approval and shipping instructions.
- Customer's Record: Records results of credit check and information that can ensure adequate customer service and documentation of business commitments.
- Shipping Orders: Documents shipments and variations of shipments from customers' orders.
- Bill of Lading: Documents items delivered and provides proof of delivery when signed by customer.
- Invoice: Bills customer and documents review procedures performed before mailing invoice (review procedures typically include reconciliation to customer's order and shipping report, recalculation of billing, checking of price, terms, and approvals, and issuance of final approval).
- Customer's Statement: Provides cumulative, monthly report to customers on both sales and collection activities (operating as check on accuracy and completeness of customers' records and encouraging payment).
- Aged Trial Balance for Accounts Receivable: Assists management in monitoring receivables and estimating uncollectibles.
- Sales Adjustments (Request for Credit Memo): Authorizes sales returns and allowances, documenting nature of problem to facilitate management's oversight.
- Sales Returns (Receiving Report): Establishes control over goods returned by customers, documenting condition of goods and subsequent handling.
- Credit Memo: Credits customers for returns and allowances.
- Open Customer Orders: Ensures timely follow-through of all customers' unfilled orders.
- Unmatched Shipping Forms: Controls risk exposure from unbilled shipments.
- Unmatched Credit Requests and Sales Returns (Receiving Reports): Ensures timely follow-through of all unfilled requests for sales returns and allowances (particularly important to maintaining good customer relations).
- Write-off and Recovery Report: Documents rationale for and authorization of write-offs and ensures proper recording of reinstated accounts.
- Deposit Slip: Documents cash receipts deposited in bank, thereby maintaining control over them.
- Daily Remittance List: Establishes control over cash receipts from customers' remittances (copies forwarded to accounts receivable for reconciliation to reported bank deposits and to treasurer for reconciliation to bank statement).
- Cash Sales Slip: Initially records cash sales and establishes control over cash receipts.
- Remittance Advice: Facilitates proper crediting of customers' payments and maintenance of up-to-date customers' addresses.
- Record of Investments: Establishes control over investment securities and related investment income.

Adapted from Wanda A. Wallace, *Handbook of Internal Accounting Controls* (Englewood Cliffs, N.J.: Prentice-Hall, 1984), pp. 152-167.

if it appears the delay caused by such a credit check may deter or defer a large sale. In recent years Sellmore's management has emphasized telephone sales. If a non-credit cardholder calls in a sale with a retail value of more than $100, the telephone operator checks with the department manager from which the merchandise is being ordered. The department manager has the authority in such instances to authorize the granting of credit.

Accounts receivable are reviewed every year by the chief accounts receivable bookkeeper. Any accounts more than six months in arrears are written off, and the customer's account is discontinued.[2]

What can go wrong in such a situation? The key risks are that excessive uncollectibles can result from too lax a credit policy, as well as from the poor controls over that policy. In particular, deficiencies in the credit-granting procedures are

1. The responsibility of granting credit is spread among many individuals.
2. The responsibility for the credit-granting function rests with individuals who have incompatible functions.
3. No limits are placed on any credit accounts.
4. Credit may be granted without proper investigation.
5. The customers' accounts are not reviewed on a timely basis.

[2]From CIA exam, May 13, 1982, part 2, question 43.

EXHIBIT 13-6
The Revenue Cycle: Things That Could Go Wrong

- Revenue may not be recorded.
- Revenues may be recorded more than once.
- Estimated revenue may be in error.
- Revenue recognition practices may not be in accordance with GAAP.
- Adverse sales commitments may not be appropriately recognized.
- Deferred income may not be appropriately recognized.
- Revenue may be incorrectly classified (e.g., short-term versus long-term receivables).
- Revenue may be recorded in the wrong period (i.e., cut-off may be improper).
- Management estimates of uncollectibles and product returns may be in error: The inability for an auditee to collect receivables could stem from customers' inability to pay, unwillingness to pay bill when due because of dissatisfaction with product or service provided, or because recorded amounts are from fictitious customers. Too liberal credit policies can create excessive amounts of uncollectibles.
- Goods returned may not be reentered into inventory books.
- Disclosure may be inadequate, particularly regarding related party transactions and pledged receivables.
- Shipments may contain more than quantity ordered.
- Billings may not be made.
- Billings may be made in error.
- Billings may not be recorded.
- False credits may be entered in sales adjustment entries.
- False credits may be entered in receivable accounts.
- Cash receipts may not be recorded.
- Cash receipts may be diverted after being recorded.

6. The decision to discontinue credit is the responsibility of the person who maintains the records—a person who probably is not trained for the function and who has an incompatible function.

The likelihood of these deficiencies resulting in more uncollectibles than the client has estimated must be determined. Besides their effects on uncollectibles, granting credit without proper investigation may increase the risk of unrecorded sales. In addition, when any single aspect of operations is poorly controlled, it can damage the control environment and other cycles' controls. And the write-off of receivables can be used to cover up fictitious receivables or the removal of cash receipts.

The next step is for the client to decide what controls to use to overcome the observed deficiencies. In our example, the following control procedures could reduce the risks of the current credit-granting practices:

1. Only one person should be responsible for granting credit.
2. Persons with credit-granting responsibility must be independent of sales, accounts receivable, and other general responsibilities.
3. All credit applications should be investigated.
4. Credit limits should be established for each account according to the results of the investigation.
5. Customer accounts should be aged monthly.
6. The aging should be done by someone with no receivables duties.
7. The write-off of accounts should be approved by someone with no receivables or cash-handling responsibilities.

With these controls, the auditor might judge compliance testing to be cost beneficial, as a basis for reducing substantive tests on the allowance for doubtful accounts and write-offs to accounts receivable. Once the relevant error types have been recognized, the relative probability of those error or irregularity conditions existing and potentially resulting in material misstatements in the financial statements must be assessed. This risk evaluation must include consideration of existing controls.

Key Risk Areas and Controls Capable of Preventing or Detecting Errors and Irregularities

Within the revenue cycle, the main assets that can be misappropriated are cash receipts, shipments, and investments. Although investments will be discussed *primarily* in the finance cycle, since both the sale of investments and income from investments are a part of the revenue cycle, a limited discussion is merited within this chapter. Given the key assets at risk have been identified, the auditor

EXHIBIT 13-7

Useful Questions to Auditor in Understanding an Auditee's Business, Particularly Its Revenue Cycle

- In what market does the auditee participate?
- What share of the market does the auditee hold?
- What are the market forecasts?
- What are the competitive conditions?
- What are the industry and company trends?
- What is the sales mix?
- How elastic is the demand for products?
- What is the seasonality of operations?
- What key market and economic shifts are likely to affect sales?
- What changes are anticipated?
- What are the nature and volume of transactions and balances?
- What are the entity's distribution channels?
- What are the client's policies regarding how sales are made and related revenue is recorded?
  - What criteria are used in determining whether a sales order is accepted?
  - Who accepts customer orders?
  - Is leasing used?
  - Is franchising used?
  - Is percentage-of-completion used?
  - What credit forms are available?
  - Who defines credit policies, and what are they?
  - What is the customer's general nature, and how do the terms of sales vary across customer classes?
  - What is the degree of concentration in the customer base?
  - Who assigns credit limits and on what basis?
  - How can credit limits be changed?
  - Who monitors credit and order acceptance activities?
  - What are the return policies?
  - Are warranties offered?
- How centralized is management?
- What are the key financial and operating statistics commonly measured in the industry, and how does the auditee compare with its competitors?
- Does the auditee have overseas operations?
- What is the regulatory environment, both at home and abroad?
- Are revenue recognition practices consistent with those of the industry, and are they particularly complex?
- Are there likely to be unrecorded liabilities, particularly regarding sales returns and allowances?
- Are collectibility problems apparent (e.g., via disputes or old receivables)?
- Is cutoff well controlled, particularly regarding foreign and domestic bank accounts?

can proceed to identify the possible means by which their misappropriations can be prevented or detected. These "desirable" controls can then be compared with the client's existing controls to assess the plausibility of control reliance and the advisability of planning compliance test work.

Cash Receipts

For example, for unrecorded cash receipts, the possible controls intended to prevent or detect their removal would include:

- ○ Using lock boxes whereby third parties collect receipts.
- ○ Using automatic registration mechanical devices.
- ○ Independently preparing prenumbered sales tickets to control receipts.
- ○ Assigning responsibility for opening mail and making collections to two persons instead of just one (thereby requiring collusion to remove receipts)—in the introductory case, such a control might have prevented the million dollar theft.
- ○ Immediate restrictive endorsement of all checks

received and deposit (at least daily) of all receipts (to limit the negotiability of receipts and accessibility to large amounts of cash receipts).

- Prenumbering remittance advices and accounting for their sequence (thus providing a completeness control over receipts).
- Comparing receipts with independently generated information about expected receipts (published dividend records like Standard & Poor's can be used for a reasonableness check on recorded receipts).

Which of these controls are expected to be present will depend, in large part, upon the type of business in which the auditee is operating. For example, an entity that made all cash sales would preclude the need for extensive controls over the incoming mail. Yet, such a client would be expected to utilize cash registers to assist in controlling and accounting for receipts.

If the auditor decides that the controls are not adequate, he or she must figure out how any misappropriations might be covered up. Controls disclosing attempts to cover up misappropriated cash receipts include requirements that

- an independent party compare the accounts receivable records with the cash receipts deposited.
- an independent party send confirmations to customers.
- an independent party handle customers' inquiries and complaints.
- tests of details, particularly tests of adjusting entries, write-offs, and returns and allowances, be performed and footings checked by an independent party.

If such controls are not present, the auditor should use confirmation and test procedures to detect possible cover-ups.

Additional controls to prevent or detect the misappropriation of recorded (as distinct from unrecorded) cash receipts, aside from the immediate restrictive endorsement of checks and timely depositing of receipts, include requiring: (1) an independent party to compare the initial listing of receipts with the books and bank deposits, (2) disbursements not to be made from cash receipts, and (3) cash verification to be synchronized with securities verification to eliminate the chance for cross-substitution. The mixing of receipts and disbursements makes it far too easy for an individual to make unauthorized disbursements from unrecorded receipts.

The principal tool for determining the reasonableness of reported cash is the bank reconciliation. The promptness with which reconciliations are prepared by an independent party will determine how effective they are as a control. If a business has many bank accounts, special care must be taken to detect improperly handled interbank transfers. Kiting occurs whenever a deposit in an interbank transfer is recorded before a disbursement is recorded; such a practice is illegal and results in an overstated cash balance.

To reinforce these ideas concerning risk and control, consider the following irregularities involving cash receipts and the "missing" controls which had they been present could have either prevented or detected the problem.

A company utilized the services of various business organizations to act as collection agencies for the convenience of customers in remote service areas. Agents were supposed to deposit cash receipts in banks for credit to the company's district office. However, one agent retained cash and made delayed deposits. This irregularity was perpetrated by transmitting false bank deposit slips with "duplicate" stamp impressions made by using a readily accessible facsimile of the bank stamp which the agent had procured.

Although bank statements were reconciled to determine that outstanding deposits in any one month were reported in the following month, control procedures did not include checking the actual dates of deposit. Hence, collections in the first week of one month could be held until the next month without detection.

A teller at a company withheld cash receipts and utilized his knowledge of cycle billing statements to time the recording of receipts. However, the timing of the belated recordkeeping was imperfect, leading to customers' complaints that their previous payments had not been credited. Had the organization established a practice of surprise rotation of tellers to a position giving no access to company cash for at least a month, the defalcation may have been deterred and would have been detected on a more timely basis.[3]

[3]Certain cases illustrated in the cycle chapters were adapted from experiences reported by the American Gas Association and *The Internal Auditor*.

These circumstances bear out (1) the need for an auditor's attention to the *specific* control procedures performed—such as the checking of days, not just months—and (2) the additional risk faced in the cash receipts area due to the assets' liquidity and the difficulty of ensuring accurate *initial* recording of cash inflows.

Shipments

The following three controls help prevent or detect misappropriated shipments:

1. An approved customer order is required to document all shipments (to ensure that all shipments are properly authorized).
2. An independent reconciliation is made of all customer orders to shipping documents and to billings (to ensure against unfilled orders, unbilled shipments, and inaccurate billings).
3. Safeguard procedures are established for storage and movement of all goods (to safeguard inventory).

Any misappropriations of shipments, if covered up, should be detectable by periodically comparing assets with detailed records, reviewing adjusting journal entries, and assigning an independent party to handle customers' complaints and inquiries. Special attention should be given to complaints of short shipments or no delivery. An interesting twist to the following case example bears out the need to direct attention to any exception noted by customers.

An entity had an invoice accompany shipments which was a five-part form: (1) file copy, (2) shipping department's copy to be matched with the delivery copy, (3) billing copy (once it is matched with the delivery copy), (4) delivery copy to be signed by the customer, and (5) customer's copy. The employee who was to deliver shipments retained a load for personal use, forged the delivery copy of the invoice, and retained the customer's invoice. When the next load was delivered to the customer, the employee left the invoice for the preceding load and then either forged the signature on the correct delivery ticket or returned it unsigned. In this manner, billings corresponded to the same invoice order as the customer's record of deliveries, although the billing to a specific date was ahead of the customer's record. When customers paid cycle billings, they would send less than billed, indicating that "invoices were not available for the later items being charged" but they did not indicate any exception with respect to delivery. The customers presumed that the cycle cut-off was weak, as it was not intended to reflect the month-end balance. The fraud was not discovered until a customer inquired as to the billing method. It is interesting to note that the accounting department had attributed the customer's notations to slow communication across the company's operating departments.

The control which would have been capable of detecting the defalcation would be for the accounting department to check whether customers' short payments corresponded to billings *other than* the last one or two deliveries on the billing. In addition, the dates of delivery per customers should correspond to the dates of delivery per books.

Investments

Finally, consider the controls to help prevent or detect the misappropriation of investments:

1. Using dual authorization procedures (thereby requiring collusion to obtain authorization of invalid transactions).
2. Safeguarding investments primarily by means of required dual access to safe deposit boxes (again, requiring collusion to remove assets).
3. Processing all investment-related cash receipts and disbursements through the normal control system (to ensure that they are as well controlled as are routine cash receipts from sales).
4. Requiring that brokers' statements and market information be reconciled to the books by an independent party (to detect any problems on a timely basis).

As with shipments, periodic comparison of records to investments can be quite effective in detecting attempts at accounting cover-ups. In addition, an independent party should review controls over adjustments, test transactions, and compare the reasonableness of the account balances to market information that is externally generated.

Investment income may be a material revenue source, for operations such as insurance companies, or a relatively immaterial source, primarily representing the temporary investment of idle working capital. The process of investing commonly involves an executive finance committee that is subject to the board of directors' approval of large transactions. Because most investments are liquid and negotiable, theft or the diversion of funds is a risk. And because investment-related transactions are not routine, they often do not have the usual controls. A far more in-depth discussion of control over investment practices, safeguarding controls, and related audit procedures is provided in Chapter 15.

Coupons

Entities often issue coupons in order to enhance sales. Because of their negotiability, many controls are needed to avoid losses from either intentional or unintentional mishandling. Specifically, when coupons are received from a printer, packages of coupons should be tested to check the accuracy of the reported quantity of coupons per package. Unused coupons should be kept under lock and key, and requisitions should be required for access to them. A perpetual record of coupons printed, issued, and on hand should be maintained and periodically compared with the physical inventory of unused coupons. The cashier's record of redemption should be matched with the mail department's record of coupons redeemed. And patterns of coupon redemption should be analytically reviewed ***[SAS 23, Section 318].*** For example, are redemptions unusually high in a certain sales area?

Complaints from customers concerning coupon redemptions should be handled by someone who is not handling cash. As suggested by the case examples for cash receipts and shipments, customers' complaints can say a lot about controls! If cash is mailed as a part of the coupon campaign, there should be safeguard controls, including minimization of the extent to which mailings that contain currency are handled. Once a coupon offering is complete, that is, when the expiration date printed on coupons has passed, any remaining coupons should be reconciled to the books and then destroyed.

Overdraft Risks

Overdrafts created by the customer service or product line of checking accounts represent a separable control concern for banks. And NSF (nonsufficient funds) checks from customers can also be a big problem for small businesses. Daily overdraft reports should be prepared and circulated among the bank's offices with daily review and approval by an authorized officer, thereby enabling management to monitor its exposure. A record of the overdrafts should be included in the monthly reports to the board of directors or its designated committee (e.g., the audit committee, should one exist).

When checks are not returned to the sender, they should be promptly charged to the respective accounts despite the resulting overdraft. There should be a system for following unpaid overdrafts, and an overdraft account should be carried on the general ledger. All overdrawn statements on larger accounts should be reviewed for irregularities.

Disclosure Issues

Disclosure issues in the revenue cycle are tied to compliance with GAAP and clarity of communication ***[SAS 32, Section 431].*** Because receivables are typically thought to represent sales to customers, any sales to employees or affiliates should be separately reported. Controls are needed to ensure the appropriate classification of receivables. Similarly, cash is thought to be available for expenditures. If compensating balances, whether informal or formal, are required, which effectively preclude unrestricted spending, they should be disclosed. These disclosure concerns are typically addressed through review and approval procedures. Issues regarding revenue recognition practices and related party transactions are the subject matter of Chapter 16.

Not-for-Profit Entities

Even not-for-profit organizations have a revenue cycle whose revenue is in the form of contributions rather than direct proceeds for specific services rendered. Controls over contributions can be strengthened by having contributors make disbursements by check instead of cash. In addition, a prenumbered receipt with a carbon copy should be used for each solicitor, and the copy should be reconciled to total receipts. A list of contributors should be maintained from year to year, with comparisons to detect missing donors or large variations in the magnitude of gifts. Letters to those not contributing may elicit information about misappropriated or unrecorded receipts. This practice, in combination with the rotation of solicitors, is likely to deter fraud. Contributions lead to far greater control problems than regular revenue does, because there is no exchange and thus no accounting trail of shipping documents or similar support of the validity of an accounting entry. In fact, consider the setting of a church and assume you were asked to audit its financial statements. It is virtually impossible to attest to the completeness of recorded cash receipts. Apparent controls are likely to be inoperative. As an example, pledge envelopes may be prenumbered with an implied objective of improving control over cash receipts, but church members cannot be relied upon to use prenumbered contribution envelopes in the proper order, without missing any weeks. While it is true that those same individuals would mail mortgage payments with the appropriate prenumbered payment cards, they would not sense the same responsibility for voluntary contributions. Moreover, the latter pose no financial penalty for nonpayment. CPAs recognize that as money is placed in an offering plate, money could also be removed and that the first effective control point over receipts is when they are deposited in the bank. For that reason your audit report would specify that your opinion related to the accountability of receipts deposited by the church.

Tests for Controls

Certain general control concepts require the auditor's attention prior to the performance of detailed compliance tests. One key concern is the adequacy with which employees' duties are segregated.

The segregation of duties within the revenue cycle should ensure that the responsibility for authorizing sales and other income-producing activities is separate from the responsibility for executing sales or investments and that each of these responsibilities is separate from the recording of transactions in order to establish a means by which the accountability of assets can be maintained. It should not be possible for a single person to perpetrate and conceal irregularities in the course of performing their routinely-assigned duties. Exhibit 13-8 outlines the key duties in the revenue cycle that ought to be segregated. As explained in Chapter 9 on internal control, authorization should be separate from custody and accounting responsibilities. Beyond considering functions that are the direct responsibility of individuals, indirect functions which may harm the effectiveness with which duties are segregated should be noted. For example, mere access to records and assets that are processed by others can pose substantial risks. Similarly, practices such as temporarily assuming others' duties during lunch or over vacation periods may thwart attempts to segregate duties. Family and related party relationships merit special attention, as they can lead to ineffective segregation of duties. The same type of risk is created when individuals are assigned responsibility to handle transactions that are known to involve conflicts of interest.

In evaluating controls over receivables, special attention should be given to separation of duties and the controls over invoices, remittance advices, credit memoranda, and noncash entries. Customers' complaints and the approval of uncollectible account write-offs should be handled by the credit department rather than by the accounting group. Typically, poorly segregated duties will not permit reliance on most detailed control procedures. For that reason, the observation of operations and of both the formal and informal division of duties is one of the first audit procedures in any engagement. To illustrate the breadth of its influence, consider an example of unsegregated duties and its potential adverse effects.

Tellers for a company were delegated the authority to waive late payment charges. Such a combination of authorization procedures with the handling of cash receipts creates a number of problems:

- the opportunity for an irregularity exists—tellers could charge customers for late payment and pocket the change by marking the penalty charge as waived.
- if the teller were to make an error and have a cash shortage, by waiving penalty charges according to the records, yet collecting the charge, the shortage could be covered.

EXHIBIT 13-8
Duties to Be Segregated in Revenue Cycle

Authorization	Custody	Accounting
Order Entry		
– Marketing/sales accepts orders. – Credit department establishes credit limits, approves all accounts for credit, and investigates overdue or unusual accounts. – Treasury department approves write-offs and confirms charge-offs 2 to 3 months later.	– Shipping prepares bills of lading and ships goods.	– Accounts receivable matches documents, prepares billings, and maintains subsidiary accounts receivable ledger. – General ledger accounting maintains control accounts, reconciling subsidiary, billings, and reports.
Adjustments to Sales		
– Marketing/sales investigates customers' complaints and approves credit memos and changes in terms.	– Receiving department controls returned goods. – Shipping department prepares bill of lading and ships goods.	– Accounts receivable accounts for sequence of credit memos, reviews credit packages, and maintains subsidiary accounts receivable ledger. – General ledger accounting maintains control accounts, reconciling subsidiary ledger.
Investments		
– Treasurer's department authorizes purchases and sales of securities.	– Treasurer's department maintains dual control over securities.	– Investment ledger is maintained. – General ledger accounting reconciles brokers' statements and investment ledger.
Cash Receipts		
– Treasury department will instruct bank not to cash checks payable to company but to accept them only for deposit.	– Receptionist/mail opener will list and restrictively endorse "For deposit only" on all receipts. – Cashier will control receipts. – Cash receipts department will make bank deposit.	– Accounts receivable will update cash receipts journal and maintain the subsidiary accounts receivable ledger. – General ledger accounting will maintain control accounts, reconciling receivables, and preparing bank reconciliation. (This reconciliation should at least be tested by the treasurer's department.)

Adapted from Wanda A. Wallace, *Handbook of Internal Accounting Controls* (Englewood Cliffs, N.J.: Prentice-Hall, 1984), pp. 146–147.

- periodic waiver of penalties could become common knowledge, resulting in numerous additional requests for waivers by customers.
- such requests of waivers can be time-consuming, resulting in slower service for all customers.

These problems could be avoided by assigning authority to the administrative office, rather than to tellers. This would also help to prevent employees from gaining an impression that the entity is lax in its control procedures. As illustrated in this example, control problems often have operating efficiency implications.

Besides evaluating the segregation of duties, certain other common controls are expected to be part of a well-controlled system. In particular, detailed records should be reconciled monthly to the control account in order to detect any problems on a timely basis. Individuals outside the accounting department should be responsible for keeping the collateral that is held on any receivables. Management's internal controls should include monitoring the age of receivables, trends in credit terms and sales, and reports on write-offs. To avoid an improper write-off of an account receivable being used to conceal a cash shortage, write-offs should be approved by a responsible officer, after reviewing the credit department's recommendations and supporting evidence. To protect assets by means of internal control, accounts receivable that have been written off should be transferred to a separate ledger, and postdated checks remitted by customers should be restrictively endorsed.

Returning to a general concern which will underlie the audit approach, attention must be directed to the nature of the client's information system. There should be an accounting trail that documents employees' operating and control duties. Controls should require documentation to be complete and available when needed, and retention policies should prevent the destruction of useful information. On the other hand, needless redundancy should be eliminated.

In generating an accounting trail, it is important that the client utilize existing documents consistently and that the order in which documents are completed and actions are taken is as prescribed. If, for example, means exist by which salespeople can authorize shipments prior to completion of a credit check, then neither credit reports nor shipping reports are being generated consistently. Furthermore, post-facto credit review has little control capability. The review process would be changed from a preventive control to a detective control. Furthermore, even if a problem were detected, the client could do little about goods that had already been shipped.

In considering safeguarding controls, you might question what actions could have been taken to "compliance test" the guard's responsibilities and anticipate that the events detailed in the introductory case could have happened. Outside of staging a similar attempt to "dupe" the guard, observation and inquiry procedures would be the key audit tools.

One of the key aspects of the control environment is making sure that the employees understand the accounting policies and procedures and job descriptions. For example, has the security guard been told how important his or her job is, the large amount of liquid assets at risk, and the necessity of taking nothing for granted? Beyond safeguard activities, credit policies should be clearly delineated, as should customer acceptance, allowable sales commitments, and acceptable transportation practices. Shipping procedures, including how over and under shipments are to be handled, should be outlined, with required authorizations delineated. Practices with respect to goods on consignment at others' locations need to be explicitly documented. A cash receipts manual and investment manual would also be expected to exist, detailing safeguarding procedures and periodic authorization and accountability practices.

Once the general controls have been reviewed, those controls which appear to be effectively designed must be evaluated from an audit perspective: Is compliance testing of that control likely to reduce the required substantive testing enough to be cost-justified?

Typical Controls and Related Compliance Tests

To reiterate those controls that are typical for most entities, in the revenue cycle, cash receipts are controlled by

- Not permitting disbursements to be made from receipts.
- Timely and regular reconciliation of bank statements by employees not handling cash receipts or disbursements, with reviews by an officer on a monthly basis. ***[SAS 45, Section 1010]***

Compliance tests would involve ensuring that all disbursements were made by check or from petty cash and examining reconciliations—recomputing amounts, checking for approval, and tying amounts to the bank statement.

To control cash receipts, prenumbered sales tickets should be used, accounting for their completeness on a daily basis. The auditor can do a sequence check and review evidence that the client periodically tested completeness. When paid, sales tickets should be stamped and later reconciled to the duplicate deposit slip from the bank by a party not involved in either granting credit or handling cash. The testing of bank reconciliation procedures and examination of stamped sales tickets can serve as compliance tests. Color coding of sales tickets can distinguish credit sales from C.O.D. transactions. These tickets can be tested for appropriate account classification. Remittances should not be held but should be deposited daily with a control listing prepared for any remittances that are not in the correct amount. Compliance tests would include the reconciliation of total remittances to deposits, the comparison of the date of remittance to the date of deposit, and investigation of any delayed deposits.

The adequacy of controls over miscellaneous receivables should be evaluated, including those over freight claims, insurance claims and refunds, royalty income, rental income, and sales from scrap or from disposals of plant, property, and equipment or other assets. Often a well-controlled system will process receipts from such nonroutine transactions the same as sales receipts, in which case compliance testing is performed over all receipts at one time. However, if the processing differs, these nonroutine transactions will need to be tested for supporting documentation, authorization, completeness, and accuracy—including the appropriateness of amount, account classification, and accounting period ***[SAS 1, Section 331]***.

Receivables are controlled by

- Adequately segregating the duties between the receivables department and the functions of billing and cash receipts (thereby separating accounting from the custody of assets).
- Performing a credit review on customers *before* granting any credit (ensuring only authorized transactions).
- Maintaining an approved customer list with credit limits specified (thereby ensuring authorization and the safeguarding of assets by limiting risk exposure).
- Regularly reconciling the receivables subsidiary ledger to the general ledger (to detect errors on a timely basis).
- Requiring approval of account write-offs by management (to ensure that authorized policies are being followed).
- Regularly preparing aged receivable trial balances and having management review them for collectibility (to evaluate the adequacy of recorded uncollectibles and monitor the quality of assets).
- Systematically calculating the allowance for doubtful accounts by using historical experience as a basis for estimation (to accurately reflect net realizable receivables).

Tied closely to controlling receivables is control over shipments. Common controls include:

- Maintaining a shipping log sequentially listing each shipping document (to ensure the completeness of recorded shipments).
- Reconciling shipping documents to sales invoices (to ensure accurate billing).
- Maintaining an open customer order file, regularly reviewing for evidence of unbilled shipments (a completeness check).

The separation of the authorization of shipping and billing is important in order to preclude the possibility of an individual initiating shipment to a personal account, then destroying the shipping and invoicing copies of documentation.

Revenues stemming from sales and investment transactions can be controlled by

- ○ Having senior management review the income statement for reasonableness and
- ○ Standardizing end-of-period processing.

A review of these control steps suggests the type of data that can be tested to provide compliance test evidence. Segregation of duties can be *observed*; evidence of credit checks, approvals, and reconciliations can be *examined*; shipping logs can be *tested* for completeness; and reports can be *read*.

Examples of compliance tests and the audit objective and question to which each pertains are provided in Exhibit 13-9. The audit objective and questions can be viewed as components of more global audit objectives to test management representations. The strength of the compliance test results will be the basis for reducing certain types of substantive test work regarding the fairness of reported balances.

As an example of a more global audit objective, let us consider investments and the desire to establish the existence of marketable securities. One substantive test is the physical inspection of stock certificates. If the compliance tests of controls indicate that access to the certificates is effectively restricted and that the signatures of those having access to them compare with the signatures of authorized personnel, then inspection can be shifted to some point before year-end. Essentially, reliance on internal controls can tie in substantive test work performed before year-end to the reported balances. Because of securities' liquidity, the inspection should not be moved back to July for a calendar-year client but may be all right in October, for example. If a trust company safeguards some investments, the auditor will perform compliance tests to gain assurance that the trust company has a good reputation and a strong financial position. Compliance tests will include examination of the formal agreement with the trust company and its auditors' report on control over securities held on behalf of third parties. Based on such tests, confirmation procedures with the trust company may be deemed to be sufficient substantive test procedures *in lieu of* inspecting securities that are held. (Note that specifics as to how investments are examined by auditors are deferred to Chapter 15 on the financing cycle, since the key concern in this chapter is with investment-related income.)

Accounts Involved and Transactions

As the transition is made from the cycle orientation of controls and compliance testing to the balance orientation of substantive test work, it is helpful to delineate the accounts affected by the types of transactions included in a particular cycle. For example, revenue, returns and allowances, accounts receivable, allowance for doubtful accounts, and cash are affected by sales, billing, and collection activities. Interest, rental, royalty, and miscellaneous income, as well as cash, are affected by investment activities and the disposal of assets other than inventory. If credit sales are made, notes receivable are directly affected by sales, billing, and collection activities, as is interest income.

Substantive Tests Including Analytical Review

Common substantive tests in the revenue cycle include

1. confirmations.
2. examination of correspondence (regarding whether customers are bona fide, whether errors have occurred, and whether collection is probable).
3. recomputation (that is, footing, checking extensions, recalculating discounts, testing interest accruals, and reviewing aged receivables).
4. comparing documents (for example, shipping documents with sales orders and invoices).
5. retracing to journals, subsidiary ledgers, and ledgers.
6. reasonableness tests, including analysis of supporting data and a review of management representations.

To provide an example of common audit approaches, an example of an audit of the revenue cycle of a bank will now be provided.

In auditing the loan balances of a finance com-

EXHIBIT 13-9

Examples of Compliance Tests and Related Audit Objectives and Questions

Audit Question to which test might relate	Compliance test
Objective: To determine that transaction dollar amounts are properly calculated. Are mathematical accuracy checks being performed, and has there been an accounting cover-up because of miscalculations?	Test extensions and footings of journal entries, journals, and ledgers.
Objective: To determine that transactions are authorized by company policy. Are designed controls over credit extension reasonable?	Discuss the auditee's established criteria for extending credit, and ascertain the reasonableness of such criteria.
Objective: To determine that controls adequately safeguard assets. Are safeguard and segregation of duties control procedures being followed?	Observe the opening of mail, prelisting of cash receipts, and the restriction of others' access to cash.
Objective: To determine that transaction accounting is complete, accurate, properly classified, and in the appropriate period. Are procedures prescribed for cash receipts, and is the bank reconciliation procedure done as an independent competent check on the handling of receipts?	Test deposit activities and the processing of receipts, including direct receipt of bank statements, and then review and test the bank reconciliation. Are all cash receipts entered in the daily remittance list, deposited intact, and recorded in the accounts receipt control account as of the date received?
Objective: To determine that all valid cash transactions are recorded and none are omitted. Are controls monitoring the agreement of balances per books and balances per banks being performed?	Review cash receipt records, and tie them into bank statements, testing them for accuracy.
Objective: To determine that transaction accounting is complete. Are the billing documents on file complete?	Check whether billing documents are prenumbered, and account for their numerical sequence.
Objective: To determine that transactions are properly authorized and accurately recorded. How adequate is the compliance with controls that are intended to ensure that only authorized sales at appropriate prices are accurately billed? Similarly, are returns and allowances controlled by compliance with designed procedures?	Select a sample of invoices and sales return and allowance memos, and test for (1) approval by the credit department, (2) appropriateness of prices per approved price listings, and (3) accuracy of extensions and footings.
Objective: To determine that recorded transactions are valid and documented and that amounts are accurate, complete, and recorded in the proper period. Were all billings appropriately supported by shipping documents, and were all credit memos similarly supported by receiving documents? Were these billings and memos accurately and completely recorded for the appropriate period? That is, were controls intended to ensure adequate supporting documentation and accurate record keeping operating effectively?	Select a sample of sales invoices and sales return and allowance memos, and trace to (1) shipping and receiving records, being attentive to the cutoff's propriety, and (2) entries in the detail records.
Objective: To determine that recorded transactions are valid, accurate, and in line with company policy. Do controls ensure billings commensurate with customers' orders, and are discount policies followed?	Compare customer's orders with copies of billings, and particularly, note propriety of discounts taken and the approval of unusual discounts. Cash receipts should be compared with invoice terms to determine that cash discounts were proper. Recalculate the discount.
Objective: To determine that recorded transactions are valid and documented. Are all recorded entries valid; that is, are they adequately supported?	Test entries in the receivable records to source documents. For example, are recorded receipts supported by remittance advices?
Objective: To determine that transactions are valid and are reasonably stated. Are confirmation procedures being executed as prescribed?	Periodically test the auditee's procedure of soliciting confirmations from customers, by observing the sending of statements and investigating any differences reported by customers.
Objective: To determine that transaction accounting is complete and accurate. Is the auditee following general control procedures, leaving an audit trail as evidence and doing so competently?	Examine the records for evidence that subsidiary journals and ledgers are periodically reconciled to the general ledger, and check the accuracy of such reconciliations. For example, are all credit sales posted to customers' individual accounts?
Objective: To determine that transaction accounting is accurate. Are control procedures intended to monitor accounts receivable being followed?	Review aging schedules for accounts receivable, noting the timeliness with which they are prepared and their accuracy.
Objective: To determine that recorded transactions are valid. Are collection procedures adequate? What risk is there that write-offs are premature, inadequately followed through, or being collected and misappropriated?	Review collectibility procedures, including efforts directed toward accounts already written off.
Objective: To determine that transactions are authorized by company policy. Are nonmerchandise sales appropriately authorized?	Examine documentation in support of scrap sales, sales of fixed assets, and other nonroutine transactions generating cash receipts, noting whether cash receipts were appropriately authorized.
Objective: To determine that transactions are properly classified. Are nonmerchandise sales classified in the appropriate accounts?	Test cash receipts for nonmerchandise sales to ensure they were posted to the proper account.

Adapted from Wanda A. Wallace, *Handbook of Internal Accounting Controls* (Englewood Cliffs, N.J.: Prentice-Hall, 1984), pp. 136-141.

EXHIBIT 13-10

An Example of the Linkage Between Internal Control Evaluation and Substantive Testing

Problem:

You are the in-charge accountant examining the financial statements of the Gutzler Company for the year ended December 31, 19X6. During late October 19X6, you, with the help of Gutzler's controller, completed an internal control questionnaire and prepared the appropriate memoranda describing Gutzler's accounting procedures. Your comments regarding cash receipts are as follows.

All cash receipts are sent directly to the accounts receivable clerk with no processing by the mail department. The accounts receivable clerk keeps the cash receipts journal, prepares the bank deposit slip in duplicate, posts from the deposit slip to the subsidiary accounts receivable ledger, and mails the deposit to the bank.

The controller receives the validated deposit slips directly (unopened) from the bank. He also receives the monthly bank statement directly (unopened) from the bank and promptly reconciles it.

At the end of each month, the accounts receivable clerk notifies the general ledger clerk by journal voucher of the monthly totals of the cash receipts journal for posting to the general ledger.

Each month, the general ledger clerk makes an entry in the general ledger cash account, to record the total debits to cash from the cash receipts journal. In addition, the general ledger clerk sometimes makes debit entries in the general ledger cash account from sources other than the cash receipts journal, e.g., funds borrowed from the bank.

You have already performed certain standard auditing procedures listed in the next column in the audit of cash receipts. The extent to which you have performed these procedures is not relevant to the question.

- Total and cross-total all columns in the cash receipts journal.
- Trace postings from the cash receipts journal to the general ledger.
- Examine remittance advices and related correspondence to support entries in the cash receipts journal.

Required:

Considering Gutzler's internal control over cash receipts and standard auditing procedures already performed, list all other auditing procedures and the reasons they should be performed to obtain sufficient audit evidence regarding cash receipts. Do not discuss the procedures for cash disbursements and cash balances and the extent to which any of the procedures are to be performed. Assume there are adequate controls to ensure that all sales transactions are recorded.

Solution:

Other audit procedures	Reason for other audit procedures	Other audit procedures	Reason for other audit procedures
1. Sources of debit entries in the general ledger cash account, other than from the cash receipts journal, should be investigated, and supporting documents should be examined.	1. Because the auditor, using standard procedures, examines only the cash receipts journal, he or she must investigate the validity of all other sources of cash receipts that are not recorded in these journals.	2. There should be a surprise examination of cash receipts. Before the accounts receivable clerk obtains the cash receipts, the auditor should make a list of them without the clerk's knowledge. The undeposited mail receipts should then be controlled after completion of their preparation for deposit and after postings have been made to the subsidiary accounts receivable ledger. The deposit slip should be totaled and compared with the remittances and the list prepared by the auditor for accuracy. Individual items on the deposit slip should be compared with postings to the subsidiary accounts receivable ledger. The auditor should then supervise the mailing of the deposit to the bank. The auditor should ask Gutzler to ask the bank to send the statement containing this deposit directly to the auditor.	2. Because there are no initial controls over cash receipts before the accounts receivable clerk obtains the cash, a surprise examination is the only method of determining whether cash receipts are being recorded and deposited properly.

EXHIBIT 13-10 (continued)

Other audit procedures	Reason for other audit procedures
3. Postings from other deposit slips should be traced to the cash receipts journal and the subsidiary accounts receivable ledger. Also, entries in the subsidiary accounts receivable ledger should be traced to the cash receipts journal and to the deposit slips.	3. Because there is no separation of duties between cash receipts and accounts receivable, the accounts receivable clerk may have been careless in performing his or her posting duties. This procedure may also disclose whether the accounts receivable clerk may have been lapping the accounts.
4. Review the subsidiary accounts receivable ledger, and confirm accounts that have abnormal transaction activity, such as consistently late payments.	4. See 3 above.
5. If Gutzler allows customers to take discounts, the amount of such discounts and the discount period should be checked.	5. Because there is no separation of duties between cash receipts and accounts receivable, the accounts receivable clerk may have appropriated discounts that could have been, but were not, taken or may have been careless in checking the appropriateness of discounts taken.
6. Dates and amounts of daily deposits per bank statements should be compared with entries in the cash receipts journal.	6. Because there are no initial controls over cash receipts before the accounts receivable clerk obtains the cash, he or she may have become careless about promptly depositing the daily receipts.
7. A proof-of-cash working paper should be prepared that reconciles total cash receipts with credits per bank statements. The opening and closing reconciliation of the proof of cash should be compared with the comparable reconciliation prepared by the controller.	7. Because internal control over cash receipts is weak, the auditor should perform this overall check to ensure that he or she has investigated all material items during his or her detail tests.
8. Prepare a ratio analysis of monthly collections to total sales of the preceding month or monthly collections to total accounts receivable at the beginning of the month and compare this analysis with a similar analysis for the preceding year.	8. Because internal control over cash receipts is weak, this overall test may highlight any irregularities
9. Visit the client on the balance sheet date or the next business day to determine whether there has been an appropriate cutoff of cash receipts.	9. Because internal control over cash receipts is weak, the auditor needs to satisfy himself or herself that cash receipts are recorded in the appropriate period.
10. For those periods for which the above audit procedures were not performed and for a period after the balance sheet date, scan the cash receipts journal and bank statements for unusual items.	10. Because internal control over cash receipts is weak, the auditor should perform this review to ensure that he or she has investigated all material items not covered during his or her other tests.

CPA exam, adapted, May 9, 1974, question 3.

pany, the first step is to use an analytical review to assess the reasonableness of recorded balances and their materiality. The second step is to evaluate controls to determine the extent of compliance and substantive tests. The third step is to prepare a schedule of loans receivable that indicates the loan number, the borrower, the date of the loan, the amount of the discount, and the face amount of the note, its term, monthly payment, and current balance. This list should be footed and tied in to the general ledger. Finally, the fourth step is to scan the general ledger control account for unusual entries warranting investigation. By examining the documentation supporting the loans, their propriety can be evaluated. Original loan disbursements should be traced to the cash disbursement records. The computation of discounts should be recomputed on a test basis and tied to interest calculations. Confirmation for a sample of accounts, including small balances, delinquent accounts, and inactive accounts, should be circularized. Cash receipts posted to loans should be compared with the cash receipts records. Delinquent accounts deserve special attention in order to evaluate the allowance for bad debts, usually done by means of inquiry procedures. Analytical review can be used to compare industry experience with reported uncollectibles, to extend reported balances by the market rate to assess the reasonableness of interest income, and to evaluate the adequacy of lending practices with respect to required collateral values.

The extent of the substantive tests, their nature, and their timing depend on the evaluation of the controls and the results of the compliance test work; such interdependence is illustrated in Exhibit 13-10. The CPA exam question describes a client's controls, audit procedures already performed, and then asks that you identify other audit procedures to be performed. The solution provided in Exhibit 13-10 (presented on pages 455 and 456) emphasizes how each suggested procedure relates back to the control system. In the example, several controls over cash receipts are weak, creating a need for additional substantive test work, with an emphasis on cut-off and "surprise" examination. The "surprise" aspect is an example of how the nature of substantive tests can be adapted to respond to varying control conditions.

Now to develop the rationale underlying the common substantive test procedures, let's consider several specific techniques in detail.

EXHIBIT 13-11

Audit Procedures for Confirming Accounts Receivable

1. Using generalized audit software, prepare and foot a detailed listing of accounts receivable, as of the confirmation date, from the subsidiary ledger.
2. Reconcile the balance of that listing with the general ledger.
3. Prepare positive confirmations for a randomly selected sample of the size determined through a mean-per-unit variables estimation.
4. Check replies to confirmations, and investigate all exceptions.
5. Send second requests for all positive confirmations for which no replies have been received within two weeks.
6. Investigate all undelivered requests by the post office, and when possible, remail using revised addresses.
7. Apply alternative auditing procedures to positive confirmation requests that cannot be delivered and to confirmation requests for which no replies are received.

Note: These audit procedures refer to the audit objective of ascertaining the propriety and collectibility of accounts receivable balances.

Confirmation Procedures

A specific audit program relating to accounts receivable confirmation is presented in Exhibit 13-11. Remember that confirmations from customers are better for detecting overstatements, rather than understatements, of accounts receivable. This fact merits consideration in preparing the audit program. CPAs must not delegate responsibility for confirmations to an outside service. GAAS require that those performing the audit be technically trained and proficient. Although the client's employees can help prepare the confirmations, the CPA must exercise thorough control. In particular, the CPA must mail the requests for confirmation and have them returned directly to him or her. A sample positive confirmation form was presented in Chapter 7. Note that exceptions to positive confirmations are to be investigated. Frequently, these stem from differing cut-offs due to in-transit items and can be reconciled with relative ease by the auditor. However, a potential problem exists which relates to those accounts which can not be confirmed.

Confirmation of receivables is a commonly applied audit technique that invariably results in numerous nonresponses ***[SAS 1, Section 331]***. To gain assurance that those receivables are reasonably stated, *alternate procedures* should be applied. This internal evidence strives to evaluate whether a valid transaction had actually occurred prior to the date of confirmation and whether payment for that obligation was received after the date of confirmation. Discussion of the account with the client's credit manager and the examination of credit files may help the auditor gain an understanding of such accounts and their likely collectibility. The evaluation also would include such audit steps as:

- Examining customers' orders or contractual terms (as evidence that a sale occurred).
- Examining the client's duplicate shipping documents (bills of lading), entries to remove inventory from books, and invoices (as evidence that delivery was made and a billing was prepared—perhaps correspondence concerning the shipment is available for review).
- Reviewing payments received from these customers subsequent to the balance sheet date (accounts receivable subsidiary and cash receipts records, checks, authenticated bank deposit slips, and customers' remittance advices—

it is assumed that subsequent payment is strong evidence that the client had a valid claim as of year-end).

Any returns and allowances would be vouched from the sales journal to supporting documents. External inquiries could be made concerning the existence and credit rating of the customer. Special attention should be given to cutoff considerations.

In audits of banks, savings and loans, and finance companies, the client may have certain customers who have requested "no correspondence" on their accounts. In such settings, in lieu of confirmation procedures, borrowers' requests for "no correspondence" should be reviewed, comparing signatures to available signature cards or loan agreements. Subsequent to year-end, collections should be reviewed, as should remittance advices to gain assurance that collections are currently being received on loans. At times, it may be permissible to contact the customer by phone.

When there is no response to a second request concerning accounts thought to be particularly unusual or material, some CPAs will mail a third request or make telephone calls in an effort to get a reply directly from the customer. Sometimes CPAs will use telegrams as effective forms of third requests for confirmation.

If the auditor has not been able to confirm certain receivables that are material, then the auditor's report should indicate this, as in the following example:

> Our examination was made in accordance with generally accepted auditing standards and thus included such tests of the accounting records and such other auditing procedures as we considered necessary in the circumstances. However, it was not practicable to confirm receivables (United States government receivables), as to which we have satisfied ourselves by means of other auditing procedures.

Note that as a matter of policy, the U.S. government will not respond to confirmation requests. If the auditor is satisfied with the validity, amount, and presentation of receivables, no exception is required in the report's opinion paragraph.

The negative form of accounts receivable confirmation might be useful when client records include a large number of relatively small balances. A sample negative confirmation form was provided in Chapter 7. Preferably, when negative confirmations are used, internal controls over accounts receivable are considered to be effective, and the auditor has reason to believe that the persons receiving the requests are likely to give them consideration. Many argue against the use of negative accounts receivable confirmations due to the fact that the inference that is drawn from receiving no reply may not be correct.

Whenever receivables have been confirmed at an interim date, it is important that the receivable control account be analyzed for unusual entries from interim to year-end. A comparison to the prior year's corresponding time period and investigation of significant variations is appropriate. Any principal entries during that period should be vouched back to underlying documents such as invoices and cash tickets. Thought should be given to the risk of entries in the sales journal not having been posted to the general ledger control accounts. At year-end, trial balances should be tested for clerical accuracy and reconciled to the control accounts. Any very significant accounts not confirmed at interim may be confirmed at year-end.

The potential flaws in confirmation procedures have been borne out by past frauds. One case in which a division manager had instructed customers to make checks payable to him, cashed the checks, and withheld proceeds nevertheless resulted in no exceptions to confirmation procedures. The manager had contacted the customers whose payments had been withheld, and told them to ignore the statements. Any customers who called concerning exceptions were told that the company knew the letters were in error, and he would correct their account. Clearly, efforts are needed by the profession to encourage customers to write exceptions to auditors, rather than directing them to the client, and *not* to follow requests by others that they ignore verification letters. This case is similar to that of the *Hochfelder* case discussed in the chapter on litigation, since in *Hochfelder* exceptions were not reported by customers who dealt directly with the CEO of an investment firm and were told not to expect either monthly statements or confirmations to reflect their "special transactions." Frauds involving fictitious accounts receivable have been covered up by the defrauder's rental of post office boxes and response to confirmations.

Of course, sloppiness by the defrauder—such as the return of all confirmations from one locale—has been detected by careful audit work (e.g., alertness to the postmark on the confirmation responses).

Attention to the Risk of Lapping

The confirmation of accounts receivable may need to be augmented if an irregularity such as lapping is suspected ***[SAS 16, Section 327]***. *Lapping* is a defalcation intended to conceal cash shortages. To perpetrate such a fraud, a cash receipt from a customer is withheld from the bank deposit. A few days later, a remittance from a second customer is credited to the first customer's account. Shortages are continuously shifted from account to account, with subsequent receipts credited to the wrong account receivable. This delaying of the crediting of cash receipts to the proper accounts receivable may be uncovered through applying the procedures presented in Exhibit 13-12.

Certain operating conditions can make it easier to perpetrate a fraud such as lapping. Consider the setting in which a manufacturer had inventory in short supply and deliveries to customers took a month or longer. Prescribed procedures were for the salesman to prepare a merchandise order form and have a receipt issued by a teller on a cash register. The order form was three part: a customer's invoice, a salesman's copy, and a notification of delivery. A salesman used the customer's knowledge of inventory shortages to his advantage. He convinced customers that if they paid cash at the time of sale, that would assist in ensuring delivery; then the salesman filled in the invoice copy of the merchandise form. Later, he set the correct merchandise order in motion, paying the money.

The control necessary to deter such lapping is eliminating the invoice copy of the order form and advising customers of delivery as part of the billing process. Even in this case, if customers are willing to accept something other than an official receipt as evidence of payment, lapping could reoccur.

EXHIBIT 13-12
Audit Procedures to Detect Lapping

- Audit the aging of accounts receivable.
- Confirm accounts receivable—particularly noting exceptions pertaining to payment dates— on a surprise basis at an interim date (expected year-end confirmations can be anticipated by a person lapping accounts and possibly be covered up by means of some alternate misstatement such as kiting), and mail positive confirmations directly to all customers with old balances.
- On a surprise basis, count cash and customers' checks on hand, control the bank deposit, and then compare details of the deposit with the cash receipts book and the accounts receivable records.
- Compare billings and monthly statements to customers with the accounts receivable subsidiary ledger.
- Make copies of duplicate deposit slips, before and after examination, and have them authenticated by the bank—not only by amounts but also by slips' detail.* Compare customers' names, dates, and amounts on these authenticated slips with remittance lists and entries in the cash receipts book and with postings to subsidiary ledger accounts. Alternatively, intercept deposits and compare the items being deposited with the deposit slip, or when microfilms of checks being deposited are made, the microfilms with the deposit slips.
- Check vouchers received with the customers' checks that often are stamped upon receipt. Compare the dates of such vouchers with stamped duplicate deposit slips and recording dates in the cash receipts book.
- Verify that noncash credits to receivables, such as write-offs, returns and allowances, and discounts, are proper.
- Foot the cash receipts journal, accounts receivable subsidiary ledger, and the accounts receivable control account, and reconcile the detail to the control.

*Often, such detail is not checked by banks. The total deposit is checked, but the details can easily be misstated. For that reason, authenticated deposit slips may be of questionable value in detecting lapping.

Note: This exhibit is adapted from AICPA exam questions on lapping that appeared in earlier CPA examinations.

Kiting

Kiting is a defalcation intended to conceal cash shortages or bank overdrafts or to pad a cash position. Such procedures take advantage of the "float" period during which a check is in transit between banks. The deposit of unrecorded, fictitious NSF checks or a transfer check drawn on another bank but not recorded as a deposit or disbursement can create the agreement between the bank and the books for a few days. Such checks can be made in an amount exceeding an intended overdraft. Whenever transfers are made from one bank to another and the deposit is recorded but the disbursement is not recorded until the following period, kiting can effectively pad the cash position. Usually the credit on the books is made to revenue and the debit to an expense account. Since kiting is very much related to cut-off (as is lapping), the discussion of how kiting might be detected is deferred to a later chapter on special audit risks (Chapter 16).

Numerical Sequence Checks

To determine that there is effective control over sales invoices, the auditor should test their numerical sequence. While the following program is tailored to invoices, it is indicative of the types of tests performed on the sequence of a great variety of accounting-related documents. A sequence check of invoices can be performed by:

- Reviewing unissued sales invoices.
- Randomly selecting a few monthly reconciliations for the numerical sequences and reviewing them for propriety, noting follow-ups of any old outstanding invoices, to gain assurance that all invoices for goods shipped are forwarded for processing.
- Reviewing the sequence of the numerical sales invoices file for the randomly selected months.
- Reviewing on a surprise basis the numerical suspense file for invoices over a month old to determine whether there has been a follow-up.

Considerations for Decentralized Operations

When cash receipts are collected at decentralized sales offices and then transferred to the home office by check, there are risks of improper cut-off, kiting, and the improper use of cash. To audit such transfers at year-end, a schedule of transfer payments should be prepared for the two-week periods before and after the fiscal year-end. Attention should be given to the dates on canceled checks, the agreement of total transfers and collections, and the date of transfers of checks issued to the home office.

If there are branch offices, the first audit decision will be to determine the principal risk areas and then how each branch is ranked accordingly. This ranking can aid in the selection of which offices are to be tested. Key questions of interest include:

- What is the general character of the office?
  - location
  - type of customers
  - experience of personnel
  - operating efficiency
- What is that office's experience in the risk areas (e.g., for branch loan offices, what is their delinquency and charge-off experience)?
- Has the office expanded or contracted in terms of volume of business?
- What condition of the office has been noted in terms of attitudes of office personnel in furnishing information, assisting auditors, and handling customers?
- What is the extent of transactions which are in some sense "special"? (This could range from related parties to banks' customers who have requested no correspondence.)

During visits to branch offices, it is possible to collect information that would improve the effectiveness of audit procedures later applied to home office. Specifically, the auditor can prepare a list of branch office employees actually observed and compare that list to payroll records at home office. She or he can review charge-offs for comparison to home office expectations, noting who was involved in granting and charging off such loans or accounts. Of course, more generally, branch office field visits provide the auditor with a good sense of the control environment.

Decentralized operations often mean small district offices which, because of their size, cannot appropriately segregate duties. Perhaps a single clerk does the billing, bookkeeping, and cashiering. In this case, an accounting supervisor should visit each district office frequently, balance the cashier's fund monthly, and approve any credit memos and daily reports by the cashier. Despite such controls, instances have arisen in which the clerk nevertheless managed to avoid reporting certain accounts, manually billed selected accounts, and pocketed cash receipts. Such experiences bear out how important it is to remove billing and bookkeeping functions from decentralized units and to centralize these operations. The district clerk ought to be responsible only for cashiering and other operating procedures.

Note that one of the few auditing procedures that might have been able to detect this type of problem would be a check of billings against the customer listing. However, if the branch office initiated customer relationships, then the central office may not have a customer listing capable of identifying the defalcation.

Adapting to Weak Controls

When duties are improperly combined, detailed tests of deposits to the cash receipts journal and the subsidiary ledger can be effective in gaining assurance that lapping is not a problem. Similarly, recomputations help assess risks from carelessness or intentional misstatement. To ensure against carelessness in handling cash receipts, the dates and amounts of deposits to the cash receipts journal should be compared, and a proof-of-cash working paper, reconciling receipts with credits for each bank statement, should be prepared. When controls over cash are weak, a ratio analysis of collections to receivables and to earlier periods can highlight irregularities. The number of days sales in receivables can also be computed and compared with expectations. In addition, special attention would need to be given to cut-off. Added assurance that material items were not missed can be provided by scanning both cash receipts and bank statements for unusual items.

Sales

Often the reasonableness of overall sales can be calculated by applying the expected markup percentage to the recorded cost of sales. The main difference between an audit of the balance sheet and an audit of the income statement is that the audit of the income statement deals with the verification of transactions. Analytical review can be useful in auditing revenues, and ratio analysis of sales to inventory purchases, production, bad debts, and receivables can be very revealing.

Procedures to audit sales should include:

- Tracing of postings from the sales journal to invoice copies (thereby testing that sales were billed to customers).
- Tracing data from sales invoices to the sales journal (thereby testing that sales were recorded).
- Determining that all shipping documents have been accounted for (a completeness check).
- Examining documents for appropriate approval, including the granting of credit, shipment of goods, and determination of price and billing (to ensure transactions were appropriately authorized).
- Determining the extent and nature of business transacted with major customers, emphasizing disclosure requirements and identification of related parties (to ensure the presentation and disclosure are adequate).
- Verifying the sales cut-off at the beginning and end of the period to determine whether the recorded sales represent revenues of the period.
- Testing of pricing by comparing invoices to the daily price list (to ensure the accuracy of recorded transactions).
- Analytical review of total recorded sales, relative to history, expectations, and industry experience.

Note that these procedures reflect a combination of compliance and substantive tests—many are dual-purpose. Those procedures answering questions as to whether a control procedure (such as authorization) was performed, by whom, and when constitute compliance tests. These tests are typically performed through inquiry, observation, and inspection procedures. Those providing information on the propriety of balances are forms of substantive evidence. The efficiency of the audit process can be enhanced by applying the computer, as described in Chapter 10. Exhibit 13-13 gives some examples of how EDP can be used to test sales.

It is important to tie audit procedures to the auditor's objective and the type of risk exposure being assessed. For example, by tracing copies of sales invoices to shipping documents, evidence can be provided that billed sales were shipped. This relates to the validity of recorded sales.

Sales cut-off should be tested by selecting representative sales transactions for the last few days of the current year and the first few days in the following year and vouching them to the related shipping documents. Then a sample for the simi-

EXHIBIT 13-13
The Computer As an Audit Tool in Testing Revenue

Substantive tests of sales can be conducted using EDP in the following manner:

- Test the extensions and footings of computerized sales records that are the basis for preparing invoices and the sales journal.
- Verify the mathematical accuracy of postings from the sales journal to the appropriate ledger accounts.
- Account for the numerical sequence of all sales invoices and other related documents.
- Review the sales journal or accounts receivable subsidiary ledger based on predetermined criteria, to select sales transactions for review (e.g., aged accounts, accounts above a certain dollar amount, and a random selection of accounts).
- Print a work paper, listing each item selected, with relevant data inserted in applicable columns.
- Select all debits posted to sales and all postings to sales that were posted from sources other than the sales journal.
- Analyze recorded sales by using ratios, percentage relationships, trends, and similar predetermined criteria both annually and periodically.
- Compare duplicate data maintained in separate files for correctness, e.g., quantities sold per client records can be compared with quantities shipped.
- Test records' completeness by checking fields of interest to assess quality of information system.
- Prepare sales analyses by quantity, product line, salesperson, territory, and customer class, and review them for overall reasonableness.

lar time frame should be traced from the shipping documents to the related entries in the records. This ties back to the auditor's concern of whether transactions are recorded in the appropriate period.

Unrecorded sales at the balance sheet date can be revealed by comparing shipping documents with sales records. This is essentially a test for completeness. In order to verify that all sales transactions have been recorded, a test of transactions should be completed on a representative sample drawn from the shipping clerk's file of duplicate copies of bills of lading.[4]

Billings

When testing the billing cycle, auditors will usually

- Select a sample of sales tickets and trace the data on those tickets to the customers' account cards (to test the accuracy of recorded transactions).
- Check the completeness of all used and unused sales ticket numbers.
- Inspect the sample of sales tickets for genuineness, that is, the presence of customers' signatures.
- Recompute extensions and footings on the tickets to test their accuracy.
- Compare the sales prices on the sales tickets with authoritative sources of price information (to ensure that the prices were properly authorized and were accurate).
- Foot daily sales tapes, if it is a retail operation, tracing totals to the billing control account (to test both accuracy and completeness).
- Foot the billing control account, scan for unusual items, and investigate unusual entries in the control account, thereby testing both accuracy and propriety.
- Examine any entries related to misfiled sales tickets or other correcting entries, emphasizing their propriety.
- Total balances on account cards and compare them with the control, investigating unusual entries and thereby testing accuracy.
- Determine whether there are any efforts to collect on overdue accounts, as one measure of the client's efforts to safeguard assets.
- Compare the posting of the data on sales tickets with the statements and account cards (to test completeness and accuracy).
- Compare the total of the postings accumulated in the billing machine register, if applicable, with the total determined from a summary of daily tapes from sales tickets (to test completeness and accuracy).
- For smaller accounts, prepare and mail negative

[4]These program steps (and those for billings) parallel those appearing in suggested solutions to various past CPA exam questions pertaining to the audit of the revenue cycle; hence, the AICPA's permission to use these materials is gratefully acknowledged.

confirmation requests under the control of the auditor, and utilize positive confirmations for larger balances, those with credit balances, delinquent accounts, and a sample of accounts written off (to test validity, completeness, accuracy, and accounting in the appropriate period).

Invoices should be compared with copies of the corresponding bills of lading to ascertain that the goods were shipped. The information on the sales order forms should be compared with that on prepared invoices to see that the customers' orders were filled. The billing prices should be checked to confirm that they are both current and correct, and then invoice prices should be tied to the unit price listing. All extensions and additions should be recalculated, providing evidence of accurate billings.

Accounts Receivable

Generalized audit software can be used to audit the validity, accuracy, and age of accounts receivable ***[SAS 48, Section 326]***. As examples, the match capability (discussed in Chapter 10) can be used to tie in accounts receivable to master files of employees, officers, directors, and affiliated companies and generate a listing for investigation of related party transactions. The authorized credit limits per customer can be compared with account balances and an exception listing of balances that exceed limits can be printed for follow-up. Files of trial balances and subsidiary ledgers can be footed and totals compared. In addition, a sample of accounts can be selected for detailed computation of ending balances by starting with the balance from the prior year's audit, and exceptions can be documented. It is a simple task to generate an aging schedule of accounts receivable to facilitate a review of collectibility.

In auditing accounts receivable, EDP can be used to

- Test extensions and footings.
- Select and print confirmation requests.
- Examine records for quality (their completeness, consistency, validity, and the like, through checks on reasonableness and completeness of fields, and limit tests).
- Summarize data and perform analyses useful to the auditor (for example, aging).
- Select and print audit samples.
- Compare duplicate data (maintained in separate files) for correctness and consistency (for example, compare catalogue prices with invoice prices).
- Compare confirmation information with company records.
- Print a work-paper listing of accounts selected.
- Compare balance with customer's history of purchases to check whether credit limits have been exceeded.

In auditing accounts receivable, a sample of entries in the detail of sales returns and allowances should be traced to the supporting approved credit memo, receiving ticket, and, when applicable, to the corresponding entry in accounts receivable. These constitute tests of the propriety of recorded transactions.

Special care should be taken with transactions involving related parties. Receivables should be confirmed and their nature, substance of terms, and plans for liquidating commitments should be investigated. Extensive discussion of related parties is postponed to Chapter 16 on special audit risks.

Uncollectibles

Auditing accounts receivable uncollectibles requires (1) tracing the write-off of bad debts to the Allowance for Doubtful Accounts, (2) testing the propriety and approval of write-offs by examining the underlying documentation, (3) confirming large or unusual accounts written off, and (4) reviewing past due accounts with a responsible official to assess their collectibility and test the adequacy of the valuation account.

The adequacy of the allowance for doubtful accounts can be determined by reviewing agings of receivables, reviewing credit and collection files, comparing previous years' and industry experiences, discussing past-due accounts with client personnel, and reviewing for subsequent collections. For large receivable balances, the customer's recent financial statements and similar data should be studied for the adequacy of control over write-offs and correspondence concerning disputes, credit reports, and bankruptcy proceedings. The better the controls, the less extensive the tracing, testing, confirming, and reviewing procedures required.

Notes Receivable

For notes receivable, there must be evidence of their existence, valuation, classification, cut-off, and disclosure adequacy. Auditing procedures include

- inspecting each note and checking its amount, maker, issue date, due date, interest rate, collateral, payee, and endorsee.
- obtaining a positive confirmation of outstanding notes—including amounts, interest rate, date, due date, and collateral on the notes—reconciling reply differences, and following up on those not answered.
- determining collectibility by assessing the value of collateral, the maker's likelihood of payment, and the adequacy of the allowance for doubtful accounts by comparing to past experience.
- for outstanding notes, tying in purchase, shipping, and invoice documents; also checking collections, write-offs, and authorizations for written-off accounts.
- testing accrued interest receivable by using interest rate data and collection information.
- asking about management policies, agreements, and unusual transactions and obtaining a representation letter covering the validity of the notes, contingent liabilities, adequacy of the allowance for bad debts, the pledging of notes as collateral to liabilities, and other material matters concerning other phases of the audit.
- evaluating of overall validity by means of ratio and trend analysis.
- separately examining related-party transactions, verifying timely repayment, and checking into renewal practices.

Dividend Income

The accuracy of recorded dividend income can be verified by comparing recorded dividends with a standard financial reporting service's record of dividends, such as Standard and Poor's or Moody's.

Putting It All Together

In reading descriptions of control considerations, possible compliance test and substantive test procedures, and detailed program steps for various phases of the revenue cycle, it is sometimes difficult to see how these aspects of auditing revenue tie together. The auditor's objectives can be expressed in terms of collecting evidence that specific errors do not exist. Then preventive and/or detective controls are considered to evaluate the potential for reliance. Of course, as the introductory case demonstrated, the definitions of preventive and detective controls often shift when actually applying control procedures. The risk of a preventive control actually being detective in operation should be an explicit consideration of an auditor in evaluating control. If the auditor believes that reliance is cost-beneficial, compliance tests are performed, then those tests are the basis for selecting substantive test procedures. Exhibit 13-14 illustrates how each of these steps ties together for four different error types, commonly of interest to the auditor. It is important to note that conclusions on each error will be drawn by considering the audit experience in other operating cycles as well. Clearly, collectibility issues interrelate with the likelihood of customer satisfaction. The cost of sales cycle encompasses the purchasing and production activities that implicitly determine the quality of goods and services provided. Similarly, the finance cycle encompasses the entire reporting function, the investment and borrowing of cash, and internal audit department activities—all of which are relevant to evaluate risks within the revenue cycle.

All audit conclusions reflect the interface of the various cycles and can be viewed as evaluations of specific error types: their probability and the likely dollar effects.

To better blend the control evaluation, computer audit, and statistical sampling tools introduced in earlier chapters, an example of one phase of an audit concerning the revenue cycle will now be provided.

EXHIBIT 13-14

The Tie-in of Possible Errors, Controls, Compliance, and Substantive Test Work in the Revenue Cycle

	Controls		Compliance Tests		Substantive Tests	
Error	Preventive	Detective	Preventive	Detective	Interim	Final
Goods shipped but not billed.	–Controlled access to shipping area. –Segregated duties. –Prenumbered shipping documents, sales orders, and invoices. –Matching of sales orders, shipping documents, and invoices.	–Independent review of sequence of prenumbered documents. –Independent review of unmatched shipping documents. –Independent review of reasonableness of sales and inventory shortages.	–Observe shipping area. –Observe separate sales orders, billings, and inventory control areas. –Examine used and unused documents for prenumbering. –Examine system of numbering incoming sales orders. –Examine logs or system in place for matching documents.	–Examine initials supporting review. –Examine evidence of separate reasonableness tests, e.g., in the internal audit work papers. –Examine evidence of separate review of inventory shortages.	–Trace shipping documents to invoices, accounting for description and quantity. –Trace sales orders to invoices to ensure all sales received were billed.	–Review all sales orders and shipping documents, determining most likely error.
Goods returned but no credit given to customer.	–Separate receiving department to handle returned goods. –Prenumbered receiving slips for returned goods. –Prenumbered credit memoranda. –Matching of receiving slips with credit memoranda.	–Independent review of sequence of prenumbered documents. –Independent review of unmatched credit memoranda and receiving slips. –Investigation of overdue accounts receivable records. –Investigation of customers' complaints.	–Examine documentation supporting write-offs. –Examine initials on write-offs indicating independent review before recording of write-offs.	–Examine initials supporting review. –Examine evidence of review of overdue accounts receivable. –Examine evidence of how customer complaints have been handled.	–Trace returned goods on receiving slips to credit memoranda. –Confirm invoices with customer, especially if overdue. –Examine correspondence from customers in credit department files.	–Confirm accounts receivable or unpaid older invoices at year end. –For last month of fiscal year, trace returned goods on receiving reports to credit memoranda.
Cash not recorded or deposited.	–Require two people to be present when mail is opened. –For over-the-counter receipts, use locked box or a cash register with standard controls.	–Separate cash receipts from accounts receivable. –Send monthly statements to customers, using a person other than the one posting detailed receivable records. –Investigate customers' complaints. –Regularly review aged trial balance and independently inquire into problems with collections.	–Observe opening of mail. –Observe system for handling over-the-counter cash receipts.	–Observe segregation of duties. –Observe practice of sending monthly statements, noting separation of duties. –Examine work papers or reports that document how customers' complaints have been handled. –Examine aged trial balance and related analyses performed.	–Confirm open accounts receivable, particularly if overdue. –Examine correspondence from customers in credit department files. –Prepare daily totals of receipts and trace to deposits, accounting for unusual variations in amounts deposited.	–Confirm year-end accounts receivable.
Unauthorized write-offs of accounts either collectible or already collected and not deposited.	–Require write-offs to be supported by documentation of collection attempts and response, if any, from customer. –Approval of write-off by someone independent from the credit granting and cash receipts functions.	–Compare amount written off against new sales to "reasonableness" benchmark (based on past experience and industry experience). –Review approvals by independent party, as well as substantiation for write-offs.	–Examine documentation supporting a reasonableness review of write-offs. –Examine initials indicating independent review was made of support for write-offs.	–Examine working papers supporting reasonableness review of write-offs. –Examine initials indicating an independent review of the support for write-offs.	–Confirm write-offs with customers. –Examine correspondence or other documentation supporting write-offs.	–Extend interim work to additional write-offs between interim date and year end.

Adapted from Jay M. Smith, "An Analysis of the Effectiveness and Efficiency of Substantive Auditing Procedures," working paper, Brigham Young University, 1980.

An Example: Analyzing Receivables

The main objective in auditing receivables is to gain assurance that they are bona fide, properly classified receivables, for which adequate allowances have been provided for related uncollectibles. In addition, any receivables that have been pledged, discounted, assigned, or sold should be properly disclosed. All significant credit balances should be reclassified to accounts payable, and any collateral held as partial security should be clearly described.

In auditing receivables, consideration of the work performed by the internal auditors, if they make periodic test confirmations of receivables, may influence the scope of work. Of course, the working papers of the internal auditors would be reviewed to assess the adequacy of their work. Assume that the auditor has evaluated controls over receivables and has performed compliance tests for the revenue cycle; further assume that controls are considered good.

An audit program for receivables was presented as Exhibit 13-11. Assuming that program was applied, how would the auditor select the sample size for circularizing receivables and proceed to evaluate the replies received? To demonstrate the process, a mean-per-unit or direct-projection sampling technique will be applied to a mini-case example.

A Statistical Sampling Application

Accounts receivable confirmations may be circularized with several objectives in mind ***[SAS 39, Section 350].*** One likely objective is to test whether accounts are materially accurate and to measure the extent of any material misstatement by using some form of classical variables sampling like the mean-per-unit estimation technique.

As an example, let us assume that an entity has a total of $20 million of accounts receivable on the books, for twenty thousand customers. Based on a generalized audit software application, the standard deviation of recorded receivables is measured as $400. The desired precision at a 90 percent confidence level is $850,000. (Note that the acceptability of 90 percent confidence rather than 95 percent reflects the auditor's planned reliance on controls.) The required sample size would be:

$$n = \left(\frac{1.65 * 400 * 20{,}000}{850{,}000}\right)^2 = 241.16$$

Rounded to 242 confirmations, assume that a random number generator was used to select the accounts to be circularized. Generalized audit software was used to print the confirmations for the selected accounts, generating a control listing for the work papers (Exhibit 13-15 offers an application chart outlining this use of generalized audit software). After second requests were mailed, a total of two hundred clean replies were received, and an additional thirty receivable balances were judged to be accurate, based on effective alternative procedures (that is, no reply was received from these thirty customers despite the second requests). Then assume that three replies indicated that there were errors. In order to analyze these results, it is useful to make analogies between the sampling experience and the population. If all twenty thousand customers had been circularized, the responses would have been expected to include about 83 percent, or 16,529 customers' receivables, with clean replies; another 12 percent or 2,479 customers' receivables, with accurate balances based on alternative procedures; 1 percent, or 248 receivables, with errors (that is, differences reported that were not due to payments in transit or other acceptable reasons that a customer might disagree with the confirmation's balance); and 4 percent, or 744 receivables, with no assurance provided through confirmation or alternative procedures. The mean of the sample was $1,011, translating into a population book value of $20,220,000 (that is, $1,011 * 20,000 items). The precision limits yield a confidence interval of $20,220,000 ± 850,000, or $19,370,000 to $21,070,000. The book value of $20,000,000 is within this acceptable range.

But what about the 4 percent of receivables that were virtually unauditable? They could be caused by customers who paid lump sums that could not be tied to the specific receivable amounts of concern or by customers who had not yet paid. Assuming a mean-per-unit extension, this represents an estimated $808,800 of book value at risk (that is, .04 * $20,220,000). If this entire amount were overstated by 78 percent, the book value would lie within the confidence interval formed around the statistical sample's mean value. Because such a large

EXHIBIT 13-15
An Accounts Receivable Application Chart Using Generalized Audit Software

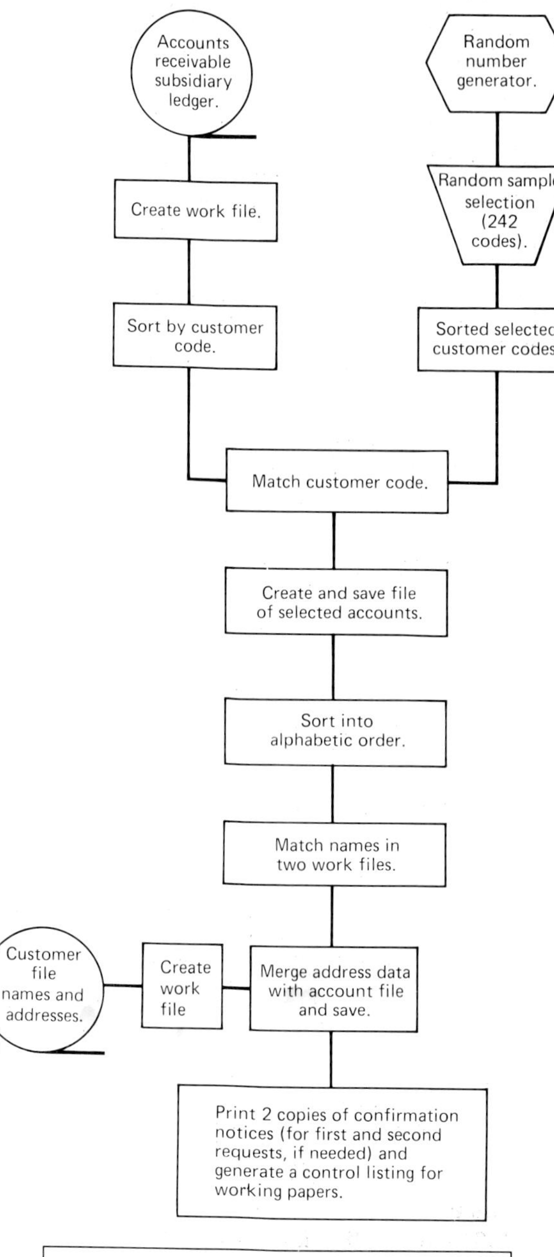

misstatement is extremely unlikely at a high level of confidence (particularly in light of the client's good internal control), the auditor should conclude that the receivables are reasonable.

The main points in this revenue cycle sampling plan are that

1. The audit objective must determine the sampling approach.
2. Low error rates preclude the use of ratio or differencing approaches.
3. The adequacy of the audit procedure should be determined in light of the auditor's planned reliance on controls, as
   a. the confirmation approach is exposed to nonresponse risk.
   b. alternative procedures commonly focus on subsequent cash receipts unlikely to have been received by all customers, and so audit coverage may not be available on all accounts.
4. Statistical sampling can be easily used by means of generalized audit software on machine-readable account balances.

The working papers that show the confirmation work should state

- whether positive or negative (or some combination thereof) confirmations were mailed.
- how the receivables were selected for testing.
- how all differences disclosed in the confirmation replies were investigated.
- what the reasons were for differences and how they were verified.
- the work done on all confirmations reporting differences obtained after the end of the last year's field work.
- how nonreplies were tested through alternative procedures.
- the tie-in of interim work to year-end balances.

The best alternative procedure when accounts receivable confirmation procedures are not applied is the examination of subsequent receipts of year-end receivables.

Besides confirmations, (1) the clerical accuracy of the receivable trial balances and the aging of receivables should be tested; (2) accounting procedures should be tested, by tracing charges to receivables to sources of the original entry; and (3) accounts with credit balances should be listed for reclassification purposes, if these accounts are expected to be numerous. The nature and extent of work performed in the receivable area should be documented, including how the allowance for doubtful accounts was reviewed. *Note that the additional results of a control evaluation, beyond accepting a lower level of confidence are that the scope of confirmation might be reduced and its timing might be shifted to an interim date.*

Note the *complementary* sources of information which exist in relation to receivables. Confirmations from banks, review of the minutes of the board of directors' meetings, and inquiries of management regarding subsequent events all can provide information about the status of receivables, their pledged and discounted nature, and the likelihood of collection. A sales cut-off test of billings similarly complements the verification of accounts receivable.

The Audit Process for the Revenue Cycle: An Overview

When auditing revenue, the auditor will first use analytical review tools to assess the reasonableness of revenue and formulate an understanding of materiality for planning purposes. Then he or she will review the system of internal control to determine the audit plan, will trace the amounts on the income statement to the general ledger, and will foot that ledger account. The idea is to see that revenues are properly accumulated and summarized in the accounts. In addition, the auditor should examine any unusual entries, test postings from books of original entry to ensure that the double-entry system is operating effectively, and trace the journal entries to the ledger on a test basis. To merit reliance on controls, the auditor would have to perform compliance tests, by drawing a sample of the customer orders or contracts that create revenue, so as to test them for proper authorization, date, amount, terms, and classification. Customer orders or contracts should be compared with shipping documents, the sales invoice, subsequent collections, and the detailed customers' records. In addition to tracing from source documents to journals to test completeness, a sample of recorded transactions should be vouched to supporting documents to test the validity of recorded sales. Finally, the daily cash records should be checked against the customer's original contract or order.

If customers are allowed to cancel their orders, the auditor should select a sample of canceled contracts and trace them back to supporting documents, including approval and notification to customers, thus confirming their cancellation.

Tests of detail usually include circularizing positive and/or negative receivable balances and testing a representative sample of shipping notices, to see that all shipments were billed. Billings should be tested for accuracy regarding customer, terms, quantities, prices, and extensions. Postings of billings should be reviewed and scanning used to identify unusual transactions which merit investigation. Analytical review procedures should be used to assess the reasonableness of revenue, perhaps through comparisons by product line, location, or customer type with industry statistics, budgeted data, or historical experience ***[SAS 23, Section 318]***. Related accounts such as sales to production or purchases should be studied for consistency. Overall tests of revenue should include evaluations of the maximum sales possible, the approximate result of extending units sold by average price, and the implications of capacity constraints for reported sales numbers.

The entire audit process will be directed at a set of audit objectives that essentially relate to ensuring against the "What Could Go Wrong?" risk exposures described earlier. Audit assurance that material misstatements stemming from those errors have not occurred in the revenue cycle form an important part of the basis for expressing an audit opinion. Internal auditors add a dimension which extends the typical external audit process: operating efficiency considerations. Often internal auditors are requested to review the effectiveness of sales efforts. Overall credit and cash management procedures can be evaluated in cost/benefit terms regarding their effects on total sales, bad debt expense, net income, and cash balances. This information can be utilized by the external auditor to evaluate the collectibility of receivables and the

EXHIBIT 13-16
Factors Affecting Audit Programs

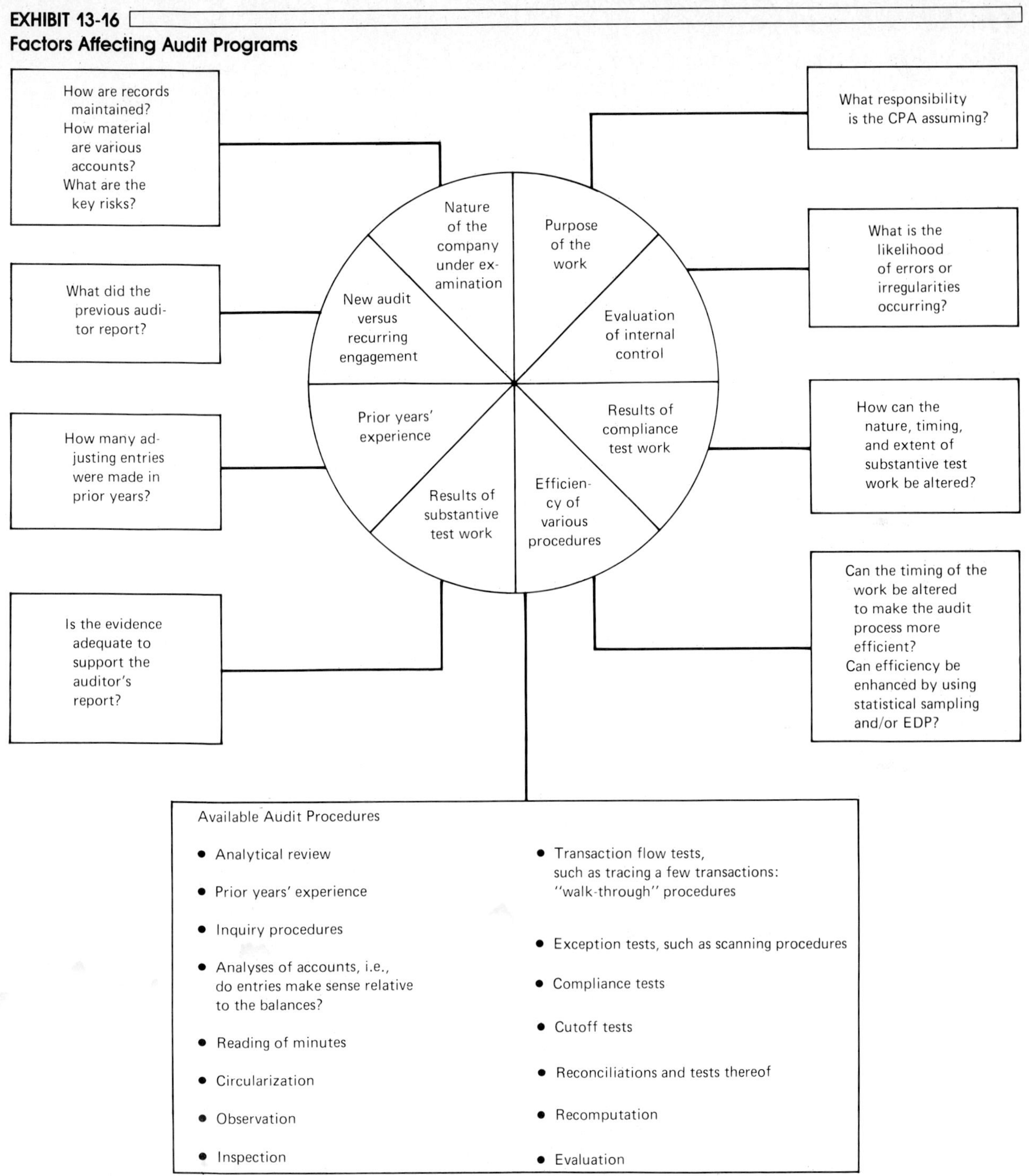

How are records maintained? How material are various accounts? What are the key risks?
What did the previous auditor report?
How many adjusting entries were made in prior years?
Is the evidence adequate to support the auditor's report?
Nature of the company under examination
Purpose of the work
Evaluation of internal control
Results of compliance test work
Efficiency of various procedures
Results of substantive test work
Prior years' experience
New audit versus recurring engagement
What responsibility is the CPA assuming?
What is the likelihood of errors or irregularities occurring?
How can the nature, timing, and extent of substantive test work be altered?
Can the timing of the work be altered to make the audit process more efficient? Can efficiency be enhanced by using statistical sampling and/or EDP?
Available Audit Procedures
• Analytical review
• Prior years' experience
• Inquiry procedures
• Analyses of accounts, i.e., do entries make sense relative to the balances?
• Reading of minutes
• Circularization
• Observation
• Inspection
• Transaction flow tests, such as tracing a few transactions: "walk-through" procedures
• Exception tests, such as scanning procedures
• Compliance tests
• Cutoff tests
• Reconciliations and tests thereof
• Recomputation
• Evaluation

reasonableness of recorded balances. When auditing receivables, the auditor must gain a knowledge of the number of receivable accounts, how those accounts are maintained, what the terms of sales are, how often statements are sent to customers, and whether these statements are transcripts of open terms or something else. An understanding of the underlying operations, accounting system, and controls are essential to the auditor in formulating an audit plan.

Open-invoice files have become increasingly common as the mode of maintaining receivable records. Specifically, they are a series of files consisting of copies of uncollected invoices in numerical, alphabetical, or geographical order that show the detail receivable record. Upon receiving payment, the invoice copies are pulled from the "open" file and placed in a "paid" file, typically filed by customer name. A tabulation of the invoices for each customer at any one time represents the equivalent of an accounts receivable trial balance. The approach to confirming receivables must adapt to such variations in accounting practices.

Similarly, *cycle billing* is often used by retailers, public utilities, and other operations dealing in a large volume of relatively small accounts. The detail accounts receivable ledger is divided into alphabetic, geographic, or account numbers in order to spread billings throughout the month. Separate control accounts are maintained for each cycle.

Since every audit engagement is unique, audit programs must be tailored to the circumstances encountered. For example, open invoice systems would require an invoice orientation when performing confirmation procedures. Confirmations would likewise have to be tailored to cycle billings. Hence, no "all purpose" audit program is feasible. Exhibit 13-16 summarizes the various factors likely to affect audit programs. As we proceed through the cost of sales and financing cycle, you will notice that per cycle, the same set of alternative procedures can be proposed, as the key difference in cycles is the actual documents analyzed or tested rather than the procedures performed ***[SAS 31, Section 326]***. Exhibit 13-16 is intended to remind us of the available audit tools; recall that these terms were introduced in earlier chapters. Each of these has been and will be referred to as we explore some of the more common audit approaches in each of the cycles.

REVIEW QUESTIONS

1. Your client has launched a big year-end sales campaign using unusual selling terms. As a result, a large quantity of goods were sold before year-end. Does this campaign require disclosure? On what assumptions is your response based? What circumstances would make you change your response?
2. What is the error analysis process of auditing?
3. What are bridging working papers?
4. Define what comprises the revenue cycle.
5. Describe the purpose of the following forms commonly used to document the revenue cycle:
   a. Bill of lading.
   b. Customer's statement.
   c. Open customer orders.
   d. Write-off and recovery report.
   e. Remittance advice.
6. What duties should be segregated in the collections or cash receipts department? Why?
7. Describe the risks in a shipping department and the controls for such risks.
8. What special control problems do coupons present, and how should they be controlled?
9. Which disclosure issues often arise within the revenue cycle?
10. How does the control of a revenue cycle for a not-for-profit entity differ from that for a profit-oriented operation?
11. What factors affect audit programs? Is an "all-purpose" audit program possible? Why or why not?
12. What is PBC? Why is such a notation made?
13. What is the difference between lead schedules and detailed schedules?
14. What should an auditor do when he or she does not get a response to a second confirmation request?
15. What is lapping, and how can an auditor detect it?
16. What is kiting?
17. How is a sequence check performed for sales invoices?
18. How does decentralization of a client's operations affect the audit process? Be specific.
19. How can EDP be used to audit accounts receivable?
20. Give an example of the tie-in of possible errors, controls, compliance tests, and substantive tests in the revenue cycle.

EXERCISES

1. The typical internal control questionnaire for cash receipts asks the following questions:

	Yes	No
a. Is incoming mail opened under dual control?	___	___
b. Is a record maintained of all items received, showing who recorded the transactions?	___	___
c. Are all checks received immediately restrictively endorsed?	___	___
d. Have banks been formally notified that they should not cash checks of others that are made payable to the company?	___	___

What is the purpose of each of the controls suggested by this questionnaire? How can an auditor test for compliance with such controls? How is the adequacy of these controls likely to affect substantive tests?

2. What does the confirmation procedure fail to indicate in regard to the accounts receivable balance?

3. An auditor uses SPS for accounts receivable but is concerned about understatements and zero balances. How can the auditor address such concerns?

4. In audits of banks, it is common to review officers', employees', and directors' accounts for propriety. These include checking, savings, CD's, and loans. Vacation schedules are reviewed and lists prepared of all bank personnel who failed to take at least two weeks' vacation at one time during the last vacation period. In addition, the directorate is studied for evidence of substantial representation by outside directors. What is the purpose of such a review? How is the list of personnel not taking vacations used?

5. Past experience indicates that bank officers and employees can systematically divert charged-off loan recoveries to their own use unless the charge-off ledger is treated as a potential asset controlled by adequate audit and internal control. In 1978, it was reported that member banks of the Federal Reserve Bank recovered over 25 percent of their charged-off loans. In other words, charged-off loans are not necessarily entirely uncollectible.[5] How can control over charged-off loans be established? Why is it a particularly difficult area to control? How can the charged-off loan area be effectively audited?

6. Dormant checking and savings accounts pose special risks for banks and savings and loans. Prepare an internal control questionnaire that an auditor can use to evaluate the controls over such accounts.

7. In reviewing working papers, a senior auditor found documentation of audit work on sales transactions performed by a young staff auditor, who inadvertently omitted a key to the tick marks. Although you intend to ask the staff auditor to complete the documentation of work performed, what explanations do you expect for each of the following tick marks, noted on the working papers presented at the bottom of this page?

a. √ **e.** √^
b. (1) **f.** √ (crossed)
c. (2) **g.** (√)
d. (3)

(Exercise 7)

W/P Ref. No.
Preparer
Date

WAJAW Corp.
Sales Transactions: Detailed Invoice Test
June 30, 19X6

Date	Customer	Invoice Number	Amount	Compared with Sales Order	Compared with Shipping Documents	Other Tests
7/15/X5	Coleman	0796	17000	√	√	√ √ (√)
12/2/X6	MaryAnne's	1796	2000	√	√	√ √ (√)
3/4/X6	Family Four	2392	5000	√	√	√ √ (√)
3/6/X6	Buddy's	2405	7000	(2)	√	√ √ (√)
4/10/X6	MAC	2707	1000	√	(3)	√ √ (√)
5/15/X6	KATIE's	2988	500	√	√	√ √ (√)
6/10/X6	JeanMarie's	3202	286.03	√	√	√ √ (√)

[5] Adapted from American Bankers Association, "Controlled Group Bonding Plan" (Washington, D.C.: American Bankers Association, 1978).

8. Several weaknesses were noted during the evaluation of controls over sales, which are expected to affect the audit plan. Give an example of how the substantive work might be altered in response to the following observed weaknesses:
   a. Cash receipts are not deposited daily in the bank.
   b. The client does not reconcile the prelisting of cash receipts to the eventual recording of receipts or to the authenticated deposit slips.
   c. There is no regular reconciliation of subsidiary ledgers to the general ledger's control account.

QUESTIONS ADAPTED FROM PROFESSIONAL EXAMINATIONS

1. You are performing your first audit of the Licitra Pest Control Company for the year ended December 31, 19X6. The company began doing business in January 19X6 and offers pest control services to industrial enterprises.
   a. The office staff consists of a bookkeeper, a typist, and the president, Tony Licitra. In addition, the company employs twenty servicemen on an hourly basis who are assigned to individual territories to make both monthly and emergency visits to customers' premises. The servicemen submit weekly time reports that include the customer's name and the time spent with each customer. The report shows time charges for emergency visits separately from the regular monthly visits.
   b. Customers are required to sign annual contracts that are prenumbered and prepared in duplicate. The original is filed in numerical order by contract anniversary date, and the copy is given to the customer. The contract entitles the customer to pest control services once each month. Emergency visits are billed separately.
   c. Fees for monthly services are payable in advance—quarterly, semi-annually, or annually—and are recorded on the books as "income from services" when the cash is received. All payments are by checks received by mail.
   d. Prenumbered invoices for contract renewals are prepared in triplicate from information in the contract file. The original invoice is sent to the customer twenty days before the due date of payment; the duplicate copy is filed chronologically by due date; and the triplicate copy is filed alphabetically by customer. If payment is not received by fifteen days after the due date, a cancellation notice is sent to the customer, and a copy of the notice is attached to the customer's contract. The bookkeeper notifies the servicemen of all contract cancellations and reinstatements and requires written acknowledgment of the receipt of such notices. Licitra approves all cancellations and reinstatements of contracts.
   e. Prenumbered invoices for emergency services are prepared weekly from information shown on the servicemen's time reports. The customer is billed at 200 percent of the serviceman's hourly rate. These invoices, prepared in triplicate and distributed as shown above, are recorded on the books as "income from services" at the billing date. Payment is due thirty days after the invoice date.
   f. All remittances are received by the typist, who prepares a daily list of collections and stamps a restrictive endorsement on the checks. A copy of the list is forwarded with the checks to the bookkeeper. A copy of the list is forwarded with the checks to the bookkeeper, who posts the date and amount received on the copies of the invoice in both the alphabetical and chronological files. After posting, the copy of the invoice is transferred from the chronological file to the daily cash receipts binder, which serves as a subsidiary record for the cash receipts book. The bookkeeper totals the amounts of all remittances received, posts this total to the cash receipts book, and attaches the daily remittance tapes to the paid invoices in the daily cash receipts binder.
   g. The bookkeeper prepares a daily bank deposit slip and compares the total with the total amount shown on the daily remittance tapes. All remittances are deposited in the bank on the day they are received. (Cash receipts from sources other than services need not be considered.)
   h. Financial statements are prepared on the accrual basis.

   Required
   a. List the audit procedures you would use to examine the Income from Services account for 19X6.
   b. You are considering using the services of a reputable outside mailing service to confirm the accounts receivable balances. The service would prepare and mail the confirmation requests and remove the returned confirmations from the envelopes and give them directly to you. What reliance, if any, would you place on the services of the outside mailing service? Discuss and state the reasons supporting your answer.

   (CPA exam adapted)

2. XYZ operates sales divisions in several cities throughout the country. In addition to other activi-

ties, the sales divisions are charged with collecting local receivables; each division maintains a bank account in which all collections are deposited intact. Twice a week these collections are transferred to the home office by check; no other checks are drawn on this bank account. Except for cash receipts and cash disbursements books, the sales offices keep no accounting books, but they retain all cash records in their files. As part of your year-end audit, you wish to include an audit of cash transfers between the sales divisions and the main office. Your representative will visit all locations.

Required:

a. What are the purposes of auditing the cash transfers?

b. Assuming that your representative understands the audit procedures for regular cash collection to which he or she will attend at each location, design only those specific audit steps that he or she will be required to perform to audit the cash transfers from each sales division to the home office.

(CPA exam adapted)

3. You are auditing the Alaska branch of Far Distributing Co. This branch has substantial annual sales which are billed and collected locally. As a part of your audit, you find that the procedures for handling cash receipts are as follows:

a. Cash collections on over-the-counter sales and COD sales are received from the customer or delivery service by the cashier. Upon receipt of cash, the cashier stamps the sales ticket "paid" and files a copy for future reference. The only record of the COD sales is a copy of the sales ticket which is given to the cashier to hold until the cash is received from the delivery service.

b. Mail is opened by the secretary to the credit manager, and remittances are given to the credit manager for review. The credit manager then places the remittances in a tray on the cashier's desk. At the daily deposit cutoff time, the cashier delivers the checks and cash on hand to the assistant credit manager, who prepares remittance lists and makes up the bank deposit; the assistant credit manager also takes the deposit to the bank. The assistant credit manager posts remittances to the accounts receivable ledger cards and verifies the cash discount allowable.

c. You also ascertain that the credit manager obtains approval from the executive office of Far Distributing Co., located in Chicago, to write off uncollectible accounts, and that as of the end of the fiscal year some remittances that are received on various days during the last month were retained in the credit manager's custody.

Required:

a. Describe the irregularities that might occur under the procedures now used for handling cash collections and remittances.

b. Recommend procedures to strengthen internal control over cash collections and remittances.

(CPA exam adapted)

4. In your examination of the financial statements of the Kay Savings and Loan Association for the year ended December 31, 19X8, you find a new account in the general ledger, Home Improvement Loans. You determine that these are unsecured loans not insured by any government agency, made on a discount basis to homeowners who are required to secure life insurance coverage provided by the association under a group life insurance policy for the outstanding amount and duration of the loan. Borrowers are issued coupon books that require monthly installment payments; however, borrowers may prepay the outstanding balance of the loan at any time in accordance with the terms of their loan contract. This account constitutes a material amount of the association's total assets at December 31, 19X8.

Required:

a. Prepare an audit program for the examination of the new account, Home Improvement Loans.

b. During your examination of the Home Improvement Loans account, the vice-president in charge of the loan department hands you a list of twenty-five accounts with balances from $300 to $8,000, representing approximately 40 percent of the total account balance. The vice-president states that confirmation requests are not to be prepared for these twenty-five accounts under any circumstances, because the borrowers have requested "no correspondence."

(1) Will you comply with the vice-president's request? Discuss.

(2) Assuming you complied with the vice-president's request and did not send confirmation requests to the "no correspondence" accounts, what effect, if any, would this compliance have on your auditor's short-form report?

(CPA exam adapted)

5. Charting, Inc., a new audit client of yours, processes its sales and cash receipts documents in the following manner:

(1) *Payment on account.* The mail is opened each morning by a mail clerk in the sales department. The mail clerk prepares a remittance advice (showing customer and amount paid) if one is not received. The checks and remittance advices are then forwarded to the sales department supervisor who reviews each check and forwards the checks and remittance advices to the accounting department supervisor.

The accounting department supervisor, who also functions as credit manager in approving new credit and all credit limits, reviews all checks for payments on past due accounts and then forwards the checks and remittance advices to the accounts receivable clerk who arranges the advices in alphabetical order. The remittance advices are posted directly to the accounts receivable ledger cards. The checks are endorsed by stamp and totaled. The total is posted to the cash receipts journal. The remittance advices are filed chronologically.

After receiving the cash from the previous day's cash sales, the accounts receivable clerk prepares the daily deposit slip in triplicate. The third copy of the deposit slip is filed by date, and the second copy and the original accompany the bank deposit.

(2) *Sales.* Sales clerks prepare sales invoices in triplicate. The original and second copy are presented to the cashier. The third copy is retained by the sales clerk in the sales book. When the sale is for cash, the customer pays the sales clerk who presents the money to the cashier with the invoice copies.

A credit sale is approved by the cashier from an approved credit list after the sales clerk prepares the three-part invoice. After receiving the cash or approving the invoice, the cashier validates the original copy of the sales invoice and gives it to the customer. At the end of each day the cashier recaps the sales and cash received and forwards the cash and the second copy of all sales invoices to the accounts receivable clerk.

The accounts receivable clerk balances the cash received with the cash sales invoices and prepares a daily sales summary. The credit sales invoices are posted to the accounts receivable ledger, and then all invoices are sent to the inventory control clerk in the sales department for posting to the inventory control cards. After posting, the inventory control clerk files all invoices numerically. The accounts receivable clerk posts the daily sales summary to the cash receipts journal and sales journal and files the sales summaries by date.

The cash from cash sales is combined with the cash received on account to make up the daily bank deposit.

(3) *Bank deposits.* The bank validates the deposit slip and returns the second copy to the accounting department where it is filed by date by the accounts receivable clerk.

Monthly bank statements are reconciled promptly by the accounting department supervisor and filed by date.

Required:
You recognize that there are weaknesses in the existing system and believe a chart of information and document flows would be helpful in evaluating this client's internal control in preparing for your examination of the financial statements. Complete the flowchart on pp. 476–477 for sales and cash receipts of Charting, Inc., by labeling the appropriate symbols and indicating information flows. The chart is complete as to symbols and document flows. The following symbols are used:

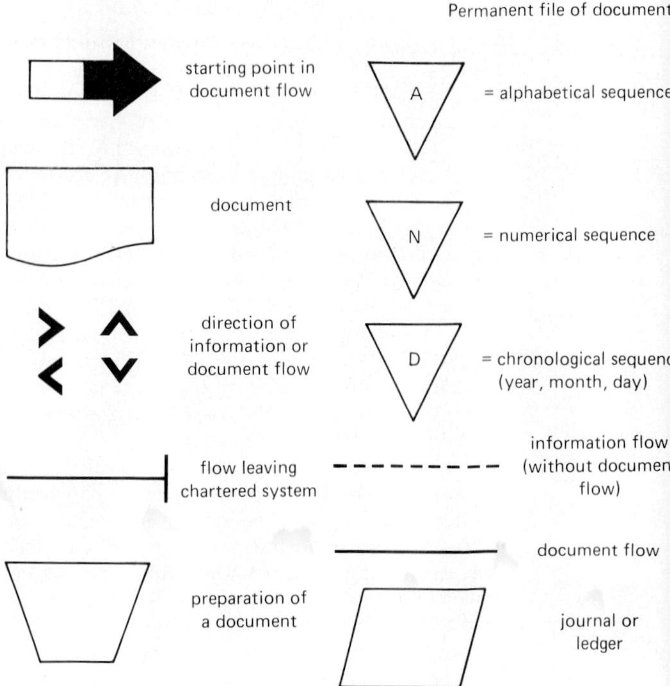

6. Dodge, a CPA, is examining the financial statements of a manufacturing company with a significant amount of trade accounts receivable. Dodge is satisfied that the accounts are properly summarized and classified and that allocations, reclassifications, and valuations are made in accordance with generally accepted accounting principles. Dodge is planning to use accounts receivable confirmation requests to satisfy the third standard of field work regarding trade accounts receivable.

a. Identify and describe the two forms of accounts receivable confirmation requests and indicate what factors Dodge will consider in determining when to use each.

b. Assume Dodge has received a satisfactory response to the confirmation requests. Describe how he could evaluate the collectibility of the trade accounts receivable.

(CPA exam adapted)

7. Toyco, a retail toy chain, honors two bank credit cards and makes daily deposits of credit card sales in two credit card bank accounts (Bank A and Bank B). Each day Toyco batches its credit card sales slips, bank deposit slips, and authorized sales return documents, and keypunches the cards for processing by its electronic data-processing department. Each week detailed computer printouts of the general ledger credit card cash accounts are prepared. Credit card banks have been instructed to make an automatic weekly transfer of cash to Toyco's general bank account. The credit card banks charge back deposits that include sales to holders of stolen or expired cards.

Toyco
Detailed General Ledger Credit Card Cash Account Printouts
for the Week Ended December 31, 19X6

	Bank A	Bank B
	Dr. or (Cr.)	
Beginning balance		
December 24, 19X6	$12,100	$ 4,200
Deposits		
December 27, 19X6	2,500	5,000
December 28, 19X6	3,000	7,000
December 29, 19X6	0	5,400
December 30, 19X6	1,900	4,000
December 31, 19X6	2,200	6,000
Cash transfer		
December 17, 19X6	(10,700)	0
Chargebacks		
Expired cards	(300)	(1,600)
Invalid deposits (physically deposited in wrong account)	(1,400)	(1,000)
Redeposit of invalid deposits	1,000	1,400
Sales returns for week ending December 31, 19X6	(600)	(1,200)
Ending balance—December 31, 19X6	$ 9,700	$29,200

Toyco
Summary of the Bank Statements
for the Week Ended December 31, 19X6

	Bank A	Bank B
	(Charges) or Credits	
Beginning balance		
December 24, 19X6	$10,000	$ 0
Deposits dated		
December 24, 19X6	2,100	4,200
December 27, 19X6	2,500	5,000
December 28, 19X6	3,000	7,000
December 29, 19X6	2,000	5,500
December 30, 19X6	1,900	4,000
Cash transfers to general bank account		
December 27, 19X6	(10,700)	0
December 31, 19X6	0	(22,600)
Chargebacks		
Stolen cards	(100)	0
Expired cards	(300)	(1,600)
Invalid deposits	(1,400)	(1,000)
Bank service charges	0	(500)
Bank charge (unexplained)	(400)	0
Ending balance—December 31, 19X6	$ 8,600	$ 0

Toyco
Bank Reconciliations
for the Week Ended December 31, 19X6

Code No.	Bank A	Bank B
	Add or (Deduct)	
1. Balance per bank statement December 31, 19X6	$8,600	$ 0
2. Deposits in transit December 31, 19X6	2,200	6,000
3. Redeposit of invalid deposits (physically deposited in wrong account)	1,000	1,400
4. Difference in deposits of December 29, 19X6	(2,000)	(100)
5. Unexplained bank charge	400	0
6. Bank cash transfer not yet recorded	0	22,600
7. Bank service charges	0	500
8. Chargebacks not recorded—Stolen cards	100	0
9. Sales returns recorded but not reported to the bank	(600)	(1,200)
10. Balance per general ledger—December 31, 19X6	$9,700	$29,200

Question 5

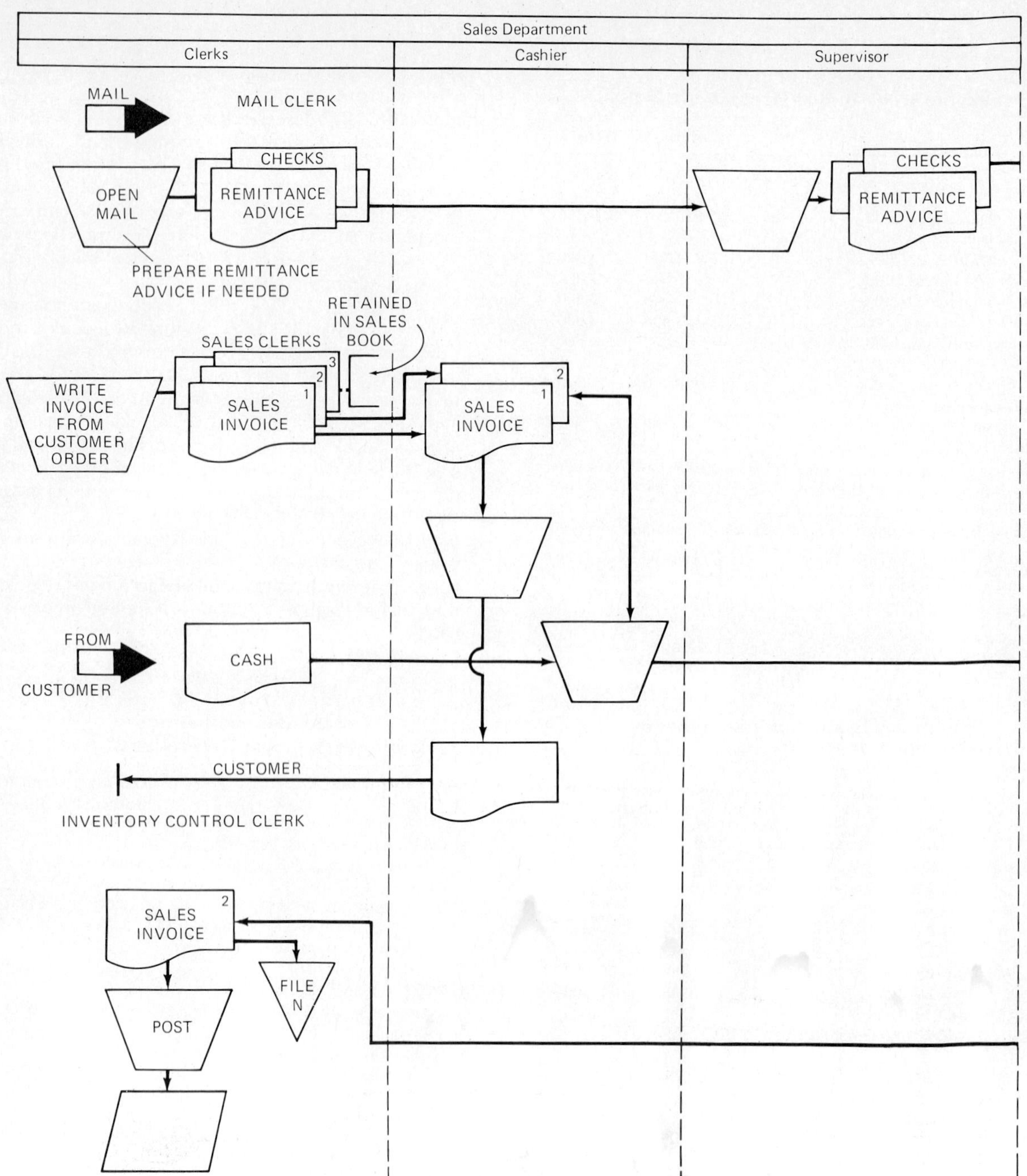

Sales Department
Clerks
Cashier
Supervisor
MAIL
MAIL CLERK
CHECKS
OPEN MAIL
REMITTANCE ADVICE
CHECKS
REMITTANCE ADVICE
PREPARE REMITTANCE ADVICE IF NEEDED
RETAINED IN SALES BOOK
SALES CLERKS
3
2
1
WRITE INVOICE FROM CUSTOMER ORDER
SALES INVOICE
2
1
SALES INVOICE
FROM
CUSTOMER
CASH
CUSTOMER
INVENTORY CONTROL CLERK
2
SALES INVOICE
FILE N
POST

Question 5 (cont'd)

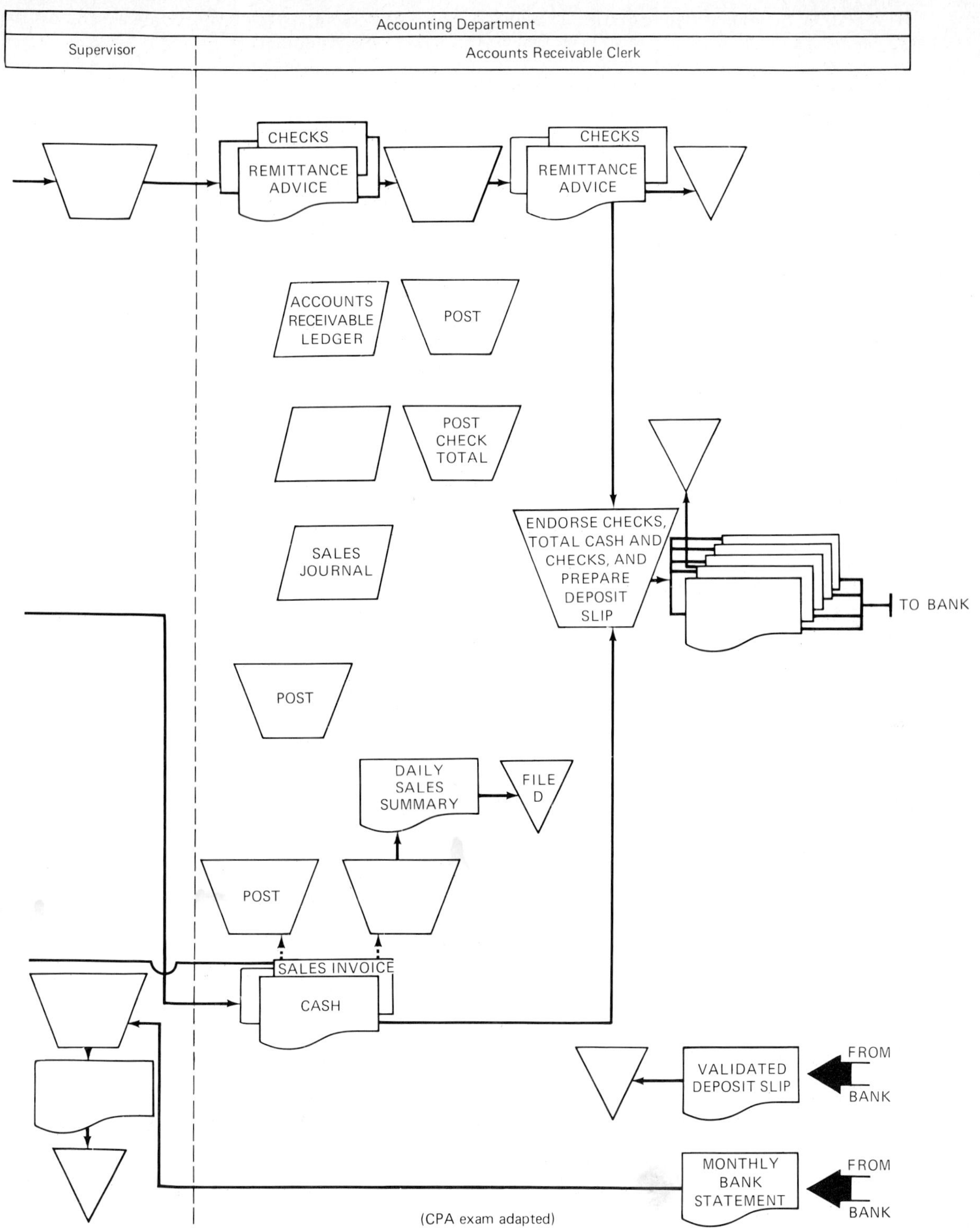

(CPA exam adapted)

The auditor examining the 19X6 Toyco financial statements has obtained the copies of the detailed general ledger cash account printouts, a summary of the bank statements, and the manually prepared bank reconciliations, all for the week ended December 31, 19X6, as shown on page 475.

Required:
Based on a review of the December 31, 19X6 bank reconciliation and the related information available in the printouts and the summary of bank statements, describe what action(s) the auditor should take to obtain audit satisfaction for each item on the bank reconciliations. Assume that all amounts are material and that all computations are accurate. Organize your answer sheet as follows using the appropriate code number for each item on the bank reconciliations:

Code No.	Action(s) to Be Taken by the Auditor to Obtain Audit Satisfaction
1.	

(CPA exam adapted)

8. You are in charge of your second yearly examination of the financial statements of Hillsboro Equipment Corporation, a distributor of construction equipment. Hillsboro's equipment sales are either outright cash sales or a combination of a substantial cash payment and one or two sixty-day or ninety-day nonrenewable interest-bearing notes for the balance. Title to the equipment passes to the customer when the initial cash payment is made. The notes, some of which are secured by the customer, are dated when the cash payment is made (the day the equipment is delivered). If the customer prefers to purchase the equipment under an installment payment plan, Hillsboro will arrange for the customer to obtain such financing from a local bank.

You begin your field work to examine the December 31 financial statements on January 5, knowing that after outlining the audit program for your assistant, you must leave temporarily for another engagement on January 7. Before leaving, you inquire about the assistant's progress in the examination of notes receivable. Among other things, the assistant shows you a working paper listing the makers' names, the due dates, the interest rates, and amounts of seventeen outstanding notes receivable totaling $100,000. The working paper contains the following notations:

1. Reviewed system of internal control and found it to be satisfactory.
2. Total of $100,000 agrees with general ledger control account.
3. Traced listing of notes to sales journal.

The assistant also informs you of plans to request positive confirmation of the amounts of all outstanding notes receivable. No other audit work has been performed in the examination of notes receivable and interest arising from equipment sales. There were no outstanding accounts receivable for equipment sales at the end of the year.

Required:

a. List the additional audit procedures that the assistant should use to audit the account for notes receivable arising from equipment sales (Hillsboro has no other notes). No subsidiary ledger is maintained.
b. You ask your assistant to examine all notes receivable on hand before you leave. The assistant returns in thirty minutes from the office safe where the notes are kept and reports that the 19X6 notes on hand total only $75,000.

   List the possible explanations that you would expect from the client for the $25,000 difference. (Eliminate fraud or misappropriation from your consideration.) Indicate beside each explanation the audit procedures you would use to determine whether each explanation is correct.

(CPA exam adapted)

9. Finney, a CPA, was engaged to audit the financial statements of Clayton Realty Corporation for the month ending January 31, 19X4. The examination of monthly rent reconciliations is a vital portion of the audit engagement.

The following rent reconciliation was prepared by the controller of Clayton Realty Corporation and was presented to Finney, who subjected it to various audit procedures:

Clayton Realty Corporation
Rent Reconciliation
for the month ended
January 31, 19X4

Gross apartment rents (Schedule A)	$1,600,800*
Less vacancies (Schedule B)	20,500*
Net apartment rentals	1,580,300
Less unpaid January rents (Schedule C)	7,800*
Total	1,572,500
Add prepaid rent collected (Apartment 116)	500*
Total cash collected	$1,573,000*

Schedules A, B, and C are available to Finney but have not been illustrated. Finney has conducted a study and evaluation of the system of internal control and found that it could be relied on to produce reliable accounting information. Cash receipts from rental operations are deposited in a special bank account.

Required:
What substantive audit procedures should Finney use during the audit in order to substantiate the validity of each of the dollar amounts marked by an asterisk(*)?

(CPA exam adapted)

10. See page 480.

11. Multiple Choice: Sales and Other Revenue, Cash, and Investments

Select the one answer that best completes the statement or answers the question.

11.1 Which of the following might be detected by an auditor's cutoff review and examination of sales journal entries for several days before and after the balance sheet date?

a. Lapping year-end accounts receivable.
b. Inflating sales for the year.
c. Kiting bank balances.
d. Misappropriating merchandise.

(CPA exam adapted)

11.2 An auditor is testing sales transactions. One step is to trace a sample of debit entries from the accounts receivable subsidiary ledger back to the supporting sales invoices. What does the auditor intend to establish by this step?

a. Sales invoices represent bona fide sales.
b. All sales have been recorded.
c. All sales invoices have been properly posted to customer accounts.
d. Debit entries in the accounts receivable subsidiary ledger are properly supported by sales invoices.

(CPA exam adapted)

11.3 Which of the following is not an auditor's objective when examining revenues?

a. To verify cash deposited during the year.
b. To study and evaluate internal control, especially the use of accrual accounting to record revenue.
c. To verify that earned revenue has been recorded and that recorded revenue has been earned.
d. To identify and interpret significant trends and variations in the amounts of various categories of revenue.

(CPA exam adapted)

11.4 Jones was engaged to examine the financial statements of the Gamma Corporation for the year ended June 30, 19X6. Having examined the investment securities, which of the following is the best method of verifying the accuracy of recorded dividend income?

a. Tracing recorded dividend income to cash receipts records and validated deposit slips.
b. Using analytical review techniques and statistical sampling.
c. Comparing recorded dividends with amounts appearing on federal information forms 1099.
d. Comparing recorded dividends with a standard financial reporting service's record of dividends.

(CPA exam adapted)

11.5 Which of the following procedures would ordinarily be expected to best reveal unrecorded sales at the balance sheet date?

a. Compare shipping documents with sales records.
b. Apply gross profit rates to inventory disposed of during the period.
c. Trace payments received after the balance sheet date.
d. Send accounts receivable confirmation requests.

(CPA exam adapted)

11.6 In order to avoid misappropriating company-owned marketable securities, which of the following is the best course of action for the management of a company with a large portfolio of marketable securities?

a. Require that one trustworthy and bonded employee be responsible for access to the safekeeping area where the securities are kept.
b. Require that employees who enter and leave the safekeeping area sign and record in a log the exact reason for their access.
c. Require that employees with safekeeping responsibilities maintain a subsidiary control ledger for securities on a current basis.
d. Require that the safekeeping of securities be assigned to a bank that will act as a custodial agent.

(CPA exam adapted)

10.

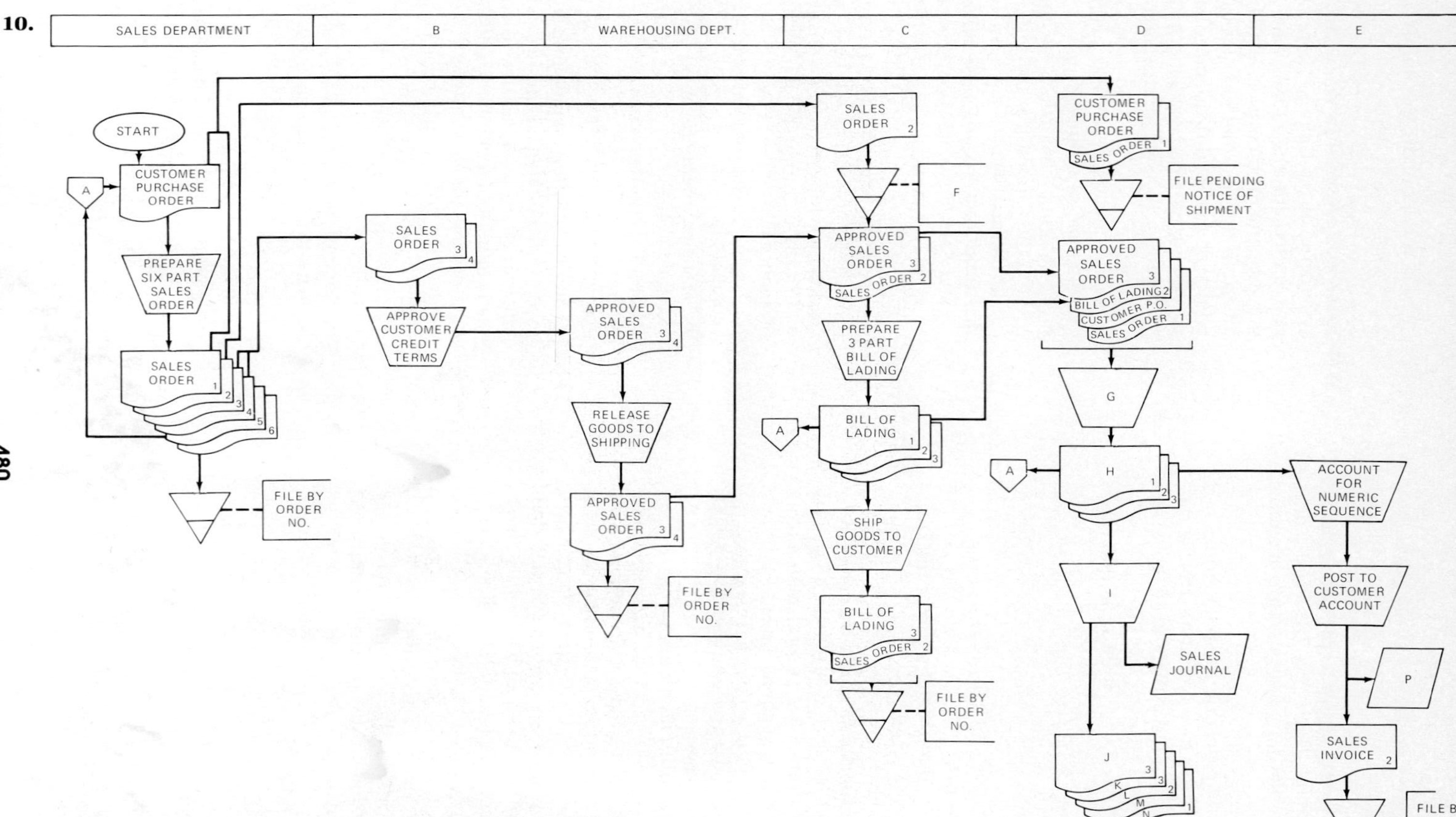

While auditing the Top Manufacturing Corporation, the auditor prepared the above flowchart of credit sales activities. In this flowchart, code letter A represents the customer.

Required:

Indicate what each of the code letters B through P represents. Do not discuss adequacies or inadequacies in the system of internal control.

(CPA exam adapted)

11.7 For proper accounting control, postdated checks remitted by customers should be
a. Restrictively endorsed.
b. Returned to customer.
c. Recorded as a cash sale.
d. Placed in the joint custody of two officers.
(CPA exam adapted)

11.8 A company policy should clearly indicate that defective merchandise returned by customers is to be delivered to the
a. Sales clerk.
b. Receiving clerk.
c. Inventory control clerk.
d. Accounts receivable clerk.
(CPA exam adapted)

11.9 During the first part of the current fiscal year, the client company began dealing with certain customers on a consignment basis. Which of the following audit procedures is least likely to bring this new fact to the auditor's attention?
a. Tracing of shipping documents to the sales journal.
b. Test of cash receipts transactions.
c. Confirmation of accounts receivable.
d. Observation of physical inventory.
(CPA exam adapted)

11.10 The primary difference between an audit of the balance sheet and an audit of the income statement is that the audit of the income statement verifies
a. Transactions.
b. Authorizations.
c. Costs.
d. Cutoffs.
(CPA exam adapted)

11.11 Of the procedures listed, which is the most likely to detect kiting?
a. Comparing the detail of cash receipts (log listings) with the cash receipts journal, accounts receivable postings, and deposit slips.
b. Investigating checks that have been outstanding for long periods.
c. Accounting for bank transfers made during the few days before and after selected dates.
d. Confirming accounts receivable balances as of a cutoff date.
e. Counting cash on hand.
(CPA exam adapted)

11.12 A sales cutoff test of billings complements the verification of
a. Sales returns.
b. Cash.
c. Accounts receivable.
d. Sales allowances.
(CPA exam adapted)

11.13 To establish illegal "slush funds," corporations may divert cash received in normal business operations. An auditor encounters the greatest difficulty in detecting the diversion of proceeds from
a. Scrap sales. **c.** Purchase returns.
b. Dividends. **d.** COD sales.
(CPA exam adapted)

11.14 Tracing copies of sales invoices to shipping documents will provide evidence that all
a. Shipments to customers were recorded as receivables.
b. Billed sales were shipped.
c. Debits to the subsidiary accounts receivable ledger are for sales shipped.
d. Shipments to customers were billed.
(CPA exam adapted)

11.15 Late in December, the Tech Products Company sold its marketable securities, which had appreciated in value, and then repurchased them on the same day. The sale and purchase transactions resulted in a large gain. Without the gain the company would have reported a loss for the year. Which of the following statements with respect to the auditor is correct?
a. If the sale and repurchase are disclosed, an unqualified opinion should be rendered.
b. The repurchase transaction is a sham, and the auditor should insist on a reversal or issue an adverse opinion.
c. The auditor should withdraw from the engagement and refuse to be associated with the company.
d. A disclaimer of opinion should be issued.
(CPA exam adapted)

11.16 To verify that all sales transactions have been recorded, a test of transactions should be completed on a representative sample drawn from
a. Entries in the sales journal.
b. The billing clerk's file of sales orders.
c. A file of duplicate copies of sales invoices for which all prenumbered forms in the series have been accounted.
d. The shipping clerk's file of duplicate copies of bills of lading.
(CPA exam adapted)

11.17 At which point in an ordinary sales transaction of a wholesaling business would a lack of specific authorization be of least concern to an auditor when conducting an audit?
- **a.** Granting of credit.
- **b.** Shipment of goods.
- **c.** Determination of discounts.
- **d.** Selling of goods for cash.

(CPA exam adapted)

11.18 As one of the year-end audit procedures, the auditor instructed the client's personnel to prepare a standard bank confirmation request for a bank account that had been closed during the year. After the client's treasurer had signed the request, it was mailed by the assistant treasurer. What is the major flaw in this audit procedure?
- **a.** The confirmation request was signed by the treasurer.
- **b.** Sending the request was meaningless because the account had been closed before the year-end.
- **c.** The request was mailed by the assistant treasurer.
- **d.** The CPA did not sign the confirmation request before it was mailed.

(CPA exam adapted)

11.19 Of the following, which is the most efficient audit procedure for verifying interest earned on bond investments?
- **a.** Tracing interest declarations to an independent record book.
- **b.** Recomputing interest earned.
- **c.** Confirming interest rate with the issuer of the bonds.
- **d.** Vouching the receipt and deposit of interest checks.

(CPA exam adapted)

11.20 As a result of analytical review procedures, the independent auditor determines that the gross profit percentage has declined from 30 percent in the preceding year to 20 percent in the current year. The auditor should
- **a.** Document management's intentions with respect to plans for reversing this trend.
- **b.** Evaluate management's performance in causing this decline.
- **c.** Require footnote disclosure.
- **d.** Consider the possibility of an error in the financial statements.

(CPA exam adapted)

12. Multiple Choice: Receivables

Select the one answer that best completes the statement or answers the question.

12.1 The audit working papers often include a client-prepared, aged trial balance of accounts receivable as of the balance sheet date. This aging is best used by the auditor to
- **a.** Evaluate internal control over credit sales.
- **b.** Test the accuracy of recorded charge sales.
- **c.** Estimate credit losses.
- **d.** Verify the validity of the recorded receivables.

(CPA exam adapted)

12.2 Once a CPA has determined that accounts receivable have increased because of slow collections in a "tight money" environment, the CPA is likely to
- **a.** Increase the balance in the allowance for bad debts account.
- **b.** Review the going concern ramifications.
- **c.** Review the credit and collection policy.
- **d.** Expand tests of collectibility.

(CPA exam adapted)

12.3 During the audit of the Third National Bank, the internal auditor found several serious deficiencies in the commercial loan files. After the internal auditor informed the bank's chief loan officer of this situation, the commercial loan department attempted to remedy the deficiencies. Which would be the appropriate follow-up procedure for the internal auditor to undertake?
- **a.** Review the corrections during next year's audit.
- **b.** Ask the chief loan officer to send a letter within sixty days to the internal auditor indicating that the corrections have been made.
- **c.** Ask the chief loan officer to send a letter within sixty days to the chief executive officer indicating that the corrections have been made.
- **d.** Ask the loan department whether the corrections were properly made.
- **e.** Conduct a follow-up audit within a short period of time.

(CPA exam adapted)

12.4 Which of the following would best protect a company that wishes to prevent the lapping of trade accounts receivable?
- **a.** Segregate duties so that the bookkeeper in charge of the general ledger has no access to incoming mail.

b. Segregate duties so that no employee has access to both checks from customers and currency from daily cash receipts.
c. Have customers send payments directly to the company's depository bank.
d. Request that customers' payment checks be made payable to the company and addressed to the treasurer.

(CPA exam adapted)

12.5 It is sometimes impractical or impossible for an auditor to use normal accounts receivable confirmation procedures. In such situations, the best alternative procedure the auditor can use is
a. Examining subsequent receipts of year-end accounts receivable.
b. Reviewing accounts receivable aging schedules prepared at the balance sheet date and at a later date.
c. Requesting that management increase the allowance for uncollectible accounts by an amount equal to some percentage of the balance in those accounts that cannot be confirmed.
d. Performing an overall analytical review of accounts receivable and sales on a year-to-year basis.

(CPA exam adapted)

12.6 Madison Corporation has a few large accounts receivable that total $1 million. Nassau Corporation has many small accounts receivable that also total $1 million. The importance of an error in any one account is, therefore, greater for Madison than for Nassau. This is an example of the auditor's concept of
a. Materiality.
b. Comparative analysis.
c. Reasonable assurance.
d. Relative risk.

(CPA exam adapted)

12.7 Which of the following internal control procedures will most likely prevent the concealment of a cash shortage resulting from the improper write-off of a trade account receivable?
a. Write-offs must be approved by a responsible officer after review of credit department recommendations and supporting evidence.
b. Write-offs must be supported by an aging schedule showing that only receivables overdue several months have been written off.
c. Write-offs must be approved by the cashier who is in a position to know if the receivables have in fact been collected.
d. Write-offs must be authorized by company field sales employees who are in a position to determine the customer's financial standing.

(CPA exam adapted)

12.8 The confirmation of the client's trade accounts receivable is a means of obtaining evidential matter and is specifically considered to be a generally accepted auditing
a. Principle. **b.** Standard.
c. Procedure. **d.** Practice.

(CPA exam adapted)

12.9 In order to safeguard assets through proper internal control, accounts receivable that have been written off are transferred to a(an)
a. Separate ledger.
b. Attorney for evidence in collection proceedings.
c. Tax deductions file.
d. Credit manager, as customers may seek to reestablish credit by paying.

(CPA exam adapted)

12.10 Johnson is auditing a utility that supplies power to a residential community. All accounts receivable balances are small, and the internal control is effective. Customers are billed bimonthly. In order to determine the validity of the accounts receivable balances at the balance sheet date, Johnson will most likely
a. Examine evidence of subsequent cash receipts instead of sending confirmation requests.
b. Send positive confirmation requests.
c. Send negative confirmation requests.
d. Use statistical sampling instead of sending confirmation requests.

(CPA exam adapted)

12.11 Which of the following is not an auditor's objective when examining accounts receivable?
a. Determining the approximate realizable value.
b. Determining the adequacy of internal controls.
c. Establishing validity of the receivables.
d. Determining the approximate time that the receivables can be collected.

(CPA exam adapted)

12.12 To conceal defalcations involving receivables, the auditor would expect an experienced

bookkeeper to charge which of the following accounts?
a. Miscellaneous income.
b. Petty cash.
c. Miscellaneous expense.
d. Sales returns.
(CPA exam adapted)

12.13 An auditor reconciles the total of the accounts receivable subsidiary ledger to the general ledger control account as of October 31, 19X6. By using this procedure, the auditor would be most likely to learn of which of the following?
a. An October invoice was improperly computed.
b. An October check from a customer was posted in error to the account of another customer with a similar name.
c. An opening balance in a subsidiary ledger account was improperly carried forward from the previous accounting period.
d. An account balance is past due and should be written off.
(CPA exam adapted)

12.14 Which of the following is the best argument against using negative accounts receivable confirmations?
a. The cost per response is excessively high.
b. There is no way of knowing if the intended recipients received them.
c. Recipients are likely to feel that the confirmation is a request for payment.
d. The inference drawn from receiving no reply may not be correct.
(CPA exam adapted)

12.15 Customers having substantial year-end past due balances fail to reply after second request forms have been mailed directly to them. Which of the following is the most appropriate audit procedure?
a. Examine shipping documents.
b. Review collections during the year being examined.
c. Intensify the study of the client's system of internal control with respect to receivables.
d. Increase the balance in the accounts receivable allowance (contra) account.
(CPA exam adapted)

12.16 In updating a computerized accounts receivable file, which one of the following would be used as a batch control to verify the accuracy of posting cash remittances?
a. The sum of net sales.
b. The sum of cash deposits less discounts taken by customers.
c. The sum of cash deposits plus discounts taken by customers.
d. The sum of net sales plus discounts taken by customers.
(CPA exam adapted)

12.17 When confirming accounts receivable, the auditor would most likely
a. Request confirmation of a sample of the inactive accounts.
b. Seek to obtain positive confirmations for at least 50 percent of the total dollar amount of the receivables.
c. Require confirmation of all receivables from agencies of the federal government.
d. Require that the confirmation request be sent within one month of the fiscal year-end.
(CPA exam adapted)

12.18 Auditors may use positive and/or negative forms of confirmation requests for accounts receivable. An auditor most likely will use
a. The positive form to confirm all balances, regardless of size.
b. A combination of the two forms, with the positive form used for large balances and the negative form for the small balances.
c. A combination of the two forms, with the positive form used for trade receivables and the negative form for other receivables.
d. The positive form when controls related to receivables are satisfactory, and the negative form when controls related to receivables are unsatisfactory.
(CPA exam adapted)

CASES FOR DISCUSSION

1. When reviewing loans in order to evaluate the reasonableness of a banking client's loan loss provision, you notice that a loan that was considered troubled last year is no longer on the books. Upon investigation, you discover that it had not been paid off by the borrower, nor had it been written off. You ask what happened to the loan, and the client explains that the bank sold it. "Who would want to buy that loan?" you ask. "As a matter of fact," your client responds, "one of our new borrowers. Apparently, the transaction has some tax advantages for him."

Although you are not a tax specialist, you cannot imagine any net tax advantage to buying a loan receivable that is known to be a bad debt. Nor do you like the idea of your banking client's selling such a loan at the same time that a loan is being extended to the same party! You suspect that the tax explanation was a smoke screen.

You decide to extend your procedures and telephone the borrower. When asked about his motive for buying the troubled loan, the borrower quickly explained, "That's the only way I could get my loan!"

a. What should the auditor do next?

b. What accounting issues arise in such a setting? If you were the borrower's auditor, how would you record the recently purchased loan receivable?

c. Discuss the ramifications of your findings for your banking client's entire audit, especially your audit of the revenue cycle.

2. A client in the construction and real estate industry has recently enjoyed a substantial increase in revenue because of a three-year expansion into the apartment and condominium business in a major metropolitan city. The client builds apartment complexes and condominiums. Then the client sells the buildings to Zachary Rentals, Inc., which rents out the apartments and sells the condominiums. Zachary Rentals, Inc. has a good reputation and is able to rent all its apartments in a reasonably short time. Once the buildings are full, your client buys back the property and manages the investments from that point on.

The past year has been tough on the real estate market. High interest rates have deterred people from buying condominiums. And depressed economic conditions have discouraged people from moving "up" in apartments, and most of your client's apartment complexes are rather expensive. As a result, two of the three buildings sold at year-end of the last fiscal period to Zachary Rentals, Inc. are still 70 percent unoccupied.

Your client, explaining how much the business values its relationship with Zachary Rentals, Inc., has just called to tell you that it has agreed to buy back the unoccupied buildings. As a result, the revenue and profit picture is not very bright for the current period.

That night, you awaken in the middle of the night. It just hit you: Your client had never really "sold" its property to Zachary Rentals, Inc.! A "convenient" transfer had been made to manipulate the revenue picture. Following up on your suspicions the next morning, your worst expectations are met. Zachary Rentals, Inc. has almost no capital base, certainly not sufficient to finance the buildings purchased over the past three years. You decide it is time to discuss the situation with your fellow partners.

a. Outline the relevant issues on which you need advice.

b. Describe how revenue realization accounting principles apply to this situation.

c. What audit procedures would have been useful in detecting this situation three years ago?

d. What should you do next?

14

The Cost of Sales or Production Cycle

Everyone expects fishermen to have their fish stories, veterans to have their war stories, and public accountants to have their inventory observation stories. Starting in their first year of public accounting, all professional staff participate in the observation of clients' physical inventories, and the stories proliferate! After a continuing education course, about eight senior- and manager-level accountants gathered for dinner and began to swap inventory stories. One told of a staff auditor, walking across some planks laid high above the production floor, who slipped and landed in a vat of pickles! Another told an almost unbelievable story about a chicken farm.

Counting chickens is not easy, because they do not stand still. So the audit team decided to take an aerial photograph and simply count the chickens in the picture. But because chickens are rather small, the photographers had to get in close for a decent shot. The solution seemed to be a helicopter. Three of the auditors boarded a helicopter with cameras in hand and instructed the pilot to fly over the chicken farm. As they descended toward the chicken pen, the auditor focusing the camera kept saying, "Get in closer, so I can get a good picture."

Suddenly there was a racket! The hens were cackling, feathers were flying, the helicopter was sputtering, and a crash was imminent! The pilot and passengers were not injured, but the helicopter had gone down so low that the inventory had been sucked into the propeller, with the expected results . . . the audit team had managed to destroy almost half of the client's inventory!

By the time the laughter had subsided, with all the CPAs left with a clear mental picture of the disaster—humorous only to a third party—another auditor mentioned that he had faced a life or death decision in a physical inventory observation. He explained that it was right before New Year's, that most of a client's chemical inventory had been observed, but that there was one more procedure. At midnight, a final review found that a sample of a particular inventory item had to be carried to an independent laboratory for testing. The auditor told one of the client's employees what he had to do. The employee nodded and asked that the auditor follow him. As he was exhausted, the staff auditor was less than pleased to see a high, ranger-station type of building, with a tall ladder along the side. When the auditor and the employee reached the top, the auditor sat down to rest and watched the employee, with some surprise. He put on an asbestos suit and hood, went to a vault, disappeared for a minute, and returned with a vial. He held it out to the auditor, signalling him to take it. The auditor confided to his colleagues at dinner that he was rather reticent about taking the vial and asked the employee, "Why the suit?"

The employee replied, "This stuff is pretty unstable; that's why we keep it way up here in this fireproof vault!"

After thinking a minute, the auditor asked, "As a chemist, would you analyze the sample and give me a report on its composition? I'd rather not have to handle it." The employee agreed and proceeded with the analysis.

There were a few chuckles, and comments like "Our firm sure knew your value as an auditor" and "Which enemy of yours planned that program step?" were tossed back and forth. Defensively, the CPA then challenged his fellow auditors: "Well, what would you have done?"

This case demonstrates both the difficulty of executing audit procedures and the nonsampling risk that can evolve as the procedures are executed by CPAs who are constantly applying individual judgment. While the pickle vat story does little beyond suggesting the physical side of a profession that constantly sends staff to unfamiliar settings, the chicken farm story brings home the role for audit planning and careful execution of audit procedures. The final tale of the chemical client strikes at the heart of the inventory observation procedure as a reasonable audit technique, as well as suggesting a role for a third-party's involvement in such procedures. I would venture to guess that few auditors would have nonchalantly taken the chemical sample to an independent lab for analysis, nor would such action be worthy of praise—due audit care is surely not synonymous with personal danger. Yet the "quick fix" of using the client's chemist to prepare a report leaves much to be desired as a source of audit evidence. What alternatives existed? For example, wouldn't it have been possible to have an independent chemist come to the client's premises to test the inventory item? What precluded the selection of one of the available alternatives? What changes to the audit plans, program steps, and approach to the audit cycle may have been effective in ensuring that adequate evidence was obtained? For example, could an independent chemist effectively review the client's chemist's lab report? These are a sample of the issues that will be addressed in this chapter, which will focus on the entire set of auditing procedures that is typically applied to the cost of sales or production cycle. One such procedure is the physical observation of inventory, a required substantive test whenever a client has a material inventory balance. As described earlier in this text, the requirement that clients' inventory be observed is directly attributable to the McKesson & Robbins fraud in which enormous amounts of fictitious inventory were entered on the books.

A Definition of What Comprises the Cost of Sales or Production Cycle

The cost of sales or production cycle would include transactions affecting inventory, manufacturing, cost accounting, scrap, and property accounts. All of these pertain to the conversion of raw materials into products or the disposition of by-products and scrap generated by production. Besides the conversion process, the cost of sales cycle contains several other types of expenditures pertaining to purchasing, transportation, receiving, trade payables, payroll, and cash disbursements.

Functions Involved in the Cost of Sales or Production Cycle

The typical information flow through the cost of sales or production cycle for an operation begins with a requisition from the control department. Based on this requisition, which reflects production plans, purchase orders are prepared, with multiple copies to facilitate the control process. The purchases are approved, the goods received, the receiving reports matched with purchases and compared with invoices from vendors, the payments approved, and the disbursements made. Exhibit 14-1 shows a typical purchasing/cash disbursements flowchart, depicting the flow of documents and the common control steps taken as such transactions are processed. Keep in mind that a manufacturer also has a cost accounting system tracking the costs of production. A key cost of operations for any type of entity is payroll; recall that Exhibit 9-7 presented a flowchart of a factory payroll system.

The information flow can be envisioned by considering the common types of forms used to document the cost of sales or production cycle, as summarized in Exhibit 14-2. These forms may be in hard-copy or machine-readable form, depending on the type of processing environment. Each form either documents a transaction or controls the flow of that transaction through the operating cycle into the accounting records.

What Can Go Wrong

In performing an audit, it is useful to consider the types of errors that can occur. For the cost of goods sold or production cycle, Exhibit 14-3 lists the possible errors or irregularities.

In order to determine which of the items in Exhibit 14-3 can actually go wrong in a particular situation, the auditor should understand the client's operations, and one means of doing so is to answer the questions presented in Exhibit 14-4. For example, assume that a junior accountant reviews a client's accounting and control procedures over raw material purchases and describes those controls as follows:

> After approval by manufacturing department foremen, material purchase requisitions are forwarded to the purchasing department supervisor who distributes such requisitions to the several employees under his control. The latter employees prepare prenumbered purchase orders in triplicate, account for all numbers, and send the original purchase order to the vendor. One copy of the purchase order is sent to the receiving department where it is used as a receiving report. The other copy is filed in the purchasing department.
>
> When the materials are received, they are moved directly to the storeroom and issued to the foremen on informal requests. The receiving department sends a receiving report (with its copy of the purchase order attached) to the purchasing department and sends copies of the receiving report to the storeroom and to the accounting department.
>
> Vendors' invoices for material purchases, received in duplicate in the mail room, are sent to the purchasing department and directed to the employee who placed the related order. The employee than compares the invoice with the copy of the purchase order on file in the purchasing department for price and terms and compares the invoice quantity with the quantity received as reported by the shipping and receiving department on its copy of the purchase order. The purchasing department employee also checks discounts, footings, and extensions and initials the invoice to indicate approval for payment. The invoice is then sent to the voucher section of the accounting department where it is coded for account distribution, assigned a voucher number, entered in the voucher register, and filed according to payment due date.[1]

What can go wrong in such a situation? The key risks pertain to unauthorized purchases and theft of inventory received in overshipments. The particular deficiencies in the purchasing procedures include

1. There is poor control over the requisitioning of materials. Foremen have custody of the materials used in production and so should not authorize purchase requisitions.
2. The receiving report should not show the

[1] CPA exam adapted, May 16, 1963, question 4.

EXHIBIT 14-1

A Typical Purchasing/Cash Disbursements Flowchart

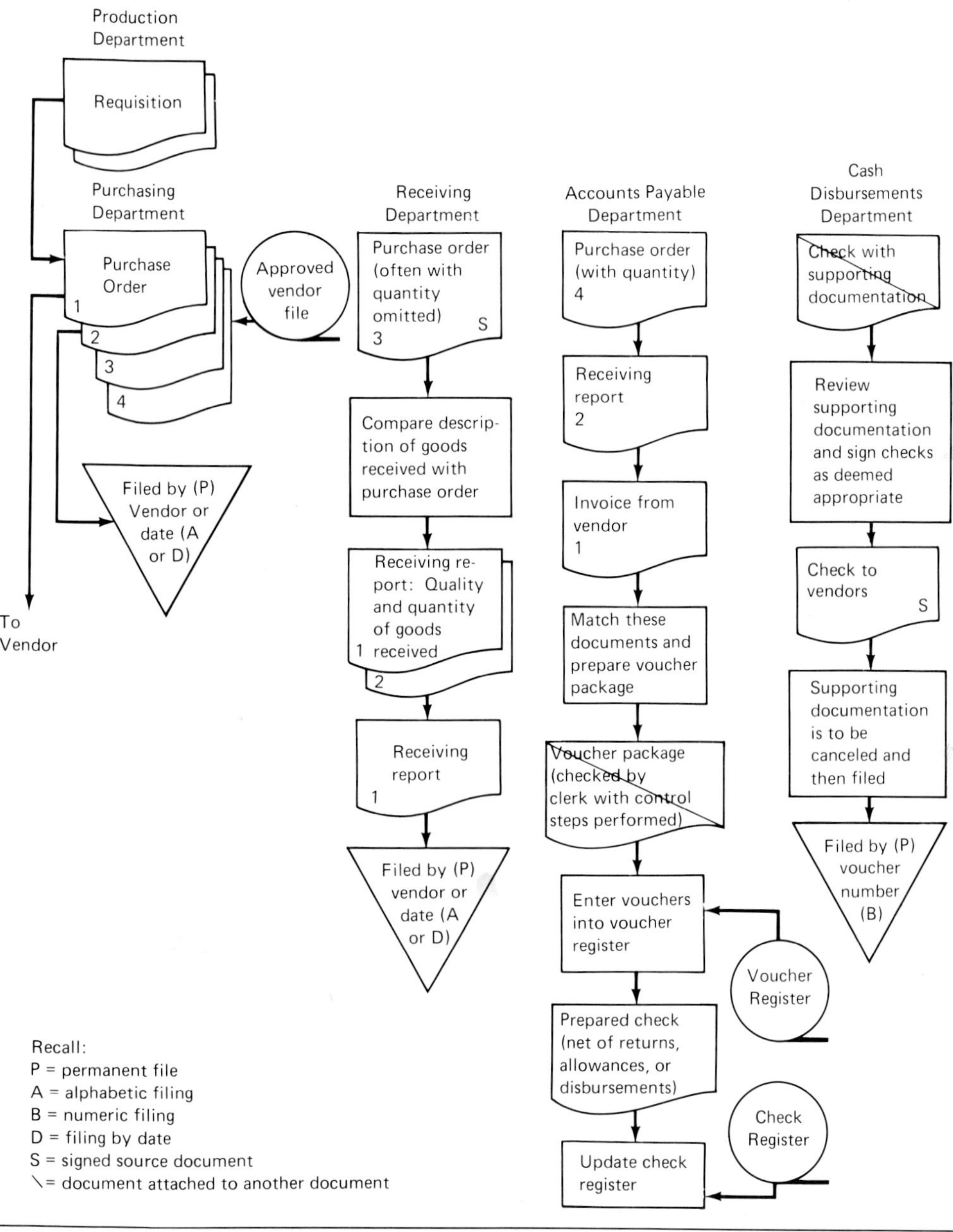

EXHIBIT 14-2

Suggested Forms for Documenting the Cost of Sales or Production Cycle

- Purchase Requisition: Authorizes purchase, documenting specifications regarding quality, price, and delivery.
- Check Requisition: Authorizes payment for services, maintenance, and repair of fixed assets; acquisition of property, plant, and equipment; and routine expenditures; and documents types, amounts, and timing of expenditures.
- Purchase Order: Initiates actual purchase, documents telephone orders, and clarifies special instructions for receiving department. (Copies are commonly distributed to vendor, receiving department, accounting department, and purchase requisitioner.)
- Buyer's Record: Documents basis for vendor selection and compliance with company policy, including long-term purchase commitment arrangements.
- Receiving Report: Documents goods received and variations from purchase orders, including performance of inspection procedures and return of damaged goods.
- Vouchers: Authorizes payment through reference to necessary supporting documents and documents performance of prescribed review duties.
- Completion Report: Authorizes payment for services by documenting completion of specified work and compliance with required inspection procedures. (When applicable, claims filed are also documented.)
- Debit Memoranda: Debit suppliers' accounts for claims, returns, and allowances and document related review procedures.
- Open Purchase Orders: Ensures timely follow-through of all unfilled purchase orders.
- Unmatched Receiving Reports: Facilitates follow-up on goods received but not yet billed by suppliers.
- Check: Makes authorized payment of funds, documenting the voucher to which payment refers. (All supporting documents should be canceled, check protector or computer should be used to print amount to deter alteration, and imprinted prenumbered checks are preferred. Often on payroll checks, a printed dollar limit and a time limit appear on check.)
- Petty Cash Voucher: Documents expenditures from petty cash, including purpose, account, and amount; the payee's signature constitutes authorization.
- Written Bank Authorization: Informs bank of authorized check signers for each bank account and provides instructions regarding unacceptable payees, dual signature requirements, and payment limits.
- Stores' Receipts of Inventory: Establishes control over goods moved from receiving to stores.
- Production Order (including self-constructed assets): Establishes control over production, documenting specifications, and inspection procedures.
- Stockroom Requisition: Establishes control over goods moved from stores to production line.
- Work Orders for Interdepartmental Movement of Materials and Fixed Assets: Establishes control over goods and fixed assets moved among departments.
- Scrap and Waste: Establishes control over and monitors magnitude of scrap, documenting its source and disposition. (Prices received for scrap should be compared with published prices.)
- Job Ticket: Documents labor on particular jobs and monitors both idle time and pieces rejected.
- Time Card: Documents each employee's hours worked and authorizes overtime.
- Personnel Authorization for Payroll: Authorizes all changes to payroll master file on related calculations (e.g., tax deductions).
- Payroll: Records payroll and documents review procedures, including tie-in to supporting documents.
- Cash Payroll Receipt: Establishes control over all cash payroll payments to employees. (Signature of employee documents that payment was made.)
- Unclaimed Wages: Establishes control over all unclaimed cash payroll payments.
- Physical Inventory Count Sheets: Documents periodic checks of quantity and condition of inventory.
- Inventory and Property Confirmation (for Assets Held by Outsiders): Documents periodic confirmation of quantity and condition of goods held on consignment or by other third parties.
- Inventory Work Sheets: Documents tie-in of physical inventory to valuation records, including performance of prescribed review procedures.
- Control over Inventory Tags, Count Sheets, and Work Sheets: Establishes numerical control over documents related to physical inventory and its extension to valuation records.
- Approval for Removal or Disassembly of Property: Authorizes removal or disassembly of property and documents its disposition.
- Insurance Coverage: Documents insurance coverage to facilitate its periodic review.
- Branch Operations Weekly Report: Establishes control over branch operations via a weekly report covering performance and expenditures.

Adapted from Wanda A. Wallace, *Handbook of Internal Accounting Controls* (Englewood Cliffs, N. J.: Prentice-Hall, 1984), pp. 203-226.

EXHIBIT 14-3

Cost of Sales or Production Cycle: Things That Could Go Wrong

- Recorded purchases may be fictitious.
- Records may indicate inventory on hand when none exists (or is otherwise misstated).
- Inventory may be overvalued and overstated owing to the misclassification of consigned-in merchandise.
- Liabilities may be incurred but not accrued.
- Expenses may be recorded more than once.
- Amounts payable to third parties may be increased or altered by employer committing fraud with third-party accomplice.
- Cash disbursements may be made but not recorded.
- Cash disbursements may be paid to unauthorized or fictitious vendors or employees or to cash or bearer for personal use.
- Prepaid expenses may not be appropriately adjusted.
- Shipments (tying back to the revenue cycle) may be made more than once in error.
- Expenses may be misclassified.
- Assets may be misclassified.
- Errors may arise from improper reconciliation of books to physical inventory.
- Cash disbursements and accruals may be recorded in wrong period.
- Recorded disbursements, purchases, and expenses, or their related liabilities, may be recorded inaccurately.
- Management's estimates of reserves for warranties, obsolete inventory, and other reserve balances may be in error.
- Inventory and assets used for production may not be accurately safeguarded or accurately recorded.
- Noncompliance with GAAP may arise in such areas as inventory recognition, recording of depreciation, accounting for leases, and capitalization of expenses.
- Incorrect or unnecessary inventory may be ordered or improper purchases be made, intended for nonbusiness use.
- Terminated employees may be paid, with other employee cashing check.
- Errors may be made in calculating pay, deductions, withholding, and taxes for payroll.
- Unauthorized production may be carried out for nonbusiness purposes.
- Incorrect requesting of materials or assignment of job skills may damage assets or lead to inefficiencies.
- Payments to bank may be intercepted.

EXHIBIT 14-4

Questions Useful to Auditor in Understanding Auditee's Business, Particularly Cost of Sales or Production Cycle

- What are the company's principal products?
- If a manufacturer, what are the manufacturing processes?
- If a manufacturer, is there a substantial amount of scrap, and does it have a market value?
- What basis of pricing inventories is in use?
- How are interplant and intercompany transfers or sales of inventory handled?
- Where are inventories stored?
- Are public warehouses being used?
- Are inventories placed on consignment?
- Where are property, plant, and equipment located?
- What is the nature of property, plant, and equipment?
- What questions arise from a tour of the plant?
- Are there policies to distinguish capitalizable items from repairs and maintenance?
- What major additions, acquisitions, or retirements have occurred in the past year?
- Are there a substantial number of small items such as tools and dies?
- What insurance coverage does the client have?
- Who are the key vendors and suppliers?
- Is supply a problem in any sense?
- Does the company have prescribed policies regarding conflicts of interest in purchasing and, in particular, the acceptance of gifts or other gratuities from vendors?
- Are all incoming purchases required to pass some control receiving point?
- Is an inspection or test of the specifications and quality of goods received performed?
- Does the client have a voucher system or an accounts payable system (note that the former would have a voucher register and the latter would have an invoice register)?
- What means are there to monitor partial shipments from vendors and to prevent duplicate payments to vendors?
- What are employment practices (e.g., are unions present; are a substantial number of part-timers employed; or are most employees on salary, as opposed to being on an hourly basis)?
- Are all payments by check or through an imprest petty cash account?
- What principal contractual obligations are there regarding product warranties, wage plans, profit sharing, and the like?

quantities ordered. At the present, the receiving personnel are not required to count incoming material in order to complete their report and so could divert overshipments to their own use without detection.

3. Without purchase order numbers being assigned to requisitions before distributing them to the employees placing orders, there is no safeguard against issuing unauthorized purchase orders.
4. There is no formal evidence that the purchase orders have been approved.
5. The purchasing department's approval of vouchers for payment could result in payments for unauthorized material or material not received.

The likelihood of these deficiencies resulting in improper purchases or loss of assets has to be evaluated.

The next step is to decide which controls the client can use to overcome observed deficiencies. For our example, the following controls could reduce the risks in the current purchasing practices:

1. Each bill of materials from the engineering department, along with a schedule of the item's planned production called for by the bill of materials, should be forwarded to a store's supervisor. The store's supervisor should be responsible for preparing the necessary purchase requisitions to maintain a supply of materials to meet the scheduled production. The foremen should draw the necessary materials from stores on a material requisition and should have no part in the purchase requisition process.
2. The copy of the purchase order that is sent to the receiving department and used as a receiving report should not show the quantities so that receiving department personnel are required to count incoming material. Receiving department personnel should also be prevented from converting overshipments to their own use.
3. The purchasing department supervisor should assign purchase order numbers to the requisitions before distribution to the employees who place the orders. He or she should also account for the sequence of purchase order numbers.
4. The purchase orders should be approved by the purchasing department supervisor to ensure that purchases are made from approved vendors at the best price for the quantity and quality requested.
5. The mail department should send the vendors' invoices to the purchasing department when they are received. The purchasing department should compare the terms and so forth, of the invoices and purchase orders and send one invoice copy to the accounting department for vouchering. The other copy should be retained in the files of the purchasing department.
6. The accounting department, rather than the purchasing department, should approve the vouchers for payment. The voucher section should receive a copy of each purchase order and receiving report and the original invoice. This section should then reconcile the purchase orders, receiving reports, and invoices; check discounts, footings, and extensions; prepare a voucher; and approve the voucher for payment. This will ensure that payment is made only for the authorized material received.
7. Beyond these changes intended to reduce the risks identified, efficiency improvements could result from merely generating additional copies of the purchase order and the receiving report. The accounting department should receive a copy of the purchase order for vouching purposes. The store's manager may want a copy of the purchase order to facilitate the planning of storage space. If stock record cards are maintained, a copy of the receiving report will be necessary. Routing a copy of each to the foreman who will use the material might help him or her in scheduling work.

If these types of controls and efficiency enhancements were established, the auditor might judge compliance testing to be cost-beneficial, as a basis for reducing substantive tests on accounts payable and raw materials.

Once the auditor recognizes the relevant error types, their relative probability of occurrence and the materiality of their effects must be evaluated. Such a risk assessment must include consideration of existing controls.

Key Risk Areas and Controls Capable of Preventing or Detecting Errors and Irregularities

Risks can be classified generally as relating to (1) the loss of documents or the introduction of bogus documents, (2) the inaccurate recording of transactions, and (3) the removal of assets. However, for an individual cycle, it is possible to be more specific as to what risks are faced, which controls can limit these risks, and which controls can help detect attempts to camouflage errors or irregularities. In the cost of sales or production cycle, the assets that can be misappropriated are cash, inventory, and fixed assets. The control objectives are to ensure that all valid transactions are recorded in the proper period and account, at the correct amounts, as authorized, and to protect the assets.

Two related risks are that improper vouchers can be prepared or unsupported checks can be issued. Requiring two check signers to examine the supporting documents and a third party to compare the paid checks with the initial cash disbursement records are the controls that can either prevent or detect problems with either vouchers or checks. If such controls are not used, the auditor should study how problems with vouchers or checks may be camouflaged. If an independent party compares disbursements with the subsidiary accounts payable ledger, reconciling them to the respective vendor, and if detailed transactions, including adjusting journal entries, are tested, camouflage attempts should be detected. Generalized audit software can be used to detect errors on blanket purchase order processing that can produce duplicate payments. The sort capability can be used to group invoices by vendor code, invoice number, date, and amount. Then an exception report can be made of all duplicate vendor codes and invoice number or date for a specified period of time. Irregularities related to improper vouchers often stem from poor control. For example, a building superintendent often has substantial latitude on a construction job, having the authority to engage contractors and approve payments for contract work and other services. In one fraud case, a building superintendent created a dummy contract with a fictitious individual, issued checks to the individual as payee, and then forged the endorsement and cashed checks with the cooperation of two cashiers with whom he was acquainted at a local bank and a discount store. This fraud might have been prevented by having more than one employee issue the contracts. And the fraud might have been detected if the internal auditors had made an on-site inspection of the records and verified the existence of the contractor. If there were no internal audit department, the company's main office could have checked the telephone book to see whether the contractor was listed and verified by phone that there was a contractual relationship. The telephone directory can be a cheap and effective control tool for both the client and the auditor.

Another risk is the possible misappropriation of signed checks. An effective preventive control is to require that the second check signer mail the checks directly to the payees. And an effective detective control is to require an independent examination of paid checks in order to uncover any unusual features. If these controls are not used, the same types of test procedures applied to the preparation of improper vouchers or the issuance of unsupported checks are likely to uncover camouflage attempts.

A risk pertaining to payroll is that payroll checks can be improperly disbursed. The relevant controls here are requiring an independent party to test the initial payroll disbursement records, compare paid checks with initial payroll disbursement records, and test payroll disbursements made to those participating in either payroll disbursements or the reconciliation of payroll bank accounts. If these controls are not used, the best way of detecting camouflage attempts is to require that an independent party prepare and handle employee earnings notifications and related employee inquiries. If the risk seems to be substantial, the auditor may send confirmations with annual employee earnings notifications. Exhibit 14-5 describes the common components of a payroll system, the risks of errors or irregularities, and the controls that clients apply to reduce such risks to an acceptable level. This CPA exam question presents a simple flowchart of direct labor payroll processing, and the solution identifies the various risks faced and the related controls which are likely to prevent or detect each

EXHIBIT 14-5

Payroll: Risks and Controls—A Case Example

Case Setting:

In connection with an examination of the financial statements of the Olympia Manufacturing Company, a CPA is reviewing procedures for accumulating direct labor hours. He learns that all production is by job order and that all employees are paid hourly wages, with time and a half for overtime hours.

Olympia's direct labor-hour input process for payroll and job-cost determination is summarized in the following flowchart:

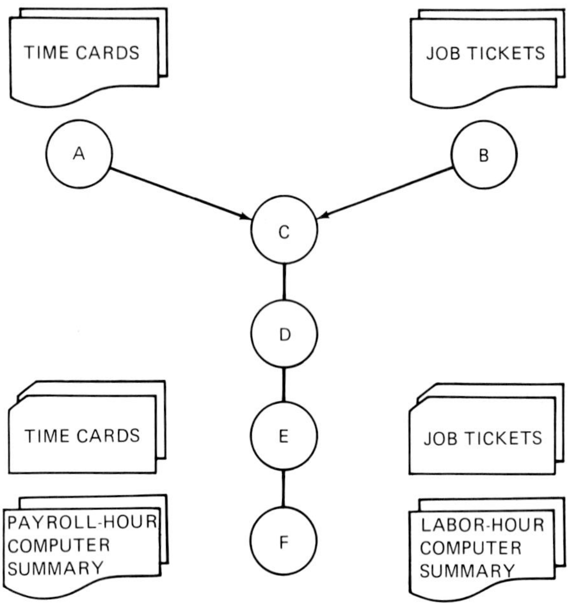

Steps A and C are performed in timekeeping, Step B in the factory operating departments, Step D in payroll auditing and control, Step E in data preparation (keypunch), and Step F in computer operations.

Required:

For each input-processing Step A through F:

1. List the possible errors or discrepancies.
2. Cite the corresponding control procedure that should be in effect for each error discrepancy.

Note: Your discussion of Olympia's procedures should be limited to the input process for direct labor hours, as shown in Steps A through F in the flowchart. Do not discuss personnel procedures for hiring, promotion, termination, and pay rate authorization. In Step F do not discuss equipment, computer program, and general computer operational controls.

Step	Possible Errors or Discrepancies	Control Procedures
A	1. Time may be improperly reported by employees.	1. a. Timekeeping for payroll hours should be an independent function. b. Time clocks should be used under the observation of timekeeping. c. Strict rules should be enforced requiring each employee to punch his or her own time card. d. Timekeeping should make periodic floor checks of employees on duty.

EXHIBIT 14-5
(continued)

Step	Possible Errors or Discrepancies	Control Procedures
	2. Payroll may be padded by timekeeper.	2. a. Employees should be paid directly by paymaster. b. Personnel department should advise payroll audit and control and the computer department of new hires and terminations.
	3. Employees may work unauthorized overtime hours.	3. A procedure for authorization of overtime should be devised, and timekeeping should determine that required authorizations are made.
B	4. Employees may not work effectively during the hours reported to timekeeping, or they may disguise inefficiencies by spreading excess hours to other jobs.	4. a. Employees should report hours by job, preferably by using a time clock. b. Supervisor should review and approve job tickets, and timekeeping should check to see that these approvals are made. (The effectiveness of this system depends on the supervisor's ability to evaluate the time spent on particular jobs and his or her conscientious review of the job tickets.) c. Employees should be instructed to assign actual hours to jobs. Either the supervisor or timekeeping should enforce this policy.
	5. Overtime work on a job may not be authorized, and the job may not be charged at the premium overtime rate.	5. Timekeeping should check required authorizations and appropriately note hours that should be charged at the premium rate.
C	6. Job tickets and time cards may not be in balance.	6. Absolute balancing may be impractical or unnecessary for cost accumulation, allocation, or control; reasonable difference limits should be established by appropriate authority. Differences can be made to fall within established limits by a. Having the timekeeper balance hours per time card with hours per job tickets and resolve differences, or b. Programming computer to zero balance total hours on job tickets with total hours on time card by employee. Differences exceeding established limits would be printed out as exceptions for follow-up by payroll audit and control and/or timekeeper.
D	7. Time cards and job tickets may be lost in transit from timekeeping to payroll audit and control.	7. a. Timekeeping should promptly forward time cards and job tickets accompanied by a transmittal slip denoting the number of employees for which time is being reported. Payroll audit and control should reconcile the number of employees reported with the master-payroll record, considering employees on vacation, out sick, and so forth. b. To ensure that all cards have been accounted for, timekeeping can prepare a hash total of employee numbers for both time cards and job tickets. These totals can be included in the transmittal slip described under (a) above.
	8. Payroll audit and control may total hours incorrectly in preparing the control total for the batch transmittal form.	8. If this is a common error, payroll audit and control should recompute all control totals. If it is an uncommon occurrence, it can be handled as an exception printout from the computer.
E	9. Time cards and job tickets may be lost in transit from payroll audit and control to data preparation.	9. Payroll audit and control should batch time cards and related job tickets. A consecutively numbered transmittal sheet should accompany each batch and contain a control total, such as total hours. This control total should be compared with total shown by keypunch machine.
	10. Keypunch operator may transcribe data incorrectly.	10. Keypunching should be verified by another operator. Errors also will be detected by using batch controls.
	11. The employee identification number may have been recorded or carried forward improperly.	11. Employee identification numbers should contain a self-checking digit, and the computer should be programmed to test the validity of each employee's number.
F	12. Time cards and job tickets may be lost in transit from data preparation to the computer.	12. Supplementing the programmed computer checks, payroll audit and control should check the computer output hours against its input log.
	13. Errors detected by programmed computer controls may not be reentered in the system.	13. Payroll audit and control should maintain an error log.

CPA exam adapted, November 2, 1972, question 3.

of the potential problems. Later in this chapter the types of compliance tests that the auditor could perform to gain assurance that such controls are operating effectively will be discussed.

Shifting to the cash underlying the transactions discussed to this point, a risk exists that cash on hand or on deposit will be misappropriated. By periodically making a surprise count of undeposited cash and imprest funds, such a problem can probably be detected. And the possibility of a cross-substitution can be prevented by requiring that the verification of cash be synchronized with the verification of securities or other liquid assets that can be converted readily into cash. Supporting documents for miscellaneous disbursements or vouchers should be independently tested, as nonroutine transactions are more often vulnerable to abuse, and perpetrators may believe that small-dollar irregularities will not be discovered. Should cash be misappropriated, any cover-ups can probably be detected by requiring that an independent party test detailed cash transactions and compare recorded disbursements with detailed payroll records.

The other risk in the cost of sales or production cycle is that tangible assets may be misappropriated. This concern for inventory and property is most effectively addressed by placing safeguarding controls over the storage and movement of assets. Should tangible assets be removed, an accounting cover-up can be detected by requiring that an independent party periodically compare tangible assets with detailed property ledgers and periodically review adjusting entries with property-related accounts.

Pilfering can be a big problem, and one hears such stories as

- how the employees at a Western cowboy boots manufacturer found that if they came to work barefoot, they could leave each day with a new pair of boots without detection.
- how theft rings operated in stores by taking orders from employees and others for desired inventory items, then placing such items in window displays, and, after taking down the displays, filling the orders without detection, because of poor control over the display items.
- the theme of a popular country song about how an employee at an auto plant stole a car by taking home one part at a time in his lunch box!

The latter bears out the fact that even large items can be subject to pilferage, given they can be disassembled. An extra problem is faced when assets are mobile. For example, construction jobs have incurred substantial losses from thieves who "hot-wired" heavy equipment and drove it away from the construction site.

Tests for Controls

As recognized in Chapter 13, general control concepts require the auditor's attention prior to the performance of detailed compliance tests. A key concern centers on the adequacy with which employees' duties are segregated.

The cost of sales or production cycle should divide the responsibilities of the purchasing department, the receiving department, and the accounts payable department. Exhibit 14-6 outlines the key duties in the cost of sales or production cycle that should be segregated. To the extent possible, duties should be segregated within each function as well. For example, the purchasing department should have one person approve purchase and check requisitions, another prepare the purchase order, a third person review and approve the purchase order, and a fourth person handle and investigate vendors' complaints.

In a sense, the first party authorizes, the second party has "custody" (over purchase orders), the third has accounting responsibility, and the fourth exercises oversight. The fourth person permits an entity to utilize vendors as a feedback loop regarding the effectiveness of controls.

There are several kinds of approvals in a purchasing operation: the initial authorization to use a particular vendor; blanket approvals for routine, small-dollar expenditures; and the approval of each order for any other purchases. To double-check the effectiveness of the authorization procedures, there should be "was–is" reports of any changes in the master files of approved vendors, for review by both the initiator of a request for change and someone else.

Because purchasing is followed by cash disbursements, an auditor must watch for improper extractions of assets by designating bogus suppliers as payees or purchasing personal items through business accounts. Both can be prevented

EXHIBIT 14-6

Duties to Be Segregated in the Cost of Sales or Production Cycle

Authorization	Custody	Accounting
Expenditures for Inventory Purchases and Services: Purchase		
– Purchasing approves purchase orders and investigates complaints. Purchase requisitions are initiated by stores or production control.	– Receiving prepares receiving report and forwards goods to warehousing.	– Accounts payable maintains voucher register, prepares checks based on matched documentation, and maintains accounts payable subsidiary ledger. – General accounting maintains control accounts and reconciles subsidiary ledger and vendor statements.
Expenditures for Inventory Purchases and Services: Payment		
– Treasury department signs checks and requires countersignature.	– Cash disbursements cancels vouchers and maintains check register.	– Accounts payable updates voucher register to reflect payments and maintains the subsidiary accounts payable ledger. – Purchase and expense ledger maintains detailed expense ledger, including prepaid items.
Expenditures: Payroll		
– Personnel approves changes in payroll. – Timekeeping maintains approved time cards.	– Cash disbursements deposits net payroll into imprest bank account.	– Payroll accounting reconciles time cards to books, prepares checks, and maintains employees' records.
– Treasury controls signature plate.	– Payroll distributes checks, returning unclaimed checks to cash disbursements.	– Accounts payable reviews payroll. – General ledger reconciles payroll clearing account, follows-up on employee complaints, and reconciles bank account.
Production Conversion		
– Production control initiates movement or transfer forms.	Warehousing and storeroom maintain safeguards and accounts for flows in and out.	– Physical inventories are taken, including cycle counts. – Cost accounting maintains manufacturing records and prepares reports. – General ledger accounting maintains control accounts, reconciling physical inventory and reports to books.
Petty Cash		
– Treasury verifies imprest basis and signs and countersigns checks for reimbursement after reviewing vouchers.	– Petty cash custodian cashes reimbursement checks and countersigns petty cash voucher.	– Accounts payable reviews petty cash vouchers and prepares check for reimbursement. – Purchase and expense ledger is updated. – General ledger accounting maintains control accounts and prepares bank reconciliation.

Adapted from Wanda A. Wallace, *Handbook of Internal Accounting Controls* (Englewood Cliffs, N.J.: Prentice-Hall, 1984), pp. 198-199.

by instituting careful authorization procedures and effective control over receiving and by avoiding potential conflicts of interest. No employee should be authorized to sign checks for disbursements to himself or herself. Therefore, if an officer requires reimbursement for travel, a third party should sign the check to reimburse that officer.

The lack of segregated duties is probably that attribute most likely to be present when an irregularity occurs. As an example, a trusted employee at a small branch office handled all responsibilities related to the working fund account: He signed checks, prepared working fund reimbursement requests, approved such requests, and reconciled the bank statement. In addition, by substituting for the regular cashier during breaks, lunch, and illnesses, he had access to cash. One of his duties was to follow up on all accounts receivable over 60 days old, and this gave him access to a computer listing of all delinquent customer receivables with both debit and credit balances. Whenever he was unable to locate a customer who had a credit balance, he issued a working fund check payable to both the former customer and the company. Then he endorsed the check with the company's "for deposit only" stamp and cashed it through the cashier's drawer. In preparing the working fund reimbursement request—the source document for the entry—he listed only the customer's name and account number. This fraud was perpetrated for about three years. Then, apparently because of an inability to gain sufficient access to the cashier's funds, the employee altered the payee on some working fund checks so that he could cash them with his signature. During an audit a staff auditor noticed such payee alteration on two checks. After further investigation, the scope of the fraud—in the millions of dollars—was uncovered. Had a few control duties been segregated, along the lines detailed in Exhibit 14-6, this fraud could have been deterred.

Beyond evaluating the segregation of duties, certain other common controls are expected to be a part of a well-controlled system. In particular, the set of subsidiary ledgers should be routinely reconciled to the general ledger, for example, the accounts payable subsidiary ledger and the perpetual or periodic inventory records should be reconciled.

In establishing an effective control environment, the accounting policies and procedures and job descriptions should be clear. For example, a purchasing manual should describe vendor selection criteria, competitive bidding practices, approval practices, coordination between purchasers and users, the right to make long-term purchase commitments, procedures for negotiation, and policies regarding employees' purchases and conflicts of interest. In addition, employees should have access to a receiving manual, inventory manual, inspection and quality control manual, production manual, payroll manual, and a cash disbursements manual. These manuals should explain (1) how partial shipments, damaged goods, obsolescence, and rework items are to be handled; (2) union relations; (3) standard costing practices; (4) hiring practices; and (5) safeguarding procedures over inventory, cash, and signature plates. Some companies have what are known as drop shipments, which are orders that a manufacturer or supplier delivers directly to an auditee's customer, instead of delivering them first to the auditee's business which typically, in turn, delivers them to the customer. Obvious control issues arise in such a setting, since the normal receiving controls cannot be exercised over such goods.

The departments must also be coordinated for efficient operations in the cost of sales cycle. For example, purchasing should be coordinated with users, transportation, receiving, inspection, accounting, management, and legal counsel to make sure that the inventory quality and quantity needs are met on a timely basis, are appropriately accounted for, and do not create legal commitments to suppliers that are inconsistent with management policies. Similarly, payroll must coordinate its activities with personnel, timekeeping, shops, cost distribution, accounts payable, cash disbursements, and general ledger accounting. Any profit sharing, pension, stock purchase, and management compensation plans will further complicate this phase of the cycle.

One of the easier controls to implement, which is frequently absent when improprieties occur in purchasing and cash disbursements, is the practice of cancelling documents. This means stamping documents as paid or processed, and even more visibly, perforating the documents as they are stamped. Such a practice deters accidental double processing of invoices or abuse of a control system by intentional recycling of certain receiving or other supporting documents.

When an auditor evaluates a client's controls, he or she should find out whether the employees understand the control policies and procedures. Often evidence of a lack of understanding is uncovered during audit tests. For example, when testing a bank reconciliation, the auditor may discover that an employee has discarded the voided checks and written checks out of sequential order. This discovery would suggest that the objective of prenumbering and the preference for a complete accounting trail of issued, unissued, and voided documents were not understood by the personnel in the cash disbursements area. Similarly, payroll employees should not mail all unclaimed payroll checks to those employees specified as payees. Rather, the employees should pick up in person the unclaimed checks from the cashier, except in unusual situations for which there should be a special approval system. Without such a practice, a defalcation involving fictitious employees is more likely to occur.

Once the auditor has reviewed the general controls, he or she must evaluate those specific controls which appear to be effectively designed from an audit perspective: Is compliance testing of that control likely to reduce the required substantive testing enough to be cost justified?

Typical Controls and Related Compliance Tests

In the cost of sales and production cycle, cash disbursements are controlled by

1. requiring that disbursements be made only on the basis of approved vouchers (to ensure that they are authorized transactions).
2. having employees not handling cash receipts or disbursements regularly reconcile the bank statements and requiring monthly reviews by an officer.
3. identifying and reclassifying any checks produced but not issued at the end of a fiscal period (to ensure that transactions are recorded in the appropriate accounting period) ***[SAS 43, Section 101].***

The auditor can examine vouchers for evidence of approval, test reconciliations, and review the dates and processing of disbursements around the cutoff date.

Inventory is controlled by

- segregating the processing of inventory records from the custodianship of inventory.
- pricing out perpetual inventory records and routinely tying them to the general ledger (to test accuracy and completeness).
- verifying the pricing of inventory in regard to clerical accuracy and GAAP compliance (to test the propriety of valuations).
- using prenumbered and controlled issue documents to monitor all withdrawals from stores (to safeguard inventory and serve as a completeness check).
- reconciling inventory received and shipped to postings in the perpetual inventory records (to test completeness and accuracy).
- documenting comprehensive cutoff procedures and marking shipping documents around cutoff as "before" or "after" the physical inventory count (to help ensure that transactions are recorded in the appropriate accounting period).
- verifying the quantity of goods held on consignment by customers or other parties (to test accuracy, completeness, and account classification).
- comparing physical inventory with perpetual records, investigating significant discrepancies, and adjusting books to the count (to test existence, accuracy, and completeness).
- regularly reviewing and updating inventory standards (to help safeguard inventory values).
- reporting on material usage and product sales (to help determine obsolete and slow-moving inventories).

Observation and inquiry are used to discover whether duties are segregated. The auditor should also consider such relevant compliance test procedures as whether to inspect and examine the books to check their tie-in, to recompute calculations, and to perform sequence checks on issue documents. Postings can be tested and cutoff documents examined for evidence of their clear classification with respect to the accounting period. The auditor will typically evaluate physical inventory procedures by means of observation techniques and then reconcile the test counts to the client's records. And inquiry and review can reveal how management monitors inventory balances and risk exposure with respect to obsolescence.

The accounts payable associated primarily with purchases are controlled by

- segregating purchasing, accounts payable, and cash disbursements.
- establishing an initiation, review, and authorization of all goods and services, by means of purchase requisitions, approved vendor files, and

the purchasing department's review and approval of purchase orders.

- linking payables and inventory so that the receipt of materials also sets up accounts payable.
- maintaining a receiving log to control receiving reports (to monitor completeness).
- comparing the goods received with the purchase order, and supplier invoices with both the purchase orders and the receiving reports (to ensure propriety and authorization).
- maintaining an open purchase order file, with a review for unreported goods or services received (to monitor completeness).
- identifying receiving reports that have not been matched with invoices at year-end, with necessary accruals made based on purchase order data (to ensure a complete recording of transactions in the appropriate accounting period).
- routinely reconciling the accounts payable subsidiary ledger to the general ledger control account (to test accuracy and completeness).
- management's reviewing intercompany items, debit balances, or other necessary reclassifications or adjustments (to ensure proper account classifications and accurate balances).

The auditor can review each of these reports, documents, and accounting records and compliance test control procedures by reperforming, on a test basis, the various reconciliations, matching procedures, and comparisons made by client personnel.

Any accrued expenses ought to be computed and evaluated routinely, with comparisons made to prior years, whereby fluctuations are investigated. Similarly, prepaid items are commonly subjected to monitoring via analytical review techniques, with year-end balances being reconciled to the general ledger, after recomputation.

Property, plant, and equipment requires controls that (1) distinguish expenses for repairs and maintenance from capitalizable items (to ensure proper account classification); (2) set minimum dollar amounts for capitalization (to communicate company policy); (3) periodically count assets and reconcile that count to detailed records (to test existence, completeness, and accuracy); (4) have management regularly review assets' lives, depreciation methods, and calculations and check consistency with GAAP (to check propriety and reasonableness); and (5) regularly balance subsidiary property records against general ledger control accounts (to test accuracy and completeness). Note that the controls over property for accountability purposes are similar for both operating and investment property. A review of company policies, tests of account classifications and reconciliations, and an examination of evidence of management's monitoring practices are the key compliance tests of such procedures.

For the expenses of producing or selling inventory, the income statement should be reviewed by senior management to identify misclassifications; the items should be analytically reviewed to assess reasonableness; a variance analysis should be conducted; standard end-of-period processing should be used to prevent and/or avoid clerical errors; and account distribution should be decided by knowledgeable personnel to protect against misclassification. Evidence of these procedures should be examined as compliance test work.

Internal control over petty cash should require that (1) all working petty cash funds be maintained on an imprest basis (to maintain accountability); (2) no cash receipts be mixed with the petty cash fund (to segregate duties); (3) responsibility for the fund be invested in one person (to establish responsibility); (4) all petty cash disbursements be made only when there is adequate supporting documentation (to ensure propriety); (5) upon reimbursement, all supporting data should be marked as paid in order to prevent duplicate payment (to protect assets); (6) checks to reimburse petty cash should be made out to the custodian of the petty cash fund (to protect assets and establish responsibility); and (7) the funds be audited by frequent and surprise counts by an internal auditor or other independent person (to check propriety and accuracy). Compliance tests are observation, inquiry, and inspection.

If a preliminary evaluation of internal control shows that the controls can be relied on and can reduce substantial audit work, then compliance tests should be performed on those procedures on which the auditor intends to rely. Exhibit 14-7 presents some examples of compliance tests and the various audit objectives and questions to which the tests pertain. Because compliance tests often produce substantive test information, many of the

EXHIBIT 14-7

Examples of Compliance Tests and Related Audit Objective and Questions

Audit Question to Which Test Might Relate	Compliance Test
Objective: To determine that transactions are authorized, accurate, and appropriately classified. Can controls be expected to result in appropriately classified and accurate recording of valid purchase transactions?	As invoices are processed, verify their account distribution, accuracy, and proper approval.
Objective: To determine propriety of recorded transactions. Are recorded transactions likely to be valid?	Trace entries to supporting documentation such as invoices, vouchers, payroll records, personnel files, canceled checks, and approved vendor listings.
Objective: To determine that transactions are recorded in appropriate period. Were purchase transactions recorded in proper period?	Examine dates on invoices, shipping reports, bills of lading, and receiving reports, and trace them to journals and perpetual records.
Objective: To determine accuracy and completeness of recorded transactions. Do control procedures requiring reconciliations of related accounts appear to have been performed?	Reconcile related accounts like work-in-process credits to finished goods debits.
Objective: To determine accuracy and completeness of recorded transactions. Are employees reconciling ledgers and journals as prescribed, and are they doing so competently?	Examine records for evidence of periodic reconciliation of subsidiary ledgers and journals to general ledger, and check accuracy of such reconciliation.
Objective: To determine propriety and accuracy of recorded transactions. Is inventory valuation reasonable, suggesting that prescribed purchasing procedures are being followed?	Compare inventory valuation with invoices, purchase commitments, pricing policies, and uncompleted contracts.
Objective: To determine reasonableness of recorded transactions. Is auditee monitoring standard cost system as prescribed, and do standard costs and overhead allocations appear reasonable?	Review variance analyses prepared by cost accounting system and analyzed by management, noting particular explanations for reported variances.
Objective: To determine whether transactions are recorded accurately, are properly classified, and are in appropriate accounting period. Is auditee complying with inventory observation procedures, suggesting likelihood of recorded inventory's being accurate?	Observe inventory observation procedures and tie in test counts, giving particular attention to cutoff and handling of consignments.
Objective: To determine that transactions are properly authorized. Is production in line with authorizations?	Examine production orders, noting appropriate approval, and compare sample of job cost sheets with production orders to ensure that authorized production has taken place.
Objective: To determine whether recorded transactions are accurate. Are physical observation results appropriately reflected in inventory records, and are inventories compiled as prescribed?	Coordinate compliance accounting with inventory records, and test accuracy of inventory compilation.
Objective: To determine propriety of recorded transactions. Are recorded property balances reflecting only the property that is owned and in use?	Observe use of property and its existence, testing evidence of ownership, including deeds and property tax receipts.
Objective: To determine accuracy and completeness of recorded transactions. Is depreciation being computed and posted as prescribed?	Test accuracy of depreciation calculations, and trace depreciation entry to ledger accounts.
Objective: To determine that transactions are properly authorized and that recorded transactions can be expected to be complete. Are controls over purchases and abandonments operating effectively?	Test property purchase and abandonment procedures.
Objective: To determine propriety of transactions. Are employees complying with prescribed procedures when distributing payroll? Did anything suspicious occur? Were unclaimed wages greater than anticipated?	Observe payroll distribution.
Objective: To determine accuracy of recorded transactions. How accurately are recorded payroll numbers likely to be recorded?	Test accuracy of payroll calculations.
Objective: To determine propriety and accuracy of recorded transactions. Is payroll appropriately classified and accurate in reflecting actual time worked?	Inspect time records and related reports and trace to payroll and production accounts. Specifically, trace sample of job-time tickets to labor reports.
Objective: To determine whether recorded transactions were authorized. Were cash disbursements properly authorized?	Trace authorizing signature to list of authorized approvers.
Objective: To determine validity, completeness, and accuracy of recorded transactions. Are recorded material costs complete and accurate?	Examine sample of reports on "materials used" for supporting documentation of material requisitions by job number and issue slips.
Objective: To determine completeness and correct classification of recorded transactions. Are all completed jobs recorded as finished goods?	Trace sample of completed job reports to finished goods and cost accounting records, and compare for completeness.

Adapted from Wanda A. Wallace, *Handbook of Internal Accounting Controls* (Englewood Cliffs, N.J.: Prentice-Hall, 1984), pp. 136-137.

procedures in Exhibit 14-7 are dual-purpose in nature.

Auditors should observe the taking of physical inventory to make sure that recorded inventory quantities are likely to be accurate. Proper planning can greatly improve the effectiveness of such procedures. In particular, auditors should encourage their clients to issue formal inventory instructions, such as those which are spelled out in Exhibit 14-8. Compliance with prescribed procedures enhances the likelihood of accurate inventory figures on the books.

In the observation of inventory, test counts are typically performed in order for the auditor to make sure that accurate counts were made by those taking inventory. Test counts tend to be a dual-purpose test, providing information about the effectiveness of the client's controls over the physical inventory process and also substantive test evidence as to inventory balances. The better controlled the process—for example, the use of two inventory teams, one checking the other—the less extensive the test counts need to be. Of course, discovery of errors would suggest a need for extended counts.

The CPA can later compare the test counts with the client's compilation of inventory, checking quantities, descriptions of inventory, conditions of inventory, and accuracy of quantities. Such documentation supports the extent of the CPA's test work.

If inventory is material, cannot be observed, and alternative procedures cannot give the auditor a satisfactory evidential base, a disclaimer is required. If the CPA is unable to observe inventory but can satisfy himself or herself by other auditing procedures, he or she must disclose this in the scope paragraph of the auditor's report.

There are service companies that perform physical inventories for clients and provide inventory certificates regarding the accuracy of the count. But such certificates cannot substitute for the CPA's audit, as the service company is effectively acting as a client when performing the services. Nevertheless, if the service company is known to be competent, its use will strengthen the controls over inventory. Although taking inventory, testing prices, and calculating inventory are still necessary, the extent of this work can be reduced. No reference should be made to the service company's certificate in the auditor's report. The service company's personnel are effectively the client's temporary employees and are not outside specialists on which an auditor can rely in the sense that they, for example, rely on other auditors' reports.[2]

If inventories are in the hands of a public warehouse or other outside custodian, the auditor or-

EXHIBIT 14-8
Formal Inventory Instructions

Inventory tags, count sheets, and work sheets should be prenumbered and controlled.

Instructions for the appropriate way of completing tags, count sheets, work sheets, and examples of each should be studied and completed.

No erasures should be made on tags. Pens should be used, and prescribed procedures for handling voided tags or count sheets should be strictly followed.

All items in inventory should be tagged.

Count teams should be used, and for large dollar items, a second count team should verify the first team's count.

Counters should be familiar with the stock being counted and able to identify and describe it.

Counters should not work excessive hours. If necessary, count teams should be rotated.

Instructions for acceptable methods of determining quantity should be studied. For example, ratio counts or weight counts are acceptable for low-cost, high-quantity items like nuts and bolts.

Receipts and deliveries of inventory should be stopped or carefully controlled to ensure an accurate count. A cut-off of receipts and deliveries should be established.

Any goods that are not a part of inventory should be segregated.

Inventory should be physically arranged to facilitate a count.

Counters should know how to report and handle damaged, obsolete, or slow-moving inventory items.

Careful control should be maintained over all documentation.

The names of the client personnel responsible for the count and the dates and times of inventory taking should be listed on the attached schedule.

There should be clear instructions for how the tags are to be compiled into final inventory listings and summaries.

There should be clear instructions for the pricing of inventory items.

[2]AICPA, *Auditing Interpretations* (New York: AICPA, July 1975), Au Section 509, 1, Section 9509.

dinarily obtains confirmation in writing from the custodian ***[SAS 1, Section 331]***. If very material amounts of inventory are involved, the CPA should review and test the client's controls for investigating and evaluating the warehouseman, obtain the warehouseman auditor's report on controls, observe physical counts, and/or confirm with lenders the detail of pledged warehouse receipts ***[SAS 43, Section 1010]***.

Compliance tests are performed in order to reduce substantive test work. As an example of how compliance tests can affect substantive work, assume that an auditor tests the accuracy of payroll expense by doing the following compliance test work:

- determining that checks are being used in numerical sequence and being accounted for.
- reviewing invoices from suppliers of checks in order to determine that all checks purchased are accounted for.
- inspecting the inventory of unused checks.
- examining the time cards for the completeness of their numerical sequence, thereby establishing numerical control.
- checking for evidence of approval on the time cards.
- asking about the designed segregation of duties and observing operations.
- unexpectedly distributing the payroll checks.

If all of these compliance tests support the controls' effectiveness, then the auditor can reduce the sample size for detailed testing or apply analytical review procedures to payroll expenses in lieu of detailed testing.

If established control procedures included the comparison of payroll to personnel files, payment by check, the use of independent payroll check signers, an independent check distribution, an independent bank statement reconciliation, an independent timekeeping operation, a rotation of payroll employees, mandatory vacations for payroll employees, and occasional surprise payoff by the internal auditors, *then* the risk of fictitious employees would be greatly reduced and the external auditor may deem it totally unnecessary to distribute payroll checks on a surprise basis. The point is that compliance test procedures will vary in response to the configuration of controls in place at a particular client's operations.

Physical Inventories Using Statistical Sampling

Consider the special circumstance in which a client uses statistical sampling to estimate year-end inventory, instead of conducting a complete annual physical count of inventory. In such cases, the auditor should review the client's procedures to evaluate their reliability and determine whether they produce substantially the same results as a 100 percent count would. The auditor should check the statistical validity of the sampling plan, its proper application, and the reasonableness of the planned precision and reliability. The client should have entered all inventory items in the perpetual records before the sample selection. The client should perform a check that this has been done and documentation of such assurance should be available for the auditor's review. The auditor should be present when the sample is drawn to confirm that the selection is random and at the actual observation to make sure that the counting procedures are properly performed. The test count may be made at any time, as long as the perpetual records are well controlled and are periodically compared with the physical counts. Finally, the auditor should review the evaluation of the statistical results and see that the estimated precision at a specified level of reliability meets the materiality requirements of the audit.

Beyond these steps, the auditor would be attentive to the procedures performed when verifying any physical quantity—(s)he would review inventory-taking procedures, observe the count, make test counts, trace selected count data to the inventory compilation, vouch from the compilation to some original count data, verify footings, trace some inventory items into the perpetual inventory records, tie compilations to the subsidiary ledger and investigate differences, test cut-off, review the handling of in-transit and consigned inventory, account for count sheets, and review the classification of inventory items, as well as the condition of inventory.

Accounts Involved and Transactions

As noted in Chapter 13, as the substantive tests are considered, it is useful to identify the accounts affected by transactions that occur within the cost of sales or production cycle. The purchasing and cash disbursements function affect inventory, accounts payable, and cash. The production function affects cost accounting records and the three classes of inventory. Both of these activities interface with the revenue cycle to produce cost of sales. Other costs of doing business involve prepaids, accrued expenses, and payroll—although any direct labor would be reflected in the inventory and cost of sales balances. Petty cash is affected by day-to-day miscellaneous disbursements related to operations.

Property, plant, and equipment are necessary inputs to any business operation and their valuation, acquisition, disposal, and depreciation are all affected by transactions within the cost of sales or production cycle. Similarly, scrap or by-products from manufacturing and their sale or disposal are facets of the cycle.

Substantive Tests, Including Analytical Review

Several substantive tests are commonly applied to the cost of sales or production cycle. The key areas for testing will now be delineated.

Unrecorded Liabilities

Unrecorded liabilities are of obvious interest to auditors. Although Chapter 16 on special audit risks will explore how an auditor searches for unrecorded liabilities in additional depth, more routine procedures are discussed herein.

Unrecorded purchases can be detected by drawing a sample of receiving reports that have not been matched with invoices. To ensure an adequate cutoff, recorded purchases should be vouched to receiving reports after the cutoff date, checking to see whether their date precedes the cutoff date. In addition, inventory quantities should be traced to the physical count. (Of course, many possibilities besides unrecorded purchases might explain any discrepancy here.) The books can be scanned to assess the reasonableness of purchase returns, with some vouching to receiving reports to clarify which inventory should be excluded from the physical count in order to obtain an appropriate cutoff.

When observing physical inventory, the auditor should note any goods that are excluded from a count and ask the reason. When deemed necessary, the recording of these purchases should be reviewed. Any items represented as being in transit during the physical count should be vouched to later receiving reports to verify that the items were in fact in transit. Any goods which are deemed to be of poor condition should be followed up as to their valuation. Generally accepted accounting principles require that such goods be presented at net realizable value. Finally, records of subsequent disposal should be reviewed, including sales documents and cash receipts.

Sometimes, unrecorded liabilities can have an unexpected effect on an operating or marketing decision. For example, consider a utility company that, before the energy crisis, decided to give out coupons for four annual maintenance checks of customers' heating systems. This campaign was meant to educate the customers and promote energy-efficient heating systems supplied by various manufacturers. At its inception, the coupons' cost was $30 per year, and the expenditures were minimal. But when the energy crisis began, many more people redeemed their coupons, and so expenditures rose threefold. Thus the long-term commitment created an unrecorded liability approaching $2 million.

Accounts Payable

The auditor usually compares a trial balance of trade accounts payable with the vendors' statements on hand or with statements requested directly from the vendor. Vouchers, cash records, and journal entries made after the closing data should be reviewed for significant items that were omitted from the accounts payable trial balance ***[SAS 23, Section 318]***. Exhibit 14-9 shows a sample audit program for trade accounts payable, and Exhibit 14-10 offers an example of an accounts payable confirmation request that may be used in testing lia-

EXHIBIT 14-9
An Audit Program for Trade Accounts Payable

1. Obtain trial balance or listing of accounts payable; and then foot and reconcile the total to the general ledger control.

2. Compare listed balances with vendors' statements:

   a. Request statements from principal suppliers when such statements are not on file, whether or not a liability to the supplier appears in the accounts.

   b. Compare vendors' statements on file and those received by us with amounts shown in the trial balance in sufficient number to determine the correctness of the individual accounts.

   c. Have client prepare reconciliations between vendors' statements and individual accounts in the trial balance. Test the larger reconciling items by reference to cash payments, merchandise in transit, and the like.

   d. Request confirmation from creditor if an important account appears to be improperly stated or is in dispute.

3. Search for unentered trade accounts payable by appropriate methods:

   a. Comparison with vendors' statements.

   b. Review of voucher records, cash records, and journal entries made after the balance sheet date.

   c. Review of debit memos and credit memos issued after the balance sheet date.

   d. Review of unentered invoices.

   e. Inquiry of operating and accounting personnel.

   f. Review of liability for sales from inventory on consignment.

   g. Review of receiving cutoff if inventory is taken at year-end.

   The schedule of unrecorded liabilities should be prepared to show source, creditor, nature, date of invoice, date goods or services were received, amount, and account to be charged.

4. Review the trial balance or listing for usable reclassifications of accounts with affiliates; amounts due to officers, directors, or stockholders; payroll; taxes; working fund reimbursements; and any significant amounts not representing usual trade accounts payable.

5. Note debit balances and investigate their nature and collectibility. Consider confirmation and reclassification.

6. Investigate past-due amounts of importance.

7. Analytical review procedures:

   - Calculate the "typical amount of payables for a short period of time," extend that amount by the number of short periods in the fiscal year, and compare with recorded purchases.

   - Multiply the total number of units returned by their average price and compare with recorded returns.

   - Compare recorded volume with current capacity and storage facilities.

   - Analyze payables by vendor.

   - Compare payables to purchases, cost of sales, production, inventory, and cash disbursements.

EXHIBIT 14-10
Example of Accounts Payable Confirmation Request

WAJAW CORPORATION
Anywhere, USA

July 12, 19X7

Vendor X
Somewhere, USA

To whom it may concern:

Our Auditors, ________CPAs, are examining our financial statements and would like you to furnish the following information as of June 30, 19X7:

1. An itemized statement of our accounts payable to you (i.e., all unpaid items);
2. An itemized statement of our notes payable and acceptances payable to you showing their
   - original date
   - due date
   - original amount
   - unpaid balance
   - discount applied
   - endorsers
3. An itemized listing of any of your merchandise that is on consignment to us.

Thank you for your cooperation in this matter. Your timely response would be most appreciated. Note that an envelope is enclosed for your response; it is important that your reply be mailed directly to our CPAs, as indicated.

Sincerely,

____
President

bilities. Such external evidence parallels the receivable confirmation procedure explored in earlier chapters. However, the effectiveness of these procedures differs according to the direction of the expected errors and the power of the evidence collected. For example, receivables are more likely to be overstated, and confirmations are usually best at detecting overstatements. In contrast, accounts payable are more likely to be understated. Of course the incentives of suppliers would encourage reports of any understatements, whereas overstated balances would not be as likely to be reported. Hence, the inherent limitation of having to use vendors' names on the clients' books for confirmation is offset to a small extent by the likelihood of understatements being reported for those accounts that are circularized.

Confirmations of accounts payable are not required, as the vendors' invoices and statements can be used to substantiate the accounts payable balance. But if the controls are weak, the client has severe working capital constraints, the physical inventory count indicates unrecorded inventory, certain vendors' statements are unavailable, or vendor accounts include unusual transactions or are pledged by assets, then the auditor may decide that the confirmation of payables to suppliers is desirable.

In selecting accounts payable balances for audit, the CPA should select accounts with relatively small or no balances, as they are more likely to be understated. In particular, vendors with whom substantial amounts of business were transacted during the year and that have small year-end balances are of primary interest. Previous-year vendors who are no longer used and new vendors used after the year-end should be circularized. Any accounts for which unusual transactions are reported or assets are pledged should be confirmed if the CPA decides to confirm accounts payable.

Related to payable and disbursement transactions is the cash balance, including petty cash. The former was discussed at length in Chapter 13 and will be elaborated upon further in Chapter 15. The latter is typically audited by making a surprise count and testing petty cash vouchers to the extent deemed necessary based on the evaluation of control.

Accrued and Prepaid Expenses

To support accrued salaries, payroll taxes, and amounts withheld from employees' compensation, the payroll is tested, and payroll tax returns are reviewed ***[SAS 44, Section 339]***. Often there are prepaid expenses on the books that must be written off as a function of time or use. Exhibit 14-11 gives an example of working-paper documentation of audit work performed on a prepaid advertising account. If prepaid insurance were being audited, the amount of the fire insurance premium, the period covered by the fire insurance policy, and the amount of expired versus unexpired insurance could be tested by examining the policy and cash disbursement. The adjusting entry would be recomputed. An account like prepaid travel advances could be tied to subsidiary records, expense reports, personnel files, and subsequent use. Confirmation procedures, inquiry, and scanning could be used. Unusual entries, particularly write-offs, should be investigated. Perhaps most important, all such balances should be subjected to analytical review: Is the balance reasonable in light of the past, the industry, and expectations?

Property, Plant, and Equipment

In auditing property, plant, and equipment (PP&E), the auditor should (1) analyze the accounts for the year; (2) examine invoices, authorizations, leases, and similar supporting documentation of major additions; (3) review depreciation and amortization, reconciling them to underlying schedules, the account analysis, and changes to expense; and (4) analyze proceeds from disposals and the accounting for related gains and losses.

Property tax accounts can be tested by examining property tax receipts and state tax returns, as well as the computations for the recorded amounts. It should be obvious that an audit of PP&E interfaces with the financing cycle—particularly with respect to outstanding liens.

Those assertions by management in which the auditor is interested are whether all fixed assets

EXHIBIT 14-11

Example of Working Paper Documenting Audit Work Related to Prepaid Advertising

W/P No.
Preparer
Date

WAJAW Corporation
Prepaid Advertising Audit
6/30/X7

Advertising Medium	Contract Number	Description	Term	Annual Charge	Prepaid Advertising 7/1/X6	Additional Advertising Prepaid	Prepaid Advertising Expensed	Prepaid Advertising 6/30/X7
KRDZ Radio	L769 ®	15, 1-minute announcements	2 years 1/X7–1/X9	30,000	-------	30,000 υ	15,000	© 15,000 CF
Channel 22 TV	X2419 ®	4, 2-minute commercials	1 year 3/X7–3/X8	90,000	-------	90,000 υ	30,000	© 60,000 CF
Bob's Billboards	A192 ®	Rental of 2 billboards	5 years 1/X4–1/X9	4,800	2,400	4,800 υ	4,800	© 2,400 CF
					2,400 √	124,800	49,800	77,400 GL
					T	T	T	T

F = foot
CF = cross-footed and verified calculation of expense
√ = tied to last year's schedule of prepaid advertising in work papers
GL = tied to general ledger
© = confirmed by advertising group; see positive confirmation filed in W/P No._____
® = reviewed contracts for agreement of terms and description
υ = vouched to underlying invoice and related voucher package

Reconciliation to GL Advertising Expense: 80,500 G/L
−49,800 (this schedule)
30,700 (tested via voucher test, see W/P No._____)

have been recorded and are in productive use—including all additions and net of all disposals—and whether repair and maintenance have been correctly expensed rather than capitalized. Related concerns are whether depreciation is accurate, taxes are fully paid to date, insurance is adequate, and an asset has been pledged as collateral. The physical observation of assets shows existence and condition, and inquiry procedures can further support the past and future plans. Directors' authorizations should be available in the minutes for large expenditures, and tracings to the ledger will ensure complete records. A physical inventory of fixed assets and confirmation procedures are not common audit procedures. But very poor controls raise questions about insured value or tax liabilities. Such a circumstance or evidential demands for "persuasive evidence" for a special extended engagement agreement can lead the auditor to use both physical count and confirmation procedures. Ownership of property and any liens or obligations can be tested by vouching to invoices, contracts, and canceled checks and tracing to the minutes and the books. Analytical review can assess the reasonableness of depreciation.

Inventory (and Cost of Sales)

In auditing both inventory and cost of sales, analytical review procedures can be very useful ***[SAS 1, Section 331]***. Comparison of ratios over the recent past and relative to the industry—such as the number of days' sales in inventory, gross profit percentage, and percent of total assets—can reveal unusual balances. Similarly, budgets, forecasts, and long-term commitments should be compared. Relationships among accounts such as receivables, sales, cost of sales, and inventory can be indicators of reasonableness. The relationship of inventory on hand to storage capabilities, production output, insurance coverage, and the balance figured from a simple periodic inventory calculation (of beginning inventory plus purchases minus cost of sales equals ending inventory) can test the fairness of the reported balance.

Detailed test work is likely to involve tracing receiving and shipping reports to the inventory records and vouching the records to the reports. Any periodic physical counts should be compared with inventory records, and adjustments should be noted. The inventory records can be recomputed to test for accuracy. Reconciliation of beginning and ending inventory, tie-in of costs to paid vouchers, and checking for consistency of accounting treatment are other common substantive tests.

The computer can be a valuable audit tool in the cost of sales or production cycle ***[SAS 48, Section 326]***. Exhibit 14-12 explains how generalized audit software can be used to audit inventory. As suggested, observation, vouching, and recalculation are critical audit procedures in tests of inventory balances, while cost of sales relies extensively on the analysis of interrelationships and only slightly upon vouching.

Ratio analysis for a retailer focuses on markdown and markup percentages, inventory shrinkage, and the relationships already discussed ***[SAS 23, Section 318]***. For a manufacturer, variance analysis, materials, labor, overhead costs, and shrinkage are of interest. Keep in mind, as with all areas of audit, key objectives are to determine validity, completeness, authorization, accuracy, ap-

EXHIBIT 14-12

The Computer As an Audit Tool in Testing Inventory

Substantive tests of inventory can be conducted by using EDP in the following manner:

- Draw a random sample of inventory items from the inventory file to be test counted during the physical inventory observation.
- Arrange test counts in a format comparable to the inventory file, and match tapes, printing any exceptions in which the test count differs from the inventory records.
- Multiply the quantity on hand times the cost per unit to test the inventory compilation and extension, and then compare the extended values with the inventory file, again printing exceptions.
- To facilitate cutoff procedures, generate a sample of inventory items purchased or sold on the day of or day before the physical count.
- To determine obsolescence, sort those items in the inventory file that are part of a group of items for which no recent sales have been made.
- List those items with unexpected balances (such as credit amounts) or unexpected fluctuations relative to the past, expectations, or industry experience.
- To facilitate physical observation or confirmation procedures, make a control list for inventory stored at places other than the client's warehouse.

propriate classification, and proper timing; the overall fairness of financial statements and the adequacy of presentation and disclosure will rest upon evaluations of each of these attributes of information generated in the cost of sales cycle.

As discussed in prior chapters, the extent, nature, and timing of substantive testing is expected to reflect the auditor's evaluation of controls and related compliance test work. To illustrate this interdependence, consider Exhibit 14-13. This illustration is similar to Exhibit 14-5, except that GAAS permit less flexibility in the inventory area. Physical observation is required; yet the scope of the test counts, the timing of the observation, and the extent to which compilations are tested all are flexible parts of substantive testing, depending on the risk, materiality, and the reliance on existing controls that have been compliance tested and found to be operating.

Scrap and by-products should be controlled in the same way that other inventory flow is. Analytical review and detailed test procedures can be used to test the handling and disposition of such materials and the reasonableness of reported balances.

Operating Efficiency

Auditors should watch for operating inefficiencies that can be reduced, if not eliminated, by changing the entity's information and control system. For example, maintaining separate perpetual inventory records for raw materials, supplies, purchased parts, work in process, finished goods, consignments out, consignments in, inventory in suppliers' hands, inventory in warehouses, inventory held for third parties, items physically on hand though routinely expensed—such as small tools—and returnable containers in customers' hands can lead to far more efficient ordering and storage practices. To reduce the cost of monitoring inventory investments, many entities use an ABC inventory classification system, analyzing values and labeling (A) items as those of high value that are critical to the production or merchandising process, (B) items as those of lower value that are also critical to operations, and (C) items of nominal value. Then cycle counts are made of A and B items, and

EXHIBIT 14-13

Example of Linkage Among Internal Control Evaluation, Compliance Test Work, and Substantive Testing

1. Evaluation of Controls over Production and Cost Accounting

Strong Controls	Weak Controls
Production orders are authorized formally by initials, as are materials and labor forms	Foreman prepares material requisitions and time summaries without any independent check
Production orders are prenumbered, sequence checks are performed, and blank forms are well controlled; the same is true for material and labor forms	Material requisitions and time cards are not prenumbered or accounted for and blank forms are not well controlled
Reports on materials used and labor are reviewed, as indicated by initials	
Both issue slips and time cards are reconciled to materials used and labor reports	Standard costs are not in use
Inventory received is reconciled to production	
All inventory entries are independently reviewed and approved	

2. Compliance Tests of Controls Deemed to Be Effectively Designed and Judged Likely to Be Cost Beneficial to Perform

Obviously, the compliance test work does not apply to the weak controls.

Control Objectives For Which Procedures Are Being Compliance Tested	
Authorization	• Examine a sample of production orders, material forms, and labor forms, noting initials.
Completeness	• Observe where and how blank forms are secured and then scan files of production orders, material forms, and labor forms for missing numbers.
Accuracy and Approval	• Examine a sample of reports on materials used and labor for initials, as evidence of an independent review.
Accuracy	• Examine reconciliations and how differences identified were resolved.
Accuracy and Approval	• Examine entries for evidence of their independent review and approval.

3. Prepare a bridging work paper for the effects of observed strengths and weaknesses of control design and the results of the compliance test work on substantive testing. The strengths of control support less-extensive test counts of finished inventory and limited testing of the linkage between use reports and journals.

The weaknesses of control suggest a need for

- more extensive test counts of work-in-process inventory.
- tracing, to jobs, from cost accounting records to test the completeness of materials and labor charges.
- vouching of materials costs to invoices and labor costs to employee contracts.
- vouching of prices used in year-end extension of inventory quantities to supporting documentation.

EXHIBIT 14-14
Overview Flowchart of Payments

Accounts Payable Department

Cash Disbursements Department

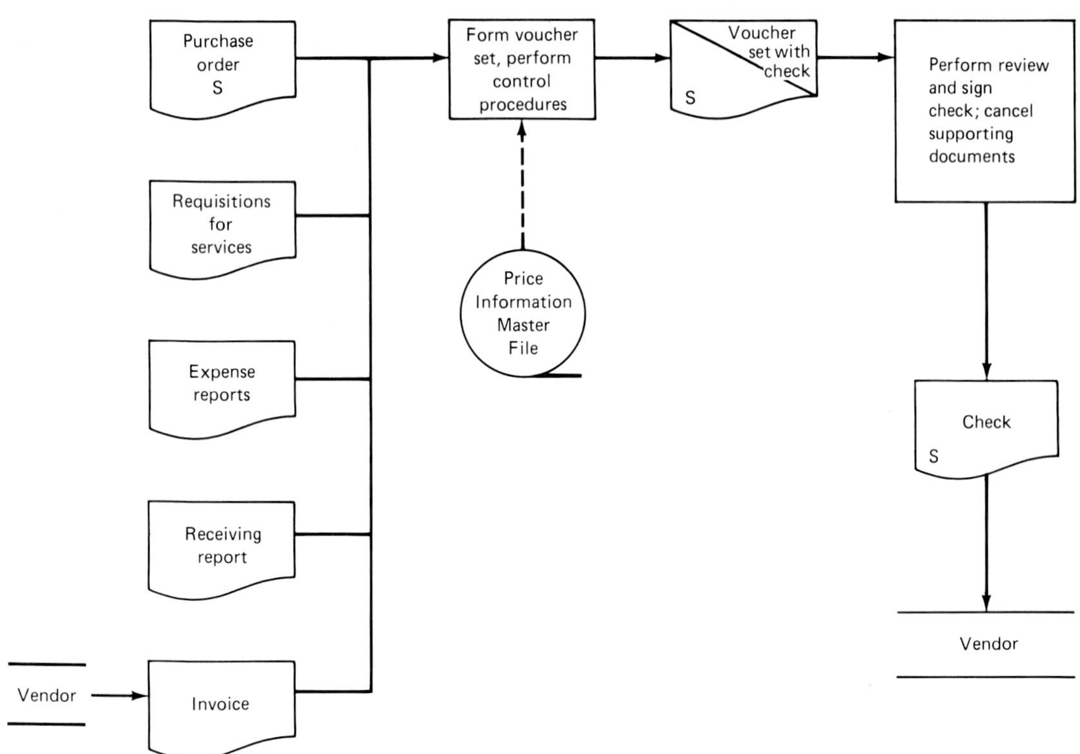

Recall: — — — means Information Flow

S means Signed

means Attached to Other Documents

means Magnetic Tape Storage of Pricing Data

means Document

means Process

C items do not have to be monitored. Besides reducing monitoring costs, inventory investments may be lowered by establishing criteria for holding inventory that are based on the sales value and turnover experience.

An Example: Analyzing Disbursements

Auditors typically perform disbursements or voucher tests on manufacturers' cost of sale or production cycle. Assume that an auditor will audit a client having $6 million in sales and $4.4 million in cost of sales. Income before income taxes is $700,000, and net income is $350,000. The client processes about five hundred invoices and two hundred vouchers a month, meaning that each voucher covers a little more than two invoices. The auditor has prepared an overview flowchart of those accounts payable department's and cash disbursements department's activities relevant to the payment of invoices. This flowchart appears in Exhibit 14-14 (see p. 511) with some reminders of the various flowcharting symbols' meanings. A preliminary evaluation suggests that the controls will justify the auditor's reliance if compliance rates are reasonable. The auditor decides that statistical sampling can be used for such compliance test work.

A Statistical Sampling Application

The first step in the sampling plan is to identify the audit objective ***[SAS 39, Section 350]***. A voucher test determines whether the prescribed controls over disbursements and their distribution to accounts are being followed and are adequate for reliance. Such a compliance test is performed using attributes estimation, so as to arrive at an estimate of the rate of deviations from prescribed procedures.

Second, the auditor must decide which detailed audit steps to perform and what will constitute an error for each audit step. Exhibit 14-15 describes the typical audit steps performed in a voucher test. In Step 1, the auditor decides what will constitute an error for each attribute. The auditor's concern here is to test compliance for each attribute rather than to determine whether a particular control error had any effect on recorded numbers. Therefore, the lack of approval is an error, even if an investigation indicates that the transaction was proper. Similarly, the absence of initials showing that a clerical check had been made is an error, even though a recomputation reveals no mathematical errors. All of these definitions of errors rec-

EXHIBIT 14-15
Audit Procedures Performed in Voucher or Cash Disbursements Test

1. Each voucher should be examined. Check the following attributes:
   - Evidence that the expenditure has proper approval.
   - Adequate supporting documentation:
     - Does the invoice appear authentic?
     - Are submitted expense reports appropriately prepared?
     - Are receiving reports attached whenever applicable?
   - Agreement across supporting documentation:
     - Does the description on the purchase order match both the invoice and the receiving report?
     - Do the quantities noted on all supporting documents match?
   - Evidence that a comparison was made between the invoice pricing and either the purchase order or some other authoritative source for the pricing of acquired goods and services.
   - Evidence that the documents were checked for clerical accuracy.
   - Indication that allowable discounts were taken.
   - Charge to the proper account was made.
   - Supporting documents were canceled to prevent their reuse.
   - Payment was made, as verified through examination of the paid check.
2. Details of the voucher should be traced to the voucher register or other appropriate records accounting for the distribution of expenses.
3. On a test basis, check the footings and cross-footings of the voucher register or other distribution records.
4. Trace the totals of the voucher register or other distribution records to the general ledger and expense ledger postings.

ognize that compliance tests are intended to assess the risk of error due to noncompliance with controls. The fact that an omitted clerical check did not result in a dollar error for a voucher examined does not remove the risk exposure from not having a consistent and effective control over clerical accuracy.

Note that the audit procedures cited in Exhibit 14-15 can be carried out by sampling either invoices or vouchers. From a statistical point of view, the fairly consistent 2-to-1 ratio of invoices to vouchers is not a problem. Either sampling unit will work from a statistical perspective. But the processing of each voucher as a separate unit and the availability of a voucher register from which vouchers can be easily sampled (or a cash disbursements record from which vouchers can be selected just as easily) combine to make the specification of vouchers as a sampling unit more practical than the selection of invoices. The population of vouchers for the year is expected to be the 200 that are processed monthly, multiplied by 12, or 2,400.

The next step in formulating a sampling plan is to determine whether a single test should be performed or whether each of the attributes summarized in (1) of Exhibit 14-15 is in fact a distinct attribute test. This would mean that nine different tests should be performed.

What are the reasons for treating the sampling plan as containing nine attribute tests rather than one? The main reason is that the different attributes may be of varying importance to the auditor. For example, although a check for clerical accuracy is important, there is far more audit risk exposure in an inadequate documentation of a transaction, as goods can be paid for without being received. If all of the attributes are combined into a single test, the error rate will be difficult to interpret—for instance, although 5 percent may be acceptable for one type of error, 3 percent may be required for another. One piece of evidence that can help the auditor decide the importance of separate tests is his or her past experience with the system being tested. What were the error rates in the past? Assume that in the past two years, the results of nonstatistical tests of vouchers identified the following errors from sample sizes of sixty vouchers:

	Last Year	**Two Years Ago**
No evidence of proper approval	1	—
No receiving report	0	1
No evidence of pricing check	2	—
Inaccurate extension, despite evidence of accuracy check	1	1
No cancellations of documents	2	1

No exceptions were noted for the remaining four attributes of interest. Thus the variability of error rates reinforces the propriety of designing the sampling plan as nine tests rather than one overall test.

But this does not mean drawing nine samples. A single random sample can be used for each of the audit tests. But because acceptable error rates vary across the attributes, the sample size requirements will also vary. As Chapter 11 indicated, it is possible to draw a sample to meet the largest sample size requirements, examine the items in the order selected, and stop at the appropriate point to draw the conclusion for each attribute, thereafter discontinuing the check for that particular attribute. However, because the client is likely to pull the vouchers in numerical order and because, once the sample is selected, the marginal cost of examining all nine attributes is very low, most auditors will perform all of the steps on the whole sample but then evaluate each test separately at the level of precision and reliability selected for that particular attribute of interest.

Multiple stopping points are preferred when different supporting documents must be examined for each sample. For example, in a voucher test, if an auditor has to refer to documents separately filed in order to confirm the pricing of invoices, he or she may stop at the smaller sample size for that particular attribute test. However, in the following example we shall assume that the largest required sample size will be used to test all nine attributes.

As explained in Chapters 11 and 12, desired precision is based on materiality, while reliability is based on the auditor's evidential needs from this particular test, weighed against audit costs. Assume that you specify the reliability and precision

EXHIBIT 14-16
Parameters for the Statistical Sampling Plan

Attribute	Desired Confidence Level	Tolerable Error Rate	Expected Error Rate	Required Sample Level
Approval	95	5%	1.0%	93
Documentation	95	5%	0.5%	93
Agreement	95	6%	1.0%	78
Pricing	90	10%	4.0%	65
Clerical	90	10%	4.0%	65
Discount	90	6%	2.0%	88
Charge	95	5%	0.5%	93
Cancel	90	10%	5.0%	78
Payment	95	5%	0.5%	93

rates reported in Exhibit 14-16 and expect the indicated error rates (the attributes are listed as key terms, which can be matched with those in Exhibit 14-15). Then the sample sizes can be determined by referring to the appropriate tables in Chapter 11. Exhibit 14-16 indicates that ninety-three items will be sampled. Clearly, the reliability will be greater than that indicated for all of those attributes requiring samples of fewer than ninety-three items.

When reviewing the precision specifications, it is important to remember that attributes testing is not a form of acceptance sampling. The precision interval will be formed around the error rate and in some sense has to be "accepted," as that is the control system in place. Other than deciding that the entity is unauditable, there is no such thing as "rejecting the system." The auditor merely adapts the audit approach to take advantage of the system's strengths and to compensate for its weaknesses.

Assume that a sample of ninety-three vouchers is randomly selected from the voucher register, and as an example, one deviation from designed approval practices is observed. This represents about a 1 percent deviation or error rate. Whenever a sample finding discloses an error rate less than or equal to expectations (as in this situation), the auditor knows that the results will meet the desired reliability level.

Note that if three invoices are attached to a voucher and one is approved but the other two are not, this will be one error because the voucher, not the invoice, is the sampling unit. However, in assessing the errors' qualitative aspects, the auditor should consider how many times more than one invoice was not approved.

Now assume that two vouchers are not supported by the receiving reports. This is a 2 percent error rate, whereas only .5 percent error was expected. To evaluate these results, refer to the appropriate exhibit in Chapter 11. The desired confidence level is 95 percent, and the closest, yet conservative, sample size in the table is 90. For two deviations, the upper limit on the risk of overreliance is 6.9 percent, a higher risk than the 5 percent specified as the tolerable rate in Exhibit 14-16.

Assume, finally, that the attributes are more narrowly defined, for example, the number of vouchers for which a receiving report was missing. Because some vouchers are for services, for which no receiving report is expected, these items are not needed to form a conclusion. Hence if out of ninety-three vouchers, only ten pertain to services, then only eighty-three will apply to this attribute. If two errors are detected, the error rate will be two out of eighty-three, not two out of ninety-three, thus increasing the possible errors even more.

Possible Reactions to Sampling Results

Two alternative reactions to the results for the compliance test and documentation practices are possible. One is for the auditor to believe that the sample of vouchers may not have been representative of the voucher system with respect to documentation practices. In other words, the inherent sampling risk of 5 percent (the complement of 95 percent reliability) affected the generalizability of the sample statistics. In this situation, the sample size is enlarged, beginning where the original sample selection left off (for example, at a particular point in the random number table). The results of the extended sample are then combined with the initial sample in the evaluation phase. Therefore, to enable the population to reflect an expected error rate of .5 percent, despite the two deviations observed, the minimum extension of the sample, if no additional errors are observed, will be 307 units. This makes it possible to observe two deviations in 400 items, producing the .5 percent occurrence rate originally expected. Two problems are evident. First, even if the auditor's expectations are correct, it will be expensive to demonstrate the veracity of that claim. Second, it is far more likely for a sample to be representative than unrepresentative, meaning that any extension of the sample is likely to confirm the original findings. For these reasons, the alternative likely to be selected is that the internal control being tested cannot be relied on to the extent expected, and so other work must be expanded. Of course, before adjusting the audit plan, a full analysis of any compliance test results requires a review of the qualitative characteristics in the errors detected. For example, did the two deviations in the receiving reports involve drop shipments? Such an evaluation may have implications for the scope of the problem and point to alternative ways of testing disbursements and purchasing practices.

The sampling results for approval practices and all other compliance tests in which the actual error rate of the sample results in an upper error limit within the tolerable range support the auditor's initial judgment that these specific controls can be relied on. In determining how to adjust the overall audit plan to the "mixed" compliance test results, the auditor should consider potential compensating controls for the inadequate procedures ***[SAS 1, Section 320]***. Some of the controls found to be effective may be secondary controls that reduce the risk exposure created by weaknesses in certain primary controls ***[SAS 45, Section 1020]***. Reliance on controls permits adjustment of the nature, timing, and extent of substantive tests ***[SAS 31, Section 326]***.

REVIEW QUESTIONS

1. What transactions are included in the cost of sales or production cycle?

2. Describe the purpose of each of the following forms:
   a. purchase requisition.
   b. buyer's record.
   c. voucher.
   d. open purchase orders.
   e. job ticket.

3. What duties should be segregated in petty cash? Why?

4. What points should be emphasized in (a) an inventory manual and (b) an inspection and quality control manual?

5. What is the purpose of canceling documents?

6. How can controls reduce the risk that tangible assets might be misappropriated?

7. What are the controls over accounts payable that are associated with purchases?

8. If inventory is material and cannot be observed, what should the CPA do?

9. If a client uses a service company to take a physical inventory, how will the client's inventory certificate affect the CPA's audit?

10. Is it acceptable for a client to use statistical sampling to estimate year-end inventory? Explain how an auditor should audit such a client's inventory.

11. What is an ABC inventory classification system?

12. If the actual error rate discovered exceeds the tolerable error rate, how should the auditor react?

EXERCISES

1. An auditor wishes to create a test deck to use in evaluating payroll processing for a large manufacturer. A review of program edit checks indicates that all payroll changes are edited for
   ○ validity of dates.
   ○ alpha name.
   ○ old pay code and rate.
   ○ whether the new rate is equal to the old rate.

In addition, any new rate greater than $100 is printed out as an exception. The rate change card format is as follows:

Card Field	Description
4–12	social security number
13–14	transaction code (04)
16	division
18–22	new hourly rate
24–29	rate change date
30	new payroll code
31–34	first four characters of last name (alpha name)
48–52	old hourly rate
75	old payroll code

Describe the types of tests you would include in the test deck.[3]

2. In 1938, an accountant's report read as follows:

> No inspection was made of the public records to verify the company's ownership of its property, the liens against such property, of the status of real estate taxes. We have not undertaken to pass upon and assume no responsibility for the legal or equitable title of the company's property. . . .[4]

   a. What are the auditor's responsibilities for determining a client's property ownership? What are the audit procedures that the auditor would probably perform?
   b. As a user of the auditor's report, how do you interpret the statement concerning property ownership?
   c. How would you revise such a report? What assumptions support your suggested revisions?

3. The typical internal control questionnaire for cash disbursements asks the following questions:

	Yes	No
a. Are unused checks sequentially numbered and adequately controlled?	___	___
b. Are spoiled checks canceled and retained?	___	___
c. Are checks over a fixed dollar amount required to be cosigned by an officer of the corporation?	___	___
d. Are all supporting documents presented to the check signer and cosigner when they sign the check?	___	___
If a facsimile machine is used,		
e. Is the key and signature plate controlled by employees who do not have access to cash?	___	___
f. Are the checks issued accounted for daily?	___	___

What is the purpose of each of the controls listed in the questionnaire? How can an auditor test for compliance with such controls? How is the adequacy of these controls likely to affect the substantive tests?

4. In reviewing working papers, a senior auditor found documentation of audit work on plant and equipment performed by a young staff auditor, who inadvertently omitted a key to his tick marks. Although you intend to ask the staff auditor to complete the documentation of work performed, what explanations do you expect for each of the following tickmarks, noted on the working papers presented?

W/P Ref. No.
Preparer
Date

WAJAW Corp.
Plant & Equipment
June 30, 19X6

Date	Voucher Number	Payee	Description	Amount
		Balance 6/30/X5		200342.40√
Additions				
7/5/X5	1492	Azny Corp.	Wrapping machine #4RB793	ξ 18322.10X
7/5/X5	1495	Freight Deliverers	Freight on wrapping machine	320.50X
7/5/X5	1502	Handiman Electronics	Installation of wiring for wrapping machine	280.10X
		Total Additions		18922.70
Deductions				
8/5/X5		Machine Corp.	Sold used wrapping machine	14000.00 CR
		Balance 6/30/X6		205265.10 GL

a. √
b. X
c. ξ
d. CR
e. GL

5. A compliance test objective is whether purchases are regularly recorded, and the related financial balance objective is whether the inventory cutoff is correct. Identify the substantive test objective that corresponds to each of the following compliance test objectives:
   a. Purchases are properly authorized.

[3] Adapted from W. Thomas Porter, "Evaluating Internal Controls in EDP Systems," *Journal of Accountancy*, August 1964, pp. 34–40.
[4] Carman G. Blough, "Accountants' Certificates," *Journal of Accountancy*, February 1938, p. 113.

b. Purchases are charged to the appropriate account.
c. All purchases are recorded.

QUESTIONS ADAPTED FROM PROFESSIONAL EXAMINATIONS

1. The client's cost system is often the focus of the CPA's examination of a manufacturing company's financial statements.

   Required:
   a. Why does the CPA review the cost system?
   b. The Summerfield Manufacturing Company uses standard costs in its cost accounting system. List the audit procedures that you would apply to satisfy yourself that Summerfield's cost standards and related variance amounts are acceptable and have not distorted the financial statements. (Confine your audit procedures to those applicable to materials.)

   (CPA exam adapted)

2. The following five financial control objectives should be achieved in regard to the acquisition of goods and services.
   a. The expenditure bears a reasonable relationship to the business's requirements.
   b. Quantities or volumes purchased are reasonable and consistent with needs.
   c. Prices and terms of the purchase are consistent with written agreements.
   d. Goods or services are received.
   e. Proper documentary evidence backs up the transaction.

   Required:
   For each of the above financial control objectives listed, describe two control techniques that can be used to achieve the objective.

   (CIA exam adapted)

3. The internal auditor is testing internal controls over the recording of payables for a manufacturing organization. The internal auditor has examined sixty unpaid vouchers entered in the voucher register during the week following the fiscal year-end and found five material items that should have been recorded as of the year-end. This finding led the internal auditor to the tentative conclusion that the system was not recording material accounts payable in the appropriate year.

   Required:
   List the additional audit procedures for the internal auditor to follow to determine whether the system is recording material accounts in the appropriate year.

   (CIA exam adapted)

4. The Jodam Manufacturing Company has about one thousand production employees who are paid hourly wage rates. The internal auditors examined records maintained by the personnel department to determine the basis of deductions from payroll. They found no system for maintaining current and proper payroll deduction authorizations in personnel files. In their sample of fifty employees, the auditors found six personnel files that did not contain the proper payroll deduction authorizations signed by employees. The internal auditors promptly reported their findings. In response, the personnel manager had the six employees sign appropriate authorization forms for payroll deductions. The personnel manager then reported to the internal auditors that the deficient condition was corrected.

   Required:
   1. Discuss the extent to which internal auditors are responsible for determining that management has taken on appropriate corrective action on the reported audit findings.
   2. What criteria should the internal auditor consider when judging the propriety of corrective action?
   3. Assess the adequacy of the personnel manager's remedial actions according to the specified criteria. (Do not focus on specific control procedures.)

   (CIA exam adapted)

5. Terra Land Development Corporation is a closely held family corporation that purchases large tracts of land, subdivides the tracts, and installs paved streets and utilities. The corporation does not construct buildings for the buyers of the land and does not have any affiliated construction companies. Undeveloped land is usually leased for farming until the corporation is ready to begin developing it.

   The corporation finances its land acquisitions by mortgages, and the mortgages require audited financial statements. This is your first audit of the company, and you have now begun the examination of the financial statements for the year ended December 31, 19X6.

   Your preliminary review of the accounts indicates that the corporation would have had a highly profitable year but the president and vice-president, his son, had not been reimbursed for exceptionally large travel and entertainment expenses.

   Required:
   The corporation has three tracts of land in various stages of development. List the audit procedures to

Question 6.

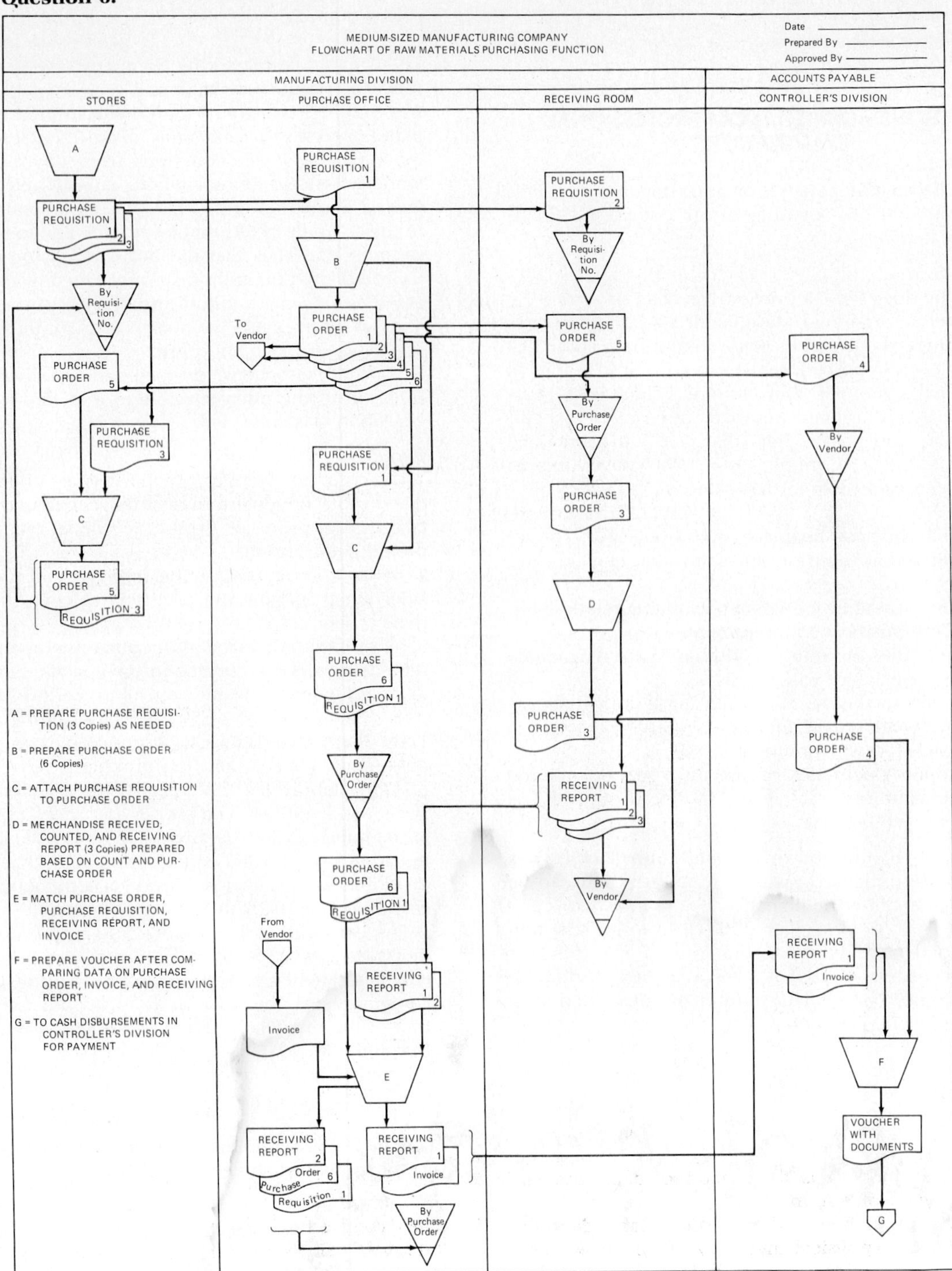

MEDIUM-SIZED MANUFACTURING COMPANY
FLOWCHART OF RAW MATERIALS PURCHASING FUNCTION
Date
Prepared By
Approved By
MANUFACTURING DIVISION
ACCOUNTS PAYABLE
STORES
PURCHASE OFFICE
RECEIVING ROOM
CONTROLLER'S DIVISION
A
PURCHASE REQUISITION 1 2 3
By Requisition No.
PURCHASE ORDER 5
PURCHASE REQUISITION 3
C
PURCHASE ORDER 5
REQUISITION 3
PURCHASE REQUISITION 1
B
To Vendor
PURCHASE ORDER 1 2 3 4 5 6
PURCHASE REQUISITION 1
C
PURCHASE ORDER 6
REQUISITION 1
By Purchase Order
PURCHASE ORDER 6
REQUISITION 1
From Vendor
Invoice
RECEIVING REPORT 1 2
E
RECEIVING REPORT 2
Order 6
Purchase
Requisition 1
RECEIVING REPORT 1
Invoice
By Purchase Order
PURCHASE REQUISITION 2
By Requisition No.
PURCHASE ORDER 5
By Purchase Order
PURCHASE ORDER 3
D
PURCHASE ORDER 3
RECEIVING REPORT 1 2 3
By Vendor
PURCHASE ORDER 4
By Vendor
PURCHASE ORDER 4
RECEIVING REPORT 1
Invoice
F
VOUCHER WITH DOCUMENTS
G
A = PREPARE PURCHASE REQUISITION (3 Copies) AS NEEDED
B = PREPARE PURCHASE ORDER (6 Copies)
C = ATTACH PURCHASE REQUISITION TO PURCHASE ORDER
D = MERCHANDISE RECEIVED, COUNTED, AND RECEIVING REPORT (3 Copies) PREPARED BASED ON COUNT AND PURCHASE ORDER
E = MATCH PURCHASE ORDER, PURCHASE REQUISITION, RECEIVING REPORT, AND INVOICE
F = PREPARE VOUCHER AFTER COMPARING DATA ON PURCHASE ORDER, INVOICE, AND RECEIVING REPORT
G = TO CASH DISBURSEMENTS IN CONTROLLER'S DIVISION FOR PAYMENT

verify the physical existence and title to the corporation's three landholdings.

(CPA exam adapted)

6. Anthony, a CPA, prepared a flowchart which portrays the raw materials purchasing function of one of Anthony's clients, a medium-sized manufacturing company, from the preparation of initial documents through the vouching of invoices for payment in accounts payable. The flowchart was part of the work performed on the audit engagement to evaluate internal control. The flowchart is presented on page 518.

Required:
Identify and explain the systems and control weaknesses evident from the flowchart. Include the internal control weaknesses resulting from activities performed or not performed. All documents are prenumbered.

(CPA exam adapted)

7. A CPA's audit working papers contain the following narrative description of a segment of the Croyden Factory, Inc.'s payroll system and an accompanying flowchart:

Narrative

The personnel department's internal control system is good and is not included in the accompanying flowchart.

At the beginning of each workweek, payroll clerk No. 1 reviews the payroll department files to determine the employment status of the factory employees, prepares the time cards, and distributes them as each individual arrives at work. This payroll clerk, who is also the custodian of the signature stamp machine, verifies the identity of each payee before delivering signed checks to the foreman.

At the end of each workweek the foreman distributes the payroll checks for the preceding workweek. At the same time, the foreman reviews the current week's employee time cards, notes on a summary form the regular and overtime hours worked, and initials the time cards. The foreman then delivers all the time cards and unclaimed payroll checks to payroll clerk No. 2.

A flowchart appears on page 520.

Required:

a. According to the narrative and accompanying flowchart, what are the weaknesses in the internal control system?
b. According to the narrative and accompanying flowchart, what inquiries should be made with respect to clarifying the existence of possible additional weaknesses in the internal control system?

Note: Do not discuss the personnel department's internal control system.

(CPA exam adapted)

8. The year-end physical inventory of a large wholesaler of automotive parts has just been completed. The internal auditor reviewed the inventory-taking instructions before the start of the physical inventory, made and recorded test counts, and observed the controls over the inventory-taking process. No significant exceptions to the process were observed. But the auditor's subsequent comparisons of the quantities shown on the count sheets with those listed on the perpetual inventory cards disclosed numerous discrepancies.

Required:

a. List five likely causes, besides theft, of such discrepancies.
b. List five inappropriate management actions that might have been taken as a result of relying on incorrect perpetual inventory data.

(CIA exam adapted)

9. David Anderson, a CPA, is examining the financial statements of Redondo Manufacturing Corporation for the year ended June 30, 19X6. Redondo's inventories at year-end include finished merchandise on consignment with consignees, and finished merchandise held in public warehouses. The merchandise held in public warehouses is pledged as collateral for outstanding debt.

Required:
Normal inventory and notes payable auditing procedures have been satisfactorily completed. What other auditing procedures should Anderson undertake with respect to:

a. Consignments out?
b. Finished merchandise in public warehouses pledged as collateral for outstanding debt?

(CPA exam adapted)

10. XYZ Corporation always has several hundred employee travel advances outstanding. Subsidiary ledger cards for individual employees are controlled by a general ledger account. Certain advances are specifically designated as "permanent"; all others are intended to be cleared at the end of each field trip. All cash transactions, that is, advances, reimbursements, or returns, and all expenses reported, are posted to the subsidiary ledger cards.

Required:
Assuming that there are no restrictions on the scope of your audit, prepare an audit program to examine the outstanding travel advances and the general ledger control account.

(CPA exam adapted)

11. In connection with the annual examination of Johnson Corp., a manufacturer of janitorial supplies, you have been assigned to audit its fixed assets. The company maintains a detailed property

Question 7.

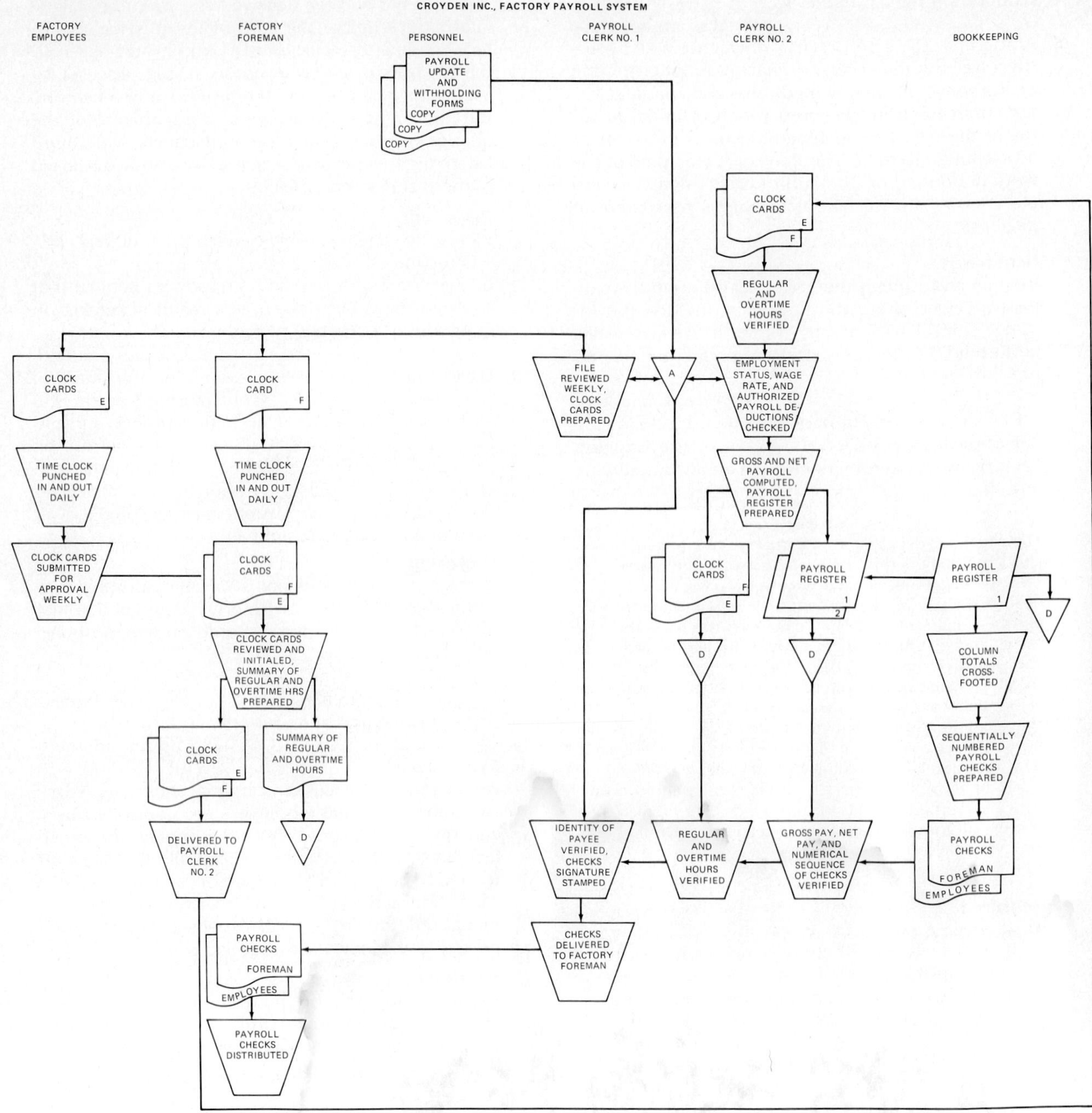

CROYDEN INC., FACTORY PAYROLL SYSTEM
FACTORY EMPLOYEES
FACTORY FOREMAN
PERSONNEL
PAYROLL CLERK NO. 1
PAYROLL CLERK NO. 2
BOOKKEEPING
PAYROLL UPDATE AND WITHHOLDING FORMS
COPY
COPY
COPY
CLOCK CARDS
E
F
REGULAR AND OVERTIME HOURS VERIFIED
CLOCK CARDS
E
CLOCK CARD
F
FILE REVIEWED WEEKLY, CLOCK CARDS PREPARED
A
EMPLOYMENT STATUS, WAGE RATE, AND AUTHORIZED PAYROLL DEDUCTIONS CHECKED
TIME CLOCK PUNCHED IN AND OUT DAILY
TIME CLOCK PUNCHED IN AND OUT DAILY
GROSS AND NET PAYROLL COMPUTED, PAYROLL REGISTER PREPARED
CLOCK CARDS SUBMITTED FOR APPROVAL WEEKLY
CLOCK CARDS
F
E
CLOCK CARDS
F
E
PAYROLL REGISTER
1
2
PAYROLL REGISTER
1
D
CLOCK CARDS REVIEWED AND INITIALED, SUMMARY OF REGULAR AND OVERTIME HRS PREPARED
D
D
COLUMN TOTALS CROSS-FOOTED
CLOCK CARDS
E
F
SUMMARY OF REGULAR AND OVERTIME HOURS
SEQUENTIALLY NUMBERED PAYROLL CHECKS PREPARED
DELIVERED TO PAYROLL CLERK NO. 2
D
IDENTITY OF PAYEE VERIFIED, CHECKS SIGNATURE STAMPED
REGULAR AND OVERTIME HOURS VERIFIED
GROSS PAY, NET PAY, AND NUMERICAL SEQUENCE OF CHECKS VERIFIED
PAYROLL CHECKS
FOREMAN
EMPLOYEES
PAYROLL CHECKS
FOREMAN
EMPLOYEES
CHECKS DELIVERED TO FACTORY FOREMAN
PAYROLL CHECKS DISTRIBUTED

ledger for all fixed assets. You prepared an audit program for the balances of property, plant, and equipment but have not yet prepared one for accumulated depreciation and depreciation expense.

Required:
Prepare a separate comprehensive audit program for the accumulated depreciation and depreciation expense accounts.

(CPA exam adapted)

12. During an examination of the financial statements of Gole Inc., Robbins, a CPA, requested and received a client-prepared property casualty insurance schedule that included the appropriate premium information.

Required:
a. Identify the other types of information that should be included in a property casualty insurance schedule.
b. What audit procedures should Robbins perform in examining the client-prepared property casualty insurance schedule?

(CPA exam adapted)

13. Trapan Retailing Inc. has decided to diversify operations by selling through vending machines. Trapan's plans call for the purchase of 312 vending machines, which will be situated at 78 different locations in one city, and the rental of a warehouse to store the merchandise. Trapan intends to sell only canned beverages at a standard price.

Management has hired an inventory control clerk to oversee the warehousing functions and two truck drivers who will periodically fill the machines with merchandise and deposit the cash collected at a designated bank. The drivers will be required to report daily to the warehouse.

Required:
What internal controls should the auditor expect to find to ensure the integrity of the cash receipts and warehousing functions?

(CPA exam adapted)

14. Review the flowchart on page 522.

Required:
Indicate what each of the letters (A) through (L) represents. Do not discuss inadequacies in the internal control system.

(CPA exam adapted)

15. Multiple Choice: Purchases, Accounts Payable, and Disbursements
Select the one answer that best completes the statement or answers the question.

15.1 An effective internal accounting control measure that protects against the preparation of improper or inaccurate disbursements is to require that all checks be
a. Signed by an officer after the necessary supporting evidence has been examined.
b. Reviewed by the treasurer before mailing.
c. Sequentially numbered and accounted for by internal auditors.
d. Perforated or otherwise effectively canceled when they are returned with the bank statement.

(CPA exam adapted)

15.2 Based on observations made during an audit, the independent auditor should discuss with management the effectiveness of the company's internal procedures that protect against the purchase of
a. Required supplies provided by a vendor who offers no trade or cash discounts.
b. Inventory items acquired based on an economic order quantity (EOQ) inventory management concept.
c. New equipment that is needed but does not qualify for investment tax credit treatment.
d. Supplies individually ordered without considering possible volume discounts.

(CPA exam adapted)

15.3 Which of the following is a standard internal accounting control for cash disbursements?
a. Checks should be signed by the controller and at least one other company employee.
b. Checks should be sequentially numbered, and the numerical sequence should be accounted for by the person preparing the bank reconciliations.
c. Checks and supporting documents should be marked "Paid" immediately after the check is returned with the bank statement.
d. Checks should be sent directly to the payee by the employee who prepares documents that authorize the check preparation.

(CPA exam adapted)

15.4 During the 19X6 audit of the local county's purchasing department, the state auditor's office found and reported to the county commissioners a lack of documentation for purchases. During the 19X7 audit, the state auditor's office wanted to determine whether steps had been taken to rectify the docu-

Question 14.

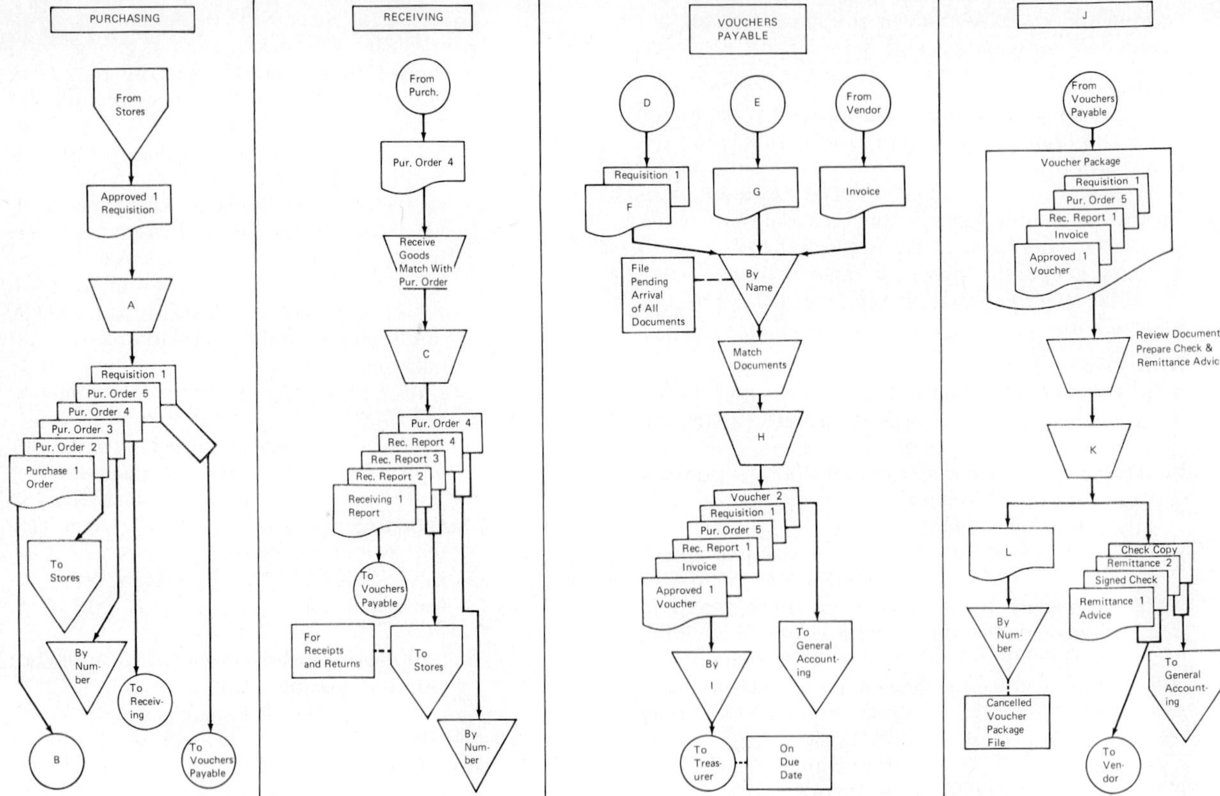

mentation deficiency. Which of the following audit procedures is most likely to disclose the failure to correct the deficiency?

a. Reviewing the purchasing procedures manual maintained in the purchasing department.
b. Examining the receiving department records to make sure that prenumbered receiving reports are issued for goods and services received.
c. Asking the departments requesting goods and services if they are receiving the ordered items.
d. Reviewing a sample of requisitions to determine whether the appropriate approvals to purchase were entered.
e. Selecting a sample of disbursement vouchers to see whether there are corresponding purchase requisitions, purchase orders, and receiving reports.

(CIA exam adapted)

15.5 Propex Corporation uses a voucher register and does not record its invoices in a subsidiary ledger. Propex will probably benefit most from the additional cost of maintaining an accounts payable subsidiary ledger if

a. There are usually invoices in an unmatched invoice file.
b. Vendors' requests for confirmation of receivables often go unanswered for several months until the paid invoices can be reviewed.
c. Partial payments to vendors are continuously made in the ordinary course of business.
d. It is difficult to reconcile the vendors' monthly statements.

(CPA exam adapted)

15.6 An auditor's confirmation of accounts payable balances at the balance sheet date may be unnecessary because

a. This is a duplication of cutoff tests.

b. Accounts payable balances at the balance sheet date may not be paid before the audit is completed.
c. Correspondence with the audit client's attorney will reveal all legal action by vendors for nonpayment.
d. There is likely to be other reliable external evidence available to support the balances.

(CPA exam adapted)

15.7 Effective internal control over the purchasing of raw materials should usually include all of the following procedures except
a. Obtaining third-party written quality and quantity reports before paying for the raw materials.
b. Determining the need for the raw materials before preparing the purchase order.
c. Systematically reporting product changes that will affect raw materials.
d. Obtaining financial approval before making a commitment.

(CPA exam adapted)

15.8 Which of the following is an internal control procedure that will prevent a paid disbursement voucher from being presented for payment a second time?
a. Vouchers should be prepared by those individuals who are responsible for signing the disbursement checks.
b. Disbursement vouchers should be approved by at least two responsible management officials.
c. The date of a disbursement voucher should be within a few days of the date that the voucher is presented for payment.
d. The official who signs the check should compare the check with the voucher and should deface the voucher documents.

(CPA exam adapted)

15.9 The audit procedures used to verify accrued liabilities differ from those used to verify accounts payable because
a. Accrued liabilities usually pertain to continuing services, and accounts payable are the result of completed transactions.
b. Accrued liability balances are less material than are accounts payable balances.
c. There is no evidence supporting accrued liabilities but there is evidence supporting accounts payable that is readily available.
d. Accrued liabilities at year-end will become accounts payable during the following year.

(CPA exam adapted)

15.10 On the last day of the fiscal year, the cash disbursements clerk drew a company check on Bank A and deposited the check in the company's account at Bank B to cover a previous theft of cash. The disbursement has not been recorded. The auditor can best detect this form of kiting by
a. Comparing the detail of cash receipts as shown by the cash receipts records with the detail on the confirmed duplicate deposit tickets for three days before and after the year-end.
b. Preparing from the cash disbursements book a summary of bank transfers for one week before and after the year-end.
c. Examining the composition of deposits in both Banks A and B after the year-end.
d. Examining paid checks returned with the bank statement of the next accounting period after the year-end.

(CPA exam adapted)

15.11 Which of the following will detect an understatement of a purchase discount?
a. Verifying footings and cross-footings of purchases and disbursement records.
b. Comparing purchase invoice terms with disbursement records and checks.
c. Comparing approved purchase orders with receiving reports.
d. Verifying the receipt of items ordered and invoiced.

(CPA exam adapted)

15.12 Budd, the purchasing agent of Lake Hardware Wholesalers, has a relative who owns a retail hardware store. Budd arranged for hardware to be delivered COD by manufacturers to the retail store, thereby enabling his relative to buy at Lake's wholesale prices. Budd was probably able to do this because of Lake's poor internal control over
a. Purchase requisitions.
b. Cash receipts.
c. Perpetual inventory records.
d. Purchase orders.

(CPA exam adapted)

15.13 An examination of the balance in the accounts payable account is ordinarily not designed to
a. Detect accounts payable that are substantially past due.
b. Verify that accounts payable were properly authorized.

c. Ascertain the reasonableness of recorded liabilities.
d. Determine that all existing liabilities at the balance sheet date have been recorded.

(CPA exam adapted)

15.14 An auditor compares the information on canceled checks with the information in the cash disbursement journal. The objective of this test is to determine that
a. Recorded cash disbursement transactions were properly authorized.
b. Proper cash purchase discounts were recorded.
c. Cash disbursements were for goods and services actually received.
d. There are discrepancies between the data on the checks and the data in the journal.

(CPA exam adapted)

15.15 Which of the following procedures regarding the examination of accounts payable can the auditor delegate entirely to the client's employees?
a. Test footings in the accounts payable ledger.
b. Reconcile unpaid invoices to vendors' statements.
c. Prepare a schedule of accounts payable.
d. Mail confirmations for selected account balances.

(CPA exam adapted)

15.16 Flowcharting a disbursements/payments cycle requires information about the use of purchase requisitions, purchase orders, receiving reports, vouchers, and
a. Bills of materials.
b. Vendors' invoices.
c. Canceled checks.
d. Economic order quantity documents.
e. Bidder's lists.

(CIA exam adapted)

15.17 In determining that purchase requisitions were authorized by appropriate personnel, the internal auditor should review
a. Procedures for selecting authorizing individuals to approve purchase requisitions.
b. Evidence of approval of the purchase by an authorized official.
c. The matching of requisitions with the corresponding purchase orders.
d. Control over the security of the requisitions process.
e. Items (a) and (b).

(CIA exam adapted)

15.18 Which of the following is usually the most important procedure that an internal auditor uses to validate a general ledger accounts payable balance as of a particular date?
a. Confirm recorded accounts payable balances with vendors.
b. Examine all vendors' statements on hand.
c. Prepare a trial balance of all open accounts payable balances.
d. Conduct a search for unrecorded accounts payable.
e. Determine that there is adequate supporting data (for example, purchase order, purchase requisitions, receiving reports).

(CIA exam adapted)

16. Multiple Choice: Payroll

Select the one answer that best completes the statement or answers the question.

16.1 Which of the following is the best reason that an auditor should consider observing a client's distribution of regular payroll checks?
a. Separation of payroll duties is not adequate for effective internal control.
b. Total payroll costs are a significant part of total operating costs.
c. The auditor did not observe the distribution of the entire regular payroll during the audit in the previous year.
d. Employee turnover is excessive.

(CPA exam adapted)

16.2 Which of the following is an effective internal accounting control used to prove that production department employees are properly validating payroll cards at a time-recording station?
a. Time cards are carefully inspected by those persons who distribute pay envelopes to the employees.
b. One person is responsible for maintaining records of employee time for which salary payment is not to be made.
c. Daily reports showing time charged to jobs are approved by the foreman and compared with the total hours worked shown on the employees' time cards.
d. Internal auditors should observe the distribution of paychecks on a surprise basis.

(CPA exam adapted)

16.3 An auditor's surprise observation of a client's regular distribution of paychecks is primarily designed to satisfy the auditor that
a. All unclaimed payroll checks are properly returned to the cashier.

b. The paymaster does not distribute the payroll checks.
c. All employees have proper employee identification.
d. Names on the company payroll are those of bona fide employees currently on the job.

(CPA exam adapted)

16.4 A CPA who reviews a client's payroll procedures would consider internal control not to be effective if a payroll department supervisor were assigned the responsibility for
a. Reviewing and approving time reports for subordinate employees.
b. Distributing payroll checks to employees.
c. Hiring subordinate employees.
d. Initiating requests for salary adjustments for subordinate employees.

(CPA exam adapted)

16.5 To check the accuracy of hours worked, an auditor usually compares clock cards with
a. Personnel records.
b. Shop job time tickets.
c. Labor variance reports.
d. Time recorded in the payroll register.

(CPA exam adapted)

16.6 In the audit of which of the following types of profit-oriented enterprises would an auditor be most likely to emphasize when testing the internal control system, the controls over proper classification of payroll transactions?
a. A manufacturing organization.
b. A retailing organization.
c. A wholesaling organization.
d. A service organization.

(CPA exam adapted)

16.7 A common audit procedure for the audit of payroll transactions is tracing selected items from the payroll journal to those employees' time cards that have been approved by supervisory personnel. This procedure is designed to provide evidence supporting the audit proposition that
a. Only bona fide employees worked and their pay was properly computed.
b. Jobs on which employees worked were charged with the appropriate labor cost.
c. Internal controls relating to payroll disbursements are operating effectively.
d. All employees worked the number of hours for which their pay was computed.

(CPA exam adapted)

16.8 Which of the following procedures would an auditor normally perform when testing payroll transactions?
a. Interview employees selected in a statistical sample of payroll transactions.
b. Trace number of hours worked as shown on payroll to time cards and time reports signed by the foreman.
c. Confirm amounts withheld from employees' salaries with proper governmental authorities.
d. Examine signatures on paid salary checks.

(CPA exam adapted)

16.9 Effective internal control over the payroll function includes which of the following?
a. Total time recorded on time-clock punch cards should be reconciled to job reports by employees responsible for those specific jobs.
b. Payroll department employees should be supervised by the management of the personnel department.
c. Payroll department employees should be responsible for maintaining employees' personnel records.
d. Total time spent on jobs should be compared with total time indicated on time-clock punch cards.

(CPA exam adapted)

16.10 A large retail enterprise has established a policy requiring the paymaster to deliver all unclaimed payroll checks to the internal auditing department at the end of each payroll distribution day. This policy was most likely adopted in order to
a. Ensure that employees who are absent on a payroll distribution day are not paid for that day.
b. Prevent the paymaster from cashing checks not claimed for several weeks.
c. Prevent a bona fide employee's check from being claimed by another employee.
d. Detect any fictitious employee who may have been placed on the payroll.

(CPA exam adapted)

17. Multiple Choice: Inventory and Production
Select the one answer that best completes the statement or answers the question.

17.1 Sanbor Corporation has an inventory of parts consisting of thousands of different items of small value individually but of great value in total. Sanbor could establish effective internal accounting control over the parts by requiring

a. Approval by a company officer of requisitions for inventory parts.
b. Maintenance of inventory records for all parts included in the inventory.
c. Physical counts of the parts on a cycle basis rather than at year-end.
d. Separation of the store-keeping function from the production and inventory record-keeping functions.

(CPA exam adapted)

17.2 The primary objective of a CPA's observation of a client's physical inventory count is to
a. Discover whether a client has counted a particular inventory item or group of items.
b. Obtain direct knowledge that the inventory exists and has been properly counted.
c. Appraise the quality of the merchandise on hand on the day of the physical count.
d. Allow the auditor to supervise the conduct of the count so as to obtain assurance that inventory quantities are reasonably accurate.

(CPA exam adapted)

17.3 To best ascertain that a company has properly included merchandise that it owns in its ending inventory, the auditor should review and test the
a. Terms of the open purchase orders.
b. Purchase cutoff procedures.
c. Contractual commitments made by the purchasing department.
d. Purchase invoices received on or around year-end.

(CPA exam adapted)

17.4 Which of the following is an internal control weakness for a company whose inventory of supplies consists of a large number of individual items?
a. Supplies of relatively little value are expensed when purchased.
b. The cycle basis is used for physical counts.
c. The storekeeper is responsible for maintaining perpetual inventory records.
d. Perpetual inventory records are maintained only for items of significant value.

(CPA exam adapted)

17.5 Which of the following is the best audit procedure for discovering damaged merchandise in a client's ending inventory?
a. Comparing the physical quantities of slow-moving items with corresponding quantities of the previous year.
b. Observing merchandise and raw materials during the client's physical inventory taking.
c. Reviewing the management's inventory representation letter for accuracy.
d. Testing overall fairness of inventory values by comparing the company's turnover ratio with the industry average.

(CPA exam adapted)

17.6 A procedure for an internal auditor to ascertain whether retail inventory thefts are occurring is to
a. Review the year-end cutoff of purchases and sales transactions.
b. Observe the taking of physical inventory and make test counts.
c. Test the pricing of merchandise inventory.
d. Investigate significant differences between physical inventory results and retail inventory estimates.
e. Talk to knowledgeable personnel.

(CIA exam adapted)

17.7 When auditing the controls over raw material quality, it is not useful to review and evaluate
a. The fire protection arrangements of the materials storage area.
b. The receiving procedures.
c. The purchasing procedures.
d. The procedures for handling materials.
e. Policies for recognizing and disposing of damaged and obsolete materials.

(CIA exam adapted)

17.8 The auditor tests the quantity of materials charged to work in process by tracing them to
a. Cost ledgers.
b. Perpetual inventory records.
c. Receiving reports.
d. Material requisitions.

(CPA exam adapted)

17.9 In verifying debits to a nonmanufacturing firm's perpetual inventory records, the auditor is most interested in examining the purchase
a. Journal.
b. Requisitions.
c. Orders.
d. Invoices.

(CPA exam adapted)

17.10 An auditor will usually trace the details of the test counts made during the observation of the physical inventory taking to a final inventory schedule. This audit procedure is undertaken to provide evidence that items physically present and observed by the auditor at the time of the physical inventory count are

a. Owned by the client.
b. Not obsolete.
c. Physically present when the final inventory schedule is prepared.
d. Included in the final inventory schedule.

(CPA exam adapted)

17.11 The accuracy of perpetual inventory records may be established, in part, by comparing the perpetual inventory records with the

a. Purchase requisitions.
b. Receiving reports.
c. Purchase orders.
d. Vendor payments.

(CPA exam adapted)

17.12 For several years a client's physical inventory count has been lower than what was shown on the books at the time of the count, so that downward adjustments to the inventory account have been required. Contributing to the inventory problem are weaknesses in internal control that led to the failure to record some

a. Purchases returned to vendors.
b. Sales returns received.
c. Sales discounts allowed.
d. Cash purchases.

(CPA exam adapted)

17.13 Effective internal control over the purchasing of raw materials should include all of the following procedures except

a. Systematic reporting of product changes that will affect raw materials.
b. Determining the need for the raw materials before preparing the purchase order.
c. Obtaining third-party written quality and quantity reports before paying for the raw materials.
d. Obtaining financial approval before making a commitment.

(CPA exam adapted)

17.14 When an auditor tests a client's cost accounting system, the auditor's tests are primarily designed to determine that

a. The quantities on hand have been computed based on acceptable cost-accounting techniques that reasonably approximate the quantities on hand.
b. The physical inventories are in substantial agreement with the book inventories.
c. The system is in accordance with generally accepted accounting principles and is functioning as planned.
d. The costs have been properly assigned to finished goods, work in process, and cost of goods sold.

(CPA exam adapted)

17.15 An auditor has accounted for a sequence of inventory tags and is now going to trace information on a representative number of tags to the physical inventory sheets. The purpose of this procedure is to make sure that

a. The final inventory is valued at cost.
b. All inventory represented by an inventory tag is listed on the inventory sheets.
c. All inventory represented by an inventory tag is bona fide.
d. Inventory sheets do not include untagged inventory items.

(CPA exam adapted)

17.16 The physical count of a retailer's inventory was higher than shown by the perpetual records. Which of the following explains the difference?

a. Inventory items had been counted, but the tags placed on the items had not been taken off the items and added to the inventory accumulation sheets.
b. Credit memos for several items returned by customers had not been recorded.
c. No journal entry had been made on the retailer's books for several items returned to its suppliers.
d. An item purchased "FOB shipping point" had not arrived at the date of the inventory count and had not been reflected in the perpetual records.

(CPA exam adapted)

17.17 Apex Manufacturing Corporation mass-produces eight different products. The controller who is interested in strengthening internal controls over the accounting for materials used in production is most likely to implement

a. An economic order quantity (EOQ) system.
b. A job order cost accounting system.
c. A perpetual inventory system.
d. A separation of duties among production personnel.

(CPA exam adapted)

17.18 If the preparation of a periodic scrap report is essential to maintain adequate control over the manufacturing process, the data for this report should be accumulated in the

a. Accounting department.
b. Production department.
c. Warehousing department.
d. Budget department.

(CPA exam adapted)

18. Multiple Choice: Property, Plant, and Equipment

Select the one answer that best completes the statement or answers the question.

18.1 Which of the following is the most important internal control over acquisitions of property, plant, and equipment?

a. Establishing a written company policy distinguishing between capital and revenue expenditures.
b. Using a budget to forecast and control acquisitions and retirements.
c. Analyzing monthly variances between authorized expenditures and actual costs.
d. Requiring acquisitions to be made by user departments.

(CPA exam adapted)

18.2 Which of the following is an internal accounting control weakness related to factory equipment?

a. Checks issued in payment of purchases of equipment are not signed by the controller.
b. All purchases of factory equipment are required to be made by the department needing the equipment.
c. Factory equipment is generally replaced when its estimated useful life, as indicated in depreciation schedules, has expired.
d. Proceeds from sales of fully depreciated equipment are credited to other income.

(CPA exam adapted)

18.3 Which of the following is the best evidence of real estate ownership at the balance sheet date?

a. Title insurance policy.
b. Original deed held in the client's safe.
c. Paid real estate tax bills.
d. Closing statement.

(CPA exam adapted)

18.4 An internal auditor made several recommendations to improve utilization of plant personnel in a large manufacturing company. Which of the following recommendations would probably have the opposite effect of that intended?

a. Use applicable time study data to specify the cost-job relationship.
b. Eliminate supervision of line personnel.
c. Rotate job responsibilities for repetitious tasks.
d. Develop detailed job performance standards.
e. Use a time clock to document the hours worked by employees.

(CIA exam adapted)

18.5 The auditor may conclude that depreciation charges are insufficient by noting

a. Insured values greatly in excess of book values.
b. Large amounts of fully depreciated assets.
c. Continuous trade-ins of relatively new assets.
d. Excessive recurring losses on assets retired.

(CPA exam adapted)

18.6 Which of the following audit procedures would be least likely to help the auditor find unrecorded fixed asset disposals?

a. Examination of insurance policies.
b. Review of repairs and maintenance expense.
c. Review of property tax files.
d. Scanning of invoices for fixed asset additions.

(CPA exam adapted)

18.7 Which of the following explanations might satisfy an auditor who discovers significant debits to an accumulated depreciation account?

a. Extraordinary repairs lengthened the life of an asset.
b. Previous years' depreciation charges were erroneously understated.
c. A reserve for possible loss on retirement was recorded.
d. An asset was recorded at its fair value.

(CPA exam adapted)

18.8 Which of the following best describes the independent auditor's approach to obtaining satisfaction concerning depreciation expense in the income statement?

a. Verifying the mathematical accuracy of the amounts charged to income as a result of depreciation expense.
b. Determining the method for computing

depreciation expense and ascertaining that it is in accordance with generally accepted accounting principles.

c. Reconciling the amount of depreciation expense to those amounts credited to accumulated depreciation accounts.

d. Establishing the basis for depreciable assets and verifying the depreciation expense.

(CPA exam adapted)

18.9 In violation of company policy, Lowell Company erroneously capitalized the cost of painting its warehouse. The auditor examining Lowell's financial statements would most likely detect this when

a. Discussing capitalization policies with Lowell's controller.

b. Examining maintenance expense accounts.

c. Observing, during the physical inventory observation, that the warehouse had been painted.

d. Examining the construction work orders supporting items capitalized during the year.

(CPA exam adapted)

18.10 Which of the following accounts should the auditor review to ensure that additions to property, plant, and equipment have not been understated?

a. Depreciation.

b. Accounts payable.

c. Cash.

d. Repairs.

(CPA exam adapted)

19. Multiple Choice: Other Topics

Select the one answer that best completes the statement or answers the question.

19.1 A normal audit procedure is to analyze the current year's repairs and maintenance accounts to provide evidence supporting the audit proposition that

a. Expenditures for fixed assets have been recorded in the proper period.

b. Capital expenditures have been properly authorized.

c. Noncapitalizable expenditures have been properly expensed.

d. Expenditures for fixed assets have been capitalized.

(CPA exam adapted)

19.2 During the 19X7 audit, the internal auditor found that 19X6 audit deficiency findings had not been acted upon with respect to receiving department procedures. What would be the most appropriate action for the auditor to take?

a. Instruct the head of the receiving department to adopt new receiving procedures.

b. Direct the plant manager to adopt new receiving procedures.

c. Ignore the situation since it had been commented on last year.

d. Repeat the comment in the 19X7 audit report and indicate that no changes have been made, despite the inclusion of the comment in the 19X6 report.

e. Report the finding immediately to the vice-president of manufacturing.

(CIA exam adapted)

19.3 In evaluating the procedures of a casualty insurance company's claims payment department, the audit step least likely to be included in the audit program is

a. Determine that the payment was within the terms of coverage.

b. Review the claims documentation.

c. Inspect the site to substantiate the extent of the claimed loss.

d. Determine that the claimants' payments on their policies are current.

e. Confirm receipt of the claims payment with the policyholder.

(CIA exam adapted)

19.4 In connection with the review of the prepaid insurance account, which of the following procedures would an auditor generally not perform?

a. Recompute the portion of the premium that expired during the year.

b. Prepare excerpts of insurance policies for the auditor's working papers.

c. Confirm premium rates with an independent insurance broker.

d. Examine support for premium payments.

(CPA exam adapted)

19.5 Patentex developed a new secret formula that is of great value because it has resulted in a virtual monopoly. Patentex has capitalized all research and development costs associated with this formula. Greene, a CPA, who is examining this account, will probably

a. Confer with management regarding transfer of the amount from the balance sheet to the income statement.

b. Confirm that the secret formula is registered and on file with the county clerk's office.
c. Confer with management regarding a change in the title of the account to goodwill.
d. Confer with management regarding ownership of the secret formula.

(CPA exam adapted)

19.6 An internal control questionnaire indicates that an approved receiving report is required to accompany every check request for payment of merchandise. Which of the following procedures offers the greatest assurance that this control is operating effectively?

a. Selecting and examining receiving reports and ascertaining that the related canceled checks are dated no earlier than the receiving reports are.
b. Selecting and examining receiving reports and ascertaining that the related canceled checks are dated no later than the receiving reports are.
c. Selecting and examining canceled checks and ascertaining that the related receiving reports are dated no earlier than the checks are.
d. Selecting and examining canceled checks and ascertaining that the related receiving reports are dated no later than the checks are.

(CPA exam adapted)

19.7 Under which of the following circumstances is an auditor most likely to intensify an examination of a $500 imprest petty cash fund?

a. Reimbursement vouchers are not prenumbered.
b. Reimbursement occurs twice each week.
c. The custodian occasionally uses the cash fund to cash employees' checks.
d. The custodian endorses reimbursement checks.

(CPA exam adapted)

19.8 Which of the following ledger accounts is an auditor most likely to analyze?

a. Service revenue.
b. Sales.
c. Repairs and maintenance expense.
d. Sales salaries expense.

(CPA exam adapted)

19.9 Which of the following is the most reliable analytical review approach to verifying the year-end financial statement balances of a wholesale business?

a. Verify depreciation expense by multiplying the depreciable asset balances by one divided by the depreciation rate.
b. Verify commission expense by multiplying sales revenue by the company's standard commission rate.
c. Verify interest expense, which includes imputed interest, by multiplying long-term debt balances by the year-end's prevailing interest rate.
d. Verify FICA-tax liability by multiplying total payroll costs by the FICA contribution rate in effect during the year.

(CPA exam adapted)

CASE FOR DISCUSSION

Your CPA firm just received a call from the SEC, which received a tip from an employee of one of your clients that a large dollar amount of recorded inventory is bogus. You tell the Commission that the news is surprising because the CPA firm has regularly observed the client's physical inventory. And that particular client has recently hired a controller who is so conservative that he wrote off over $1 million of inventory last year, which included a number of pharmacy items with expired shelf lives, and the client destroyed these items. But the Commission informs you that an investigation team has been sent to the client's warehouses.

As partner of the engagement, you gather the audit team members for a conference. The staff auditors report that they made numerous test counts during the physical inventory and that everything looked fine. When asked about the destruction of the inventory items, the manager winced. "Well, as a matter of fact, that was a little strange. When the assistant controller asked me about the client's intention to destroy inventory, I asked him to tell me the date, time, and location of the destruction, as we would need to observe the process. He assured me that he would, but one month later I got a call. He explained that he had been to Hawaii on business for three weeks and that someone had destroyed the inventory without giving him advance notification."

"So, we didn't actually see the destruction process?" the partner asked. "I'm afraid not," responded the manager.

"Well, our problem doesn't appear to be inventory that isn't on the books. Our problem supposedly is that fictitious inventory has been recorded."

Later that day, the SEC contacts the partner to inform him that the inventory was in fact misstated. The investigators discovered a lot of empty bottles in boxes at the warehouses. Apparently, these boxes had been counted and erroneously valued according to their labels. When the controller was interviewed, he admitted that he became aware of the inventory defalcation when hired but had been unwilling to absorb the entire write-off on the company's books in a single year. Therefore, his plan had been to "destroy" the nonexistent inventory as "spoiled," over a three- to five-year period. He admitted that the auditors had posed a problem when the assistant controller was asked to inform them of the date of destruction so that they could observe it. "We had no inventory to destroy!" the controller explained. "But by sending the assistant controller to Hawaii for three weeks, we were able to claim ignorance. We just apologized to the CPAs, assuring that it would not happen again."

Analyze this case setting in terms of its implications for auditors.

15

The Financing Cycle

James was assigned to do a physical count of the contents of a client's safety deposit box. Two client officers accompanied him to the bank and watched him as he inspected each security and matched it to the description obtained earlier from the client's records. While examining one security, he noted that the serial number did not match his listing. As he turned to ask the client's treasurer about it, the treasurer fell to the floor in a faint. The other client officer exclaimed, "It must be his heart; quick, get a doctor." James ran out to the bank's lobby, explained the emergency, and phoned for an ambulance.

When he returned, the treasurer had revived, and his colleague looked relieved. When told that an ambulance was coming, the treasurer assured them it was unnecessary. But, James persuaded him that it would be a good idea if he went. The treasurer insisted on being accompanied to the hospital, so James was left alone with the safety deposit box. Seeing no reason not to continue, James resumed his inspection. Much to his surprise, the serial number of the security now matched the listing. He decided that he must have made an error earlier.

After completing the count, James returned the box to its appropriate place in the vault and saw that it was locked. He then instructed the bank to lift the freeze that the CPA firm had requested on the box for the first two weeks of January.

Upon returning to his office, James explained to the manager what had happened. The manager asked, "Did you notice anything unusual before the treasurer collapsed?" James mentioned the serial number that had not matched at first. The manager then asked, "Did you have a client employee or a bank officer attest to the contents of the box before returning it to the vault?"

James replied, "No, they both went in the ambulance."

The manager then asked, "Is the freeze still on the box to prevent anyone from reentering it?" At the "no" response, the manager picked up the phone, called the bank, and reinstated the freeze.

"James, I think we'd better extend some of our cutoff procedures and pay special attention to the client's liquid assets and those line items that can easily be made into liquid assets, like the cash surrender value of life insurance."

Puzzled, James asked, "What should we be watching for?"

The manager explained, "I think it's possible that the fainting was staged so that the client could replace a missing security, most likely, the security whose serial number didn't match. If it was, then the money necessary to buy it had to come from somewhere. The cutoff may have been manipulated, and we now have a clue to the magnitude of the problem and the timing of its cover-up."

"Do you mean that everything was a hoax? I thought they were a solid client."

"Yes, they have been. However, lately they've had some rather severe working capital problems, and it's possible that they had used that security as collateral on an unrecorded liability. Most likely, that collateral was substituted or the obligation was temporarily retired in some creative manner."

James left the manager's office but still had a lot of questions:

- Why did it matter whether someone else attested to the contents of the safety deposit box before it was put back?
- Why had the manager reinstated the freeze on the safety deposit box?
- If there had been a manipulation of the cutoff, how could it be detected?
- Of what use could the security have been, even if it were on temporary loan to the client, as the identical serial number had to be retrieved for the year-end physical inspection?

Suddenly, some of the answers became obvious:

- Someone might accuse James of tampering with the box's contents.
- An employee might retrieve the security and use it again for an unrecorded transaction to enhance working capital.
- If there was a cutoff problem, there should be a cash receipt for the improper use of the security. A cash disbursement in the last few days may account for the client's ability to replace the missing security.
- The most obvious use of the security would be as collateral for some unrecorded debt, just as the manager thought. And that would make year-end retrieval possible. Now that he had some of the answers, the task at hand was clear. . . .

In this chapter, the methodology of physical inspections of securities and numerous other audit tests of the finance cycle will be discussed. Periodically, these discussions will tie back to this case which bears out the risk that arises from highly negotiable investments and easy substitution across various types of assets. Although the case presents the client in a far more adversary position than is typically the case in an audit setting, it manages to communicate the full depth of auditor responsibility for the guarded execution of all audit procedures. Sloppy procedures, or a moment of less than full attention to one's actions, can have serious ramifications for an auditor. Of course, internal controls exist mainly to prevent and detect *errors* and audit procedures are similarly directed at errors, since "honest mistakes" far exceed the incidence of irregularities. The introductory cases' discussion of fraud is not intended to imply that such events are other than rare occurrences.

A Definition of What Comprises the Financing Cycle

The financing cycle incorporates debt and equity transactions with their related dividend, interest, and miscellaneous expense items, as well as the management of cash balances. In addition, nonroutine transactions, like adjusting and nonstandard journal entries, financial reporting and general control management responsibilities, and internal auditing activities are usually considered as part of the financing cycle. As explained in Chapter 13, investment activities are the subject matter of both the revenue and financing cycles.

Functions Involved in the Finance Cycle

The typical information flow through the finance cycle is an initial plan by top management that identifies financing needs and desired working capital balances. Then market information and ratios are analyzed to decide whether debt or equity markets offer the better opportunity for raising capital. Of course, consideration is given to control of the company and dilution of ownership whenever the type of financing is selected. The monitoring of debt, equity, and investment transactions, along with the entire accounting information system, thus requires detailed journals and ledgers, with many completeness and accuracy controls, such as periodic reconciliations. The accounting trail for the financing cycle is shown in Exhibit 15-1, which presents some forms for documenting the finance cycle and describes how such forms are used. These documents can be in both computerized and hard-copy form. They document the nature of transactions and related control procedures.

EXHIBIT 15-1

Suggested Forms for Documenting the Financing Cycle

- Loan Compliance Checklist: Documents compliance with debt covenants or the receipt of a waiver for any covenants not met.
- Chart of Accounts: Documents all authorized accounts for use in the financial reporting system.
- Standard Journal Entry Form: Establishes control over all journal entries, cross-referencing or attaching supporting documentation and requiring approval.
- Standard Elimination and Reclassification Form: Establishes control over all elimination and reclassification entries, cross-referencing or attaching supporting documentation and requiring approval.
- Control Sheet over Closing Entries: Ensures booking of all authorized closing entries while documenting the review process.
- Control Listing of Reports Issued: Establishes control over all reports, documenting authorizations as to who receives which reports.
- Standard Reporting Forms: Makes the preparation of monthly financia statements more efficient.
- Checklist of Additional Disclosures Required: Ensures that disclosures are complete.
- Standard Transaction and Consolidation Forms: Makes the preparation of consolidated financial statements more efficient.
- Stock Certificates: Documents ownership of stock.
- Debentures; Notes; Commercial Paper; Similar Debt Instruments: Documents existence and terms of debt obligations.

Adapted from Wanda A. Wallace, *Handbook of Internal Accounting Controls* (Englewood Cliffs, N.J.: Prentice-Hall, 1984), pp. 256-261.

What Can Go Wrong

Exhibit 15-2 lists the possible errors or irregularities in the financing cycle. The auditor can determine a client's vulnerability to each of these risks by studying the client's operations. Consider the following situation:

> The treasurer performs all the investment activities for a company and works very closely with a brokerage house in making investment decisions. There is no management policy specifying a certain return on investment, risk level, liquidity, or diversification.[1]

This description suggests several risks that the client is not controlling:

1. An investment loss due to the lack of a management investment policy.

[1] See CIA Exam, November 10, 1983, question 41.

2. Loss of securities and cash due to inadequate safeguarding procedures; that is, there appear to be no accounting procedures or internal accounting controls for the physical security and cash disbursement for investments.
3. Highly fluctuating cash flow resulting from the lack of a management policy regarding cash levels.
4. Inability to meet capital needs due to the absence of any guidelines on liquidity.
5. Unreasonably valued securities due to the lack of diversification policies or return on investment requirements.
6. The potential for collusion between the treasurer and stockbroker, resulting in the loss of company assets.

The client can limit the exposure to such risks by establishing the following policies and control procedures:

1. A formal investment policy, establishing a minimum expected return, a limit on the equity interest (in percentage terms) acquired in an

EXHIBIT 15-2
The Financing Cycle: Things That Could Go Wrong

- Liabilities may be incurred but not accrued.
- Transactions may be recorded more than once.
- Transactions may be incorrectly classified.
- Clerical errors may cause calculation, extension, footing, and posting errors.
- Accruals of interest and dividends may be recorded in the wrong period.
- Management estimates of reserves may be in error.
- Noncompliance with GAAP may be a problem in such areas as disclosing debt as long term when it is current, changing accounting principles and not recording the change appropriately, or omitting required disclosures.
- Investment assets and cash balances may be inadequately safeguarded.
- Both blank forms related to debt and equity issues and treasury stock may be inadequately safeguarded.
- Disbursement checks may be diverted.
- Bank reconciliations may be falsified.
- Investment securities may be used as collateral for personal loans.
- Sales or purchases of securities may be made at an improper price for personal gain.
- Proceeds from borrowings may be diverted.
- Dividend and interest receipts or payments may be misappropriated.
- Debt or equity covenants may not be honored.
- Excessive costs may be incurred in filing unnecessary reports.

EXHIBIT 15-3
Questions Useful to Auditor in Understanding Auditee's Business, Particularly Its Financing Cycle

- Is the entity closely held and, if so, by what group? What is the profile of the current stockholders?
- What affiliations are there between the entity and major stockholders, board members, customers, suppliers, creditors, or other third parties?
- What is the corporate structure?
- Is the entity regulated? With which regulatory agencies are reports filed?
- What types of communications have gone to stockholders and the public? For example, what is the content of recent news releases and proxy statements?
- What do analysts say about the company's securities?
- What is the level and trend of market price, trading volume, and such operating ratios as the debt-to-equity ratio, times interest earned, and the price-earnings ratio?
- How does the entity's borrowing rate compare with the average market rates?
- What types of forecasting and budgeting procedures are applied day to day and over the long term? For example, is there a formal capital expenditures five-year plan?
- What debt covenants presently restrict debt, equity, or other transactions?
- Who maintains capital stock records?
- What is the entity's level of investment activity?

investment in another country, minimum credit ratings on purchased commercial paper, and similar criteria.
2. An established responsibility for custody of the evidence of ownership and monitoring of the reasonableness of recorded purchases and sales of investments through the use of analytical review procedures.
3. Review and constant updating of cash flow projections.
4. Formal timetable of intended borrowings, loan and equity payouts, and investments of funds.
5. Written approval of investments and verification of recorded value.
6. Competitive selection of a brokerage house, with formal approval by the board of directors and/or the investment committee.

If controls were in place, the auditor might judge compliance testing to be cost beneficial, as a basis for reducing substantive tests of investments.

In order to identify which of the errors and irregularities in Exhibit 15-2 a particular client may commit, the auditor should understand the client's operations. One way to do this is to answer the questions presented in Exhibit 15-3. Once the relevant error types have been recognized, the probability of their occurring and the possibility of their resulting in material misstatements in the financial statements must be assessed. Such a risk evaluation will include consideration of existing controls.

Key Risk Areas and Controls Capable of Preventing or Detecting Errors and Irregularities

There are three key risks in the financing cycle. The first is the possibility that cash on hand or on deposit will be misappropriated. But by requiring an independent party to perform a surprise count of the funds handled by the cash management group and requiring some periodic testing of the supporting documentation for transactions, this risk can be controlled. However, if cash still is misappropriated, an independent party's comparison of recorded activity in the cash account with detailed records and that party's testing of detailed cash transactions should uncover any attempts to cover it up.

The second risk is that tangible assets (such as machinery, trucks, furniture, and investments) will be misappropriated. The establishment of safeguarding procedures for the storage and movement of assets can help prevent such losses. An independent party's periodic comparisons of tangible assets with detailed property ledgers and a periodic review of general and adjusting journal entries affecting property-related accounts are the primary means by which attempts to cover up misappropriations of tangible assets can be detected.

The third risk is that the financial position will be misrepresented. To control this risk, compliance with record-keeping control procedures is essential. Both the establishment of an internal audit group and the examination by external auditors are ways that entities can control risks of financial statement misrepresentations.

Care must be taken to apply GAAP consistently in reporting. In addition, if consolidated statements are to be presented, intercompany transactions must be correctly classified and adjusted. If the accounting system is not effectively controlled, there may be unexplained differences in the subsidiary ledgers' reconciliation to the general ledger. Similarly, the imprest dividend account should be reconcilable to the ledger but, in a poor control environment, may contain discrepancies.

If an entity is regulated and files many public reports, one risk is that unnecessary reports will be filed resulting in excessive costs. For example, a public utility entity had its internal auditors survey reports given to federal, state, and city agents, and the auditors discovered that redundant, unnecessary reports were being filed and that certain reports were being issued too frequently. By seeking the approval of some governmental agencies to modify or eliminate certain filings, the entity saved over $200,000.

Tests for Controls

Certain general control concepts require the auditor's attention before the performance of detailed compliance tests ***[SAS 1, Section 320]***. As with the revenue and cost of sales or production cycles,

EXHIBIT 15-4
Duties to Be Segregated in the Financing Cycle

Authorization	Custody	Accounting
Management of Cash Balances: Budget is prepared and approved by financial management.	– Cashier handles cash.	– A reporting function should quantify opportunity cost of idle cash and prepare cash flow report. – General ledger accounting reviews journal entries, prepares bank reconciliation, and ties cash flow report to books.
Financing Activities – Debt: Treasury department negotiates and seeks authorization of debt agreements.	– Treasurer's department controls prenumbered debt instruments. – Independent trustee oversees sinking fund.	– Liabilities group should monitor bond covenants and report on cost of debt, maintaining payment schedule. – General ledger accounting maintains control accounts, tests interest calculations, and reconciles to board of directors' minutes.
Financing Activities – Equity: Treasury department authorizes stock transactions, signing certificates and ensuring cancellation of stock being replaced.	– Treasurer's department controls prenumbered stock certificates. – An independent transfer agent, registrar, and dividend payment agent often are employed.	– Equities group maintains certificate book and stockholder ledger, and accrues dividends. – General ledger accounting reconciles stockholder ledger and agents' reports to board minutes and control accounts.
Financial Reporting: Board of directors authorizes a chart of accounts.	– Secretary maintains control listing over reports and collects supplementary data.	– Reporting function prepares financial statements and related information. – Controller reviews reports, checking compliance with GAAP.
Internal Auditing: Board of directors authorizes charts, standards, reporting status, and audit plan.	– Board of directors grants to internal auditors full, unrestricted access to assets and records.	– Internal audit prepares reports and follows up on responses, with approval by director and reporting link to board.
Other General Controls: Board of directors or top management authorizes policies and procedures, organization chart, and long-range plans. Treasurer approves board minutes.	– Accounting maintains control over forms.	– General accounting records journal entries and reserve accounts. – General ledger accounting maintains balances and closes books.

Adapted from Wanda A. Wallace, *Handbook of Internal Accounting Controls* (Englewood Cliffs, N.J.: Prentice-Hall, 1984). pp. 252-253.

the financing cycle's control effectiveness depends on the adequate segregation of duties which, for the financing cycle, is depicted in Exhibit 15-4.

Unfortunately, duties that appear to be segregated in form, do not always accomplish their objective in substance. Consider a recently publicized fraud in which $16 million was embezzled from a brokerage firm. The fraud involved false computer entries, check kiting, counterfeit stock certificates, and even a takeover of the company by the embezzlers. The auditors settled charges of negligence for $300,000, noting that they had done nothing wrong, and the SEC stated that its staff was not adequate to ferret out fraud, particularly in the complex computerized securities industry. In explaining how the fraud was perpetrated, the embezzler cited many practices pertaining to the abuse of designed controls. For example:

- When booking "unusual entries" to cover up thefts, such as inflating stockholdings or erasing debt, the embezzler would slip some of them into other clerks' stacks of entries to be processed, returning later to retrieve and destroy the paper work.
- To cover his thefts, the embezzler obtained blank stock certificates from publishing houses and counterfeited lightly traded stocks that did not pay dividends, and although the firm required two people to be present when stock was put into or removed from the bank vault, in the words of the embezzler, he had no problems stuffing the vault with counterfeit shares to cover equity shortages—he simply chose clerks to accompany him who were, as he put it, "too busy or too dumb" to ask questions.
- The embezzler became an active broker but retained responsibility for monitoring margin accounts, despite the treasurer's complaints to the CEO.
- The embezzler also started keeping stock certificates in his desk instead of the vault, despite objections by the treasurer.
- Knowing the date of the annual audit, the embezzler was careful to forge enough stock to cover equity shortages; he pointed out that he had observed auditors merely reading the stock names out loud and comparing the names against the computer's inventory of stocks rather than inspecting the certificates thoroughly (nonetheless, the embezzler had called companies to make sure he had the right officers' names for the certificate, and the signatures were made by an accomplice who signed once with each hand).
- After the annual audit, the embezzler would retrieve the phony certificates from the vault to prevent them from being inadvertently used as collateral for loans.

Upon news of investigation by the Internal Revenue Service, the embezzler turned himself in.[2] As with many fraud cases, the ease of access, unknowing assistance by colleagues, deterioration of control practices, and anticipation of audit procedures facilitated the defalcation. Such tales point to the importance of observation and inquiry procedures to assess whether employees understand the importance of such control practices as dual access to vaults or batch controls and sequence checks on documents processed. Moreover, the auditor should exercise healthy skepticism and resist approaching routine audit procedures in a mundane manner. The similarity of signatures across certificates, the evaluation of the percent of stock holdings which generate no dividend income, and a dominance of unfamiliar stocks which are lightly traded were all potential telltale signs of a problem.

Because of the liquidity of many of the assets exchanged in financing transactions, dual authorization procedures are preferred. The effectiveness of these procedures requires that two persons check the propriety of the transaction being authorized and the compliance with established policies and procedures. Control over issued and unissued documents is critical. Stock certificates and debentures and standardized journal entry forms can substantially influence both the level of assets and the accountability for assets. One way of controlling certain aspects of the financing cycle is to use independent third parties as custodians. Trustees, transfer agents, registrars, and dividend-paying agents often provide such services for debt and equity holdings and investments. These agents, plus an effective internal audit department, can reduce risk exposure. Nonetheless, the company has primary responsibility for complying with all legal, accounting, and record-keeping needs pertaining to the company's ownership and must keep in mind that these agents carry only a portion of that responsibility.

[2]John Curley, "Rise and Fall: How a Clerk Built Up a Brokerage Business by Hook or by Crook," *Wall Street Journal*, February 7, 1985, p. 1.

Operating manuals describing budgeting, investment, and reporting policies, accounting policies and procedures, and job descriptions should be available for cash planning, financing, general accounting procedures, and internal audit activities. These manuals should also discuss preferred sources of credit, negotiation procedures, long-term planning, the acceptability of particular types of debt covenants, and the desired debt-to-equity mix. To ensure an effective internal auditing group, its organizational status should ensure independence. In addition, full access to records and assets should be formally granted to the professional internal audit staff. If an entity consolidates its reports, trades internationally, and faces currency translation–reporting requirements, or is expected to provide supplementary disclosures in accordance with generally accepted accounting principles or regulatory requirements, such practices should also be detailed in the general accounting procedures manual.

The staff should be kept abreast of any changes in accounting, legal, regulatory, and tax requirements. The investment program should address three key risks: unsafe investments, lack of liquidity, and the inadequacy of return relative to the cost of funds, that is, unfavorable leverage. Proper management of these risks requires timely market information and familiarity with innovative analysis and investment techniques. For the investment area, there should be written policies outlining objectives, identifying permissible types of investments, providing diversification guidelines to prevent undue concentration, outlining maturity schedules, identifying quality limitations (such as investments requiring a certain minimum bond rating), and

EXHIBIT 15-5

Control Checklist for Investments, Securities, and Real Estate Holdings, with Related Objectives

	Yes	No
1. Validity: Does the entity maintain documentation to support account entries, e.g., broker's advice and journal entries?	___	___
2. Completeness: Is an investment security ledger maintained, detailing all securities held and all security transactions?	___	___
3. Accuracy: Is the investment security ledger regularly balanced to the general ledger, with respect to both principal and accrued interest totals?	___	___
4. Safeguarding and Proper Period: Have procedures been established to ensure prompt collection of all coupon interest income or other income due on the investment security portfolio? (*Note*: This relates to the revenue cycle.)	___	___
5. Accuracy, Validity, and Disclosure: Are there established procedures to identify related parties, including any association between brokers and officers, directors, or employees?	___	___
6. Authorization and Safeguarding: Have procedures been established to control the officers' authority to purchase and sell securities?	___	___
7. Validity: Are routine legal procedures followed that will produce valid titles, and evidence thereof, to all property?	___	___
8. Accuracy: Is real estate promptly appraised?	___	___
9. Safeguarding: Is a current appraisal obtained for real estate to be sold, as a basis for establishing a sales price?	___	___
10. Existence and Valuation: Are properties periodically inspected?	___	___
11. Existence and Valuation: Do inspections indicate both the condition of the property and its occupancy status?	___	___
12. Safeguarding and Valuation: Are maintenance procedures in effect, ensuring that properties will retain their market value?	___	___
13. Classification: Are separate subsidiary records maintained for each parcel, documenting items capitalized, expenses, rentals, and the like?	___	___
14. Accuracy and Completeness: Are subsidiary ledgers for real estate balanced monthly to the general ledger?	___	___
15. Completeness and Validity: Are complete files maintained for each parcel of real estate?	___	___
16. Safeguarding: Is effective control maintained over rental income? (*Note*: This relates to the revenue cycle.)	___	___
17. Propriety: Does the entity's advertising for the sale or rental of real estate holdings comply with regulations, including governmental agencies' advertising guidelines?	___	___
18. Safeguarding: Are agents bonded who manage properties and collect rent?	___	___
19. Safeguarding: Are security deposits properly controlled?	___	___
20. Safeguarding: Are negotiable securities held under dual control?	___	___
21. Safeguarding: Is the accounting function separate from the security transactions?	___	___
22. Existence and Completeness: Are negotiable securities periodically counted and verified with the general ledger?	___	___

providing for exceptions to standard policy. These policies should be reviewed at least annually for possible revision in light of changing conditions. Exhibit 15-5 (see page 539) is a control checklist that can be useful in analyzing a client's controls over investments, securities, and real estate holdings. The general control objective to which each question relates is highlighted.

Hand in hand with investment activities is their financing and the financing of overall operations. The board of directors should formulate a policy regarding its objectives in borrowing, its philosophy with respect to risks (for example, liquidity-income concerns versus leverage-growth considerations), and its intent to diversify risks by staggering maturities. Borrowings should be limited by the amount outstanding, specific type of borrowing, and/or total interest expense allowable. The execution of borrowings by officers should be limited, with subsequent approval by the board. These actions will place a ceiling on risk exposure caused by a single person. A system of reporting requirements should be in place to help monitor borrowing activities. All established policies, including the stated objectives of top management, should be reviewed annually and revised as appropriate to ensure they are relevant to present market conditions.

In evaluating the controls over stockholders' equity, the auditor should look into the role of the board of directors. For example, in a well-controlled environment, all transfers to and from the net worth accounts should be reviewed by management and approved by the board of directors. The board should designate an individual to control the stockholder records and to sign stock certificates. All transactions involving equity accounts should be clearly explained and adequately documented. Any stock certificates surrendered should be canceled in such a way that prohibits their reuse.

The board of directors should establish policies regarding who is to sign certificates, maintain custody of unissued certificates, sign dividend checks, and maintain journals and records. Unissued stock certificates should be kept under dual control to reduce the risk of misuse in the absence of collusion. A stock certificate book should be maintained, with certificates numbered serially by the printer to assist in maintaining control. Those handling the certificates and debentures should not be responsible for recording transactions, as this would combine custody and accounting, a basic flaw in any control system. There should be a policy for handling lost or stolen certificates so as to prevent their misuse. All capital transactions should be independently verified before certificates are issued. The stockholders' ledger should separately account for each class of authorized and outstanding capital stock and should list the name of the registered owner and the balance of shares owned. At least quarterly, someone other than the person who transfers certificates or makes entries in the stockholders' ledger should prepare a trial balance of outstanding shares from the stockholders' ledger.

For any capital stock transfers, the officer authorized to sign new certificates should inspect the surrendered certificate and make entries in the stockholders' ledger. Surrendered stock certificates should be perforated to prevent possible reuse and attached to related issue stubs in the stock certificate books. A trial balance of open stubs in the stock certificate books should be taken at least annually to test completeness. Once these types of controls have been evaluated from a design perspective, the auditor will decide which controls will reduce the required substantive testing enough to justify the cost of performing compliance tests.

Typical Controls and Related Compliance Tests

Those controls pertaining to investments include (1) a review of maturities at year-end to determine that debt is appropriately classified, (2), the control of securities by a trustee or an officer, and (3) the routine reconciliation of detailed investment records to the general ledger ***[SAS 43, Section 101].*** These controls can be compliance tested by observation and inquiry procedures. Evidence that the review and reconciliation were performed should be available for inspection. Debt transactions may require renegotiation or repayment, and related interest requires monitoring. Proper classification as to maturity and the clerical accuracy

EXHIBIT 15-6

Examples of Compliance Tests and Related Audit Objectives and Questions

Audit Question to Which Test May Relate	Compliance Test
Completeness: Are stock certificates controlled so as to ensure accountability over all such certificates?	Ascertain whether stock certificates are prenumbered, and account for their numerical sequence.
Safeguarding: Are unissued and redeemed securities controlled to prevent unauthorized use?	Examine evidence of effective control over redeemed notes and bonds, canceled equity securities, and unissued securities.
Completeness: Are all issues and dividends recorded?	Trace documentation of stock issues and dividends to records.
Completeness and Accuracy: Are all proceeds and disbursements recorded?	Trace proceeds and disbursements to records, and check their accuracy.
Proper Period: Does the client have controls to ensure timely payment of debt obligations?	Review client's calendar of principal payments and interest payments.
Safeguarding: Are controls over dividend payments effective, or is there a substantial risk of excess payment?	Examine policies regarding use of imprest bank account for dividend payments, and test compliance with such policies.
Authorization: Are charges to equity accounts authorized and accurate?	Review summary of changes in equity balances, recompute, test for board of directors' approval, and reconcile to the entity's records.
Propriety and Safeguarding: Is there regulatory or legal exposure for improper financing activities?	Review lawyer's opinion that the entity's equity and debt issuances have complied with the state's and the SEC's requirements.

of interest calculations need to be tested. Evidence of review and recomputation can be inspected and control procedures reperformed.

For stockholders' transactions, movements in stock accounts and retained earnings should be reconciled, recomputed, and checked by knowledgeable personnel, and entries to such accounts must be approved. Evidence of reconciliation, recomputation, and approval can be inspected in compliance test work.

Disclosure problems for investments center on lower of cost or market valuation, short-term versus long-term classification of marketable securities, and the possibility of investments being made for the purpose of control, shifting to an equity method of accounting and a consolidation basis. Inquiry procedures, stated policies, and the minutes can reveal management's intentions with respect to investments.

Exhibit 15-6 offers some examples of compliance tests that might be performed in the financing cycle, along with an audit objective and question to which each test is related. Keep in mind that many of these tests also provide substantive test evidence and would more accurately be classified as dual-purpose tests.

Compliance tests are performed in order to reduce substantive tests. For example, if an entity uses independent transfer agents and registrars and an imprest bank account for dividend payments, then the auditor can omit examining the stock book and rely entirely on confirmation procedures. In addition, this would provide a basis for reducing the sample size for examining dividend payments.

The minutes of meetings are a formal documentation of the board of directors' important decisions regarding a corporation's operations and activities. By examining the minutes, the auditor can verify whether top management's directives are being fulfilled and whether significant transactions were properly authorized. For example, bonuses, pay increases to officers and employees, charitable contributions, and pension and profit-sharing plans all would require authorization by the board of directors. In addition to noting the agreement between accounting records and the minutes, the CPA should ascertain that the minutes reviewed were complete, verify key points with appropriate corporation officers, obtain formal letters of representation from responsible officials, and review the corporate charter and bylaws to ensure that the actions taken were authorized. To obtain evidence that all minutes are accounted for, the auditor might (1) obtain a letter from the secretary listing all the meeting dates of the board of directors and stockholders during the period of the examination, (2) refer to the approval of the minutes of the preceding meeting (date) in each set of minutes, (3) review the usual meeting schedule, and (4) analyze the fees paid to directors for attending the meeting. If minutes are missing due to their untimely

EXHIBIT 15-7
Corporate Actions That Typically Require Stockholders' Approval and Should Be Recorded in Minutes of Stockholders' Meetings

- Election of directors.
- Stock issuances and retirements.
- Stock voting arrangements.
- Authorization of new classes of securities.
- Waiving of preemptive rights.
- Sale of all or significant parts of business.
- Merger of business.
- Significant acquisitions of other companies.
- Meeting arrangements.
- Stock option, bonus, or profit-sharing plans for key personnel.
- Selection of independent auditors (unless delegated to board of directors).
- Amendments to articles of incorporation and bylaws.
- Liquidation of corporation.

preparation, they need to be prepared and signed. Those actions that an auditor would expect to be approved by stockholders and recorded in the minutes of the stockholders' meetings are summarized in Exhibit 15-7. If approval was not obtained for a significant transaction, the CPA should consult with counsel about the legal significance of failing to properly authorize the transaction and should consider the need for a qualified audit opinion.

Accounts Involved and Transactions

As noted in the prior cycle chapters, the transition from the cycle orientation of compliance tests to the balance orientation of substantive tests requires identification of those accounts which are affected by the types of transactions included in a particular cycle. Investment activities affect marketable securities, long-term accounts like Investments in Unconsolidated Subsidiaries, cash, and related income accounts. Financing activities affect cash, notes payable, and other forms of debt like mortgages and bonds payable. Fixed assets may be affected as collateral for borrowings, requiring certain disclosures. Equity financing relates to stockholder equity accounts, as well as outstanding rights to obtain equity, including stock options, stock appreciation rights, and similar performance plans tied to stock. Dividend policies affect dividends payable, retained earnings, and cash. Donated capital may be received, affecting the contributed capital account and various asset accounts. Finally, an entity may decide to reacquire its own stock, thereby affecting the treasury stock account and cash.

Substantive Tests, Including Analytical Review

When examining investment securities, the auditor should look at brokers' advices and other independent corroborating evidence to verify the sales of securities. Dividend rates can be verified by referring to public records such as Standard & Poor's record of dividend declarations.

In taking an inventory of a client's securities, the auditor's first step should be to obtain a copy of the client's records to use in the count and documentation in the working papers. The second step should be to arrange for a count when a client representative—preferably the treasurer—can accompany the auditor. The reason for the auditor's wanting the treasurer to be present during the count is that in case any securities are missing, there will be a witness who knows that the auditor did not remove such valuables while counting them. Note that this concern ties back to the introductory case. Some auditors will get a signed statement that all investments were returned, with a note of the date of the count. Because the cutoff of liquid assets is extremely important, access to securities should be frozen from year-end to the count period. If securities are stored in a bank, this can easily be done by having the client not authorize any access for the relevant time period and then

EXHIBIT 15-8
Examination of Securities: Watch for . . .

- Name of registered owner.
- Signed power of attorney for collateral held.
- Comparison of date stamped on certificates with cash disbursement—an unreasonable time lag during which funds might have been diverted merits investigation.
- Class of security, face value and, serial number—possible substitutions affecting market valuations.
- Interest and dividend rates and payment dates—use in testing income from investments.
- Maturity dates.
- Coupon bonds' dates—no past due interest coupons and no coupons missing.
- Alterations—possible forgeries.
- Endorsements for transfer—should be rare and require authorization.
- Worthless security status—should not be missing but should be well controlled.

reviewing the bank's records to confirm that no such access has been granted.

The auditor's third step is the actual examination of the securities, and Exhibit 15-8 summarizes those attributes of securities that the auditor should inspect.

In auditing notes payable, the auditor will prepare a schedule of notes payable transactions for the year, showing originating and maturity dates, lenders, amounts, interest rates, and the computation of interest paid and accrued. The amounts due, dates of maturity, and rates of outstanding notes as of the balance sheet date will be confirmed with the lenders. Loan agreements will be reviewed, and compliance with their provisions will be investigated. If a client has a cash surrender value of life insurance as of the balance sheet date, it should be confirmed by direct correspondence with the insurers. The confirmation usually also requests that the insurance company verify the name of the beneficiary and who has the right to make any changes. In addition, the insurer is asked to inform the auditor if any policy loans are in effect. Note that the approximate average debt outstanding multiplied by the average interest rate is expected to tie into interest expense ***[SAS 23, Section 318].***

In auditing stockholders' equity, the auditor should read the minutes of the meetings held by stockholders and directors, noting excerpts of pertinent data. Any changes in the charter or capital stock structure should be reviewed. Total balances of the outstanding preferred and common stock for smaller companies can be prepared fairly easily from the stock certificate stubs. Inquiry procedures are used to identify and review stock options and stock reservations granted during the period. Analytical review procedures may include multiplying the total shares by the approximate average market price and comparing the result with the recorded balances.

The auditor then analyzes the entries to equity accounts and refers to the minutes to determine that declared dividends were paid or approximately reported as a liability. There should be control over the preparation, mailing, and accounting for dividend checks. Dividend checks should be serially numbered and issued sequentially, and all outstanding dividend checks should be independently reconciled at least monthly. The total dividends should be reconcilable to the total number of outstanding shares on the date of record multiplied by the dividend rate approved by the board of directors.

The auditor should ask management about any contingent liabilities, and he or she should ask the company's counsel for written information about any pending litigation, claims, and unasserted claims ***[SAS 12, Section 337].*** Contingencies will be discussed in far greater depth in Chapter 16.

When auditing federal taxes, the auditor should compute the current provision for income taxes and ascertain the tax status for previous years. Risks under the Internal Revenue Code, such as possible exposure to the accumulated earnings tax, should be considered. Accounting income multiplied by the status of the income tax rate can serve as a test of reasonableness.

In a well-controlled system, management will prepare formal plans in the form of a budget and then monitor whether it has achieved its goals. The budget would be reviewed and approved by appropriate managerial personnel and/or the Board of Directors. It would be periodically reviewed and updated to reflect changed conditions. Periodic statements would be prepared, comparing the budget to actual operations, with explanations of variances provided; such statements would be reviewed by management. In this manner, problems can be addressed on a timely basis and the reasons for success can be identified and those procedures applied to other aspects of operation.

Auditors are expected to be alert to opportunities for improving clients' efficiency. In the financing cycle, CPAs will frequently be asked to comment on the entity's working capital and investment policies. The basis for advice will most often be industry experience, that is, how the client's practices compare with those of its industry. Common mechanisms for minimizing working capital commitments include the offering of cash discounts, the tightening of credit standards, and the use of lock boxes at dispersed locations with one-day deposit to a central location.

With this general overview, let's direct attention to some of the key account areas of concern in the finance cycle, tests of the statement of changes in financial position, review of subsequent events, unique considerations in the audit of a partnership, and coordination activities between the CPA and other auditors.

Cash

To summarize the nature and extent of reconciling items in the cash accounts as of the balance sheet date, the auditor may choose to prepare a lead schedule similar to that in Exhibit 15-9. Such a summary is often supported by detailed reconciliations, which are prepared by both the client and the auditor. For each bank statement, the person preparing the reconciliation

- traces the balance for each bank to the bank statement, the cutoff bank statement (that statement after year-end, covering about fifteen days and mailed directly to the auditor), and the confirmation from the bank.
- examines authenticated (by the bank) duplicate deposit slips for deposits in transit, noting dates, details, and computational accuracy.

EXHIBIT 15-9
Lead Schedule for Cash in Bank—Summary of Reconciliations

W/P No.
Preparer
Date

WAJAW Corporation
Cash
Audit 6/30/X6

Name of Bank (account number)	Balance per Books 6/30/X5	Balance per Books 6/30/X6	Reconciling Items, 6/30/X6				Balance per Bank 6/30/X6
			Outstanding Checks	Deposits in Transit	Bank Charges	Other Items	
7964	80,460.02	92,364.80	7,460.10	12,000.00	20.00	-----	87,804.90
3169	45,965.40	42,565.40	3,000.00	42,000.00	-----	-----	3,565.40
	.	.	.	.	.	.	.
	.	.	.	.	.	.	.
	.	.	.	.	.	.	.

- foots outstanding checks, ties those clearing to the cutoff bank statement, and investigates older outstanding items of a material amount.
- traces bank charges to bank statement and banks.
- traces the balance for each bank to the general ledger.
- checks the clerical accuracy of the reconciliation.

When auditing a bank reconciliation, the auditor sends a standard bank confirmation to confirm bank balances. All exceptions noted on the confirmation should be investigated. The auditor should arrange to obtain the cutoff bank statement directly from each bank that will have banking-related documents for the weeks after year-end through the auditor's cutoff date. Any items in transit should be tied to bank statements to ascertain that all deposits have been properly credited. The auditor should recompute the totals, as defalcations or errors can be camouflaged by underfooting outstanding checks.

A standard confirmation inquiry form was illustrated in Chapter 7. It requests information on contingent liabilities related to notes receivable which have been discounted by the bank. In addition, information on collateral is requested.

Cutoff bank statements should be requested separately from the bank confirmations, as each item will probably be handled by different departments in the bank. The letter requesting the cutoff bank statement should list the bank accounts and account numbers for which statements are requested. Whenever an entity has several bank accounts, the auditor should watch for kiting.

Cash counts of undeposited cash receipts and cash working funds should be made simultaneously with a count of significant amounts of negotiable securities on hand, in order to minimize the possibility of their being used temporarily to obtain funds to add to the cash on hand. It is concern for cash cutoff, in part, that prompted the manager in the introductory case to reinstate the freeze on access to the client's investments, held for safekeeping in a bank safety deposit box.

Investments

Increases in long-term investments (net allowances) and the allowance for unrealized losses on noncurrent marketable equity securities can be audited by tying (1) the increases to changes in the previous year's and the current year's balance sheets, (2) the net unrealized loss to the stockholders' equity section of the balance sheet and to the statement of stockholders' equity, and (3) the net of purchases and sales at cost to the long-term investment section of the audit working papers ***[SAS 1, Section 332]***.

Notes Payable to Officers

A zero balance in an account does not mean that no attention need be given to that balance, for the magnitude and nature of transactions passing through the account can be significant. For example, even if Notes Payable to Officers had a zero balance, the auditor should see that all notes issued during the period were properly executed, that proceeds were used for company operations, that notes paid during the period were canceled, and that there had not been some sort of window dressing or smoothing. Audit tests can reveal excess interest paid on notes, unrecorded notes at year-end, and the like. The related-party nature of officers demands attention to the account, and tests are important as a double check on the balancing part of the entry recorded in that account.

Long-term Debt

The audit objectives in an audit of long-term debt are to determine that all genuine obligations are recorded, are properly classified, and have been properly authorized. The proper computation of interest expense and amortization should be tested. The auditor should also determine whether the client has violated any loan agreements. Finally, disclosure should be reviewed to ensure the adequate reporting of all pledged assets.

To meet these objectives, the auditor must examine loan agreements, confirm terms and balances with the creditor, trace the receipt of funds into the cash receipts book and the bank statement, test interest computations, and tie the debt issuance to authorizations in the minutes ***[SAS 45, Section 1020]***. For all debt agreements involving related parties, the auditor should understand the business purpose of the loans, test that payments were made, review the adequacy of disclosure, and obtain a management representation letter. Lease obligations pose special classification, valuation, and disclosure issues that must be evaluated.

In testing a client's compliance with debt covenants, both form and substance should be emphasized. Consider the following situation:

A company has a debt agreement requiring that capital structure not be changed and that cash dividends not be paid without the creditor's prior consent. Nevertheless, the company altered its certificate of incorporation to change its authorized capital structure and to issue a special "Class B" stock to a selected number of officers. Cash dividends were paid to the holders of the special stock.

Apparently, the client believed that the officers' stock and its dividends were sufficiently different from the other stock outstanding that it was not included in the "form" of the restrictive covenant. Management felt that the change in the certificate of incorporation ensured compliance with existing debt agreements.

However, the substance of the covenant had certainly been violated, and there was the risk that the creditor would declare the loan immediately payable or advance the due date. In this situation, the creditor should be told the facts, and a waiver should be obtained on the covenant provisions with respect to the "Class B" stock transactions. It is advisable to confer with the client on the importance of complying with the substance of loan restrictions or obtaining formal waivers of any provisions with which noncompliance is anticipated.

Investments in Unconsolidated Subsidiaries

To audit an investment in an unconsolidated subsidiary, net of cash dividends paid, the auditor should tie the balance into the subsidiary's net income. To do so, the net income must be adjusted for intercompany items, cash dividends as reported on the statement of retained earnings, and the client's proportionate ownership. In addition, the client's income statement should be tied to the subsidiary's income and adjusted for dividends.

Sometimes, the auditor may be asked to evaluate the need for an equity basis of accounting ***[SAS 1, Section 331]***. A client may claim not to have a controlling interest in an entity though be able indirectly to dictate the voting of 20 percent of the stock. Because the SEC requires disclosure of transactions with controlling persons, the judgment presents a substantial risk exposure. Often it is useful to investigate why the client does not want to use the equity basis of accounting, as it may uncover valuation problems. Some widely publicized misstatements of operating conditions have been facilitated by siphoning off those segments of the business that have incurred large losses or extensive debts to related parties that are not adequately disclosed in the client's financial statements.

Stock Options

Proceeds from an exercise of stock options should be tied to the amount credited on the statement of stockholders' equity to the common stock and paid-in capital accounts. All transactions related to options and stock appreciation rights should be tested for compliance with GAAP, including disclosure requirements.

Dividends Paid

Cash dividends paid on common and preferred stock should agree with the amount in the dividend schedule of the stockholders' equity section of the audit working papers and the amounts included in the statement of stockholders' equity. Like dividend and interest income, payments can also be verified from newspapers and dividend records.

Pensions

Because pension fund liabilities require very complex actuarial calculations, auditors usually have an independent actuary evaluate their reasonableness ***[SAS 11, Section 336]***. Due to the discretion necessary in reporting liabilities—such as the expected rate of return on pension assets—the risk exposure can be substantial. Note that this is related to the cost of sales cycle, as it is effectively another dimension of payroll.

Capital Stock

The stock and paid-in capital accounts are audited together. Their existence and completeness can be addressed by examining the stock certificate stub book and tying the total of open stubs to the general ledger. Canceled stock certificates also should be examined, by comparing the details on the stubs with the Capital Stock Account. In performing a sequence check on certificates, the CPA may choose to confirm the number of certificates printed with the printer. The stockholders' names in the stub book should be compared with those in the stockholders' ledger. Finally, there should be a test of original issue and capital stock transfer taxes to see that they are accurate and appropriately affixed to the stubs and canceled certificates. Valuation questions can be addressed by tracing cash transfers and property into the journals. Proper accounting for treasury stock requires testing, and the auditor should determine whether any state laws have been violated. Presentation and disclosure issues can be evaluated by examining the articles of incorporation, bylaws, and minutes.

Retained Earnings

To audit retained earnings, the account should be reviewed from its inception. Transactions should be traced to the minutes for authorization, recomputed in the case of dividends, and compared with closing entries to verify the effects of income. One concern is whether items have been charged directly to retained earnings that are not prior period adjustments and represent noncompliance with GAAP. Another concern is the effective reflection of covenant constraints through appropriations of retained earnings.

Statement of Changes in Financial Position

To examine the statement of changes in a company's financial position, the following audit procedures are commonly performed:

- Reviewing the statement for its compliance with GAAP.
- Checking clerical accuracy.
- Ascertaining that the format of the statement is the most informative (for example, cash versus working capital).
- Verifying that all important aspects of the company's financing and investing activities and important sources and uses of funds are disclosed.
- Ascertaining that the statement's format is correct, prominently showing funds provided from operations and funds provided from or used for extraordinary and similar items.
- Verifying that the statement ties to balances on the other audited financial statements.
- Analytically reviewing the transactions in nonfund accounts for possible effects on the statement of changes in financial position, in order to assess reasonableness.
- Ascertaining that a statement of changes in financial position is presented for each period for which an income statement is presented and is consistent with those of previous years.
- Tracing, matching, or agreeing statement amounts and like amounts in other financial statements and/or in audit working papers to test accuracy and completeness.
- Reviewing the statements to obtain significant information for helping management with its sources and uses of funds.

The adequacy of disclosure with respect to this and other financial statements is a key concern of the finance cycle ***[SAS 32, Section 431].*** Presentation should be compared with GAAP.

Subsequent Events

Subsequent events are often discovered by

- talking to officers, key personnel, and legal counsel (this is one reason that management's letter of representation is one of the last audit steps) ***[SAS 19, Section 333].***
- examining the minutes of meetings of the board of directors and stockholders.
- reading local newspapers.
- preparing tax returns for the client or its managers.
- scanning transactions in the month following year-end.

- reading the client's representation letter.
- observing operations.
- inspecting contracts or agreements on which actions are pending.
- reviewing subsequent period's financial statements.

These need to be carefully considered in terms of their effect on the financial statements, including required footnote disclosure.

Audits of Partnerships

If a CPA is auditing a partnership, he or she should take special care in reviewing withdrawals. Should the CPA become aware of excessive withdrawals by a particular partner, he or she should (1) discuss the matter with the managing partner, (2) insist on full disclosure to all partners, and (3) withdraw from the engagement if the managing partner refuses to make the information available, with a written withdrawal letter telling the partners the reason for the withdrawal. The key here is that the client is in a partnership with all of the partners, not merely the managing partner, and so the CPA is responsible for making full disclosure to all the partners, without exception. No disclosure to outsiders would be required. Informing other partners in the described setting would not be necessary if the partnership agreement specifically states that a partner's drawings may exceed his or her pro rata share of the earnings. This usually happens when there is no true partnership or when the partners of large professional firms do not have the same status as the executive committee or the managing partner.

Coordinating Work with Other Auditors

The audit of each cycle should include consideration of how the audit plan might be made more efficient and effective if other auditors' work were used. If clients encourage cooperation between external auditors and regulatory agencies' auditors, they also should understand that the latter cannot substitute for the former's work without a disclaimer or a limitation on audit scope. Nevertheless, the internal and external audit departments should work together and gather information from all auditors of the client's operations ***[SAS 9, Section 322]***.

While the audit procedures described herein are "typical," all audit programs are tailored to client settings, permitting a wide variety of mixes in compliance and substantive tests. Moreover, audit results from testing the revenue and cost of sales or production cycles will provide evidence on the control environment and the operation of the overall accounting system ***[SAS 31]***. The better the control setting, the more reliable the evidence, and the further substantive test work can be reduced and reliance on controls increased ***[SAS 31, Section 326]***. Hence, each of the cycle examinations overlaps the other two in reaching an overall audit judgment.

An Example: Analyzing Securities

An auditor may have clients for which, owing to their large securities portfolio, a 100 percent examination, confirmation, and evaluation of securities are impractical. Dollar coverage of such highly negotiable assets may be desirable, and so the auditor may decide on sampling proportionate to size. If the client's records are computerized, sampling software can be used to select a representative sample and to print test-count sheets and confirmations.

To determine the necessity of a security count, the auditor should consider the materiality of security transactions, controls, custodians' access to cash and other negotiable instruments, and the possibility of substitution across liquid assets. If securities are held in safekeeping by an independent reputable custodian, the auditor can rely on confirmations. Of course, the CPA would need to be satisfied as to the custodian's reliability.

To further demonstrate how an audit of the financing cycle proceeds, a specific example of how a client's investments might be audited will be provided. The example applies statistical sampling as well as generalized audit software.

A Sampling Application

If the auditor selects dollar-unit sampling, how does he or she proceed? By means of generalized audit software, the auditor can create a cumulative dollar record of the securities portfolio's master file ***[SAS 39, Section 350].*** The auditor then determines how that portfolio was ordered, to decide whether systematic selection was appropriate. If the client's records are computerized, random selection is very easy, and so any ordering of the file at all, which could have a bearing on the objective of reaching a conclusion as to whether the reported security balances were overstated, points to the selection through a random number table or generator. For example, the ordering of an investment file by date of acquisition, type of security, or the broker through whom the securities were purchased all can influence the representativeness of the sample tested if systematic selection is used. This is true even though systematic sampling based on dollars has less risk exposure to underlying patterns in populations than does systematic sampling of physical units (in this case, individual securities).

Assume that the cumulative field of the EDP-generated work file reports a total balance of marketable securities of $3 million and that a random number generator is used to select which dollar bills from 1 to 3,000,000 will be tested. The sample size is calculated using dollar-unit sampling:

$$n = \frac{\text{UEL factor}}{\text{UEL rate}}$$

where

n is the sample size.

UEL factor is the appropriate upper error limit factor for the desired confidence level and the anticipated number of errors (that is, dollar bills in error).

UEL rate is the upper error limit expressed as a decimal, that is, materiality in dollars divided by the population in dollars.

The auditor decides that the population of $3 million has a related materiality of $60,000 and the desired confidence level is 95 percent. It is expected that no more than one error will be found. The upper error limit factor at 95 percent with one sample error is 4.75 (from widely available tables). Because $60,000 divided by $3 million is 2 percent, the UEL rate is .02, which means that

$$n = \frac{4.75}{.02} = 237.50$$

Note that this calculation is just a different algebraic form of the sampling interval calculation given in Chapter 12. Based on this calculation, the random number generator is used to select 238 numbers from 1 to 3 million.

The numbers selected are sorted from lowest to highest. A matching routine is then used that compares each dollar selected randomly with the cumulative dollar column of the securities file. The algorithm used is as follows:

- Is the cumulative amount less than the selected dollar? If so, check the next cumulative amount and determine whether it is less than the selected dollar.
  —If both of these are less, continue.
  —If the first is less but the next is greater, select the former security for the sample and then proceed.

Note that multiple listing of a single security is possible, as large balances can include more than one of the dollar bills sampled. Any selected securities should be copied (with all details noted on the master file) onto a newly created file to be used for testing.

At this point, the auditor should use the generalized audit software to make the planned inspection of securities as efficient as possible ***[SAS 48, Section 326].*** Assume that inquiry procedures have identified five different locations at which securities are held. At two locations, the securities are arranged alphabetically in the name of the issuer, and at three locations the securities are arranged in the order of acquisition. With proper planning, it is simple to have the computer perform the following steps:

- Sort by the five locations.
- Sort two of those location subfiles alphabetically.
- Sort the other three location subfiles by acquisition date.
- Print five different control sheets for the inspection.

The auditor should decide how the control sheets will be printed. What attributes of the securities will be checked, and in what order will they be checked? For example, if the front and then the back of the securities is inspected, then the control sheet will first print information from the front on the left side of the control sheet, and then information from the back on the right side of the control sheet. The columns should indicate what each information field represents, and there should be space for tick marks documenting the various audit procedures to be performed. Exhibit 15-10 illustrates a possible format for the security count work sheet at one of the five locations. The note regarding the lack of entry into the safety deposit box recognizes the importance of planning audit procedures in a manner which guards against the substitution of securities already counted for other securities or assets which should be on hand but are not. Assume that before the sample selection, the auditor was aware that certain securities were being held by creditors as collateral. He or she will thus want to confirm any such securities that may be selected through the statistical sampling procedures. To find out whether the sample includes any of these securities held as collateral, the software's if-then exception reporting capability can be used to check the field of each security record that will contain a "C" if held as collateral. The exception report indicates that no such securities have been selected for inspection.

At this point, the auditor should reconsider whether separate evidence is needed for securities held as collateral. Although they were a part of the total population and had a chance, proportional to their dollar magnitude, to be selected, none was chosen. To assess the possible dollar risk from collateral holdings, the auditor uses the generalized audit software to identify collateral securities and foot their total. Assume that they total $80,000. Be-

EXHIBIT 15-10
Count Work Sheet for Security Investments

W/P No.
Preparer
Date

Client's Name
Security Count
12/31/X6

Location A		Front of Security						Back of Security	Audit Tick Marks
Name of Registered Owner	Date Prepared	Corporate Name and Class of Security	Face Value	Serial Number	Interest Rate	Maturity Date	Coupons	Endorsements	
Client	3/10/X4	ANNE Corp. Common Stock	$100	Y07932	N/A	N/A	N/A	None	√
.	.	.	.	.	.	.	.	.	
.	.	.	.	.	.	.	.	.	
.	.	.	.	.	.	.	.	.	

√ Inspected certificates, noting agreement of all details and no endorsements.

This inspection was performed in the presence of the treasurer and returned to her intact on 1/2/X7 at 2:00 P.M. This is formally acknowledged by her signature, which follows: ________________

Note: Bank entry records indicate that no one has entered the safety deposit box since 12/15/X6.

cause this exceeds the $60,000 materiality amount, the auditor decides that he or she wishes some representation from the collateral securities but does not believe that their size or occurrence merits a separate statistical sampling application. So the auditor will "oversample" the securities using a nonstatistical extension of the original set of 238 selected securities. That is, he or she will use "directed sampling," intended to address two objectives. First, the auditor wants representation from a cross section of the creditors who hold securities as collateral. Because 90 percent of such securities are held by two creditors, confirmations will be mailed to those two. In addition, the largest single-security collateral holding in dollars is held by a third creditor and in the interest of dollar coverage, a confirmation will also be mailed to that creditor.

The generalized audit software can again be used to print the three positive confirmations to creditors holding securities as collateral. The auditor can make copies for control documentation in the working papers and there should be a "to do" note to ascertain that proper disclosure of securities held as collateral is made in the client's financial statements. All of the generalized audit software applications described to this point are summarized in the program flowchart in Exhibit 15-11.

From the auditor's inspection, one exception was noted: A past-due interest coupon was not clipped, indicating the possible understatement of interest income or that interest is in default and the principal may be uncollectible. Investigation by the auditor finds that the interest was not in default but had been understated.

To evaluate the DUS results, the auditor can use the following formula:

$$\text{UEL rate} = \frac{\text{UEL factor}}{n}$$

Because the UEL factor at 95 percent for 1 error was 4.75 and the sample size was 238

$$\text{UEL rate} = \frac{4.75}{238} = .02$$

Note that .02 times $3,000,000 converts to the $60,000 precision initially specified. This is no surprise, as the sample results were exactly as expected: one error.

Conceptually, the DUS approach supports the conclusion that the precision was even better than $60,000. This is because of the role of tainting, that is, the ratio of the error amount to the reported book value of the physical unit in which it occurs. For attest audits, tainting is defined as follows:

$$\text{Tainting} = \frac{\text{effect of error in overstating or understating pretax income}}{\text{reported book value of the physical unit in which it occurs}}$$

If the past-due interest coupon represents a 10 percent tainting, then the sample evaluation will result in an upper error limit somewhere between zero errors and one error, as, in effect, it indicates that less than a full 100 percent of the physical unit's dollars are in error. Note that the 95 percent confidence level produces a 3.0 factor at zero errors and a 4.75 factor at one error. In the sample evaluation formula, if zero errors were found, the UEL rate would be

$$\frac{3.00}{238} = .013$$

The tainting means that instead of raising the UEL rate from .013 to .02, only 10 percent of that increase will be observed, that is, 10 percent of the difference between .02 and .013, or .0007. This means that the upper error limit is .013 plus .0007, or .0137. When multiplied by $3,000,000, this means a precision of $41,100, which is clearly better than the $60,000 required. Note that the tainting concept is far more complex as multiple errors are observed.

The auditor now turns to the confirmation procedures. Two confirmations are received without exception. The third, which is the confirmation of the large-dollar single security, has not been returned. The auditor calls that creditor who confirms the holding, apologizes for not having returned the confirmation, and assures the auditor that it will be mailed today. The auditor then documents the phone conversation in the working papers and posts a "to do" note to attach the formal written confirmation to the documentation of the verbal evidence when it is received.

EXHIBIT 15-11
Program Flowchart of Application of Generalized Audit Software to Investment Securities

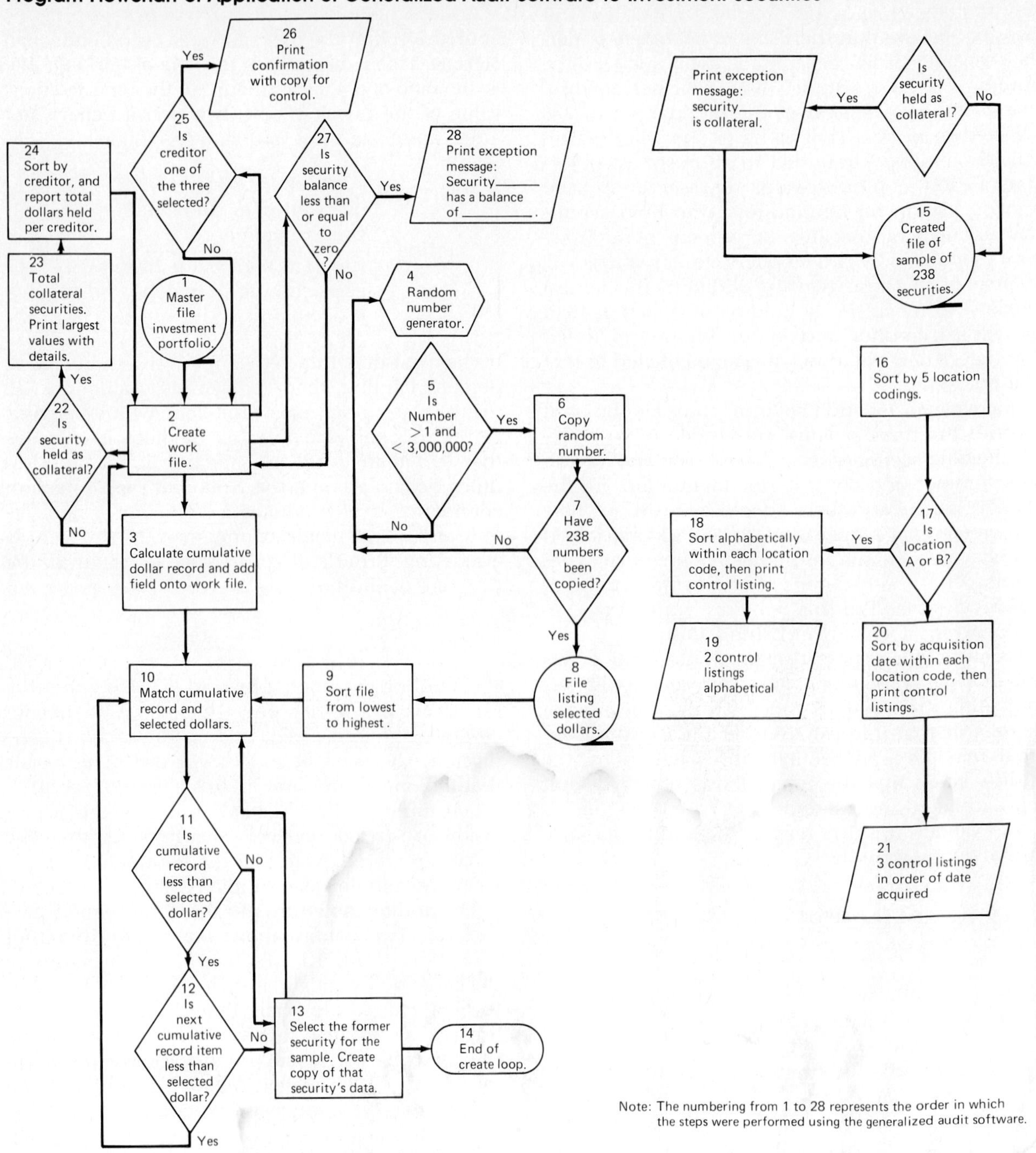

Note: The numbering from 1 to 28 represents the order in which the steps were performed using the generalized audit software.

Although the auditor has very effective evidence that the marketable securities are not overstated, possible understatements should be considered. The audit risk of this is tied to management's incentives to understate assets, possible problems of cash handling being "covered up" by transfers from reported security values to other accounts, and internal control quality. Recognizing DUS's inherent limitations, the auditor knows that no zero or credit balances on the security file have any chance of being selected. Because worthless securities may be on the file, the auditor decides to list all securities with zero or credit balances, by using generalized audit software. There are no credit balances and only two worthless securities. Note that this additional generalized audit software application is also depicted in Exhibit 15-11. Because these securities have been worthless for some time, the auditor can tie them into the previous year's working papers and do no further work on them. If there had been many such securities, separate sampling for their inspection would have been necessary.

With the audit assurances from the evaluation of the client's control environment, the tests of cash disbursements, and the specific dual controls established over all transactions related to investment securities, no further work was deemed to be necessary.

The working papers for investments document the inspection and confirmation work performed on securities, with special emphasis on how the auditor accounted for items in transit. The receipt for the return of all securities that the auditor counted should be included in the working papers. The valuation of securities should have been tested, in accordance with their classification as short or long term, and a concise conclusion as to the fair presentation of investments should appear in the working papers.

REVIEW QUESTIONS

1. Define what comprises the financing cycle.
2. What is dual control?
3. Explain the purpose of the following forms:
   a. standard journal entry form.
   b. control sheet over closing entries.
   c. commercial paper.
4. To ensure an effective internal auditing group, what organizational status should that group have?
5. What are the three risks that should be addressed by an investment program?
6. What financing duties—related to both debt and equity transactions—should be segregated?
7. Explain the role of the board of directors in controlling the financing cycle.
8. What types of errors can occur in the financing cycle?
9. What are the main disclosure issues related to investments?
10. How does an auditor use the minutes of the board of directors' meetings?
11. Outline the steps taken in performing an inventory of a client's securities.
12. How can a client minimize working-capital commitments?
13. What information is requested on the standard bank confirmation?
14. Is it appropriate not to perform audit procedures on the account "Notes Payable to Officers" if it has a zero balance? Why or why not?
15. How does an auditor examine the client's statement of changes in financial position?
16. How can an auditor find out whether there have been subsequent events that may influence the client's financial statements and related disclosure requirements?
17. In auditing a partnership, to whom is the CPA responsible?
18. How should the external auditor work with regulatory agencies' auditors and with internal auditors?

EXERCISES

1. The typical internal control questionnaire for the general ledger and journal entries asks the following questions:

	Yes	No
a. Are postings to the general ledger made by an employee who does not have access to cash?	___	___
b. Are all journal vouchers approved in writing by someone other than the vouchers' originator?	___	___
c. Does a proper explanation appear on the journal voucher?	___	___
d. Are all subsidiary ledgers proved to the general ledger at least monthly?	___	___

What is the purpose of each of these controls? How can the auditor test for compliance with such controls? How is the adequacy of these controls likely to affect the substantive tests?

2. In reviewing working papers, a senior auditor finds documentation of a bank reconciliation performed by a young staff auditor, who did not include a key to his tick marks. Although you intend to ask the staff auditor to complete the documentation of work performed, what explanations do you expect for each of the following tick marks, noted on the working papers presented?

W/P Ref. No.
Preparer
Date

WAJAW Corp.
Bank Reconciliation
June 30, 19X6

Trust bank account #349-6721-3901		
Balance per bank statement 6/30/X6		C 43,972.69 √
Add: Deposits in transit (receipts of 6/29/X6)	5,200.19 ✗̸ CR	
Bank charge incorrectly booked by bank	15.00 (√)	5,215.19
Total		49,187.88
Less outstanding checks—see attached list √^		19,240.34
Balance per general ledger 12/30/X6		29,947.54 GL

a. C
b. √
c. ✗̸
d. CR
e. (√)
f. √^
g. GL

3. A client has recently replaced its batch-processing EDP system with an on-line processing system. This on-line system is used to record transactions in the financing cycle. Describe how you would (a) compliance test the entry of the on-line transactions and (b) test the controls related to the EDP system. Explain how your approach to on-line systems differs from that used in previous years for the batch system.

4. While many employees were on vacation, that employee authorized to buy and sell investments for a client was assigned the additional duties of cashier. All investment proceeds were channeled to this employee, who also prepared investment transaction reports and maintained cash and total investment controls. The employee falsified entries in the cash book from individual investment sales reports generated to him and other employees, making the totals agree with the deposits. Then he altered the inventory control over investment reports and underlying transaction documentation to show all such documents as being reported or being on hand. How can the auditor detect this defalcation?

5. Protective covenants in loan agreements are generally in one of three groups:
(1) general provisions—vary to fit the situation.
(2) routine provisions—used in most agreements, do not usually vary.
(3) specific provisions—used according to the situation.

Routine provisions include a requirement that borrowers furnish financial statements, maintain adequate insurance, pay taxes and liabilities when due, not sell a substantial portion of their assets, not pledge or mortgage certain assets, not discount or sell its receivables, not enter into leasing agreements beyond a certain dollar amount, and not incur other contingent liabilities. What do you think are the common general provisions and specific provisions? How does the auditor test compliance with these covenants?

6. How can the audit of interest expense help identify unrecorded liabilities, and how can the audit of rental expense help identify unrecorded liabilities?

QUESTIONS ADAPTED FROM PROFESSIONAL EXAMINATIONS

1. a. At the beginning of your examination of the financial statements of Efel Insurance Company, the president of the company requested that in the interest of efficiency, you coordinate your audit procedures with the audit being conducted by the state insurance examiners for the same fiscal year. The state examiners audited the company's asset accounts, and you audited the accounts for liabilities, stockholders' equity, income, and expenses. In addition you obtained confirmations of the accounts receivable and were satisfied with the results of your audit tests. Although you had no supervisory control over the state examiners, they allowed you to review and prepare extracts from their work papers and report. After reviewing the state examiners' work papers and report to your complete satisfaction, you are now preparing your short-form report.

Required:

What effect, if any, will these circumstances have on your auditor's short-form report?

b. During your annual audit of the Cook Manufacturing Co., your assistant reports to you that although a number of entries were made during the year in the general ledger account, Notes Payable to Officers, she decided that it was not necessary to audit the account because it had a zero balance at year-end.

Required

Do you agree with your assistant's decision? Discuss.

(CPA exam adapted)

2. A client, without consulting its CPA, changed its accounting so that it now is not in accordance with generally accepted accounting principles. During the regular audit engagement, the CPA discovers that the statements based on the accounts are so grossly misleading that they might be considered to be fraudulent.

a. Discuss what the CPA should do.

b. In this situation, what obligation does the CPA have to outsiders if he or she is replaced?

c. In this situation, what obligation does the CPA have to a new auditor if he or she is replaced?

(CPA exam adapted)

3. In connection with your examination of the financial statements of Olars Mfg. Corporation for the year ended December 31, 19X6, your post-balance sheet date review disclosed the following items:

(1) *January 3, 19X7:* The state government approved a plan for the construction of an express highway. The plan will result in the appropriation of a portion of the land area owned by Olar Mfg. Corporation. Construction will begin in late 19X7. No estimate of the condemnation award is available.

(2) *January 4, 19X7:* Mr. Olars obtained the funds, from a loan on his personal life insurance policy, for a $25,000 loan to the corporation made on July 15, 19X6. The loan was recorded in the account Loan from Officers. Mr. Olars's source of funds was not disclosed in the company records. The corporation pays the premiums on the life insurance policy and Mrs. Olars is the beneficiary.

(3) *January 7, 19X7:* The mineral content of a shipment of ore en route on December 31, 19X6, was determined to be 72 percent. The shipment was recorded at year-end at an estimated content of 50 percent by a debit to Raw Material Inventory and a credit to Accounts Payable in the amount of $20,600. The final liability to the vendor is based on the actual mineral content of the shipment.

(4) *January 15, 19X7:* Culminating a series of personal disagreements between Mr. Olars, the president, and his brother-in-law, the treasurer, the latter resigned, effective immediately, under an agreement whereby the corporation would purchase his 10 percent stock ownership at book value as of December 31, 19X6. Payment is to be made in two equal amounts in cash on April 1 and October 1, 19X7. In December the treasurer divorced his wife, who is Mr. Olars's sister.

(5) *January 31, 19X7:* Because of reduced sales, promotion was curtailed in mid-January, and some workers were laid off. On February 5, 19X7, all the remaining workers went on strike. To date the strike has not been settled.

(6) *February 10, 19X7:* A contract was signed in which Mammoth Enterprises purchased from Olars Mfg. Corporation all of the latter's fixed assets (including rights to receive the proceeds of any property condemnation), inventories, and the right to conduct business under the name "Olars Mfg. Division." The effective date of the transfer is March 1, 19X7. The sale price was $500,000, subject to adjustment following the taking of a physical inventory. Important factors contributing to the decision to enter into the contract were the policy of the board of directors of Mammoth Industries to diversify the firm's activities and the report of a survey conducted by an independent market appraisal firm that revealed a declining market for Olars's products.

Required:

Assume that these items came to your attention before completing your audit work on February 15, 19X7, and that you will render a short-form report. For each of the above items:

a. Name the audit procedures, if any, that would have brought the item to your attention. Indicate other sources of information that may have revealed the item.

b. Discuss the disclosure that you would recommend for the item, listing all the details that should be disclosed. Indicate those items or details, if any, that should not be disclosed. Give your reasons for recommending or not recommending disclosure of the items or details.

(CPA exam adapted)

4. The inspection of the minutes of meetings is an integral part of a CPA's examination of a corporation's financial statements.

Required:

a. A CPA should determine whether there is any disagreement between the transactions recorded in the corporate records and the actions approved by the corporation's board of directors. Why is this so, and how is it accomplished?

b. Discuss the effect that each of the following situations would have on specific audit steps in a CPA's examination and on his or her auditor's opinion:

1. The minute book does not show approval for the sale of an important manufacturing division which was consummated during the year.
2. Some details of a contract negotiated during the year with the labor union are different from the outline of the contract included in the minutes of the board of directors.
3. The minutes of a meeting of directors held after the balance sheet date have not yet been written, but the corporation's secretary shows the CPA his notes from which the minutes are to be prepared when the secretary has time.

c. What corporate actions should be approved by stockholders and recorded in the minutes of the stockholders' meetings?

(CPA exam adapted)

5. In connection with his examination of the financial statements of Belasco Chemicals, Inc., Kenneth Mack, a CPA, is considering inspecting marketable securities on the balance sheet date, May 31, 19X6, or at some other date. The marketable securities held by Belasco include negotiable bearer bonds, which are kept in a safe in the treasurer's office, and miscellaneous stocks and bonds, which are kept in a safe deposit box at the Merchants Bank. Both the negotiable bearer bonds and the miscellaneous stocks and bonds are material to the proper presentation of Belasco's financial position.

Required:

a. What factors should Mr. Mack consider in determining the necessity for inspecting these securities on May 31, 19X6, as opposed to other dates?

b. Assume that Mr. Mack plans to send a member of his staff to Belasco's offices and the Merchants Bank on May 31, 19X6, to make the security inspection. What instructions should he give to his staff member as to the conduct of the inspection and the evidence to be included in the audit working papers? (**Note:** Do not discuss the valuation of securities, the income from securities, or the examination of information in the company's books and records.)

c. Assume that Mr. Mack cannot send a member of his staff to Belasco's offices and the Merchants Bank on May 31, 19X6. What other procedures can he use to ensure that the company had physical possession of its marketable securities on May 31, 19X6, if the securities are inspected on (1) May 28, 19X6?, or on (2) June 5, 19X6?

(CPA exam adapted)

6. You are auditing the financial statements of the Sandy Core Company for the year ended December 31, 19X6. Sandy Core Company sells lumber and building supplies at wholesale and retail. It has total assets of $1 million and a stockholders' equity of $500,000.

The company's records show an investment of $100,000 for one hundred shares of common stock of one of its customers, the Home Building Corporation. You learn that Home Building Corporation is closely held and that its capital stock, consisting of one thousand shares of issued and outstanding common stock, has no published or quoted market value.

Examination of your client's cash disbursements record reveals an entry of a check for $100,000 drawn on January 23, 19X6, to Felix Wolfe, who is said to be the former holder of the one hundred shares of stock. Mr. Wolfe is president of the Sandy Core Company. Sandy Core Company has no other investment.

Required:

a. List the auditing procedures you would use for your client's $100,000 investment in the capital stock of the Home Building Corporation.

b. Discuss the presentation of the investment on the balance sheet, including its valuation.

(CPA exam adapted)

7. You were engaged to examine the financial statements of the Ronlyn Corporation for the year ended June 30, 19X6. On May 31, 19X6, the corporation borrowed $500,000 from Second National Bank to finance plant expansion. The long-term note agreement provided for the annual payment of principal and interest over five years, and the existing plant was pledged as security for the loan.

Owing to unexpected difficulties in acquiring the building site, the plant expansion had not begun at June 30, 19X6. To make use of the borrowed funds, management decided to invest in stocks and bonds, and on May 16, 19X6 the $500,000 was invested in securities.

Required:

a. What are the audit objectives in examining long-term debt?

b. Prepare an audit program for the examination of the long-term note agreement between Ronlyn and the Second National Bank.

c. How can you verify Ronlyn's security position at June 30, 19X6?

d. In your audit of investments, how would you

1. Verify the dividend or interest income recorded?
2. Determine market value?
3. Establish the authority for security purchases?

(CPA exam adapted)

8. You have been engaged to examine the financial statements of the Elliott Company for the year ended December 31, 19X6. You performed a similar examination as of December 31, 19X5. The following is the trial balance for the company as of December 31, 19X6:

	Dr.(Cr.)
Cash	$ 128,000
Interest receivable	47,450
Dividends receivable	1,750
6.5 percent secured note receivable	730,000
Investments at cost:	
Bowen common stock	322,000
Investments at equity:	
Woods common stock	284,000
Land	185,000
Accounts payable	(31,000)
Interest payable	(6,500)
8 percent secured note payable to bank	(275,000)
Common stock	(480,000)
Paid-in capital in excess of par	(800,000)
Retained earnings	(100,500)
Dividend revenue	(3,750)
Interest revenue	(47,450)
Equity in earnings of investments carried at equity	(40,000)
Interest expense	26,000
General and administrative expense	60,000

You have obtained the following data concerning certain accounts:

- The 6.5 percent note receivable is due from the Tysinger Corporation and is secured by a first mortgage on land sold to Tysinger by Elliott on December 21, 19X5. The note was to have been paid in twenty equal quarterly payments plus interest, beginning on March 31, 19X6. Tysinger, however, is in very poor financial condition and has not made any principal or interest payments to date.
- The Bowen common stock was purchased on September 21, 19X5, for cash in the market where it is actively traded. It is used as security for the note payable and is held by the bank. Elliott's investment in Bowen represents approximately 1 percent of the total outstanding shares of Bowen.
- Elliott's investment in Woods represents 40 percent of the outstanding common stock that is actively traded. Woods is audited by another CPA and has a December 31 year-end.
- Elliot neither purchased nor sold any stock investments during the year other than that noted above.

Required:
For the following account balances, discuss (1) the types of evidence you should obtain and (2) the audit procedures you should perform during your examination.

a. 6.5 percent secured note receivable.

b. Bowen common stock.

c. Woods common stock.

d. Dividend revenue.

(CPA exam adapted)

9. Andrews, a CPA, has been engaged to examine the financial statements of the Broadwall Corporation for the year ended December 31, 19X6. During the year, Broadwall obtained a long-term loan from a local bank for a financing agreement that provided that the

1. Loan was to be secured by the company's inventory and accounts receivable.
2. Company was to maintain a debt-to-equity ratio not to exceed two to one.
3. Company would not pay dividends without permission from the bank.
4. Monthly installment payments would commence on July 1, 19X6.

In addition, during the year the company also borrowed from the president of the company, on a short-term basis, including substantial amounts just before the year-end.

Required:

a. For the audit of the Broadwall Corporation's financial statements, what procedures should Andrews use to examine the described loans? Do not discuss internal control.

b. What are the financial statement disclosures that Andrews should expect to find with respect to the loans from the president?

(CPA exam adapted)

10. The schedule at the bottom of this page was prepared by the controller of World Manufacturing Inc., for use by the independent auditors during their examination of World's year-end financial statements. All procedures performed by the audit assistant were noted at the bottom "Legend" section, and it was properly initialed, dated and indexed, and then submitted to a senior member of the audit staff for review. Internal control was reviewed and is considered to be satisfactory.

Required:

a. What information essential to the audit of marketable securities is missing from this schedule?

b. What are the necessary audit procedures that were not noted as having been performed by the audit assistant?

(CPA exam adapted)

11. Public accounting firms often use a questionnaire to investigate and record their inquiries into the client's internal control system, in order to determine whether there are weaknesses in internal control.

Required:

Prepare an internal control questionnaire pertaining to securities (short-term and long-term investments) held by a medium-sized manufacturing company.

(CPA exam adapted)

12. The client-prepared bank reconciliation on page 559 is being examined by Kautz, a CPA, during an examination of the financial statements of Cynthia Company.

Required:

Indicate one or more audit procedures that Kautz should perform in gathering evidence supporting items (a) through (f).

(CPA exam adapted)

Question 10.

World Manufacturing, Inc.
Marketable Securities
Year Ended December 31, 19X6

Description of Security			Serial No.	Face Value of Bonds	Gen. Ledger 1/1	Purch. in 19X6	Sold in 19X6	Cost	Gen. Ledger 12/31	12/31 Market	Dividend and Interest: Pay date(s)	Amt. Rec.	Accruals 12/31
Corp. Bonds	**%**	**Yr. Due**											
											1/15	300b,d	
A	6	96	21-7	10000	9400a				9400	9100	7/15	300b,d	275
D	4	89	73-0	30000	27500a				27500	26220	12/1	1200b,d	100
G	9	104	16-4	5000	4000a				4000	5080	8/1	450b,d	188
Rc	5	91	08-2	70000	66000a		57000b	66000					
Sc	10	105	07-4	100000		100000e			100000	101250	7/1	5000b,d	5000
					106900	100000	57000	66000	140900	141650		7250	5563
					a,f	f	f	f	f,g	f		f	f
Stocks													
											3/1	750b,d	
P 1,000 shs.			1044		7500a				7500	7600	6/1	750b,d	
Common											9/1	750b,d	
											12/1	750b,d	250
U 50 shs.			8530		9700a				9700	9800	2/1	800b,d	
Common											8/1	800b,d	667
					17200				17200	17400		4600	917
					a,f				f,g	f		f	f

Legends and comments

a = Beginning balances agree to 19X5 working papers.
b = Traced to cash receipts.
c = Minutes examined (purchase and sales approved by the board of directors).
d = Agreed to 1099.
e = Confirmed by tracing to broker's advice.
f = Totals footed.
g = Agreed to general ledger.

Question 12. (continued)

Cynthia Company
Bank Reconciliation
Village Bank Account 2
December 31, 19X6

Balance per bank (a)		$18,375.91
Deposits in transit (b)		
12/30	$1,471.10	
12/31	2,840.69	4,311.79
Subtotal		$22,687.70
Outstanding checks (c)		
837	$6,000.00	
1941	671.80	
1966	320.00	
1984	1,855.42	
1985	3,621.22	
1987	2,576.89	
1991	4,420.88	(19,466.21)
Subtotal		$ 3,221.49
NSF check returned		
12/29 (d)		200.00
Bank charges		5.50
Error check no. 1932		148.10
Customer note collected by the bank ($2,750 plus $275 interest) (e)		(3,025.00)
Balance per books (f)		$ 550.09

13. When examining the annual financial statements of Amis Manufacturing, Inc., the company's president, Alderman, and the auditor, Luddy, reviewed matters that were supposed to be included in a written representation letter. Upon receipt of the following client representation letter, Luddy contacted Alderman to state that it was incomplete.

To E. K. Luddy, CPA:

In connection with your examination of the balance sheet of Amis Manufacturing, Inc., as of December 31, 19X6, and the related statements of income, retained earnings, and changes in financial position for the year then ended, for the purpose of expressing an opinion as to whether the financial statements present fairly the financial position, results of operations, and changes in financial position of Amis Manufacturing, Inc. in conformity with generally accepted accounting principles, we confirm, to the best of our knowledge and belief, the following representations made to you during your examination. There were no:

- Plans or intentions that may materially affect the carrying value or classification of assets and liabilities.
- Communications from regulatory agencies concerning noncompliance with, or deficiencies in, financial reporting practices.
- Agreements to repurchase assets previously sold.
- Violations or possible violations of laws or regulations whose effect should be considered for disclosure in the financial statements or as a basis for recording a loss contingency.
- Unasserted claims or assessments that our lawyer has advised are probable of assertion and must be disclosed in accordance with Statement of Financial Accounting Standards No. 5.
- Capital stock repurchase options or agreements or capital stock reserved for options, warrants, conversions, or other requirements.
- Compensating balance or other arrangements involving restrictions on cash balances.

R. Alderman, president

Amis Manufacturing, Inc.

March 14, 19X7

Required:
What other matters should Alderman's representation letter confirm?

(CPA exam adapted)

14. **Multiple Choice**
Select the one answer that best completes the statement or answers the question.

14.1 If a company employs a capital stock registrar and/or transfer agent, the registrar or agent, or both, should confirm directly to the auditor the number of shares of each class of stock

a. Surrendered and canceled during the year.
b. Authorized at the balance sheet date.
c. Issued and outstanding at the balance sheet date.
d. Authorized, issued, and outstanding during the year.

(CPA exam adapted)

14.2 A company issued bonds for cash during the year under audit. To ascertain that this transaction was properly recorded, the auditor's best course of action is to

a. Request a statement from the bond trustee as to the amount of the bonds issued and outstanding.
b. Confirm the results of the issuance with the underwriter or investment banker.
c. Trace the cash received from the issuance to the accounting records.

d. Verify that the net cash received is credited to an account entitled Bonds Payable.

(CPA exam adapted)

14.3 In an examination of bonds payable, an auditor would expect to find in a trust indenture

a. The issue date and maturity date of the bond.
b. The names of the original subscribers to the bond issue.
c. The yield to maturity of the bonds issued.
d. The company's debt-to-equity ratio at the time of issuance.

(CPA exam adapted)

14.4 The auditor's program for the examination of long-term debt should include steps that require the

a. Verification of the bondholders' existence.
b. Examination of any bond trust indenture.
c. Inspection of the accounts payable subsidiary ledger.
d. Investigation of credits to the bond interest income account.

(CPA exam adapted)

14.5 An audit program for the examination of the related earnings account should include verification of the

a. Gain or loss resulting from disposition of treasury shares.
b. Market value used to charge retained earnings to account for a two-for-one stock split.
c. Authorization for both cash and stock dividends.
d. Approval of the adjustment to the beginning balance as a result of a write-down of an account receivable.

(CPA exam adapted)

14.6 During its fiscal year, a company issued, at a discount, a substantial amount of first-mortgage bonds. When performing an audit in connection with the bond issue, the independent auditor should

a. Confirm the bondholders' existence.
b. Review the minutes for authorization.
c. Trace the net cash received from the issuance to the bond payable account.
d. Inspect the records maintained by the bond trustee.

(CPA exam adapted)

14.7 The main reason for preparing a reconciliation between interest-bearing obligations outstanding during the year and interest expense presented in the financial statements is to

a. Evaluate the internal control over securities.
b. Determine the validity of prepaid interest expense.
c. Ascertain the reasonableness of imputed interest.
d. Detect unrecorded liabilities.

(CPA exam adapted)

14.8 When no independent stock transfer agents are employed and the corporation issues its own stocks and maintains stock records, canceled stock certificates should

a. Be defaced to prevent reissuance and attached to their corresponding stubs.
b. Not be defaced but segregated from other stock certificates and retained in a canceled certificates file.
c. Be destroyed to prevent fraudulent reissuance.
d. Be defaced and sent to the secretary of state.

(CPA exam adapted)

14.9 During an examination, Wicks learns that the audit client was granted a three-month waiver of the repayment of principal on the installment loan with Blank Bank without an extension of the maturity date. With respect to this loan, the audit program used by Wicks would be least likely to include a written verification of the

a. Interest expense for the year.
b. Balloon payment.
c. Total liability at year-end.
d. Installment loan payments.

(CPA exam adapted)

14.10 The auditor can best verify a client's bond sinking fund transactions and year-end balance by

a. Confirmation with the bond trustee.
b. Confirmation with individual holders of the retired bonds.
c. Recomputation of interest expense, interest payable, and amortization of bond discount or premium.
d. Examination and count of the bonds retired during the year.

(CPA exam adapted)

14.11 Once satisfied that the balance sheet and income statement are fairly presented in accordance with generally accepted accounting principles, an auditor who is examining the statement of changes in financial position would be most concerned with details of transactions in

a. Cash. **b.** Trade receivables.
c. Notes payable.
d. Dividends payable.

(CPA exam adapted)

14.12 The auditor is concerned with establishing that dividends are paid to stockholders of the client corporation owning stock as of the
a. Issue date.
b. Declaration date.
c. Record date.
d. Payment date.

(CPA exam adapted)

14.13 During an examination of a publicly held company, the auditor should obtain written confirmation regarding debenture transactions from the
a. Debenture holders.
b. Client's attorney.
c. Internal auditors.
d. Trustee.

(CPA exam adapted)

14.14 Treetop Corporation acquired a building and arranged mortgage financing during the year. Verification of the related mortgage acquisition costs would be least likely to include an examination of the related
a. Deed.
b. Canceled checks.
c. Closing statement.
d. Interest expense.

(CPA exam adapted)

14.15 A company guarantees the debt of an affiliate. Which of the following best describes the audit procedure that would make the auditor aware of the guarantee?
a. Reviewing the minutes and resolutions of the board of directors.
b. Reviewing the previous year's working papers with respect to such guarantees.
c. Reviewing the possibility of such guarantees with the chief accountant.
d. Reviewing the legal letter returned by the company's outside legal counsel.

(CPA exam adapted)

14.16 During the year under audit, a company has completed a private placement of a substantial amount of bonds. Which of the following is the most important step in the auditor's program for the examination of bonds payable?
a. Confirming the amount issued with the bond trustee.
b. Tracing the cash received from the issue to the accounting records.
c. Examining the bond records maintained by the transfer agent.
d. Recomputing the annual interest cost and the effective yield.

(CPA exam adapted)

14.17 In an audit of both registered and bearer securities, the auditor should
a. Conduct the physical examination within five days after the cash has been counted and reconciled.
b. Make a surprise count of the securities without the custodian or other designated official being present.
c. Value the securities at market value to conform to current valuation methods.
d. Secure written confirmation of securities held by others as collateral.
e. Ascertain the cost of the stock investment in each wholly owned subsidiary.

(CIA exam adapted)

14.18 When auditing contingent liabilities, which of the following procedures would be the least effective?
a. Reading the minutes of the board of directors.
b. Reviewing the bank confirmation letter.
c. Examining customer confirmation replies.
d. Examining invoices for professional services.

(CPA exam adapted)

14.19 Ajax Inc. is an affiliate of the audit client and is audited by another firm of auditors. Which of the following is an auditor most likely to use to obtain assurance that all guarantees of the affiliate's indebtedness have been detected?
a. Sending the standard bank confirmation request to all of the client's lender banks.
b. Reviewing client's minutes and obtaining a representation letter.
c. Examining supporting documents for all entries in intercompany accounts.
d. Obtaining written confirmation of indebtedness from the affiliate's auditor.

(CPA exam adapted)

CASES FOR DISCUSSION

1. The American Bankers Association's Controlled Group Bonding Plan (December 1978) explicitly cited some relationships representing common circumstances which would contribute to an internal auditor's position not being an independent relationship. These include:

a. If bank operational officers are on the audit committee.

b. If the internal auditor owns more than 5 percent of the bank's outstanding shares of common stock.

c. If the internal auditor is closely related to any employee of the bank, particularly the directors or other officers.

d. If the board of directors does not establish and regulate the internal auditor's salary (and bonus, if any).

e. If the internal auditor does not report directly to the board of directors or its audit committee.

Describe the possible risks of these circumstances. What could be the implications for the external auditor, should any of these circumstances arise?

2. A CPA reviews his client's investments and notices that a large certificate of deposit (CD) is in a foreign bank. Being unfamiliar with the bank, he calls the firm's industry specialist in banking. She tells him that she, too, is unfamiliar with that bank and warns him to be careful when evaluating the CD, because banking in that particular country is totally unregulated. "Some banks are nothing more than a front window and some stationery," she explained.

The CPA thanked the specialist and decided to send a letter of confirmation to the bank holding the CD. The confirmation was returned, verifying with a signature by a bank officer that the CD was, indeed, on deposit.

Eight months later, the client declared bankruptcy, and investigation by the creditors revealed that no CD really existed. The bank had been one of the "window only" institutions described by the industry specialist.

A litigation suit is now pending against the CPA. He intends to defend himself on the premise that he followed generally accepted auditing standards. "The confirmation is," he points out, "the strongest evidential source when received by a third party, such as a creditor, supplier, customer, broker, or banker. I used due audit care, and I share no responsibility for the poor business practices of my client that led to its failure."

Assume that you have been asked to serve as an expert witness for the court. Describe your testimony.

16

Special Concerns Posing Audit Risk

Two students are talking with their intermediate accounting professor about SFAS No. 5 on contingencies.

Sean. I remember reading about Penn Square Bank and how it had given a tacit guarantee that any Penn Square loans sold to major "upstream" banks would be repurchased on demand. The regulators claimed this loan buy-back agreement was an unrecorded contingent liability on the part of the lender, making Penn Square's books inaccurate.

I'm trying to reconcile that account with our discussion today. How would an informal takeout agreement be handled according to SFAS No. 5?

Professor Smith. You would need to apply the probability and estimable criteria of SFAS No. 5, just as we discussed.

Janice. But what about enforceability? Is a "tacit guarantee" the same as a contractual buy-back commitment?

Sean. Well, as I recall, there was a letter from Continental Illinois's vice-president to Penn Square's executive vice-president that stated that he had assured a group that had purchased Penn Square loans that Penn Square would take the credits out at maturity or whenever they felt unconfident. But the newspaper accounts say that the bank's accountants actually made a notation at the end of that letter proposing "no disclosure" of the so-called "informal takeout agreement."

Professor Smith. One interesting aspect of that case is that Penn Square was a $500 million bank with about $2.5 billion of participation loans outstanding after it was closed. There seems to be a feasibility issue here: How could such a buy-back commitment be credible?

Sean. But does credibility matter if the claim can be made against the $500 million in assets? I guess the real question is what type of disclosure might have been made? How can a reserve be estimated? With the bank's scale of business, the reserve probably would have exceeded the bank's net worth!

Janice. I remember reading about Penn Square. I remember that their valuation problems went far beyond the buy-back agreement. There was also widespread abuse of insider loans, which reportedly were a major factor in the bank's collapse.

Professor Smith. Related-party problems complicate the recording of transactions in any business. But the judgmental nature of lending decisions are especially open to such abuse.

Sean. It doesn't help when illegalities are rampant at an institution. Reportedly, all of the directors and their related interests had been given extensions of credit in violation of federal laws. I find such widespread fraud hard to imagine. You'd think that someone would have questioned the practices and have come forward and told the regulators.

Professor Smith. Unfortunately, Penn Square is not unique. Just a couple of months ago, it was reported that at McCormick & Co., a "substantial number" of a division's approximately 2,500 employees, including that division's top management, either participated in accounting irregularities or knew of them. The irregularities went on from 1977 to 1980 without detection.

Janice. I remember hearing about that. Weren't some invoices altered? In that situation, I don't know how the accounting department can be expected to assign proper values to transactions. The supporting documentation of even arm's-length transactions can't be relied on!

Professor Smith. Despite the media coverage, fraud is still a rare event—and so is the intentional distortion of financial statements. Most companies want to report on their operations fairly, but it's not always clear what "fairly" is.

Sean. I guess that's why SFAS No. 5 requires that only the minimum point in the range of estimated losses be booked, rather than the average value. As long as the user of the financial statements understands what the entity is supposed to book, it seems reasonable. But how understanding are users when the high point of that range is actually reached? Is the FASB "setting up" accountants?

Professor Smith. There are certainly those who think so. Let's talk about that more on Thursday.[1]

This account highlights some special risk areas faced by auditors that will be discussed in this chapter. Contingencies, judgmental valuations, related party transactions, and fraud all pose problems for auditors, and in some cases, the standard-setting bodies appear to have made the problems even more acute—sometimes by their actions and sometimes by their inaction. The chapter's discussion focuses first on technical auditing issues and then addresses environmental issues which pose special audit risk.

The accounting or audit trail of numerous rou-

[1]Adapted from Jeff Gerth, "Penn Square Had Secret Loan Pact," *New York Times,* August 17, 1982, p. 4, Section D; and Betsy Morris, "McCormick & Co. Division Is Found to Use Dubious Accounting Methods to Boost Net," *Wall Street Journal,* June 1, 1982, p. 8.

tine economic transactions, even in an EDP environment, can be made visible and be audited in a rather systematic manner which is capable of producing tight precision on recorded financial data. For example, when a sale of inventory occurs, a customer order form, an invoice, a shipping report, and subsequent collection are available for reference by the auditor. Often the market price is easily verified. Yet numerous transactions do not have an analogous trail or have a trail that is in some sense "suspect," because of the possible involvement of related parties. Some accounting entries are not tied directly to exchange transactions, but involve estimations that are indirectly linked to past or future transactions or economic events. Underlying the recording of accounting transactions are concepts of matching, realization, going concern presumptions, and reporting periods with recognized cut-offs intended to result in comparability of financial reports over time. These concepts require judgment and may or may not be easily supported by an accounting trail. Top management directs judgments within an entity; the auditor will want to consider management's incentives as well as the direction which management has set for the organization via prescribed policies, controls, and performance evaluation schemes.

The audit process has been described as the collection of a sufficient amount of evidence to enable the auditor to form an opinion about the fairness of the financial presentations. This process is guided by a joint consideration of materiality and audit risk. Certain aspects of the client's operations and account areas may pose special concerns for an auditor when assessing risk and attempting to form an opinion.

Risk problems include an inability to realize assets, an inappropriate application of generally accepted accounting principles (GAAP), overly optimistic or pessimistic views of judgmental matters, improper cutoffs, unrecorded liabilities, unrecognized adverse commitments, and a failure to identify significant related-party transactions and pledged assets. Seven key technical auditing issues will now be described, in tandem with suggestions as to how an auditor can control related audit risks. Then the additional risk dimension posed by environmental issues will be discussed.

#1) Judgmental Account Areas

Perhaps of foremost concern are accounts that are inherently subjective, requiring judgment to reach the valuations for the financials. These are sometimes referred to as "softer" accounts, as the precision with which these numbers can be estimated or audited is much wider in range than what is feasible in recording, for example, a loan transaction.

Reserves

Reserves span a range of subjectivity, from account areas that have a long history of experience with estimation and that are comparable to industry norms, to areas that are primarily future oriented, whose amounts depend on highly uncertain future outcomes, often outside the client's control or influence. A good example of the first type of account area would be warranty accounts related to well-established product lines, and an example of the second is the estimation of loss reserves for personal injury claims from a transportation company, such as a railroad or airline. Although such claims are expected in the normal course of business, the actual liability that results will depend heavily on the courts' determinations, which, in turn, will be influenced by social norms and expectations—difficult to project for the future decade.

Reserves have been a common source of or element in litigation involving auditors, typically the reserves' inadequacy. Remember that the Penn Square Bank's failure involved a dispute over the adequacy of loan loss reserves. Recall that this bank was the focal point of discussion in this chapter's introductory case.

Bank auditors are expected to review loan files and collections when evaluating reserves; yet such routine approaches to evaluating uncollectibles can sometimes lead the auditor away from the considerations that could cause him or her to question the adequacy of reserves. Even comparisons with historical experience can be problematic for a fast-growing client. For Penn Square, the evaluation that could have revealed the audit risk was linking of a thorough understanding of the client's operations to its market, and the risk in its approach to lending. A comparison of Penn Square's loan loss reserves with those of other banks may well have failed to flag an "unreasonable" reserve, because the industry norm was not the same type of loan portfolio that Penn Square held. A business understanding of the client's operations, particularly how they compare with those of the other industry participants, is, obviously, essential.

Inherent Subjectivity. The more subjective the accounting is for a client's operations and, consequently, the greater the management's ability to influence the accounting results, then the greater the audit risk will be. The auditor must estimate the extent to which each area of the audit will require management judgments. For example, work in process can entail an elaborate cost system and projections of the final completion costs and revenues. When evaluating an allowance for doubtful accounts, consider who establishes the allowance, the extent to which collection is monitored, and the amounts that are written off.

And when reviewing the allowance for uncollectibles, the auditor should evaluate the collectibility of receivables in light of the nature of the charge and the collateral held. For example, is the nature of the charges the routine credit basis for sales, or are most sales on a cash basis with exceptions on credit? Are all receivables unsecured? Once these questions have been answered, the aging of receivables, after testing its accuracy, and the credit and collection files ought to be reviewed. Past-due balances should be discussed with knowledgeable client personnel. Significant receivables that have been confirmed but pertain to a customer whose credit standing is not readily apparent should be investigated by checking into the customer's ability to pay. The past-due balances ought to be compared with the previous years' balances, and subsequent collections should be reviewed. The entity's past loss experience and current industry, geographical, and economic trends also warrant consideration.

Control over written-off receivables should be established and large write-offs tied to supporting documentation and confirmations. The need to establish an allowance for returns, credits, or discounts should also be considered.

Obsolete, slow-moving, and excess stock reviews should include inventory held outside and inventory held for outsiders. Physical inventories of work in process are often not practicable for major construction projects. In this situation, the auditor should visit major construction projects to ensure that they exist, but often he or she will also want to consult a qualified engineer in addition to examining job-cost records, to gain assurance as to the reasonableness of the recorded balances.

Both judgment and ingenuity are required in order to detect obsolescence and slow-moving, excess inventory. A comparison of sales with expectations, rates of usage, turnover statistics, and industry experience can be useful. While performing normal audit procedures, the auditor should watch for deteriorated conditions; old prices (in other than a LIFO situation); changing marketing, products, and sales requirements; and the age of inventory and inactivity on jobs, all of which can flag problems. Reserves for inventory losses and scrap must be evaluated, often in relation to past experiences.

A product liability reserve can mean significant risk exposure, due to uncertainty inherent in the estimation process. The auditor will make a specific review of the status of each known exposure and obtain legal representation letters from outside counsel.

Liabilities for estimated amounts payable in the future under pension or profit-sharing plans, self-insurance programs, product warranties, deferred income taxes, and the like must be tested for reasonableness. These accounts lend themselves to matching. Companies make actuarial and statistical studies of their own and others' experiences to formulate estimates, and so in reviewing the accounts, the auditor should prepare a summary analysis based on management's studies and then analyze the company's experience and the reasonableness of the estimates.

All of these techniques provide systematic means of analyzing inherently subjective accounts such as reserves. Just as judgmental as reserve balances are, so too are the valuation and disclosure issues surrounding contingencies and revenue realization.

Contingencies

Financial statements appear far more precise than the known uncertainties which underlie them. The general contingencies faced by all businesses are described in Exhibit 16-1. But there are also the special contingencies that can influence reported financial statements and that require disclosure in accordance with SFAS No. 5 (as cited in the introductory case).

Uncertainties may take the form of gain or loss contingencies or realization issues. Loss contingencies most commonly involve litigation claims, warranty-related claims, tax matters, or collectibility problems with receivables. These claims frequently stem from catastrophies, accidents, examinations by the Internal Revenue Service (IRS), investigations by agencies other than the IRS, changes in regulation, changes in laws, ambiguities in court decisions, cancellations of contracts, or failure by others to meet debt obligations. They are not resolved until the settlements are negotiated, the payments are collected, and the investigations are completed, or the assets are disposed of and the extent of loss can be determined. Recording gain contingencies involves less uncertainty than do loss contingencies because of their timing for reporting purposes—rarely are they recorded before realization.

Realization issues arise from the risk of bankruptcy and fluctuations in market value and, generally, related contingencies include

- assessment or possible assessment of additional taxes or other claims.
- legal actions.
- guarantees of debt.
- guarantees of contractual performance of others.
- agreements to repurchase receivables sold or discounted.

EXHIBIT 16-1
General Contingencies Confronted by Business

- Will debtors pay?
- Will inventory be sold?
- How long will fixed assets be useful?
- Allocations are based on assumptions as to future events; thus will experience invalidate such assumptions?
- How will changes in regulation affect business?
- How will tax law changes affect income?

To identify contingent liabilities and commitments, letters are obtained from the entity's legal counsel and its management. Often, bank confirmations and replies to accounts payable circularization letters will indicate contingencies and disputes. Rental expenses may flag significant loan agreements, and minutes may indicate authorization for plant expansion, contractual agreements, and other commitments. An analysis of legal expenses may reveal lawsuits, and inquiry of officers and employees may uncover additional commitments.

Since risks and contingencies relate to regulators' actions, it is interesting to note the following claim by a past executive of Seafirst: "The SEC investigation was a 'routine' probe prompted by the share drop in the price of the company's stock."[2] Given the SEC-defined estimates of liability damages relate to the decline in market value from the date of the error to the date of claim, the SEC may assess companies experiencing large declines as having far greater risk of being sued for financial statement "misstatements." If accurate, this anecdote suggests the wisdom of CPAs monitoring clients' stock prices when assessing audit risk.

When evaluating contingencies, again the question arises of who monitors claims and potential litigation and who determines reserves and in consultation with whom? Have reserves been reasonable in other years? Corporate counsel and outside counsel will be asked to review the status of outstanding claims and lawsuits. When a reasonable estimate of claims is extremely uncertain,

[2] Victor F. Zonana and Ken Wells, "Penn Square Probe Is Widened to Seafirst, Continental Illinois, Other Loan Buyers," *Wall Street Journal*, June 15, 1983, p. 2.

pressures are exerted on the auditor to issue a qualified opinion, as discussed in the *Wall Street Journal,* using examples of Union Carbide's exposure to claims stemming from the accident in Bhopal, India, and Manville's exposure to asbestos litigation (December 17, 1984, p. 4: "Auditor Is Likely to Be Under Pressure to Qualify Union Carbide's Statement"). Such difficulties stem in part from the fact that many claims have not even been filed as of the audit report date.

Unasserted claims are situations involving possible litigation claims or assessments in which there has been no manifestation of awareness of such a claim by a potential claimant. Determining whether an assertion or a loss is probable and whether that loss can be estimated can be difficult. Furthermore, the client will probably not want this revealed, owing to the self-fulfilling prophecy of such reporting, creating potential liability against the auditor for inadequate disclosure. SFAS No. 5 seems to permit accrual without disclosure.[3] Even obtaining information on unfavorable or adverse outcomes on claims or legal suits is likely to be difficult:

> The central concern of lawyers is the fear that legal counsel may be exposed to possible liabilities and a company's defense may be compromised by too much disclosure of sensitive information, whereas the central concern of the auditors is the fear that the auditor may be exposed to liabilities and the users of financial statements may be misled by too little or inadequate disclosure.[4]

EXHIBIT 16-2
Audit Procedures Regarding Contingencies and Uncertainties

- Inquiry procedures, directed at managers with administrative, financial, and accounting responsibilities related to the risk areas.
- Gaining a thorough understanding of the entity's business, operating characteristics, industry, general economic conditions, and government regulations that are related to the risks being analyzed.
- Review correspondence to provide background information, as well as insights regarding entities' current status and future prospects and the amount of potential loss.
- Examine contracts, correspondence with legal counsel, minutes of the board of directors, and tax examiner's report or notice of assessment, as applicable to the risk area.
- Review accounting records and financial statements, alert to assets that may be impaired or liabilities that may have been incurred.
- Confirm with outside parties the details of agreements underlying unconditional purchase obligations.
- Confirm details as to both methods and assumptions about loss estimates with specialists.
- Review SAS No. 12, "Inquiry of a Client's Lawyer Concerning Litigation, Claims and Assessments," SAS No. 19, "Client Representations," and SAS No. 34, "The Auditor's Considerations When a Question Arises About an Entity's Continued Existence," and perform the appropriate procedures related to uncertainties.

AICPA, Auditing Standards Board, "Consideration of Elimination of the 'Subject to' Qualification," Public Meeting, June 30, 1982.

Clients should be asked about outstanding purchase and sales commitments—particularly possible losses, as disclosed by comparing market values with committed purchase prices. Disclosure may be required, and any evident losses should be booked.

Effects on audit planning are observed for advance sales commitments, transactions with related parties, bill and hold arrangements—peculiar to certain industries, nonrecurring revenues, and pledged or discounted receivables. Exhibit 16-2 outlines audit procedures likely to be useful in identifying and quantifying contingencies and uncertainties. Should there be buy-back commitments such as the one extended by Penn Square, there should be an investigation of whether a commitment in fact exists, and if it does, at the very least, this should be disclosed in a footnote.

Realization Issues

The literature recommends greater attention be given to assets as economic resources, liabilities as legal and substantive claims, and an overall objec-

[3] Raymond J. Clay, Jr., and William W. Holder, "Unasserted Claims: Accounting Measurement and Disclosure," *CPA Journal,* October 1977, pp. 83–85.

[4] W. McRae, "Representation Letters from a Company's Legal Counsel—Auditing and Reporting Considerations," *Journal of Accountancy,* November 1973, pp. 76–77.

tive of reflecting value in financial statement data. In so doing, transactions would not be the critical test for income recognition if they failed to reflect changes in the value of net economic resources. The percentage-of-completion means of recognizing a long-term earnings process would be used more, and if risks of sales were transferred before shipping, the recognition of revenue might be recorded on an earlier date. The value approach to recognizing income emphasizes (1) the transfer of ownership risks, (2) the timing of the earnings process, and (3) the existence of viable claims. For example, the retention of ownership risks by a lessor, a plan to construct that has not begun, and a mere option to purchase, would not generate income.[5]

In evaluating revenue recognition, auditors must determine whether

- an exchange has taken place.
- the risks of ownership have been transferred.
- the sales transaction can be considered "closed."
- the earnings process is substantially complete.
- the sale has substance rather than being a sale only in form.

Problems arise in these determinations because of the common contractual complications that affect the decision of when it is appropriate to recognize revenue. Some of these complications are summarized in Exhibit 16-3.

EXHIBIT 16-3
Problems in Determining Appropriate Timing of Revenue Recognition

- Both parties to a transaction often retain or assume certain risks and benefits, making it difficult to determine whether the risks of ownership have in fact been transferred.
- The selling party may have a continuing interest or involvement even after a business transaction has been completed, making it difficult to determine whether the transaction is actually "closed."
- Objective means of quantifying revenue and related cost are not always available once this problem is further complicated by the involved parties' lack of independence.
- The enforceability of contractual terms is often not clear-cut, and again, related party status may preclude effective enforceability of terms.
- It is often difficult to distinguish between a transaction's legal form and its economic substance, and this distinction can be most blurred in exchanges between related parties.

Percentage-of-Completion. Contract revenue recognition can be particularly problematic, as it relies on estimates of future costs and future events that the auditor must determine to be reasonable. Whatever methods are used to account for long-term contracts ought to be consistently applied to all contracts; otherwise they will be distorted. If the completed-contract method is used, a consistent set of criteria should be established to determine the point of substantial completion. Otherwise, manipulation of income could be substantial through arbitrary selection of the point of completion.

Percentage-of-completion is susceptible through distortions of cost estimates or stage-of-completion estimates. In addition, changes in estimates may be motivated more by a desire to control the reported results of operations than by new information. But delays in adjusting to new information can also lead to distortion.

Auditors should review both incurred costs and estimated costs of completion. Foreseeable losses may not be recorded appropriately if (1) a client is observed to not be making periodic estimates of progress and total contract costs, (2) the client is determining the percentage of completion on the basis of costs incurred without regard for physical progress, or (3) contract inventories are observed to be increasing without any apparent increase in contracting activity.

For percentage-of-completion to be acceptable, there must be a written contract with clearly specified terms; the buyer must be able to satisfy the obligations to which he or she is committed; and the seller must be able to perform his or her contractual obligations, have an adequate estimating process, and have a cost accounting system that can adequately accumulate and allocate costs. The key audit procedures used to evaluate percentage-of-completion accounting are shown in Exhibit 16-4.

[5] *Objectives of Financial Statements for Business Enterprises* (Chicago: Arthur Andersen & Co., 1972).

EXHIBIT 16-4

Audit of Percentage-of-Completion Contracts

- Examine a sample of contracts.
- Confirm the contract provisions with the buyer.
- Evaluate the contract's provisions, with the assistance of a specialist, if necessary.
- Be alert to substantial changes in original contracts, a large number of contract cancellations, disputes between parties, increases in contracting at year-end, related party transactions, and clients' attempts to limit the scope of confirmation procedures.
- Review the client's procedures for checking the financial substance of primary contractors; typical procedures include a statement of financial condition, an interim construction loan agreement with a bank, or interim progress payments.
- Be alert to increases in unbilled contract receivables, exceeding increases in contracting activity, uncollected progress billings, and depressed industry conditions for buyers.
- Review past contracting practices, and evaluate risks that contracts will not be completed—this risk is deemed to be greater if the items to be constructed differ from the contractor's past experience.
- Be alert to signs that a client's resources and financial position are insufficient to fulfill contracts, problems with the technological feasibility of completing contracts, significant turnover of personnel or inadequate personnel, and difficulties with subcontractors' completing their obligations.
- Evaluate the assumptions underlying the client's estimation process and related controls, by
    - -- reviewing estimates with managers.
    - -- discussing with supervisors.
    - -- reviewing management information systems.
    - -- making on-site observations.
    - -- considering changes in circumstances affecting estimates.
    - -- performing both substantive and compliance tests of the system.
- Be alert to an absence of variance analysis and interim estimation practices, inadequate records for cost estimates, and an absence of consideration of uncontrollable factors as estimates are developed.
- Determine that documentation permits comparisons of estimated costs with actual costs as each phase of the project is completed.
- Test detailed cost estimates to purchase orders, purchase commitments, and independent price lists, and compare subcontractors' cost with the final contract.
- Evaluate labor costs relative to past experience and performance to date on the contract in progress.
- Be alert to inadequate documentation costs in excess of estimates, lack of review process over estimates, inexperienced personnel, and significant revisions in the estimated cost of completion.
- Gain assurance that costs are accumulated and allocated on a timely basis and dovetail into the management information system for variance analysis which, in turn, the client uses to update and reevaluate cost estimates on a timely basis.
- Be alert to insufficiency of detail in the cost accounting system for allowing early identification of cost overruns, allocation on a group basis—rather than on a contract-by-contract basis—no tie-in of invoices for materials and services and labor costs by contract, no comparison of actual and estimated costs, and weak controls over purchasing of materials and their handling.

Real Estate. Some of the most publicized abuses of revenue recognition practices have been in the real estate area. An article, "Castles of Sand?" authored by Abraham J. Briloff, appeared in *Barron's*[6] and pointed out the then prevalent practice of land development companies to record 100 percent of revenue from land sales in the year a contract was signed, in spite of an average of 9 years of life remaining on the contract, 90 percent of the payment being outstanding, and the prevalence of cancellations. At the opposite end of the spectrum was an implicit practice of submerging values.[7]

Real estate transactions have raised accounting problems largely because of the lack of emphasis on their values and changes therein. For example, if land valued at $20,000 is acquired, appreciates to $2 million, and then is transferred to a corporation for real estate development, and if the same owners of the land also own the corporation, then the contribution of the land will be recorded at $20,000. Of course, the $1.98 million misstatement will gradually be reflected in the corporation's earnings per share—emitting an impressive image of a successful operation, even if the entity, in fact, were mismanaged and gradually eroding the original "principal" of $2 million.[8] Such submerging of real values clearly distorts reports of operating performance. While some accounting changes have curbed abuses in the real estate area, these examples help to highlight the joint audit risk of "too rapid" or "too deferred" revenue recognition practices.

#2) Unrecorded Liabilities

Because so many audit procedures are based on recorded transactions, the auditor should pay special attention to unrecorded transactions. As most companies prefer to present favorable financial statements, a critical risk area is the possibility of unrecorded liabilities. A check for unrecorded liabilities includes a review of expenditures booked from the date of the balance sheet to the last day of field work, as well as inquiries of management about disputed items involving suppliers, creditors, and tax agencies, including the status of tax returns for previous years which are still open. In addition, the status of renegotiable business should be raised. A review of the minutes can be an important source of information about unrecorded liabilities, and the account balances for the current period should be compared with those of the preceding year.

To determine the risk of unrecorded liabilities, the auditor should look at cash payments for a period after the year-end and match them with the corresponding invoices and receiving reports, as well as review the correspondence with the principal suppliers.

Searches for unrecorded liabilities for a calendar-year client mean inspecting invoices paid from January 1 to February 15—if February 15 is the intended report date—which are for an amount in excess of a dollar figure such as $50,000. This is sometimes referred to as a review of the unentered vendors' invoice file.

Indentures and loan agreements for outstanding obligations should be examined to determine whether commitments, contingencies, and guarantees have been made but not recorded and whether significant liabilities were incurred after the balance sheet date. Any existing contracts and agreements can reveal possible unrecorded liabilities. Of similar interest is the question of whether the entity is in compliance with all covenants and restrictions. Discussions with employees, representations from management, and the attorney's bills and letter of representation can be good sources of information about unrecorded liabilities.

An effective way of testing to detect unrecorded liabilities is to analyze reciprocal populations. For example, audit tests of the cutoff date for such reciprocal accounts as inventory and fixed assets can be tied to related liabilities. Sending confirmation

[6] February 2, 1970, pp. 3, 15, 16.

[7] See "Gimme Shelter" by Abraham J. Briloff, *Barron's* (October 25, 1971) for development of some industry examples.

[8] Adapted from *Objectives of Financial Statements for Business Enterprises* (Chicago: Arthur Andersen & Co., 1972).

requests to lenders with whom the company has done business in the recent past—even if no liability balance is shown as of the confirmation date—can be an important test which is often a part of the audit work in the cash area. Vouching open purchase orders, talking to purchase personnel, and confirming with suppliers all help detect commitments to repurchase inventories at fixed prices. And such commitments may represent unrecorded liabilities or undisclosed contingencies and may be uncovered while performing cutoff tests on inventory or reviewing controls.

#3) Cutoff Practices

There is also the concern that recorded transactions have been booked in the wrong period; hence many audit procedures are directed toward the client's cutoff practices. Cutoff tests should be coordinated among the client's locations, and if they are not done concurrently by the CPA firm, any intercompany transactions during the intervening period should be reviewed for their effect on the financial statements.

Cash

Because it is liquid, cash is of special concern when evaluating the effectiveness of a client's cutoff practices. Cutoff bank statements are obtained for the period after the year-end during which most reconciling items are expected to clear. The auditor should receive these directly from the bank and then should study the outstanding checks, deposits in transit, bank charges, and similar items used to reconcile bank to book balances at year-end.

If for some reason the auditor does not receive the cutoff statement directly from the bank, he or she should

- check the cancellation stamp for the appropriate date and its apparent validity.
- foot all contents (even those in an apparently unopened envelope) to check the completeness of canceled checks and debit memos and their tie-in to the bank statements.
- review the bank statement for alterations or erasures and confirm with the bank that any changes detected were made by the bank.
- confirm with the bank the balance as of the end of cutoff.

The cutoff statements' cleared checks dated before the year-end should be (1) traced to the outstanding check list; (2) compared with the cash disbursements journal for agreement; (3) investigated if payable to officers, known employees, subsidiaries and affiliated companies, banks, cash, or an unusual payee, or if drawn in an unusual amount or for an unusual purpose; (4) compared for a match between the checks' signers and an authorized listing; (5) examined for check endorsements and investigated if unusual items are noted, such as second endorsements or unusual deposit practices; (6) assessed as to the reasonableness of the time lapse from the date of the first bank endorsement or the date of cancellation to the issuance date, for signs that the cash disbursements were "held open" for issuance of checks after the balance sheet date but recorded before the year-end.

Any canceled checks dated after year-end and returned with the cutoff statement should be checked to make sure that the first bank endorsement did not precede the audit date, suggesting they were issued before the year-end but not recorded. Again, unusual payments and related-party checks, as well as those payable to banks and cash, are to be investigated.

Similarly, deposits in transit should be reviewed for unusual delays, and authenticated duplicate deposit slips should be traced to the cash receipts book, as one means of detecting the substitution of cash items and delayed crediting of collections, or lapping. If several deposits in transit are involved, an alternative approach such as counting undeposited cash receipts at year-end should be used. All other reconciling items will need to be traced to corrections in the books or supporting documentation. It is important that the auditor trace individual items on the deposit slips to the books, not just the column totals on the deposit slips to the general ledger, for the concern is with the substitution of one customer's payment for another's. Because lapping may occur throughout the period and be "caught up" at year-end, the auditor must be careful to perform tests of receipt handling at other than the balance sheet date.

Any reconciling items not clearing the bank should be reviewed by using alternative auditing procedures. The cash disbursement journal and supporting documents should be studied, and if a very long time has passed and an unusual material amount is involved, the client may be requested to contact the payee, requesting a reply to be addressed directly to the auditor. For an ongoing engagement, the auditors in the next period should test such "nonclearing" items in their preliminary work in order to gain assurance as to the propriety of the cash cutoff.

Interbank and intrabank transfers should be tested to ensure that the date withdrawn and date deposited are appropriate and that there has been no kiting—recording transfers as deposits in one period and as disbursements in the subsequent period. Because kiting is far more likely to occur around the balance sheet date, the auditor should perform tests around this time. In contrast, lapping tests can be performed at any time and, in fact, may be more effective at a time other than year-end.

Any bank accounts reported to be closed should be formally closed, and the confirmations should be mailed to make sure that there have not been any transactions since the closing and that the bank was in fact notified of the account's closing.

Incorrect cutoffs of cash receipts and disbursements can result in misstatements of cash, receivables, payables, and related ratios. The misappropriation of cash income may be an omission of cash receipts from the records or a substitution of checks for currency in the books and records. The misappropriation of cash disbursements may be checks payable to cash, to a third party whose endorsement is forged or obtained under false pretense—or who is an accomplice—or to banks for drafts or cashier's checks. The accounting may be covered up by manipulating accounts or falsifying footings, postings, balances, or entries.

Sales

Untimely cutoffs of sales or cash receipts from credit sales will misstate receivables. Delays in shipping, mishandling of consigned goods shipped as sales, retroactive posting of cash received after the year-end, or "holding open" the cash book all are sources of cutoff misstatements. Sales cutoff is checked by selecting invoices for a short period before and after the balance sheet date and tracing them to actual shipments in the appropriate period. Fictitious or duplicate invoices can cause a misstatement in sales, and so the auditor should watch for alterations of invoices or an apparent reuse of documentation. Care in segregating accounts from notes receivable, current from noncurrent items, debit from credit balances, and receivables from customers from others' receivables can go far to prevent misstatements.

Lapping, or the practice of abstracting cash, not recording that cash receipt, but waiting for the next customer's receipt before giving the first customer credit for payment, is the most common irregularity in receivables. Confirmation procedures, adequate follow-up of exceptions, and review of records for manipulations of various types can detect lapping problems.

Inventory

Cutoff tests for inventory typically include a review of receiving, work-in-process classifications, and sales of finished goods. When looking at sales for anything unusual, the auditor should focus on the last month of the year.

The client should have established procedures for obtaining accurate receiving, shipping, and production cutoffs. Inventory observation, the testing of inventory compilation, and the testing of costs recorded in inventory offer evidence of cutoff. During physical inventory, the company's procedures to obtain accurate cutoffs must be observed. If the reports are not prenumbered, copies of several of the receiving and shipping reports just before and just following the inventory date ought to be obtained for later testing in relation to recorded costs. The appropriate dating of the accounting records in relation to receiving and shipping reports will be checked; a testing to vendors' and sales invoices may be required. Any records relating to inventory movement during the cutoff period ought to be tested.

If the physical inventory is taken at an interim date, the accuracy of the cutoff should be tested at both interim and year-end. Cutoff tests for purchasing should match the materials in the inventory with the recording of the invoice costs as a liability. The receiving records for several days before and after year-end should be matched with the dates on which the vendors' invoices were recorded.

#4) Smoothing Incentives

One reason that cutoff practices deserve much of the auditor's attention is that managers often have incentives to smooth the earnings.

Smoothing of earnings is defined in the literature as the intentional control over fluctuations in earnings in order to report some "normal earnings level" and is accomplished by management via a reduction of abnormal variations in earnings through selecting among generally accepted accounting principles as well as by making discretionary management decisions. This practice has been deemed as desirable by some but is clearly open for abuse. This is particularly so when the discretion is exercised to systematically bias reported numbers in a single direction. Management's incentives for smoothing the earnings are to report steady upward trends in performance measures and to maximize compensation through bonus plans that typically have both ceilings and floors—making it advantageous not to have abnormal fluctuations in earnings.

Cutoff manipulations are one means of smoothing income in an unacceptable manner. While it is important to recognize the risk of smoothing, it is also imperative that the auditor recognize those forces which constrain managers' discretion to misstate operating performance:

- the market for goods and services.
- the market for finance and for corporate control.
- the market for managerial services.
- internal and external monitoring systems.[9]

The last limitation includes auditors' tests to prevent material misstatements of financial position.

#5) Related Parties

Related parties played a visible role in Continental Vending, U.S. Financial, Westec, Republic National Life Insurance, Allied Crude Vegetable Oil, BarChris, Cenco, CIT Financial, Equity Funding, Four Seasons, Home-Stake, McKesson & Robbins, Penn Central, Stirling Homex, Talley Industries, Vesco, Westgate, and other "front page" reporting problems. Transactions involving related parties, as discussed in earlier chapters, pose special audit risks which merit direct evaluation by the auditor.

A related party is management, owners, or any person or entity in a position to influence significantly the management or the operating policies of either the reporting entity or the other party to a transaction. The substance or exchange value of the transactions may be determined by a desire to achieve some management objective apart from the economic substance of that economic dealing.

Members of the immediate family of both owners and managers are related parties, including spouses, parents, children, residents of these individuals' households, brothers and sisters and their spouses, and perhaps other relatives. In assessing the controlling interest, common ownership or management is to be considered, unless geographic location or some other factor precludes its ability to affect the entity's business. The key test of related-party relationships is whether either of the transacting parties may be prevented from fully pursuing its own separate interests.

Auditors' key concerns in identifying and evaluating related-party situations are summarized in Exhibit 16-5. Note that disclosure concerns include not only actual transactions but also potential transactions. For example, Statement of Financial Accounting Standards No. 57, "Related Party Disclosures" (FASB, 1982, par. 14), notes:

> Sometimes two or more enterprises are under common ownership or management control but do not transact

[9] George J. Benston, "Accounting and Corporate Accountability," working paper, University of Rochester, June 1981.

EXHIBIT 16-5
Auditor's Concern in Identifying and Evaluating Related-Party Situations

- Is the transaction's economic substance being reflected?
- Are the transactions' terms equivalent to those likely to be observed in an arm's length transaction?
- Are the buyer's identity and substance in purchase transactions clear?
- Can the buyer "put back" the property purchased, thereby negating the transaction?
- Is the buyer financed by the seller directly or indirectly?
- Are transactions unduly complex, concentrated at the end of the period, or do they have a questionable business purpose?

business with each other. The common control, however, may result in operating results or financial position significantly different from that which would have been obtained if the enterprises were autonomous. For example, two or more enterprises in the same line of business may be controlled by a party that has the ability to increase or decrease the volume of business done by each. Disclosure of information about certain control relationships and transactions with related parties helps users of financial statements form predictions and analyze the extent to which those statements may have been affected by that relationship.

This disclosure provision complicates the auditor's task, as he or she cannot count the actual transactions to reveal all of the required disclosures.

Officers should be requested to provide a list of subsidiaries, affiliates, and other known related parties with whom the entity may transact business, as well as a description of the types of such transactions and the basis of pricing or setting the contractual terms.

It is useful to formulate a profile of the sales to or receivables from related parties in regard to amount, pricing, and collectibility. Product transfers for intracompany and intercompany sales are frequently priced above cost for internal purposes but must be net of unrealized profits for financial statements. Both routine and unusual transactions with related parties should be explored, and if there are significant transactions not involving accounting recognition—such as providing certain services without charge—they should be disclosed. The extent of the disclosure will depend in part on the minority shareholdings.

Management's representations should be corroborated by means of other audit procedures. An audit program to determine the existence of related parties and identify related-party transactions, and a summary of disclosure requirements for related-party transactions are presented in Exhibit 16-6.

Transactions may also involve concealed related parties. If there are unusual transactions pertaining to sales and loans, the other party to the transaction should be identified. These investigations may entail special studies to discover the names of partners, officers, directors, and principal shareholders—and possibly to secure credit reports. The *business purpose* of material transactions must be understood and may very well require the use of specialists.

Auditing Issues Raised When Reporting on Personal Financial Statements

An audit engagement that often poses special problems in both identifying the related parties and gauging their effects on asset valuation is one involving personal financial statements. Although GAAS for such audits are the same, the auditor should pay special attention to auditing the estimated current values of assets and the current amounts of liabilities, as they are required accounting disclosures for personal financial statements. Once the auditor is satisfied that these estimated current values in the financial statements present fairly the individual's financial condition and changes in net worth in conformity with generally accepted accounting principles applied consistently and that accounting methods are adequately disclosed, he or she should issue an unqualified opinion. Its general form is similar to that of the standard auditor's report. But the most common difficulty in reaching such an opinion is that the accounting records are inadequate for audit purposes. At a minimum, this will lead to a scope limitation, and at a maximum, a disclaimer must be issued. The second most common prob-

EXHIBIT 16-6

Disclosure Requirements for Related Party Transactions and an Audit Program to Comply with SAS No. 6 in Determining Existence of Related Parties and the Identification of Related Party Transactions

Staff should be satisfied as to the adequacy of disclosure about related party transactions. Sufficient evidence should be gathered to provide an understanding of the relationship of the parties, the substance of the transactions and the effects on the financial statements. Adequate disclosure should include the following:

- The nature of the relationship(s).
- A description of the transactions (summarized when appropriate) for the reported period, including amounts and such other information necessary to an understanding of the effects on the financial statements.
- The dollar volume of transactions and the effects of any change in the method of establishing terms from that used in the preceding period (consistency of treatment).
- Amounts due from or to related parties and, if not otherwise apparent, the terms and manner of settlement.*

Audit procedures. Each of the following procedures should be reviewed and initialed by the staff:

1. Evaluate internal accounting controls over management activities.
2. Evaluate the company's procedures for identifying and properly accounting for related party transactions.
3. Ask appropriate management personnel for the names of all related parties and any transactions with these parties during the period.
4. Review the reporting entity's filings with the SEC and with other regulatory agencies for the names of related parties and for other businesses in which officers and directors occupy directorships or management positions.
5. Determine the names of all pension and other trusts established for the benefit of employees and the names of the officers and trustees thereof. (If the trusts are managed by or under the trusteeship of management, they should be deemed to be related parties.)
6. Review stockholder listings of closely held companies in order to identify principal stockholders.
7. Review workpapers of prior years for the names of known related parties.
8. Ask predecessor, principal, or other auditors of related entities about their knowledge of existing relationships and the extent of management's involvement in material transactions.
9. Review material investment transactions during the period under examination to determine whether the nature and extent of investments during the period create related parties.
10. A list of known related parties should be provided to all audit personnel working on the engagement so that they may become aware of transactions with such parties during their examinations.
11. Review the minutes of meetings of the board of directors and executive operating committees for information as to material transactions authorized or discussed at their meetings.
12. Review proxy and other material filed with the SEC and comparable data filed with other regulatory agencies for information as to material transactions with related parties.
13. Review conflict-of-interest statements obtained by the company from its management.
14. Review the extent and nature of business transacted with major customers, suppliers, borrowers and lenders for indications of previously undisclosed relationships.
15. Consider whether any transactions are occurring that are not being given accounting recognition, such as receiving or providing accounting, management, or other services at no charge or a major stockholder's absorbing corporate expenses.
16. Review accounting records for large, unusual or nonrecurring transactions or balances, paying particular attention to transactions recognized at or near the end of the reporting period.

EXHIBIT 16-6 (continued)

17. Review confirmations of compensating balance arrangements for indications that balances are or were maintained for or by related parties.

18. Review invoices from law firms and response to lawyers' inquiry letters for indication of the existence of related parties or related party transactions.

19. Review confirmations of loans receivable and payable for indications of guarantees. When guarantees are indicated, determine their nature and the relationships, if any, of the guarantors to the reporting entity.

20. In examining related party transactions, obtain an understanding of the business purpose of the transaction (a discussion of the purpose of certain transactions with the specific parties involved may be necessary to a full understanding).

21. Examine invoices, executed copies of agreements, contracts and other pertinent documents, such as receiving reports and shipping documents.

22. Determine whether related party transactions have been approved by the board of directors or other appropriate officials.

23. Test for reasonableness the compilation of amounts to be disclosed, or considered for disclosure, in the financial statements.

24. Arrange for the audits of inter-company account balances to be performed as of concurrent dates, even if fiscal years differ. Ensure examination of specified, important and representative related party transactions by the auditors of each of the parties, with an appropriate exchange of relevant information.

25. Inspect or confirm and obtain satisfaction as to the transferability and value of collateral supporting related party transactions.

26. When necessary to fully understand the business purpose or substance of related party transactions, perform the following extended procedures:

a. Confirm transaction amount and terms, including guarantees and other significant data, with the other party(ies) to the transaction.

b. Inspect evidence in possession of the other party(ies) to the transaction.

c. Confirm or discuss significant information with intermediaries, such as banks, guarantors, agents, or attorneys.

d. Refer to financial publications, trade journals, credit agencies, and other sources if there is reason to believe that customers, suppliers, or other enterprises with which material amounts of business have been transacted may be financially unstable.

e. For material uncollected balances, guarantees, and other obligations, obtain information as to the financial capability of the other party(ies) to the transaction (such information may be obtained from audited financial statements, unaudited financial statements, income tax returns, and reports issued by regulatory agencies, taxing authorities, financial publications, or credit agencies).

* "Auditing Interpretations," *Journal of Accountancy,* March 1976, p.70
Courtenay L. Granger and Thomas D. Hubbard, "An Audit Program for Related Party Transactions," *Journal of Accountancy,* September 1977, pp. 50, 52, 54.

lem with personal statements is gathering enough evidence to test the assets' estimated current values. Even though testing actual market prices is no problem for assets like marketable securities, closely held business investments and similar assets and obligations (particularly those obtained in related-party transactions) often require the use of price indexes, appraisals, liquidation values, capitalization of past and prospective earnings, discounted amounts of projected cash receipts and payments, and, concurrently, careful analysis of the specialists' work and the assumptions used to generate the estimated values. Thus when the audit report states "such other auditing procedures as we considered necessary in the circumstances," it probably is referring to these procedures. In addition, because individuals' records are often informal, good sources of information are likely to be checkbooks, brokers' statements, property insurance policies and schedules, wills, leases, lists of vault or safety deposit box contents, real estate and personal property tax returns, income tax returns, financial records of other entities such as closely held businesses, and inquiry procedures.[10]

#6) Going Concern Issues

Bankruptcies have been occurring at an increasing rate in the 1980s, relative to the prior decade, as indicated in Exhibit 16-7. Such proceedings are extremely complicated, as reflected in the 1976 estimate by bankruptcy experts that the average duration of a bankruptcy proceeding was about seven years. Yet, exceptions occur such as the 1963 bankruptcy of Continental Vending which was still in court in 1976.[11] It is not a coincidence that the name Continental Vending is familiar from earlier discussions of auditor litigation. In fact, Exhibit 16-8 offers a sample of auditor litigation cases that included the announcement of bankruptcy. When investors and creditors are faced with losses, they are apt to sue the auditor. Of course, the risk of financial statements being claimed to be unreasonable increases as related party transactions are involved and also when reporting practices seem to have miscommunicated the ill-effects or risks attached to rapid expansion. This overlap of the special risk areas discussed to this point is evident via footnotes incorporated in Exhibit 16-8. The auditor's concern for a client's risk of bankruptcy stems from the obvious liability exposure as well as the effect of such an event on asset valuation.

EXHIBIT 16-7
Bankruptcy Filings over Time

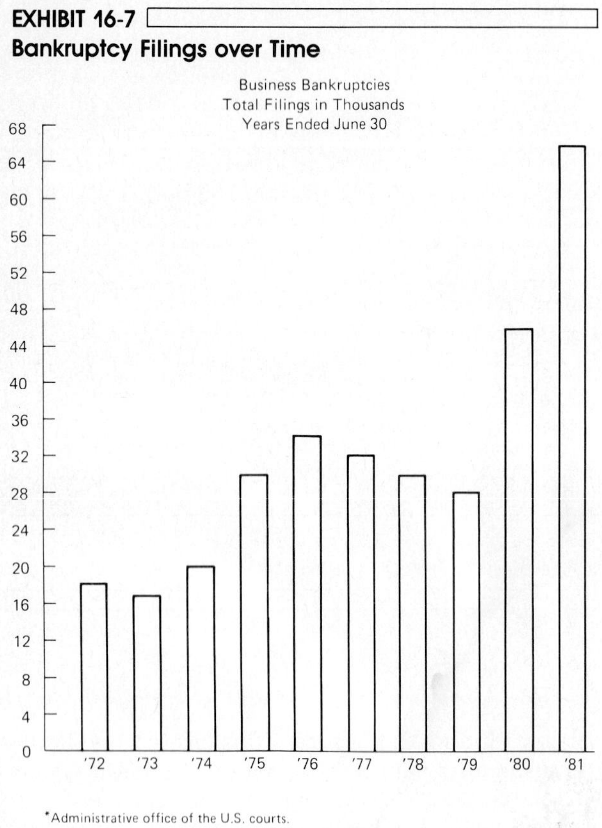

The going concern principle has been cited as the reason for distinguishing between realized and unrealized profits and losses. If, indeed, an entity is to be in operation for a long time, temporary or short-term market changes and the distress values of recorded assets will be irrelevant ***[SAS 34, Section 340].*** Many an example can be offered of entities holding large amounts of natural resources and land at historical cost valuations on the financials, which have enormous market values. However, going the less conservative direction, railroads argued that their unused rail lines and similar assets should not be written down, as the going-concern nature of the business could well create new value for such resources. In the aftermath of Penn Central, the credibility of such a claim is suspect; yet, accounting principles were vague as to how and when the going concern presumption was to be modified. New direction was provided by SAS No. 34.

An auditor is expected to assess the client's ability to continue to meet its obligations without having to liquidate assets, restructure debt, or be forced by outsiders to revise its operations. The auditor's reasons for questioning the client's going concern

[10] A discussion of the "Accounting and Financial Reporting for Personal Financial Statements," see Statement of Position 82-1 (New York: AICPA, October 1, 1982). In addition, auditing issues are addressed in an AICPA publication entitled *Personal Financial Statements Guide* (1983).

[11] Dana L. Thomas, "Painful Chapter, The Books Aren't Yet Closed on Continental Vending," *Barron's*, June 21, 1976, pp. 3–12.

EXHIBIT 16-8
Litigation Cases in Which Bankruptcy Was Filed

Client Involved	CPA Firm	Bankruptcy Announcement
Continental Vending*	C & L	7/15/63
R. Hoe & Co., Inc.	C & L	7/ 7/69
Penn Central*@	PMM & Co.	6/21/70
Four Seasons Nursing Centers of America, Inc.*@	AA & Co.	6/29/70
Black Watch@	AA & Co.	9/ 8/70
Viatron	AA & Co.	2/24/71
Blair & Co.	AY & Co.	4/15/71
Beck Industries	E & E (now E & W)	5/24/71
Stirling Homex*@	PMM & Co.	1972
Visual Electronics	PMM & Co.	1/12/72
Ancorp National Services	PMM & Co.	3/24/73
Equity Funding*@	TR & Co.	4/ 5/73
Cartridge Television	AY & Co.	7/ 2/73
Dolly Madison	TR & Co.	7/ 3/73
U.S. Financial Inc.*	TR & Co.	7/25/73
Co-Build	L & H	7/31/73 (technical default)
Westgate-California*@	AG & Co. TR & Co.	1974
Beverly Hills BanCorp & Western Diversified Equities	E & W	1/17/74
Omega-Alpha Inc. & Transcontinental Investing Corporation	TR & Co.	3/22/74
Investors Funding Corp.	PMM & Co.	10/ 4/74
W.T. Grant	E & W	1975
Wheatheart	PMM & Co.	1/24/75
King Resources	AA & Co.	1977
Mego International	JKL & Co.	1982

* Related party transactions were involved.
@Extremely rapid expansion was observed.

Key: AA & Co. = Arthur Andersen
AG & Co. = Alexander Grant
AY & Co. = Arthur Young
C & L = Coopers & Lybrand
E & W = Ernst & Whinney
JKL & Co. = J.K. Lasser & Co. (later, merged with TR & Co.)
L & H = Laventhol & Horwath
PMM & Co. = Peat, Marwick, Mitchell & Co.
TR & Co. = Touche Ross & Co.

From W. Steve Albrecht and Marshall B. Romney, "Auditing Implications Derived from a Review of Cases and Articles Relating to Fraud," *Auditing Symposium V* (Lawrence: University of Kansas Press, 1980), pp. 101-119.

status are a loss of key personnel, principal customers, critical supply sources, and primary revenue-producing assets. Solvency problems may be indicated by negative trends, defaults, difficulties in complying with capital requirements or acquiring debt, and external problems like litigation, uninsured catastrophes, union strikes, or problematic long-term commitments. These types of events should be considered as contrary evidence, that is, evidence that suggests that the normal going concern assumption may be in error. The auditor should also recognize any factors that may mitigate the significance of such information, including management's plans. Such factors are listed in Exhibit 16-9.

The key issue is whether there are means by which the client can remain a going concern. The initial mitigating factors in Exhibit 16-9 relate to solvency concerns, while the management plans deal with problems involving solvency and similar critical operating issues which need attention within the next year. In evaluating management plans, the sensitivity of forecasts and projections should be considered, as should their correspondence to historical experience. In forming an opinion as to the going concern status of a client, the auditor may be called upon to evaluate a forecast or management plan. In doing so, Monte Carlo simulation may be useful. Such an approach effectively tests the sensitivity of projections or forecasts to various assumptions or possible sources of error in estimation, so that risk can be more effectively evaluated. Simulation may also be useful in evaluating the degree of uncertainty in various reserve estimates.[12] Joint consideration of contrary information and the items cited in Exhibit 16-9, including sensitivity analysis of proposed plans, form the basis for an audit judgment as to required disclosure.

Accounting Changes

Much research has been directed to improving ways of gauging the risk of bankruptcy, finding a possible correlation between accounting changes

[12] Davis L. S. Chang and Shu S. Liao, "Measuring and Disclosing Forecast Reliability," *Journal of Accountancy*, May 1977, pp. 76–87.

EXHIBIT 16-9

Information That Might Mitigate Significance of Information Contrary to the Going Concern Assumption

Mitigating Factors

Asset factors:

- Disposability of assets not operationally interdependent.
- Capability of delaying the replacement of assets consumed in operations or of leasing rather than purchasing certain assets.
- Possibility of using assets for factoring, sale-leaseback, or similar arrangements.

Debt factors:

- Availability of unused lines of credit or similar borrowing capacity.
- Capability of renewing or extending the due dates of existing loans.
- Possibility of entering into debt restructuring agreements.

Cost factors:

- Separability of operations producing negative cash flows.
- Capability of postponing expenditures for such matters as maintenance or research and development.
- Possibility of reducing overhead and administrative expenditures.

Equity factors:

- Variability of dividend requirements.
- Capability of obtaining additional equity capital.
- Possibility of increasing cash distributions from affiliates or other investees.

Management Plans

Plans to liquidate assets:

- Apparent marketability of the assets that management plans to sell.
- Restrictions on the disposal of assets, such as covenants limiting such transactions in loan or similar agreements or encumbrances against assets.
- Possible direct and indirect effects of the disposal of assets.

Plans to borrow money or restructure debt:

- Availability of debt financing, including existing or committed credit arrangements, such as lines of credit and arrangements for factoring receivables or sale-leaseback of assets.
- Existing or committed arrangements to restructure or subordinate debt or to guarantee loans to the entity.
- Possible effects on management's borrowing plans of existing restrictions on additional borrowing and the sufficiency of available collateral.

Plans to reduce or delay expenditures:

- Apparent feasibility of plans to reduce overhead and administrative expenditures, to postpone maintenance or research and development projects, or to lease rather than purchase assets.
- Possible direct and indirect effects of reduced or delayed expenditures.

Plans to increase ownership equity:

- Apparent feasibility of plans to increase ownership equity, including existing or committed arrangements to raise additional capital.
- Existing or committed arrangements to reduce current dividend requirements or to accelerate cash distributions from affiliates or other investees.

Statement in Auditing Standards No. 34, "The Auditor's Considerations When a Question Arises About an Entity's Continued Existence" (New York: AICPA, March 1981).

and the existence of corporate financial distress. In a study of 149 distressed companies compared with 163 healthy companies, the former were observed to make four times as many discretionary changes in accounting that had a material positive effect on income. These changes pertained to depreciation, inventory, expense and revenue recognition, income tax, deferrals and credits, pension, bad debt provisions, and warranty provisions.[13]

A widely publicized financially troubled company epitomizes the potential abuse of accounting changes by failing entities. Chrysler Corporation reported fourth-quarter profits in 1978 of $43.2 million after adding an estimated $50 million to quarterly profits by increasing the assumed rate of return on pension assets (that is, one of the pension actuarial assumptions). However, this was not the first discretionary accounting change that had a positive effect on reported earnings. In 1970, Chrysler changed from LIFO to FIFO, raising reported earnings by $20 million (simultaneously increasing taxes by $56 million—an accounting change that's been questioned widely as to what possible rationale could exist for such a switch). In 1979, revision of pension actuarial assumptions increased reported earnings by $11 million. In 1975, a change from the deferral method of accounting for the investment tax credit to the flow-through method created a $23 million increase in reported earnings. In 1975, asset life assumptions were revised so that the estimated service lives of certain assets were increased, creating a $50 million increase in earnings.[14]

Other examples are available. Gelco Corporation which leased and rented trucks and containers was able to report $50 million of earnings in the year it had financial difficulties, due in large part to the $20 million created from

- changing from the deferral method to the flow-through method.
- revising estimated service lives of assets.
- changing the method of recognizing income on vehicles purchased for lease.

Similarly, Nashua Corporation, which manufactures office systems and supplies and computer equipment, changed from the deferral to flow-through method and revised pension assumptions to double 1975 reported earnings. Yet, in 1975, bonds were downgraded due to that corporation's financial problems.[15] The implication of such research for auditors is that actions by clients to make discretionary accounting changes may signal financial difficulties. This possibility is reinforced by research results that indicate that the market appears to distinguish between companies making discretionary versus nondiscretionary accounting changes. The former are accompanied by lower relative market values.[16] In fact, a study of 80 companies that reported discretionary accounting changes during 1965 to 1970 indicated that their reported earnings per share for those years exhibited a poorer pattern or trend than a random sample of companies which reported no accounting changes during that same period.[17] Of course, accounting changes may not be indicative of a going concern problem, since there are many legitimate reasons for changing accounting methods.

Ratios

There are also more traditional means of evaluating the risk of failure, including ratio analysis. Some studies have indicated that financial ratios can signal increases in the probability of business failure for as much as five years before a firm's actual failure.[18] An analysis of Penn Central Transportation Company's ratios indicated significant differences between that entity and the industry average—for example, the cash flow to total debt was .0295 for Penn Central and .1442 for the indus-

[13] Kenneth B. Schwartz, "Accounting Changes by Corporations Facing Possible Insolvency," *Journal of Accounting, Auditing & Finance*, Fall 1982, pp. 32–43.

[14] Ibid. [15] Ibid.

[16] Tom Harrison, "Different Market Reactions to Discretionary and Nondiscretionary Accounting Changes," *Journal of Accounting Research*, Spring 1977, pp. 84–107.

[17] Wayne G. Bremser, "The Earnings Characteristics of Firms Reporting Discretionary Accounting Changes," *The Accounting Review*, July 1975, pp. 563–573.

[18] William H. Beaver, "Financial Ratios As Predictors of Failure," *Empirical Research in Accounting: Selected Studies* (University of Chicago: 1966), pp. 71–111.

try average (significantly different at a .01 level or at a 99 percent level of confidence). A comparison of fourteen ratios yielded lower-than-desired ratios, at a significant level for eleven ratios of Penn Central relative to the other railroads, suggesting that its failure was certainly possible.[19]

Liquidity and equity deficiencies, debt defaults, and fund shortages, as well as operating problems plagued by losses, cutbacks in operations, and poor control all have been cited as indicative of a going concern problem. Bankruptcy models using measures of these attributes have been cited as potentially useful in helping auditors determine their clients' risk of failure. For thirty-four companies entering bankruptcy proceedings during 1970 to 1973, auditors reported going concern qualifications two years prior for 21 percent of the entities, one year prior for 46 percent of the entities, and in the report last available prior to bankruptcy for 44 percent. In contrast, one proposed bankruptcy model flagged 58 percent, 82 percent, and 82 percent, respectively.[20] This type of analysis suggests that auditors may be able to improve their ability to assess the risk of bankruptcy by applying modeling techniques. But one problem with these models is they often create many Type I or alpha errors, mistakenly indicating a high risk of failure. In addition, the populations of firms analyzed in studies of bankruptcy models often contain a higher percentage of bankrupt firms than would normally occur in the marketplace, resulting in very inflated measures of how effective the model is at predicting pending bankruptcy.

#7) Auditability Questions

> [T]here seems to be a tendency for new management to replace auditors associated with the previous management, particularly where there is a question of fraud or improper financial statements and a potential for auditor culpability.[21]

The new auditor thus needs to talk to the predecessor auditor about

- management's integrity.
- any differences of opinion between the client and the auditor.
- whether a report on material accounting control weaknesses has been sent to the client (in line with SAS No. 16, which states that a possible sign of irregularities is management's inaction with respect to a material weakness).
- the adequacy of working capital or credit.
- the industry's experience with failures.
- the client's economic dependence on a few customers or suppliers.
- the existence of necessary accounting records.
- the company's maintenance of a relationship with an attorney that is sufficient to permit the proper evaluation of claims, litigation, and assessments.

All of these questions address the prospective auditor's main concern: Is the entity auditable? Probably the greatest difficulty is created by an unfavorable response to the question about management's integrity. Any evidence of unethical business practices may well impugn management's reliability and preclude a cost-effective audit.

In 1976, about 250 American companies notified the Securities and Exchange Commission that they had made illegal or questionable payments in the United States and abroad. The SEC investigations revealed that 300 companies out of the 900 it investigated had slush funds. Obviously, such funds pose significant control problems and substantially increase the auditors' risk. Yet, to retain perspective, it is useful to consider a quote from the former Secretary of the Treasury W. Michael Blumenthal:

> People in business have not suddenly become immoral. What has changed are the contexts in which corporate decisions are made, the demands that are being made on business, and the nature of what is considered proper corporate conduct. Corporation executives today are held accountable to many different constituents and overseers—the board of directors, other members of management, shareholders, customers, employees, the news

[19] Paul E. Dascher, "The Penn Central Revisited: A Predictable Situation," *Financial Analysts Journal*, March–April 1972, pp. 61–64.

[20] Edward I. Altman and Thomas P. McGough, "Evaluation of a Company as a Going Concern," *Journal of Accountancy*, December 1974, pp. 50–57.

[21] Arthur G. Hendricks, "The Initial Audit Engagement," *Michigan CPA*, July–August 1979, pp. 51–56.

media and others. In short, business has become everybody's business.[22]

Responsibility for Detecting Fraud

If one reviews *auditors' responsibility for detecting fraud,* it is possible to generalize that

- in the early 1900s, a primary objective was the detection of fraud.
- in the late 1940s, the auditor considered it to be a "responsibility not assumed."
- in the 1960s, the auditor acknowledged responsibility for detecting fraud that would normally be uncovered by an examination performed in accordance with GAAS.
- by the early 1980s, the auditor had responsibility to search for fraud which may have a material effect on the financial statements (required by ***SAS No. 16,*** Section 327, on "The Independent Auditor's Responsibility for the Detection of Errors or Irregularities," and reflected in ***SAS No. 6*** on "Related Party Transactions," ***SAS No. 17,*** Section 328, "Illegal Acts by Clients," ***SAS No. 19,*** "Client Representations," ***SAS No. 20,*** "Required Communication of Material Weaknesses in Internal Accounting Control").

The best way of detecting fraud is to know the client, the business, and the industry in which the client operates. Concerns for fraud increase if there are related-party transactions or bankruptcy proceedings (of course, this emphasis on risk after proceedings are under way is likely to be overshadowed by the risk of fraud occurring before any bankruptcy proceedings have begun). Fraud can be intentional improper transfer pricing that misstates the valuation of goods exchanged between related parties. Or it can be a planned demise by means of bankruptcy in order to gain advantages such as the abrogation of certain contracts. The national news media have cited such actions to prevent litigation and to alter labor contracts. Of course, the more serious risk when financial trouble strikes is fraud perpetrated to delay or avert bankruptcy. As noted in the introductory case, recent frauds have depicted a willingness by large groups of employees to pool their efforts in perpetrating such operating cover-ups.

In several fraud cases reviewed by The Cohen Commission (p. 40), direct confirmations from outside parties did not provide the expected assurance because outsiders ignored incorrect information, actively cooperated with management in giving incorrect confirmation, or were not even aware of incorrect information but responded anyway. Attention needs to be given to the effectiveness of traditional audit tools and to the development of new ones in light of these experiences. Remember that confirmations are better at detecting overstatements than understatements when confirming assets, particularly accounts receivable.

Lessons from Past EDP Frauds

As discussed in prior chapters, auditors can learn from past frauds. The "red flag" literature evolved from studying past litigation and fraud discoveries.

EXHIBIT 16-10
Lessons from Past Computer Frauds

- Industry groups which are expected to have large inventory shrink may indirectly encourage frauds in the inventory area.
- Analysis of 150 cases indicated that 40 percent of corporate fraud involved fraudulent payments
  - to creditors (disbursements)
  - to employees via payroll
  - to other individuals (typically pension or insurance claims).
- Manipulation of incoming funds is most often tied to some means of permanently eliminating receivables from accounts through unauthorized adjustment.
- Manipulation of transactions that are most common include:
  - adding unauthorized transactions (e.g., phony purchase orders),
  - altering transactions (e.g., posting deposits to another account), and
  - not processing transactions (e.g., interest income).
- Ordinary managers and clerks have perpetrated more of the discovered computer fraud than computer experts.
- Means of detection of fraud are often suspicions by fellow employees or excessive greed that prompts an investigation.

Brandt Allen, "The Biggest Computer Frauds: Lessons for CPAs," *Journal of Accountancy,* May 1977, pp. 52-62.

[22] "Management Fraud, Preventive Actions for Business," *Coopers & Lybrand Newsletter,* April 1970.

An area that will merit special attention in the future is fraud in EDP environments.

When evaluating risks, it is useful to know where frauds have occurred in the past in EDP environments. The systematic analysis of computer frauds has determined that the principal area of risk is in the generation and flow of input transactions. In most large fraud cases, the perpetrators either added bogus transactions or altered transactions. Exhibit 16-10 (which appears on page 583) summarizes other lessons from past experiences.

Environmental Issues

Besides these seven key technical auditing issues, three environmental issues create increased special audit risk: media attention, disclosure aspects, and standard-setting activities.

"Bad" Press

Abe Briloff tells the story of a corporation shopping for an auditor:

"The president figured he'd make the rounds, asking CPA firms how much is two plus two. Invariably, they all said four. Finally, when he gets to the last firm on his list, he poses the question again: How much is two plus two? This time the response is more to his liking, 'What did you have in mind?' "[23]

This sort of "bad" press increases the auditor's liability risk and also indirectly affects the level of the profession's due audit care and the degree of independence it can retain if new entrants in the profession come to believe such assertions.

An article in the *Wall Street Journal* reported that

> . . . the SEC challenged InterFirst's claim of $54 million in tax benefits from a net operating loss carry-forward. The SEC questioned the claim, which was supported by InterFirst's outside auditor, Arthur Andersen & Co., starting in "the latter part of the fourth quarter," the company said.[24]

This is indicative of the close, advocate-type relationship depicted by the media between auditors and their clients, which emphasizes disagreements with regulators and government agencies.

The very real ill effects of bad press is evidenced in the media. A *Fortune* article on July 17, 1978, reported that from May 1973 to April 1977, Peat, Marwick's client portfolio decreased a net of 95 clients and cites that bad publicity and tougher client acceptance procedures which stemmed, in part, from troubles with the Securities and Exchange Commission were the likely cause of the decline.

The Cohen Commission, an independent group that studied the accounting profession in order to suggest ways of improving audit quality, stated that increased time pressures had led to sloppy work, that out of 1,100 practitioners, 58 percent had indicated that they had signed off on a required audit step without completing the work or noting the omission. These results were widely quoted.[25]

Yet this research had flaws, since later inquiry uncovered respondents' tendency to make literal interpretations of the questions posed by the Cohen Commission, rather than responding to the substance of the question. Often auditors feel that an audit objective has been met prior to completion of each audit program step, due to the overlapping nature of audit procedures and the evolutionary nature of the audit process. Hence, they will initial those steps related to that achieved objective. While the program should, instead, have been adjusted to reflect actual work performed, the inferences drawn from the Cohen Commission's survey were unrepresentative of practice.

Media has accused auditors of too often looking the other way and paying only lip service to full and fair disclosure, yet the Chairman of Peat, Marwick, Mitchell & Co. responded to such assertions as follows:

> The real fact of life is that auditors frequently challenge management and require that something be presented differently in the company's financial statements in order for the auditor to express an unqualified opinion on those financial statements. The multitude of occurrences like this are never publicized.[26]

[23] Mark Stevens, *The Big Eight* (New York: Macmillan, 1981), p. 68.
[24] "InterFirst's Chief Resigns, Profit Fell in 4th Period," January 19, 1984, p. 4.
[25] For example, see *Fortune*, July 17, 1978, p. 96.
[26] Thomas L. Holton, "Limits of Auditor's Ledger Domain," *Wall Street Journal*, February 2, 1984, p. 27.

In "What Are Earnings? The Growing Credibility Gap,"[27] it is noted:

> The accountants maintain that they are not the pawns of management. "We had over a hundred cases last year where we had to say 'no' to management," says Richard D. Baker, managing partner of Ernst & Ernst. Even the SEC's Chief Accountant, Andrew Barr, backs them up on this contention. "Believe me," he says, "we see plenty of cases where accountants have stood up to management. These cases never hit the newspapers." Adds Queenan of Haskins & Sells: "No single client makes up more than a tiny portion of our total billings. We can afford to lose a big client if it comes to that."

It is often claimed that the likelihood of an opposing stance by a CPA is small due to the client's ability to simply change auditors. This idea is exemplified by an account in a local newspaper which echoes the national stories that have posed questions about the accounting profession. *Dallas Times Herald,* on August 29, 1982, ran an article by Irwin Frank entitled "Auditors: Not Detectives," which noted: "The heat is on auditors these days. Businesses are going belly up at record rates. And frequently the employees and the stockholders of these fragile firms are the last to know" (p. N–1). The article references the Penn Square debacle, noting that Arthur Young seemed to be suspicious of the firm in 1980 when it qualified its report due to the possible inadequacy of loan loss reserves. However, the article continues: "Penn Square promptly fired Arthur Young and, looking for someone to provide a clean bill of financial health, brought in Peat, Marwick" (p. N–1). This impression that "shopping around for auditors is effective" is far too common a message of the media. Yet, numerous reasons exist why such "shopping" is unlikely to prevail. One reason was, in fact, cited in the news article. Public companies which fire auditors must report to the SEC why. While Penn Square was not publicly held, companies which are would likely try to minimize the attention by the SEC that could result from firing their auditor. The deterrence power of this reporting requirement is enhanced by the fact that the auditing firm has the right to review the letter to the SEC and state whether or not it agrees with the client's explanation of why the auditor was fired. The requirement being described is the filing of 8-K's.

Accounting Series Release No. 165 (now known as FRRs) requires that clients report via Form 8-K whenever an audit change occurs as to whether in the prior two years

> there were any disagreements with the former accountant on any matter of accounting principles or practices, financial statement disclosure or auditing scope or practice, which disagreements if not resolved to the satisfaction of the former accountant would have caused him to make reference in connection with his report on the subject matter of the disagreement. [12(b) of Form 8-K]

In addition, Section 12(c) asks for the past two years' audit opinion if it was other than a clean audit report. Disagreements involving primary and secondary auditors of material numbers would be reportable, as would reservations as to an entity's auditability either due to poor controls or questions of management integrity.[28]

In addition to 8-K's, the other deterrent to auditor change for the purpose of "shopping for an auditor" is that clients are unlikely to find an "agreeable" CPA, regardless of the media's contentions to the contrary. Several research studies have supported the consistency with which the Big Eight firms apply generally accepted reporting practices. One research study tested for differences in the incidence of consistency exceptions by CPA firms when accounting changes occurred. If it can be assumed that auditing conditions and the frequency of accounting changes is similar per Big-8 firm, the results support the similarity of firms in their report qualification practices. An average of 9.3 percent of clients receive consistency qualifications per firm. Such evidence suggests that clients will not systematically discover more lax disclosure practices by their auditors' chief competitors.[29]

[27] *Forbes,* May 15, 1967.

[28] "Disagreements Under Accounting Series Release No. 165," *Journal of Accountancy,* October 1976, pp. 75–82.

[29] Carl S. Warren, "Characteristics of Firms Reporting Consistency Exceptions—A Cross-Sectional Analysis," *The Accounting Review,* January 1977, pp. 150–161.

There has also been research on the consistency with which auditing standards are used, which focused on the percentage of qualified audit reports versus clean reports and the various types of qualified reports. The study assumed that the Big Eight CPA firms had similar client portfolios and analyzed 1,543 SEC-filed 10-K reports. But it found no significant difference in the percentage of qualified opinions that each firm issued: On the average, 25.5 percent of the reports issued were qualified, and there was no statistically significant variation in the type of qualifications observed across auditing firms.[30]

Another study found that the average riskiness of client portfolios differs across the Big 8 firms and that the issuance of qualified opinions is strongly related to riskiness. The finding that more high-risk clients (as evaluated through an analysis of market data) receive qualified opinions is expected and suggests that report qualifications relate to real economic differences across clients. The findings support the comparability of audit "quality" across CPA firms since the opinion qualifications do appear to be consistently applied to higher risk clients regardless of the particular firm under analysis. A total of 2,716 companies were studied from 1972 to 1975.[31]

Of particular interest is an analysis of 1,226 annual reports which indicated that 12.1 percent of the audit opinions were qualified. This sizable incidence of qualifications has been attributed to:

- increased litigation.
- increased reluctance by attorneys to state that clients have good defenses against major lawsuits.
- increased conservatism of auditors, concerned as to their liability exposure.
- SEC pressure for auditors to be more "hard nosed" toward their clients.[32]

Empirical evidence clearly supports the profession's maintaining a quality standard, which makes highly suspect the claim that clients change auditors to obtain more favorable audit reports. There are many reasons for changing auditors that are fairly unrelated to the possibility that disagreements between management and the auditors precipitated the change. My own research found that 10 to 15 percent of those companies changing their auditors were also changing their management. Acquired companies frequently switch to the acquirer's CPA firm. In fact, from 1973 to 1975, 10 to 20 percent of acquired firms were observed to change auditors—a much higher percentage than for companies in general at that time. In addition, litigation suits involving the auditor can lead to a lack of independence, as clients are often cited for contributory negligence. In fact, 27 to 33 percent of companies whose auditors are involved in litigation were observed to change auditors from 1973 to 1976. Other explanations of changes are reductions in audit fees and preferences for particular auditors' methodologies, client-service levels, or personality—all of which could be considerations in spite of equivalent quality audits per CPA firm. The competitive environment is cited as a key explanation for 523 publicly traded companies changing auditors in 1984—a 9 percent increase from 1983 and 75 percent from 1981.[33]

Judgmental Disclosure Dilemmas

The profession has been cited as having strayed from professionalism, trading in a "rule book" for the appropriate exercise of judgment. Such rules invite "gamesmanship," in which loopholes are sought out and minimum standards decay.

An example of transactions that judgmentally appear to represent rights and obligations but that under current standards are not recorded is exe-

[30] Carl S. Warren, "Uniformity of Auditing Standards," *Journal of Accounting Research*, Spring 1975, pp. 162–176.

[31] John K. Shank and Richard J. Murdock, "Comparability in the Application of Report Standards: Some Further Evidence," *The Accounting Review*, October 1978, pp. 824–835.

[32] " 'Qualified' opinions rise along with cost of audits," *Journal of Accountancy*, October 1977, p. 7.

[33] Wanda A. Wallace, "Discussant Comments: Some Consideration on Auditor Turnover," *Proceedings of the 1979 American Accounting Association Annual Meeting Held in Hawaii* (Sarasota, Fla.: AAA, 1979). The statistics on auditor changes were compiled by *Public Accounting Report* (an Atlanta newsletter) and reported by Lee Berton, in an article entitled "Auditor Changes by Public Companies Set High as Accountants Compete More," in the *Wall Street Journal*, January 29, 1985, p. 12.

cutory contracts such as processing agreements, through-put agreements, and take-or-pay contracts. Other than for some leases, assets and liabilities are not recorded at the time that a contract is initiated.[34] Yet such firm commitments appear to meet the definition of benefits and obligations that underlies recorded assets and liabilities. The CPA thus must constantly grapple with judgment versus established standards. Recall the litigation chapter's discussion of Continental Vending and Bar Chris in which the auditor was challenged for complying with the form of GAAP, rather than the substance of GAAP. The practical problem is clients' familiarity with GAAP and ability to pressure CPAs to comply with the "letter" of GAAP. Obviously, the preferred approach would be to have GAAP reflect the *substance* of transactions. Yet, dilemmas have been repeatedly created by both actions and inaction of standard-setting bodies. Regulators' intervention has resulted in so-called RAAP (regulatory accepted accounting principles), which continually drift away from GAAP, creating additional problems for accountants. One example is reflected in a headline from the *Wall Street Journal:* "Accountants Decry U.S. Plan for Thrifts to Use 'Mark-to-Market' Loan Method" (October 13, 1982, p. 10). This hotly debated issue, according to critics, "created" net worth for ailing thrift institutions. The problem faced by the profession is well summarized by an official at the SEC: "The savings and loan industry isn't going to be saved by ruining the credibility of the accounting profession." Ironically, on March 21, 1985, the front-page headline read "Accounting at Thrifts Provokes Controversy as Gimmickry Mounts" and the profession, predictably, was criticized that GAAP was masking problems.

Paradoxical FASB Approaches

Accounting for the development and sale of computer software is an example of a current problem being addressed by an AICPA task force which is presently being faced by auditors in practice. Representative of the issues involved are:

- When is research and development complete?
- When is it appropriate to capitalize software construction costs?
- Should the recoverability of software construction costs be probable before capitalization is permitted?
- Should capitalization of software costs be required, or should it be an option?

Because two hundred publicly held computer service companies receive a substantial portion of their revenue from software products, additional accounting guidance is needed. A July 1982 survey reported that of 231 computer service companies, 58 reported some costs of internally developed software as assets; 13 of these 58 were publicly held companies. A review of 30 publicly held computer software companies' financial statements indicated that 4 disclosed capitalization of some internally developed software, and 2 capitalized enhancements and improvements of current products. This diversity in practice is due to ambiguities in FASB Statement No. 2, which have only recently been addressed by a later pronouncement. The magnitude of costs typically involved can be assessed by considering the reported average new product costs of $550,584 for mainframes and $212,185 for micros. Unsuccessful products account for 39 to 45 percent of the average cost of successful products. Three to ten percent failure rates are reported. The critical importance of this issue is reflected in a *Wall Street Journal* article entitled "Two Systems & Computer Officers Quit After Clash with Auditor Over Revenue"—the clash focused on the recognition of revenue for the computer software company.[35]

In addition to the lack of clarity in past pronouncements by FASB, the FASB's delays in reacting to new accounting techniques that distort financial statements have created other problems for auditors when evaluating risks and forming an audit opinion. For example, Morgan Guaranty Trust developed instantaneous defeasance, which is a technique to reduce debt on balance sheets by creating a trust to service it. A $400 million zero-

[34] *Objectives of Financial Statements for Business Enterprises* (Chicago: Arthur Andersen & Co., 1984).

[35] Adapted from Issues Paper entitled, "Accounting for Software Costs," Prepared by Task Force on Accounting for the Development and Sale of Computer Software (AICPA: January 16, 1984). The *Wall Street Journal* article appeared on January 29, 1985, p. 18.

coupon Eurobond might bring in proceeds of $41.5 million, be matched by stripped treasury securities at a cost of $38.2 million, and thereby generate $3.3 million of money (often cited as illusory profits) that would not otherwise be available. Although in February 1984 the FASB initially questioned the practice, the issue was only recently resolved.[36]

To more specifically illustrate the paradox presented by FASB actions and inaction, the topics of leases, consolidations, and management compensation practices will be discussed.

Leases

When a company decides to lease rather than purchase, it may be because of financing issues or income-tax advantages. But if existing debt covenants prevent the entity from obtaining additional loans, the reason for leasing may be avoiding showing debt on the balance sheet. Financial Accounting Standard No. 13 on leases can be used to achieve the entity's objective, as it specifies that one of four criteria must be met in order for the capitalization of leases to be required: (1) the ownership is transferred; (2) a bargain purchase option is offered; (3) the term for the lease is equal to or greater than 75 percent of the useful life of the item being leased; and (4) the present value of lease payments is equal to or greater than 90 percent of the value of the item being leased. The first two criteria can be easily avoided, and by simply setting the lease term at 74 percent of the useful life, with payments that represent 89 percent of the value of the item being leased, the company can ensure treatment of the transaction as an operating lease.

Most auditors prefer a SFAS that emphasizes substance over form, so that a transaction that they know instinctively is more of a purchase transaction than an operating lease transaction can be capitalized. But the FASB's checklist approach effectively precludes an emphasis on substance, directing all of its attention to form.

Creditors' concern for the substance of leasing transactions has been reflected in bond indentures and term-loan agreements containing provisions that all lease obligations be discounted or that rentals be capitalized as an additional liability when calculating working capital and checking compliance with debt restrictions. Some have contended that footnote disclosures are sufficient without capitalization; yet if total lease assets and lease liabilities are major assets and obligations, why should they be omitted from the financial statements any more than property, plant, and equipment with its related financing should?

Consolidation Principles

Similar to the artificial criteria governing leases are the guidelines for whether a combination should be accounted for as a pooling or a purchase. Because pooling means that assets and liabilities are combined at their book values, whereas purchasing requires a fair value recording of net assets—often with goodwill being recorded—the reporting effects of the two accounting methods are different. Carrying goodwill as an asset then results in annual charges against income from amortization.

A 1963 Accounting Research Study (No. 5) written by Arthur R. Wyatt and published by the AICPA concluded: "A business combination which is basically an exchange transaction between independent parties should be accounted for in a manner similar to other exchange transactions."[37] The study stated that there is no basis for pooling-of-interests if such an exchange occurs and that the assets acquired should be accounted for at their fair value. A later Accounting Research Study (No. 10)[38] stated that standards emphasizing whether stock or cash was used in the combination represented an emphasis on "substitute forms of consideration" rather than a substantive difference. Similarly, the American Accounting Association's 1966 report of the Committee to Prepare a Statement of Basic Accounting Theory recommended "that the pooling-of-interests technique be disallowed."

[36] Lee Berton and Ann Monroe, "FASB Mulls Ban on Defeasance Method in Which Firms Issue Debt to Post Gains," *Wall Street Journal*, September 12, 1984, p. 6; and FAS No. 76.

[37] *A Critical Story of Accounting for Business Combinations.*

[38] George R. Catlett and Norman O. Olson, *Accounting for Goodwill* (New York: AICPA, 1968).

The evasion of the criteria set for qualifying a combination as a pooling thus has become a game. The criteria are arbitrary and are linked to past abuses rather than sound theory. For example, why does the nature of consideration—the express exclusion of voting convertible preferred stock—matter? Why aren't earn-out arrangements, designed for legitimate business purposes, permitted? How does the requirement of no significant disposals of assets as an approach to prohibiting "instant earnings" accomplish anything other than precluding what may well be the exercise of sound business judgment? What of pooling's result that all financials are restated on a combined basis as though the companies were always together? The economic substance of combinations is that one entity is the acquirer and assets are negotiated for transfer at fair value—not out-of-date book values.

Also, in regard to goodwill, the arbitrary amortization charges are not related to the current period's income, and so the buildup of goodwill as an asset is misleading. A reduction of stockholders' investments for the amount of goodwill is far more consistent conceptually with the substance of the transaction than is the creation of the intangible asset of goodwill. This is because goodwill has no reliable relationship to cost, relates to the business as a whole, is not reasonably matched to particular periods, and, as it is not tax deductible when amortized, can have twice the effect on current reported income of other charges.[39]

Management Compensation

Management compensation in the form of stock options typically leads to no charge against income, but if stock appreciation rights (SARs) are issued, income is charged as the stock market price changes (both debited and credited), leading to sizable differences in income for entities that have, in substance, similar management compensation practices. There are many examples of the magnitude of SARs' effect in the letters submitted to the FASB when it formulated Interpretation No. 28.

> Time Incorporated distributed $2,722,000 of compensation expense, utilizing the measurement rules in the FASB proposal, over the period from second quarter, 1975 to the first quarter, 1978. The largest quarter charge was $1,601,000 and the largest adjustment to compensation expense was ($469,000), with annual charges fluctuating from ($66,000) to $2,335,000.

Such fluctuations can represent as much as 14 percent of quarterly income.

My own empirical research supports the hypotheses that the accounting treatment of SARs

- has deterred companies with stock option plans from adopting SARs.
- has deterred smaller companies more than larger companies from adopting SARs.
- has had a discernible "bad news" effect on the market.
- has affected the form of those SAR plans that have been adopted.

Delays by accounting policy setters in reconciling the accounting treatment of stock options and stock appreciation rights had all of these effects and placed auditors in the undesirable position of inconsistently treating two economically equivalent events. Again, form prevailed over substance, only this time through the FASB's inaction.[40]

Concluding Remarks

You have no doubt noticed that the various technical and environmental issues discussed in this chapter overlap with prior chapters' coverage. Rather than integrate each of these topics in depth in earlier cycle chapters, their in-depth discussion was presented in this chapter in order to highlight particular sources of high audit risk. Since many of these risks permeate a number of asset, liability, revenue, and expense accounts, they can be more effectively addressed as potential problems stemming from an underlying characteristic such as a

[39] Adapted from Arthur Andersen & Co., *Accounting and Reporting Problems of the Accounting Profession*, 4th ed., August 1973.

[40] See Wanda A. Wallace, "The Effects of Delays by Accounting Policy-Setters in Reconciling the Accounting Treatment of Stock Options and Stock Appreciation Rights," *Accounting Review*, April 1984, pp. 325–341.

judgmental basis of estimation or a related-party dimension to the transactions producing reported balances. An attempt has also been made to bear out the difficulty which an auditor may have in applying the "substance" of GAAP.

REVIEW QUESTIONS

1. What is meant by "inherent subjectivity," and how does it pertain to audit risk?
2. What audit procedures are useful in identifying and quantifying contingencies and uncertainties?
3. What special problems do unasserted claims pose?
4. How can completed contract accounting be manipulated? Does completed contract or percentage-of-completion accounting have a greater audit risk? Explain.
5. Give two examples of the revenue realization questions that real estate transactions can raise.
6. Audit sampling is typically applied to recorded transactions to draw conclusions about the reasonableness of reported balances. Can it be applied to detect unrecorded liabilities? Why or why not?
7. What is meant by cutoff, and which are the critical areas of operations in which cutoff practices are of particular importance to an auditor?
8. What procedures should be performed if an auditor does not receive the cutoff bank statement directly?
9. How are the risks of kiting and lapping controlled?
10. **a.** What is smoothing, and how can management be prevented from smoothing?

    b. A 1932 article in *Fortune,* "Certified Public Accountants," reported:

    > One mistake and a CPA's career is ended. . . . CPAs are by nature skeptical, cool, cautious, and conservative; to them understatement is a golden virtue and overstatement almost the equivalent of fraud. (June 1932, p. 63)

    Is this a valid assertion today?
11. Define *related party.* Why does a related party offer increased audit risk?
12. Why should an auditor care that a client may go bankrupt?
13. How should auditors evaluate the significance of information that is contrary to the going concern assumption?
14. How can an analysis of clients' accounting changes improve audit effectiveness?
15. What is the auditor's responsibility for detecting fraud?
16. How can an analysis of past EDP frauds help an auditor assess risk?
17. What does Accounting Series Release No. 165 (now an FRR) require?
18. What evidence is available to support the existence of a firm's uniform quality standard for the auditing profession? How does this evidence relate to some of the unfavorable press for the profession?
19. Give an example of a FASB statement that stresses form over substance.
20. How has FASB's inaction created a paradox for the auditor?

EXERCISES

1. When describing auditing standards in 1947, an AICPA publication addressed the CPA's disclosure responsibilities:

    > Disclosure should not be considered to require the publicizing of certain kinds of information that would be detrimental to the company or its stockholders. For example, the threat of a patent infringement suit might impel a conscientious management to set up an ample reserve for possible loss, even though it would expect to fight the issue vigorously; but publicity given to such a loss provision might inure to the harm of the company or its stockholders, for courts have held that a reserve for patent infringements constituted an allocation of infringement profits (where ready determination otherwise was not feasible) notwithstanding a refusal on the part of the company or its management to concede that such an amount might be an equitable allotment of the profits in dispute.[41]

    Contrast this position with the CPA's current disclosure responsibilities, with special attention to SFAS No. 5, concerning contingencies. What attention should the CPA pay to how detrimental a particular disclosure is likely to be?
2. The criticisms of the accounting profession arise in part because people grant to the accounting function a degree of certainty that it does not have and never can attain. George O. May is credited with recognizing that "accounting can rise no higher than the scale of certainty of the events which it reflects."[42] Discuss the validity of these assertions, and

[41] Special Report by the Committee on Auditing Procedure, "Tentative Statement of Auditing Standards—Their Generally Accepted Significance and Scope" (New York: AICPA, 1947), p. 42.

[42] Alvin R. Jennings, "Present-Day Challenges in Financial Reporting," *Journal of Accountancy,* January 1958, p. 28.

give some examples of when practice appears both to support and contradict these claims.

3. But the accountant knows that things hoped for are not always received, and among those receivables he spots some uncollectibles. . . . A slightly less conservative accountant would reach a slightly different total. It is a matter of opinion. That almost all accountants are conservative by nature, that all accountants take delight in discounting chickens before they are hatched, is what stabilizes the opinion.[43]

   Do auditors have such a conservative bias when reviewing the various special audit risk areas described in this chapter? Give examples of situations in which it does and does not seem to be applicable.

4. The thrift industry, it has been speculated, would have had many failing entities in the absence of FSLIC or FDIC assistance, due to its operating practices of lending long and borrowing short. How should auditors evaluate going concern risks for clients in the thrift industry? What disclosure practices are appropriate?

5. Dear Fellow Shareholders:
   After showing seven consecutive years of profits, we regret to announce that your company filed for bankruptcy last month.[44]

   How is such an announcement possible? Can you give some examples? How does the statement's veracity affect audit risk?

6. "No one can audit a liar or a crook!"[45] How does this statement pertain to the auditability question?

7. In a 1926 statement, United States Rubber Company reported the balance of an account as $7,338,305.19. As one review noted: "This time, thanks be, the figures are carried out to the last penny, so that we may be assured exactly how things stand. Isn't it about time that such open and shut methods were brought to an end?"[46] Does the writer have a point? How could the profession more effectively communicate with users?

8. Consider the following headlines:

   "Data General: Troubled 'Soul'—Company Lag Follows Years of Growth," Thomas J. Lueck, *New York Times*, June 21, 1982, Section D, pp. 1,3.

   "Long-term U.S. Rates Ease: 30-Year Issue Yields 14.12%," Vartanig G. Vartan, *New York Times*, June 25, 1982, p. D5.

   "Market Fell Out for Steel: Recession Chopped Production in Half and Smothered the Industry's Hopes for a New Vitality," Lydia Chavez, *New York Times*, June 20, 1982, p. 1.

   How should an auditor use such information when evaluating audit risk? Be specific.

9. In "The Numbers Game,"[47] then Securities and Exchange Commissioner A. A. Sommer was quoted as saying: "The application of GAAP does not guarantee there will be fair presentation." John Shank, then associate professor of accounting and finance at the Harvard Business School, stated: "No matter how detailed the accounting rules, the mind of the enterprising entrepreneur can always conceive of a transaction consistent with the rules, but inconsistent with the spirit behind them."[48] Do you agree with these statements? Why or why not?

10. Firing auditors is not solely a news item in public accounting; it has also obtained media coverage with respect to internal auditing. For example, on May 31, 1979, the *Wall Street Journal* reported on two former auditors in the real estate department of the J. C. Penney Co. who had lost a $10 million suit in which they had alleged they had been fired in June 1977 as part of a cover-up of their investigation into kickbacks and payoffs to some officers.[49] How can information about such firings help an external auditor? How can such information be obtained?

QUESTIONS ADAPTED FROM PROFESSIONAL EXAMINATIONS

1. You were in the final stages of your examination of the financial statements of the Ozine Corporation for the year ended December 31, 19X6 when you were consulted by the corporation's president who believes there is no point to your examining the 19X7 voucher register and testing data in support of 19X7 entries. He stated that (a) bills pertaining to 19X6 that were received too late to be included in the December voucher register were recorded as of the year-end by the corporation by journal entry, (b) the internal auditor made tests after the year-end, and (c) he would give you a letter certifying that there were no unrecorded liabilities.

[43] "Certified Public Accountants," *Fortune*, 1932.

[44] Kenneth B. Schwartz, "Accounting Changes by Corporations Facing Possible Insolvency," *Journal of Accounting, Auditing & Finance*, Fall 1982, p. 32.

[45] William C. Foster, "Related-Party Transactions—Some Considerations," *CPA Journal*, May 1975, p. 18.

[46] William Z. Ripley, "Stop, Look and Listen!" *Atlantic Monthly*, September 1926, p. 390.

[47] *Forbes*, August 1, 1975, pp. 31–32.

[48] Ibid.

[49] "Ex-Auditors of Penney Lose Suit over Firing; Cover-up Was Alleged," p. 16.

Required:

a. Should a CPA's test for unrecorded liabilities be affected if the client made a journal entry to record 19X6 bills that were received late? Explain.

b. Should a CPA's test for unrecorded liabilities be affected if a letter is obtained in which a responsible management official certifies that to the best of his or her knowledge all liabilities have been recorded? Explain.

c. Should a CPA's test for unrecorded liabilities be eliminated or reduced because of the internal audit tests? Explain.

d. Assume that the corporation handled some government contracts but had no internal auditor and that an auditor for a federal agency spent three weeks auditing the records and was just completing his work at this time. How would the CPA's unrecorded liability test be affected by the work of the auditor for a federal agency?

e. What sources in addition to the 19X7 voucher register should the CPA consider in order to locate possible unrecorded liabilities?

(CPA exam adapted)

2. During the year the Strang Corporation began to encounter cash flow difficulties, and a cursory review by management revealed receivable collection problems. Strang's management engaged Stanley, a CPA, to perform a special investigation. Stanley studied the billing and collection cycle and noted the following:

a. The accounting department employs one bookkeeper who receives and opens all incoming mail. This bookkeeper is also responsible for depositing receipts, filing daily remittance advices, recording receipts in the cash receipts journal, and posting receipts in the individual customer accounts and the general ledger accounts. There are no cash sales. The bookkeeper prepares and controls the mailing of monthly statements to customers.

b. The concentration of functions and the receivable collection problems caused Stanley to suspect that a systematic defalcation of customers' payments through a delayed posting of remittance (lapping of accounts receivable) is present. Stanley was surprised to find that no customers had complained about receiving erroneous monthly statements.

Required:

What procedures should Stanley perform to determine whether lapping exists? Do not discuss deficiencies in the internal control system.

(CPA exam adapted)

3. The internal auditing department was told that two employees had been terminated for falsifying their time records. The two employees had altered overtime hours on their time cards after their supervisors had approved the hours actually worked. Several years ago, the company discontinued the use of time clocks. Since then, the plant supervisors have been responsible for manually posting the time cards and approving the hours for which their employees should be paid. The postings are usually entered in pencil by the supervisors or their secretaries. After the postings for the week are complete, the time cards are approved and placed in the mail racks outside the supervisors' offices for the timekeepers to pick up. But sometimes the timekeepers do not pick up the time cards promptly.

Required:

Assuming the company does not wish to return to using time clocks, give three recommendations to prevent a recurrence of this situation. For each recommendation, indicate how it will deter fraudulent reporting of hours worked.

(CIA exam adapted)

4. Multiple Choice

Select the one answer that best completes the statement or answers the question.

4.1. Which of the following is the most efficient audit procedure for detecting unrecorded liabilities at the balance sheet date?

a. Confirm large accounts payable balances at the balance sheet date.

b. Compare cash disbursements in the subsequent period with the accounts payable trial balance at year-end.

c. Examine purchase orders issued for several days before the close of the year.

d. Obtain an attorney's letter from the client's attorney.

(CPA exam adapted)

4.2. During 19X6, a bookkeeper perpetrated a theft by preparing erroneous W-2 forms. The bookkeeper's FICA withheld was overstated by $500, and the FICA withheld from all other employees was understated. Which of the following audit procedures would detect such a fraud?

a. Multiplication of the applicable rate by the individual gross taxable earnings.

b. Using Form W-4 and withholding charts to determine whether the deductions authorized for each pay period agree with amounts deducted for each pay period.

c. Footing and cross-footing of the payroll register followed by tracing postings to the general ledger.

d. Vouching canceled checks to federal tax forms 941.

(CPA exam adapted)

4.3. Which of the following statements best describes the auditor's responsibility regarding the detection of fraud?

a. The auditor is responsible for failing to detect fraud only when such failure clearly results from the nonperformance of audit procedures specifically described in the engagement letter.

b. The auditor must extend auditing procedures to actively search for evidence of fraud in all situations.

c. The auditor must extend auditing procedures to actively search for evidence of fraud when the examination indicates that there may be fraud.

d. The auditor is responsible for failing to detect fraud only when an unqualified opinion is issued.

(CPA exam adapted)

4.4. When auditing a public warehouse, which of the following is the most important audit procedure with respect to disclosing unrecorded liabilities?

a. Confirming negotiable receipts with holders.

b. Reviewing outstanding receipts.

c. Inspecting receiving and issuing procedures.

d. Observing inventory.

(CPA exam adapted)

4.5. When auditing contingent liabilities, which of the following procedures would be the least effective?

a. Abstracting the minutes of the board of directors.

b. Reviewing the bank confirmation letters.

c. Examining customer confirmation replies.

d. Examining invoices for professional services.

(CPA exam adapted)

4.6. For the examination of financial statements, an independent auditor can be held responsible for failing to detect a material fraud if

a. Statistical sampling techniques were not used on the audit engagement.

b. The auditor planned the work hastily and inefficiently.

c. The accountant performing important parts of the work failed to discover a close relationship between the treasurer and the cashier.

d. The fraud was perpetrated by one client employee, who circumvented the existing internal controls.

(CPA exam adapted)

4.7. When an independent auditor's examination of financial statements discloses special circumstances that make the auditor suspect fraud, the auditor's initial course of action should be to

a. Recommend that the client pursue the suspected fraud to a conclusion that is agreeable to the auditor.

b. Extend the normal audit procedures in an attempt to detect the full extent of the suspected fraud.

c. Reach an understanding with the proper client representative as to whether the auditor or the client will investigate to determine whether there is a fraud.

d. Decide whether the fraud, if in fact it should exist, might be of such a magnitude as to affect the auditor's report on the financial statements.

(CPA exam adapted)

4.8. Which of the following audit procedures would be the least effective for detecting contingent liabilities?

a. Abstracting the minutes of the meetings of the board of directors.

b. Reviewing the bank confirmation letters.

c. Examining confirmation letters from customers.

d. Confirming pending legal matters with the corporate attorney.

(CPA exam adapted)

4.9. A major difference of opinion concerning an accounting issue has arisen between an assistant on an audit engagement and the auditor with final responsibility for the engagement. If after consultation the assistant believes it necessary to disassociate himself or herself from the resolution of the matter, both the auditor and his or her assistant must

a. Document details of the disagreement and the basis of resolution.

b. Inform management of the nature of the disagreement.

c. Inform the company's audit committee of the nature of the disagreement.

d. Refer the matter to the firm's peer review committee.

(CPA exam adapted)

4.10. Which of the following audit procedures is the least likely to detect an unrecorded liability?

a. Analyzing and recomputing interest expense.

b. Analyzing and recomputing depreciation expense.
c. Mailing standard bank confirmation forms.
d. Reading the minutes of the meetings of the board of directors.

(CPA exam adapted)

CASES FOR DISCUSSION

1. Even if auditors reason by analogy properly, different auditors may nevertheless conclude on occasion that different accounting principles are appropriate in similar circumstances. This has sometimes led to the selection of auditors on the basis of their acceptance or rejection of a particular accounting principle. Selection of auditors on this basis could result in a deterioration of accounting principles and a tendency for auditors to abstain from judgments they are competent to make. Such a result can only serve to erode users' confidence further, and modification is needed in the means by which independent auditors are appointed.[50]

Comment on the legitimacy of the Cohen Commission's claims. Support your analysis, and state how you believe the appointment of independent auditors might be changed to improve the profession.

2. The chairman of Peat, Marwick, Mitchell & Co. noted that auditors are effectively given stockholders' power of attorney to override management on accounting and disclosure matters through the use of qualified opinions on financial statements: "It is very unusual for management to accept a qualified opinion instead of making the necessary corrections or disclosures."[51]

Do you agree that auditors effectively hold such power? Can you propose any changes within the profession or by regulators that would enhance such power?

3. A local utility client intends to build a nuclear power plant. The "pronukes and antinukes" controversy looms both locally and nationally, reinforced by the Three-Mile Island incident and such movies as *The China Syndrome.* Nevertheless, the plans are continuing. Your client has been awarded the construction contract, estimating the total cost to be $400 million on the $410 million contract. The project should take five years to complete, and your client has agreed to a rather stiff penalty should construction not be completed in five years. Your client uses percentage-of-completion contract methods; however, most contracts require only two to three years to complete. How would you evaluate the audit risk in this situation, and how would your evaluation be likely to affect your audit plans?

4. A manufacturer of mobile homes arranges a large sale to an aggressive home furnishings company by promising informally that any unsold mobile homes can be returned. The revenue from the sales was $500,000, with recorded profits of $52,000. What audit risks does this type of transaction create? How should it be recorded by the manufacturer's auditor?

5. The accounting profession as a whole contributed to the debacle [of Penn Central] by making acceptable practices that are an open invitation to distortions and outright fraud.[52]

The bookkeeping problems included covering normal operating expenses out of capital instead of income, crediting uncollectible freight charges to income, treating real estate sales and securities sales as normal income, treating asset write-offs as extraordinary items to avoid depreciation, and booking large profits on assets sold to a financial subsidiary. The result was reported income before extraordinary items in 1969 of $4.4 million, which is speculated to have disguised the true operating results of a loss of as much as $120 million.[53] Does the profession have any defense?

[50] Cohen Commission Report.
[51] Thomas L. Holton, "Limits of Auditor's Ledger Domain," *Wall Street Journal*, February 2, 1984, p. 31.
[52] Rush Loving, Jr., "The Penn Central Bankruptcy Express," *Fortune*, August 1970, p. 171.
[53] Ibid., p. 164.

17

Other Types of Engagements

We have stressed the importance of communicating the nature of a CPA's engagement and the CPA's opinion and degree of responsibility for the financial statements presented. To ensure that these requirements are met, there must be quality control over all types of engagements and the related materials given to clients. The consequences of failing to exercise such control and the difficulty in relying on third parties to evaluate and comprehend the materials prepared by CPAs without the desired disclosures are spelled out in the following true story. The names of the borrower and bank involved have been omitted.

A business owner talked with Singer, Lewak, Greenbaum & Goldstein, a CPA firm in Beverly Hills, California, about becoming a client, and during their discussion, the accounting firm gave the owner a set of specimen financial statements. The owner did become the CPA firm's client. But several months later, the owner called Andrew Hillas, a partner of the CPA firm, and complained that the financial statements for the business made no sense. The company's name was missing, replaced by a string of x's and the numbers were wrong!

Puzzled, Hillas told him that his firm had not yet prepared financial statements for the business, and after talking for a while, it became clear that the owner was looking at the specimen financial statements. The owner explained that the statements had just been returned by a big bank to which he had submitted them when applying for a $50,000 loan. The specimen financial statements were rather vague about the company's business, saying only, "Company is a California corporation engaged in the promotion and sale of XXXXX." Of course, the results did not in any way correspond with the borrowing company's earlier years' results. Nevertheless, the owner got the loan![1]

[1]Adapted from Sanford Jacobs, "Bank Gives Loan to Concern Selling X's," *Wall Street Journal*, November 14, 1983, p. 29.

Some might read this account and wonder at whether users read CPAs' reports, but others may well point out that it is the weight of the CPA's stationery and opinion that inspire users' confidence and hence particular care must be taken with how CPAs use their trusted titles. For example, if a CPA is asked to express an opinion on a software package that figures odds for racetrack betting, what would be appropriate participation by the CPA? To what attributes of the software can and should the CPA attest? It surely would not be desirable to imply that users will make a fortune betting on horse races as a result of using the software. Imagine the liability consequences in such a setting as users begin to lose. This type of issue, and the wide expanse of engagements that are acceptable for CPAs to perform, but in which extreme care is needed in reporting professional responsibilities, will be explored in this chapter.

Unaudited Financial Statements

Reporting standards require that whenever a CPA is associated with financial statements, a report containing a clear indication of the character of the CPA's examination be issued. The accountant is *associated* with financial statements when he or she has consented to the use of his or her name in a report, document, or written communication containing the statements ***[SAS 2, Section 509].*** In the case of unaudited statements, the CPA is to issue a disclaimer as follows:

> The accompanying balance sheet of Company XYZ as of December 31, 19X4, and the related statements of income, retained earnings, and changes in financial position for the year then ended were not audited by us and, accordingly, we do not express an opinion on them.
> (signature and date)[2]

In addition to the disclaimer, each page of the financial statements should be clearly and conspicuously marked as unaudited. This kind of disclaimer is intended to show that the CPA is responsible only for reading over the financial statements for obvious material errors. No procedures are to be applied if there are no obvious material errors, and any procedures that are applied should not be disclosed.

Except in either a letter to an underwriter or a review engagement (to be described later in this chapter), the CPA is not permitted to include expressions of assurance on the absence of departures from GAAP or any negative assurances.

Should the CPA lack independence, the disclaimer will be identical, except that before the first sentence, the CPA should add: "We are not independent with respect to Company XYZ" ***[SAS 26, Section 504].*** Neither the reasons for the lack of independence nor the procedures performed should be described, as they might confuse the users of the financial statements.

The standard of the profession requiring GAAP disclosures in unaudited financial statements has been criticized, particularly as it pertains to closely held corporations. It has been contended, for example, that earnings per share, deferred income taxes, statement of changes in financial position, imputed interest, and the equity method are irrelevant to closely held corporations and are unduly expensive disclosures to produce. This controversy is often referred to as the "Big GAAP–Little GAAP" issue, which involves a dispute over the propriety of differential disclosure standards based on size. A survey of about 240 chief commercial lending officers indicated that 57.5 percent strongly agreed that any known departures from GAAP should be disclosed and that the earnings-per-share disclosure, price-level–adjusted information, product-line reporting, and projection information were relatively unimportant for closely held companies. Yet, the information was perceived as being of equal importance in audited and unaudited statements, for the various items surveyed.[3] This type of research is credited with changing the earnings-per-share reporting requirements, as well as spurring discussion of the adequacy of professional services available to smaller, closely held entities. Many ar-

[2] Statement on Auditing Standards No. 38, "Unaudited Financial Statements" (New York: AICPA, September 1967).

[3] Haim Falk, Bruce C. Gobdel, and James H. Naus, "Disclosure for Closely Held Corporations," *Journal of Accountancy,* October 1976, pp. 85–91.

gued that entities were having to turn to people other than CPAs for write-up services in order to avoid costly GAAP disclosures not felt to be meaningful by either the company or its creditors.

Compilation and Review Services

The profession responded by creating compilation and review services ***[SSARS 1].*** A description of the details of these services and their implication for bankers and other creditors is provided in the reprint of a 1979 article presented in Exhibit 17-1.

A compilation report should state the service performed, the limitation of such a service, and a clear disclaimer. The following form is suggested by Statement on Standards for Accounting and Review Statements No. 1 (as amended by ***SSARS No. 5***):

> I (we) have compiled the accompanying balance sheet of ——— Company as of December 31, 19X6, and the related statements of income, retained earnings, and changes in financial position for the year then ended in accordance with standards established by the American Institute of Certified Public Accountants.
>
> A compilation is limited to presenting in the form of financial statements information that is the representation of management (owners). I (we) have not audited or reviewed the accompanying financial statements and, accordingly, do not express an opinion or any other form of assurance on them.[4]

Of course, a compilation report on a single financial statement is permitted.

If the accountant has been asked to omit substantially all GAAP disclosures, a third paragraph should be added to the compilation report, as follows:

> Management has elected to omit substantially all of the disclosures (and the statement of changes in financial position) required by generally accepted accounting principles. If the omitted disclosures were included in the financial statements, they might influence the user's conclusions about the company's financial position, results of operations, and changes in financial position. Accordingly, these financial statements are not designed for those who are not informed about such matters. (par. 2)

When an accountant is asked to compile statements included in a prescribed form (for example, the form used by industry trade associations, credit agencies, and regulatory bodies) that calls for departure from GAAP, he or she may do so by changing the report to emphasize the financial statements' conformance with the requirements prescribed, differing from GAAP. The report, as specified in Statement on Standards for Accounting and Review Services No. 3, "Compilation Reports on Financial Statements Included in Certain Prescribed Forms,"[5] should state: "These financial statements are not designed for those who are not informed about such differences" (that is, the differences in prescribed standards and GAAP).

If the CPA is not independent according to the code of ethics, the final paragraph of the report should state:

> I am (we are) not independent with respect to ——— Company.

The recommended report form for a review engagement ***[SSARS 1]*** is as follows:

> I (we) have reviewed the accompanying balance sheet of ——— Company as of December 31, 19X6, and the related statements of income, retained earnings, and changes in financial position for the year then ended, in accordance with standards established by the American Institute of Certified Public Accountants. All information included in these financial statements is the representation of the management (owners) of ——— Company.
>
> A review consists principally of inquiries of company personnel and analytical procedures applied to financial data. It is substantially less in scope than an examination in accordance with generally accepted auditing standards, the objective of which is the expression of an opinion regarding the financial statements taken as a whole. Accordingly, I (we) do not express such an opinion.
>
> Based on my (our) review, I am (we are) not aware of any material modifications that should be made to the accompanying financial statements in order for them to

[4] AICPA, December 1978, par. 17, amended July 1982.
[5] AICPA, December 1981.

EXHIBIT 17-1
New AICPA Standards for Smaller Companies

CPA reports on unaudited financial statements of smaller businesses should now be more meaningful to lenders, without added costs to the borrower.

A new pronouncement by the American Institute of Certified Public Accountants will affect the alternative sources of financial information available to the banking community. CPAs will be permitted to perform compilations and reviews of financial statements, beginning this month.

Basically, these services provide a substitute for the internally generated financial statement, without the imposition of fees for disclosure in compliance with generally accepted accounting principles (GAAP) in which the banker may lack interest or for which he has alternative information sources.

Compilation Service

The Statement on Standards for Accounting and Review Services (SSARS) #1 permits CPAs to present financial statements (F/S) information that is the representation of management (owners) without audit or review. Any accountant who has knowledge of the accounting principles and practices of the industry in which the entity operates, either through previous experience or by consulting professional publications and knowledgeable individuals, is permitted to perform the compilation service.

To fulfill the engagement, the CPA will gain a general understanding of (1) the nature of the clients' business transactions, (2) the form of its accounting records, (3) the stated qualifications of its accounting personnel, (4) the accounting basis on which the financial statements are to be presented, and (5) the form and content of the financial statements. This understanding will be obtained through experience with the entity or inquiry of the entity's personnel. The CPA is not required to verify, corroborate, or review the client's information by means of any other procedures. The client may choose to omit substantially all disclosures required under GAAP; in this case, the auditor's report will state:

> Management has elected to omit substantially all of the disclosures (and the statement of changes in financial position, if omitted) required by GAAP. If the omitted disclosures were included in the F/S, they might* influence the user's conclusions about the company's financial position, results of operations, and changes in financial position. Accordingly, these financial statements are not designed for those who are not informed about such matters.

If the client instead chooses to comply with GAAP, the compilation service does not provide assurance of compliance. If the CPA becomes aware of noncompliance, he/she will state the known departure and its effects if provided by management. One other facet of the compilation reporting function of which the user should be aware is that a CPA who lacks independence can still perform the service, provided he/she informs the user of the lack of independence in the compilation report.

Review Service

An alternative service described in SSARS #1 involves the performance of inquiry and analytical procedures that provide the accountant with a reasonable basis for expressing limited assurance there are no material modifications† that should be made to the statements in order for them to be in conformity with GAAP or, if applicable, with another comprehensive basis of accounting.‡ For this service, the CPA must be independent; other than this distinction, the qualifications of the CPA and his/her task of becoming acquainted with a client are identical to the description of the compilation service.

However, in addition to the accountant's more extensive inquiries of the client, limited§ analytical procedures are performed by the CPA. These involve (A) comparison of the F/S with statements for comparable prior period(s), (B) comparison of the F/S with anticipated results, if available (for example, budgets and forecasts), and (C) study of the relationships of the elements of the financial statements that would be expected to conform to a predictable pattern based on the entity's experience (e.g., the relationship of changes in sales and changes in accounts receivable).

The review does not contemplate a study and evaluation of internal accounting control, nor tests of accounting records and of responses to inquiries by obtaining corroborating evidential matter. Hence, there is a significant difference in the limited assurance of the review function and the assurance provided by an audit.

Potential Role

When the banker sets information requirements for loan applicants, he/she is cognizant of the costs imposed on the client. The requirement of a CPA's involvement in the past meant the client would have to comply with GAAP, or provide information on the effect of any noncompliance in order to obtain unaudited financial statements with a CPA's disclaimer.

EXHIBIT 17-1 (continued)

In light of the numerous disclosure requirements of GAAP—disclosures concerning pensions, leases, contingencies, accounting changes, and related parties are often cited as particularly burdensome for smaller companies—the costs‖ of unaudited F/S may well exceed their benefit to a small company and impose greater risk on the loan decision due to the decreased value of the firm.

The alternatives in the past have been the use of a non-CPA for F/S preparation and/or the use of internally generated F/S by loan applicants. Discussions with bankers indicate a concern over F/S preparation by loan applicants' employees. Now an alternative is available that will not impose a high cost on the applicant, but will provide an independent preparer who has the recognized skills of a CPA.

It would appear the extended services of CPAs offer flexibility to the banker. He/she can require firms to provide compilation reports and/or review reports as information sources. The banker can designate disclosures required under GAAP that are unimportant to the loan decision or which relate to information known by the banker due to past experience or alternative information sources. These disclosures can be omitted and highlighted in the CPA's report without incurring the cost of the CPA's disclosure of the omitted data. SSARS #1 permits the CPA to report that information is omitted, with the statement:

> . . . the effects of this departure from GAAP on financial position, results of operations, and changes in financial position have not been determined.

From Wanda A. Wallace, *Bankers Monthly Magazine,* August 15, 1979, pp. 30-31: discusses the details of compilation and review services and the implication of such services to bankers and other creditors.

*The accountant may compile such F/S only if the report is not, to his/her knowledge, undertaken with the intention of misleading those who might reasonably be expected to use it.

†Any known departure will be described in the accountant's report.

‡Any basis other than GAAP would be specified in both the compilation and review reports, e.g., a basis of accounting the reporting entity uses to comply with the requirements on financial reporting provisions of a government regulatory agency.

§SSARS #1 does not include all of the analytical procedures relevant to an audit function as described in Statement on Auditing Standards #23.

‖These include the opportunity cost of not using other CPA services, such as budgeting and management advisory services, which could improve a borrower's operations and thereby lower a lender's level of risk assumption.

be in conformity with generally accepted accounting principles.

Each page of the financial statements should be marked "See Accountant's Compilation Report" or "See Accountant's Review Report," as appropriate, to indicate the nature of the accountants' engagement. Engagement letters are strongly encouraged to ensure that a clear understanding of services to be performed exists, particularly their inability to be relied on for the disclosure of errors, irregularities, or illegal acts.

Just as comparative financial statements are desirable in audited engagements, they are also useful in compilation and review engagements. Statement on Standards for Accounting and Review Services No. 2, "Reporting on Comparative Financial Statements," states that continuing accountants should update their preceding year's report by reexpressing previous conclusions, altered as required by subsequently obtained information. However, if the previous year's level of service was higher than the current period's, then the previous year's responsibility should be expressly described in a separate paragraph in the current report. Or, the CPA may reissue the earlier report. Reissuance means that a subsequent event review is performed and the report is dual dated to reflect this review. Whenever a new CPA wishes to report on comparative financial statements, compilation and review services are required for the previous year, unless a predecessor auditor can reissue his or her report or the current auditor can refer to the earlier report. These issues are discussed in SSARS No. 2.

Many practitioners have questioned: where does a review end and an audit begin? Although practice and legal liability cases usually answer this

EXHIBIT 17-2

Inquiries Made When Reviewing Financial Statements

The inquiries to be made in a review of financial statements are a matter of the accountant's judgment. In determining his inquiries, an accountant may consider (a) the nature and materiality of the items, (b) the likelihood of misstatement, (c) knowledge obtained during current and previous engagements, (d) the stated qualifications of the entity's accounting personnel, (e) the extent to which a particular item is affected by management's judgment, and (f) inadequacies in the entity's underlying financial data. The following list of inquiries is for illustrative purposes only. The inquiries do not necessarily apply to every engagement, nor are they meant to be all-inclusive. This list is not intended to serve as a program or checklist in the conduct of a review; rather it describes the general areas in which inquiries might be made. For example, the accountant may feel it is necessary to make several inquiries to answer one of the questions listed below, such as item 3(a).

1. General
   a. What are the procedures for recording, classifying, and summarizing transactions (relates to each section discussed below)?
   b. Do the general ledger control accounts agree with subsidiary records (for example, receivables, inventories, investments, property and equipment, accounts payable, accrued expenses, noncurrent liabilities)?
   c. Have accounting principles been applied on a consistent basis?

2. Cash
   a. Have bank balances been reconciled with book balances?
   b. Have old or unusual reconciling items between bank balances and book balances been reviewed and adjustments made where necessary?
   c. Has a proper cutoff of cash transactions been made?
   d. Are there any restrictions on the availability of cash balances?
   e. Have cash funds been counted and reconciled with control accounts?

3. Receivables
   a. Has an adequate allowance been made for doubtful accounts?
   b. Have receivables considered uncollectible been written off?
   c. If appropriate, has interest been reflected?
   d. Has a proper cutoff of sales transactions been made?
   e. Are there any receivables from employees and related parties?
   f. Are any receivables pledged, discounted, or factored?
   g. Have receivables been properly classified between current and noncurrent?

4. Inventories
   a. Have inventories been physically counted? If not, how have inventories been determined?
   b. Have general ledger control accounts been adjusted to agree with physical inventories?
   c. If physical inventories are taken at a date other than the balance sheet date, what procedures were used to record changes in inventory between the date of the physical inventory and the balance sheet date?
   d. Were consignments in or out considered in taking physical inventories?
   e. What is the basis of valuation?
   f. Does inventory cost include material, labor, and overhead where applicable?
   g. Have write-downs for obsolescence or cost in excess of net realizable value been made?
   h. Have proper cutoffs of purchases, goods in transit, and returned goods been made?
   i. Are there any inventory encumbrances?

5. Prepaid Expenses
   a. What is the nature of the amounts included in prepaid expenses?
   b. How are these amounts amortized?

6. Investments, including Loans, Mortgages, and Intercorporate Investments
   a. Have gains and losses on disposal been reflected?
   b. Has investment income been reflected?
   c. Has appropriate consideration been given to the classification of investments between current and noncurrent, and the difference between the cost and market value of investments?
   d. Have consolidation or equity accounting requirements been considered?
   e. What is the basis of valuation of marketable equity securities?
   f. Are investments unencumbered?

7. Property and Equipment
   a. Have gains or losses on disposal of property or equipment been reflected?
   b. What are the criteria for capitalization of property and equipment? Have such criteria been applied during the fiscal period?
   c. Does the repairs and maintenance account only include items of an expense nature?
   d. Are property and equipment stated at cost?
   e. What are the depreciation methods and rates? Are they appropriate and consistent?
   f. Are there any unrecorded additions, retirements, abandonments, sales, or trade-ins?
   g. Does the entity have material lease agreements? Have they been properly reflected?
   h. Is any property or equipment mortgaged or otherwise encumbered?

EXHIBIT 17-2 (continued)

8. Other Assets
   a. What is the nature of the amounts included in other assets?
   b. Do these assets represent costs that will benefit future periods? What is the amortization policy? Is it appropriate?
   c. Have other assets been properly classified between current and noncurrent?
   d. Are any of these assets mortgaged or otherwise encumbered?

9. Accounts and Notes Payable and Accrued Liabilities
   a. Have all significant payables been reflected?
   b. Are all bank and other short-term liabilities properly classified?
   c. Have all significant accruals, such as payroll, interest, and provisions for pension and profit-sharing plans been reflected?
   d. Are there any collateralized liabilities?
   e. Are there any payables to employees and related parties?

10. Long-term Liabilities
    a. What are the terms and other provisions of long-term liability agreements?
    b. Have liabilities been properly classified between current and noncurrent?
    c. Has interest expense been reflected?
    d. Has there been compliance with restrictive covenants of loan agreements?
    e. Are any long-term liabilities collateralized or subordinated?

11. Income and Other Taxes
    a. Has provision been made for current and prior-year federal income taxes payable?
    b. Have any assessments or reassessments been received? Are there tax examinations in process?
    c. Are there timing differences? If so, have deferred taxes been reflected?
    d. Has provision been made for state and local income, franchise, sales, and other taxes payable?

12. Other Liabilities, Contingencies, and Commitments
    a. What is the nature of the amounts included in other liabilities?
    b. Have other liabilities been properly classified between current and noncurrent?
    c. Are there any contingent liabilities, such as discounted notes, drafts, endorsements, warranties, litigation, and unsettled asserted claims? Are there any unasserted potential claims?
    d. Are there any material contractual obligations for construction or purchase of real property and equipment and any commitments or options to purchase or sell company securities?

13. Equity
    a. What is the nature of any changes in equity accounts?
    b. What classes of capital stock have been authorized?
    c. What is the par or stated value of the various classes of stock?
    d. Do amounts of outstanding shares of capital stock agree with subsidiary records?
    e. Have capital stock preferences, if any, been disclosed?
    f. Have stock options been granted?
    g. Has the entity made any acquisitions of its own capital stock?
    h. Are there any restrictions on retained earnings or other capital?

14. Revenue and Expenses
    a. Are revenues from the sale of major products and services recognized in the appropriate period?
    b. Are purchases and expenses recognized in the appropriate period and properly classified?
    c. Do the financial statements include discontinued operations or items that might be considered extraordinary?

15. Other
    a. Are there any events that occurred after the end of the fiscal period that have a significant effect on the financial statements?
    b. Have actions taken at stockholder, board of directors, or comparable meetings that affect the financial statements been reflected?
    c. Have there been any material transactions between related parties?
    d. Are there any material uncertainties? Is there any change in the status of material uncertainties previously disclosed?

From Statement on Standards for Accounting and Review Services No. 1, "Compilation and Review of Financial Statements" (New York: AICPA, 1979), pp. 20-23.

question more definitively, an appendix to SSARS No. 1 lists questions about the subjects covered in a review engagement. This list, not intended to be all-inclusive and not sufficient for use as an audit program, is presented in Exhibit 17-2 (see pages 600 and 601). Numerous inquiries per item are likely, rather than a single audit step. Besides answering the questions in Exhibit 17-2, the accountant performing a review service should obtain a letter of representation from the client. As emphasized in the exhibit, no study and evaluation of internal accounting control is contemplated, nor are tests of accounting records or corroboration of the responses to the inquiries anticipated. A successor accountant is not required to communicate with a predecessor accountant in connection with accepting a compilation or review engagement ***[SSARS 4]***. But if he or she chooses to do so, the client's permission should be obtained, and the predecessor accountant, when granted permission, should respond promptly and fully in ordinary circumstances.

Reviews of Interim Financial Statements

Due to the desired timeliness of interim financial reporting, CPAs are commonly asked to review interim numbers rather than to audit them ***[SAS 36, Section 722]***. And because of the information's interim nature, many costs and expenses are estimated to a greater extent than is annual financial information, suggesting that such review procedures are likely to be more cost beneficial than audit procedures are. An accountant's report accompanying interim financial information that has been reviewed should

1. State that the review was made in accordance with accepted standards.
2. Specify what interim information was reviewed.
3. Describe the procedures for a review.
4. State that a review is substantially less in scope than an audit would be.
5. State whether the accountant is aware of any material modifications that should be made to gain conformance with GAAP. Each page of the interim data should be clearly marked as unaudited. Additional information concerning such reports is available in SAS No. 36, "Review of Interim Financial Information."[6]

[6]AICPA, April 1981.

Presentations Not in Accordance with GAAP

In some circumstances, the CPA will be asked to report on a comprehensive basis of accounting other than generally accepted accounting principles ***[SAS 14, Section 621]***. Government regulatory agencies sometimes specify financial reporting provisions, such as state insurance commissions' accounting guidelines and the Interstate Commerce Commission's uniform system of accounts for railroad companies. An entity's tax basis of accounting, a cash basis (or a modification thereof) or a basis of accounting for which there are criteria that have substantial support like a price-level basis is acceptable as a comprehensive basis of accounting. If any of these bases are used, the auditor's report is expected to contain a paragraph identifying the financial statements and stating whether the examination was performed in accordance with GAAS, as well as a paragraph that states—or, preferably, refers to a footnote that states—the comprehensive basis of accounting. This footnote should indicate how the basis differs from GAAP, although a monetary effect of the difference is not required. This paragraph should also state that the financial statements are not intended to be presented in conformity with GAAP. The opinion paragraph should clearly indicate whether the financial statements are in compliance with the comprehensive basis of accounting, considering the completeness of the disclosures provided. If the auditor does not consider the statements to be presented fairly, he or she should state the principal reasons for that conclusion and appropriately modify the opinion. The report should also comment on the consistency with which the basis of accounting is applied. Note that this type of auditor's report can be issued only in accordance with the provisions of a government regulatory agency if the financial statements are intended solely for filing with a regulatory agency or if additional distribution is recognized as appropriate by an AICPA accounting or audit guide or auditing interpretation.

When an accountant is associated with unaudited financial statements prepared in accordance with a comprehensive basis of accounting other than GAAP, the disclaimer of opinion should also identify the financial statements and explain how the presentation differs from GAAP (again, monetary effects need not be stated) ***[SAS 26, Section 504].***

Of special interest to the concept of fairness is the debate before the issuance of SAS No. 5, Section 411, "The Meaning of 'Present Fairly in Conformity with Generally Accepted Accounting Principles' in the Independent Auditor's Report."[7] For example, a 1966 survey found the following perceptions:[8]

	Financial Community	Accounting Profession
Statements are both fair and in conformity with GAAP	44%	34%
Statements are fair because they are in conformity with GAAP	22%	30%
Statements are fair only to the extent that GAAP are fair	28%	20%
Other	6%	16%

The first interpretation suggests that members of the profession are concerned with the fairness of accounting principles per se.[9] The same concern arises in reporting on a comprehensive basis of accounting other than GAAP; apart from compliance with an "accepted" alternative to GAAP, the auditor must also determine the fairness of the statement. The concept is analogous to the option available under Rule 203 of the code of ethics: acknowledgment that financial statements are not misleading.

EXHIBIT 17-3

Auditor's Report on Financial Statements Prepared on the Entity's Income Tax Basis

We have examined the statement of assets, liabilities, and capital-income tax basis of Johanna and Jim, Partnership as of December 31, 19X4, and the related statements of revenue and expenses-income tax basis and changes in partners' capital accounts-income tax basis for the year then ended. Our examination was made in accordance with generally accepted auditing standards and, accordingly, included such tests of the accounting procedures as we considered necessary in the circumstances.

As described in Note 10, the Partnership's policy is to prepare its financial statements on the accounting basis used for income tax purposes; consequently, certain revenue and the related assets are recognized when received rather than when earned, and certain expenses are recognized when paid rather than when the obligation is incurred. Accordingly, the accompanying financial statements are not intended to present financial position and results of operations in conformity with generally accepted accounting principles.

In our opinion, the financial statements referred to above present fairly the assets, liabilities, and capital of Johanna and Jim, Partnership as of December 31, 19X4, and its revenue and expenses and changes in its partners' capital accounts for the year then ended, on the basis of accounting described in Note 10, which basis has been applied in a manner consistent with that of the preceding year.

From SAS No. 14, "Special Reports" (New York: AICPA, December 1976).

To demonstrate the special reports that can be issued in accordance with a comprehensive basis other than GAAP, Exhibit 17-3 provides an auditor's report on financial statements prepared on the entity's income tax basis.

Communication

Because of the various responsibility and service levels for limited assurance engagements, it is imperative that a clear understanding of the service to be performed is communicated to clients by CPAs. When engagements begin, it is suggested that a formal engagement letter be drafted, describing the terms, nature, and limitations of the service to be performed. If the CPA intends to rely on an independent agent's information and representa-

[7] AICPA, July 1975.

[8] Abraham J. Briloff, "Old Myths and New Realities in Accounting," *Accounting Review*, July 1966, p. 485.

[9] Geraldine F. Dominiak and Joseph G. Louderback III, " 'Present Fairly' and Generally Accepted Accounting Principles," *CPA Journal*, January 1972, pp. 45–49.

tions when performing the engagement, the letter should state the auditee's agreement that such reliance is appropriate. The client should sign a copy of the engagement letter, acknowledging his or her agreement, understanding, and approval of the planned scope. The CPA's bills for services should also be clear as to the nature of the engagement. Similarly, the CPA should discourage a client from

EXHIBIT 17-4
A Typical Comfort Letter

June 30,19X6

(Addressee)
Dear Sirs:

We have examined the consolidated balance sheets of the Blank Company, Inc. (the company) and subsidiaries as of December 31, 19X5 and 19X4, and the consolidated statements of income, retained earnings, and changes in financial position for each of the three years in the period ended December 31, 19X5, and the related schedules all included in the registration statement (no. 2-00000) on Form S-1 filed by the company under the Securities Act of 1933 (the act); our reports with respect thereto are also included in the registration statement. The registration statement, as amended on June 23, 19X5, is herein referred to as the registration statement.

In connection with the registration statement:

1. We are independent certified public accountants with respect to the Blank Company, Inc., within the meaning of the act and the applicable published rules and regulations thereunder.

2. In our opinion (include the phrase "except as disclosed in the registration statement," if applicable), the consolidated financial statements and schedules examined by us and included in the registration statement comply in form in all material respects with the applicable accounting requirements of the act and the related published rules and regulations.

3. We have not examined any financial statements of the company as of any date or for any period subsequent to December 31, 19X5; although we have made an examination for the year ended December 31, 19X5, the purpose (and therefore the scope) of the examination was to enable us to express our opinion on the consolidated financial statements as of December 31, 19X5, and for the year then ended, but not on the financial statements for any interim period within that year. Therefore, we are unable to and do not express any opinion on the unaudited consolidated condensed balance sheet, as of March 31, 19X6, and unaudited consolidated condensed statements of income, retained earnings, and changes in financial position for the three-month periods ended March 31, 19X6 and 19X5, included in the registration statement, or on the financial position, results of operations, or changes in financial position as of any date or for any period subsequent to December 31, 19X5.

4. For purposes of this letter we have read the 19X6 minutes of meetings of the stockholders, the board of directors, and (include other appropriate committees, if any) of the company and its subsidiaries as set forth in the minute books at June 25, 19X6, officials of the company having advised us that the minutes of all such meetings through that date were set forth therein; and have carried out other procedures to June 25, 19X6 (our work did not extend to the period from June 26, 19X6, to June 30, 19X6, inclusive), as follows:

a. With respect to the three-month periods ended March 31, 19X6 and 19X5, we have
   i. Read the unaudited consolidated condensed balance sheet as of March 31, 19X6, and unaudited consolidated condensed statements of income, retained earnings, and changes in financial position for the three-month periods ended March 31, 19X6 and 19X5, included in the registration statement; and
   ii. Made inquiries of certain officials of the company who have responsibility for financial and accounting matters regarding (1) whether the unaudited consolidated condensed financial statements referred to under a(i) comply in form in all material respects with the applicable accounting requirements of the Act and the related published rules and regulations thereunder and (2) whether those consolidated condensed financial statements are in conformity with generally accepted accounting principles applied on a basis substantially consistent with that of the audited consolidated financial statements included in the registration statement.

b. With respect to the period from April 1, 19X6, to May 31, 19X6, we have
   i. Read the unaudited consolidated financial statements of the company and subsidiaries for April and May of both 19X5 and 19X6 furnished us by the company, officials of the company having advised us that no such financial statements as of any date or for any period subsequent to May 31, 19X6, were available; and
   ii. Made inquiries of certain officials of the company who have responsibility for financial and accounting matters regarding whether the unaudited financial statements referred to under b(i) are stated on a basis substantially consistent with that of the audited financial statements included in the registration statement.

EXHIBIT 17-4 (continued)

The foregoing procedures do not constitute an examination made in accordance with generally accepted auditing standards. Also, they would not necessarily reveal matters of significance with respect to the comments in the following paragraph. Accordingly, we made no representations regarding the sufficiency of the foregoing procedures for your purposes.

5. Nothing came to our attention as a result of the foregoing procedures, however, that caused us to believe that

a. (i) The unaudited consolidated condensed financial statements described in 4a(i), included in the registration statement, do not comply in form in all material respects with the applicable accounting requirements of the Act and the related published rules and regulations and (ii) the unaudited consolidated condensed financial statements are not in conformity with generally accepted accounting principles applied on a basis substantially consistent with that of the audited consolidated financial statements; or

b. (i) At May 31, 19X6, there was any change in the capital stock or long-term debt of the company and subsidiaries consolidated or any decreases in consolidated net current assets or net assets as compared with amounts shown in the March 31, 19X6, unaudited consolidated condensed balance sheet included in the registration statement or (ii) for the period from April 1, 19X6, to May 31, 19X6, there were any decreases, as compared with the corresponding period in the preceding year, in consolidated net sales or in the total or per-share amounts of income before extraordinary items or of net income, except in all instances for changes or decreases that the registration statement discloses have occurred or may occur.

6. As mentioned under 4b, company officials have advised us that no consolidated statements as of any date or for any period subsequent to May 31, 19X6, are available; accordingly, the procedures carried out by us with respect to changes in financial statement items after May 31, 19X6, have, of necessity, been even more limited than those with respect to the periods referred to in 4. We have made inquiries of certain company officials who have responsibility for financial and accounting matters regarding whether (a) there was any change at June 25, 19X6, in the capital stock or long-term debt of the company and subsidiaries consolidated or any decreases in consolidated net current assets or net assets as compared with amounts shown on the March 31, 19X6, unaudited consolidated condensed balance sheet included in the registration statement or (b) for the period from April 1, 19X6, to June 25, 19X6, there were any decreases, as compared with the corresponding period in the preceding year, in consolidated net sales or in the total or per-share amounts of income before extraordinary items or of net income. On the basis of these inquiries and our reading of the minutes as described in 4, nothing came to our attention that caused us to believe that there was any such change or decrease, except in all instances for changes or decreases that the registration statement discloses have occurred or may occur.

7. This letter is solely for the information of the addressees and to assist the underwriters in conducting and documenting their investigation of the affairs of the company in connection with the offering of the securities covered by the registration statement, and it is not to be used, circulated, quoted, or otherwise referred to within or without the underwriting group for any other purpose, including but not limited to the registration, purchase, or sale of securities, nor is it to be filed with or referred to in whole or in part in the registration statement or any other document, except that reference may be made to it in the underwriting agreement or in any list of closing documents pertaining to the offering of the securities covered by the registration statement.

From Statement on Auditing Standards No. 49, "Letters for Underwriters" (New York: AICPA, September 1984), pp. 27-30.

using misleading account titles (for example, fees for write-up services should not be called audit fees). Similar to this concern for telltale signs of clients' misunderstanding, accountants doing limited assurance engagements should be alert to any potential problem areas, such as evidence of missing documentation. Upon noticing any problems, accountants should tell the client of the problem and suggest that it be followed up. If it is expected to be material, either the client or the CPA, before expressing an opinion, should investigate it. If the problem pertains to valuation issues that indicate noncompliance with generally accepted accounting principles, the CPA should request disclosure by the client. If the client refuses, the CPA must determine the materiality of the distortion and, if it is material, issue an adverse opinion.

Letters for Underwriters

Although the securities acts do not expressly require letters for underwriters and these letters are not filed with the SEC, most underwriting agreements either formally require or lead to the request that accountants furnish a comfort letter ***[SAS 49, Section 631]***. Such a letter gives the underwriters evidence that they have performed a "reasonable investigation" of the unaudited financial information contained in a registration statement. Because CPAs are also subject to the reasonable investigation of unaudited information contained in a registration statement containing audited financial statements, they are normally willing to help the underwriters. The underwriters are expected to determine what constitutes reasonable investigation and to ask the CPAs to comment only on matters requiring the CPA's expertise.

The comfort letter can provide no more than negative assurance. This means that nothing came to the CPA's attention causing him or her to believe that specified matters did not meet a specified standard, even though they may, nevertheless, fail to meet the standard. Exhibit 17-4 (on pages 604 and 605) shows a typical comfort letter, as presented in Statement on Auditing Standards No. 49, "Letters for Underwriters."[10] The focus on negative assurance, with a clear description of the scope of work performed, is evident, as is the restricted purpose of the letter.

Reports on Compliance

One special reporting function that CPAs often perform concerns clients' compliance with contractual provisions or regulatory requirements ***[SAS 14, Section 621].*** Frequently creditors will require borrowers to provide assurance from the independent auditor that the borrower is complying with all covenants in the loan agreement that relate to accounting or auditing matters. The auditor is permitted to provide negative assurance that the covenants are met, provided that he or she has examined the financial statements to which the contractual arrangements or regulatory requirements relate. The common covenants reviewed include sinking fund provisions, interest payments, the maintenance of a certain working-capital level and current ratio, specified uses of proceeds from sales of property, and restrictions on dividend payments or executive bonus plans.

The negative assurance may be given as a separate report or as an additional paragraph in the auditor's report that accompanies the financial statements. In either case, the connection of the expression of negative assurance with an examination of the financial statements should be specified. A statement that the examination was not directed primarily toward obtaining information regarding compliance is recommended by the professional standards. Whenever a separate report is issued, it should include a paragraph that states that the financial statements were examined, the date of the auditor's report of the examination, and whether the examination was made in accordance with GAAS. Exhibit 17-5 gives a sample report on compliance. But if the compliance report is made part of the auditor's report, the second paragraph of the report in Exhibit 17-5 should be added after the opinion paragraph of the auditor's report.

Sometimes the compliance reports requested will pertain to one or more specified elements, accounts, or items of the financial statement. For example, the 1980 statutory annual statement to be filed with state regulatory agencies by property and liability insurance companies requires a statement by a qualified loss reserve specialist that expresses an opinion on the loss and loss adjustment expense reserves. A CPA familiar with loss reserve evaluation is qualified to express such an opinion.

EXHIBIT 17-5

Report on Compliance with Contractual Provisions Given in a Separate Report

We have examined the balance sheet of Wayne Corporation as of December 31, 19X6, and the related statements of income, retained earnings, and changes in financial position for the year then ended, and have issued our report thereon dated February 16, 19X7. Our examination was made in accordance with generally accepted auditing standards and accordingly included such tests of the accounting records and such other auditing procedures as we considered necessary in the circumstances.

In connection with our examination, nothing came to our attention that caused us to believe that the Company was not in compliance with any of the terms, covenants, provisions, or conditions of sections 24 to 36, inclusive, of the Indenture dated July 21, 19X5, with Stalwart Bank. However, it should be noted that our examination was not directed primarily toward obtaining knowledge of such noncompliance.

From Statement on Auditing Standards No. 14, "Special Reports" (New York: AICPA, December 1976).

[10] AICPA, September 1984.

EXHIBIT 17-6
Opinion on Company's Loss and Loss Adjustment Expense Reserves

To: Board of Directors
ATOP Property and Liability
Insurance Company

We are members of the American Institute of Certified Public Accountants (AICPA) and are the independent public accountants of ATOP Property and Liability Insurance Company. We acknowledge our responsibility under the AICPA's Code of Professional Ethics to undertake only those engagements which we can complete with professional competence.

We have examined the financial statements prepared in conformity with generally accepted accounting principles (or prepared in conformity with accounting practices prescribed or permitted by the insurance department of the state of_____) of ATOP Property and Liability Insurance Company as of December 31, 19X4, and have issued our report thereon dated March 1, 19X5. Our examination was made in accordance with generally accepted auditing standards and, accordingly, included such tests of the accounting records and such other auditing procedures as we considered necessary in the circumstances. In the course of our examination, we have examined the estimated liabilities for unpaid losses and unpaid loss adjustment expenses of ATOP Property and Liability Insurance Company as of December 31, 19X4, as set forth in the accompanying schedule including consideration of the assumptions and methods relating to the estimation of such liabilities.

In our opinion, the accompanying schedule presents fairly the estimated unpaid loss adjustment expenses of ATOP Property and Liability Insurance Company, that could be reasonably estimated at December 31, 19X4, in conformity with accounting practices prescribed or permitted by the insurance department of the state of _____ on a basis consistent with that of the preceding year.

This report is intended solely for filing with regulatory agencies and is not intended for any other purpose.

Signature
Date

From AICPA Auditing Interpretations 9a, questions .40-.46, AU 9621.42, May 1981.

The report would be expected to take a form similar to that in Exhibit 17-6. The accompanying schedule should list the liability for losses, the liability for loss adjustment expenses, and notes explaining the basis of the presentation and the extent of reinsurance.

The CPA is expressly forbidden from providing assurance that an entity is in compliance with the provisions of the Foreign Corrupt Practices Act. This is because such an opinion must be a legal determination, beyond the auditor's expertise.[11]

Another dimension of compliance reporting ties into internal control evaluations. For example, special-purpose reports on internal accounting control at service organizations may cover design considerations and the results of certain compliance tests. These types of compliance-related reports will be discussed later in this chapter, with an explanation of engagements to review internal accounting control.

In an internal auditing environment, compliance audits are similar to compliance-related special reports. They test whether auditees are in compliance with the organization's prescribed policies and procedures, which often entail compliance with regulation and requirements established in contractual arrangements with third parties. A routine compliance audit is the internal auditors' review of the purchasing department's operations so as to ensure that personnel were complying with competitive bidding procedures and acquiring materials that met the standards prescribed by customers and regulators. Obviously, the orientation of internal auditors toward oversight responsibility for the operation of controls lends itself to extensive compliance audits and related reporting.

Operational Audits

The concept of operational auditing is credited to the General Accounting Office (GAO) and is defined in the "Standards for Audit of Governmental Organizations, Programs, Activities, and Function," presented in an appendix to this chapter, Exhibit 17-A. (Note that the standards related to reporting were presented at the beginning of this book in Chapter 2 and are not repeated in the appendix.) Compliance audits, control-oriented reviews, effi-

[11] AICPA Auditing Interpretation No. 5, "Compliance with the Foreign Corrupt Practices Act of 1977," Question 10, AU§9642.10, issued October 1978, modified August 1980.

EXHIBIT 17-7
Audit Program: Material and Component Availability

1. Are schedules or shop orders checked to make certain that materials are available before authorizing the start of production?

2. If component parts and subassemblies are produced, do their production schedules tie in with end-product schedules?

3. Verify that records provide adequate visibility concerning obligated material.

4. Is it necessary to "stage" production in order to determine whether all parts are on hand or can the formal inventory records be relied upon?

5. If production is "staged" is it "destaged" when the due date is set back?

6. If you utilize a checkout (staging) system, are there written procedures:

   - Defining when checkout (or staging) is to take place?

   - Limiting checkout to no more than a specified number of days in advance of production?

7. Is there a time limit as to how long material may remain in the checkout (or staging) area?

8. Verify that material staging does not occur too far in advance of production.

9. Perform an aging of staged materials in total, if possible, or of a sample basis otherwise.

10. Are schedules for receiving materials already ordered used in production scheduling?

11. Are shortages hampering production? If so, are they caused by shortages in purchased items or in component parts manufactured by the firm?

12. Determine whether consideration is given to on-hand assembled units and safety stocks before initiating production orders.

    Select a representative number of production orders and compare the quantity to the quantity available at the production order date per Production Control records (See schedule which follows).

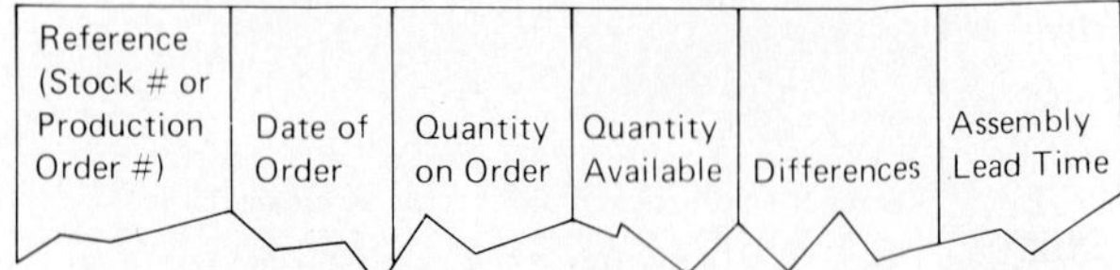

Reference (Stock # or Production Order #)	Date of Order	Quantity on Order	Quantity Available	Differences	Assembly Lead Time

    Discuss results of review with Production Control supervisors and obtain explanations where consideration apparently was not given to inventory quantities.

13. Ascertain that the status report compares inventory on hand and on order with requirements for ensuing periods and determine that it is:

    - Frequent enough for control action
    - Issued promptly following the cutoff date
    - Used for requisitioning
    - Used for expediting
    - Used regularly by Accounting for evaluating inventories and reserves

14. Obtain a copy of the format of the status report for reference purposes and include in the work papers.

From Gary L. Holstrum and William A. Collins, *Operational Audits of Production Control, Research Report No. 20* (Altamonte Springs, Fla: Institute of Internal Auditors, 1978), pp. 40-42.

ciency and effectiveness assessments, and the overall program results of various operations all are included in the GAO's audit process.

Such auditing is also within the purview of internal auditors, who often, for example, perform operational audits of production control. Their objective is to determine whether the production control function has met its responsibility for determining that material, labor, and machines are available to produce the optimum production quantity to meet customer needs based on sales forecasts. To demonstrate how such an assessment is made, an audit program for one part of this type of audit is presented in Exhibit 17-7. This audit program on material and component availability reflects the auditors' concern that objectives are being met and operations are being routinely monitored to identify inefficiencies in the system. Once this type of program is carried out, the internal audit report is written. Recall from the chapter which introduced audit reports that they have six key components:

- an overall summary.
- an introduction.
- a statement of purpose.
- a statement of scope.
- a statement of opinion.
- findings.

In reporting findings, a summary of the factual finding, criteria used for measurement, an assessment of conditions, the effect of the finding, its cause, and recommendations on means of addressing problems should be clearly presented.

As various aspects of operations are reviewed, the operational auditor will focus on what generally are regarded as essential facets of the management process: planning, implementing, controlling, decision making, and communication. Although the GAO and internal auditing have been most involved in this form of auditing, external auditors are expanding their services toward what has been referred to as *comprehensive auditing*, combining a financial and operational auditing approach. Exhibit 17-8 shows the type of report that may result from the audit program in Exhibit 17-7. The detail of such reports tends to vary widely. Exhibit 17-8 is in summary form whereas many GAO reports

EXHIBIT 17-8

Internal Auditor's Report on Material and Component Availability

Foreword

There are four employees responsible for material and component availability for the production process. These employees handle 100 different types of material and components, the average total value of which is about $500,000. Management has requested us to perform an operational audit, as no such prior exam has been performed.

Purpose

The purpose of the audit was to evaluate the efficiency and effectiveness of ordering, monitoring, scheduling, and issuing activities related to materials and components used in the production process.

Scope

We did not review purchasing procedures; only the scheduling of purchases and the determination of quantities to be ordered were reviewed.

Opinion

While ordering, scheduling, and issuing activities appear to be reasonably effective and efficient, the monitoring activities are unsatisfactory in terms of effectively controlling materials returned, after being checked out.

Statement of Condition

The prescribed procedures state that when excess materials are returned by the production department, they are to be entered on the records to enable accurate monitoring of the levels of inventory on hand and available for issuance.

Yet, our tests indicated that in the past three months, no supplies returned from production have been entered in the records. This inaccurate monitoring led to the carrying of excess materials costing about $50,000.

The employee who should have entered returns into the records was new; the old employee quit three months ago, without notice. As a result, no on-the-job-training was available to clarify the new employee's responsibilities.

Recommendation

The records should be brought up-to-date, and the new employee ought to receive some on-the-job training by a supervisor. Steps should be taken to advise supervisors of their responsibility to orientate newly hired employees who were not trained by the employee whom they are replacing.

From Gary L. Holstrum and William A. Collins, *Operational Audits of Production Control, Research Report No. 20* (Altamonte Springs, Fla.: Institute of Internal Auditors, 1978).

would detail the program steps and both positive and negative findings.

Before issuing a report like that in Exhibit 17-8, internal auditors will hold an *exit conference* with the auditee, to discuss the findings of the audit, planned recommendations, plausible alternative means of meeting objectives, and the expected content of the internal audit report. Not only does this type of meeting enhance the auditor's rapport with auditees, but it can also improve the overall quality of the auditor's report, since unreasonable recommendations or misinterpretations of findings are unlikely to go unchallenged. The manager of the audited operation should decide who will attend the conference. In conducting such interviews, attempts should be made to establish open lines of communication. If an auditee disagrees with proposed audit report language, auditors should ask for suggested revisions and discuss those suggestions. Auditees' managers should be asked if they would like to provide written comments for inclusion in the internal audit report. During the exit conference, the internal auditor should ask the managers if there are any areas in which they would like additional field work performed. If there are, the managers should be made aware of internal auditors' practice of identifying that aspect of the audit as having been performed at the auditee's request.

Reviews of Internal Accounting Control

A report can be issued on the auditor's evaluation of internal accounting controls, based solely on that study and evaluation performed as part of the audit service ***[SAS 30, Section 642].*** In addition, CPAs can be hired separately or in addition to the audit function to perform a comprehensive review of internal accounting controls. Besides these two services, CPAs are often requested to provide reports based on regulatory agencies' preestablished criteria, such as reports on the controls of broker-dealers, as prescribed by the SEC. Finally, CPAs may be asked to prepare special-purpose reports that address special information requests and involve only a portion of the control system. This diversity of services is shown in Exhibit 17-9, which describes the various purposes, scopes, uses, and opinions expressed in these engagements. Essentially, a comprehensive review engagement requires all aspects of control which could have a material effect on the financial statements to be reviewed and compliance tested to facilitate an expression of an opinion on the system, as a whole.

The comprehensive review process begins with gaining an understanding of the client's operations and asking about control objectives and system design. Either the client or the auditor must document the system of controls, identifying the major control areas. Once the general controls have been evaluated and tested, the auditor must decide whether any observed weaknesses are being compensated for by other controls. If there are material weaknesses in the general controls, the client should be advised and encouraged to take prompt corrective action. If the general controls are adequate, the auditor will identify specific control objectives and examine the key control procedures. The effects of general control on specific controls will influence the compliance tests to be performed. Again, compensating controls must be considered and a determination made as to whether material weaknesses exist in specific controls. The combined effect of immaterial weaknesses also must be weighed to make sure that they do not together constitute a material weakness. Finally, the auditor must decide whether any observed material weaknesses are sufficiently pervasive to require an adverse opinion.[12]

Clients frequently use service organizations to execute transactions and maintain related accountability and/or to record transactions and process related data. Common examples are bank trust departments' investment of assets for employee benefit plans and EDP service centers. Depending on their relationship to clients' financial statements, service organizations may be asked to provide a report on the design of their system and compliance test results of specific objectives of in-

[12]Adapted from Wanda A. Wallace, *Handbook of Internal Accounting Controls* (Englewood Cliffs, N.J.: Prentice-Hall, 1984).

EXHIBIT 17-9

Distinction Between Evaluation of Internal Accounting Controls for Opinion on Financial Statements, Review of Internal Accounting Controls for Report on System, and Other Internal Control-Related Engagements

Report Forms Related to Internal Accounting Control:	Opinion on Entity's System of Internal Accounting Control As of Specified Date During Specified Period of Time	Report on Entity's System Based Solely on Study and Evaluation of Internal Accounting Control As Part of Audit	Report on All or Part of Entity's System Based on Regulatory Agencies' Preestablished Criteria	Special-Purpose Reports on All or Part of Entity's System
Purpose	To determine whether management has reasonable assurance that assets are safeguarded, financial records are reliable, and financial statements can be prepared.	Intermediate step in forming opinion on financial statements, which provides basis for determining nature, timing, and extent of audit procedures.	To meet regulators' reporting requirements.	To meet special information requests that do not require opinion on system taken as a whole.
Scope	To assess susceptibility of entity's assets to be misused, entity's overall control environment, effect of recent operating and control changes, significance of classes of transactions and related assets; and to use available knowledge of entity to – conclude whether entity's control procedures are suitably designed to achieve objectives of internal control, – determine whether such prescribed procedures are being applied, – evaluate total system.	Whereas entire system is reviewed, testing of system is limited to those prescribed control procedures on which auditor relies. No testing is performed on – procedures not satisfactory for auditor's purposes, or – procedures for which audit effort required to test compliance exceeds reduction in audit effort possible through control reliance.	According to regulatory agency's specifications.	According to specifications of party engaging accountant.
Use	No restrictions on use of this report. May serve as basis for auditor's reliance on internal accounting controls, as procedures are same.	Use restricted to management, specified regulatory agencies, or other specified third parties.	Use restricted to management or specified regulatory agencies.	Use restricted to management, specified regulatory agencies, or other specified third parties.
Opinion	Scope. Date. Responsibilities of management. Objectives – Report does not affect audit report. Inherent limitations. Opinion that system as whole prevents or detects material errors or irregularities. In accordance with AICPA standards. Disclose material weaknesses (and immaterial weaknesses, if desired). Qualify report for scope restrictions, or disclaim, if substantial restrictions. State if management believes costs exceed benefits – do not express a related opinion but issue disclaimer if desired. Do not mention corrective actions unless design is reviewed and application is tested.	Restricted use. Limited purpose (GAAS). Disclaim opinion on whole. Would not necessarily disclose all material weaknesses in the system. Negative assurance regarding material weaknesses. Material weaknesses considered in determining audit tests – report does not affect audit report. If immaterial weaknesses are included in some Reports and excluded from others, be able to justify any exclusion.	Restricted use. Matters covered by study. Whether tests of compliance were performed. Objectives and limitations of both internal accounting control and accountant's evaluation. Conclusions based on criteria, i.e., adequate for agency's purpose (study and audit). Material weaknesses disclosed even if not material by agency's criteria (but not responsible for comprehensiveness of agency's criteria.) Can disclose immaterial weaknesses, recommendations for corrective actions, and description of actions taken if reviewed and tested.	Restricted use. Scope and nature of accountant's procedures. Disclaimer on System as whole. State accountant's findings.

ternal accounting control procedures on which the auditor intends to rely. Any CPA asked for a special-purpose report as the auditor of a service organization is expected to comply with the profession's general standards and relevant GAAS guidelines. However, the auditor of the service organization may lack independence with respect to client organizations using the service. Reports on

EXHIBIT 17-10

Recent Proposals, Pronouncements, and Regulations Related to Internal Accounting Control

Securities and Exchange Commission (SEC) (Securities Exchange Act Release No. 13185)	– Proposed requirement that management maintain an adequate system of internal control	January 19, 1977
	– Expressed interest in requiring internal control reports to shareholders	
The Commission on Auditors' Responsibilities (Report of Tentative Conclusions) (see also the Report, Conclusions, and Recommendations, 1978)	– Recommended auditor's report on material weaknesses to management, "including, if appropriate, the audit committee or the full board" (p. 39)	1977
	– Recommended a report by management on internal controls and management's response to the auditor's suggestions for correction of weaknesses	
	– Recommended a report by the auditor "on whether he agrees with management's description of the company's controls" that would also "describe material uncorrected weaknesses not disclosed in that report" (p. 61)	
American Institute of Certified Public Accountants (AICPA) Auditing Standards Board (Statement on Auditing Standards No. 20)	– Required communication of material weaknesses in internal accounting controls	August, 1977
Congress [Foreign Corrupt Practices Act of 1977 (FCPA)]	– Required public companies to maintain adequate systems of internal accounting controls	December 19, 1977
Securities and Exchange Commission (Accounting Series Release No. 242)	– Advised companies to "review their accounting procedures, systems of internal accounting controls and business practices in order that they may take any actions necessary to comply with the requirements contained in the Act" (FCPA) (43FR7752)	February 16, 1978
Financial Executives Institute (FEI) (Guidelines for Preparation of A Statement of Management Responsibility for Financial Statements)	– Endorsed the furnishing of management reports, including "Management's assessment of the effectiveness of the internal accounting control system" (p. 1)	June, 1978
AICPA, Reports by Management Special Advisory Committee (Tentative Conclusions and Recommendations)	– Tentatively concluded that annual reports to shareholders should include a management report which should discuss internal accounting control	December 8, 1978
Securities and Exchange Commission (Statement of Management on Internal Accounting Control; delayed for 1979 per AICPA [December 10, 1979, p. 1])	– Proposed rules that would require a management statement and an auditor's opinion on internal accounting control by all SEC registrants	April, 1979
AICPA, Auditing Standards Board (Exposure draft: Reporting on Internal Accounting Control)	– Provides guidance on reports made as part of an engagement to study and evaluate internal accounting control, as well as reports based solely on the review of controls made as part of an audit	December 31, 1979
Securities and Exchange Commission (Statement on Withdrawal of Proposal to Require Reports on Internal Accounting Controls)	– Withdrew rules proposed in April, 1979, and announced the SEC's intention to monitor voluntary private-sector initiatives in this area through the spring of 1982 and then to reconsider regulatory action	June 6, 1980

From Wanda A. Wallace, "Internal Control Reporting Practices in the Municipal Sector," *Accounting Review,* July 1981, p. 667.

design, design and compliance, or just a segment of a service organization can be issued, depending on the client auditors' requirements, in line with SAS No. 30.[13]

The opinion types shown in Exhibit 17-9 are described in Statement on Auditing Standards No. 30, "Reporting on Internal Accounting Control" (July 1980). The diversity of services is, in part, due to the disagreement over the users' desire for extensive information on internal controls. Exhibit 17-10 gives an overview of the various proposals, pronouncements, and regulations related to the internal accounting controls instituted between 1977 and 1980. The SEC proposed that internal accounting control reports be audited and required for publicly held companies. But after receiving over 950 letters protesting this, the SEC withdrew its proposal and encouraged voluntary disclosures of the adequacy of entities' control systems. SAS No. 30 was issued in large part to show the various types of voluntary reporting.

Internal accounting control reports are publicly available for some banks' trust departments, broker-dealers, and service centers. But, other types of clients have not requested such services, despite the SEC's interest in control-related disclosures. The reasons include possible competitive harm from disclosing control-related secrets, increased risk exposure stemming from disclosing material weaknesses, and the questionable information content of such disclosures without a detailed understanding of clients' operations.

Forecasts

The association of accountants with management forecasts is being encouraged by the SEC, FASB, and AICPA. In the past, the SEC prohibited forecasts in prospectuses but now allows forecasts under broad standards and disclosure requirements and provides a safe-harbor rule intended to reduce any liability consequences attendant to prospective statements.[14]

Accountants' Service Regarding Prospective Financial Statements

Whenever an accountant submits to a client, or others, prospective financial statements (either financial forecasts or projections) that he or she has assembled or helped assemble or provides reports on prospective financial statements that are, or reasonably might be, expected to be used by another (third) party, he or she should perform an examination, compilation, or an engagement to apply agreed-upon procedures and should issue a report. The degree of responsibility should be clear. Disclosures regarding the prospective statements must be sufficient, including a summary of the significant assumptions underlying the forecasts.

Exhibit 17-11 summarizes the accountant's considerations when performing compilation services on prospective financial statements. These guidelines do not apply to engagements involving prospective financial statements used solely in connection with litigation support services, although they may be used for them. Likewise, "internal-use only" statements are separate from the requirements for compilation reports. Keep in mind that the following discussion is based on a proposed authoritative statement that may be modified before being issued as a guide to CPAs for services regarding prospective financial statements. The recommended standard report form for the compilation of prospective financial statements appropriate for use by third parties (adjusted to reflect Statement on Standards for Accountants' Services on Prospective Financial Information, issued October 1985) is as follows:

> We have compiled the accompanying forecasted/projected balance sheet statements of income, retained earnings, and changes in financial position of XYZ Company as of December 31, 19XX, and for the year then ending, in accordance with standards established by the American Institute of Certified Public Accountants.
>
> A compilation is limited to presenting in the form of a forecast/projection information that is the representation of management and does not include evaluation of the support for the assumptions underlying the fore-

[13]SAS No. 44, "Special-Purpose Reports on Internal Accounting Control at Service Organizations" (New York: AICPA, December 1982).

[14]See Releases 33-5992, 34-15305, 34-6084, 34-15944, 35-21115, and 39-532.

EXHIBIT 17-11

Considerations When Performing Compilation Service on Prospective Financial Statements

Susceptibility to Review

Is there suitable support for the underlying assumptions?
- Did the client identify key factors?
- Were assumptions developed per factor?
- Were multiple effects of assumptions considered?
- Are other than the responsible party's representations available as support?

Assistance to Entity

Although the CPA can help in identifying assumptions, information gathering, or assembly, the client is still responsible for the preparation and presentation of prospective financial statements, particularly the underlying assumptions.

The CPA's report should in no way allude to his or her involvement in its preparation.

Other Information

The CPA should read other information for material consistency with the information in prospective financial statements.

Inconsistent information is flagged by phrases like
- "cannot be predicted at this time"
- "unlikely to occur"

Compilation Procedures

Establish understanding with client of services to be performed, preferably by means of an engagement letter.

Ask about accounting principles used and compare with historical financials and plans for future historical cost statements. If client is new, ask about consistency of principles with industry practice and future plans for reporting on historical basis.

Ask about process for identifying key factors and developing assumptions.

Obtain a list of assumptions and consider
- Their completeness.
- Whether they contain any obvious internal inconsistencies.
- Whether they are obviously inappropriate in light of expected conditions and course of action in prospective period.

Perform or test mathematical accuracy of computations that translate assumptions into prospective financial statements.

Read the prospective financial statements and summary of significant assumptions for appropriateness and compliance with AICPA presentation guidelines applicable to prospective financial statements.

If significant part of prospective period has expired, compare the forecast or projection with historical results.

Obtain written representations from responsible party
- Documenting that party's responsibility for assumptions and belief that they are expected.
- Stating that projections are based on expected set of conditions and course of action (or expected course of action if projection, as distinct from forecast).

Decide whether there is any basis for withdrawal.

Reports

State that CPA assumes no responsibility for updating report for events and circumstances occurring after date of report.

Point out lack of assurance regarding attainment of prospective results.

Adapted from "Proposed Authoritative Statement: Prospective Financial Statements," AICPA, File Ref. No. 2660, Draft of February 15, 1985.

cast/projection. We have not examined the forecast/projection and, accordingly, do not express an opinion or any other form of assurance on the accompanying statements or assumptions. Furthermore [for a projection, describe hypothetical assumptions, for example, "even if the financing of $1 million is obtained as described in the accompanying summary of significant assumptions"; for a multiple projection, describe hypothetical assumptions, for example, "even if the actual occupancy rate attained is within the range shown as described in the accompanying summary of significant assumptions"], there will usually be differences between the forecasted/projected and actual results because events and circumstances frequently do not occur as expected, and those differences may be material. We have no responsibility to update this report for events and circumstances occurring after the date of this report.[15]

Each set of slashes is mutually exclusive, relating either to forecasted statements or to projected statements. A *financial forecast* is a presentation of prospective financial information that describes, to the best of the responsible party's knowledge and belief, an entity's expected financial position, results of operations, and changes in financial position. A *financial projection* is a presentation of prospective financial information that describes, to the best of the responsible party's knowledge and belief, given one or more hypothetical assumptions, an entity's expected financial position, results of operations, and changes in financial position. For example, a projection is often prepared for one or more "what if" scenarios.

An examination of prospective financial statements enables a CPA to report on the conformity of these statements with AICPA presentation guidelines and whether the assumptions provide a reasonable basis for the responsible party's forecast (or projection, given the hypothetical assumptions). The CPA must make sure that the responsible party has explicitly identified all factors expected to affect materially the entity's operations during the prospective period (in the case of a projection, if the hypothetical assumptions were to materialize). The accountant can conclude that underlying assumptions are suitably supported if the preponderance of information supports each significant assumption (in the case of a projection, given the hypothetical assumption). The reliability of information used in developing the assumptions should be considered. The accountant would be likely to concentrate on those assumptions that are material to the prospective amounts, particularly sensitive to variations, deviations from historical trends, and especially uncertain. An example of a sensitive assumption is the income tax treatment of future transactions. The CPA should weigh the sufficiency of support for assumptions, the consistency of assumptions, the comparability or incomparability of historical data, and the logical arguments or theory.

The CPA's standard report on an examination of prospective financial statements appropriate for use by third parties (adjusted to reflect Statement on Standards for Accountants' Services on Prospective Financial Information, issued October 1985) is as follows:

We have examined the accompanying forecasted/projected balance sheet, statements of income, retained earnings, and changes in financial position of XYZ Company as of December 31, 19XX, and for the year then ending. Our examination was made in accordance with standards for an examination of a forecast/projection established by the American Institute of Certified Public Accountants and, accordingly, included such procedures as we considered necessary to evaluate both the assumptions used by management and the preparation and presentation of the forecast/projection.

In our opinion, the accompanying forecast/projection is presented in conformity with guidelines for presentation of a forecast/projection established by the American Institute of Certified Public Accountants and the underlying assumptions provide a reasonable basis for management's forecast [for a projection, describe the hypothetical assumption, for example, "given the passage of the referendum as described in the summary of significant assumptions"; for a multiple projection, describe hypothetical assumptions, for example, "given the occupancy rates of 60 percent and 80 percent of available apartments as described in the summary of significant assumptions"]. However [for a projection, describe hypothetical assumption, for example, "even if the referendum is passed"; for a multiple projection, describe hypothetical assumptions, for example, "even if the actual occupancy rate achieved is within the range shown"], there will usually be differences between the forecasted/projected and the actual results because events and circumstances frequently do not occur as expected, and those differences may be material. We have no responsibility to update this report for events and circumstances occurring after the date of this report.[16]

Note that the caveat is essential, as many conditions can affect the actual outcome, including (1)

[15] "Proposed Authoritative Statement: Prospective Financial Statements" (AICPA, File Ref. No. 2660, Draft on February 15, 1985); updated to reflect Statement on Standards for Accountants' Services on Prospective Financial Information (New York: AICPA, October 1985).

[16] "Proposed Authoritative Statement: Prospective Financial Statements" (AICPA, File Ref. No. 2660, Draft on February 15, 1985); updated to reflect Statement on Standards for Accountants' Services on Prospective Financial Information (New York: AICPA, October 1985).

realization may depend on the client's intentions, which cannot be reviewed; (2) assumptions are inherently uncertain; (3) there is likely to be contradictory information about some assumptions; and (4) different yet similarly reasonable assumptions can be derived from the same information.

If a CPA believes that one or more significant assumptions do not provide a reasonable basis for presentation, he or she should issue an adverse report.

When using the AICPA guidelines, the CPA must decide whether a forecast is reasonable. One well-known technique used in "futurism research" is called the *Delphi technique.* This approach systematically elicits and compares the opinions of experts who are not known to one another. After each round of eliciting opinions, the experts are told about the others' forecasts, and in light of this additional information, the experts may change their own forecasts. Presumably, a series of "rounds" will lead to a consensus forecast. Alternative means of eliciting such opinions and of analyzing the results are described in existing literature.[17]

Based on current research proposals, forecasts may become more important to accountants. For example, Yuji Ijiri proposed a "triple-entry bookkeeping system" in which the third dimension is a budget or future projection or some measure of the force or rate of change in income accounts.[18]

But a 1981 study of 405 corporate participants found that only 42 companies publicly disclosed their internal forecasts. The respondents indicated their lack of confidence in the forecasts' reliability, their apprehensions of the legal liability for inaccurate forecasts, and the possible adverse effects from disclosure on stock market prices.[19]

Fraud Detection

Although the auditor's examination, based on the selective testing of data, cannot guarantee that material errors or irregularities will be detected, extended testing may be able to find enough evidence to reveal the existence and effects of material errors or irregularities ***[SAS No. 16, Section 327].*** In fact, it is common, when discovering fraud, to ask a CPA firm to investigate in order to determine the effect of the fraud and to prepare revised financial statements.

When a fraud is expected, auditors perform *threat analysis*, which means that they examine what assets are held and how those assets can be taken. Then, the auditors strive to "outsmart the crooks." In a fraud situation, there is often no audit trail, as the records have been destroyed, are inadequate, have been misstated, or have been intentionally altered. Thus, auditors must often reconstruct the flow of accounting numbers and assets.

One audit technique that can help find the people involved in the fraud is inquiry. By asking questions whose answers the auditor already knows, he or she can ascertain the interviewee's truthfulness and desire to cooperate. In a fraud investigation, auditors may actually create errors to see whether they can travel through the control system, in the hopes that the way the fraud was perpetrated can be found. The entire approach to fraud auditing is detailed in nature, due to the necessity of finding that which has been intentionally hidden.

Levels of Assurance

As discussed in earlier chapters, numerous levels of assurance are currently being provided by CPAs. An example of a recent request received by CPAs from creditors is to issue a letter providing some assurance as to the solvency of the prospective borrower. To date, this demand is limited to a subset of borrowers with financial statements that raise some valuation issues as to whether net worth is positive or negative. Another recent type of as-

[17] See also Robert E. Jensen, "Reporting of Management Forecasts: An Eigenvector Model for Elicitation and Review of Forecasts," *Decision Sciences*, January 1982, pp. 15–37; and Robert E. Jensen, "Rosy Scenarios: Scaling and Analysis of Cross-Impacts of Assumptions of Financial Forecasts and Performance," monograph (Sarasota, Fla.: American Accounting Association, 1983).

[18] Yuji Ijiri, "Triple-Entry Bookkeeping and Income Momentum," Studies in Accounting Research #18 (Sarasota, Fla.: American Accounting Association, 1982).

[19] Frances A. Lees, *Public Disclosure of Corporate Earnings Forecasts* (New York: Conference Board, 1981), p. 3.

surance requested of CPAs is an expression of an opinion as to what various computer software packages are capable of analyzing. Little doubt exists that CPAs will be asked to offer widely divergent levels of assurance as to both financial and nonfinancial attributes of clients.

Formulation of Estimates for Tax Purposes

CPAs offer a wide variety of tax services, including assistance in formulating estimates for tax purposes. All accruals for income taxes are to be appropriately documented. Because of the IRS's efforts to gain access to tax accrual work papers, some clients have restricted their auditors' access to tax-planning documentation or have asked them not to keep copies of the work papers. The former is a restriction of scope and must be evaluated in terms of its effects on the sufficiency of the audit evidence, but the latter is permitted, provided that there is enough memoranda evidence to form an opinion. Some clients have even suggested that they give their legal counsel or tax counsel tax contingency information and ask him or her to give the auditor an opinion on the adequacy of the tax accrual. But because an audit of income tax accounts combines tax expertise and knowledge of the client's business, reliance on only such a legal opinion is not appropriate.

Due to the nature of income tax accruals, CPAs are sometimes asked to report on the adequacy of a provision for income taxes ***[SAS 14, Section 621]***. This type of service is encompassed in the CPA's ability, under GAAS, to report on specified elements, accounts, or items of a financial statement. Although this reporting function may be accepted as a separate engagement for most items, an opinion on the adequacy of tax provisions can be issued only in conjunction with an examination of financial statements. However, if an adverse opinion or disclaimer is issued on financial statements, only specified items that do not constitute a major amount of the financials can be covered by a special report. To guard against issuing what may appear as a piecemeal opinion, such special reports must not accompany the entity's financials. Because the auditor expresses an opinion on the specified items, he or she should measure their materiality in relation to these items rather than to the financial statements taken as a whole. For that reason, the examination of such items is typically more extensive than in an audit engagement. An example of a report on the adequacy of a provision for income taxes is as follows:

Board of Directors
ABC Company, Inc.

We have examined the financial statements of ABC Company, Inc., for the year ended June 30, 19X6, and have issued our report thereon dated August 15, 19X6. Our examination was made in accordance with generally accepted auditing standards and, accordingly, included such other auditing procedures as we considered necessary in the circumstances.

In the course of our examination, we examined the provision for federal and state income taxes for the year ended June 30, 19X6, included in the company's financial statements referred to in the preceding paragraph. We also reviewed the federal and state income tax returns filed by the company that are subject to examination by the respective taxing authorities.

In our opinion, the company has paid or has provided adequate accruals in the financial statements referred to above for the payment of all federal and state income taxes and has provided for related deferred income taxes, applicable to fiscal 19X6 and prior fiscal years, that could be reasonably estimated at the time of our examination of the financial statements of ABC Company, Inc., for the year ended June 30, 19X6.[20]

Overview

Limited assurance engagements are often based on auditing knowledge and review procedures. Some services involve agreed-upon procedures at the discretion of either the user or the auditor. Certain engagements do not presume prior audit knowledge and prescribe specific steps to meet generally accepted standards. The communication devices used range from disclaimers with implicit negative assurance, to positive opinions. Reports of findings and exception reporting are common, often accompanied by a disclaimer. The report forms sometimes have a restricted distribution (for example, comfort letters and the application of agreed-

[20] SAS No. 14, "Special Reports" (New York: AICPA, December 1976).

upon procedures to either specific accounts [see SAS 35] or the financial statements as a whole [see SAS 26]). These are the circumstances in which detailed descriptions of the procedures applied are required. The emphasis is on the engagement's reporting limitations, including a scope smaller than that of the audit function, the possibility of the scope's not being sufficient to meet the users' needs, the inherent limitations of the control systems, the fact that audits are not directed at finding noncompliance with contracts or regulations, and the expectation that the actual results will differ from the forecasts.

The auditor's attest function is continually being extended. An example cited earlier is accountants' reports on computer software. These reports typically indicate that the software was reviewed and tested to determine that certain aspects of the system are accurate and conform to existing guidelines in engineering, statistics, tax, or accounting. The procedures performed tend to be presented in some detail in the report, which bears a specific date indicating that the opinion refers to a single point in time when the testing was carried out. The users are often advised that reports do not constitute warranties, have no applicability to future needs or revisions, and should be evaluated along with other factors affecting software selection in a particular business situation. Opinions are frequently accompanied by a supplemental report describing the software package under review.

"Subject to" reports regarding limitations of packages have been observed, as have reports which acknowledge that consistency with certain laws does not necessarily mean that a package is complete in meeting legal and regulatory needs.

In approaching such limited assurance engagements and others which are likely to evolve over time, accountants should carefully consider:

- required expertise.
- extent of reliance on outside specialists.
- ability to relate reports to existing authoritative standards in various areas.
- freedom from bias.
- independence issues.
- the ability to clearly communicate information and related responsibility to user groups.

Appendix

Exhibit 17-A presents the audit standards of the General Accounting Office.

REVIEW QUESTIONS

1. What is the CPA's responsibility for unaudited financial statements?

2. What is the Big GAAP–Little GAAP controversy? How did it affect the services offered by CPAs?

3. What are the differences between compilation and review services? Can a CPA who lacks independence perform such services? How does the compilation service differ from an association with unaudited financial statements?

4. How does a review engagement differ from an audit?

5. What are the acceptable "comprehensive bases of accounting," other than GAAP, on which a CPA may express an opinion? How must the auditor's report be altered for such a reporting basis?

6. What types of special reports cannot be issued separately if an audit has not been performed?

7. What is a comfort letter?

8. What types of special reports on compliance are commonly requested of CPAs? Which type of compliance report is a CPA forbidden to issue?

9. What is operational auditing? What is the recommended report form for operational audits? What are an exit conference and its objective?

10. What are the various types of internal accounting control reports that can be issued? How do the scopes that underlie these reports differ?

11. Explain how a comprehensive review engagement is performed.

12. What is a service organization?

13. Give an historical account of the proposals, pronouncements, and regulations that have affected internal accounting control since 1977.

14. What are the past and present attitudes toward forecasts in prospectuses and the accountants' association with such forecasts?

15. What are an accountant's major considerations when performing compilation services on prospective financial statements?

16. What are the differences between forecasts and projections?

17. What assurances can be provided by an examination of prospective financial statements that do not result from a compilation service?

18. On which assumptions that underlie a set of prospective financial statements should the examination of these statements concentrate?

EXHIBIT 17-A

Standards for Audit of Governmental Organizations, Programs, Activities, and Functions

Introduction

Purpose

This statement contains a body of audit standards that are intended for application to audits of all government organizations, programs, activities, and functions—whether they are performed by auditors employed by Federal, State, or local governments; independent public accountants; or others qualified to perform parts of the audit work contemplated under these standards. These standards are also intended to apply to both internal audits and audits of contractors, grantees, and other external organizations performed by or for a governmental entity. These audit standards relate to the scope and quality of audit effort and to the characteristics of a professional and meaningful audit report.

The American Institute of Certified Public Accountants (AICPA) has adopted standards and procedures that are applicable to audits performed to express opinions on the fairness with which financial statements present the financial position and results of operations.* These standards are generally accepted for such audits and have been incorporated into this statement. However, the interests of many users of reports on government audits are broader than those that can be satisfied by audits performed to establish the credibility of financial reports. To provide for audits that will fulfill these broader interests, the standards in this statement include the essence of those prescribed by the American Institute of Certified Public Accountants and additional standards for audits of a broader scope as will be explained subsequently.

Scope

A fundamental tenet of a democratic society holds that governments and agencies entrusted with public resources and the authority for applying them have a responsibility to render a full accounting of their activities. This accountability is inherent in the governmental process and is not always specifically identified by legislative provision. This governmental accountability should identify not only the objects for which the public resources have been devoted but also the manner and effect of their application.

This concept of accountability is woven into the basic premises supporting these standards. These standards provide for a scope of audit that includes not only financial and compliance auditing but also auditing for economy, efficiency, and achievement of desired results. Provision for such a scope of audit is not intended to imply that all audits are presently being conducted this way or that such an extensive scope is always desirable. However, an audit that would include provision for the interests of all potential users of government audits would ordinarily include provision for auditing all the above elements of the accountability of the responsible officials.

Definitions of the three elements of such an audit follow.

1. Financial and compliance—determines (a) whether financial operations are properly conducted, (b) whether the financial reports of an audited entity are presented fairly, and (c) whether the entity has complied with applicable laws and regulations.

2. Economy and efficiency—determines whether the entity is managing or utilizing its resources (personnel, property, space, and so forth) in an economical and efficient manner and the causes of any inefficiencies or uneconomical practices, including inadequacies in management information systems, administrative procedures, or organizational structure.

3. Program results—determines whether the desired results or benefits are being achieved, whether the objectives established by the legislature or other authorizing body are being met, and whether the agency has considered alternatives which might yield desired results at a lower cost.

The audit standards are intended to be more than the mere codification of current practices, tailored to existing audit capabilities. Purposely forward-looking, these standards include some concepts and areas of audit coverage which are still evolving in practice but which are vital to the accountability objectives sought in the audit of governments and of intergovernmental programs. Therefore the audit standards have been structured so that each of the three elements of audit can be performed separately if this is deemed desirable.

It should be recognized that a concurrent audit of all three parts would probably be the most economical manner of audit, but often this may not be practical. Furthermore, it may not be practical or necessary to perform all three elements of the audit in particular circumstances. For most government programs or activities, however, the interests of many potential government users will not be satisfied unless all three elements are performed.

In memoranda of engagements between governments and independent public accountants or other audit organizations, the arrangement should specifically identify whether all, or specifically which, of the three elements of the audit are to be conducted. Such agreements are needed to ensure that the scope of audit to be made is understood by all concerned.

EXHIBIT 17-A (continued)

Basic Premises

The following certain basic premises underlie these standards and were considered in their development.

1. The term "audit" is used to describe not only work done by accountants in examining financial reports but also work done in reviewing (a) compliance with applicable laws and regulations, (b) efficiency and economy of operations, and (c) effectiveness in achieving program results.

2. Public office carries with it the responsibility to apply resources in an efficient, economical, and effective manner to achieve the purposes for which the resources were furnished. This responsibility applies to all resources, whether entrusted to the public officials by their own constituency or by other levels of government.

3. A public official is accountable to those who provide the resources he uses to carry out governmental programs. He is accountable both to other levels of government for the resources such levels have provided and to the electorate, the ultimate source of all governmental funds. Consequently he should be providing appropriate reports to those to whom he is accountable. Unless legal restrictions or other valid reasons prevent him from doing so, the auditor should make the results of audits available to other levels of government that have supplied resources and to the electorate.

4. Auditing is an important part of the accountability process since it provides independent judgments of the credibility of public officials' statements about the manner in which they have carried out their responsibilities. Auditing also can help decisionmakers improve the efficiency, economy, and effectiveness of governmental operations by identifying where improvements are needed.

5. The interests of individual governments in many financially assisted programs often cannot be isolated because the resources applied have been commingled. Different levels of government share common interests in many programs. Therefore, an audit should be designed to satisfy both the common and discrete accountability interests of each contributing government.

6. Cooperation by Federal, State, and local governments in auditing programs of common interest with a minimum of duplication is of mutual benefit to all concerned and is a practical method of auditing intergovernmental operations.

7. Auditors may rely upon the work of auditors at other levels of government if they satisfy themselves as to the other auditors' capabilities by appropriate tests of their work or by other acceptable methods.

An inherent assumption that underlies all the standards is that governments will cooperate in making audits in which they have mutual interests. For many programs that are federally assisted, it would be neither practical nor economical to have every auditor at every level of government do his own background research on the laws, regulations, objectives, and goals of his segment of the program. Therefore, to provide the auditor with the necessary background information and to guide his judgment in the application of the accompanying standards, Federal or State agencies that request State, local, or other levels to make audits are expected to prepare broad, comprehensive audit instructions, tailored to particular programs or program areas.

The content of such audit guidance should include a digest of, or as a minimum, citations to applicable statutes, regulations, instructions, manuals, grant agreements, and other program documents; identification of specific audit objectives and reporting requirements in terms of matters of primary interest in such areas as program compliance, economy, and effectiveness; and other audit guidelines covering specific areas in which the auditor is expected to perform.

General Standards

1. The full scope of an audit of a governmental program, function, activity, or organization should encompass:

   a. An examination of financial transactions, accounts, and reports, including an evaluation of compliance with applicable laws and regulations.

   b. A review of efficiency and economy in the use of resources.

   c. A review to determine whether desired results are effectively achieved.

   In determining the scope for a particular audit, responsible officials should give consideration to the needs of the potential users of the results of that audit.

2. The auditors assigned to perform the audit must collectively possess adequate professional proficiency for the tasks required.

EXHIBIT 17-A (continued)

3. In all matters relating to the audit work, the audit organization and the individual auditors shall maintain an independent attitude.

4. Due professional care is to be used in conducting the audit and in preparing related reports.

Examination and Evaluation Standards

1. Work is to be adequately planned.

2. Assistants are to be properly supervised.

3. A review is to be made of compliance with legal and regulatory requirements.

4. An evaluation is to be made of the system of internal control to assess the extent it can be relied upon to ensure accurate information, to ensure compliance with laws and regulations, and to provide for efficient and effective operations.

5. Sufficient, competent, and relevant evidence is to be obtained to afford a reasonable basis for the auditor's opinions, judgments, conclusions, and recommendations. . . . (Reporting standards are given in Chapter 2.)

Supplemental Standards

1. The auditor shall actively participate in reviewing the design and development of new data-processing systems or applications, and significant modification thereto, as a normal part of the audit function.

2. The auditor shall review general controls in data-processing systems to determine that (A) controls have been designed according to management direction and legal requirements, and (B) such controls are operating effectively to provide reliability of, and security over, the data being processed.

3. The auditor shall review application controls of installed data-processing applications to assess their reliability in processing data in a timely, accurate, and complete manner.

From Comptroller General of the United States, Standards for Audit of Governmental Organizations, Programs, Activities, and Functions (Washington, D.C.: U.S. General Accounting Office, 1972).

*The basic standards are included in "Statements on Auditing Standards," issued by the American Institute of Certified Public Accountants.

19. What is the Delphi Technique? How can it be useful to a CPA when examining prospective financial statements?
20. What is triple-entry bookkeeping?
21. What does a CPA do to detect fraud?
22. What kinds of assurances have been requested of CPAs in the marketplace?
23. How have clients dealt with the Internal Revenue Service's trying to get access to tax accrual work papers? How can the CPA prevent such actions?
24. How does a report on specified elements, accounts, or items consider materiality? Under what circumstances can such a report not be issued as the result of a separate engagement?

EXERCISES

1. If the same CPA were engaged to perform an audit and a comprehensive review of internal accounting controls, how could the client save money?
2. SSARS No. 1's encouraging CPAs to issue engagement letters that clearly state the inability of compilation and review services to be relied on for the disclosure of errors and irregularities or illegal acts has been criticized as being deceptive and leading to a false hope of decreased liability exposure. Do you believe that this criticism is valid? Why or why not?
3. For years, Arthur Andersen & Co. worded its audit

opinions as "present fairly . . . and were prepared in conformity with generally accepted accounting principles."[21] Why is such wording significant?

4. The literature has suggested that a serious problem with publishing forecasts is the unwarranted credibility likely to be attached to them. In addition, should previously issued forecasts be revised from time to time as the year passes? Because of liability considerations, many believe that forecasts issued to the public by entities are likely to be more conservative than warranted. Such fears are encouraged by the experience of Monsanto, one of the first entities to make its forecast public. When the forecast was not achieved, Monsanto was sued. Although the company was able to demonstrate the reasonableness of its approach to the forecast and did win the case, its experience in no way encouraged other entities' experimentation.
   - **a.** How valid are the concerns expressed in past literature with regard to publicly available forecasts? What has been done to deter such apprehensions?
   - **b.** Some have suggested that CPAs give information to the public about the company's forecasting performance; that is, how did past forecasts compare with the actual results? Do you believe such disclosure is advisable? Support your response with the professional literature and your understanding of the nature of CPAs' professional services.

QUESTIONS ADAPTED FROM PROFESSIONAL EXAMINATIONS

1. A supervisory auditor is reviewing the audit report of the team that made an internal audit of the company printshop. A paragraph of the report states:

   We have reviewed the printshop's charges to user departments and find that these charges do not adequately cover costs. We compared the charges for printing jobs with prices on similar jobs from a commercial printer and determined that the printshop's charges are lower. We, therefore, recommend that the printshop charges to user departments be increased.

   After reading the report, the supervisor asked the lead auditor:
   - **a.** Why did you check the charges?
   - **b.** Who sets the amount to be charged?
   - **c.** Who approves the amount?
   - **d.** How much do the charges differ from commercial rates?
   - **e.** What is the effect of the charges on the user departments?
   - **f.** What costs are included in the comparison? (direct, indirect)
   - **g.** How much should the charges be increased?
   - **h.** Does this situation apply to all the printshop output?
   - **i.** Do our departments buy printing from commercial printers?
   - **j.** To whom are you recommending an increase in charges?

   Required:
   - **a.** What are the seven attributes of an unfavorable audit finding?
   - **b.** Write on your answer sheet the letter for each of the supervisor's questions (a to j), and after each letter, indicate the attribute to which the question applies.

   (CIA exam adapted)

2. An internal auditor is preparing for an exit conference. The auditee manager has been very defensive, has refused to participate in the interim discussions of findings, has discouraged discussions with lower-level supervisors, and has cooperated as little as possible during the audit.

   Below are ten statements pertaining to the auditor's actions in conducting and controlling the exit conference.
   - **a.** You should invite the manager's subordinate supervisors to attend the exit conference.
   - **b.** You should adopt the manager's firm attitude in order to impress him or her.
   - **c.** The conference should be conducted in such a manner that the manager will be discouraged from injecting his opinions.
   - **d.** If you and the manager do not agree on the audit report language, ask him or her to suggest a revision.
   - **e.** Ask the manager if he or she would like to provide written comments for inclusion in the audit report.
   - **f.** Ask the manager if there are any areas that he or she would like you to audit as an extension of the field work.
   - **g.** Orally present the audit findings in the least offensive manner so as to create no waves, even

[21] Geraldine F. Dominiak and Joseph G. Louderback III, "'Present Fairly' and Generally Accepted Accounting Principles," *CPA Journal*, January 1972, p. 46; the authors cite the Carrier Corporation's annual reports from 1953 through 1958 as an example.

though the findings may be presented more forcefully in the report.

h. If the manager suggests another area of audit, tell him or her that your report will specify the audit as being done at his or her suggestion.

i. To overcome the manager's anticipated strong antagonism, point out findings that management omitted.

j. Tell the manager that any corrective measures taken to resolve the audit findings should be cleared with you.

Required:
List the identifying letter of each of these actions that would hinder rather than help the auditor–auditee relations. Explain why you selected each response.

(CIA exam adapted)

3. The limitations on the CPA's professional responsibilities when he or she is associated with unaudited financial statements are often misunderstood. But these misunderstandings can be substantially reduced by carefully following professional pronouncements in his or her work and taking other appropriate measures.

Required:
The following list describes seven situations the CPA may encounter or contentions he or she may have to deal with in his or her association with and preparation of unaudited financial statements. Briefly discuss the extent of the CPA's responsibilities and, if appropriate, the actions he or she should take to minimize any misunderstandings. Label your answers according to the letters in the list.

a. The CPA was engaged by telephone to perform write-up work, including the preparation of financial statements. His or her client believes that the CPA has been engaged to audit the financial statements and examine the records accordingly.

b. A group of businessmen who own a farm managed by an independent agent engages a CPA to prepare quarterly unaudited financial statements. The CPA prepares the financial statements from information given to him or her by the independent agent. Subsequently, the businessmen find the statements to be inaccurate because their independent agent was embezzling funds. The businessmen refuse to pay the CPA and blame him or her for not detecting the situation, contending that he or she should not have relied on representations from the independent agent.

c. In comparing the trial balance with the general ledger, the CPA finds an account labeled "audit fees" in which the client has accumulated the CPA's quarterly billings for accounting services, including the preparation of quarterly unaudited financial statements.

d. Unaudited financial statements were accompanied by the following letter of transmittal from the CPA:

> We are enclosing your company's balance sheet as of June 30, 19X6, and the related statements of income and retained earnings and changes in financial position for the six months then ended which we have reviewed.

e. To determine appropriate account classification, the CPA reviewed a number of the client's invoices. The CPA noted in the working papers that some invoices were missing but did nothing else because he or she felt they did not affect the unaudited financial statements he or she was preparing. When the client subsequently discovered that the invoices were missing, the client contended that the CPA should not have ignored the missing invoices when preparing the financial statements and had a responsibility to at least inform the client that they were missing.

f. The CPA has prepared a draft of unaudited financial statements from the client's records. While reviewing this draft with his or her client, the CPA learns that the land and building were recorded at appraisal value.

g. The CPA is engaged to review without audit the financial statements prepared by the client's controller. During this review, the CPA learns of several items that according to generally accepted accounting principles require adjustment of the statements and footnote disclosure. The controller agrees to make the recommended adjustments to the statements but says that he or she is not going to add the footnotes because the statements have not been audited.

(CPA exam adapted)

4. Loman, a CPA, who has examined the financial statements of the Broadwall Corporation, a publicly held company, for the year ended December 31, 19X6, was asked to perform a limited review of the financial statements of the Broadwall Corporation for the period ending March 31, 19X6. The engagement letter stated that a limited review does not provide a basis for the expression of an opinion.

Required:

a. Explain why Loman's limited review will not provide a basis for the expression of an opinion.

b. What are the review procedures that Loman should use, and what is the purpose of each? Include in your response a list of procedures and a list of the purposes of the procedures.

(CPA exam adapted)

5. On January 11, 19X7, at the beginning of your annual audit of the Grover Manufacturing Company's financial statements for the year ended December 31, 19X6, the company president confides in you that an employee is living on a scale in excess of that which his salary would support.

The employee has been a buyer in the purchasing department for six years and has charge of purchasing all general materials and supplies. He is authorized to sign purchase orders for amounts up to $200. Purchase orders in excess of $200 require the countersignature of the general purchasing agent.

The president understands that the usual examination of financial statements is not designed, and cannot be relied on, to disclose fraud or conflicts of interest, although their discovery may result. The President authorizes you, however, to expand your regular audit procedures and to apply additional audit procedures to determine whether there is any evidence that the buyer has been misappropriating company funds or has been engaged in activities that are a conflict of interests.

Required:

a. List the audit procedures that you would apply to the company records and documents in an attempt to

1. Discover evidence within the purchasing department of defalcations being committed by the buyer. Give the purpose of each audit procedure.

2. Provide leads as to possible collusion between the buyer and suppliers. Give the purpose of each audit procedure.

b. Assume that your investigation disclosed that some suppliers have been charging the Grover Manufacturing Company more than their usual prices and apparently have been making kickbacks to the buyer. The excess charges are material in amount. What effect, if any, would the defalcation have on (1) the financial statements prepared before the defalcation was uncovered and (2) your auditor's report?

(CPA exam adapted)

6. The Generous Loan Company has one hundred branch loan offices. Each office has a manager and four or five subordinates who are employed by the manager. Branch managers prepare the weekly payroll, including their own salaries, and pay employees from cash on hand. The employee signs the payroll sheet signifying the receipt of his or her salary. Hours worked by hourly personnel are inserted in the payroll sheet from time cards prepared by the employees and approved by the manager.

The weekly payroll sheets are sent to the home office along with other accounting statements and reports. The home office compiles employee earnings records and prepares all federal and state salary reports from the weekly payroll sheets.

Salaries are established by home office job-evaluation schedules. Salary adjustments, promotions, and transfers of full-time employees are approved by a home office salary committee based on the recommendations of the branch managers and area supervisors. Branch managers advise the salary committee of new full-time employees and terminations. Part-time and temporary employees are hired without referral to the salary committee.

Required:

a. Based on your review of the payroll system, how could the funds for payroll be diverted?

b. Prepare a payroll audit program that the home office could use to audit the branch office payrolls of the Generous Loan Company.

(CPA exam adapted)

7. When you arrive at your client's office on January 11, 19X7, to begin the December 31, 19X6, audit, you discover that the client has been drawing checks as creditors' invoices became due but not necessarily mailing them. Because of a working capital shortage, some checks may have been held for two or three weeks.

The client informs you that unmailed checks totaling $27,600 were on hand at December 31, 19X6. He states that these December-dated checks were entered in the cash disbursements book and charged to the respective creditors' accounts in December because the checks were prenumbered. Heavy collections permitted him to mail the checks before your arrival.

The client wants to adjust by $27,600 the cash balance and accounts payable at December 31 because the cash account had a credit balance. He objects to submitting to his bank your audit report showing an overdraft of cash.

Required:

a. Submit a detailed audit program listing the procedures you would use to satisfy yourself of the accuracy of the cash balance on the client's statements.

b. Discuss the propriety of reversing the indicated amount of outstanding checks.

(CPA exam adapted)

8. Describe the audit steps that would generally be

followed in establishing the propriety of the recorded liability for federal income taxes of an established corporation that you are auditing for the first time. You should consider the status of (a) the liability for previous years and (b) the liability arising from the current year's income.

(CPA exam adapted)

9. Jones and Todd, a local CPA firm, received an invitation to bid for the audit of a local, federally assisted program. The audit is to be conducted in accordance with the audit standards published by the General Accounting Office (GAO), a federal auditing agency. Jones and Todd has become familiar with the GAO standards and recognizes that they are not inconsistent with generally accepted auditing standards (GAAS). The GAO standards, unlike GAAS, are concerned with more than the financial aspects of an entity's operations. The GAO standards broaden the definition of auditing by establishing that an audit's full scope should encompass the following elements:

a. An examination of financial transactions, accounts, and reports, including an evaluation of compliance with applicable laws and regulations.

b. A review of efficiency and economy in the use of resources, such as personnel and equipment.

c. A review to determine whether the desired results have been achieved (program results).

Jones and Todd has been engaged to perform the audit of the program, and the audit is to cover all three elements.

Required:

a. Jones and Todd should perform sufficient audit work to satisfy the financial and compliance element of the GAO standards. What should such audit work determine?

b. After making appropriate review and inquiries, what uneconomical practices or inefficiencies should Jones and Todd be alert to, in satisfying the efficiency and economy element of the GAO standards?

c. After making appropriate review and inquiries, what should Jones and Todd consider in order to satisfy the program results element of the GAO standards?

(CPA exam adapted)

10. Brown, a CPA, received a telephone call from Calhoun, the sole owner and manager of a small corporation. Calhoun asked Brown to prepare the financial statements for the corporation and told Brown that the statements were needed in two weeks for external financing purposes. Calhoun was vague when Brown inquired about the intended use of the statements. Brown was convinced that Calhoun thought Brown's work would constitute an audit. To avoid confusion, Brown decided not to explain to Calhoun that the engagement would be only to prepare the financial statements. Brown, with the understanding that a substantial fee would be paid if the work were completed in two weeks, accepted the engagement and started the work at once.

During his work, Brown discovered an accrued expense account labeled "professional fees" and learned that the balance in the account represented an accrual for the cost of Brown's services. Brown suggested to Calhoun's bookkeeper that the account name be changed to "fees for limited audit engagement." Brown also reviewed several invoices to determine whether accounts were being properly classified. Some of the invoices were missing. Brown listed the missing invoice numbers in the working papers with a note indicating that there should be a follow-up on the next engagement. Brown also discovered that the available records included the fixed asset values at estimated current replacement costs. Based on the records available, Brown prepared a balance sheet, income statement, and statement of stockholders' equity. In addition, Brown drafted the footnotes but decided that any mention of the replacement costs would only mislead the readers. Brown suggested to Calhoun that readers of the financial statements would be better informed if they received a separate letter from Calhoun explaining the meaning and effect of the estimated replacement costs of the fixed assets. Brown mailed the financial statements and footnotes to Calhoun with the following note included on each page:

The accompanying financial statements are submitted to you without complete audit verification.

Required:

Explain what Brown did wrong and what he should have done to avoid each inappropriate action.

Organize your answer sheet as follows:

Inappropriate Action	What Brown Should Have Done to Avoid Inappropriate Action

(CPA exam adapted)

11. The following is part of an interim internal audit report:

Subject: Controls over the Billing of Charges for Parts-Repair Work

Current procedures provide for using prenumbered sales order forms and recording sales orders for repairs in manually maintained logs. Those procedures also provide for creating manually serialized shipping documents and recording such shipping documents in the sales order log. Recording the shipping document numbers in the sales order log serves to close the sales order and may give rise to a billing for the repair work (some work is done on a "no-charge" basis).

Our examination of the sales order log disclosed a significant number of sales order numbers unmatched by shipping document numbers for the past two years. As a result, it is not clear whether the repair work performed had been authorized for those orders. Specifically, we found that the sales order logs showed "no entry" for seventy-one (about 18 percent) sales order serial numbers spread randomly over a range of about four hundred serial numbers covering a recent twelve-month period. This indicated that the billing personnel had not received sales orders for, or information about, the disposition of those serial numbers. Further investigation disclosed that fifty of the serial numbers showing "no entry," referred to sales orders that had been voided or referred to billings that had been closed at no charge. In addition, sixteen other serial numbers referred to sales orders that had been issued and were still open. However, we were unable to account for the remaining fifteen serial numbers.

Required:

The internal auditor made several errors in the interim audit report, involving numbers, computations, and logic. Identify three errors made by the internal auditor, and state how you would correct each.

(CIA exam adapted)

12. Current internal auditing literature suggests that internal auditors should recognize and take into account the following attributes when reporting an audit finding requiring corrective action:

a. Criteria—What should be done?
b. Facts—What was wrong?
c. Cause—What created the deficiency?
d. Effect—The potential or actual adverse results and their materiality.
e. Recommendation—The action needed or taken to correct the deficiency.
f. Action—The action taken before the report was issued.

The following ten sentences were selected from an auditor's working papers. Some are relevant to the formulation of an audit finding. The sentences are numbered for ready identification.

(1) After the reconciliations were made, four bank errors that had not been detected for as long as five months were disclosed.
(2) Accounting Procedure 101.1 calls for the General Accounting Department to make monthly reconciliations of all bank accounts.
(3) The bank statements and canceled checks are delivered to General Accounting on the fifth of each month.
(4) We found that the last reconciliation of the payroll account had been made six months before the date of our audit.
(5) The differences between the bank balance and the ledger balances totaled $19,876.
(6) A discovery sample of 437 canceled payroll checks gave us a 94.5 percent assurance that we would have found an improper item, assuming the existence of 25 improper items.
(7) We discussed the matter with the manager of the General Accounting Department, and as a result, he or she issued instructions to have the bank and ledger accounts promptly reconciled.
(8) Before we completed our audit, the accounts were reconciled.
(9) The manager of the General Accounting Department had given a low priority to bank reconciliations.
(10) A senior accounting clerk was made responsible for keeping the reconciliations current.

Required:

You are asked to construct an audit finding that includes all sentences essential to an understanding of the finding but that excludes matters that, though interesting, are not directly relevant. List the sentence numbers 1 to 10 on your answer sheet. After each number, show the letter of the attribute represented by the sentence. If a sentence is irrelevant to the finding, write the letter g after the number.

(CIA exam adapted)

13. Young and Young, CPAs, completed an examination of the financial statements of XYZ Company, Inc., for the year ended June 30, 19X3, and issued a standard unqualified auditor's report dated August 15, 19X3. At the time of the engagement the board of directors of XYZ requested a special report attesting to the adequacy of the provision for federal and state income taxes and the related accruals and deferred income taxes as presented in the June 30, 19X3, financial statements. Young and Young submitted the appropriate special report on August 22, 19X3.

Required:

Prepare the special report that Young and Young should have submitted to XYZ Company, Inc.

(CPA exam adapted)

14. Multiple Choice: Special Reports
Select the one answer that best completes the statement or answers the question.

14.1 A CPA has been engaged to audit financial statements that were prepared on a cash basis. The CPA
a. Must ascertain that there is proper disclosure of the fact that the cash basis was used, the general nature of material items omitted, and the net effect of such omissions.
b. May not be associated with such statements that are not in accordance with generally accepted accounting principles.
c. Must render a qualified report explaining the departure from generally accepted accounting principles in the opinion paragraph.
d. Must restate the financial statements on an accrual basis and then render the standard (short-form) report.
(CPA exam adapted)

14.2 The term *special reports* may include all of the following except reports on financial statements
a. Of an organization that has limited the scope of the auditor's examination.
b. Prepared for limited purposes, such as a report that pertains to only certain aspects of financial statements.
c. Of a not-for-profit organization that follows accounting practices differing in some respects from those followed by business enterprises organized for profit.
d. Prepared in accordance with a cash basis of accounting.
(CPA exam adapted)

14.3 An auditor is reporting on cash-basis financial statements. These statements are best referred to in his or her opinion by which one of the following descriptions?
a. Financial position and results of operations arising from cash transactions.
b. Assets and liabilities arising from cash transactions, and revenue collected and expenses paid.
c. Balance sheet and income statement resulting from cash transactions.
d. Cash balance sheet and the source and application of funds.
(CPA exam adapted)

14.4 Whenever special reports, filed on a printed form designed by the authorities, call on the independent auditor to make an assertion that the auditor believes is not justified, the auditor should
a. Submit a short-form report with explanations.
b. Reword the form or attach a separate report.
c. Submit the form with the questionable items omitted.
d. Withdraw from the engagement.
(CPA exam adapted)

14.5 An auditor's report would be designated as a special report when it is issued in connection with which of the following?
a. Financial statements for an interim period that are subjected to a limited review.
b. Financial statements that are prepared in accordance with a comprehensive basis of accounting other than generally accepted accounting principles.
c. Financial statements that purport to be in accordance with generally accepted accounting principles but do not include a presentation of the statement of changes in financial position.
d. Financial statements that are unaudited and are prepared from a client's accounting records.
(CPA exam adapted)

14.6 Which of the following best describes an auditor's report on supplementary financial statements prepared in accordance with a price-level basis of accounting that has substantial support?
a. A supplementary report.
b. An unaudited report.
c. A report on limited review of financial information.
d. A special purpose report.
(CPA exam adapted)

14.7 Auditors' reports issued in connection with which of the following are generally not considered to be special reports or special purpose reports?
a. Specified elements, accounts, or items of a financial statement.
b. Compliance with aspects of contractual agreements pertaining to audited financial statements.
c. Financial statements prepared in conformity with the price-level basis of accounting.
d. Compiled financial statements prepared

in accordance with appraised liquidation values.

(CPA exam adapted)

14.8 An auditor's report on financial statements that are prepared in accordance with a comprehensive basis of accounting other than generally accepted accounting principles should preferably include all of the following, except

a. Disclosure of the fact that the financial statements are not intended to be presented in conformity with generally accepted accounting principles.

b. An opinion as to whether the use of the disclosed method is appropriate.

c. An opinion as to whether the financial statements are presented fairly in conformity with the basis of accounting described.

d. An opinion as to whether the disclosed basis of accounting has been applied in a manner consistent with that of the preceding period.

(CPA exam adapted)

15. Multiple Choice: Compilations and Review

Select the one answer that best completes the statement or answers the question.

15.1 A report based on a limited review of interim financial statements would include all of the following elements except

a. A statement that an examination was performed in accordance with generally accepted auditing standards.

b. A description of the procedures performed or a reference to procedures described in an engagement letter.

c. A statement that a limited review would not necessarily disclose all matters of significance.

d. An identification of the interim financial information reviewed.

(CPA exam adapted)

15.2 When making a limited review of interim financial information, the auditor's work consists primarily of

a. Studying and evaluating limited amounts of documentation supporting the interim financial information.

b. Scanning and reviewing client-prepared, internal financial statements.

c. Making inquiries and performing analytical procedures concerning significant accounting matters.

d. Confirming and verifying significant account balances at the interim date.

(CPA exam adapted)

15.3 If as a result of a limited review of interim financial information, a CPA concludes that such information does not conform with generally accepted accounting principles, the CPA should

a. Insist that the management ensure that the information conforms with generally accepted accounting principles and, if this is not done, resign from the engagement.

b. Adjust the financial information so that it conforms with generally accepted accounting principles.

c. Prepare a qualified report that refers to the lack of conformity with generally accepted accounting principles.

d. Advise the board of directors of the respects in which the information does not conform with generally accepted accounting principles.

(CPA exam adapted)

15.4 Which of the following procedures is not included in a review engagement of a nonpublic entity?

a. Inquiries of management.

b. Inquiries regarding events subsequent to the balance sheet date.

c. Any procedures designed to identify relationships among data that appear to be unusual.

d. A study and evaluation of internal control.

(CPA exam adapted)

15.5 In performing a compilation of financial statements of a nonpublic entity, the accountant decides that modification of the standard report is not adequate to indicate deficiencies in the financial statements taken as a whole, and the client is not willing to correct the deficiencies. The accountant should therefore

a. Perform a review of the financial statements.

b. Issue a special report.

c. Withdraw from the engagement.

d. Express an adverse audit opinion.

(CPA exam adapted)

15.6 An accountant's compilation report should be dated as of the date of

a. Completion of field work.

b. Completion of the compilation.

c. Transmittal of the compilation report.
d. The latest subsequent event referred to in the notes to the financial statements.
(CPA exam adapted)

15.7 A CPA who is not independent may issue a
a. Review report.
b. Comfort letter.
c. Qualified opinion.
d. Compilation report.
(CPA exam adapted)

15.8 When an auditor performs a review of interim financial statements, which of the following steps would not be a part of the review?
a. Review of computer controls.
b. Inquiry of management.
c. Review of ratios and trends.
d. Reading the minutes of the stockholders' meetings.
(CPA exam adapted)

15.9 During a review of financial statements of a nonpublic entity, the CPA would be least likely to
a. Perform analytical procedures designed to identify relationships that appear to be unusual.
b. Obtain written confirmation from management regarding loans to officers.
c. Obtain reports from other accountants who reviewed a portion of the total entity.
d. Read the financial statements and consider conformance with generally accepted accounting principles.
(CPA exam adapted)

15.10 The objective of a review of interim financial information is to give the CPA a basis for
a. Expressing a limited opinion that the financial information is presented in conformity with generally accepted accounting principles.
b. Expressing a compilation opinion on the financial information.
c. Reporting whether material modifications should be made to such information to make it conform with generally accepted accounting principles.
d. Reporting limited assurance to the board of directors only.
(CPA exam adapted)

15.11 Which one of the following is generally more important in a review than in a compilation?
a. Determining the accounting basis on which the financial statements are to be presented.
b. Gaining familiarity with industry accounting principles and practices.
c. Obtaining a signed engagement letter.
d. Obtaining a signed representation letter.
(CPA exam adapted)

15.12 Each page of the financial statements compiled by an accountant should include a reference such as
a. See accompanying accountant's footnotes.
b. Unaudited, see accountant's disclaimer.
c. See accountant's compilation report.
d. Subject to compilation restrictions.
(CPA exam adapted)

16. Multiple Choice: Reports on Internal Accounting Control and Prospective Statements, and Other Issues

Select the one answer that best completes the statement or answers the question.

16.1 The accountant's report expressing an opinion on an entity's system of internal accounting control should state that the
a. Establishment and maintenance of the system of internal control are the responsibility of management.
b. Objectives of the client's system of internal accounting control are being met.
c. Study and evaluation of the system of internal control were conducted in accordance with generally accepted auditing standards.
d. Inherent limitations of the client's system of internal accounting control were examined.
(CPA exam adapted)

16.2 Under which of the following circumstances could an auditor consider rendering an opinion on pro forma statements that make proposed transactions effective?
a. When the proposed transactions are subject to a definitive agreement among the parties.
b. When the time interval between the date of the financial statements and the consummation of the transactions is relatively long.
c. When certain subsequent events may interfere with the consummation of the transactions.
d. When the pro forma statements include amounts based on financial projections.
(CPA exam adapted)

16.3 Which of the following narrative disclosures appearing in notes to financial statements would an auditor be most likely to consider inappropriate?

a. The related party transaction was consummated on terms no less favorable than those that would have been obtained if the transaction had been with an unrelated party.

b. The accounts of subsidiaries in which the corporation has more than 50 percent ownership are fully consolidated.

c. Legal and other costs associated with the covenant not to compete will be amortized using the straight-line method during the next three years.

d. Minor fluctuations in foreign currency exchange rates are not reflected in the accompanying financial statements.

(CPA exam adapted)

16.4 Which of the following is not an acceptable way of designating that an estimated figure was used in preparing a federal income tax return?

a. State expressly that an amount has been estimated.

b. Use a round amount.

c. Use an amount suggested in a treasury department guideline.

d. Modify the tax preparer's declaration on the return before signing the tax return.

(CPA exam adapted)

16.5 When a CPA is associated with the preparation of forecasts, all of the following should be disclosed except the

a. Sources of information.

b. Character of the work performed by the CPA.

c. Major assumptions in the preparation of the forecasts.

d. Probability of achieving estimates.

(CPA exam adapted)

16.6 Whenever a CPA gives negative assurance, it is based on

a. An absence of nullifying evidence.

b. A presence of substantiating evidence.

c. An objective examination in accordance with generally accepted auditing standards.

d. A judgmental determination in accordance with guidelines promulgated by the AICPA.

(CPA exam adapted)

16.7 When financial statements examined by the independent auditor contain notes captioned "unaudited" or "not covered by the auditor's report," the auditor

a. May refer to these notes in the auditor's report.

b. Has no responsibility with respect to information contained in these notes.

c. Must refer to these notes in the auditor's report.

d. Cannot refer to these notes in the auditor's report.

(CPA exam adapted)

16.8 Which of the following reports indicates the CPA's changing role and calls for an extension of the auditor's attest function?

a. Report on annual comparative financial statements.

b. Report on internal control based on an audit.

c. Report on separate balance sheet of a holding company.

d. Report on balance sheet and statements of income, retained earnings, and changes in financial position prepared from incomplete financial records.

(CPA exam adapted)

16.9 Which of the following must accompany unaudited financial statements prepared by a CPA?

a. Only a disclaimer of opinion.

b. Either a disclaimer of opinion or an adverse opinion.

c. Either a disclaimer of opinion or a qualified opinion.

d. A disclaimer of opinion, an adverse opinion, or a qualified opinion.

(CPA exam adapted)

16.10 Which of the following techniques should the internal auditor use to obtain evidence of inefficiencies pertaining to personality conflicts?

a. Interview employees to obtain their opinions of the productivity of peers.

b. Invite employees to sign and return questionnaires identifying causes of inefficient operations.

c. Discuss possible personality conflicts with the leaders of the informal organizations.

d. Interview selected individuals about the causes of inefficiencies.

e. Ask suspected workers to identify existing intradepartment personality conflicts that cause inefficiencies.

(CIA exam adapted)

16.11 Negative assurance is not permissible in

a. Letters required by security underwriters for data pertinent to SEC registration statements.
b. Reports pertaining to the results of agreed-upon procedures for one or more specified elements, accounts, or items of a financial statement.
c. Reports based on a review engagement.
d. Reports based on an audit of the interim financial statements of a closely held business entity.

(CPA exam adapted)

16.12 When an auditor issues an unqualified opinion on an entity's system of internal accounting control, it implies that the

a. Entity has not violated provisions of the Foreign Corrupt Practices Act.
b. Likelihood of management fraud is minimal.
c. Financial records are sufficiently reliable to permit the preparation of financial statements.
d. Entity's system of internal accounting control is in conformity with criteria established by its audit committee.

(CPA exam adapted)

16.13 A typical objective of an operational audit is for the auditor to

a. Determine whether the financial statements fairly present the entity's operations.
b. Evaluate the feasibility of attaining the entity's operational objectives.
c. Make recommendations for improving performance.
d. Report on the entity's relative success in attaining profit maximization.

(CPA exam adapted)

16.14 The evaluation of audit field work of an operating unit should answer the following questions:

1. Why are the results what they are?
2. How can performance be improved?
3. What results are being achieved?

What is the chronological order in which these questions should be answered?

a. 3-1-2.
b. 1-3-2.
c. 3-2-1.
d. 1-2-3.
e. 2-3-1.

(CIA exam adapted)

16.15 During an audit, independent CPAs are often asked to give informal advice on many diverse questions. This type of service differs from management advisory services in that it is informal and therefore

a. The independent CPA does not make any warranties with respect to the competence of the extemporaneous advice.
b. The independent CPA is not exposed to liability as a consequence of the extemporaneous advice.
c. No presumption should exist that all pertinent facts have been identified and considered.
d. No presumption should exist that the advice will affect the operations of the business enterprise.

(CPA exam adapted)

16.16 A CPA who is associated with the financial statements of a public entity but has not audited or reviewed such statements should

a. Insist that they be audited or reviewed before publication.
b. Read them to determine whether there are obvious material errors.
c. State these facts in the accompanying notes to the financial statements.
d. Issue a compilation report.

(CPA exam adapted)

16.17 An auditor's report on internal accounting control is least likely to be issued as a result of a (an)

a. Audit of the financial statements of a governmental agency.
b. Review of the annual financial statements of a large corporation.
c. Special study of a proposed system of internal accounting control.
d. Special study of related-party transactions.

(CPA exam adapted)

16.18 Governmental auditing often extends beyond examinations leading to the expression of opinion on the fairness of financial presentation and includes audits of efficiency, effectiveness, and

a. Internal control.
b. Evaluation.
c. Accuracy.
d. Compliance.

(CPA exam adapted)

16.19 An auditor's report on internal control of a publicly held company would ordinarily be of least use to

a. Shareholders.

b. Officers.
c. Directors.
d. Regulatory agencies.

(CPA exam adapted)

16.20 The accountant's report expressing an opinion on an entity's system of internal accounting control would not include a
a. Description of the engagement's scope.
b. Specific date that the report covers, rather than a period of time.
c. Brief explanation of the broad objectives and inherent limitations of internal accounting control.
d. Statement that the entity's system of internal accounting control is consistent with that of the previous year after subsequent changes are made effective.

(CPA exam adapted)

CASES FOR DISCUSSION

1. The Securities and Exchange Commission issued a proposal in April 1979 to require a statement from management on its internal accounting control. But on June 6, 1980, the SEC withdrew its proposal, stating that at a later date it would monitor voluntary disclosure practices and reassess the need for required reports on control. I wrote an article entitled "Internal Control Reporting—950 Negative Responses" about those who opposed the proposed requirement, and it appeared in *The CPA Journal* (January 1981, pp. 33–38). A few excerpts follow:

The purpose of this article is to provide evidence of primary flaws in the SEC's analysis of the value of internal accounting control disclosures and consequent problems with the SEC's expectations and proposed means of monitoring "private-sector initiatives for public reporting on internal accounting control." Literature citations, market evidence, and survey findings provide support for the critique.

Reliable Financial Statements in Spite of Inadequate Control

In the SEC's 1979 proposal, the Commission states: "An effective system of internal accounting control has always been necessary to produce reliable financial statements," and the Withdrawal reiterates this assertion.

While difficult to evaluate with such ambiguous language as "effective," "necessary" and "reliable," these statements seem to contradict the accounting and auditing literature. It is widely recognized that a clean audit report can be issued to a company with a poor internal control system.

It should be understood that when an auditor gives a certificate on the financial statements of a company, he is not necessarily endorsing, or completely satisfied with, the system of internal check and control he finds in effect. He has to take it as he finds it for the current examination, and determine how far it should influence the scope and extent thereof.[22]

While influencing the risk of the auditor, a poor control system will be compensated for through substantive tests to assure that the auditor has the evidential base required to attest to financial statement reliability.

The ability of auditors to compensate for poor controls is supported by the infrequency of audit opinions which are qualified due to problems involving internal accounting control systems. A review of the *Disclosure Journal* indicates that out of all the filings with the SEC, including disclaimers and qualified opinions by auditors, less than ten companies annually have inadequacies in the internal control system which influence the audit opinion. The SEC Proposal and Withdrawal overstate the "need" for control reports when they claim such controls are essential for reliable financial statements. Further, due to the judgment involved in selecting reporting practices which can significantly affect financial statement reliability, the mere existence of an adequate control system does not preclude the preparation of unreliable financial reporting.

Evidence Is Available on Costs and Benefits

The SEC in its Withdrawal refers to the costs and benefits "asserted" by commentators and points to its intention to evaluate voluntary efforts of registrants to engage independent auditors to examine and publicly report on their system of internal accounting control as a basis for evaluating the actual costs of such examinations. The inference that only assertions as to the cost/benefit tradeoffs exist ignores the ability to measure such cost and benefits by observing the current market equilibrium and the current demand for and related costs of providing internal control reports to commercial lending officers and private placement debt officers.

It is an empirical fact that market forces have led to accountants' reports on internal control in only two companies' annual reports: J. P. Morgan & Co., Incorporated, and Bankers Trust New York Corporation. This indicates that auditors can furnish these reports but there is little market demand for them. The existence of only two such public disclosures reflects consumers' cost-based valuation of internal control reports.

Even stronger support for the low valuation of auditors' reports on internal control is provided by the fact that commercial lending officers and private placement analysts, in a position to demand internal control reports without the inclusion of such information in annual reports, rarely require them (based on interview and survey evidence collected by the author). Even management letters, normally available to managers and potentially available to such third parties at nominal or no cost to the borrowers, are rarely

[22] Walter A. Staub, *Auditing Developments During the Present Century* (Cambridge, Mass.: Harvard University Press, 1942).

requested. Based on discussions with loan officers, they are only requested from small to medium-sized companies considered high-risk investment prospects, and the reports are then only useful in raising the right questions. Most officers state that the report would be meaningless without direct access to management to discuss the issues addressed in the management letters.

A direct measure of demand for internal control related information is available from the examination of bonding indentures and covenants. Since companies are rewarded for contracting to supply information for monitoring bonding covenants at the times of entering into covenants, i.e., by being able to sell the securities at higher prices with the convenants than without them, the companies have incentives to fill information requests by third parties and to provide the most useful means of monitoring their performance to third parties. Yet, the required types of reports specified in bond covenants do not include management letters or other internal accounting control reports.

[Certain relevant cost factors related to public reporting on controls have not been considered. Can the following assumptions be expected to hold and are they valid?]

- Management should be placed in a defensive position when not correcting material weaknesses, i.e., it is desirable to pressure management to implement controls to correct cited "material weaknesses";
- Some benefit is derived from the implied "bad information" that material weaknesses exist in the internal control system;
- A description of a material weakness can be understood without thorough knowledge of the internal accounting control system of the entity;
- Users will comprehend that a material weakness does not translate to a probable loss;
- Such reported weaknesses cannot be utilized to "rip-off" resources;
- Significant competitive disadvantages will not result;
- Users comprehend auditors' current responsibility, particularly the absence of a cost/benefit analysis of controls; and
- There is a significant problem with weaknesses in the control systems of corporations and this information is of value.

If any one of these assumptions is in error, extensive "misinformation" will be communicated through public reporting of material weaknesses. The third and fourth points may well be the most critical.

The risk exposure due to a given control weakness is a judgment which may differ across business managers and across auditors. There are even cases where a material weakness is also a material strength to a control system. The classic example is in the owner-managed company where owner participation replaces numerous controls involving segregation of duties in larger entities. Yet from a creditor's perspective, the dependence primarily on the owner can be an extremely risky proposition. In the auditing literature, decisions that are matters of judgment are rarely described because of the professional expertise and information required to evaluate the circumstances. Ordinarily, an opinion is "better left unexplained." For instance, when an auditor lacks independence, he simply states that fact, not explaining, for example, that the lack of independence is based on his wife's ownership of five percent of the client's stock. Such an explanation could confuse the user, implying that he should reassess whether the auditor is indeed lacking independence. A measure of overall system adequacy or risk exposure appears to be a superior means of discussing internal controls when compared with the proposed alternative of listing material weaknesses, which implies users have some basis for evaluating the importance of the individual weaknesses.

A survey by the author in 1979 indicates there is substantial diversity in the interpretation of the effect of internal control points on report users' assessment of management. This observed diversity suggests that the report form of a management letter or a listing of material weaknesses alone is inadequate to provide a basis for evaluation of a company's management. The respondents noted that it was impossible to evaluate the internal control points without knowing more about the company and the context of the control suggestion.

Similarly, description of the means of evaluating internal accounting controls implies that the user of the report can meaningfully incorporate such information in an investment decision. Yet, without in-depth knowledge of an entity, evaluating the appropriateness of a review technique is extremely difficult. The disclosure of the basis for the management opinion, suggested in the original SEC proposal and in the Withdrawal statement, will likely be uninformative and its effect will be much like an advertising marketing reaction: what "sounds" best. For example, if one company has a periodic inventory system with six spot-checks a year, while another firm has a perpetual inventory system but poor control over the accessibility of inventory, which firm's description of the approach to controlling inventory is preferred? If one firm follows "common industry practices" while another "unlike other companies in this industry . . ." adopts a unique control or approach to controls, how can this be evaluated? To give an adequate description of internal control, the length of disclosures would be excessive. To give less, particularly with *some* description, is misleading in the inference that "information" is being made available; data perhaps, but certainly not *information*.

The questionable information content of proposed disclosures is supported empirically by a survey (reported in the *Financial Analysts Journal*, May–June 1980) of 112 Chartered Financial Analysts, 60 to 70 percent of whom believed that a report on internal accounting controls could not lead

> to valid inferences about the quality of management, the likelihood of embezzlement or other impropriety, the reliability of audited financial statements (in addition to the auditor's opinion), the reliability of unaudited financial information or compliance with the FCPA (p. 79—Survey by Holzmann).

In light of such questionable benefits, the costs related to internal control regulation of registrants would be expected to affect the capital formation process by encouraging more private debt placements.

An investigation of financial disclosure in a competitive economy indicates that disclosures interfering with management's legitimate right to make decisions (in this case, the selection of internal control policies), should be viewed as "disfunctional" and as having a harmful effect on capital formation. In addition, the disclosure of material weaknesses in control systems can have a competitive impact. Despite the problems with such reports in terms of information content, some users will evaluate such disclosures as "bad news" and reallocate resources. Further, there is some possibility that the information will be used to "beat the control system" of the entity, and thereby "rip-off" assets of a company which otherwise were adequately safeguarded. Some "trade secrets" may be disseminated in control related disclosures.

The application of the ruling to all companies will clearly alter the relative wealth positions of small and large ones as well as those in industries with differing control practices. Business conditions can be expected to lead to adequate controls for large companies, with those businesses with very liquid assets necessarily having more extensive control systems. Hence, the relative costs of conforming with regulations are not uniform across companies. Competitive disadvantages from financial disclosure are possible when the costs of disclosure fall unevenly on competing companies. Consideration should be given to the cumulative costs to the company (of disclosure) as well as to the effects of disclosure on hardship cases which may be so severe as to imperil some companies' survival.

What are the arguments made in these passages? What counterarguments can you suggest? What do you think about the SEC's requiring management reports on internal accounting control? Explain your answer.

2. A survey of various users and producers of financial reports to find out what form of report on internal accounting control they preferred resulted in such comments as

None of these reports would be particularly useful to the public. In fact, they could be misleading in that the public might view them as an auditor's assurance that fraud cannot take place within the firm.

Too much information is worse than not enough (from a private placement officer).

I cannot rate these. And do not wish to. Most stockholders and probably most investors would not read a report including so much additional and technical comment and could easily misinterpret them (from a common stock investment officer).

The whole concept of "a report" is foolish and the concept of trying to synthesize the conditions prevailing in our 1,500 legal entities produces an exercise in madness.

Please, SIRS, SUMMARIZE *THE ENCYCLOPAEDIA BRITANNICA* IN ONE SENTENCE (from a board of directors and audit committee member).

Alternative report forms on which respondents were asked to comment in addition to providing rank orderings were

a. An auditor's opinion that a company's internal accounting control system adequately provides reasonable assurance that there is control over errors or irregularities that could be material to the financial statements.

b. An auditor's opinion that a company's internal accounting control system adequately provides reasonable assurances of achievement of each of the objectives of internal accounting control (that is, cost-benefit considerations are not limited to amounts material to the financial statements).

c. A description of the existing internal accounting controls by management (not over five pages for the annual report).

d. The external auditor's letter of control recommendations (that is, the management letter).

e. The auditor's list of primary strengths and weaknesses of internal accounting controls (not over five pages).

f. Management's opinion on the adequacy of the internal accounting control system.

g. Management's opinion attested to by an independent auditor, taking the form of (a).

h. Management's opinion attested to by an independent auditor, taking the form of (b).

The survey included members of boards of directors and audit committees, common-stock investment officers, certified financial analysts, mutual fund analysts, government employees, commercial lending officers, certified public accountants, controllers for companies, and private placement investment officers. How diverse do you believe their opinions were in regard to the desirable form of reporting on internal control, if such reports were to be made available? What report form do you prefer?[23]

[23] Adapted from Wanda A. Wallace, "How Not to Communicate Material and Immaterial Weaknesses in Accounting Controls," *Auditing Symposium VI, Proceedings of the 1982 Touche Ross University of Kansas Symposium on Auditing Problems*, edited by Donald R. Nichols and Howard F. Stettler (Lawrence: School of Business, University of Kansas, 1982).

18

Issues Facing the Profession

Setting. Auditing classroom.
Professor. I know no better way to describe the regulators' views of the accounting profession than to quote from the public record of a federal subcommittee that investigated the profession in the mid-1970s. In the cover letter to the Metcalf Report, formally called *The Accounting Establishment: A Staff Study* and issued on December 7, 1976, Lee Metcalf reported:

> Late last year, this subcommittee began a study of the federal government's role in establishing accounting practices which are used by publicly-owned corporations in reporting financial and other information to the public. The study was precipitated by continual revelations of previously unreported wrongdoing by major corporations, as well as a series of corporate failures and financial difficulties which have come to light in recent years. In many cases, the problems which occurred were caused or aggravated by the use of accounting practices that failed to reflect accurately the substance of corporate business activities. . . .
>
> The SEC's failure to exercise its authority on accounting matters has led to many of the problems which have caused a serious erosion of public confidence in the accuracy and usefulness of information reported by corporations. . . .
>
> In particular, I am disturbed by two of the study's major findings. The first is the extraordinary manner in which the SEC has insisted upon delegating its public authority and responsibilities on accounting matters to private groups with obvious self-interests in the resolution of such matters. The second is the alarming lack of independence and lack of dedication to public protection shown by the large accounting firms which perform the key function of independently certifying the financial information reported by major corporations to the public.

In summarizing the report, the subcommittee made the following observations:

- Accounting practices ultimately involve social issues that affect the nation's economic welfare. . . .

- The "Big Eight" are often called "public accounting firms" or "independent public accounting firms." This study finds little evidence that they serve the public or that they are independent in fact from the interests of their corporate clients. For that reason, this study refers to the "Big Eight" simply as accounting firms. . . .
- The concentration of major corporations as clients of the "Big Eight" indicates a need for an investigation of possible anti-competitive effects. . . .
- Involvement [in management advisory services] creates a professional and financial interest by the independent auditor in a client's affairs which is inconsistent with the auditor's responsibility to remain independent in fact and in appearance. . . . An independent auditor . . . may be placed in the position of auditing its own work. . . .
- "Big Eight" firms have advocated the interests of corporate clients on substantive political issues regarding taxation of corporations. . . .
- The "Big Eight" accounting firms readily identify with the self-interests of corporate managements on many other controversial issues. . . .
- The "Big Eight" firms effectively control the power structure, and use the AICPA to advance their collective interests.
- The AICPA . . . advocates legislation to limit the legal liability of CPAs for performing faulty or incomplete audits. . . .
- Long association between a corporation and an accounting firm may lead to such close identification of the accounting firm with the interests of its client's management that truly independent action by the accounting firm becomes difficult. . . .
- Accounting standards involve social and economic issues which can only be resolved effectively through the processes of government responsible solely to the public. . . .
- Direct or indirect representation of clients' interests and performance of non-accounting management advisory services for public or private clients are two activities which are particularly incompatible with the responsibilities of independent auditors and should be prohibited by federal standards of conduct.[1]

Student 1. Why does government equate bigness with a lack of competitiveness? Aren't the Big Four auto makers competitive? What's the big deal about a Big Eight?

Student 2. After all the merger discussions, how would Congress react if we became the Big Four?

Student 3. How can the Metcalf Report support its assertions? I thought that individuals belonged to the AICPA and that firms belonged to the sections, and in either case, the Big Eight are far outnumbered by non-Big Eight. How is the AICPA controlled?

Student 4. If a handful of failures mean overall bad performance, shouldn't the government stop its operations, given its repeated failure to account for its resources without a loss of assets due to fraud? What about mailing of social security checks to dead people, problems with the food stamp program, and the inability to collect on student loans? Why are they not worse than Penn Central?

[1] Subcommittee on Reports, Accounting and Management of the Committee on Government Operations, United States Senate, *The Accounting Establishment: A Staff Study* (Washington, D.C.: U.S. Government Printing Office, December 1976), excerpts from pp. 1–24.

After all, the General Accounting Office isn't being blamed in the way the Big Eight are, despite the similar "apparent audit failures." Or are there two sets of rules, one for the public sector and another for the private?

Student 5. Why would the SEC have done nothing if the profession had been guilty? After all, it represents the government and does have the power to intervene.

Student 6. I find it strange that Congress wants to "muzzle" the accounting profession on tax and related issues. Why that's our specialty, and though I understand the government might not want to be challenged, in a democratic society, the qualified populace should have a forum without being told that such actions are incompatible with professional responsibilities. I don't think that inaction and apathy by CPAs on such matters is in the public interest!

Student 7. Though I can understand the perception that MAS and audit services are incompatible, don't these regulators know that GAAS, enforced in the courtroom, are a reason for CPAs to monitor their own activities and maintain their independence?

Student 8. I have the most difficulty with the synonymous treatment of independence and the rotation of auditors. Long-term relationships are claimed to be harmful. How then does Congress explain the prevalence of audit problems in the first or second year of an audit? Given the infamous logrolling and vote swapping of Congress, perhaps a proposal should be made that no congressman serve more than four years, given the obvious mutual dependence that grows *across* representatives, creating a potential problem in directing adequate attention to the electorate's preferences. Surely, just as power concurrently grows with longer terms in Congress, auditors' power increases over time as they gain a more thorough understanding of clients' operations.

Student 9. What struck me is the negative view of the profession. How did we avoid regulation, with these attitudes?

Student 10. Will we be able to avoid it in the future?

As the class discussion was pursued, the topics described in this chapter were explored. Specifically, details of the *Metcalf and Moss reports,* the *Cohen Commission's conclusions,* influential legislation like the *Foreign Corrupt Practices Act,* and SEC activities are provided. Then, the reaction of the profession to such events, via the *Public Oversight Board* and the AICPA is described. Actions by the private sector and individual auditing firms to improve communication links between auditors and report users are discussed. The Congressional Dingell Hearings of the mid-80's are recognized as being a part of the profession's environment, likely to be very influential in determining whether the profession will be able to retain a self-regulated status. The objective of the introductory case and this chapter is to create an *awareness* of the public's demands upon the profession and the possible shape of things to come.

The increasing attention paid by regulators to the accounting profession can be traced to the litigation of the 1970s. In 1976, the Moss Commission proposed that the Financial Accounting Standards Board be abolished. The December 1976 Metcalf Report was followed by the March 1977 Cohen Commission Report. Senator Eagleton pursued a questionnaire directed at actions which had been taken pursuant to the Metcalf Report, and a NOSECA was proposed, i.e., national organization of securities and exchange commission accountants, to register CPAs, review audits, and mete out discipline. The organization was envisioned as setting all the standards for the profession. Then, in part to address some of the concerns raised and in part to prevent government action, the AICPA restructured its organization, creating the SEC and private practice sections. The SEC's subsequent report to Congress resulted in mixed signals for the profession.

Of interest to one attempting to gain an appreciation of the attention directed to the profession in the 1970s, consider the following expectations verbalized in 1978 by an AICPA officer:

- When Congress convenes in January, Mr. Moss intends to refile the bill originally proposed in 1978;
- Congressman Eckhardt, the chair of a subcommittee of the House Interstate and Foreign Commerce Committee, has stated an intent to hold hearings in 1979 to monitor the profession's progress toward self-regulation;
- Senator Eagleton indicated that the subcommittee on Governmental Efficiency and the District of Columbia would hold similar hearings; Mr. Jack Chesson, a member of the staff of the subcommittee is expected to seek legislation to regulate the profession;
- The SEC will file a progress report with Congress in July, meaning pressure to adopt at least one of the recommendations of the SEC:
  - requiring audit committees at SEC companies,
  - giving the SEC full access to peer review working papers,
  - restricting MAS services,
  - subjecting audit work outside the United States on U.S. engagements to peer review.[2]

To avoid regulation, there had to be a representative number of peer reviews, and the program of self-regulation had to be supported by the profession, as demonstrated by firms' joining these two sections.

An example of the dissension in the profession was the filing of a lawsuit by eighteen members of the AICPA which sought to suspend the Division for Firms because of its competitive disadvantage effects. Some of this dissent was dissipated by the AICPA's decision to study the future prospects and viability of small- and medium-sized firms (the special committee chaired by Sam Derieux) and to pressure the FASB to agree that some types of disclosures need not be required for private companies, such as earnings per share.

The Metcalf Report

The Metcalf Report, named after the committee's chairman Senator Lee Metcalf and issued by the Senate Subcommittee on Reports, Accounting, and Management of the Committee on Government Affairs, summarizes an investigation of the Big Eight accounting firms. Taking into account (1) the social reform of the 1960s, (2) several widely publicized audit failures, and (3) revelations of corporate illegal payments, the subcommittee noted:

> Accounting practices ultimately involve social issues that affect the nation's economic welfare. . . . If past abuses are to be prevented in the future, it is important that the accounting establishment, which has permitted many abuses to occur, be understood. Accounting issues are too important to be left to accountants alone.

As indicated in the introductory case to this chapter, the subcommittee's criticism centered on the CPA firms' perceived lack of independence and the management advisory services' inconsistency with the professional responsibility of auditing. In addition, the Metcalf Report claimed that the Big Eight controlled the AICPA, the SEC, the Financial Accounting Foundation, and the FASB.

In investigating the major CPA firms and their relation to the FASB and the AICPA, Senator Metcalf sent two separate letters and questionnaires to the Big Eight to collect information on those firms' clientele, degree of influence in professional and standard-setting affairs, and relationships with the federal government. What inspired this investigation? Some point to the following two events:

1. Congressional consideration of energy legislation involving questions about the reliability of the financial information provided by the oil and gas industry, with blame placed by Congress-

[2] See Wallace E. Olson, "Eye of the Storm," address to the Tax Division in San Diego, California, December 4, 1978.

man John E. Moss and others on the public accounting profession's failure to establish proper accounting and reporting standards and to insist on clients' full and fair disclosure. The cause of such failure was attributed to a lack of independence from the large and powerful oil companies that were clients. Moss proposed that the GAO establish accounting and reporting standards for the oil and gas industry and then audit both the oil companies and their auditors.

2. Scores of revelations of corporate illegal political contributions, bribes, and unrecorded funds alarmed congressmen and made them ask where the auditors were and what they were doing to prevent the repetition of such practices.[3]

EXHIBIT 18-1
Chart of Control Proposed by Metcalf Report

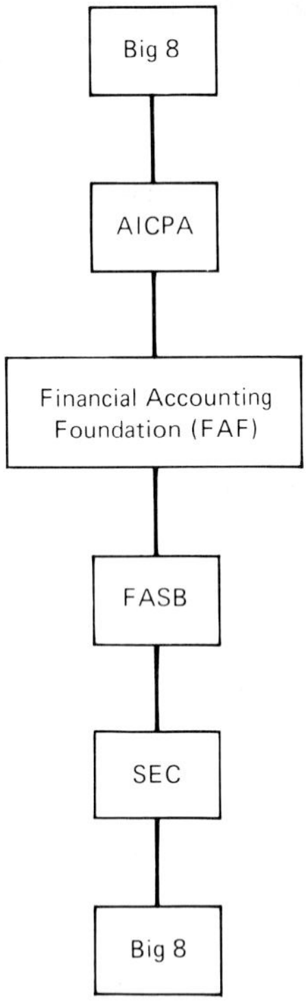

Big 8
AICPA
Financial Accounting Foundation (FAF)
FASB
SEC
Big 8

Adapted from United States Senate, Subcommittee on Reports, Accounting and Management of the Committee on Government Operations, *The Accounting Establishment: A Staff Study*, (Washington, D. C.: U. S. Government Printing Office, December 1976), chart 1, p. 3.

The Metcalf Report was flawed in three primary ways. Two of these were alluded to by students in the introductory case to this chapter. First, the accountant asked to testify at the hearings was Abraham Briloff, who is well known for his criticism of the profession, and there was no attempt to balance Briloff's views. Second, there was little information in the report to support its proposals. And third, deficiencies in the recommendations were not reported. For example, the conclusion that the Big Eight firms were too big and should be pared down ignored the reason for their size. The size of public accounting firms is determined in part by the large companies' demand for accounting services. For instance, one of Price Waterhouse's clients, with sales in excess of $3.5 billion, has locations in forty foreign countries and throughout the United States. Its audit requires approximately twenty-six labor-years and personnel from thirty-eight U.S. and thirty-five foreign offices.[4]

One major error in the Metcalf Report was in the chart of control within the profession, shown in Exhibit 18-1. Its claim that the Big Eight are a unified body is debatable, as they often disagree, as documented in past decisions of the Accounting Principles Board, comments on accounting matters published by each of the Big Eight firms, and even legal cases. Moreover, there is no evidence that the SEC is ruled by either the Big Eight or the FASB. The SEC endorses the FASB but clearly exercises its prerogative on various reporting problems. Their investigative and disciplinary actions against the Big Eight firms make it extremely difficult to identify any credible hierarchy of power which would resemble Exhibit 18-1. By the same token, the claim that the Big Eight firms control the AICPA ignores the fact that all CPAs, not just Big Eight CPAs, can

[3]See Wallace Olson, "Who Accounts for Accountants?" address to the Mountain States Conference, Scottsdale, Arizona, April 23, 1976.

[4]Arnold and Porter, "Memorandum to John C. Biegler, Price Waterhouse & Co., re: Recommendations on 'Concentration' and 'Competition' Included in the Staff Study of the Senate Subcommittee on Reports, Accounting and Management," Appendix E in Statement of John C. Biegler, May 4, 1977, pp. E4–5.

vote on rules as members of the AICPA. And the numbers clearly suggest a dominance by non-Big Eight members.

The AICPA had 70,000 active CPAs as members in the mid-70's: 21 percent were in one-member firms, 30 percent were in firms with 2 to 9 members, 11 percent in firms with 10 or more members except the largest 25 firms, and 38 percent in the largest 25 firms. The "Big Eight" accounting firms employ 15 percent of the AICPA's members.[5]

To illustrate the lack of consensus among the Big Eight firms, consider the following views expressed at the Metcalf hearings. Arthur Andersen favored a requirement that CPA firms produce audited financial statements and quality control information, whereas Touche Ross endorsed disclosure of limited financial and operational data, plus voluntary financial reports. Price Waterhouse advocated a quality control review by another firm, following regulations set by the SEC, but Touche Ross wanted an AICPA voluntary quality control program. Coopers & Lybrand favored the requirement of audit committees by the SEC, and Deloitte Haskins & Sells thought that the formation of audit committees should be encouraged. Both Arthur Andersen and Touche Ross promoted the prohibition of executive recruiting, whereas Deloitte Haskins & Sells encouraged an individual firm effort to drop nonaccounting services. Price Waterhouse favored the SEC-required rotation of partners, and the Associated Accounting Firms International spokesperson opposed any rotation of firms, pointing out that it would lead to the displacement of smaller firms with regard to auditing standards. Price Waterhouse, Arthur Young, and Touche Ross all pushed for a full-time auditing standards board, but Coopers and Lybrand wanted to try to strengthen AudSEC before establishing a full-time board.

To demonstrate the gap between the CPAs' and the government participants' views in the Metcalf hearings, consider the following:

Senator Metcalf

- Government authorities should participate in quality control reviews of CPA firms.
- Broader representation and public access to the accounting and auditing standard-setting process are needed.

Representative Moss

- All management advisory services performed should be disclosed by the CPA firms.
- FASB and AudSEC should issue pronouncements within a framework established by the SEC.
- The *Hochfelder* decision is anticonsumer and should be remedied.

The Moss Bill

The Moss Bill was named after John E. Moss, then chairman of the House Commerce Committee's Subcommittee on Oversight and Investigations, and is officially named H.R. 13175, "Public Accounting Regulatory Act." It proposed government regulation of the accounting profession, specifically, the establishment of the aforementioned national organization of securities and exchange commission accountants. CPA firms would have been required to register with the commission and to furnish audit reports related to the SEC's financial statement filings. Every three years, the commission would have reviewed the CPA firms' work, watching for "acts of omissions" by the firms or principals in the firms that were contrary to the interests of the investor public. The commission would have been empowered to take disciplinary action against the firms and their principals, including economic sanctions, fines, and suspension or expulsion from registration.

The Moss Bill would also have affected the auditors' liability exposure:

> Any independent accounting firm should be liable for any damages sustained by any private party as a result of such party's reliance on an audit report by such firm with respect to a financial statement, report, or other document filed with the Commission under any federal securities law, if such accounting firm was negligent in the preparation of such audit report.

[5] Staff Study, *The Accounting Establishment*, prepared by the Subcommittee on Reports, Accounting and Management of the Committee on Governmental Affairs, U.S. Senate (Washington, D.C.: U.S. Government Printing Office, December 1976).

Congressman Moss introduced HR 13175 before he retired, which (1) would have created a federal agency to regulate the accounting profession which, in turn, (2) would have required a continuing investigation of the firms' audits, making the results of such investigations public, (3) would have abolished the FASB and Auditing Standards Board, and (4) would have required the SEC to establish GAAP and GAAS. Even though the bill was much criticized, the threat of such legislation persists.

The Cohen Commission

The Commission on Auditors' Responsibilities—widely known as the Cohen Commission and named after its chairman, Manuel F. Cohen—was an independent body charged to investigate an alleged gap between the public's expectations and the auditors' responsibilities. If such a gap were found, the commission was to recommend ways of bridging it. The commission met from November 1974 to March 1977, when its *Report of Tentative Conclusions* was published in order to solicit comments and suggestions before the final report was issued. After holding a public meeting and analyzing both written and oral responses, the final report was issued in 1978. The commission's conclusions in its final report and its recommendations are presented in Exhibits 18-A and 18-B, in the appendix to this chapter.

One finding of the Cohen Commission's investigation of past court cases involving auditors and its interviews of auditors was that audit failures were due to mistakes in judgment because of excessive reliance on client representations. The Cohen Commission analyzed a number of past court cases and concluded that several of them, including *Escott* v. *BarChris*, revealed auditors' tendency to accept, without support, false accounting representations from client managers who previously had been employed by the audit firm. In particular, Peat, Marwick, Mitchell & Co. (PMM & Co.), which had audited BarChris from 1958 to 1969, knew that Kircher, a CPA and former employee of PMM & Co., was the treasurer of BarChris and that Trilling, a CPA and PMM & Co's senior accountant on the BarChris audit of 1959, was the controller. Knowing that Kircher and Trilling supervised the accounting records and financial statement preparations, PMM & Co. was confident that the audit team would be kept fully informed of material facts and events. With the benefit of hindsight, undue reliance was placed on the integrity and good faith of those key management personnel who had been former employees. Such findings made CPAs more alert to the attendant risks of overreliance on client personnel, regardless of their past audit positions. Presumably, these insights and others cited in Exhibit 18-A and 18-B in the appendix contribute to progressive steps toward overall improvement of the profession.

A summary of projects that had been undertaken by the Auditing Standards Board since 1978 attributed the reason for the following projects to be the Cohen Commission:

- Exposure Draft to revise auditors' reports began 12/77; dropped after exposure draft 3/81; explanatory booklet issued 1982,
- Standards for reviews of corporate policy statements, began 12/77 but disbanded in 1979 due to negligible demand,
- Review of small companies' needs with respect to GAAS; SAS 32, Adequacy of Disclosure—1980,
- SAS 30, Reporting on Internal Control,
- Public hearing in June 1982 to consider eliminating the 'subject to' opinion; abandoned and guidance on applying this type of qualifier is being developed.

Of interest is the nonacceptance or lack of demand for three of the suggestions to which the profession attempted to respond. Nevertheless, the SASs, both SAS No. 30 and SAS No. 32, can be tied directly to the Cohen Commission report.[6]

Regulation

The Foreign Corrupt Practices Act (FCPA), passed in late 1977, requires internal accounting controls sufficient to ensure that transactions are executed as authorized and can be reported as being in

[6] Report of the Auditing Standards Structure Committee, initiated 1982 (AICPA), Appendix B.

compliance with GAAP and maintaining accountability for assets. In addition, the FCPA requires that access to assets be permitted only as authorized and that the books be compared periodically with the records. Violation of these provisions can lead to $1,000 fines and five years imprisonment for those company officials who are responsible. The act's bribery prohibitions provide for $1,000,000 fines for companies and the same penalties for the officials as in the act's control provisions.

The FCPA led to many companies' complaints regarding uncertainties in the law. But the SEC refused to give advisory opinions to companies on the legality of planned actions through 1980. Finally in February 1980, the SEC requested companies' comments on actual problems with the FCPA for potential follow-up.[7] The attitude of such bodies, reflected in comments by the Justice Department, too often holds that maximum uncertainty promotes maximum conformity and therefore provides the best enforcement.[8]

Although illegal payments in the private sector are widely criticized and in large part led to the FCPA and its related uncertainties, government has had substantial fraud as well. Known fraud against the government over a thirty-month period ending on March 31, 1979, ran anywhere from $150 million to $220 million, excluding fraud in regard to welfare, Medicaid, and food stamps. Of the 77,211 cases studied by the General Accounting Office, most were petty offenses, and about 1,348 involved kickbacks, bribes, or extortion.[9] Nonetheless, increased government regulation of the private sector was cited as the "solution" to the illegal payments problem.

As might be guessed, the auditor's communication of material weaknesses (SAS No. 20) was feared as possibly violating the FCPA, and thus it has been speculated that the FCPA has discouraged certain types of formal communication between the auditor and the client, specifically suggestions for improvement of internal control.

In addition to the Metcalf subcommittee's investigation citing concerns over market competitiveness, the Federal Trade Commission (FTC) has also investigated potential restrictive anticompetitive practices in the profession, focusing on the implementation of CPA requirements by the state boards of accountancy and the design of the Uniform CPA Examination. The FTC's study indicated that the national average pass rate on the CPA exam climbed from 13 percent in 1921 to approximately 20 percent between 1973 and 1976. The FTC collected statistics on the success rate in four states of "serious candidates," that is, those taking and retaking the exam up to six times. The result was that with perseverance, 80 to 90 percent of such candidates passed. Clearly, the study supported the idea that the exam is a competency test and not an effective barrier to entry.[10]

Between 1976 and 1978, the Justice Department investigated restrictions of the profession's ethical rules, leading to repeal of the prohibition on encroachment and the softening of both advertising and solicitation guidelines. Hence, numerous regulations have had an effect on the profession beyond those of the SEC.

An interesting aspect of some of the antitrust implications for the profession has to do with the effects of litigation. The expansion of legal actions to the full limits of foreseeable users can be expected to increase the concentration of audit markets. This is because the expanding auditor liability may virtually squeeze out those accounting firms that lack so-called deep pockets.

Regulation is by no means unique to the United States. For example, Taiwan's Securities and Exchange Commission required in 1983 that any firm auditing a listed company employ at least 3 CPAs and 9 other professional staff, at least 3 of which must hold college degrees in accounting. Two CPAs are required to sign financial statements, and firms must be willing to have a team of outside accountants examine their auditing methods and workpapers. Furthermore, auditors of publicly listed companies must take continuing education

[7] "SEC Asks for Comments on Foreign-Payoffs Ban," *Wall Street Journal*, February 22, 1980, p. 2.

[8] Jerry Landauer, "U.S. Will Clarify Statute on Corrupt Acts by American Firms Operating Overseas," *Wall Street Journal*, September 21, 1979, p. 20.

[9] "Known Fraud," *Wall Street Journal*, May 8, 1981, p. 1.

[10] N. Dopuch and D. Simunic, "Competition in Auditing: An Assessment," *Audit Symposium*, University of Illinois, October 1980.

courses.[11] Hence, the regulatory environment for the accounting profession encompasses many bodies through the world. Of course, one of the most visible domestically is the United States' Securities and Exchange Commission (SEC).

The SEC

The SEC chairman Harold Williams in 1980 emphasized a "keep their feet to the fire" approach to dealing with the accounting profession and the AICPA's self-regulatory program. In its 1982 Report to Congress on Oversight of the Accounting Profession, the SEC called for all accounting firms auditing public companies to join the SEC Practice Section. It also began requiring visible evidence that the Special Investigations Committee was taking disciplinary actions against member firms involved in litigation. Such use of sanctions was cited as critical to demonstrating the effectiveness of the profession's self-regulation.

A key source of information about the SEC's position on matters is the expression of view points in speeches and interviews. As an example, SEC Commissioner James C. Treadway, Jr., in an interview with the *Bureau of National Affairs* in the fall of 1984, noted that the SEC's enforcement cases were focusing on issuers rather than the accountants. He noted that specific audit failures do not translate to inadequate standards or to an epidemic problem, particularly in light of the small number of audit failures relative to the 10,500 companies reporting to the SEC annually. In expressing his high regard for the accounting profession, he nevertheless acknowledged that enough audit failures do occur to merit some question of whether they represent an institutional defect in a firm or in the profession. The intent of the Commission to go after even isolated instances was made clear, as such action "serves to keep everybody on notice that we're serious about it."[12]

The SEC has also influenced the generally accepted auditing standards. In a summary of projects undertaken since 1978 by the Auditing Standards Board, the reason for the project was cited to be the SEC for

- development of criteria for compilations and reviews of forecasts and projections leading to the issued guide in 1980 and to Statement on Standards for Accountants' Services on Prospective Financial Information (October 1985).
- consideration of new forms of reporting by means of comfort letters and interim reviews, resulting in SAS No. 36, "Review of Interims" (1981); No. 37, "Filing Under Federal Security Statutes" (1981); No. 38, "Letters to Underwriters" (1981); and No. 42, "Reporting on Condensed Financial Statements" (1982).
- development of guidance in response to the SEC's practice developments, begun in October 1982 and still in progress.[13]

Often the SEC's pressure is informal. For example, after newspapers reported that the audit committee of National Telephone had never held a meeting before the company was placed in the hands of a court-appointed receiver, the SEC was reported to be encouraging active audit committees by pressing accountants not to accept as clients any public corporations that lacked such committees. The New York Stock Exchange, prodded by the SEC, adopted an audit committee requirement that took effect in June 1978. Interference in corporate governance by states has been discussed as well, perhaps that states should require companies to have a certain number of "really independent" directors.[14]

In a sense, the SEC's pressure for audit committees has given more power to the CPAs when interacting with management, because of their direct reporting link with outside directors. The general definition of an audit committee, its responsibili-

[11] "Taiwan Adopts Tighter Rules For Auditors," *Wall Street Journal*, July 12, 1983, p. 33.

[12] "SEC Commissioner Treadway Discusses Wide Range of Business Issues," Deloitte Haskins & Sells, *The Week in Review* (September 28, 1984), p. 1.

[13] Report of the Auditing Standards Structure Committee, initiated 1982 (AICPA), Appendix B.

[14] Burt Schorr, "Board Breakup: Corporate Directors Scorned for Lax Scrutiny of Managements' Acts—SEC and Others Seek Curbs on Conflicts of Interest; Firms Slow to Respond," *Wall Street Journal*, April 10, 1978, p. 1.

EXHIBIT 18-2
Audit Committees

- Audit committees are typically composed of three to five directors who are outside directors; preferably at least one member will have financial experience.

- Responsibilities should include
  - the nomination of the independent accountants and discussion of their work with them.
  - the review and evaluation of reports on control weaknesses.
  - follow-up to ascertain whether management has taken appropriate action on these recommendations.
  - a review of financial statements and interim reports with the independent accountants.
  - establishing a direct line of communications between the directors and independent accountants.
  - appraisal of the effectiveness of the audit effort, including discussion of scope, opinion, and desirable areas for special emphasis.
  - determination that management placed no restrictions on the auditors.
  - inquiry into the effectiveness of the company's management in financial and accounting functions and the absence of illegal or improper payments.
  - evaluation of the internal audit department's effectiveness.
  - review of limited review engagements, including asking about large or unusual transactions, the adequacy of disclosure, accounting developments affecting reporting practices, and changes in accounting and operating controls.

- To discharge such responsibilities, three to four meetings a year are commonly held, and those present may include legal counsel and others with information relevant to auditing, accounting, and disclosure issues. Auditors should be permitted to request a special meeting with the audit committee to discuss topics requiring special attention. Assuming four meetings a year, the likely agenda for each meeting would be
  1. the objectives and scope of the audit process, including attention to reporting requirements, recent developments in financial reporting, and the overall audit plan.
  2. the audit's status after interim work and problems needing attention before year-end.
  3. review of the financial statements to be submitted to the board, including a review of the auditor's report and consideration of the independent accountants' need to meet with the board.
  4. a final review of the audit and preparation of a committee report to the full board.

Adapted from Price Waterhouse, *The Audit Committee: The Board of Directors and the Independent Accountant* (New York: Price Waterhouse, 1976), pp. 1-12.

ties, and its typical means of discharging committee responsibilities are outlined in Exhibit 18-2.

Practitioners have said that both sensitivity and numbness have resulted from the current regulation of the profession. Accounting Series Release No. 264 (note again that ASRs have been replaced with FRRs—Financial Reporting Releases—and enforcement rulings) objected to the Public Oversight Board's findings, stressing that great care was needed in hiring independent auditors for nonaudit services, owing to the independence problem. The ASR's predictable effect was a feeling by many clients that rather than have to justify the purchase of accounting services from their auditor, they might as well hire another accounting firm for nonaudit services. This effect on the marketing of nonaudit services has been cited as being particularly harmful to the smaller CPA firms. The profession has observed that ASR 264 violates the Administrative Procedures Act because it was not issued as an exposure draft for comment, yet represents an intent to restrain trade. But no legal cases have been filed, reportedly because the profession feels that it cannot win.

The SEC's effects on public accounting are substantial. First, it can censure auditing practices when it investigates specific cases. As an example, ASR 19 (1940) involving McKesson & Robbins criticized nonconfirmation of receivables and the lack of required physical observation of inventories. Similarly, the *Interstate Hosiery Mills, Inc.* case (4 SEC 706, 1939) established the necessity of an accounting firm to review the work done by subordinates. ASR 64 (1948) involving Drayer-Hanson emphasized the necessity of having auditors examine the client's system of internal control and cost systems. ASR 144 (1973) regarding Touche, Ross & Co. and ASR 173 (1975) regarding Peat, Marwick, Mitchell & Co. criticized auditing practices and led to required professional reviews of both firms. Beyond such effects, the SEC has the power under Rule 2(e) to disqualify a firm or practitioner from representing SEC entities. In addition, the SEC can increase auditors' power over their clients through disclosure requirements such as 8-Ks.

The SEC's or any other government agency's promulgation of auditing and reporting standards, such as asserted by Metcalf and Moss, can be challenged on the basis of past failures by government in its analogous activities. Specifically, the inconsistency of the Internal Revenue Service's and the SEC's LIFO reporting preferences and congressional and the SEC's actions regarding investment credit and oil and gas accounting that led to less uniformity than promoted by private sector standard setters contradict the government's supposed ability to improve reporting consistency. As of 1979, (1) the U.S. government had generally failed to publish consolidated financial statements on an accrual basis; (2) the Interstate Commerce Commission had used an antiquated chart of accounts for railroads; (3) the Federal Communications Commission, because of its poor accounting system, was unable to devise a system that could meet a court order to justify its fees; and (4) the audit guides and procedures for federal programs tended to be untimely and confusing. All of these conditions challenge the contention that the government's takeover of accounting and audit services would be an improvement over private sector control.[15]

The SEC has repeatedly sought access to peer review working papers, as well as the work papers of the audit firm being reviewed. The latter has been opposed by the profession for fear that the SEC might go on a fishing expedition. Clients may well leave were such access granted or may simply refuse to make their work papers available for their CPA's peer reviewers. In 1982 a compromise seemed to have been reached, though negotiation between the SEC and the private sector's self-regulation program is continuing.

The SEC's plan for the 1980's has been likened to an expectation that "in tandem—in constructive tension—the profession and the SEC will enhance the usefulness, and the concomitant responsibilities and prestige, of the accounting and auditing functions."[16] Harold M. Williams in an address to the Accounting Research Center, Northwestern University in Evanston, Illinois on April 23, 1980, entitled "The First Thousand Days—and Beyond," warned

> guard against the tendency to become complacent, or to develop an attitude that enough or too much, has already been done—or that much of what is being done is not substantively necessary or cost justifiable, but rather a mandatory title to keep powerful, but misguided external forces at bay.[17]

The friction will continue, and the profession should be alert to the SEC's willingness to intervene should the AICPA relax its self-regulatory efforts. A key aspect of such efforts is the operation of the Public Oversight Board or POB and its communications with the SEC.

The Public Oversight Board

The Public Oversight Board (POB) of the SEC Practice Section of its division of CPA firms is intended to increase self-regulation by being authorized to report any information, findings, or recommendations based on its oversight activities to the section's executive committee, the SEC, the appropriate congressional committees, or the public at large. The POB is expected to judge the accounting profession's self-regulatory program from close up and with an unbiased, objective view. The first board had five members, including two former SEC chairmen, a lawyer, and two former CEOs.

[15] This discussion has been adapted from a paper on the conclusions and recommendations in the Metcalf report: George J. Benston, "The Market for Public Accounting Services: Demand, Supply, and Regulation," working paper, University of Rochester, April 24, 1979.

[16] George C. Mead, "The Accounting Profession in the 1980's—Some SEC Perspectives," *Auditing Symposium V;* Proceedings of the 1980 Touche Ross/University of Kansas Symposium on Auditing Problems, Editors Donald R. Nichols and Howard F. Stettler (University of Kansas, 1980), p. 158.

[17] Cited on p. 157 by George C. Mead, "The Accounting Profession in the 1980's—Some SEC Perspectives," *Auditing Symposium V;* Proceedings of the 1980 Touche Ross/University of Kansas Symposium on Auditing Problems, Editors Donald R. Nichols and Howard F. Stettler (University of Kansas, 1980), pp. 147–158.

The first board met at least monthly, testified three times before Congress, and has had numerous meetings with the SEC Practice Section's executive committee and the SEC commissioners and staff members. Owing to the importance of the SEC's support for the profession's self-regulatory process, the POB is often referred to as offering a shuttle diplomacy between the SEC and the profession.

MAS—Questions of Independence

Besides its involvement in peer review, the POB investigated the question of the proper scope of management advisory services that an auditor can perform, an investigation prompted by the disagreements between the profession and the SEC. The POB read different views on the subject, issued a notice of a public hearing, and called for both written and oral testimony. Over 150 written comments were received, and 31 oral presentations were made at the two-day public hearings in August 1979. The self-serving nature of consultants' testimony was evident: Executive search firms felt that CPA firms should be prohibited from offering personnel placement; data-processing firms testified that CPAs could not design systems and software packages and then objectively audit the results; and actuaries recommended that CPA firms be prevented from offering actuarial services to audit clients. The board's conclusions and the SEC Practice Section's actions, based on an analysis of testimonies and written comments, are summarized in Exhibit 18-3. Nonetheless, as cited in the earlier discussion on the SEC, ASR No. 264 (now an FRR) was issued, stressing the independence problem.

Effects on GAAS

Just as the SEC has affected GAAS, so has the POB. A recommendation by the Public Oversight Board resulted in ***SAS No. 46, Section 390,*** "Consideration of Omitted Procedures After the Report Date."[18]

This provided direction as to what should be done if peer review activities indicate that inadequate work has been performed in a past audit. Essentially, if deemed necessary to support the audit opinion, omitted procedures are to be applied by the auditor.

The AICPA

To reduce the possibility of government regulation, the profession has taken actions to self-regu-

EXHIBIT 18-3

Summary Findings of POB Regarding Questions of MAS and the Profession's Reaction

- The existing Code of Ethics and the MAS Standards provide sufficient assurance that auditor independence will be maintained.
- Clients should not be denied the benefits that accrue from their auditors rendering MAS unless there is a strong showing of actual or potential detriment.
- Limitation should be placed on MAS only if such services impair the auditor's independence or present a strong likelihood of doing so.
- An accounting firm can serve as auditor for a company and as auditor and actuary of its employee benefit plan. The Board recommended, however, that the same firm cannot provide primary actuarial advice to and then audit an insurance company.
- Executive recruiting services are proscribed because such services are perceived by many as having a strong likelihood of impairing independence and have no offsetting benefit.
- No arbitrary rules should be imposed on any other service simply because it may not be compatible with public accounting.

Reaction by the SEC Practice Section

(1) The SEC Practice Section is not adopting any artificial limitations on MAS except executive recruiting, psychological testing, public opinion polls, and merger and acquisition assistance for a finder's fee; (2) it is prohibiting the rendering of primary actuarial services to insurance company audit clients; (3) it is requiring disclosure of tax and MAS fees received from SEC audit clients; and (4) it is expanding the scope of peer reviews to determine whether MAS engagements impaired independence.

From Louis W. Matusiak, "The Role of the Public Oversight Board in the Accounting Profession's Self-regulatory Program," *Ohio CPA,* Autumn, 1979 pp. 144-152.

[18] Report of the Auditing Standards Structure Committee, initiated in 1982 (AICPA), Appendix B.

late. On September 17, 1977, the AICPA established the SEC Practice Section and the Private Companies Practice Section. Exhibit 18-C in the appendix shows the latter's organizational structure and functions. CPA firms joining either of the sections demonstrate their willingness to:

- undergo mandatory continuing education.
- have a peer review every three years.
- accept sanctions.
- file related information for the public's use.
- carry liability insurance.
- report disagreements with management to the board or audit committee.
- report other services and fees to the board or audit committee.
- rotate their audit partners every five years.

The AICPA also formed committees to study the problems shown in Exhibit 18-4.

A pamphlet distributed by the AICPA's Private Companies Practice Section, entitled *Your Printed Image,* by Norman Rachlin, provides numerous examples of CPA firms' newsletters to clients publicizing their peer review. The benefits of peer review commonly cited in such newsletters are given in Exhibit 18-5, showing that some CPAs have used the institute's self-regulation efforts to their advantage.

EXHIBIT 18-4
AICPA Committees' Assignments

- Scope of management advisory services: Independence issues.
- Reports by management: Their role and content.
- Importance of establishing audit committees and advice about how such a committee's meetings should be conducted.
- How to set auditing standards.
- How should the auditor's report be revised?
- What are the standards for internal accounting control?
- How should uncertainties be disclosed?
- What policies are desirable with respect to corporate conduct?
- What is the nature of frauds and audit failures?
- What are the criteria for Rule 203 departures, concerning preferability?
- What accounting and review services can be provided, and how?

EXHIBIT 18-5
Benefits of Peer Review Commonly Publicized to Clients

- The peer review program is a system to sustain a quality practice.
- The peer review program checks the organization of the firm in terms of the effectiveness of its management and performance.
- Participation in peer review has qualified the firm for a liability insurance discount.
- Reduced liability exposure results from undergoing peer review.
- The peer review program illustrates that the profession and our firm do it ourselves, without outside monitors and regulators.
- The peer review exemplifies our dedication to a united professionalism.
- The peer review activity provided us with a competitive edge, in part through advertising the results of the peer review activity—often including publishing the peer review report—Examples of newsletter headlines are
  a. "______ CPAs Receive a Glowing Report on Their System of Quality Control"
  b. "It's Our Turn! We Passed!"
  c. "Quality! Quality! Quality!"
  d. "______, CPA Meets Accounting Profession's Highest Standards"

From Norman S. Rachlin, CPA, "Your Printed Image" (Distributed by private companies' practice section division for CPA firms) (New York: AICPA, 1982).

However, there has been sharp disagreement within the AICPA, with smaller and medium-sized CPA firms expressing dissatisfaction with the mounting number of technical standards that have forced them to charge their clients for unwanted services. The partners of such firms have claimed, at times, that the Institute is the captive of the large firms; this complaint, ill-informed and directed at accounting standard-setting, is taken out of context in investigations by governmental agencies.

The credibility of *self-regulation of the profession* would seem to rest on actions such as

- the Commision on Auditors' Responsibilities, chaired by Manny Cohen.

- the operation of an effective quality control review program.
- an effective system of discipline, with integration of the Institute's efforts with those of the State Boards.
- enforcement of the code of professional ethics.
- a visible role in continuing professional education.
- technical standard-setting.
- attention to GAAP for small company considerations.
- an examination of alternative services, including compilations and reviews.

The profession has taken many overt acts to ensure that self-regulation maintains its credibility. As just one example, when Price Waterhouse was criticized for having Deloitte Haskins & Sells perform its peer review, due to the fact that the two firms had begun merger discussions, PW selected KMG Main Hurdman to review the peer review by DH & S and render an opinion on the peer review. (Note that PW and DH & S later abandoned negotiations related to a possible merger.) This move by PW regarding its peer review meant the KMG Main Hurdman could do the entire peer review over again if judged to be necessary.[19]

Ironically, a testimonial as to auditors' typical conservatism in enforcing the spirit of accounting practices was provided by SEC Commissioner James C. Treadway, Jr., in a speech before the Financial Executives Institute in Chicago, Illinois (February 16, 1984), entitled "Accounting Shenanigans and The Commission's 1984 Response." While citing an exception, it was noted that out of 4,000 companies sampled, only that single company had recognized the future tax benefits from a net operating loss carry forward in current income.[20] Such careful attention to the substance of GAAP by auditors can only serve to facilitate self-regulation.

The AICPA's practice review was educational and not punitive before 1978, but its ability to identify substandard work requiring discipline has been well recognized, as described by Wallace E. Olson in his address to the Ethics Conference in Chicago on November 3, 1978. The SEC has encouraged the profession's discipline of its members. The state boards' surveillance of CPAs has been joined by that of ethics committees of state societies, and a third disciplinary or regulatory level is the institute's ethics division and trial board.

The range of possible sanctions that the profession's organizations can impose against members or firms for the private practice section are also presented in Exhibit 18-C. Note that these are an additional layer of discipline over legal liability, SEC sanctions, and the possible suspension by state boards of accountancy. But despite many CPAs' claim that the threat of unlimited legal liability is sufficient by itself to ensure that the profession will exercise due care to avoid audit failures, the public has shown no willingness to accept the profession's abdication of disciplinary responsibility.

As of October 21, 1981, over 2,000 CPA firms belonged to the AICPA Division for CPA Firms and 500 were members of the SEC Practice Section. These 500 firms audit over 90 percent of the publicly owned corporations regulated by the SEC.[21] This participation level has been applauded by the SEC.

Pressure from the Private Sector

The accounting profession's uniqueness as a private group which affects the entire society via developing and reporting financial data that are used to make economic decisions makes it a target for government control. Of the 2,641 corporations listed on the two major stock exchanges, the Big Eight firms audit 92 percent of the companies listed on the New York Stock Exchange and 76 percent of the companies listed on the American Stock Exchange.[22] This concentration has been publicized and has attracted attention in the private sector.

[19] "Questioned CPA Review to Get New Examiner," *Wall Street Journal,* October 15, 1984, p. 10.

[20] Loomis, "Behind the Aetna," *Fortune,* November 15, 1982, p. 56.

[21] Public Oversight Board SEC Practice Section, Division for CPA Firms, *Annual Report 1981–82* (AICPA, June 30, 1982).

[22] Subcommittee on Reports, Accounting and Management of the Committee on Governmental Affairs, United States Senate, *The Accounting Establishment* (Washington, D.C.: U.S. Government Printing Office, December 1976), pp. 5–6.

EXHIBIT 18-6
Common Questions Asked by Shareholders

Overall Operations

- How is the company performing relative to the industry and the economy in general?
- What is being done to reduce costs?
- At what percentage of capacity does the company operate?
- Why has the stock price changed in the manner that it has relative to market averages?
- Are labor negotiations planned during this year, and what are management's expectations?
- How did actual results compare with budgets and forecasts?
- What has been the effect of the recent press coverage of your competitor's problems?
- Who are your major customers, and are they financially stable?
- Have charitable donations been increased, and what organizations have received funds?
- By industry segment or product line, did sales and profit meet expectations?
- What percentage of total sales was generated from foreign markets?
- What actions have been taken to minimize the effects of changes in foreign exchange rates and to compensate for certain countries' high inflation?
- How have technological advances and the gradual shift from heavy industry to a service economy affected the company's operations and future plans?

Future Expectations

- Will the company diversify operations?
- Will dividend policies change?
- Do you plan to issue debt or stock?
- Will the company issue financial forecasts? If so, when, and if not, why not?

Management and Directors

- What types of compensation packages are offered, and who determines them?
- Does the company have any "golden parachute" arrangements with its executives? What are the possible tax consequences?
- Does the company intend to add more outside directors?
- Is there a plan for management succession?
- Does the board receive adequate information for monitoring performance?

Audit Committees and Independent Auditors

- What are the audit committee's responsibilities, and how does the committee interact with management, the internal auditors, and the external auditors?

EXHIBIT 18-6 (continued)

Internal Control

- Is the system of internal control adequate overall?
- How is unauthorized access to your EDP system prevented?
- Have any major frauds been discovered? If so, what actions have been taken?
- Given the proliferation of microcomputers, what security precautions has the company implemented regarding confidential information?

Financial Reporting Matters

- What is the composition of particular line items, and why have certain amounts changed?
- Does the company follow common industry accounting practices and can they be characterized as liberal or conservative?
- What are the company's debt-to-equity ratio and book value?
- How much does the annual report cost?
- What is the difference between generally accepted auditing standards and generally accepted accounting principles?

Tax Matters

- How has the company been affected by recent tax legislation?
- Do the independent auditors prepare the tax return (or review it)?
- What is the company doing to reduce its taxes?

Adapted from Ernst & Whinney "1984 and 1985 Shareholder Meetings—Financial Questions That May Be Asked" (Ernst & Whinney, 1984 and 1985; U.S.A., E & W No. 42247, 1984 and 1985).

The private sector has called for the accounting profession to be more stringently controlled. In the mid-1970s, a coalition of public interest groups, assisted by Ralph Nader's organization, filed a petition with the SEC seeking an amendment of Regulation S-X to invoke more stringent SEC control of the accounting profession. The amendment would have required the rotation of auditors every three years for all registered companies, presumably to enhance their independence.[23]

Auditors need to take action to communicate with the private sector, in order to alleviate the types of misapprehensions that must have encouraged this amendment. A study by Georgeson & Co., a New York investor-relations firm, indicated that 40 percent of corporate shareholders either do not read the annual report or spend only one to five minutes with it, and 26 percent spend six to fifteen minutes reading it.[24] A more effective forum for such communications therefore may be stockholders' meetings. The financial questions likely to be asked at shareholders' meetings can be anticipated, and, public accounting firms print pamphlets of these questions and answers to help management and directors prepare for such meetings. Exhibit 18-6 (see page 649) gives excerpts from one such pam-

[23] Adapted from Wallace Olson, "Who Accounts for Accountants?" address to the Mountain States Conference, Scottsdale, Arizona, April 23, 1976.

[24] Ronald Alson, "Annual Reports Now Doing Double Duty for Many Concerns: They Are Used to Promote Sales, Morale, Lobbying and Regional Chauvinism," *Wall Street Journal,* March 16, 1978, p. 1.

phlet. By demonstrating an understanding of operations and an independence in addressing inquiries, meetings with stockholders can help to establish a rapport with the community which CPAs serve.

Activism by shareholders is probably most evident with respect to merger offers. Shareholders have filed suits in an attempt to force managers to disclose to shareholders any reasonable offers for an entity's stock which provide big "premiums" over existing market prices and then permit the shareholders to decide whether to sell.[25] Little doubt exists that should stockholders perceive a need for particular disclosures or auditing practices, forums do exist in which they can air their preferences.

What the Future Holds

The mid-1980s promise a *déjà vu* experience for the accounting profession. At the time of this writing, the House Subcommittee on Oversight and Investigation, chaired by Representative John Dingell, is holding hearings on the accounting profession to review the profession's progress since the Metcalf hearings. The Dingell Committee has hired John Chesson, a former staffer for Senator Lee Metcalf, as counsel to the subcommittee and has cited twelve to fifteen issues of interest, including the success of peer review, the Public Oversight Board's role, whether auditors can offer MAS and remain independent, whether FASB is serving its purpose, and the role that the SEC has played in policing the profession.

The SEC has increased pressure on the profession by using more than 40 percent of its enforcement staff to pursue financial fraud. John Shad, chairman of the SEC, and John Fedders, director of the division of enforcement, have their staffs scrutinizing financial statements from 1980 to 1982, watching for "cooked books," accounting irregularities, reckless application of GAAP and GAAS, and improprieties stemming from shopping for auditors' opinions. Concern exists that some CPAs have interpreted GAAP and GAAS too liberally.[26]

Hence, little doubt exists that regulators' interest in the profession and active oversight by the SEC will continue into the future. The struggle for self-regulation in lieu of governmental regulation beyond the status quo will be continuing and its resolution is difficult to anticipate. Some have suggested that the self-regulation is not the clearly preferred alternative, because of its significant costs, yet it would appear that the majority of the profession has a clear preference for doing whatever appears necessary in a self-regulatory program in order to deter government control. In 1979, SEC Chairman Harold Williams endorsed the use of a voluntary organization to set corporate accountability and ethics standards, along the lines of the National Advertising Review Board—composed of 10 advertisers, 10 representatives of ad agencies, and 10 representatives of the public and sponsored by the Council of Better Business Bureaus, Inc. That Board reviews complaints about the truth and accuracy of ads; the group envisioned as a corporate accountability board would be an independent source of standards that if not met by companies would lead to questioning by analysts, lenders, creditors, and other interested parties. The emphasis on companies putting their own houses in order, as opposed to the government, is an implicit encouragement of the type of self-regulatory activities which the profession has taken. Audit committees were cited as needing oversight by such a voluntary group, to ensure substance rather than merely form or "window dressing."[27]

As a result, the sole prediction which seems indisputable is that regulation over the profession will increase, whether it comes in the form of self-regulation or increased government intervention.

International Auditing Standards

As technological and commercial links have made the world smaller, international auditing stan-

[25] Priscilla S. Meyer, "Shareholder Actions Seeking the Right to Force Sale of Firm by Management," *Wall Street Journal*, January 21, 1980, p. 6.

[26] "Congress to Review Profession's Progress over Last Decade," *Public Accounting Report*, August 1984.

[27] "SEC Chief Suggests Voluntary Policing on Business Ethics—Other Industry Groups Cited as Examples on Corporate Accountability, Standards," *Wall Street Journal*, October 25, 1979, p. 19.

EXHIBIT 18-7
Proposed International Auditing Standards

Standards of Independence, Integrity, and Objectivity

- in fact and appearance
- no financial or functional relationship
- to be applied with utmost rigor

Standard of Knowledge and Expertise

- their validation

Standards on Evidence and the Collection and Evaluation Thereof

- adequate supervision and control
- if more than one auditor involved, how to proceed
- use of experts from other professions
- reliance on internal control

Standards of Communication

- clear and unequivocal reporting
- opinion as to the "fairness"

Standard of the Financial Statement on Enforcement

- places responsibility on the professional body in the country in which the auditor is located

Adapted from Edward Stamp and Maurice Moonitz, "International Auditing Standards—Part I," *CPA Journal*, June 1982, pp. 24-32.

dards are likely to increase in both their role and their importance. The International Accounting Standards Committee was formed in 1973; the International Federation of Accountants (IFAC) was formed in 1977 at the World Congress of Accountants in Munich; and the Auditing Practices Committee of IFAC was formed in early 1978. As of May 1982, this committee had issued seven international auditing guidelines and four exposure drafts.

The nature of international auditing standards proposed in past literature is summarized in Exhibit 18-7. But enforcing the independence standards has been difficult because of different perceptions of independence among countries and the various attitudes toward enforcement. This diversity of practice and attitudes is reviewed in Exhibit 18-8. It would appear that consensus needs to be reached as to what constitutes independence. Enforcement would need to include preventive measures directed at education and training requirements pre and postcertification, as well as some sort of disciplinary body dealing with failures to comply with standards. The essential role of standards is expressed in the recognition that just as auditing gives credibility to financial reporting, auditing standards give credibility to auditing.[28]

Another Big Eight?

The changing face of the profession may well include a redefinition of the Big Eight. For example, on September 12, 1984, a headline of the *Wall Street Journal* read "Price Waterhouse, Deloitte Tell Staffs of Possible Merger" (p. 7). Although the merger of these two Big Eight CPA firms would have produced the biggest CPA firm in the United States, based on 1983 revenue statistics, the merger talks were abandoned. Considering the fact that Price Waterhouse has 90 U.S. offices and 260 offices in 94 other nations, while Deloitte has 103 U.S. offices and about 300 offices in about 70 other nations, the size of the resulting entity would have literally dwarfed the organizations attracting Metcalf's attention in the mid-1970s.

Of course, such a proposed merger did not go unnoticed, and the executive director of the National CPA Group—a group of forty local and medium-sized accounting firms—stated that such a merger would violate antitrust law. Indeed, before the merger negotiations broke up, Representative John D. Dingell urged the FTC and Justice Department to investigate the competitive implications of such a merger, expressing the fear that a wave of mergers might result in the Big Four CPA firms and noting that such concentration would be "unacceptable and inimical to the normally competitive nature of the accounting industry."

Yet Charles Cordry, deputy assistant director of the FTC's bureau of competition, points out that antitrust violations are difficult to prove against professional firms, particularly against private

[28] Edward Stamp and Maurice Moonitz, "International Auditing Standards—Parts I and II," *CPA Journal*, June and July, 1982, pp. 24–32, 48–53.

EXHIBIT 18-8

Overview of International Auditing Practices Concerning Standards, Independence, and Enforcement Activities

Western Europe:	Prefer standards to include compliance with laws and regulations and pressure for an audit of management.
European Economic Community:	Support for international harmony.
France:	Statutory auditors can only audit and cannot perform tax and MAS, whereas contractual auditors are not so restricted. There are regional councils with appeal available to a national council, with each having two qualified auditors and one judge. Over statutory auditors there is an organization patterned after the SEC which examines work papers and can approve or disapprove statutory auditors for a company. Although the company can ignore such disapproval, the reporting of such action to shareholders is required, and the regulators can refuse that company's prospectus.
Canada:	Objective state of mind.
Australia, New Zealand, and United States:	Auditors commonly serve as directors on the boards of nonclient companies.
West Germany:	Auditors cannot own shares in their clients but can do management consulting work.
France and Belgium:	Statutory auditors can own shares in their clients but cannot perform tax or consulting work for audit clients.
United Kingdom:	No direct financial interest but nonbeneficial interests, like being a trustee of an estate, are acceptable. No prohibition of tax or MAS but cannot serve as officers or directors of client companies. If a cause of action is possible in the courts, the institute is advised by legal counsel not to act.
Japan:	CPAs cannot hold a financial interest except shareholdings of about $1,000 or less in U.S. dollars or debt of less than $2,000. Cannot audit a company in which the CPA or spouse had been an officer or employer or had other important interest within the last year. The Tokyo Stock Exchange requires all new listings to be audited by a major auditing firm and has the power to examine working papers. Standards are believed to evolve in their general acceptance, and consensus will evolve into effective enforcement.
New Zealand:	Auditing standards are felt to be self-enforcing owing to legal consequences of nonadherence. Firms' quality control practices are also cited as effectively self-policing. Law requires its society to discipline its members and grants subpoena powers.
Netherlands:	Enforcement is likely to stress form over substance. The emphasis should be on independence. A disciplinary board and court of appeal, separate from the institute, have power of subpoena, and testimony is made under oath. Disciplinary hearings are not delayed by civil actions but run concurrently, often ending first. Board can order that auditor provide working papers for review. Penalties range from warnings to expulsion. Both lawyers and auditors serve on the board.
Australia:	Institute actions are delayed until after any legal proceedings; often this is an eight-year delay.

Adapted from Edward Stamp and Maurice Moonitz, "International Auditing Standards—Parts I and II," *CPA Journal,* June-July 1982, pp. 24-32, 48-53.

partnerships where public information is not readily available.[29]

If changes eventually occur via merger, regulators are likely to play a role in determining the degree of concentration that results. Moreover, smaller CPA firms are likely to vocalize their concerns through such mechanisms as the advertisement that "Bigness Is Not Goodness!" which appeared in the *Wall Street Journal* on October 1, 1982 (page 2).

New Audit Approaches

Twelve of the fourteen largest public accounting firms in the United States have developed a new

[29] Lee Berton, "Merger Issue Is Dividing CPA Firms," *Wall Street Journal,* October 16, 1984, Section 2, p. 37.

audit process within the recent few years, and the other two have development projects in progress. With this attention to applied research, the audit process of the 1990s may be entirely different from that of the 1980s.[30]

Industry Concentrations

A study of audit clients in 1971 indicated that Price Waterhouse audited 48.04 percent of amusements, 70.42 percent of office equipment, 44.20 percent of oil, and 60.79 percent of steel and coal. Deloitte Haskins & Sells audited 46.46 percent of the gas utilities; Touche Ross & Co. audited 38.95 percent of retailing; and Coopers & Lybrand audited 41.85 percent of metals (aluminum, copper, and fabricating) and 62.18 percent of the telephone industry.[31] But in the future, this specialization—in light of regulators' interests, changing audit procedures, and increased competitiveness—may change radically.

Scope of Services

Besides future regulatory changes, there are likely to be even greater changes in attest services. In October 1978, the AICPA's bylaws gave the Auditing Standards Board the following directive:

> The board shall be alert to new opportunities for auditors to serve the public, both by the assumption of new responsibilities and by improved ways of meeting old ones, and shall as expeditiously as possible develop standards and procedures that will enable the auditor to assume these responsibilities.

SAS No. 30, on "Reporting on Internal Accounting Control," and SAS No. 36, "Review of Interim Financial Information," are examples of standards covering new attest services. But to avoid a piecemeal development of such standards, the board is now reconsidering new standards of attestation to replace the ten generally accepted auditing standards, which date back to September 1948 and November 1949. The proposed definition of an *attest engagement* is

> one in which a certified public accountant either is engaged to issue, or does issue, a written communication that (1) expresses a conclusion with respect to the reliability of an assertion that is the responsibility of one party and (2) is or reasonably might be expected to be used by another (third) party. [p. 3]

The third party refers to anyone not responsible for the preparation and presentation of the assertion. This definition excludes: accounting service, tax, and management consulting engagements for the client; advocacy roles such as representation before the Internal Revenue Service; and expert witness activities. The reasons for the proposed adoption of attestation standards is to ensure that the GAAS (including review services) are covered by such standards and provide boundaries within which auditors' services can be expanded. The proposed attestation standards are summarized in Exhibit 18-9.[32] A comparison of the new proposed standards to current GAAS reveals that all references to financial statements and GAAP have been removed. The language accommodates the expansion of attestation services beyond historical financial statements and recognizes the growth of attest services beyond the traditional positive opinion (that is, the diverse levels of assurance currently provided). Another conspicuous change is deletion of the second standard of field work concerning internal control. That is, in part, due to its lack of relevance to many attestation engagements and also due to the fact that the notion is encompassed in the concept of sufficient evidence. Rather than restricting attestation to specific areas, financial information, or quantifiable data, the board is

[30] See James K. Loebbecke, "Auditing Research State of the Art: Auditing Approaches, Methods, Programs and Procedures," presented at the Peat, Marwick, Mitchell & Co. Audit Research Conference, May 26–27, 1981.

[31] John Grant Rhode, Gary M. Witsell, and Richard L. Kelsey, "An Analysis of Client–Industry Concentrations for Large Public Accounting Firms," *Accounting Review*, October 1974, pp. 772–787. Also see John W. Eichenseher and Paul Danos, "The Analysis of Industry-Specific Auditor Concentration: Towards an Explanatory Model," *Accounting Review*, July 1981, pp. 479–492.

[32] "Proposed Attestation Standards: Their Significance and Scope," File Ref. No. 3450 (New York: AICPA, December 19, 1984).

EXHIBIT 18-9
Proposed Attestation Standards

General Standards

1. The engagement shall be performed by a person or persons having adequate technical training and proficiency as an attester.

2. The engagement shall be performed by an attester or attesters having adequate knowledge in the subject matter of the assertion.

3. The attester shall perform an engagement only if he or she has reason to believe that the following two conditions exist:
   - the assertions are capable of evaluation against reasonable criteria which either have been established by a recognized body or are stated in the presentation of the assertions in a sufficiently clear and comprehensive manner for a reader to be able to understand them, and
   - the assertions are capable of reasonably consistent estimation or measurement using such criteria; that is, competent persons using the same or similar measurement or disclosure criteria should obtain materially similar estimates or measurements.

4. In all matters relating to the attest engagement, an independence in mental attitude shall be maintained by the attester or attesters.

5. Due professional care shall be exercised in the performance of the engagement.

Standards of Field Work

1. The work shall be adequately planned and assistants, if any, shall be properly supervised.

2. Sufficient evidence shall be obtained to provide a reasonable basis for the conclusion that is expressed in the attest report.

Standards of Reporting

1. The attester's report shall identify the assertions being reported on and state the character of his or her engagement.

2. The report shall state the attester's conclusion as to whether the assertions are presented in conformity with established or stated criteria against which they were measured.

3. The report shall state all of the attester's significant reservations about the engagement and the presentation of assertions.

4. The report on an engagement to evaluate an assertion that has been prepared in conformity with agreed-upon criteria or on an engagement to apply agreed-upon procedures should contain a statement limiting its use to the parties who have agreed upon such criteria or procedures.

"Proposed Attestation Standards: Their Significance and Scope," File Ref. No. 3450 (New York: AICPA, December 19, 1984).

proposing an emphasis on the consistency of estimation and the attester's competency in the subject matter. Clearly, these boundaries permit the expansion of attestation services far beyond today's activities.

Management Audits

One area in which the scope of auditing has expanded is management auditing, particularly in the utility industry. Many regulatory state commissions have imposed "management efficiency audits" on the utilities they oversee, to demonstrate that they are making utilities operate efficiently as a condition for rate relief. Management auditors review areas like personnel costs, capital structure, controls over EDP and plans for EDP activities, customer relations, environmental requirements and productivity practices.[33] *Management auditing* has been defined as the process of lending credibility to managements' representations. Such representations can be (1) financial in nature—such as number of stores or number of stockholders—(2) marketing related—such as shares of the market and advertising plans—(3) innovation related—such as research and development personnel (number

[33] Marvin E. Ray, "A New Twist for the Management Audit and Bond Ratings," *Public Utilities Fortnightly*, January 17, 1980, pp. 34–38.

and skills) and training programs—and (4) social-external—such as litigation cases, pollution control, and safety programs.[34]

In a management audit, the auditor judges whether managers have enough relevant information and techniques to identify and evaluate alternatives. But the auditor does not decide whether management is making the right strategic or operative decision.[35]

The management audit would appear to be feasible in light of the eight tentative postulates of auditing put forth by Mautz and Sharaf in *The Philosophy of Auditing:*

1. financial statements and data are verifiable—emphasis of means should permit such verifiability.
2. no necessary conflict of interest between the auditor and the management of the enterprise under audit—by setting up industry benchmarks, fairly objective analysis is possible.
3. financial statements and other information submitted for verification are free from collusive and other unusual irregularities—this risk can be assessed through control evaluation.
4. a satisfactory system of internal control eliminates the probability of irregularities—the focus would be upon management controls.
5. N/A; only tied to financial audits.
6. in the absence of clear evidence to the contrary, what was held true in the past for the enterprise under examination will hold true in the future—though the auditor should be unbiased in the approach to the examination.
7. when examining financial data for the purpose of expressing an independent opinion thereon, the auditor acts exclusively in the capacity of an auditor—via reliance on experts and development of management audit skills.
8. the professional status of the independent auditor imposes commensurate professional obligations—actions will have to be taken to ensure competency in areas being audited.[36]

Audits of the management process would focus on planning, implementation, control, decision, and communication process controls and are detailed in publications such as *Guide to an Audit of the General Management Process.*[37] In fact, the term *comprehensive auditing* has been applied to an examination that focuses on both financial and management controls and offers an objective and constructive assessment of the extent to which financial, human, and physical resources are managed economically, efficiently, and effectively and accountability relationships are reasonably served.

Governmental auditors have cited how little difference exists in the practice of auditing in one area of management performance, that is, financial statement exams, and a review of efficiency, economy, and effectiveness of an organization.[38] Further development of management auditing and operational auditing techniques is likely to occur over the next decade.

Helping Shape the Future

A former SEC chief accountant, John C. Burton wrote an article in *The New York Times* on April 13, 1980 under the title "Where Are the Angry Young CPAs?" in which he criticized the profession for not fulfilling its social function. As noted in an expansion of that article entitled "New Frontiers in Accounting,"

> In general, with a few exceptions, the profession has not been in the front lines of political, social or economic change, and our tools have frequently been ignored in the decisions which have shaped and are shaping our society.[39]

[34] Jack C. Robertson and Robert W. Clarke, "Verification of Management Representations: A First Step Toward Independent Audits of Management," *Accounting Review*, July 1971, pp. 562–571.

[35] John C. Burton, "Management Auditing," *Journal of Accountancy*, May 1968, pp. 4–46.

[36] Robert K. Mautz and Hussein A. Sharaf, *The Philosophy of Auditing* (American Accounting Association, Monograph No. 6, 1961).

[37] Treasury Board of Canada, Comptroller General, Interdepartmental Advisory Committee on Internal Audit, Ottawa, Ontario, March 1983.

[38] Leo Herbert, "An Historical Perspective of Government Auditing—With Special Reference to the U.S. General Accounting Office," University of Kansas Symposium on Auditing Problems (May 22–23, 1980).

[39] John C. Burton, "New Frontiers in Accounting," *CPA Journal*, September 1980, p. 16.

It is interesting to review this criticism alongside the introductory case in which the Metcalf Report faulted the profession for its involvement in testifying before Congress on taxation and other economic issues. The profession is likely to continue its activity politically, yet will no doubt be conservative in its participation due to the political liability of extensive involvement. As a result, such criticism from those who would have the profession do more is likely to persist alongside those who would have the profession remove itself totally from such activities. The future may well be in the hands of "angry young CPAs" who are forced to change hats and become politicians so that their accounting and auditing skills can be brought to bear on government matters. Though very much a minority, some CPAs have become state legislators and members of Congress, and they report that a great deal of education is needed for legislators to understand and use accounting and audit reports to improve overall accountability.

Appendix

EXHIBIT 18-A
Major Conclusions of the Cohen Commission

- Users expect the auditor to be concerned with the possibilities of both fraud and illegal behavior.
- Users expect more than they believe they are receiving.
- Independent audits are necessary because of the inherent potential conflict between an entity's management and users of its financial statements.
- Audited statements help ensure the market's efficiency by limiting the life of inaccurate information.
- Management's and the employees' conduct may be influenced positively by anticipation of the audit.
- Financial statements cannot be more accurate or reliable than GAAP permit.
- The traditional division of responsibility in which management is directly responsible for financial statements, and the auditors are responsible for expressing an opinion thereon is sound and should remain.
- Judgment is essential to apply properly the generally accepted accounting principles.
- Alternative accounting methods frequently are established before authoritative bodies have addressed the practice problems.
- Auditors are not more able to predict the likelihood of liquidation or other uncertainties than are financial statement users.
- Certain traditional audit steps, such as direct confirmation procedures, do not always produce the assurances that they are intended to provide.
- There is a substantial gap between some corporate behavior and society's view of appropriate corporate conduct.
- The audit function must be broader than the traditional association of the auditor with financial statements.
- Research indicates that many users misunderstand the auditor's role and responsibilities and that the present standard report only adds to the confusion.
- Many new accountants find that their formal education has not adequately prepared them for the responsibilities they face after graduating.
- A four-year liberal arts undergraduate program and a three-year graduate professional program, similar to law school, is necessary to permit accounting to compete on an equal footing for students making career decisions after college graduation.
- The Uniform CPA Examination appears to be a reasonable measure of the qualifications for initial admission to practice.

EXHIBIT 18-A (continued)

- It would be impractical to recommend that companies be prevented from hiring individuals who were previously employed by their public accounting firms, although measures to avoid the appearance of conflicts of interest are expected to be taken.
- When an accounting firm employs a specialist to perform specialized services for an audit client, the need to perform comprehensive audit procedures directed to such services is not eliminated.
- Except in the Westec case, the commission's research did not find instances in which the auditor's independence appeared to be compromised by providing other services.
- Increased scrutiny of changes of auditors is desirable.
- Rotation of firms should not be required. Many of the asserted advantages of rotating firms can be achieved by rotating personnel assigned to an engagement.
- Time and budget pressures frequently cause substandard auditing and are often due to excessive price competition.
- Excessive time pressure is one of the most pervasive factors leading to audit failures. Such pressures are an often-cited factor in judgment errors.
- No need has been established for removing the auditing standards–setting function from the domain of the accounting profession; the relationship between the SEC and AICPA has worked well.
- There should be no differences in the auditing standards applied to publicly owned corporations and to private entities.
- The oversight of professional practice should remain within the profession, and the concept of individual firms' having responsibility for the quality of their own practices should be retained. Voluntary peer reviews, provision of related reports to concerned parties, and the establishment of an oversight group to supervise the peer review process could improve overall quality control.
- Peer reviews of large, complex firms are probably better performed by another CPA firm that has the experience and ability to conduct a large and complex audit, although an AICPA local firm quality review team is a feasible alternative.
- Excessive secrecy is a serious weakness in the profession's disciplinary process.
- Disciplinary actions by the profession should not be restrained when litigation arises, unless the pending litigation is directly related to the misconduct charges and it is likely that the litigation would be unduly influenced by the disciplinary action.
- Some form of statutory limitation of monetary damages is essential to the continued healthy existence of the public accounting profession in the private sector, although that limit should provide significant penalties and redress.
- It does not appear that a comprehensive federal mechanism for regulating the profession would be superior to the present system, nor is a complete restructuring of the profession required.
- The less desirable effects of the present litigious environment is a reluctance by auditors to accept expanded responsibilities and the profession's unwillingness to define auditing standards more rigorously for fear of providing a basis for additional litigation.
- The commission endorses the use of court-appointed masters to make impartial expertise available whenever litigation is complex.
- "Safe-harbor rules" should be passed to cover auditors when they extend responsibilities into new, untried high-risk areas; such rules would require the plaintiff to prove that a specific standard was not met.

Adapted from Cohen Commission, "Summary of Conclusions and Recommendations," The Commission on Auditors' Responsibilities: Reports, Conclusions and Recommendations (New York: AICPA, 1978).

EXHIBIT 18-B

Recommendations of the Cohen Commission

Lines of Communication

- Closer, more active cooperation among boards of directors, independent auditors, and internal auditors is desirable and can be expected to strengthen corporate accountability.

Reporting and Accounting Alternatives

- Delete the phrase "present fairly" from the auditor's report, as it is unnecessary.

- When selecting among alternative GAAP, choose the principle that is most applicable to the transaction. The auditor should not merely accept management's selection but should evaluate the cumulative effect of management's judgment in the presentation of financial statements.

- "Subject to" qualifications for material uncertainties should be eliminated. Instead, a footnote on uncertainties, complying with SFAS No. 5, should be provided.

Auditor's Objectives

- Design audits to provide reasonable assurance that the financial statements are not affected by material fraud and that management is accountable for material amounts of corporate assets.

Selection of Clients and Audit Risk Assessment

- Auditors should feel no obligation for accepting or retaining a client about whose integrity he or she has reservations; such clients should be rejected.

- Due care includes understanding a client's business, methods of operations, significant practices, and regulatory requirements.

- A study and evaluation of controls to prevent and detect fraud should be a part of due care, and material weaknesses should be reported to management and the board (or the audit committee) and then followed up to ensure their elimination.

Fraud

- The AICPA should establish means for the regular dissemination of information on developments in perpetration and detection of fraud.

Effectiveness of Audit Techniques

- The AICPA and auditors should concentrate on the effectiveness of conventional auditing techniques and the development of new techniques.

- Auditors should not undertake special engagements to detect fraud without obtaining full understanding, by themselves and their clients, of the inherent limitations of such engagements.

Codes of Conduct

- Corporations should be required to adopt policy statements regarding the conduct that will not be tolerated, distribute them to shareholders and employees, and monitor compliance with the statements.

- Management's reports should state whenever a corporate code of conduct exists and should note that procedures have been implemented to monitor compliance. The auditor's report should state that the code and monitoring procedures have been reviewed, with conclusions regarding those aspects that can be audited.

Illegal Acts

- Upon discovering illegal or questionable acts, the auditor should not use quantitative ideas to assess materiality but should see that the problem is addressed by top management. If it is not, disclosure should be requested, and if refused, the auditor's report should disclose the matter.

Uncertainties

- Managers and legal advisers should report directly to users concerning the adequacy with which material uncertainties have been accounted for and disclosed, including the treatment of material uncertainties.

The Changing Profession

- When society perceives needs for new services, the public accounting profession should attempt to meet them.

- The auditor's association should be limited to accounting and financial information.

Internal Control

- The auditor should expand the study and evaluation of controls over the accounting system in order to determine whether they provide reasonable, though not absolute, assurance that the system is free of material weaknesses.

EXHIBIT 18-B (continued)

- Management's report should disclose the condition of controls and responses to auditors' suggestions that certain weaknesses be corrected, with the auditor reporting agreement or disagreement with management's description and disclosing material uncorrected weaknesses not noted in management's report.

Continuous Audits

- Continuous auditing is expected, so that all significant financial information released regularly during the year is audited. This can be facilitated by increasing the attention to controls, although users will need to understand the limitations of an audit function at an interim date.

Review of Other Information

- Auditors should read all other information accompanying audited financial statements, watching for inconsistencies requiring modification or disclosure in the audit report. The auditor's report should describe work performed on such information and conclusions reached.

Forecasts

- By standardizing forecast preparation, reviews of the process by auditors should be possible. Standards need to detail the type of information required for input and the means by which such information is to be recorded and documented.

Operational Auditing

- Information about efficiency, economy, and effectiveness of corporate programs, including social programs, that is produced by the accounting system and required to be disclosed should be subject to audit. However, separate evaluations of the degree to which a corporate activity is efficient, economic, or effective should not be provided by auditors.

Disclosure Issues and the Auditor's Report

- The auditor's report should describe his or her work, note that technical elements are involved in an audit, and express findings. Additional messages regarding other information in the annual report, association with interim information, internal accounting controls, corporate codes of conduct, and meetings with the audit committee of the company's board of directors should be included in the report. No reference to consistency should be made in the auditor's report, as that is appropriately a part of management's disclosures.

- APB No. 20 should be amended to require a standard note to the financial statements covering accounting changes.

- Audit reports should not refer to other auditors' work. Either enough work should be performed to take full responsibility, or management should present the other auditors' reports.

- Auditors should report on all unaudited financial information with which he or she is associated.

Information to Users

- Auditors should be present at stockholders' meetings and at due diligence meetings before the issuance of securities, so as to encourage contact between themselves and users. Auditors' attendance at such meetings should be announced.

Education

- Economics suggests that graduate professional accounting schools would be an effective intermediate step toward the creation of professional schools of accounting.

Educators' Involvement in the Profession

- The AICPA and state CPA societies should develop associate membership for accounting educators who are not CPAs—passing the CPA exam is a reasonable prerequisite for such membership.

CPA Exam

- As the quality of graduates improves, the level of the Uniform CPA Examination can be commensurately advanced.

Independence

- Professional standards should be expanded to cover the provision of advice on accounting principles in a manner that avoids jeopardizing perceived independence.

- In all advocacy engagements, CPAs should clearly communicate that their opinions are not presented in the capacity of independent auditors.

- CPA firms should not engage in employment recruiting or placement of individuals who would be directly involved in the decision to select or retain the independent auditors.

Other Services

- Auditors should inform the board or its audit committee of all services performed, fees for those services, the relationship of those services to the audit function, and the fact that information acquired in providing other services must be considered by the auditor in performing the audit function.

EXHIBIT 18-B (continued)

- Public accounting firms should establish procedures that ensure that knowledge gained while performing other services is communicated to the partner in charge of the audit.

- If the management report fails to disclose other services performed by the auditor, then the audit report should provide such information.

Selection of Auditors
- The board of directors, preferably including independent directors and having an audit committee, should control recommendations to shareholders on the appointment of the independent auditor and should regularly evaluate the relationship between auditors and management. In addition, the board should make cost quality evaluations of audit arrangements.

- Management reports should make 8-K type disclosures when changing auditors.

Early Earnings Releases
- Early press releases of earnings information should be accompanied by a statement like the following: "The accompanying results have been prepared by management; they may be subject to revision upon examination by the independent auditors."

"Low Balling"
- The practice of accepting an audit engagement with the expectation of offsetting early losses or lower revenues with later audits' fees threatens independence and should be considered by the AICPA's ethics division.

Ethical Issues
- Audit firms should draw up rules, and the AICPA should provide more definitive guidelines as to what amounts of client gifts or favors can be considered "token."

GAAS
- Additional guidance is needed regarding how smaller entities are to be audited.

- GAAS should offer more specific guidance.

Progress
- Rather than treating technological and methodological advances in auditing as proprietary, they should be quickly and widely disseminated to ensure maximum progress by the profession.

Standard-Setting Practices
- The present AudSEC should be replaced by a smaller, full-time committee compensated by the AICPA, with support provided by task forces and subcommittees of AICPA members and staff.

- Auditing standards ought to incorporate a statement of the auditor's role with timely updating, as needed.

- Standard setters should include outside participants and should encourage responses to exposure drafts.

Improving the Profession's Quality
- The profession's self-disciplinary efforts should be strengthened.

- Public accounting firms should experiment with voluntarily disclosing information.

- Greater activity and aggressiveness by state boards could usefully augment the total system of regulating auditors. Uniformity in state regulation is encouraged.

- Penalties imposed by disciplinary bodies should be well publicized.

Research
- The AICPA and CPA firms should establish a mechanism for timely and continuing analyses of audit failures as they move through the judicial or regulatory system and dissemination of these published analyses to practitioners, teachers, and others.

Litigation
- Appropriate legislation should be enacted to deter nuisance or strike suits against auditors.

Adapted from Cohen Commission, "Summary of Conclusions and Recommendations," The Commission on Auditors' Responsibilities: Reports, Conclusions and Recommendations (New York: AICPA 1978).

EXHIBIT 18-C

Structure and Functions of the Private Companies Practice Section of the AICPA's Division of CPA Firms

I. Source of Authority

The section was established by a resolution of the Council of the AICPA adopted on September 17, 1977.

II. Name

The name of the section shall be the "Private Companies Practice Section" of the AICPA Division of CPA Firms.

III. Objectives

The objectives of the section shall be to achieve the following:

1. Improve the quality of services by CPA firms to private companies through the establishment of practice requirements for member firms.
2. Establish and maintain an effective system of self-regulation of member firms by means of mandatory peer reviews, required maintenance of appropriate quality controls and the imposition of sanctions for failure to meet membership requirements.
3. Provide a better means for member firms to make known their views on professional matters, including the establishment of technical standards.

IV. Membership

1. Eligibility and Admission of Members

All CPA firms all of whose partners, shareholders or proprietors are members of the AICPA are eligible for membership in the section. To become a member, a firm must submit to the section a written application agreeing to abide by all of the requirements for membership and submitting such non-financial information about the firm as the executive committee may require.

The membership of the section shall consist of all firms which meet the admission requirements and continue to maintain their membership in good standing.

2. Termination of Members

Membership of a CPA firm may be terminated:

a. By submission of a resignation providing the firm is not the subject of a pending investigation or recommendation of the Peer Review Committee for sanctions or other disciplinary action by the Executive Committee.
b. By action of the Executive Committee for failure to adhere to the requirements of membership.

3. Requirements of Members

Member firms shall be obligated to abide by the following:

a. Ensure that all partners, shareholders or proprietors have a valid and unrevoked license or permit to practice as a CPA and are members of the AICPA.
b. Adhere to AICPA Quality Control Standards established by the AICPA Quality Control Standards Committee.
c. Submit to peer reviews of the firm's accounting and audit practice every three years or at such additional times as designated by the Executive Committee, the reviews to be conducted in accordance with review standards established by the section's Peer Review Committee.
d. Ensure that all professionals in the firm resident in the United States, including CPAs and non-CPAs, participate in at least 40 hours of continuing professional education annually.
e. Maintain such minimum amounts and types of accountants' liability insurance as shall be prescribed from time to time by the Executive Committee.
f. Pay dues as established by the Executive Committee and comply with the rules and regulations of the section as established from time to time by the Executive Committee and with the decisions of the Executive Committee in respect of matters within its competence, to cooperate with the Peer Review Committee in connection with its duties, including disciplinary proceedings, and to comply with any sanction which may be imposed by the Executive Committee.

V. Governing Bodies

The activities of the section shall be governed by an Executive Committee having senior status within the AICPA with authority to carry out the activities of the section. Such activities shall not conflict with the policies and standards of the AICPA.

At the discretion of the Executive Committee all activities of the section may be subject to the oversight and public reporting thereon by a Public Oversight Board appointed by the Executive Committee with the approval of the AICPA Board of Directors.

VI. Executive Committee

1. Composition and Terms

a. The Executive Committee shall be composed of representatives of 21 member firms.
b. The terms of Executive Committee members shall be for three years with initial staggered terms to provide for seven expirations each year.
c. Executive Committee members shall continue in office until their successors have been appointed.

2. Appointment

a. The members of the Executive Committee shall be appointed by the AICPA Chairman with the approval of the AICPA Board of Directors.

EXHIBIT 18-C (continued)

b. All appointments after the initial Executive Committee is established shall also require approval of the then existing Executive Committee.
c. Nominations for appointments of representatives of member firms to the Executive Committee shall be provided to the Chairman of the AICPA by a nominating committee. The nominating committee shall be elected by the AICPA Council and shall consist of individuals drawn from seven of the member firms of the section. It is intended that nominations shall adhere to the principle that the Executive Committee shall at all times include at least fourteen representatives of firms with no SEC clients.

3. Election of Chairman

The Chairman of the Executive Committee shall be elected from among its members to serve at the pleasure of the Executive Committee but in no event for more than three one-year terms.

4. Responsibilities and Functions

The Executive Committee shall:

a. Establish general policies for the section and oversee its activities.
b. Amend requirements for membership as necessary but in no event shall such requirements be designed so as to unreasonably preclude membership by any CPA firm.
c. If necessary, establish budgets and dues requirements to fund activities of the section such as special projects or a public oversight board. Staffing of the section will be provided for in the AICPA general budget. Any dues shall be scaled in proportion to the size of member firms.
d. Determine sanctions to be imposed on member firms based upon recommendations of the Peer Review Committee of the section.
e. Receive, evaluate and act upon other complaints received with respect to actions of member firms.
f. If the Executive Committee decides to appoint a Public Oversight Board, select public persons to serve on it and establish its functions and compensation with the approval of the AICPA Board of Directors.
g. Appoint persons to serve on such committees and task forces as necessary to carry out the functions of the section.
h. Make recommendations to other AICPA boards and committees for their consideration.
i. Organize and conduct annual regional conferences covering appropriate practice subjects.

5. Quorum, Voting, Meetings and Attendance

a. Fourteen members of the Executive Committee or their designated alternates must be present and represented to constitute a quorum.
b. Eleven affirmative votes shall be required for action on all matters except for items 4(b) and (d) under "Responsibilities and Functions" for which fourteen affirmative votes shall be required.
c. Meetings of the Executive Committee shall be held at such time and in such locations as the chairman shall determine.
d. Representatives of member firms of the section may attend meetings of the Executive Committee as observers under rules established by the Executive Committee except when the committee is considering disciplinary matters.

VII. Public Oversight Board

1. Type of Members, Selection and Appointment

If it chooses to, the Executive Committee may, with the approval of the AICPA Board of Directors, select and appoint a five-member Public Oversight Board and establish its functions and compensation. Members of such Board shall be drawn from among prominent individuals of high integrity and reputation including but not limited to former public officials, lawyers, bankers, securities industry executives, educators, economists and business executives.

2. Chairman and Terms of Members

a. The Chairman shall be appointed by the Executive Committee.
b. The terms of members shall be for a period of three years renewable at the pleasure of the Executive Committee.

3. Responsibilities and Functions

The Executive Committee may require a Public Oversight Board to:

a. Monitor and evaluate the regulatory and sanction activities of the Peer Review and Executive Committees to assure their effectiveness.
b. Determine that the Peer Review Committee is ascertaining that firms are taking appropriate action as a result of peer reviews.
c. Conduct continuing oversight of all other activities of the section.
d. Make recommendations to the Executive Committee for improvements in the operations of the section.
e. Publish periodic reports on results of its oversight activities.
f. Engage staff to assist in carrying out its functions.
g. Have the right for any or all of its members to attend any meetings of the Executive Committee.

VIII. Peer Reviews

1. Review Requirements

Peer reviews of member firms shall be conducted every three years or at such additional times as designated by the Executive Committee.

2. Peer Review Committee

a. Composition and Appointment

The Peer Review committee shall be a continuing committee appointed by the Executive Committee and shall consist of 15 individuals selected from member firms.

EXHIBIT 18-C (continued)

b. Responsibilities and Functions
The Peer Review Committee shall:
1. Administer the program of peer reviews for member firms.
2. Establish standards for conducting reviews.
3. Establish standards for reports on peer reviews and publication of such reports.
4. Recommend sanctions and other disciplinary decisions (including whether the name of the affected firm is published) to the Executive Committee.
5. Keep appropriate records of peer reviews which have been conducted.

3. Peer Review Objectives
The objectives of peer reviews shall be to determine that:
a. Member firms, as distinguished from individuals, are maintaining and applying quality controls in accordance with standards established by the AICPA Quality Control Standards Committee. Reviews for this purpose shall include a review of working papers rather than specific "cases." (The existence of "cases" in a firm might raise questions concerning its quality controls.)
b. Member firms are meeting membership requirements.

IX. Sanctions Against Firms
1. Authority to Impose
The Executive Committee shall have the authority to impose sanctions on member firms either on its own initiative or on the basis of recommendations of the Peer Review committee and shall establish procedures designed to assure due process to firms in connection with disciplinary proceedings.
2. Types of Sanctions
The following types of sanctions may be imposed on member firms for failure to maintain compliance with the requirements for membership:
a. Require corrective measures by the firm including consideration by the firm of appropriate actions with respect to individual firm personnel.
b. Additional requirements for continuing professional education.
c. Accelerated or special peer reviews.
d. Admonishment, censure or reprimand.
e. Monetary fines.
f. Suspension from membership.
g. Expulsion from membership.

X. Financing and Staffing of Section
1. Section Staff and Meeting Costs
a. The President of the AICPA shall appoint a staff Director and assign such other staff as may be required by the section.
b. The costs of the section staff and normal meeting costs shall be paid out of the general budget of the AICPA.
2. Public Oversight Board and Special Projects
a. The costs of a Public Oversight Board, if appointed, and its staff shall be paid out of the dues of the section.
b. The cost of special projects shall be paid out of the dues of the section.

XI. Relationship to Other AICPA Segments
Nothing in the organizational structure and functions of this section shall be construed as taking the place of or changing the operations of existing senior committees of the AICPA or the status of individual CPAs as members of the AICPA.

From "Organizational Structure and Functions of the Private Companies Practice Section of the AICPA Division of CPA Firms," *Journal of Accountancy*, November 1977, pp. 116-117.

REVIEW QUESTIONS

1. What apparently prompted the Metcalf Report?
2. Compare and contrast the activities of the Metcalf Committee and the Moss Commission.
3. Which of the Cohen Commission's recommendations have been adopted?
4. With which conclusions of the Cohen Commission do you disagree, and why?
5. Besides the SEC's, what other types of regulation have influenced the accounting profession?
6. What has the SEC's position been with respect to the profession's self-regulatory efforts?
7. What is the role of the Public Oversight Board?

8. Who appears to have prevailed in the dispute over the performance of management advisory services? Support your position.
9. How has the AICPA acted to deter government regulation? Be specific.
10. In what sense has the private sector affected the accounting profession?
11. What is the purpose of an audit committee and what are its responsibilities?
12. How can auditors improve their communication with financial statement users?
13. How do you think the profession's standards will change over the next ten years?
14. What is the expressed intent of Dingell's investigation? How does it compare with the experiences of the 1970s?
15. How diverse are international auditing standards? Provide two examples.
16. Define attestation.
17. Compare and contrast the proposed standards of attestation and the current ten generally accepted auditing standards (that is, the general, fieldwork, and reporting standards).
18. What is a management audit?

EXERCISES

1. "To those who say accountants are fulfilling their role responsibly, I say, what is their role? They are making the debits equal the credits—yes. But is that enough? No." (Abraham Briloff, professor of accounting at Baruch College and a tenacious critic of the accounting profession)

   Respond to Briloff's questions.
2. "Accounting issues are too important to be left to accountants alone." (Metcalf Report) Do you agree? Why or why not?
3. In a speech before the Mountain States Conference in Scottsdale, Arizona (April 23, 1976), Wallace Olson stressed that governmental intervention affected the entire profession, not merely the Big Eight, and repeated Ben Franklin's famous warning: "We must hang together or we shall surely hang separately."[40] What did Wallace Olson mean? Has the profession heard Franklin's warning? How has it reacted?
4. Given the reports of litigation in the financial press that allege accounting or auditing failure, how can one claim that peer review and self-regulation activities have been effective?
5. It has been pointed out that there is no way to estimate what might have gone wrong had there been no self-regulatory action by the profession. What do you think would have been the result of inaction?
6. In the fiscal year ended June 30, 1983, Peat, Marwick, Mitchell had 1,375 partners, 12,500 other employees, 100 offices, U.S. revenue of $810 million, and worldwide revenue of $1.2 billion. The international firm has 82 firms, 2,340 partners, 25,460 other employees, and 328 offices in 82 countries.[41] Do you believe that the size of a Big Eight firm should be troublesome to government regulators? Why or why not?
7. In 1977, the Arthur Andersen World Wide Organization was audited by Deloitte Haskins & Sells. In that same year, Price Waterhouse issued unaudited annual reports. Since that time, financial reports by CPAs have become less commonplace. Do you concur with the Cohen Commission's conclusion that the sources of demand for such disclosures are not apparent? Why or why not? What is the desirability of the issuance of (a) an annual report and (b) audited financials?
8. Accountants seem to be changing. It is becoming easier for many practitioners to speak of the "accounting industry" or "business" rather than "the profession." . . . Professor Briloff is not the only party concerned with whether the growth of the aggressive consultant mentality may be affecting the "typical auditor."[42] Do you see a problem with the image of the profession, as described above? Explain your response.

QUESTIONS ADAPTED FROM PROFESSIONAL EXAMINATIONS

1. **Multiple Choice**

   Select the one answer that best completes the statement or answers the question.

   1.1 Which of the following is a conclusion reached by the Commission on Auditors' Responsibilities, the independent commission established by the American Institute of Certified Public Accoun-

[40] In his speech entitled "Who Accounts for Accountants?".

[41] Lee Berton, "Who's News: Peat Marwick Elects Horner as Chairman of Domestic Firm," *Wall Street Journal*, October 11, 1984, p. 20.

[42] George C. Mead, "The Accounting Profession in the 1980's—Some SEC Perspectives," *Auditing Symposium V; Proceedings of the 1980 Touche Ross, University of Kansas Symposium on Auditing Problems*, edited by Donald R. Nichols and Howard F. Stettler (Lawrence: University of Kansas, 1980), p. 148.

tants to study the role and responsibilities of independent auditors?

- **a.** Different auditing standards should apply to audits of publicly owned and private entities.
- **b.** The AICPA Auditing Standards Executive Committee should be replaced by a larger, part-time group.
- **c.** The oversight of professional practice should remain with the accounting profession.
- **d.** "Safe harbors" should be made available for all work done by an auditor.

(CPA exam adapted)

1.2 A CPA who is seeking to sell an accounting practice must

- **a.** Not allow a peer review team to look at working papers and tax returns without permission from the client before consummation of the sale.
- **b.** Not allow a prospective purchaser to look at working papers and tax returns without permission from the client.
- **c.** Give all working papers and tax returns to the client.
- **d.** Retain all working papers and tax returns for a period of time sufficient to satisfy the statute of limitations.

(CPA exam adapted)

CASES FOR DISCUSSION

1. The British journal *Accountancy* offered some projections for the year 2080, as follows:

> What is certain, brothers, is that you cannot extrapolate the future from the present, and hope to get it right. For instance, if I extrapolate demographic trends and the rise in the chartered institute's membership, then I get to the point somewhere around 2031 when the entire population will be chartered accountants. Now I do not find that an unsatisfactory future, for it would be nice if everyone were quietly spoken and soberly dressed and tied their shoelaces neatly. Nor do I find it wholly implausible, since accountants have an infinite capacity for generating work for each other. But I know that future cannot happen, because I know that some great big social discontinuity is bound to drop out of the sky and send us off in some other direction. If you want to see the future, first choose your discontinuity.
>
> Given the range of possible discontinuities, I felt that it would be unfair to present you with a single future, and I now offer you [two] futures—the first is very happy and the last is very sad. These set the extremes, for there can be nothing happier or sadder.
>
> A very happy future. The world is a very happy place. Even the humblest Bushman has two helicopters on his heliport and a personal robot to clip his toe-nails. Life expectancy has more than doubled over the past century, but overcrowding has been avoided through the colonisation of a group of planets a little bit beyond Alpha Centauri, each of which proved to be temperate and fertile and capable of making every one who settled on them, well, very happy too. Over the past century, everyone became so wealthy that there was a massive increase in the demand for auditing services.
>
> Some centi-sexagarians still prefer to have a review, but most of the population would no more do without the security of an annual audit of their affairs than they would walk out in the rain without switching on their field force. In turn, most of the population are only too eager to take advantage of the wide range of non-audit services now offered by accountants—services which started with personal financial counselling towards the end of the past century and moved successively into computer-based fortune telling, interior design consultancy and psychotherapy. As a result all chartered accountants are now incredibly wealthy. They are also very happy. . . .
>
> A very sad future. By the year 2050, the de-industrialisation of the West was complete. All manufactured products were imported, and the only exports were invisibles. (Food exports from North America had ceased by 2030 when all food production, surplus to the weekly ration requirements, was converted into alcohol fuel.) The most visible of these invisibles was accounting services.
>
> In 2055, mutual accusations of dumping led to a tariff war over accounting services between the North American Federation (as the U.S. and English-speaking parts of Canada had by then become) and Engwales (as the UK had become after the Great Secessions). From that point on, the commercial battle for accounting work in the Third World grew bitter.
>
> The flash-point came in 2065. The NAF accused Engwales of winning the audit of the Lower Chad Solar Energy Authority, by means of a secret guarantee that the Authority would be spared any audit qualification for a period of five years. Engwales responded by ordering the expulsion of a visiting Peer Group Review Team. Over the following five years relationships deteriorated to the point where as a final step in the escalation of accounting conflict, NAF banned the import of goods from any company which did not comply with NAF Financial Accounting Standards.
>
> The rest is history. Five minutes after NAF customs officers turned away a hydro-freighter carrying a cargo of pornographs from a Micronesian company audited by McQuibble, McQuery in accordance with Engwales Accounting Standards, a nuclear strike devastated all major cities and missile sites in North America. By then, of course, the retaliatory missiles had raced as far as Rockall.
>
> In the Post-Holocaust world, the surviving accountants were treated by the surviving non-accountants as lower than the mutants. Driven out from the villages, the accountants formed little communes in the desert. At night they would huddle round small fires of small twigs, and recite as much as they could remember of the standard audit report.
>
> During the day, the bolder, more fleet of foot among them, would squat outside the gate of the nearest village hoping—pathetically—that someone might come out and offer them a Reporting Accountant's Investigation, or even some write-up work on incomplete records. But the world was tired of

accountants and they would be driven away by stones and by those fierce dogs which had survived.[43]

Share your reactions to these extreme projections, and then formulate your own idea of what the auditing profession will be like in the year 2080. Give the reasons for your forecast, and when possible, support the assumptions for your projections.

2. In an article discussing the role of the Public Oversight Board, Chief Staff Officer Louis W. Matusiak noted:

> To begin, it seems appropriate to put the accounting profession's problems in perspective. To many of us, it may seem that everyone is picking on us accountants to the exclusion of everyone else. An objective view, however, leads to a different conclusion. Not too long ago, members of all professions were held in general high esteem. The doctor's image was that of a person dedicated solely to the well-being of his patients serving their needs during all hours of the day and night; the teacher was a devoted, selfless pedagogue, who was paid primarily in psychic rather than monetary income; the lawyer was a defender of the poor and downtrodden, working unselfishly to see that justice was done. Accountants were not generally understood but were considered austere and unfathomable but valuable advisors to business. Today, however, most professions are under attack. The aura of the professional person who with an inner sense of ethics works for the common good is replaced by the portrait of a tainted person who puts self-interest above public interest and whose ethics leave something to be desired. It is evident that all the learned professions are not the splendid companies, held in awe and respect, that they once were.
>
> Doctors are now seen as profiteers, often of doubtful competence. Lawyers have never been popular, but now they are often thought to be neglectful and extortionate and often dishonest. Latest on the carpet, we accountants are being viewed as masters of misrepresentation. Rather than being honored and respected, "the professional man" is more and more spoken of with criticism and contempt.
>
> But if a profession is to be judged rightly, it cannot be done from afar. It must be done by someone with knowledge of the facts.[44]

Do you agree with Matusiak's observations? How do you believe the accounting profession can be judged "rightly"?

3. The Metcalf staff report accused the profession of an antitrust conspiracy and criticized the structure of the profession and its role in big business. The report concluded that the Big Eight are too powerful, dominate the AICPA and the FASB, strengthen their hold on audit clients by selling additional advisory services, represent clients on legislative matters, and are part of a conspiracy by which *Fortune* 500 companies through their auditors and through interlocking directorates dominate the American economy. These more radical staff criticisms, for whatever reasons, did not find their way into the official Senate Subcommittee report.[45]

What reactions do you have to such criticisms? How can the profession curb such perceptions and attitudes? What has already been done that may help alter such attitudes?

4. Consider the following testimony in the following hypothetical case:

Plaintiff's attorney. Mr. CPA, what were you engaged to perform for Small Manufacturing?

CPA. I was retained by the company's president to compile its calendar 19X2 financial statements.

Attorney. What do you mean by compile?

CPA. According to our professional standards, financial statements are compiled when a CPA presents in financial statement format financial information that is the representation of management without undertaking to express any assurance on the statements. The CPA isn't required, beyond information he may have acquired as a result of performing other services for the client, to make inquiries or otherwise corroborate or review information supplied by the entity, although he might consider it necessary to perform some accounting services to enable him to compile the statements.

Attorney. Did the company president understand what you meant by this compiling process?

CPA. I explained it very carefully.

Attorney. Then in your opinion, your client knew that you were not verifying these statements in any way?

CPA. I'm sure he understood.

Attorney. Did you submit an engagement letter to your client explaining what you were going to do and what you weren't going to do?

CPA. No, I felt that he understood my oral explanation.

Attorney. You heard Mr. Small, the president, testify that he has always expected CPA-prepared statements to have a significant degree of reliability, no matter how the CPA describes his or her services.

CPA. That isn't how I explained my role to him, and I felt at that time that he understood what I meant.

[43] "Accounting Odyssey—2080," *Accountancy*, May 1980, pp. 65, 67.

[44] Louis W. Matusiak, "The Role of the Public Oversight Board in the Accounting Profession's Self-Regulatory Program," *Ohio CPA*, Autumn 1979, p. 144.

[45] Ibid., p. 145.

Attorney. And you decided not to describe your role in writing?

CPA. I felt that the compilation report spoke for itself.

Attorney. Isn't it now true that the statements turned out to be significantly in error?

CPA. Yes. We later found out that the inventory was overstated.

Attorney. Shouldn't this have been disclosed by the procedures you performed?

CPA. No. I performed only those procedures required by our standards, plus one or two additional tests.

Attorney. Do your working papers document this?

CPA. My notes certainly do.

Attorney. What are the schedules with various percentages listed on them that we found in your papers?

CPA. They were tests of some monthly gross profit percentages, and they were varied, but the variations didn't seem significant.

Attorney. Why didn't these varied percentages arouse your suspicions?

CPA. The client requested a compilation and not an audit. Also, as I indicated, the variations didn't appear excessive.

Attorney. Was there anyone in Small Manufacturing's accounting department capable of preparing those statements?

CPA. The company's accountant is a CPA, so he probably could have done it.

Attorney. Why was Mr. Small willing to pay to have the work done when his own accounting staff could have done it?

CPA. Creditors like your client often prefer an outside CPA, for obvious reasons.

Attorney. Why would a bank rely on financial statements with which you were associated when they were not verified?

CPA. My report clearly stated that the statements were compiled and we didn't hold out to do anything other than what the client asked us to do.

Is the foregoing dialogue[46] an imaginative conjecture or could it actually occur?

An accountant's exposure to the risk of legal liability results in part from an "expectation gap" between the perceived and the actual responsibilities assumed by an accountant. While the expectations gap cited here relates to compilation and review services, do you perceive a similar expectations gap for other aspects of CPAs' professional services? How might the gap depicted in the case be addressed?

5. In describing questions asked by stockholders about accountants, a legend was provided for illustrations showing the management's reactions. The legend for the face depicted in the following excerpt [*not reprinted here*] was "An embarrassing question—one that management cannot answer gracefully or would rather not be confronted with at the annual meeting." If you were the auditor and asked to respond to these questions, how would you answer the stockholders?

- Do auditing firms allow their partners to serve as directors for client corporations?
- Do the company's auditors make suggestions in writing regarding the company's system of internal check and control? If so, to whom are such suggestions directed and have such suggestions been adopted by the company?
- Are the auditors satisfied that the company's budgetary and accounting systems are adequate to provide necessary information for management decisions?
- Do the auditors' responsibilities extend to the stockholders as well as to the officers and directors?
  (The answer to this is yes. The auditors' responsibilities extend to any third party who relies on the company's financial statements on which the auditors have expressed an opinion.)
- Have the auditors had any serious disagreements with the company's officers during the year and, if so, who prevailed?
- Do the auditors consider it a duty to reveal to anyone other than their client the fact that they are aware that information previously published by management is not correct?
  (This would depend on the nature of the finding. Before taking a further step, such as disclosure in a joint statement to the public, the matter would be thoroughly discussed with top management.)[47]

[46] Adapted from examples provided in various articles appearing in the *Journal of Accountancy* and *CPA Journal.*

[47] "What Stockholders Are Asking About Accountants," *The Practical Accountant,* January–February 1974, p. 56.

Appendix

A Brief Topical Outline of Statements on Auditing Standards

Statement on Auditing Standards	Date Issued	Title/Outline of Content
1	November 1972	**Codification of Auditing Standards and Procedures**
Section 110		**Responsibilities and Functions of the Independent Auditor** I. The objective of an ordinary examination is an opinion on the fairness with which it presents financial position, results of operations, and changes in financial position in conformity with GAAP. II. The financial statements are management's representations. III. Which audit procedures are necessary in the circumstances is to be an informed judgment of a qualified professional person with the education and experience to practice as an independent auditor. IV. The auditor is responsible for complying with accepted standards.
Section 150		**Generally Accepted Auditing Standards** I. Auditing procedures refer to acts to be performed, whereas standards refer to the objectives of the procedures, the quality of the performance, and the judgment exercised in performing an examination. II. GAAS include general standards requiring adequate training and proficiency, independence in mental attitude, and the exercise of due professional care; field work standards requiring adequate planning and supervision, a proper study and evaluation of internal control, and sufficient competent evidential matter; and reporting standards requiring a statement on the accordance with GAAP, recognition of consistency, adequate disclosure, and an opinion or an assertion that an opinion cannot be expressed and the reasons why. III. Materiality and relative risk assessments are the basis for applying GAAS.
Section 201		**Nature of General Standards** I. General standards apply to field work and reporting.
Section 210		**Training and Proficiency of the Independent Auditor** I. Proper education and experience in the field of auditing are essential to meet GAAS. II. Proficiency in accounting and auditing requires a continual awareness of professional developments.
Section 220		**Independence** I. Independence implies judicial impartiality, intellectual honesty, and freedom from any obligation to or interest in the client, its management, or its owners. II. Independent auditors should avoid situations that may lead to others' doubt as to their independence. III. The institute's Code of Professional Ethics has the force of professional law for the independent auditor.
Section 230		**Due Care in the Performance of Work** I. All auditors are to observe the standards of field work and reporting and perform their work with due care. II. Critical review is required at every level of supervision of work done and judgment exercised.
Section 310		**Relationship Between the Auditor's Appointment and Planning** I. Early appointment enables expeditious planning and interim audit work. II. Appointment near or after the year-end date is acceptable, but auditors should discuss with clients before accepting the engagement the possible necessity of a qualified opinion or disclaimer.

Statement on Auditing Standards	Date Issued	Title/Outline of Content
Section 320		**The Auditor's Study and Evaluation of Internal Control** I. The purpose of the auditor's study and evaluation of internal control is to establish a basis for reliance thereon in determining the nature, extent, and timing of audit tests to be applied in the examination of the financial statements. II. Definitions of transactions, administrative controls, accounting controls, basic concepts of control, the role of data processing, the nature of compliance tests, and the relationship of control evaluation to other audit procedures are provided.
Section 331		**Receivables and Inventories** I. Confirmation of receivables and observation of inventories are generally accepted auditing procedures, and if not employed by the independent auditors, they have the burden of justifying the opinion they express. II. Guidelines are provided on how to confirm receivables, how to observe inventories, and in particular, how to confirm inventories held in public warehouses.
Section 332		**Long-term Investments** I. Auditors should examine sufficient competent evidential matter supporting the existence, ownership, cost, and carrying amount of investments, income and losses, and related disclosures. II. Evidential matter is often in the form of audited financial statements, unaudited financial statements, market quotations, appraisals, and collateral. III. To audit investments recorded using the equity method of accounting, management must be asked whether it has significant influence over the entity.
Section 410		**Adherence to Generally Accepted Accounting Principles** I. The auditor should express an opinion as to whether financial statements conform to GAAP (i.e., a statement of fact is not required).
Section 420		**Consistency of Application of Generally Accepted Accounting Principles** I. Accounting changes that affect consistency, requiring disclosure in the auditor's report, include changes in accounting principle, corrections of errors in principle, changes in principles that are inseparable from changes in estimate, and changes in the reporting entity. II. If the auditee is in its first year of operation, no reference should be made to consistency. III. If only the current year is reported, consistency refers to the preceding year; if two or more years are reported, consistency is reported regarding the preceding year if there are financial statements on which the auditor is reporting for that year.
Section 530		**Dating of the Independent Auditor's Report** I. Generally, the date of the audit report should coincide with the date of the field work's completion. II. If there are later events that require disclosure, the auditors may either dual date their report or use the later date. III. Reissued reports commonly bear the original reporting date.
Section 542		**Other Conditions Which Preclude the Application of Necessary Auditing Procedures** I. If opening inventories cannot be adequately examined, the auditor should either disclaim an opinion on the statement of income or qualify the opinion. II. Similarly, scope limitations affecting the audit of long-term investments can lead to a qualified opinion or disclaimer.
Section 543		**Part of Examination Made by Other Independent Auditors** I. Principal auditors must decide whether to refer to examinations made by other auditors. If such reference is made, the responsibility should be clearly divided. II. Whenever other auditors are involved, the other auditors' professional reputation and independence should be verified.

Statement on Auditing Standards	Date Issued	Title/Outline of Content
Section 544		**Lack of Conformity with Generally Accepted Accounting Principles** I. Regulated companies' financial statements for purposes other than filings with their regulators should be dealt with in the same manner as are unregulated companies' statements with respect to reporting on noncompliance with GAAP.
Section 545		**Inadequate Disclosure** I. If information required by GAAP is omitted, a qualified or adverse opinion should be issued, and the information should be given in the audit report.
Section 546		**Reporting on Inconsistency** I. Any changes in accounting should be indicated in the auditor's report, with a statement as to the auditor's concurrence with the change. II. In the initial exam, the auditor must ensure that the same accounting principles are used in the current and the preceding year.
Section 560		**Subsequent Events** I. Information received after the date of the balance sheet about conditions that existed at the date of the balance sheet should be used to adjust estimates in the financial statements. II. Subsequent events relating to conditions that did not exist at the balance sheet date should be disclosed if the financial statements would otherwise be misleading; such events include the loss of a plant or inventories in a fire or flood, purchase of a business, and a sale of a bond or capital stock issue. III. To identify subsequent events, auditors should review interim statements; ask officers and other executives about contingencies, significant changes in stock, debt, or working capital, and unusual adjustments; read available minutes; talk to legal counsel; and obtain letters of representation regarding significant matters.
Section 561		**Subsequent Discovery of Facts Existing at the Date of the Auditor's Report** I. If such information is judged to affect a past report, on which persons are relying, it should be investigated to assess its reliability. The auditee's management (including the board of directors) should be notified, with a concurrent request for cooperation. II. If the subsequent report is imminent, disclosure can be made in the new financial statements regarding revisions; if not imminent, revised financials and auditor's report should be issued. III. If the effect of the subsequently discovered information cannot be quickly determined, known users of the past report should be notified. IV. If an auditee refuses to take the necessary steps for adequate disclosure, the auditors should notify each of the directors that they will take action to notify users in the absence of disclosure by the client. Such action should include notifying the client that the auditor's report can no longer be associated with the financial statements and notifying regulatory agencies and known users. V. It is recommended that auditors seek an attorney's advice when handling these matters.
Section 901		**Public Warehouses — Controls and Auditing Procedures for Goods Held** I. An independent auditor of a warehouse person should study and evaluate accounting and administrative controls, test records and warehouse receipts for accountability, observe physical counts of goods in custody, and confirm accountability. II. Definitions of types of warehouses, warehouse receipts, regulation, internal controls, and audit procedures are provided for both the warehouse person and for those storing goods in public warehouses.
2 (Section 509)	October 1974	**Reports on Audited Financial Statements** I. The types of audit reports, the circumstances in which each is appropriate, and examples are detailed. II. The fourth standard of reporting determines the language of the auditor's report. III. Departures from the auditor's standard report include scope limitations, use of other auditors, departure from GAAP, inconsistent application of principles, uncertainties, and the emphasis of a matter regarding the financial statements.

Statement on Auditing Standards	Date Issued	Title Outline of Content
3	December 1974	**Superseded by SAS 48.**
4	December 1974	**Superseded by SAS 25.**
5 (Section 411)	July 1975	**The Meaning of "Present Fairly in Conformity with Generally Accepted Accounting Principles" in the Independent Auditor's Report** I. Essentially financial statements prepared in compliance with GAAP are fairly presented. II. GAAP includes pronouncements, widely accepted practices, and other accounting literature. III. The substance of transactions should determine the form of recording transactions.
6	July 1975	**Superseded by SAS 45.**
7 (Section 315)	October 1975	**Communications Between Predecessor and Successor Auditors** I. Before accepting an engagement, the successor auditor should ask the prospective client to authorize the predecessor auditor to respond fully to inquiries. If a client refuses, the reasons for such refusal should be obtained and their implications for the successor auditor evaluated in deciding whether to accept the client. II. Predecessor auditors should be asked about management's integrity, disagreements on accounting or auditing matters, and the reasons for the change of auditors. Predecessor auditors should inform the successor if only a limited response is being given to that auditor. III. Successor auditors should likewise ask clients to authorize the predecessor to allow a review of past working papers. Once permission is granted, which working papers are made available is the predecessor auditor's choice.
8 (Section 550)	December 1975	**Other Information in Documents Containing Audited Financial Statements** I. Auditors should read other information to determine its consistency with the financial statements or its expression of a material misstatement of fact. II. Material inconsistencies should be discussed with the client, and if revision is not forthcoming, inclusion of an explanatory paragraph in the audit report, withholding of the report, or withdrawal from an engagement may be appropriate. III. Material misstatements of fact should be brought to the client's attention, and the auditor should seek legal counsel if they are not corrected.
9 (Section 322)	December 1975	**The Effect of an Internal Audit Function on the Scope of the Independent Auditor's Examination** I. Internal auditors' work cannot be substituted for an independent auditor's work but should be considered in determining the nature, timing, and extent of audit procedures. II. If the independent auditor's work is to be adjusted according to internal audit work, the internal auditors' competency and objectivity, as well as their work, should be evaluated. III. Internal auditors can directly assist in the independent auditor's exam, provided they are competent, objective, and are supervised (a process that includes testing the work performed). IV. All judgment areas are to be evaluated by the independent auditor rather than the internal auditors.
10	December 1975	**Superseded by SAS 24.**
11 (Section 336)	December 1975	**Using the Work of a Specialist** I. A specialist is a person (or firm) possessing special skill or knowledge in a particular field other than auditing or accounting, such as actuarial science, appraisal skills, legal issues, engineering expertise, or geology. II. The auditor should ask about the specialists' professional qualifications and reputation and determine whether their methods or assumptions are suitable as corroboration. III. The auditor should not refer to the specialists' work or findings in the auditor's report.

Statement on Auditing Standards	Date Issued	Title/Outline of Content
12 (Section 337)	January 1976	**Inquiry of a Client's Lawyer Concerning Litigation, Claims and Assessments** I. To identify contingencies, the auditor should talk to management, examine related documents, and request that management send a letter of inquiry to lawyers with whom the company has consulted. II. The content of the letter of audit inquiry is described. III. A lawyer's refusal to furnish requested information represents a limitation on scope that is sufficient to preclude an unqualified opinion. IV. A lawyer's inability to respond on a matter will lead to a qualified opinion if the effect of that matter on the financial statements can be material. V. An appendix provides an illustrative audit inquiry letter to legal counsel.
13	May 1976	**Superseded by SAS 24.**
14 (Section 621)	December 1976	**Special Reports** I. Financial statements prepared in accordance with a comprehensive basis of accounting other than generally accepted accounting principles, as well as the nature of the related auditor's report are defined. II. Specified elements, accounts, or items of a financial statement on which an opinion is expressed may include rentals, royalties, a profit participation, or a provision for income taxes. The form of the auditor's report is described. III. Requests for reports on compliance with aspects of contractual agreements or regulatory requirements related to audited financial statements are normally satisfied by giving negative assurance. The form of such reports is described. IV. Financial information presented in prescribed forms or schedules that require a prescribed form of auditor's report often must be reworded or replaced by a separate report in order to ensure that all of the auditor's assertions are justified.
15 (Section 505)	December 1976	**Reports on Comparative Financial Statements** I. The fourth standard of reporting refers to the financial statements taken as a whole and is intended to apply both to the current period and to those of one or more earlier periods that are presented for comparison. II. Updating reports, issuing differing opinions across the years being compared, and reissuing reports are explained, with several examples provided.
16 (Section 327)	January 1977	**The Independent Auditor's Responsibility for the Detection of Errors or Irregularities** I. Errors are unintentional mistakes, and irregularities are intentional distortions of the financial statements. II. The independent auditor has the responsibility to plan the examination to search for errors or irregularities that would have a material effect on the financial statements. This requirement is met by the usual approach to performing an audit, unless the auditor's examination indicates that there may be material errors or irregularities. III. An attitude of professional skepticism should direct the auditor's scope. IV. Additional details are provided concerning internal accounting control substantive tests, evaluation of the integrity of management, inherent limitations of an audit, and procedures to apply when an examination indicates that errors or irregularities may exist.
17 (Section 328)	January 1977	**Illegal Acts by Clients** I. When detected, illegal political contributions, bribes, and other violations of laws and regulations should be communicated to clients in order to facilitate action. II. If such acts are material and are improperly accounted for or disclosed, auditors should qualify their opinion or express an adverse opinion. III. If a client refuses to accept the auditor's report, the auditor should withdraw from the current engagement, indicating in writing to the board of directors the reason for withdrawing. IV. A GAAS exam cannot be expected to ensure that illegal acts will be detected. If such acts are detected, the auditor is not obligated to notify other than client personnel.
18	May 1977	**Withdrawn by Auditing Standards Board**

Statement on Auditing Standards	Date Issued	Title/Outline of Content
19 (Section 333)	June 1977	**Client Representations** I. Independent auditors must obtain written representations from management to complement other auditing procedures. II. The typical content of such representation letters, addressed to the auditor, is described, and an illustrative letter is presented. III. Management's refusal to furnish written representations constitutes a scope limitation that is sufficient to preclude an unqualified opinion.
20 (Section 323)	August 1977	**Required Communication of Material Weaknesses in Internal Accounting Control** I. The auditors must communicate to senior management and the board of directors or its audit committee material weaknesses in internal accounting control that come to their attention during an examination of financial statements made in accordance with GAAS. The form of communication is optional. II. A weakness in control is material when there is more than a relatively low level of risk of finding errors or irregularities in amounts that would be material in regard to the financial statements being audited and which may not be detected within a timely period by employees in the normal course of performing their assigned functions.
21 (Section 435)	December 1977	**Segment Information** I. The materiality of segment information is evaluated primarily by relating the dollar magnitude of the information to the financial statements taken as a whole. II. The procedures to apply to segment information are detailed; reporting effects are described; and disclosures regarding misstatements or omissions, inconsistencies, and scope limitations are illustrated. III. If requested to report separately on segment information, the auditor should evaluate materiality of the segment information, not the financial statements as a whole.
22 (Section 311)	March 1978	**Planning and Supervision** I. Audit planning means developing an overall strategy for the expected conduct and scope of the examination and preparation of a written audit program in sufficient detail to ensure that the examination's objectives can be achieved. II. Supervision refers to the direction of the assistants' efforts to determine whether the objectives of the examination have been accomplished. A review and an evaluation of results are required to ensure their consistency with the auditor's report. III. The planning of an audit requires a knowledge of the entity's business, just as the extent of supervision requires an understanding of the complexity of the subject matter under audit and the qualifications of the individuals performing the work.
23 (Section 318)	October 1978	**Analytical Review Procedures** I. Analytical review procedures are substantive tests of financial information made by a study and comparison of relationships among data. II. Any combination of tests of details of transactions and balances and analytical review procedures can be used as the basis for auditors' reliance on substantive tests. III. Analytical review procedures may be performed in the initial planning stage, during the examination as substantive test work, and at or near the conclusion of the audit as a final review. IV. Procedures include comparison with earlier periods, anticipated results (such as budgets and forecasts), predictable patterns and trends, industry data, and nonfinancial information.
24	March 1979	**Superseded by SAS No. 36.**

Statement on Auditing Standards	Date Issued	Title/Outline of Content
25 (Section 161)	November 1979	**The Relationship of Generally Accepted Auditing Standards to Quality Control Standards** I. Rule 202 of the Rules of Conduct of the Code of Professional Ethics of the American Institute of Certified Public Accountants requires members to comply with such standards when associated with financial statements. II. To comply with GAAS in conducting an audit practice, a firm should establish quality control policies and procedures appropriate to its size, operating autonomy, nature of its practice, organization, and cost-benefit analysis. III. Such policies should provide reasonable assurance of conformance with GAAS in its audit engagements.
26 (Section 504)	November 1979	**Association with Financial Statements** I. An accountant is associated with financial statements when he or she has consented to use his or her name in a report, document, or written communication containing the statements or when he or she submits to his or her client or others financial statements that he or she has prepared or assisted in preparing, even though his or her name is not appended to the statements. II. If an accountant has not audited or reviewed the financial statements, a disclaimer of opinion should be issued. III. If an accountant lacks independence, a disclaimer of opinion must be issued. IV. If the accountant is aware of nonconformity with GAAP, he or she should suggest revision and, if not appropriately revised, should describe the departure in the disclaimer. V. Reports are illustrated, including those on statements in comparative form; negative assurance is not appropriate except for letters to underwriters or similar special report engagements that meet similar applicable requirements.
27 (Section 553)	December 1979	**Supplementary Information Required by the Financial Accounting Standards Board** I. For required supplementary information, the auditor should apply inquiry procedures, check consistency with the financial statements and other available knowledge, and apply any procedures specifically prescribed. II. Deficiencies in or the omission of required supplementary information, and the inability to complete the prescribed limited procedures should be reported. Otherwise, the auditor's report does not need to be expanded.
28 (Section 554)	June 1980	**Supplementary Information on the Effects of Changing Prices** I. Auditor's inquiry procedures should be directed to judgments made concerning measurement and presentation, including information sources, assumptions made, and rationale for selecting a particular method to estimate the recoverable amount of inventory and property, plant, and equipment. II. The auditor should read narrative explanations of disclosures to assess their consistency with the financial statements and the possibility of a material misstatement of fact, either of which would require disclosure in the audit report.
29 (Section 551)	July 1980	**Reporting on Information Accompanying the Basic Financial Statements in Auditor-submitted Documents** I. Some additional details or explanations of items in or related to the basic financial statements, consolidating information, historical summaries of items extracted from the basic financial statements, statistical data, and other material may be from sources outside the accounting system or outside the entity. But all are outside the basic financial statements in the sense that they are not considered necessary to GAAP presentation. II. The auditor should express an opinion on whether the information is fairly stated or issue a disclaimer on some or all of such information. The opinion or disclaimer can be a part of the standard report or may appear separately. III. Reporting examples are provided. If an auditor describes procedures applied, they should be separate from management's representations and neither contradict nor detract from the scope paragraph of the standard report.

Statement on Auditing Standards	Date Issued	Title/Outline of Content
30 (Section 642)	July 1980	**Reporting on Internal Accounting Control** I. An accountant may express an opinion on an entity's system of internal accounting control as of a specified date or for a period of time. The report forms vary according to the intended user and the scope of the review work. II. The general considerations, study and evaluation, and the various forms of the accountant's report are described, including the report form possible based solely on the study and evaluation of control made as part of an audit.
31 (Section 326)	August 1980	**Evidential Matter** I. Management's assertions can be classified as relating to existence or occurrence, completeness, rights and obligations, valuation or allocation, and presentation and disclosure. II. Based on these assertions, an auditor defines specific audit objectives and then identifies those audit procedures that are capable of providing evidence to meet each objective (examples of objectives and related substantive tests are provided). III. Underlying accounting data and all corroborating information available to the auditor is evidential matter and should be evaluated in terms of its competency, that is, both its validity and relevancy. IV. Evidence is sufficient when it gives the auditor a reasonable basis for forming an opinion. It should be persuasive but need not be convincing.
32 (Section 431)	October 1980	**Adequacy of Disclosure in Financial Statements** I. Adequate disclosure encompasses the form, arrangement, and content of the financial statements and their appended notes, including, for example, the terminology used, the amount of detail given, the classification of items in the statements, and the bases of amounts set forth. II. Omitted disclosures required by GAAP should be provided in the auditor's report if practicable, i.e., reasonably obtainable from management's records; yet the provision of which does not make the auditor assume the position of the preparer of the financial information. III. Ordinarily, the auditor should not make information not required by GAAP available to report users without the client's permission.
33	October 1980	**Superseded by SAS 45**
34 (Section 340)	March 1981	**The Auditor's Considerations When a Question Arises About an Entity's Continued Existence** I. Without information to the contrary, an entity's continuation is usually assumed in financial accounting. Should the auditor detect contrary information, it should be evaluated along with any factors that tend to mitigate that information or management's plans that pertain to the conditions underlying that information. II. Indicators of solvency problems, examples of mitigating factors, and means of evaluating the effect of management's plans are discussed. III. Effects on the auditor's report are described.
35 (Section 622)	April 1981	**Special Reports – Applying Agreed-upon Procedures to Specified Elements, Accounts, or Items of a Financial Statement** I. An accountant can agree to a scope limited to one or more specified elements, accounts, or items and a set of agreed-upon procedures, provided the parties involved understand the procedures to be performed and the distribution of the report is restricted to the named parties involved. II. The second and third standards of field work do not apply to such limited engagements. Illustrations of report forms are provided.

Statement on Auditing Standards	Date Issued	Title/Outline of Content
36 (Section 722)	April 1981	**Review of Interim Financial Information** I. A review of interim financial information should give the accountant, via analytical review procedures and inquiries, a basis for reporting whether there should be material modifications for the information to conform with GAAP. II. The extent of audit procedures depends on the accountant's knowledge of accounting and reporting practices, weaknesses in internal accounting control, changes in the nature or volume of activity or accounting changes, the issuance of accounting pronouncements, accounting records maintained at multiple locations, and questions raised in performing other procedures. III. The accountant's report on a review of interim financial information and modifications of the report form are described.
37 (Section 711)	April 1981	**Filings Under Federal Securities Statutes** I. The inclusion of an accountant's report in registration statements, proxy statements, or periodic reports filed under the securities statutes entails the same responsibility as in other reporting, except that the nature and extent of this responsibility are specified in some detail in risks and regulations and the auditor's responsibility extends to the effective date of the registration statement. II. At or near the effective date, the auditor should read the entire prospectus and other pertinent portions of the registration statement and obtain written representation from management, making certain that the auditor's name is not being used in a way that indicates that responsibility exceeds the intended level.
38	April 1981	**Superseded by SAS 49.**
39 (Section 350)	June 1981	**Audit Sampling** I. Audit sampling means applying an audit procedure to some of the items in an account balance so as to see a characteristic of that balance. II. Statistical and nonstatistical sampling are described, with guidance on planning, performing, and evaluating audit samples. III. An appendix relates the risk of incorrect acceptance for a substantive test of details to other sources of audit reliance.
40 (Section 556)	February 1982	**Supplementary Mineral Reserve Information** I. An auditor's inquiries should be directed at management's understanding of the specific requirements for disclosing the supplementary mineral reserve information. II. In addition, the auditor should make inquiries as to the expertise of the individual making estimates of reserve quantities and the documentation of the methods and bases for estimates. III. Reserve information should be compared with recent production, depletion, and amortization information, financial statement data on production, and purchased or sold mineral reserves. IV. The auditor should ask about the method and bases used to calculate the market information disclosed.
41 (Section 339)	April 1982	**Working Papers** I. The principal record of the work performed and the auditor's conclusions is contained in the working papers. II. Beyond supporting observance of the standards of field work, working papers help the auditor conduct and supervise the engagement. III. Working papers are the auditor's property, but the auditor's rights of ownership are subject to ethical limitations pertaining to the confidential relationship with clients. IV. The auditor should adopt reasonable procedures for the safe custody of working papers.

Statement on Auditing Standards	Date Issued	Title/Outline of Content
42 (Section 552)	September 1982	**Reporting on Condensed Financial Statements and Selected Financial Data** I. An auditor may be engaged to report on condensed financial statements that are derived from audited financial statements, but he or she cannot report in the same manner as on the complete statements, as necessary disclosures are likely to have been omitted. II. Report forms are illustrated.
43 (Section 1010)	August 1982	**Omnibus Statement on Auditing Standards** I. The ten GAAS, to the extent that they are relevant in the circumstances, apply to all services other than examinations of financial statements unless a statement specifies otherwise. II. A minimum study and evaluation of the system of internal accounting control may be limited to obtaining an understanding of the control environment and the flow of transactions, and the documentation need record only the auditor's reasons for not extending the review of controls beyond the minimum level. III. If inventories represent a significant proportion of total or current assets, an additional potential audit procedure is to obtain an independent accountant's report on the warehouse person's system of internal accounting control. IV. The variations in presentation of Statement of Changes in Financial Position that need not be reported as inconsistencies are described. V. "Subject to" qualifications should not be accompanied by references to "the effects, if any," on the financial statements "of the ultimate resolution." VI. The order of authority of sources of established accounting principles that an auditor should follow in determining GAAP is clarified; the removal of the phraseology "presents fairly" from letters for underwriters expressing negative assurance is specified; and the effective date of SAS No. 39 on audit sampling is postponed one year.
44 (Section 324)	December 1982	**Special-Purpose Reports on Internal Accounting Control at Service Organizations** I. Guidance is offered regarding the independent auditor's use of a special-purpose report on certain aspects of internal accounting control of an organization that offers certain services to a client whose financial statements the auditor has been engaged to examine. II. Factors are discussed affecting the decision to obtain a service auditor's report, considerations in using such a report, and responsibilities of service auditors for special-purpose reports.
45 (Section 1020)	August 1983	**Omnibus Statement on Auditing Standards — 1983** I. Additional guidance is offered regarding the auditor's considerations before applying substantive tests to the details of asset or liability accounts at interim dates, including the relationship between internal accounting control and such tests. II. SAS No. 6 is superseded, and guidance is offered regarding accounting considerations and audit procedures intended to help in determining and disclosing the existence of related parties and material related-party transactions. III. The supplementary oil and gas reserve information in SAS No. 33 was technically revised to reflect FASB Statement No. 69.
46 (Section 390)	September 1983	**Consideration of Omitted Procedures After the Report Date** I. When an auditor concludes that an auditing procedure considered necessary at the time of the examination in the circumstances then prevailing was omitted, its importance should be evaluated in light of the possibility that other work compensated for the omission. II. Legal counsel is recommended, and if the omitted procedure materially impairs the basis for expressing an opinion, the omitted procedure or alternative yet equivalent procedures should be applied.

Statement on Auditing Standards	Date Issued	Title/Outline of Content
47 (Section 312)	December 1983	**Audit Risk and Materiality in Conducting Audit** I. Audit risk and materiality should be considered together in determining the nature, timing, and extent of auditing procedures and in evaluating the results of these procedures. II. Audit risk may be assessed in quantitative or nonquantitative terms but should be limited to a low level through audit planning. III. Audit risk includes inherent risk – susceptibility to error when there are no related internal accounting controls – and control risk – the possibility of errors not being prevented or detected by controls – and detection risk – the possibility of errors not being detected by audit procedures. IV. The auditor should aggregate errors to arrive at a best estimate of the most likely error and should include the effect on the current period's financial statements of the earlier period's likely errors when evaluating the possibility of materially misstated financial statements.
48 (Section 321)	July 1984	**The Effects of Computer Processing on the Examination of Financial Statements** I. Aspects of computer processing affect the planning of an audit examination, and the availability of computer-generated data may affect the selection of analytical review procedures. II. Some characteristics of EDP affect the system of internal accounting control but do not affect the objective of controls. III. Audit evidence is not affected by the use of computer processing.
49 (Section 631)	September 1984	**Letters for Underwriters** I. Those areas on which it is or is not proper for independent CPAs to comment and the acceptable form of these comments are identified. II. Suggestions are offered regarding the form of comfort letters. III. Ways of reducing or avoiding uncertainties are described. For example, care should be taken to reduce the risks of misunderstanding the scope of work performed, and the accountant should state that he or she cannot ensure the sufficiency of the procedures for the underwriter's purposes.

Name Index

Subject Index

Italicized page number indicates page on which term is defined.